National University *of* Ireland, Galway
Ollscoil na hÉireann, Gaillimh

Leabharlann James Hardiman

Níl sé ceadaithe an leabhar seo a choinneáil thar an dáta is déanaí atá luaite thíos.

This book must be returned not later than the last date stamped below.

3 1 JAN 2002

1 0 AUG 2004

2 0 JUL 2004

Gearrfar cáin i gcomhar gach lá nó cuid de lá a coinneofar an leabhar seo thar an dáta atá luaite thuas.

A fine will be charged for each day or part of a day this book is retained beyond the date due for return.

Handbook of
INDUSTRIAL, WORK AND ORGANIZATIONAL PSYCHOLOGY

Volume 1
Personnel Psychology

Handbook of
INDUSTRIAL, WORK
AND ORGANIZATIONAL
PSYCHOLOGY

Volume 1
Personnel Psychology

Edited by

NEIL ANDERSON
DENIZ S. ONES
HANDAN KEPIR SINANGIL
CHOCKALINGAM VISWESVARAN

SAGE Publications
London • Thousand Oaks • New Delhi

First published 2001

SAGE Publications Ltd
6 Bonhill Street
London EC2A 4PU

SAGE Publications Inc
2455 Teller Road
Thousand Oaks, California 91320

SAGE Publications India Pvt Ltd
32, M-Block Market
Greater Kailash – I
New Delhi 110 048

British Library Cataloguing in Publication data

A catalogue record for this book is available from the British Library

ISBN Volume 1 0 7619 6488 6
     Volume 2 0 7619 6489 4

Library of Congress Control number available

Typeset by SIVA Math Setters, Chennai, India
Printed in Great Britain by The Cromwell Press Ltd., Trowbridge, Wiltshire

To Mavis Anderson, my mother, and George Anderson (deceased), my father,
for teaching me the meaning of conscientiousness in life (NA)

To my parents Drs Saime Ülker Öneş and Somer Öneş for continuing
to inspire me with their talent and achievements (DSO)

To my dear parents Sevinç and Mustafa Kepir for their everlasting
love and support (HKS)

To Sankaravadivoo (deceased), my mother, and S. P. Chockalingam, my father,
for their confidence in me and for all their encouragement (CV)

Contents of Volume 1

Contents of Volume 2

Biographic Profiles

Editors

Neil Anderson is Professor of Work Psychology at Goldsmiths College, University of London. He is Founding Editor of the *International Journal of Selection and Assessment*. His research interests include recruitment and selection, organizational and work group socialization, innovation at work, and organizational climate. He has co-authored and edited a number of books including the *International Handbook of Selection and Assessment*, and his work has appeared in several scholarly journals including *Journal of Applied Psychology*, *Human Relations*, *Journal of Organizational Behavior*, *Journal of Occupational and Organizational Psychology*, and the *International Journal of Selection and Assessment*. Neil has on-going research projects, either collaboratively or alone, into interviewer and applicant decision-making in assessment interviews, work group socialization of graduates, the structure and psychometric properties of popular 'Big Five' measures of personality, telephone-based interviewing procedures, and the practitioner–researcher divide in work and organizational psychology. Committed to an international perspective in work psychology, Neil has been Visiting Professor to the University of Minnesota (USA) and the Free University of Amsterdam (The Netherlands). Neil is a fellow of the British Psychological Society and the Society for Industrial and Organizational Psychology.

Deniz S. Ones is an international expert in personality and integrity testing for personnel selection and personality assessment for workplace applications. She received her PhD from the University of Iowa in 1993 and was previously a faculty member of the University of Houston. Currently, she is the holder of the Hellervik Endowed Professorship in Industrial and Organizational Psychology at the Department of Psychology of the University of Minnesota. Dr Ones is the author of over 60 articles and over 200 international/national conference papers and published abstracts on topics ranging from the reliability of performance ratings to influences of social desirability on personality test validity to discipline problems at work. Her research has appeared in the *Annual Review of Psychology, Journal of Applied Psychology*, *Personnel Psychology*, and *Psychological Bulletin*, among others. In 1994, Dr Ones received the Society of Industrial and Organizational Psychology's (Division 14 of the American Psychological Association) S. Rains Wallace Best Dissertation Award. In 1998, she received the Ernest J. McCormick Early Career Contributions Award from the Society for Industrial Organizational Psychology (Division 14 of the American Psychological Association), making her one of two people to ever receive both awards. Her current research and teaching interests include personality as it relates to job performance, integrity testing, and the application of meta-analytic techniques in the social sciences. Dr Ones is a Fellow of the American Psychological Association (Divisions 5 and 14) and the Society for Industrial and Organizational Psychology and serves on the editorial boards of *Personnel Psychology, International Journal of Selection and Assessment,* and *European Journal of Work and Organizational Psychology.* Recently, she has edited special issues for two prestigious journals (*Human Performance* on ability testing, and *International Journal of Selection Assessment* on counterproductive work behaviors).

Handan Kepir Sinangil is Professor of Work and Organizational Psychology at Marmara University, Organizational Behaviour Graduate Program, and Adjunct Professor at Bogazici University. She is the General Secretary of the European Association of Work and Organizational Psychology (EAWOP) and a member of the American Psychological Association (APA), the Society for Industrial and Organizational Psychology (SIOP, APA Division 14), the International Association of Applied Psychology (IAAP), and the International Association of Cross-Cultural Psychology (IACCP). Dr Sinangil's international and national publications exceed 70 as book chapters and conference papers. She is also associate editor of the *International Journal of Selection and Assessment (IJSA).* Her ongoing research projects, either with international collaboration or alone include expatriate management, organizational culture and change, performance appraisal and selection. Additionally, her current teaching interests include assessment, training and development, and psychology of management.

Chockalingam (Vish) Viswesvaran is an international expert in performance measurement, modeling performance determinants, personality and integrity testing, personnel selection and meta-analysis. He received his PhD from the University of Iowa in 1993. Currently, he is an Associate Professor at the Department of Psychology of the Florida International University. Dr Viswesvaran is the author of over 70 articles and over 200 international/national conference papers and published abstracts. His research has appeared in the *Journal of Applied Psychology, Personnel Psychology, Journal of Vocational Behavior* and *Educational and Psychological Measurement,* among others. In 1995, Viswesvaran received the Society of Industrial and Organizational Psychology's (Division 14 of the American Psychological Association) S. Rains Wallace Best Dissertation Award. In 1998, he received the Ernest J. McCormick Early Career Contributions Award from the Society for Industrial Organizational Psychology (Division 14 of the American Psychological Association), making him one of two people to ever receive both awards. His current research and teaching interests include job performance assessment, personality as it relates to job performance, integrity testing, and the application of meta-analytic techniques in the social sciences. Viswesvaran is a Fellow of the Society for Industrial and Organizational Psychology and serves on the editorial boards of *Personnel Psychology* and *Educational and Psychological Measurement.* Recently, Viswesvaran has edited a special issue for *Human Performance* on ability testing.

Authors

Herman Aguinis (http://www.cudenver.edu/~haguinis) received his PhD (1993) in industrial/organizational psychology from the University at Albany, State University of New York. He is currently an Associate Professor of Management and Director of the MS in Management Program at the University of Colorado at Denver. His research interests include personnel selection, social power and influence, estimation of interaction effects, meta-analysis, and research methods. He has been a visiting scholar in universities in Europe, Asia and Latin America, has written over 40 articles in refereed journals, and delivered over 100 refereed and invited presentations. His articles have appeared in *Academy of Management Journal, American Psychologist, Journal of Applied Psychology, Personnel Psychology*, and elsewhere. He currently serves as an associate editor for *Organizational Research Methods*, and as an elected member of the Executive Committee of the Human Resources Management Division of the Academy of Management.

Karen Arnold, PhD, is a member of the Psychology Department, University of Wales, Swansea. She is a Director of KADO Associates, Specialists in User Needs Analysis, and has successfully applied her expertise to a number of European R&D projects and is the Project Manager for the Developing Employment in the Information Society (DEIS) project.

Zeynep Aycan is an Assistant Professor of Industrial and Organizational Psychology at Koc University, Istanbul, Turkey. Dr Aycan received her PhD from Queen's University, Kingston, Canada in 1996 where she worked under the supervision of Professor John W. Berry. She then continued working with Professor Rabindra N. Kanungo at McGill University on a number of cross-cultural research projects on organizational behavior. Her research interests mainly focus on the impact of culture on organizational behavior and HRM practices; indigenous concepts of management and leadership; cross-cultural perspectives on women's workforce participation and the work–family interface. She has published two edited books on expatriate management as well as indigenous management, leadership and HRM practices (the latter is in Turkish). She is the co-editor (with Terrence Jackson) of the *International Journal for Cross-Cultural Management* and she serves on the editorial boards of a number of professional journals such as *Applied Psychology: An International Review*. She is an executive committee member of the International Association for the Study of Work and Organizational Values whose conference she organized in Istanbul in 1998. She also has consulting experience with some large-scale multinational and local organizations.

Talya N. Bauer, PhD, Purdue University, is an Associate Professor of Organizational Behavior and Human Resource Management at Portland State University, Portland, Oregon, USA. Her experience training, consulting, and conducting research with organizations includes work with such organizations as Bristol-Meyers Squibb, NASA, Subaru-Isuzu, Hewlett-Packard, Intel, and the Los Angeles Unified School District. Her teaching and research interests include socialization, leadership, and applicant reactions to selection. She is a member of the *Journal of Applied Psychology* editorial board and is the program chair for the year 2001 Society for Industrial and Organizational Psychologist's Annual Conference in San Diego, California. Her work appears in outlets such as *Academy of Management Journal, Personnel Psychology, Journal of Applied Psychology, Research in Personnel and Human Resource Management, Group and Organization Management, Journal of Career Planning and Employment, Journal of Applied Social Psychology*, and *Journal of Business and Psychology*.

Philip Bobko is Professor of Management and Psychology at Gettysburg College. He is the author of over 60 publications on topics including test fairness, moderated regression analysis, validation methods, goal-setting, decision-making, utility analysis, and performance standard setting. He has authored two chapters in Dunnette and Hough's *Handbook of Industrial and Organizational Psychology* and has published a book on the topic of correlation and regression. He has been scientific advisor or principal scientist for government contracts totaling approximately $50 million, and he has served as co-editor of the *Academy of Management Journal* and editor of the *Journal of Applied Psychology*.

Marise Born is Associate Professor of Work Psychology at the Vrije Universiteit Amsterdam. She is associate editor of the *International Journal of Selection and Assessment*. Her research interests include recruitment and selection, the assessment center, personality, gender issues, entrepreneurship, and the method of meta-analysis. Her work has appeared in several Dutch and international journals including the *International Journal of Selection and Assessment, Journal of Cross-Cultural Psychology, Journal of Business and Psychology*, and *Educational Psychology*. Her on-going research projects, either collaboratively or alone, include job search behavior, construct validity issues of the assessment center, gender differences in applicant decision-making, entrepreneurship and personality, and application of the Social Relation Model (Kenny) to personnel selection. Marise has been Visiting Professor to the University of Houston (USA).

John P. Campbell is Professor of Psychology and Industrial Relations at the University of Minnesota where he received his PhD (1964) in Psychology. From 1964 to 1966 he was Assistant Professor of Psychology, University of California, Berkeley, and has been at Minnesota from 1967 to the present. He was elected President of the Division of I/O Psychology of the APA in 1977/78 and from 1974 to 1982 served as associate editor and then editor of the *Journal of Applied Psychology*. He is the author of *Managerial Behavior, Performance, and Effectiveness* (with M. Dunnette, E. Lawler, and K. Weick, 1970), *Measurement Theory for the Behavioral Sciences* (with E. Ghiselli and S. Zedeck, 1978), *What to Study: Generating and Developing Research Questions* (with R. Daft and C. Hulin, 1984), *Productivity in Organizations* (with R. Campbell, 1988), and *Exploring the Limits of Personnel Selection and Classification* (with D. Knapp, 2001). He was awarded the Society of I/O Psychology Distinguished Scientific Contribution Award in 1991. From 1982–94 he served as Principal Scientist for the Army's Project A research program. Current research interests are in performance measurement, personnel selection and classification, and modeling the person/job match.

Thomas R. Carretta received his PhD in psychology in 1983 from the University of Pittsburgh. Currently, he is a Research Psychologist in the Crew Systems Development Branch of the Human Effectiveness Directorate of the Air Force Research Laboratory in Dayton, Ohio. Prior to his current position, he spent over 10 years in the Manpower and Personnel Research Division of the Air Force Research Laboratory in San Antonio, Texas, working on aircrew selection and classification issues. His professional interests include personnel measurement, selection, and individual and group differences.

Nicole Cunningham-Snell is Assessment and Psychology Manager at Shell International and works in the 'Talent Identification and Leadership Development Team'. She provides selection and assessment methodology advice to the Shell Group of Companies globally and is directly involved in the design and delivery of Shell's assessment products. She obtained her PhD from Goldsmiths College, University of London and continues to actively research in the area of applicants' reactions to selection procedures.

Cynthia J. DeVore is a doctoral student in the I/O Psychology program at the University of Minnesota, Twin Cities campus. She received her BA in Computer Studies in 1983 at Macalester College. Her research interests include motivation, work stress, and organizational change.

Clive Fletcher is Professor of Occupational Psychology at Goldsmiths College, University of London. He is a Fellow of the British Psychological Society and a former Chair of its occupational psychology section. Dr Fletcher has authored 6 books and over 100 other publications on assessment centres, psychological testing, 360 degree feedback, performance appraisal, performance management and related topics. He has also acted as a consultant in these areas to a wide range of major organizations in the UK and internationally.

Christine A. Henle received her PhD (2001) in industrial/organizational psychology from Colorado State University. She is currently an Assistant Professor of Management at the University of North Carolina at Charlotte. Her research interests include counterproductive work behaviors, employment law, and human resource management systems.

Sarah A. Hezlett is a doctoral student in industrial and organizational psychology at the University of Minnesota, where she has taught courses on motivation and individual behavior in organizations. As a Senior Research Scientist & Consultant at Questar Data Systems, she designs organizational assessments and 360-degree feedback systems, helping individuals and organizations to interpret and take action on the results. Her research, which focuses on individual development, 360-degree feedback, and measurement issues, has appeared in *Psychological Bulletin*, *Personnel Psychology*, and *Human Resource Management*. She has an MA in I/O psychology from the University of Minnesota and an AB in Politics from Princeton University.

Leaetta Hough is an internationally recognized expert in the design and implementation of human resource management systems such as selection, training, and performance management for companies such as Sony, Microsoft, and Verizon. She is also an expert in the development and use of personality inventories in work settings. Her work with personality variables during the 1980s has been recognized as instrumental in reviving the role of personality variables in the field of industrial, work, and organizational psychology as respectable and highly useful individual difference variables in understanding and predicting human behavior in the workplace. She is co-editor, along with Marvin Dunnette, of the four-volume *Handbook of Industrial and Organizational Psychology*, is senior author of the personnel selection chapter in the 2000 *Annual Review of Psychology*, and has contributed hundreds of other pieces in a variety of settings and outlets. She received her PhD from the University of Minnesota in 1981 and is a fellow of the American Psychological Society, the American Psychological Association, as well as its Divisions 5 (Evaluation, Measurement, and Statistics) and 14 (Society for Industrial and Organizational Psychology). Dr Hough is currently president of Dunnette Group, Ltd.

John E. (Jack) Hunter (PhD, University of Illinois) is a professor in the Department of Psychology at Michigan State University. He has co-authored two books, *Meta-Analysis and Mathematical Models in Attitude Change*, and has published over 200 articles on a wide variety of topics. His current research in personnel focuses on the determinants of job performance, and in meta-analysis on the extension of meta-analytic methods to correct for artifacts not yet handled. He is also doing research in psychometric theory. Professor Hunter is a Fellow of the Society for Industrial and Organizational Psychology, the American Psychological Society and the American Psychological Association. He has received distinguished scientific contributions awards (with Frank Schmidt) from both the American Psychological Association and the Society for Industrial and Organizational Psychology.

Rabindra N. Kanungo is Professor Emeritus in Management and Organizational Behavior, Faculty of Management, McGill University, Montreal, Canada. He has published widely in both basic and applied areas of psychology and management. His publications include more than 200 professional articles, and 19 books. His latest book is *Charismatic Leadership* (co-authored with Jay A. Conger) published in 1998. He is a Fellow of the Canadian Psychological Association, past President of the International Association for the Study of Work and Organizational Values, and acts on several editorial boards of professional journals.

Véronique De Keyser is a Professor in Work and Organizational Psychology, and Director of the Work and Organizational Psychology Department at the University of Liège, Belgium. She is also President of the European Association for Work and Organizational Psychology and Co-director of the French revue 'Le Travail Humain'. She is an expert for national authorities, FNRS (B) and CNRS (FR), and for the European Commission, Telematics (DRIVE), FAST, SCIENCE, HCM, BRITE-EURAM. Her team is involved in field and laboratory studies, basic and applied research in cognitive psychology and ergonomics. Her basic research is mainly focused on temporal reasoning, implicit learning, and

I.A. modeling. Her applied research in industrial sectors (mainly process control, aeronautics, anesthesiology, transport) concerns the evaluation and design of man–machine interfaces – including the design of computer-based technologies for cooperative work – safety and human reliability.

Nathan R. Kuncel is a doctoral student in I/O psychology at the University of Minnesota, where he received both an MA in I/O psychology and a BA in psychology. He held a three year National Science Foundation Graduate Fellowship and currently holds the Eva O. Miller Fellowship. His research is focused on personnel selection, educational selection, personality measurement, and the relations between ability, knowledge, skills, and job performance. His work on these topics has appeared in the *Psychological Bulletin*, the *American Psychologist*, and various conference papers. His work experience also includes several research positions at Personnel Decisions International.

Edward L. Levine grew up in the Red Hook section of Brooklyn NY before its current gentrification began. After being named valedictorian of Public School 27, he attended the prestigious Stuyvesant High School where he excelled in Latin and in Lunch. His abilities in the latter allowed him to become a member of the honor society and to graduate with honors. An early advocate of diversity his best buddies in high school were an Italian, who is now a university Dean, and a Greek, who, last he heard owned a Greek Diner in New York City. Having won a Regents College Scholarship, he decided he could make money on it if he lived at home and attended Brooklyn College. Despite some questioning of his decision to stay at home by his father, he started strong there as pre-med, but soon decided, after exposure to pungent odors and cloudy reagent bottles in Organic Chemistry, that Psychology was for him even after getting a D in intro-psych during his identity crisis. The identity crisis resolved itself once he met his Dulcinea, who in his case did not quite share some of the pedestrian characteristics of the original. As a senior he took a course in I/O psychology, which convinced him he could become a psychologist and still make a living. He received his PhD in Psychology from New York University with honors, and his career, which early on was focused on issues related to equal employment opportunity, led him to positions with the State of Arizona where he served as Chief of the Selection Resource Center, which provided job analysis, screening and selection services to state and local government agencies, and ultimately with the University of South Florida. He currently holds the position of Professor and Chairperson of the Department of Psychology, and has served as major professor for 13 PhD graduates of the I/O program to date, including the gifted Dr Juan I. Sanchez. Luckily they all still talk to him and even collaborate with him on projects such as the chapter in this handbook. A husband of his Dulcinea and proud father of a budding I/O psychologist, a budding pharmacist, and a budding slacker, who is determined to deplete all of his papa's retirement savings, Dr Levine holds a diplomate in I/O Psychology from the American Board of Professional Psychology, and has published widely in job analysis and related topics.

Hunter Mabon received his PhD degree (1974) in Human Resource Management from the Stockholm School of Economics. He is a Professor at the Stockholm

School of Business and has had his own business consultancy for many years. He has written eight textbooks which have been widely used in Swedish universities, one of which, *Personnel Administration* (1984), received the book of the year award. He has been Chairman of the Swedish Society for Human Resource Consultants and of the Personnel Economics Institute at Stockholm University. He has also been guest editor of the *Journal of Human Resource Costing and Accounting*. At present he is chairman of the board of Psykologiförlaget, the leading Swedish test publishing company. His primary research interests are costing human resource interventions, especially concerning selection and downsizing, as well as psychological testing in selection situations, and he has published a number of articles within these fields.

Cynthia D. McCauley is Vice President of New Initiatives at the Center for Creative Leadership, North Carolina. Her work at the Center has focused on enhancing leadership development knowledge and practice in the areas of 360-degree feedback, developmental relationships, challenging job assignments, and feedback-intensive programs. She has developed management assessment tools and is co-editor of *The Center for Creative Leadership Handbook of Leadership Development*. She holds a PhD in Industrial and Organizational Psychology from the University of Georgia.

Anne-Sophie Nyssen received a PhD in Work Psychology in 1997, from the University of Liège (Belgium), supported by the National Research Fund Foundation, under the direction of Professor V. De Keyser. The primary goal of her research focused on human errors in anaesthesia using interviews, questionnaires, and observations in the operating room as data sources. Progressively, the research extended its scope and an evaluation methodology was developed to assess the impact of technology changes on practitioner cognition. For the last four years, she has contributed to the use of a full-scale anesthesia simulator for training and research on expertise. In 1999, she received a grant from NATO to carry out post-PhD research at Stanford University. In the same year, her research project to develop a systemwide healthcare critical incident reporting system in Belgium was approved for funding by the Office of the Prime Minister of Belgium.

David Oborne is Professor and Head of the Department of Psychology at the University of Wales, Swansea. He has been the Prime Contractor for an ORA project (PATRA – Psychological Aspects of Teleworking in Rural Areas) and the Lead Contractor for an EU Horizon project (EDIT – Employment Development through Innovative Technologies). He has been a Partner and Associate Partner in TIDE and ORA projects, and the lead contractor in a Department of Trade and Industry (DTI) multimedia project. He is currently leading four other projects in Wales: SWIG (South Wales Information Gateway – ERDF), DEIS (Developing Employment in the Information Society – ESF), TeleTrain (Telematics-based Training System – Welsh Development Agency/Wales Information Society Initiative), and RMI (a Remote Multimedia Interviewing system – EPSRC). He has been an auditor, evaluator and raporteur for the European Union's ACTS programme. He has produced over 12 books on aspects of ergonomics and HCI and has written more than 30 articles in learned journals.

Cheri Ostroff received her PhD (1987) in industrial/organizational psychology from Michigan State University. She is currently Associate Professor of Psychology and Education at Teachers College, Columbia University. Her research interests include levels of analysis issues, person–environment fit, and human resource management systems. Her articles have appeared in journals such as *Academy of Management Journal*, *Journal of Applied Psychology*, *Personnel Psychology*, and *Organizational Behavior and Human Decision Processes*. She has received the Ernest J. McCormick Award for Early Career Contributions from the Society of Industrial Organizational Psychology, and the American Psychological Association's Distinguished Scientific Award for Early Career Contributions in Applied Research.

Sharon K. Parker is at the Australian Graduate School of Management, The University of New South Wales. She obtained her PhD from the Institute of Work Psychology, University of Sheffield, UK. Her current research interests concern how work design and related practices affect the development of flexible role orientations, proactivity, and role breadth self-efficacy amongst employees. Other research interests include stress, safety, performance, and equal opportunities. Her research has appeared in leading journals such as the *Journal of Applied Psychology* and the *Academy of Management Journal*. She is the co-author of a book entitled *Job and Work Design: Organizing Work to Promote Well-being and Effectiveness*.

Elissa L. Perry is an Assistant Professor of Psychology and Education at Teachers College, Columbia University. She received an MS and PhD in Organizational Behavior and Theory from Carnegie Melon University. Professor Perry has research interests in the role of demographic variables in human resource judgements, sexual harassment, and older workers. She has published articles in journals such as *Academy of Management Review*, *Journal of Applied Psychology*, and *Journal of Applied Social Psychology*.

Malcolm James Ree received his PhD in psychometrics in 1976 from the University of Pennsylvania. He is Associate Professor on the faculty of the Center for Leadership Studies at Our Lady of the Lake University, San Antonio, Texas. Formerly he was the Senior Scientist in the Space Warfighter Training Branch of the Human Effectiveness Directorate of the Air Force Research Laboratory. His professional interests include human abilities, individual differences, the intelligence–job performance nexus, and the history of statistics.

Philip L. Roth is Professor of Management at Clemson University. His research areas include personnel selection and research methods. His selection interests are in the areas of interviewing, grades as predictors of organizational outcomes, and utility analysis. His methods and interests are primarily in missing data and meta-analysis. He publishes in journals such as the *Journal of Applied Psychology*, *Personnel Psychology*, *Journal of Management*, and *Organizational Research Methods*.

Paul R. Sackett (Ohio State, 1979) is Professor of Psychology at the University of Minnesota. He served as the editor of *Personnel Psychology* from 1984 to 1990, as President of the Society for Industrial and Organizational Psychology (Div. 14), as co-chair of the Joint Committee on the 1999 Standards for Educational and Psychological Testing, as a member of the National Research Council's Board on Testing and Assessment, as chair of APA's Committee on Psychological Tests and Assessments, and as chair of APA's Board of Scientific Affairs. He is a fellow of Divisions 5 and 14, and serves on many editorial boards, including *Psychological Bulletin* and the *Journal of Applied Psychology*.

Jesus F. Salgado is Professor of Organizational Psychology in the Faculty of Psychology at the University of Santiago de Compostela, Spain. He has been a visiting fellow at the Goldsmiths College of the University of London. He has authored over 50 articles published in leading psychology and management journals, including *Academy of Management Journal, Applied Psychology, Human Performance, International Journal of Selection and Assessment, International Review of Industrial and Organizational Psychology, Journal of Applied Psychology,* and *Journal of Occupational and Organizational Psychology*. He also has authored two books *Comportamiento Organizational* (Organizational Behavior) and *Entrevista Conductual Estructurada* (Structured Behavioral Interview). His research is mainly on the criterion validity and the international validity generalization of personnel selection procedures.

Juan I. Sanchez earned his PhD in Industrial/Organizational Psychology from the University of South Florida, Tampa. He currently holds an appointment of Associate Professor of Psychology at Florida International University in Miami. He has 17 years of experience in job analysis, assessment development, employment interview, and validation services. He is a member of the American Psychological Association, the Society for Industrial and Organizational Psychology, and the Academy of Management. He has consulted with multiple organizations in the US, Latin America, and Europe. He has also consulted with government agencies such as the Federal Aviation Administration (FAA), the US Army, and the US Department of Labor. His research has been awarded by the International Personnel Management Association and the National Society for Performance and Instruction. He is currently a consulting editor of the leading journal in the field of industrial/ organizational psychology, the *Journal of Applied Psychology*, and has published in refereed journals such as the *Academy of Management Journal*, the *Academy of Management Executive*, the *Journal of Applied Psychology*, the *Journal of Organizational Behavior*, the *Journal of Occupational and Organizational Psychology, Group and Organization Management*, the *Journal of Vocational Behavior*, the *Journal of Applied Social Psychology*, the *Journal of Quality Management*, the *Journal of Business and Psychology, Educational and Psychological Measurement,* and *Human Resources Management Review*, among others. He is the author of a widely used measure of customer service skills commercialized by NCS/London House. Dr Sanchez occasionally serves as an expert witness in cases involving personnel selection and human resource assessment disputes.

Frank Schmidt (PhD, I/O psychology, Purdue 1970) is the Ralph L. Sheets Professor of Human Resources at the University of Iowa. He has published numerous articles on validity generalization and practical utility in personnel selection and general articles on quantitative research methods. He is co-author of a widely used text on meta-analysis and has authored numerous journal articles on meta-analysis. He has received distinguished scientific contributions awards (with John Hunter) from both the American Psychological Association and the Society for Industrial and Organizational Psychology.

Paul E. Spector is Professor of Industrial/Organizational (I/O) Psychology and Director of the I/O Doctoral Program at the University of South Florida. He has over 100 publications concerning both content and methodology in the field. He has conducted research on employees of hundreds of organizations worldwide. Professor Spector has also written three books on research methodology. His scientific writing has been recognized by the Institute for Scientific Information in their list of the top 50 psychology scholars (out of 102,000) worldwide. He currently holds two editorships for top journals of the field, the *Journal of Organizational Behavior* and the *Journal of Occupational and Organizational Behavior*, and he is on the editorial board of six other major scientific journals in the field, including *Journal of Applied Psychology* and *Journal of Management*.

James Steindl is a doctoral student in psychometrics and statistics at the University of Texas at Austin and a newly commissioned Ensign in the United States Navy. He is an Arab linguist as well as a psychometrician. His professional interests include individual differences, statistics, and personnel selection.

Sully Taylor, PhD, University of Washington, is an Associate Professor of International Management at Portland State University. She has conducted consulting, training or research with such organizations as Boeing, Dow Chemical, British Telecommunications, NEC, Mitsubishi, Tellabs, Fujitsu, and has received Fulbright research awards to Japan and to Chile. Her teaching and research interests are in international management, international human resource management, and global learning organizations. She is a member of the JAI *Advances in International Comparative Management* series editorial board, and is the program chair for the International Western Academy of Management meeting in Japan, 2000. She is the co-author (with Nancy Napier) of the book *Western Women Working in Japan: Breaking Corporate Barriers*, and her work has appeared in such outlets as *Academy of Management Review*, *Human Resource Management*, *Sloan Management Review*, *Advances in International Comparative Management*, and *Human Resource Planning*.

Toby D. Wall is a Professor of Occupational Psychology at the University of Sheffield, UK. He is Director of the University's Institute of Work Psychology and of the UK's Economic and Social Research Council's Centre for Organisation and Innovation. He received his PhD in psychology from the University of Nottingham. His current research interests encompass the effects of modern technologies, management practices and work organization on performance, strain and innovation. His research has appeared in the *Journal of Applied Psychology* as well as other leading journals. He is the author or editor of several books, including *The Human Side of Advanced Manufacturing Technology*.

Preface
Toward a Global Science of IWO Psychology

From scientific management to human relations movement, from cottage industries to craft guilds, from the industrial age to the informational society, the issues that have dominated the field of Industrial, Work and Organizational (IWO) Psychology have changed over the years. In the 21st century, IWO Psychology is becoming a global science and an arena for professional practice. In editing these two volumes, our objectives were (1) to cover recent research on work and organizational psychology by leading experts around the globe and (2) to develop a psychology of work principles that are applicable across international boundaries.

Volume 1 primarily focuses on individuals in organizations and covers personnel psychology issues. Volume 2 primarily covers organizational psychology topics that have a greater emphasis on the group, inter-group, and organizational level analyses. Both volumes include chapters on topic areas stipulated in the SIOP (Society for Industrial and Organizational Psychology), EAWOP (European Association for Work and Organizational Psychology), and Australian I/O psychology teaching syllabi, as well as topics commonly laid down by national bodies and associations in IWO Psychology.

It was our intention, as editors of this Handbook, to produce a globally contributed, globally oriented, and globally relevant collection of chapters which comprehensively covered the major topics comprising our field into the 21st Century. Such lofty ideals may well occur to the reader as having a somewhat grandiose flavor to them, so much so that in reality it is impossible to produce a truly 'global' treatise given such manifest cross-cultural, socio-economic, and historical differences. We were indeed highly conscious that this aim set our sights high, but we were equally determined not to allow a drift downward into parochial, single nation, local issues and perspectives to dominate this Handbook. The very title *Handbook of Industrial, Work and Organizational Psychology* reflects these aspirations on the part of the editors. Credit is due to our esteemed colleague Paul Sackett who proposed this internationally encompassing title for our field as a combination of Industrial–Organizational (I/O) Psychology in the USA, and Work and Organizational (W/O) Psychology in Europe and other countries worldwide. It is our sincere hope that IWO Psychology becomes the embracing, internationally recognized title for our field as it develops into a global arena for science and practice into the next millennium.

One important question that arises immediately from this simple issue over our choice of a title for these volumes is 'to what extent is IWO Psychology presently a global science and professional practice?'. As editors of this two-volume set, our view is that our field is fast becoming precisely this, a global science and practice. Let us consider the scientific and practitioner wings briefly in turn.

First, scientific findings in IWO Psychology generated predominantly in the USA have been increasingly subjected to validation in other countries around the world. No area has been more exposed to such a trend toward verification of the international validity generalization of American findings as that of recruitment and selection. Selection researchers in Europe, and elsewhere, have begun to suggest that results for certain effects found in the USA do indeed possess generalizability to other countries and cultures, countering earlier challenges that the science of IWO Psychology is merely an artifact of American culture rather than a truly global science.

Second, we have witnessed the emergence of an entirely new sub-discipline within IWO Psychology concerned exclusively with cross-national and international issues. The growth of international assignments, expatriate selection and management issues has further fueled this field, with organizations and scientists in IWO Psychology becoming concerned with cross-national moves, issues of leadership style, and re-acculturation in post-overseas assignment of personnel back into their countries of origin. These developments have shifted the perceptual, analytical, and disciplinary boundaries of IWO Psychology forever away from parochial, within-country studies; our zone of proximal development, so to speak, has been inexorably driven by these environmental changes toward international concerns and challenges.

With regard to the practice of IWO Psychology, alongside this diversification of scientific focus, simultaneous changes in the practice of organizational psychology have also taken on an increasingly multi-national shape and size. Several consultancies now boast a multi-national presence and practice with IWO Psychologists being moved between different country offices where and whenever appropriate. The largest consultancies, including Personnel Decisions International, SHL, SRA, Aon and Gallup have indeed possessed this global presence for some years now; the inevitable implication of which has been a move toward a more synonymous and standardized practice across rather than within countries. Whether there is yet a single, global market for IWO consultancy is a moot point; national and cultural differences clearly still play some part in the professional practice of our discipline. But what is inescapable is that the move toward global players on the practitioner wing of our discipline has resulted in significantly greater collaboration and sharing of expertise across countries in IWO Psychology.

In this two-volume series, we set out to summarize the major principles learnt over the years in IWO Psychology. The chapters are written by internationally eminent authors based in a variety of countries worldwide, including the USA, UK, Spain, Australia, Belgium, China, The Netherlands, Turkey, Italy, and Canada. This eclectic mix of countries of author origin was intentional on the part of the editors, in part to ensure a truly global set of contributions to this Handbook. This is especially the case at the organizational level of analysis, where the globalization of international business and work organizations has created strikingly similar issues to come to the fore in many countries worldwide over more recent years. To neglect these inescapable inter-linkages would be to neglect the globalization of business markets, and it is therefore entirely appropriate that IWO psychology embraces these trends and insurgent patterns.

The chapters in both volumes are geared to consolidate the research and theory on topics that IWO psychologists study, drawing upon research and practice across the globe, to build theory. The ideas presented herein, hopefully, reflect and satisfy the demands of an increasingly global science and practice of IWO Psychology in the 21st century.

Handan Kepir Sinangil, Istanbul
Deniz S. Ones, Minneapolis
Chockalingam Viswesvaran, Miami
Neil Anderson, London/Amsterdam

March, 2001

Acknowledgments

Co-editing a major, globally relevant *Handbook of Industrial, Work and Organizational Psychology* required much collaboration and effort from all of us. We also experienced, first hand, what is possible in working with a team whose members were on different continents, and from varied cultural backgrounds. First, and foremost thanks are due to each other for making this a fun team to be part of. We have provided each other intellectual challenges and social support through the past three years. We have been good for each other, and hopefully good for these volumes. The order of authorship listed for the two volumes (Anderson, Ones, Sinangil, and Viswesvaran) is alphabetical. We truly shared the work equally.

For the actualization of the Handbook with 43 chapters across 2 volumes, our gratitude goes to the 79 eminent authors across 14 countries. They accepted our invitation with enthusiasm, and devoted considerable amount of effort to this project. Not only did they produce outstanding chapters, but also were timely with their revisions.

The volume of administrative work on this undertaking turned out to be much greater than anticipated. In hindsight, working with individuals across 14 different time zones is not an easy task. Our support staff at the University of Minnesota's Psychology Department, where our Administrative Headquarters was located, were more helpful and important for this project than they will ever realize. We would like to express our gratitude to Jocelyn Wilson and Jeanette Shelton, who were our chief editorial assistants during 2000–2001 and 1999–2000, respectively. Their efficiency, professionalism, and enthusiasm made our editorial work a little easier and a little less distressing. During especially hectic times, Barbara Hamilton, Rachel Gamm and Jennifer Benka also lent helping hands and we are thankful for that. Partial financial support for the Handbook editorial office was provided by the Department of Psychology of the University of Minnesota, as well as the Hellervik Chair endowment.

We also would like to extend our sincerest thanks to the original commissioning editor of these volumes, Naomi Meredith and the SAGE (publishing) team. During the various phases of the Handbook, we relied on opinions of many colleagues and students at the University of Minnesota, Marmara University, Goldsmiths College, and Florida International University. The intellectual stimulation and care that they so freely gave proved to be invaluable.

Those closest to us, perhaps gave the most and suffered the greatest during the completion of this project. To them, we offer genuine apologies for the neglect they had to endure and for the encouragement, they, nonetheless, provided, while we labored long hours during nights and weekends. For this, Deniz would like to thank Ates Haner (my dear husband, and an extraordinarily wonderful man), Handan would like to thank Sinan Sinangil (my good friend and husband), and Vish would like to thank Saraswathy Viswesvaran (my invaluable wife and best friend).

It is our sincere hope that these two volumes prove useful to the field of IWO Psychology.

Deniz S. Ones
Handan Kepir Sinangil
Neil Anderson
Chockalingam (Vish) Viswesvaran

Where We Have Been, Where We Are, (and Where We Could Be)

CHOCKALINGAM VISWESVARAN,
HANDAN KEPIR SINANGIL
DENIZ S. ONES and NEIL ANDERSON

AN IWO PSYCHOLOGY ODYSSEY

Work – the expenditure of effort and energy to achieve a goal – has been around since the Big Bang. The celestial bodies worked their way to the present configuration. The molecules and atoms did work. As the first unicellular organisms appeared on the face of this planet, work was an essential component. As multicellular organisms evolved, the nature of work changed. Whereas work for the unicellular organisms like ameba consisted of the simplistic task of synthesizing material for survival, more complex differentiated functions had to be completed by the evolving multicellular organisms. As the thinking organism emerged underscoring the supremacy of the brain, apes and humans faced more complicated sequences of activities to accomplish their goals, but work as a concept has been around even before such complications arose.

Given the natural climate of the prehistoric days, humans found value in numbers. First, as families, then as tribes humans began to organize. The first *organizations* were more varied and were different from what we think of as organizations now, but they nevertheless were organizations. Those who studied behavior and prescribed interventions in such groups may not have been psychologists, but the chieftains, head priests and alpha males were nevertheless using psychological principles (perhaps ineffective sometimes) when they designed and led their groups. But as group-living in tribes became the norm, the nature of work for the survival of the group became too complicated for an individual.

Various forms of structure and parceling of work became necessary and were tried out. Perhaps the first job analytic techniques were invented then!

As the eons passed by, humans with their intellectual powers began to harness the raw and unabated fury of nature. As humans became more successful in surviving the vagaries of nature, they began to aggrandize. Perhaps some would argue that this aggrandizement was what enabled humans to survive natural disasters. Empires were born. The Roman Empire, the city states of Greece, the majestic ruins of Mohenjo-daro and Harappa in the Indus valley, the pyramids of Egypt, all attest to the glory of organizations.

Thus, organizations have also had a long and hoary history. The principles of structure, leadership theories, and motivational theories, may not have been known to the Roman, Ottoman and British generals in the form we see in textbooks today, but they nevertheless existed in some rudimentary form (George, 1972; Wren, 1994). In short, both *work and organizations* have been with us for a long time.

Human curiosity has propelled us to codify the principles that govern the behavior of organisms and movements of objects. The growth of sciences has been accelerating for the past eight centuries. At first, the growth was more pronounced in the physical and biological sciences. The knowledge about the principles of the atom, chemical properties of elements, movements of celestial bodies, and the functioning of biological organisms were codified. One can arguably state that by the middle of the nineteenth century, we started codifying the knowledge we had of human behavior. The observations of Darwin on emotions, the recording of individual differences by Galton and Cattell, and the laboratory work of Wundt and Tichner, started the science of psychology – broadly defined as the study of behavior.

The late nineteenth century and the early twentieth century saw the advent of the first big *industrial* organizations. In this arrangement, we had humans who spent time – a considerable part of the day – with other humans with whom they may have had no other contact outside of work. This impersonal nature of the relationships did not lessen the importance of what they did together in industrial organizations. The welfare of the society depended on the effective functioning of these industrial organizations. The quality of life of individuals also depended on it. Thus, there was an urgent need to study, understand, and prescribe how industrial work is to be effectively organized. Frederick Taylor investigated how to organize work in industries (Taylor, 1911). Stalwarts like Scott, Munsterberg, Bingham and Yerkes studied how to select individuals for the various jobs and motivate them to performance. Volumes have been written about Industrial, Work and Organizational (IWO) psychology since then. This is the first attempt to the editors' knowledge to produce a globally oriented, unifying Handbook covering our field.

In this two-volume series, our over-riding objective as editors was to ask internationally eminent authors to provide state-of-the-art summaries of their respective fields in terms of theory, research and practice, and thus to summarize the major principles learnt over the years in IWO psychology. There are three themes that resurface in multiple chapters of this Handbook: globalization, the scientist-practitioner model, and technological advances. We first elaborate on these three themes using specific examples of how the chapters in these volumes relate to these themes. Next, we provide an introduction to and overview of the chapters in this volume.

GLOBALIZATION

The principles of IWO psychology, like humans, have evolved with variations in different geographical regions that reflect the variations in local conditions. As long as the variations were localized and could not mix with the rest of the world, the variations were safe – all that mattered was that they fit with the local conditions. When the different variants came into contact, the survival of the fittest ensued.

In a similar vein, as the different organizations and organizing principles remained incommunicado, all that mattered was their fit to local conditions. The local tyrant king was safe as long as his subjects did not come to know of democratic societies (or no one envisioned such an organizational variant in their geographical area). But the technological advances of the recent years in transportation and communication have rendered such islands implausible (Toffler, 1981). Organizational principles from different parts of the world are coming into contact, clashing and commingling with preset principles (Hage, 1988). What we have had in the past few decades is a dynamic explosion of knowledge, which is probably likely to continue.

Against this background, we need to consider our knowledge of IWO psychology from a global perspective (see also Reich, 1991). With this in mind we have invited scholars from different countries to contribute chapters to this volume. Where possible we asked individuals from different cultural backgrounds to contribute to a topic. (We even asked some colleagues who did not know each other to collaborate on chapters.)

Globalization has also affected how work is accomplished in organizations. Economists conceptualize labor and capital as components of a production function, where the goal is to maximize the utility of the production function. With globalization, all components of the production function have become more mobile (Johnston & Packer, 1987). Organizations are attempting to exploit time zone differences across the world by moving work to different regions, so as to ensure continuous work. We have instances of software engineers working on a product in Bangalore, India who e-mail their work at the end of their workday to San Francisco where their colleagues are just coming in to work (Cascio, 1995).

Another characteristic feature of globalization for IWO psychology is the necessity of incorporating workplace diversity in our traditional functions. Many areas of IWO psychology are touched by diversity concerns. Conflict resolution skills are becoming more paramount (Olson-Buchanan, Drasgow, Moberg, Mean, Keenan & Donovan, 1998). Arguments have been made that organizations should value diversity in their selection (Murphy, in press) practices. Researchers have documented cultural differences in acceptance of teamwork (Kirkman & Shapiro, 1997). Compensation practices must take into account the different valences that individuals from different demographic groups have for the various rewards. Differences in reward allocation preferences have been noted between American and Chinese employees (Chen, 1995; Kim, Park & Suzuki, 1990). The aging workforces in some countries (Kim & Feldman, 2000) also underscores the need to revisit our intervention techniques.

SCIENTIST–PRACTITIONER MODEL

IWO psychology has been an applied endeavor for most of its recorded history. The problems faced by industrial organizations in the management of work have been the focus in IWO psychology, and most of our interventions have been based on scientific testing, experimentation and study. The dichotomy and the resulting acrimony found with our clinical counterparts have not affected us to the same degree (Raimy, 1950; Rice, 1997). In fact, Kehoe (2000) argues that as far as personnel selection is concerned both research and practice share the same governing principles and professional identity. The presence and emergence of global consulting firms in the last two decades also reflects this healthy integration of theory and practice in IWO psychology.

Nevertheless, concerns continue to be expressed over the apparent growing disparity between research and practice in some areas of IWO psychology (e.g., Anderson, Herriot & Hodgkinson, in press; Sackett, 1994). But such concerns are not new. In Dunnette's seminal *Handbook of Industrial and Organizational Psychology* published almost exactly 25 years ago (Dunnette, 1976), it is intriguing to note that precisely the same theme was addressed in his editorial introduction chapter (as indeed was also the case in the Dunnette & Hough, 1991 four-volume successor handbook). Dunnette foresaw the scientist–practitioner model as we would now refer to it some two decades later. Emphasizing the benefits to be gained by both wings of our discipline working in synergy, he professed a cautiously optimistic future:

> I believe that success for the field … is just around the corner. Industrial and Organizational Psychology is today an academic discipline, an emerging blend of research, theory, and practice. The blend offers great promise, in the years ahead, for further developing and extending our knowledge of those behavioral processes which are critical to an understanding of interactions between persons and the institutions and organizations of society.
>
> (Dunnette, 1976, pp. 11–12)

IWO psychology has come a long way since these comments 25 years ago; the 'great promise' of blending practice and science has to a great extent been realized. Our sincere hope is that this current two-volume set provides the reader with a timely overview of our field, whether approaching this from the basis of being a practitioner, an established researcher, or a student new to this burgeoning field of inquiry into human behavior in the workplace.

ROLE OF TECHNOLOGY

The third main characteristic theme of these volumes is the increasing role of technology in the design, execution and evaluation of work. IWO principles and practices are affected by technology (Howard, 1995). Some have argued that changes in

technology have rendered questionable the concept of jobs (Bridges, 1994; Pearlman, 1995). A new employee is emerging in the networked organization with distinctly different psychological contracts from the employee of the previous generations (Munk, 1998). Recruitment trends are changing (cf. Rynes, Orlitzky and Bretz, 1997).

Technology has moved the emphasis from brawn to brain. The role of cognitive ability has increased, and in fact the complexity of modern work is such that teams of specialists are sometimes needed to get the project completed. Despite some concerns about routinization and job simplification due to automation, the expectations of Babbage and Taylor have not been realized. What we have is more challenging and cognitively complex work (Ackerman, 1992). Technology has reduced geographical boundaries and the advances in communications technology have resulted in truly global work. Technology has also raised the concerns for an ecologically embedded IWO psychology (Whiteman & Cooper, 2000). Many chapters in these volumes illustrate the roles of technology and complexity in reshaping work behavior.

PREAMBLE TO VOLUME 1

In this, the first volume of the *Handbook of Industrial, Work and Organizational Psychology*, the focus is mainly on personnel psychology and more individual levels of analysis. The 20 chapters in this volume can be broadly classified into three groups. The first group consists of Chapters 1–3 with focus on research methods, data collection, data analysis, and interpretation of results. The second group, which makes up the largest part of this volume (Chapters 4–17), focuses on the various functions of IWO psychology. The last three chapters focus on the impact of globalization in IWO psychology.

The 20 chapters in this volume cover a diversity of topics, including methodology, measurement, job analysis, work design, job performance, selection, training, development, and cross-cultural issues. The chapters are written by authors based in a variety of countries worldwide including the USA, UK, Sweden, Spain, Turkey, Canada, The Netherlands, and Belgium.

In addition to the main themes involving globalization, and expanding technologies, the chapters of this volume also relate to themes of building theory, integration of various traditional functions, and consequences of expanding the criterion domain.

Traditional mainstays of IWO psychology have started to change in the global environment. Job analysis has to take into account technical as well as temperamental characteristics essential for success (Raymark, Schmit & Guion, 1997). Work design must accommodate the flextime and flexspace (i.e., telecommuting) workers (Dannhauser, 1988). Performance assessment has to incorporate not only task specific performance but also contextual performance (Borman & Motowidlo, 1993) and counterproductive behaviors (Ones, Viswesvaran & Schmidt, 1993; Sanchez, Williams & Viswesvaran, 2000).

There was a time when IWO psychology was more tuned to prediction than explanation of the process mechanisms by which our interventions achieve their utility. As a science matures, professionals in that field (both scientist and practitioner), more confident of their place in the pantheon of sciences, move beyond the need to establish the utility of their science to understanding the principles that guide their work (Landy, 1986; Schmidt & Kaplan, 1971). IWO psychology is no exception. At first, professionals were more concerned with demonstrating the utility of what they did. Once effectiveness had been demonstrated, researchers (e.g., Schmidt & Hunter, 1992) attempted to develop explanatory models of how and why.

A similar trend can be seen in all sub-areas of IWO psychology. In this volume, Parker and Wall present theories of organizations (e.g., sociotechnical systems) to guide work design. Sackett and DeVore integrate diverse streams of literature in explicating the counterproductivity domain of job performance. Salgado, Viswesvaran and Ones review several path models examining how the various predictors contribute to individual job performance. Anderson, Born, and Cunningham-Snell integrate the empirical findings on personnel selection from an applicant's perspective, and conclude by proposing a general model of applicant decision-making in selection upon which future research can be based and derived. Ree, Carretta and Steindl review the theoretical basis of one of the best predictors (Schmidt & Hunter, 1998) of personnel selection – general mental ability – whereas Hough and Ones present a comprehensive review of the theoretical underpinnings of the use of personality in IWO psychology.

The search for underlying theory and explication of process and causal mechanisms has spawned two characteristic trends in the last two decades. First, researchers have stressed the need to clearly distinguish between the different levels of analyses (Klein, Dansereau & Hall, 1994). The constructs used and conclusions derived from one level, say the individual level, may or may not hold at different levels, say team or organizational or industry level. Different composition models may hold and different analytic strategies are needed (Jones & Lindley, 1988). Aguinis, Henle and Ostroff summarize the issues involved here, and Spector provides an introduction to hierarchical linear regression in his chapter. All authors are cognizant of this issue in their chapters. For example, Fletcher and Perry stress the importance of performance assessment at

the group level and Salgado et al., cover the issues in team selection. Team selection has been a hot topic (Barry & Stewart, 1997; Campion, Medsker & Higgs, 1993; Stevens & Campion, 1994) and promises to continue to be one for the next couple of decades.

Related to the levels of analysis issue is the need to expand the criterion domain. This theme is also evident in many chapters. Parker and Wall stress the need to expand our research beyond the motivational effects of work design. The notion that cognitive ability predicts task performance, whereas personality constructs predict contextual performance, has gained currency in personnel selection (Guion, 1998). Fletcher and Perry underscore the need to consider the relationships between individual job performance and team or organizational performance. To some extent, IWO psychologists have attempted to link individual job performance to organizational level outcomes (Terpstra & Rozell, 1993), and Roth, Bobko and Mabon do an excellent job of summarizing this literature on utility estimation. Sackett and DeVore address the link between organizational behavior and misbehavior. Nyssen and DeKeyser as well as Oborne and Arnold expand our focus to an investigation of errors in work performance.

The chapters in this volume also reflect the role of technology in the science and practice of IWO psychology. Spector as well as Aguinis et al., present the issues involved in using the Internet in data collection. The use of technology to collect job analytic data as well as performance data is summarized in the respective chapters by Sanchez and Levine, and Fletcher and Perry. The use of virtual reality technology in personnel selection is described in Salgado et al. The dark side of technology for IWO psychology is underscored to emphasize the need for adequate precautions in the chapters on error analysis by Nysson and DeKeyser, and Oborne and Arnold. Campbell and Kuncel take a more positive view of technology and suggest that technology will facilitate the optimal aptitude by treatment interaction for training program designs. It is clear that technology is bound to play a major role in how work is done in organizations, and how the science and practice of IWO psychology is affected. Recruitment, selection, socialization, work processes, performance appraisal, and training will be affected, and we are as everyone else curious and excited about what the future will bring. Hopefully, the authors have sketched some interesting scenarios for all of us to ponder.

STRUCTURE OF THIS VOLUME

Research methods define what we do as professionals (Scandura & Williams, 2000). Spector, in the first chapter in the volume, provides an excellent summary of the rationale for, and succinct descriptions of, the common tools used by IWO psychologists. He stresses how IWO professionals have to balance the rigor of research and ethical concerns, given that our laboratory setting is more often the field where control is harder to achieve. The readers will glean invaluable insights on appropriate data collection strategies in our field. In an interesting comparison of trends in two main journals in IWO psychology (*Journal of Organizational and Occupational Psychology, JOOP* and *Journal of Applied Psychology, JAP*), Spector notes that: (1) *JAP* publishes almost one third of its research with student samples, whereas *JOOP* is almost exclusive in its investigation of employees and applicants, and (2) more importantly, 82% of the samples in *JAP* articles have used American samples, whereas the samples used in *JOOP* articles have tended to be more globally diverse. Further, it is heartening to note how over the past two decades IWO psychologists have replicated some of the earlier substantive conclusions (e.g., antecedents of commitment) in increasingly multivariate designs. Spector concludes with a review of techniques for assessing measurement equivalence in cross-cultural research.

Aguinis, Henle and Ostroff continue the topic of measurement equivalence in cross-cultural research in Chapter 2, and provide a succinct summary of psychological measurement. They discuss the steps of defining the purpose of measurement, clarifying the attributes to be measured, developing a measurement plan, creating items, conducting item analysis, establishing norms, and assessing the reliability and validity of the measures. An easily accessible but a comprehensive overview of the issues is provided. The authors stress the importance of the different types of reliability coefficients and their appropriate use (Guilford, 1954; Schmidt & Hunter, 1996; Schmidt, Viswesvaran & Ones, 2000; Viswesvaran, Ones & Schmidt, 1996), and also cover the important issue of how the level of analysis should be kept in mind for both data collection as well as data analysis. Finally, they compare the recent literature in measurement-oriented journals such as *Educational and Psychological Measurement* (*EPM*) and *Applied Psychological Measurement* (*APM*), and find a healthy increase in research on assessing cross-cultural equivalence of measures. Truly, our field has come a long way in assessing the applicability of constructs and measures across cultures.

Data collection with various research designs and different analytic techniques are designed to yield substantive information about the science and practice of IWO psychology. However, data comes encrypted (Hunter & Schmidt, 1990; Schmidt, 1992) and the information yield in many studies is low owing to the small sample sizes. In many studies, the nature of the subject is such that large samples are unavailable. The techniques of meta-analysis can help us correct for bias in research findings, cumulate results across several research studies, and interpret broad patterns of covariations between the different constructs. Meta-analysis has generated a paradigm shift in personnel selection as well as in different subareas of IWO psychology.

Schmidt and Hunter in Chapter 3 note how traditional significance testing has resulted in an illusion of conflicting findings. They explode the myth of the perfect study and suggest how meta-analyses can be used to establish the empirical relations between constructs that then need to be explained by theory. The necessity of meta-analysis becomes more apparent as we move from simple questions of whether there is a relationship between two variables (or an effect) (the null hypothesis in traditional significance testing) to an accurate estimation of the effect size (for theory development and for testing alternate theories). The statistical power requirement for accurate parameter estimation necessitates the use of very large samples. This chapter provides a useful guide to the methods of meta-analysis.

The next 14 chapters focus on the traditional functions in IWO psychology. In Chapter 4, Sanchez and Levine summarize the current thinking in job analytic approaches. They argue for an emphasis on work analysis instead of the more narrow focus on the job. Taxonomies of job classifications are reviewed. Methods of data collection, sources of data, and types of data that need to be collected are discussed. The authors highlight the need for strategic job analysis that incorporates the rapid technological changes occurring in the workplace. The need to broaden our analyses to identify not only ability requirements but also personality requirements for contextual performance is noted.

Parker and Wall continue the discussion on work design in Chapter 5, and describe how work design principles have evolved from an exclusive focus on job simplification in the days of Taylor, Smith and Babbage to the integrated approaches that take into account ergonomic, biological and motivational concepts in the design of work. They call for an expansion of the set of antecedents examined, to include contextual factors such as supervisory style and uncertainty in the environment, and also for an increasing focus to be placed on outcomes other than motivational concepts. The need to explore outcomes of work design on learning and individual development, as well as stressors, is underscored. Finally, they also point to the importance of contingencies and call for research into understanding the meaning of work (i.e., alternatives to positivistic analysis of work). This call for a phenomenological approach to understanding work is also noted by Sanchez and Levine when they state that job analytic tools are predominantly rationalistic in the US, whereas the tools are more eclectic globally (e.g., phenomenological prism in Sweden).

Individual job performance is a central construct in IWO psychology. Chapters 6, 7, and 8 focus on this construct and its measurement. Viswesvaran provides a concise and thorough review of the different models of job performance dimensions, and methods used to measure performance. An overview of the psychometric quality of performance assessments as found in the extant literature is also provided. Viswesvaran notes how the different measures used to assess individual job performance can be conceptualized as a hierarchy, with a general factor at the apex of a three level hierarchy with group and specific factors comprising the second and third lower levels. The different models of job performance differ in the number and breadth of the group factors at the second level.

Fletcher and Perry do an outstanding job of discussing the issues, both measurement and social factors, which influence performance appraisal in work organizations. They invoke the cultural dimensions of power distance and individualism–collectivism in which national differences have been noted, to develop some propositions about the factors influencing performance appraisal in different countries. Specifically, they argue that differences in power distance and individualism and collectivism will be reflected in differences in who appraises (e.g., multi-source feedback is more likely in low power distance cultures), the style and process of appraisal (e.g., appeals are more likely in low power cultures), content of evaluation (e.g., more task oriented in high power distance cultures, more positive feedback in collectivist cultures), and purpose of appraisal (e.g., less emphasis on individual merit pay in collectivistic cultures). They note how increasing globalization could bring charges of national discrimination, and how the rapidly evolving technology could change the content of performance appraisals (e.g., electronic monitoring of performance).

Sackett and DeVore complete the triad of chapters on job performance assessment. They direct attention to a growing body of literature that focuses on organizational misbehavior (i.e., counterproductivity). This chapter is a timely summary of a burgeoning area. The authors argue that counterproductive behaviors are distinct from both task and contextual performance (Borman & Motowidlo, 1993). They summarize both situational and individual differences variables that influence counterproductive behaviors. The emerging technology and globalization of business with its attendant increase in autonomy and telecommuting are probably likely to see an increase in the study of counterproductive behaviors in the coming decades.

Salgado, Viswesvaran and Ones review the available selection techniques in Chapter 9. Results from the first validity generalization studies outside of the US are presented. The authors discuss the prevalence, measurement and construct validity issues, criterion-related validity, incremental validity, and group differences for each of the predictors. Cognitive ability, physical and perceptual abilities, personality, interviews, assessment centers, biodata, are some of the predictors discussed. Issues in team selection, combining predictors, and societal issues pertaining to selection are highlighted. The role of technology in developing new predictors is also reviewed.

In Chapter 10 Anderson, Born and Cunningham-Snell summarize the findings on personnel selection from an applicant's perspective, and review five different models of applicant decision making (rational–economic, rational–psychological, person–organization fit, individual differences, and negotiation process models), as the basis for developing their 'general model' of applicant decision making in selection. They call for a renewed interest in underlying theory stating that 'selection involves more than merely predicting in statistical terms the suitability of an individual for a job', and invoke attribution theory, primarily used to explain empirical findings with the employment interview, to study the findings pertaining to tests, personality and work sample testing. The possible impact of culture on justice perceptions, as well as the potential for interaction between procedural and distributive justice concepts, are delineated again from the applicant's perspective in terms of applicant decision making in the selection process.

Ree, Carretta and Steindl (Chapter 11) provide an authoritative summary of the research on general mental ability (cognitive ability). They note how the importance of cognitive abilities was stressed even in the days of Aristotle, Descartes, and several other thinkers. For example, Descartes defined humans by their ability to think (I think, therefore I am). The authors summarize the different models of cognitive ability and conclude that there is overwhelming evidence for a hierarchical model with a general factor at the apex. Several physiological and behavioral correlates of cognitive ability are presented and the importance of this construct for work settings is discussed.

Although IWO psychologists have generally accepted that cognitive ability has high predictive validity (Schmidt & Hunter, 1998), concerns have been expressed in both the USA (e.g., Murphy, 1989) and Europe (e.g., Herriot & Anderson, 1997) that a large portion of variance in individual job performance remains unexplained by cognitive ability. Researchers have used personality variables in explaining organizational behavior (Barrick & Mount, 1991; Salgado, 1997). Hough and Ones, prominent among researchers in this area, summarize the exciting resurgence of personality assessment in IWO psychology in Chapter 12. They stress the importance of a construct oriented approach to the study of personality in IWO psychology, and address several methodological concerns such as the use of ipsative measurement, strategies to mitigate faking, and the effects of social desirability in personality assessment. They also offer an overview of the influence of personality on career and occupational choice, organizational choice, training, satisfaction, leadership, and occupational health and safety. They conclude that research on the role of personality in work behavior should include, but not be limited to, personnel selection.

In Chapter 13 Campbell and Kuncel discuss the critical training needs for the new millennium. The rapidly evolving technology implies that continuous training is needed for all employees. The resulting stress, uncertainty and challenges have to be addressed. On the positive side, the authors note how emerging technology can also result in optimally designed training programs that are tailored to individual needs, and they envision the realization of the optimal aptitude by treatment interaction. They express the view that: 'Multimedia intelligent tutoring systems could customize the training experience down to virtually the optimal level'. Three paths by which training is linked to organizational effectiveness are noted. After discussing the universals in training design (needs assessment, specifying content, instructional methods), the authors address the factors influencing the optimality of training interventions (goal difficulty, goal specificity, feedback, practice, etc.). Issues in transfer of training as well as specific topics such as cross-cultural training, leadership training, are considered. This chapter is indeed a tour de force in summarizing the extant training research.

Continuing this topic of individual development is a thorough chapter by McCauley and Hezlett (Chapter 14). The authors posit three approaches to understanding individual development: behavioral change, self-centered learning, and adult development. They review the literature on six popular practices (360-degree feedback, executive coaching, developmental assignments, action learning, social support for learning, and communities of practice). Recent technological and societal changes have transferred the locus of development from the organization to the individual. The authors stress that individual development is not limited to improved task performance but also encompasses relational skills. They note the differences between individual development and training as well as career development, and conclude by identifying five factors critical for individual development. Their discussion of the issues is thought provoking and truly innovative. The chapter makes informative reading and the reader is likely to glean invaluable insights from the authors' review.

The topic of human-machine interaction is covered in Chapter 15. The rapid changes in technology and the ever increasing complexity of the tools render this a timely topic. Oborne and Arnold stress the centrality of the human in the interaction. According to the authors: 'Rather than concentrating simply on ways of improving the information flow between components within the system, person-centered ergonomics takes as its central point the need to accommodate the human attributes that the person brings to the system'. This emphasis on the person is also reflected in the writings of Toffler (1981) on the cravings of society for human touch in the new technologies. The authors vividly show the implications of human purposivity, likes/dislikes, and communication limits, on this interaction. IWO psychology is likely to spend more resources in this area in the coming decades.

The role of error prevention tools in IWO psychology is elaborated in Chapter 16 by Nyssen and De Keyser. The authors invoke the Russian Activity Theory to identify six principles that could be used in work design. Different ways of classifying errors (slots that ignore cognitive processes, classifications based on mental actions, etc.) are presented. They discuss the different error reporting systems, training simulators and operator aids that could be pressed into service here, and stress the need to integrate these design features with other human resource interventions, such as work design, selection, training and performance appraisal. Excellent illustrations have been provided by the authors. The chapter concludes with potent suggestions for improvements to research in this area.

The globalization of IWO psychology and emerging technological uncertainties have reduced the error margin for organizations. IWO psychologists are called upon to document the value of their interventions. Utility analysis has been a useful framework to study the cost–benefit tradeoffs of different options. Roth, Bobko and Mabon present, in Chapter 17, the historical development of utility analysis in IWO psychology. Their chapter reflects an international collaboration that is a hallmark of this Handbook. They discuss the potential for multiattribute models of utility. Different methods of estimating individual variability in performance (both inter- and intra-individual variability) are summarized. Several measurement issues as well as user reactions to the presentation of utility data are presented. The authors also stress the inevitable interactions between the different interventions and the futility of trying to tease out independent effects.

The last three chapters of this volume take a global perspective on IWO psychology. Aycan and Kanungo provide an integrated future-oriented framework to understand how socio-cultural context influences organizational phenomena. They argue that in addition to examining the unilateral effects of culture on organizations, we should also explore the effects of industrialization on culture.

This is akin to what Hage (1988) calls the effects of the post industrial organization on societal values. Aycan and Kanungo argue that the logic of industrialization can affect social structures.

Bauer and Taylor focus on how organizations can foster organizational identification and unique organizational values in an era of globalization. Organizational socialization is a process by which newcomers to an organization learn about the organization's values and develop a common identity with other employees in that organization. The empirical literature to guide organizations in this endeavor is scant; most of the socialization research is within-country research. The authors present several propositions, which future research needs to explore. They adopt a cautiously critical approach to reviewing the whole gamut of the extant literature. The next few decades may see advances in this area of IWO psychology. In this chapter Bauer and Taylor have laid the foundation for many new research streams.

Finally, in the last chapter of this volume Sinangil and Ones address the issue of expatriate management with aplomb. The logic of globalization necessitates the need for expatriates. Issues in adjustment to new cultures, work–family conflicts, and personality characteristics of successful expatriates, as well as the training needed for expatriates, are discussed.

CONCLUDING THOUGHTS

Personnel psychology has evolved greatly over the past few decades. We have come a long way. The changing nature of work (Howard, 1995) is perhaps a reflection of our history as a species. In our odyssey as a science, several exciting turns are ahead and we hope this volume captures some of the excitement in our field.

REFERENCES

Ackerman, P.L. (1992). Predicting individual differences in complex skill acquisition: Dynamics of ability determinants. *Journal of Applied Psychology, 77*, 598–614.

Anderson, N., Herriot, P., & Hodgkinson, G. (in press). The practitioner–researcher divide in Industrial, Work and Organizational psychology: Where are we now and where do we go from here. *Journal of Occupational and Organizational Psychology.*

Barrick, M.R., & Mount, M.K. (1991). The Big Five personality dimensions and job performance: A meta-analysis. *Personnel Psychology, 44*, 1–26.

Barry, B., & Stewart, G.L. (1997). Composition, process, and performance in self-managed groups: The role of personality. *Journal of Applied Psychology, 82*, 62–78.

Borman, W.C., & Motowidlo, S.J. (1993). Expanding the criterion domain to include elements of contextual performance. In W.C. Borman, & N. Schmitt (Eds), *Personnel selection in organizations* (pp. 71–98). San Francisco: Jossey Bass.

Bridges, W. (1994). *Job shift: How to prosper in a world without jobs.* Reading, MA: Addison-Wesley.

Campion, M.A., Medsker, G.J., & Higgs, A.C. (1993). Relations between work group characteristics and effectiveness: Implications for designing effective work groups. *Personnel Psychology, 46*, 823–850.

Cascio, W.F. (1995). Whither industrial and organizational psychology in a changing world of work? *American Psychologist, 50*, 928–939.

Chen, C.C. (1995). New trends in reward allocation preferences: A Sino-US Comparison. *Academy of Management Journal, 38*, 408–428.

Dannhauser, C.A.L. (1988, November). The invisible worker. *Working Woman*, p. 38.

Dunnette, M.D. (1966). Fads, fashions, and folderol in psychology. *American Psychologist, 21*, 343–352.

Dunnette, M.D. (1976). *Handbook of industrial and organizational psychology.* Chicago: Rand McNally.

Dunnette, M.D., & Hough, L.M. (Eds) (1991). *Handbook of industrial and organizational psychology* (2nd ed.). Palo Alto, CA: Consulting Psychologists Press.

George, C. (1972). *History of management thought* (2nd ed.). Englewood Cliffs, NJ: Prentice-Hall.

Guilford, J.P. (1954). *Psychometric methods* (2nd ed.). New York: McGraw-Hill.

Guion, R.M. (1998). *Assessment, measurement, and prediction for personnel decisions.* Malawah, NJ: Lawrence Erlbaum Associates.

Hage, J. (1988). *The future of organizations.* Lexington, MA: Heath.

Herriot, P., & Anderson, N. (1997). Selecting for change: How will personnel and selection psychology survive?, in N. Anderson, & P. Herriot (Eds.), *International Handbook of Selection and Assessment* (pp. 1–38), West Sussex, UK: Wiley.

Howard, A. (Ed.) (1995). *The changing nature of work.* San Francisco, CA: Jossey-Bass.

Hunter, J.E., & Schmidt, F.L. (1990). *Methods of meta-analysis: Correcting for error and bias in research findings.* Newbury Park, CA: Sage.

Johnston, W.B., & Packer, A.E. (1987). *Workforce 2000.* Indianapolis: Hudson Institute.

Jones, R.G., & Lindley, W.R. (1988). Issues in the transition to teams. *Journal of Business and Psychology, 13*, 31–40.

Kehoe, J.F. (2000). Research and practice in personnel selection. In J.F. Kehoe (Ed.), *Managing selection in changing organizations* (pp. 397–437). San Francisco, CA: Jossey-Bass.

Kim, S., & Feldman, D.C. (2000). Working in retirement: The antecedents of bridge employment and its consequences for quality of life in retirement. *Academy of Management Journal, 43*, 1195–1210.

Kim, K.I., Park, H., & Suzuki, N. (1990). Reward allocation in the United States, Japan, and Korea: A comparison of individualistic and collectivistic cultures. *Academy of Management Journal, 33,* 188–198.

Kirkman, B.L., & Shapiro, D.L. (1997). The impact of cultural values on employee resistance to teams: Toward a model of globalized self-managing work team effectiveness. *Academy of Management Review, 22,* 730–757.

Klein, K.J., Dansereau, F., & Hall, R.J. (1994). Levels issues in theory development, data collection, and analysis. *Academy of Management Review, 19,* 195–229.

Landy, F.J. (1986). Stamp collecting versus science: Validation as hypothesis testing. *American Psychologist, 41,* 1183–1192.

Munk, N. (1998, March, 16). The new organization man. *Fortune,* pp. 63–74.

Murphy, K.R. (1989). Is the relationship between cognitive ability and job performance stable over time? *Human Performance, 2(3),* 183–200.

Murphy, K.R. (in press). Can conflicting perspectives on the role of g in personnel selection be resolved? *Human Performance.*

Olson-Buchanan, J.B., Drasgow, F., Moberg, P.J., Mean, A.D., Keenan, P.A., & Donovan, M.A. (1998). Interactive video assessment of conflict resolution skills. *Personnel Psychology, 51,* 1–24.

Ones, D.S., Viswesvaran, C., & Schmidt, F.L. (1993). Comprehensive meta-analysis of integrity test validities: Findings and implications for personnel selection and theories of job performance [Monograph]. *Journal of Applied Psychology, 78,* 679–703.

Pearlman, K. (1995, May). Is Job dead? Implications of changing concepts of work for I/O Science and practice. Panel discussion conducted at the tenth annual conference of the Society for Industrial and Organizational Psychology, Orlando, FL.

Raimy, V. (Ed.) (1950). *Training in clinical psychology.* Upper Saddle River, NJ: Prentice-Hall.

Raymark, P.H., Schmit, M.J., & Guion, R.M. (1997). Identifying potentially useful personality constructs for employee selection. *Personnel Psychology, 50,* 723–736.

Reich, R.B. (1991). *The work of nations: Preparing ourselves for the 21st century capitalism.* New York: Knopf.

Rice, C.E. (1997). Scenarios: The scientist–practitioner split and the future of psychology. *American Psychologist, 52,* 1173–1181.

Rynes, S.L., Orlitzky, M.O., & Bretz, R.D., Jr. (1997). Experienced hiring versus college recruiting: Practices and emerging trends. *Personnel Psychology, 50,* 309–339.

Sackett, P.R. (1994). The content and process of the research enterprise within industrial and organizational psychology. Presidential address to the Society for Industrial and Organizational Psychology conference, Nashville, TN, April 1994.

Salgado, J.F. (1997). The Five Factor Model of personality and job performance in the European Community. *Journal of Applied Psychology, 82,* 30–43.

Sanchez, J.I., Williams, M., & Viswesvaran, C. (2000 April). What separates contextual from task performance in customer service jobs? In C. Viswesvaran (Chair), *Expanding the role of personality in explaining organizational behavior: New Horizons.* Symposium conducted at the 15th Annual Conference of SIOP, New Orleans, LA.

Scandura, T.A., & Williams, E.A. (2000). Research methodology in management: Current practices, trends, and implications for future research. *Academy of Management Journal, 43,* 1248–1264.

Schmidt, F.L. (1992). What do data really mean? Research findings, meta-analysis, and cumulative knowledge in the social sciences. *American Psychologist, 47,* 1173–1181.

Schmidt, F.L., & Hunter, J.E. (1992). Development of a causal model of processes determining job performance. *Current Directions in Psychological Science, 1,* 89–92.

Schmidt, F.L., & Hunter, J.E. (1996). Measurement error in psychological research: Lessons from 26 research scenarios. *Psychological Methods, 1,* 199–223.

Schmidt, F.L., & Hunter, J.E. (1998). The validity and utility of selection methods in personnel psychology: practical and theoretical implications of 85 years of research findings. *Psychological Bulletin, 124,* 262–274.

Schmidt, F.L., & Kaplan, L.B. (1971). Composite versus multiple criteria: A review and resolution of the controversy. *Personnel Psychology, 24,* 419–434.

Schmidt, F.L., Viswesvaran, C., & Ones, D.S. (2000). Reliability is not validity and validity is not reliability. *Personnel Psychology, 53,* 901–912.

Stevens, M.J., & Campion, M.A. (1994). The knowledge, skill, and ability requirements for teamwork: Implications for human resource management. *Journal of Management, 20,* 503–530.

Taylor, F.W. (1911). *Principles of scientific management.* New York: Harper.

Terpstra, D.E., & Rozell, E.J. (1993). The relationship of staffing practices to organizational level measures of performance. *Personnel Psychology, 46,* 27–48.

Toffler, A. (1981). *The third wave.* New York: Bantam Books.

Viswesvaran, C., Ones, D.S., & Schmidt, F.L. (1996). Comparative analysis of the reliability of job performance ratings. *Journal of Applied Psychology, 81,* 557–574.

Whiteman, G., & Cooper, W.H. (2000). Ecological embeddedness. *Academy of Management Journal, 43,* 1265–1282.

Wren, D. (1994). *The evolution of management thought.* New York: Wiley.

1

Research Methods in Industrial and Organizational Psychology: Data Collection and Data Analysis with Special Consideration to International Issues

PAUL E. SPECTOR

This chapter covers research methods in industrial/organizational psychology focusing primarily on data collection and data analysis. The first section discusses various research designs including quasi-experimental, cross-sectional, longitudinal, observational, and survey designs. Internal validity and issues concerning causal conclusions are included. The second section covers both new and popular statistical methods for data analysis. This includes multiple regression, logistic regression, analysis of variance, factor analysis, structural equation modeling, hierarchical linear modeling, and item response theory. Issues concerning appropriate use of statistical controls are discussed. The third section is concerned with special challenges in conducting international research, especially with samples of people who speak different languages. The last section offers the advice for sound methodological practice from the American Psychological Association's committee on significance testing: Report complete statistical results, avoid premature theory, practice statistical parsimony (use the simplest statistical method that accomplishes the objective), and use only those methods you fully understand.

The nature of the industrial/organizational (I/O) psychology field produces significant challenges to the conduct of research. First, as a field concerned with the study of human behavior, we share with other areas of psychology the ethical and practical issues that provide barriers to the sorts of research we can conduct on human beings. Second, as an applied field concerned with the workplace, accessibility problems further limit the research methods that can be used. Combined, both aspects of I/O psychology make doing research extremely challenging, as we are rarely in a position to conduct the sort of research we would like to conduct in the places

we would like to be. Compromises must be made at every turn, which necessitates the strong focus our field places on issues of methodology. We must be flexible and ready to apply a variety of data collection and analysis approaches to the problems we wish to address, as we must take advantage of opportunities that are presented.

In this chapter I will cover some basic issues of research methodology in I/O psychology. I will cover both data collection (research design) and analysis (statistics). A short chapter such as this cannot be more than a general overview of methodology, so I offer some suggested sources for further details. In particular this chapter will look at current trends in methodology, and current practices seen in the major I/O journals. Furthermore, given the international focus of this book, particular attention will be given to issues specific to cross-national research.

DATA COLLECTION

As an empirical/scientific field, the basis of I/O inquiry is data derived from systematic data collection procedures. Such procedures include the instrumentation and operationalization of variables, as well as the design or structure of data collection. The data collection approach is determined by a combination of the researcher's purpose, and practical limitations in potential research settings available. Each study is very much a compromise between what should be done from a scientific perspective to address the question of interest, and what can be done from an ethical and practical standpoint. I/O psychology is a quantitative science, and most of our research follows in this tradition. Recent advances in qualitative methods (Cassell & Symon, 1994) have seen only occasional use in our field to date, but can be found more often in other social sciences. Furthermore, I/O psychologists typically use such methods for data collection, and then apply procedures to quantify qualitative observations.

Descriptive Versus Hypothesis-Testing Research

A good study is based firmly on an explicit purpose or research question. The question is most typically an explicit statement of relations among two or more variables, such as 'what's the relation between job satisfaction and job performance?', or 'does working overtime lead to physical illness?' Of course, with most published research, questions are typically more complex and involve more than two variables. It is possible to raise a purely descriptive question, such as 'how many physicians working for a health maintenance organization like their jobs?' Often such questions can be important, but are far more likely to be encountered in applied work than in published research that demands more complex and theoretically based questions.

Often research studies are designed to test specific hypotheses that are derived from prior research and theory. Such hypotheses are statements about the expected outcomes of studies in terms of relations among variables, for example, '...contingent reward leadership is positively related to performance' (Geyer & Steyrer, 1998: 401). Sometimes rather than simple relations among variables, entire causal models are proposed. Such models display a chain of relations unfolding over time, and are intended to illustrate a causal process of certain variables leading to other variables, that lead to still others.

Descriptive research can also be found in which prior hypotheses are not formulated and tested. Such studies provide answers to many practical and theoretical questions, and should serve as the raw material for theory development. New areas of inquiry will normally begin with purely descriptive research which provides basic data concerning the phenomena of interest. As patterns and relations among variables are uncovered, theories can be built that will be subject to scientific testing with hypothesis-driven approaches.

The current trend in the I/O journals has been to discourage descriptive research (with some exceptions) in favor of hypothesis and theory-driven research. However, a great deal of research done in practice settings is of the descriptive variety in order to answer an immediate, practical question, such as 'how do employees feel about the new incentive system?' This has contributed to an unfortunate schism between academic researchers and practitioners. Much of the more theoretical research has little immediate applicability in organizational settings, and much of the research conducted in organizations addresses issues that are not of interest to the academic community that dominates the journals. However, both a healthy practice and science need both forms of research. Descriptive data provide the raw material for theories and theories provide a basis for new innovations, so both should be equally valued by both constituencies.

Assessment and the Operationalization of Variables

Every empirical investigation involves the operationalization of variables. This means that each variable in the study must be somehow quantified, which can involve the creation of levels of a variable, as in experiments. More frequently it involves the measurement of variables that are not manipulated. Operationalizations refer to all of the ways we quantify our variables, and include psychological scales and tests that are the basis of much I/O research. Researchers have a choice between using existing instruments and operationalizations or developing new ones. Often the development of a new operationalization (instrument) is the purpose of a piece of research. The psychometrics chapter in this book will cover the major issues concerned in the operationalization process, so they do not need repeating here.

Research Design

Design refers to the basic structure of a study. It describes the variables to be assessed, and when they are assessed. For those designs in which individual participants are treated differently, it shows how those participants are assigned to research conditions. Designs can be classified into experimental and nonexperimental. Experimental designs are those in which participants are randomly assigned to treatment conditions typically (but not always) created by the researcher. Nonexperimental designs are those in which observations are taken on a group of people, but no assignment to conditions occurs; for example, a group of people are asked to complete a survey. There also exist quasi-experimental designs which may approximate experiments, but are not true experiments, as will be discussed later.

Another aspect of design is the setting in which the investigation occurs. The laboratory is a setting in which we study behavior where it would not otherwise occur. In other words, we create an artificial setting in which to study people's reactions. The field is a setting in which behavior is studied where it is naturally occurring. For the I/O psychologist, this is usually the workplace. The laboratory provides a highly controlled setting in which experiments can be conducted so that we can draw confident inferences that our created or manipulated variable had certain effects. However, it typically lacks obvious generalizability or external validity. Without further testing in the field, we cannot be certain that the same effects would occur. The field will typically have greater external validity, since we are studying the phenomenon in its natural setting, but it is at the cost of control that allows for internal validity. In other words, we cannot be certain that the relations we observe are causal. This is not because of the field setting itself, of course, but rather is due to the limits on research designs in the field.

One of the distinguishing features of I/O psychology is that researchers use a variety of experimental and nonexperimental methods in both the field and laboratory. Schaubroeck and Kuehn (1992) analyzed the methodologies of all articles from three of the major I/O journals for two years. They found that 63% of studies were conducted in the field but 37% were in the laboratory. The majority of field studies (77%) were nonexperimental, whereas 90% of laboratory studies were experiments. What determined to a great extent both the design and setting was the research topic. Studies of motivation tended to be experiments (76%), and were conducted in the laboratory (56%). By comparison, studies of job attitudes and job satisfaction were almost all field studies (92%), and were mostly nonexperimental (69%).

For this chapter, I have followed Schaubroeck and Kuehn's (1992) approach and categorized some of the methodological features of all the 1997 and 1998 (last two complete years) articles in the *Journal of Applied Psychology* (*JAP*) and the *Journal of Occupational and Organizational Psychology* (*JOOP*). I chose these two journals in order to contrast the methodology found in the US-based *JAP* with the more international, UK-based *JOOP*. Only articles related to the I/O field were included in the analysis. For the *JAP*, results were not too different from what Schaubroeck and Kuehn found in terms of types of studies. About a third of articles used student samples, mostly in laboratory studies. The remaining two thirds used employed samples mostly in field studies. The editorial policy at *JOOP* is to discourage publication of studies using nonemployed student samples, and in these two years 100% of studies had employed samples. Interestingly, *JAP* samples were almost entirely American (82%), whereas *JOOP* samples were much more diverse, with 20% American, 22% Australian, 15% English, 11% Dutch, and the remainder from a variety of countries in Asia, Europe, and the Middle-East.

Experimental and Quasi-Experimental Designs

What distinguishes the experiment from other designs is that participants are randomly assigned to conditions (the independent variable), typically by the researcher, although at times such assignment can occur naturally without researcher intervention (e.g., a psychologist is able to study the effects of a workplace intervention conducted by management in which employees are randomly assigned to participate). In most cases the researcher also creates the treatment conditions, but this is not necessary for a study to be an experiment. In the simplest case there are two treatment conditions (e.g., receive training vs. not receive training or control), participants are randomly assigned to one or the other conditions, and effects on one or more dependent variables are assessed.

A quasi-experiment is a study that approximates an experiment, but does not have true random assignment of participants to levels of the independent variable. This might occur because there is only one condition in the study, or because participants were not randomly assigned to conditions. It is typically the case in workplace field settings that participants cannot be placed into various treatment conditions for practical reasons. For example, in a study of the effects of training, financial and logistical considerations might not allow researchers to pick a random sample of employees from the organization for training, especially if those employees are spread throughout the country or world. At best, the organization might only allow the training of all employees at one location, leaving perhaps a second location as a nontrained control group, if there is a control group at all. There are far too many specific quasi-experimental designs to discuss in one short chapter, so I will only cover two major types after first discussing the general issue of drawing inferences from designs or internal validity.

Internal validity of designs   The ultimate goal of most researchers is to draw conclusions about causal relations among variables, in other words, did one variable cause another? The experiment is a powerful tool that allows such inferences. When properly designed, we can have confidence in the conclusion (assuming we found supporting evidence in our data) that the independent variable *caused* the dependent variable. This is because the structure of the experiment, with random assignment of participants to conditions, allows us to rule out or control outside influences that might have been the real cause of our results. Of course, it is possible that our statistical results were due to chance (Type 1 error), and that there really is not a relation, causal or otherwise, between our variables. But assuming this was not the case, we will have confidence in drawing a causal conclusion. It should be kept in mind that our confidence in such internal validity has little bearing on the issue of generalizability or external validity, and it might only be in the specific setting of our study that the causal link occurs.

Nonexperimental designs make drawing such causal inferences more difficult. If all we know is that two variables assessed at the same time were related, we have little basis upon which to conclude that one causes the other. It is likely in many cases that additional 'third variables' (Zapf, Dormann & Frese, 1996) not assessed are the real cause. Thus if we ask participants to indicate their level of job satisfaction and their level of organizational commitment, finding the two variables are related says little about the cause. Perhaps factors (variables) that lead to one, lead to the other, although it is conceivable these two variables are somehow directly linked causally.

The problem with nonexperimental and quasi-experimental designs is that there are alternative possible mechanisms that threaten causal inference, or what Cook and Campbell (1979) refer to as threats to internal validity (see Cook and Campbell for a detailed explanation of threats in various designs). These are things that can occur that produce relations among variables other than possible causal connections between them. Some of these threats are problems when data are collected over time, for example, as when we assess people before and after some organizational change, such as a training program. This is the simple pre-test–post-test design in which the same participants are assessed twice over time. Other threats occur when we compare different groups of people who were not randomly assigned to conditions.

Nonequivalent group designs   With nonequivalent group designs there is no random assignment process, but rather participants find themselves in different treatment conditions due to other reasons. For example, suppose there are employee attitude problems in an organization that are believed to be caused by poor supervision. Management might decide to try supervisory training to solve the problem, and might wish to evaluate the effects by conducting a study. A nonequivalent group design might consist of training all the managers at one facility, say in Dallas, and comparing them to another facility, say in Philadelphia, that is used as a control. The dependent variable could be the level of job satisfaction assessed in employees after training has been completed in Dallas, and at the same time in Philadelphia. In this design there is an independent variable that is manipulated, but there is not random assignment. It is also possible to have a nonequivalent group design in which no manipulation occurred at all. In other words, the researcher might find that certain groups of people fit a certain category, for example had completed voluntary work training, and this might serve as the independent variable (trained vs. not trained).

It is difficult to draw strong inferences about the effects of the independent variable on the dependent variable in the nonequivalent group design because the groups are initially different. In the above training example, if the Dallas employees are more satisfied with their jobs, how do we know that they were not more satisfied initially? For all we know, the training might have even had a detrimental effect. Only knowing that one group was trained and the other was not, and the job satisfaction scores after training tells us little about the effects of training. We need additional information to draw that conclusion. Had our design been experimental with random assignment, we would have felt confident in attributing job satisfaction differences between groups to the training, because we would be able to assume that the groups were statistically equivalent before training, that is, differences among groups would be attributable merely to chance. A better approach if it is not possible to randomly assign individual managers would be to choose several facilities and randomly assign some of them to training and some not. Another improvement would be to assess employee job satisfaction before and after training, using a pre-test–post-test design in combination with the nonequivalent group design, as will be covered in the next section.

Designs over time   Some designs involve assessment of the same variables repeatedly over time. The simplest is the single group pre-test–post-test design in which a sample of participants is assessed before and after some event occurs, such as an organizational change (implement flextime) or training. This sort of design can be a true experiment, where there is random assignment, or a quasi-experiment where there are treatment conditions but no random assignment (nonequivalent group design). It can have two assessments, or many assessments, for example before training, immediately after training, and then quarterly for a year. Adding extra assessments over time can be a good strategy because often changes have only short-term transitory effects. People who are sent to extensive training often return to work with a high level of motivation to implement what they learned. However, such motivation often wanes as they find limited support for and many impediments to change.

The single group pre-test–post-test design is a weak design that leaves open many alternative possible explanations for results. Suppose we find that scores on a dependent variable are higher after a treatment than before it. We cannot be certain that there were not other events that occurred that are the real explanation for the change. Going back to the management training example, suppose job satisfaction is assessed in Dallas before and after the supervisors receive their training. Any number of other changes that occurred at work (e.g., announcing future expansion, awarding annual merit raises, distributing bonuses, or implementing flextime) might have been the real cause. As time frames become longer, there are more and more opportunities for extraneous factors to have an impact on employee job satisfaction.

The multi-group design helps solve this problem to the extent that all participants might be exposed to the same events. Thus having a control group adds an important feature. However, it is critical that all groups have equal exposure to all events. If Dallas is a more productive office and gets bonuses that Philadelphia does not get, the advantage of the control group is compromised. This is a further problem with the nonequivalent group design. Not only are there possible initial differences that are important, but ongoing things can occur that influence results of a study.

Nonexperimental Designs

A nonexperimental design is one in which data are collected on one or more variables, but no treatment conditions occur. In other words the researcher only collects observations of variables that already exist. Such designs are often called correlational because typically they involve continuous variables and correlations are computed to reflect possible relations among them. This term is unfortunate in that it encourages thinking of a connection between design and statistics that does not exist, specifically the old saying that correlation (the statistic) does not indicate causality. Statistics themselves have little to say about causality, as such conclusions are allowed or not by the design itself. I will discuss two

types of nonexperimental designs – observational designs and survey designs. Although we distinguish them, the major difference concerns how data are collected, with the observational design having observers record data on participants, whereas the survey design involves having participants themselves directly provide data.

Observational designs As the name implies, observational designs involve taking observations of some sort on a sample of participants. Typically one or more observers are trained to assess some characteristic of people or their job situation. They can focus on individual employees, and it is common to have an observer spend an hour or more with each subject in the study. The observations can be unstructured, where observers watch for a period of time, and then make ratings along given dimensions. For example, after watching an employee work for an hour, the observer might rate the complexity of the job or the extent to which the person interacts with others. A more structured approach might have observers record each instance of a particular behavior. For example, the observer might note each time the subject speaks to another person or each time the person is given a direction by a supervisor.

It is also possible to use an unobtrusive approach (Webb, Campbell, Schwartz, Sechrest & Grove, 1981), where observers watch and record behavior without the participant's knowledge. Although more popular in social psychology, this approach can be used in I/O psychology to assess employee behavior without the possibility of the observer's presence affecting people's reactions. However, there are limits to the use of this method because of concerns over privacy rights. The use of this approach is limited to observations of public behavior in public places, for example having observers in the parking lot record how many employees drive alone or carpool. Although it might be legal for organizations to use hidden cameras to watch their employees, psychologists would have concerns about ethical issues in using such approaches unless employees are aware they are or might be observed.

An important issue with observers is assuring that their observations are replicable. It is important that data are not idiosyncratic to the particular observer, or that ratings are inaccurate and error prone. A procedure that can be used to establish this is to have two or more observers make the same observations independently, and then compare them. This is referred to as interrater agreement (Tinsley & Weiss, 1975), which means that data are the same across observers, or that there is consensus. Agreement suggests that ratings are independent of the particular individual observers and that they are systematic. In other words all observers are collecting data the same way.

There are two limitations of using observers. First, this can be an expensive and inefficient means of collecting data. Typical studies require 100 subjects or more, and if each one requires several hours of observer time, data collection becomes labor intensive. Furthermore, few researchers have access to financial support of their research (grants), making the hiring of observers prohibitively expensive. This problem is compounded if two or more observers are required to assure agreement. A second limitation is that observer ratings are not always very accurate when they are asked to make ratings of dimensions, such as the complexity or difficulty of a job (Frese & Zapf, 1988). In fact studies that have compared observers with employees themselves have found that observers are unable to make the fine distinctions among different dimensions, as reflected in high correlations among dimensions, that are made by employees themselves, who had much lower inter-dimension correlations (e.g., Glick, Jenkins & Gupta, 1986; Spector, Fox & Van Katwyk, 1999).

Survey designs The most popular method for conducting field research in I/O psychology is the survey. There are many ways of conducting them, including self-administered questionnaires, group administered questionnaires, telephone interviews, face-to-face interviews, and more recently the e-mail and web-based questionnaire. All involve asking participants to answer questions about themselves and their jobs. Most surveys have closed-ended questions in which respondents are given fixed response choices, and are asked to pick one (usually) from a list; for example, 'I like my job' might have choices *strongly disagree, slightly disagree, slightly agree, strongly agree*. Often they form a continuum, as in this case.

It is also possible to have open-ended questions, in which respondents are free to answer how they wish. Questions tend to be much more general, and often there are several on the topic of interest. For example, several researchers have used this method to study causes of and responses to job stress (e.g., Keenan & Newton, 1985; Narayanan, Menon & Spector, 1999). Keenan and Newton (1985) asked respondents to describe an incident at work that was stressful, and how they responded to it. Such responses can be quantified with content analysis (Weber, 1990). This is a procedure in which responses are read by trained judges and are placed into categories based on similarities. The goal is to produce categories that describe the sorts of responses given. For example, the above question concerning job stress produced categories of *people wasted my time* and *conflicts with other people*. As with observers, multiple judges are used to assure agreement.

Questionnaires are by far the most popular method for doing surveys. This is because they are a very cheap and efficient means of data collection. It is possible to survey large numbers of employees

in a very short time period, with relatively little labor. There are four main ways such surveys are conducted. First, regular mail can be used to deliver questionnaires to either a home or work address. Often organizations can provide mailing lists, so little effort would be involved unless there are a large number of employees. The biggest expense is typically postage. Second, a cheaper alternative to regular mail is to use organizational mail to deliver questionnaires to the work location, as it is usually free. Third, questionnaires can be hand delivered to individuals at their workplace. In most circumstances this takes more time than mail, unless there are a small number of employees who are in a fairly small location. With each of these three methods, questionnaires are returned either to a drop box located somewhere at work or via mail. A problem is that often response rates are not very good, as it is not uncommon for fewer than 50% (and sometimes no more that 10% to 15%) of respondents will return questionnaires. Sometimes hand delivery can help, particularly if the person delivering the questionnaire returns to collect it later. The fourth approach, administering questionnaires to groups of employees who fill them out at a meeting, is more effective in gaining a high response rate, often as high as 100%, as even when people do not have to complete the questionnaire, they will generally do so as time has been set aside for it.

A new approach to survey administration is to use the internet, either via e-mail or the world wide web. E-mail can be an alternative means of administering questionnaires. It is cheap, as there is little cost for sending an e-mail, and efficient as it is easy to send e-mails to large numbers of people at one time. However, in my experience response rates are quite low compared to alternatives, as most people tend to ignore such requests. Furthermore, many people do not check their e-mail regularly, and may never receive the request. The web can be used by putting the questionnaire on a website where respondents can go to complete it online. This approach works best where access is limited to the population of interest, for example, by placing it on a company's intranet, and when employees are required to log on and either complete the questionnaire, or at least indicate they have considered the request. Putting a questionnaire on an open site in the hopes of having people complete it makes data collection too uncontrolled. Individuals can complete the scale more than once, and one cannot be certain about the response rate, or what percentage of people who saw the questionnaire completed it. Furthermore, the nature of the underlying population of people who are being surveyed is not clear.

Interviews can be an effective means of data collection, but this is a more time consuming procedure than questionnaires. The main advantage is the ability to collect more in-depth data, and to probe for more information if an answer is incomplete or vague. Telephone interviews are more efficient in terms of time required to complete each interview, but such interviews have to be kept short, as most people will not tolerate being kept on the telephone for long periods. Face-to-face is inefficient, but is appropriate when in-depth information is needed that will take a long time to acquire. Interviews are not as good as questionnaires if there are many closed-ended questions. Respondents can become quite impatient at being asked to answer orally when a written form is easier. However, this can be a good procedure for people who have poor written language or who otherwise cannot do a written questionnaire. Interviews are better for cases where at least some of the questions are open-ended, and where some prompting may be necessary to have respondents give complete answers.

Although most questionnaires gather information from people about themselves via self-reports, this method can also be used to gather information about others. Perhaps the most frequent use of this is to survey supervisors about the job performance (or other information) of subordinates. Often such data are tied to the subordinate's self-reports about themselves, and allow for investigations of how employee feelings and perceptions relate to performance, at least as seen by supervisors. It is also possible to tie the survey to other sources of data, creating a hybrid design of observation and survey. Glick et al. (1986) for example, compared observers ratings of job characteristics with employee's own ratings.

Multisource designs   Multisource or hybrid designs combine data from an employee survey with other sources of data; for example, archival sources such as company records, observer ratings, or supervisor survey. This is a common design in studies of employee behavior, such as absence or job performance. With absence studies, organizational records are used to provide absence data whereas for studies of job performance, supervisors are asked to rate each employee. This design is particularly useful where some variables are factual or objective in nature, such as whether or not the person comes to work (i.e., absence or lateness).

Multisource designs help get around one of the biggest criticisms of the employee survey – mono-method bias or method variance. It is often assumed that variables assessed within the same questionnaire will produce inflated correlations because of common biases that affect all scales completed by participants. However, evidence that inflation generally occurs has not been found (Spector, 1987). Furthermore, common biases do not necessarily inflate correlations, but are more likely to attenuate them (Williams & Brown, 1994). Finally, as illustrated by Spector and Brannick (1995) specific biases tend to affect specific variables, so general

mono-method bias normally does not occur. Rather bias occurs via complex processes that involve both the specific method used and the nature of what is being assessed. For example, socially sensitive questions about very personal issues (trait anxiety or psychopathology) are likely influenced by social desirability tendencies of respondents, but questions about non-ego threatening things (job satisfaction or skills required for doing a job) are not.

The biggest advantage of multisource designs is their greater objectivity. As I/O psychologists, we are generally interested in determining the effects and relations of the work environment with people's reactions. Self-report surveys shed light on how people's perceptions and feelings relate, but they cannot tell us how those person variables relate to the objective environment. Finding that perceptions of a job condition (e.g., job complexity) relate to job satisfaction does not automatically mean that people who have more objectively complex jobs will be more satisfied. To determine that we need to objectively assess job complexity through the use of non-incumbent sources of data.

Cross-sectional designs   Observational designs can involve assessment of all variables for each subject at the same time (cross-sectional) or with variables assessed at different times (longitudinal). The cross-sectional design is the more popular because it is easier to accomplish, as data are collected all at one time, for example in the same questionnaire. Data can be collected anonymously, which means participants will feel more free to be candid. In addition the researcher does not have to be concerned with ethical issues of protecting participant identity. This can be of particular concern for professionals working inside organizations in that superiors might demand to see who said what in an employee survey in which people are identified. Of course, in a hybrid design in which data are collected from more than one source (e.g., from an employee questionnaire and from supervisors), there must be some way of matching data on participants across sources.

The problem with the cross-sectional design is that it does not allow for causal conclusions that certain variables caused others. All that can generally be concluded is that variables are related to one another. This can be helpful, in that the first step in determining causality is showing that variables are related. However, a relation is a necessary but not sufficient condition for causality, and determining causality is normally our ultimate objective in organizational science. Cross-sectional designs are typically used at the beginning stages of research on a topic as they can indicate whether or not it's worth continuing to address a research question using more conclusive, but less efficient methods.

Longitudinal designs A longitudinal design involves repeated measurements over time on the same subjects, often on the same variables. It is one of the most powerful tools available for the study of many organizational phenomena that cannot be studied experimentally. For example, such designs are quite popular in turnover research, where job satisfaction and other variables are assessed at one time, and six months to a year later turnover is determined. The longitudinal design has important advantages in being better able to shed light on causal relations among variables. This is because it allows us to see if a variable at one time can predict a subsequent variable, such as job satisfaction predicting turnover. The strength of this conclusion is that the turnover did not occur until after the person reached the observed state of satisfaction, meaning the direction of causality must have been from time 1 (job satisfaction) to time 2 (turnover). If it is not certain, however, that the time 2 variable reached its state subsequent to time 1, causal conclusions are compromised.

Longitudinal designs do not automatically indicate causality; that is, one should not expect that merely assessing a variable subsequently indicates that that variable was an effect of what was assessed previously if there is a relation. Causality can only be inferred if it can be shown that the state of the 'effect' variable at time 2 did not occur until after the 'cause' variable at time 1 reached a certain state, or what Davis (1985) calls freezing. Furthermore, the appropriate time period for variable 1 to cause variable 2 must be chosen (Zapf et al., 1996), which is quite difficult to anticipate. Choosing two arbitrary points in time to conduct assessments will not necessarily be helpful. It is likely that even if one variable causes another, after a period of time the causal process would be completed, so that observations of both variables could not show which one caused the other. For example, assume for the sake of argument that job satisfaction causes organizational commitment, that is people who like their jobs become committed to their employers. Further assume that for a new employee, job satisfaction freezes during the first week, but it takes two months for it to affect commitment. If we were to assess commitment and satisfaction after one month and then after two months, what we would expect to see is that at one month there's little relation between satisfaction and commitment, because the process has not yet occurred. Commitment at one month would not have much relation with satisfaction at two months, because commitment does not affect subsequent satisfaction. However, satisfaction at one month would be correlated with commitment at two months because it is a cause. Merely finding that job satisfaction and commitment are related at two months tells us little about causality, as such a relation can be caused by either one causing the other as well as

by extraneous or 'third' variables causing both. Furthermore, if we assess commitment at 4 months and job satisfaction at 6 months, we will not be able to determine which caused which because the causal process has been completed. However, we might erroneously conclude that commitment caused job satisfaction because there would likely be a relation over time.

Unfortunately, we rarely have a basis for hypothesizing what the appropriate time frame should be for a causal process (Zapf et al., 1996), and in most longitudinal studies times are chosen arbitrarily or based on practical considerations (e.g., the organization where the research is being done conducts annual employee surveys). A different strategy, however, can be very useful, and that is assessing variables on either side of an event or change. For example, Spector and O'Connell (1994) used this strategy by assessing personality traits in a sample of college students and work variables (job stressors and job strains) 18 months after students graduated and began their careers. This design allowed for more confident causal conclusions that personality somehow had a causal role in the job stress process because when personality was assessed the students had not yet begun their jobs. Of course, the exact nature of that process is uncertain, and it is still possible that third variables at play over the entire time of the study affected all variables. Without controlled experiments, drawing strong causal conclusions is difficult and requires many different approaches that will hopefully converge on a common conclusion.

Although there are advantages to longitudinal designs, they are not often a researcher's first choice because of practical limitations. As noted above, participants must be identified so that assessments at each time period can be matched. This limits the sorts of things that can be studied, as sensitive topics such as employee sabotage and theft, may be out of bounds. Furthermore, participant attrition is a problem, as the longer the time period, the more difficult it will be to locate participants to take the next assessment. Furthermore, with several retestings, participants may become tired of the study and quit. Finally, conducting such studies requires more time and resources. It represents a bigger commitment on the part of the organization where it is being conducted, and it is not uncommon for an organization to quit in the middle of such a study. Because of participant attrition, larger numbers must be initially recruited, resulting in higher costs for questionnaire administration (e.g., copying and postage). Finally, there is the time involved in waiting the interval between assessments. All of these factors discourage researchers from conducting such studies. Professors, who conduct most of the published research, are under pressure for publication productivity, and are hesitant to invest a great deal of time into a project that is high risk in not producing a publication. Practitioners who conduct applied research for their employing organizations typically find that management is not willing to wait for longitudinal studies to provide answers to questions that need immediate attention.

DATA ANALYSIS

I/O psychology tends to be a statistical science, meaning the nature of our data lends itself to the use of statistical methods. In addition our studies are typically data intensive; we collect many numbers both by having many variables and large sample sizes. With hundreds and often thousands of observations in a study, we need to use a variety of statistical methods and tests to help us draw inferences. We want to know if variables are related to one another and ultimately if those relations might be causal. The former question can be answered with statistical tests that tell us the likelihood that variables are related to one another. The latter issue of causality has little to do with statistics themselves. Rather those conclusions are based on interpretation of the statistical results (relations among variables) in light of the study's design. In other words, there are statistical tests for relations, but there is no statistical test for causality.

Hundreds of different statistical procedures exist, but only a handful see frequent use in I/O psychology. As is true of all fields, certain procedures come into common use for a variety of good and bad reasons. Traditions arise due in large part to the nature of data, designs, and research questions, as new potentially useful methods are developed. Unfortunately, acceptable procedures can be quite trendy, and too often choice of statistic is dictated more by what is believed to enhance a paper's publication chances than by careful consideration of what might be the best approach to answering the purpose of the study. Furthermore, there is a frequent overreliance on complex data analysis as a means of overcoming weak design, often leading to misapplication and misinterpretation of the most complex statistics when simpler approaches would provide clearer answers to the question being addressed.

There are a handful of statistical methods that have enjoyed long and widespread use in our field. Correlation, multiple regression, analysis of variance, and factor analysis have been particularly popular fundamental methods. Beginning in the late 1960s, the computer encouraged the use of more complex methods, including multivariate analogues (see Tabachnick & Fidell, 1996 for a readable guide) to many univariate statistics (e.g., canonical correlation, discriminant analysis, and multivariate analysis of variance, MANOVA and multivariate

analysis of covariance, MANCOVA) as well as development of new procedures, such as structural equation modeling (SEM) and Hierarchical Linear Modeling (HLM). In a very real sense, the prior two decades has been a period in our history in which we have seen old research merely replicated with more complex statistical methods, often reaching similar conclusions.

New and/or Popular Analyses Used in I/O Psychology

Correlation/Regression

As noted earlier, a great deal of I/O research is non-experimental and has as its major purpose the investigation of relations among variables. Furthermore, most I/O research is quantitative in nature, and our variables are assessed along a continuum from low to high. This allows us to use Pearson product-moment correlation (hereafter just called correlation), and parametric methods that are based on correlation, for example multiple regression. These methods allow a great deal of flexibility in exploring relations among two or more variables at a time, and they allow for additive vs. nonadditive (interactive or multiplicative) and linear vs. nonlinear tests. We see correlation used a great deal in I/O research, as it provides the basic building blocks for many more complex methods. For additional discussion of correlation methods, there are several classic texts such as Cohen and Cohen (1983) and Pedhazur (1997).

Correlation is most often used in field research where cross-sectional survey designs dominate. Unfortunately, such designs greatly limit the sorts of conclusions that can be drawn from data. We might only be able to reasonably conclude that variables are related, but our ultimate objective is to understand the causal process underlying those relations. When the design does not allow for such conclusions, we often turn to statistics. They can assist us by providing a means of control, or by allowing us to test hypotheses, but such analyses must be applied carefully.

Correlation methods with control of other variables The correlation itself can indicate only relations between two variables. Control can be introduced through the use of partialing of additional variables. A partial correlation indicates the relation between two variables with the statistical effect of a third held constant. For example, suppose we do a study in which we find a correlation between job complexity and job performance in a diverse sample of employees from a large organization. We can certainly conclude that people in more complex jobs perform better, but perhaps it is not due to the complexity but something associated with complexity, such as cognitive ability (CA). If CA correlates with complexity and job performance, we can statistically control its effect by partialing it from the complexity–performance correlation. If the result is a sharp reduction in magnitude of correlation, then we can statistically attribute the relation to the effect of CA. If the partial is not much different from the original correlation, we would conclude that the relation cannot be attributable to CA.

There is an important caution in the interpretation of partials, as well as other forms of statistical control. One should not draw causal conclusions from the statistics alone (Davis, 1985). Note that in the prior example I used the term, to *statistically attribute* the relation. This means one can note that it is possible for the partialled variable, CA to be the cause of the relation between the other two variables, but this does not mean we can draw that conclusion. To do that requires more evidence than just the observed pattern of correlations and partials. In point of fact there are many possible causal flows that might result in a given observed pattern of relations. Failure to find an expected pattern is solid evidence against the hypothesized causal flow. Finding it merely provides evidence that the conclusion is plausible. Unfortunately, in our field in which we have severe limits on the controls we can apply in our designs, it is very tempting to apply statistical controls in the hope of being able to stretch conclusions beyond what is reasonable. Severe limitations in interpreting partials has been discussed by Meehl (1971), which should be required reading for all researchers who use statistical controls.

Multiple regression Multiple regression can be used for a variety of purposes, and is one of the most widely applied statistics in the I/O field. Perhaps the most popular use in research is to test hypotheses concerning complex relations among variables. It can be used to control certain variables while testing for statistical effects of others. This is a commonly used procedure to see if we can attribute the relation of two variables to a third variable or variables. For example, White and Spector (1987) used this approach to test hypotheses that the relation of age and job satisfaction could be attributed to several factors, including salary level and person–job fit.

Multiple regression can also be found in practice settings. A common use is to choose the best subset of predictors from a larger set. For example, one might have a large number of questions on a biographical inventory that can be analyzed using multiple regression to reduce the inventory to a smaller size. Those questions that best predict performance can be chosen, and those that do not add significant predictability would be deleted. Procedures for variable selection can be very useful, such as forward,

backward, and stepwise (see Pedhazur, 1997, for details).

As with partialing (which is related), one must be careful not to over-interpret results from multiple regression. This method can be very useful for testing hypotheses, but it cannot in and of itself tell us if one variable is the cause of relations among others. Finding that a variable becomes nonsignificant in the presence of another when entered into the analysis tells us that a certain causal pattern is possible, but not that it is certain. Additional variables not in the analysis might have been the real cause. Furthermore, multiple regression and other commonly used statistics provide optimized solutions (according to a statistical criterion) for the sample of data being analyzed. With the sizes of samples typically available, there can be variability of results from replication to replication of the study, and this variability gets worse as the number of predictors increases and the size of intercorrelations among predictors increases. So we must be cautious in rushing to conclusions based on what might be unstable results. Multiple regression is a valuable tool, but it cannot substitute for sound research design.

Moderated regression Some of the most interesting hypotheses that we address with multiple regression involve complex interactions among variables. Moderated regression, which is analogous to interaction in analysis of variance, tests for the joint effects of two or more predictors. Specifically, it tests if the relation of one predictor to a criterion varies across levels of the other predictor. For example, we might wish to test if negative affectivity (NA, a personality variable) moderates the relation between workload and headaches. Our hypothesis might be that high NA people will be more sensitive to stress, and for them there will be a positive relation between workload and headache. For individuals low in NA, there will be no relation. The procedure for conducting the moderated regression is beyond our scope, but can be found in any number of sources (e.g., Arnold, 1982).

Mediator tests A mediator is an intervening variable in a causal chain that is the effect of one variable and the cause of another. It plays an explanatory role in theories of why two variables are related, and represents a common type of hypothesis to test. Mediator analyses can be conducted with either partial correlation or multiple regression using procedures described by Kenny (1979). As with other analyses of causal processes, these procedures provide evidence that either refutes or supports mediation. They should not be considered *tests* of mediation per se, as they do not specifically indicate that relations are causal. However, they can be useful in helping to build a case for a mediator hypothesis.

Logistic regression Multiple regression is based on several assumptions that are often not met in practice. It assumes that the criterion variable is continuous, but often our criterion is dichotomous – for example hired vs. not hired. Such criterion variables can be analyzed with multiple regression, but there are two problems that can occur. First, if the split between the two possible values deviates from 50/50, the possible range of correlations is attenuated, and the bigger the deviation the greater the attenuation. Extreme splits, such as 90/10 can make finding significant results difficult, and can distort results. Second, with multiple regression, there is no limit on the values of predicted variables, so a multiple regression equation might predict values of the criterion for some cases to be less than the lower bound or higher than the upper bound. For example, if the values for the criterion variable are 1 and 2, predicted values can be less than 1 or greater than 2.

Logistic regression uses a different approach, based on treating the values of the criterion variable as two categories, and then predicting likelihood of cases falling into each one. It does not require an assumption of equal numbers of cases in each category, and it does not produce predicted values outside of the possible range. For some problems it produces results that are more easily interpretable as it indicates probabilities of falling into categories. This can be quite useful, for example, with turnover research as the criterion will be shown as probabilities of turnover or no turnover. One limitation with this method that has not received sufficient attention is the relative statistical power of logistic regression versus multiple regression. Logistic approaches are designed for large samples, and with sample sizes of a few hundred typical in our studies, power is low. Menard (1995) and Pedhazur (1997, chapter 17) provide overviews of logistic regression.

Analysis of variance Analysis of variance or ANOVA is a procedure that allows one to investigate the relations of the dependent variable (DV) to each of the independent variables (IV), providing both a significance test of the relation and the magnitude of the relation. It is mathematically related to multiple regression, both of which are variations of the same underlying general linear model. Thus it is possible to use a multiple regression program to compute an ANOVA (see Pedhazur, 1997, for the procedure). There is little advantage to doing so, however, since results will be the same (assuming the same analyses are conducted). However, the ANOVA is easier to set up and interpret in most cases.

The most common use of ANOVA is to analyze data from an experiment or quasi-experiment. However, it can be used for any situation in which one variable can be setup as a continuous dependent-type variable and the other/s as independent-type categorical variables. For example, we might investigate ethnic/racial differences in test performance using an ANOVA to show us if there is a relation, as reflected in group differences in means. One can easily expand the analysis by adding other variables, such as gender, job classification, or religion.

When ANOVA is used to analyze data from experiments, results can be given a causal interpretation. Thus when we refer to independent variables as 'effects', this is meant in a causal sense of the IV causing the DV. It should be kept in mind, however, that the ability to draw causal conclusions has nothing to do with the type of data analysis, but rather with the use of an experimental design. In a cross-sectional survey in which we use ANOVA for categorical variables, conclusions can be no more causal than if a correlation were computed.

Factor Analysis

A common problem in I/O research is reducing a large number of variables to a smaller number of more interpretable dimensions. This can be done in a purely exploratory way to investigate the structure of some variables. It can also be done in a confirmatory way to see if variables conform to a hypothesized structure. Factor analysis is most frequently applied to this problem. The relatively recent development of structural equation modeling (SEM) methods has seen a shift toward the use of confirmatory factor analysis (CFA), and in fact it has become quite difficult in many I/O journals to publish factor analysis results without it being a CFA. For example, I found that in the *Journal of Applied Psychology* during 1997 and 1998, only 3% of studies used EFA, while 26% used some form of SEM, not all of which were CFAs. Results were quite different in the *Journal of Occupational and Organizational Psychology* where an equal number of papers (20%) used EFA and SEM.

The appropriate use of CFA vs. EFA has produced considerable debate (e.g., Hurley et al., 1997). These authors point out that although methodologists have stated clearly that CFA is appropriate only in cases where there's a strong theoretical basis for a hypothesized factor structure, journal reviewers tend to force the use of CFA rather than EFA. This contributes to a practice of using confirmatory methods in an exploratory way, by setting an initial structure and when it fails to confirm, modifying it again and again until a confirmable structure is found. Unfortunately, details of the iterative process are often not found in the paper, either because the author/s failed to fully disclose their methods, or because editors and reviewers did not want to waste journal space and asked that it be removed. Hurley et al. (1997) provide clear guidance about conditions under which CFA and EFA are appropriate and useful.

Structural Equation Modeling

It can be quite frustrating to be an I/O researcher because we want to understand the causal processes underlying the phenomena we study in the workplace, but the limits on our ability to do experiments often leaves us studying mere covariation among variables. It is no surprise that the introduction of methods to test causal processes or causal models from information about relations alone have been so strongly embraced. The idea of testing causal models is far from new, but the introduction of such methods began in earnest in the early 1980s using multiple regression to conduct path analysis. Soon software to conduct more complex structural equation modeling (SEM) became available, with the most popular programs being LISREL (Jöreskog & Sörbom, 1992) and EQS (Bentler, 1992). Additional sources on these methods include Bollen and Long (1993); Hoyle (1995); James, Mulaik, and Brett (1982); Pedhazur (1997, chapters 18 and 19).

SEM allows for the a priori specification of a set of relations among variables that would be expected if a certain causal flow is true. Data can then be analyzed to determine how well it fits the hypothesized structure. Failure to find good fit is evidence that the hypothesized model is probably incorrect. However, finding good fit is not in and of itself strong support for the model's veracity. Unfortunately, there can be many alternative causal processes that will produce a given pattern of relations (the model equivalence problem). So the best that can be concluded is that a given model is feasible, given the data. We need additional information to rule out alternative explanations.

Another issue concerns the determination of model fit. There have been many statistical indicators developed, and no consensus has been reached about which is best to use. The chi-square provides a traditional statistical test of significance comparing the observed variances and covariances among the variables in the analysis with the estimated variances and covariances given the model being assessed. It is well-known that this test has serious limitations due to its sensitivity to sample size and violation of assumptions (Hu & Bentler, 1995) as well as the number of parameters in the model being estimated (Jöreskog, 1993). Furthermore, it can only be used when variances/covariances and not correlations are analyzed (Pedhazur, 1997). More than a dozen alternative fit indices that provide descriptive information (but no statistical test) about the degree of fit are available. They can be classified into absolute vs. comparative or incremental (Hu & Bentler, 1995), as well as discrepancy indices. The absolute indices compare how well the observed data matches what would be expected based on the model being evaluated. The incremental indices compare the model in question with an alternative model to see how much better it fits. The usual standard is a model in which none of the variables are related. Discrepancy indices compare each element of the correlation or variance/covariance matrix being analyzed with one that is estimated by the program. The different indices vary in the extent to which they take into account sample size, number of parameters estimated, variability in the index over repeated sampling from the same population, and violation of assumptions. Table 1.1 contains a list of some of the most commonly used indices, along with the standard typically used for a good fit. Advantages and disadvantages are also noted in the last column of the table. This information was compiled from several sources, as shown at the bottom of the table.

The strength of conclusions reached in an SEM study is based on the soundness of both design and underlying theory. Design attributes can help rule out alternative explanations; for example, longitudinal designs can eliminate possibilities of later variables being the cause of earlier variables. Strong theories, based on sound research, can help eliminate other possibilities as well as support hypothesized causes. For example, there have been widely accepted causal conclusions reached concerning the effects of job dissatisfaction on turnover through the use of longitudinal designs.

As with CFA, however, there has been a rush to use SEM methods to test 'causal' models in hope of enhancing publishability of studies. In some cases there has been an overinterpretation of results, inappropriately hinting at causal conclusions. As with CFA, many times the confirmatory study has become exploratory, as the initial model hypothesized must be modified again and again until good fit is achieved. Such a practice results in specification of one of many possible models that might represent the true causal process, and absolutely no basis to rule out any of them.

SEM can be a useful tool if applied appropriately. What is required is a sound underlying theoretical basis for the model being tested, and ideally a design that allows for the elimination of at least some alternative explanations. The use of longitudinal designs and multiple sources of data can be helpful in this regard. Experimental and quasi-experimental designs can also be used, for example, where one variable is manipulated and its possible effects on subsequent variables assessed over time. Such data analyzed with SEM methods can provide good support for a hypothesized causal flow.

Hierarchical Linear Modeling (HLM)

With field data, subjects are often found in a hierarchy of categories or groups. Employees might be

Table 1.1   *Summary of SEM fit statistics*

Index		Index type	Criterion for good fit	Advantages/limitations
GFI	Goodness of fit index	Absolute	.90	Inaccurate with small samples
AGFI	Adjusted goodness of fit index	Absolute	.80	Adjusts for number of parameters
NFI	Normed fit index	Incremental	.90	Tends to show poor fit with small samples
NNFI	Non-normed fit index	Incremental	.90	Adjusts for number of parameters; high variability in results
IFI	Incremental fit index	Incremental	.90	Less-variable results than NNFI
CFI	Comparative fit index	Incremental	.90	Does well in small samples
PSI	Parsimony index	Incremental	.90	Adjusts for parameter to sample size ratio
RMSEA	Root mean square error of approximation	Discrepancy	.05 or .08	Criterion not well-established
RMR	Root mean square residual	Discrepancy	.05	For correlation matrix input
RMR	Standardized	Discrepancy	.05	For variance/covariance matrix input

Source: Compiled from Browne and Cudeck (1993); Hu and Bentler (1995); Pedhazur (1997); Tabachnick and Fidell (1996).

found in different work groups that are organized into departments that are organized into divisions of a company. Each of these levels in the hierarchy can have effects on the variables of interest. Furthermore, sometimes we are interested in data at more than one level, such as individual attitudes (employee level) versus overhead costs (department level). One should be extremely cautious in doing cross-level data analysis, as mixing data across levels can produce erroneous results, referred to as an aggregation bias. As Bryk and Raudenbush (1992) explain, this can occur because the effects of a variable can be different from level to level. To paraphrase their example, socioeconomic status (SES) of employees at an organization level can represent something different than at an employee level. At the organization level it may represent the type of product and/or service provided, as well as management philosophy (i.e., different kinds of organizations have different kinds of employees). At the employee level it may represent the characteristics of the job held, such as complexity. Thus relating organization level SES to some other variable may indicate something quite different from relating the same variables at the employee level.

Although there are many ways to approach the hierarchical problem, Hierarchical Linear Modeling (HLM; Bryk & Raudenbush, 1992) has been receiving recent attention. It allows for analysis of multiple levels at the same time, decomposing statistical effects into the individual versus higher levels. Thus one might determine that some of the variance in job performance can be attributable to work group, while other variance is attributable to the employee. Work group in particular is a level

likely to see attention using HLM in future studies, especially with increased use of teams in modern organizations.

Item Response Theory (IRT)

A relatively new approach to the development and evaluation of psychological tests is based on Item Response Theory (see the psychometrics chapter in this volume for a more thorough discussion). A number of methodological procedures have been devised to apply this approach that allows one to investigate the characteristics of each item in relation to respondents' standing on the underlying trait of interest. Most applications have involved ability tests for which each item has several choices and one correct answer. With such tests, an item-characteristic curve (ICC) can be plotted for each item relating the probability of answering correctly against the respondent's trait score.

IRT has been of particular interest in the area of personnel selection (Schuler & Guldin, 1991) to deal with two issues. First, IRT has been used to investigate test fairness by investigating possible bias in individual test items (McIntire & Miller, 2000). Comparisons of ICCs and their parameters (mathematical characteristics) across ethnic subgroups can be useful in test development to minimize unfairness. IRT has also been useful for adaptive testing (Bartram, 1994; Hesketh, 1993), in which the items presented to each respondent are tailored specifically to that person's ability level. This provides the same information with a shorter test, as each respondent does not have to take all items.

INTERNATIONAL RESEARCH

With the rapid globalization of the world economy and organizations, there is increasing interest in expanding our research base from a limited number of English-speaking countries to the rest of the world. Conducting research in countries with different cultures and languages produces special methodological challenges that make it difficult to disentangle the effects of culture and nationality from language and other factors. Two particular problems concern equivalence of translation of instruments and equivalence of samples.

The widely used back-translation method (Van de Vijver & Leung, 1997) can be used to achieve equivalence of meaning between versions of instruments in two languages. An instrument is translated from the source language to the target by a bilingual individual sufficiently fluent in both languages. It is then translated back from target to source independently by another bilingual. Discrepancies in meaning between the source and the back-translated source can be resolved by rephrasing in the target language, and then back-translating again as a double check. This procedure can be effective, but it does not guarantee perfect equivalence even when the source and back-translated source are identical. This is because there might not be a one-to-one correspondence in exact meaning between words that translate into one another between languages. Furthermore, often words in one language carry additional connotative meaning not shared by others. Concerns have been raised about nonequivalence problems in back-translated scales, but research has been inconsistent in demonstrating the problem.

Two sophisticated methods have been used to investigate equivalence. Confirmatory factor analysis can be applied to compare factor structures across samples that took the instruments in different languages. Jöreskog and Sörbom (1992) provide a hierarchy of tests that can be conducted to explore equivalence. Item response theory can also be used to determine if items that work well in one sample will work equally well or be biased in another (Ellis, 1989; Van de Vijver & Leung, 1997).

A second problem is maintaining equivalence in samples when comparisons are made across countries (Matsumoto, 1994). Often studies confound country with other characteristics of samples, such as type of job or organization. Unfortunately, it is not always possible to find directly comparable samples. For example, a comparison of many jobs between the US with China is likely to confound country with company size, as well as economic sector. Furthermore, job conditions are likely to vary. In the US many jobs are done by independent contractors/consultants that might be done by government employees elsewhere. Some of this can be controlled through careful choice of jobs, but many countries are so different, that exact equivalence cannot be achieved. Even when the job itself is the same, the relative salary and status can be quite different.

Perhaps the most reasonable solution is to rely on convergence of results across independently done studies. If, say, Chinese workers are always higher than Americans on a variable, regardless of the jobs/organizations compared or the instruments used, we could have confidence in the conclusion that there is a difference attributable to country. More extensive research would be needed to determine the reasons. Thus it will be important to amass enough studies to be able to compile results, perhaps by using meta-analytic procedures which are discussed in a separate chapter in this volume. Of course, things are no different with our typical mono-country studies, as our almost complete reliance on convenience samples makes the amassing of many studies with diverse samples essential for exploring the limits of generalizability.

RECOMMENDATIONS FOR CONDUCTING APPLIED RESEARCH

The fact that often it goes ignored, does not seem to stop those of us who write about methodology from offering advice about how it should be done. There seems to be somewhat of a divide between the textbook procedures and the realities of what it is like in the field. So although everyone (presumably) learns from the same sources, experience with journals and practical limitations quickly distorts things. Concerns about misuse and poor use of methodology led to a report by a distinguished American Psychological Association committee, headed by Jacob Cohen, Robert Abelson, and Robert Rosenthal. Although concerned about psychology in general, their advice is quite appropriate for I/O. They provided four basic principles that should be the basis for everyone's personal research practice (American Psychological Association, 1996):

- *Avoid potential misrepresentation of findings* The committee noted that too often researchers provide incomplete results, making it difficult for reviewers and readers to fully evaluate results. This is particularly problematic with SEM studies in which only parameter estimates and fit statistics from the program's output are provided. At a minimum the means, standard deviations, ranges, and correlations among variables in the analysis should be shown. An exception might be in factor analysis studies of scales where there are too many variables (items) to put in an article. In those cases, full information should be available from the author, as mentioned in a footnote. Complete reporting avoids misinterpretation of results and allows the reader to draw his or her own conclusions. It also potentially enhances the value of a paper to the field, as often a reader is interested in simpler statistics, such as when compiling correlations for a meta-analysis.

- *Avoid the use of premature theory* A theory can be a useful tool in science, but to be really useful a theory should have some solid foundation. Usually this means basing a theory on sound observation. As I noted earlier, in our field there is prejudice against descriptive research, cutting off the best source of raw material for theory. The committee pointed out that the emphasis on theory results in people rushing to use confirmatory methods, often resulting in misrepresentation of what is in reality an exploratory study. They call for an equal emphasis and respect for descriptive/ exploratory versus confirmatory studies.

- *Adopt the principle of analytical parsimony* One of the byproducts of the computer age is the tendency among researchers to use the most complex methods available. In part this is caused by editors and reviewers who demand that simpler methods be replaced with the latest, cutting-edge methods, as if this in and of itself represents advancement of our science. The committee calls for adoption of the analytical parsimony principle – use the simplest methodology that is necessary to meet the research objective. Sometimes this requires the most sophisticated methods, but at other times it might require something quite simple. They note three reasons for this advice. First, the simplest methods tend to have the fewest and least-restrictive assumptions. Often complex methods are used with little attention given to important but untested (or untestable) assumptions. Second, simpler analyses are less prone to error. A correlation is quite easy to run with any of a number of statistical programs. LISREL, however, requires considerable expertise to run the model hypothesized, and it is quite easy to run the wrong model without realizing it. Third, results of simple analyses are easier to communicate. Since the goal of publication is to communicate results, this should be a concern.

- *Be competent in a computer program before using it* Although computers can make complex data analysis easy to conduct, and perhaps too easy, it requires expertise to use them properly. The committee observed that the use of state-of-the-art computer programs has not necessarily resulted in scientific advancement. They recommend that people do not use computer programs without understanding the statistical method they are using. This means learning about a method itself before using it, and not just directions for running the software. They also advise not taking results of an analysis on faith as being correct. One should review results to see if they are reasonable, and even conduct some analyses by hand if feasible (or perhaps with different software) to check results.

SUMMARY AND CONCLUSIONS

A good research study begins with a solid design. Where experiments are not possible, a variety of approximations or quasi-experiments might be used. Unfortunately, in too many cases a cross-sectional survey may be our only available choice. There is always a temptation in such instances to apply the most advanced statistics to such data in hope of rescuing the simple design. It should be kept in mind, however, that such designs mainly indicate existence of relations among variables (although statistical controls can provide important insights and support for hypothesized possibilities), but that even this can be an important contribution. Not every study should be asked to address causal issues or test theoretical hypotheses.

Researchers in I/O like to use a variety of statistical methods. It is best to conduct analyses in stages from the simplest to the most complex. This can facilitate interpretation, and minimize the chances of errors. Begin with descriptive statistics; that is, means, standard deviations, and ranges. Look for anomalies, such as means being higher than the maximum possible score on a variable. Look at distributions to see if there are outliers or skewed distributions. If results look in order, move on to the next level, and then the next. For a multiple regression study, first inspect correlations. Interpret multiple regression results in combination with correlations, as this can indicate the existence of suppressors – that is predictors that are unrelated to a criterion but because they relate to another predictor contribute to the multiple regression results. They are easy to overlook and easy to misinterpret.

Considering the severe limits on our research procedures, it is vital that we apply the principle of converging operations by using a variety of methods. We might begin with the easiest approaches, such as the cross-sectional survey, and then expand to more and more difficult methods. Longitudinal designs and multisource designs can be particularly helpful. Of course such approaches do not always yield converging results, making it necessary to devise new strategies to resolve the inconsistencies. Laboratory experiments can also be helpful, and will often provide additional support for field findings.

Research in I/O psychology and related fields can be quite difficult. Although some of us may conduct laboratory research with college students, most I/O studies are conducted in the field with employees. Not only are these subjects difficult to access, but their employers are not usually willing to allow experimentation. We must remain opportunistic and vigilant, looking for creative ways and places to conduct our research. This produces extra problems, but the challenge is also what makes doing I/O research so interesting and rewarding.

REFERENCES

American Psychological Association (1996). Task Force on Statistical Inference Initial Report. [Online] available: http://www.apa.org/science/tfsi.html, October 20, 1999.

Arnold, H.J. (1982). Moderator variables: A clarification of conceptual, analytic, and psychometric issues. *Organizational Behavior and Human Performance, 29,* 143–174.

Bartram, D. (1994). Computer-based assessment. In C.L. Cooper & I.T. Robertson (Eds.), *International Review of Industrial and Organizational Psychology 1994 Volume 9* (pp. 31–69). Chichester, UK: John Wiley.

Bentler, P.M. (1992). *EQS structural equations program manual.* Los Angeles: BMDP Statistical Software.

Bollen, K.A., & Long, J.S. (Eds.) (1993). *Testing structural equation models.* Thousand Oaks, CA: Sage.

Browne, M.W., & Cudeck, R. (1993). Alternative ways of assessing model fit. In K.A. Bollen & J.S. Long (Eds.), *Testing structural equation models* (pp. 136–162). Thousand Oaks, CA: Sage.

Bryk, A.S., & Raudenbush, S.W. (1992). *Hierarchical linear models: Applications and data analysis methods.* Thousand Oaks, CA: Sage.

Cassell, C., & Symon, G. (Eds.) (1994). *Qualitative methods in organizational research: A practical guide.* Thousand Oaks, CA: Sage.

Cohen, J., & Cohen, P. (1983). *Applied multiple regression/ correlation analysis for the behavioral sciences* (2nd ed.). Hillsdale, NJ: Lawrence Erlbaum Associates.

Cook, T.D., & Campbell, D.T. (1979). *Quasi-experimentation: Design and analysis issues for field settings.* Chicago: Rand McNally.

Davis, J.A. (1985). *The logic of causal order.* Sage University Paper series on Quantitative Applications in the Social Sciences, series no. 07–55. Thousand Oaks, CA: Sage.

Ellis, B.B. (1989). Differential item functioning: Implications for test translations. *Journal of Applied Psychology, 74,* 912–921.

Frese, M., & Zapf, D. (1988). Methodological issues in the study of work stress: Objective vs. subjective measurement of work stress and the question of longitudinal studies. In C.L. Cooper & R. Payne (Eds.), *Causes, coping and consequences of stress at work* (pp. 375–411). Chichester, UK: John Wiley.

Geyer, A.L.J., & Steyrer, J.M. (1998). Transformational leadership and objective performance in banks. *Applied Psychology: An International Review, 47,* 397–420.

Glick, W.H., Jenkins, G.D., Jr., & Gupta, N. (1986). Method versus substance: How strong are underlying relationships between job characteristics and attitudinal outcomes? *Academy of Management Journal, 29,* 441–464.

Hesketh, B. (1993). Measurement issues in industrial and organizational psychology. In C.L. Cooper & I.T. Robertson (Eds.), *International Review of Industrial and Organizational Psychology 1993 Volume 8* (pp. 133–172). Chichester, UK: John Wiley.

Hoyle, R.H. (Ed.) (1995). *Structural equation modeling: Concepts, issues, and applications.* Thousand Oaks, CA: Sage.

Hu, L.T., & Bentler, P.M. (1995). Evaluating model fit. In R.H. Hoyle (Ed.), *Structural equation modeling: Concepts, issues, and applications.* Thousand Oaks, CA: Sage.

Hurley, A.E., Scandura, T.A., Schriesheim, C.A., Brannick, M.T., Seers, A., Vandenberg, R.J., & Williams, L.J. (1997). Exploratory and confirmatory factor analysis: Guidelines, issues, and alternatives. *Journal of Organizational Behavior, 18,* 667–683.

James, L.R., Mulaik, S.A., & Brett, J.M. (1982). *Causal analysis: Assumptions, models, and data.* Thousand Oaks, CA: Sage.

Jöreskog, K.G. (1993). Testing structural equation models. In K.A. Bollen & J.S. Long (Eds.), *Testing structural equation models* (pp. 294–316). Thousand Oaks, CA: Sage.

Jöreskog, K.G., & Sörbom, D. (1992). *LISREL VIII: A guide to the program and applications.* Mooresville, IN: Scientific Software.

Keenan, A., & Newton, T.J. (1985). Stressful events, stressors, and psychological strains in young professional engineers. *Journal of Organizational Behavior, 6,* 151–156.

Kenny, D.A. (1979). *Correlation and causality.* New York: Wiley.

Matsumoto, D. (1994). *Cultural influences on research methods and statistics.* Pacific Grove, CA: Brooks Cole.

McIntire, S.A., & Miller, L.A. (2000). *Foundations of psychological testing.* New York: McGraw-Hill.

Meehl, P.E. (1971). High school yearbooks: A reply to Schwarz. *Journal of Abnormal Psychology, 77,* 143–148.

Menard, S. (1995). *Applied logistic regression analysis.* Sage University Paper series on Quantitative Applications in the Social Sciences, series no. 07–106. Thousand Oaks, CA: Sage.

Narayanan, L., Menon, S., & Spector, P.E. (1999). Stress in the workplace: A comparison of gender and occupations. *Journal of Organizational Behavior, 20,* 63–73.

Pedhazur, E.J. (1997). *Multiple regression in behavioral research: Explanation and prediction* (3rd ed.). Fort Worth, TX: Harcourt Brace.

Schaubroeck, J., & Kuehn, K. (1992). Research design in industrial and organizational psychology. In C.L. Cooper & I.T. Robertson (Eds.), *International Review of Industrial and Organizational Psychology*

1992 Volume 7 (pp. 99–121). Chichester, UK: John Wiley.

Schuler, H., & Guldin, A. (1991). Methodological issues in personnel selection research. In C.L. Cooper & I.T. Robertson (Eds.), *International Review of Industrial and Organizational Psychology 1991 Volume 6* (pp. 213–264). Chichester, UK: John Wiley.

Spector, P.E. (1987). Method variance as an artifact in self-reported affect and perceptions at work: Myth or significant problem? *Journal of Applied Psychology, 72*, 438–443.

Spector, P.E., & Brannick, M.T. (1995). The nature and effects of method variance in organizational research. In C.L. Cooper & I.T. Robertson (Eds.), *International Review of Industrial and Organizational Psychology 1995 Volume 10* (pp. 249–274). Chichester, UK: John Wiley.

Spector, P.E., Fox, S., & Van Katwyk, P.T. (1999). The role of negative affectivity in employee reactions to job characteristics: Bias effect or substantive effect? *Journal of Occupational and Organizational Psychology, 72*, 205–218.

Spector, P.E., & O'Connell, B.J. (1994). The contribution of personality traits, negative affectivity, locus of control and Type A to the subsequent reports of job stressors and job strains. *Journal of Occupational and Organizational Psychology, 67*, 1–11.

Tabachnick, B.G., & Fidell, L.S. (1996). *Using multivariate statistics* (3rd ed.). New York: HarperCollins.

Tinsley, H.E., & Weiss, D.J. (1975). Interrater reliability and agreement of subjective judgments. *Journal of Counseling Psychology, 22*, 358–376.

Van de Vijver, F., & Leung, K. (1997). *Methods and data analysis for cross-cultural research.* Thousand Oaks, CA: Sage.

Webb, E.J., Campbell, D.T., Schwartz, R.D., Sechrest, L., & Grove, J.B. (1981). *Nonreactive measures in the social sciences* (2nd ed.). Boston: Houghton Mifflin.

Weber, R.P. (1990). *Basic content analysis* (2nd ed.). Sage University Paper series on Quantitative Applications in the Social Sciences, series no. 07–49. Thousand Oaks, CA: Sage.

White, A.T., & Spector, P.E. (1987). An investigation of age-related factors in the age–job satisfaction relationship. *Psychology and Aging, 2*, 261–265.

Williams, L.J., & Brown, B.K. (1994). Method variance in organizational behavior and human resources research: Effects on correlations, path coefficients, and hypothesis testing. *Organizational Behavior and Human Decision Processes, 57*, 185–209.

Zapf, D., Dormann, C., & Frese, M. (1996). Longitudinal studies in organizational stress research: A review of the literature with reference to methodological issues. *Journal of Occupational Health Psychology, 1*, 145–169.

2

Measurement in Work and Organizational Psychology

HERMAN AGUINIS,
CHRISTINE A. HENLE,
and CHERI OSTROFF

The goals of this chapter are to (a) provide an overview of measurement and the process of measure development, and (b) describe recent and future trends in the field of measurement in work and organizational psychology. First, we define measurement, discuss some of its benefits, and describe scales of measurement. Second, we describe the process of measure development. This section includes topics such as defining the purpose of measurement and the attribute(s) to be measured, the development of a measurement plan, creating items, conducting a pilot study and item analysis, selecting items, establishing norms, and assessing the reliability and validity of a measure. Finally, we address a selective set of recent and future trends in measurement including issues pertaining to levels of analysis, the impact of technology on measurement, cross-cultural measurement transferability, emerging legal and social issues in measurement, and the globalization of measurement.

Measurement is pervasive in our everyday lives. As we go through our daily activities we glance at our watches to check the time, step on the scale to assess our weight, and look at the speedometer to see how fast we are driving. In addition, schools grade our knowledge, employers test our intelligence and personality, and medical doctors evaluate our health. In sum, we are continually measuring and being measured by others. Not only does measurement influence our daily lives, but also the science and practice of work and organizational (W&O) psychology rely on good measurement. Without good measurement as a foundation, our field could not advance or provide a valuable service to the business community.

As W&O psychologists, we continuously make many decisions that rely on accurate measurement. In practice, we use our knowledge to make decisions, for example, about employee selection, classification, placement, and guidance. These decisions rely on solid measurement of employee attributes, skills,

interests, and values. If we do not have reliable and valid measures of employee characteristics, the decisions we make are not justified and numerous lives may be affected negatively. Thus, as practitioners, we have a responsibility to our clients to ensure that we base our recommendations and decisions on sound measurement.

The decisions we make in practice also rely on research we have conducted in both laboratory and field settings. The accuracy of this research relies on sound measurement of the variables examined. Measurement is essential to our research because it allows us to describe, predict, explain, diagnose, and make decisions about the issues under investigation. If our research lacks good measurement, results will be meaningless and unable to inform the practice of W&O psychology.

Measurement is the cornerstone of both the science and practice of W&O psychology. Without solid measurement, our research is misleading and our practice is haphazard. We must focus on measurement because it can provide accurate and relevant information that leads to informed decision-making.

This chapter is organized as follows. First, we define measurement, discuss some of its benefits, and describe scales of measurement. Then, we describe the process of measure development. This section includes topics such as defining the purpose of measurement and the attribute(s) to be measured, the development of a measurement plan, creating items, conducting a pilot study and item analysis, selecting items, establishing norms, and assessing the reliability and validity of a measure. The last section of the chapter addresses a selective set of recent and future trends in measurement including issues pertaining to levels of analysis, the impact of technology on measurement, cross-cultural measurement transferability, emerging legal and social issues in measurement, and the globalization of measurement.

DEFINITION OF MEASUREMENT

Measurement is the assignment of numbers to attributes or properties of people, objects, or events based on a set of rules (Stevens, 1968). From this definition we can derive several characteristics of measurement. First, measurement focuses on *attributes* of people, objects, or events not actual people, objects, or events. Second, measurement uses a set of rules to quantify these attributes. Rules must be standardized, clear, understandable, and easy and practical to apply. Third, measurement consists of two components, scaling and classification. Scaling is the assignment of numbers to attributes of people, objects, or events in order to quantify them (i.e., determine how much of a particular attribute is present). Classification refers to defining whether people, objects, or events fall into the same or different categories based on a given attribute.

The above definition alludes to a process of measurement. First, we need to determine the purpose of measurement (e.g., prediction, classification, decision-making). Second, we must identify and define the attribute we intend to measure. A definition must be agreed upon before the attribute is measured or different rules may be applied, resulting in varying numbers assigned to the attribute. The purpose of the measurement should guide the definition. Next, we determine a set of rules, based on the definition, to quantify the attribute. Finally, we apply the rules in order to translate the attribute into numerical terms.

BENEFITS OF MEASUREMENT

We asserted above that the science and practice of W&O psychology cannot exist without sound measurement. Science cannot progress any faster than the measurement of important variables in the field. By following the process of measurement outlined above, we can develop good measures which, in turn, reap several benefits (Nunnally, 1978). First, measurement contributes to objectivity. It minimizes subjective judgment from scientific observation and allows theories to be tested because attributes being examined can be adequately assessed and measured (Aguinis, 1993). Second, measurement leads to quantification. By quantifying the attributes we are exploring, more detail can be gathered than with personal observations and judgments. In addition, more subtle effects can be observed and more powerful methods of statistical analysis can be used, which enables us to make precise statements about the patterns of attributes and their relationships among each other (Pedhazur & Pedhazur Schmelkin, 1991). Third, standardized measures result in better communication because they create a common language and understanding of attributes, thus research can be compared. Fourth, sound measures save time and money by allowing researchers and practitioners to focus their energy elsewhere because less-trained individuals can administer and score standardized measures.

Arguably, the most important benefit of measurement is better decision-making about individuals and groups. Measurement provides relevant and accurate information that decision-makers can use to make sound and informed decisions. Thus, measurement provides an important set of tools for improving the information available to decision-makers regarding employee selection, placement, classification, guidance, training and development, compensation, and so forth.

SCALES OF MEASUREMENT

As mentioned earlier, measurement uses a set of rules to quantify attributes of people, objects, or events. The type of measurement scale places a limit on the statistical analyses that can be applied to the quantification of attributes. Stevens (1951) proposed four types of measurement scales: Nominal, ordinal, interval, and ratio. As the measurement of attributes progresses from nominal to ratio, more sophisticated quantitative analyses can be implemented.

Nominal Scales

A nominal scale is the most basic and it involves assigning numbers as labels to individual objects (e.g., telephone numbers) or categories of objects (e.g., sex, organizational unit). Nominal scales determine whether objects belong in the same or different categories (e.g., male or female) based on a given attribute (e.g., sex). Thus, nominal scales classify people or objects.

Data collected using nominal scales have a limited number of transformations and statistics available. First, each category may be assigned any number as long as it is different from other category numbers. For example, men may be labeled 1 and women 2 or men could be labeled 123 and women 654. The categories are not ordered; one is not more than the other, but they are different from each other. Second, the amount of difference between categories is unknown and the only permissible statistics for nominal scales are those based on counting the number of subjects in each category (i.e., frequencies) and proportions.

Ordinal Scales

Ordinal scales involve assigning numbers to people or objects so that their rank order can be determined. That is, ordinal scales help decide if one person is equal to, greater than, or less than another based on a given attribute. For example, a supervisor believes María is a better performer than Bob, thus María is given a 2 while Bob is assigned a 1 to show María has a higher performance ranking than Bob. However, this does not indicate the magnitude of the difference between María's and Bob's performance levels, we just know that María is better than Bob.

Monotonic transformations are permissible for ordinal scales. This means that the transformation must maintain the rank order of individuals or categories. Categories labeled 1, 2, and 3 can be transformed to any numbers as long as their order is preserved (e.g., 4, 5, 6 or 10, 20, 30 is permissible, but 6, 5, 4 is not). Permissible statistics for data collected using ordinal scales include the median and the mode; the mean cannot be calculated because a different mean will be obtained whenever the categories are recoded while the median and mode categories will stay the same. Percentile ranks, correlation coefficients based on ranks (e.g., Spearman's rho and Kendall's W), and rank-order analysis of variance can also be used.

Interval Scales

Interval, like ordinal scales, assign numbers to reflect whether individuals or objects are greater than, less than, or equal to each other. However, interval scales also indicate the difference between objects on a particular attribute. A common example of an interval scale is Celsius temperature. If one city has a temperature of 20° and another has a temperature of 40°, we not only know that the second city has a warmer temperature than the first, but that it is 20° warmer than the first. Thus, interval scales use constant units of measurement so that differences between objects on an attribute can be expressed and compared. However, the absolute magnitude of the attribute is not known because the zero point on an interval scale is arbitrarily determined (e.g., zero point on Celsius scale is set arbitrarily at the freezing point of water). Most measures used in W&O psychology include interval scales.

Linear transformations (e.g., $X' = a + b X$) are permissible with interval scales where X' is the transformed score, X is the score to be transformed, and a and b are constants. For example, Celsius temperature can be transformed to Fahrenheit using the following linear transformation: $F = 32 + 1.8C$. Arithmetic means, variance, and Pearson product-moment correlation are permissible on data collected using interval scales.

Ratio Scales

Ratio scales have a true zero point. The true zero point is the point at which no amount of the attribute is present. Because a zero point can be determined, the ratio between actual scores of an attribute can be examined. Weight and height are two good illustrations of ratio scales. Using length as an example, let's say three rulers have lengths of 10, 20, and 60 centimeters (i.e., approximately 3.94, 7.87, and 23.62 inches, respectively). We can state the second ruler is twice as long as the first and the third is three times as long as the second because length is measured on a ratio scale. Unfortunately, ratio scales are rare in W&O psychology, but they do exist. One example is reaction time on performance tests.

A transformation allowed with ratio scales is $X' = b X$. Scores may be multiplied by a constant b, which changes the units of measurement, but not the ratio between two objects because this transformation does not change the zero point. Permissible statistics include the geometric mean.

So far, we have defined measurement, discussed some of the benefits of measurement, and described the four types of measurement scales. Now, we turn to the process of developing measures.

MEASURE DEVELOPMENT

While data can often be gathered using previously developed measures, W&O psychologists are often faced with a situation in which a new measure needs to be developed (e.g., because a previously developed measure lacks strong psychometric properties or because there is no measure for a specific attribute). The careful construction of measures ensures that they are dependable and accurate assessments of the attributes examined. If precautions are taken during measure development, fewer revisions will have to be made later to increase the measure's usefulness. There are many types of measures, some of which require special steps or processes during their development. However, we will limit our discussion to the general process of constructing a measure. This general process involves determining the purpose of measurement, defining the attribute to be measured, developing a measure plan, writing items, conducting a pilot study and item analysis, selecting items, establishing norms, and determining the reliability and validity of the measure.

Determining a Measure's Purpose

The first step in developing a measure is to determine its purpose. Measures may be designed to assess an attribute for research purposes (e.g., measure of perceived social power and its relationship with various outcomes; Nesler, Aguinis, Quigley, Lee & Tedeschi, 1999), predict future performance (e.g., measure of cognitive ability used to select applicants most likely to succeed on the job), evaluate performance adequacy (e.g., measure of reading ability to assess proficiency), diagnose individual strengths and weaknesses (e.g., measure of performance completed by supervisor), evaluate programs (e.g., measure of participant attitudes towards a training program), or give guidance or feedback (e.g., measure of vocational interests used for career development). The intended use of the measure will guide the development by dictating factors like thoroughness of attribute definition, types of items included, and length and complexity of the measure. Clearly stating the purpose before constructing the measure will help ensure that the measure does what it was intended to do.

Defining the Attribute

The second step is to define precisely the attribute to be measured. Without a clear definition, it will be difficult to be sure the measure is assessing the desired attribute. To clarify the attribute, it is necessary to state what concepts are included in the attribute as well as what is excluded. For example, a measure of perceived social power in dyadic relationships may include power bases such as expert power, coercive power, and legitimate power, but exclude trustworthiness (Nesler et al., 1999). Also, it is helpful to explain the psychological processes underlying the attribute. Continuing with the social power example, a process may be that the display of specific nonverbal behaviors leads to a supervisor being perceived as having high coercive power (Aguinis & Henle, forthcoming; Aguinis, Simonsen & Pierce, 1998), resulting in a dissatisfactory relationship with his or her subordinate which, in turn, may adversely affect subordinate

performance (Aguinis, Nesler, Quigley, Lee & Tedeschi, 1996). Further, it is important to state a theory describing the properties of the attribute (e.g., overall or global social power may be broken down into various power bases; Aguinis & Adams, 1998). A thorough description of the attribute provides a domain of content for writing items for the measure. Without a precise and clear definition of the attribute in question, we do not know what is to be measured or if it has been measured well (Guion, 1998).

Developing a Measure Plan

After the purpose of the measure is specified, and the attribute is defined, the next step is to establish the measure plan. The measure plan is a blueprint of the content, format, items, and administrative conditions for the measure to ensure it will be well constructed. First, the measure plan must include an outline of content to be included in the measure, which is derived from the attribute definition and will enable adequate coverage of important aspects of the attribute. Next, a description of the target population, who will be responding to the measure, including their demographics and reading level, is needed. Then, based on the target population, a description of the types of items to be used (e.g., multiple choice, true/false, short answer, essay, verbal responses), number of items, and examples of the items is written. Further, administrative procedures like instructions, how long the measure will take to administer, how it will be administered and by whom, and how it will be scored and interpreted, is outlined. Once the measure plan is written, experts and potential users should review it. A well thought-out plan enables appropriate items to be written and indicates intentions to design a good measure.

Writing Items

Next, using the definition of the attribute and the measure plan as guidelines, items are written. The closer these guidelines are followed, the more likely it is that items will measure the intended attribute. At this stage, twice the number of items desired for the final measure should be written because items will be discarded or revised. Although it is hard to know ahead of time how many items will be needed, Nunnally (1978) advises that at least 30 items are needed for a measure to have high reliability and, thus, initially at least 60 items should be written (we will discuss reliability later in the chapter). Note, however, that many measures in W&O psychology include fewer than 30 items and, nevertheless, estimates of their reliability are acceptable. Thus, given other things equal, although the number of items improves reliability, the number of items needed to reliably measure an attribute depends on the attribute in question.

There are many guidelines for writing good items (e.g., Berk, 1984; Flaugher, 1990; Thorndike, Cunningham, Thorndike & Hagen, 1991). In general, items should be written as simply and clearly as possible, should not be vague or ambiguous, never contain double negatives, have the appropriate level of complexity given the target population, avoid sexist or otherwise offensive language, and when using negatively phrased items, the negative word should be capitalized, bolded, or underlined.

Conducting a Pilot Study and Item Analysis

After the items are written, they need to be reviewed, with the attribute definition and target population in mind, for appropriateness, difficulty, and clarity (Nunnally, 1978). The measure is then administered, following the procedures outlined in the measure plan, to a sample that is representative of the target population in terms of age, gender, ability level, and so forth. Also, the sample must be large in order to sufficiently evaluate the measure (e.g., at least five times as many subjects as items; Nunnally, 1978). Respondent reactions are gathered to evaluate the clarity of items and administrative procedures as well as to determine if the time limit is adequate.

Gathering feedback from respondents will provide information about the clarity of items and procedures. In addition, to gather more in-depth information about the quality of the items, an item analysis can be conducted. Item analysis helps eliminate items that are poorly written as well as items that are not relevant to the targeted attribute. Thus, item analysis can explain why a measure has a certain level of reliability or validity (Murphy & Davidshofer, 1998). The following three types of indicators can be computed to better understand item functioning: (a) distractor analysis, (b) item difficulty, and (c) item discrimination. In addition, Item Response Theory can be used to conduct a comprehensive item analysis. We discuss these issues next.

Distractor Analysis

Distractor analysis evaluates multiple choice items that may appear on measures of achievement or ability. The frequency that respondents choose each response is calculated to determine the effectiveness of distractors (i.e., incorrect responses). The frequencies for the distractors should be about equal. If a distractor is chosen less frequently than the others, it may be too transparent and should be replaced. Alternatively, if a distractor is selected more often than the others, it may be tapping partial knowledge of the item or indicate that the item is misleading.

Item Difficulty

Item difficulty evaluates how difficult it is to answer an item correctly. An indicator of item difficulty, known as the *p* value, can be calculated to determine the percentage of respondents answering the item correctly. The *p* value is computed by dividing the number of individuals answering the item correctly by the total number responding to the item. A high *p* value indicates that most respondents answered the item correctly, and thus the item may be too easy. In contrast, a low *p* value indicates a difficult item since few were able to answer the item correctly. Ideally, the mean item *p* value should be about .5, which indicates a moderate difficulty level for the measure. Extreme *p* values do not discriminate among individuals, and items with such extreme values should be omitted or revised. However, an average *p* value of .5 may not be optimal for all measurement purposes (e.g., assessing the cognitive ability of applicants for an engineering position may require a measure with difficult items and thus a low mean *p* value).

Item Discrimination

Item discrimination analysis is appropriate for most measures and it evaluates whether the response to a particular item is related to responses on the other items. It determines which items are best measuring the attribute and whether the items are differentiating between those who do well on the measure and those who do not. That is, those who do well on a measure overall should answer an item correctly while those performing poorly on a measure should answer the item incorrectly. There are several statistics that serve this purpose, but we will limit our discussion to the discrimination index and the item–total score correlation.

The discrimination index *d* compares the number of respondents who answered an item correctly in the high scoring group with the number who answered it correctly in the low scoring group. If an item is discriminating adequately, more respondents with high scores should answer the item right as compared to respondents with low scores. To calculate *d*, the top and bottom scoring groups are selected (this can be done by taking the top and bottom quarters or thirds), and *d* is computed using Equation 2.1:

$$d = \frac{p_u}{n_u} - \frac{p_l}{n_l} \qquad (2.1)$$

where p_u and p_l are the number of individuals passing the item in the upper and lower scoring groups, and n_u and n_l are the size of the upper and lower groups, respectively. Items with large, positive *d* scores are good discriminators; that is, the item is harder for the lower scoring group and easier for the higher scoring group. An item with a negative *d* score should be discarded because negative scores indicate the item is easier for those who do poorly on the measure overall.

The second and most popular method for determining the ability of an item to discriminate is the correlation between an item and the total score on a measure. Items with high, positive item–total score correlations are related to the attribute the measure is examining and, thus, contribute to the measure's reliability. These items also have more variance than items with low item–total score correlations, which allows the measure to discriminate between individuals who do well on the measure and those who do not. Any items with item–total score correlations that are low or near zero should be revised, omitted, or replaced. Item–total correlations above .30 are preferred (Nunnally, 1978).

Item Response Theory

In addition to the statistics described above, Item Response Theory (IRT) can be used to conduct a comprehensive item analysis. IRT explains and analyzes the relationship between responses to individual items and the attribute being measured (Hulin, Drasgow & Parsons, 1983; Lord, 1980; Thissen & Steinberg, 1988). Specifically, IRT explains how individual differences on a particular attribute affect the behavior of an individual when he/she is responding to an item. That is, individuals with a large amount of the attribute will be more likely to respond correctly to an item requiring more of that attribute. Thus, the amount of an attribute can be estimated based on how an individual responds to items on the measure.

IRT holds assumptions about the mathematical relationship between an individual's level of the attribute and the likelihood that he/she will answer an item in a certain way. These assumptions and responses to the measure combine to form an item-characteristic curve (ICC). The ICC is a graphical representation of the probability of selecting the correct answer on an item due to an individual's level of the attribute. If an item is assessing the attribute, the probability of choosing the correct answer should increase as the level of the attribute does (Drasgow & Hulin, 1991).

By examining the ICC, we can determine item difficulty, discrimination, and the probability of answering correctly by guessing. Item difficulty is evaluated by examining the position of the curve. If the item is difficult, which is defined as requiring a large amount of the attribute in order to answer the item correctly, the curve starts to rise on the right side of the ICC plot. Alternatively, for easy items the curve begins to rise on the left side of the plot. Item discrimination is assessed by the steepness of the ICC. The flatter the curve, the less the item discriminates among individuals. Finally, from the ICC the probability of guessing the correct answer when an individual is low on the attribute can be

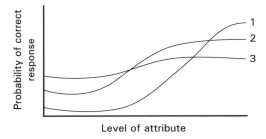

Figure 2.1   *Illustration of item-characteristic curve (ICC) for three hypothetical items*

determined. The higher the lower asymptote of the curve is, the easier it is to guess correctly on that item. That is, the higher the curve begins on the *y*-axis, the higher the probability of guessing.

Consider the ICC shown in Figure 2.1. Items 2 and 3 are easier than 1 because their curves begin to rise further to the left on the plot. Item 1 is the most discriminating while item 3 is the least because its curve is relatively flat. Finally, item 3 is the most susceptible to guessing because it begins higher on the *y*-axis.

Selecting Items

Based on the results of the pilot study and item analysis, items are selected and revised. A common method for selecting items uses the results of the item analysis to rank items based on their item–total score correlations from highest to lowest (Nunnally & Bernstein, 1994). A group of the top items is selected (e.g., 30 items) and the reliability of the items is calculated using coefficient alpha (reliability will be discussed more thoroughly in the next section). If the reliability, of those items is high (e.g., $\geq$ .80), no more items are selected. If the reliability is not high enough, then five to ten more items are added, depending on the gap between current and desired reliability, and then reliability is re-computed for the new set of items. This iterative process is repeated until the desired level of reliability is reached. Note that items with low item–total score correlations (i.e., below .20) should not be added because they do not improve reliability. Also, if reliability is no longer increasing or it is decreasing, the process of adding items should stop.

Once the desired reliability level is reached, a frequency distribution of scores on the entire instrument is plotted. A normal distribution is ideal, but if the distribution is skewed, adjustments can be made. When the distribution is positively skewed (i.e., scores cluster at the lower end of the plot), the items are too hard. Thus, items with low *p* values should be replaced with ones that have higher *p* values. Alternatively, when the distribution is negatively skewed (i.e., scores cluster at the high end of the plot), the items are too easy and items with high *p* values should be replaced with ones that have lower *p* values.

Establishing Norms

If the measure will be used to make decisions about individuals, norms should be established. Norms are used to provide standards for interpreting the scores of individuals, and are determined by gathering scores on the measure from a representative cross-section of individuals who are members of the target population (e.g., women and men, various levels of socioeconomic status; see Angoff, 1971 for more details). Norms are typically expressed in either standard scores (i.e., *z*) or percentiles. Standard scores are scores on a measure referenced to the normal distribution (i.e., $z = [X - M]/SD$, where *X* is an individual's score on the measure and *M* and *SD* are the measure's mean and standard deviation, respectively). Percentiles indicate the percentage of individuals in the sample who score below a particular score.

Determining Reliability

Reliability refers to the extent that a measure is dependable, stable, and consistent over time. If a measure is reliable, there is consistency between two sets of scores on a measure. For example, if a personality measure is administered to a job candidate and the candidate does not get the job, but applies for a similar position 6 months later and takes the measure again, the scores from the two administration periods should be similar if the measure is reliable. If the scores are considerably different, they may contain errors of measurement.

The concept of reliability assumes that scores obtained from a measure include a 'true' score or accurate representation of an individual's level of the attribute being measured. For example, if we give a typing test to job applicants, we assume that the test is assessing their true ability to type. However, in addition to the true component, measures in W&O psychology contain error. Errors of measurement are unsystematic or random and affect the obtained score on a measure, but are not related to the attribute being measured. Errors of measurement can be the result of changes in individuals responding to the measure (e.g., fatigue, anxiety) that affect their scores at one administration but not at another, or the result of changes in administrative conditions (e.g., noise, poor lighting). These errors prevent direct measurement of true scores and force us to rely on obtained scores as estimates of true scores. Thus, a score obtained from a measure has a true score component as well

Table 2.1 *Sources of error in the different reliability estimates*

Method of estimating reliability	Source of error
Test–retest	Time sampling
Parallel forms (immediate)	Content sampling
Parallel forms (delayed equivalent)	Time and content sampling
Split-half	Content sampling
Cronbach's α	Content sampling
Kuder–Richardson 20	Content sampling
Interrater agreement	Interrater consensus
Interclass correlation	Interrater consistency
Intraclass correlation	Interrater consistency

as an error component. Equation 2.2 demonstrates this relationship:

$$X_{\text{obtained score}} = X_{\text{true score}} + X_{\text{error}} \qquad (2.2)$$

In order to increase the reliability of a measure, errors of measurement must be minimized. Ideally, they should be completely eliminated. By decreasing error and subsequently increasing reliability, it is more likely the measure will reflect an individual's true possession of the attribute measured. If the measure contains a substantial amount of error, we cannot be confident that it is measuring the attribute. However, what constitutes errors of measurement varies from one situation to another depending on the purpose of measurement. Different methods of estimating reliability treat some factors as error while others do not. In sum, what is classified as errors of measurement depends on the purpose of measurement and subsequently, the method used to estimate reliability.

Methods for Estimating Reliability

Methods for estimating the reliability of a measure use the correlation coefficient to assess the relationship or degree of consistency between two sets of scores. The reliability coefficient can range from 0 to 1, with numbers closer to one indicating high reliability and little measurement error, and values closer to zero indicating low reliability and a large amount of measurement error.

Next, we discuss the following four methods for estimating reliability: Test–retest, parallel forms, internal consistency, and interrater. Each method calculates a reliability coefficient, but they differ regarding what they define as error (see Table 2.1 for a summary). Thus, the choice for a method to estimate reliability depends on the purpose of the measure as well as what is considered to be an important source of error.

Test–retest reliability involves giving the measure to the same group of individuals at different points in time. Scores are correlated from Time 1 and Time 2 to get a reliability coefficient referred to as coefficient of stability, which assesses the amount of error due to random fluctuations in scores over time. Thus, error is defined as changes in individuals (e.g., anxiety, fatigue, mood, health) and changes in measure administration (e.g., lighting, noise, distractions) that affect scores at one time but not at the other. The coefficient of stability can assess if a measure given now will be representative of the same individuals at a later time. In sum, this method should be used to estimate reliability when the attribute being measured is believed to be stable over time because this method can determine if the measure is free from error associated with the passage of time.

If the measure is reliable, scores should only change slightly from Time 1 to Time 2 and the rank order of individuals should stay the same. However, the reliability coefficient may differ depending on the length of time between administrations. If the time period is too short, the effects of memory may inflate the reliability coefficient because respondents may be able to recall how they answered the measure the first time. However, if the time period is too long, learning may affect the reliability coefficient. If individuals learn the answers to the items on the measure or if they learn information that changes how they respond to the measure, reliability may be underestimated because their scores will have changed from one administration to another. Although there is no magical number for the time interval between measure administrations, there should be at least 8 weeks between administrations (Nunnally, 1978), but not more than 6 months.

Parallel forms, also called alternate or equivalent forms, is a second method for estimating reliability. This method examines the consistency with which an attribute is measured across different versions of a measure. This is achieved by calculating the correlation between two forms to obtain a coefficient of equivalence. The two forms can be administered close together but, to prevent order effects, half of those taking the measure should be given form A first and the other half form B. Error using this method is defined as content sampling or samples of items that are nonequivalent. That is, high coefficients of equivalence indicate that the content sampled on the two versions of the measure are equivalent and, thus, measuring the same attribute. This method can be modified to assess error due to both content and time sampling. The modified version, labeled *delayed equivalent forms*, estimates reliability by increasing the amount of time between administrations (like test–retest) to get a coefficient of stability and equivalence by computing the correlation between one form given at Time 1 and the other form given at Time 2.

Unfortunately, it is hard to design equivalent measures. To be equivalent, measures must have the same number and type of items, same difficulty level, and the means and standard deviations of the scores obtained by respondents on both forms should be the same. Because it is hard to design equivalent forms of a measure, reliability coefficients determined by this method will be conservative estimates of reliability. Despite the difficulties associated with this method, parallel forms is useful for measures that are likely to be administered repeatedly (e.g., achievement measures).

The above discussion of measurement equivalence focused on parallel forms (Lord & Novick, 1968). Parallel measures have equal regressions of observed scores on true scores and equal error variances, and they can be used interchangeably. However, there are additional, less stringent, types of measurement equivalence. First, Tau-equivalent measures have equal regressions of observed scores on true score, but possibly different error variances (Jöreskog, 1971). Second, congeneric measures assess the same underlying construct (i.e., they are linearly related), but have different regressions of observed scores on true scores as well as different error variances (Jöreskog, 1971) (we refer readers to Vandenberg and Lance, 2000, for a more detailed discussion of measurement equivalence).

Internal consistency is a third method for estimating reliability. Internal consistency determines the degree to which various items of a measure correlate with each other. Error is defined as item heterogeneity; the more homogenous the items, the lower the error. This is important because items that are highly intercorrelated indicate they are measuring the same attribute. Three popular methods of determining internal consistency (i.e., split-half, Cronbach's coefficient alpha, and Kuder–Richardson 20) are discussed below.

The split-half method estimates internal consistency by administering a measure once and splitting it into two equivalent halves after it has been given to get two scores for each individual. This method is based on the premise that any item or group of items should be equivalent to any other item or group. The correlation between the two halves is a coefficient of equivalence that demonstrates the similarity of responses between the two halves. Thus, error is defined as inconsistency in content sampling between the halves for the attribute being measured. However, this reliability coefficient is based on a single administration of the test, so it does not take into account errors of measurement that occur over time (e.g., changes in individuals or administration) and, thus, it provides a liberal estimate of reliability.

Like parallel forms, equivalent halves need to be equal in terms of content, difficulty, and means and standard deviations of responses. The measure can be divided by placing the odd items in one half and even items in the other or, preferably, by random selection of items. The resulting coefficient of equivalence from the split-halves is the reliability of a measure half the length of the original one, which underestimates reliability because reliability increases as number of items does. Therefore, the Spearman–Brown prophecy formula shown in Equation 2.3 is used to determine the reliability of the entire measure:

$$r_{nn} = \frac{nr_{11}}{1 + (n-1)r_{11}} \qquad (2.3)$$

where n is the factor by which a measure is increased (e.g., $n = 2$ indicates the measure is doubled in size), r_{11} is the obtained reliability coefficient, and r_{nn} is the estimated reliability of a measure n times as long. For example, a mathematical ability measure is divided into two halves with odd items in one and even in the other. The correlation between the two halves is .68, which represents the reliability for a measure half the length of the original. If we use these values in Equation 2.3, the estimated reliability for the entire measure is:

$$r_{nn} = \frac{2(.68)}{1 + (2-1)(.68)} = .81$$

The second method for estimating internal consistency is Cronbach's α (see Cortina, 1993, for a review). Like split-half, Cronbach's α indicates the degree that items on a measure are correlated with each other. However, this method recognizes that there are many ways to divide a measure, so it takes the average of all possible split-halves of a measure (Kuder & Richardson, 1937). Cronbach's α is computed when there is a range of responses to items on a measure (e.g., 'always,' 'sometimes,' 'occasionally,' 'never'). As noted above, this type of reliability coefficient is determined by taking the average of all the possible split-halves of the measure so that it can assess how similar items are to each other and, thus, whether they are measuring the same attribute. If reliability is low, the measure may be assessing more than one attribute. The equation for computing Cronbach's α is the following:

$$r_{tt} = \frac{k}{k-1}\left(\frac{\sigma_t^2 - \Sigma\sigma_i^2}{\sigma_t^2}\right) \qquad (2.4)$$

where k is number of items included in the measure, σ_t^2 is the variance of total scores on the measure, and $\Sigma\sigma_i^2$ is the sum of the variances of item scores.

A special case of Equation 2.4 occurs when responses to items are binary in nature (i.e., two responses such as true or false, and right or wrong). For this special case, Kuder and Richardson (1937) developed the following variation of Equation 2.4 (i.e., KR-20):

$$r_{tt} = \frac{k}{k-1}\left(\frac{\sigma_t^2 - \Sigma pq}{\sigma_t^2}\right) \qquad (2.5)$$

where k and σ_t^2 are defined in Equation 2.4, and Σpq is the sum of all the products of p and q for each item, with p representing the number of individuals who pass the item and q representing number of individuals who fail the item.

Interrater reliability is a fourth method for estimating reliability. This method is useful when a measure is subjectively scored (e.g., observational data, ratings) and judgment is involved because raters' biases and inconsistencies (e.g., raters interpret rating standards differently or inconsistently) may influence ratings (Kraiger & Aguinis, 2001). Interrater reliability determines the consistency among raters and whether characteristics of the raters are determining the ratings instead of the attribute being measured.

In general, interrater reliability determines the degree of consistency across raters when rating objects or individuals. A distinction is made, however, between interrater consensus (i.e., absolute agreement between raters on some dimension), and interrater consistency (i.e., interrater reliability, or similarity in the ratings based on correlations or similarity in rank order) (Kozlowski & Hattrup, 1992). We discuss the following three ways to calculate interrater reliability: Interrater agreement, interclass correlation, and intraclass correlation.

Interrater agreement focuses on exact agreement between raters on their ratings of some dimension. The most commonly used statistics are (a) percentage of rater agreement, (b) Tinsley and Weiss's (1975) index of agreement T, (c) Kendall's (1948) coefficient of concordance W, and (d) Cohen's (1960) kappa (κ)[26]. When a group of judges rates a single attribute (e.g., organizational climate), the degree of rating similarity can be assessed by using James, Demaree and Wolf's (1984, 1993) r_{wg} index. All of these indices focus on the extent to which raters agree on the level of the rating or make essentially the same ratings.

Interclass and intraclass correlations are indices of consistency, are correlational in nature, and refer to proportional consistency of variance among raters (Kozlowski & Hattrup, 1992; Lahey, Downey & Saal, 1983; Lawlis & Lu, 1972; Shrout & Fleiss, 1979). Interclass correlation is used when two raters are rating multiple objects or individuals (e.g., performance ratings). Pearson product-moment correlation r and Cohen's (1960) weighted kappa (κ)[29] are the two most commonly used statistics. Intraclass correlation (ICC) is typically used when multiple raters are rating objects or individuals. This method determines how much of the differences among raters are due to differences in individuals on the attribute being measured and how much is due to errors of measurement.

There are six different forms of intraclass correlations, which allow for assessing situations including a group of raters and a single and/or multiple dimensions. Intraclass correlation is typically expressed as the ratio of the variance associated with targets (e.g., objects or individuals being rated in performance evaluations) over the sum of the variance associated with targets plus error variance based on the results of an analysis of variance (see Lahey et al., 1983 or Shrout & Fleiss, 1979, for the formulae for computing each of the six forms of intraclass correlations). ICC(1,1) is used to evaluate the reliability of multiple raters making judgements about multiple targets on a single dimension; ICC(2,1) is appropriate when the judges are randomly sampled from the larger population of judges, but each judge rates each of the targets; ICC(3,1) is used when each target is rated by each of the same judges and there are no other possible judges of interest; ICC(2,1) differs from ICC(3,1) in that ICC(2,1) allows one to generalize reliability to other judges while ICC(3,1) is used when there is an interest in the reliability of only a single judge or a fixed set of judges. The remaining three forms of intraclass correlations are identical to the above but include cases when multiple dimensions are rated for each target.

Interpreting Reliability Coefficients

Reliability coefficients are the means to an end. The end is to produce scores that measure attributes consistently across time, forms of a measure, items within a measure, or raters. We compute a reliability coefficient to understand if our scores are consistent. But, what exactly do the reliability coefficients tell us? What constitutes an acceptable level of reliability for our measure?

A reliability coefficient can be translated as the percentage of score variance on a measure that results from 'true' differences in the attribute being measured. For example, if a measure of cognitive ability has a reliability coefficient of .92, this means that 92% of score variance can be accounted for by differences in cognitive ability among respondents, and 8% can be attributed to errors of measurement. The acceptable size of a reliability coefficient depends on the purpose of the measure. If the measure is used to compare individuals (e.g., selection measure), the reliability coefficient should be greater than .90 (Nunnally, 1967). But, .70 may be sufficient for most measures in W&O psychology and even lower coefficients may be acceptable for research purposes.

Standard Error of Measurement

Reliability estimates provide information about the consistency of most individuals' scores on a measure. However, they do not provide information about the consistency of a given individual's score on the measure (Aguinis, Cortina & Goldberg, 1998). Rather, reliability reflects the error associated with a particular measure. To gather information about how much error we can expect for an individual's score on a measure, we can calculate the standard error of measurement. Standard error of measurement provides an estimate of the standard

deviation of a normal distribution of scores that an individual would obtain if he/she responded to the measure an infinite number of times. The standard error of measurement σ_{Meas} is computed as follows:

$$\sigma_{Meas} = \sigma_x \sqrt{1 - r_{xx}} \qquad (2.6)$$

where σ_x is the standard deviation of the distribution of obtained scores, and r_{xx} is the reliability estimate for the measure. Using the standard error of measurement, we can derive confidence intervals that estimate the range of scores that will, at a certain probability level, include an individual's true score (cf. Equation 2.2). If the standard error of measurement for a reading measure is 2.21 and an individual obtained a score of 60 on the measure, by adding and subtracting the standard error from the obtained score (60 ± 2.21), a confidence interval of 57.79 to 62.21 is derived. This range of scores can be interpreted as if the individual was given the test 100 times, the reading scores would fall between 57.79 and 62.21 about 68 times (i.e., 68% confidence interval). Note that the level of confidence can be increased from 68% to 95% by adding and subtracting two standard errors from the obtained score (i.e., the interval would go from a low of $60 - 4.42 = 55.8$ to a high of $60 + 4.42 = 64.42$).

The standard error of measurement can aid decision-making about individuals in several ways. For example, if we are deciding whether to hire Sarah by comparing her score of 60 to a cutoff score of 65, the standard error of measurement can help with this decision. Sarah's score is only five points away from the cutoff, but when we examine the 68% confidence interval calculated earlier (i.e., 57.79 to 62.21), we estimate that it is not likely that she will meet this cutoff upon retesting. Further, the standard error can be used to assess whether two applicants' scores on the reading test are different from one another (cf. Aguinis, Cortina & Goldberg, 2000). For instance, Sarah scored a 60 and Rachel scored a 62. The standard error is 2.21 and the difference between the candidates is only 2 points; therefore, upon retesting, Sarah may score higher than Rachel. The standard error can also be used to evaluate scores between groups. For example, it can determine if scores for men and women differ significantly.

Improving Reliability Coefficients

We want the reliability of our measures to be as large as possible to ensure that our measures are dependable, consistent, and stable over time. However, the size of reliability coefficients may be limited by several factors and if we are not aware of these factors and do not take them into consideration, we may over or underestimate reliability. First, the method for estimating reliability can affect the size of the obtained coefficient. As described above, the various methods for estimating reliability define error differently and, consequently, the reliability coefficient for a measure differs depending on the method used. Some methods are more liberal (e.g., split-half), which may overestimate reliability, while others are more conservative (e.g., parallel forms), which may underestimate reliability.

Second, variability in scores can influence the size of reliability coefficients. If we administer a measure of perceived social power (i.e., ability to influence) in a flat organization where all employees have the ability to influence each other, there will be no variance in scores because everyone will score very high. Variability among measure scores allows for differentiation among the individuals taking the measure. If all respondents score a 20, we cannot differentiate among them based on social power. However, if there is a wide range of scores (e.g., 20, 17, 13, 12, 9, 7, 6, 1), we are able to make many differentiations among pairs or groups of individuals. In addition, variability can be affected by individual differences. As individual differences (i.e., variability) among scores increase, so does the correlation between them, which makes it easier for the measure to differentiate among individuals. Thus, other things equal, the greater the variability, the greater the reliability.

Third, as the length of a measure increases, so does its reliability. If the number of items relevant to measuring a particular attribute increases, we are able to obtain a more accurate picture of an individual's true score on that attribute. We can use Spearman–Brown's prophecy formula (i.e., Equation 2.3) to demonstrate the relationship between measure length and reliability. Assume we are using a measure of extroversion, which contains 15 items and has a reliability of .80, and we double the size of the measure. Entering these values in Equation 2.3 yields:

$$r_{nn} = \frac{2(.80)}{1 + (2-1)(.80)} = .89$$

By doubling the number of items on the extraversion measure to 30, we increased its reliability from .80 to .89. However, a caveat must be made. Indiscriminately adding items will not increase the reliability, especially internal consistency. Of course, additional items must be similar to previous ones and be relevant to the attribute being measured.

Fourth, the characteristics of the sample used also affect reliability. Sample size will influence the magnitude of the reliability coefficients because larger samples will have less sampling error than small samples (Aguinis, forthcoming), thus providing a better estimate of reliability. In addition, the sample must be representative of the population the measure is going to be used for or reliability will be over or underestimated.

Generalizability Theory

Our discussion of reliability thus far has followed a classical approach. However, an alternative approach

to reliability is generalizability theory (Cronbach, Gleser, Nanda & Rajaratnam, 1972), which is a process of determining the limits of the generalizability of inferences derived from measures. That is, it assesses the situations (e.g., different people, places, and times) to which inferences made from a measure can be applied and, thus, evaluates how well a measure is assessing an attribute.

The classical approach to reliability that we have discussed also explores issues of generalizability, but only in a limited way. For instance, the coefficient of stability assesses generalizability over time while internal consistency determines the extent to which inferences generalize across items on a measure. However, generalizability theory takes into account many sources of error simultaneously instead of examining one at a time and shows how much total variance is a result of each source of error.

Generalizability theory uses experimental studies to determine how much variance is attributable to different sources of error. A *generalizability study* is designed to evaluate the extent to which results obtained using a measure are consistent despite different administrative conditions. Information is collected from individuals responding to the measure under different circumstances to determine a coefficient of generalizability. A *decision study* evaluates decisions made based on a measure's scores. Thus, it tells us how sound are the conclusions made using a measure. For a more detailed discussion of generalizability theory, we refer readers to Cronbach et al. (1972) and Brennan (1992).

In sum, scores gathered using a measure are affected by numerous sources of error. As shown in Equation 2.2, observed scores have a true score as well as an error component. A reliability analysis allows us to estimate the extent to which observed scores are influenced by a random error component. A large reliability coefficient (i.e., small standard error of measurement, cf. Equation 2.6) suggests that scores are consistent. However, consistency does not ensure accuracy. For example, a scale may be consistently off by 20 pounds. The scale lacks random measurement error and, thus, scores are very consistent. However, scores do not represent true weight, and therefore decisions made based on these scores (e.g., change patterns of eating behavior) may be incorrect. The issues of whether scores, and decisions made based on scores, are accurate are issues of validity. We discuss this topic next.

Gathering Evidence of Validity

Validity refers to the utility of the inferences made from a measure's scores. Inferences made from measures can involve measurement issues (e.g., Is this measure of leadership effectiveness really assessing who is an effective leader?) or decisions (e.g., Can the measure of leadership effectiveness help predict who will be successful as a manager?). Thus, the process of validation evaluates whether a measure is assessing the attribute it is supposed to and if a measure can be used to make accurate decisions. The measure itself is not validated, rather the inferences about what the measure is assessing and decisions made from the scores are. Empirical investigations are conducted to gather evidence to support these inferences. Evidence is continually gathered to evaluate a measure and to revise it if it is not fulfilling its intended purposes. Therefore, validation is an ongoing process. In sum, validity provides evidence attesting to what attribute a measure is assessing, how well it measures that attribute, and what decisions can be made from a measure's scores.

Originally it was posited that there was a particular type of validity that was appropriate for a given type of measure. The specific measurement purpose dictated which type of validity was used to establish validity. However, validity is now viewed as a unitarian concept. There are not different types of validity, rather different types of evidence for determining the validity of a measure (Binning & Barrett, 1989; Cronbach, 1988; Landy, 1986). Thus, many types of evidence should be gathered to support the inferences and decisions that are made based on a measure's scores. Next, we discuss the following three types of validity evidence: Content, criterion, and construct. Although they are discussed separately, they are interrelated and a combination of them is necessary to determine what inferences can be made from a measure's scores.

Content-Related Evidence

Content-related validity evidence examines the adequacy of domain sampling; that is, whether a measure is assessing the attribute it is intended to measure. This is demonstrated when the content of a measure (i.e., items) is judged to be a representative sample of the content of the attribute under consideration. Thus, this method of gathering evidence of validity relies on judgments of potential users and experts.

Establishing content-related evidence begins during the construction of a new measure. Developing a well thought-out plan for measure construction (as described earlier in the chapter) and adhering to that plan provides evidence of content validity. When potential users of a measure and experts of the attribute being measured agree the plan was well developed and implemented, the measure is most likely to be a representative sample of the content of the attribute. Thus, following the steps outlined previously for developing a measure will help establish content-related evidence.

The content validation process starts with a description of the content domain. The content domain is the total set of items that could be used to measure an attribute (Guion, 1977), and there are

three parts to the content domain. First, a definition of the domain or attribute to be measured must be clarified. For example, if we are developing a measure of job satisfaction, a definition may be 'An individual's affective reaction to his/her job.' Next, the different areas or categories of the attribute to be included in the measure must be specified. For our job satisfaction measure, we may include the following categories of satisfaction: Pay, supervision, coworkers, and the work itself. Finally, the relative importance of the categories must be established. For example, if we believe that satisfaction with pay and the work itself are more important than satisfaction with supervision and coworkers, we must weigh them more heavily so that they will comprise a larger portion of the measure (e.g., pay = 30%, work itself = 30%, coworkers = 20%, supervision = 20%).

After the content domain has been described, and items have been written following this description, we can compare the content of the measure to the content domain to provide evidence of content validity. Each item on the measure is evaluated against the definition and classified into a category to determine if it falls within the domain of the attribute. The measure as a whole is also compared to the content domain to evaluate if the measure samples all the areas of the attribute and if there are more items representing the areas that were ranked as more important. The closer the measure matches the content domain, the stronger the evidence regarding content validity.

The extent to which experts agree on the content validity of a measure can be calculated using Lawshe's (1975) Content Validity Ratio (CVR). To compute CVR, experts who are familiar with the attribute measured (e.g., recognized researchers in the field of job satisfaction) rate whether each item is essential, useful but not essential, or not necessary for measuring the attribute. Their ratings are used in Equation 2.7:

$$\text{CVR} = \frac{n_e - N/2}{N/2} \qquad (2.7)$$

where n_e is the number of experts that rated the item as essential, and N is the total number of experts. The resulting CVR represents the overlap between the content of the attribute and the content of the measure. For example, if 10 experts rate an item of a measure and eight of them believe the item is essential, CVR is:

$$\text{CVR} = \frac{8 - 10/2}{10/2} = .6$$

CVR can range from − 1 to + 1 with values closer to + 1 indicating that more experts agree the item is essential. In the above example CVR is .6, which is close to 1, so most experts believed that there was overlap between the content of the item and the content of the attribute. Further, CVRs for all the items on a measure can be averaged to determine the extent that experts believe the entire measure overlaps with the attribute content.

Criterion-Related Evidence

As mentioned throughout this chapter, measurement is used to make important decisions about individuals. The second type of evidence, criterion-related, is particularly suited to determine if a measure can be used to make predictions and/or decisions. Thus, a measure demonstrates criterion-related evidence of validity if it can be used to make accurate decisions. Criterion-related evidence involves correlating scores on a predictor (i.e., measure of an attribute) with some criterion (e.g., measure of decision outcome or level of success) to determine if accurate decisions can be made from scores. There are two types of studies, predictive and concurrent, that can be designed to test the relationship between a predictor and a criterion.

Predictive validation studies focus on the prediction of future behavior. Predictive studies begin with obtaining scores from a random sample of the population in which decisions will be made, thus ensuring study results are generalizable. Next, decisions are made without using scores from the measure. After the decision is made, scores on a criterion are gathered and the correlation between the measure and criterion is calculated. An example of a predictive validation study is when job applicants are given a measure of integrity and selected for the job without considering their scores. After applicants have been hired and on the job for a period of time, information on absenteeism, theft, and other counterproductive behaviors is gathered and correlated with the integrity measure to determine its predictive ability.

Unfortunately, predictive studies are not as practical as concurrent studies because they require not using the measure to make decisions and a time delay before the criterion data are collected. Thus, *concurrent validation studies* are more commonly implemented to determine whether using a measure leads to accurate decisions. Concurrent evidence evaluates if an individual's level of an attribute is adequate to achieve the criterion at the present time. Concurrent validation studies gather scores on the predictor and criterion at about the same time from a preselected population. Then, the correlation between predictor and criterion scores is obtained. For example, current employees could complete the integrity measure and their employment files could be checked at the same time to determine how often they are absent, if they have been disciplined for theft, and any other information regarding counterproductive behaviors. The predictor and the criteria are then correlated to determine the predictive value of the integrity measure. Although concurrent studies are more practical than predictive, they may not

be generalizable to the broad population because these studies rely on a preselected sample instead of randomly selecting from the target population.

Note that in both types of criterion-related validation studies (i.e., predictive and concurrent), there is an artificial reduction in the variance in one or more of the variables under consideration. This artificial reduction in variance, often labeled range restriction or censorship, deserves attention because it might have an impact on correlation coefficients, regression coefficients, and means. For example, a reduction in variance decreases the size of validity coefficients so that results obtained using restricted samples may underestimate actual validity coefficients. There are three types of range restriction (see Thorndike, 1949: 169–180 for a more detailed discussion regarding range restriction). Cases I and II are often labeled 'direct or explicit restriction', and Case III is often labeled 'indirect or implicit restriction'. Case I is a situation in which we are interested in the relationship (e.g., correlation) between predictor variable X and criterion variable Y, variable X's range is restricted, and we have information regarding variable Y's variance in both the restricted (sample) and unrestricted (population) groups, and information regarding variable X's variance in the restricted group only. This situation is not likely to be encountered by most W&O psychologists. Case II involves a situation in which we are also interested in the correlation between X and Y, variable X's range is restricted, and we have information regarding X's variance in both the restricted (sample) and unrestricted (population) groups, and information regarding variable Y's variance in the restricted group only. This situation is more frequently encountered by W&O psychologists, and it is particularly common in the personnel selection literature. Finally, Case III involves a situation in which we are also interested in the correlation between X and Y, but restriction of range has taken place on a third, or more, of often unspecified variables which are correlated with X and Y. Because of the correlations between X and the unspecified variable(s), and Y and the unspecified variable(s), we have variance information regarding both X and Y for the restricted groups only (Aguinis & Whitehead, 1997). Case III is the most pervasive type of range restriction in the personnel selection literature (Aguinis & Whitehead, 1997; Thorndike, 1949).

Construct-Related Evidence

Construct-related evidence is the third type of evidence that can be used to determine if inferences made from a measure's scores are valid. Construct, like content-related evidence, is the process of accumulating evidence to establish whether the measure is assessing the attribute it is intended to assess. However, instead of evaluating the measure plan and determining whether the measure includes a representative sample of the content of the attribute,

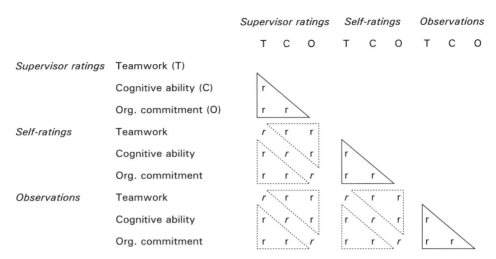

Figure 2.2   *Illustration of the multitrait–multimethod matrix for hypothetical study on the relationship among measures of teamwork, cognitive ability, and organizational commitment*

construct-related evidence investigates hypothesized relationships between a construct and other constructs to assess if actual relationships are similar to predicted ones. A construct is an abstract characteristic or attribute that a measure is believed to be assessing. Conscientiousness, extraversion, social power, job satisfaction, and intelligence are examples of constructs. Because we cannot observe these constructs, we need measures to be concrete and operational indicators of them. Thus, construct-related evidence involves conducting studies to support that a measure is indeed assessing the proposed construct by relating a measure to measures of other constructs.

The process of gathering construct-related evidence begins with defining the construct and identifying observable behaviors that operationally define the construct. Upon determination of observable behaviors of the construct, relationships among the different behaviors are investigated. If the observable behaviors are good indicators of the construct, they should be highly intercorrelated indicating that they are measuring the same concept. Once the internal consistency of the behaviors has been established, a nomological network is constructed (Cronbach & Meehl, 1955). A nomological network is a pattern of proposed relationships between the construct, its observable behaviors, and other constructs and observable behaviors. This network specifies variables to which the construct should and should not be related. Studies are then conducted to determine the degree that actual relationships match the expected ones delineated in the nomological network. The closer the match between the hypothesized nomological network and the actual relationships, the stronger the evidence of construct validity.

There are different types of studies that can be designed to support the hypothesized relationships between the construct and other variables. The more evidence accumulated from different sources, the more confident we can be that the measure is assessing the construct. One type of study that examines several types of evidence of construct validity is the multitrait–multimethod approach developed by Campbell and Fiske (1959). To conduct a study using this approach, data must be gathered on at least two constructs each measured by at least two different methods (e.g., supervisor ratings, observations, self-reports). Correlations among the different constructs measured by different methods are calculated to form a multitrait–multimethod matrix. The matrix shown in Figure 2.2 includes hypothetical correlations among measures of teamwork, cognitive ability, and organizational commitment using supervisor ratings, self-ratings, and observer ratings.

The first type of evidence provided by the matrix is convergent validity, which examines whether different methods of assessing the construct produce similar results. If results obtained using different methods are highly correlated, we can be more confident that our measures are assessing the intended construct. Convergent validity is determined by examining the italicized correlations in the matrix.

Next, we can assess divergent validity; that is, whether measures hypothesized not to be related are not related. Examining the correlations within the dashed triangles provides evidence regarding divergent validity.

Then, we can evaluate method bias, which is the inflation of correlations due to a common method of measurement. This is determined by investigating the correlations between different constructs using the same method, which are contained in the solid-lined triangles. If these correlations are higher than correlations between different constructs measured by different methods, method bias exists.

Finally, we should note that structural equation modeling (SEM) can be used to gather construct-related evidence. SEM can be used to assess convergent and discriminant validity simultaneously (e.g., Pierce, Aguinis & Adams, 2000).

Improving the Size of Validity Coefficients

Similar to the reliability coefficient, there are several factors that affect the magnitude of the validity coefficient. First, to obtain high validity coefficients there must be variability among scores on both the predictor and criterion. If respondents have approximately the same scores, it will be hard for the measure to differentiate among individuals based on the criterion. Also, as described above, in many situations in W&O psychology, the variability in a sample is artificially smaller than that in the population (e.g., personnel selection research; Aguinis & Stone-Romero, 1997; Aguinis & Whitehead, 1997). Range restriction can occur in the predictor when criterion data are available only for those who are hired. Low scorers on the predictor are not hired and thus are not represented in the sample. Likewise, restriction in the criterion may occur as a consequence of terminations, turnover, or transfers that occur before data on the criterion are gathered. Note that when a sample is affected by range restriction in the predictor, the criterion, or both, there are formulae and computer programs available to determine what the validity coefficient would be in the absence of range restriction (Johnson & Ree, 1994).

Second, validity can be enhanced if the influence of factors unrelated to scores on the criterion is minimized. Criterion contamination occurs when factors that are unrelated to the criterion affect scores on the criterion and, consequently, lower validity. For example, an organization uses a general cognitive ability measure to predict job performance. However, if factors such as availability of resources, quality of equipment, or supervisory liking unduly influence supervisory ratings of performance, the validity of the cognitive ability measure will decrease. We are no longer just measuring cognitive ability but, in addition to cognitive ability, we are assessing differences in resources, equipment, and likeability.

Third, validity estimated using the correlation coefficient depends on the relationship between the measure and a criterion being linear. When the relationship is linear, the predictor can accurately predict both high and low scores. If this statistical assumption is violated (e.g., the relationship between the predictor and criterion is curvilinear), the validity coefficient is underestimated.

Finally, if the relationship between the measure and a criterion differs for various groups (e.g., men vs. women), the measure is not similarly valid for these groups (Aguinis, 1995; Aguinis & Stone-Romero, 1997). Thus, prediction of outcomes based on a measure's scores will differ depending on group membership (Aguinis & Pierce, 1998b; Aguinis, Petersen & Pierce, 1999). Consequently, the overall predictive accuracy of a measure will be diminished (Aguinis & Pierce, 1998a; Aguinis, Pierce & Stone-Romero, 1994).

In sum, this section reviewed the process of measure development. We discussed the determination of the purpose of measurement, the definition of the attribute to be measured, the measure development plan, writing items, conducting a pilot study and item analysis, selecting items, establishing norms, and the assessment of reliability and validity. Next, we discuss our views on recent and future trends in the field of measurement in W&O psychology.

RECENT AND FUTURE TRENDS IN MEASUREMENT IN W&O PSYCHOLOGY

This section of the chapter is devoted to a selective set of issues that constitute what in our view are recent and future trends in the field of measurement in W&O psychology. Admittedly, due to space limitations, the following is only a subset of issues that we could describe. However, we hope that discussing these issues will provide an appreciation for what we believe are some important changes affecting the field. First, we discuss issues pertaining to levels of analysis. Specifically, we describe basic concepts regarding levels of analysis, different relationships at different levels, and measurement issues and aggregation. Second, we discuss the impact of technology on measurement. Third, we provide a brief overview of issues regarding cross-cultural measurement transferability. Fourth, we discuss legal and social issues in measurement. Finally, we describe the proliferation of measurement worldwide.

Levels of Analysis and Measurement

As noted above, the first step in the measurement process is to determine the purpose of our measurement. For example, is our purpose to draw conclusions about individuals in a particular organizational setting, individuals in general, groups, or organizations as a whole? Consideration of these different hierarchical 'levels' is important for developing appropriate measures and drawing appropriate conclusions.

For many years, researchers in W&O psychology have been conducting research and developing techniques for recruitment, selection, training and compensation of employees, for dealing effectively with unions, for enhancing productivity and job satisfaction, for reducing turnover, and so forth. Hundreds of studies have been directed at examining and refining these practices resulting in numerous recommendations for the most effective means of dealing with human resources in organizations. That is, based on the results of these studies, researchers and authors have assumed that organizations will be more effective if we follow practices that are deemed technically superior regarding the management of individuals. Yet, this may not be the case (Ostroff & Bowen, 2000). It is inappropriate to assume that what applies when we study individual differences in organizations also applies to entire groups, divisions, organizational systems, industries or even countries (Klein, Dansereau & Hall, 1994; Ostroff, 1993). Thus, in designing measurement systems, we must attend to 'levels of analysis issues'.

Traditionally, W&O psychologists have focused primarily on the individual level of analysis. Much of our research has been conducted by gathering data from individuals, typically within a single organization, and examining relationships with individual-level performance, behaviors, and attitudes. This focus on individual differences is important and useful provided we only draw conclusions about individuals and do not assume that these same results would apply to all individuals across organizations, or to groups or organizations as a whole.

Basic Levels Concepts

It has long been recognized that multiple, interdependent levels in organizations exist and that understanding the interrelations within and between levels is critical to understanding organizations and organizational behavior (e.g., House, Rousseau & Thomas-Hunt, 1995; Roberts, Hulin & Rousseau, 1978). Individuals comprise groups, groups comprise organizations, organizations comprise industries or markets, and so forth. Interdependencies exist among these levels as, for example, individuals interact with others in their group, groups within the organization interact with other groups, and organizations interact with other organizations. For the purposes here, we will focus primarily on individuals, groups and organizations to illustrate our points, but these issues are also relevant to dyads (e.g., supervisor and subordinate pairs), industries, markets, countries, and other relevant groupings.

Single-level studies are common in organizational research. For example, an individual-level study might be conducted to examine the relationship between employees' perceived job autonomy and their job performance, and an organizational-level study might be conducted to examine the relationship between technology and productivity of organizations. In cross-level studies, a higher-level and a lower-level construct are examined simultaneously. For example, a cross-level study might investigate the impact of organizational climate (an organizational construct) on individual-level satisfaction and behavior. In multi-level studies, two or more levels are examined simultaneously. Cross-level and multi-level examinations fall under the rubric of the meso paradigm (House et al., 1995) because they pertain to the study of at least two levels simultaneously.

Problems are encountered when the level of theory, measurement, statistical analysis, and interpretation are not consistent (Dansereau, Alluto & Yammarino, 1984; Rousseau, 1985). The *level of theory* is the 'target' level or the level that we aim to explain (e.g., individuals, groups, or organizations). The *level of measurement* refers to the source of the data we gather (e.g., survey of individuals, supervisory measure of group performance). The *level of statistical analysis* pertains to the level at which we analyze our data during statistical analyses (e.g., if we gather data from individuals, but then average those data to form aggregate scores for each group during our analyses, then our level of statistical analysis is the group). Finally, the *level of interpretation* refers to the level at which we draw conclusions. For example, if we measure group morale and analyze our data at the group level by using aggregate scores for the group, then we can only draw conclusions about groups. Drawing inferences from our data about any other level, such as how individuals or organizations respond, is inappropriate. Attributing results to a different level than the one from which theory and corresponding analytical techniques were drawn results in the fallacy of the wrong level (Roberts et al., 1978).

Different Relationships at Different Levels

We noted above that different relationships among variables exist at different levels of analysis (individual, group, or organization). How can this be explained? First, consider Figure 2.3. Each oval represents an organization, each small dot represents an individual, and each square represents the average score among individuals within the organization. The solid line represents the correlation across all individuals, the dashed line represents the correlation among the aggregated (average) scores, and the solid line within an oval represents the correlation among individuals within an organization.

In the left panel of the figure we see that if we measured individuals within an organization we would find very little relationship between the two constructs. However, if we measured individuals across organizations we would find a positive relationship, and if we measured aggregated (averaged) scores at the organizational level we would find a strong positive relationship between the two constructs. How could this happen? Suppose, for example, that we are examining the relationship between satisfaction and performance. It may be difficult to

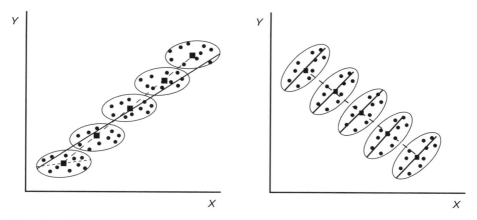

Figure 2.3   *Correlations of different magnitudes at different levels (left panel) and correlations in opposite directions at different levels (right panel)*

predict the relationship between any one individual's satisfaction and his/her performance within an organization. Lower performance is only one possible response to dissatisfaction. A dissatisfied employee may, for example, file a grievance, sabotage the workplace, ask for a transfer and so forth. In contrast, a satisfied employee could work harder, engage in more citizenship behaviors, improve skills or make suggestions for improvements in work processes. While the relationship between individual-level satisfaction and performance may be weak, collective organizational effects can be much stronger due to the cumulative interactions among employees and the cumulative impacts of the behaviors and responses of satisfied or dissatisfied employees overall (Ostroff, 1992).

A different scenario is presented in the right panel of Figure 2.3. Here, the relationship when we study individuals within a single organization is negative, but the relationship at the organizational level (among aggregated mean scores) is positive. How can a case like this be explained? Suppose we are examining the relationship between cognitive ability (*X*) and performance (*Y*). It may be that those organizations who rely primarily on cognitive ability tests have more intelligent employees, but they may be missing other critical employee attributes such as interpersonal skills, conscientiousness, or citizenship behaviors, thereby causing lower productivity for the organization.

There are many different configurations that can emerge when examining relationships across levels. The examples here serve to illustrate how different relationships can occur at different levels and the importance of considering one's theoretical interests and aligning them with one's measurement. These notions are explained in more detail in the following section.

Measurement Issues and Aggregation

The level of measurement refers to the level at which data are collected. Individual-level constructs should be collected at the individual level. Higher-level constructs (e.g., group, organization) may be assessed by gathering individual level data and aggregating individual scores to represent the higher level or by collecting a global measure for that level. For many constructs (e.g., group or organizational performance) a global index for the higher-level construct is preferable (e.g., objective measures, expert sources to provide a rating for each group). Frequently, researchers do not have a global index of the higher-level constructs of interest. Further, for some constructs such as organizational climate or group norms, which are based on shared perceptions of members, it is appropriate to gather data from the individuals within the unit and aggregate them to represent the higher level.

One question that arises when relying on aggregated (or averaged) data from individuals to represent the higher-level construct pertains to the extent of 'agreement' among individuals in the focal unit on the construct. While the focus of some debate, it has been generally assumed that individuals within the same focal unit should have relatively similar scores. Individual-level measures should not be aggregated to represent a higher-level construct unless some degree of within-unit agreement can be demonstrated. This is particularly critical for constructs that rely on notions of shared perceptions such as organizational climate, group norms, and cohesiveness (Kozlowski & Klein, 2000).

It is highly unlikely that the variation in responses among individuals within a unit will be close to zero. One issue that arises is how to treat the variance within a unit. One argument is that the aggregate (mean) response per group or organization is a more accurate representation of the organizational characteristics (Glick, 1985; James, 1982). Intragroup or intraorganizational variance in responses is viewed as a source of inaccuracy or random error. Individual deviations from the mean of their focal unit are not of substantive interest, except in terms of measurement accuracy. Aggregation results in a more stable assessment of the constructs. For example, if one is interested only in examining whether there is a relationship between training of employees and organizational productivity at the organizational level, then issues of individual variation may be irrelevant.

Alternatively, a researcher could view individual variation within a group as partly a result of random error, but also as a reflection of systematic variance or real individual differences. Here, a researcher might examine whether there is a relationship between the constructs among individuals and also among organizations, and whether the relationship at the organizational level is stronger or weaker than the one at the individual level (Ostroff, 1993).

It is likely that some, but not all, of the individual deviation from the mean score of their group is random error. The individual's score is the group true score (mean score for the group) plus some systematic individual variation from the mean plus some random measurement error (cf. Equation 2.2). Given these assumptions, the correlation among the mean scores will differ from the correlation among individuals. This is because measurement error attenuates or reduces the correlation among individuals. However, the correlation among the mean scores is not affected by individual-level random measurement error because the random errors essentially 'average out' in the aggregated score. Hence, before comparing a correlation at the individual level to a higher-level correlation among aggregated scores, it is important to first correct the individual-level score for random measurement error (Ostroff, 1993). Once this has been accomplished, the magnitude of the individual correlation and group or organizational level can be compared. If they are similar, the same processes and relationships exist among individuals as they do for groups (or organizations); if they differ, then different processes are operating at the different levels and more investigation is needed to determine the cause of the differences (Ostroff, 1993).

Finally, there are additional issues that must be considered in constructing items from a multi-level perspective. Clearly, if one is interested in individuals, then the referent for the items should be the individual. However, if one is interested in groups for example, the referent in the items might be better focused on the group. For example, rather than phrase an item as 'I think...' or 'My work...', the item could be phrased as 'Members of this group think...' or 'Our work...'. This referent-shift (Chan, 1998) may result in greater within-group agreement

on the construct (Kozlowksi & Klein, 2000) and is preferable if the unit of theory is the group or a higher level.

IMPACT OF TECHNOLOGY ON MEASUREMENT

Improvements in technology are leading to many advances in the area of measurement. Specifically, computers and the Internet have produced new methods for assessing attributes. Measures can be administered online and computers can be used to instantly score measures, store the results, and interpret the meaning of scores through computer-generated reports. Although there are costs associated with hardware and software, the benefits of computerized measurement may outweigh the initial investment. Computers provide standardized and easy administration, quick scoring procedures, efficient storage of results, and less error and chance of cheating. Further, computer unfamiliarity and anxiety are decreasing as the technology becomes more available (Nunnally & Bernstein, 1994).

Computers can administer attribute measures in the exact format as paper and pencil versions. Thus, the computer acts as an electronic page turner. However, an additional advantage of computer technology is that measures of cognitive ability and knowledge can be administered as computerized adaptive tests (CATs). Unlike conventional paper and pencil measures, which require high-ability respondents to waste time answering a number of easy items and low-ability respondents to become frustrated answering many difficult items, CATs are tailored to the ability level of each respondent. CATs use item response theory (discussed earlier in the chapter) to determine the difficulty and discriminability of items. Using the information derived from item response theory, CATs begin with an item of moderate difficulty and the next item administered is determined by a respondent's answer. If a respondent answers correctly, a more difficult item is selected while an incorrect response results in the selection of a less difficult item. The test continuously estimates each respondent's ability level, chooses items appropriate for that level, and uses responses to items to revise the ability estimate (Weiss & Davinson, 1981). This process continues until a certain number of items is administered or the estimate of ability stops changing. In sum, computerized adaptive testing is an efficient method because it measures ability with fewer items (Drasgow & Hulin, 1991) and, thus, can be administered in less time.

Measures can also be administrated via the Internet. Attribute measures can be e-mailed to a targeted population (e.g., attitude measures e-mailed to current employees) or they can be posted on a web page with either open access to the page (e.g., measure of customer satisfaction) or restricted access using a password (e.g., cognitive ability measure administered to job applicants passing initial screening). Posting measures on a web site and collecting responses through the Internet can be less expensive and time consuming than conventional paper and pencil measures (Schmidt, 1997). Few, if any, proctors are needed; data entry and errors associated with it are eliminated; many individuals from various locations can respond at their leisure; and, unlike e-mailed measures, confidentiality is guaranteed. Unfortunately, when open access to a measure administered through a web page exists, the Internet may not attract a representative sample. The Internet may lead to samples overrepresenting males and professionals, and higher educated and more computer literate individuals (Nicholson, White & Duncan, 1998; Stanton, 1998).

In spite of the advantages of using computers to administer measures, the following caveat is in order. Although converting a conventional paper and pencil measure to a computerized version may allow for quicker and more efficient collection of information, it may also change the meaning of scores. Stated differently, respondents may not obtain similar scores on the paper and pencil and computerized versions of a measure due to the format in which the measure is presented. Mazzeo and Harvey (1988) asserted that differences between the two formats may depend on whether the measure is speeded, contains graphics, has items requiring passages to be read that do not fit on the same screen as the items, and whether respondents can omit or return to items. However, in a meta-analysis comparing paper and pencil to computerized versions of cognitive ability measures, Mead and Dragow (1993) found that the two methods were equivalent for power or computerized adaptive tests of cognitive ability, but not for speeded measures. Further, King and Miles (1995) found that computerized and paper and pencil versions of attitude and personality measures were equivalent. Although these results are promising, others have found that some personality measures may not be measuring the intended attribute (e.g., Davis & Cowles, 1989) because respondents may have a stronger tendency to fake good (i.e., present themselves in a favorable light) on computerized versions of the measures. More recently, Richman, Kiesler, Weisband & Dragow (1999) conducted a meta-analytic review and ascertained that, overall, computer-administered measures are not more adversely affected by social desirability distortion than paper and pencil measures.

While technology has advanced the field of measurement, there are still several unresolved issues. First, measures that are translated from a paper and pencil to a computerized version may not be equivalent, that is, they may not be measuring the same attribute. Second, measures that are administered through the Internet with open access may not result in representative samples. Finally, although the availability of computers and the Internet has increased and individuals have become more competent at using these technologies, their use is still not widespread and there are marked differences across countries. Administering measures through these technologies may exclude certain populations (e.g., lower social-economic statuses) and induce anxiety in those who are not familiar with this medium. However, computerized measurement is growing worldwide as evidenced by recent international publications on the topic (e.g., *Applied Psychology: An International Review*, vol. 36, issues 3–4, as cited in Murphy and Davidshofer, 1998).

CROSS-CULTURAL MEASUREMENT TRANSFERABILITY

As interest in measurement increases worldwide, the questions of the transferability of a measure designed in one culture to another and the feasibility of comparing different cultures on the same attribute become important (Cheung & Rensvold, 1999). Concern has been expressed about transferring measures from one culture to another without modifying them to account for cultural differences (Hofstede, 1993). Thus, a measure developed in one type of culture (e.g., individualistic) may not be applicable to a different culture (e.g., collectivistic). Many factors can affect the validity of a measure used in different cultures. Different cultural beliefs, political structures, languages, economies, technologies, and acceptability of and familiarity with measures, may influence the effectiveness of measures. Thus, it is important to cross-validate measures developed in one culture before using them in another culture to ensure that decisions based on measurement are sound. Further, additional explanation and instructions, practice items, and proctor training may be required for cultures not accustomed to particular types of measurement.

The first step in transferring a measure to another culture is establishing translation equivalence. Blind back-translation assesses the equivalence of the wording of a measure that has been translated into a different language (Brislin, Lonner & Thorndike, 1973). The process begins with an individual translating the measure from the original language to another. Next, a second individual, who has not seen the original measure, translates it back to the original language. Finally, the second version of the measure is compared with the original and discrepancies are discussed and resolved.

Unfortunately, translation equivalence does not ensure transferability of the measure to another culture. Stated differently, the measure must also have conceptual equivalence, which is when the attribute being measured has similar meaning across cultures (Brett, Tinsley, Janssens, Barsness & Lytle, 1997). Measures must produce the same conceptual frame of reference in different cultures, which means different cultures are defining the attribute in the same way (Riordan & Vandenberg, 1994). Some items on a measure or even the attribute in general may have different meanings in different cultures. For instance, a measure of initiative asking questions about individual contributions may be interpreted as boastful or arrogant in a collectivistic culture instead of as a sign of initiative. Further, respondents must interpret response options on the measure similarly (Riordan & Vandenberg, 1994). For example, the response option of 'neither disagree nor agree' may be interpreted as indifference in one culture and as slight agreement in another. In sum, before measures developed in one culture can be used in another, translation and conceptual equivalence must be established or the measure cannot be used to make accurate decisions.

EMERGING LEGAL AND SOCIAL ISSUES IN MEASUREMENT

In the United States (US) measurement is strongly influenced by employment law (for more detail, see AERA, APA & NCME, 1999; SIOP, 1987). Various laws require that measures used in work settings do not discriminate against applicants or current employees on the basis of, for example, race, color, sex, religion, national origin, age, and disability status. If measures do discriminate against a protected group, it must be demonstrated that the measure is related to job performance and that decisions made based on the scores are valid. Thus, measurement in the US focuses on establishing measures that are nondiscriminatory against protected groups and valid for making decisions about individuals.

The influence of the legal system on measurement is increasingly becoming a global phenomenon, as evidenced by the proposal or enactment of similar laws in other countries. For instance, South Africa recently implemented the Employment Equity Act (EEA) of 1998. EEA provides equal opportunity and fair treatment in employment by eliminating unfair discrimination. More importantly, EEA mandates, among other things, that psychological measures used in employment settings be prohibited unless they are reliable and valid. Of course, the passage of equal opportunity laws does not necessarily mean that these laws are strictly enforced. In the US, a government office (i.e., Equal Employment Opportunity Commission) is responsible for such enforcement; however, similar government offices are not common in other countries. Nevertheless, as equal employment opportunity laws are proposed and passed in other countries, measurement adhering to

the principles and processes discussed in this chapter will become essential.

GLOBALIZATION OF MEASUREMENT

To support the aforementioned claim regarding the increasing importance of measurement worldwide, we reviewed all articles written by authors with affiliations outside of the US in *Educational and Psychological Measurement* and *Applied Psychological Measurement* from January 1995 to December 1999. This is an admittedly selective review, particularly in light of the fact that these journals are published in English. Consequently, non-English speaking W&O psychologists may not be able, or even wish, to submit their work for publication consideration in these outlets. Nevertheless, results of this selective 5-year review suggest that measure development is increasing in importance. More specifically, many studies described the construction and validation of a variety of measures (e.g., Bessant, 1997; Chang, 1996; Koustelios & Bagiatis, 1997). Moreover, there were numerous studies examining the reliability and validity of existing measures (e.g., Byrne, Baron & Balev, 1998; Cheung, 1996; Mateo & Fernandez, 1995; Tharenou & Terry, 1998). In addition, the goal of many of these studies was to validate a measure cross-nationally.

An additional finding of our selective review is that many of the topics discussed in this chapter are currently being studied in several countries. Computerized adaptive testing is a popular topic, especially in the Netherlands (e.g., Eggen, 1999; Meijer & Nering, 1999; van der Linden, 1998). Another popular topic is Item Response Theory with researchers in the Netherlands, Belgium, Canada, Spain, and Australia exploring this issue (e.g., Andrich, 1995; Janssen & De Boeck, 1997; Maranon, Barbero-Garcia & Costas, 1997; Sijtsma & Verweij, 1999; Zumbo, Pope, Watson & Hubley, 1997). Other topics investigated outside of the US include reliability and validity (e.g., Raykov, 1997), measurement equivalence (e.g., Rensvold & Cheung, 1998; Sukigara, 1996), item analysis (e.g., El-Korashy, 1995), generalizability theory (e.g., Chang, 1997), and the multitrait–multimethod matrix (e.g., Massey, 1997), among others.

In sum, this review is encouraging because it demonstrates that measurement and the issues we have discussed in this chapter are growing in importance worldwide.

In closing, we set two ambitious goals for this chapter. First, our goal was to discuss basic issues in measurement. Second, we also wanted to go beyond basic concepts and discuss a selective set of present and future trends in the field of measurement in W&O psychology. As noted throughout the chapter, sound measurement is a *sine qua non* condition for the science and practice of W&O

psychology. Changes in technology and the legal environment worldwide suggest several challenges as well as the globalization of the field of measurement in W&O psychology. We certainly hope W&O psychologists around the world will continue to appreciate the criticality of sound measurement in their science as well as their practice.

ACKNOWLEDGEMENTS

We thank Charles A. Pierce (Montana State University) for helpful comments on previous drafts. Portions of the research reported herein were conducted while Herman Aguinis was on sabbatical leave from the University of Colorado at Denver and holding visiting appointments at China Agricultural University-International College of Beijing (People's Republic of China), City University of Hong Kong (People's Republic of China), Nanyang Technological University (Singapore), University of Science Malaysia (Penang, Malaysia), and University of Santiago de Compostela (Spain). This research was supported, in part, by grants from the Graduate School of Business Administration (University of Colorado at Denver) and the Institute for International Business (University of Colorado at Denver) to Herman Aguinis.

REFERENCES

Aguinis, H. (1993). Action research and scientific method: Presumed discrepancies and actual similarities. *Journal of Applied Behavioral Science, 29,* 416–431.

Aguinis, H. (1995). Statistical power problems with moderated multiple regression in management research. *Journal of Management, 21,* 1141–1158.

Aguinis, H. (forthcoming). Estimation of sampling variance of correlations in meta-analysis. *Personnel Psychology.*

Aguinis, H., & Adams, S.K.R. (1998). Social-role versus structural models of gender and influence use in organizations: A strong inference approach. *Group and Organization Management, 23,* 414–446.

Aguinis, H., Cortina, J.M., & Goldberg, E. (1998). A new procedure for computing equivalence bands in personnel selection. *Human Performance, 11,* 351–365.

Aguinis, H., Cortina, J.M., & Goldberg, E. (2000). A clarifying note on differences between the W.F. Cascio, J. Outzz, S. Zedeck, & I.L. Goldstein (1991) and H. Aguinis, J.M. Cortina, and E. Goldberg (1998) banding procedures. *Human Performance, 13,* 199–204.

Aguinis, H., & Henle, C.A. (forthcoming). Effects of nonverbal behavior on perceptions of a female employee's power bases. *Journal of Social Psychology.*

Aguinis, H., Nesler, M.S., Quigley, B.M., Lee, S., & Tedeschi, J.T. (1996). Power bases of faculty supervisors and educational outcomes for graduate students. *Journal of Higher Education, 67,* 267–297.

Aguinis, H., Petersen, S.A., & Pierce, C.A. (1999). Appraisal of the homogeneity of error variance assumption and alternatives to multiple regression for estimating moderating effects of categorical variables. *Organizational Research Methods, 2,* 315–339.

Aguinis, H., & Pierce, C.A. (1998a). Heterogeneity of error variance and the assessment of moderating effects of categorical variables: A conceptual review. *Organizational Research Methods, 1,* 296–314.

Aguinis, H., & Pierce, C.A. (1998b). Statistical power computations for detecting dichotomous moderator variables with moderated multiple regression. *Educational and Psychological Measurement, 58,* 668–676.

Aguinis, H., Pierce, C.A., & Stone-Romero, E.F. (1994). Estimating the power to detect dichotomous moderators with moderated multiple regression. *Educational and Psychological Measurement, 54,* 690–692.

Aguinis, H., Simonsen, M.M., & Pierce, C.A. (1998). Effects of nonverbal behavior on perceptions of power bases. *Journal of Social Psychology, 138,* 455–469.

Aguinis, H., & Stone-Romero, E.F. (1997). Methodological artifacts in moderated multiple regression and their effects on statistical power. *Journal of Applied Psychology, 82,* 192–206.

Aguinis, H., & Whitehead, R. (1997). Sampling variance in the correlation coefficient under indirect range restriction: Implications for validity generalization. *Journal of Applied Psychology, 82,* 528–538.

American Educational Research Association, American Psychological Association, and National Council on Measurement in Education (1999). *Standards for Educational and Psychological Testing.* Washington, DC: American Educational Research Association.

Andrich, D. (1995). Distinctive and incompatible properties of two common classes of IRT models for graded responses. *Applied Psychological Measurement, 19,* 101–119.

Angoff, W.H. (1971). Norms, scales, and equivalent scores. In R.L. Thorndike (Ed.), *Educational Measurement* (2nd ed.). Washington, DC: American Council on Education.

Berk, R.A. (1984). *A Guide to Criterion-referenced Test Construction.* Baltimore: Johns Hopkins University Press.

Bessant, K.C. (1997). The development and validation of scores on the mathematics information processing scale (MIPS). *Educational and Psychological Measurement, 57,* 841–857.

Binning, J.F., & Barrett, G.V. (1989). Validity of personnel decisions: A conceptual analysis of the inferential and evidential base. *Journal of Applied Psychology, 74,* 478–494.

Brennan, R.L. (1992). *Elements of Generalizability Theory* (2nd ed.). Iowa City, IA: American College Testing Program.

Brett, J.M., Tinsley, C.H., Janssens, M., Barsness, Z.I., & Lytle, A.L. (1997). New approaches to the study of culture in industrial/organizational psychology. In P.C. Earley and M. Erez (Eds.), *New Perspectives on International Industrial/Organizational Psychology.* (pp. 75–129) San Francisco: New Lexington Press.

Brislin, R.W., Lonner, W., & Thorndike, R.M. (1973). *Cross-cultural Research Methods.* New York: Wiley.

Byrne, B.M., Baron, P., & Balev, J. (1998). The Beck Depression Inventory: A cross-validated test of second-order factorial structure for Bulgarian adolescents. *Educational and Psychological Measurement, 58,* 241–251.

Campbell, D.T., & Fiske, D.W. (1959). Convergent and discriminant validation by the multitrait-multimethod matrix. *Psychological Bulletin, 56,* 81–105.

Chan, D. (1998). Functional relations among constructs in the same content domain at different levels of analysis: A typology of composition models. *Journal of Applied Psychology, 83,* 234–246.

Chang, L. (1996). Quantitative Attitudes Questionnaire: Instrument development and validation. *Educational and Psychological Measurement, 56,* 1037–1042.

Chang, L. (1997). Dependability of anchoring labels of Likert-type scales. *Educational and Psychological Measurement, 57,* 800–807.

Cheung, S. (1996). Reliability and factor structure of the Chinese version of the Depression Self-Rating Scale. *Educational and Psychological Measurement, 56,* 142–154.

Cheung, G.W., & Rensvold, R.B. (1999). Testing factorial invariance across groups: A reconceptualization and proposed new method. *Journal of Management, 25,* 1–27.

Cohen, J. (1960). A coefficient of agreement for nominal scales. *Educational and Psychological Measurement, 10,* 37–46.

Cortina, J.M. (1993). What is coefficient alpha? An examination of theory and applications. *Journal of Applied Psychology, 78,* 98–104.

Cronbach, L.J. (1988). Five perspectives on validity argument. In H. Wainer & H.I. Braun (Eds.), *Test Validity* (pp. 3–17). Hillsdale, NJ: Lawrence Erlbaum.

Cronbach, L.J., Gleser, G.C., Nanda, H., & Rajaratnam, N. (1972). *The Dependability of Behavioral Measurements: Theory of Generalizability for Scores and Profiles.* New York: Wiley.

Cronbach, L.J., & Meehl, P.E. (1955). Construct validity in psychological tests. *Psychological Bulletin, 52,* 281–302.

Dansereau, F., Alluto, J., & Yammarino, F.J. (1984). *Theory Testing in Organizational Behavior: The Variant Approach.* Englewood Cliffs, NJ: Prentice Hall.

Davis, C., & Cowles, M. (1989). Automated psychological testing: Method of administration, need for approval, and measures of anxiety, *Educational and Psychological Measurement, 49,* 311–337.

Drasgow, F., & Hulin, C.L. (1991). Item response theory. In M. Dunnette & L. Hough (Eds.), *Handbook of Industrial and Organizational Psychology.* Vol. 1, 2nd ed. (pp. 577–636) Palo Alto, CA: Consulting Psychologists Press.

Eggen, T.J.H.M. (1999). Item selection in adaptive testing with the sequential probability ratio test. *Applied Psychological Measurement, 23,* 249–261.

El-Korashy, A. (1995). Applying the Rasch model to the selection of items for a mental ability test. *Educational and Psychological Measurement, 55,* 753–763.

Flaugher, R. (1990). Item pools. In H. Wainer (Ed.), *Computerized Adaptive Testing: A Primer* (pp. 41–63). Hillsdale, NJ: Lawrence Erlbaum.

Glick, W.H. (1985). Conceptualizing and measuring organizational and psychological climate: Pitfalls in multilevel research. *Academy of Management Review, 10,* 601–616.

Guion, R.M. (1977). Content validity – the source of my discontent. *Applied Psychological Measurement, 1,* 1–10.

Guion, R.M. (1998). *Assessment, Measurement, and Prediction for Personnel Decisions.* Mahwah, NJ: Lawrence Erlbaum.

Hofstede, G. (1993). Cultural constraints in management theories. *Academy of Management Executive, 7,* 81–94.

House, R., Rousseau, D.M., & Thomas-Hunt, M. (1995). The meso paradigm: A framework for the integration of micro and macro organizational behavior. *Research in Organizational Behavior, 17,* 71–114.

Hulin, C.L., Drasgow, F., & Parsons, C.K. (1983). *Item Response Theory: Application to Psychological Measurement.* Homewood, IL: Dow Jones-Irwin.

James, L.R. (1982). Aggregation bias in estimates of perceptual agreement. *Journal of Applied Psychology, 57,* 219–229.

James, L.R., Demaree, R.G., & Wolf, G. (1984). Estimating within-group interrater reliability with and without response bias. *Journal of Applied Psychology, 69,* 1–98.

James, L.R., Demaree, R.G., & Wolf, G. (1993). r_{wg}: An assessment of within-group interrater agreement. *Journal of Applied Psychology, 78,* 306–309.

Janssen, R., & De Boeck, P. (1997). Psychometric modeling of componentially designed synonym tasks. *Applied Psychological Measurement, 21,* 37–50.

Johnson, J.T., & Ree, M.J. (1994). RANGEJ: A Pascal program to compute the multivariate correction for range restriction. *Educational and Psychological Measurement, 54,* 693–695.

Jöreskog, K.G. (1971). Statistical analysis of sets of congeneric tests. *Psychometrika, 36,* 109–133.

Kendall, M.G. (1948). *Rank Correlation Methods.* London: Griffin.

King, W.C., & Miles, E.W. (1995). A quasi-experimental assessment of the effect of computerizing noncognitive paper-and-pencil measurements: A test of measurement equivalence. *Psychological Science, 6,* 203–211.

Klein, K.J., Dansereau, F., & Hall, R.J. (1994). Levels issues in theory development, data collection, and analysis. *Academy of Management Review, 19,* 195–229.

Koustelios, A.D., & Bagiatis, K. (1997). The Employee Satisfaction Inventory (ESI): Development of a scale to measure satisfaction of Greek employees. *Educational and Psychological Measurement, 57,* 469–476.

Kozlowksi, S.W.J., & Hattrup, K. (1992). A disagreement about within-group agreement: Disentangling issues of consistency versus consensus. *Journal of Applied Psychology, 77,* 161–167.

Kozlowski, S.W.J., & Klein, K.J. (2000). A multilevel approach to theory and research in organizations: Contextual, temporal, and emergent processes. In

K.J. Klein & S.W.J. Kozlowski (Eds.), *Multilevel Theory, Research, and Methods in Organizations* (pp. 512–553). San Francisco: Jossey-Bass.

Kraiger, K., & Aguinis, H. (2001). Training effectiveness: Assessing training needs, motivation, and accomplishments. In M. London (Ed.), *How People Evaluate Others in Organizations* (pp. 203–220). Mahwah, NJ: Lawrence Erlbaum.

Kuder, G., & Richardson, M. (1937). The theory of the estimation of test reliability. *Psychometrika*, 2, 151–160.

Lahey, M., Downey, R.G., & Saal, F.E. (1983). Intraclass correlations: There's more there than meets the eye. *Psychological Bulletin*, 93, 586–595.

Landy, F. (1986). Stamp collecting versus science: Validation as hypothesis testing. *American Psychologist*, 41, 1183–1192.

Lawlis, G.F. & Lu, E. (1972). Judgement of counseling process: Reliability, agreement, and error. *Psychological Bulletin*, 78, 17–20.

Lawshe, C.H. (1975). A quantitative approach to content validity. *Personnel Psychology*, 28, 563–575.

Lord, F.M. (1980). *Applications of Item Response Theory to Practical Testing Problems*. Hillsdale, NJ: Erlbaum.

Lord, F.M., & Novick, M.R. (1968). *Statistical Theories of Mental Test Scores*. Reading, MA: Addison Wesley.

Maranon, P.P., Barbero-Garcia, M.I., & Costas, C.L. (1997). Identification of nonuniform differential item functioning: A comparison of Mantel-Haenszel and item response theory analysis procedures. *Educational and Psychological Measurement*, 57, 559–568.

Massey, A.J. (1997). Multitrait–multimethod/multiform evidence for the validity of reporting units in national assessments in science at age 14 in England and Wales. *Educational and Psychological Measurement*, 57, 108–117.

Mateo, M.A., & Fernandez, J. (1995). Evaluation of the setting in which university faculties carry out their teaching and research functions: The ASEQ. *Educational and Psychological Measurement*, 55, 329–334.

Mazzeo, J., & Harvey, A.L. (1988). *The Equivalence of Scores from Automated and Conventional Educational and Psychological Tests: A Review of the Literature* (College Board Report No. 88–8). Princeton, NJ: Educational Testing Service.

Mead, A.D., & Drasgow, F. (1993). Equivalence of computerized and paper-and-pencil cognitive ability tests: A meta-analysis. *Psychological Bulletin, 114,* 449–458.

Meijer, R.R., & Nering, M.L. (1999). Computerized adaptive testing: Overview and introduction. *Applied Psychological Measurement*, 23, 187–194.

Murphy, K.R., & Davidshofer, C.O. (1998). *Psychological Testing* (4th ed.). Upper Saddle River, NJ: Prentice Hall.

Nesler, M.S., Aguinis, H., Quigley, B.M., Lee, S., & Tedeschi, J.T. (1999). The development and validation of a scale measuring global social power based on French and Raven's (1959) power taxonomy. *Journal of Applied Social Psychology*, 29, 750–771.

Nicholson, T., White, J., & Duncan, D. (1998). Drugnet: A pilot study of adult recreational drug use via the WWW. *Substance Abuse, 19,* 109–121.

Nunnally, J.C. (1967). *Psychometric Theory*. New York: McGraw-Hill.

Nunnally, J.C. (1978). *Psychometric Theory* (2nd ed.). New York: McGraw-Hill.

Nunnally, J.C., & Bernstein, I.H. (1994). *Psychometric Theory*. 3rd edn. New York: McGraw-Hill.

Ostroff, C. (1992). The relationship between satisfaction, attitudes, and performance: An organizational level analysis. *Journal of Applied Psychology*, 77, 963–974.

Ostroff, C. (1993). Comparing correlations based on individual-level and aggregated data. *Journal of Applied Psychology, 78,* 569–582.

Ostroff, C., & Bowen, D.E. (2000). Moving HR to a higher level: HR practices and organizational performance. In K.J. Klein and S.W.J. Kozlowski (Eds.), *Multilevel Theory, Research and Methods in Organizations* (pp. 211–266). San Francisco: Jossey-Bass.

Pedhazur, E.J., & Pedhazur Schmelkin, L. (1991). *Measurement, Design, and Analysis*. Hillsdale, NJ: Lawrence Erlbaum.

Pierce, C.A., Aguinis, H., & Adams, S.K.R. (2000). Effects of a dissolved workplace romance and rater characteristics on responses to a sexual harassment accusation. *Academy of Management Journal*, 43, 869–880.

Raykov, T. (1997). Estimation of composite reliability for congeneric measures. *Applied Psychological Measurement*, 21, 173–184.

Rensvold, R.B., & Cheung, G.W. (1998). Testing measurement model for factorial invariance: A systematic approach. *Educational and Psychological Measurement*, 58, 1017–1034.

Richman, W.L., Kiesler, S., Weisband, S., & Drasgow, F. (1999). A meta-analytic study of social desirability distortion in computer-administered questionnaires, traditional questionnaires, and interviews. *Journal of Applied Psychology*, 84, 754–775.

Riordan, C.M., & Vandenberg, R.J. (1994). A central question in cross-cultural research: Do employees of different cultures interpret work-related measures in an equivalent manner? *Journal of Management*, 20, 643–671.

Roberts, K.H., Hulin, C.L., & Rousseau, D.M. (1978). *Developing an Interdisciplinary Science of Organizations*. San Francisco: Jossey-Bass.

Rousseau, D.M. (1985). Issues of level in organizational research: Multi-level and cross-level perspectives. *Research in Organizational Behavior*, 7, 1–38.

Schmidt, W.C. (1997). World-wide web survey research: Benefits, potential problems, and solutions. *Behavior Research Methods, Instruments, & Computers, 29,* 274–279.

Shrout, P.E., & Fleiss, J.L. (1979). Intraclass correlations: Uses in assessing rater reliability. *Psychological Bulletin*, 86, 420–428.

Sijtsma, K., & Verweij, A.C. (1999). Knowledge of solution strategies and IRT modeling of items for transitive reasoning. *Applied Psychological Measurement*, 23, 55–68.

Society for Industrial and Organizational Psychology, Inc. (1987). *Principles for the Validation and Use of Personnel Selection Procedures* (3rd ed.). College Park, MD: Author.

Stanton, J.M. (1998). An empirical assessment of data collection using the Internet. *Personnel Psychology, 51,* 709–725.

Stevens, S.S. (1951). Mathematics, measurement, and psychophysics. In S.S. Stevens (Ed.), *Handbook of Experimental Psychology* (pp. 1–49). New York: Wiley.

Stevens, S.S. (1968). Measurement, statistics, and the schemapiric view. *Science, 161,* 849–856.

Sukigara, M. (1996). Equivalence between computer and booklet administrations of the new Japanese version of the MMPI. *Educational and Psychological Measurement, 56,* 570–584.

Tharenou, P., & Terry, D.J. (1998). Reliability and validity of scores on scales to measure managerial aspirations. *Educational and Psychological Measurement, 58,* 475–492.

Thissen, D., & Steinberg, L. (1988). Data analysis using item response theory. *Psychological Bulletin, 104,* 385–395.

Thorndike, R.L. (1949). *Personnel Selection*. New York: John Wiley & Sons.

Thorndike, R.M., Cunningham, G.K., Thorndike, R.L., & Hagen, E. (1991). *Measurement and Evaluation in Psychology and Education* (5th ed.). New York: Macmillan – now Palgrove.

Tinsley, H.E., & Weiss, D.J. (1975). Interrater reliability and agreement of subjective judgments. *Journal of Counseling Psychology, 22,* 358–376.

Vandenberg, R.J., & Lance, C.E. (2000). A review and synthesis of the measurement invariance literature: Suggestions, practices and recommendations for organizational research. *Organizational Research Methods, 3,* 4–69.

van der Linden, W.J. (1998). Optimal assembly of psychological and educational tests. *Applied Psychological Measurement, 22,* 195–211.

Weiss, D.J., & Davinson, N.L. (1981). Test theory and methods. *Annual Review of Psychology, 32,* 629–658.

Zumbo, B.D., Pope, G.A., Watson, J.E., & Hubley, A.M. (1997). An empirical test of Roskam's conjecture about the interpretation of an ICC parameter in personality inventories. *Educational and Psychological Measurement, 57,* 963–969.

3

Meta-Analysis

FRANK L. SCHMIDT
and JOHN E. HUNTER

The small sample studies typical of I/O psychology produce seemingly contradictory results, and reliance on statistical significance tests causes study results to appear even more conflicting. Meta-analysis is needed to integrate the findings across such studies to reveal the simpler patterns of relations that underlie research literatures, thus providing a basis for theory development. Meta-analysis can correct for the distorting effects of sampling error, measurement error, and other artifacts that produce the illusion of conflicting findings. This chapter discusses these artifacts and the procedures used to correct for them. Several different approaches to meta-analysis are discussed. Applications of meta-analysis in I/O psychology and other areas are discussed and evidence is presented that meta-analysis is transforming not only research in I/O psychology, but in psychology in general.

WHY WE NEED META-ANALYSIS

The goal in any science is the production of cumulative knowledge. Ultimately this means the development of theories that explain the phenomena that are the focus of the scientific area. One example would be theories that explain how personality traits develop in children and adults over time and how these traits affect their lives. Another would be theories of what factors cause job and career satisfaction and what effects job satisfaction in turn has on other aspects of one's life. But before theories can be developed, we need to be able to pin down the relations between variables. For example, what is the relation between peer socialization and level of extroversion? Or the relation between job satisfaction and job performance?

Unless we can precisely calibrate such relations among variables, we do not have the raw materials from which to construct theories; there is nothing for a theory to explain. For example, if the relationship between extroversion and popularity of children varies capriciously across different studies from a

strong positive to a strong negative correlation and everything in between, we cannot begin to construct a theory of how extroversion might affect popularity. The same applies to the relation between job satisfaction and job performance.

The unfortunate fact is that most research literatures do show conflicting findings of this sort. Some studies find statistically significant relationships and some do not. In many research literatures, this split is approximately 50–50 (Cohen, 1962; 1988; Schmidt, Hunter & Urry, 1976; Sedlmeier & Gigerenzer, 1989). This has been the traditional situation in most areas of the behavioral and social sciences, including I/O psychology, and hence it has been very difficult to develop understanding, theories and cumulative knowledge.

THE MYTH OF THE PERFECT STUDY

Before meta-analysis, the usual way in which scientists attempted to make sense of research literatures was by use of the narrative subjective review. But in many research literatures there were not only conflicting findings, there were also large numbers of studies. This combination made the standard narrative-subjective review a nearly impossible task – one far beyond human information processing capabilities (Hunter & Schmidt, 1990b: 468–469). How does one sit down and make sense of, say, 210 conflicting studies?

The answer as developed in many narrative reviews was what came to be called the myth of the perfect study. Reviewers convinced themselves that most – usually the vast majority – of the studies available were 'methodologically deficient' and should not even be considered in the review. These judgments of methodological deficiency were often based on idiosyncratic ideas: One reviewer might regard the Jagnathan Personality Inventory as 'lacking in construct validity' and throw out all studies that used that instrument. Another might regard use of that same inventory as a prerequisite for methodological soundness and eliminate all studies not using this inventory. Thus, any given reviewer could eliminate from consideration all but a few studies and perhaps narrow the number of studies from 210 to, say, seven. Conclusions would then be based on these seven studies.

It has long been the case that the most widely read literature reviews are those appearing in textbooks. The function of textbooks is to summarize what is known in a given field, but no textbook can cite and discuss 210 studies on a single relationship. Often textbook authors would pick out what they considered to be the one or two 'best' studies and then base their conclusions on just those studies, discarding the vast bulk of the information in the research literature. Hence the myth of the perfect study.

But in fact there are no perfect studies. All studies contain measurement error in all measures used, as discussed later. Independent of measurement error, no study's measures have perfect construct validity, and there are typically other artifacts that distort study findings. Even if a hypothetical (and it would have to be hypothetical) study suffered from none of these distortions, it would still contain sampling error – typically a substantial amount of sampling error, since sample sizes are rarely very large. Hence no single study or small selected subgroup of studies can provide an optimal basis for scientific conclusions about cumulative knowledge. As a result, reliance on 'best studies' did not provide a solution to the problem of conflicting research findings. This procedure did not even successfully deceive researchers into believing it was a solution – because different narrative reviewers arrived at different conclusions because they selected a different subset of 'best' studies. Hence the 'conflicts in the literature' became 'conflicts in the reviews.'

SOME RELEVANT HISTORY

By the middle 1970s the behavioral and social sciences were in serious trouble. Large numbers of studies had accumulated on many questions that were important to theory development and/or social policy decisions. Results of different studies on the same question were typically conflicting. For example, are workers more productive when they are satisfied with their jobs? The studies did not agree. Do students learn more when class sizes are smaller? Research findings were conflicting. Does participative decision making in management increase productivity? Does job enlargement increase job satisfaction and output? Does psychotherapy really help people? The studies were in conflict. As a consequence, the public and government officials were becoming increasingly disillusioned with the behavioral and social sciences especially in the United States and to some extent in all other countries, and it was becoming more and more difficult to obtain funding for research. Then in 1981, the Director of the Federal Office of Management and Budget in the United States, David Stockman, proposed an 80% reduction in federal funding for research in the behavioral and social sciences. Such proposed cuts are typically trial balloons in the United States sent up to see how much political opposition they arouse. Even when proposed cuts are much smaller than a draconian 80%, constituencies can be counted on to come forward and protest the proposed cuts. This usually happens, and many behavioral and social scientists in the United States expected it to happen. But it did not. The behavioral and social sciences, it turned out, had no constituency among the public; the public did not care (see 'Cuts raise new social science query', 1981). Finally, out of desperation, the American Psychological Association took the lead in forming the Consortium of Social Science Associations to lobby against the proposed cuts. Although this super-association had some success in getting these cuts reduced (and even, in some areas, getting small increases in research funding in subsequent years), these developments should make us look carefully at how such a thing could happen.

The sequence of events that led to this state of affairs was much the same in one research area as another. First, there was initial optimism about using social science research to answer socially important questions. Do government-sponsored job training programs work? We will do studies to find out. Does Head Start really help disadvantaged kids? The studies will tell us. Does integration increase the school achievement of Black children? Research will provide the answer. Next, several studies on the question are conducted, but the results are conflicting. There is some disappointment that the question has not been answered, but policy-makers – and people in general – are still optimistic. They, along with the researchers, conclude that more research is needed to identify the supposed interactions (moderators) that have caused the conflicting findings. For example, perhaps whether job training works depends on the age and education of the trainees. Maybe smaller classes in schools are beneficial only for lower-IQ children. It is hypothesized that psychotherapy works for middle-class but not working-class patients. That is, the conclusion at this point is that a search for moderator variables is needed.

In the third phase, a large number of research studies are funded and conducted to test these moderator hypotheses. When they are completed, there is now a large body of studies, but instead of being resolved the number of conflicts increases. The moderator hypotheses from the initial studies are not borne out; no one can make sense of the conflicting findings. Researchers conclude that the question that was selected for study in this particular case has turned out to be hopelessly complex, and they turn to the investigation of another question hoping that this time the question will turn out to be more tractable. Research sponsors, government officials, and the public become disenchanted and cynical. Research funding agencies cut money for research in this area and in related areas. After this cycle has been repeated enough times, social and behavioral scientists themselves become cynical about the value of their own work, and they publish articles expressing doubts about whether behavioral and social science research is capable *in principle* of developing cumulative knowledge and providing general answers to socially important questions (e.g., see Cronbach, 1975; Gergen, 1982; Meehl, 1978).

Clearly, at this point there is a critical need for some means of making sense of the vast number of accumulated study findings. Starting in the late 1970s, new methods of combining findings across studies on the same subject were developed. These methods were referred to collectively as *meta-analysis*. Applications of meta-analysis to accumulated research literatures showed that research findings are not nearly as conflicting as had been thought and that useful and sound general conclusions can in fact be drawn from existing research. Cumulative theoretical knowledge is possible in the behavioral and social sciences, and socially important questions can be answered in reasonably definitive ways. As a result, the gloom and cynicism that had enveloped many in the behavioral and social sciences has been lifting.

META-ANALYSIS VS. SIGNIFICANCE TESTING

A key point in understanding the effect that meta-analysis has had is that the illusion of conflicting findings in research literatures resulted mostly from the traditional reliance of researchers on statistical significance testing in analyzing and interpreting data in their individual studies (Cohen, 1994). These statistical significance tests typically had low power to detect existing relationships. Yet the prevailing decision rule has been that if the finding was statistically significant, then a relationship existed; and if it was not statistically significant, then there was no relationship (Oakes, 1986; Schmidt, 1996). For example, suppose that the population correlation between a certain familial condition and juvenile delinquency is .30. That is, the relationship in the population of interest is $\rho = .30$. Now suppose 50 studies are conducted to look for this relationship, and each has a statistical power of .50 to detect this relationship if it exists. (This level of statistical power is typical of many research literatures.) Then approximately 50% of the studies (25 studies) would find a statistically significant relationship; the other 25 studies would report no significant relationship, and this would be interpreted as indicating that no relationship existed. The researchers in these 25 studies would most likely incorrectly state that because the observed relationship did not reach statistical significance, it probably occurred merely by chance. Thus half the studies report that the familial factor was related to delinquency and half report that it had no relationship to delinquency – a condition of maximal apparent conflicting results in the literature. Of course, the 25 studies that report that there is no relationship are all incorrect. The relationship exists and is always $\rho = .30$.

Traditionally, however, researchers did not understand that a statistical power problem such as this was even a possibility, because they did not understand the concept of statistical power. In fact, they believed that their error rate was no more than 5% because they used an alpha level (significance level) of .05. But the 5% is just the Type I error rate (the alpha error rate) – the error rate that would exist if the null hypothesis were true and in fact there was no relationship. They overlooked the fact that if a relationship did exist, then the error rate would be 1.00 minus the statistical power (which here is $1.00 - .50 = .50$). This is the Type II error rate: the probability of failing to detect the relationship that exists. If the relationship does exist, then it is impossible to make a Type I error; that is, when there is a relationship, it is impossible to falsely conclude that there is a relationship. Only Type II errors can occur – and the significance test does not control Type II errors.

Now suppose these 50 studies were analyzed using meta-analysis. Meta-analysis would first compute the average *r* across the 50 studies; all *r*s would be used in computing this average regardless of whether they were statistically significant or not. This average should be very close to the correct value of .30, because sampling errors on either side of .30 would average out. So meta-analysis would lead to the correct conclusion that the relationship is on the average $\rho = .30$.

Meta-analysis can also estimate the real variability of the relationship across studies. To do this, one first computes the variance of the 50 observed rs, using the ordinary formula for the variance of a set of scores. One next computes the amount of variance expected solely from sampling error variance, using the formula for sampling error variance of the correlation coefficient. This sampling variance is then subtracted from the observed variance of the rs; after this subtraction, the remaining variance should be approximately zero. Thus the conclusion would be that all of the observed variability of the rs across the 50 studies is due merely to sampling error and does not reflect any real variability in the true relationship. Thus one would conclude correctly that the real relationship is always .30 – and not merely .30 on the average.

This simple example illustrates two critical points. First, the traditional reliance on statistical significance tests in interpreting studies leads to false conclusions about what the study results mean; in fact, the traditional approach to data analysis makes it impossible to reach correct conclusions (Hunter, 1997; Hunter & Schmidt, 1990b; Schmidt, 1996). Second, by contrast, meta-analysis leads to the correct conclusions about the real meaning of research literatures. These principles are illustrated and explained in more detail in Hunter and Schmidt (1990a); for a shorter treatment, see Schmidt (1996).

The reader might reasonably ask what statistical methods researchers should use in analyzing and interpreting the data in their individual studies. If reliance on statistical significance testing leads to false conclusions, what methods should researchers use? The answer is point estimates of effect sizes (correlations and d-values) and confidence intervals. The many advantages of point estimates and confidence intervals are discussed in Hunter and Schmidt (1990b), Hunter (1997), and Schmidt (1996). A recent APA Task Force report on statistical methods in research also discusses the advantages of confidence intervals over significance tests (Wilkinson and the Task Force on Statistical Inference, 1999).

Our example here has examined only the effects of sampling error variance and low statistical power. There are other statistical and measurement artifacts that cause artifactual variation in effect sizes and correlations across studies – for example, differences between studies in measurement error, range restriction, and dichotomization of measures. Also, in meta-analysis, mean correlations (and effect sizes) must be corrected for downward bias due to such artifacts as measurement error and dichotomization of measures. There are also artifacts such as coding or transcriptional errors in the original data that are difficult or impossible to correct

for. These artifacts and the complexities involved in correcting for them are discussed later in this chapter and are covered in more detail in Hunter and Schmidt (1990a; 1990b) and Schmidt and Hunter (1996). This section is an overview of why traditional data analysis and interpretation methods logically lead to erroneous conclusions and why meta-analysis can solve this problem and provide correct conclusions.

A common reaction to the above critique of traditional reliance on significance testing goes something like this: 'Your explanation is clear but I don't understand how so many researchers (and even some methodologists) could have been so wrong so long on a matter as important as the correct way to analyze data? How could psychologists and others have failed to see the pitfalls of significance testing?' Over the years, a number of methodologists have addressed this question (Carver, 1978; Cohen, 1994; Guttman, 1985; Meehl, 1967; Oakes, 1986; Rozeboom, 1960). For one thing, in their statistics classes young researchers have typically been taught a lot about Type I error and very little about Type II error and statistical power. Thus they are unaware that the error rate is very large in the typical study; they tend to believe the error rate is the alpha level used (typically .05 or .01). In addition, empirical research suggests that most researchers believe that the use of significance tests provides them with many nonexistent benefits in understanding their data. For example, most researchers believe that a statistically significant finding is a 'reliable' finding in the sense that it will replicate if a new study is conducted. For example, they believe that if a result is significant at the .05 level, then the probability of replication in subsequent studies (if conducted) is $1.00 - .05 = .95$. This belief is completely false. The probability of replication is the statistical power of the study and is almost invariably much lower than .95 (e.g., typically .50 or less). Most researchers also falsely believe that if a result is nonsignificant, one can conclude that it is probably just due to chance, another false belief, as illustrated in our delinquency research example. There are other widespread but false beliefs about the usefulness of information provided by significance tests (Carver, 1978; Oakes, 1986). A discussion of these beliefs can be found in Schmidt (1996).

During the 1980s and accelerating up to the present, the use of meta-analysis to make sense of research literatures has increased dramatically, as is apparent from reading research journals. Lipsey and Wilson (1993) found over 350 meta-analyses of experimental studies of treatment effects alone; the total number is many times larger, because most meta-analyses are conducted on correlational data (as was our hypothetical example above). The overarching meta-conclusion from all these efforts is that cumulative, generalizable knowledge in the behavioral and social sciences is not only possible but is increasingly a reality. In fact, meta-analysis has even produced evidence that cumulativeness of research findings in the behavioral sciences is probably as great as in the physical sciences. Psychologists have long assumed that their research studies are less replicable than those in the physical sciences. Hedges (1987) used meta-analysis methods to examine variability of findings across studies in 13 research areas in particle physics and 13 research areas in psychology. Contrary to common belief, his findings showed that there was as much variability across studies in physics as in psychology. Furthermore, he found that the physical sciences used methods to combine findings across studies that were 'essentially identical' to meta-analysis. The research literature in both areas – psychology and physics – yielded cumulative knowledge when meta-analysis was properly applied. Hedges's major finding is that the frequency of conflicting research findings is probably no greater in the behavioral and social sciences than in the physical sciences. The fact that this finding has been so surprising to many social scientists points up two facts. First, psychologists' reliance on significance tests has caused our research literatures to appear much more inconsistent than they are. Second, we have long overestimated the consistency of research findings in the physical sciences. In the physical sciences also, no research question can be answered by a single study, and physical scientists must use meta-analysis to make sense of their research literature, just as psychologists do.

Another fact is relevant at this point: The physical sciences, such as physics and chemistry, do not use statistical significance testing in interpreting their data. It is no accident, then, these sciences have not experienced the debilitating problems described earlier that are inevitable when researchers rely on significance tests. Given that the physical sciences regard reliance on significance testing as unscientific, it is ironic that so many psychologists defend the use of significance tests on grounds that such tests are the objective and scientifically correct approach to data analysis and interpretation. In fact, it has been our experience that psychologists and other behavioral scientists who attempt to defend significance testing usually equate null-hypothesis statistical significance testing with scientific hypothesis testing in general. They argue that hypothesis testing is central to science and that the abandonment of significance testing would amount to an attempt to have a science without hypothesis testing. They falsely believe that null-hypothesis significance testing and hypothesis testing in science in general are one and the same thing. This belief is tantamount to stating that physics, chemistry, and the other physical sciences are not legitimate sciences because they are not built on hypothesis testing. This belief implies that prior to the introduction of null-hypothesis significance testing by Fisher (1932) in the 1930s, no legitimate scientific research was possible. The fact, of course, is that there are many ways to test scientific hypotheses – and that significance testing is one of the least effective methods of doing this (Schmidt & Hunter, 1997).

IS STATISTICAL POWER THE SOLUTION?

Some researchers believe that the only problem with significance testing is low power and that if this problem could be solved there would be no problems with reliance on significance testing. These individuals see the solution as larger sample sizes. They believe that the problem would be solved if every researcher before conducting each study would calculate the number of subjects needed for 'adequate' power (usually taken as power of .80) and then use that sample size. What this position overlooks is that this requirement would make it impossible for most studies ever to be conducted. At the start of research in a given area, the questions are often of the form, 'Does Treatment A have an effect?' (e.g., Does interpersonal skills training have an effect? Or: Does this predictor have any validity?). If Treatment A indeed has a substantial effect, the sample size needed for adequate power may not be prohibitively large. But as research develops, subsequent questions tend to take the form, 'Is the effect of Treatment A larger than the effect of Treatment B?' (e.g., Is the effect of the new method of training larger than that of the old method? Or: Is predictor A more valid than predictor B?). The effect size then becomes the *difference* between the two effects. Such effect sizes will often be small, and the required sample sizes are therefore often quite large – often 1,000 or 2,000 or more (Schmidt & Hunter, 1978). And this is just to attain power of .80, which still allows a 20% Type II error rate when the null hypothesis is false – an error rate most would consider high. Many researchers cannot obtain that many subjects, no matter how hard they try; either it is beyond their resources or the subjects are just unavailable at any cost. Thus the upshot of this position would be that many – perhaps most – studies would not be conducted at all.

People advocating the power position say this would not be a loss. They argue that a study with inadequate power contributes nothing and therefore should not be conducted. But in fact such studies contain valuable information when combined with others like them in a meta-analysis. In fact, very precise meta-analysis results can be obtained based on studies that *all* have inadequate statistical power individually. The information in these studies is lost if these studies are never conducted.

The belief that such studies are worthless is based on two false assumptions: (a) the assumption that every individual study must be able to justify a conclusion on its own, without reference to other studies, and (b) the assumption that every study should be analyzed using significance tests. One of the contributions of meta-analysis has been to show that no single study is adequate by itself to answer a scientific question. Therefore each study should be considered as a data point to be contributed to a later meta-analysis. And individual studies should be analyzed using not significance tests but point estimates of effect sizes and confidence intervals.

How, then, *can* we solve the problem of statistical power in individual studies? Actually, this problem is a pseudoproblem. It can be 'solved' by discontinuing the significance test. As Oakes (1986: 68) notes, statistical power is a legitimate concept only within the context of statistical significance testing. If significance testing is not used, then the concept of statistical power has no place and is not meaningful. In particular, there need be no concern with statistical power when point estimates and confidence intervals used to analyze data in studies and meta-analysis are used to integrate findings across studies.

Our critique of the traditional practice of reliance on significance testing in analyzing data in individual studies and in interpreting research literatures might suggest a false conclusion: the conclusion that if significance tests had never been used, the research findings would have been consistent across different studies examining a given relationship. Consider the correlation between job satisfaction and job performance. Would these studies have all had the same findings if researchers had not relied on significance tests? Absolutely not: the correlations would have varied widely (as indeed they did). The major reason for this variability in correlations is simple sampling error – caused by the fact that the small samples used in individual research studies are randomly unrepresentative of the populations from which they are drawn. Most researchers severely underestimate the amount of variability in findings that is caused by sampling error.

The law of large numbers correctly states that large random samples are representative of their populations and yield parameter estimates that are close to the real (population) values. Many researchers seem to believe that the same law applies to small samples. As a result they erroneously expect statistics computed on small samples (e.g., 50 to 300) to be close approximations to the real (population) values. In one study we conducted (Schmidt, Ocasio, Hillery & Hunter, 1985), we drew random samples (small studies) of $N = 30$ from a much larger data set and computed results on each $N = 30$ sample. These results varied dramatically from 'study' to 'study' – and all this variability was due solely to sampling error (ibid.). Yet when we showed these data to researchers they found it hard to believe that each 'study' was a random

draw from the larger study; they did not believe simple sampling error could produce that much variation. They were shocked because they did not realize how much variation simple sampling error produces in research studies.

A major advantage of meta-analysis is that it controls for sampling error. Sampling error is random and nonsystematic – over and underestimation of population values are equally likely. Hence averaging correlations or *d*-values (standardized mean differences) across studies causes sampling error to be averaged out, producing an accurate estimate of the underlying population correlation. As noted earlier, we can also subtract sampling error variance from the between-study variance of the observed correlations (or *d*-values) to get a more accurate estimate of real variability across studies. Taken together, these two procedures constitute Bare Bones meta-analysis – the simplest form of meta-analysis. Bare Bones meta-analysis is discussed in more detail in a later section.

Most other artifacts that distort study findings are systematic rather than random. They usually create a downward bias on the obtained study *r* or *d*-value. For example, all variables in a study must be measured and all measures of variables contain measurement error. (There are no exceptions to this rule.) The effect of measurement error is to downwardly bias every correlation or *d*-value. However, measurement error can also contribute to differences between studies: If the measures used in one study have more measurement error than those used in another study, the observed *r*s or *d*s will be smaller in the first study. Thus meta-analysis must correct for both the downward bias and the artifactually created differences between different studies. Corrections of this sort are discussed below under the heading 'More Advanced Methods of Meta-Analysis'.

ORGANIZATION OF REMAINDER OF THIS CHAPTER

Different methodologists have developed somewhat different approaches to meta-analysis (Glass, McGaw & Smith, 1981; Hedges & Olkin, 1985; Hunter, Schmidt & Jackson, 1982; Hunter & Schmidt, 1990b; Rosenthal, 1991). In this chapter we first examine the Hunter–Schmidt methods, followed by an examination of the other approaches. Finally, we look at the impact of meta-analysis over the last 20 years on the research enterprise in psychology.

BARE BONES META-ANALYSIS

Bare Bones meta-analysis corrects only for the distorting effects of sampling error. It ignores all other statistical and measurement artifacts that distort

Table 3.1

Table 3.1 *21 validity studies (N = 68 each)*

Study	Observed validity	Study	Observed validity
1	.04	12	.11
2	.14	13	.21
3	.31*	14	.37*
4	.12	15	.14
5	.38*	16	.29*
6	.27*	17	.26*
7	.15	18	.17
8	.36*	19	.39*
9	.20	20	.22
10	.02	21	.21
11	.23		

*$p < .05$, two-tailed

study findings. For this reason we do not recommend Bare Bones meta-analysis for use in the final integration of research literatures; its primary value is that it allows illustration of some of the key features of more complete methods of meta-analysis. We illustrate Bare Bones meta-analysis using the data shown in Table 3.1, which shows 21 observed correlations, each based on a sample of 68 US Postal Service letter sorters. Each study presents the estimated correlation between the same aptitude test and the same measure of accuracy in sorting letters by zip code. Values range from .02 to .39 and only eight of the 21 (38%) are statistically significant. Both these facts suggest a great deal of disagreement among the studies.

We first compute the average correlation using the following formula:

$$\bar{r} = \frac{\sum [N_i r_i]}{\sum N_i} = \bar{\rho}_{xy} = .22$$

where $\bar{r}$ estimates $\bar{\rho}_{xy}$, the population mean correlation. Note that this formula weights each correlation by its sample size – because studies with larger Ns contain more information. (However, in this case all $N = 68$, so all studies are weighted equally.) The mean value of .22 is the meta-analysis estimate of the mean population correlation.

We next compute the variance of the observed correlations using the following formula:

$$S_r^2 = \frac{\sum [N_i (r_i - \bar{r})^2]}{\sum N_i} = .0120$$

This formula also weights by sample size. The next step is to compute the amount of variance in the observed correlations expected across these studies due solely to sampling error variance:

$$S_e^2 = \frac{(1 - \bar{r}^2)^2}{\bar{N} - 1} = .0135$$

Finally, we estimate the amount of between-study variance that is left after we subtract out expected sampling error variance:

$$S_{\rho_{xy}}^2 = S_r^2 - S_e^2$$
$$S_{\rho_{xy}}^2 = .0120 - .0135 = -.0015$$

In this case there is slightly less variance in the observed r than is predicted from sampling error. (This deviation from zero is called second-order sampling error; Hunter & Schmidt, 1990b, chapter 9). Hence we conclude that $\bar{\rho}_{xy} = .22$ and $SD_{\rho_{xy}} = 0$. That is, we conclude that sampling error accounts for all the observed differences between the studies. We conclude that the population ρ_{xy} value underlying every one of the studies is .22.

This example illustrates how meta-analysis sometimes reveals that all of the apparent variability across studies is illusory. Sometimes, however, there can be considerable variability remaining after correcting for sampling error. Often this remaining variability will be due to other variance-producing artifacts that have not been corrected for. But sometimes some of it might be 'real'. Suppose the researcher hypothesizes (say, based on evolutionary psychology theory) that the results are different for males and females. He or she can then check this hypothesis by subgrouping the studies into those conducted on males and those conducted on females. If sex is indeed a real moderator, then the mean correlations will be different for males and females. The average within group $SD_{\rho_{xy}}$ will also be smaller than the overall $SD_{\rho_{xy}}$. Later we will discuss other methods of checking for moderator variables.

OTHER ARTIFACTS AND THEIR EFFECTS

Bare Bones meta-analysis is deficient and should not be used without further refinement in integrating research literatures. It is deficient because there is no research literature in which the only source of distortion in study findings is sampling error. Since there are no scales that are free of measurement error, the findings of every study are distorted by measurement error – in both the independent variable measure and the dependent variable measure. In addition, independent of measurement error, no measure has perfect construct validity; all measures, even good ones, have at least some construct deficiency (something left out) and some construct contamination (something included that should not be). The findings of most studies are also distorted by other artifacts.

Table 3.2 lists ten of these additional artifacts. Measurement error in the independent and dependent variable measures biases obtained correlations or *d*-values downwards, with the amount of downward bias depending on the size of the reliabilities

Table 3.2 *Study artifacts beyond sampling error that alter the value of outcome measures (with examples from personnel research)*

1. Error of measurement in the dependent variable:
    Study validity will be systematically lower than true validity to the extent that job performance is measured with random error.

2. Error of measurement in the independent variable:
    Study validity for a test will systematically understate the validity of the ability measured since the test is not perfectly reliable.

3. Dichotomization of a continuous dependent variable:
    Turnover – the length of time that a worker stays with the organization is often dichotomized into 'more than...' or 'less than...' where ... is some arbitrarily chosen interval such as one year or six months.

4. Dichotomization of a continuous independent variable:
    Interviewers are often told to dichotomize their perceptions into 'acceptable' versus 'reject'.

5. Range variation in the independent variable:
    Study validity will be systematically lower than true validity to the extent that hiring policy causes incumbents to have a lower variation in the predictor than is true of applicants.

6. Attrition artifacts: Range variation in the dependent variable:
    Study validity will be systematically lower than true validity to the extent that there is systematic attrition in workers on performance, as when good workers are promoted out of the population or when poor workers are fired for poor performance.

7. Deviation from perfect construct validity in the independent variable:
    Study validity will vary if the factor structure of the test differs from the usual structure of tests for the same trait.

8. Deviation from perfect construct validity in the dependent variable:
    Study validity will differ from true validity if the criterion is deficient or contaminated.

9. Reporting or transcriptional error:
    Reported study validities differ from actual study validities due to a variety of reporting problems: inaccuracy in coding data, computational errors, errors in reading computer output, typographical errors by secretaries or by printers.
    Note: These errors can be very large in magnitude.

10. Variance due to extraneous factors:
    Study validity will be systematically lower than true validity if incumbents differ in job experience at the time their performance is measured.

of the measures. For example, if both measures have reliability of .70, the downward bias from this artifact alone will be 30%. In addition, differences in reliability between studies will cause differences in findings between studies.

Either or both of the continuous independent and dependent variable measures may be dichotomized (typically at the median). If both measures are dichotomized at the median or mean, the underlying correlation will be reduced by the factor $.80 \times .80$ or .64 (Hunter & Schmidt, 1990a).

Either or both of the variables may be affected by range variation. For example, only the top 50% of test scorers might be hired, producing a downward bias of around 30% due to range restriction on the independent variable. In addition, those with poor job performance might be fired, producing range restriction on the dependent variable, and a further downward bias.

Deviation from perfect construct validity in the two measures produces an additional independent downward bias. Construct validity is defined as the correlation between the actual construct one is attempting to measure and true scores on the scale one uses to measure that construct.

Errors in the data are not systematic in their effect on the mean correlation or mean *d*-value; the distortion produced in the correlation can be in either direction. Across studies such errors increase the amount of artifactual variation. Sometimes data errors can be detected and corrected but usually this is not possible in meta-analysis.

Consider the following example. Suppose the construct-level correlation between two personality traits A and B is .60. ($\rho_{AB} = .60$.) This is the correlation that we as researchers are interested in, the correlation between the two constructs themselves. Measure *x* is used to measure trait A and measure *y* is used to measure trait B. Now suppose we have the following situation:

$a_1 = .90 =$ the square root of the reliability of x;
$\quad r_{xx} = .81$;
$a_2 = .90 =$ the square root of the reliability of y;
$\quad r_{yy} = .81$;
$a_3 = .90 =$ the construct validity of x;
$a_4 = .90 =$ the construct validity of y;
$a_5 = .80 =$ the attenuation factor for splitting x at the median; and
$a_6 = .80 =$ the attenuation factor for splitting y at the median.

This is not an extreme example. Both measures have acceptable reliability (.81 in both cases). Both measures have high construct validity; for each measure, its true scores correlate .90 with the actual construct. Both measures have been dichotomized into low and high groups, but the dichotomization is at the median, which produces less downward bias than any other split.

The total impact of the six study imperfections is the total attenuation factor A:

$$A = (.90)(.90)(.90)(.90)(.80)(.80) = .42$$

Hence the attenuated study correlation – the expected observed study correlation – is:

$$\rho_{xy} = .42\rho_{AB} = .42(.60) = .25$$

That is, the study correlation is reduced to less than half the value of the actual correlation between the two personality traits.

This realistic example illustrates the power of artifacts other than sampling error to severely distort study results. These artifacts produce serious distortions and must be taken seriously. This example contains six artifacts; the first four of these are always present in every study. Dichotomization does not occur in every study, but in many studies in which it does not, other artifacts such as range restriction do occur, and the overall attenuation factor, A, is often smaller than our .42 here.

This example illustrates a single study. The different studies in a research literature will have different levels of artifacts and hence different levels of downward bias. Hence these artifacts not only depress the overall mean observed correlation, they also create additional variability in correlations across studies beyond that created by sampling error.

MORE ADVANCED METHODS OF META-ANALYSIS

More advanced forms of meta-analysis correct for these artifacts. First, they correct for the overall downward bias produced by the artifacts. Second, they correct for the artifactual differences between studies that these artifacts create. These more advanced meta-analysis methods take two forms: methods in which each observed study correlation (or d-value) is corrected individually, and methods in which distributions of artifact values are used to correct the entire distribution of observed correlations (or d-values) at one time. Both of these advanced meta-analysis methods are referred to as psychometric meta-analysis methods, and they are now discussed in the following two sections.

Methods that Correct Each *r* or *d*-value Independently

We will describe this form of meta-analysis for correlations but the same principles apply when the

statistic being used is the d-value. The method that corrects each statistic individually is the most direct form of the more complete methods of meta-analysis. In this method, each individual observed correlation is corrected for each of the artifacts that have biased it. This is most easily illustrated using our example from the last section, in which the underlying construct level correlation is .60 ($\rho_{AB} = .60$). But the total downward bias created by the six artifacts operating on it reduced it to .25:

$$\rho_{xy} = .42\rho_{AB} = .42(.60) = .25$$

The total attenuating or biasing factor is .42. Now in a real study if we can compute this total biasing factor, we can correct our observed value of .25 by dividing it by this factor:

$$\rho_{AB} = .25/.42 = .60$$

A correction of this sort is applied to each of the observed correlations included in the meta-analysis. This correction reverses the downwardly biasing process and restores the correlation to its actual construct level value. In the population (that is, when N is infinite), this correction is always accurate, because there is no sampling error. In real studies, however, sample sizes are not infinite, so there is sampling error. The effect of this sampling error is that corrections of this kind are accurate only on the average. Because of sampling error, any single corrected value may be randomly too large or too small, but the average of such corrected values is accurate. It is the average of these corrected values across all the studies in the meta-analysis that is the focus of the meta-analysis. So our estimate of $\bar{\rho}_{AB}$ is accurate in expectation. There will be no downward or upward bias.

Meta-analysis also has a second focus: on the variability of these corrected correlations. The variance of these corrected correlations is inflated by sampling error variance. In fact, the corrections actually increase the amount of sampling error variance. This sampling error variance is subtracted from the variance of the corrected rs to estimate the real variance of the construct-level correlations:

$$S^2_{\rho_{AB}} = S^2_{\hat{\rho}_{AB}} - S^2_{e\hat{\rho}_{AB}}$$

In this equation, $S^2_{\hat{\rho}_{AB}}$ is the variance of the corrected correlations. This variance contains sampling error, and the amount of that sampling error is $S^2_{e\hat{\rho}_{AB}}$. Hence the difference between these two figures, $S^2_{\rho_{AB}}$, estimates the real (i.e., population) variance of $\hat{\rho}_{AB}$. The square root of $S^2_{\rho_{AB}}$ is the estimate of $SD_{\rho_{AB}}$. Hence we have $\bar{\rho}_{AB}$ and $SD_{\rho_{AB}}$ as the products of the meta-analysis. That is, we have estimated the mean and the SD of the underlying construct-level correlations. This is a major improvement over Bare Bones meta-analysis, which estimates the mean and SD of the downwardly biased correlations ($\bar{\rho}_{xy}$ and $SD_{\rho_{xy}}$) and hence does not tell us anything about the correlation between actual constructs or traits.

If $SD_{\rho_{AB}}$ is zero or very small, this indicates that there are no moderators (interactions) producing different values of ρ_{AB} in different studies. Hence there is no need to test moderator hypotheses. If $SD_{\rho_{AB}}$ is larger, this variation may be due to other artifacts – such as data errors – that you have not been able to correct for. However, some of the remaining variation may be due to one or more moderator variables. If there is theoretical evidence to suggest this, these hypotheses can be tested by subgrouping the studies and performing a separate meta-analysis on each subgroup. It may turn out that $\bar{\rho}_{AB}$ really is different for males and females, or for higher vs. lower management levels. If so, the moderator hypothesis has been confirmed. Another approach to moderator analysis is correlational: the values of $\hat{\rho}_{AB}$ can be correlated with study characteristics (hypothesized moderators). Multiple regression can also be used. Values of $\hat{\rho}_{AB}$ can be regressed on multiple study characteristics. In all forms of moderator analysis, there are statistical problems in moderator analysis that the researcher should be aware of. We discuss these problems later.

What we have presented here is merely an overview of the main ideas in this approach to meta-analysis. A detailed discussion can be found in Hunter and Schmidt (1990b). In that book, chapter 3 discusses application of this method to correlations and chapter 7 to d-values. The actual formulas are considerably more complicated than in the case of Bare Bones meta-analysis and are beyond the scope and length limitations of this chapter. Several computer programs have been created for these methods. These programs are in the public domain and are available to anyone.

Meta-Analysis Using Artifact Distributions

Most meta-analyses do not use the method described above; they do not correct each r or d statistic individually for the artifactual biases that have affected it. Probably less than 10% of advanced level meta-analyses correct each r or d-value individually. The reason for this is that most studies do not present all of the information on artifacts that is necessary to make these corrections. For example, many studies do not present information on the reliability of the scales used, or do not present information of the degree of range restriction present in the data. The same is true for the other artifacts.

However, artifact information is usually present sporadically in the studies included in the meta-analysis. Some studies present reliability information on the independent variable measures and some on the dependent variable measures. Some present range restriction information but not reliability information. In addition, information on artifact levels typical of the research literature being analyzed is often available from other sources. For example, test or inventory manuals often present information on scale reliability. Information on typical levels of range restriction can be found in the personnel selection literature. Using all such sources of artifact information, it is often possible to compile a distribution of artifacts that is representative of that research literature; for example, a distribution of inter-rater reliabilities of supervisory ratings of job performance; a distribution of reliabilities typical of spatial ability tests; or a distribution of reliabilities of job satisfaction measures.

Artifact distribution meta-analysis is a set of quantitative methods for correcting artifact-produced biases using such distributions of artifacts. Correlations are not corrected individually, instead, a Bare Bones meta-analysis is first performed and then the mean $(\bar{\rho}_{xy})$ and SD $(SD_{\rho_{xy}})$ produced by the Bare Bones analysis are corrected for artifacts other than sampling error. The formulas for this form of meta-analysis are even more complex than those used when each correlation is corrected individually. These methods are presented in detail in Hunter and Schmidt (1990b), in chapter 4 for correlations and in chapter 7 for the d-value statistic. Approximately 90% of advanced level meta-analyses use artifact distribution meta-analysis methods. Again, several public domain computer programs are available for implementing this method of meta-analysis.

In addition to methods developed by the present authors, artifact distribution-based meta-analysis methods have been developed by Callender and Osburn (1980) and Raju and Burke (1983). Computer simulation studies have shown that all of these methods are quite accurate. In data sets in which artifact information is available for each correlation, it is possible to apply both methods of advanced level meta-analysis to the same set of studies. That is, each correlation can be corrected individually and artifact distribution-based meta-analysis can also be applied in a separate analysis. In such cases, the meta-analysis results have been essentially identical, as would be expected.

Moderator hypotheses may also be examined when using artifact distribution meta-analysis. With this method of meta-analysis, subgrouping of studies is the preferred method of moderator analysis. Regression of study correlations onto study characteristics (potential moderators) works less well because the study correlations in this case have not been corrected individually for artifacts and hence the correlations are (differentially) biased as indices of actual study findings. Hence they lack construct validity as measures of true study correlations or effect sizes.

OTHER APPROACHES TO META-ANALYSIS

Descriptive Meta-Analysis Methods

Glass (1976) advanced the first meta-analysis procedures and coined the term meta-analysis to designate the analysis of analyses (studies). For Glass, the purpose of meta-analysis is descriptive; the goal is to paint a very general, broad, and inclusive picture of a particular research literature (Glass, 1977; Glass, McGaw & Smith, 1981). The questions to be answered are very general; for example, does psychotherapy – regardless of type – have an impact on the kinds of outcomes that therapy researchers consider important enough to measure, regardless of the nature of these outcomes (e.g., self-reported anxiety, count of emotional outbursts, etc.)? Thus Glassian meta-analysis often combines studies with somewhat different independent variables (e.g., different kinds of therapy) and different dependent variables. As a result, some critics have criticized these methods as combining apples and oranges. Glassian meta-analysis has three primary properties:

1. *A strong emphasis on effect sizes rather than significance levels.* Glass believed the purpose of research integration is more descriptive than inferential, and he felt that the most important descriptive statistics are those that indicate most clearly the magnitude of effects. Glassian meta-analysis typically employs estimates of the Pearson *r* or estimates of *d*. The initial product of a Glassian meta-analysis is the mean and standard deviation of observed effect sizes or correlations across studies.

2. *Acceptance of the variance of effect sizes at face value.* Glassian meta-analysis implicitly assumes that the observed variability in effect sizes is real and should have some substantive explanation. There is no attention to sampling error in the effect sizes. The substantive explanations are sought in the varying characteristics of the studies (e.g., sex or mean age of subjects, length of treatment, and more). Study characteristics that correlate with study effect are examined for their explanatory power. The general finding has been that few study characteristics correlate significantly with study outcomes. Problems of capitalization on chance and low statistical power associated with this step in meta-analysis are discussed in Hunter and Schmidt (1990b; chapter 2).

3. *A strongly empirical approach to determining which aspects of studies should be coded and tested for possible association with study outcomes.* Glass (1976, 1977) felt that all such questions are empirical questions, and he de-emphasized the role of theory in determining which variables should be tested as potential moderators of study outcome (see also Glass, 1972).

One variation of Glass's methods has been labeled *study effects meta-analysis* by Bangert-Drowns (1986). It differs from Glass's procedures in several ways. First, only one effect size from each study is included in the meta-analysis, thus ensuring statistical independence within the meta-analysis. If a study has multiple dependent measures, those that assess the same construct are combined (usually averaged), and those that assess different constructs are assigned to different meta-analyses. Second, study effects meta-analysis calls for the meta-analyst to make some judgments about study methodological quality and to exclude studies with deficiencies judged serious enough to distort study outcomes. In reviewing experimental studies, for example, the experimental treatment must be at least similar to those judged by experts in the research area to be appropriate, or the study will be excluded. This procedure seeks to calibrate specific relationships rather than to paint a broad Glassian picture of a research area and in this sense is quite different from Glass methods. However, this approach is like the Glass method in that it does not acknowledge that much of the variability in study findings is due to sampling error variance. That is, it takes observed correlations and *d*-values at face value. Some of those instrumental in developing and using this procedure are Mansfield and Busse (1977), Kulik and his associates (Bangert-Drowns, Kulik & Kulik, 1983; Kulik & Bangert-Drowns, 1983–1984), Landman and Dawes (1982), and Wortman and Bryant (1985). In recent years, few published meta-analyses have used Glassian methods or study effects meta-analyses.

Meta-Analysis Methods that Focus on Sampling Error

As noted earlier, numerous artifacts produce the deceptive appearance of variability in results across studies. The artifact that typically produces more false variability than any other is sampling error variance. Glassian meta-analysis and study effect meta-analysis implicitly accept variability produced by sampling error variance as real variability. There are two types of meta-analyses that move beyond Glassian methods in that they attempt to control for sampling error variance.

Homogeneity Test-Based Meta-Analysis

This approach was advocated independently by Hedges (1982b; Hedges & Olkin, 1985) and by Rosenthal and Rubin (1982). Hedges (1982a) and Rosenthal and Rubin (1982) proposed that chi-square statistical tests be used to decide whether study outcomes are more variable than would be expected from sampling error alone. If these chi-square tests of homogeneity are not statistically significant, then the population correlation or effect size is accepted as constant across studies and there is no search for moderators. Use of chi-square tests of homogeneity to estimate whether findings in a set of studies differ more than would be expected from sampling error variance was originally proposed by Snedecor (1946).

The chi-square test of homogeneity typically has low power to detect variation beyond sampling error (National Research Council, 1992). Hence the meta-analyst will often conclude that the studies being examined are homogeneous when they are not; that is, the meta-analyst will conclude that the value of ρ_{xy} or δ_{xy} is the same in all the studies included in the meta-analysis when, in fact, these parameters actually vary across studies. A major problem here is that under these circumstances, the fixed effects model of meta-analysis is then used in almost all cases. Unlike random effects meta-analysis models, fixed effects models assume zero between-study variability in ρ_{xy} or δ_{xy} in computing the standard error of the $\bar{r}$ or $\bar{d}$, resulting in underestimates of the relevant standard errors of the mean. This in turn results in confidence intervals around the $\bar{r}$ or $\bar{d}$ that are erroneously narrow – sometimes by large amounts. This creates an erroneous impression that the meta-analysis findings are much more precise than in fact they really are. This problem also results in Type I biases in all significance tests conducted for $\bar{r}$ or $\bar{d}$, and these biases are often quite large (Hunter & Schmidt, 2000). As a result of this problem, the National Research Council (1992) report on data integration recommended that fixed effects models be replaced by random effects models which do not suffer from this problem. We have also made that recommendation (Hunter & Schmidt, 2000). However, the majority of published meta-analyses using the Rosenthal–Rubin methods and the Hedges–Olkin methods have used their fixed effects models. For example, most of the meta-analyses that have appeared in the *Psychological Bulletin* are fixed effects meta-analysis, and most of these analyses employ the Hedges and Olkin (1985) fixed effect meta-analysis model.

Both Rosenthal and Rubin and Hedges and Olkin have presented random effects meta-analysis models as well as fixed effects methods, but meta-analysts have rarely employed their random effects methods. The Hunter–Schmidt methods, described earlier in this chapter, are all random effects methods.

Hedges (1982b) and Hedges and Olkin (1985) extended the concept of homogeneity tests to develop a more general procedure for moderator analysis based on significance testing. It calls for breaking the overall chi-square statistic down into the sum of within- and between-group chi-squares. The original set of effect sizes in the meta-analysis is divided into successively smaller subgroups until the chi-square statistics within the subgroups are non-significant, indicating that sampling error can explain all the variation within the last set of subgroups.

Homogeneity test-based meta-analysis represents an ironic return to the practice that originally led to the great difficulties in making sense out of research literatures: reliance on statistical significance tests. As noted above, the chi-square test typically has low power. Another problem is that the chi-square test has a Type I bias. The chi-square test allows only for sampling error; but there are other purely artifactual sources of variance between studies in effect sizes. These include computational, transcriptional, and other data errors, differences between studies in reliability of measurement, and in levels of range restriction, and others, as discussed earlier. Thus, even when true study effect sizes are actually the same across studies, these sources of artifactual variance will create variance beyond sampling error, sometimes causing the chi-square test to be significant and hence to falsely indicate heterogeneity of effect sizes. This is especially likely when the number of studies is large, increasing statistical power to detect small amounts of such artifactual variance. Another problem is that even when the variance beyond sampling error is not artifactual, it often will be small in magnitude and of little or no theoretical or practical significance. Hedges and Olkin (1985) recognized this fact and cautioned that researchers should not merely look at significance levels but should evaluate the actual size of the variance; unfortunately, however, once researchers are caught up in significance tests, the usual practice is to assume that if it is statistically significant it is important (and if it is not, it is zero). Once the major focus is on the results of significance tests, effect sizes are usually ignored.

Bare Bones Meta-Analysis

The second approach to meta-analysis that attempts to control only for the artifact of sampling error is what we referred to earlier as *bare bones meta-analysis* (Hunter, Schmidt & Jackson, 1982; Hunter & Schmidt, 1990b; Pearlman, Schmidt & Hunter, 1980). This approach can be applied to correlations, *d*-values or any other effect size statistic for which the standard error is known. For example, if the statistic is correlations, the mean *r* is first computed. Then the variance of the set of correlations is computed. Next the amount of sampling error variance is computed and subtracted from this observed variance. If the result in zero, then sampling error accounts for all the observed variance, and the *r* value accurately summarizes all the studies in the meta-analysis. If not, then the square root of the remaining variance is the index of variability remaining around the mean *r* after sampling error variance is removed. Earlier in this chapter we presented examples of bare bones meta-analysis.

Because there are always other artifacts (such as measurement error) that should be corrected for, we have consistently stated in our writings that the bare bones meta-analysis method is incomplete and unsatisfactory. It is useful primarily as the first step in explaining and teaching meta-analysis to novices. However, studies using bare bones methods have been published; the authors of these studies have invariably claimed that the information needed to correct for artifacts beyond sampling error was unavailable to them. This is in fact rarely the case, since estimates of artifact values (e.g., reliabilities of scales) are usually available from the literature, from test manuals, or from other sources, as indicated earlier.

Psychometric Meta-Analysis

This is a third type of meta-analysis which corrects not only for sampling error (an unsystematic artifact), but for other systematic artifacts such as measurement error, range restriction or enhancement, dichotomization of measures, and so forth. These other artifacts are said to be systematic because, in addition to creating artifactual variation across studies, they also create systematic downward biases in the results of all studies. For example, measurement error systematically biases all correlations downward. Psychometric meta analysis corrects not only for the artifactual variation across studies, but also for the downward biases. Psychometric meta-analysis is the only meta-analysis method that takes into account both statistical and measurement artifacts. Two variations of these procedures were described earlier in this chapter in the section 'More Advanced Methods of Meta-Analysis'. A detailed presentation of these procedures can be found in Hunter and Schmidt (1990b) or Hunter, Schmidt and Jackson (1982).

UNRESOLVED PROBLEMS IN META-ANALYSIS

In all forms of meta-analysis, there are unresolvable problems in the search for moderators. First, when effect size estimates are regressed on multiple-study characteristics, capitalization on chance operates to increase the apparent number of significant associations for those study characteristics that have no actual associations with study outcomes. Because the sample size is the number of studies and many study properties may be coded, this problem is often severe (Hunter & Schmidt, 1990b, chapter 2). There is no purely statistical solution to this problem. The problem can be mitigated, however, by basing choice of study characteristics and final conclusions not only on the statistics at hand, but also on other theoretically relevant empirical findings (which may be the result of other meta-analyses) and on theoretical considerations. Results should be examined closely for substantive and theoretical meaning. Capitalization on chance is a

threat whenever the (unknown) correlation or regression weight is actually zero or near zero. When there is in fact a relationship, there is another problem: Power to detect the relation is often low (Hunter & Schmidt, 1990b, chapter 2). Thus, true moderators of study outcomes (to the extent that such exist) may have only a low probability of showing up as statistically significant. In short, this step in meta-analysis is often plagued with all the problems of small-sample studies. Other things being equal, conducting separate meta-analyses on subsets of studies to identify a moderator does not avoid these problems and may lead to additional problems of confounding of moderator effects (Hunter & Schmidt, 1990b, chapter 13).

Although there are often serious problems in detecting moderator variables in meta-analysis, there is no approach to moderator detection that is superior to meta-analysis. In fact, all alternative methods have even more serious problems and hence are inferior to meta-analysis. Moderator detection is difficult because a large amount of information is required for clear identification of moderators. Even sets of 40–50 studies often do not contain the required amounts of information.

THE ROLE OF META-ANALYSIS IN THEORY DEVELOPMENT

As noted at the beginning of this chapter, the major task in the behavioral and social sciences, as in other sciences, is the development of theory. A good theory is a good explanation of the processes that actually take place in a phenomenon. For example, what actually happens when employees develop a high level of organizational commitment? Does job satisfaction develop first and then cause the development of commitment? If so, what causes job satisfaction to develop and how does it have an effect on commitment? How do higher levels of mental ability cause higher levels of job performance? Only by increasing job knowledge? Or also by directly improving problem solving on the job? The researcher is essentially a detective; his or her job is to find out why and how things happen the way they do. To construct theories, however, researchers must first know some of the basic facts, such as the empirical relations among variables. These relations are the building blocks of theory. For example, if researchers know there is a high and consistent population correlation between job satisfaction and organization commitment, this will send them in particular directions in developing their theories. If the correlation between these variables is very low and consistent, theory development will branch in different directions. If the relation is highly variable across organizations and settings, researchers will be encouraged to advance interactive or moderator-based theories.

Meta-analysis provides these empirical building blocks for theory. Meta-analytic findings tell us what it is that needs to be explained by the theory. However, meta-analysis has been criticized because it does not directly generate or develop theory (Guzzo, Jackson & Katzell, 1986). This is like criticizing typewriters or word processors because they do not generate novels on their own. The results of meta-analysis are indispensable for theory construction; but theory construction itself is a creative process distinct from meta-analysis.

As implied in the language used here, theories are causal explanations. The goal in every science is explanation, and explanation is always causal. In the behavioral and social sciences, the methods of path analysis (e.g., see Hunter & Gerbing, 1982) can be used to test causal theories when the data meet the assumptions of the method. The relationships revealed by meta-analysis – the empirical building blocks for theory – can be used in path analysis or structural equation modeling to test causal theories even when all the delineated relationships are observational rather than experimental. Experimentally determined relationships can also be entered into path analyses along with observationally based relations by transforming d values to correlations. Path analysis can be a very powerful tool for reducing the number of theories that could possibly be consistent with the data, sometimes to a very small number, and sometimes to only one theory (Hunter, 1988). For examples, see Hunter (1983) and Schmidt (1992). Every such reduction in the number of possible theories is an advance in understanding.

META-ANALYSIS IN INDUSTRIAL-ORGANIZATIONAL PSYCHOLOGY AND OTHER APPLIED AREAS

There have been numerous applications of meta-analysis in industrial-organizational (I/O) psychology, the most extensive and detailed of which have been in the study of the generalizability of the validities of employment selection procedures (Schmidt, 1988; Schmidt & Hunter, 1981). The findings have resulted in major changes in the field of personnel selection. Validity generalization research is described in more detail below.

The meta-analysis methods presented in this chapter have also been applied in other areas of I/O psychology and organizational behavior. Between 1978 and 1998, there have been approximately 80 published non-selection applications, and the following are some examples: (a) correlates of role conflict and role ambiguity (C.D. Fisher & Gittelson, 1983; Jackson & Schuler, 1985); (b) relation of job satisfaction to absenteeism (Hacket & Guion, 1985;

Terborg & Lee, 1982); (c) relation between job performance and turnover (McEvoy & Cascio, 1987); (d) relation between job satisfaction and job performance (Iaffaldono & Muchinsky, 1985; Petty, McGee & Cavender, 1984); (e) effects of nonselection organizational interventions on employee output and productivity (Guzzo, Jette & Katzell, 1985); (f) effects of realistic job previews on employee turnover, performance and satisfaction (McEvoy & Cascio, 1985; Premack & Wanous, 1985); (g) evaluation of Fiedler's theory of leadership (Peters, Hartke & Pohlmann, 1985); and (h) accuracy of self-ratings of ability and skill (Mabe & West, 1982).

The applications have been to both correlational and experimental literatures. As of the mid-1980s, sufficient meta-analyses had been published in I/O psychology that a review of meta-analytic studies in this area was published. This lengthy review (Hunter & Hirsh, 1987) reflected the fact that this literature had already become quite large. It is noteworthy that the review denoted considerable space to the development and presentation of theoretical propositions; this was possible because the clarification of research literatures produced by meta-analysis provides a foundation for theory development that previously did not exist. It is also noteworthy that the findings in one meta-analysis were often found to be theoretically relevant to the interpretation of the findings in other meta-analyses. A second review of meta-analytic studies in I/O psychology has since been published (Tett, Meyer & Roese, 1994).

The examples cited here applied meta-analysis to research programs, and the results of such programs can sometimes be used as a foundation for policy recommendations. But meta-analysis can be applied more directly in the public policy arena. Consider one example. The Federation of Behavioral, Psychological and Cognitive Sciences sponsors regular Science and Public Policy Seminars for members of the United States Congress and their staffs. In one seminar, the speaker was Eleanor Chelimsky, for years the director of the General Accounting Office's (GAO) Division of Program Evaluation and Methodology. In that position she pioneered the use of meta-analysis as a tool for providing program evaluation and other legislatively significant advice to the United States Congress. Chelimsky (1994) stated that meta-analysis has proven to be an excellent way to provide the United States Congress with the widest variety of research results that can hold up under close scrutiny under the time pressures imposed by Congress. She stated that the General Accounting Office has found that meta-analysis reveals both what is known and what is not known in a given topic area, and distinguishes between fact and opinion 'without being confrontational'. One application she cited as an example was a meta-analysis of studies on the merits of producing binary chemical weapons (nerve gas in which the two key ingredients are kept separate for safety until the gas is to be used). The meta-analysis did not support the production of such weapons. This was not what officials in the Department of Defense wanted to hear, and the Department of Defense disputed the methodology and the results. But the methodology held up under close scrutiny, and in the end the United States Congress eliminated funds for binary weapons. By law it is the responsibility of the General Accounting Office to provide policy-relevant research information to the United States Congress. So the adoption of meta-analysis by the General Accounting Office provides a clear and even dramatic example of the impact that meta-analysis can have on public policy.

As noted above, one major application of meta-analysis to date has been the examination of the validity tests and other methods used in personnel selection. Meta-analysis has been used to test the hypothesis of situation-specific validity. In personnel selection it had long been believed that validity was specific to situations; that is, it was believed that the validity of the same test for what appeared to be the same job varied from employer to employer, region to region, across time periods, and so forth. In fact, it was believed that the same test could have high validity (i.e., a high correlation with job performance) in one location or organization and be completely invalid (i.e., have zero validity) in another. This belief was based on the observation that obtained validity coefficients for similar tests and jobs varied substantially across different studies. In some such studies there was a statistically significant relationship, and in others there was no significant relationship – which, as noted earlier, was falsely taken to indicate no relationship at all. This puzzling variability of findings was explained by postulating that jobs that appeared to be the same actually differed in important but subtle (and undetectable) ways in what was required to perform them. This belief led to a requirement for local or situational validity studies. It was held that validity had to be estimated separately for each situation by a study conducted in that setting; that is, validity findings could not be generalized across settings, situations, employers, and the like (Schmidt & Hunter, 1981). In the late 1970s, meta-analysis of validity coefficients began to be conducted to test whether validity might in fact be generalizable (Schmidt & Hunter, 1977; Schmidt, Hunter, Pearlman & Shane, 1979); these meta-analyses were therefore called *validity generalization* studies. If all or most of the study-to-study variability in observed validities was due to sampling error and other artifacts, then the traditional belief in situational specificity of validity would be seen to be erroneous, and the conclusion would be that validity did generalize.

Meta-analysis has now been applied to over 500 research literatures in employment selection, each one representing a predictor–job performance combination. These predictors have included nontest

procedures, such as evaluations of education and experience, employment interviews, and biographical data scales, as well as ability and aptitude tests. As an example, consider the relation between quantitative ability and overall job performance in clerical jobs (Hunter & Schmidt, 1996). This substudy was based on 223 correlations computed on a total of 18,919 people. All of the variance of the observed validities was traceable to artifacts. The mean validity was .50. Thus, integration of these data leads to the general (and generalizable) principle that the correlation between quantitative ability and clerical performance is .50, with no true variation around this value. Like other similar findings, this finding shows that the old belief that validities are situationally specific is false.

Today many organizations use validity generalization findings as the basis of their selection-testing programs. Validity generalization has been included in standard texts (e.g., Anastasi, 1988) and in the *Standards for Educational and Psychological Tests* (American Educational Research Association, 1999). A report by the National Academy of Sciences (Hartigan & Wigdor, 1989) devoted a chapter (chapter 6) to validity generalization and endorsed its methods and assumptions.

WIDER IMPACT OF META-ANALYSIS ON PSYCHOLOGY

Some have viewed meta-analysis as merely a set of improved methods for doing literature reviews. Meta-analysis is actually more than that. By quantitatively comparing findings across diverse studies, meta-analysis can discover new knowledge not inferable from any individual study and can sometimes answer questions that were never addressed in any of the individual studies contained in the meta-analysis. For example, no individual study may have compared the effectiveness of a training program for people of higher and lower mental ability; but by comparing mean *d*-value statistics across different groups of studies, meta-analysis can reveal this difference. That is, moderator variables (interactions) never studied in any individual study can be revealed by meta-analysis. But even though it is much more than that, meta-analysis is indeed an improved method for synthesizing or integrating research literatures. The premier review journal in psychology is the *Psychological Bulletin*. In viewing that journal's volumes from 1980 to 2000, the impact of meta-analysis is apparent. Over this time period, a steadily increasing percentage of the reviews published in this journal are meta-analyses and a steadily decreasing percentage are traditional narrative subjective reviews. Most of the remaining narrative reviews published today in *Psychological Bulletin* focus on research literatures that are not developed well enough to be amenable to quantitative treatment. It is not uncommon for narrative review manuscripts to be returned by editors to the authors with the request that meta-analysis be applied to the studies reviewed.

As noted above, most of the meta-analyses appearing in *Psychological Bulletin* have employed fixed effects methods, resulting in many cases in overstatement of the precision of the meta-analysis findings. Despite this fact, these meta-analyses produce findings and conclusions that are far superior to those produced by the traditional narrative subjective method. Many other journals have shown the same increase over time in the number of meta-analyses published. Many of these journals, such as the *Journal of Applied Psychology*, had traditionally published only individual empirical studies and had rarely published reviews up until the advent of meta-analysis in the late 1970s. These journals began publishing meta-analyses because meta-analyses came to be viewed not as 'mere reviews' but as a form of empirical research in themselves. Between 1978 and 1997, the *Journal of Applied Psychology* published 60 meta-analysis-based articles, which contained a total of 1647 separate meta-analyses. As a result of this change, the quality and accuracy of conclusions from research literatures improved in a wide variety of journals and in a corresponding variety of research areas in psychology. This improvement in the quality of conclusions from research literatures has expedited theory development in a wide variety of areas in psychology.

The impact of meta-analysis on psychology textbooks has been positive and dramatic. Textbooks are important because their function is to summarize the state of cumulative knowledge in a given field. Most people – students and others – acquire most of their knowledge about psychological theory and findings from their reading of textbooks. Prior to meta-analysis, textbook authors faced with hundreds of conflicting studies on a single question subjectively and arbitrarily selected a small number of their preferred studies from such a literature and based the textbook conclusions on only those few studies. Today most textbook authors base their conclusions on meta-analysis findings – making their conclusions and their textbooks much more accurate. It is hard to overemphasize the importance of this development in advancing cumulative knowledge in psychology.

The realities revealed about data and research findings by the principles of meta-analysis have greatly influenced our views of the individual empirical study, the nature of cumulative research knowledge, and the reward structure in the research enterprise.

Meta-analysis has explicated the role of sampling error, measurement error, and other artifacts in determining the observed findings and statistical power of individual studies. In doing this, it has revealed how little information there is in any single study. It has shown that, contrary to previous belief, no single primary study can provide more than tentative evidence on any issue; multiple studies are required to draw solid conclusions. The first study done in an area may be revered for its creativity, but sampling error and other artifacts in that study will often produce a fully or partially erroneous answer to the study question. The quantitative estimate of effect size will almost always be erroneous. The shift from tentative to solid conclusions requires the accumulation of studies and the application of meta-analysis to those study results.

Furthermore, adequate handling of other study imperfections such as measurement error – and especially imperfect construct validity – may also require separate studies and more advanced meta-analysis. Because of the effects of artifacts such as sampling error and measurement error, the data in studies come to us encrypted, and to understand their meaning we must first break the code. Doing this requires meta-analysis. Therefore any individual study must be considered only a single data point to be contributed to a future meta-analysis. Thus the scientific status and value of the individual study is necessarily reduced. Ironically, however, the value of individual studies in the aggregate is increased.

Because multiple studies are needed to solve the problem of sampling error, it is critical to ensure the availability of all studies on each topic. A major problem is that many good replication articles are rejected by our primary research journals. Journals currently put excessive weight on innovation and creativity in evaluating studies and often fail to consider either sampling error or other technical problems such as measurement error. Many journals will not even consider 'mere replication studies' or 'mere measurement studies'. Many persistent authors eventually publish such studies in journals with lower prestige, but they must endure many letters of rejection and publication is delayed for a long period.

To us this clearly indicates that we need a new type of journal – whether hard-copy-based or electronic – that systematically archives all studies that will be needed for later meta-analyses. The American Psychological Association's Experimental Publication System in the early 1970s was an attempt in this direction. However, at that time the need subsequently created by meta-analysis did not yet exist; the system apparently met no real need at that time and hence was discontinued. Today, the need is so great that failure to have such a journal system in place is retarding our efforts to reach our full potential in creating cumulative knowledge in psychology and the social sciences. The Board of Scientific Affairs of the American Psychological Association is currently studying the feasibility of such a system.

CONCLUSIONS

Until recently, psychological research literatures were conflicting and contradictory. As the number of studies on each particular question became larger and larger, this situation became increasingly frustrating and intolerable. This situation stemmed from reliance on defective procedures for achieving cumulative knowledge: the statistical significance test in individual primary studies in combination with the narrative subjective review of research literatures. Meta-analysis principles have now correctly diagnosed this problem, and, more important, have provided the solution. In area after area, meta-analytic findings have shown that there is much less conflict between different studies than had been believed, that coherent, useful, and generalizable conclusions can be drawn from research literatures, and that cumulative knowledge is possible in psychology and the social sciences. These methods have also been adopted in other areas such as medical research. A prominent medical researcher, Thomas Chalmers (as cited in Mann, 1990), has stated, '[Meta-analysis] is going to revolutionize how the sciences, especially medicine, handle data. And it is going to be the way many arguments will be ended' (p. 478). In concluding his oft-cited review of meta-analysis methods, Bangert-Drowns (1986: 398) stated:

> Meta-analysis is not a fad. It is rooted in the fundamental values of the scientific enterprise: replicability, quantification, causal and correlational analysis. Valuable information is needlessly scattered in individual studies. The ability of social scientists to deliver generalizable answers to basic questions of policy is too serious a concern to allow us to treat research integration lightly. The potential benefits of meta-analysis method seem enormous.

REFERENCES

American Educational Research Association, American Psychological Association, and National Council on Measurement in Education (1999). *Standards for educational and psychological testing*. Washington, DC: American Psychological Association.

Anastasi, A. (1988). *Psychological testing* (7th ed.). New York: Macmillan – now Palgrave.

Bangert-Drowns, R.L. (1986). Review of developments in meta-analytic method. *Psychological Bulletin, 99*, 388–399.

Bangert-Drowns, R.L., Kulik, J.A., & Kulik, C.-L.C. (1983). Effects of coaching programs on achievement test performance. *Review of Educational Research, 53*, 571–585.

Baum, M.L., Anish, D.S., Chalmers, T.C., Sacks, H.S., Smith, H., & Fagerstrom, R.M. (1981). A survey of clinical trials of antibiotic prophylaxis in colon surgery: Evidence against further use of no-treatment controls. *New England Journal of Medicine, 305*, 795–799.

Callender, J.C., & Osburn, H.G. (1980). Development and test of a new model for validity generalization. *Journal of Applied Psychology, 65*, 543–558.

Carver, R.P. (1978). The case against statistical significance testing. *Harvard Educational Review, 48*, 378–399.

Chelimsky, E. (1994, October 14). *Use of meta-analysis in the General Accounting Office*. Paper presented as the Science and Public Policy Seminars, Federation of Behavioral, Psychological and Cognitive Sciences. Washington, DC.

Cohen, J. (1962). The statistical power of abnormal-social psychological research: A review. *Journal of Abnormal and Social Psychology, 65*, 145–153.

Cohen, J. (1988). *Statistical power analysis for the behavioral sciences*. (2nd ed.) Hillsdale, NJ: Erlbaum.

Cohen, J. (1990). Things I learned (so far). *American Psychologist, 45*, 1304–1312.

Cohen, J. (1994). The earth is round ($p < .05$). *American Psychologist, 49*, 997–1003.

Cronbach, L.J. (1975). Beyond the two disciplines of scientific psychology. *American Psychologist, 30*, 116–127.

Cuts raise new social science query: Does anyone appreciate social science? (1981, March 27). *Wall Street Journal*, p. 54.

Fisher, C.D., & Gittelson, R. (1983). A meta-analysis of the correlates of role conflict and ambiguity. *Journal of Applied Psychology, 68*, 320–333.

Fisher, R.A. (1932). *Statistical methods for research workers* (4th ed.). Edinburgh, Scotland: Oliver & Boyd.

Fisher, R.A. (1935). *The design of experiments*. London: Oliver & Boyd.

Fisher, R.A. (1973). *Statistical methods and scientific inference* (3rd ed.). Edinburgh: Oliver & Boyd.

Gaugler, B.B., Rosenthal, D.B., Thornton, G.C., & Bentson, C. (1987). Meta-analysis of assessment center validity. *Journal of Applied Psychology, 72*, 493–511.

Gergen, K.J. (1982). *Toward transformation in social knowledge*. New York: Springer-Verlag.

Glass, G.V. (1972). The wisdom of scientific inquiry on education. *Journal of Research in Science Teaching, 9*, 3–18.

Glass, G.V. (1976). Primary, secondary and meta-analysis of research. *Educational Researcher, 5*, 3–8.

Glass, G.V. (1977). Integrating findings: The meta-analysis of research. *Review of Research in Education, 5*, 351–379.

Glass, G.V., McGaw, B., & Smith, M.L. (1981). *Meta-analysis in social research*. Beverly Hills, CA: Sage.

Guttman, L. (1985). The illogic of statistical inference for cumulative science. *Applied Stochastic Models and Data Analysis, 1*, 3–10.

Guzzo, R.A., Jackson, S.E., & Katzell, R.A. (1986). Meta-analysis analysis. In L.L. Cummings & B.M. Staw (Eds.), *Research in organizational behavior* (Vol. 9, pp. 407–442). Greenwich, CT: JAI Press.

Guzzo, R.A., Jette, R.D., & Katzell, R.A. (1985). The effects of psychologically based intervention programs on worker productivity: A meta-analysis. *Personnel Psychology*, 38, 275–292.

Hackett, R.D., & Guion, R.M. (1985). A re-evaluation of the absenteeism-job satisfaction relationship. *Organizational Behavior and Human Decision Processes*, 35, 340–381.

Halvorsen, K.T. (1986). Combining results from independent investigations: Meta-analysis in medical research. In J.C. Bailar & F. Mosteller (Eds.), *Medical uses of statistics*. Waltham, MA: New England Journal of Medicine Books.

Hartigan, J.A., & Wigdor, A.K. (1989). Fairness in employment testing: Validity generalization, minority issues, and the General Aptitude Test Battery. Washington, DC: National Academy Press.

Hedges, L.V. (1982a). Estimation of effect size from a series of independent experiments. *Psychological Bulletin*, 92, 490–499.

Hedges, L.V. (1982b). Fitting categorical models to effect sizes from a series of experiments. *Journal of Educational Statistics*, 7, 119–137.

Hedges, L.V. (1987). How hard is hard science, how soft is soft science: The empirical cumulativeness of research. *American Psychologist*, 42, 443–455.

Hedges, L.V., & Olkin, I. (1985). *Statistical methods for meta-analysis*. Orlando, FL: Academic Press.

Hunter, J.E. (1979, September). *Cumulating results across studies: A critique of factor analysis, canonical correlation, MANOVA, and statistical significance testing.* Invited address presented at the 86th Annual Convention of the American Psychological Association. New York.

Hunter, J.E. (1983). A causal analysis of cognitive ability, job knowledge, job performance, and supervisory ratings. In F. Landy, S. Zedeck & J. Cleveland (Eds.), *Performance measurement and theory* (pp. 257–266). Hillsdale, NJ: Erlbaum.

Hunter, J.E. (1988). A path analytic approach to analysis of covariance. Unpublished manuscript, Department of Psychology, Michigan State University, East Lansing.

Hunter, J.E. (1997). Needed: A ban on the significance test. *Psychological Science*, 8, 3–7.

Hunter, J.E., & Gerbing, D.W. (1982). Unidimensional measurement, second order factor analysis and causal models. In B.M. Staw & L.L. Cummings (Eds.), *Research in organizational behavior* (Vol. 4, pp. 267–320), Greenwich, CT: JAI Press.

Hunter, J.E., & Hirsh, H.R. (1987). Applications of meta-analysis. In C.L. Cooper & I.T. Robertson (Eds.), *International review of industrial and organizational psychology 1987* (pp. 321–357). London: Wiley.

Hunter, J.E., & Schmidt, F.L. (1990a). Dichotomization of continuous variables: The implications for meta-analysis. *Journal of Applied Psychology*, 75, 334–349.

Hunter, J.E., & Schmidt, F.L. (1990b). *Methods of meta-analysis: Correcting error and bias in research findings*. Newbury Park, CA: Sage.

Hunter, J.E., & Schmidt, F.L. (1994). The estimation of sampling error variance in meta-analysis of correlations: The homogenous case. *Journal of Applied Psychology*, 79, 171–177.

Hunter, J.E., & Schmidt, F.L. (1996). Cumulative research knowledge and social policy formulation: The critical role of meta-analysis. *Psychology, Public Policy, and Law*, 2, 324–347.

Hunter, J.E., & Schmidt, F.L. (2000). Fixed effects vs. random effects meta-analysis models: Implications for cumulative knowledge in psychology. *International Journal of Selection and Assessment*, 8, 275–292.

Hunter, J.E., Schmidt, F.L., & Jackson, G.B. (1982). *Meta-analysis: Cumulating research findings across studies*. Beverly Hills, CA: Sage.

Iaffaldono, M.T., & Muchinsky, P.M. (1985). Job satisfaction and job performance: A meta-analysis. *Psychological Bulletin*, 97, 251–273.

Jackson, S.E., & Schuler, R.S. (1985). A meta-analysis and conceptual critique of research on role ambiguity and role conflict in work settings. *Organizational Behavioral and Human Decision Processes*, 36, 16–78.

Joreskog, K.G., & Sorbom, D. (1979). *Advances in factor analysis and structural equation models*. Cambridge, MA: Abt Books.

Kulik, J.A., & Bangert-Drowns, R.L. (1983–1984). Effectivness of technology in precollege mathematics and science teaching. *Journal of Educational Technology Systems*, 12, 137–158.

Landman, J.T., & Dawes, R.M. (1982). Psychotherapy outcome: Smith and Glass' conclusions stand up under scrutiny. *American Psychologist*, 37, 504–516.

Law, K.S., Schmidt, F.L., & Hunter, J.E. (1994a). Nonlinearity of range corrections in meta-analysis: A test of an improved procedure. *Journal of Applied Psychology*, 79, 425–438.

Law, K.S., Schmidt, F.L., & Hunter, J.E. (1994b). A test of two refinements in meta-analysis procedures. *Journal of Applied Psychology*, 79, 978–986.

Lipsey, M.W. & Wilson, D.B. (1993). The efficacy of psychological, educational, and behavioral treatment: Confirmation from meta-analysis. *American Psychologist*, 48, 1181–1209.

Mabe, P.A. III, & West, S.G. (1982). Validity of self evaluations of ability: A review and meta-analysis. *Journal of Applied Psychology*, 67, 280–296.

Maloley et al., v. Department of National Revenue (1986, February). Canadian Civil Service Appeals Board, Ottawa, Ontario, Canada.

Mann, C. (1990). Meta-analysis in the breech. *Science*, 249(4968), 476–480.

Mansfield, R.S., & Busse, T.V. (1977). Meta-analysis of research: A rejoinder to Glass. *Educational Researcher*, 6, 3.

McDaniel, M.A., Schmidt, F.L., & Hunter, J.E. (1988). A meta-analysis of training and experience ratings in personnel selection. *Personnel Psychology*, 41, 283–314.

McDaniel, M.A., Whetzel, D.L., Schmidt, F.L. & Maurer, S.D. (1994). The validity of employment interviews: A comprehensive review and meta-analysis. *Journal of Applied Psychology, 79,* 599–616.

McEvoy, G.M., & Cascio, W.F. (1985). Strategies for reducing employee turnover: A meta-analysis. *Journal of Applied Psychology, 70,* 342–353.

McEvoy, G.M., & Cascio, W.F. (1987). Do poor performers leave? A meta-analysis of the relation between performance and turnover. *Academy of Management Journal, 30,* 744–762.

Meehl, P.E. (1967). Theory-testing in psychology and physics: A methodological paradox. *Philosophy of Science, 34,* 103–115.

Meehl, P.E. (1978). Theoretical risks and tabular asterisks: Sir Karl, Sir Ronald, and the slow progress of soft psychology. *Journal of Consulting and Clinical Psychology, 46,* 806–834.

National Research Council (1992). *Combining information: Statistical issues and opportunities for research.* Washington, DC: National Academy of Science Press.

Oakes, M. (1986). *Statistical inference: A commentary for the social and behavioral sciences.* New York: Wiley.

Pearlman, K., Schmidt, F.L., & Hunter, J.E. (1980). Validity generalization results for tests used to predict job proficiency and training success in clerical occupations. *Journal of Applied Psychology, 65,* 373–406.

Peters, L.H., Hartke, D., & Pohlmann, J. (1985). Fiedler's contingency theory of leadership: An application of the meta-analysis procedures of Schmidt and Hunter. *Psychological Bulletin, 97,* 274–285.

Petty, M.M., McGee, G.W., & Cavender, J.W. (1984). A meta-analysis of the relationship between individual job satisfaction and individual performance. *Academy of Management Review, 9,* 712–721.

Premack, S., & Wanous, J.P. (1985). Meta-analysis of realistic job preview experiments. *Journal of Applied Psychology, 70,* 706–719.

Raju, N.S., & Burke, M.J. (1983). Two procedures for studying validity generalization. *Journal of Applied Psychology, 68,* 382–395.

Ramamurti, A.S. (1989). A systematic approach to generating excess returns using a multiple variable model. In F.J. Fabozzi (Ed.), *Institutional investor focus on investment management.* Cambridge, MA: Ballinger.

Rosenthal, R. (1991). *Meta-analytic procedures for social research* (2nd ed.). Newbury Park, CA: Sage.

Rosenthal, R., & Rubin, D.B. (1982). Comparing effect sizes of independent studies. *Psychological Bulletin, 92,* 500–504.

Rozeboom, W.W. (1960). The fallacy of the null hypothesis significance test. *Psychological Bulletin, 57,* 416–428.

Sacks, H.S., Berrier, J., Reitman, D., Ancona-Berk, V.A., & Chalmers, T.C. (1987). Meta-analysis of randomized controlled trials. *New England Journal of Medicine, 316,* 450–455.

Schmidt, F.L. (1988). Validity generalization and the future of criterion-related validity. In H. Wainer & H.I. Braun (Eds.), *Test validity* (pp. 173–292). Hillsdale, NJ: Erlbaum.

Schmidt, F.L. (1992). What do data really mean? Research findings, meta-analysis, and cumulative knowledge in psychology. *American Psychologist, 47,* 1173–1181.

Schmidt, F.L. (1996). Statistical significance testing and cumulative knowledge in psychology: Implications for the training of researchers. *Psychological Methods, 1,* 115–129.

Schmidt, F.L., Gast-Rosenberg, I., & Hunter, J.E. (1980). Validity generalization results for computer programmers. *Journal of Applied Psychology, 65,* 643–661.

Schmidt, F.L., & Hunter, J.E. (1977). Development of a general solution to the problem of validity generalization. *Journal of Applied Psychology, 62,* 529–540.

Schmidt, F.L., & Hunter, J.E. (1978). Moderator research and the law of small numbers. *Personnel Psychology, 31,* 215–232.

Schmidt, F.L., & Hunter, J.E. (1981). Employment testing: Old theories and new research findings. *American Psychologist, 36,* 1128–1137.

Schmidt, F.L., & Hunter, J.E. (1996). Measurement error in psychological research: Lessons from 26 research scenarios. *Psychological Methods, 1,* 199–223.

Schmidt, F.L., & Hunter, J.E. (1997). Eight common but false objections to the discontinuation of significance testing in the analysis of research data. In L. Harlow, S. Muliak & J. Steiger (Eds.), *What if there were no significance tests?* (pp. 37–64). Mahwah, NJ: Erlbaum.

Schmidt, F.L., & Hunter, J.E. (1999). Comparison of three meta-analysis methods revisited: An analysis of Johnson, Mullen, and Salas. *Journal of Applied Psychology, 84*(1), 144–148.

Schmidt, F.L., Hunter, J.E., Pearlman, K., & Shane, G.S. (1979). Further tests of the Schmidt–Hunter Bayesian validity generalization procedure. *Personnel Psychology, 32,* 257–281.

Schmidt, F.L., Hunter, J.E., & Urry, V.E. (1976). Statistical power in criterion-related validation studies. *Journal of Applied Psychology, 61,* 473–485.

Schmidt, F.L., Law, K.S., Hunter, J.E., Rothstein, H.R., Pearlman, K., & McDaniel, M. (1993). Refinements in validity generalization methods: Implications for the situational specificity hypothesis. *Journal of Applied Psychology, 78,* 3–13.

Schmidt, F.L., Ocasio, B.P., Hillery, J.M., & Hunter, J.E. (1985). Further within-setting empirical tests of the situational specificity hypothesis in personnel selection. *Personnel Psychology, 38,* 509–524.

Sedlmeier, P., & Gigerenzer, G. (1989). Do studies of statistical power have an effect on the power of the studies? *Psychological Bulletin, 105,* 309–316.

Snedecor, G.W. (1946). *Statistical methods* (4th ed.). Ames: Iowa State College Press.

Terborg, J.R., & Lee, T.W. (1982). Extension of the Schmidt–Hunter validity generalization procedure to the prediction of absenteeism behavior from knowledge of job satisfaction and organizational commitment. *Journal of Applied Psychology, 67,* 280–296.

Tett, R.P., Meyer, J.P., & Roese, N.J. (1994). Applications of meta-analysis: 1987–1992. In *International Review of Industrial and Organizational Psychology*, Vol. 9 (pp. 71–112). London: Wiley.

Wilkinson, L., & the Task Force on Statistical Inference (1999). Statistical methods in psychology journals: Guidelines and explanations. *American Psychologist, 54*, 594–604.

Wortman, P.M., & Bryant, F.B. (1985). School desegregation and black achievement: An integrative review. *Sociological Methods and Research, 13*, 289–324.

Yusuf, S., Simon, R., & Ellenberg, S.S. (1986). Preface to proceedings of the workshop on methodological issues in overviews of randomized clinical trials, May 1986. *Statistics in Medicine, 6*, 217–218.

4

The Analysis of Work in the 20th and 21st Centuries

JUAN I. SANCHEZ
and EDWARD L. LEVINE

Although the flexibility demanded by the new economy is blurring the boundaries that used to define the responsibilities of a job, the analysis of work continues to be of invaluable help in designing and staffing organizations. It is therefore not surprising that early efforts to classify occupational requirements such as the US Department of Labor's *Dictionary of Occupational Titles* are being transformed into electronic systems such as the Occupational Network or O*NET. New business trends demand new forms within each one of the traditional blocks of work analysis: type, source, data collection method, and level of information, as well as new thinking about the manner of storing, retrieving, and disseminating information. The evaluation of work-analytic data, however, should take a hard look at the extent to which such data fruitfully support the inferences and outputs that benefit other human resource functions such as selection and training, as well as the extent to which inferences and decisions prove capable of sustaining legal challenges. Choosing among the many methodologies available should be facilitated by this focus on the purpose of work analysis. Finally, the definition of work requirements should look beyond individual responsibilities and incorporate the organization's mission, values, and strategy without sacrificing sound measurement. The role of these and other macro variables in defining work requirements is of utmost importance when organizations have to compete in the global economy.

IS THE DEFINITION OF JOB ANALYSIS CHANGING?

Traditionally, job analysis has referred to the process of gathering, analyzing, and structuring information about a job's components, characteristics, including environmental contexts, and job requirements (Gael, 1988; Levine, 1983; McCormick, 1976). Recent changes in the dynamic nature of current work assignments have led some to announce 'the end of the job' as a fixed and stable set of predetermined responsibilities (Bridges, 1994). Although it is questionable that the notion of the job will go away, clearly job boundaries are blurring in many

work settings. In line with the evolving nature of work, Sanchez (1994) and Sanchez and Levine (1999) argued in favor of the term 'work analysis' in lieu of 'job analysis', to emphasize that the focus of the analysis of work should shift from the definition of rigid job boundaries to the facilitation of organizational effectiveness. Along the same lines, Visser, Altink and Algere (1997) have suggested employing the term 'work profiling' instead of job analysis. Although it might be still useful to think about 'jobs', the analysis of work should not necessarily use the 'job' as the primary or even the best unit of analysis. The term 'job' in 'job analysis' may soon be obsolete, just like the term 'Industrial' in the US designation of what in Europe is referred to as 'Work' Psychology. The US nomenclature is reminiscent of a time when work psychologists were concerned primarily with manufacturing operations. In this chapter, we use the term 'job analysis' in its broad sense of work analysis.

Our focus in this chapter is mainly human resource (HR) applications of work analysis; however, readers should be aware of the fact that work analysis is also an important tool in non-HR applications, such as the ergonomic design of machinery and equipment. In fact, a work analysis pioneer like Ernest McCormick was also an early leader of the field of human factors or ergonomic design.

It has been argued that the derivation of human attributes or job specifications demanded by the job should not be included within the rubric of 'job analysis' (Harvey, 1991), despite the fact that early definitions of job analysis included data concerning skills, abilities, and personality traits (McCormick, 1976: 652–653). We definitely agree on the need to distinguish between the observable, behavioral aspect of job analysis, which merely describes job activities and the work environment, and the inferential function centered upon the derivation of human attributes required for job performance. However, we do consider the derivation of human attributes to be an integral component of job analysis. This 'translation' of job activities into human attributes is what makes job analysis a psychological endeavor, and one at which those without a psychological background often fail. Regardless of semantic distinctions in its definition, job analysis provides the basis for a host of organizational processes ranging from traditional human resource functions such as selection, training, job classification, performance appraisal, and compensation, to those concerning the latest trends like downsizing and workflow reengineering.

The following two scenarios, one from Europe and the other from the US, illustrate how strategic usages of job analysis can provide answers to the challenges posed by today's and tomorrow's dynamic organizational environment. Facing the task of creating a local police force in a territory where nationalist sentiments and anti-police attitudes were running high, the Basque Government decided that the Basque Police Force's responsibilities should match the security needs that residents of the Basque territory had previously expressed in a large-scale survey. Task analysis was used to monitor how well the newly created Basque Police was focusing on the Basque people's mandate. The analysis focused on the correspondence between the citizens' desired goals and the actual distribution of time spent on job tasks (Gorriti, 1996).

Now let us turn to the example from the US. The US Army is concerned about how changes in technology will affect the job requirements that should be demanded from soldiers in the twenty-first century. Night-vision goggles, body armor, hand-sized portable computers, and other electronic devices are radically changing modern warfare. A future-oriented job analysis methodology is being considered as more and more tasks become automated or influenced by electronic devices, because it is probable that job requirements will change as well.

Work analysis, like any other scientific descriptive effort, has had, as one of its goals the development of a taxonomic system for clustering jobs, occupations, or components of these. In the next section, we focus on the classification schemes used to form clusters that themselves may serve useful human resource objectives.

CLASSIFICATION OF OCCUPATIONS AND JOBS

In 1921, the International Labor Organization (hereafter referred to as ILO) detected the need to establish an international classification of occupations. The *Uniform International Classification of Occupations* was first produced by the ILO in 1958 (International Labor Organization, 1991), and it is updated every 10 years. The classification serves the purposes of facilitating cross-country statistics, occupational migration patterns, and helps in developing national classifications. Thus, countries have the need to develop 'cross-walk maps' that allow them to turn their national occupational codes into those used by the ILO's classification.

The *Dictionary of Occupational Titles* (DOT) (US Department of Labor, 1977) has been the national occupational classification system in the US, and it was produced by the Department of Labor. The original goal of the DOT was to improve job placement and counseling for unemployed individuals registering at offices of the employment service. The DOT classifies jobs using a nine-digit code. The first three digits specify the occupational code, the title of the job, and the industry; the next three digits indicate the extent to which the job incumbent has responsibility and judgment over data (e.g., coordinating), people (e.g., negotiating), and things (e.g., handling); and the last three digits are used to classify the job alphabetically within that occupational group with the same level of complexity.

O*NET

The Occupational Information Network or O*NET is a new classification effort sponsored by the US Department of Labor. O*NET is intended to replace the DOT by providing an automated database and a set of ready-to-use instruments for collecting, describing, storing, and disseminating reliable and valid occupational information (Peterson, Mumford,

Borman, Jeanneret & Fleishman, 1999). O*NET is positioned to become an important tool for acquiring and exchanging occupational information in the twenty-first century. Perhaps the most novel aspect of O*NET is its usage of 'multiple windows' or different kinds of descriptors ranging from fine-grained to broad and from generic to occupation-specific that could be used to address different issues. To facilitate the description of occupations across the economy, the developers of O*NET chose cross-job descriptors that could be used to describe multiple jobs over job-specific descriptors like task statements. For instance, O*NET uses 'generalized work activities', which are broader than traditional task statements so that the same descriptors can be used across jobs. However, occupation specific information is available in the database for use in accomplishing some objectives.

The O*NET content model also distinguishes between worker requirements such as skills and knowledge, and worker characteristics such as abilities and values. O*NET employs a modified version of Fleishman's Ability Requirement Scales (ARS) to identify job specifications. New categories such as occupational values and interests are also captured by ARS-like scales. Whether this 'holistic' approach to job specification ratings provides information that is as valid as that derived from simpler descriptors warrants further research.

Other Taxonomies of Work

Several researchers have attempted the development of a taxonomy or classification of work. Such efforts have included both work activities and worker attributes, as well as the linkages between these two domains (i.e., what attributes are needed to perform which activities). For instance, Fleishman and his colleagues (Theologus & Fleishman, 1973) showed that abilities map onto performance dimensions. Second, the work of McCormick and his associates on the Position Analysis Questionnaire (McCormick, Jeanneret & Mecham, 1972) tied job elements to worker attribute profiles via factor analysis.

Still another noteworthy taxonomic effort is Holland's (1973). He postulated six major interest areas describing both work environments and types of people. According to Holland, the optimal vocational choice involves matching people with their proper environmental type. These six areas or themes are: realistic, investigative, artistic, social, enterprising, and conventional. Holland's taxonomy has been incorporated in vocational guidance instruments such as the Strong–Campbell Vocational Inventory, which are routinely used to match people and occupations. Meta-analytic research has generally been supportive of Holland's taxonomy (Tracey & Rounds, 1993).

THE BUILDING BLOCKS OF JOB ANALYSIS

Job analysis can be said to involve four facets or 'building blocks' (Levine, 1983; McCormick, 1976): (1) the type of information to be collected, (2) the source of information to be employed, (3) the method of collecting information, and (4) the level of analysis or detail to be observed in the analysis. We add here a fifth, namely the manner of storing, retrieving, and disseminating data. The job analyst needs to decide among the various options or choices that exist within each one of these building blocks. In the next sections, we will review how traditional choices within these five building blocks should be reconsidered according to the changing rules of today's business environment.

Types of Work-Analytic Information

Work-analytic data can be classified into two primary kinds: descriptions of the characteristics of the people doing the work and descriptions of the work itself. Often, several types of data are collected in the work analysis.

Almost all systematic job analysis methods collect data on the machines, tools, and work aids used. More complete analyses also include a record of contextual factors of the job (e.g., physical working conditions, environmental hazards, contact with co-workers). Some job analysis methods also provide information on work performance standards (e.g., quality and quantity standards, error analysis) and specific customer requirements, which can be helpful in documenting and supporting personnel decisions based on performance appraisal such as terminations, assignment to training, or promotion.

Descriptors of worker attributes that reflect the new strategic and team-oriented aspects of work are needed (Klimoski & Jones, 1995). Consider the case of customer service, which is a central element in today's service-oriented economy. Job descriptions have typically emphasized task performance or the technical component of customer service (Motowidlo & Van Scotter, 1994), but have ignored contextual aspects of performance such as organizational citizenship and service-oriented behavior (Organ, 1988). In general, work analysis has given insufficient attention to describing the dynamics of interpersonal behavior, which are not fully represented in task inventories incorporating only within-job activities or activities involving a single job title. Given an increasing reliance upon interdependent work processes in modern organizations, job analysis should emphasize the description of between-worker interfaces. Methodologies that describe dynamic processes, such as work process mapping can be a helpful supplement to traditional job descriptions (Levine & Baker, 1991). Work process mapping relies on flowcharting to describe work processes. A work process map represents the flow of how work gets done to achieve specific goals (Galloway, 1994). A process map illustrates alternative paths thereby providing useful ideas for reengineering the tasks and decisions made in the process of transforming inputs into outputs. Processes are likely to become even more important as the basis of a work analysis as more organizations accomplish work through teams. Processes may usefully be explored in the team context because they include a clear terminal goal, multiple skills and competencies to complete a team task, and interdependence among value-added stages of the work.

The surging interest in personality factors called for by jobs and organizations is certainly congruent with current management trends such as employee empowerment, team-based organizations, and the prescription of emotional labor (e.g., employees of theme parks and even theme restaurants in the US are required to represent certain emotions). In his review of personnel selection methods, Salgado (1999) notes that the surging interest in personality led the French researchers Rolland and Mogenet (1994) to develop a job analysis system termed the 'Description in Five Dimensions' (D5D) based on the five-factor model of personality. Rolland has later expanded on this methodology by asking French soldiers who were part of the NATO's forces in the former Yugoslavian republics to describe their event-related emotions along the Big Five personality factors. In the US, Raymark, Schmit and Guion (1997) developed the Personality-Related Position Requirements Form (PPRF), which also attempts to identify Big-Five personality antecedents of job performance.

Sources of Job Analytic Information

Although job incumbents have been the traditional Subject Matter Experts (SMEs) in job analysis, the frequency and intensity of interpersonal interaction demanded by today's changing assignments, which often require crossing functional boundaries, demand the inclusion of internal and external customers as sources of job analysis information (Bernardin, 1992). It is possible to select different sources of information regarding distinct aspects of the jobs, in a sort of a 360-degree approach to job analysis. That is, the recipients of each major job function should be first identified and then employed as sources of information on those particular functions. In the retail industry, for example, professional 'mystery shoppers' regularly visit branches armed with checklists of critical behaviors that employees should perform in their interactions with customers. Such professional shoppers are likely to provide a wealth of information concerning customer service.

Alternate sources of work information like mystery shoppers should supplement rather than replace job incumbents, who have direct and continuous information about the job, and are therefore best suited to inform others about them. However, incumbents cannot be presumed to be the best informants for every single piece of job-analytic information. For example, the difficulty of learning various KSAOs (knowledges, skills, abilities and other personal characteristics) may be best judged by training or education specialists, and psychological requirements like tolerance for stress may be best assessed by those holding a psychological background (Jones et al., in press). Sanchez, Zamora and Viswesvaran (1997) found that agreement between incumbents and non-incumbents was moderated by job complexity and job satisfaction, with agreement being highest when jobs were not complex and incumbents were not highly satisfied. Such findings reinforce the notion that job analytic judgments are affected by cognitive and affective factors and, therefore, a multi-source evaluation is more informative than a single source assessment.

An interesting issue that has been the object of recent research is the sampling of job analysis respondents. In other words, do relatively small panels of respondents provide job analytic information equivalent to that provided by large samples of respondents. Although the evidence suggests that panels may provide very similar information to larger samples (Tannenbaum & Wesley, 1993; Ash, Levine, Higbee & Sistrunk, 1982), we believe that this question is not fully answered by comparing the responses provided by the panel and the larger group. This kind of question can be addressed also by validating the job analytic information against a criterion of job success. That is, the convergence between panel and larger groups bears more on reliability of data than validity. It would be instructive to learn if the panel's data lead to outcomes as successful as those based on large samples of respondents.

The question also arises as to whether panel or team dynamics affect the quality of work analysis data. In the only study on this issue known to the authors, Levine and Sanchez (1998) studied group-level variables such as median age, group size, functional diversity, gender, racial and ethnic diversity. Across 14 diverse jobs (e.g., activity therapist, maintenance equipment operator and patient records technician) and several scales applied both to tasks on the one hand and knowledges, skills, abilities and other personal characteristics (KSAOs) on the other, the group variables appeared to have had little impact on various indicators of group member agreement or other indexes of data quality. This study was clearly exploratory, and more such research is indicated.

Methods of Collecting Information

Traditional methods of data collection have included job observation, individual or group interviews, examination of diaries or records of critical incidents and work documents, and questionnaires. Although occupations cut across organizations and are therefore broader than job titles, relevant occupational descriptions listed in the *Dictionary of Occupational Titles* (DOT) can also be reviewed (US Department of Labor, 1977). According to Borman, Hanson and Hedge (1997), the person–job fit feature of O*NET will allow assessments of person–job fit by comparing person attributes and occupational requirements.

In the US, there are legal reasons to document interviews, job observations, and other data collection activities very carefully, in order to facilitate an independent verification of what was done as mandated by the *Uniform Guidelines on Employee Selection Procedures* (1978). Applicants' rights to challenge selection or promotion decisions exist in every democratic society and, therefore, careful documentation of job analysis procedures is advisable where such challenges may be expected.

Traditional data collection methods assume that SMEs have prior experience on the job. However, when jobs are new or are changing, incumbents lack direct job experience. To guide this kind of future-oriented job analysis, Schneider and Konz (1989) suggest comparing present vs. future-oriented job analytic ratings as a means to ascertain trends in how the job will change over time. The validity of such SMEs' future-oriented ratings, however, should be evaluated in longitudinal designs rather than taken for granted.

Hypothetical scenarios can be designed to facilitate forecasts of future job requirements. Scenarios may involve the demographic and socio-technical factors affecting the job (London, 1988: 203). For instance, in the job of air traffic controller, tasks that used to be accomplished from the control tower are being shifted to computer screens operated in a 'dark room environment'. Simulations of such hypothetical scenarios are feasible and should be helpful in envisioning changes in job requirements. Subject matter experts charged with forecasting the requirements of tomorrow's air traffic controller may concentrate on currently computerized tasks, and then visualize themselves performing all tasks in a similar manner. Thinking about what will be different under the new paradigm may help SMEs formulate inferences about future-oriented work requirements.

In Sweden, Sandberg (2000) has advocated a phenomenological approach to the analysis of work, where work and worker are seen as one entity formed through the lived experience of work. This approach contrasts with the rationalistic view of the job as separate from the job incumbent that has dominated the practice of work analysis in the US. Under the phenomenological prism, work analysts should strive to decipher the variations in the ways in which workers frame their work experience. Such an understanding facilitates the description of what constitutes job competence. In other words, work is described through conceptions of work, rather than 'verifiable' work attributes. Sandberg also argues for different kinds of validity and reliability criteria to evaluate a work analysts's interpretation of work competence. Specifically, he alludes to communicative and pragmatic validity, and to reliability as interpretative awareness. Although it seems unlikely that this kind of phenomenological validation will be well-received in countries with a positivistic tradition like the US, Sandberg's approach may serve to increase awareness about data-collection procedures such as in-depth interviews, which may shed light on the manner in which workers experience and conceive their work. Such insights may prove valuable in ascertaining the emotional and attitudinal requirements of work.

Level of Analysis

Basic movements constitute the smallest unit of job analysis. The time-and-motion studies characteristic of the division of labor/scientific management approach focused on such movements. As most routine manufacturing and packaging operations become automated through computer-aided manufacturing, electronic commerce, digital phone menus and so forth, time-and-motion studies have lost ground. Still, the job analyst is often left with the decision of how broad the job descriptors should be. In the US, describing jobs at the task level has become common, probably because quasi-legal regulations such as the *Uniform Guidelines on Employee Selection Procedures* (1978) advocate the identification of important and critical work behaviors (in contrast, the Society for Industrial and Organizational Psychology's Principles do not explicitly call for important behavior identification in job analysis). Job tasks of the type employed in the task inventory approach, however, are too job-specific and do not allow cross-job comparisons. To circumvent this problem, McCormick (1976) suggested describing jobs using worker-oriented descriptors, which involve more generic yet behavioral descriptors than task statements. The advantage over the task inventory is that the same set of limited worker-oriented elements can be used to describe quite different jobs. The downside, of course, is that some job specificity is lost in the job description.

Job analysis has traditionally chosen to decompose jobs at the level of tasks and human attributes. However, the dynamic nature of today's jobs renders job descriptions obsolete very quickly in many business environments. Excessively detailed or molecular job analyses are being replaced by descriptions that use broader descriptors of both work behaviors and human attributes. In line with this argument, the O*NET project decided in favor of Generalized Worker Activities (GWAs) that parallel the broadly defined business processes characteristic of today's work assignments (Cunningham, 1996; Jeanneret, Borman, Kubisiak & Hanson, 1999). The question of whether these broad descriptors can provide sufficient information to inform human resource systems is an empirical one. The answer depends to some extent on the purpose of the job analysis, which will be discussed in a subsequent section.

Storing, Retrieving, and Disseminating Data

It is striking that whereas all areas of work are rapidly changing due to technological advancements, the practice of traditional job analysis remains virtually untouched by modern technology. That is, face-to-face interviews and paper-and-pencil surveys are still the normal data-gathering procedures in most applications of traditional job analysis. Not surprisingly, today's cost-conscious organizations object to standard job analytic practices such as convening large panels of SMEs to provide task or KSAO ratings. Convening these panels is particularly impractical in today's highly distributed and decentralized organizations, where many organizational agents operate from remotely distant locales. For instance, the director of operations of a large telecommunications company in Brazil noted the difficulties inherent in arranging any kind of face-to-face meeting with his subordinates in the interior part of the country. A round-trip air ticket from the corporate headquarters in Sao Paulo to the interior part of the country is still twice as expensive as a round-trip ticket from Sao Paulo to Miami, USA., thereby rendering face-to-face meetings with corporate representatives in the interior land of Brazil very expensive.

It is noteworthy that traditional job analysis has not taken advantage of potentially rich sources of work information such as the data provided by electronic performance monitoring. For example, mobile maintenance units are equipped with telecommunication devices that allow headquarters to track their operations, such as number of stops, time spent on each service call, and so on. Similarly, transportation companies have on-board computers synchronized to the truck's engine, and are therefore capable of recording performance data such as speed and idle time. Call centers represent another industry where electronic performance monitoring keeps records of important work parameters such as the number of calls handled and the time spent on each call. Call center technology allows even live monitoring of calls through the use of electronic switchboards.

It is paradoxical that, in traditional job analysis, many of these parameters of work that are nowadays electronically recorded by monitoring systems are instead estimated by SMEs. For example, task frequency and time spent are two task dimensions normally incorporated in task analysis surveys that may be more objectively ascertained by examining electronic records of performance over time. To illustrate how this may be done, an example from the US military may be instructive. As stated previously, the US Army is rapidly incorporating technology for the job of soldier in the twenty-first century. Night-vision goggles, body armor, hand-sized portable computers, and other electronic devices are radically changing modern warfare. A 'battle' map is periodically updated and maintained on-line by soldiers assigned to surveillance tasks; these soldiers use their portable computers to send relevant information such as changes in the coordinates of the enemy's position. The 'cookie files' or electronic records of these computers can be read to gather information such as the frequency and time spent on certain tasks. Electronic records are also left by e-commerce transactions between business to business (B2B) and business to consumer (B2C). Technical complexity and the potential for violations of individual privacy make the analysis of electronic records a challenge for work analysts.

Interviews and surveys may, however, remain an integral component of work analysis, because the data gathered electronically often lack the rich, qualitative dimension that is gained through more traditional formats such as one-on-one interviews. However, the expenses associated with face-to-face interviews and paper-and-pencil surveys can be significantly reduced by employing electronic media. Tele-conferencing and commercial 'groupware' supported by intranets are two examples of platforms that remain underutilized by traditional job analysts.

Internet capabilities allow access to a variety of data banks containing job and occupational data. For instance, O*NET will contain data on at least 950 occupations in the US economy. Among the on-line capabilities planned for O*NET, skill searches will be feasible, so that all the occupations that require a given level of a certain skill could be rapidly downloaded using O*NET's online search engine. Requests for a specific job description are also common in e-mail lists of human resource specialists. As more organizations become willing to exchange this information for benchmarking purposes, a virtual database of 'just-in-time' job descriptions may become available on-line, thereby eliminating the need to 'reinvent the wheel' every time a job analysis is needed. Within organizations, human resource activities such as recruitment can trigger an update of job specifications contained in a database. Before the recruitment campaign begins, for example, hiring supervisors may be sent the specifications in the files and asked to comment or to revise them as needed.

Criteria That Ought to Guide the Choice for Each Building Block of Job Analysis

Several job analysis experts agree that these choices have to be guided by the purpose of the job analysis (Levine, 1983; Levine, Thomas & Sistrunk, 1988; Sanchez & Levine, 1999); that is, one needs to examine the intended application of the job analysis (e.g., the design of a selection procedure, a performance appraisal system, a training program, a job evaluation system), and make the choices within each building block that are best suited for such a purpose. Because job analysis can be time-consuming, job analysis experts have favored a multipurpose job analysis where multiple types of information are gathered so the job analysis can be used later on to support more than one application (Levine, Ash, Hall & Sistrunk, 1983). The O*NET system is designed on that basis (Peterson et al., 1999). Thus, even though the organization may not intend to use the job analysis to support training design, enough information is collected so that, if a decision is made to do so in the future, the information would be available and the organization would not need to redo the job analysis.

In addition to the purpose of the job analysis, the type of job under analysis as well as the educational level and background of the job incumbents should be taken into account when deciding among the various options within each building block. For instance, choosing a questionnaire as the method of data collection may not be the best approach when analyzing a job that involves primarily a physical element, especially when incumbents are not used to filling out surveys and forms. Similarly, job observation may not be the best choice of methodology when analyzing the job of certified public accountant, because the tasks carried out by the incumbent are primarily directed toward internalized cognitive information processing, and are not readily observable. Other, more pragmatic issues may also be considered (Levine, 1983). Factors like cost and time to complete an analysis can be important in determining which of the options to employ.

As stated, a primary factor influencing work-analytic choices is the purpose of the work analysis. Such purposes are often embedded in the kinds of inferences that work analysis should support. Let us now turn to this issue.

INFERENTIAL LEAPS INFORMED BY JOB ANALYSIS

As noted by Gatewood and Feild (1994), the main inferential leaps from job-analytic data to applications supported by job analysis are:

- Work–worker attribute leap. Work activity information (e.g., tasks, work behaviors, critical incidents) is used to derive human attributes or KSAOs.
- Worker attribute–intervention leap. Human attributes or KSAOs are used to select instruments (e.g., tests, interviews, assessment centers), devise training programs, enrich jobs, or develop other interventions that presumably build on those KSAOs.
- Work–performance measure leap. Work-related information such as tasks and critical incidents are used to design job-related performance measures.

Inferences vary along a continuum ranging from those immediately supported by job analysis such as KSAOs inferred from a task inventory to inferences distally supported by job analysis such as inferring the validity of a selection instrument by computing its correlation with a performance measure. This classification of job analytic inferences is consistent with the distinction between immediate and intermediate criteria drawn by Thorndike (1949). The ultimate criterion of job performance is often unavailable, and therefore researchers examine only immediate and intermediate consequences of job analytic data. For instance, studying whether difficulty-of-learning ratings for tasks affect the content of training programs relies on a less distal criterion than examining the indirect effect of these job analytic ratings on performance gains derived from the training program.

Consequence-oriented evaluations of work analysis are rare. For instance, Levine, Ash and Bennett (1980) showed that different job descriptions put together through different job-analytic methods led personnel specialists to develop very similar selection exams. This study uncovers an important issue in job analysis. That is, a very detailed or molecular job analysis may not always provide a significant return on investment. A particular job–analytic methodology may provide a wealth of information, but the rules governing the manner in which such job analytic information is used in making inferences may fail to capitalize on this abundance of data. In the next section, we review different rules that have been employed to make the inferences supported by job analysis.

The Rules that Govern Job Analytic Inferences

We have just suggested that job analytic methodologies varying in the degree of detail may fail to produce significantly different outcomes. One such instance in addition to the example just discussed relating to human resource selection is in the area of job classification (Cornelius, Schmidt & Carron, 1984; Sackett, Cornelius & Carron, 1981). These findings do not mean that a detailed work analysis yields results that are necessarily equivalent to those of a cursory work analysis. The lack of significant differences between the outcomes generated by the two methodologies may be a function of the rather simple goals of the target inferences (e.g., create job groupings or families). When making more complex inferences such as those concerning the content of training programs, rules regarding the crafting of linkages between job analytic data and training content may pay off.

Consider the example of Goldstein's (1993) elaborate procedures for linking job analytic data and training programs. Such procedures if supported by properly designed research may produce more effective training programs. Other rules governing job analytic inferences involve setting cut-off scores on KSAO scales (Levine, 1983). These cut-off scores may be more effectively established via these rules than by leaving these choices to loosely defined 'professional judgment'. The decision charts employed by Fleishman and colleagues to help identify whether an ability underlies performance on a given task are another example of rules regarding job analytic inferences (Fleishman & Reilly, 1992). Still another example of an inference-making aide is the two-way matrix to facilitate the generation of linkages between job activities and KSAOs or between KSAOs and selection procedures (Arvey, Salas & Gialluca, 1992; Drauden & Peterson, 1974; Guion, 1980; Sanchez & Fraser, 1994). In short, inferential rules are as important as the quality and level of detail of job analytic data, because good data accompanied by inadequate rules may result in ineffective inferences.

When serving as expert witnesses in cases of selection procedures facing legal challenges, we have encountered instances where very molecular or detailed job analyses were not accompanied by rules through which to turn such data into job-related selection procedures. Levine, Sistrunk, McNutt and Gael (1991) have called for the development of standards concerning rules governing job analysis inferences. The absence of such a body of rules is of concern because the potential outcomes of time-consuming job analyses may fail to crystallize into such outcomes as better selection procedures. In addition, failing to demonstrate that molecular job analyses make a difference may raise skepticism about the need to invest in such labor-intensive procedures.

LEGAL RELEVANCE OF JOB ANALYSIS

In the US, the enactment of the Civil Rights Act in 1964 and subsequent court rulings dealing with equal employment opportunity as defined in that law fueled an increased interest in job analysis. In particular, the [US] Supreme Court's seminal decisions in *Griggs v. Duke Power* and *Albemarle Paper Company v. Moody* emphasized the importance of demonstrating the 'job-relatedness' of employer selection systems. Despite accusations of being a 'legalistic nuisance', job analysis continues to play a pivotal role in many legal challenges of selection procedures. The legal mandate for a job analysis may not be as firm in other countries as it is in the US, but the need to justify the business necessity of human resource decisions cuts across national boundaries. In the US, such business necessity is closely associated with the job-relatedness of the selection procedure. Job-relatedness, in turn, can be demonstrated by content validity informed by a job analysis or by an empirical association between predictors and criteria of job success.

Quasi-legal standards enacted by National enforcement agencies such as the US Equal Employment Opportunity Commission (EEOC) also focus on the need for job analysis. The EEOC's *Uniform Guidelines on Employee Selection Procedures* (1978) demand that selection procedures be linked to important and critical job behaviors, which are identified through job analysis. Court cases like *EEOC v. Atlas Paper Co.* illustrate the risks of not conducting an on-site job analysis. There are a number of court cases which focus on the results of (or the nonexistence of) a job analysis. For example, women have challenged the physical ability tests (e.g., push-ups, sit-ups) mandated in past years for entry into some police or firefighters' academies.

In the US, when prima facie evidence of discrimination is established, the burden of proof then rests with the employer to show that the selection device or job specification (e.g., the test, test score, educational requirement) is 'job-related' or a 'business necessity'. In one case involving physical abilities, firefighter candidates in Dallas, Texas were required to climb a fence six feet in height in a prescribed amount of time. Because a higher percentage of women were unable to scale the fence than men, the court asked the city to show how climbing this fence was 'job-related'. The city presented job analysis data which demonstrated that the average fence in the jurisdiction was six feet in height and that scaling fences was a frequent activity which must be performed by competent firefighters.

In the US, legal challenges to job specifications involving physical attributes (e.g., strength, speed) and mental attributes have increased under the Americans with Disabilities Act (ADA). The ADA specifies that employers must make 'reasonable accommodations' that would allow qualified disabled workers to perform the 'essential functions' of the job. The determination of such essential functions is clearly a job analytic activity (Brannick, Brannick & Levine, 1992; Mitchell, Alliger & Morfopoulos, 1997).

However, not all work analysis methods are equal to the task of providing legal defensibility; and legal defensibility, it seems, is largely a function of whether an impartial observer can place confidence in the inferences arising from a job analysis. More specifically, when work analysis data are (1) collected from a representative sample of job incumbents and other informed sources (e.g., supervisors and administrators), (2) represent the full breadth of tasks to be completed on a job, (3) are reduced to written form, (4) are current, and (5) specify the level of competency necessary for entry-level work, there is greater likelihood that the subsequent inferences about what KSAOs are needed to perform the job will stand up to legal challenges (Thompson & Thompson, 1985).

JOB ANALYSIS OUTPUTS

Different job analysis methods yield different outputs or products; however, the most common outputs of job analysis are 'job descriptions' and 'job specifications'. Job descriptions define the primary job responsibilities or job functions. Job descriptions may also describe work aids, and equipment to be used on the job, working conditions, relationships with co-workers, and whether the job incumbent is responsible for people, cash, expensive equipment, and so forth. Job descriptions are often summarized in classified employment ads and Internet-based job placement services.

Job specifications consist of the human attributes or KSAOs needed to carry out the job tasks and duties. Educational requirements and minimum qualifications (e.g., Ph.D., MD, MBA, Ed.D., MSW, years and kinds of work experience), certifications or licenses (e.g., CPA, CFP), or other credentials are often listed in job specifications.

Job specifications may be contested because they may deny access to the job to individuals or groups who are protected by anti-discrimination laws. Thus, inferences regarding minimum qualifications should be backed by content or criterion-based evidence both of which rest on a foundation of job analysis (Levine, Maye, Ulm & Gordon, 1997). Unnecessarily inflated job specifications will result in higher labor costs and, at least in the US, are likely to be closely scrutinized by the courts. However, the courts have observed some flexibility in the need for an on-site job analysis in the case of police officers, where possessing a high level of education perhaps equivalent to a college degree in the US is in the view of some an obvious requirement:

> A police officer today is poorly equipped for his job if he does not understand the legal issues involved in his everyday work, the nature of the societal problems he constantly encounters, the psychology of people whose attitudes towards the law differ from his. Such understanding is not easy to acquire without the kind of broad general knowledge that a higher education imparts.
>
> (*Davis v. City of Dallas*, 1990)

JOB ANALYSIS METHODOLOGIES

There are many job analysis methodologies available today. The two-volume *Job Analysis Handbook for Business, Industry, and Government* (Gael, Cornelius, Levine & Salvendy, 1988) describes 18 different job analysis methodologies. *Everything You Always Wanted to Know About Job Analysis* (Levine, 1983) provides hands-on, practical descriptions of selected methodologies. In Europe, Fernández Ríos (1995) provides a comprehensive summary of the historical evolution of job analysis as well as descriptions of multiple job analytic methodologies. In fact, methodologies are not immune to the psychological theories that were dominant at the time of their development. For instance, the emphasis on tasks and work behaviors of the Functional Job Analysis, task inventory, and DOT approaches has a parallel in the behavioral analysis paradigm, whereas the Position Analysis Questionnaire's conceptualization of work in terms of inputs, mental processes, and outputs is indicative of cognitive and systems theories. Critical incidents also fall into the tradition of behaviorism, while the job elements approach may be linked to structuralism. Next, some of the most widely used methodologies will be summarized, but note that this list does not exhaust the large number of job analysis methodologies available.

Functional Job Analysis (FJA)

Functional Job Analysis is a worker-oriented job analytic approach that was first formulated in 1951–52 and used as a basis for the third edition of the DOT in 1965 (Fine, 1988). Fine (1989) continues to expand the number of function scales in the FJA, which initially included only 26 functions.

The basic unit of FJA is the task. Fine noted that what passed for tasks in some job descriptions was often a miscellany of phrases referring not only to activities but also knowledge, skills, and abilities (1989). In an attempt to standardize the language of task descriptions, FJA uses the basic structure of the English sentence as a model. Thus, the basic structure of a task statement in FJA includes the action verb, the object of the action, the source of information or instruction, and the results. These elements are combined in task statements of the DOT, where activities (action verb and object of the action) and outcomes (products and/or purposes) are matched (e.g., 'Operates grader following work order for haul road'). However, FJA task statements such as the ones found in DOT occupational descriptions are typically broader than those developed using other methods, and so they tend to be fewer in number. Indeed some may call these statements of major duties of a job or occupation.

> The original assumptions of the FJA scales were that:
> Workers relate to a universe of objects represented by Data, People, and Things.
> Workers relate to these objects through their physical, mental, and interpersonal potential. (Fine, 1989)

Skills can be represented as action verbs or functions, which can be in turn classified hierarchically within each object category (i.e., Data, People, Things). In this classification, each level includes those below it, and therefore identifying the three highest functions within each object category provides an accurate description of the job.

The People scale refers to interactions between people, communication, and interpersonal actions. Mentoring, for example, may be a job's most complex relationship involving people, whereas taking instructions is at the lowest end. The Data scale measures facts, ideas, mental operations, and knowledge of conditions. Synthesizing is at the highest end of this continuum, whereas comparing is at the lowest end. The Things scale assesses interaction with and response to tangibles and images visualized spatially. 'Setting up' is the action defined as the highest end of the Things continuum, whereas 'handling' is at the lowest end.

The Task Inventory

The task inventory is a widespread job analysis approach that involves defining a list of tasks or activities carried out on the job. This methodology was pioneered by the work of Christal and his associates at the Air Force Human Resource Laboratory (Christal, 1974). The approach was initially designed for collecting and organizing task-level information for hundreds of occupations. The task inventory has become the job analytic methodology of choice of many organizations in the US, probably because of its high face validity and the mandate to reflect important and critical job behaviors in human resource systems. Task statements are usually worded using the elements of the basic English sentence as in Fine's FJA. However, the items that appear in many task inventories are better characterized as

work activities, since they often lack the structure required by FJA task statements.

Once the products are defined and the tasks and activities have been identified, they can be rated according to their importance, frequency, time spent, difficulty of learning, and so on. Research on the choice of scales for task analysis suggests that ratings of task importance, time spent, and difficulty of learning provide relatively independent information. When interested in identifying the most important tasks, relatively complex formulas that combine these ratings (e.g., criticality × time spent + difficulty) do not appear worthy as the most important tasks can be simply identified by adding ratings of criticality (consequences of error) and ratings of difficulty of learning (Sanchez & Fraser, 1992; Sanchez & Levine, 1989). Harvey (1991) argued against the use of 'relative' scales (i.e., those that require within-job comparisons, such as asking how important a task is relative to all other tasks of the job), because such ipsative scales do not allow cross-job comparisons. However, Manson, Levine and Brannick (2000) found high levels of convergent validity and some discriminant validity among task constructs regardless of whether the scale was absolute or relative.

The term 'essential job functions' has been popularized by the language employed in the Americans with Disabilities Act passed by the US Congress. Thus, job analysis scales may be reworded so that respondents are asked to indicate whether a task meets several criteria as outlined by Brannick, Brannick and Levine (1994) to be labeled essential. As mentioned, the determination of the most important and critical tasks is also advocated by the *Uniform Guidelines on Employee Selection Procedures* (1978), and it has been supported by the US courts. The Society for Industrial and Organizational Psychology's *Principles,* in contrast, do not explicitly recommend the identification of important behaviors. Harvey (1991) argues that this is a shortcoming in the *Principles* because it opens the doors to unwarranted inferences about human attributes required for job performance.

Task inventories can be long and therefore the process of rating a large number of tasks on multiple scales can be tedious. How many tasks should a task inventory have? The answer depends on the kind of job under consideration, and on whether the inventory has been prepared to cover one or multiple jobs. A simple job may be described with a few dozen tasks, whereas more complex jobs may require hundreds of tasks. Of course, the number of tasks also depends on the level of detail observed in the task description. Because today's jobs change rapidly, it may be preferable to keep tasks at a relatively broad level of detail (Cunningham, 1996). Management philosophies like Total Quality Management and the trend towards a team-based organization also argue against establishing rigid boundaries among jobs defined through detailed job descriptions. In addition, long inventories are tedious to complete and can lead to distorted responses due to fatigue. However, statements of tasks, or more exactly work activities, should not be so broad that they do not facilitate inferences regarding the requirements of a position. For instance, the statement 'handles citizen complaints' does not really indicate the degree of involvement of a police officer in this task; one is left wondering whether the incumbent simply records the complaint or tries to solve the complaint and, if so, how much autonomy the incumbent enjoys in finding an answer to the citizen's complaint.

Unfortunately, detailed job analyses have often been justified in the US by the need to safeguard against potential legal challenges, particularly in these litigious times. Job analysis, however, was not intended to be just a litigation tool. In fact, the primary purpose of job analysis continues to be aiding in the development of useful business applications like selection procedures, training programs, and performance evaluations.

The Job Element Method

This job analytic methodology is characterized by an identification of the critical knowledges, skills, abilities, and other personal characteristics (or KSAOs) necessary to perform the tasks (Primoff, 1959). Knowledge refers to an organized body of information, usually of a factual or procedural nature applied directly to the performance of a function. For example, computer programmers may need knowledge of specific languages such as C++ or Visual Basic.

An ability refers to a demonstrated competence to perform an observable behavior or a behavior that results in an observable product. Firefighters, for example, are required to possess the physical ability to climb a ladder or the cognitive ability to understand and complete reports from the previous shift. A skill is a competence to perform a learned, psychomotor act, and may include a manual, verbal, or mental manipulation of data, people, or things. Examples are driving skill or skill in operating and maintaining a weapon.

Finally, other personal characteristics include personality factors, attitudes, and values needed to perform the job. Even something as simple as being courteous to civilians plays an important role in determining how well police officers perform their jobs. When firefighters do not tolerate stressful circumstances, or when police officers act impulsively thereby destroying evidence at a crime scene, they demonstrate some shortcoming on personal characteristics such as personality that affect their job performance. Being able to handle an irate customer and control one's temper may be critical in customer-contact jobs. The personal characteristics

and attitudes that qualify someone to work in teams are also examples of an 'other' attribute that is critical in many team-based organizations.

Each 'element' or KSAO is rated using four basic scales, which have been very influential in job analysis:

Barely acceptable: What relative proportion of even barely acceptable workers is good in the element?
Superior: How important is the element in picking out the superior worker?
Trouble: How much trouble is likely if the element is ignored when choosing among applicants?
Practical: To what extent can the organization fill its openings if the element is demanded?

Ratings are provided using three categories that can be scored as follows: $+ = 2$, $\checkmark = 1$, $0 = 0$. The scale 'Superior,' which tries to identify the profile that distinguishes the superior from the average worker, illustrates the lasting influence of the job element method on such current human resource practices as competency modeling (Lucia & Lepsinger, 1999).

A&Os ('abilities' and 'other') are the basic foundations upon which K&Ss ('knowledge' and 'skills') are built. K&Ss are typically acquired through formal instruction and practice whereas A&Os are less easily acquired through experience and are also more stable over time. This point illustrates why screening on ability and other characteristics are so important for many jobs. Because A&Os (such as personality traits) are not easy to acquire through formal training, organizations need to be extremely careful in identifying job candidates who possess the requisite A&Os for subsequent job training success. Even professional standards like the Society for I/O Psychology's *Principles* (1987) warn against relying on easy to learn K&Ss when designing selection procedures, which should emphasize more difficult to learn A&Os.

An interesting component of the job elements method is its ability to provide an estimate of the validity of a test battery based on ratings of job elements and on prevalidated weights of the test elements. This validity estimate is expressed in mathematical form through the J-coefficient. The J-coefficient can be helpful in the many field situations that, due to small sample sizes and other practical constraints, preclude local criterion-related validation.

Position Analysis Questionnaire (PAQ)

The Position Analysis Questionnaire (PAQ) is a standardized questionnaire which assesses activities using 187 items in six categories. These are (1) Information Input (where and how does the worker obtain the information needed to perform the job? e.g., use of visual or sensory input); (2) Mental Processes (what reasoning, planning, decision-making or information processing activities are necessary to perform the activities?); (3) Work Output (what physical activities are performed, and what tools are used?); (4) Relationships with Other People (what relationships with other people are required to perform the job?; e.g., negotiating, performing supervisory activities); (5) Job Context (in what physical and social contexts is the work performed?; e.g., hazards, stress); and (6) Other Job Characteristics (what other activities or characteristics are relevant to the job; e.g., apparel required, work schedule, salary basis).

Items on the PAQ are rated using several different scales matched to the item including importance, amount of time required, extent of use, possibility of occurrence, applicability, and difficulty. The PAQ can be completed in about two and a half hours. The completed questionnaires are then shipped to PAQ services headquarters for computerized scoring. Each job is scored on 32 dimensions, and a profile is constructed for the job. Norms are provided so that the job profile can be compared to profiles of 'benchmark' jobs. Usually, a computer printout is prepared for each job which illustrates the job dimension scores and profile, estimates of aptitude test data (e.g., the average scores expected for incumbents on standardized tests), and job evaluation points for compensation purposes.

The PAQ must usually be completed by trained job analysts rather than incumbents since the language in the questionnaire is difficult and at a fairly high reading level. The instrument also lacks the specificity which can be gained by a task inventory developed within the company for one or more particular positions. In computing interrater agreement of PAQ ratings, researchers have warned about the spurious effects of does-not-apply items. That is, relatively high indices of agreement can be obtained simply because raters agree on which items do not apply, rather than on the value or rank-order of items' importance for the job (Cornelius, DeNisi & Blencoe, 1984; Friedman & Harvey, 1986; Smith & Hakel, 1979).

The extensive research that has been conducted with the PAQ makes it one of the most useful of the standardized job analysis instruments, particularly for selection and compensation purposes. PAQ results can help to set a wage for a new job or to reclassify jobs and to identify the most valid tests for selecting personnel for the job. In fact, the PAQ provides job component validity (Jeanneret, 1992), which represents a synthetic validity estimate that is highly similar to empirically-derived validity coefficients of cognitive ability tests (Hoffman & McPhail, 1998).

Ability Requirements Scales

Fleishman and his colleagues (Fleishman & Reilly, 1992) developed the Ability Requirements Scales to gain insights about common processes demanded by different types of tasks. Abilities were empirically determined through the relationships among abilities across these separate performance domains. In other words, factor-analytic studies or other clustering methods based on the correlations across diverse task performances help in identifying these separate ability dimensions. The development of this taxonomy of human abilities started with laboratory research in which tasks were specifically designed to test certain hypotheses about abilities in a certain range of tasks. Then, Fleishman and his colleagues proceeded to develop a rating scale methodology by means of which the ability requirements of tasks could be described. An interesting feature of these scales is the use of decision flow diagrams intended to simplify decisions by observers when estimating the ability requirements of a task. These diagrams represent an aid to facilitate binary decisions such as 'is the respondent required to choose between stimuli or responses?' or 'does the task require fine muscular adjustments?'

Evidence supporting Fleishman's Ability Requirements Scales includes controlled studies of performance in vigilance tasks, and predictive validity studies where judges' ability ratings were correlates of actual task performance (Theologus & Fleishman, 1973). The *Handbook of Human Abilities* (Fleishman & Reilly, 1992), which is often used with the Fleishman Job Analysis Survey (F-JAS), lists 21 cognitive abilities (e.g., originality, speed of closure), ten psychomotor abilities (e.g., arm-hand steadiness), nine physical abilities (e.g., trunk strength), and 12 sensory/perceptual abilities (e.g., depth perception). As stated, the F-JAS approach has been very influential in the development of O*NET, whose scales parallel the content and format of the Ability Requirements Scales (Peterson et al., 1999).

Critical Incident Technique (CIT)

This technique was originally developed during the Second World War as a training needs assessment and performance appraisal tool (Flanagan, 1954). In this regard, individuals recalled and reported specific behavioral examples of incidents that reflected exceptionally good or exceptionally poor performance (Bownas & Bernardin, 1988). However, not every description of a situation qualifies as a critical incident. Contrary to the kinds of descriptions that are sometimes claimed to fall in this category, a critical incident should possess four characteristics: it should be specific, focus on observable behaviors that have been exhibited on the job, describe the context in which the behavior occurred, and indicate the consequences, outcomes or products of the behavior. The following is an example of a well-written critical incident:

The parents arrive at the emergency room with their young son. The boy has a small scalp laceration requiring stitches. The parents demand that their son be seen immediately. However, there are more serious patients requiring immediate life-saving attention. The parents were informed of this, but this incited their anger. The nurse in charge listened to their concerns, assured them that their son would be seen as quickly as possible, and then checked back with them periodically. The parents found the nurse's explanations reassuring, and calmed down considerably.

Critical incidents are an excellent approach for the development of situational and behavioral interviews (Taylor & O'Driscoll, 1995), and also low-fidelity tests administered via paper-and-pencil or electronic platforms (Sanchez & Fraser, 1993). Experts can provide the examples or benchmark responses to the situation representing effective and ineffective performance, which are then used to develop the assessment instruments.

Job Components Inventory (JCI)

In the UK, Banks (1988) developed the JCI as a tool for curriculum development and occupational and vocational assessment. Its primary goal is to provide information on job requirements to facilitate career development and planning. The JCI involves 132 items classified in six section: tools and equipment, physical and perceptual requirements, mathematical knowledge, communication skills, decision-making and responsibility, and working conditions.

Task and Demands Analysis (Arbeitswissenschaftliches Erhebungsverfahren zur Tätigkeitsanalyse – AET)

In Germany, Rohmert (1988) developed the AET methodology. Contrary to the methodologies developed in the US that often take the job's design for granted, the AET examines the degree of adjustment between the incumbent and the job. Its focus is on ergonomic stress or the extent to which job demands provoke the experience of stress on the incumbent. To evaluate stress, the AET examines the technological, technical, ergonomic, and organizational design where the incumbent works. In line with the philosophy of adapting work to the incumbent, this methodology takes into account the limitations of human physiology. The AET methodology involves a 216-item questionnaire that can be supplemented with additional sections focusing on specific requirements such as word processing and incumbent disabilities. The contrast between the focus of this European methodology and the ones developed in the US is noteworthy. That is, whereas American methodologies focus on maximizing performance by identifying an incumbent that best fits the job requirements,

the AET acknowledges that, in spite of individual differences, some work designs are likely to overwhelm even the most apt incumbent.

CHOOSING AMONG JOB ANALYSIS METHODOLOGIES

A few studies have examined the relative effectiveness of specific job analysis methods. For example, one study asked experienced job analysts to indicate the extent to which four methods accomplished the various purposes for job analysis (Levine, Ash, Hall & Sistrunk, 1983). In addition, they were asked to evaluate the amount of training required for use of the method, the sample sizes required for deriving reliable results, and the cost to administer and score the job analysis method. The results indicated that, of the methods evaluated, if the purpose is to generate a job description or to do job classification or job design, one of the best job analysis methods is the Functional Job Analysis Method (FJA).

Their results also suggest that CIT is probably not as good for job classification purposes. The best methods for job evaluation as reported in that study are FJA and the PAQ. The PAQ is also an excellent method for the selection of the best test to use for hiring. If the purpose of the job analysis is to develop a performance appraisal instrument or to develop training programs, the recommended method is CIT. No method is ideal in terms of legal compliance, including compliance with the Americans with Disabilities Act or its precursors. For companies in need of highly detailed information about a job, the development of their own job analysis method is probably preferable to an 'off-the-shelf' type such as the PAQ which would not provide the level of detail in describing the job that may be needed to, for example, design a training program. However, as mentioned before, experts agree that the choice of job analysis method depends upon the purposes to be served by the data and the desired product. There is no 'one best way' to conduct a job analysis. The practicality and cost of the various methods for particular organizations must be considered as well (Levine et al., 1988). The most definitive finding from the research on the relative effectiveness of the various methods is that multiple methods of job analysis should be used whenever possible.

DOING WORK ANALYSIS IN A CHANGING ENVIRONMENT

Due to changing technology and markets, job analyses may need to be conducted in situations where jobs do not already exist such as when a new business is started or where jobs are changing dramatically as might result from moving to an electronic commerce environment. In instances where a job is being created or where it is undergoing significant change, job analysis becomes a predictive rather than descriptive tool. This approach has been termed 'strategic job analysis' as it intends to forecast what a job may be like in a new environment with new strategic goals, with different work aids (e.g., e-commerce), increased customer contact, or expanded duties (Schneider & Konz, 1989). In essence, strategic job analysis involves a comparison between present and future job descriptions to ascertain the extent to which job requirements may change. For instance, the Federal Aviation Administration has recently developed a job analysis methodology to identify changes in job requirements of the Air Traffic Controller job. As noted earlier, air traffic control tasks that used to be performed visually from the control tower are being shifted to a 'dark room environment' or computer room where traffic is controlled through electronic devices. The FAA was concerned about the extent to which these technological changes would modify the air traffic controller's job. Scenarios of future-oriented job performance can be simulated or recreated to gain insight into the job requirements needed for future job performance, so that selection procedures and training programs can be adapted to the new demands. This approach requires direct involvement from industry experts and organizational members, often from different functional areas. One of the risks of this approach is that it might degenerate into 'armchair job analysis' or mere speculation about what the future may bring.

In a way, future-oriented work analysis is not necessarily strategic. That is, when SMEs merely speculate about what the future may bring, they are not thinking strategically. Strategic work analysis should be proactive in the sense that, in addition to forecasting future work requirements, it should ensure the presence of the KSAOs needed to accomplish the strategic goals of the organization. The recent literature on strategic human resource management offers interesting insights into how organizations may engage in truly 'strategic' job analysis (Barney & Wright, 1998; Porter, 1985; Wright & McMahan, 1992). For instance, Schippmann (1999) describes how organizations wishing to achieve a competitive advantage by virtue of flexibility and speed may seek teamwork skills such as tolerance of ambiguity, whereas those whose competitive advantage is predicated on low cost may seek conscientiousness and dedication.

COMPETENCY MODELING

The notion of 'competencies' and the practice of 'competency modeling' have acquired a great deal of popularity in recent years (Lucia & Lepsinger, 1999;

Schippmann, 1999). However, there is a wide range of variation in the definition of competencies. The term competency was made popular by Prahalad and Hamel's (1990) work on organizational core competencies, even though it was probably first enunciated by McClelland (1973) when he argued for the replacement of intelligence testing with competence testing. Some definitions hint that the line separating competency modeling from job analysis is a blurry one: 'an individual characteristic that can be reliably measured or counted and that can be shown to differentiate superior from average performers' (Spencer, McClelland & Spencer, 1994).

The need for competency modeling has been questioned (Barrett & Callahan, 1997; Pearlman, 1997). In closer examination, the main difference between job analysis and competency modeling may lie in the level of analysis, with competencies being broader human attributes than traditional knowledge, skills, and abilities (KSAs). However, the methodology employed in developing competency models seems at times a watered-down version of traditional job analysis methodology. Despite its less than rigorous methodology, we believe that the competency modeling trend should serve as a wake-up call to job analysis researchers and practitioners. Indeed, competency modeling includes an effort to understand the organization's mission, values, strategy, and broad goals and to incorporate those into the individual competency requirements. Such an effort is unfortunately missing in traditional job analysis formats.

One of the problems shared by a majority of approaches to competency modeling lies in the difficulty of measuring the focal constructs or competencies. That is, mapping these competencies in behavioral terms is not a straightforward task, primarily because the 'nomological net' of relationships with other variables (i.e., convergent and discriminant validities) is not always well understood. For instance, employees of a retail chain of office supplies expressed their concerns about being evaluated on competencies such as 'maturity,' whose behavioral referents seem fuzzy at best.

Unlike traditional worker attributes, competencies do not always have straightforward behavioral referents in prescribed job tasks (Jackson & Schuler, 1990; Kerr, 1982; Snow & Snell, 1993). In fact, competencies are often considered to be organizational rather than job bound. Thus, inferences about competencies cannot follow solely from the analysis of prescribed job activities. This need not be a drawback because sticking to a narrowly defined set of work activities may not be the ideal methodology to describe the attributes associated with today's ever-changing task assignments (Cannon-Bowers, Tannenbaum, Salas & Volpe, 1995; Stevens & Campion, 1994). For instance, competencies should also be informed by organizational variables such as strategic and core business values. Making and justifying these inferential leaps on the slippery floor of behaviorally-fuzzy competencies is certainly a methodological challenge that deserves further attention. In advance of the empirical work that might support organization-wide and generic as opposed to job-specific and fine-grained sets of human requirements, Behling (1998) has provided a rationally derived set of guidelines which set forth conditions calling for one vs. the other.

ANALYZING WORK IN THE GLOBAL ECONOMY

Globalization adds to the challenge faced by those who would analyze work. Although globalization affects the requirements of virtually every job, its influence is most obvious among international assignees. These expatriates should possess not only the technical requirements demanded by the job, but also the adaptability demanded by a new set of cultural rules. Four areas have been deemed equally important for expatriate work: technical skills, family situation, relational skills, and motivation. However, 90% of all companies appear to base their international selection solely on technical expertise. This widespread practice ignores that technically qualified candidates are not always capable of adjusting to critical cultural differences such as those involving social status and group dependence (Teagarden & Gordon, 1995).

When ascertaining the requirements of international assignments, cultural values and norms should be examined. In a way, culture analysis becomes an extension of work analysis when cultural boundaries are crossed. Theoretical frameworks distinguishing between cultural dimensions like uncertainty avoidance, individualism-collectivism, and power distance are available (e.g., Hofstede, 1984), and they provide a potentially useful list of cultural requirements demanded by expatriate assignments.

Openness to the profound personal transformation that awaits the expatriate executive is perhaps the most fundamental sign of expatriate readiness. It is not surprising that courage and risk-taking are among the core characteristics of successful expatriates who, knowing themselves, are willing to revisit their most deeply held assumptions. Authoritarianism, rigidity, and an ethnocentric attitude hinder a successful adaptation to a foreign culture. Because these are deeply ingrained personality traits that are not easily changeable, candidates should probably possess these characteristics from 'day one' on the job. Although traditional personality inventories have not proven very effective at predicting expatriate success, available measures specifically designed to evaluate expatriate potential appear promising (Spreitzer, McCall & Mahoney, 1997).

EVALUATING WORK ANALYSIS DATA

Much of the success of work analysis efforts is a function of the extent to which the inferences one draws about job requirements lead to valid and useful selection procedures, training programs, and so on. One underlying objective of work analysis is to minimize the 'inferential leaps' required to arrive at conclusions regarding job requirements and specifications. Traditionally, it has been assumed that better inferences are made when the following work analysis practices are observed:

1 *Description of work behaviors.* In the US, quasi-legal standards such as the *Uniform Guidelines on Employee Selection Procedures* (1978) require that the KSAOs measured by the selection procedure be linked to important job behaviors. This link between important behaviors and KSAOs is also mandated by professional regulations concerning the practice of assessment centers (Task Force on Assessment Center Guidelines, 1989), although not, as we have stated, mandated by the Society for Industrial and Organizational Psychology's *Principles for the Validation and Use of Personnel Selection Procedures* (1987). Case law generated by US courts also suggests that an on-site job analysis that identifies the most important and critical job behaviors is necessary (*EEOC v. Atlas Paper Box Co.*, 1989; Williamson, Campion, Malos, Roehling & Campion, 1997). Sometimes the behavior necessary for successful performance is not directly observable, but the products or outcomes, kinds of materials or work aids used, and the people included in the decision process can be reported.

2 *Work analysis records.* The organization must maintain adequate records of the work analysis and document the linkages between the work analysis and human resource systems. The organization should be able to justify the inferences or judgments that work analysis supports. The data must be reliable, which is often measured by showing that different sources agreed on judgements about the work. Although agreement among SMEs formulating ratings of the same job is desirable, within-job title disagreement should be carefully explored. Disagreement is often interpreted as evidence that incumbents are biased in their reports or are actually performing different jobs. However, disagreement may also suggest differences in the manner in which the same job is performed among incumbents. Understanding such differences can provide meaningful information. For instance, Sanchez, Prager, Wilson and Viswesvaran (1998) identified a difference of

over $50,000 in sales between two patterns of task ratings followed by SMEs holding the job of sales representative.

There has been considerable research on the extent to which job analytic data are vulnerable to bias (see Morgeson & Campion, 1997 for a review of potential sources of bias in job analysis). In the absence of a better criterion to evaluate job analytic data, disagreement among job incumbents of the same job title has, as we just suggested, been interpreted as a sign of bias. Instead of focusing on disagreement, it has been argued that evaluations of job analytic data should focus on the extent to which the data facilitate the formation of valid inferences regarding selection, training, and other decisions (Sanchez & Levine, 2000).

US courts have often been critical of the racial/sexual composition of work analytic panels of experts. The assumption behind this criticism is that, for example, a job specification stipulated by an all-white, male panel of job experts would somehow be biased against minorities and females. Although potential racial and gender bias should not be ignored, post hoc examinations of rating differences as a function of demographic factors such as race and gender are not likely to clarify the meaning of disagreement. That is, statistically significant differences are elusive and their practical significance questionable (Arvey, Davis, McGowen & Dipboye, 1982; Arvey, Passino & Lounsbury, 1977; Landy & Vasey, 1991; Schmitt & Cohen, 1989). Because disagreement may not always represent spurious variation, scrutinizing such differences may yield fruitful insights for human resource programs. We agree with Harvey's (1991) recommendation regarding the need to understand within-job disagreement Specifically, a generalizability theory frame of mind is needed to reveal the sources of variance explaining within-job variance. As stated previously, Sanchez, Zamora and Viswesvaran (1997) found that incumbent– nonincumbent agreement was moderated by job complexity and job satisfaction, such that agreement was highest when jobs were simple and incumbents were relatively dissatisfied. Such findings show that understanding the origins of disagreement may be more informative than simply quantifying the level of disagreement.

SUMMARY

Work analysis supports a variety of applications such as selection, training, performance appraisal, and compensation. However, as a result of technology, the flattening of organizational structures, and the dynamic global markets, jobs are no longer as static as they once were. The boundaries distinguishing the responsibilities of one job from another continue to blur. It is not surprising that the analysis of work is shifting towards generalized work activities and broad dimensions that apply across a broad spectrum of jobs, while moving away from task-based descriptions that are very specific to a limited group of jobs.

Work analysis faces the challenge of producing enough information so that selection tests, levels of compensation, training and development efforts, and performance standards are demonstrably relevant to job success, and yet flexible enough to be applied to the study of dynamic work arrangements in continuous flux.

Despite rhetoric to the contrary, work analysis remains an essential tool in the repertoire of work psychologists. The 'de-jobbing' of organizations (Bridges, 1994) makes the analysis of work even more significant. Regardless of the plasticity of work assignments, studying current and possible arrangements of work process is *sine qua non* in the design of virtually every human resource system including downsizing, reengineering, recruitment, selection, training and career planning, performance appraisal, job redesign, compensation, and occupational health and safety. Even if the legal mandate for a work analysis did not exist in the US at least, the reliance upon work analysis is positive inasmuch as it improves the effectiveness of human resources practices. In this sense, the legal mandate for work analysis is fortunate, because it forces businesses to design human resource systems that are likely to improve organizational performance. In conclusion, although static 'jobs' may be a thing of the past, studying work processes and arrangements continues to be the foundation of any human resource system today and in the foreseeable future.

REFERENCES

Arvey, R.D., Davis, G.A., McGowen, S.L., & Dipboye, R.L. (1982). Potential sources of bias on job analytic processes. *Academy of Management Journal, 25,* 618–629.

Arvey, R.D., Passino, E.M., & Lounsbury, J.W. (1977). Job analysis results as influenced by sex of incumbent and sex of analyst. *Journal of Applied Psychology, 62,* 411–416.

Arvey, R.D., Salas, E., & Gialluca, K.A. (1992). Using task inventories to forecast skills and abilities. *Human Performance, 5,* 171–190.

Ash, R.A., Levine, E.L., Higbee, R.H., & Sistrunk, F. (1982). *Comparison of task ratings from subject matter experts vs. job incumbents.* Paper presented at the Southeastern Psychological Association Annual Meeting, New Orleans, March.

Banks, M.H. (1988). Job components inventory. In S. Gael, E.T. Cornelius, III, E.L. Levine & G. Salvendy (Eds.),

The job analysis handbook for business, industry and government, Vol II (pp. 960–974). New York: John Wiley.

Barney, J., & Wright, P.M. (1998). On becoming a strategic partner: The role of human resources in gaining competitive advantage. *Human Resource Management, 37*(1), 31–46.

Barrett, G.V., & Callahan, C.M. (1997). Competencies: The Madison Avenue approach to professional practice. In R.C. Page (Chair), *Competency Models: What Are They and Do They Work?* Practitioner Forum presented at the 12th Annual Conference of the Society for Industrial and Organizational Psychology, St. Louis, Missouri, April.

Behling, O. (1998). Employee selection: Will intelligence and conscientiousness do the job? *Academy of Management Executive, 12*, 77–86.

Bernardin, H.J. (1992). An analytic framework for customer-based performance content development and appraisal. *Human Resources Management Review, 2*, 81–102.

Borman, W.C., Hanson, M.A., & Hedge, J.W. (1997). Personnel selection. *Annual Review of Psychology, 48*, 299–337.

Bownas, D., & Bernardin, H.J. (1988). The critical incident method. In S. Gael, E.T. Cornelius, III, E.L. Levine & G. Salvendy (Eds.), *The job analysis handbook for business, industry and government,* Vol. II (pp. 1120–1137). New York: John Wiley & Sons.

Brannick, M.T., Brannick, J.P., & Levine, E.L. (1992). Job analysis, personnel selection and the ADA. *Human Resource Management Review, 2*, 171–182.

Bridges, W. (1994). *Jobshift.* Reading, MA: Addison-Wesley.

Cannon-Bowers, J.A., Tannenbaum, S.I., Salas, E., & Volpe, C.E. (1995). Defining competencies and establishing team training requirements. In R.A. Guzzo, E. Salas & Associates (Eds.), *Team effectiveness and decision-making in organizations* (pp. 333–380). San Francisco: Jossey-Bass.

Christal, T.E. (1974). The U.S. Air Force occupational research projects. *JSAS Catalog of Selected Documents in Psychology, 4*, 61.

Cornelius, E.T., DeNisi, A.S., & Blencoe, A.G. (1984). Expert and naive raters using the PAQ: Does it matter? *Personnel Psychology, 37*, 453–464.

Cornelius, E.T., Schmidt, F.L., & Carron, T.J. (1984). Job classification approaches and the implementation of validity generalization results. *Personnel Psychology, 37*, 247–260.

Cunningham, J.W. (1996). Generic job descriptors: A likely direction in occupational analysis. *Military Psychology, 8*, 247–262.

Davis v. City of Dallas (1990). 56 Fair Empl. Prac Cas. (BNA) 669.

Drauden, G.M., & Peterson, N.G. (1974). *A domain approach to job analysis.* St. Paul: Minnesota Department of Personnel, Test Research and Development Section.

EEOC v. Atlas Paper Box Co. (1989). 868 F.2d 1487.

Fernández Ríos, M. (1995). Análisis y descripción de puestos de trabajo [Analysis and description of jobs]. Madrid: Díaz de Santos.

Fine, S.A.. (1988). Functional job analysis. In S. Gael, E.T. Cornelius, III, E.L. Levine & G. Salvendy (Eds.), *The job analysis handbook for business, industry, and government*, Vol. II (pp. 1019–1035). New York: John Wiley & Sons.

Fine, S.A. (1989). *Functional job analysis scales.* Milwaukee, Wisconsin: S.A. Fine Associates.

Flanagan, J.C. (1954). The critical incident technique. *Psychological Bulletin, 51*, 327–358.

Fleishman, E.A., & Reilly, M.E. (1992). *Handbook of human abilities.* Palo Alto, CA: Consulting Psychologists Press, Inc.

Friedman, L., & Harvey, R.J. (1986). Can raters with reduced job descriptive information provide accurate position analysis questionnaire (PAQ) ratings? *Personnel Psychology, 39*, 779–789.

Gael, S. (Ed.), Cornelius, E.T. III, Levine, E.L., & Salvendy, G. (Assoc. Eds.) (1988). *The job analysis handbook for business, industry and government*, Vols I, II. New York: John Wiley & Sons.

Galloway, D. (1994). *Mapping work processes.* Milwaukee, WI: ASQC Quality Press.

Gatewood, R.D., & Feild, H.S. (1994). *Human resource selection* (3rd ed.). Ft. Worth, TX: Dryden.

Goldstein, I.L. (1993). *Training in organizations* (3rd ed.). Pacific Grove, CA: Brooks/Cole.

Gorriti, M. (1996). Determining content of training programs at the Basque Police: A worker oriented job analysis procedure. In R.G. Jones (Chair), *Answers about the use of job analysis for training decisions.* Symposium presented at the 11th Annual Conference of the Society for Industrial and Organizational Psychology, San Diego, CA.

Guion, R.M. (1980). *Job analysis and validation procedures: Applications to construct identification.* Third Annual Conference on EEO Compliance and Human Resource Utilization. Chicago, IL, May.

Harvey, R.J. (1991). Job analysis. In M.D. Dunnette & L.M. Hough (Eds.), *Handbook of industrial and organizational psychology*, Vol. 2 (2nd ed.) (pp. 71–163). Palo Alto, CA: Consulting Psychologists Press.

Hoffman, C.C., & McPhail, S.M. (1998). Exploring options for supporting test use in situations precluding local validation. *Personnel Psychology, 51*, 987–1003.

Hofstede, G. (1984). *Culture's consequences.* Newbury Park, CA: Sage.

Holland, J.L. (1973). *Making vocational choices: A theory of careers.* Englewoods Cliffs, NJ: Prentice-Hall.

International Labor Organization (1991). *Uniform International Classification of Occupations-88.* Geneva: International Labor Organization.

Jackson, S.E., & Schuler, R.S. (1990). Human resource planning: Challenges for I/O psychologists. *American Psychologist, 45*, 223–239.

Jeanneret, P.R. (1992). Applications of job component/synthetic validity to construct validity. *Human Performance, 5*, 81–96.

Jeanneret, P.R., Borman, W.C., Kubisiak, U.C., & Hanson, M.A. (1999). Generalized work activities. In N.G. Peterson, M.D. Mumford, W.C. Borman,

P.R. Jeanneret & E.A. Fleishman (Eds.), *An occupational information system for the 21st century: The development of O*NET*. Washington, DC: American Psychological Association.

Jones, R.G., Sanchez, J.I., Parameswaran, G., Phelps, J., Shoptaugh, C., Williams, M., & White, S. Selection or Training? (in press). A two-fold test of the validity of job-analytic ratings of trainability. *Journal of Business and Psychology.*

Kerr, J.L. (1982). Assigning managers on the basis of the life-cycle. *Journal of Business Strategy, 2*, 56–65.

Klimoski, R., & Jones, R.G. (1995). Staffing for effective group decision making: Key issues in matching people and teams. In R.A. Guzzo, E. Salas & Associates (Eds.), *Team effectiveness and decision-making in organizations* (pp. 333–380). San Francisco: Jossey-Bass.

Landy, F.J., & Vasey, J. (1991). Job analysis. The composition of SME samples. *Personnel Psychology, 44*, 27–50.

Levine, E.L. (1983). *Everything you always wanted to know about job analysis*, Tampa, FL: Mariner Publishing. [Now available from the author.]

Levine, E.L., Ash, R.A., & Bennett, N. (1980). Exploratory comparative study of four job analysis methods. *Journal of Applied Psychology, 65*, 524–535.

Levine, E.L., Ash, R.A., Hall, H., & Sistrunk, F. (1983). Evaluation of job analysis methods by experienced job analysts. *Academy of Management Journal, 26*, 339–348.

Levine, E.L., & Baker, C.V. (1991). *Team task analysis: A procedural guide and test of the methodology*. Paper presented at the 6th Annual Conference of the Society for Industrial and Organizational Psychology. St. Louis, MI, April.

Levine, E.L., Maye, D.M., Ulm, R.A., & Gordon, T.R. (1997). A methodology for developing and validating minimum qualifications (MQS). *Personnel Psychology, 50*, 1009–1023.

Levine, E.L., & Sanchez, J.I. (1998). Sources of inaccuracy in job analysis and suggestions for remediation. Paper presented as part of the symposium, *Job analysis inaccuracy: Cracks in the foundation of HR management?*, co-chaired by F.P. Morgeson & M.A. Campion, 13th Annual Meeting of the Society of Industrial and Organizational Psychology, Dallas, April.

Levine, E.L., Sistrunk, F., McNutt, K.J., & Gael, S. (1991). Exemplary job analysis systems in selected organizations: A description of process and outcomes. In J.W. Jones, B.D. Steffy, & D.W. Bray (Eds.), *Applying psychology in business: The manager's handbook*. Lexington, MA: Lexington Books.

Levine, E.L., Thomas, J.N., & Sistrunk, F. (1988). Selecting a job analysis approach. In S. Gael (Ed.), E.T. Cornelius (III), E.L. Levine, & G. Salvendy (Associate Eds.), *The job analysis handbook for business, industry and government*, Vol. I (pp. 339–352). New York: Wiley.

London, M. (1988). *Change agents. New roles and innovation strategies for human resource professionals.* San Francisco: Jossey-Bass.

Lucia, A.-D., & Lepsinger, R. (1999). *The art and science of competency models*. San Francisco: Jossey-Bass.

Manson, T.M., Levine, E.L., & Brannick, M.T. (2000). The construct validity of task inventory ratings: A multitrait–multimethod analysis. *Human Performance, 13*, 1–22.

McClelland, D.C. (1973). Testing for competence rather than for intelligence. *American Psychologist, 28*, 1–14.

McCormick, E.J. (1976). Job and task analysis. In M.D. Dunnette (Ed.), *Handbook of industrial and organizational psychology* (pp. 651–696). Chicago, IL: Rand-McNally.

McCormick, E.J., Jeanneret, P.R., & Mecham, R.C. (1972). A study of job characteristics and job dimensions as based on the Position Analysis Questionnaire (PAQ). *Journal of Applied Psychology, 56*, 347–368.

Mitchell, K.E., Alliger, G.M., & Morfopoulos, R. (1997). Toward an ADA-appropriate job analysis. *Human Resource Management Review, 7*, 5–26.

Motowidlo, S.J., & Van Scotter, J.R. (1994). Evidence that task performance should be distinguished from contextual performance. *Journal of Applied Psychology, 79*, 475–480.

Morgeson, F.P., & Campion, M.A. (1997). Social and cognitive sources of potential inaccuracy in job analysis. *Journal of Applied Psychology, 82*, 627–656.

OIT (1958). Clasificación internacional uniforme de ocupaciones [Uniform international classification of occupations]. Geneve: OIT.

Organ, D. (1988). *Organizational citizenship behavior: The good soldier syndrome*. Lexington, MA: Lexington Books.

Pearlman, K. (1997). Competencies: Issues in their application. In R.C. Page (Chair), *Competency models: What are they and do they work?* Practitioner Forum presented at the 12th Annual Conference of the Society for Industrial and Organizational Psychology, St. Louis, Missouri.

Peterson, N.G., Mumford, M.D., Borman, W.C., Jeanneret, P.R., & Fleishman, E.A. (Eds.) (1999). *An occupational information system for the 21st century: The development of O*NET*. Washington, DC: American Psychological Association.

Porter, M.E. (1985). *Competitive advantage*. New York: Free Press.

Prahalad, C.K., & Hamel, G. (1990). The core competence of the corporation. *Harvard Business Review, May–June*, 79–91.

Primoff, E. (1959). The development of processes for indirect or synthetic validity: IV. Empirical validations of the J-coefficients. A symposium. *Personnel Psychology, 12*, 413–418.

Raymark, P.H., Schmit, M.J., & Guion, R.M. (1997). Identifying potentially useful personality constructs for employee selection. *Personnel Psychology, 50*, 723–736.

Rohmert, W. (1988). AET. In S. Gael (Ed.), E.T. Cornelius, III, E.L. Levine, & G. Salvendy (Associate Eds.) *The job analysis handbook for business, industry and government* (pp. 843–859). New York: John Wiley.

Rolland, J.P., & Mogenet, J.L. (1994). Manuel d'application, Systéme D5D d'aide à l'évaluation des personnes [User manual. D5D Assistance system for people assessment] Paris, France: Les Editions du Centre de Psychologie Appliquée.

Sackett, P.R., Cornelius, E.T., & Carron, E.T. (1981). A comparison of global judgment vs. task-oriented approaches to job classification. *Personnel Psychology*, *34*, 791–804.

Salgado, J.F. (1999). Personnel selection methods. *International Review of Industrial and Organizational Psychology*, *14*, 1–54.

Sanchez, J.I. (1994). From documentation to innovation: Reshaping job analysis to meet emerging business needs. *Human Resource Management Review*, *4*, 51–74.

Sanchez, J.I., & Fraser, S.L. (1992). On the choice of scales for task analysis. *Journal of Applied Psychology*, *77*, 545–553.

Sanchez, J.I., & Fraser, S.L. (1993, May). *Development and validation of the Corporate Social Style Inventory: A measure of customer service skills*. Report No. 93–108.

Sanchez, J.I., & Fraser, S.L. (1994). An empirical approach to identify job duty-KSA linkages in managerial jobs: A case example. *Journal of Business and Psychology*, *8*, 309–325.

Sanchez, J.I., & Levine, E.L. (1989). Determining important tasks within jobs: A policy-capturing approach. *Journal of Applied Psychology*, *74*, 336–342.

Sanchez, J.I., & Levine, E.L. (1999). Is job analysis dead, misunderstood, or both? New forms of work analysis and design. In A. Kraut & A. Korman (Eds.), *Evolving Practices in Human Resource Management* (pp. 43–68). The SIOP Practice Series, San Francisco: Jossey-Bass.

Sanchez, J.I., & Levine, E.L. (2000). Accuracy or consequential validity: Which is the better standard for job analysis data? *Journal of Organizational Behavior*, *21*, 809–818.

Sanchez, J.I., Prager, I., Wilson, A., & Viswesvaran, C. (1998). Understanding within-job title variance in job-analytic ratings. *Journal of Business and Psychology*, *12*, 407–420.

Sanchez, J.I., Zamora, A., & Viswesvaran, C. (1997). Moderators of agreement between incumbent and non-incumbent ratings of job characteristics. *Journal of Occupational and Organizational Psychology*, *70*, 209–218.

Sandberg, J. (2000). Understanding human competence at work: An interpretative approach. *Academy of Management Journal*, *43*, 9–25.

Schmitt, N., & Cohen, S.A. (1989). Internal analysis of task ratings by job incumbents. *Journal of Applied Psychology*, *74*, 96–104.

Schippmann, J.S. (1999). *Strategic job modeling*. Mahwah, New Jersey: Lawrence Erlbaum.

Schneider, B., & Konz, A.M. (1989). Strategic job analysis. *Human Resources Management*, *28*, 51–63.

Smith, J., & Hakel, M.D. (1979). Convergence among data sources, response bias, and reliability and validity of a structured job analysis questionnaire. *Personnel Psychology*, *32*, 677–692.

Snow, C.C., & Snell, A.A. (1993). Staffing as strategy. In N. Schmitt, W.C. Borman, & Associates (Eds.), *Personnel Selection in Organizations* (pp. 448–480). San Francisco: Jossey-Bass.

Society for Industrial and Organizational Psychology, Inc. (1987). Principles for the validation and use of personnel selection procedures (3rd ed.). College Park, MD: Society for Industrial and Organizational Psychology, Inc.

Spencer, L.M., McClelland, D.C., & Spencer, S. (1994). *Competency assessment methods: History and state of the art*. Boston: Hay McBer Research Press.

Spreitzer, G.M., McCall, Jr. M.W., & Mahoney, J.D. (1997). Early identification on international executive potential. *Journal of Applied Psychology*, *82*, 6–29.

Stevens, M.J., & Campion, M.A. (1994). The knowledge, skill, and ability requirements for teamwork: Implications for human resource management. *Journal of Management*, *20*, 503–530.

Tannenbaum, R.J., & Wesley, S. (1993). Agreement between committee-based and field-based job analyses: A study in the context of licensure testing. *Journal of Applied Psychology*, *78*, 975–980.

Task Force on Assessment Center Guidelines (1989). Guidelines and ethical considerations for assessment center operations. Pittsburgh, PA: Development Dimensions International.

Taylor, P.J., & O'Driscoll, M.P. (1995). *Structured employment interviewing*. Hampshire, U.K.: Grower.

Teagarden, M.B., & Gordon, G.D. (1995). Corporate selection strategies and expatriate manager success. In J. Selmer (Ed.), *Expatriate Management. New Ideas for International Business* (pp. 17–36). Westport, Connecticut: Quorum.

Theologus, G.C., & Fleishman, E.A. (1973). Development of a taxonomy of human performance: Validation study of ability scales for classifying human tasks. *JSAS Catalog of Selected Documents in Psychology*, *3* (29) (Ms. no. 326).

Thompson, D.E., & Thompson, T.A. (1985). Court standards for job analysis in test validation. *Personnel Psychology*, *35*, 865–874.

Thorndike, R.L. (1949). *Personnel selection: Test and measurement techniques*. New York: Wiley.

Tracey, T.J., & Rounds, J.B. (1993). Evaluating Holland's and Gati's vocational interest models: A structural meta-analysis. *Psychological Bulletin*, *113*, 229–246.

Uniform Guidelines on Employee Selection Procedures (1978). *Federal Register*, *43*, (166), 38290–38309.

U.S. Department of Labor (1977). *Dictionary of occupational titles* (4th ed.). Washington, D.C: U.S. Government Printing Office.

Visser, C.F., Altink, W.M.M., & Algere, J.M. (1997). From job analysis to work profiling: Do traditional procedures still apply? In N. Anderson & P. Herriot (Eds.), *International handbook of selection and assessment*. Oxford: Wiley.

Williamson, L.G., Campion, J.E., Roehling, M.V., Malos, S.B., & Campion, M.A. (1997). Employment interview on trial: Linking interview structure with litigation outcomes. *Journal of Applied Psychology*, *82*, 900–912.

Wright, P.M., & McMahan, G.C. (1992). Theoretical perspectives for strategic human resource management. *Journal of Management*, *18*, 295–320.

5

Work Design: Learning from the Past and Mapping a New Terrain

SHARON K. PARKER
and TOBY D. WALL

In this article, we review the practice and theory of work design with the aim of learning from the past and looking to the future. Starting from the Industrial Revolution and job simplification, we outline major practical and theoretical developments in work design. We describe established theories, including Hackman and Oldham's Job Characteristics Model (1976) and the socio-technical systems approach, as well as complementary theoretical perspectives. We suggest that work design theory can be usefully expanded via the inclusion of work design antecedents, a broader set of work characteristics and outcomes, consideration of mechanisms and contingencies, and attention to work design processes. We also propose key implications for work design research in the light of the changing workplace. These include: the recurrent issue of job simplification; the continued importance of uncertainty as an antecedent and contingency variable; interdependence, team working and social complexity as increasingly important work features; a greater emphasis on cognitive demands and knowledge aspects at work; and the effect of demographic and contractual changes on work design.

Consider a company that is in the process of planning to introduce team working. Those responsible ask themselves the following questions: Will the advantages of teamwork outweigh the costs? How self-managing should the team be? If the team is self-managing, who will take responsibility in an emergency? How should the team be led? Similarly, if the company were considering setting up individual jobs, the questions might include: What range of tasks should be combined to make up a job? What kind of feedback should be provided? and, How much discretion should the job incumbent have in deciding how to work?

All these questions concern work design. They are important because the decisions made can affect the performance of employees, as well as their stress, motivation, commitment, and even their learning and development. Thus work design is concerned with choices made about the nature or content of peoples' jobs, and how these choices affect individual and organizational outcomes such as employee well-being and productivity. In some respects, of course, work design choices can be constrained. They are affected by the nature of the product or service in question, the supporting technology, and other organizational aspects such as culture and supervisory style. Yet none of these is deterministic or immutable, all leave considerable latitude, especially with regard to the range of tasks undertaken by individuals or groups and the amount of discretion they have in carrying them out. This is the domain of work design.

Our aim in this chapter is to provide an overview of the practice and theory of work design, to learn from the past and look to the future.

EARLY WORK DESIGN: JOB SIMPLIFICATION

Historically, the dominant approach to work design has been that of job simplification. This can be traced back to views that emerged in Great Britain during the Industrial Revolution from 1760 to around the mid-1830s. As people came together to work in factories, the question arose of how to organize their activities. Adam Smith (1776) offered an answer. He advocated breaking down complex jobs into simpler and narrower ones, arguing that this would lead to employees becoming more dexterous, and time being saved through their not having to move to different tasks. Charles Babbage (1835) added to these ideas, and pointed out that an additional advantage of job simplification is that it requires less skilled, and therefore cheaper, labor.

At the turn of the twentieth century, the idea of job simplification was given much momentum through the contributions of two key individuals – Frederick Taylor and Henry Ford. Taylor (1911) developed a work design method called 'Scientific Management', which involved identifying the most efficient ways of carrying out particular tasks (e.g., eliminating all false, slow or unnecessary movements), and reconstituting the job on the basis of those 'best ways'. Thus, while the emphasis of Smith and Babbage was on the horizontal division of labor, on breaking work down into narrower sets of tasks, Taylor was also concerned with the vertical division of labor, of removing from employees the discretion they had over how to carry out the tasks. This was to be determined 'scientifically' and enforced by management.

Henry Ford's contribution was to take this approach further through the development of the moving assembly line, which he introduced in 1914 at his automobile factory in Michigan in the United States. Having broken up a complex task into a set of simpler ones, it was a logical development to use the technology of the day (e.g., transporters, conveyors) to move the work between stages and so eliminate 'unproductive' time spent in carrying. The outcome was simplified jobs that were paced by the speed of the resultant assembly line.

Job simplification and assembly line work spread to other companies in the United States, both in the automobile industry and outside, and crossed the Atlantic to Europe. Davis, Canter and Hoffman (1955) illustrated the pervasiveness of the practice in a survey of personnel responsible for designing jobs in US companies. Asked about the importance of a range of different work design criteria, respondents rated the single most important factor as 'minimizing the time required to perform operation', closely followed by 'minimizing skill requirements'. Later studies showed the continuing dominance of job simplification ideas within manufacturing (Braverman, 1974; Taylor, 1979), as well as their extension into administrative domains. Even today, despite much rhetoric about empowerment, the thinking behind scientific management is still firmly embedded in the structure and culture of many organizations. Indeed it may even be the 'natural' response, as suggested by Campion and Stevens' (1991) study showing that naive participants (college students) in work design simulations intuitively opt for job simplification.

DESIGNING WORK: ESTABLISHED THEORY AND PRACTICE

Early Research and Practice

At the time that job simplification was taking hold in industry, studies began to emerge supporting intuitive views about its psychological costs. Over nearly three decades, investigations in the UK of such jobs as bicycle chain assembly showed that simplified work was dissatisfying and not necessarily more productive (e.g., Wyatt & Ogden, 1924), and could even damage mental health (Fraser, 1947). Research conducted in the US resulted in similar conclusions (e.g., Walker & Guest, 1952).

The main recommendations for job 'redesign' to which the above research gave rise were for job rotation and horizontal job enlargement. *Job rotation* involves employees moving at regular intervals between (simplified) jobs. The jobs remain unchanged, but people are not tied to one narrow set of tasks. This form of job redesign can reduce employees' boredom, provide physical relief from repetitive movements, and enhance workforce flexibility. In contrast, *horizontal job enlargement* involves expanding the range of activities in a given job. For example, an office employees' job might be changed from carrying out only filing for many clients to carrying out all key clerical tasks (filing, mail, typing, etc.) for fewer clients.

Another example of job enlargement is to expand the content of machine operators' jobs so that they not only load and unload their equipment, but also set up their machines and inspect the quality of their work. Walker (1950) evaluated just such an initiative within an American IBM plant, and found that the redesign resulted in positive outcomes such as improved quality and much reduced set-up and inspection times. Many similar programs and outcomes were reported around this time in different national contexts (e.g., Thornley & Valentine, 1968). On the whole, job enlargement was shown to have positive, albeit not especially marked, effects for employees and organizations (Davis & Canter, 1956). A limitation, however, is that although the approach expands the range of tasks it does little to put the 'thinking' back into 'doing' the job.

Major Theoretical and Practical Developments: 1950s to 1980s

Herzberg's Two-Factor Theory and Job Enrichment

It was not until the mid-twentieth century that theories of work design began to be formulated. An early influential example is the Two-Factor (or Motivation-Hygiene) Theory (Herzberg, 1966; Herzberg, Mausner & Snyderman, 1959). Herzberg and colleagues used a critical incidents technique to obtain evidence on peoples' causal attributions for times when they had been particularly satisfied and dissatisfied at work. It was found that the reasons for satisfaction were typically intrinsic to the work itself (e.g., opportunity for achievement), whereas those associated with dissatisfaction were extrinsic (e.g., company policy). This led to the idea that the determinants of satisfaction (motivator factors) differed from those that determined dissatisfaction (hygiene factors).

The simplicity of this idea made it amenable to application. From it emerged the notion of *job enrichment*, described by Paul and Robertson (1970: 17) as 'building into peoples' jobs, quite specifically, greater scope for personal achievement, recognition (and) more challenging and responsible work'. In other words, to obtain positive effects it was necessary to capitalize on intrinsic rather than extrinsic factors. In contrast to job rotation or horizontal job enlargement, job enrichment entails enhancing the discretion people exercise in carrying out their work, thus reversing the vertical division of labor that Taylor sought to achieve. For example, an enriched job could involve an employee making their own decisions about the methods and timing of their tasks, rather than a supervisor making these decisions. It is in putting this vertical dimension back on the agenda that the significance of Herzberg's work lies.

Paradoxically, the Two Factor Theory and the practice of job enrichment to which it gave rise, have fared very differently. The theory lost credibility as subsequent studies using different methods failed to replicate the original results (Wall & Stephenson, 1970). The idea of job enrichment, however, has survived, and is central to contemporary notions such as that of empowerment.

The Job Characteristics Model

A theory that has better stood the test of time, and also promoted job enrichment, is Hackman and Oldham's (1976, 1980) Job Characteristics Model. Drawing on earlier work (Turner & Lawrence, 1965; Hackman & Lawler, 1971), these authors identified five *core job characteristics*: skill variety (requiring different skills; SV), task identity (completing a whole piece of work, TI), task significance (having an impact on other people, TS), autonomy (having choice and discretion, A), and feedback (obtaining feedback about performance from the job, F).

These job characteristics were posited to result in three *critical psychological states*: the first three leading to *experienced meaningfulness* of the work; autonomy promoting *experienced responsibility*; and feedback determining *knowledge of results* of work activities. The critical psychological states in turn were suggested collectively to promote work satisfaction, internal work motivation, work performance, and to reduce absence and turnover. Additionally, an individual's *growth need strength* (i.e., desire for challenge and personal development) was proposed to moderate the relationships, with stronger effects predicted for individuals with stronger growth needs. Other moderators (knowledge and skill, and satisfaction with the work context) were added in later formulations of the model (Oldham, 1996).

A feature of the model was that the five core job characteristics were combined into a single index of the overall potential of a job to promote work motivation (the *motivating potential score* (MPS). This formula $[MPS = (SV + TI + TS)/3 \times A \times F)]$ weights autonomy and feedback more heavily than the other core job characteristics. The researchers also developed a set of measures for the variables in the model (the Job Diagnostic Survey; Hackman & Oldham, 1975), which contributed to the popularity of the approach.

There is no doubt that the Job Characteristics Model was an important development. Indeed, many of its principles are central to current notions of empowerment (e.g., Spreitzer, 1995) and high involvement management (Lawler, 1992). However, as with the Two-Factor Theory, not all of the model's predictions have been supported (for reviews see: Fried & Ferris, 1987; Parker & Wall, 1998; Roberts & Glick, 1981). Some of the key problems are that the mediating role of the critical psychological states has not been confirmed; the five job characteristics have not always been shown to be distinctive; a simple additive score has proved to be as strongly related to outcomes as the complex MPS score, if not more so; the assumed positive interrelationships among the outcome variables are not consistent with other research findings (e.g., job satisfaction and performance are only weakly correlated); and the model considers only narrow range of work characteristics and outcomes. We expand on this last criticism later.

Although incorrect in some of its finer points, the core proposition of the model, that the specified job characteristics can be important determinants of the outcomes, has been supported. On the whole, stronger and more consistent effects have been demonstrated for attitudinal outcomes (job satisfaction and internal work motivation) than for behavioral ones (performance, absence) (see Fried & Ferris, 1987;

Kelly, 1992). Growth need strength has also been found to be an important moderating variable.

The Socio-Technical Systems Approach and Autonomous Work Groups

The Two-Factor Theory and the Job Characteristics Model both concern individual work design. The sociotechnical systems (STS) approach, in contrast, reflects a broader organizational perspective with the focus on group work design. The approach originated at the Tavistock Institute of Human Relations in London during the 1950s (Trist & Bamforth, 1951), and is based on a distinction between the social and technical subsystems of organizations, and the proposal that there should be joint optimization and parallel design of the two (also taking account of the fit with the external environment). More specific principles include that methods of working should be minimally specified, and that variances in work processes (e.g., breakdowns) should be handled at source (Cherns, 1976).

Applied to work design, the STS approach gave rise to the idea of *autonomous work groups* (alternative terms include self-managing or self-directed groups or work teams). It is significant that the recommended work properties for such groups, independently specified, parallel those of the Job Characteristics Model. For example, it was proposed that groups should have a variety of meaningful tasks to complete, and a clear area of decision-making authority. The latter was expected to include members being able to decide among themselves on the work methods to use and to manage most operational problems. Group members were also expected to have responsibility beyond the task itself, such as making collective decisions about training team members and managing group resources. Changes in supervision style, selection, training, payment and information systems often accompany this form of work redesign.

A notable example of the use of autonomous work groups is that of Volvo in Udvella, Sweden, where, breaking away from assembly-line work which dominates car making, teams of around nine employees were responsible for assembling a whole car. Later examples include Levi Strauss, AT & T, and Xerox (Appelbaum & Batt, 1994).

The effects of autonomous work groups on employee and organizational outcomes have been widely investigated (for reviews see: Beekun, 1989; Cummings, Molloy & Glen, 1977; Guzzo, Jette & Katzell, 1985; Pasmore, Francis, Haldeman & Shani, 1982). Many positive outcomes have been documented, such as: reduced costs; decreased absenteeism and turnover; reduced accidents; enhanced organizational commitment; increased perceived opportunities for skill use; improved mental health; and faster customer service. However, only a handful of studies have had comparative or longitudinal research designs. These have generally shown positive effects of autonomous groups on job satisfaction (e.g., Cohen & Ledford, 1994; Cordery, Mueller & Smith, 1991; Goodman, 1979; Wall, Kemp, Jackson & Clegg, 1986). As was the case with job enrichment, however, results are less consistent in relation to the effects of autonomous work groups for other outcomes such as mental health and particularly performance (Goodman, Devadas & Griffith-Hughson, 1988; but see Pasmore, 1988). As we describe later, we believe clearer findings will be obtained when we better understand the circumstances affecting the viability of such work design initiatives.

Criticisms have been levelled at the STS approach to work design (e.g., Kompier, 1996). Problems include the rather vague recommendations about work characteristics and their expected consequences; an overemphasis on mass production; a tendency to see autonomous work groups as the only solution; and insufficient attention to organizational culture or individual differences. Another criticism is that the STS approach does not deal directly with the political issues surrounding the balancing of human and efficiency criteria (Moldaschl & Weber, 1998). Nevertheless, there is no doubt that the sociotechnical systems approach is one of enduring value, and the practical idea of autonomous work groups has been one of the major contributors to work redesign practice.

BEYOND ESTABLISHED WORK DESIGN THEORY

Despite their differences, the approaches to work design described above have much in common. They are all based on the premise that job characteristics affect individual and organizational outcomes, and they show convergence with regard to the particular characteristics and outcomes of interest. This allows consideration of their common limitations. The most general criticism is that they are narrowly conceived. Perhaps this reflects the context of job simplification against which the approaches were developed. Nonetheless, it is the case that these approaches do not systematically consider the antecedents or context of work design; focus on a limited set of work characteristics and outcomes; assume motivation to be the main or even sole mechanism underlying the relationship between job characteristics and outcomes; do not fully identify individual or organizational factors that might influence the effectiveness or appropriateness of particular work designs; and do not consider the process of work redesign. In this section, we consider ways to constructively extend work design theory to address these limitations (see Parker & Wall, 1998 for a more detailed discussion).

Antecedents

A long-standing criticism of work design research is that it has failed to take account of contextual factors that influence and constrain the choice of work design (Clegg, 1984). Many of these are internal organizational factors, such as managerial or supervisory style (e.g., close, directive supervision implies low autonomy); the nature of technology and tasks (e.g., assembly lines limit the potential for job variety and autonomy; the type of task affects job complexity, Wood, 1986); and organizational strategy, structure, culture, reward systems, and human resource policies (e.g. individual bonus payment systems inhibit group work design; and information systems can negate autonomy, Clegg & Fitter, 1978). Separately or in combination, these factors can help shape and influence work design.

Work design antecedents can also be external to the organization, such as the nature of the environment (e.g., greater uncertainty about type of output required may increase cognitive demands); political and labor institutions (e.g., industry-based demarcation lines can prevent some forms of work design); the availability of new technology; social customs; economic circumstances; and the nature of the labor market (Burns & Stalker, 1961; Frenkel, Korczynski, Shire & Tam, 1999). In the latter case, for example, a lack of skill in the labor market may limit the extent to which enriched work design is feasible. Indeed, it is not a coincidence that job simplification arose at a time when, because factory work was a new departure, relevant skills were by definition scarce.

Finally, as implicit in the discussion of labor markets above, attention might also be paid to individual level antecedents of work design. Virtually no attempt has been made to determine the extent to which work design is influenced by the characteristics of employees. Yet it is reasonable to assume that the degree of autonomy in a job will at least in part reflect the abilities of people to respond to such an opportunity, and that people with more to offer may mould the nature of the work to their own abilities. Research has shown, for example, that more proactive individuals are likely to expand their task domain through a process of role making (e.g., Graen, 1976).

There are, therefore, various organizational, environmental and individual antecedents of work design that vary in their proximity and the nature of their influence. Incorporating these antecedents into work design theory will allow better prediction of the likely work designs found in particular settings, as well as better prediction of the feasibility of alternative forms of work design for these contexts. It also reminds us that there may be ways of changing work design in ways other than by directly manipulating job characteristics, such as by running leadership development programs or introducing flexible technologies.

An Expanded Set of Work Characteristics and Outcomes

A further limitation of the work characteristics approach as developed so far is the narrow range of independent and dependent variables it encompasses. For example, as noted by many (e.g., Oldham, 1996; Wall & Martin, 1987), there are important job features over and above the five identified in the Job Characteristics Model. These relate to physical characteristics, such as work load and physical context; job security; the opportunity for skill acquisition; social aspects, such as social contact, social interaction and social support; various types of demands such as cognitive demand, the costs associated with error, performance monitoring pressures, and home–work conflict; and role features such as role ambiguity, role conflict, role overload. As we shall expand upon later, many of these additional characteristics have become more important because of the changes occurring in the workplace. For example, the opportunity to acquire skills (especially those that are transferable) is likely to become increasingly salient as downsizing and related changes result in employees needing to move from one organization to another more frequently.

Although there has been research demonstrating that the above factors affect well-being and performance at work, they have not been integrated into work design theory. As a consequence we do not know whether such factors add to, interact with or are accounted for by the traditional focus on variables such as autonomy and variety. Extending the range of work characteristics we investigate, and looking at how they relate to existing work design variables, is necessary to more fully understand the effects of modern changes on job content, and to design jobs that promote desired outcomes.

A particular weakness in the current approaches to work design concerns an imbalance in the types of work characteristic measures available. Considerable effort has been devoted to developing measures of individual job properties, but much less to team work properties. Team work is becoming increasingly popular in practice, and there is considerable value in examining group level work characteristics. This means not only covering the work design dimensions of traditional concern at the group level (e.g., team autonomy), but also properties that are a function of groups or teams per se, such as the degree of cohesion among members. This line of development will gain from considering models of group effectiveness (e.g., Campion, Medsker & Higgs, 1993) that focus attention on a broader range of predictors than just the nature of the tasks, such as the organizational context (e.g., rewards, training) and group diversity.

Interactions between work characteristics have also rarely been considered in traditional job design research. The demand–control model of job stress (Karasek, 1979) has taken the lead in this respect. A high level of demands is proposed to result in only average strain when one also has high autonomy (a so-called *active job*), but if the high demands co-occur with low autonomy then a *high strain* job results. Evidence regarding the hypothesized interaction effect is mixed, but the idea remains an appealing one since the implication is that demands can be increased without causing stress so long as autonomy is also increased.

On the other side of the coin, the outcomes of traditional interest are narrowly drawn, and need not be so limited. Whereas job satisfaction, motivation, attendance behavior, and performance will remain central to the agenda, individual or group work characteristics are also likely to affect other outcomes such as safety behavior, industrial relations attitudes, grievances, outside work relationships, leisure activities, and even individual learning and development.

Regarding the latter, research has traditionally focused mostly on how people react to job content in the short term, but a growing body of research suggests work redesign affects people in the longer term. Studies have shown a link between enhanced autonomy and cognitive development (Kohn & Schooler, 1978); the application and development of knowledge (Wall, Jackson & Davids, 1992); the greater use of personal initiative (Frese, Kring, Soose & Zempel, 1996); the development of more proactive role orientations (Parker, Wall & Jackson, 1997); and increased self-efficacy (Parker, 1998). This evidence suggests that work redesign is not just a motivational technique, as it is often narrowly construed, but is an intervention that promotes learning and growth. Such a perspective is entirely consistent with Action Theory, a German development (Hacker, Skell & Straub, 1968) that has recently been made accessible in English (Frese & Zapf, 1994). We cannot do justice to the theory here, but its basic tenet, that work is goal-directed and action-oriented, leads to an emphasis on learning and employee personality development through work redesign.

The above is a long list of additional independent and dependent variables to be considered in future research. We are not arguing that any one study or even theory should attempt to cover them all. Rather, the message is that the time is now ripe to expand the horizons of work design research along the above lines, as well as to take on board the additional issues discussed next.

Mechanisms

A weakness of contemporary approaches is their failure to specify the mechanisms through which work design has its effects. It might be argued that the Job Characteristics Model can be excluded from this charge, as it includes critical psychological states as mediators. However, these have not been shown to account for the effects of work characteristics on outcomes as predicted (Fried & Ferris, 1987), and indeed these states have been found to be unnecessary as mediators (Wall, Clegg & Jackson, 1978).

Fundamentally, the assumption underpinning current work design theory is that the mechanism is motivational, at least as far as performance effects are concerned. This is certainly explicit in the Two Factor Theory, though perhaps less so in the Job Characteristics Model (where, oddly, motivation is categorized as a joint outcome with performance). In the sociotechnical systems approach the mechanisms are even less clear.

So why should jobs designed to enhance employee autonomy or self-management enhance performance? Kelly (1992) suggested several possibilities, including some that elaborate on the motivational theme. One was that job redesign might entail improved goal-setting which is known to have motivational properties; or alternatively it may create closer perceived links between effort, performance, and valued rewards. Clearly, a motivational component in the link between work design and outcomes has to be assumed, but there are several other pathways to consider. One mechanism, implicit in the sociotechnical principle that variances should be controlled at source, is that giving employees responsibility for tasks otherwise completed by support staff means that employees can deal with disruptive events as and when those arise. Thus increased responsibility for problem management can enable quicker responses to performance threatening events.

Employee learning and development also potentially explain performance gains as a result of work design initiatives. As we described above, studies have shown that increased autonomy can promote changes in role orientation (e.g., greater internalization of quality concerns), self-efficacy, personal initiative and cognitive development; and these types of changes are highly likely to lead to better performance. Indeed, two studies of work redesign for operators of complex manufacturing technology have shown how performance benefited from the prevention of operational problems that previously had not been resolved. In other words, employees were not working harder, but 'smarter' (Jackson & Wall, 1991; Wall, Jackson & Davids, 1992). Performance gains that occur as a result of work redesign might therefore be due as much to quicker responses and learning as to motivational benefits, or the combination of all three.

Similar questions about mechanisms apply to the relationship between work content and other outcomes such as job strain and safety. Frese (1989;

see also Jackson, 1989) proposed several ways that autonomy might prevent job strain, such as by enabling employees to directly reduce stressful work aspects (for example, having the control to shut a noisy door) or by reducing the negative impact of stressful work aspects (for example, having the autonomy to take rest breaks could reduce the impact of repetitive work). Strain might also be reduced via a learning mechanism, as Karasek and Theorell (1990) proposed in an extension to the demand–control model of strain. They suggested that well-designed jobs promote mastery, which in turn helps people to cope with the strain caused by the job.

The above suggestions are largely speculative, being supported by very limited empirical data. The key point is that the nature of the mechanisms underlying the effects of work design have been mostly neglected by researchers. We know *that* work design can affect behavior and attitudes at work, but we have little systematic evidence of *why*. Yet if we ascertain why a given work characteristic or more general work design affects outcomes, it will be easier to judge the circumstances under which a particular form of work design will and will not be effective. The significance of this last point emerges in the following section.

Contingencies

Work design theory has been largely universalistic in nature. Yet it is plausible to assume that alternative forms of work design will be more or less effective under different conditions. In other words, there will be contingencies that affect the appropriateness and outcomes of work design.

At the individual level, the contingency factor that has received the most attention is that of *growth need strength*. Most research has confirmed that job enrichment is most likely to lead to positive outcomes for individuals high in growth need strength (Spector, 1985). Studies of other individual level moderator variables (e.g., need for achievement, the Protestant Work Ethic), however, have produced less consistent results. In addition, some potentially important individual difference variables like proactivity, self-efficacy, and tolerance of ambiguity have received little attention. A study by Parker and Sprigg (1999), for example, showed that proactive personality moderated the interactive effect of job autonomy and demands on job strain.

Though knowledge of individual differences as contingencies is scant, that for organizational factors has a stronger theoretical base. Cummings and Blumberg (1987) proposed three variables that affect the choice of work design. The first is *technical interdependence*, or the degree of required cooperation to make a product or service. When there is high technical interdependence, and employees need to interact and share information to get the job done (as in a hockey team), work should be designed at the group level to facilitate the coordination of interrelated tasks. Low technical interdependence, such as in the job of a lighthouse keeper, implies a need for individual job redesign such as enlargement or enrichment because there is little need for cooperation. The implication is that a mismatch between the form of work design and the degree of interdependence will lead to underperformance or employee dissatisfaction (see Sprigg et al., 2000, for an example study).

The second factor is *technical uncertainty*, or the amount of information processing and decision-making required when executing the task. Software developers using computer tools that are frequently being updated, for example, experience such uncertainty in that they have to keep changing how they complete the work. In these situations, decision-making should be devolved to the employees because it is not possible to specify rules or procedures for all the uncertainties that arise; neither is it possible for a supervisor or manager to make all, or the best, decisions. Control can be achieved by setting and monitoring goals, and by establishing norms of appropriate behavior, whilst allowing considerable discretion over how these are achieved (Ouchi, 1977). In contrast, when there is low technical uncertainty, such as when an employee is producing a highly standardized product on a very reliable machine, control can be achieved through rules and procedures or direct supervisory control (Clegg, 1984).

Cummings and Blumberg (1987) made similar arguments in relation to *environmental uncertainty*, that is variability from external sources such as change in customer requirements or market demand. To the extent that this affects requirements for employees (e.g., to deliver services to different specifications), the implication is that more autonomous work designs are best. This argument reflects the tenets of more general organizational theory, which proposes that 'mechanistic' structures involving routinized tasks and centralized decision-making are appropriate for stable and predictable conditions, and that 'organic' structures with decentralized decision-making are best for more uncertain and complex environments (e.g., Burns & Stalker, 1961).

Both technical and environmental uncertainty can be manifest at the job level in equivalent ways, so for work design purposes they can sensibly be considered as together as *operational uncertainty*. The implication for work design is that more autonomous forms will be most appropriate where there is high operational uncertainty, whereas more simplified forms of work design will be effective where operational uncertainty is low. Empirical support for this proposition comes from a study by Wall, Corbett, Martin, Clegg and Jackson (1990), who compared the effect of enhanced operator control over complex technology characterized by different levels of operational uncertainty. For machines with low uncertainty, no performance benefits were recorded. In contrast, where machines were liable to frequent operational problems (e.g., because of the delicacy of the product they dealt with), the increase in operator control led to substantial performance gains. A complementary study of group work design showed similar results (Cordery, Wright, Morrison & Wall, in preparation), and although we are aware of no studies that have tested this, parallel arguments have been made in relation to empowerment within white collar settings (Bowen & Lawler, 1992).

It is interesting to note how operational uncertainty as a contingency relates to the earlier discussion of learning-based mechanisms (see p. 95). Essentially, uncertainty means a lack of knowledge about when problems will arise and how best to deal with them (Jackson, 1989). Thus in conditions of low operational uncertainty, events are predictable and the means of dealing with them known; the 'one best way' of doing the job can therefore be determined and enforced. Where there is high operational uncertainty, in contrast, problems are less predictable as are the means of solving them. This implies that, in uncertain situations, structuring work in a way that promotes learning and enables this to be applied will be both possible and important. In the words of Wall and Jackson (1995: 163), 'production uncertainty is important as a contingency because it defines the conditions under which knowledge development and application can occur and affect performance'.

From the above evidence it is clear that operational uncertainty is a strong candidate as an organizational contingency variable linking work design to performance, one which needs to be integrated into theory. The failure to do so may well explain the apparently inconsistent performance effects of work design recorded to date. In addition there are other organizational factors that can affect whether job redesign leads to the predicted outcomes, such as those concerned with the process of introducing work redesign; adequacy of training; appropriateness of reward systems; level of job security; management style; and culture. Regarding the latter, for example, work design theory is largely derived from studies of industrialized Western jobs, and therefore theory and practice are likely to need adapting for other cultures (e.g., Nicholls, Lane & Brechu, 1999). The general point is that we need to establish which contingencies are important, and incorporate them into our theoretical frameworks. Until then, the practice of work redesign will remain a very inexact and unpredictable process, and research findings will continue to be inconsistent. We turn to the particular importance of understanding the process of introducing work redesign next.

Work Design and Redesign Processes

Most of the above criticisms of existing work design theory concern the 'what' and 'why' of work design. A further challenge concerns giving greater attention to the 'how' of work design, or the processes involved in successfully designing and redesigning work roles. Work redesign is rarely a straightforward or short-term intervention, particularly as it typically involves a redistribution of responsibility and power. Redesigning work roles requires careful consideration of implications for multiple stakeholders (e.g., employees, supervisors, managers, support staff, unions), as well as alignment between the work design system and other human resources, control, information, and technology systems (Parker & Wall, 1998). It is also a dynamic and evolving intervention that requires considerable learning and adjustment (Mohrman, Cohen & Mohrman, 1995).

Despite the complexity of work redesign processes, there is remarkably little research-based guidance to inform practitioners about how to achieve this type of change successfully (Hackman & Oldham, 1980; Oldham, 1996). For example, to what extent should employees participate in work redesign and how should this process be managed? How do you motivate employees who have been in long-term simplified jobs to be interested in enrichment? How do the expectations and needs of employees change over the work design process?

To investigate these and other such questions, we advocate studies that are designed specifically to investigate work design change processes (e.g., Campion and Stevens, 1991); the wider reporting of process issues in studies assessing the outcome of work redesign; the development of research-based tools and guidelines to assist practitioners in redesigning work (see Franklin, Pain, Green & Owen, 1992, for a human-centered approach to redesign); and a more pluralistic research approach including qualitative methods and drawing on perspectives from disciplines other than psychology (e.g., sociology, anthropology, management, and engineering). Regarding the latter point, there is likely to be value in complementing the dominant positivist tradition to consider other methods of inquiry. For example, Hardy and Leiba-O'Sullivan (1998: 472) criticized mainstream approaches to the study of empowerment, which they argued 'skirt the issue of power' and, in so doing, make employees vulnerable to its abuse. These researchers recommended a more critical approach informed by postmodern perspectives in which power is put back into the equation.

Work design theory has therefore not developed much in regard to understanding the processes involved in implementing and sustaining work redesign. Researchers recommending redesign will be in a stronger position to influence practice if they can simultaneously give theoretically-sound and empirically-derived advice about how to manage the change process.

Summary

The aim of this section has been to suggest avenues along which work design theory should be developed; these suggestions are summarized in Table 5.1. Of course, there are also alternatives to the job characteristics approach that have informed our knowledge of work design, and we describe these next.

COMPLEMENTARY APPROACHES IN WORK DESIGN RESEARCH

As well as the dominant theories of work design described thus far, there are complementary theoretical perspectives which serve to broaden the agenda for work design research. We have already noted above two approaches that have implications for work design theory; German action theory and the demand–control model of strain. Additional contributions come from the social information processing approach, an interdisciplinary perspective on job design, and models of group effectiveness.

Social Information Processing Approach

The job characteristics theories assume that there are 'objective' job characteristics that employees perceive and react to. However, the Social Information Processing Approach (Salancik & Pfeffer, 1977) questions this assumption, and proposes that social cues determine reactions to jobs (e.g., Griffin, 1983; O'Reilly & Caldwell, 1979, 1985). Put simply, the argument is that if an employee is told by others that the job is interesting and autonomous, s/he will believe it. Many studies have investigated this proposition by simultaneously manipulating social cues and objective job properties (e.g., Griffin, Bateman, Wayne & Head, 1987). Meta-analyses of these studies show that, although social information does indeed affect employees' job ratings, objective job features have a much stronger effect on how people see their jobs (Taber & Taylor, 1990). Changing objective features of jobs is thus more likely to result in positive outcomes such as job satisfaction than simply manipulating social cues, although these studies show that it is nevertheless important to consider social aspects (such as supervisory communications) when redesigning work.

An Interdisciplinary Perspective on Work Design

Campion and colleagues (Campion, 1988, 1989; Campion & Berger, 1990; Campion & McClelland, 1991, 1993; Campion & Thayer, 1985, 1987) summarized four distinct models of work design from the literature, each varying in their derivation, recommendations for design, and anticipated costs and benefits. Two of these approaches we have already discussed. The *motivational approach* refers to the job characteristics theories and is basically concerned with designing enriched jobs. The benefits of motivational work design are proposed to include satisfaction, motivation, better job performance, and lower absenteeism, while anticipated costs include longer training times, more chance of error, and a greater likelihood of mental overload and stress. The *mechanistic approach* derives from classic industrial engineering and is basically concerned with designing simplified and Taylorized jobs. Benefits include faster training times, less chance of error, and less chance of overload, while costs include lower satisfaction, motivation and higher absence.

The two additional models summarized by Campion and colleagues are the *biological* and the *perceptual-motor* approaches. The former emerged from fields such as bio-mechanics, work physiology, and ergonomics. The aim is to minimize employee physical stress and strain, by improving the ergonomic design of work stations. Expected benefits include lower fatigue, better physical health, fewer aches and pains, and fewer injuries; whereas costs include the expenses associated with modifying equipment and making changes to the environment. The *perceptual-motor* approach is concerned with ensuring cognitive capabilities are not exceeded by job demands. This approach arose out of research in such areas as human factors engineering, skilled performance and human information processing. Benefits of jobs designed in this way include a reduced likelihood of errors and accidents, reduced mental overload, fatigue, stress and boredom and lower training times. An important cost, however, may be decreased job satisfaction due to a lack of stimulating mental demands.

Investigations by Campion and colleagues show that the different approaches to job design largely give rise to the costs and benefits they proposed (Campion & Thayer, 1985; Campion, 1988), although there are methodological limitations of many of these studies (Parker & Wall, 1998). A methodologically improved study (Campion & McClelland, 1993) showed more complex results of the motivational approach than the model proposed. There were benefits when jobs were expanded in terms of the number of products employees had to understand ('knowledge enlargement'), but when employees did more tasks with the same product

Table 5.1   *An expanded framework for work design research and theory*

	Traditional work design theory	Recommended extensions	Advantages of extended approach
Antecedents	• Little or no consideration of contextual or individual factors that constrain or shape work design	• Consider internal organizational factors that shape work design (e.g., management style, culture, reward systems) • Consider external factors that shape work design (e.g., environmental uncertainty, social customs, labor markets) • Consider individual-level factors that shape work design (e.g., proactive employees take on broader roles)	• Better predicts what work designs will occur in particular contexts (e.g., different cultures) • Better predicts feasibility of alternative work designs • Links work design theory into broader organizational and labor process literatures • Highlights ways that work designs can be changed
Range of work characteristics and outcomes	• Narrow focus on core individual-level work characteristics (autonomy, skill variety, task identity, task significance, task feedback) • Narrow set of outcomes, most focus on affective reactions (e.g., job satisfaction and strain)	• Consider a broader range of work characteristics (e.g., physical aspects, role conflict, cognitive demands, performance monitoring, work load, time pressure), investigate interactions between work characteristics, and consider group-level work characteristics • Consider a wider range of outcomes (e.g., contextual performance; accidents and safety; learning and development outcomes such as initiative, knowledge and self-efficacy; and non-work effects such as family relationships)	Including more salient work features: • enhances prediction of outcomes and therefore enables the design of better jobs • allows fuller understanding of the effects of new work practices and technologies Including additional outcomes: • promotes understanding of full range of consequences of work design for individuals and organizations • highlights use of work design to promote outcomes traditionally seen as unrelated to work design
Mechanisms linking work characteristics and outcomes	• Assumed performance gains derive from extra effort (i.e. motivational mechanism) • Assumed well-being gains are based on motivation, need fulfillment and intrinsic interest	• Consider additional performance mechanisms (e.g., the 'quick response'; learning and development, such as promoting performance through knowledge acquisition) • Consider learning and development pathways for well-being (e.g., job design promotes a sense of mastery which helps individuals to cope with job demands)	• Promotes understanding of why work design has the effects it does • Enables predictions about the circumstances under which various forms of work design will be effective

(Contd.)

Table 5.1 *(Contd.)*

	Traditional work design theory	Recommended extensions	Advantages of extended approach
Contingencies	• Most attention to individual difference factors, especially growth need strength	• Expand the range of individual differences considered (e.g., tolerance of ambiguity, preference for group work) • Consider organizational factors (e.g., production uncertainty; interdependence; support for training and type of rewards; methods of implementation)	• Identifies who will benefit most from particular forms of work design • Predicts what types of work design will be most appropriate for particular contexts • Explains inconsistencies in findings linking work characteristics to outcomes
Processes	• Little attention given to the processes involved in redesigning work	• Consider processes involved in redesigning work (e.g., effect of employee participation) • Consider dynamic nature of work design (e.g., changing employee expectations and needs)	• Influences practice by providing practitioners with research-based tools and guidance for successfully redesigning work • Links work design theory into wider organizational change and development theories

Source: Adapted from Parker and Wall, 1998, p. 30.

('task enlargement') there were long-term costs such as lower satisfaction and more errors.

This latter study highlights the importance of distinguishing between different types of motivational work design. However, such distinctions were not built into Campion and colleagues' description of the motivational model. Perhaps a necessary trade-off given the breadth of the interdisciplinary orientation, the motivational approach is rather oversimplified in this and other respects. In addition, the proposed outcomes are not necessarily supported in the literature (e.g., there is little evidence that mental overload and stress occur as a result of motivational work redesign), and some important benefits of motivational job redesign are not indicated (such as faster response time to problems, employee learning and greater flexibility). Parker and Wall (1998) proposed that one way to develop the interdisciplinary approach is to build organizational contingencies into the framework. The different models, or combinations of them, might suit different contexts. For example, as proposed earlier, the motivational approach to work design might be most suited to highly uncertain environments.

An important contribution of this interdisciplinary perspective is that it makes clear how different professionals are likely to have contrasting underlying values and assumptions about how best to design jobs. It suggests the need to reduce the compartmentalization within organizations to help avoid the problem of specialists approaching topics such as work design purely from their own narrow framework (Campion & Thayer, 1985).

Models of Group Effectiveness

To date, we have described the sociotechnical systems perspective on designing work groups. However, other models have been developed to further elaborate how group work should be designed and supported to maximize its effectiveness (e.g., Campion, Medsker & Higgs, 1993; Cohen & Ledford, 1994; Cohen, Ledford & Spreitzer, 1996; Gladstein, 1984; Hackman, 1987). For example, Hackman's (1987) Normative Model of Group Effectiveness proposes that, assuming the necessary material resources are present, an increase in various *process criteria* (i.e., effort, knowledge, and appropriateness of task performance strategies) will lead to more effective work group. There are three levers, or inputs, that affect the process criteria. The first is *group design*, comprising organizing tasks so that members have a good work design (e.g., job variety and autonomy), designing an appropriate group composition (e.g., the right number and diversity of people), and ensuring the group has appropriate norms about performance. The other two levers concern the *organizational context*, or having the appropriate

reward, education, and information systems to support and reinforce effective performance, and *group synergy*, that is ways to help the group to interact effectively.

Models such as Hackman's (1987) are important developments on the earlier sociotechnical systems approach to group work design. They include a more precise delineation of how various group features link to outcomes, and they also encompass aspects that have received less attention in traditional research on autonomous work groups, such as consideration of the broader organizational systems and the role of group processes. There is general support for the main components of these models. For example, Campion, Papper and Medsker (1996) reported that team effectiveness was most strongly predicted by various process characteristics (such as the degree of social support and communication within the team) and job design features (the degree of self-management, variety, etc.). Contextual characteristics and the level of interdependence were predictive to a lesser extent, and various composition characteristics (such as group heterogeneity) were inconsistently related to effectiveness.

One issue, however, is that most investigations of team effectiveness models remain cross-sectional. They suffer from many of the methodological problems that have long been observed in work design research. Moreover, with some recent exceptions (e.g., Druskat & Kayes, 1999), most of the tests of the models do not examine the specific mediating or moderating pathways that have been proposed. Parker and Wall (1998) recommended conceptual development and refinement of these models. They also recommended, along with Cordery (1996), more attention to the social and cognitive processes within groups. A recent study, for example, has shown the importance of teams having shared mental models for effective group processes and ultimately team effectiveness (Mathieu, Heffner, Goodwin, Salas & Cannon-Bowers, 2000).

WORK DESIGN IN THE FUTURE

The call for a more comprehensive approach to work design is given added weight and direction by changes currently underway in the world of work. New technologies, practices and forms of work make it clear that traditional concerns with job simplification remain salient, but at the same time they give substance to the view that there is a need to broaden the approach. In this section, we look at some developments in the nature of work, and the directions these suggest for the future of work design theory and practice. We start with the wider context.

The Developing Work Context

Spurred by a global marketplace, more demanding customers, new enabling technologies, and various economic and political developments, many organizations are changing in fundamental ways in their attempt to maintain or increase their competitiveness. Traditional distinctions between departments are disappearing, and organizations are becoming more integrated and 'boundaryless' in order to enable the rapid delivery of low cost, high quality and customized products (Dean & Snell, 1991) and to provide customers with seamless service (Davis, 1995). Many organizations are becoming leaner through downsizing and the growth of a large contingent workforce. Boundaries between organizations are also blurring, as shown by a growth in new forms such as network organizations in which independent firms work together through joint ventures, subcontracting, franchising, strategic partnerships and the like.

Developments in information technology in particular are beginning to have major implications for work (Van der Spiegel, 1995). Faxes, modems, the Internet, notebook computers, and other such computer-based systems allow employees to share information even though they are separated by time and space. Thus for many kinds of service, employees no longer need to work in a designated 'office'. Telecommuters can now operate from elsewhere, such as at home (teleworking), and employees in different locations and on different schedules can work together as 'virtual teams' (Mohrman & Cohen, 1995). People freed from the constraints of an office can work a 'waking week' rather than the traditional 'working week'.

There are also changes occurring in employment structures. The introduction of labor saving technologies in manufacturing, a growing demand for services, and the loss of lower-skilled production work to lower-wage countries have all led to a decline in manufacturing jobs and a rise in service work. Over the period 1974 to 1994, service sector employment increased by 9%, to 73%, in the United States; by 13% to 71%, in Australia, and by 10% to 60%, in Japan (Organization for Economic Cooperation and Development, 1996). 'Front-line work', that concerned with direct contact with customers, has also grown considerably, as a result of service-based competition now being seen as more than twice as important as cost-based competition (Osterman, 1997).

Future Work Design Priorities

The changes taking place in work have many implications for the development of work design theory and practice. Here we outline five key implications, ranging from more established to newer themes. They concern: the recurrent issue of job simplification; the continued importance of operational uncertainty as an antecedent and contingency variable; interdependence, team working and social complexity as increasingly important work features; a greater emphasis on cognitive demands and knowledge aspects at work; and the effect of demographic and contractual changes on work design.

The Recurrent Job Simplification Issue

The question of job simplification has always been at the center of work design, and looks set to remain so. A widely expressed concern is that new technologies, practices and forms of work will reinforce job simplification. This concern has been most clearly articulated in relation to manufacturing, where the argument can be traced back more than 25 years to Braverman's (1974) analysis of the precursor to current advanced manufacturing technology, the numerically controlled machine tool. In essence, Braverman argued that traditional operator expertise is built into the computer program, making it possible to limit operators to the more mundane tasks of loading, unloading, and monitoring.

The concern that new technology will simplify skilled jobs has been generalized to the more sophisticated forms of computer-based technology that have followed, such as computer-numerically-controlled machines, robots and groupings of such equipment into flexible manufacturing systems. The concern of job simplification has also been raised in relation to complementary initiatives such as just-in-time and total quality management practices (e.g., Delbridge & Turnbull, 1992). For instance, it has been argued that the removal of buffer stocks central to just-in-time reduces employees' autonomy to leave the workstation; and that the standardization of processes involved leads to reduced employee discretion over work methods. To illustrate the latter, Delbridge and Turnbull (1992: 62) cited a training manual that is used at Nissan in which employees are instructed 'you should never change the work procedure at your discretion' because otherwise '[you] may put the process before or after that process in jeopardy, or increase the cost'.

Though starting in manufacturing, concerns about work simplification are not limited to that context; equivalent arguments are now being raised in other domains. A case in point is the fast expanding world of call centers where, in many instances, agents are required to respond to customer inquiries on the basis of computer delivered protocols. This means that the way in which they perform their work is closely prescribed. Additionally, the number of calls agents complete, and how they deal with customers, is often automatically recorded. In effect, information technology can be used to control, monitor and constrain the detail of interactions with customers in ways that would not be possible with traditional technologies (e.g., face-to-face or traditional telephone contact). In a similar way, computer technology can be used to monitor the performance of teleworkers, thereby reducing autonomy and even threatening their privacy.

It is clear, therefore, that job simplification can be perpetuated or accelerated by the changes occurring in the workplace, and the issue remains an important one in future work design research. Nevertheless, this is not the whole story. Some commentators are highly optimistic about the effects of modern changes on work design. For example, it has been argued that the new work practices can reunite conceptual and manual tasks (Abernathy, Clark & Kantrow, 1981); that teleworkers removed from the traditional office will have greater discretion about how and when they do their work (Feldman & Gainey, 1997); and that information technology increases individuals' and teams' access to information (such as customer databases), which means they are able to act more autonomously and make decisions at the point of action (Mohrman & Cohen, 1995).

These two perspectives, that new initiatives at work will lead to the simplification or enrichment of jobs, may not be as contradictory as they first appear. Both may be correct in different cases, and we may expect to see instances of job simplification and enrichment side by side, within and across organizations in the future. Consistent with others (e.g., Dean & Snell, 1991), we suggest that the effect of modern technologies and initiatives on work design depends on the nature of the systems involved, the organizational context (such as the level of uncertainty), and the choices made in organizing work. Research supports this view. For instance, although it is clear that the potential exists for just-in-time to reduce individual autonomy, studies have shown it can enhance group autonomy (Mullarkey, Jackson & Parker, 1995), and that the effects can be influenced by the extent to which operators are involved in designing and implementing the changes (Parker, Myers & Wall, 1995). Likewise, studies have shown mixed effects of information technology on work design, and a range of factors that can influence the nature of the associated work design such as individual difference and demographic variables, system characteristics, and the implementation process.

It is clear there are currently no definitive answers to the question of whether developments in the world of work will lead to greater job simplification. Nor do we expect there to be, for this is probably the wrong question. Rather, the issue is under what circumstances does job simplification arise and when is it most and least effective for different outcomes? We describe next the importance of operational uncertainty in this respect. At this stage, the conclusion to be drawn is that job simplification, along with its antecedents and contingencies,

remains as salient to the future of work design research and practice as it has always been.

Uncertainty as an Antecedent and Contingency

One of the most powerful ideas for guiding the design of work to meet future challenges is likely to remain the principle that the effect of work enrichment is contingent on uncertainty. We presented evidence earlier showing how the impact of enhanced autonomy on performance increased as uncertainty increased, both in the case of individual and group work redesign (see p. 96).

We raise this idea again because many commentators have argued that today's organizations face greater operational uncertainty than they have in the past. For example, the existence of more flexible technology supports meeting more differentiated market demand through greater product customization, and therefore more frequent changes in design and smaller batches. The trend towards more variability and complexity in work processes, and hence in operational uncertainty, looks set to continue. Thus job enrichment and self-management initiatives are put forward as general recipes for future work design (e.g., Hayes, Wheelwright & Clark, 1988). Greater operational uncertainty has therefore been suggested as an antecedent factor that is leading to the wider introduction of autonomous forms of work design.

There is nevertheless a danger of misreading the nature and scale of these trends. Even if there is a move towards greater operational uncertainty, there will be many organizations, and areas of work within organizations, characterized by relatively stable and certain operating conditions. It should not be forgotten that the objective of many initiatives is to reduce uncertainty. In call centers, developments in telecommunications that enable customers to route their calls according to their nature, reduce the range of problems encountered by any one agent. Similarly, quality management programs aim to reduce errors; engineers strive to build ever more reliable machines; supply-chain partnering is designed to eliminate variability in component availability and quality; and lean production aims to eliminate unpredictability (Graham, 1988). Thus, although some forces may be leading towards greater operational uncertainty, developments in technology and various management practices are likely to counteract, and may even sometimes reverse, the effect.

The effect of new technologies and practices on work design, and indeed the choice of work design, is therefore likely to depend partly on the uncertainty of the situation. Niepce and Molleman (1998) argued that lean production methods, which aim to reduce production uncertainty, are most likely to be successful if the tasks are stable, repetitive and uncomplicated. However, they suggested that sociotechnical work designs such as autonomous work groups will be more appropriate if there is high uncertainty because these contexts require 'knowledge about the product and the process as a whole, a larger analytical capability and problem-solving capacities' (p. 277). In this regard, it is interesting to note that critical theorists who have reported deskilling as a result of just-in-time and related initiatives (e.g., Delbridge & Turnbull, 1992) have mostly focused their attention on cases of mass production, such as the automobile industry, where the uncertainties are fewer. Bratton (1993) also showed that cellular manufacturing was likely to lead to deskilling in low uncertainty mass production situations, but was likely to lead to, and require, job enrichment in high uncertainty, small-batch settings.

This does not mean to say that organizations always make the right choices about work design. There is already ample evidence that the frequent failure of new technologies and practices to realize their potential (e.g., Waterson et al., 1999) is often due, not to the initiatives themselves, but to deficiencies in the associated work design (e.g., Hayes et al., 1988). Most often, simplified work designs are retained or introduced in spite of highly uncertain and unpredictable contexts. We can thus expect work designs to be introduced which are not in tune with circumstances, which means that considering operational uncertainty as a contingency variable will continue to be a central issue for the foreseeable future.

Interdependence, Team Working, and Social Complexity

As we described earlier, interdependence is a key criterion on which to distinguish the choice of work design (see page 96); with group-based strategies being most appropriate when there is a high level of interdependence and a strong need for cooperation. We raise interdependence as an issue again here because this feature of work is accentuated in the modern workplace, which in turn creates a need for more group-based forms of work design, and the use of various other lateral integration mechanisms. Interdependence is therefore emerging as an important work characteristic in its own right.

A key feature of the various production technologies and techniques that are being deployed to improve competitiveness (e.g., just-in-time, advanced manufacturing technology) is that they serve to integrate previously separate stages and functions of production (Dean & Snell, 1991). For example, just-in-time involves removing buffers between processes, and hence closer coordination is required than before. Nevertheless, the trend towards increased interdependence is not just restricted to manufacturing, and may be even stronger elsewhere. For example, with complex knowledge-work such as that involving software development or complex product design, the need to integrate separate areas of expertise to arrive at the end product creates a high level of interdependence. The uncertainty about the process signals not only the need for groups, but also teams with sufficient autonomy and information to manage the complex environment (Goodman et al., 1988). However, this is far from a complete picture. As Mohrman et al. (1995) argued, it will not be enough to install teams, we will also need much greater specification of team processes and their interface with the larger organization.

On top of this, to reduce development or design lead times, an emerging practice is for work to be passed electronically between teams working within different time zones across the world. Thus the work process is continuous over 24 hours, even though particular teams work normal hours. Existing work design theory has little to say about this level and kind of interdependence, which is an area manifestly requiring attention. Commentators agree that theory will need development and reorientation to apply to these types of work practices (Mohrman et al., 1995).

Interdependence leads to the identification of another aspect of work likely to play an increasingly important role, that is social and emotional demands (Stevens & Campion, 1994). Work practices such as supply-chain partnering, integration across traditional departments, 24-hour product designs, and virtual team working all place social interaction and communication in key roles. The growth of front-line customer service work also highlights this issue. Such work is people-oriented and involves employees being 'on stage' and carrying out tasks that involve emotional labor (Hochschild, 1989). Employees are expected to display resilience and flexibility in the face of frequent internal and external uncertainties (Frenkel et al., 1999). Thus emotional demands are likely to be very salient in these contexts, and control and support to help manage these demands is likely to be an important work design issue (Frenkel et al., 1999).

Cognitive Demands and Knowledge Aspects at Work

In contrast to the continuities with traditional concerns discussed above, emerging technologies and forms of work underwrite the need for work design approaches to incorporate work characteristics and outcomes hitherto largely ignored. One area of such development to be emphasized is that of cognitive demand. As Howard (1995: 23) observed: 'In the post-industrial information age, the balance of work has tipped from hand to head, from brawn to brain'. For example, it has been suggested that new production technologies emphasize two types of cognitive demand: attentional demand, as a result of increased vigilance requirements (e.g., Van Cott, 1985); and problem-solving demand, because of the need for fault prevention and active diagnosis of errors (e.g., Dean & Snell, 1991). We need to understand the impact of both, as high attentional demand is likely to have a negative impact on employee well-being, while problem-solving demand can add challenge to a job.

The emphasis on understanding the impact of cognitive demand is especially true in nonproduction settings, such as in research and development, sales and service, and new product development. Information technology often absorbs what is referred to as 'routine knowledge work' (such as processing accounts), and emphasizes complex problem-solving, or 'nonroutine knowledge work' (Mohrman et al., 1995). Likewise, greater product variety and more frequent policy and procedural changes are predicted to enhance the complexity of service work. Front-line workers will be increasingly expected to play multiple roles, such as to provide information, generate revenue through selling, and perform an intelligence-gathering role (Frenkel et al., 1999: 272). As these researchers observed, the cognitive demands will be much greater for service workers of the future who 'will be required to possess more higher-order contextual knowledge (i.e., about industry and market developments) to deal with more complex customer queries and to demonstrate more pervasive selling techniques'.

More generally, the emphasis on knowledge in service and professional settings requires a reorientation of existing work design theory to address questions such as 'What forms of knowledge and expertise are designed into (and out of) work organizations? Why? How does knowledge and expertise get shared and developed?' (Clegg, Waterson & Axtell, 1996: 247). In a related vein, Mohrman et al. (1995) argued that we need greater understanding about what can be done to help people cope with greater cognitive complexity, such as by improving people's ability to process complex information, or by developing 'cognitive' tools to support collaborative decision-making.

Demographic and Contractual Changes

Against the background of short-term employment contracts and careers affected by downsizing, we have pointed to the rising salience for work design of aspects such as the opportunity to gain transferable skills. The growth of temporary contract and part-time work, as well as flexible work patterns such as job share, also highlights the importance of work design issues such as job security and autonomy over working hours. The actual composition of the workforce is also changing in ways that have significance for the design of work. Howard (1995: 33) succinctly captured this idea when she noted that the current US workforce is becoming 'less young, less male, and less white'; a characterization that applies to most Western countries. Yet work design theory is virtually

silent on the effect of demographic issues (Parker & Wall, 1998).

There are several important ways the demographic considerations influence work design practice and theory. First, the changing composition of the workforce will render salient work characteristics beyond those traditionally considered. For example, research suggests that, compared with men, working women are more likely to experience home-work conflict (e.g., Hochschild, 1989), and are therefore likely to value autonomy over working hours (i.e., flexible working patterns) as it enables them to more easily juggle the demands of home and work (Thomas & Ganster, 1995). Second, there may be different relationships between work characteristics and outcomes as a function of age, gender, and race; both in terms of the strength of these relationships and in terms of the underlying mechanisms. For example, autonomy for older workers in physically demanding work settings might be especially important in this situation, not for the usual reasons, but because it allows them to rest and alleviate any physical strain.

A third set of implications of the changing workforce concerns the effect of factors such as age, gender and ethnic status on the antecedents and processes of work design. For example, compared with men, women tend to be employed in lower-paid part-time positions; their knowledge and skill tend to be devalued, and their access to technology is often restricted (Franklin, Pain, Green & Owen, 1992). Many of the same discriminating processes apply to members of ethnic minority groups, and it is therefore important to consider the potentially restricted opportunities for work design that might arise for members of different groups as a consequence of negative stereotypes, structural barriers (e.g., home-work conflict), or other issues (e.g., language problems).

Summary

Looking at the implications of developments in the world of work, the narrowness of existing work design approaches becomes increasingly obvious. If we are to meet the challenges of the future, we need to expand our horizons. Although job simplification will remain a core concern, as will the role of uncertainty as a contingency, there is a need to take account of many other work content factors such as cognitive demand, interdependence, social interaction, emotional demand, home-work conflict, and job security. This is not to say that there will be increases on all these dimensions in the future, but rather that these will be among the factors that will distinguish between different forms of work, and will be important in understanding their consequences. The workforce for whom we are designing work is also changing, and we need to incorporate important demographic contingencies such as race, gender, and age into work design theory.

CONCLUSION: THE CHALLENGES FOR PRACTICE AND THEORY

Our aim in this chapter was to set out what is known about work design and what remains to be discovered. Applying what is known presents the main challenge for practitioners. Thus, we know from an extensive body of research that enriched work designs will promote positive outcomes for individuals and organizations, especially in those (increasingly prevalent) circumstances characterized by complexity and uncertainty. A challenge for practitioners is to put work enrichment on the agenda rather than taking for granted job simplification as the only option. Part of this challenge is to recognize that work redesign can be a way to achieve strategic objectives relating to a range of outcomes (e.g., performance, safety and learning) and can be a way to maximize the potential of new work practices, such as information technology. Work design is too swiftly categorized as a narrow motivational technique when its potential benefits are much wider.

It is equally a challenge for practitioners to choose appropriate work designs and implement them successfully. Many organizations are jumping on the empowerment and self-managing bandwagon without making sensible work design choices for the context (e.g., considering the level of interdependence and uncertainty) and without careful planning for implementing and sustaining the change. The challenge for practitioners, therefore, lies largely in putting into place what we already know about work design.

For researchers, the challenge is to discover those important things we do not know. We have outlined some long-standing questions that continue to be important, as well as some new questions that arise because of the types of changes occurring in the workplace and the workforce. Investigating such questions will be helped by adopting an expanded work design framework, such as by considering a broader range of antecedents, work characteristics, mechanisms, contingencies, and processes. Rigorous methodologies and research designs will also help to meet this challenge (a feature that has unfortunately been all too rare in work design research to date), as will a willingness to complement the dominant positivist tradition with alternative modes of inquiry.

REFERENCES

Abernathy, W., Clark, K., & Kantrow, A. (1981). The new industrial competition. *Harvard Business Review*, 59, 51–68.

Applebaum, E., & Batt, R. (1994). *The New American Workplace: Transforming Work Systems in the United States*. Ithaca, NY: ILR Press.

Babbage, C. (1835). *On the Economy of Machinery and Manufacturers*. London: Charles Knight.

Beekun, R.I. (1989). Assessing the effectiveness of sociotechnical interventions: Antidote or fad? *Human Relations*, 10, 877–897.

Bowen, D.E., & Lawler, E.E. (1992). The empowerment of service workers: What, why, how, and when. *Sloan Management Review*, Spring, 31–39.

Bratton, J. (1993). Cellular manufacturing: Some human resource implications. *International Journal of Human Factors in Manufacturing*, 3, 381–399.

Braverman, H. (1974). *Labour and Monopoly Capital: The Degradation of Work in the Twentieth Century*. New York: Monthly Review Press.

Burns, T., & Stalker, G.M. (1961). *The Management of Innovation*. London: Tavistock.

Campion, M.A. (1988). Interdisciplinary approaches to job design: A constructive replication with extensions. *Journal of Applied Psychology*, 73, 467–481.

Campion, M.A. (1989). Ability requirement implications of job design: An interdisciplinary approach. *Personnel Psychology*, 42, 1–24.

Campion, M.A., & Berger, C.J. (1990). Conceptual integration and empirical test of job design and compensation relationships. *Personnel Psychology*, 43, 525–553.

Campion, M.A., & McClelland, C.L. (1991). Interdisciplinary examination of the costs and benefits of enlarged jobs: A job design quasi-experiment. *Journal of Applied Psychology*, 76, 186–198.

Campion, M.A., & McClelland, C.L. (1993). Follow-up and extension of the inter-disciplinary costs and benefits of enlarged jobs. *Journal of Applied Psychology*, 78, 339–351.

Campion, M.A., Medsker, G.J., and Higgs, A.C. (1993). Relations between work group characteristics and effectiveness: Implications for designing effective work groups. *Personnel Psychology*, 46, 823–850.

Campion, M.A., Papper, E.M., & Medsker, G.J. (1996). Relations between work team characteristics and effectiveness: A replication and extension. *Personnel Psychology*, 49, 429–452

Campion, M.A., & Stevens, M.J. (1991). Neglected questions in job design: How people design jobs, task-job predictability, and influence of training. *Journal of Business and Psychology*, 6(2), 169–191.

Campion, M.A., & Thayer, P.W. (1985). Development and field evaluation of an interdisciplinary measure of job design. *Journal of Applied Psychology*, 70, 29–43.

Campion, M.A., & Thayer, P.W. (1987). Job design: Approaches, outcomes, and trade-offs. *Organizational Dynamics*, 15, 66–79.

Cherns, A.B. (1976). The principles of socio-technical design. *Human Relations*, 29, 783–792.

Clegg, C.W. (1984). The derivation of job designs. *Journal of Occupational Behaviour*, 5, 131–146.

Clegg, C.W., and Fitter, M.J. (1978). Information systems: The Achilles heel of job design. *Personnel Review*, 7, 5–11.

Clegg, C.W., Waterson, P.E., and Axtell, C.M. (1996). Software development: Knowledge-intensive work organizations. *Behaviour and Information Technology*, *15*(4), 237–249.

Cohen, S.G., & Ledford, G.E., Jr. (1994). The effectiveness of self-managing teams: A quasi-experiment. *Human Relations*, *47*, 13–43.

Cohen, S.G., Ledford, Jr., G.E., & Spreitzer, G.M. (1996). A predictive model of self-managing work team effectiveness. *Human Relations*, *49*, 643–676.

Cordery, J.L. (1996). Autonomous work groups and quality circles. In M.A. West (Ed.), *Handbook of Work Group Psychology* (pp. 225–246). Chichester, UK: John Wiley & Sons.

Cordery, J.L., Mueller, W.S., & Smith, L.M. (1991). Attitudinal and behavioral effects of autonomous group working: A longitudinal field study. *Academy of Management Journal*, *43*, 464–476.

Cordery, J.L., Wright, B.M., Morrison, D., & Wall, T.D. (manuscript in preparation). Production uncertainty as a moderator of the effectiveness of self-managing work team interventions: A field study.

Cummings, T.G., & Blumberg, M. (1987). Advanced manufacturing technology and work design. In T.D. Wall, C.W. Clegg & N.J. Kemp (Eds.), *The Human Side of Advanced Manufacturing Technology* (pp. 37–60). Chichester, Sussex: Wiley.

Cummings, T.G., Molloy, E.S., & Glen, R. (1977). A methodological critique of fifty eight selected work experiments. *Human Relations*, *30*, 675–708.

Davis, D.D. (1995). Form, function and strategy in boundaryless organizations. In A. Howard (Ed.), *The Changing Nature of Work* (pp. 112–138). San Francisco: Jossey Bass.

Davis, L.E., & Canter, R.R. (1956). Job design research. *Journal of Industrial Engineering*, *7*, 275–282.

Davis, L.E., Canter, R.R., & Hoffman, J. (1955). Current job design criteria. *Journal of Industrial Engineering*, *6*, 5–11.

Dean, J.W., & Snell, S.A. (1991). Integrated manufacturing and job design: Moderating effects of organizational inertia. *Academy of Management Journal*, *34*, 774–804.

Delbridge, R., & Turnbull, P. (1992). Human resource maximisation: The management of labour under just-in-time manufacturing systems. In P. Blyton & P. Turnbull (Eds.), *Reassessing Human Resource Management*. London: Sage.

Druskat, V.U., & Kayes, D.A. (1999). The antecedents of team competence: Toward a fine-grained model of self-managing team effectiveness. In R. Wageman (Ed.) et al., *Research on Managing Groups and Teams: Groups in Context*, Vol. 2 (pp. 201–231). Stamford, CT, US: Jai Press Inc.

Feldman, D.C., & Gainey, T.W. (1997). Patterns of telecommuting and their consequences: Framing the research agenda. *Human Resource Management Review*, *7*(4), 369–388.

Franklin, I., Pain, D., Green, E., & Owen, J. (1992). Job design within a human centred (system) design framework. *Behaviour and Information Technology*, *11*, 141–150.

Fraser, R. (1947). *The Incidence of Neurosis Among Factory Workers*. Report No. 90, Industrial Health Research Board. London: HMSO.

Frenkel, S.J., Korczynski, M., Shire, K.A., & Tam, M. (1999). *On the Front Line: Organization of Work in the Information Economy*. London: Cornell University Press.

Frese, M. (1989). Theoretical models of control and health. In S.L. Sauter, J.J. Hurrell, Jnr., & C.L. Cooper (Eds.), *Job Control and Worker Health* (pp. 108–128). New York: Wiley.

Frese, M., Kring, W., Soose, A., & Zempel, J. (1996). Personal initiative at work: Differences between East and West Germany. *Academy of Management Journal*, *39*, 37–63.

Frese, M., & Zapf, D. (1994). Action as the core of work psychology: A German approach. In H.C. Triandis, M.D. Dunnette & J.M. Hough (Eds.), *Handbook of Industrial and Organizational Psychology*, Vol. 4 (2nd ed.) (pp. 271–340). Palo Alto, CA: Consulting Psychologists Press.

Fried, Y., & Ferris, G.R. (1987). The validity of the job characteristics model: A review and meta-analysis. *Personnel Psychology*, *40*, 287–322.

Gladstein, D. (1984). Groups in context: A model of task group effectiveness. *Administrative Science Quarterly*, *29*, 499–517.

Graen, G.B. (1976). Role making processes within complex organizations. In M.D. Dunnette (Ed.), *Handbook of Industrial and Organizational Psychology* (pp. 1201–1245). Stokie, IL: Rand McNally.

Griffin, R.W. (1983). Objective and social sources of information in task design: A field experiment. *Administrative Science Quarterly*, *28*, 184–200.

Griffin, R.W., Bateman, T.S., Wayne, S.J., & Head, T.C. (1987). Objective and social factors as determinants of task perceptions and responses: An integrated perspective and empirical investigation. *Academy of Management Journal*, *30*, 501–523.

Goodman, P.S. (1979) *Assessing Organizational Change: The Rushton Quality of Work Experiment*. New York: Wiley.

Goodman, P.S., Devadas, R., & Griffith-Hughson, T.L. (1988). Groups and productivity: Analysing the effectiveness of self-managing teams. In J.P. Campbell, R.J. Campbell & Associates (Eds.), *Productivity in Organizations* (pp. 295–327). San Francisco: Jossey-Bass.

Graham, I. (1988). Japanisation as mythology. *Industrial Relations Journal*, *19* (Spring), 69–75.

Guzzo, R.A., Jette, R.D., & Katzell, R.A. (1985). The effects of psychologically based intervention programs on worker productivity: A meta analysis. *Personnel Psychology*, *38*, 275–292.

Hacker, W., Skell, W., & Straub, W. (1968). *Arbeitspychologie und Wissenschaftlich-techische Revolution*, Berlin: Deutscher Verlag der Wissenschaften.

Hackman, J.R. (1987). The design of work teams. In J. Lorsch (Ed.), *Handbook of Organizational Behavior* (pp. 315–342). Englewood Cliffs, NJ.: Prentice-Hall.

Hackman, J.R., & Lawler, E.E. (1971). Employee reactions to job characteristics. *Journal of Applied Psychology, 55,* 259–286.

Hackman, J.R., & Oldham, G. (1975). Development of the Job Diagnostic Survey. *Journal of Applied Psychology, 60,* 159–170.

Hackman, J.R., & Oldham, G. (1976). Motivation through the design of work: Test of a theory. *Organizational Behavior and Human Performance, 16,* 250–279.

Hackman, J.R., & Oldham, G.R. (1980). *Work Redesign.* Reading, MA.: Addison-Wesley.

Hardy, C.H., & Leiba-O'Sullivan, S. (1998). The power behind empowerment: Implications for research and practice. *Human Relations, 51,* 451–483.

Hayes, R.H., Wheelwright, S.C., & Clark, K.B. (1988). *Dynamic Manufacturing: Creating the Learning Organization.* New York: The Free Press.

Herzberg, F. (1966). *Work and the Nature of Man.* Cleveland, OH: World Publishing.

Herzberg, F., Mausner, B., & Snyderman, B. (1959). *The Motivation to Work.* New York: Wiley.

Hochschild, A. (1989). *The Second Shift.* New York: Viking.

Howard, A. (1995). A framework for work change. In A. Howard (Ed.), *The Changing Nature of Work* (pp. 3–44). San Francisco: Jossey-Bass.

Jackson, S.E. (1989). Does job control control job stress? In S.L. Sauter, J.J. Hurrell, Jnr. & C.L. Cooper (Eds.), *Job Control and Worker Health.* Chichester, England: Wiley.

Jackson, P.R., & Wall, T.D. (1991). How does operator control enhance performance of advanced manufacturing technology? *Ergonomics, 34,* 1301–1311.

Karasek, R.A. (1979). Job demands, job decision latitude and mental strain: Implications for job redesign. *Administrative Science Quarterly, 24,* 285–308.

Karasek, R.A., & Theorell, T. (1990). *Healthy Work: Stress, Productivity, and the Reconstruction of Working Life.* New York: Basic Books.

Kelly, J.E. (1992). Does job re-design theory explain job re-design outcomes? *Human Relations, 45,* 753–774.

Kohn, M.L., & Schooler, C. (1978). The reciprocal effects of the substantive complexity of work on intellectual complexity: A longitudinal assessment. *American Journal of Sociology, 84,* 24–52.

Kompier, M.A.J. (1996). Job design and well-being. In M.J. Schabracq, J.A.M. Winnubst & C.L. Cooper (Eds.), *Handbook of Work and Health Psychology* (pp. 349–368). New York: John Wiley & Sons.

Lawler, E.E. (1992). *The Ultimate Advantage: Creating the High Involvement Organization.* San Francisco: Jossey-Bass.

Mathieu, J.E., Heffner, T.S., Goodwin, G.F., & Salas, E, Cannon-Bowers, J.A. (2000) The influence of shared mental models on team process and performance. *Journal of Applied Psychology, 85,* 273–283.

Mohrman, S.A., & Cohen, S.G. (1995). When people get out of the box: New relationships, new systems. In A. Howard (Ed.), *The Changing Nature of Work* (pp. 365–410). San Francisco: Jossey-Bass.

Mohrman, S.A., Cohen, S.G., & Mohrman, A.M. Jnr. (1995). *Designing Team-based Organizations: New Forms for Knowledge and Work.* San Francisco: Jossey-Bass.

Moldaschl, M., & Weber, W.G. (1998). The 'three waves' of industrial group work: Historical reflections on current research on group work. *Human Relations, 51,* 347–388.

Mullarkey, S., Jackson, P.R., & Parker, S.K. (1995). Employee reactions to JIT manufacturing practices: A two-phase investigation. *International Journal of Operations and Production Management, 15,* 62–79.

Nicholls, C.E., Lane, H.W., & Brechu, M.B. (1999). Taking self-managed teams to Mexico. *The Academy of Management Executive, 13,* 15–25.

Niepce, W., & Molleman, E. (1998). Work design issues in lean production from a sociotechnical systems perspective: NeoTaylorism or the next step in sociotechnical design. *Human Relations, 51*(3), 259–287.

Oldham, G.R. (1996). Job design. In C.L. Cooper, & I.T. Robertson (Eds.), *International Review of Industrial and Organizational Psychology,* Vol. 11 (pp. 35–60). New York: John Wiley & Sons.

O'Reilly, C.A., & Caldwell, D.F. (1979). Informational influence as a determinant of perceived task characteristics and job satisfaction. *Journal of Applied Psychology, 64,* 157–165.

O'Reilly, C.A., & Caldwell, D.F. (1985). The impact of normative social influence and cohesiveness on task perceptions and attitudes: A social information processing approach. *Journal of Occupational Psychology, 59,* 193–206.

Organization for Economic Cooperation and Development (1996). *Employment Outlook.* Paris.

Osterman, P. (1997). Work organization. In P.E. Cappelli et al. (Eds.), *Change At Work* (pp. 89–121). New York: Oxford University Press.

Ouchi, W.G. (1977). The relationship between organizational structure and organizational control. *Administrative Science Quarterly, 22,* 95–113.

Parker, S.K. (1998). Role breadth self-efficacy: Relationship with work enrichment and other organizational practices. *Journal of Applied Psychology, 83,* 835–852.

Parker, S.K., Myers, C., & Wall, T.D. (1995). The effects of a manufacturing initiative on employee jobs and strain. In S.A. Robertson (Ed.), *Contemporary Ergonomics 1995* (pp. 37–42). London: Taylor & Francis.

Parker, S.K. & Sprigg, C.A. (1999). Minimizing strain and maximizing learning: The role of job demands, job control, and proactive personality. *Journal of Applied Psychology, 84,* 925–939.

Parker, S.K., Wall, T.D., & Jackson, P.R. (1997). That's not my job: Developing flexible employee work orientations. *Academy of Management Journal, 40,* 899–929.

Parker, S.K. & Wall, T.D. (1998). *Job and Work Design: Organizing Work To Promote Well-Being and Effectiveness.* CA: Sage.

Pasmore, W.A. (1988). *Designing Effective Organizations: The Sociotechnical Systems Perspective*. New York: Wiley.

Pasmore, W., Francis, C., Haldeman, J., & Shani, A. (1982). Socio-technical systems: A North American reflection on the empirical studies of the seventies. *Human Relations, 35*, 1179–1204.

Paul, W.P., & Robertson, K.B. (1970). *Job Enrichment and Employee Motivation*. London: Gower.

Roberts, K.H., & Glick, W. (1981). The job characteristics approach to job design: A critical review. *Journal of Applied Psychology, 66*, 193–217.

Salancik, G.R., & Pfeffer, J. (1977). A social information processing approach to job attitudes and task design. *Administrative Science Quarterly, 23*, 224–253.

Smith, A. (1776). *The Wealth of Nations*. Republished in 1974. Harmondsworth, Middx: Penguin.

Spector, P.E. (1985). Higher-order need strength as a moderator of the job scope-employee outcome relationship: A meta-analysis. *Journal of Occupational Psychology, 58*, 119–127.

Spreitzer, G.M. (1995). Psychological empowerment in the workplace: Dimensions, measurement, and validation. *Academy of Management Journal, 38*, 1442–1465.

Sprigg, C.A., Jackson, P.R., & Parker, S.K. (2000). Production team-working: The importance of interdependence for employee strain and satisfaction. *Human Relations, 53*(11), 1519–1543.

Stevens, M.J. and Campion, M.A. (1994). The knowledge, skills, and ability requirements for teamwork: Implications for human resource management. *Journal of Management, 20*, 503–530.

Taber, T.D., & Taylor, E. (1990). A review and evaluation of the psychometric properties of the Job Diagnostic Survey. *Personnel Psychology, 43*, 467–500.

Taylor, F.W. (1911). *The Principles of Scientific Management*. New York: Harper.

Taylor, J.C. (1979). Job design criteria twenty years later. In L.E. Davis & J.C. Taylor (Eds.), *Design of Jobs* (2nd ed.). Santa Monica, California: Goodyear.

Thomas, L.T., & Ganster, D.C. (1995). Impact of family-supportive work variables on work-family conflict and strain: A control perspective. *Journal of Applied Psychology, 80*, 6–15.

Thornley, D.H., & Valentine, G.A. (1968). Job enlargement: Some implications of longer cycle jobs on fan heater production. *Phillips Personnel Management Review*, 12–17.

Trist, E.L., & Bamforth, K.W. (1951). Some social and psychological consequences of the long-wall method of coal-getting. *Human Relations, 4*, 3–38.

Turner, A.N., & Lawrence, P.R. (1965). *Industrial Jobs and the Worker*. Cambridge, MA: Harvard University Press.

Van Cott, H.P. (1985). High technology and human needs. *Ergonomics, 28*, 1135–1142.

Van der Spiegel, J. (1995). New information technologies and changes in work. In A. Howard (Ed.), *The Changing Nature of Work* (pp. 97–111). San Francisco: Jossey-Bass.

Wall, T.D., Clegg, C.W., & Jackson, P.R. (1978). An evaluation of the Job Characteristics Model, *Journal of Occupational Psychology, 51*, 183–196.

Wall, T.D., Corbett, M.J., Martin, R., Clegg, C.W. & Jackson, P.R. (1990). Advanced manufacturing technology, work design and performance: A change study. *Journal of Applied Psychology, 75*, 691–697.

Wall, T.D., & Jackson, P.R. (1995). New manufacturing initiatives and shopfloor work design. In A. Howard (Ed.), *The Changing Nature of Work* (pp. 139–174). San Francisco: Jossey-Bass.

Wall, T.D., Jackson, P.R., & Davids, K. (1992). Operator work design and robotics system performance: A serendipitous field study. *Journal of Applied Psychology, 77*, 353–362.

Wall, T.D., Kemp, N.J., Jackson, P.R., & Clegg, C.W. (1986). An outcome evaluation of autonomous work groups: A long-term field experiment. *Academy of Management Journal, 29*, 280–304.

Wall, T.D., & Martin, R. (1987). Job and work design. In C.L. Cooper & I.T. Robertson (Eds.), *International Review of Industrial and Organisational Psychology* (pp. 61–91). Chichester: Wiley.

Wall, T.D., & Stephenson, G.M. (1970). Herzberg's two-factor theory of job attitudes: A critical evaluation and some fresh evidence. *Industrial Relations Journal, 1*, 41–65.

Walker, C.R. (1950). The problem of the repetitive job. *Harvard Business Review, 28*, 54–58.

Walker, C.R., & Guest, R. (1952). *The Man on the Assembly Line*. Cambridge, MA: Harvard University Press.

Waterson, P.E., Clegg, C.W., Bolden, R., Pepper, K., Warr, P.B., & Wall, T.D. (1999). The use and effectiveness of modern manufacturing practices: A survey of UK industry. *International Journal of Production Research, 37*, 2271–2292.

Wood, R.E. (1986). Task complexity: Definition and construct. *Organizational Behavior and Human Decision Processes, 37*, 60–82.

Wyatt, S., & Ogden, D.A. (1924). *On the Extent and Effects of Variety and Uniformity in Repetitive Work*. Report No. 26, Industrial Fatigue Research Board. London: HMSO.

6

Assessment of Individual Job Performance: A Review of the Past Century and a Look Ahead

CHOCKALINGAM VISWESVARAN

Job performance is a central construct in work psychology. The methods of assessing individual job performance, the factor structure of the construct, criteria for evaluating the criterion, as well as path models explaining individual job performance, are reviewed. The factor structure of job performance is best conceptualized as a hierarchy, with the general factor at the apex and several group factors at the second, lower level. The number and nature of the group factors varies according to the theorist. Issues of bias in ratings as well as contamination and deficiency in nonratings measures are summarized. The evidence for the reliability and construct validity of individual job performance assessment (both for overall assessments as well as dimensional assessments) are presented. The changing nature of work and its impact on the conceptualization and assessment of individual job performance are noted.

Job performance is an important construct in industrial/organizational psychology (Arvey & Murphy, 1998; Austin & Villanova, 1992; Campbell, 1990; Murphy & Cleveland, 1995; Schmidt & Hunter, 1992). In fact, most of what industrial-organizational psychologists do is geared to have a positive impact on job performance. The importance of assessment of individual job performance is probably reflected in the volume of literature devoted to it, and many leading researchers in our field have written on the topic of individual job performance.

Individual job performance plays a central role in what we do as researchers and practitioners. For example, one question in recruitment is whether the different sources of recruitment result in attraction of individuals who differ in job performance levels (Barber, 1998). In personnel selection, attempts are made to identify individual differences variables that are related to individual differences in job performance, and select individuals based on those

characteristics (Guion, 1998). Organizations require that the expenses associated with training programs (e.g., socialization or orientation programs, skills training) be justified with evidence that such training improves individual job performance. In short, individual job performance is a central construct in our field.

Individual job performance data can be used in numerous ways. Cleveland, Murphy and Williams (1989) identified several uses of individual job performance data, classifying these uses into four categories: (1) between-person decisions, (2) within-person decisions, (3) systems maintenance, and (4) documentation. Between-persons decisional uses included the use of individual job performance data for salary administration purposes, making promotion decisions, and to design merit pay systems. Within-person decisions included providing feedback to individuals so as to identify individual strengths and weaknesses – data that is used for assessing training and placement needs. The systems maintenance category refers to the use of individual job performance assessments for human resources planning and reinforcement of authority structures in organizations. Finally, individual job performance data are also used for legal documentation purposes.

Cascio (1991) groups these uses into three main categories: administrative, feedback, and research purposes. Administrative use refers to the use of individual job performance assessment for making administrative decisions such as pay allocation, promotions, and layoffs. Individual job performance assessment can also be used to provide feedback to individuals by identifying their strengths and weaknesses, and finally, it is required for research purposes – be it validation of a selection technique or evaluating the efficacy of a training program.

That individual job performance assessments are used in a variety of ways has also been found in several studies. For a long time, administrative uses have been known (Whisler & Harper, 1962), and DeVries, Morrison, Shullman and Gerlach (1986) report that surveys conducted in the 1970s in both the United States and the United Kingdom indicated the prevalence of individual job performance assessment for the purpose of making administrative decisions. In fact, these surveys suggested that more than 50% of the use of individual job performance assessment was for the purpose of making administrative decisions. DeVries et al. (1986) noted that the use of such assessments in Great Britain can be classified into three categories: (1) to improve current performance, (2) to set objectives, and (3) to identify training and development needs.

In this chapter, I review the research on individual job performance. There are four sections. The first deals with the different methods of assessment, and following this I summarize the studies conducted to explicate the content domain of individual job performance. Factor analytic studies as well as theoretical and rational analyses of what constitutes individual job performance are reviewed. In the third section, I review the criteria for assessing the quality of individual job performance assessments along with a discussion of such studies. Finally, in the fourth section, I summarize some of the causal path models postulated to explain the determinants and components of individual job performance.

METHODS OF ASSESSMENT

Methods used to assess individual job performance can be broadly classified into (1) organizational records, and (2) subjective evaluations. Organizational records are considered to be more 'objective' in contrast to the subjective evaluations that depend on a human judgment. Subjective evaluations could either be criterion referenced (e.g., ratings) or norm-referenced (e.g., rankings). The distinction between organizational records and subjective evaluations has a long history. Burtt (1926) and Viteles (1932) grouped criterion measures into objective and subjective classes. Farmer (1933) grouped criteria into objective measures, judgments of performance (judgments based on objective performance), and judgments of ability (judgments based on traits). Smith (1976) distinguished between hard criteria (i.e., organizational records) and soft criteria (i.e., subjective evaluations).

Methods of assessments should be distinguished from types of criteria. Thorndike (1949) identifies three types of criteria: immediate, intermediate, and ultimate criteria. The ultimate criterion summarizes the total worth of the individual to the organization over the entire career span. The immediate criteria on the other hand is a measure of individual job performance at that particular point in time. Intermediate criteria summarize performance over a period of time. Note that both organizational records and subjective evaluations can be used to assess, say, an intermediate criterion. Similarly, Mace (1935) argued that measures of individual job performance can stress either capacity or will to perform. This distinction is a forerunner to the distinction between maximal and typical performance measures (e.g., DuBois, Sackett, Zedeck & Fogli, 1993; Sackett, Zedeck & Fogli, 1988). Maximal performance is what an individual can do if highly motivated whereas typical performance is what an individual is likely to do in a typical day. The distinction between ultimate, intermediate, and immediate criteria or between maximal and typical performance refers to types of criteria. Both organizational records and subjective evaluations (methods) can be used to assess them.

Organizational records can be further classified into direct measures of productivity and personnel data (Schmidt, 1980). Direct measures of productivity stress the number of units produced. Also included are measures of quality such as the number of errors, scrap material produced, and so forth. Personnel data, on the other hand, do not directly measure productivity but inferences of productivity can be derived based on them. Lateness or tardiness, tenure, absences, accidents, promotion rates, and filing grievances can be considered as indirect measures of productivity – there is an inferential leap involved in using these personnel data as a measure of individual job performance. Organizational records, by focusing on observable, countable, discrete outcomes, may overcome the biasing influences of subjective evaluations but may be affected by criterion contamination and criterion deficiency. Contamination occurs in that outcomes could be due to factors beyond the control of the individuals; deficiency results as the outcomes assessed may not take into account important aspects of individual job performance. I will discuss the literature on the construct validity of organizational records after presenting the criteria for the job performance criterion in the third section of this chapter.

Subjective evaluations can be either ratings or rankings of performance. Ratings are criterion-referenced judgments where an individual is evaluated without reference to other individuals. The most common form of rating scale is a graphic rating scale (GRS), which typically involves presenting the rater with a set of dimensions or task categories with several levels of performance and requiring the raters to choose the level that best describes the person being rated. There are several formats of GRS. The different formats differ in the number of levels presented, the clarity in demarcating the different levels (e.g., asking the rater to circle a number vs. asking them to indicate a point in a line the end points of which are described), and the clarity in identifying what behaviors constitute a particular level. Smith and Kendall (1963) designed the Behaviorally Anchored Rating Scales (BARS) to explicitly tie the different levels to behavioral anchors. Steps involved in the construction of BARS include generating a list of behaviors depicting different performance levels of a particular dimension of performance, checking the agreement across raters (retranslation), and designing the layout of the scale. A variant of the BARS is the Behavioral Observation Scale (BOS) where the rater merely notes whether a behavior was displayed by the ratee (Latham Fay, & Saari, 1980) and the Behavioral Evaluation Scale (BES) where the rater notes the likelihood of the ratee exhibiting a particular behavior (Bernardin, Alvares & Cranny, 1976).

Researchers have also addressed, by developing checklists, the reluctance of raters to judge the performance of others. The rater merely indicates whether a particular behavior has been exhibited, and either a simple sum or weighted combination is then computed to assess performance. There are several types of these summated rating scales in existence. To address the problem that raters could intentionally distort their ratings, forced choice scales and mixed standard scales (MSS) have also been developed. In a forced choice assessment, raters are provided with two equally favorable statements of which only one discriminates between good and poor performers. The idea is that the rater who wants to give lenient ratings may choose the favorable but nondiscriminating statement as descriptive of the rater. The MSS comprises of three statements for each dimension of performance rated with the three statements depicting an excellent, an average and a poor performance, respectively on that dimension. The rater rates the performance of each ratee as better than, equal to or worse than the performance depicted in that statement. Scoring rules are developed and MSS can identify inconsistent or careless raters (Blanz & Ghiselli, 1972).

Several research studies have been conducted over the years to compare the quality of the different rating scales. Symonds (1924) investigated the optimal number of scale points and recommended seven categories as optimal. Other researchers (e.g., Bendig, 1954; Lissitz & Green, 1975) present conflicting conclusions. Schwab Heneman and DeCotiis (1975) questioned the superiority of BARS over other formats, and finally, Landy and Farr (1980) in an influential article concluded that rating formats and scales do not alter the performance assessments, and guided researchers away from the unprofitable controversies of which scale and rating format is superior to investigations of the cognitive processes underlying performance assessments.

In contrast to ratings which are criterion-referenced assessments, rankings are norm-referenced assessments. The simplest form of ranking is to rank all ratees from best to worst. The ranking will depend on the set of ratees and it is impossible to compare the rankings from two different sets of individuals; the worst in one set may be better than the best in second set of ratees. A modified version, called alternate ranking, involves (1) picking the best and worst ratees in the set of ratees under consideration, (2) removing the two chosen ratees, (3) picking the next best and worst from the remaining ratees, and (4) repeating the process until all ratees are ranked. The advantage of the alternate ranking method is that it reduces the cognitive load on the raters. Yet another approach is to compare each ratee to every other ratee, a method of paired comparisons that becomes unwieldy when the number of ratees increases. Finally, forced distribution methods can be used where a fixed percentage of ratees are placed in each level. Forced distribution methods can be useful to generate the desired distribution (mostly normal) of assessed scores.

With subjective evaluations (ratings or rankings), the question of who should rate arises. Typically, in traditional organizations the supervisors of the employees provide the ratings. Recent years have seen an increase in the use of 360 degree feedback systems (Church & Bracken, 1997) where rating assessments can be made by self (the ratee himself or herself), subordinates, peers, and customers or clients. I discuss the convergence among the different sources as well as the convergence between subjective evaluations and organizational records under the section on the construct validity of performance assessments.

EXPLICATING THE CONSTRUCT DOMAIN OF INDIVIDUAL JOB PERFORMANCE

Job performance is an abstract, latent construct. One cannot point to one single physical manifestation and define it as job performance; there are several manifestations of an abstract construct. Explicating the construct domain of individual job performance involves specifying what is included when we talk of the concept (Wallace, 1965). Further, keeping with the abstract nature of constructs, there are several manifestations of individual job performance with the actual operational measure varying across contexts; explication of the construct involves identifying dimensions that make up the construct. The dimensions generalize across contexts whereas the exact measures differ. For example, interpersonal competence is a dimension of individual job performance that could be relevant in several contexts, but the actual behavior could vary depending on the construct. One measure of interpersonal competence for a professor may be how polite the professor is in replying to reviewers. For a bank teller, a measure of interpersonal competence is how considerate they are of customer complaints or the extent to which they smile at customers.

To explicate a construct domain, it is optimal to start with a definition of the construct. In this chapter, I define individual job performance as evaluatable behaviors. Although I use the term behaviors, I would stress that the difference between behaviors and outcomes is not clear-cut in many instances. Some researchers (Campbell, 1990) insist on a clear demarcation between behaviors and outcomes whereas others (Austin & Villanova, 1992; Bernardin & Pence, 1980) deemphasize this difference. The reason for emphasizing this difference between behaviors and outcomes is the alleged control an individual has over them. The argument is that the construct of individual job performance should not include what is beyond the individual's control. The distinguishing feature is whether the individual has control over what is assessed. If the individual does have such control, it is included under the individual job performance construct.

Consider the research productivity of a professor. Is the number of papers *published* a measure of individual job performance? Surely, several factors beyond the control of the professor affect the publishing of the paper. Is the number of papers *written*, a measure of individual job performance? Again, surely we can think of several factors that could affect the number of papers written that are not under the control of the professor. Thus, for every measure or index of individual job performance, the degree of control the individual has is a matter of degree. As such the distinction between behaviors and outcomes is also a question of degree and not some absolute distinction. Whether one defines performance and related constructs as behaviors or outcomes depends on the attributions one makes and the purpose of the evaluation.

How have researchers and practitioners defined the construct domain of individual job performance in their studies? Generally they have applied some combination of the following three approaches.

First, researchers have reviewed job performance measures used in different contexts and attempted to synthesize what dimensions make up the construct. This rational method of synthesizing and theory building is however affected by the personal bias of the individual researchers.

Second, researchers have developed measures of hypothesized dimensions, collected data on these measures, and factor analyzed the data (e.g., Rush, 1953). This empirical approach is limited by the number and type of measures included in the data collection phase. Recently, Viswesvaran (1993) invoked the lexical hypothesis from personality literature (Goldberg, 1995) to address this limitation. The lexical hypothesis states that practically significant individual differences in personality are encoded in the language used, and therefore a comprehensive description of personality can be obtained by collating all the adjectives found in the dictionary. Viswesvaran, Ones and Schmidt (1996) extended this principle to job performance assessment and argued that a comprehensive specification of the content domain of the job performance construct can be obtained by collating all the measures of job performance that had been used in the extant literature.

Third, researchers (e.g., Welbourne, Johnson & Erez, 1998) have invoked organizational theories to define what the content of the job performance construct should be. Welbourne et al., used role theory and identity theory to explicate the construct of job performance. Another example of invoking a theory of work organization to explicate the construct of job performance comes in the distinction made between task and contextual performance (Borman & Motowidlo, 1993). Distinguishing between task and contextual performance parallels the social and technical systems that are postulated to make-up the organization. Of these three approaches, most of the extant literature employs either rational synthesis or factor analytic approaches. Therefore, I review these two set of studies separately.

Rational Synthesis of Job Performance Dimensions

Toops (1944) was one of the earliest attempts to hypothesize what dimensions comprise the construct of job performance, arguing a distinction between accuracy (quality or lack of errors) and volume of output (quantity). Toops (1944) lists units of production, quality of work, tenure, supervisory and leadership abilities as dimensions of individual job performance. Wherry (1957), on the other hand, lists listed six dimensions: output, quality, lost time, turnover, training time or promotability, and satisfaction. The last two decades have seen several rational analyses (of the individual job performance construct) based on the plethora of factor analytic studies that have been conducted over the years. In this section, I present three such frameworks.

Bernardin and Beatty (1984) define performance as the record of outcomes produced on a specified job function or activity during a specified time period. Although a person's job performance depends on some combination of ability, motivation and situational constraints, it can be measured only in terms of some outcomes. Bernardin and Beatty (1984) then consider the issue of dimensions of job performance. Every job function could be assessed in terms of six dimensions (Kane, 1986): quality, quantity, timeliness, cost-effectiveness, need for supervision, and interpersonal impact. Some of these dimensions may not be relevant to all job activities. Bernardin and Russell (1998) emphasize the need to understand the interrelationships among the six dimensions of performance. For example, a work activity performed in sufficient quantity and quality but not in time may not be useful to the organization.

Campbell (1990) describes the latent structure of job performance in terms of eight dimensions. According to Campbell (1990) and Campbell, McCloy, Oppler and Sager (1993), the true score correlations between these eight dimensions are small, and hence any attempt to cumulate scores across the eight dimensions will be counterproductive for guiding research and interpreting results. The eight factors are: job-specific task proficiency, nonjob-specific task proficiency, written and oral communication, demonstrating effort, maintaining personal discipline, facilitating peer and team performance, supervision, and management or administration.

Job-specific task proficiency is defined as the degree to which the individual can perform the core substantive or technical tasks that are central to a job and which distinguish one job from another. Nonjob-specific task proficiency, on the other hand, is used to refer to tasks not specific to a particular job, but is expected of all members of the organization. Demonstrating effort captures the consistency or perseverance and intensity of the individuals to complete the task, whereas maintenance of personal discipline refers to the eschewment of negative behaviors (such as rule infractions) at work. Management or administration differs from supervision in that the former includes performance behaviors directed at managing the organization that are distinct from supervisory or leadership roles. Written and oral communications reflect that component of the job performance that refers to the proficiency of an incumbent to communicate (written or oral) independent of the correctness of the subject matter. The description of these eight dimensions are further elaborated in Campbell (1990) and Campbell et al. (1993). Five of the eight dimensions were

found in a sample of military jobs (Campbell, McHenry & Wise, 1990). Further details about these dimensions may be found in Campbell (1990).

Murphy (1989) describes the construct of job performance as comprising of four dimensions: downtime behaviors, task performance, interpersonal, and destructive behaviors. Task performance focuses on performing role-prescribed activities whereas downtime behaviors refer to lateness, tardiness, absences or, broadly, to the negative pole of time on task (i.e., effort exerted by an individual on the job). Interpersonal behaviors refer to helping others, teamwork ratings, and prosocial behaviors. Finally, destructive behaviors correspond to compliance with rules (or lack of it), violence on the job, theft, and other behaviors counterproductive to the goals of the organization. The four dimensions are further elaborated in Murphy (1989).

Factor Analytic Studies

In a typical factor analytic study, individuals are assessed on multiple measures of job performance. Correlations are obtained between the measures of job performance and factor analysis is used to identify the measures that cluster together. Based on the commonalities across the measures that cluster together, a dimension is defined. For example, when absence measures, lateness measures, and tenure cluster together, a dimension of withdrawal is hypothesized. I review below some representative studies; the actual number of studies is too numerous to even list, let alone describe in a book chapter.

An important point needs to be stressed here. Factor analyses of importance ratings of task elements, frequency of tasks performed, and time spent on tasks done on the job, are not reviewed. The dimensions identified in such studies do not capture dimensions of individual job performance (Schmidt, 1980; Viswesvaran, 1993). Consider a typical job analytic study that obtains importance ratings of task statements from raters. The correlation between these ratings (e.g., the correlation between task i and task j) are computed and the resulting correlation matrix is factor analyzed. Tasks that cluster together are used to identify a dimension of job performance. But because all raters are rating the same stimulus (say task i), the true variance is zero (Schmidt & Hunter, 1989). Any observed variability across raters is the result of random errors, disagreements between raters, and differences between raters in leniency and other rater idiosyncrasies. Correlating the rating errors in pairs of variables (importance ratings of tasks i and j) and factor analyzing the resulting correlations cannot reveal individual differences dimensions of job performance (Schmidt, personal communication, June 25, 1993). Therefore, in this section I focus only on studies that obtained individual job performance data on different measures, correlated the measures, and factor analyzed the resulting correlation matrix to identify dimensions of performance.

Rush (1953) factor analyzed nine rating measures and three organizational records-based measures of job performance for 100 salespeople. He identified the following four factors: objective achievement, learning aptitude, general reputation, and proficiency of sales techniques. A sample size of 100 for analyzing a 12 × 12 matrix of correlations would probably be considered inadequate by present-day standards, but this was one of the first studies to employ factor analytic techniques to explicate the underlying dimensions and factor structure of the individual job performance construct.

Baier and Dugan (1957) obtained data on 346 sales agents on 15 objective variables and two subjective ratings. Factor analysis of the 17 × 17 intercorrelation matrix resulted in one general factor. Several different measures such as percentage sales, units sold, tenure, knowledge of products, loaded on this general factor. In contrast, Prien and Kult (1968) factor analyzed a set of 23 job performance measures and found evidence for seven distinct dimensions. Roach and Wherry (1970) using a large sample of (N = 900) salespersons found evidence for a general factor. Seashore, Indik and Georgopoulos (1960) using comparably large samples (N = 975) found no evidence for a general factor.

Ronan (1963) conducted a factor analysis of a set of 11 job performance measures. Four of the measures were objective records including measures of accidents and disciplinary actions. The factor analysis indicated a four-factor solution. One of the four factors reflected the 'safe' work habits of the individual (e.g., index of injuries, time lost due to accidents); acceptance of authority and adjustment constituted two other factors. The fourth factor was uninterpretable (Ronan, 1963).

Gunderson and Ryman (1971) examined the factor structure of individual job performance in extremely isolated groups. The sample analyzed involved scientists spending their winter in Antarctica. Three factors were identified: task efficiency, emotional stability, and interpersonal relations. Klimoski and London (1974) obtained data from different sources (e.g., supervisors, peers) to avoid monomethod problems, and reported evidence for the presence of a general factor, a finding that is interesting when considered in the wake of arguments (cf. Borman, 1974) that raters at different levels of job performance construe the content domain of job performance differently.

Factor analytic studies in the last two decades (1980–99) have used much larger samples and refined techniques of factor analysis, and the use of confirmatory factor analysis has enabled researchers to combine rational synthesis and empirical partitioning of variance. For example, Borman, Motowidlo, Rose and Hansen (1985) developed a model of soldier effectiveness based on data collected during Project A. Project A is a multi-year effort undertaken by the United States Army to develop a comprehensive model of work effectiveness. As part of that landmark project, Borman et al., developed a model of job performance for first-tour soldiers that are important for unit effectiveness. Borman et al., noted that in addition to task performance, there were three performance dimensions: allegiance, teamwork, and determination, and that each of these three dimensions could be further subdivided. Thus, allegiance involved following orders, following regulations, respect for authority, military bearing, and commitment. Teamwork comprised of cooperation, camaraderie, concern for unit morale, boosting unit morale, and leadership. Determination involved perseverance, endurance, conscientiousness, initiative, and discipline.

Hunt (1996) developed a model of generic work behavior applicable to entry-level jobs especially in the service industry. Using performance data from over 18,000 employees primarily from the retail sector, Hunt identified nine dimensions of job performance that do not depend on job-specific knowledge. The nine dimensions were: adherence to confrontational rules, industriousness, thoroughness, schedule flexibility, attendance, off-task behavior, unruliness, theft, and drug misuse. Adherence to confrontational rules reflected an employee's willingness to follow rules that might result in a confrontation between the employee and a customer (e.g., checking for shoplifting). Industriousness captured the constant effort and attention towards work while on the job. Thoroughness was related to the quality of work whereas schedule flexibility reflected the employees' willingness to change their schedule to accommodate demands at work. Attendance captured the employee's presence at work when scheduled to work, and punctuality. Off-task behavior involved the use of company time to engage in nonjob activities. Unruliness referred to minor deviant tendencies as well as abrasive and inflammatory attitudes towards co-workers, supervisors, and work itself. Finally, theft involved taking money or company property, or helping friends steal property whereas drug misuse referred to inappropriate use of drugs and alcohol.

Another trend discernible in the last two decades is the focus on specific performance aspects other than task performance. Smith, Organ and Near (1983) popularized the concept of 'Organizational Citizenship Behavior' (OCB) into the job performance literature. OCB was defined as individual behavior that is discretionary, not directly or explicitly recognized by the formal reward system, and that in the aggregate promotes the effective functioning of the organization (Organ, 1988). Factor analytic studies have identified distinct sub-dimensions of OCB: altruism, courtesy, cheerleading, sportsmanship, civic virtue, and conscientiousness.

Over the years several concepts related and overlapping with OCB have been proposed. George and Brief (1992) introduced the concept of 'organizational spontaneity', defining organizational spontaneity as voluntarily performed extra-role behavior that contributes to organizational effectiveness. Five dimensions were postulated: helping co-workers, protecting the organization, making constructive suggestions, developing oneself, and spreading goodwill. Organizational spontaneity is distinguished from OCB partly on account of reward systems being designed to recognize organizational spontaneity.

Van Dyne, Cummings and Parks (1995) argued for the use of 'Extra-Role Behavior' (ERB). Based on role theory concepts developed by Katz (1964), ERB has been hypothesized to contribute to organizational effectiveness. Brief and Motowidlo (1986) introduced the related concept of Prosocial Organizational Behavior (POB), which has been defined as behavior performed with the intention of promoting the welfare of individuals or groups to whom the behavior has been directed. POB can be either role-prescribed or extra-role, and it can be negative towards organizations although positive towards individuals.

Finally, Borman (1991) as well as Borman and Motowidlo (1993) describe the construct of job performance as comprising task and contextual performance. Briefly, task performance focuses on performing role-prescribed activities whereas contextual performance accounts for all other helping and productive behaviors (Borman, 1991; Borman & Motowidlo, 1993). The two dimensions are further elaborated in Borman and Motowidlo (1993). Motowidlo, Borman and Schmit (1997) developed a theory of individual differences in task and contextual performance. Some researchers (e.g., Van Scotter & Motowidlo, 1996) have argued that individual differences in personality variables are linked more strongly than individual differences in (cognitive) abilities to individual differences in contextual performance. Cognitive ability was hypothesized to be more predictive of task performance than contextual performance. Although persuasive, empirical support for this argument has been mixed. Conscientiousness, a personality variable, has been linked as strongly as cognitive ability to task performance in some studies (Alonso, 2000).

Behaviors that have negative value for organizational effectiveness have also been proposed as constituting distinct dimensions of job performance, and organizational misbehavior has become a topic of research interest. Clark and Hollinger (1983) discussed the antecedents of employee theft on organizations. Our work on integrity testing (Ones, Viswesvaran & Schmidt, 1993) as well as the works of Paul Sackett and colleagues (cf. Sackett & Wanek, 1996) have identified the different forms of counterproductive behaviors such as property damage, substance abuse, violence on the job. Withdrawal behaviors have long been studied by work psychologists in terms of lateness or tardiness, absenteeism, and turnover. Work psychologists and social psychologists have explored the antecedents and consequences of social loafing, shirking or the propensity to withhold effort (Kidwell & Bennett, 1993).

A major concern in evaluating the different factor analytic studies in the job performance domain is the fact that the dimensions identified are a function of the measures included. To ensure a comprehensive specification of the content domain of the job performance construct, Viswesvaran (1993) invoked the lexical hypothesis which was first introduced in the personality assessment literature (see also Viswesvaran et al., 1996). A central thesis of this lexical approach is that the entire domain of job performance can be captured by culling all job performance measures used in the extant literature. This parallels the lexical hypothesis used in the personality literature which, as first enunciated by Goldberg, holds that a comprehensive description of the personality of an individual can be obtained by examining the adjectives used in the lexicon (e.g., all English language words that could be obtained/culled from a dictionary).

Viswesvaran (1993) listed job performance measures (486 of them) used in published articles over the years. Two raters working independently then derived 10 dimensions by grouping conceptually similar measures. The 10 dimensions were: overall job performance, job performance or productivity, effort, job knowledge, interpersonal competence, administrative competence, quality, communication competence, leadership, and compliance with rules. Overall job performance captured overall effectiveness, overall work reputation, or was the sum of all individual dimensions rated. Job performance or productivity included ratings of quantity or ratings of volume of work produced. Ratings of effort were statements about the amount of work an individual expends in striving to do a good job. Interpersonal competence was assessments of how well an individual gets along with others whereas administrative competence was a ratings measure of the proficiency exhibited by the individual in handling the coordination of the different roles in an organization. Quality was an assessment of how well the job was done and job knowledge was a measure of the expertise demonstrated by the individual. Communication competence reflected how well an individual communicated regardless of the content. Leadership was a measure of the ability to successfully bring out extra performance from others, and compliance with or acceptance of authority assessed the perspective the individual has about rules and regulations. Illustrative examples as well as more elaborate explanations of these dimensions are provided in Viswesvaran et al. (1996).

Although the lexical approach is promising, it should be noted that there are two potential concerns here. First, it can be argued that just as the technical nuances of personality may not be reflected in the lexicon, some technical but important aspects of job performance have never been used in the literature – thus, not covered in the 10 dimensions identified. Second, it should be noted that generating 10 dimensions from a list of all job performance measures used in the extant literature involved the judgmental task of grouping conceptually similar measures.

Of these two concerns, the first is mitigated to the extent that the job performance measures found in the extant literature were identified by industrial-organizational psychologists and other professionals (in consultation with managers in organizations). As such the list of measures can be construed as a comprehensive specification of the entire domain of the construct of job performance. The second concern, the judgmental basis on which the job performance measures were grouped into 10 conceptual dimensions, is mitigated to the extent that inter-coder agreement is high (the intercoder agreement in grouping the conceptually similar measures into the 10 dimensions was reported in the 90%s, Viswesvaran, 1993).

A comprehensive specification of the job performance construct involves many measures, the inter-correlation among which is needed to conduct the factor analyses. Estimating the correlations among all variables with adequate sample sizes may not be feasible in a single study. Fortunately, meta-analysis can be used to cumulate the correlations across pairs of variables, and the meta-analytically constructed correlation matrix can be used in the factor analyses (cf. Viswesvaran & Ones, 1995). Conway (1999) developed a taxonomy of managerial behavior by meta-analytically cumulating data across 14 studies, and found a three-level hierarchy of managerial performance. Viswesvaran (1993) cumulated results from over 300 studies that reported correlations across the 10 dimensions. Both interrater and intrarater correlations, as well as nonratings-based measures were analyzed. The 10 dimensions showed a positive manifold of correlations, suggesting the presence of a general factor across the different dimensions (Campbell, Gasser & Oswald, 1996).

CRITERIA FOR ASSESSING THE QUALITY OF INDIVIDUAL JOB PERFORMANCE ASSESSMENTS

For over a century, researchers have grappled with the issues involved in assessment of individual job performance (cf. Austin & Villanova, 1992, for a summary). It is no wonder that several researchers have advanced criteria for evaluating these assessments. Freyd (1926) argued that measures of individual job performance assessments should be validated. While Freyd argued for the importance of establishing the construct validity of criteria, Farmer (1933) stressed the need for assessing the reliability of measures. Burtt (1926) provided a list of variables (e.g., opportunity bias) that could affect organizational records or objective performance. Brogden and Taylor (1950) discussed the different types of criterion bias, specifically differentiating between bias that is correlated with predictor variables and biases that are unrelated to predictors.

Bellows (1941) identified six criteria that he grouped into statistical, acceptability, and practical effects categories. Bechtoldt (1947) introduced three criteria: (1) reliability and discriminability, (2) pertinence and comprehensiveness, and (3) comparability. Reliability is the consistency of measurement (Nunnally, 1978) and a good measure of assessment of individual job performance should discriminate across individuals. Pertinence refers to job-relatedness, and comprehensiveness requires that all important aspects of job performance are included in the assessment. Comparability focuses on the equivalence across the different dimensions assessed (e.g., time, place).

Thorndike (1949) proposed four criteria: (1) relevance, (2) reliability, (3) freedom from discrimination, and (4) practicality. Relevance is the construct validity of the measures, and can be construed as the correlation between the true scores and the construct (i.e., job performance). Given that this correlation can never be empirically estimated, relevance or construct validity is assessed by means of a nomological net of correlations with several related measures (see section on construct validity in Chapter 2 by Aguinis et al., in this volume). Relevance is the lack of criterion contamination (the measure includes what it should not include) and criterion deficiency (measure lacks what it should include). Note that Thorndike's use of the term 'discrimination' differs from use of the term by Bechtoldt (1947). For Thorndike discrimination is unfair distinctions made based on (demographic) group memberships. All measures designed to assess individual job performance should discriminate – the question is whether the discrimination is relevant to job performance or is unrelated to it.

Ronan and Prien (1966) argued that reliability of assessments is the most important factor in evaluating the quality of individual job performance assessments. Guion (1976), on the other hand, stressed the importance of assessing the construct validity of the performance assessments. Smith (1976) identified relevance (construct validity), reliability, and practicality as criteria for evaluating job performance assessments. Blum and Naylor (1968) summarize the conclusions of many researchers on criteria. Across the different classifications, the common criteria can be stated as (1) discriminability across individuals, (2) practicality, (3) acceptability, (4) reliability, (5) comprehensiveness (lack of criterion deficiency), and (6) construct validity (or relevance or job relatedness or pertinence or freedom from bias such as contamination).

Of these six criteria, voluminous research has focused on issues of reliability and construct validity. Methods to assess job relatedness (pertinent) has been covered in other chapters (see Chapter 4 by Sanchez & Levine, this volume). Criteria such as discriminability and practicality pertain to administration issues and may depend on the context. For example, how well an individual counts can be a good measure of job performance for entry-level clerks in a grocery store but not for high-level accountants. Finally, there has been some limited research on user acceptability as a criterion. In light of this, I devote the rest of this section to these two issues – reliability and construct validity of individual job performance assessments – after briefly summarizing the research on user acceptability.

User Acceptability

Some recent research in the past 20 years has focused on user acceptability of peer ratings of individual job performance. Researchers (e.g., King, Hunter & Schmidt, 1980) have noted that raters were unwilling to accept nontransparent rating instruments such as the mixed standard scales and forced choice measures. Bobko and Colella (1994) summarize the research on how users make meaning and set acceptable performance standards. Dickinson (1993) reviews several factors that could affect user reactions. Folger, Konovsky and Cropanzano (1992) present a due process model based on notions of organizational justice to explain user reactions. User reactions were more favorable when adequate notice was given by the organization about the performance assessment process, a fair hearing was provided, and standards were consistently applied across individuals. Peer ratings were more accepted when peers were considered knowledgeable and have had opportunity to observe the performance.

Earlier research by Borman (1974) had suggested that involvement in the development of rating scales produced more favorable user reactions. This is consistent with the idea that the ability to provide input into a decision process enhances perceptions of procedural justice. Notions of informational and interactional justice (see Chapter 8 in Volume 2 by Gilliland & Chan) also affect user reactions. Taylor, Tracey, Renard, Harrison and Carroll (1995) found that when rater–ratee pairs were randomly formed with some raters trained in due process components, ratees assigned to the trained raters expressed more favorable reactions even though their performance evaluations were more negative compared to the ratees assigned to untrained raters. Several researchers (e.g., Villanova, 1992) have advanced a stakeholder model that explicitly takes into account the values which underlie performance assessments.

Reliability of Individual Job Performance Assessments

Reliability is defined as the consistency of measurement (Nunnally, 1978; Schmidt & Hunter, 1996). Mathematically it can be defined as the ratio of true to observed variance, and depending on what part of observed variance is construed as true variance and what is construed as error variance we have different reliability coefficients (Pedhazur & Schmelkin, 1991; Schmidt & Hunter, 1996). The three major types of reliability assessments that pertain to individual job performance are (1) internal consistency, (2) stability estimates, and (3) interrater reliability estimates. These reliability estimates can be computed for either overall job performance assessments or for each dimension assessed. Some of these estimates (e.g., interrater) are applicable to only some methods of assessments (e.g., subjective evaluations such as ratings) whereas other types of reliability estimates (e.g., stability) are applicable to all methods of assessment (subjective evaluations such as ratings and organizational records).

Consider a researcher interested in assessing the dimension of interpersonal competence in individual job performance. The researcher could develop a list of questions that relate to interpersonal competence and require knowledgeable raters to evaluate individuals in each of the questions. Either an unweighted or weighted sum of the responses to all questions is taken as a measure of interpersonal competence. Now in considering the observed variance across individuals, each question has a specific or unique variance as well as a shared variance with other items. To estimate what proportion of the observed variance is common or shared across items, we employ measures of internal consistency. The most commonly used measure of internal consistency is Cronbach's alpha (Cronbach, 1951).

Internal consistency estimates are also appropriate when organizational records are used to assess individual job performance. If several operational measures of absenteeism are obtained and absenteeism is defined as the common or shared variance across these different operationalizations, then an estimate of internal consistency of organizational records can be computed.

Stability estimates can be obtained as the correlation between measures obtained at times 1 and 2. Here true performance is construed as what is common to both time periods. The greater the time interval, the more likely that true performance will change. Coefficients of stability can be assessed for both organizational records as well as for subjective evaluations such as ratings. With ratings, the same rater has to evaluate the individual at both times of assessment; if different raters are used, stability estimates of ratings confound rater differences with temporal instability.

To estimate the extent to which two raters will agree in their ratings, the interrater reliability is assessed as the correlation between the ratings provided by two raters of the same group of individuals. In reality, different sets of two raters are used to estimate different individuals; under such circumstances the interrater correlation also takes into account rater leniency. Interrater reliability is less applicable with measures based on organizational records, unless the interest is on estimating how accurately the performance has been recorded (better designated as interobserver or intercoder or interrecorder reliability). Interrater reliability can be assessed for overall job performance assessments as well as for specific dimensions of individual job performance.

Interrater reliability can be assessed for different types of raters: supervisors, peers, subordinates, clients/customers. One question that could be raised is whether there are two 'parallel' supervisors. That is, to estimate interrater agreement among supervisors, we need ratings of a group of individuals from at least two supervisors. In many organizations we have only one 'true' supervisor and a second individual (perhaps the supervisor to the supervisor) is included to assess interrater reliability. It could be argued that these two sets of ratings are not parallel. Although conceptually sound, the evidence we review below for interrater reliability of job performance assessments shows that this is not the case. The interrater reliability for peer ratings is lower than that for supervisor ratings (and presumably there are parallel peers).

The different types of reliability estimates for job performance assessments were explained in terms of correlations. However, analysis of variance models can also be used (Hoyt & Kerns, 1999). In fact, generalizability theory (Cronbach, Gleser, Nanda & Rajaratnam, 1972) has been used as a framework to assess the variance due to different sources. Depending on how error variance is conceptualized, different generalizability coefficients can then be proposed. Some researchers (e.g., Murphy & DeShon, 2000) have mistakenly argued that generalizability theory alone estimates these different reliability estimates. In reality, correlational methods and analysis of variance models based on classical measurement theory can be (and were) used to estimate the different reliability estimates (generalizability coefficients). There is not much difference across the different frameworks when properly estimated and interpreted (Schmidt, Viswesvaran & Ones, 2000).

Several studies that had evaluated individual job performance report internal consistency estimates. Consistent with the predominance of cross-sectional studies in the literature compared to longitudinal studies, fewer studies have estimated stability coefficients. Further, more reliability estimates have been reported for subjective evaluations such as ratings than for measures of organizational records. Rather than reviewing each study (which is impossible even in a book-length format), I will summarize the results of major studies and meta-analyses conducted on this topic.

Rothe (1978) conducted a series of studies to assess the stability of productivity measures for different samples of chocolate dippers, welders, and other types of workers. Hackett and Guion (1985) report the reliability of absenteeism measures. Accident measures at two different time periods have been correlated.

Viswesvaran et al. (1996) conducted a comprehensive meta-analysis cumulating results across studies reporting reliability estimates for peer and supervisor ratings. Coefficient alphas, stability estimates, and interrater reliability estimates were averaged separately. The reliability was reported both for assessments of overall job performance as well as for nine dimensions of performance. For supervisory ratings of overall job performance, coefficient alpha was .86, the coefficient of stability was .81, and interrater reliability was .52. It appears that the largest source of error variance was due to rater-specific variance. This finding compares with the generalizability estimates obtained by Greguras and Robie (1998) as well as meta-analysis of the generalizability studies by Hoyt and Kerns (1999).

The reliability estimates for supervisory ratings of different dimensions of job performance are also summarized in Viswesvaran et al. (1996). The sample size weighted mean estimates (along with total number of estimates averaged and total sample size across averaged estimates) are provided below. Interrater reliability estimates were .57 ($k = 19$, $N = 2,015$), .53 ($k = 20$, $N = 2,171$), .55 ($k = 24$, $N = 2,714$), .47 ($k = 31$, $N = 3,006$), and .53 ($k = 20$, $N = 14,072$), for ratings of productivity, leadership, effort, interpersonal competence, and job knowledge, respectively. Coefficient alphas for ratings of productivity, leadership, effort, interpersonal competence were .82, .77, .79, and .77, respectively.

Viswesvaran et al. (1996) also report the sample size weighted average reliability for peer ratings. For ratings of overall job performance, interrater reliability was .42 and coefficient alpha was .85. Reliabilities for peer ratings of leadership, job knowledge, effort, interpersonal competence, administrative competence, and communication competence are also reported (see Viswesvaran et al., 1996). Average coefficient alphas for peer ratings of leadership, effort, and interpersonal competence were .61, .77, and .61, respectively.

Viswesvaran et al. (1996) focused on peer and supervisor ratings, whilst recent studies have explored the reliability of subordinate ratings, for example Mount (1984) as well as Mount, Judge, Scullen, Stysma and Hezzlett (1998). Interrater reliability of subordinate ratings have been found to vary between .31 to .36 for the various dimensions of performance. Scarce data exist for assessing the reliability of customer ratings of performance, and research in the new millennium should remedy this deficiency in the literature.

Further research should also explore the effects of contextual variables in reliability assessments. Churchill and Peter (1984) as well as Petersen (1994) investigated the moderating effects of 13 variables on the reliability estimates of different variables (including job performance). No strong moderator effects were found. Rothstein (1990) reported that the interrater reliability of supervisor ratings of job performance is moderated by the length of exposure the rater has to the ratees. Similar effects such as opportunity to observe should be explored for their effects on reliability estimates. However, these moderating variables can also be construed as variables affecting the construct validity of ratings. It is erroneous to argue that since several variables could potentially affect ratings, interrater reliability estimates do not assess reliability. Reliability is not validity and validity is not reliability (Schmidt et al., 2000). I now turn to a discussion of the construct validity of individual job performance assessments.

Construct Validity of Individual Job Performance Assessments

The construct validity of a measure can be conceptualized as the correlation between the true scores from the measures and the underlying construct (i.e., individual job performance). This correlation can never be empirically estimated, and several lines of evidence are analyzed to assess construct validity. A major component of construct validity is to assess the convergent validity between different methods of assessing the same construct. Heneman (1986) meta-analytically cumulated the correlation between subjective evaluations of job performance provided by supervisors with organizational records-based measures of individual job performance. Heneman (1986) cumulated results across 23 studies (involving a total sample of 3,718) and found a corrected mean correlation of .27 between supervisory ratings and organizational records. Heneman used a reliability estimate of .60 for supervisory ratings and a test–retest stability estimate of .63 for output measures. Using a value of .52 for the reliability of supervisory ratings results in a correlation of .29.

Heneman's (1986) analyses were updated by Bommer, Johnson, Rich, Podsakoff and Mackenzie (1995), who also introduced refinements to the estimation of the convergent validity. Bommer et al. (1995) computed composite correlations across

conceptual replications and cumulated the composite correlations. Composite correlations are more construct-valid than average correlations (see Viswesvaran, Schmidt & Ones, 1994, for a mathematical proof). Bommer et al., estimated the convergence validity between supervisory ratings and organizational records as .39, a value that agrees with the correlations estimated by Viswesvaran (1993). Both Heneman (1986) and Bommer et al. (1995) concluded that rating format and rating scale do not moderate the convergent validity.

McEvoy and Cascio (1987) estimated the correlation between turnover and supervisory ratings of job performance as −.28. This estimate of −.28 was based on a cumulation of results across 24 studies involving 7,717 individuals. McEvoy and Cascio (1987) had used a reliability estimate of .60 for supervisory ratings; using an estimate of .52, results in a correlation of −.30. Bycio (1992) meta-analyzed the results across studies reporting a correlation between absenteeism and job performance. Across 49 samples involving 15,764 datapoints, the correlation was −.29. This estimate of −.29 averaged results across studies that used either time lost or frequency measures of absenteeism. When the cumulation was restricted to time lost measures of absenteeism, the correlation was −.26 (28 samples, 7,704 individuals); when restricted to frequency measures of absenteeism, the estimate was −.32 (21 samples, 8,060 individuals).

In addition to investigating the convergence between supervisory ratings of job performance and organizational records of (1) productivity, and (2) personnel data such as turnover and absenteeism, researchers have explored the overlap between organizational records of productivity and personnel data (e.g., absenteeism, promotions etc.). Bycio (1992) reports a correlation of .24 between organizational records of performance indices and absenteeism (23 samples, 5,204 individuals). The correlation was −.28 (11 samples, 1,649 individuals) when time lost measures of absenteeism were considered; with frequency-based measures of absenteeism (12 samples, 3,555 individuals) the meta-analyzed correlation was −.22.

The meta-analytic results summarized so far focused on supervisory ratings and on ratings of overall job performance. Viswesvaran (1993) reports correlations between organizational records of productivity and 10 dimensions of rated job performance. The convergent validity of ratings and records-based measures were analyzed for peers and supervisors. In general, the convergent validity was higher for supervisory ratings than they were for peer ratings. Organizational records seem to reflect the supervisory perspective more than the peer perspective.

The convergence among the different sources of ratings have been explored, and two reviews of this literature have been reported. Mabe and West (1982) presented the first review of this literature which was subsequently updated by Harris and Schaubroeck (1988). Harris and Schaubroeck (1988) found a correlation of .62 between peer and supervisory ratings of overall job performance (23 samples, 2,643 individuals). The correlation between self and supervisor or peer ratings were much lower. Whilst Harris and Schaubroeck focused on overall ratings of job performance, Viswesvaran, Schmidt and Ones (2000) meta-analyzed the peer–supervisor correlations for overall as well as eight dimensions of job performance. Viswesvaran et al. (2000) reported a mean observed peer–supervisor correlation of .40, .48, .38, .34, .35, .36, .41, and .49, for ratings of productivity, effort, interpersonal competence, administrative competence, quality, job knowledge, leadership, and compliance with authority, respectively. Research suggests (e.g., Harris, Smith & Champagne, 1995) that ratings obtained for administrative and research purposes are comparable.

Most of the extant literature reported correlations between self ratings, peer ratings, supervisor ratings, and organizational records. Recent research has started exploring the convergence between other sources of ratings (e.g., subordinates, customers). Mount et al. (1998) report correlations between subordinate ratings and peer or supervisor ratings for overall as well as three dimensions of performance. More research is needed in the future to make robust conclusions of convergent validity across these sources.

In addition to investigating the convergent validity across sources with correlations, researchers have used the multitrait–multimethod matrix (Campbell & Fiske, 1959) of correlations between different methods and performance dimensions to tease out the trait and method variance. Cote and Buckley (1987) as well as Schmitt and Stults (1986) provide elaboration of this approach as well as a summary of the application to performance assessment. Conway (1996) used an MTMM matrix and confirmatory factor analyses to support the construct validity of task and contextual performance measures. Mount et al. (1998), however, caution that previous applications of this approach had neglected within-source variability, and once this source is taken into account substantive conclusions vary.

Convergence across sources is one aspect of construct validity. Assessment of construct validity also involves assessing the potential and presence of several sources of variance that is unrelated to the construct under investigation. From as early as the 1920s researchers have been developing lists of factors that could affect the construct validity of job performance assessments. Burtt (1926) drew attention to the potential for criterion contamination and deficiency in organizational records, whilst Thorndike (1920) introduced the concept of halo error in ratings.

The last half of the twentieth century has seen an explosion of research on judgmental errors that could affect ratings. Lance, LaPointe and Stewart (1994) identified three definitions of halo error. Halo could be conceptualized as (1) a general evaluation that affects all dimensional ratings, (2) a salient dimension that affects ratings on other dimensions, and (3) insufficient discrimination among dimensions (Solomonson & Lance, 1997). Cooper (1981) discusses the different measures of halo as well as strategies designed to mitigate the effects of halo. Distributional problems such as leniency, central tendency, and stringency have been assessed. Judgmental errors such as the fundamental attribution error, representativeness and availability heuristics, and contrast effects in assessments have been studied. Wherry and Bartlett (1982) present a model incorporating many of the potential influences on ratings. Recent methodological advances such as combining meta-analysis and structural equations modeling, meta-analysis and generalizability theory (Hoyt, 2000; Hoyt & Kerns, 1999), have enabled researchers to assess the effects of these judgmental processes on the construct validity of job performance assessments.

Finally, investigations of the construct validity of ratings have been explored by estimating the effects of demographic variables on assessments. Kraiger and Ford (1985) reported differences between racial groups of almost one half of a standard deviation unit. However, the Kraiger and Ford (1985) meta-analyses included laboratory-based experimental studies as well as field studies. More importantly, ratee ability was not controlled. Pulakos, White, Oppler and Borman (1989) found in a large sample study of job performance assessment in a military setting, that once ratee ability is controlled, the biasing effects of race are small. Similar findings were found with civilian samples of over 36,000 individuals across 174 jobs (Sackett & Dubois, 1991). The effects of age and gender of the ratees and raters have also been investigated (see Cascio, 1991, for a summary). The biasing effects of demographic variables has not been found to be substantial. The dynamic nature of criteria has also been investigated, and empirical evidence suggests that although mean levels of individual job performance changed over time, rank ordering of individuals did not (Barrett, Cladwell & Alexander, 1989). Although potential exists for distortion, most well-constructed and administered performance assessments systems result in construct-valid data on individual job performance.

CAUSAL MODELS FOR JOB PERFORMANCE DIMENSIONS

In the last section of this chapter, I review models of work behavior that postulate how different individual differences variables are linked to different aspects of performance. The search for explanation and understanding suggests a step beyond mere prediction (Schmidt & Kaplan, 1971). Hunter (1983) developed and tested a causal model where cognitive ability was a direct causal antecedent to both job knowledge and job performance. Job knowledge was an antecedent to job performance. Both job knowledge and job performance contributed to supervisory ratings. These findings suggest that cognitive ability contributes to overall job performance through its effects on learning job knowledge and mastery of required skills. Borman, Hanson, Oppler, Pulakos and White (1993) extended the model to explain supervisory performance.

McCloy, Campbell and Cudeck (1994) argued that all individual differences variables affect performance in any dimension by their effects on either procedural knowledge or declarative knowledge or motivation. Barrick, Mount and Strauss (1993) tested and found support for a model where conscientiousness predicted overall performance by affecting goal setting. Ones and Viswesvaran (1996) argued that conscientiousness has multiple pathways by which it affects overall performance. First, conscientious individuals are likely to spend more time on the task and less time daydreaming. This investment of time will result in greater acquisition of job knowledge, which in turn will result in greater productivity and which in turn will result in positive ratings. Further, conscientious individuals are likely to engage in organizational citizenship behaviors which in turn might enhance productivity and ratings. Finally, conscientious individuals are expected to pay more attention to detail and profit more via vicarious learning (Bandura, 1977) which would result in higher job knowledge and productivity.

Borman and Motowidlo (1993) postulated that ability will predict task performance more strongly than individual differences in personality. On the other hand, individual differences in personality were hypothesized to predict contextual performance better than ability. Motowidlo et al. (1997) developed a more nuanced model where contextual performance was modeled as dependent on contextual habits, contextual skills, and contextual knowledge. Although habits and skills were predicated on personality, contextual knowledge was influenced both by personality and cognitive ability. Similarly, task performance is influenced by task habits, task skill and task knowledge. Whereas task skill and task knowledge are influenced solely by cognitive ability, task habits are affected by both cognitive ability and personality variables. Thus, this more nuanced model implies that both ability and personality have a role in explaining task and contextual performance. The bottom line appears to be that each performance dimension is complexly determined so that it is impossible to specify different individual differences variables as sole cause or antecedent of a particular dimension of job performance. This is also to be expected given the positive correlations across the various dimensions.

CONCLUSIONS

Job performance is a central construct in our field. Voluminous research has been undertaken to assess (1) the factor structure of the construct, (2) refine the methods of assessment, (3) assess user reactions, reliability, and construct validity of assessments of individual job performance, and (4) develop models of work behavior that delineate the antecedents of individual job performance. A century of research suggests that the factor structure of job performance can be summarized as a hierarchy with a general factor at the apex with group factors at the next level. The breadth and range of the group factors differ across authors.

Several methods of assessments have been proposed, evaluated, and used. Research on user reactions has invoked justice theory concepts. Interrater reliability, internal consistency estimates, and stability assessments have been examined for assessments of overall performance as well as for several dimensions of performance. Correlational, Anova and generalizability models have been used in reliability estimation. The construct validity of individual job performance assessment has been assessed with emphasis on judgmental errors such as halo, group differences, convergences between different methods of assessments. Finally, path models have been specified to link antecedents to the different job performance dimensions.

Impressive as the existing literature is on assessments of individual job performance, several trends in the workplace call for additional research. The changing nature of work (Howard, 1996) brings with it the changes in assessment of performance (Ilgen & Pulakos, 1999); and the use of electronic monitoring and other technological advances may change the nature of what we measure (Hedge & Borman, 1995). Assessments of performance of expatriates will also gain in importance (see Chapter 20 by Sinangil & Ones in this volume). In short, a lively phase is ahead for researchers and practitioners.

REFERENCES

Alonso, A. (2000). The relationship between cognitive ability, the Big Five, Task and Contextual Performance: A meta-analysis. Unpublished Masters Thesis, Florida International University, Miami, FL.

Arvey, R.D., & Murphy, K.R. (1998). Performance evaluation in work settings. *Annual Review of Psychology*, *49*, 141–168.

Austin, J.T., & Villanova, P. (1992). The criterion problem: 1917–1992. *Journal of Applied Psychology*, 77, 836–874.

Baier, D.E., & Dugan, R.D. (1957). Factors in sales success. *Journal of Applied Psychology*, 41, 37–40.

Bandura, A. (1977). *Social learning theory*. Englewood Cliffs, NJ: Prentice-Hall.

Barber, A.E. (1998). *Recruiting employees: Individual and organizational perspectives*. Thousand Oaks, CA: Sage.

Barrett, G.V., Cladwell, M.S., & Alexander, R.A. (1989). The predictive stability of ability requirements for task performance: A critical reanalysis. *Human Performance*, 2, 167–181.

Barrick, M.R., Mount, M.K., & Strauss, J. (1993). Conscientiousness and performance of sales representatives: Test of the mediating effects of goal setting. *Journal of Applied Psychology*, 78, 715–722.

Bechtoldt, H.P. (1947). Factorial investigation of the perceptual-speed factor. *American Psychologist*, 2, 304–305.

Bellows, R.M. (1941). Procedures for evaluating locational criteria. *Journal of Applied Psychology*, 25, 499–513.

Bendig A.W. (1954). Reliability and the number of rating-scale categories. *Journal of Applied Psychology*, 38, 38–40.

Bernardin, J.H., Alvares, K.M., Cranny, C.J. (1976). A recomparison of behavioral expectation scales to summated scales. *Journal of Applied Psychology*, 61(5), 564–570.

Bernardin, H.J., & Beatty, R. (1984). *Performance appraisal: Assessing human behavior at work*. Boston: Kent-PWS.

Bernardin, H.J., Pence, E.C. (1980). Effects of rater training: Creating new response sets and decreasing accuracy. *Journal of Applied Psychology*, 65(1), 60–66.

Bernardin, H.J., & Russell, J.E.A. (1998). *Human resource management: An experiential approach* (2nd ed.). Boston, MA: McGraw-Hill.

Blanz, F., & Ghiselli, E.E. (1972). The mixed standard scale: A new rating system. *Personnel Psychology*, 25, 185–199.

Blum, M.L., & Naylor, J.C. (1968). *Industrial Psychology: Its theoretical and social foundations*. New York: Harper & Row.

Bobko, P., & Colella, A. (1994). Employee reactions to performance standards: A review and research propositions. *Personnel Psychology*, 47, 1–29.

Bommer, W.H., Johnson, J.L., Rich, G.A., Podsakoff, P.M., & MacKenzie, S.B. (1995). On the interchangeability of objective and subjective measures of employee performance: A meta-analysis. *Personnel Psychology*, 48, 587–605.

Borman, W.C. (1974). The rating of individuals in organizations: An alternate approach. *Organizational Behavior and Human Performance*, 12, 105–124.

Borman, W.C. (1991). Job behavior, performance, and effectiveness. In M.D. Dunnette, & L.M. Hough (Eds.), *Handbook of industrial and organizational psychology*

(2nd ed., Vol. 2, pp. 271–326). Palo Alto, CA: Consulting Psychologists Press.

Borman, W.C., Hanson, M.A., Oppler, S.H., Pulakos, E.D., & White, L.A. (1993). Role of early supervisory experience in supervisor performance. *Journal of Applied Psychology*, 78, 443–449.

Borman, W.C., & Motowidlo, S.J. (1993). Expanding the criterion domain to include elements of contextual performance. In N. Schmitt & W.C. Borman (Eds.), *Personnel selection in organizations* (pp. 71–98). San Francisco, CA: Jossey-Bass.

Borman, W.C., Motowidlo, S.J., Rose, S.R., & Hansen, L.M. (1985). *Development of a model of soldier effectiveness*. Minneapolis, MN: Personnel Decisions Research Institute.

Borman, W.C., White, L.A., Pulakos, E.D., Oppler, S.H. (1991). Models of supervisory job performance ratings. *Journal of Applied Psychology*, 76, 863–872.

Brief, A.P., & Motowidlo, S.J. (1986). Prosocial organizational behavior. *Academy of Management Review, 11*, 710–725.

Brogden, H., & Taylor, E.K. (1950). The dollar criterion: Applying the cost accounting concept to criterion construction. *Personnel Psychology*, 3, 133–154.

Burtt, H.E. (1926). *Principles of employment psychology*. Boston: Houghton-Mifflin.

Bycio, P. (1992). Job performance and absenteeism: A review and meta-analysis. *Human Relations, 45*, 193–220.

Campbell, J.P. (1990). Modeling the performance prediction problem in industrial and organizational psychology. In M. Dunnette & L.M. Hough (Eds.), *Handbook of industrial and organizational psychology* (Vol. 1, 2nd ed., pp. 687–731). Palo Alto, CA: Consulting Psychologists Press.

Campbell, D.T., & Fiske, D.W. (1959). Convergent and discriminant validation by means of the multitrait-mutimethod matrix. *Psychological Bulletin, 56*, 81–105.

Campbell, J.P., Gasser, M.B., & Oswald, F.L. (1996). The substantive nature of job performance variability. In K.R. Murphy (Ed.), *Individual differences and behavior in organizations* (pp. 258–299). San Francisco: Jossey-Bass.

Campbell, J.P., McCloy, R.A., Oppler, S.H., & Sager, C.E. (1993). A theory of performance. In N. Schmitt & W.C. Borman (Eds.), *Personnel selection in organizations* (pp. 35–70). San Francisco, CA: Jossey-Bass.

Campbell, J.P., McHenry, J.J., & Wise, L.L. (1990). Modeling job performance in a population of jobs. *Personnel Psychology, 43*, 313–333.

Cascio, W.F. (1991). *Applied psychology in personnel management* (4th ed.). Englewood Cliffs, NJ: Prentice-Hall.

Church, A.H., & Bracken, D.W. (1997). Advancing the state of the art of 360 degree feedback. *Group and Organization Management, 22*, 149–161.

Churchill, G.A., Jr., & Peter, J.P. (1984). Research design effects on the reliability of rating scales: A meta-analysis. *Journal of Marketing Research, 21*, 360–375.

Clark, J.P., & Hollinger, R.C. (1983). *Theft by employees in work organizations: Executive summary*. Washington, DC: National Institute of Justice.

Cleveland, J.N., Murphy, K.R., & Williams, R.E. (1989). Multiple uses of performance appraisal: Prevalence and correlates. *Journal of Applied Psychology*, *74*, 130–135.

Conway, J.M. (1996). Analysis and design of multitrait-multirater performance appraisal studies. *Journal of Management*, *22*, 139–162.

Conway, J.M. (1999). Distinguishing contextual performance from task performance for managerial jobs. *Journal of Applied Psychology*, *84*, 3–13.

Cooper, W.H. (1981). Ubiquitous halo. *Psychological Bulletin*, *90*(2), 218–244.

Cote, J.A., & Buckley, M.R. (1987). Estimating trait, method and error variance: Generalizing across seventy construct validation studies. *Journal of Marketing Research*, *24*, 315–318.

Cronbach, L.J. (1951). Coefficient alpha and the internal structure of tests. *Psychometrika*, *16*, 297–334.

Cronbach, L.J., Gleser, G.C., Nanda, H., & Rajaratnam, N. (1972). *The dependability of behavioral measurements: Theory of generalizability for scores and profiles*. New York: Wiley.

DeVries, D.L., Morrison, A.M., Shullman, S.L., & Gerlach, M.L. (1986). *Performance appraisal on the line*. Greensboro, NC: Center for Creative Leadership.

Dickinson, T.L. (1993). Attitudes about performance appraisal. In H. Schuler, J.L. Farr & M. Smith (Eds.), *Personnel selection and assessment: Individual and organizational perspectives* (pp. 141–162). Hillsdale, NJ: Erlbaum.

DuBois, C.L., Sackett, P.R., Zedeck, S., & Fogli, L. (1993). Further exploration of typical and maximum performance criteria: Definitional issues, prediction, and white-black differences. *Journal of Applied Psychology*, *78*, 205–211.

Farmer, E. (1933). The reliability of the criteria used for accessing the value of vocational tests. *British Journal of Psychology*, *24*, 109–119.

Folger, R., Konovsky, M.A., & Cropanzano, R. (1992). A due process metaphor for performance appraisal. In B.M. Staw & L.L. Cummings (Eds), *Research in Organizational Behavior* (Vol. 14, pp. 129–177). Greenwich, CT: JAI Press.

Freyd, M. (1926). What is applied psychology? *Psychological Review*, *33*, 308–314.

George, J.M., & Brief, A.P. (1992). Feeling good–doing good: A conceptual analysis of the mood at work-organizational spontaneity relationship. *Psychological Bulletin*, *112*, 310–329.

Goldberg, L.R. (1995). What the hell took so long? Donald Fiske and the big-five factor structure. In P.E. Shrout & S.T. Fiske (Eds.), *Advances in personality research, methods, and theory: A festschrift honoring Donald W. Fiske*. New York, NY: Erlbaum.

Greguras, G.J., & Robie, C. (1998). A new look at within-source interrater reliability of 360-degree feedback ratings. *Journal of Applied Psychology*, *83*, 960–968.

Guion, R.M. (1976). Recruiting, selection, and job placement. In M.D. Dunnette (Ed.), *Handbook of industrial and organizational psychology* (pp. 777–828). Chicago: Rand McNally.

Guion, R.M. (1998). *Assessment, measurement, and prediction for personnel selection*. Mahwah, NJ: Lawrence Erlbaum.

Gunderson, E.K.E., & Ryman, D.H. (1971). Convergent and discriminant validities of performance evaluations in extremely isolated groups. *Personnel Psychology*, *24*, 715–724.

Hackett, R.D., & Guion, R.M. (1985). A re-evaluation of the absenteeism-job satisfaction relationship. *Organizational Behavior and Human Decision Processes*, *35*, 340–381.

Harris, M.M., & Schaubroeck, J. (1988). A meta-analysis of self-supervisor, self-peer, and peer-supervisor ratings. *Personnel Psychology*, *41*, 43–62.

Harris, M.M., Smith, D.E., & Champagne, D. (1995). A field study of performance appraisal purpose: Research-versus administrative-based ratings. *Personnel Psychology*, *48*, 151–160.

Hedge, J.W., & Borman, W.C. (1995). Changing conceptions and practices in performance appraisal. In A. Howard (Ed.), *The changing nature of work* (pp. 451–481). San Francisco, Jossey-Bass.

Heneman, R.L. (1986). The relationship between supervisory ratings and results-oriented measures of performance: A meta-analysis. *Personnel Psychology*, *39*, 811–826.

Howard, A. (Ed.) (1996). *The changing nature of work*. San Francisco, Jossey-Bass.

Hoyt, W.T. (2000). Rater bias in psychological research: When is it a problem and what can we do about it? *Psychological Methods*, *5*, 64–86.

Hoyt, W.T., & Kerns, M.D. (1999). Magnitude and moderators of bias in observer ratings: A meta analysis. *Psychological Methods*, *4*, 403–424.

Hunt, S.T. (1996). Generic work behavior: An investigation into the dimensions of entry-level, hourly job performance. *Personnel Psychology*, *49*, 51–83.

Hunter, J.E. (1983). *Test validation for 12,000 jobs: An application of job classification and validity generalization to General Aptitude Test Battery* (USES Test Research Report no. 45). Washington, DC: United States Department of Labor.

Ilgen, D.R., & Pulakos, E.D. (1999). *The changing nature of performance: Implications for staffing, motivation, and development*. San Francisco: Jossey-Bass.

Kane, J.S. (1986). Performance distribution assessment. In R.A. Berk (Ed.), *Performance assessment* (pp. 237–273). Baltimore: Johns Hopkins University Press.

Katz, D. (1964). The motivational basis of organizational behavior. *Behavioral Science*, *9*, 131–146.

Kidwell, R.E., & Bennett, N. (1993). Employee propensity to withhold effort: A conceptual model to intersect three avenues of research. *Academy of Management Review*, *18*, 429–456.

King, L.M., Hunter, J.E., & Schmidt, F.L. (1980). Halo in a multidimensional forced-choice performance evaluation scale. *Journal of Applied Psychology*, *65*, 507–516.

Klimoski, R., & London, M. (1974). Role of the rater in performance appraisal. *Journal of Applied Psychology*, *59*, 445–451.

Kraiger, K., & Ford, J.K. (1985). A meta-analysis of ratee race effects in performance ratings. *Journal of Applied Psychology, 70,* 56–65.

Lance, C.E., LaPointe, J.A., & Stewart, A.M. (1994). A test of the context dependency of three causal models of halo rater error. *Journal of Applied Psychology, 79,* 332–340.

Landy, F.J., & Farr, J.L. (1980). Performance rating. *Psychological Bulletin, 87,* 72–107.

Latham, G.P., Fay, C., & Saari, L.M. (1980). BOS, BES, and baloney: Raising Kane with Bernardin. *Personnel Psychology, 33,* 815–821.

Lissitz, R., & Green, S.B. (1975). Effect of the number of scale points on reliability: A Monte Carlo approach. *Journal of Applied Psychology, 60,* 1–10.

Mabe, P.A. III, & West, S.G. (1982). Validity of self-evaluation of ability: A review and meta-analysis. *Journal of Applied Psychology, 67,* 280–296.

Mace, C.A. (1935). *Incentives: Some experimental studies.* (Report 72). London: Industrial Health Research Board.

McCloy, R.A., Campbell, J.P., & Cudeck, R. (1994). A confirmatory test of a model of performance determinants. *Journal of Applied Psychology, 79,* 493–505.

McEvoy, G.M., & Cascio, W.F. (1987). Do good or poor performers leave? A meta-analysis of the relationship between performance and turnover. *Academy of Management Journal, 30,* 744–762.

Motowidlo, S.J., Borman, W.C., & Schmit, M.J. (1997). A theory of individual differences in task and contextual performance. *Human Performance, 10,* 71–83.

Mount, M.K. (1984). Psychometric properties of subordinate ratings of managerial performance. *Personnel Psychology, 37,* 687–702.

Mount, M.K., Judge, T.A., Scullen, S.E., Stysma, M.R., & Hezlett, S.A. (1998). Trait, rater, and level effects in 360-degree performance ratings. *Personnel Psychology, 51,* 557–576.

Murphy, K.R. (1989). Dimensions of job performance. In R. Dillon & J. Pelligrino (Eds.), *Testing: Applied and theoretical perspectives* (pp. 218–247). New York: Praeger.

Murphy, K.R., & Cleveland, J.N. (1995). *Understanding performance appraisal: Social, organizational, and goal-based perspectives.* Thousand Oaks, CA: Sage.

Murphy, K.R., & DeShon, R. (2000). Inter-rater correlations do not estimate the reliability of job performance ratings. *Personnel Psychology, 53,* 873–900.

Nunnally, J.C. (1978). *Psychometric theory* (2nd ed.). New York: McGraw Hill.

Ones, D.S., & Viswesvaran, C. (1996). A general theory of conscientiousness at work: Theoretical underpinnings and empirical findings. In J.M. Collins (Chair), *Personality predictors of job performance: Controversial issues.* Symposium conducted at the eleventh annual meeting of the Society for Industrial and Organizational Psychology, San Diego, CA, April.

Ones, D.S., Viswesvaran, C., & Schmidt, F.L. (1993). Comprehensive meta-analysis of integrity test validities: Findings and implications for personnel selection and theories of job performance. *Journal of Applied Psychology, 78,* 679–703.

Organ, D.W. (1988). *Organizational citizenship behavior.* Lexington, MA: D.C. Heath.

Pedhazur, E.J., & Schmelkin, L.P. (1991). *Measurement, design, and analysis: An integrated approach.* Hillsdale, NJ: Erlbaum.

Peterson, R.A. (1994). A meta-analysis of Cronbach's coefficient alpha. *Journal of Consumer Research, 21,* 381–391.

Prien, E.P., & Kult, M. (1968). Analysis of performance criteria and comparison of a priori and empirically-derived keys for a forced-choice scoring. *Personnel Psychology, 21,* 505–513.

Pulakos, E.D., White, L.A., Oppler, S.H., & Borman, W.C. (1989). Examination of race and sex effects on performance ratings. *Journal of Applied Psychology, 74,* 770–780.

Roach, D.E., & Wherry, R.J. (1970). Performance dimensions of multi-line insurance agents. *Personnel Psychology, 23,* 239–250.

Ronan, W.W. (1963). A factor analysis of eleven job performance measures. *Personnel Psychology, 16,* 255–267.

Ronan, W.W., & Prien, E. (1966). *Toward a criterion theory: A review and analysis of research and opinion.* Greensboro, NC: Smith Richardson Foundation.

Rothe, H. (1978). Output rates among industrial employees. *Journal of Applied Psychology, 63,* 40–46.

Rothstein, H.R. (1990). Interrater reliability of job performance ratings: Growth to asymptote level with increasing opportunity to observe. *Journal of Applied Psychology, 75,* 322–327.

Rush, C.H. (1953). A factorial study of sales criteria. *Personnel Psychology, 6,* 9–24.

Sackett, P.R., & DuBois, C.L. (1991). Rater-ratee race effects on performance evaluations: Challenging meta-analytic conclusions. *Journal of Applied Psychology, 76,* 873–877.

Sackett, P.R., & Wanek, J.E. (1996). New developments in the use of measures of honesty, integrity, conscientiousness, dependability, trustworthiness and reliability for personnel selection. *Personnel Psychology, 49,* 787–830.

Sackett, P.R., Zedeck, S., & Fogli, L. (1988). Relations between measures of typical and maximum job performance. *Journal of Applied Psychology, 73,* 482–486.

Schmidt, F.L. (1980). The measurement of job performance. Unpublished manuscript.

Schmidt, F.L., & Hunter, J.E. (1989). Interrater reliability coefficients cannot be computed when only one stimulus is rated. *Journal of Applied Psychology, 74,* 368–370.

Schmidt, F.L., & Hunter, J.E. (1992). Causal modeling of processes determining job performance. *Current Directions in Psychological Science, 1,* 89–92.

Schmidt, F.L., & Hunter, J.E. (1996). Measurement error in psychological research: Lessons from 26 research scenarios. *Psychological Methods, 1,* 199–223.

Schmidt, F.L., & Kaplan, L.B. (1971). Composite versus multiple criteria: A review and resolution of the controversy. *Personnel Psychology, 24,* 419–434.

Schmidt, F.L., Viswesvaran, C., & Ones, D.S. (2000). Reliability is not validity and validity is not reliability. *Personnel Psychology, 53,* 901–912.

Schmitt, N., & Stults, D.M. (1986). Methodology review: Analysis of multitrait–multimethod matrices. *Applied Psychological Measurement, 10*(1), 1–22.

Schwab, D.T., Heneman, H.G. III., & DeCotiis, T. (1975). Behaviorally anchored rating scales: A review of the literature. *Personnel Psychology, 28*, 549–562.

Seashore, S.E., Indik, B.P., & Georgopoulos, B.S. (1960). Relationships among criteria of job performance. *Journal of Applied Psychology, 44*, 195–202.

Smith, C.A., Organ, D.W., & Near, J.P. (1983). Organizational citizenship behavior: Its nature and antecedents. *Journal of Applied Psychology, 68*, 655–663.

Smith, P.C. (1976). Behavior, results, and organizational effectiveness: The problem of criteria. In M.D. Dunnette (Ed.), *Handbook of industrial and organizational psychology* (pp. 745–775). Chicago: Rand McNally.

Smith, P.C., & Kendall, L.M. (1963). Retranslation of expectations. *Journal of Applied Psychology, 47*, 149–155.

Solomonson, A.L., & Lance, C.E. (1997). Examination of the relationship between true halo and halo error in performance ratings. *Journal of Applied Psychology, 82*, 665–674.

Symonds, P. (1924). On the loss of reliability in ratings due to coarseness of the scale. *Journal of Experimental Psychology, 7*, 456–461.

Taylor, M.S., Tracey, K.B., Renard, M.K., Harrison, J.K., & Carroll, S.J. (1995). Due process in performance appraisal: A quasi-experiment in procedural justice. *Administrative Science Quarterly, 40*, 495–523.

Thorndike, E.L. (1920). A constant error in psychological ratings. In J.P. Porter & W.F. Book (Eds.), *The Journal of Applied Psychology, 4*, 25–29.

Thorndike, R.L. (1949). *Personnel selection: Test and measurement techniques*. New York: Wiley.

Toops, H.A. (1944). The criterion. *Educational and Psychological Measurement, 4*, 271–297.

Van Dyne, L., Cummings, L.L., & Parks, J.M. (1995). Extra-role behaviors: Its pursuit of construct and definitional clarity (a bridge over muddied waters). In L.L. Cummings & B.M. Staw (Eds.), *Research in organizational behavior* (Vol. 17, pp. 215–285). Greenwich, CT: JAI Press.

Van Scotter, J.R., & Motowidlo, S.J. (1996). Interpersonal facilitation and job dedication as separate facets of contextual performance. *Journal of Applied Psychology, 81*, 525–531.

Villanova, P. (1992). A customer-based model for developing job performance criteria. *Human Resource Management Review, 2*, 103–114.

Viswesvaran, C. (1993). Modeling job performance: Is there a general factor? Unpublished doctoral dissertation, University of Iowa, Iowa City, IA.

Viswesvaran, C., & Ones, D.S. (1995). Theory testing: Combining psychometric meta-analysis and structural equations modeling. *Personnel Psychology, 48*, 865–885.

Viswesvaran, C., & Ones, D.S. (2000). Perspectives on models of job performance. *International Journal of Selection and Assessment, 8*, 216–226.

Viswesvaran, C., Ones, D.S., & Schmidt, F.L. (1996). Comparative analysis of the reliability of job performance ratings. *Journal of Applied Psychology, 81*, 557–574.

Viswesvaran, C., Schmidt, F.L., & Ones, D.S. (1994). Examining the validity of supervisory ratings of job performance using linear composites. Paper presented in F.L. Schmidt (Chair), *The construct of job performance*. Symposium conducted at the ninth annual meeting of the Society of Industrial and Organizational Psychologists, Nashville, Tennessee, April.

Viswesvaran, C., Schmidt, F.L., & Ones, D.S. (2000). The moderating influence of job performance dimensions on convergence of supervisory and peer ratings of job performance: Unconfounding construct-level convergence and rating difficulty. Unpublished manuscript.

Viteles, M.S. (1932). *Industrial psychology*. New York: Norton.

Wallace, S.R. (1965). Criteria for what? *American Psychologist, 20*, 411–417.

Welbourne, T.M., Johnson, D.E., & Erez, A. (1998). The role-based performance scale: Validity analysis of a theory-based measure. *Academy of Management Journal, 41*, 540–555.

Wherry, R.J. (1957). The past and future of criterion evaluation. *Personnel Psychology, 10*, 1–5.

Wherry, R.J., Bartlett, C.J. (1982). The control of bias in ratings: A theory of rating. *Personnel Psychology, 35*, 521–551.

Whisler, T.L., & Harper, S.F. (Eds.) (1962). *Performance appraisal: Research and practice*. New York: Holt.

7

Performance Appraisal and Feedback: A Consideration of National Culture and a Review of Contemporary Research and Future Trends

CLIVE FLETCHER and ELISSA L. PERRY

This chapter critically reviews the direction of research on performance appraisal and multi-source feedback systems. In view of the increasing internationalization of work, it offers a detailed analysis of appraisal from a cross-cultural perspective. Two dimensions – power distance and individualism/collectivism – are discussed in terms of their influence on (1) who appraises, (2) the style/process used, (3) the content of evaluation, and (4) the purpose of appraisal. Some implications of this analysis for the generalizability of US/Western appraisal research are considered. Finally, the chapter looks to the future of appraisal in light of changes in organizations, legislation and – in particular – information technology. The potential role and contribution of organizational psychology in the face of these changes are discussed.

Performance appraisal (PA) is the term applied to a variety of processes that generally involve the assessment and development of an individual and their performance at work, both in terms of their existing effectiveness and their potential for advancement. PA has been with us, as a formal process of one kind or another, for the best part of a century. It is found almost universally in large organizations, and has been subject to much research by psychologists. Yet for all that, it remains a problematic area. It is often perceived as being not as successful as it should be; 80% of companies reported dissatisfaction with their appraisal scheme in one UK survey (Fletcher, 1997a). The purpose of the present chapter is to consider where PA is now and how it arrived there, and to project forward by discussing its likely future development. In the process of this, we will focus on a specific theme which we feel has been unduly neglected in the appraisal literature,

namely, cross-cultural perspectives on the PA process. It has been estimated that 90% of studies in industrial and organizational psychology have used data from Northwestern Europe and North America despite the fact that these samples represent no more than 15% of the world's population (Triandis, 1989).

Formal PA systems were well established by the 1950s; at that time, personality-based appraisal systems were quite common on both sides of the Atlantic, associated with a belief in the importance of feedback as an aid to learning and as a motivating mechanism. Much of the development of appraisal practice from then until the 1990s is arguably American in origin. McGregor's (1957) 'uneasy look' at PA highlighted the growing concerns about the use of personality-based ratings and the reluctance of managers to actually carry out appraisals during this period. With considerable prescience, he advocated a more participative and performance-based approach, incorporating a strong element of self-appraisal. McGregor's vision of PA as a goal-directed process that looked forward more than it looked backward was also supported by other writers (Maier, 1958; Meyer, Kay & French, 1965). So, with the additional influence of the Management By Objectives movement, appraisal practice moved through the 1960s with a greater emphasis on goal-setting and the assessment of performance-related abilities.

The 1970s were marked chiefly by the growing impact of legislation on PA. Appraisal practices became more open to both individual and public scrutiny as a result. Organizations in the US and some European countries had to be able to prove that their appraisal ratings were job related, reliable, and nondiscriminatory. One consequence of this was that numerous cases were brought to court (Holley & Field, 1975); another was that research on rating scales and their use – always a favored field for psychologists – increased considerably, and has continued to be a major element in the PA literature to the present day. An additional trend emerging first in the 1960s but gathering momentum in the 1970s and early 1980s was the increasing use of psychometric tests and assessment centers (see Chapters 2 and 9) for identifying management potential. Assessing promotability and potential had been one of the functions of appraisal, but the subjective nature of such judgments had long been recognized, and as a result of the growing confidence in these (i.e., tests and assessment centres) alternative approaches this tended to become a less prominent part of the appraisal process.

In the 1980s and early 1990s, pressures on western economies from Pacific Rim competition, cheaper labor costs in some of the less developed countries and various other factors brought numerous changes in organizations (such as delayering and downsizing), which in turn led to a stronger than ever focus on performance. The concept of performance management became fashionable, representing a more holistic approach to generating motivation, improving performance and managing human resources (Williams, 1998). PA was a key element in this, and in better examples of performance management systems it was linked more effectively with other human resource management processes than had often been the case previously (IPM, 1992). Less positively, though, the same period saw a de-emphasis on the short to medium term developmental function of appraisal; so many organizations were downsizing that there was little interest in developing staff for a future in the company that was either unpredictable or nonexistent.

However, once this phase had passed and economies started coming out of the recession in the early 1990s, development was once again back as an integral part of the appraisal agenda. Also, organizational cultures in general had shifted markedly to become more dynamic, flexible and open (Cascio, 1995). These changes, by reducing the hierarchical nature of many companies, paved the way for the most prominent recent trend in appraisal – namely the introduction of multi-source, multi-rater (MSMR) feedback systems, often referred to as 360-degree feedback systems (see below). Overall, then, the way PA has developed in the last three decades has mainly been in response to wider social, economic, and legal changes and their impact on organizations.

CURRENT PERFORMANCE APPRAISAL RESEARCH

There has been no shortage of research on appraisal, and there are a number of reviews that have been published (e.g., Landy & Farr, 1980; Latham, Skarlicki, Irvine & Siegel, 1993; Arvey & Murphy, 1998). However, the research has not always moved us forward as far as might be hoped (Banks & Murphy, 1985), maybe because the dominant theme of much of the work has been assessment accuracy, either in terms of rating scale formats or the effects of rater errors and how to overcome them. Despite the greater time and effort required to construct more objective scales (e.g., Behaviorally Anchored Rating Scales), the results have sometimes been disappointing (Jacobs, Kafry & Zedeck, 1980). The work on rater errors has resulted in a number of different strategies for training raters to increase accuracy – focusing on sensitizing them to the kinds of errors that can be made, giving them behavioral observation training, training them in the use of performance dimensions and so on. These have met with mixed and far from overwhelming success. The most effective has been 'frame of reference' training, which is oriented towards establishing a common understanding of performance standards and how they are defined (Woehr & Huffcutt, 1994).

The concern with accuracy in appraisal and how to increase it has also been associated with attempts to improve our knowledge of the underlying cognitive processes involved in making performance judgments. The most thorough program of work carried out in this area has been that of DeNisi and his colleagues (DeNisi, 1996). Their research looked at the information acquired by the rater, how the information is stored and retrieved, and how it is integrated with other information to arrive at an assessment. Taken in isolation, cognitive approaches to modeling assessment decisions tend to view PA as a disinterested desire to give an accurate rating of performance against some clear-cut criteria; the appraiser is neutral and would rate accurately if possessed with the skills to do so – although accuracy is recognized as an unattainable goal. The fact that this approach often overlooks the complexity of real world situations – in terms of the appraiser's attitudes and motivations, the aims of the exercise, and the nature of the performance criteria – has been increasingly recognized. Bernardin and Villanova (1986) reported a survey of staff involved in the appraisal process which showed that the majority believed the deliberate distortion of ratings was a more significant influence on accuracy than were cognitive errors. Cleveland and Murphy (1992) go as far as to suggest that what would traditionally be seen as rater errors are often not errors as such but consciously-adopted and adaptive responses to the wider situation. Taking a social, motivational and organizational perspective on PA – rather than an exclusively cognitive one – is likely, ultimately, to be a more fruitful line for research and practice. It is to this theme that the rest of this section addresses itself.

Recognition that the appraisal situation is one that is laden with varying and often conflicting motivations of participants is scarcely new; however, it has received more attention in recent years. Cleveland and Murphy (1992) list several goals that influence appraisers' ratings, including projecting a favorable image of their unit (which in turn reflects favorably on them as the manager) and avoiding confrontation and conflict with subordinates that might arise if unfavorable ratings are given. The *political* nature of PA is a theme that has been addressed by a number of writers. Longenecker and Gioia (1988) found deliberate manipulation of PA assessments for political purposes (e.g., getting rewards for subordinates). Longenecker, Sims and Gioia (1987) reported how managers felt it was both in their own best interests and entirely justifiable in some circumstances to give lenient or overly-favorable ratings to their staff to maintain group harmony or to protect their staff from adverse consequences. Work such as this has prompted the development of questionnaires to measure perceived political considerations in PA (e.g., Tziner, Latham, Price & Haccoun, 1996). It is perhaps worth noting here that not all appraisal is concerned with managerial positions, and it is possible that the impact of political influences is less in the assessment of lower level jobs in the organization e.g., for clerical or operative staff. (Gioia & Longenecker, 1994). In cultural contexts (and their associated legal frameworks) outside the USA and Western Europe, the political influences on appraisal may simply be different.

The notion that the complexity of managerial work makes its appraisal more susceptible to manipulation can be looked at in a slightly different way. The kinds of changes that have overtaken organizations have affected the nature of work itself, and the continuing rate of change means that the definition of what a job is, what it contains and what represents good performance is also less stable. Borman and Motowidlo (1993) capture this move to a more dynamic concept of jobs and roles by discriminating between task performance (proficiency at core technical activities) and *contextual* performance – which deals with the manner and extent to which an individual contributes to the organizational, social and psychological environment in accomplishing goals. Factors such as communication and teamwork skills, stress and conflict reduction, handling of emotion, and conscientiousness are involved in contextual performance. Thus, where organizations previously relied heavily on task-based job descriptions that placed considerable emphasis on qualifications and knowledge, they now increasingly use competency frameworks as the vehicles for defining what is required in any particular role at any given time; such frameworks better capture and describe the nature of some of the elements of contextual performance. Arvey and Murphy (1998) in reviewing the PA literature indicate that there is evidence for a distinction between task and contextual performance, and that while cognitive factors are more strongly associated with the former, personality variables are more critical for the latter. There is an interesting echo here of the popular concept of emotional intelligence (Goleman, 1998; Higgs & Dulewicz, 1999). Emotional intelligence, or 'EQ' has been the subject of a good deal of research (Salovey & Mayer, 1990; Schutte et al., 1998) and is claimed to be more important than any other factor in determining outstanding performance (Goleman, 1998). EQ essentially includes noncognitive factors such as self-awareness, social awareness, social skills and so on; in other words, very much part of the domain covered in discussions of contextual performance. The importance of personality factors in contextual performance is perhaps part of the explanation of the correlations found between appraisal ratings and appraisee personality trait scores. For example, Fletcher (1995) found that questionnaire-measured attributes of the person appraised, such as Optimism, correlated with appraisal ratings across nearly all the (mainly task-oriented) performance dimensions assessed. It may be that in instances of this kind appraisers are actually making assessments of contextual performance but letting these influence their ratings across the board.

Awareness of the complexity of appraisal and of its political dimension has also lead to some formal ethical analysis of PA (Banner & Cooke, 1984; Longenecker & Ludwig, 1990) and a growing interest in viewing PA from an organizational justice standpoint (Folger & Greenberg, 1985). The latter has been applied quite widely in selection settings (e.g., Gilliland, 1993; Ployhart & Ryan, 1997) but a little less so in relation to appraisal. Perhaps unsurprisingly, it is advocated (Folger, Konovsky & Cropanzano, 1992) and found (Taylor, Tracy, Renard & Harrison, 1995) that procedural justice in the form of making explicit the performance standards and nature of the appraisal process, giving those appraised a fair hearing and seeking to apply standards in a consistent manner all increase the likelihood of positive attitudes toward appraisal. The importance of the fair hearing element has been demonstrated in the research for some time – though not specifically in the context of organizational justice theory – by studies showing the influence of "voice" or levels of appraisee participation in the appraisal process. Cawley, Keeping and Levy (1998) carried out a meta-analysis on 27 studies that looked at participation in the PA process. They differentiated between instrumental participation that allows an employee to influence the outcomes of appraisal and value-expressive participation that allows the individual to voice their opinions irrespective of the influence this may have. The analysis demonstrated a strong relationship between participation and appraisee reactions, especially satisfaction, and that value-expressive participation seemed to be the most important.

The political dimension from the appraiser's point of view has, as we have seen, received attention. But since Maier (1958) few writers have gone beyond the issue of employee participation to examine appraisees' motives and how they might guide their attitudes and responses to appraisal. Thompson and Dalton (1970) noted the potential threat posed by appraisal to the appraisee's self-esteem, and Pearce and Porter (1986) showed that being rated as 'satisfactory' did not make many subordinates happy – which is to be expected given that most self-ratings show leniency effects. Dulewicz and Fletcher (1989) suggested that appraisee motives may include getting feedback, presenting a positive impression, trying to sustain a good relationship with the appraiser, seeking career development opportunities, mounting a defense against criticism and protecting self-esteem. Some of these motives may conflict with each other, with the appraiser's motives and with the organization's aims. Small wonder, then, that PA seldom achieves all that is hoped of it. Even the fundamental assumption that underpins much of appraisal practice, that giving feedback will improve performance, is unsafe. Kluger and DeNisi (1996) in their comprehensive review and meta-analysis of feedback found that feedback interventions often do not improve performance and in over one-third of cases actually decreased it. The basic conditions for feedback in appraisal to have a positive effect include:

- a balanced review of performance, covering positive and negative aspects;
- discussion of not more than two limitations in any one interview;
- a participative approach allowing the person appraised ample chance to put across their views; and

- a good level of communication between appraiser and appraisee on a day-to-day basis outside of the appraisal.

But the requisite conditions seldom seem to have all been met in the past, judging from the research (Fletcher, 1994).

The most notable contemporary shift in PA research and practice is towards involving other parties in the appraisal process through the use of 360 degree feedback. Because of its growing significance, it is dealt with in a separate section here.

360-Degree Feedback in Performance Appraisal

Multi-source, multi-rater (MSMR), or 360-degree feedback systems generally entail a process whereby a target manager is rated on various behavioral dimensions or competencies by one or more bosses, peers, subordinates and – sometimes – customers. The dimensions rated usually focus on interpersonal attributes – in particular leadership and team working – and in most systems these ratings are aggregated and compared against the target's self-rating in a written report; the process may be paper-based or completed via specifically designed software packages. MSMR systems spread quickly across a whole range of public and private sector organizations in both the US. (Antonioni, 1996) and the UK in the early 1990s, though they were adopted less frequently in the rest of Europe. Such systems are quite often linked to appraisal in the US. London and Smither (1995) reported that 50% of the consultancy companies and MSMR system providers they contacted said that at least some of their clients used the systems for administrative purposes. Whilst in the UK. the emphasis is still more on developmental use, the trend is for organizations there also to move in the direction of applying 360-degree feedback in the context of PA and performance-related pay (Handy, Devine & Heath, 1996).

Although there is a considerable practitioner literature offering advice on how to develop and run 360-degree feedback systems, little of this guidance is empirically-based; the speed with which this approach has been taken up seems to have left research some way behind. There are some findings, however, on the outcomes achieved by using MSMR assessment as an input to appraisal and development. One criterion measure of the impact of giving employees feedback of this kind is what effect it has on subsequent ratings of their performance. The assumption made is that if ratings from colleagues become more favorable on successive applications of MSMR procedures, this indicates performance improvement. Another aspect of rating change is the change in rater–ratee agreement (congruence) over time. This may be independent of whether raters have identified any improvement in the target; it is possible for greater congruence to result from the raters' assessments remaining the same on separate occasions while self-ratings move from a more lenient, less congruent level to a less lenient and more congruent level as a result of repeated feedback exercises. Such a measure can be thought of as reflecting the extent to which self-awareness is enhanced – something that may be thought of as a desirable end in itself (London & Smither, 1995).

London & Wohlers (1991) found that there was a significant increase in agreement between self-ratings and subordinate ratings, from .28 on the first administration of a set of ratings to .34 a year later. Atwater, Roush and Fischthal (1995) looked at both changes in ratings and changes in congruence resulting from successive feedback episodes in a large sample of subjects. They found that, overall, raters' assessments of targets increased in favorability, and that targets' self-ratings increased in congruence. Smither, London, Vasilopoulos, Reilly, Millsap and Salvemini (1995) reported a study where self and subordinate ratings of a sample of junior to middle managers were taken on two occasions six months apart. Managers whose initial performance ratings from subordinates were moderate or low obtained significantly improved ratings on the second feedback application.

One of the problems of using changes in ratings as an outcome measure for MSMR schemes is that different rating groups may have very differing perspectives, or they may sample different aspects of the individual ratee's behavior. Thus, Bernardin, Hagan & Kane (1995) found that with a one-year gap between feedback exercises, a group of managers showed higher ratings from peers and subordinates but not from bosses or customers. Another problem is that aggregating ratings from various rater groups may obscure discrepancies between them, and give a misleading picture of the effects of feedback provision. It can be argued that neither of the measures mentioned provide proof of actual performance improvement. More favorable assessments from raters or greater congruence could result from enhanced impression management tactics, such as ingratiation (Giacalone & Rosenfeld, 1989), rather than from any fundamental behavior change. Objective measures of performance change following MSMR applications are difficult to find, but since research on conventional performance appraisal have produced few examples of objective measures of performance change, it is probably optimistic to expect that the literature on 360-degree feedback will produce them.

In terms of behavior change, then – as far as this can be identified through shifts in successive sets of feedback ratings and in rating congruence – the picture is of consistent but rather modest degrees of change. There is little research on the psychometric qualities of 360-degree feedback systems,

but what there is suggests that whatever their other advantages over conventional PA, better quality of ratings is not one of them (Fletcher, Baldry & Cunningham-Snell, 1998). But the use of MSMR assessment does offset some of the main problems with traditional PA; it is inherently fairer (providing a more rounded assessment, not dependent on one perspective) and as a consequence represents a form of feedback that is more difficult to ignore or fail to respond to. However, although the volume of research on 360-degree feedback is growing rapidly (Fletcher & Baldry, 1999) and there are a number of theoretical formulations to guide it (e.g., London & Smither, 1995; Atwater & Yammarino, 1997), it is still not large by comparison with that of PA in general.

Summary

The shift of research focus in the final decade of the twentieth century away from purely measurement issues to social and motivational aspects of appraisal is surely a move in the right direction, as are the changes in the nature of appraisal schemes themselves – including more reliance on more objective methods (tests and assessment centers) for assessing potential and promotability and the adoption of MSMR input to appraisal. Perhaps the fact that 360 degree feedback has spread so widely and so quickly is an indicator of the very considerable shift in organizational culture that has taken place – such feedback systems may be more a symptom or expression of change than a factor in its causation. The nature of organizations in the future and the implications of this for how PA operates is something that will be discussed in the final section of this chapter. Before that, though, we will look at one of the most neglected aspects of PA, namely the impact of national cultural differences.

A CROSS-CULTURAL PERSPECTIVE

Due to the increasing internationalization of the workplace, national culture is an important influence in organizational life. National culture and associated work-related values may influence the performance expectations that employees develop and the role that performance feedback plays in organizations (Bretz, Milkovich & Read, 1992). Some have suggested that PA research which has assumed a predominantly western approach may be culturally bound (Bretz et al., 1992). There is evidence of frequent failures to replicate American social psychology research findings to other national cultures (Smith, Dugan & Trompenaars, 1996). Moreover, systematic differences in work-related values across countries have led some to caution that management techniques developed in one country may not be applicable and acceptable in other countries (Elenkov, 1998; Love, Bishop, Heinisch & Montei, 1994). However, despite these potential difficulties, relatively little cross-cultural research has explored the performance feedback and appraisal process (Vance, McClaine, Boje & Stage, 1992) and we are aware of only one theoretical paper (Milliman, Nason, Gallagher, Huo, Von Glinow & Lowe, 1998) that has explored the impact of national culture on the PA process. This section, then, seeks to extend the examination of this perspective on PA.

Theoretical Framework

Research has found systematic differences in work-related values across countries (e.g., Elenkov, 1998; Hofstede, 1980; Fernandez, Carlson, Stepina & Nicholson, 1997; Smith et al., 1996). Two dimensions of culture that have received considerable research attention are power distance and individualism/collectivism (e.g., Early, 1986; Early, 1994; Elenkov, 1998; Fernandez et al., 1997; Hofstede 1980, 1991; Smith et al., 1996). Hofstede's 1980 study is one of the most frequently cited works on the relationship between national culture and work-related values (Fernandez et al., 1997). Hofstede (1980) found that the dimensions of power distance and individualism/collectivism differed across a large number of countries. The individualism/ collectivism dimension is increasingly being used as an explanatory concept in cross-cultural psychology (Kagitcibasi & Berry, 1989). Smith et al. (1996) noted that a number of studies exploring cultural value dimensions, including their own, have found a factor related to individualism/collectivism. In addition, Hofstede's power distance dimension has been found to correlate with theoretically similar factors in other studies of cross-cultural values (Smith et al., 1996). There is some evidence that power distance and individualism are in fact correlated (Hofstede, 1980). However, for ease of presentation, we treat these dimensions independently in this chapter. Whilst national cultures are likely to differ on a variety of dimensions, we will focus on these two because there is theoretical and empirical evidence that they are useful in explaining differences across national cultures; other cultural value dimensions may be equally important, but space limitations prevent their being considered here.

Power Distance in the Workplace

This concerns how less powerful organizational members accept and expect that power is distributed unequally. When power distance is large, supervisors and subordinates consider themselves unequal and subordinates are more dependent on their supervisors. In addition, employees are afraid to express disagreements with their supervisors and supervisors tend to have (and it is preferred that they have) an autocratic or paternalistic management style. Subordinates are expected to be told what to do and contact between the supervisor and subordinate is supposed to be initiated by the supervisor. Large power distance is also associated with greater centralization of power in the organization and the absence of assumptions that abuses of power by a supervisor will or should be redressed. By contrast, small power distance is associated with more limited dependence of subordinates on their supervisors and the use of and preference for a consultative or participatory style of management. In addition, when power distance is small so too is emotional distance resulting in subordinates' greater willingness to approach and contradict their supervisors.

Individualism/Collectivism in the Workplace

This concerns the extent to which the interests of the individual prevail over the interests of the group. In an individualist culture, employees act in their own interest and the relationship between the employee and employer is conceived as a business relationship. Emphasis is often placed on individualism, personal freedom of choice, and individual initiative; companies are not expected to get involved in the personal lives of their employees. By contrast, in a collectivist culture, the interests of the group prevail over the interests of the individual. Employers hire individuals who belong to an in-group and employees act in accordance with the interests of this group. It is important to reduce differences between members of the collective and to maintain group harmony. The relationship between the employer and employee typically involves protection in exchange for loyalty.

Application of Theoretical Framework to the Performance Appraisal Process

The dimensions of power distance and individualism/collectivism may influence several aspects of the PA process – who provides the feedback and appraisals, the process or style used to deliver the feedback and appraisals, the content and the purpose or aim of the feedback and appraisals. Table 7.1 summarizes the primary effects of individualism/collectivism and power distance on the PA process. In their conceptual paper, Milliman et al. (1998) similarly considered the impact of individualism and power distance on the PA process. However, they did not consider the influence of culture on who provides feedback and evaluation and its intended purpose. In this chapter, we consider the influence of power distance and individualism/collectivism on four aspects of the PA process, but

Table 7.1   *The effect of individualism/collectivism and power distance (P.D.) on the PA process*

Cultural dimension	PA process			
	Who	How	Content	Purpose
Low P.D.	Multi-source (e.g., peer, subordinate)	Participatory two-way communication Employee-initiated Appeals process	Unspecified	Unspecified
High P.D.	Supervisor (someone with relatively more power)	Directive Supervisor initiated No appeals process	Unspecified	Unspecified
Collectivist	Supervisor Third party	Subtle/indirect	Group level More positive tone Relationship-focused (criteria include loyalty; seniority; cooperativeness)	Developmental (increase loyalty)
Individualist	Unspecified	Direct/open	Individual level Job focused	Administrative (make personnel decisions)

Note: Cells labelled 'unspecified' indicate that there was little empirical or conceptual evidence of how the dimension would influence the PA process.

we also acknowledge that cultural differences may influence whether countries value feedback and even have formal appraisal systems.

Power Distance

Who

Power distance may influence who provides performance feedback and appraisals in the organization. In large power distance cultures, power is centralized and employees are dependent on their supervisors. This suggests that employee appraisal will most often be conducted by a person with relatively more power than the appraisee (e.g., the employee's immediate supervisor). In addition, because there is a perception that managers and employees are unequal, it may be particularly inappropriate to have individuals in positions of power evaluated by individuals who hold less power (e.g., managers evaluated by their subordinates). In contrast, employees in small power distance cultures are less dependent on their supervisors and multi-rater feedback systems including upward appraisals may be more acceptable and likely. In support of this, Fletcher and Baldry (1999) noted that the history of multi-rater feedback is longer in North America,

which includes relatively low power distance cultures such as the US, than elsewhere. Lepsinger and Lucia (1997) suggested that 360-degree feedback is most effective in participative compared to authoritative environments. Gregersen, Hite and Black (1996) noted that supervisors' requests for feedback from subordinates may undermine supervisors' authority in Latin American countries where power distance tends to be high. Finally, Huo and Von Glinow (1995) noted that peer evaluation was virtually nonexistent in China (see Chow, 1988 for an exception), a relatively high power distance culture, in part because only leaders are seen as sufficiently qualified to evaluate subordinates' performance.

How

Power distance may influence the style and process by which performance feedback and appraisals are delivered in the organization. In high power distance cultures employees tend to be more satisfied with a directive or persuasive supervisor, while those in low power distance cultures tend to be more satisfied with a participative supervisor (Triandis, 1989). Consequently, in the former, supervisors are expected to initiate feedback and employees are less likely to seek feedback from their superiors. In addition, feedback providers are expected to deliver feedback using a more directive and autocratic style; two-way communication and joint problem-solving between supervisors and employees are less likely (Mendonca & Kanungo, 1996). In small power distance cultures, feedback may be initiated by the supervisor, but because emotional distances are small, employees may also be more willing to approach and contradict their supervisors. In addition, feedback providers in such cultures are expected to use a more consultative and participatory style in the context of the feedback and appraisal process. Employees, who are less dependent on their supervisors, may expect and prefer to participate in the performance appraisal process. Finally, appeal processes might be more likely in low power distance cultures than high power distance cultures where there are no assumptions that abuses by employers will be redressed.

There is some indirect evidence that national culture may influence how performance feedback and appraisals are given. Williams, Walker and Fletcher (1977) found some evidence that the extent of participation in the performance appraisal process varied across countries. In Latin America, where power distance is high, participation as a management technique has not been successful (Triandis, 1989). Elenkov (1998) found that Russian managerial culture is more characterized by higher power distance than American managerial culture and suggested that American concepts of subordinate participation in managerial decisions (e.g., in performance appraisal) may be incompatible with Russian culture. Huo and Von Glinow (1995) observed that due to the large power distance found in China, Chinese managers are reluctant to engage in two-way communication or provide counseling in the performance appraisal process. As a result, participation by employees has been low in most Chinese organizations. Mendonca and Kanungo (1990) suggested that high power distance in developing countries is not compatible with joint problem-solving and the development of an employee–supervisor partnership in performance management. In a general management survey of perceptions of national management style, Vance et al. (1992) found evidence of less employee involvement in performance appraisal in Malaysia compared to Thailand, Indonesia and the US; Hofstede (1991) identified Malaysia as having greater power distance than the other countries.

Research evidence suggests that managerial style may influence a manager's approach to the performance appraisal *interview*. Wexley and Klimoski (1984) observed that managers with a directive style and those interested in controlling subordinates' behavior are more likely to use a tell and sell or tell and listen approach in the interview. Managers with a more participatory style will tend to use a problem-solving or mixed model approach.

To the extent that managerial style is influenced by national culture (Kagitcibasi & Berry, 1989), this research suggests that national culture may affect the manner and style in which performance feedback and appraisals are given. Wexley and Klimoski (1984) observed that appraisees who are more dependent on their supervisors may expect a more directive approach in the performance appraisal interview. If subordinates in large power distance cultures are more dependent on their supervisors, they may expect and wish to receive performance feedback in a more directive manner.

Content

There is little theoretical or empirical evidence that power distance influences the content of performance feedback and evaluation. For example, Early and Stubblebine (1989) found that American and English production workers did not significantly differ in the reported type (e.g., positive, negative) or amount of feedback received from their supervisors, despite a significant difference in reported power distance between the two countries. However, the authors found that the effect of feedback characteristics (e.g., sign) on performance differed as a function of country of origin and power distance beliefs. Specifically, feedback characteristics were more strongly related to performance in the US, where workers tend to have lower power distance beliefs than in England. The authors suggested that lower power distance American workers tend to be more open to feedback from their supervisors while English workers are less trusting of such feedback and perceived sources of influence. Bochner and Hesketh (1994) found that individuals who identified with higher power distance cultures tended to be more task oriented. This may have implications for what is assessed (the content of appraisals) in performance appraisal. In other words, higher power distance cultures may evaluate task accomplishment to a greater extent than lower power distance cultures.

Purpose

There is some evidence that perceptions of the importance of feedback vary across national cultures (Early, 1986). This may suggest that the purposes for which feedback is used will also differ across national cultures. However, we found no research that directly explored the relationship between power distance and the purpose of performance feedback and appraisal.

Individualism/Collectivism

Who

Individualism/collectivism may influence who provides performance feedback and from whom feedback is preferred. Collectivist societies tend to be hierarchical and collectivists tend to accept and respond more positively to authoritarian leadership styles than individualists (Early & Gibson, 1998; Triandis, 1989). This may suggest that employees in collectivist societies expect and prefer feedback from their supervisors. However, others have suggested that feedback to individuals in collectivist cultures is often given by a third party to avoid loss of face. This apparent inconsistency may be understood if third parties are used to provide informal feedback and supervisors formal feedback.

Early (1986) found that collectivism was positively related to perceptions of trust in supervisors and that perceptions of trust partially mediated the effect of feedback on performance. Greater trust in their supervisors may lead members of collectivist cultures to consider supervisors as psychologically close and therefore more informative sources of feedback (Greller & Herold, 1975). Huo and Von Glinow (1995) suggested that Chinese workers may be reluctant to evaluate their peers for fear of threatening the harmony of the group and interpersonal relationships with co-workers. Finally, Seddon (1987) observed that third parties were used to provide informal feedback in many parts of Africa which tend to score low on individualism.

How

Individualism/collectivism may influence how PA is delivered in organizations. Feedback in individualist cultures is likely to be direct and blunt, and negotiation and open discussion between the parties is expected. In collectivist cultures, confrontation is avoided as open discussions may reduce group harmony and result in the loss of face (Hofstede, 1991). As a result, feedback in collectivist cultures is likely to be communicated more subtly, indirectly, and privately versus publicly. Williams et al. (1977) found that openness in performance appraisals (e.g., the amount of information appraisers shared with appraisees) varied across countries. Elenkov (1998) suggested that direct feedback is perceived as undesirable in Russia, which is more collectivist than America. Americans expect performance to improve if people receive direct feedback about their performance. Russian culture views open and direct feedback as potentially harmful to group harmony, the employee's self-image, and loyalty to the organization. In a case study based on data from senior executives, Seddon (1987) observed that members of developing countries (e.g., Kenya) which tend to be more collectivist may not engage in discussions in the performance appraisal interview.

Content

Performance appraisals in individualistic cultures assume that most of the variance in job performance is due to individual factors with little consideration given to situational and group factors (Triandis, 1989). Performance appraisals in individualistic cultures are based on the individual and his or her personal achievements (Erez, 1994). Therefore, feedback givers are likely to provide, and recipients are likely to prefer, feedback that focuses on the individual's performance. In collectivist cultures, feedback and evaluation are likely to focus on group rather than individual performance (Erez, 1994). In addition, feedback in collectivist cultures may be more positive in tone to avoid loss of face, to maintain the harmony of the group, and because relationships are perceived to be more important than the task. The focus in individualistic cultures is on the accomplishment of job objectives while greater attention is given to relationships associated with the job in collectivist cultures (Mendonca & Kanungo, 1996).

There is some evidence that individualism/ collectivism influences employees' preferences for different types of feedback. Erez (1994) observed that Japanese models of human resource management (HRM) focus on the group level while American models focus on the individual level. Elenkov (1998) suggested that Russians who score higher on collectivism than Americans will respond more positively to performance appraisals that focus on the objectives and achievements of work teams. Similarly, Waldman (1997) found that collectivist norms were associated with preferences for performance evaluations and rewards oriented at the group level. Vance et al. (1992) found that Indonesian managers focused on group and company performance rather than individual performance to a greater extent than Thai and Malay managers. This is consistent with Hofstede's identification of Indonesia as a relatively more collectivist country than the latter. In their study of a multicultural workforce in an Australian bank, Bochner and Hesketh (1994) found that collectivists believed more strongly that personal advancement was dependent on group performance than individualists although this difference was not statistically significant. In contrast, Smither, Wohler and London (1995) found that their US sample generally preferred some individualized feedback compared to normative only feedback. This finding is consistent with the fact that the US tends to score high on individualism.

Individualism/collectivism may also have implications for giving and responding to positive and negative feedback. Early (1986) found that English workers responded more positively to praise than criticism, while Americans (lower on collectivism) responded equally to both forms of feedback. Seddon (1987) observed that Malaysians, who score low on individualism, tend to avoid negative feedback. Chow (1988) indicated that performance evaluations of Chinese cadres tended to be lenient and positive – consistent with the notion that feedback and evaluations may be more positive in tone in collectivist cultures where saving face and maintaining group harmony are important.

Performance criteria may also vary across individualist and collectivist cultures. Smith et al.'s (1996) study of work-related values across 43 countries suggests that in collectivist cultures, loyalty and seniority considerations are the focus of evaluation and form the basis for personnel decisions. Consistent with this, Ramamoorthy and Carroll (1998) found that collectivism was negatively related to preferences for merit-based promotion systems. Seddon (1987) observed that loyalty was an important part of appraisal in Malaysia and Kenya, countries identified as low on individualism. There is also research evidence that collectivist cultures (e.g., Japan, China) may evaluate and reward cooperativeness in the workplace (Chow, 1988; Rosenstein, 1985). Mendonca and Kanungo (1990) suggested that individuals' priorities in developing countries, which tend to score low on individualism, are on the relationships generated by the job rather than job accomplishments.

Purpose

There is some evidence that the effectiveness of a given purpose of PA may vary across countries (Milliman, Nason, Lowe, Kim & Huo, 1995). Individualist cultures view the employee–employer relationship as a business transaction and may be more likely to use feedback for improving performance and evaluating the individuals' fulfillment of the employee contract (Seddon, 1987). The focus in individualist cultures is often on competition and the individual's accomplishments. Consequently, in individualist cultures, appraisals may be used to differentiate between employees and make personnel decisions (e.g., promotion, pay) accordingly. In contrast, in collectivist cultures, performance feedback and appraisals may be used to increase employees' loyalty to the organization. The focus in collectivist cultures is on minimizing differences between group members. Therefore, feedback and appraisals may be used for developmental more than evaluative purposes in collectivist cultures. A survey of civil service employees in the Democratic Republic of the Sudan (Siegel, 1984) found that the majority of respondents (over 70%) perceived that performance appraisal should be developmental rather than evaluative in nature. This is consistent with the low levels of individualism found in a number of African countries (Hofstede, 1991). Love et al.'s (1994) research revealed that there was no formal PA system in a Japanese owned and likely more collectivist oriented firm located in the US. This suggests that performance feedback in this organization was not used for formal evaluation purposes.

IMPLICATIONS FOR THE GENERALIZABILITY OF US AND WESTERN-BASED PA RESEARCH AND PRACTICE

We make two general cautions about the interpretation of the previously reviewed research. First, it is important not to overgeneralize study results when few studies exploring the PA process have been conducted in a given country (e.g., Russia). Second, it is important to be mindful that studies may be time sensitive and results found in a particular study may have limited generalizability when countries undergo rapid political and economic changes. However, even with these caveats made, it appears reasonable to conclude that to the extent that the majority of PA research has been conducted in the US and other western countries, and has only infrequently considered the role of national culture, its results may be culturally bound. For example many studies, mostly of US origin, have considered the role of employee participation in the PA process and indicated that participation has positive effects on employee reactions and – sometimes – on actual performance (e.g., Burke, Weitzel & Weir, 1978; Cawley et al., 1998; Dipboye & de Pontbriand, 1981; Klein & Snell, 1994; Korsgaard & Roberson, 1995; Nathan, Mohrman & Milliman, 1991). However, as we noted earlier, it may not be the case that employees from larger power distance cultures expect or desire to participate in the feedback and evaluation process. Employees who are more dependent on their managers for guidance may expect and prefer a more directive approach. Similarly, a number of American writers and researchers have advocated the use of MSMR systems. However, little research has considered the role that cultural differences may play in these systems. In cultures where power distance is large, managers may be unwilling to accept feedback from their employees, and employees likewise may feel uncomfortable and unwilling to provide their superiors with feedback. Therefore, it is important to explore the role of national culture in preference for and responsiveness to – among other things – participation and feedback source in the PA process. Mendonca and Kanungo (1990) warned that uncritically transplanting performance management processes developed in North America to developing countries would doom such processes to failure. Managerial systems and techniques may be most effective when they are congruent with a country's cultural values (Erez, 1994; Triandis, 1989).

The problems of cultural differences can, of course, also arise within a single organization, when the feedback provider and feedback recipient are from different national cultures. Kikoski (1999) observed that face to face communication such as occurs in the context of performance appraisal will become significantly more complicated and problematic as the workforce becomes more culturally diverse. Triandis and Brislin (1984) noted that when a supervisor from one culture appraises the performance of a subordinate from another, the accuracy of appraisal is likely to be lower, in part due to the fact that the appraiser is not aware of the norms in the other culture that govern certain behaviors. Two examples will serve to illustrate how national culture differences between appraisers and appraisees may cause difficulties.

An appraiser from a culture lower on power distance than an appraisee may seek the appraisee's self-assessments and their views on how to solve job problems. However, the appraisee may feel reluctant to participate in the performance appraisal process in this manner and feel it is not their place to do so. The appraisee may also view the appraiser's request for input as a sign of weakness.

An appraiser from a culture higher on individualism than the appraisee may focus on the personal contribution of the employee and pay less attention to team issues. The appraisee, in contrast, may emphasize their role in the team and fail to highlight their personal achievements.

Such cultural differences can result in misunderstandings that negatively influence employee and employer relationships, reactions to the appraisal system, and performance and performance ratings.

THE FUTURE OF PERFORMANCE APPRAISAL

The vision we have of PA in the future puts development and motivation as the principal aims, rather than assessment and administration purposes, and places more responsibility on the person appraised to own the process. At managerial levels, the change in the psychological contract means that generating and maintaining commitment and effort will depend more than ever on transformational management styles and on offering individuals good development opportunities. The increasing proportion of knowledge workers, the wider geographical dispersion of business and the greater autonomy of individual managers are all part of the backdrop to this. As a consequence of these changes, and partly due to the frustration felt with the failure of traditional appraisal methods to deliver what was asked of them, performance appraisal systems have begun to take on a very different appearance in some organizations. The monolithic appraisal system, which typically involved a universally-applied process with a heavy emphasis on appraisal forms and on using the process primarily for assessment purposes, is becoming an endangered species; in our view, it will eventually become extinct. The familiar concept of appraisal seems to be breaking down into separate processes dealing with performance review, competency development and the assessment and growth of potential.

Another important future trend is likely to be that the elements constituting what we normally think of as PA will increasingly be properly integrated into the human resource policies of the organization – using the same competency framework for all HR processes, linking individual objectives with team and business unit objectives, framing the input of appraisal to promotion assessment in an appropriate manner, and so on. Embedding appraisal in a wider approach to selection and development makes it a more effective mechanism and less of an annual ritual that appears to exist in a vacuum. The research evidence shows that such integrated HR policies do make an impact on employee attitudes and organizational commitment (Caldwell, Chatman & O'Reilly, 1990; Kinicki, Carson & Bohlander, 1992; Fletcher & Williams, 1996), which in turn can impact organizational performance (Ostroff, 1992; Patterson, West, Lawthom & Nickell, 1998). However, the continued usefulness of the term performance appraisal must be questioned; increasingly, it does not necessarily connote either a single process or a specific and exclusive focus on appraisal. Should we abandon the term in future, it might help discourage the futile notion of a single annual event achieving a series of conflicting aims, and help liberate thinking about this area of activity and study.

The changes in the nature of work and organizations seen so far are probably small compared to those that will be seen in the early part of the twenty-first century, and in particular those arising from advances in information technology (IT) – which not only impact on what can be done, but also the speed at which it happens and the geographical location of where it happens. Such changes and their implications for organizational psychologists have been discussed by a number of writers (e.g., Cascio, 1995; Prieto & Simon, 1997; Herriot & Anderson, 1997). The future, as ever, is unclear. On the one hand, there are likely to be more home-based teleworkers, working fairly independently, and increasing reliance on the internet for marketing and selling. The actual physical location of many employees will not matter greatly. The challenge for performance appraisal is that independent, geographically scattered employees are likely to be harder to monitor and assess except, perhaps, in terms of outputs. On the other hand, the likely continued growth of call centers offers a different picture, with the potential to record and assess almost all aspects of an individual's performance and to control the work environment very closely. At managerial and professional levels, however, the most likely picture is one of greater flexibility, with the boundaries of job roles continually changing, and individuals frequently working in a series of project teams of short duration – thus placing more emphasis on capacity and inclination for teamwork. Under the 'new deal' (Rousseau, 1995; Herriot & Pemberton, 1996; Herriot & Anderson, 1997) managers may expect to stay with any one organization for a limited period only, rather than serve out a career there. Indeed, the notion of a single career that lasts for life – except in some professions – is increasingly questioned.

For performance appraisal to have any relevance in such a radically different world, it too has to evolve further. What will be the criteria by which to judge performance in the circumstances outlined? As pointed out, it may become difficult to gauge any individual manager's inputs and results obtained in some cases. In others, the nature of the work and the objectives may vary greatly within an annual review period, as will the colleagues with whom an individual has worked, thus raising questions as to who should be appraising performance, and when, and making relative judgement or assessment more difficult. One likely consequence is an increasing use of self-appraisal, since the one person who is always present to observe his or her performance is the individual. Although self-assessment has often been noted to be dogged by leniency effects (Harris & Schaubroek, 1988), there are conditions under which these may be minimized (Mabe & West, 1982; Fox, Caspy & Reisler, 1994). The use of other sources of assessment and feedback, through MSMR systems, is already with us and is almost certain to grow with the greater reliance on teamworking. It may be that appraisal in the future will be a more reflective process, where greater emphasis than hitherto is placed on the individual looking at their own self-assessment against the perceptions of others, and where the focus of that exercise is increasingly on performance against competency standards rather than on comparisons with others at the same level. This would fit with the growing interest in the concept of emotional intelligence and how it can be enhanced as an attribute; insight and sensitivity to the reactions of others are integral to the notion of 'EQ'. The emphasis on enhancing self-awareness and on seeking and using feedback (London & Smither, 1995; Fletcher, 1997b; Atwater & Yammarino, 1997) will continue to be a key feature of appraisal in 'learning organizations' which recognize the importance of continuous employee development in fast-developing, flexible work environments. Where assessment is needed for fundamental decisions on promotion and fast-track potential, it is difficult not to conclude that the reliance on a new generation of psychometric measures making use of enhanced computer-presented simulation techniques, assessment centers and development centers will increase still further, because of their greater objectivity and more sophisticated measurement potential.

On another theme, the impact of legislation on appraisal practices is likely to grow rather than recede. So far, the majority of the literature on legal issues surrounding the PA process comes from the US, which may in part be a function of the cultural values of the US relative to other countries. However, the development of the legal framework for the European Union could well yield a fresh crop of issues in this domain. Werner and Bolino (1997) found that most US legal cases of performance appraisal involved some form of discrimination, but less than 11% of these involved charges of discrimination based on national origin or creed. As the workplace continues to become internationalized, opportunities for discrimination based on national origin will rise. Cultural differences may create uncertainty about whether discrimination has occurred. Many authors have provided prescriptions for sound and legally defensible performance appraisal systems (e.g., Austin, Villanova & Hindman, 1996; Barrett & Kernan, 1987; Bernardin & Cascio, 1988). These prescriptions include but are not limited to some of the following: a formal system of review or appeal; the use of multiple raters; avoidance of a single overall global ranking or rating; provision of instructions to raters; documentation of extreme ratings; the use of job analysis; performance counseling or corrective guidance; application of the system fairly and consistently; frequent performance evaluations; communication of performance standards; and a focus on job-related behaviors versus global trait descriptions. Research that finds that courts and arbitrators are concerned with the procedural fairness aspects of the performance appraisal system suggests that prescriptions related to due process issues may be most important from a legal perspective. However, organizations should not be unconcerned with the validity of their performance appraisal systems. The point here is that a focus on rating accuracy and validity to the exclusion of due process issues is likely to be problematic. Further, as has been indicated, the changing nature of work and rater limitations make the achievement of error free evaluations difficult at best. It is important, however, to be mindful that recommendations for legally defensible PA systems are based on the US experience.

The impact of new technology on organizations, and hence on the context of PA, has been mentioned several times here. But IT has something to offer more directly to PA, and this is discussed below.

The Role of IT Developments in the PA Process

Computers are increasingly being used in and affecting the practice of performance appraisal in organizations (Reinhardt, 1985; Sulsky & Keown, 1998). They can generate feedback such as when they are used to monitor performance and count employee activities (e.g., number of keystrokes). Computers can also be used to mediate feedback; recording and compiling performance appraisal ratings and making them available on-line. An increasing number of software packages are available that help managers structure their performance appraisals (Adams, 1995; McCune, 1997). Some of these programs include a section in which managers can comment about individuals throughout the year in preparation for the annual formal review. One software company estimates that by 2001, between four and six million managers will use people management software to conduct human resources tasks such as performance evaluations (McCune, 1997).

There are a number of potential advantages to bringing performance appraisals on-line. Performance feedback provided on-line can be made available to employees even when evaluators are not available to provide important performance feedback. This may be particularly helpful in the context of 360-degree feedback when a target individual must be evaluated by multiple raters. It may also facilitate feedback between individuals working in geographically dispersed locations (e.g., across countries). In addition, a computer based system can greatly reduce the amount of paperwork that is necessary in the PA process, make it easier for raters to edit and revise their comments, and monitor raters' responses for logic, completeness, and problematic phraseology. A computer based performance feedback system is fairly easy to develop and use. In many organizations it could take advantage of technology that is already available and in use.

Research suggests that computers can play a positive role in the performance feedback and appraisal process. There is some evidence that individuals are more likely to seek feedback from a computer (e.g., a feedback giver using electronic mail) than from a feedback giver face-to-face (Ang & Cummings, 1994; Kluger & Adler, 1993). Concerns about loss of face and evaluation apprehension may be lessened when feedback can be sought from an inanimate and relatively nonevaluative and unemotional feedback source (i.e., the computer). In addition, there is some evidence that the accessibility of the feedback source can increase the likelihood of feedback-seeking behavior (Ashford & Cummings, 1983; Vancouver & Morrison, 1995). As suggested previously, computer based feedback may be more accessible than feedback from other sources (e.g., busy managers). Research finds that individuals trust feedback that they obtain on the computer more than feedback provided by their supervisor (Early, 1988). The credibility of the feedback source has been found to be positively related to perceptions of feedback accuracy and feedback seeking (Fedor, 1991; Fedor, Rensvold, & Adams, 1992).

There is also evidence that feedback provided by computer results in better work performance and learning than when the same feedback is provided by a human (Early, 1988; Schneider & Shugar, 1990). Finally, less social information is conveyed on-line (electronic mail) than in other forms of communication technology (e.g., telephone, voice mail) (Hinds & Kiesler, 1995). A computer based system that focuses raters' attention on job-relevant behaviors and which, by virtue of the medium, reduces the salience of demographic and cultural cues, may help to limit bias in the PA process.

It is important to acknowledge that the use of computers in the performance appraisal process may not always have positive consequences. Relatively little research so far has directly explored the role that computer technology may play in the performance appraisal process. A computer based system will only be effective if management and the organizational culture support it and employees are held accountable for its successful implementation (Levine, 1986). Computer based systems may reduce the potential for bias, but they will not eliminate it. Although these systems can be designed to cue evaluators' attention to job-relevant dimensions, they cannot prevent the influence of job-irrelevant dimensions in the final performance appraisal. In addition, although performance feedback conveyed on-line may reduce face to face confrontation and be less affectively laden, it may still lead to disagreement and resentment. This may occur in part because individuals tend to be less polite and show less concern for others when communicating over electronic media and raters may be less able to assess how ratees initially react to the feedback (Sproull & Kiesler, 1991).

If computers are to be brought into the PA process they should facilitate not replace face to face feedback. Some have suggested that the effects of feedback source (e.g., computer vs. person-based) on performance may be influenced by the level of experience individuals have with computer systems (Early, 1988). Computer based performance feedback systems may be most effective when employees frequently use and have access to computer technology. It is also important to offer training that helps appraisers provide constructive feedback and appraisees interpret feedback on-line. Finally, it is important to consider the role that national culture may play in individuals' willingness to use computers in the performance appraisal process. For example, collectivists may perceive the computer as a nonevaluative third party feedback provider that allows them to save face with their supervisor. Alternatively, the impersonal nature of interacting with a computer may be particularly unsatisfactory for collectivists who value personal relationships.

DIRECTIONS FOR FUTURE RESEARCH AND THE CONTRIBUTION OF WORK AND ORGANIZATIONAL PSYCHOLOGY

On the basis of the analysis offered here, we offer a number of suggestions for future research. The organizational psychology research agenda for appraisal should give a high priority to self-assessment and self-awareness and the circumstances that increase their utility. It might also pay more attention to placing appraisal practices in the context of developments in motivation theory, for although PA is often perceived as a motivational device, there is little discussion of this aspect of it in the literature other than in terms of objective-setting. Less investigation of rating methods and the cognitive processes underlying the rating of performance, and more focus on the dynamics of appraisal might prove fruitful. The latter might include the conduct of the appraisal interview itself, a topic surprisingly neglected in recent years; given the political and social influences on the appraisal situation mentioned earlier, it would seem to be important to delve further into the nature of interview interaction and its impact on outcomes. Much of the guidance given to managers on how to conduct appraisal interviews rests on experience and judgment rather than any empirically-derived basis. Yet how the interview is handled, to some extent perhaps irrespective of the nature of the appraisal scheme, is likely to exert a crucial effect on the subsequent attitudes and motivation of the person appraised.

Another increasingly important focus will be cross-cultural issues in relation to performance appraisal. To what extent does national origin discrimination occur in the PA process? What are the specific cultural dimensions that result in differences in the PA process across cultures and how do they influence the PA process? Future research is necessary to assess the extent to which the predominantly US-based performance appraisal research generalizes to other cultures. In addition, future research and theory should expand on the ideas presented here. We suggest several important directions. Greater consideration should be given to the joint effects of cultural dimensions on the PA process. For example, how do individuals from a high collectivist and low power distance culture conduct appraisals? It is also necessary to acknowledge that cultural differences are not dichotomies but continua (Hermans & Kempen, 1998). While research has typically studied countries at the extremes of the continuum, it is also important to consider the PA process in countries that fall toward the middle of cultural value dimensions. Also, it needs to be recognized that there are a number of factors that may influence the PA process (e.g., individual differences, economic factors, organizational culture) – it is important to determine the *relative* influence of national cultural differences and when they are most influential in the PA process. For example, to what extent do centralized HR policies in multi-national corporations reduce the influence of national culture differences in the PA process? It is possible that strong corporate cultures provide a unifying framework for employees that reduces the influence of preexisting national differences. However, little is known about the interplay between national and corporate culture and their consequent effects on the feedback process.

Finally, additional research is needed to explore the role of computers in the operation of PA systems. Specifically, research is needed to assess organizations' and employees' responsiveness to using such systems in the PA process. It is also important to assess the extent to which computer systems influence feedback giving and seeking behaviors, the quality of supervisor/subordinate relationships, and ultimately performance on the job.

In framing these research themes, it is perhaps as well to bear in mind that the research of work and organizational psychologists has probably not had as much impact as they might wish. Their chief contribution has, in a sense, been to identify the shortcomings of traditional PA, and to devise alternative approaches to achieve some of its functions. In particular, the application of assessment centers and development centers to the task of identifying and enhancing promotability and potential have helped substantially and demonstrate superior validity (see Chapters 9 and 14). More recently, the advent of 360-degree feedback is providing a fresh impetus to research and model-building in relation to appraisal and feedback generally (see, for example, London & Smither, 1995; Atwater & Yammarino, 1997). This research stream looks to be especially promising in that it is tending to raise its sights above simple measurement issues. However, there is no room for complacency. Many organizations with appraisal schemes have almost certainly (a) not consulted a psychologist in devising them, and (b) not employed anyone who has ever read any psychological texts on the subject. Human resource management professionals who act as consultants to some of these companies may have been exposed to psychological literature on the subject, and so it may have had an indirect influence. One of the key objectives for work and organizational psychology, then, should be the more effective dissemination of its findings and an enhanced capacity to influence organizations to take note of them. Without this, there is a danger that the research we do will remain of largely academic interest and confined to a culturally similar audience of our fellow psychologists.

REFERENCES

Adams, J.T. (1995). Four performance appraisal packages add ease and speed to evaluations. *HR Magazine, 40*(5), 151–155.

Ang, S., & Cummings, L.L. (1994). Panel analysis of feedback-seeking patterns in face-to-face, computer-mediated, and computer-generated communication environments. *Perceptual and Motor Skills, 79*, 67–73.

Antonioni, D. (1996). Designing an effective 360-degree appraisal feedback process. *Organizational Dynamics, 25*, 24–38.

Arvey, R.D., & Murphy, K.R. (1998). Performance evaluation in work settings. *Annual Review Psychology, 49*, 141–168.

Ashford, S.J., & Cummings, L.L. (1983). Feedback as an individual resource: Personal strategies of creating information. *Organizational Behavior and Human Performance, 32*, 370–398.

Atwater, L., Roush, P., & Fischthal, A. (1995). The influence of upward feedback on self-ratings and follower ratings of leadership. *Personnel Psychology, 48*(1) 35–59.

Atwater, L.E. & Yammarino, F.J. (1997). Self-other rating agreement: A review and model. *Research in Personnel and Human Resource Management, 15*, 121–174.

Austin, J.T., Villanova, P., & Hindman, H.D. (1996). Legal requirements and technical guidelines involved in implementing performance appraisal systems. In G.R. Ferris & M.R. Buckley (Eds.), *Human Resource Management: Perspectives, context, functions, and outcomes* (pp. 271–288). Englewood Cliffs, NJ: Prentice Hall.

Banks, C.G., & Murphy, K.R. (1985). Toward narrowing the research-practice gap in performance appraisal. *Personnel Psychology, 38*, 335–345.

Banner, D.K., & Cooke, R.A. (1984). Ethical dilemmas in performance appraisal. *Journal of Business Ethics, 3*, 327–333.

Barrett, G.V., & Kernan, M.C. (1987). Performance appraisal and terminations: A review of court decisions since Brito v. Zia with implications for personnel practices. *Personnel Psychology, 40*, 489–503.

Bernardin, H.J., & Cascio, W.F. (1988). Performance appraisal and the law. In R.S. Schuler, S.A. Youngblood & V.L. Huber (Eds.), *Readings in personnel and human resource management* (3rd ed., pp. 235–247). St. Paul: West Publishing.

Bernardin, H.J., Hagan, C., & Kane, J.S. (1995). The effects of a 360-degree appraisal system on managerial performance: No matter how cynical I get I can't keep up. In W.W. Tornow (Chair). *Upward Feedback. The ups and downs of it.* Symposium conducted at the Tenth Annual Conference of the Society for Industrial and Organizational Psychology, Orlando, FL, May.

Bernardin, H.J., & Villanova, P. (1986). Performance Appraisal. In E. Locke (Ed.), *Generalizing from Laboratory to Field Settings*. Lexington, MA: Lexington Books.

Bochner, S., & Hesketh, B. (1994). Power distance, individualism/collectivism, and job-related attitudes in a culturally diverse work group. *Journal of Cross-Cultural Psychology, 25*, 233–257.

Borman, W.C., & Motowidlo, S.J. (1993). Expanding the criterion domain to include elements of contextual performance. In N. Schmitt & W.C. Borman & Associates (Eds.), *Personnel Selection in Organizations*. San Francisco: Jossey-Bass.

Bretz, R.D., Milkovich, G.T., & Read, W. (1992). The current state of performance appraisal research and practice: Concerns, directions, and implications. *Journal of Management, 18*, 321–352.

Burke, R.J., Weitzel, W., & Weir, T. (1978). Characteristics of effective employee performance review and development interviews: Replication and extension. *Personnel Psychology, 31*, 903–920.

Caldwell, D.F., Chatman, J.A., & O'Reilly, C.A. (1990). Building organizational commitment: A multifirm study. *Journal of Occupational Psychology, 63*, 245–261.

Cascio, W.F. (1995). Whither industrial and organizational psychology in a changing world of work? *American Psychologist, 50*, 928–939.

Cawley, B.D., Keeping, L.M., & Levy, P.E. (1998). Participation in the performance appraisal process and employee reactions: A meta-analytic review of field investigations. *Journal of Applied Psychology, 83*, 615–631.

Chow, K.W. (1988). The management of Chinese cadre resources: The politics of performance appraisal (1949–84). *International Review of Administrative Sciences, 54*, 359–377.

Cleveland, J.N., & Murphy, K.R. (1992). Analyzing performance appraisal as goal-directed behavior. *Research in Personnel and Human Resources Management, 10*, 121–185.

DeNisi, A.S. (1996). *Cognitive Approach to Performance Appraisal: A Programme of Research*. Routledge: London.

Dipboye, R.L., & de Pontbriand, R. (1981). Correlates of employee reactions to performance appraisals and appraisal systems. *Journal of Applied Psychology, 66*, 248–251.

Dulewicz, S.V., & Fletcher, C. (1989). The Context and Dynamics of Performance Appraisal. In P. Herriot (Ed.), *Assessment and Selection in Organisations*. London: John Wiley & Son.

Early, P.C. (1986). Trust, perceived importance of praise and criticism, and work performance: An examination of feedback in the United States and England. *Journal of Management, 12*, 457–473.

Early, P.C. (1988). Computer-generated performance feedback in the magazine-subscription industry. *Organizational Behavior and Human Decision Processes, 41*, 50–64.

Early, P.C. (1994). Self or group? Cultural effects of training on self-efficacy and performance. *Administrative Science Quarterly, 39*, 89–117.

Early, P.C., & Gibson, C.B. (1998). Taking stock in our progress on individualism-collectivism: 100 years of solidarity and community. *Journal of Management, 24,* 265–304.

Early, P.C., & Stubblebine, P. (1989). Intercultural assessment of performance feedback. *Group and Organization Studies, 14,* 161–181.

Elenkov, S.E. (1998). Can American management concepts work in Russia? A cross-cultural comparative study. *California Management Review, 40,* 133–156.

Erez, M. (1994). Toward a model of cross-cultural industrial and organizational psychology. In H.C. Triandis, M.D. Dunnette & L.M. Hough (Eds.), *Handbook of Industrial and Organizational Psychology* (2nd ed., Vol. 4, pp. 557–607). Palo Alto, CA: Consulting Psychologists Press, Inc.

Fedor, D.B. (1991). Recipient responses to performance feedback: A proposed model and its implications. *Research in Personnel and Human Resources Management, 9,* 73–120.

Fedor, D.B., Rensvold, R.B., & Adams, S.M. (1992). An investigation of factors expected to affect feedback seeking: A longitudinal field study. *Personnel Psychology, 45,* 779–805.

Fernandez, D.R., Carlson, D.S., Stepina, L.P., & Nicholson, J.D. (1997). Hofstede's country classification 25 years later. *The Journal of Social Psychology, 137,* 43–54.

Fletcher, C. (1994). The effects of performance review in appraisal: Evidence and implications. In C. Mabey & P. Iles (Eds.), *Managing Learning.* London: Routledge/Open University.

Fletcher, C. (1995). New directions for Performance Appraisal; Some findings and observations. *International Journal of Selection and Assessment, 3,* 191–196.

Fletcher, C. & Williams, R. (1996). Performance management, job satisfaction and organisational commitment. *British Journal of Management, 7,* 169–179.

Fletcher, C. (1997a). *Appraisal: Routes to Improved Performance* (2nd ed.). London: Institute of Personnel and Development.

Fletcher, C. (1997b). Self-Awareness – A neglected attribute in selection and assessment? *International Journal of Selection and Assessment, 5*(3), 183–187.

Fletcher, C., & Baldry, C. (1999). Multi-source feedback systems: A research perspective. In C. Cooper & I.T. Robertson (Eds.), *International Review of Organizational and Industrial Psychology,* Vol. 14, New York & London: Wiley & Sons.

Fletcher, C., Baldry, C., & Cunningham-Snell, N. (1998). The Psychometric Properties of 360 Degree Feedback: An empirical study and cautionary tale. *International Journal of Selection and Assessment, 6,* 19–34.

Folger, R., & Greenberg, J. (1985). Procedural justice: An interpretive analysis of personnel systems. In K. Rowland & G. Ferris (Eds.), *Research in Personnel and Human Resources Management,* Vol. 3 (pp. 141–183). Greenwich, CT: JAI Press.

Folger, R., Konovsky, M., & Cropanzano, R. (1992). A due process metaphor for performance appraisal. In B. Staw & L. Cummings (Eds.), *Research in Organizational Behavior,* Vol. 14 (pp. 127–148). Greenwich, CT: JAI Press.

Fox, S., Caspy, T., & Reisler, A. (1994). Variables affecting leniency, halo, and the validity of self-appraisal. *Journal of Occupational and Organizational Psychology, 67,* 45–56.

Giacalone, R.A., & Rosenfeld, P. (1989). The effect of sex and impression management on future salary estimations. *Journal of General Psychology, 116*(2), 215–219.

Gilliland, S.W. (1993). The perceived fairness of selection systems: An organizational perspective. *Academy of Management Review, 18,* 694–734.

Gioia, D.A., & Longenecker, C.O. (1994). Delving into the dark side: The politics of executive appraisal. *Organizational Dynamics, 22,* 47–58.

Goleman, D. (1998). *Working with Emotional Intelligence.* London: Bloomsbury.

Gregersen, H.B., Hite, J.M., & Black, J.S. (1996). Expatriate performance appraisal in U.S. multinational firms. *Journal of International Business Studies, 27,* 711–738.

Greller, M.M., & Herold, D.M. (1975). Sources of feedback: A preliminary investigation. *Organizational Behavior and Human Performance, 13,* 244–256.

Handy, L., Devine, M., & Heath, L. (1996). *Feedback: Unguided Missile or Powerful Weapon?* Report published by the Ashridge Management Research Group, Ashridge Management College.

Harris, M.M. & Schaubroeck, J. (1988). A meta-analysis of self-supervisor, self-peer and peer-supervisor ratings. *Personnel Psychology, 41,* 43–62.

Hermans, H.J.M., & Kempen, H.J.G. (1998). Moving Cultures: The perilous problems of cultural dichotomies in a globalizing society. *American Psychologist, 53,* 1111–1120.

Herriot, P., & Anderson, N. (1997). Selecting for change: How will personnel and selection psychology survive? In N. Anderson & P. Herriot (Eds.), *International Handbook of Selection and Assessment.* Chichester: Wiley.

Herriot, P., & Pemberton, C. (1996). Contracting careers. *Human Relations, 49,* 757–790.

Higgs, M., & Dulewicz, V. (1999). *Making Sense of Emotional Intelligence.* Windsor: NFER-NELSON.

Hinds, P., & Kiesler, S. (1995). Communication across boundaries: Work, structure, and use of communication technologies in a large organization. *Organization Science, 6,* 373–393.

Hofstede, G. (1980). *Culture's consequences: International differences in work-related values.* Beverly Hills, CA: Sage.

Hofstede, G. (1991). *Cultures and organizations.* London: McGraw-Hill.

Holley, W.H., & Field, H.S. (1975). Performance appraisal and the law. *Labor Law Journal, 26,* 423–430.

Huo, Y.P., & Von Glinow, M.A. (1995). On transplanting human resource practices to China: A culture driven approach. *International Journal of Manpower, 16,* 3–15.

IPM (1992). *Performance Management in the UK: An Analysis of the Issues*. London: Institute of Personnel Management.

Jacobs, R., Kafry, D., & Zedeck, S. (1980). Expectations of Behaviourally Anchored Rating Scales. *Personnel Psychology*, *33*, 595–640.

Kagitcibasi, C., & Berry, J.W. (1989). Cross-cultural psychology: Current research and trends. *Annual Review Psychology*, *40*, 493–531.

Kikoski, J.F. (1999). Effective communication in the performance appraisal interview: Face-to-face communication for public managers in the culturally diverse workplace. *Public Personnel Management*, *28*, 301–323.

Kinicki, A.J., Carson, K.P., & Bohlander, G.W. (1992). Relationship between an organization's actual human resource efforts and employee attitudes. *Group and Organization Management*, *17*, 135–152.

Klein, H.J., & Snell, S.A. (1994). The impact of interview process and context on performance appraisal interview effectiveness. *Journal of Managerial Issues*, *VI*, 160–175.

Kluger, A.N., & Adler, S. (1993). Person- versus computer-mediated feedback. *Computers in Human Behavior*, *9*, 1–16.

Kluger, A.N., & DeNisi, A. (1996). The effects of feedback interventions on performance: A historical review, a meta-analysis, and a preliminary feedback intervention theory. *Psychological Bulletin*, *119*, 254–284.

Korsgaard, M.A., & Roberson, L. (1995). Procedural justice in performance evaluation: The role of instrumental and non-instrumental voice in performance appraisal discussions. *Journal of Management*, *21*, 657–669.

Landy, F.J., & Farr, J.L. (1980). Performance Rating. *Psychological Bulletin*, *87*, 72–107.

Latham, G.P., Skarlicki, D., Irvine, D., & Siegel, J.P. (1993). The increasing importance of performance appraisals to employee effectiveness in organizational settings in North America. In C. Cooper & I.T. Robertson (Eds.), *International Review of Industrial and Organizational Psychology*, *8*, 87–132.

Lepsinger, R., & Lucia, A.D. (1997). 360° feedback and performance appraisal. *Training*, *34*, 62–70.

Levine, H.Z. (1986). Performance appraisals at work. *Personnel*, *63*, 63–71.

London, M., & Smither, J.W. (1995). Can multi-source feedback change perceptions of goal accomplishment, self-evaluations and performance related outcomes? Theory-based applications and directions for research. *Personnel Psychology*, *48*, 803–839.

London, M., & Wohlers, A.J. (1991). Agreement between subordinate and self-ratings in upward feedback. *Personnel Psychology*, *44*, 2, 375–390.

Longenecker, C.O., & Gioia, D.A. (1988). Neglected at the top: Executives talk about executive appraisal. *Sloan Management Review*, Winter, 41–47.

Longenecker, C.O., & Ludwig, D. (1990). Ethical dilemmas in performance appraisal. *Journal of Business Ethics*, *9*, 961–969.

Longenecker, C.O., Sims, H.P. Jr. & Gioia, D. (1987). Behind the mask: The politics of employee appraisal. *The Academy of Management Executive*, *1*, 183–193.

Love, K.G., Bishop, R.C., Heinisch, D.A., & Montei, M.S. (1994). Selection across two cultures: Adapting the selection of American assemblers to meet Japanese job performance demands. *Personnel Psychology*, *47*, 837–846.

Mabe, P.A., & West, S.G. (1982). Validity of self-evaluation of ability – a review and meta-analysis. *Journal of Applied Psychology*, *67*, 280–296.

Maier, N.R.F. (1958). Three types of appraisal interview. *Personnel*, March/April, 27–40.

McCune, J. C. (1997). Employee appraisals the electronic way. *Management Review*, *86*, 44–46.

McGregor, D. (1957). An uneasy look at performance appraisal. *Harvard Business Review*, *35*, 89–94.

Mendonca, M., & Kanungo, R.N. (1990). Work culture in developing countries: Implications for performance management. *Psychology and Developing Societies*, *2*, 137–164.

Mendonca, M., & Kanungo, R.N. (1996). Impact of culture on performance management in developing countries. *International Journal of Manpower*, *17*, 66–75.

Meyer, H.H., Kay, E., & French, J.R.P. (1965). Split roles in performance appraisal, *Harvard Business Review*, *43*, 123–129.

Milliman, J., Nason, S., Gallagher, E., Huo, P., Von Glinow, M.A., & Lowe, K.B. (1998). The impact of national culture on human resource management practices: The case of performance appraisal. *Advances in International Comparative Management*, *12*, 157–183.

Milliman, J.F., Nason, S., Lowe, K., Kim, N., & Huo, P. (1995). An empirical study of performance appraisal practices in Japan, Korea, Taiwan, and the US. In *Proceedings of the Academy of Management Conference* (pp. 812–186). Vancouver, Canada, August.

Nathan, B.R., Mohrman, A.M. Jr. & Milliman, J. (1991). Interpersonal relations as a context for the effects of appraisal interviews on performance and satisfaction: A longitudinal study. *Academy of Management Journal*, *34*, 352–369.

Ostroff, C. (1992). The relationship between satisfaction, attitudes and performance: An organizational level analysis. *Journal of Applied Psychology*, *77*, 963–974.

Patterson, M., West, M., Lawthom, R., & Nickell, S. (1998). *Issues in People Management*. IPD Report no. 22. London: Institute of Personnel and Development.

Pearce, J.L., & Porter, L.W. (1986). Employee responses to formal appraisal feedback. *Journal of Applied Psychology*, *71*, 211–218.

Ployhart, R.E., & Ryan, A.M. (1997). Applicants' reactions to the fairness of selection procedures: The effects of positive rule violations and time of measurement. *Journal of Applied Psychology*, *83*, 3–16.

Prieto, J.M., & Simon, C. (1997). Network and its implications for assessment. In N. Anderson & P. Herriot (Eds.), *International Handbook of Selection and Assessment*. Chichester: Wiley & Sons.

Ramamoorthy, N., & Carroll, S.J. (1998). Individualism/collectivism orientations and reactions toward alternative human resource management practices. *Human Relations, 51,* 571–588.

Reinhardt, C. (1985). The state of performance appraisal: A literature review. *Human Resource Planning, 8,* 104–110.

Rosenstein, E. (1985). Cooperativeness and advancement of managers: An international perspective. *Human Relations, 38,* 1–21.

Rousseau, D. (1995). *Psychological Contracts in Organizations.* California: Sage.

Salovey, P., & Mayer, J.D. (1990). Emotional intelligence. *Imagination, Cognition and Personality, 9,* 185–211.

Schneider, H.G., & Shugar, G.J. (1990). Audience and feedback effects in computer learning. *Computers in Human Behavior, 6,* 315–321.

Schutte, N.S., Malouff, J.M., Hall, L.E., Haggerty, D.J., Cooper, J.T., Golden, C.J., & Dornheim, L. (1998). Development and validation of a measure of emotional intelligence. *Personality and Individual Differences, 25,* 167–177.

Seddon, J. (1987). Assumptions, culture, and performance appraisal. *Journal of Management Development, 6,* 47–54.

Siegel, G.B. (1984). Performance appraisal for development of human resources in the democratic republic of the Sudan. *Public Personnel Management Journal, 13,* 147–155.

Smith, P.B., Dugan, S., & Trompenaars, F. (1996). National culture and the values of organizational employees: A dimensional analysis across 43 nations. *Journal of Cross-Cultural Psychology, 27,* 231–264.

Smither, J.W., London, M., Vasilopoulos, M.L., Reilly, M.R., Millsap, R.E., & Salvemini, N. (1995). An examination of the effects of an upward feedback program over time. *Personnel Psychology, 48*(1), 1–34.

Smither, J.W., Wohler, A.J., & London, M. (1995). A field study of reactions to normative versus individualized upward feedback. *Group and Organization Management, 20,* 61–89.

Sproull, L., & Kiesler, S. (1991). Two-level perspective on electronic mail in organizations. *Journal of Organizational Computing, 2,* 125–134.

Sulsky, L.M., & Keown, J.L. (1998). Performance appraisal in the changing world of work: Implications for the meaning and measurement of work performance. *Canadian Psychology, 39,* 52–59.

Taylor, M.S., Tracy, K.B, Renard, M.K., & Harrison, J.K. (1995). Due process in performance appraisal: A quasi-experiment in procedural justice. *Administrative Science Quarterly, 40,* 495–523.

Thompson, P.H., & Dalton, G.W. (1970). Performance appraisal: Managers beware. *Harvard Business Review, 48,* 149–57.

Triandis, H.C. (1989). Cross-cultural industrial and organizational psychology. In H.C. Triandis, M.D. Dunnette & L.M. Hough (Eds.), *Handbook of Industrial and Organizational Psychology* (2nd ed., Vol. 4, pp. 103–172). Palo Alto, CA: Consulting Psychologists Press.

Triandis, H.C., & Brislin, R.W. (1984). Cross-cultural psychology. *American Psychologist, 39,* 1006–1017.

Tziner, A., Latham, G.P., Price, B.S., & Haccoun, R. (1996). Development and validation of a questionnaire for measuring perceived political considerations in performance appraisal. *Journal of Organizational Behavior, 17,* 179–190.

Vance, C.M., McClaine, S.R., Boje, D.M., & Stage, H.D. (1992). An examination of the transferability of traditional performance appraisal principles across cultural boundaries. *Management International Review, 32,* 313–326.

Vancouver, J.B., & Morrison, E.W. (1995). Feedback inquiry: The effect of source attributes and individual differences. *Organizational Behavior and Human Decision Processes, 62,* 276–285.

Waldman, D.A. (1997). Predictors of employee preferences for multirater and group-based performance appraisal. *Group and Organization Management, 22,* 264–287.

Werner, J.M., & Bolino, M.C. (1997). Explaining U.S. courts of appeals decisions involving performance appraisal: Accuracy, fairness, and validation. *Personnel Psychology, 50,* 1–24.

Wexley, K.N., & Klimoski, R. (1984). Performance appraisal: An update. *Research in Personnel and Human Resources Management, 2,* 35–79.

Williams, R. (1998). *Performance Management.* London: International Thomson Business Press (Essential Business Psychology Series).

Williams, R., Walker, J., & Fletcher, C. (1977). International review of staff appraisal practices: Current trends and issues. *Public Personnel Management, 6,* 5–12.

Woehr, D.J., & Huffcutt, A.I. (1994). Rater training for performance appraisal: A quantitative review. *Journal of Occupational and Organizational Psychology, 67,* 189–206.

8

Counterproductive Behaviors at Work

PAUL R. SACKETT and
CYNTHIA J. DeVORE

The unifying theme of this chapter is a broad focus on the range of counterproductive behaviors by organization members, in contrast with the long tradition of specialized literatures focusing on individual behaviors or behavior domains (e.g., theft, absence). Our first theme is the dimensionality of counterproductive behavior, where we review the literature and find consistent patterns of intercorrelations among various counterproductive behaviors, and suggest a hierarchical perspective with both a broad construct of counterproductive behavior as well as more specific subconstructs. We also examine the relationship of counterproductive behavior to other facets of job performance, including task performance and citizenship behavior. Our second theme is an examination of antecedents of counterproductive behavior. We posit that there is no incompatibility between person-oriented and situation-oriented perspectives on antecedents of counterproductive behavior. We review large bodies of literature showing consistent relationships between individual difference variables and various counterproductive behaviors, and also review literature linking various categories of situational variables to counterproductive behaviors. We posit that common links of person and situation variables to various counterproductive behaviors support taking a broad and inclusive perspective on these behaviors.

Counterproductive workplace behavior at the most general level refers to any intentional behavior on the part of an organization member viewed by the organization as contrary to its legitimate interests. Here we offer a set of observations about this rough definition.

First, we distinguish 'counterproductive behavior' from 'counterproductivity', viewing the latter as the tangible outcomes of counterproductive behavior. We view counterproductive behavior as a facet of job performance. Consistent with current conceptualizations of job performance (e.g., Campbell, McCloy, Oppler & Sager, 1993), we view performance as reflecting behaviors, rather than outcomes. Thus the intentional violation of safety procedures is an example of a counterproductive

behavior, as such behaviors put the individual and the organization at risk. The number and cost of injuries resulting from such counterproductive behaviors might serve as a measure of counterproductivity. In a given time period, violation of safety procedures (behaviors) may not result in any injuries (outcomes), thus illustrating the distinction between counterproductive behavior and counterproductivity.

Second, the set of behaviors falling under this umbrella rubric partially overlap with a set of related terms and concepts, such as illegal, immoral, or deviant behaviors. Those three labels each have differing connotations, with illegal behaviors defined in terms of the laws of the jurisdiction in which the organization functions, immoral behaviors in terms of a particular value system, perhaps religious and perhaps secular, and deviant behaviors defined as deviating from a norm, thus requiring that an organizational or societal norm exist for a given behavior. All three of these terms generally carry connotations of wrongdoing, a connotation perhaps shared with the term 'counterproductive behavior'.

Our definition of counterproductive behavior clearly takes the perspective of the organization. We do this in order to make clear that a behavior can be performed by many employees in a given organization (e.g., a setting where taking sick leave when not actually sick has become widespread), and hence the behavior is not deviant in the norm-violation sense. The behavior may still, however, be viewed by the organization as counterproductive. We do note, though, that there are limits to taking the organization's view: some behaviors (e.g., leaving one's job for career improvement) are counterproductive in the sense of being contrary to the organization's interests, yet do not carry the connotation of wrongdoing that accompanies behaviors viewed as illegal, immoral, or deviant. Similarly, it may be in an organization's interests to have employees willing to routinely work 14-hour days without extra compensation; again, an unwillingness to do so does not carry connotations of wrongdoing. Hence we include the term 'legitimate' in the definition of counterproductive behavior as behavior contrary to the organization's legitimate interests.

Third, as noted by Robinson and Greenberg (1998), attempts at domain definition in this area commonly imply a focus on intentional behavior. We concur, in the sense that 'intentional' is viewed as synonymous with 'voluntary' or 'purposeful'. An important distinction is between whether an action was intentional and whether an outcome was intentional. A common rationale given for restricting the domain to intentional behavior is to rule out accidental acts. An accidental slip and fall resulting in an injury, despite following all safety regulations, is excluded by the current view of intentionality. On the other hand, an accident resulting from an employee choosing to disregard safety procedures would be intentional, as it is the unsafe act that constitutes counterproductive behavior, not the undesired outcome.

Intentionality has an additional connotation in some treatments, namely, intent to harm the organization. We concur that intent to harm is an important variable in understanding counterproductive behavior, but do not view it as a defining feature. For example, an unexcused absence may reflect an intent to retaliate against a supervisor, or it may reflect giving higher priority to an activity other than work (e.g., a ball game), without any consideration of bringing harm to the organization. We view both absences as intentional, in the sense that they are voluntary behaviors. These examples (absence as retaliation vs. absence to go to a ball game) highlight the fact that intent generally cannot be inferred from behavior. All that is directly observed is that an individual was not present at work; only via self-report might it be possible to separate retaliatory absence from other forms of absence.

Counterproductive behavior encompasses a broad number of domains. Gruys (1999) identified 87 separate counterproductive behaviors appearing in the literature (Baron & Neuman, 1996; Hollinger, 1986; Hollinger & Clark, 1982, 1983a; Hollinger, Slora & Terris, 1992; Hunt, 1996; Jones, 1980; Mangione & Quinn, 1975; Raelin, 1994; Robinson & Bennett, 1995; Robinson & O'Leary-Kelly, 1996; Ruggiero, Greenberger & Steinberg, 1982; Skarlicki & Folger, 1997; Slora, 1989; Terris & Jones, 1982), and used a rational sort and factor analytic techniques to produce 11 categories of counterproductive behaviors. We present those categories here as an overview of the range of behaviors included in the counterproductive behavior domain:

- Theft and related behavior (theft of cash or property, giving away of goods or services, misuse of employee discount);
- Destruction of property (deface, damage, or destroy property; sabotage production);
- Misuse of information (reveal confidential information, falsify records);
- Misuse of time and resources (waste time, alter time card, conduct personal business during work time);
- Unsafe behavior (fail to follow safety procedures, failure to learn safety procedures);
- Poor attendance (unexcused absence or tardiness, misuse sick leave);
- Poor quality work (intentionally slow or sloppy work);
- Alcohol use (alcohol use on the job, coming to work under the influence of alcohol);
- Drug use (possess, use, or sell drugs at work);
- Inappropriate verbal actions (argue with customers, verbally harass coworkers);
- Inappropriate physical actions (physically attack coworkers, physical sexual advances toward coworker).

We offer several comments about this categorization scheme. First, this list is presented to give a sense of the range of behaviors in this domain, rather than as an exhaustive list. Gruys did find some behaviors that did not fall cleanly into one of these categories (e.g., fake an injury to avoid work duties). Second, a central theme of the chapter is the need for an understanding of the covariance structure of counterproductive behaviors. There has been a tendency to treat each form of counterproductive behavior as discrete, resulting in separate literatures on behavior categories such as theft, drug and alcohol use, absenteeism, and unsafe behaviors. This tradition is reflected in the fact that this Handbook includes chapters on absenteeism and turnover by Johns (Chapter 12, Volume 2), and on safety by Nyssen and De Keyser (Chapter 16, this volume). As a complement to these behavior-specific literatures, we believe that there is great value in understanding the pattern of interrelationships among various forms of counterproductive behavior. One possibility is that these truly are independent behaviors, with separate sets of antecedents. Another is that some, or perhaps all, of these behaviors are substantially interrelated, with each a behavioral manifestation of a latent trait with common individual difference and/or situational antecedents. Understanding the pattern of interrelationships would shed light on the possibility of integrating these distinct literatures. There does appear to have been a recent movement toward more integrative treatments of the range of counterproductive behaviors, as reflected in Hollinger and Clark (1983b), Griffin, O'Leary-Kelly and Collins (1998), and Robinson and Greenberg (1998).

Thus the first major theme in this chapter is an integrative focus on counterproductive behavior. As just noted, one key issue is the interrelationships among various forms of counterproductive behavior. Another aspect of this integrative focus is the treatment of counterproductive behavior as a facet of job performance, where performance is defined as all employee workplace behavior relevant to organizational outcomes. Here we will consider the relationship between counterproductive behavior and various forms of productive behavior, such as task performance and organizational citizenship.

The second major theme of the chapter is the role of personal and situational factors as antecedents to counterproductive behavior. Researchers with differing orientations have emphasized one of these categories of antecedents, often to the exclusion of the other. We explore person, situation, and interactionist perspectives, with person perspectives focusing on stable individual difference variables (e.g., personality traits) as key determinants of counterproductive behavior and situational perspectives focusing on features such as group norms, organizational culture, organizational policies and practices, and control systems as key determinants of counterproductive behavior. Interactionist perspectives, as the name implies, examine the interaction of person and situation factors as determinants of counterproductive behavior.

THE DIMENSIONALITY OF COUNTERPRODUCTIVE BEHAVIORS

A seminal body of work examining a broad range of counterproductive behaviors is that of Hollinger and Clark (1983b) who developed a broad list of counterproductive behaviors, provided a conceptual framework for interrelating those behaviors, and collected self-report data from large employee samples in three industries. They proposed that counterproductive behaviors could be grouped into two broad categories. The first is 'property deviance', involving misuse of employer assets. Examples include theft, property damage, and misuse of discount privileges. The second is 'production deviance', involving violating norms about how work is to be accomplished. This includes not being on the job as scheduled (absence, tardiness, long breaks) and behaviors that detract from production when on the job (drug and alcohol use, intentionally slow or sloppy work).

Robinson and Bennett (1995) noted that the set of behaviors examined by Hollinger and Clark did not include interpersonal counterproductive behaviors, such as sexual harassment, and set out to expand upon the Hollinger and Clark framework. They had workers generate a large number of critical incidents of counterproductive behavior, obtained ratings of the similarity between pairs of behaviors, and subjected the resulting pairwise similarity matrix to multidimensional scaling. They obtained a two-dimensional solution, with one dimension differentiating behavior toward the organization (Hollinger & Clark's production and property deviance) from interpersonal behavior toward other organizational members (e.g., harassment, gossip, verbal abuse), and the other dimension representing a continuum from minor to serious offenses. Arraying behaviors in this two-dimensional space, Robinson and Bennett labeled the resulting four quadrants as property deviance (organizational – serious), production deviance (organizational – minor), personal aggression (interpersonal – serious, including behaviors such as harassment, and theft from coworkers), and political deviance (interpersonal – minor, including behaviors such as favoritism, gossip, and blaming others for one's mistakes).

It is critical to note that this categorization scheme was based on workers' perceptions of the similarity of pairs of behaviors. When asked to judge the similarity of pairs of behaviors, respondents were not constrained as to the basis for their similarity judgments. The purpose of the multidimensional scaling technique is to identify dimensions underlying similarity judgments, and the study findings indicate that, in the aggregate, respondents used the two dimensions of organization as target vs. other person as target and minor offense vs. serious offense as the basis for their similarity judgments. While it is useful to know what dimensions underlie perceptions of similarity between counterproductive behaviors, we posit here that the key issue for understanding interrelationships among various forms of counterproductive behavior is the covariance of occurrence among these behaviors. The question is whether individuals who engage in one form of counterproductive behavior are also likely to engage in others. It is possible that the pattern of co-occurrence among counterproductive behaviors is quite different from the pattern of perceived similarity emerging from the Robinson and Bennett perceptual similarity task. For example, theft from a coworker and verbal abuse of a customer are located close together in the multidimensional space emerging from Robinson and Bennett's analysis, in that both are serious offenses that target another person. However, the two behaviors may differ on a variety of other dimensions (e.g., a public vs. private dimension, a planned vs. unplanned dimension), making the rate of co-occurrence of the two an open question.

How might one get insight into the rate of co-occurrence of counterproductive behaviors? While the ideal would be the objective measurement of each form of counterproductive behavior, we acknowledge what has been viewed as the Achilles heel of counterproductivity research, namely, that while some forms of counterproductive behavior are public (e.g., absence), many are acts by employees who do not wish to be detected (e.g., theft, sabotage, harassment). In the face of the difficulties of direct observation, data on the covariance of counterproductive behaviors come from three sources: (a) self-report of the rate of occurrence, (b) judgments by others (e.g., supervisors) of the rate of occurrence, and (c) direct judgments about the rate of co-occurrence of counterproductive behaviors. We offer the caveat that both self-report and other-report data are, like direct observational data, subject to interpretational difficulties. The correlations among self-reports could conceivably be inflated as a result of social desirability in responding, and the correlations among supervisor ratings may be inflated as a result of halo error. As none of these strategies is clearly ideal, we review exemplars of each of these in turn, and comment on the convergence of findings across strategies.

The first example of the use of a self-report strategy comes from Bennett and Robinson (2000). The goal of the study was to develop a self-report instrument to assess the degree to which individuals engaged in counterproductive behavior. An extensive instrument development and refinement process was used, and the effort was guided by the conceptual framework developed in the Robinson and Bennett (1995) study described above. Specifically, the goal was an instrument with separate scales to assess behaviors aimed at the organization and behaviors aimed at other individuals. The final instrument, based on responses from a broad spectrum of 352 working adults, had a 12-item organizational deviance scale and a 7-item interpersonal deviance scale; internal consistency reliabilities for the two were .81 and .78 respectively.

Correlations between individual behaviors are not reported, but several useful insights can be gained about the interrelationships among behaviors. First, we can use the reported internal consistency reliabilities and the Spearman Brown formula to ascertain that the mean correlation is .26 among the organizational deviance items and .34 among the interpersonal deviance items. Thus intercorrelations among self-reports of individual behaviors are positive, but modest in magnitude, as is common with intercorrelations among individual behaviors. Second, Bennett and Robinson reported that the correlation between the organizational deviance scale and the interpersonal deviance scale is .68. Correcting this for unreliability results in a corrected correlation of .86. Thus when one moves from correlations between individual behaviors to composites of behaviors within a category (i.e., organizational vs. interpersonal), the composite correlations between the two scales are very high. We do not argue that the two forms of counterproductivity are, in fact, inseparable: to the contrary, Bennett and Robinson did show differential patterns of relationships with a number of other constructs (e.g., a courtesy scale is more highly related to the interpersonal deviance scale than to the organizational deviance scale.)

Ashton (1998) reported a similar set of findings from a study of college students with work experience. Individual self-report items dealing with eight counterproductive behaviors all falling into the organizational deviance category used by Bennett and Robinson (e.g., absence, tardiness, alcohol use, safety violations, theft) were used; the mean intercorrelation among the eight was .30, and the internal consistency reliability for a composite of the eight was .77. These findings closely parallel Bennett and Robinson's.

A different approach to self-reports of counterproductive behavior was taken by Gruys (1999). First, she noted that many individual counterproductive behaviors were specific to certain work contexts, and that some respondents might never have had the opportunity to engage in some of the behaviors (e.g., one cannot abuse an employee discount if one has not worked in a setting where such a discount is available). Thus Gruys asked respondents to consider that range of circumstances under which one could work and respond to behaviors using a scale anchored from 'no matter what the circumstances, I would not engage in the behavior' to 'in a wide variety of circumstances, I would engage in the behavior'. Second, ratings of 87 behaviors were obtained, and composite scores were obtained for the 11 behavior categories presented at the opening of this chapter (theft, destruction of property, misuse of information, misuse of time and resources, unsafe behavior, poor attendance, poor quality work, alcohol use, drug use, inappropriate verbal actions, inappropriate physical actions). Thus correlations were reported not between individual behaviors, but between behavior categories.

Highly similar findings emerged from a sample of 115 students and a sample of 343 college alumni; we focus here on the alumni sample. The mean correlation among the 11 behavior category composites was .50; we interpret the higher values than those found in studies of individual behaviors as reflecting the higher reliability of composites. Combining the 11 category composite into an overall grand composite results in an internal consistency reliability of .92.

A second strategy for insight into the covariance of counterproductive behaviors comes from ratings made by others (e.g., supervisors) of the degree to which individuals engage in various counterproductive behaviors. Hunt (1996) reported the largest scale study using this strategy that we are aware of, involving ratings of over 18,000 employees in 36 companies. Individual ratings items were combined into composites, and Hunt reported correlations among the composites. Five of the dimensions rated fall into the counterproductivity domain: attendance, off-task behavior (e.g., unauthorized breaks, personal business on work time), unruliness, theft, and drug misuse. The mean correlation among the composite measures for these five dimensions was .50 – a figure that corresponds precisely to the mean correlation reported in Gruys's study using composites obtained from self-reports of counterproductivity.

A final strategy for insight into the covariance of counterproductive behaviors involves obtaining direct judgments about the likelihood of co-occurrence of various counterproductive behaviors. Gruys (1999) employed this strategy in addition to the self-report research described above. Like Robinson and Bennett (1995), she obtained direct judgments of the similarity of counterproductive behaviors. However, while Robinson and Bennett permitted respondents to construe 'similarity' in whatever fashion they chose, Gruys explicitly presented respondents with the task of making judgments of the likelihood that a person who engaged in one form of counterproductivity on the job would also engage in another. Gruys reported two dimensions underlying these likelihood judgments. Like Robinson and Bennett, a dimension emerged distinguishing acts that primarily harm the organization (e.g., theft, absence) from acts that primarily harm other individuals (e.g., verbal and physical acts toward others). In contrast to Robinson and Bennett's minor vs. serious dimension, Gruys's second dimension differentiated acts that detract from job performance (e.g., absence, intentionally doing poor quality work, safety violations) from harmful acts in the workplace not directly related to job performance (e.g., theft). The direct judgments of likelihood of co-occurrence did not translate into a correlational metric, thus not permitting a direct comparison of these results with those obtained using self-report or other-report. However, because Gruys had the same respondents perform both the paired comparison likelihood of co-occurrence task and the self-rating task described earlier, it is possible to compare the matrix of co-occurrence ratings with the correlation matrix from the self-report ratings, as both tasks involved the same 11 behavior categories previously outlined. The correlation between the elements of the co-occurrence matrix and the elements of the self-report correlation matrix was −.17, which was not significantly different from zero. Thus perceptual data about likelihood of co-occurrence does not produce a similar pattern of interrelationships among counterproductive behaviors from that resulting from self-report. At a more general level, though, the results do match one aspect of the data emerging from self-report and other-report research, namely, a pattern of positive relationship among counterproductive behaviors. On a scale where 1 means that two behaviors are very unlikely to co-occur and 7 means that two behaviors are very likely to co-occur, the average rating was 4.2.

Thus self-report, other-report, and direct judgments of likelihood of co-occurrence support the notion of positive interrelationships among counterproductive behaviors. Self-report data indicated positive correlations in the range of .30 between individual counterproductive behaviors, but higher correlations of about .50 between composites of related behaviors, a finding replicated with data using supervisor ratings. It appears reasonable to think in terms of an overall counterproductivity construct, as the true score correlation between Bennett and Robinson's two domains of organizational and interpersonal deviance is .86, the reliability of a grand overall composite across Gruys's 11 behavioral domains is .92, and the reliability of a grand composite across five behavioral domains in Hunt's work is .83.

In proposing an overall counterproductivity construct, we are not arguing against research focusing on more specific forms of counterproductivity. We suggest a hierarchical model, with a general counterproductivity factor at the top, a series of group factors, such as the organizational deviance and interpersonal deviance factors identified by Bennett and Robinson (2000), below this general factor, and specific behavior domains, such as theft, absence, safety, and drug and alcohol use below these group factors. Researchers and practitioners may focus at different levels of this hierarchy for different applications. We suggest that in many personnel selection settings organizations are interested in identifying prospective employees who will not engage in the broad range of counterproductive behaviors, and thus may focus on the broad counterproductivity construct. In contrast, an intervention may be sought that will deal effectively with a single specific problem behavior (e.g., widespread violation of safety procedures). Our perspective is that the decision as to where to focus one's intervention and/or measurement efforts on this continuum from general factor to specific behaviors is best made recognizing the interrelationships among counterproductive behaviors.

COUNTERPRODUCTIVE BEHAVIORS AND JOB PERFORMANCE

The prior section focused on interrelationships among different forms of counterproductive behavior. We turn now to the relationship between counterproductive behaviors and other behaviors making up the broad domain of job performance. The most prominent contemporary framework for viewing job performance is that of Campbell (Campbell et al., 1993), who offered eight performance components: job-specific task proficiency, nonjob-specific task proficiency, written and oral communication, demonstrating effort, maintaining personal discipline, facilitating peer and team performance, supervision/leadership, and management/administration. The maintaining personal discipline dimension reflects the counterproductivity domain as discussed here.

A series of interrelated frameworks have been offered that focus on a set of behaviors variously labeled as citizenship behaviors (Smith, Organ & Near, 1983), prosocial behaviors (Brief & Motowidlo, 1986), and contextual performance (Borman & Motowidlo, 1993). What these have in common is a focus on positive behaviors that contribute to organizational effectiveness, but that do not reflect core job tasks. These include helping others, persistence and extra effort, and supporting the organization. While there are differences in emphasis in these different frameworks (e.g., some frameworks require that a behavior be discretionary, i.e., not formally rewarded by the organization, while others do not include this restriction), the behavioral domains covered by these frameworks are largely overlapping. An emerging literature differentiates and contrasts the task performance domain and the citizenship/prosocial/contextual performance domain (referred to as citizenship, as a term to reflect the broad domain) (e.g., Conway, 1999; Motowidlo & Van Scotter, 1994). Adding the counterproductive behavior domain that is the focus of this chapter leads to a broad conception of three primary performance domains: task performance, citizenship performance, and counterproductive behavior, and prompts questions as to relationships between counterproductive behavior and the other two domains.

We focus primarily on three large multi-sample data sets in examining this issue. The first is the US Army Selection and Classification Project, commonly referred to as Project A (Campbell, 1990; McHenry, Hough, Toquam, Hanson & Ashworth, 1990). Project A investigated a broad array of predictor and criterion variables across a set of military jobs. Of great interest is the focus on the careful identification of constructs underlying measured variables. Thirty-two different criterion measures were obtained; and factor analytic work was done to identify a set of five criterion constructs underlying these measures. These constructs include core technical proficiency, general soldiering proficiency, effort and leadership, physical fitness and military bearing, and maintaining personal discipline. The two soldiering proficiency measures reflect the task performance domain; effort and leadership the citizenship domain, and maintaining personal discipline the counterproductive behavior domain. Construct-level scores were obtained by combining different measures, including work samples, supervisor ratings, and indicators from administrative records, including the number of disciplinary infractions. Criterion scores were obtained for 4,039 soldiers in nine military enlisted jobs.

The key findings were observed uncorrected mean correlations of $-.19$ and $-.17$ between counterproductivity and the general and specific task performance dimensions, and a mean correlation of $-.59$ between counterproductive behavior and the effort/leadership construct. Thus the relationship between counterproductive behavior and quantity and quality of task performance is quite low; in contrast to the relationship between counterproductive behavior and effort/leadership, which is quite high.

The second large data set is the work of Hunt (1996), referenced earlier in the context of the interrelationship among various forms of counterproductive behavior. Hunt's focus was on what he termed 'generic work behavior', namely, behaviors common across jobs and not specific to the tasks of any given jobs. Our earlier discussion focused on five dimensions of counterproductive behavior; also relevant here are two dimensions labeled industriousness and persistence, which correspond conceptually to the effort/leadership dimension in Project A, and to the broad construct we are labeling citizenship. Hunt derived composite measures of these dimensions using a sample of over 18,000 supervisory ratings across 36 organizations.

We use the psychometric theory of composites to estimate the correlation between a citizenship composite made up of Hunt's industriousness and persistence dimensions and a counterproductive behavior composite, made up of Hunt's five counterproductive behavior dimensions. The resulting correlation is $-.67$, which is quite similar to the value of $-.59$ obtained in Project A.

The final source is a meta-analysis by Viswesvaran, Schmidt and Ones (1999) of the interrelationships among supervisor ratings. They sorted ratings from the published literature into eight dimensions. Sample sizes varied by dimensions, and ranged from roughly 2,000 to 11,000. Here we combine ratings of job knowledge, quantity of output and quality of output into the broad dimension of task performance, ratings of interpersonal competence, effort, and leadership into the broad dimension of citizenship, and ratings of compliance/acceptance of authority corresponded to the domain of counterproductive behavior. The mean unobserved correlation between counterproductive behavior and ratings in the citizenship and task domains was − .57 and − .54 respectively.

There is clear convergence with respect to the relationship between counterproductive behavior and the citizenship domain: mean observed *r* is −.59 in Project A, − .67 in Hunt, and − .57 in Viswesvaran et al. In contrast, findings regarding the relationship between counterproductive behavior and task performance are quite discrepant: a mean *r* of − .18 in Project A and a mean *r* of − .54 in the Viswesvaran et al., meta-analysis. We posit that these differences reflect differences in the conceptualization and measurement of task performance in the two studies. The task performance measures in Project A were work sample and job knowledge measures. They reflect measures of maximum performance: what the individual 'can do' when performance is closely monitored. In contrast, the Viswesvaran et al., study was restricted to supervisor ratings, which can generally be seen as reflecting measures of typical performance: what the individual 'will do' over an extended period of time (Sackett, Zedeck & Fogli, 1988). The 'can do' measures are primarily a function of knowledge and skill, while the 'will do' measures are also influenced by the full range of individually and situationally driven motivational factors − factors that also affect counterproductive behavior. Thus counterproductive behavior would be expected to correlate more highly with typical task performance than with maximum task performance.

A key question at this point is whether the citizenship and counterproductive behavior domains are so highly negatively correlated that they should be viewed as a single dimension, with citizenship reflecting the positive pole and counterproductive behavior the negative pole (Puffer, 1987). Our perspective is that while two negatively correlated variables may usefully be combined into a composite for some purposes, the treatment of the two as reflecting a single continuum has implications of mutual exclusivity, namely, that the fact that an individual with high standing on citizenship cannot also be high in counterproductive behavior, and vice versa. There are ready examples of the highly productive employee who is also engaging in extensive counterproductive behavior (as when a high performer viewed as beyond suspicion is caught embezzling). The fact of a high correlation between the two domains can be usefully used in research on common antecedents, and a composite of the two reflecting an individual's contribution to the organization can be created without adopting a bipolar single dimensional view.

Antecedents of Counterproductive Behaviors

We note that researchers who state the goal of understanding counterproductive behavior in work settings may, in fact, have quite different goals in mind. We suggest two important dimensions here. The first is the level of analysis: whether the interest is the behavior of an individual or the aggregate behavior of multiple individuals. The second is time frame, moving from focusing on a single behavior at a single point in time to patterns of behavior over an extended period of time. Crossing these two dimensions creates four combinations: individual − single behavior (e.g., was Joe absent today?), individual − extended time period (e.g., what is Joe's rate of absenteeism over the past year?), aggregate − single behavior (e.g., what proportion of the workforce was absent today?), and aggregate − extended time period (e.g., what is the average daily absenteeism rate over the past year?)

Various theoretical perspectives on counterproductive behavior align themselves with different cells in this two-dimensional matrix. Perspectives that focus on individual differences as antecedents to counterproductive behavior clearly take the individual level of analysis. If the individual-level variables of interest are those viewed as stable over time (e.g., personality variables), the tendency will be to focus on outcome variables over an extended period of time (e.g., examining whether individuals high in conscientiousness tend to consistently have lower levels of absenteeism over time). If the individual-level variables of interest are those viewed as changing over time (e.g., mood), the tendency will be to focus on outcome variables in the short term.

In contrast, perspectives that focus on situational characteristics as antecedents to counterproductive behavior lend themselves to an aggregate level of analysis. Perspectives focusing on the effects of relatively stable characteristics (e.g., organizational policies regarding the consequences of detected counterproductive behavior, or control systems, such as the use of security cameras) tend to focus on outcome variables over an extended period of time. Perspectives focusing on triggering events (e.g., departures from a steady state such as a round of downsizing or a labor dispute) tend to focus on outcome variables in the short term.

One interesting feature of the literature on counterproductive behavior is presence of different communities of scholars, some who focus solely on personal factors (e.g., personality traits) as antecedents of counterproductive behaviors, and others who focus solely on situational factors (e.g., organizational culture, fairness of treatment by supervisors). In some cases, this may reflect personal preference or disciplinary background. In other cases it may reflect differences in the nature of the question the researcher is addressing. For example, a researcher interested in the question 'can I identify individuals prior to hire who are likely to engage in counterproductive behaviors if hired?' is likely to focus on individual difference variables measurable prior to hire. The level of analysis is the individual, and the focus is typically within-organization. The goal is to explain variability in counterproductive behavior among individuals for whom at least some situational factors are constant (e.g., control systems, organizational reward and punishment policies), though others may vary (e.g., fairness of treatment by supervisors). In contrast, another researcher may be interested in the question 'why does the rate of employee theft differ across organizations?' The level of analysis is the organization, and the focus is across-organization. The focus is likely to be on situational factors, though individual difference variables aggregated to the level of the organization may be of interest. Thus in some cases the rationale for a differential focus on personal and situational variables is clear and reasonable.

We note the person vs. situation issue is at times presented as competing perspectives, from which will eventually emerge a winner and a loser. Our sense is that there is no necessary competition between the perspectives: while situational factors may affect the mean level of counterproductive behavior in a specific organization, the variance in behavior in that situation is of interest to the student of individual differences.

These differing perspectives on the level of analysis and on the role of person and situation variables are among the factors that contribute to the lack of a generally accepted theory of counterproductive behaviors. Another factor is the tendency to focus on individual counterproductive behaviors. Detailed conceptual models of the antecedents of specific forms of counterproductive behavior exist, e.g., absenteeism (Sheridan, 1985), safety (Guastello, 1991; Steffy, Jones, Murphy & Kunz, 1986), violence (Mack, Shannon, Quick & Quick, 1998; Martinko & Zellars, 1998), and sexual harassment (Gutek, Cohen & Konrad, 1990). While there are commonalities, no integrative model is as yet generally accepted.

Yet another factor is that conceptualizations of the antecedents of counterproductivity differ on a proximal–distal continuum. Distal antecedents would include situational features, such as job characteristics, group norms, organizational policies and practices, and control systems. Proximal antecedents would include perceptual variables, such as inequity, need, acceptability, and risk. Such perceptual variables may be the mechanisms mediating the relationship of distal variables to counterproductive behaviors. For example, group norms may affect an individual's perceptions as to the acceptability of various forms of counterproductive behavior, or a specific organizational action may lead to perception of inequity.

In light of all of these factors, we will not propose an integrative theory here. What we have done is to review theories dealing with specific forms of counterproductive behaviors and extracted broad categories of distal determinants (e.g., individual and situational variables) that are implicated as antecedents of multiple forms of counterproductive behaviors. We focus largely on these distal determinants, as they are features potentially amenable to intervention (e.g., a selection system can be designed to screen in individuals with particular individual difference characteristics, control systems can be implemented or modified, or interventions to change organizational culture can be undertaken).

While focusing on distal antecedents, we note that more proximal antecedents may mediate the relationship between the distal antecedents we have been discussing and the outcome variables of interest. One can readily posit internal states, such as attitudes or emotions that may result from distal antecedents. We note that researchers may productively work on various linkages, e.g., from organizational events to perceived injustice to frustration to counterproductive behavior. While focusing on distal antecedents as features more directly amenable to intervention, we do not mean to imply by this choice that understanding mediating processes is not valuable. Thus we briefly outline a few exemplars of research on internal states as mediators of the relationship between organizational events and counterproductive behaviors.

We first focus on individual attitudes as antecedents of counterproductive behavior. In contrast with the personality variables, which will be treated subsequently as a category of distal antecedents, we view these as attributes of an individual that are more readily influenced by the situation, and thus are not viewed as inherently stable or permanent. Hollinger (1986) used a sample of over 9,000 randomly selected employees to test the applicability of social bonding theory in the prediction of counterproductive behaviors. The respondents were all from retail, service, or manufacturing business sectors to represent the United States most densely populated business segments. Using two categories of counterproductive behaviors, property deviance (e.g., theft, misuse of information, time, and resources), and production deviance (e.g., poor attendance, poor quality work, and alcohol or drug use), Hollinger found that property deviance could be predicted from intention to leave and age and production deviance could be predicted from job satisfaction.

Job satisfaction recurs as a work attitude variable that researchers have associated with specific counterproductive behaviors. Klein and her colleagues (Klein, Leong & Silva, 1996) hypothesize that job satisfaction is related to sabotage in their biopsychosocial model of employee sabotage while Hackett (1989) evaluated three meta-analyses that determined the relationship between job satisfaction and absenteeism. In reconciling the differences between the three meta-analyses, Hackett found strong links ($r = -0.21$ for absence frequency and work satisfaction; $r = -0.23$ for absence duration and overall job satisfaction).

As another example of more proximal antecedents to counterproductive behaviors, other researchers see the occurrence of counterproductive behavior as an outcome of stress (e.g., Leiter & Robichaud, 1997; Mack et al., 1998; Steffy et al., 1986). According to the stress model, counterproductive behaviors are simply dysfunctional coping mechanisms (Lennings, 1997). The chain of events is a familiar one: an individual perceives a set of stressors, from some or all of three typical areas, environmental, organizational, and personal (Mack et al., 1998). These stressors build up and the individual believes that he or she does not have adequate resources at his or her disposal to restore balance in his or her life and thus exhibits a stress response as evidenced at the individual and/or organizational level. Steffy et al. (1986) hypothesize the work attitudes and stressors of work load and role conflict are distal causes of alcoholism. In an empirical study based on the responses of 157 Canadian Forces personnel, Leiter and Robichaud (1997) found withdrawal behaviors related to all three dimensions of burnout (exhaustion $r = .57$, cynicism $r = .62$, and professional efficacy $r = -.36$).

Our framework for discussing distal antecedents of counterproductive behaviors expands upon the frameworks of other researchers. Robinson and Greenberg (1998) described antecedents in three different categories, namely individual factors (i.e., personality and demographics), social and interpersonal factors (i.e., norms of deviance and unfair interpersonal treatment), and organizational factors. Griffin et al. (1998) mentioned six categories: individual evaluative criteria, pathological characteristics, norms of the organization and group, culture, the reward system, and the control system. Building on these frameworks and a review of empirical research on antecedents of counterproductive behavior, we offer the following as major categories of antecedents: (1) personality variables, (2) job characteristics, (3) work group characteristics, (4) organizational culture, (5) control systems, and (6) injustice.

A key characteristic of these categories is that they are hypothesized to be linked to multiple forms of counterproductive behavior. We note that there are additional antecedents that we view as idiosyncratic, namely, antecedents relevant to only a single type of counterproductive behavior. For example, a model of employee tardiness may include transportation issues as important antecedent variables (Bardsley & Rhodes, 1996). But conceptually, there is no clear basis for linking commuting difficulties to, say, theft or drug use. Thus we acknowledge that there are likely to be idiosyncratic determinants of each specific type of counterproductive behavior. Our focus here, though, is on the commonalities in antecedents across types of counterproductive behavior.

1. Personality Variables as Antecedents to Counterproductive Behaviors

Robinson and Greenberg (1998) claimed that little or no support has been found for associations between personality and counterproductive behavior. Our goal in this section is to provide a concise overview of bodies of evidence linking individual difference measures to various counterproductivity criteria. We rely primarily on meta-analytic evidence, rather than describing individual studies, as the body of work on this topic is far too voluminous to do justice to individual studies. We focus on three sources: (1) meta-analyses of integrity tests as predictors of counterproductive behaviors, (2) meta-analyses of personality measures, organized using the Big 5 framework, as predictors of counterproductive behaviors, and (3) the large-scale US Army Project A, which examined various personality measures as predictors of counterproductive behavior in a military setting.

Integrity Tests as Predictors of Counterproductive Behaviors

Integrity tests are paper-and-pencil instruments designed to identify individuals likely to engage in counterproductive behaviors. Two categories of tests have emerged, which Sackett, Burris and Callahan (1989) labeled 'overt' and 'personality-oriented' tests. Overt integrity tests (alternately labeled 'clear purpose tests') commonly consist of questions about beliefs about the frequency and extent of theft, punitiveness toward theft, ruminations about theft, perceived ease of theft, endorsement of common rationalizations for theft, and assessments of one's own honesty, in addition to requests for admissions of theft and other wrongdoing. Applicants are asked to describe the frequency and amount of theft and other illegal and/or counterproductive activity. Personality-oriented measures (alternately labeled 'disguised purpose tests') are closely linked to normal-range personality assessment devices, such as the California Psychological Inventory. They are considerably broader in focus, and are not explicitly aimed at theft. They include items dealing with dependability, conscientiousness, social conformity, thrill-seeking, trouble with authority, and hostility.

A large body of research on these tests has emerged over the last two decades, as documented in a series of reviews by Sackett and colleagues (Sackett et al., 1989; Sackett & Decker, 1979;

Sackett & Harris, 1984; Sackett & Wanek, 1996). While research has shown linkages between these tests and both overall job performance and measures of counterproductivity, the focus here is solely on the relationships with measures of counterproductivity. One theme emerging in this body of research is that methodological choices have a large effect on the findings emerging from validity studies. Larger validity coefficients are found when self-report measures are used as criteria, and when concurrent rather than predictive designs are used. Ones, Viswesvaran and Schmidt (1993a) presented a large-scale meta analysis of the integrity test validity literature, in which they argued that the most persuasive studies were those using a predictive design, applicant samples, and nonself-report criteria. Table 8.1 contains the subset of studies from their meta-analysis that meet these criteria. It is critical to note that all correlations in the table are reported in a format whereby a positive correlation indicates a relationship in the expected direction (e.g., a positive correlation would indicate that a favorable integrity test score is linked to a favorable outcome, e.g., a low absenteeism rate)

Note that the mean correlation with theft criteria is low (.09). This has been the focus of some critics, who assert that theft is the prototypical behavior these tests were designed to predict, and these low correlations indicate that the tests are ineffective (Guastello & Rieke, 1991). Sackett and Wanek (1996) point out, however, that these low correlations are the inevitable result of attempting to predict behaviors with low base rates: mathematically, the maximum possible correlation between a predictor and a dichotomous criterion with a 95–5 split (e.g., 5% of the sample is detected stealing) is .47; with a 98–2 split the maximum is .39. Thus the mean correlation of .09 can be rescaled to roughly .20 if the observed correlation is viewed as a ratio of the observed correlation to the maximum possible correlation (e.g., .09 where the maximum possible is .40 is roughly analogous to .20 where the maximum possible is 1.0).

Table 8.1 also shows the relationships between both overt and personality-based integrity tests and a broad category of 'non-theft' criteria. This category aggregates all forms of counterproductivity other than theft. Both types of tests show sizable relationships with this aggregate criterion. Ones and colleagues later attempted to better differentiate this 'non-theft' criterion, and report separate meta-analyses using absence, substance abuse, and workplace violence as criteria. As Table 8.1 shows, integrity tests show sizable relationships to each of these forms of counterproductive behavior. Thus a very large body of literature links integrity tests to both broad and specific measures of counterproductivity.

Personality, the Big 5, and Counterproductive Behaviors

The seminal meta-analysis of the personality literature for personnel selection was reported by Barrick and Mount (1991), who were the first to organize the voluminous literature on personality in the workplace in terms of the Big 5 framework which has come to dominate personality research. Different terminology is sometimes used to label Big 5 dimensions; we use the terms emotional stability (sometimes labeled neuroticism), extraversion, agreeableness, conscientiousness, and openness to experience (sometimes labeled intellectance) in our treatment here. The Barrick and Mount meta-analysis focused on job performance criteria; two subsequent meta-analyses focused on counterproductive behavior criteria: Hough (1992) and Salgado (2000).

Hough (1992) argued for an expanded form of the Big 5, including nine personality dimensions. Relevant to the discussion here is the separation of conscientiousness into two subfacets (achievement and dependability) and the separation of extraversion into two subfacets (affiliation and potency). Hough differentiated between eight different criterion constructs (e.g., technical proficiency, teamwork); the criterion construct relevant here is what she termed 'irresponsible behavior', defined as including poor attendance, counterproductive behavior, disciplinary actions, not following directions, unauthorized absence, and drug and alcohol use on the job. The analysis did not differentiate between these different behaviors making up the irresponsible behavior category. Hough also made no attempt to correct observed correlations for unreliability or range restriction, and thus only observed correlations are reported.

Table 8.1 reports the results of Hough's meta analysis. The dominant feature, in terms of both the sheer amount of data and the nature of the results, is the finding of a mean correlation of .24 for dependability, based on 69 independent samples. Achievement, emotional stability, and openness to experience also produce mean correlations of .15 or higher, though based on much smaller samples.

Salgado (2000) noted the combining of various forms of counterproductive behavior in Hough's meta-analysis, and undertook a follow-up analysis incorporating both American and European studies done since Hough's earlier work with the goal of treating various forms of counterproductive behavior separately. He reported separate analyses for four criteria in this domain: absence, accidents, counterproductive behaviors (theft and disciplinary problems), and turnover. The results are included in Table 8.1. None of the personality dimensions were related to either absence or accidents. Conscientiousness and agreeableness were related to the counterproductivity criterion, and four of five (all but openness to experience) were related to turnover.

The finding of no relationship with absenteeism is puzzling. We noted earlier that Ones et al. (1993c) reported relationships between integrity tests and absence. Research on the constructs underlying

Table 8.1   *Do individual difference variables predict counterproductive behavior?*

Measure	# of sample	Total N	Mean observed r	Mean corrected r
A. *Integrity tests*				
1. Ones et al. (1993a)				
Overt tests – theft criteria	7	2,434	.09	.13
Overt tests – nontheft criteria	10	5,598	.27	.39
Personality-based tests – nontheft criteria	62	90,092	.20	.29
2. Viswesvaran et al. (1992)				
Overt integrity tests – absence criteria	10	8,357	.06	.09
Personality-based tests – absence criteria	18	5,345	.25	.36
3. Schmidt et al. (1997)				
Substance abuse criteria – applicant samples	10	22,091	.17	.23
4. Ones et al. (1994)				
Honesty scales – workplace violence as criteria	17	11,079	.18	.26
Violence scales – workplace violence as criteria	7	522	.32	.46
B. *Big 5 personality measures*				
1. Hough (1992) – counterproductive behavior criteria				
Achievement	4	19,476	.19	
Dependability	69	98,676	.24	
Emotional stability	9	21,431	.15	
Extraversion	14	38,578	.06	
Agreeableness	4	24,259	.08	
Openness to experience	2	1,414	.15	
2a. Salgado (2000) – absence criteria				
Emotional stability	12	2,491	.03	.04
Extraversion	10	1,799	.05	.08
Openness to experience	8	1,339	.00	.00
Agreeableness	8	1,339	.03	.04
Conscientiousness	10	2,155	− .04	− .06
2b. Salgado (2000) – accidents as criteria				
Emotional stability	5	2,121	.04	.08
Extraversion	7	2,341	.02	.04
Openness to experience	5	1,660	− .05	− .09
Agreeableness	4	1,540	.00	.01
Conscientiousness	6	2,094	.03	.06
2c. Salgado (2000) – counterproductivity criteria				
Emotional stability	15	3,107	.04	.06
Extraversion	12	2,383	− .01	− .01
Openness to experience	8	1,421	− .10	− .14
Agreeableness	9	1,299	.13	.20
Conscientiousness	10	1,737	.18	.26
2d. Salgado (2000) – turnover as criteria				
Emotional stability	4	554	.25	.35
Extraversion	4	554	.14	.20
Openness to experience	4	554	.11	.14
Agreeableness	4	554	.16	.22
Conscientiousness	5	748	.23	.31
C. *Project A*				
McHenry et al. (1990) – 'maintaining personal discipline' as criteria				
Achievement	9	4,039	.18	
Dependability	9	4,039	.30	
Adjustment	9	4,039	.11	

integrity tests showed them to be essentially a composite of conscientiousness, agreeableness, and emotional stability (Ones, Viswesvaran & Schmidt, 1993b). Thus we would have expected these three dimensions to be related to absenteeism. The relationships with counterproductive behavior mirror Hough's earlier findings, supporting in particular the relationship between conscientiousness and counterproductive behavior. Recall that Hough separated conscientiousness into separate achievement and dependability facets, while Salgado reports findings in terms of the broad dimension of conscientiousness. Finally, while Salgado reports relationships between four personality dimensions and turnover, the findings are hard to interpret without more information about the context in which the data were collected. We do not know the point in an individual's tenure where turnover was assessed, and thus it is unclear, for example, whether the studies dealt with predicting survival of an initial probationary period for news hires, or with turnover over an extended period of time among experienced employees. It is also worth noting an earlier discussion of whether turnover belongs within the counterproductivity domain: while leaving may be contrary to the organization's interest, pursuit of better career options would generally be viewed as perfectly legitimate self-interested behavior on the part of an employee.

The Army Project A and Counterproductive Behaviors

Among the most comprehensive investigations of the relationships between individual difference variables and job performance is the US Army Selection and Classification Project, commonly referred to as Project A (Campbell, 1990), some aspects of which were discussed earlier on the treatment of relationships between counterproductive behavior and other facets of job performance. Project A investigated a broad array of predictor and criterion variables across a set of military jobs. Of great interest is the focus, on both the predictor and criterion sides of the equation, on the careful identification of constructs underlying measured variables. On the criterion side, factor analytic work was done to identify a set of five criterion constructs underlying these measures; of interest here is the construct of maintaining personal discipline, reflecting the domain of counterproductive behavior. A construct-level score was obtained by combining different measures, including supervisor ratings of maintaining discipline, following regulations, and exhibiting integrity, and indicators from administrative records, including the number of disciplinary infractions. On the predictor side, three composite scores were created from a multidimensional personality inventory, yielding scores for achievement orientation, dependability, and adjustment. Predictor and criterion scores were obtained for 4,039 soldiers

in nine military enlisted jobs. Table 8.1 reports the mean validity across jobs for each of these personality composites; note that dependability (mean $r = .30$) and achievement orientation (mean $r = .18$) exhibit sizable validity coefficients.

Conclusions Regarding Personality Variables and Counterproductive Behavior

We find the pattern of evidence summarized in Table 8.1 to be compelling: meta-analytic evidence from the integrity testing literature, the Big 5 literature, and the literature on the prediction of military performance all makes clear that some personality dimensions show consistent relationships to counterproductive behaviors. The strongest findings are for the dimension of conscientiousness. First, integrity tests showed sizable relationships (mean observed $r = .27$ and .20 for two different types of integrity tests) with counterproductive behaviors, and research on the constructs underlying integrity tests showing that conscientiousness was the single largest source of variance in integrity tests (Ones et al., 1993b). Second, Hough separated the Big 5 conscientiousness dimension into dependability and achievement subfacets and reported similar relationships with counterproductivity criteria (mean observed $r = .19$ and .24 for achievement and dependability). Third, the military's Project A similarly separated dependability and achievement and reported comparable findings (mean observed $r = .18$ and .30 for achievement and dependability). These conclusions were based on well over 100 studies of several hundred thousand individuals. These findings refute Robinson and Greenberg's (1998) conclusion that little or no support has been found for associations between personality and counterproductive behavior.

2. Job Characteristics as Antecedents to Counterproductive Behavior

Several lines of inquiry suggest that job characteristics are linked to the likelihood of engaging in counterproductive behavior. Hackman and Oldham's (1976, 1980) well-known Job Characteristics Model suggested that a set of core job characteristics (skill variety, task identity, task significance, autonomy, and feedback from the job) led to a set of critical psychological states (experienced meaningfulness of the work, experienced responsibility for outcomes of the work, and knowledge of the results of the work activities), which led to a set of outcomes, including performance, satisfaction, internal work motivation, and absence and turnover. While the theory itself listed only a small piece of the counterproductivity domain (i.e., absence and turnover) as outcomes of job characteristics, one can readily hypothesize links between low meaningfulness of work and low responsibility for work outcomes and a variety of forms of counterproductive behavior.

Rentsch and Steel (1998), investigated the robustness of job characteristics as predictors of attendance over an extended period. Beginning with 475 civilian, white collar, professional, and clerical men and women working in the US Department of Defense, and ending with 339 of the original respondents six years later, they measured job characteristics, job competence, and need for achievement in year 1 and year 6. Two absenteeism measures were calculated for each of the six years of the study. One measure was for time lost and the other for frequency of absence. Rentsch and Steel found that even controlling for demographic variables of age, sex, tenure, and educational level, job characteristics predicted absence scores. Skill variety, task identity, and autonomy each correlated between − .25 and − .20 with each measure of absence.

Klein et al. (1996) proposed the development of a biopsychosocial model of sabotage. Broader than its name implies, the biopsychosocial model incorporates psychopathology, non-occupational stress, injustice and social information processing (both to be discussed in upcoming sections) and the proximal factors of organizational commitment and job satisfaction as predictors of sabotage. Like Rentsch and Steel (1998) they also looked to job design, proposing that skill variety and autonomy are particularly relevant. According to Klein et al., sabotage can be the outgrowth of employees trying to make their jobs more interesting. Although this assertion is not directly supported or proposed by the studies cited for their examples of employees engaging in playful interactions to make the jobs more tolerable (Hamper, 1991) and in individual and group activities to make jobs less boring (Roy, 1960), the authors propose that in the absence of condoned diversions, bored individuals might engage in sabotage. The authors further propose that sabotage can result from horseplay (Duncan, Smeltzer & Leap, 1990; Dwyer, 1991).

Klein and her associates (Klein et al., 1996) reported links between self-reported sabotage and perceived lack of autonomy (Sprouse, 1992). Those who committed acts of sabotage reported an increase in this counterproductive behavior when their superiors watched them too closely and when the employees were not allowed to complete their work according to their own plans and insights.

3. Work Group Characteristics as Antecedents to Counterproductive Behaviors

For some theorists, the self does not exist except in relation to others (e.g., Goffman, 1959). 'We're only as good as the company we keep' goes the folk saying and when considering the antecedents of counterproductive behaviors at work, the literal 'company' we keep, the work group, can have great influences on the behavior of an individual. In this section we describe theories and empirical evidence that inform our knowledge of others' impact on an individual's pattern of counterproductive behavior.

According to Attraction-Selection-Attrition Theory (Schneider, 1975), people will be attracted to, and selected into organizations with which they share attitudes. People who have ideas at odds with the rest of the organization will either not be a candidate, not be hired, or if hired, will not stay. For example, if Joe likes to put in short hours on the job, he might choose an organization that does not use time cards. If Joe were hired into an organization valuing putting in long hours, Joe would be compelled to change or leave.

The mechanism for change according to Social Information Processing Theory (Salancik & Pfeffer, 1978) begins with an individual seeking information from his or her immediate surroundings to help interpret events. Using those in the immediate surroundings as examples, the individual develops attitudes that align with those of the group. If we take Joe and put him in a work group wherein the members come in late and leave early and show no concern for this counterproductive behavior, Joe is more likely to engage in putting in short hours.

In classical conditioning, individuals repeat or decrease behaviors based on direct consequences for actions (i.e., we repeat behaviors for which we are rewarded and decrease behaviors that result in our being punished). Social Learning Theory (Bandura, 1977) proposes that individuals adapt their behavior based on the consequences not experienced directly, but that are observed for significant others. If Joe sees that his coworker Jane is severely reprimanded for coming in late and leaving early, Joe might change his behavior in order to avoid future consequences.

Robinson and O'Leary-Kelly (1998) combined the theories of Attraction-Selection-Attrition (i.e., people who wish to engage in counterproductive behaviors will be attracted to and be selected into organizations that support those behaviors and those who are not of the same mind will leave), Social Information Processing Theory (i.e., individuals will adjust their views of counterproductive behaviors through continued exposure to the behaviors of the group), and Social Learning Theory (i.e., individuals observe the behaviors of others and see the consequences for their behaviors) to explain how individuals behave relative to their cohorts. The particular behaviors they expressly measured include destruction of property, poor quality work, unsafe behaviors, and inappropriate verbal actions. In a sample of 187 men and women from 35 work groups from clerical, professional, and technical occupations each participant provided information about his/her involvement in antisocial behaviors as well as tenure in the group, task interdependence, perceived likelihood of punishment, and perceived closeness of supervision. Robinson and O'Leary-Kelly controlled for job satisfaction, perceived control over the environment, and a variety of demographic variables. They created a measure of the level of counterproductive behavior in the group by aggregating individual self-reported counterproductive behaviors, excluding the target individual. Thus they created independent measures of individual counterproductive behavior and the aggregate level of counterproductive behavior of other members of each individual's workgroup.

The key finding reported by Robinson and O'Leary-Kelly is that after including the demographic and other control variables mentioned above in a regression model, the group aggregate measure of counterproductive behavior had a significant effect on individual counterproductive behavior. This otherwise admirable study is made difficult to interpret due to some questionable aspects of the reported data analysis. For example, the squared multiple correlation decreases when additional variables are added to the regression equation in their table 2, and reported degrees of freedom are inconsistent with the described data analyses. We reanalyzed the data based on the correlation matrix included in the article, and were not able to replicate the reported findings; in our reanalysis, the aggregate group counterproductive behavior variable does not add significantly to the prediction of individual antisocial behavior. Thus this issue clearly merits additional inquiry.

Another theoretical perspective that posits a link between deviance of work group members and various counterproductive behaviors is Hirschi's social bonding theory. According to Hollinger (1986), social bonding theory is applicable to counterproductive behaviors in that to the extent an individual is bonded with and connected to their work community the individual will not engage in counterproductive behaviors. Social bonding theory has been used extensively in the explication of juvenile delinquency (e.g., Edwards, 1996). Typically, social bonding is defined along four dimensions: attachment, commitment, involvement, and belief. In the context of deviant behavior, attachment is seen as an indication of the closeness an individual feels toward non-deviant others. Hollinger hypothesized that the greater the attachment an employee has toward the nondeviant exemplars in an organization, the less likely that individual is to engage in deviant behaviors. The second factor, commitment, reflects how much is risked in the future if the individual engages in counterproductive behaviors and is reprimanded for those behaviors. The third factor in social bonding theory is involvement. Colloquially speaking, involvement precludes

deviant behaviors through continuous activity. In other words, if idle hands are the devil's playthings, involvement keeps the hands busy. The fourth element, belief, implies a common opinion about the legal system. Hollinger excludes the fourth element, belief, on the grounds that employees engaging in deviant behaviors do not see themselves as doing criminal or illegal acts. If the fourth component of Hirschi's control theory is interpreted as the 'belief in a common value system' (Lasley, 1988: 348), then perhaps deviant employees do share a common value system that sees the behaviors as permissible and legal.

Another aspect of counterproductive behavior in which work group influences have been exampled is absenteeism. As an exemplar, we summarize a study by Gellatly (1995) of 166 Canadian hospital workers, in which he measured actual absenteeism at the individual and work-group level, the employees' perceptions of the absence norm of the work group, affective and continuance commitment, interactional justice as well as organizational tenure and age. Gellatly found that the perceived absence norm was positively related to absence frequency ($r = 0.18$) and total days absent ($r = 0.35$).

In this section, we explored the mechanisms by which the group can influence the behaviors of the individual. In the next section, we explore the influence the organizational culture has on the behaviors of individuals.

4. Organizational Culture as an Antecedent to Counterproductive Behavior

While there are similarities between group influences and organizational culture in the sense that both constitute social influences on individuals in the workplace, culture is a broader phenomenon, influenced by factors outside the immediate workgroup, such as management (e.g., Thompson, Hilton & Witt, 1998).

One area that has been the focus of investigation is the concept of an organization's 'climate of honesty'. Two different conceptualizations of climate have been used. Cherrington and Cherrington (1985) sought employee perceptions of the presence or absence of a strong company code of ethics, the level of honesty of top management, the adequacy of internal accounting controls, and the discipline and publicity accompanying the detection of employee theft or fraud. Shrinkage in three companies was examined; greater shrinkage was found in companies where a code of ethics was not well defined, where good internal accounting controls were not present, and where a punitive system of discipline was present in which those caught stealing were openly punished as a deterrent to others.

A different approach was taken by Jones and Terris (1983), who operationalized honesty climate as the mean integrity test score of present employees. This index was computed for eight home improvement centers and used as a predictor of counterproductive behaviors for new applicants. The climate index proved predictive of supervisory ratings of a variety of counterproductive behaviors, such as taking extended work breaks.

We turn from 'honesty climate' to similar issues surrounding sexual harassment. Fitzgerald and her colleagues (Fitzgerald, Drasgow, Hulin, Gelfand & Magley, 1997), in a study on the antecedents and consequences of sexual harassment, analyzed responses from 459 women working for a utility company, and found their perception of the organizational acceptance for sexual harassment to be related to their reported experiences of gender harassment, unwanted sexual attention, and sexual coercion ($r = .45$). The scale used to quantify organizational tolerance for sexual harassment (Hulin, Fitzgerald & Drasgow, 1996) measured three facets: the risk associated with reporting, likelihood of being taken seriously, and probability of sanctions. Each of these facets can be influenced by management example and intervention.

Gutek and her associates (Gutek et al., 1990) posited that three factors, gender, contact with the other gender, and sexualization of the work environment, led to perceived sexual harassment and perceived nonharassing sexual behavior. In their study of 827 women and 405 men, Gutek et al., measured perceived sexualization of the workplace and the contact each respondent had with the opposite gender. Gutek et al., found consistent relationships between contact and nonharassing sexual behavior ($r = .294$) and between contact and sexual harassment ($r = .142$). Similar relationships were found between sexualization of the work environment and nonharassing sexual behavior and sexual harassment ($r = .182$ and $r = .244$, respectively).

5. Control Systems as Antecedents to Counterproductive Behavior

Control systems are physical or procedural entities within the workplace, meant specifically to diminish the occurrence of counterproductive behaviors through increasing the risk of detection or increasing the penalties for counterproductive behaviors. First implemented through supervisory oversight, then advancing with the use of technology in continuous flow production, to bureaucratic control since the Second World War, methods of control permeate the workplace (Sewell, 1998). Some of the common control practices are security systems (i.e., audits, computer applications, and surveillance), drug testing, employee training, environmental design, time clocks, and logbooks (e.g., Murphy, 1993; Murphy, Thornton & Prue, 1991; Rosenbaum & Baumer, 1985; Sewell, 1998). There is little

sound empirical evidence on the effectiveness of various control techniques, which Rosenbaum and Baumer (1985) attributed to organizations' belief that acknowledgment of the use of a specific control technique is an admission of vulnerability to theft and sabotage and a sign of weakness in the face of competition. Bearing this in mind, we discuss the control systems for which we have found empirical justification.

The problem of employee theft in the retail industry is more costly than that of shoplifting in the retail industry, with 60% of shortages being attributed to employee theft, 30% ascribed to outside shoplifters, and 10% to accounting errors (Cherrington & Cherrington, 1985). Murphy (1993) described several options for deterring theft, including security audits, computer applications, surveillance and spies, posting signs, rewarding 'whistleblowers', and providing employees the opportunity to take merchandise that is dated, partially damaged or cannot be sold.

We note that the existence of sophisticated security systems does not prevent all counterproductive behaviors. In fact, the technology can be used in the commission of counterproductive behaviors. For instance, although computer programs can be used to flag discrepancies between a physical and accounting inventory, they can, however, be used by the savvy individual as the means to commit an act of sabotage, falsify records, or acquire and pass on proprietary company information (e.g., Lasley, 1988; Murphy, 1993; Shapiro, 1990).

The physical systems described above are focused primarily on prevention of counterproductive behavior by offering the possibility of 'catching people in the act'. One might think that the likelihood of getting caught and thereby risking sanction or termination is sufficient deterrence, however the perceived ability to commit theft or to defraud the organization was not related to actual theft in the three companies in the Cherrington and Cherrington study (Cherrington & Cherrington, 1985).

In addition to security systems, organizations can use policies and procedures as another set of control mechanisms. Policies describe consequences of drug use (e.g., Ambrose, 2000; Stone & Kotch, 1989), absenteeism (e.g., Gellatly, 1995), and sexual harassment (e.g., Dekker & Barling, 1998), among others. Researchers of the phenomena of sexual harassment report that the absence of policies could be construed as a lack of concern for the issue (Dekker & Barling, 1998). In a study of 278 Canadian male university faculty and staff, those who saw the sexual harassment policy as 'weakly enforced or without prohibitive sanctions' showed higher levels of gender ($r = -.22$) and sexualized ($r = -.24$) harassment (p. 9).

Control systems are commonly used in the area of drug and alcohol use. Random drug testing is one method of finding employees who may be impaired on the job (Cook, Back & Trudeau, 1996). The topic of drug testing of incumbent employees has sparked much discourse and empirical research, much of it based on the acceptance of the procedure by the employees (e.g., Ambrose, 2000; Konovsky & Cropanzano, 1991; Murphy et al., 1991; Normand, Salyards & Mahoney, 1990; Stone & Kotch, 1989; Tepper, 1994). Although the incidence of drinking or drug use during work hours is suspected to be minimal, the incidence of drinking or drug use *before* work hours is of great concern, especially in the transportation industry (Shain, 1982). Researchers found that the general public is supportive of preemployment drug screening because applicants have the power to withhold their applications if they object to testing (Ambrose, 2000). Support also exists for testing job incumbents, who are in occupations that are dangerous or put the public at risk if the employee were impaired by drugs or alcohol (Murphy et al., 1991). This last study highlights the great variability in opinions over drug testing in any particular job.

6. Injustice as Antecedent of Counterproductive Behavior

There is a certain poetry in behaving badly in response to some perceived injustice, a situation eloquently summarized by Aristotle who wrote, 'Men regard it as their right to return evil for evil – and, if they cannot, feel they have lost their liberty.' Organizational justice theory and equity theory have been used to describe this phenomenon. We present a description of the theory and provide empirical support for the connection between injustice and counterproductive behaviors.

Equity theory claims that people compare the rewards for their efforts with the rewards others receive for their efforts. If the effort/reward ratios are not proportional, inequity exists, with the possibility of some individuals experiencing overreward and others underreward. When ratios are equivalent, the condition of equity results (Greenberg, 1990b). For instance, if Joe receives a bonus of $100 for completing a project early and John receives a bonus of $80 for completing the same project, Joe is hypothesized to feel guilty for being overpaid and John is predicted to feel anger for being underpaid.

Organizational justice incorporates the idea of imbalance, but goes further to define the types of norms that are violated in various situations. Organizational justice incorporates a variety of subfacets, the two most studied being distributive justice and procedural justice. Distributive justice refers to the equitable allocation of rewards or punishments, while procedural justice refers to fairness in the way the decisions were made (Greenberg, 1990b). If, for our previous example, management

announced that bonuses varied by time on the project (and Joe had been on the project longer than John), then both Joe and John should feel the sense of procedural justice. In spite of the unequal rewards (a violation of the equity norm), the difference was reasonable as explained. Procedural justice can be viewed as two distinct forms: fairness of formal procedures and quality of interpersonal treatment, also known as interactional justice (Skarlicki & Folger, 1997).

In a classic experiment, Greenberg (1990a) measured reactions to a pay cut using three sites: one site received an 'inadequate' explanation, the second received an adequate explanation, and the third served as a control and did not have a pay cut. Greenberg measured theft at all three sites. Greenberg found that the event alone (e.g., a pay cut) was not sufficient for inducing deviant behaviors (e.g., theft). The combination of pay cut and an inadequate explanation was required for employees to react by increased levels of theft and poor attendance. Note that in this experiment the theft rate increased during the pay cut period for both groups that experienced the pay cut, and the rate for the group with an inadequate explanation was higher than that for the group with the adequate explanation that was itself higher than the steady state rate of theft as measured by the control group.

One research stream focused on a specific event precipitating feelings of injustice or frustration (e.g., the Greenberg pay cut study). At other times instead of focusing on a single event, researchers directly examined feelings of frustration and linked these to various counterproductive behaviors. For example, Spector (1975) surveyed 82 men and women from clerical, professional, and manual jobs. Each respondent completed measures: organizational frustration and actual reactions to frustration. In factor analyzing the responses to frustration, Spector found six factors (e.g., aggression against others, sabotage, wasting of time and materials, interpersonal hostility and complaining, interpersonal aggression, and apathy about the job) that coincide with Gruys' (1999) categories of destruction of property, misuse of time and resources, poor attendance, poor quality work, and inappropriate verbal and physical behavior. Using the measure of reactions to frustration developed in the above study, Storms and Spector (1987) surveyed 160 men and women in supervisory and nonsupervisory roles in a mental health facility. In addition, participants responded to three other measures: situational constraints, frustration, and locus of control. Consistent with the earlier study, acts of aggression, sabotage, hostility and complaining, and withdrawal correlated moderately with situational constraints and perceived frustration. This study also presented interactions between justice and counterproductive behaviors. The additional variable, locus of control, was found to affect the types of responses individuals exhibited; 'internals' did not react as much to either high or low frustration as 'externals', and 'externals' engaged in more counterproductive behaviors when frustration was high than when frustration was low (Storms & Spector, 1987). This work illustrated the potential for integrating an individual differences (e.g., personality) perspective and a situational perspective, as it posited and found that reactions to frustrating organizational events vary as a function of individual difference variables.

More recent work by Fox and Spector (1999) similarly found links between the experiencing of frustrating events and self-reports of a wide range of counterproductive behaviors. In this same tradition, Aquino, Lewis and Bradford (1999) related perceptions of distributive, procedural, interpersonal, and interactive justice to self-reports of organizational and interpersonal deviance.

In previous examples, the organization created the triggering event through its own policies and practices. In an example of a societal triggering event, the United Kingdom's No Smoking Day to get smokers to quit or abstain from smoking for a day, the accident rate increased on that day (Waters, Jarvis & Sutton, 1998). Of course we cannot presume that any or all of the accidents on that day were due to unsafe behaviors; however, we mention this as a reminder that spikes in organizationwide deviance can be caused by events outside of the organization.

CONCLUDING COMMENTS

In this chapter we have been necessarily selective in our focus. One overarching theme has been a call for a broad perspective on counterproductive behaviors as a supplement to the tradition of focusing on a single type of behavior (e.g., theft, absenteeism). In support of that theme we have done a number of things. First, we focused extensively on the dimensionality and structure of counterproductive behavior. We noted the growing body of research that works toward a taxonomic structure for counterproductive behavior, and reviewed research on the intercorrelations among various forms of counterproductive behavior. We noted the strong evidence for consistent patterns of positive correlations among various forms of behavior, and noted that stronger relationships are observed using multi-item scales than when single items are used. Second, we offered a brief and selective overview of research on antecedents of counterproductive behavior, including personality variables, group norms, organizational culture, organizational control systems, and specific triggering events linked to perceptions of injustice. One key message from this selective review is that each of these broad categories of antecedents has surfaced repeatedly in the literatures on specific forms of counterproductive behaviors. It is not the case that researchers in the theft domain, for example, have identified markedly different sets of antecedents than researchers in the absenteeism domain. Thus we point to both the pattern of positive intercorrelations among counterproductive behaviors and the recurrence of common categories of antecedents in support of an integrative perspective on counterproductive behavior.

A second overarching theme is one of the need for attention to both individual and situational antecedents of counterproductive behavior. We developed conceptual arguments as to why there is no necessary competition between individual and situational perspectives, and noted reasons why different communities of scholars may legitimately focus in one domain or the other. But we believe that the research reviewed here makes a persuasive case that a full understanding of counterproductive behavior requires both domains. We believe that the large bodies of literature that we summarize in the personality domain refute claims that individual difference variables are not systematically related to counterproductive behavior. We also believe that bodies of literature that we are only able to selectively review similarly make a strong case for a broad array of situational antecedents.

We conclude by reiterating our proposal of a hierarchical model of counterproductive behavior. We suggest a general counterproductivity factor at the top, a series of group factors, such as the organizational deviance and interpersonal deviance factors identified by Bennett and Robinson (2000) below this general factor, and specific behavior domains, such as theft, absence, safety, and drug and alcohol use below these group factors. Researchers and practitioners may focus at difference levels of this hierarchy for different applications. Our perspective is that the decision as to where to focus one's intervention and/or measurement efforts on this continuum from general factor to specific behaviors is best made recognizing the interrelationships among counterproductive behaviors.

REFERENCES

Ambrose, M.L. (2000). Drug testing and procedural fairness: The influence of situational variables. *Social Justice Research*, *13*(1), 25–40.

Aquino, K., Lewis, M.U., & Bradfield, M. (1999). Justice constructs, negative affectivity, and employee deviance: a proposed model and empirical test. *Journal of Organizational Behavior*, *20*, 1073–1091.

Ashton, M.C. (1998). Personality and job performance: the importance of narrow traits. *Journal of Organizational Behavior*, *19*, 289–303.

Bandura, A. (1977). *Social learning theory*. Englewood Cliffs, NJ: Prentice-Hall.

Bardsley, J.J., & Rhodes, S.R. (1996). Using the Steers–Rhodes (1984) framework to identify correlates of employee lateness. *Journal of Business and Psychology, 10*(3), 351–365.

Baron, R.A., & Neuman, J.H. (1996). Workplace violence and workplace aggression: Evidence on their relative frequency and potential causes. *Aggressive Behavior, 22*, 161–173.

Barrick, M.R., & Mount, M.K. (1991). The big five personality dimensions: A meta-analysis. *Personnel Psychology, 44*, 1–26.

Bennett, R.J., & Robinson, S.L. (2000). The development of a measure of workplace deviance. *Journal of Applied Psychology, 85*(3), 349–360.

Borman, W.C., & Motowidlo, S.J. (Eds.) (1993). *Expanding the criterion domain to include elements of contextual performance*. San Francisco: Jossey-Bass.

Brief, A.P., & Motowidlo, S.J. (1986). Prosocial organizational behaviors. *Academy of Management Review, 11*, 710–725.

Campbell, J.P. (1990). An overview of the Army selection and classification project (Project A). *Personnel Psychology, 43*, 231–239.

Campbell, J.P., McCloy, R.A., Oppler, S.H., & Sager, C.E. (Eds.) (1993). *A theory of performance*. San Francisco: Jossey-Bass.

Cherrington, D.J., & Cherrington, J.O. (1985). The climate of honesty in retail stores. In W. Terris (Ed.), *Employee Theft: Research, Theory, and Applications* (pp. 51–65). Chicago: London House Press.

Conway, J.M. (1999). Distinguishing contextual performance from task performance for managerial jobs. *Journal of Applied Psychology, 84*, 3–13.

Cook, R.F., Back, A., & Trudeau, J. (1996). Substance abuse prevention in the workplace: Recent findings and an expanded conceptual model. *The Journal of Primary Prevention, 16*(3), 319–339.

Dekker, I., & Barling, J. (1998). Personal and organizational predictors of workplace sexual harassment of women by men. *Journal of Occupational Health Psychology, 3*(1), 7–18.

Duncan, W.J., Smeltzer, L.R., & Leap, T.L. (1990). Humor and work: applications of joking behavior to management. *Journal of Management, 16*, 255–278.

Dwyer, T. (1991). Humor, power and change in organizations. *Human Relations, 44*, 1–19.

Edwards, W.J. (1996). A measurement of delinquency differences between a delinquent and nondelinquent sample: What are the implications? *Adolescence, 31*(124), 973–989.

Fitzgerald, L.F., Drasgow, F., Hulin, C.L., Gelfand, M.J., & Magley, V.J. (1997). Antecedents and consequences of sexual harassment in organizations: A test of an integrated model. *Journal of Applied Psychology, 82*(4), 578–589.

Fox, S., & Spector, P.E. (1999). A model of work frustration-aggression. *Journal of Organizational Behavior, 20*, 915–931.

Gellatly, I.R. (1995). Individual and group determinants of employee absenteeism: Test of a causal model. *Journal of Organizational Behavior, 16*, 469–485.

Goffman, E. (1959). *The presentation of self in everyday life*. New York: Anchor Books Doubleday.

Greenberg, J. (1990a). Employee theft as a reaction to underpayment inequity: The hidden cost of pay cuts. *Journal of Applied Psychology, 75*(5), 561–568.

Greenberg, J. (1990b). Organizational justice: Yesterday, today, and tomorrow. *Journal of Management, 16*(2), 399–432.

Griffin, R.W., O'Leary-Kelly, A., & Collins, J. (1998). Dysfunctional work behaviors in organizations. In C.L. Cooper & D.M. Rousseau (Eds.), *Trends in Organizational Behavior* (Vol. 5, pp. 65–82): John Wiley & Sons.

Gruys, M.L. (1999). *The dimensionality of deviant employee performance in the workplace*. Unpublished doctoral dissertation, University of Minnesota, Minneapolis, MN.

Guastello, S.J. (1991). Psychosocial variables related to transit safety: The application of catastrophe theory. *Work & Stress, 5*(1), 17–28.

Guastello, S.J., & Rieke, M.L. (1991). A review and critique of honesty test research. *Behavioral Sciences and the Law, 9*(4), 501–523.

Gutek, B.A., Cohen, A.G., & Konrad, A.M. (1990). Predicting social-sexual behavior at work: A contact hypothesis. *Academy of Management Journal, 33*(3), 560–577.

Hackett, R.D. (1989). Work attitudes and employee absenteeism: A synthesis of the literature. *Journal of Occupational Psychology, 62*, 235–248.

Hackman, J.R., & Oldham, G.R. (1976). Motivation and the design of work: Test of a theory. *Organizational Behavior and Human Performance, 16*, 250–279.

Hackman, J.R., & Oldham, G.R. (1980). *Work Redesign*. Reading, MA: Addison-Wesley.

Hamper, B. (1991). *Rivethead: tales from the assembly line*. New York: Warner Books.

Hollinger, R.C. (1986). Acts against the workplace: Social bonding and employee deviance. *Deviant Behavior, 7*(1), 53–75.

Hollinger, R.C., & Clark, J.P. (1982). Employee deviance: A response to the perceived quality of the work experience. *Work and Occupations, 9*(1), 97–114.

Hollinger, R.C., & Clark, J.P. (1983a). Deterrence in the workplace: Perceived certainty, perceived severity and employee theft. *Social Forces, 62*(2), 398–418.

Hollinger, R.C., & Clark, J.P. (1983b). *Theft By Employees*. Lexington, MA: DC Heath & Co. Lexington Books.

Hollinger, R.C., Slora, K.B., & Terris, W. (1992). Deviance in the fast-food restaurant: Correlates of employee theft, altruism, and counterproductivity. *Deviant Behavior: An Interdisciplinary Journal, 13*(2), 155–184.

Hough, L.M. (1992). The 'Big 5' personality variables-construct confusion: description vs. prediction. *Human Performance, 5*, 139–155.

Hulin, C.L., Fitzgerald, L.F., & Drasgow, F. (1996). Organizational influences on sexual harassment. In M. Stockdale (Ed.), *Sexual Harassment in the Workplace* (Vol. 5, pp. 127–150). Thousand Oaks, CA: Sage.

Hunt, S.T. (1996). Generic work behavior: An investigation into the dimensions of entry-level, hourly job performance. *Personnel Psychology, 49*, 51–83.

Jones, J.W. (1980). Attitudinal correlates of employees' deviance: Theft, alcohol use, and nonprescribed drug use. *Psychological Reports, 47*, 71–77.

Jones, J.W., & Terris, W. (1983). Predicting employees' theft in home improvement centers. *Psychological Reports, 522*, 187–201.

Klein, R.L., Leong, G.B., & Silva, J.A. (1996). Employee sabotage in the workplace: A biopsychosocial model. *Journal of Forensic Sciences, 41*(1), 52–55.

Konovsky, M.A., & Cropanzano, R. (1991). Perceived fairness of employee drug testing as a predictor of employee attitudes and job performance. *Journal of Applied Psychology, 76*(5), 698–707.

Lasley, J.R. (1988). Toward a control theory of white-collar offending. *Journal of Quantitative Criminology, 4*(4), 347–362.

Leiter, M.P., & Robichaud, L. (1997). Relationships of occupational hazards with burnout: An assessment of measures and models. *Journal of Occupational Health Psychology, 2*(1), 35–44.

Lennings, C.J. (1997). Police and occupationally related violence: A review. *Policing: An International Journal of Police Strategies and Management, 20*(3), 555–566.

Mack, D.A., Shannon, C., Quick, J.D., & Quick, J.C. (1998). Stress and the preventive management of workplace violence. In R.W. Griffin & A. O'Leary-Kelly (Eds.), *Dysfunctional Behavior in Organizations: Violent and Deviant Behavior* (Vol. 23, pp. xxiii, 288). Stamford, CT, USA: Jai Press, Inc.

Mangione, T.W., & Quinn, R.P. (1975). Job satisfaction, counterproductive behavior, and drug use at work. *Journal of Applied Psychology, 60*(1), 114–116.

Martinko, M.J., & Zellars, K.L. (1998). Toward a theory of workplace violence and aggression: A cognitive appraisal perspective. In R.W. Griffin & A. O'Leary-Kelly (Eds.), *Dysfunctional Behavior in Organizations: Violent and Deviant Behavior* (Vol. 23, pp. 1–42). Stamford, CT, USA: Jai Press.

McHenry, J.J., Hough, L.M., Toquam, J.L., Hanson, M.A., & Ashworth, S. (1990). Project A validity results: The relationship between predictor and criterion domains. *Personnel Psychology, 43*, 335–354.

Motowidlo, S.J., & Van Scotter, J.R. (1994). Evidence that task performance can be distinguished from contextual performance. *Journal of Applied Psychology, 79*, 475–480.

Murphy, K.R. (1993). *Honesty in the workplace.* Pacific Grove, CA: Brooks/Cole Publishing.

Murphy, K.R., Thornton, G.C., & Prue, K. (1991). Influence of job characteristic on the acceptability of employee drug testing. *Journal of Applied Psychology, 76*(3), 447–453.

Normand, J., Salyards, S.D., & Mahoney, J.J. (1990). An evaluation of preemployement drug testing. *Journal of Applied Psychology, 75*(6), 629–639.

Ones, D.S., Viswesvaran, C., & Schmidt, F. (1993a). Comprehensive meta-analysis of integrity test validities: Findings and implications for personnel selection and theories of job performance. *Journal of Applied Psychology Monograph, 78*(4), 679–703.

Ones, D.S., Viswesvaran, C., & Schmidt, F. (1993b). *Integrity tests predict substance abuse and aggressive behaviors at work.* Paper presented at the American Psychological Association Convention, Toronto, Canada.

Ones, D.S., Viswesvaran, C., & Schmidt, F.L. (1993c). *Personality characteristics and absence taking behavior: The case of integrity.* Paper presented at the 1992 Annual meeting of Academy of Management, Personnel/Human Resources Division, Las Vegas.

Ones, D.S., Viswesvaran, C., Schmidt, F.L., & Reiss, A.D. (1994). *The validity of honesty and violence scales of integrity tests in predicting violence at work.* Paper presented at the Annual Meeting of the Academy of Management, Dallas, TX.

Puffer, S.M. (1987). Prosocial behavior, noncompliant behavior, and work performance among commission sales people. *Journal of Applied Psychology, 72*, 615–621.

Raelin, J.A. (1994). Three scales of professional deviance within organizations. *Journal of Organizational Behavior, 15*(6), 483–501.

Rentsch, J.R., & Steel, R.P. (1998). Testing the durability of job characteristics as predictors of absenteeism over a six-year period. *Personnel Psychology, 51*, 165–189.

Robinson, S.L., & Bennett, R.J. (1995). A typology of deviant workplace behaviors: A multidimensional scaling study. *Academy of Management Journal, 38*(2), 555–572.

Robinson, S.L., & Greenberg, J. (1998). Employees behaving badly: Dimensions, determinants and dilemmas in the study of workplace deviance. In C.L. Cooper & D.M. Rousseau (Eds.), *Trends in Organizational Behavior* (pp. 1–30). New York: John Wiley & Sons.

Robinson, S.L., & O'Leary-Kelly, A. (1996). *Monkey see, monkey do: The role of role models in predicting workplace aggression.* Paper presented at the Academy of Management Best Paper Proceedings, Pleasantville, MY.

Robinson, S.L., & O'Leary-Kelly, A.M. (1998). Monkey see, monkey do: The influence of work groups on the antisocial behavior of employees. *Academy of Management Journal, 41*(6), 658–672.

Rosenbaum, D.P., & Baumer, T.L. (1985). Measuring and controlling employee theft: A national assessment of the state-of-the art. In W. Terris (Ed.), *Employee Theft: Research, Theory, and Applications.* Chicago: London House Press.

Roy, D.F. (1960). Banana time: job satisfaction and informal interaction. *Human Organization, 18*, 158–168.

Ruggiero, M., Greenberger, E., & Steinberg, L.D. (1982). Occupational deviance among adolescent workers. *Youth and Society, 13*(4), 423–448.

Sackett, P.R., Burris, L.R., & Callahan, C. (1989). Integrity testing for personnel selection: An update. *Personnel Psychology, 42*, 491–529.

Sackett, P.R., & Decker, P.J. (1979). Detection of deception in the employment context: A review and critique. *Personnel Psychology, 32,* 487–506.

Sackett, P.R., & Harris, M.M. (1984). Honesty testing for personnel selection: A review and critique. *Personnel Psychology, 37,* 221–245.

Sackett, P.R., & Wanek, J.E. (1996). New developments in the use of measures of honesty, integrity, conscientiousness, dependability, trustworthiness, and reliability for personnel selection. *Personnel Psychology, 49,* 787–829.

Sackett, P.R., Zedeck, S., & Fogli, L. (1988). Relations between measures of typical and maximum performance. *Journal of Applied Psychology, 73,* 482–486.

Salancik, G.J., & Pfeffer, J. (1978). A social information processing approach to job attitudes and task design. *Administrative Science Quarterly, 23,* 224–253.

Salgado, J.F. (2000). *The big five personality dimensions as predictors of alternative criteria.* Paper presented at the 15th Annual Conference of the Society for Industrial and Organizational Psychology, New Orleans, LA.

Schmidt, F.L., Viswesvaran, C., & Ones, D.S. (1997). Validity of integrity tests for predicting drug and alcohol abuse: A meta-analysis. In W.J. Bukoski (Ed.), *Meta-Analysis of Drug Abuse Prevention Programs* (pp. 69–95). Rockville, MD: NIDA Press.

Schneider, B. (1975). Organizational climates: An essay. *Personnel Psychology, 28,* 447–480.

Sewell, G. (1998). The discipline of teams: The control of team-based industrial work through electronic and peer surveillance. *Administrative Science Quarterly, 43,* 397–428.

Shain, M. (1982). Alcohol, drugs and safety: An updated perspective on problems and their management in the workplace. *Accident Analysis and Prevention, 14*(3), 239–246.

Shapiro, S.P. (1990). Collaring the crime, not the criminal: Reconsidering the concept of white-collar crime. *American Sociological Review, 55,* 346–365.

Sheridan, J.E. (1985). A catastrophe model of employee withdrawal leading to low job performance, high absenteeism, and job turnover during the first year of employment. *Academy of Management Journal, 28*(1), 88–109.

Skarlicki, D.P., & Folger, R. (1997). Retaliation in the workplace: The roles of distributive, procedural, and interactional justice. *Journal of Applied Psychology, 82*(3), 434–443.

Slora, K.B. (1989). An empirical approach to determining employee deviance base rates. *Journal of Business and Psychology, 4*(2), 199–218.

Smith, C.A., Organ, D.W., & Near, J.P. (1983). Organizational citizenship behavior: Its nature and antecedents. *Journal of Applied Psychology, 68,* 653–663.

Spector, P.E. (1975). Relationships of organizational frustration with reported behavioral reactions of employees. *Journal of Applied Psychology, 60*(5), 635–637.

Sprouse, M. (Ed.). (1992). *Sabotage in the American workplace: Anecdotes of dissatisfaction, mischief and revenge.* San Francisco, CA: Pressure Drop Press.

Steffy, B.D., Jones, J.W., Murphy, L.R., & Kunz, L. (1986). A demonstration of the impact of stress abatement programs on reducing employees' accidents and their costs. *American Journal of Health Promotion, 1*(2), 25–32.

Stone, D.L., & Kotch, D.A. (1989). Individuals' attitudes toward organizational drug testing policies and practices. *Journal of Applied Psychology, 74*(3), 518–521.

Storms, P.L., & Spector, P.E. (1987). Relationships of organizational frustration with reported behavioural reactions: The moderating effect of locus of control. *Journal of Occupational Psychology, 60*(3), 227–234.

Tepper, B.J. (1994). Investigation of general and program-specific attitudes toward corporate drug-testing policies. *Journal of Applied Psychology, 79*(3), 392–401.

Terris, W., & Jones, J. (1982). Psychological factors related to employees' theft in the convenience store industry. *Psychological Reports, 51,* 1219–1238.

Thompson, R.C., Hilton, T.F., & Witt, L.A. (1998). Where the safety rubber meets the shop floor: A confirmatory model of management influence on workplace safety. *Journal of Safety Research, 29*(1), 15–24.

Viswesvaran, C., Ones, D.S., & Schmidt, F.L. (1992). *Appropriateness of self-reported criteria for integrity tests validities: Evidence from beyond.* Paper presented at the Annual Meeting of the Society for Industrial and Organizational Psychology, Montreal, Canada.

Viswesvaran, C., Schmidt, F.L., & Ones, D.S. (1999). The role of halo error in interdimensional ratings: The case of job performance ratings examined via meta-analysis. *Manuscript submitted for publication.*

Waters, A.J., Jarvis, M.J., & Sutton, S.R. (1998). Nicotine withdrawal and accident rates. *Nature, 394*(6689), 137.

9

Predictors Used for Personnel Selection: An Overview of Constructs, Methods and Techniques

JESÚS F. SALGADO,
CHOCKALINGAM VISWESVARAN
and DENIZ S. ONES

We review and summarize the literature on personnel selection as well as provide an overview of global trends in practice. The first section of our review covers different predictors (constructs and methods) that have been used in and studied in personnel selection contexts. Cognitive ability tests, psychomotor and perceptual ability tests, personality inventories, assessment centers, biodata, interviews and so forth are reviewed. In reviewing each, we cover: (1) prevalence of use, (2) measurement and construct validity issues, (3) criterion-related validity, (4) issues of incremental validity, and (5) group differences. In the second section of this chapter, we include a brief discussion of some issues in designing and administering selection systems.

Personnel selection is one of the central topics in the study of work behavior (Guion, 1998), and aims to identify the individuals who will constitute the workforce in an organization. 'People make the place' (Schneider, 1987) and selecting the right people for the right jobs constitutes a source of competitive advantage for organizations. Matching individual abilities and needs to organizational rewards and demands has been a concern for human resource development experts. The financial health of an organization is predicated on the optimal selection and placement of employees (Hunter, Schmidt & Judiesch, 1990). In this chapter we review and summarize the literature on personnel selection as well as provide an overview of global trends in the practice of personnel selection.

The organization of the chapter is as follows. There are two main sections. The first section reviews the different predictors that have been used and studied in personnel selection contexts. Cognitive ability tests, psychomotor and perceptual ability tests, personality tests, assessment centers, biodata, interviews and so on are reviewed. A separate subsection is devoted to each predictor. In reviewing each predictor, we organize the available literature into five main areas covering the following topics: (1) prevalence of use, (2) measurement and construct validity issues, (3) criterion-related validity, (4) issues of incremental validity, and (5) group differences. The existing literature for some predictors is sparse and in some instances this results in very short subsections (e.g., group differences in assessment centers). For these, we merely note the lack of empirical evidence and conclude with calls for more research.

In the second section to this chapter, we include a brief discussion of some issues in designing and administering selection systems. First, we discuss the various ways to combine data from different predictors and the literature on these different approaches. The use of compensatory versus non-compensatory systems (multiple hurdle, multiple cut-off), shrinkage in validation, and cross-validation are discussed. Second, we address and clarify issues around test fairness such as adverse impact, group differences, bias, and single group validity. Here we also aim to answer questions of how group differences in predictors may be handled (e.g., banding). Third, we summarize the literature on some special topics in personnel selection that have gained visibility in recent years. Here we discuss areas such as team selection and computerized assessment. A summary of process models that have been developed to explain and understand the validities of different predictors is included. Methodological issues such as method bias and appropriateness of correlation as an index of validity are also covered. Although we present these diverse issues in the second section in a sequential manner, it should be noted that the realities of designing a personnel selection system is such that these steps are dynamically interrelated and influence one another simultaneously.

AN OVERVIEW OF PREDICTORS USED IN PERSONNEL SELECTION

Personnel selection begins by identifying what individual characteristics are likely to be related to job performance. To do this, two sources of information are needed. First, we need to understand what is done in a job by an individual, under what conditions, and for what purposes. This information is obtained through job analysis, and Sanchez and Levine in their chapter in this Handbook cover the different job-analytic techniques available. Second, information is needed to identify what is valued. That is, we should identify the criterion used to judge performance on the job. Several chapters in this Handbook have been devoted to this important topic of performance assessment. Once we know what individual characteristics are needed on the job and how we are going to assess performance, we can specify links between those individual characteristics and job performance measures. Once the links are specified, we can proceed to the actual measurement of those individual characteristics and administration issues involved with that measurement.

The different individual characteristics used in personnel selection are generally referred to as 'individual differences' variables. These are variables on which individuals differ and such differences are linked to differences in job performance. These characteristics need to be measured, and different methods can be used for this purpose. For example, cognitive ability is a trait that can be measured by different methods such as paper and pencil tests, interviews, assessment centers, certain biodata items, and so forth. For purposes of our review, we refer to any unique combination of an individual difference characteristic and a method of assessing it as a predictor. In this section, we review the literature on commonly used predictors. In this overview, ideally, we would have liked to devote subsections to all constructs that have been used in personnel selection, comparing and contrasting different measurement methods to assess these. It is preferable to focus on constructs (i.e., traits) for a better scientific understanding (Hough & Paullin, 1994; Schmitt & Chan, 1998). However, the state of the literature is such that we had to organize our review based on particular predictors (construct-method combinations). There simply is too little research in the literature to compare multiple methods of assessing the same construct (Hough & Oswald, 2000). Future research in personnel selection would be more profitable if a theory based approach to understanding constructs and methodological issues is emphasized.

For each predictor, we first review the prevalence of their use. Survey results indicating how widely that predictor is employed in personnel selection (and for what types of jobs and occupations) are presented. Measurement and construct validity issues that are specific to each predictor (e.g., general vs. specific abilities for cognitive ability, structure of specific abilities, etc.) are reviewed next. The criterion-related validity for different criteria is summarized followed by a discussion of how much incremental validity that predictor adds when combined with other predictors. Finally, we discuss group differences in mean scores and discuss implications for hiring rates for various groups. In discussing group differences, we clearly distinguish between group differences, adverse impact, discrimination, bias, single-group validity, differential validity, differential item functioning, and fairness. These are related, but distinct, concepts. Ideally, it would have been excellent if there were research evidence on group differences, adverse impact, single-group validity, differential validity, differential item functioning, and bias for each predictor. Similarly demographic groups can be formed based on several characteristics including race, ethnicity, gender, age, and combinations of these. Again, ideally we would have liked to present research evidence on group differences, adverse impact, and differential item functioning for each predictor and for each pair of defined groups. In discussing predictive bias, we would have liked to have evidence for each predictor – criterion combination for every group of interest. In discussing single-group and differential validity, we would have liked to present evidence for each predictor and for each pair of defined groups for every criterion of interest (e.g., Is there evidence of differential validity of cognitive ability tests for whites and blacks for the criterion of productivity?). Unfortunately, such a comprehensive database does not exist in the literature. Therefore, our review attempts to cover as much evidence as is *available* under the topic of group differences for each predictor.

1. Ability and Aptitude Tests

Prevalence

Aptitude and ability tests have been commonly used over the years as a tool of personnel selection. However, the frequency of use varies substantially from one country to another. In the last few years, several surveys were carried out in order to evaluate the extent to which typical instruments for selecting personnel are used. For example, Gowing and Slivinski (1994) reported on a survey carried out in the USA, which found that 16% of companies administer cognitive ability (or general mental ability, GMA) tests and 42% administered specific aptitude tests for selection purposes. They also reported that 43% of companies in Canada use aptitude tests. In another US survey, Marsden (1994) reported that 7.4% of companies used mental ability for hiring decisions in nonmanagerial occupations and 9.1% in managerial jobs. A survey conducted in 12 European countries, members of the European Community, showed that the percentage of use of psychometric tests (GMA tests) by companies ranged from 6% of companies in Germany to 74% of companies in Finland (Dany & Torchy, 1994; cited by Cook, 1998). The average for these 12 countries was 34%. In this same survey, it was reported that 8% of companies in Germany and 72% of companies in Spain use aptitude tests. In another survey conducted in five European countries, Shackleton and Newell (1994; see also Shackleton & Newell, 1997) showed that the percentage use of cognitive tests ranged from 20% of Italian companies to 70% of companies based in United Kingdom. Di Milia, Smith and Brown (1994) reported that cognitive tests are used by 56.2% of companies in Australia. Similar results were reported by Taylor, Mills and O'Driscoll (1993) for New Zealand and by Baron, Ryan and Page (1998) for 15 countries from all continents. Taken together, these surveys suggest that GMA tests and aptitude tests have been used in a generalized way across the world.

Measurement and Construct Validity Issues

Most aptitude and ability tests measure more than a single ability (Ree & Carretta, 1997, 1998). Furthermore, different batteries have been developed to measure cognitive abilities in both civil and military settings. The best known batteries are the Air Force Officer Qualification Test (AFOQT), Armed Services Vocational Aptitude Battery (ASVAB), Army Classification Test (ACT), Differential Aptitude Test (DAT), Employee Aptitude Survey (EAS), General Aptitude Test Battery (GATB), and the Flanagan Classification Test (FCT).

Despite the multiple subfactors and abilities measured in these batteries, most of the variance of these measures is due to a general factor called g or General Mental Ability (GMA) (see Jensen, 1998; Ree & Carretta, 1997). This result has been found for both paper-and-pencil ability tests and computerized cognitive tests (Kranzler & Jensen, 1991; Kyllonen, 1993). Given the widespread applicability of general mental ability tests, more research should be directed at understanding its theoretical underpinnings (Campbell, 1996; Lubinski, 2000). Future research should continue to explore the presence of specific abilities, and more importantly, attempt to identify any jobs/settings where a specific ability may be more appropriate for personnel selection than the general factor. Thus far the evidence for the incremental validity of specific abilities over GMA is very poor (Schmidt, Ones & Hunter, 1992; see below also).

Criterion-Related Validity

Several meta-analyses have been carried out on the criterion-related validity of GMA. For example, in one of earliest quantitative syntheses on the issue, Ghiselli (1973) grouped validity coefficients from thousands of studies and found an average validity correlation of .25 (uncorrected) for predicting job performance ratings. Another meta-analysis was carried out by Pearlman, Schmidt and Hunter (1980), who showed that GMA was a valid predictor of job performance for clerical occupations and its validity generalized across job families and organizations. A third comprehensive meta-analysis was conducted by Hunter and Hunter (1984) with a database consisting of 515 studies ($n = 38,620$) carried out using the GATB database of the US Employment Service (USES). They presented the results for two criteria: job performance ratings and training success. Hunter and Hunter corrected the mean validity for criterion unreliability and range restriction using .60 as an estimate of criterion reliability for a single rater, .80 for training reliability, and .80 as the ratio between the standard deviation of the selected group and the standard deviation of the applicant group. They found an average operational validity of .45 for job performance ratings and .54 for training success.

Hunter and Hunter's work has subsequently been replicated by the USA National Research Council (Hartigan & Wigdor, 1989). However, this new study contains some differences with Hunter and Hunter's meta-analysis. The three main differences were that the number of studies in the 1989 study was larger by 264 validity coefficients ($n = 38,521$), the estimate of job performance ratings reliability was assumed to be .80 and range restriction was not corrected for. Under these conditions, the panel found an estimate of the average operational validity of .22 ($k = 755$, $n = 77,141$) for predicting job performance ratings. Interestingly, the analysis of the 264 new studies showed an average observed validity of .20. Recent results by Rothstein (1990), Salgado and Moscoso (1996), and Viswesvaran, Ones and Schmidt (1996) have shown that Hunter and Hunter's estimate of job performance ratings reliability is very accurate. These studies showed that the interrater reliability for a single rater is lower than .60. If Hunter and Hunter's figures were applied to the mean validity found by the panel, the average operational validity would be .38, a figure closer to Hunter and Hunter's result for GMA predicting job performance ratings.

A fifth meta-analysis was carried out by Schmitt, Gooding, Noe and Kirsch (1984) who, using studies published between 1964 and 1982, found an average validity of .22 (uncorrected) for predicting job performance ratings. Correcting this last value using Hunter and Hunter's figures for criterion unreliability and range restriction, the average operational validity resulting is essentially the same in both studies (see Hunter & Hirsh, 1987).

Meta-analysis of the criterion-related validity of cognitive ability has also been explored for specific jobs. For example, Schmidt, Hunter and Caplan (1981) meta-analyzed the validities for craft jobs in the petroleum industry. Hirsh, Northrop and Schmidt (1986) summarized the validity findings for police officers. Hunter (1986) in his review of studies conducted in the United States military estimated GMA validity as .63. The validity for predicting objectively measured performance was .75.

Levine, Spector, Menon, Narayanan and Canon-Bowers (1996) conducted another relevant meta-analysis for craft jobs in the utility industry (e.g., electrical assembly, telephone technicians, mechanical jobs). In this study, a value of .585 was used for range restriction corrections and .756 for reliability of job performance ratings. Levine et al. found an average observed validity of .25 and an average operational validity of .43 for job performance ratings. For training success the average observed validity was .38 and the average operational validity was .67. Applying Hunter and Hunter's estimates for criteria reliability and range restriction, the results show an operational validity of .47 for job performance ratings and .62 for training success. These two results indicate a great similarity between Hunter and Hunter's and Levine et al.'s findings.

Two single studies using large samples must also be commented on. In 1990, the results of Project A, a research project carried out in the US Army, were published. Due to the importance of the project, the journal *Personnel Psychology* devoted a special issue to this project; according to Schmidt,

Ones and Hunter (1992), Project A has been the largest and most expensive selection research project in history. McHenry, Hough, Toquam, Hanson and Ashworth (1990) reported validities of .63 and .65 for predicting ratings of core technical proficiency and general soldiering proficiency. The second large-sample study was carried out by Ree and Earles (1991), who showed that a composite of GMA predicted training performance, finding a corrected validity of .76.

All the evidence discussed so far were carried out using studies conducted in the USA and Canada, although there is some cross-national data assessing the validity of cognitive ability tests. In Spain, Salgado and Moscoso (1998) found cognitive ability to be a predictor of training proficiency in four samples of pilot trainees. In Germany, Schuler, Moser, Diemand and Funke (1995) found that cognitive ability scores predicted training success in a financial organization (validity corrected for attenuation = .55). In the United Kingdom, Bartram and Baxter (1996) reported positive validity evidence for a civilian pilot sample.

In Europe, Salgado and Anderson (2001) have recently meta-analyzed the British and Spanish studies conducted with GMA and cognitive tests. In this meta-analysis, two criteria were used: job performance ratings and training success. The results showed average operational validities of .44, and .65 for job performance ratings and training success, respectively. Salgado and Anderson also found that GMA and cognitive tests were valid predictors for several jobs, including clerical, driver and trade occupations. The finding of similar levels or generalizable validity for cognitive ability in the UK and Spain is the first large-scale cross-cultural evidence that ability tests retain validity across jobs, organizations and even cultural contexts.

GMA also predicts criteria other than just job performance ratings, training success, and accidents. For example, Schmitt et al. (1984) found that GMA predicted turnover ($r = .14$; $n = 12,449$), achievement/grades ($r = .44$, $n = 888$), status change (promotions) ($r = .28$, $n = 21,190$), and work sample performance ($r = .43$, $n = 1,793$). However, all these estimates were not corrected for criterion unreliability and range restriction. Brandt (1987) and Gottfredson (1997) have summarized a large number of variables that are correlated with GMA. From a work and organizational psychological point of view, the most interesting of these are the positive correlations between GMA and occupational status, occupational success, practical knowledge, and income, and GMA's negative correlations with alcoholism, delinquency, and truancy. Taking together all these findings, it is possible to conclude that GMA tests are one of the most valid predictors in IWO psychology. Schmidt and Hunter (1998) have suggested the same conclusion in their review of 85 years of research in personnel selection.

Incremental Validity

Several studies have been conducted to investigate whether or not specific cognitive abilities showed incremental validity over GMA. Numerous specific abilities have been postulated in the literature. Carroll (1993) has reported results of over 300 studies that had explored the different types of specific abilities. However, Ree and Earles (1991) and Ree, Earles and Teachout (1994) have shown that specific abilities did not account for any additional variance beyond GMA for job performance ratings and training success. In fact, the average increase by adding specific abilities to GMA was .02 across 89 training studies. In another study, Olea and Ree (1994) showed that specific abilities showed an incremental validity over GMA of .08 and .02 for pilots and navigators, respectively. Thus, in summarizing the current evidence it would appear that specific abilities do not incrementally predict job performance ratings and training success.

Although researchers have argued that specific abilities do not add much more predictive validity beyond general mental ability, other predictors (e.g., personality) have been found to add incremental validity to general mental ability. For example, LePine, Hollenbeck, Ilgen and Hedlund (1997) reported the importance of personality variables in predicting performance in team-settings. Barrick, Stewart, Neubert and Mount (1998) related member ability and personality to work-team processes and team effectiveness. Schmidt and Hunter (1998) after reviewing 85 years of research in personnel selection concluded that it would be a profitable venture to explore the incremental validity of other predictors (e.g., integrity tests and interviews) over cognitive ability. In discussing individual predictors below, we will note studies that examined the incremental validity of each predictor over general mental ability.

Group Differences

It is well known that general mental ability tests show subgroup differences, for example when black and white individuals are compared. It is known that there is about a 1 standard deviation difference between American blacks and whites, with blacks scoring lower (Hunter & Hunter, 1984). Recently, Schmitt, Clause and Pulakos (1996) reviewed the subgroup differences in the more frequently used procedures for personnel selection, including GMA and cognitive ability tests. When blacks and whites are compared on cognitive ability tests, Schmitt et al. found a difference of -0.83 SD units, indicating that black performance was lower on these tests. They also found effect sizes of -0.55 and -0.64 for verbal ability and mathematical ability, respectively. The subgroup effect sizes are smaller if US Hispanics and white peoples are compared and also when the comparisons are between male and female groups. For Hispanic-Americans,

Schmitt et al. found effect sizes ranging from $-.45$ to -0.58. For gender comparisons, the male–female comparison showed an effect size of -0.09 for GMA and cognitive ability tests, with females showing slightly lower performance. However, in the case of mathematical ability females showed a higher performance than males (effect size $= 0.27$).

Despite these differences, Schmidt, Ones and Hunter (1992) suggested that such differences were not due to any bias in the tests as predictors of job performance. They affirmed that research evidence supports that GMA tests are predictively fair for minorities and that the validity coefficients are comparable. The evidence for single group validity (i.e., tests being valid only for whites) is weak in black–white and Hispanic–white comparisons for overall job performance (Boehm, 1977; Hunter, Schmidt & Hunter, 1979). A meta-analytic cumulation of the differential validity of cognitive ability tests also found little support (Hunter et al., 1979). Predictive fairness for other racial groups and cultures around the world has not been examined.

2. Physical, Psychomotor and Perceptual Ability Tests

Fleishman's taxonomy (Fleishman and Quaintance, 1984; Fleishman and Reilly, 1991), grouped abilities in four categories: (a) cognitive, (b) psychomotor, (c) perceptual, and (d) physical. Most of the empirical research conducted in workplace settings has focused on cognitive ability tests. This is perhaps attributable to the widespread applicability of cognitive ability tests in the workplace. Cognitive ability tests are related to job performance in many more jobs than are physical ability tests. Psychomotor abilities and physical abilities are critical in only a limited number of jobs (e.g., firefighters, security personnel) compared to the wide applicability of cognitive ability tests. Given this state of the literature, we present a combined review of psychomotor, perceptual, and physical ability tests.

Prevalence

There is little data regarding the use of physical ability tests in personnel selection. Surveys mentioned before suggest that physical ability tests are used in less than 10% of companies and that they are restricted to physically demanding occupations (e.g., police). There are no data on prevalence of psychomotor and perceptual ability test use.

Measurement and Construct Validity Issues

Usually, physical ability tests are highly intercorrelated. Fleishman and Mumford (1991) found nine factors underlying physical proficiency: Dynamic strength, trunk strength, static strength, explosive strength, extent flexibility, dynamic flexibility, gross body coordination, balance, and stamina. J. Hogan (1991) studied the physical requirements of occupational tasks, showing that muscular strength, cardiovascular endurance and movement quality described those requirements. The three-component structure was found in both job analyses and test performance data. Furthermore, this structure was independent of jobs, raters and incumbents' performance levels. Arvey, Landon, Nutting and Maxwell (1992) factor analyzed eight physical ability tests and found two constructs: strength and endurance. J. Hogan and Quigley (1994) showed that training preparation was capable of maximizing selection opportunities of qualified applicants for physically demanding jobs.

For a long time, it has been considered that psychomotor abilities consist of several independent factors and that there is no general psychomotor ability factor (Cronbach, 1970; Fleishman, 1954; Fleishman & Quaintance, 1984). For example, Fleishman's taxonomy of abilities includes 11 psychomotor abilities. However, recent evidence by Ree and Carretta (1994, Carretta & Ree, 1997; 2000; Chaiken, Kyllonen & Tirre, 2000) suggest that there are several lower-order psychomotor factors and a general higher-order psychomotor ability factor.

Criterion-Related Validity

Two meta-analyses have investigated the predictive validity of physical abilities. Schmitt et al. (1984) found that physical abilities predicted turnover ($r = 0.15$ $n = 852$), achievement/grades ($r = .28$ $n = 976$), status change ($r = .61$, $n = 245$), and work sample performance ($r = .42$, $n = 959$). None of these validities were corrected for unreliability and range restriction. A more recent meta-analysis carried out by Blakeley, Quiñones, Crawford and Jago (1994) quantitatively integrated the results of six studies in which isometric strength tests were used as selection procedures. They found that these tests predicted supervisory ratings of physical performance as well as performance on work simulations. For the first criteria, Blakeley et al. (1994) reported an average operational validity of .32 and for the second criteria an operational validity of .55.

Few meta-analytic studies have been directed at investigating the predictive validity of psychomotor and perceptual abilities. For example, Hunter and Hunter (1984) reported on two independent studies in which these abilities were investigated. In the first study, Hunter and Hunter reanalyzed Ghiselli's (1973) validity coefficients and found that perceptual abilities showed validities ranging from .22 for sales clerks to .46 for clerk occupations, with the average validity being .35. Psychomotor abilities showed predictive validities ranging from .17 for sales clerks to .44 for vehicle operators. The average predictive validity for psychomotor abilities was .30. In the second study, Hunter and Hunter meta-analyzed the 515 studies of the GATB database of

the US Employment Service. The GATB includes both perceptual tests and psychomotor tests. Hunter and Hunter found that a composite of perceptual ability tests showed an operational predictive validity of .38. They also found that a composite of psychomotor ability tests showed a predictive validity of .35. Hunter and Hunter noted that as job complexity increases the validity of psychomotor tests for predicting job performance decreases.

The meta-analysis conducted by the NRC panel using the 264 new studies carried out with the GATB showed an observed validity of .17 for a composite of perceptual abilities and an observed validity of .13 for a composite of psychomotor abilities. If these validities are corrected for criterion unreliability and range restriction using Hunter and Hunter's figures, the resulting operational validities would be .32 and .24 for the perceptual and psychomotor composites, respectively.

In the meta-analysis of crafts jobs in the utility industry, commented on in the prior section, Levine et al. (1996) found that perceptual tests had an average operational validity of .34 for predicting job performance and .36 for predicting training criteria. For psychomotor tests, Levine et al., found an average operational validity of .34 for performance ratings and .35 for training success.

In a meta-analysis of validity studies carried out in Spain using psychomotor tests as predictors, Salgado (1994) found an average observed validity of .36. In this study, type of criterion was used as a moderator. Salgado found an observed validity of .20 for predicting training success and .33 for predicting accident rates. There are no meta-analyses in which criteria other than job performance, training, and accidents have been used.

Incremental Validity

In a reanalysis of Ghiselli's (1973) summary of aptitude test validity, Hunter and Hunter (1984) found that for nine different occupational families, psychomotor and clerical ability tests did not show any substantial incremental validity. The NRC panel (Hartigan & Wigdor, 1989) found a similar result in the case of perceptual abilities. In another study, Carretta and Ree (1994) showed that the BAT, a psychomotor test battery, added a small incremental validity beyond the validity of cognitive tests. They suggested that this small incremental validity was a consequence of the commonality of measurement. Therefore, the evidence seems to suggest that for at least medium or high complexity jobs, the tests of psychomotor and perceptual abilities add little incremental validity beyond that of cognitive ability tests.

Group Differences

J. Hogan (1991) did not find differences between blacks and whites on physical ability tests but found differences between males and females for the majority of physical abilities assessed (e.g., muscular endurance, power, tension, and cardiovascular activity). These differences ranged between 1 and 4 standard deviations, the largest for any personnel selection predictor studied. However, J. Hogan (1991) found that females performed better than males in flexibility tests.

With regard to group differences, little research has been carried out on spatial ability. Schmitt et al. (1996) found that African-Americans showed lower performance in spatial ability than whites (effect size − 0.66). Similar results were also found for mechanical comprehension (effect size = − 0.40). Sackett and Wilk (1994) also summarize group differences found in perceptual, mechanical and physical ability tests. Although very little evidence has been reported for bias, more research is needed before definitive inferences can be drawn.

3. Personality Scales

Unlike ability measurement, personality measurement in psychology has had a checkered history. During the 1960s and 1970s, even personality psychologists themselves believed that situations were more potent determinants of behavior. During the past decade, however, a series of studies in work psychology have demonstrated the usefulness of personality variables in selection systems (Barrick & Mount, 1991; Hogan & Hogan, 1989; Hough, Eaton, Dunnette, Kamp & McCloy, 1990; Hough & Oswald, 2000; Ones, Viswesvaran & Schmidt, 1993; Ones & Viswesvaran, 2001a, 2001b; Sackett, Burris & Callahan, 1989). There are two main reasons behind this comeback: (1) applications of the techniques of meta-analysis to the fragmented personality validity literature; and (2) emerging consensus on the structure of personality domain (see sections below for detailed overviews of these points).

Personality predictors used in personnel selection can be roughly divided into two categories. First, there are general measures of adult personality. Examples of these inventories are the NEO-PI, Personality Research Form, and 16PF. The primary purpose in the construction of these was the accurate *description* of individual differences in personality. That is, they were initially constructed to provide a broad description of personality that could be used in a wide variety of settings. Researchers and practitioners have used these general purpose personality inventories in selection work. However, it is important to note that the usage of these inventories for personnel screening and selection is only one of their many applications. The second category of personality measures used in personnel selection can loosely be referred to as 'measures of personality at work'. The initial purpose in construction of these has been the accurate *prediction* of individual differences in *work behaviors* of interest. Integrity tests, violence scales, drug and alcohol scales, sales potential scales,

and managerial potential scales can all be grouped under the broad umbrella of measures of personality at work. Some of these measures of personality at work have been constructed for the prediction of specific criteria (e.g., drug and alcohol abuse on the job, theft, customer service ratings, violence at work, stress tolerance). Others have been constructed for specific occupational groups (e.g., sales, managers, clerical workers). In our overview below, we will aim to summarize work on general purpose personality inventories for comparison purposes with other selection instruments. Much more detailed information is provided on these scales in the personality chapter in this volume (see Hough and Ones, Chapter 12, this volume). Detailed reviews of criterion-focused occupational personality scales may be found in Ones and Viswesvaran (2001a, 2001b).

Prevalence of Use

The previously held erroneous belief that personality measures had unacceptably low validities resulted in fairly low levels of their use in many countries. At the beginning of 1990s, Levy-Leboyer (1994) noted that personality tests were perceived to be low in validity and acceptability by most researchers and practitioners. However, given the past decade of persuasive research documenting validity for these measures (e.g., Barrick & Mount, 1991; Hough, 1992; Ones, Viswesvaran & Schmidt, 1993; Salgado, 1997), there has been a steady rise in usage levels.

In North America, a number of surveys have reported on personality test usage. For the United States, for example, in 1983, an American Society of Personnel Administrators (ASPA) survey (ASPA, 1983) across 437 responding companies found only 9% reporting personality test use for external selection, and found only 4% reporting personality test use for internal selection/promotion use. A later survey conducted by the Bureau of National Affairs (1988) suggested that personality testing has been increasing in the US between 1983 and 1988. In 1988, 17% of 245 employers surveyed reported using personality tests. Finally, in 1990, a study by Harris, Dworkin and Park (1990), found that 20% of 186 surveyed organizations indicated that they used personality tests. In Canada, a 1987 survey (Thacker & Catteneo, 1987) of 581 organizations found 21% reporting personality test use. Similar longitudinal data are not available for Australia or New Zealand. However a 1994 survey of 240 companies in Australia (Di Milia, Smith & Brown, 1994) found only 39% of companies indicated never using personality measures for personnel selection. For New Zealand, Taylor, Mills & Driscoll (1993) surveyed 129 organizations and consulting companies and found that 67% reported using personality measures. According to Taylor et al. (1993), personality inventories were being used more frequently for managerial selection than for nonmanagement selection.

In Europe, earlier studies suggested little if any use of personality inventories. For the United Kingdom, Robertson and Makin (1986) stated that 64% of 108 companies reported never using personality scales in personnel selection. Further, in the Institute of Manpower Studies' survey of 320 British employers (Bevan & Fryatt, 1988) 78.3% indicated that they never used personality measures; while 19.5% indicated that they used them for a few jobs. More recent surveys by Shackleton and Newell (1991, 1994) compared usage of personnel selection procedures across four European countries. In Great Britain, France and the French-speaking portion of Belgium only 38% of companies surveyed reported never using them. In the Flemish part of Belgium, the figure for not using them at all was even lower, 17%. On the other hand, in Germany and Italy, over 80% of organizations surveyed indicated that personality tests were never used in selection. In Turkey, across over 200 organizations surveyed, 28% reported personality test use (Sinangil, Ones & Jockin, 1999).

Most recently, in their survey of organizations from 20 countries and 959 organizations across the globe, Ryan, McFarland, Baron and Page (1999) found that personality questionnaires were on average used 'occasionally' in personnel selection (21–50%). However, there was variance across the countries studied. In this survey, the highest levels of usage were reported for Spain, Belgium, Sweden, South Africa, New Zealand, the United Kingdom and France.

In general, taken together, the surveys reviewed above suggest two trends: (1) personality test usage around the globe is increasing, and (2) personality measures are used more frequently for managerial and professional selection. As such, personality measures appear to be used for personnel selection across the world in varying degrees.

Measurement and Construct Validity Issues

Over the years personality has been conceptualized from various taxonomic viewpoints. In fact, there have been so many personality concepts, and so many scales used to measure them that, the characterization of a '... Babel of concepts and scales ...' seems appropriate for the personality domain (John, 1990). It is true that '... the world does not come to us in neat little packages' (Gould, 1981: 158), but without a generally accepted taxonomy, personality research cannot properly communicate empirical findings, let alone systematically cumulate them.

In the field of personality structure, one needs to make the distinction between the development of factor analytic models for representing latent variables underlying individual differences in personality structure and the development of taxonomies of trait descriptive terms of how personality characteristics are encoded in language (Wiggins & Pincus, 1992). The starting place for a common descriptive

taxonomy of personality has been with the latter model: the natural language of personality description. The rationale behind this approach is that most important individual differences in human behaviors are encoded in languages. This is the fundamental lexical hypothesis (Goldberg, 1990). Fortunately, the last ten years has seen the convergence for the structure of personality from these two distinct streams of research.

In efforts to arrive at taxonomies of the personality trait domain, hundreds of factor structure investigations have been carried out for decades. That is, starting in the first half of the twentieth century, researchers have relied on factor analysis to uncover basic personality traits. Most of these studies have yielded evidence for three to seven major personality dimensions (Goldberg, 1993). Examples include Eysenck's three-factor model (Eysenck, 1990, 1991a, 1991b, 1994a, 1994b, 1998), the Big Five dimensions of personality (Costa & McCrae, 1992a, 1992b; Goldberg, 1990, 1992), and Tellegen's seven-factor model (Algamor, Tellegen & Waller, 1995).

Of various personality models, the most extensive recent attention has been directed at the Big Five model. Initially, Tupes and Christal's (1961) factor analyses of Cattell's bipolar scales in an attempt to predict officer effectiveness in the Air Force yielded five factors: Surgency, Agreeableness, Dependability, Emotional Stability, and Culture. During the last two decades, a large body of literature has accumulated which provides compelling evidence for the robustness of the five-factor model of personality: across different theoretical frameworks (Goldberg, 1993); using different instruments (e.g., Conley, 1985; Costa & McCrae, 1988; Lorr & Youniss, 1973; McCrae, 1989; McCrae & Costa, 1985, 1987); in different cultures (e.g., Bond, Nakazato & Shiraishi, 1975; Borkenau & Ostendorf, 1990; Noller, Law & Comrey, 1987, Yang & Bond, 1990); using ratings obtained from different sources (e.g., Digman & Takemoto-Chock, 1981; Fiske, 1949; McCrae & Costa, 1987; Norman, 1963; Norman & Goldberg, 1966; Watson, 1989); and with a variety of samples. (See McCrae & John, 1992; Digman, 1990; John, 1990; Goldberg, 1990; Wiggins & Pincus, 1992, for more detailed discussions.) Based on the results of several studies using comprehensive sets of trait terms, using multiple replications, and different factor analytic techniques, Goldberg (1990) summarized the state of the research in the following way: 'It now seems reasonable to conclude that analyses of any reasonably large sample of English trait adjectives in either self or peer descriptions will elicit a variant of the Big Five Structure, and therefore virtually all such terms can be represented within this model' (p. 1223). Digman and Takemoto-Chock (1981) summarized their conclusions as: 'Regardless of whether teachers rate children, officer candidates rate one another, college students rate one another, or clinical staff members rate graduate trainees, the results are pretty much the same' (pp. 164–165).

It is widely agreed that the first dimension is Extroversion/Introversion, although it has also been called Surgency. Traits associated with it include sociability, talkativeness, and assertiveness (on the high end) and being retiring, silent, reserved and cautious (on the low end). The second factor is most frequently called Emotional Stability, or Neuroticism, and is usually defined from the negative pole. Common traits associated with this factor include anxiety, depression, anger, embarrassment, emotion, worry, fearfulness, instability, and insecurity. The third dimension has generally been interpreted as Agreeableness or Likability. Traits associated with this dimension include courteousness, flexibility, trust, good-naturedness, cooperativeness, forgiveness, empathy, soft-heartedness, and tolerance. The fourth dimension has most frequently been called Conscientiousness, although it has also been called Conformity or Dependability. Because of its relationship to a variety of educational achievement measures and its association with volition, it has also been called 'Will to Achieve'. Traits associated with this dimension reflect both dependability – carefulness, thoroughness, responsibility, organization, efficiency, planfulness, and volition – hard work, achievement-orientation and perseverance. The last dimension has been interpreted frequently as Openness to Experience, Intellect, or Culture. Traits commonly associated with this dimension include imagination, curiosity, originality, broad-mindedness, intelligence, and artistic sensitivity.

Among others, Costa and McCrae (1985) demonstrated the presence of the Big Five in a multitude of personality inventories (e.g., Eysenck Personality Questionnaire, Jackson Personal Research Form, Myers–Briggs Type Indicator, California Q-Set). Only the MMPI was identified as having four dimensions rather than five with Conscientiousness absent. Even though disagreements still exist about the Big Five (e.g., Block, 1995; Eysenck, 1991b), the considerable consensus that the personality of an individual can be described in terms of the Big Five factors and their facets has provided a workable taxonomy, thereby facilitating literature integration. Despite criticisms and suggested modifications, the Big Five dimensions of personality have provided psychologists with a lexicon to describe the meaning of scores on a multitude of personality scales.

When personality measures are intended for use in personnel selection settings, it is important to document potential response distortion influences on factor structure. There have been a number of investigations of social desirability influences on the factor structure of personality inventories in applied settings (e.g., Cellar, Miller, Doverspike & Klawsky, 1996; Hogan & Hogan, 1991; Livneh &

Livneh, 1989) as well as direct factor structure comparisons between applicant and nonapplicant groups (Michaelis & Eysenck, 1971; Schmit & Ryan, 1993).

For example, Cellar et al.'s (1996) confirmatory factor analyses of two Big Five measures (Goldberg Five Factor Markers [Goldberg, 1992], and NEO-Personality Inventory [Costa & McCrae, 1985]) using data from flight attendant trainees indicated a better fit for a six-factor solution to the data, compared to a five-factor solution. Hogan and Hogan's (1991) principal components analysis of another Big Five-based inventory, the Hogan Personality Inventory, based on data from employees revealed the presence of eight components. Livneh and Livneh (1989) used a non-Big Five inventory, the Adjective CheckList (Gough & Heilbrun, 1983) in gathering data from human service providers. They were unable to extract a five-factor solution. Michealis and Eysenck (1971) compared the factor structures and factor intercorrelations for personality scale scores using data from both job applicants and nonapplicants. Differences between job applicants and nonapplicants were found in factor pattern matrices and factor intercorrelations. More recently, Schmit and Ryan (1993) also compared the factor structures and factor intercorrelations for a Big Five inventory (NEO-PI) for both job applicants and nonapplicants (students). While the five-factor solution fits the data from nonapplicants, exploratory factor analysis indicated a better fit for a six-factor solution to the applicant data. This sixth factor was labeled 'an ideal employee' factor. Also, the factor intercorrelations in the applicant sample were larger than those obtained for nonapplicants. Finally, Costa (1996) interpreted the results from these investigations as follows: 'Effects of evaluation bias on the structure of the NEO-FFI are relatively modest' (p. 231).

Most recently, Ellingson (1999) provided the largest scale and the most thorough examination of the impact of naturally occurring social desirability on personality factor structure. Large-scale databases for the Army Background and Life Experiences (ABLE) personality questionnaire ($N = 39,352$ newly enlisted soldiers), California Psychological Inventory (CPI) ($N = 13,730$ job applicants screened by a consulting firm), and 16PF ($N = 39,879$ applicants and employees) were used. According to Ellingson (1999) '…multiple group confirmatory factor analysis indicated that responding in a socially desirable manner did little to alter the factor structures underlying the ABLE, the CPI, and the 16PF' (p. 82).

Measurement error in the Big Five personality dimensions across inventories was recently examined by Viswesvaran & Ones (2000), who used meta-analysis to cumulate the results across studies examining the reliability of personality scale scores. A total of 848 coefficients of stability and 1,359 internal consistency reliabilities were cumulated for the Big Five factors of personality. The frequency weighted mean observed internal consistency reliabilities were .78 for emotional stability ($K = 370$), .78 for extraversion ($K = 307$), .73 for openness to experience ($K = 251$), .75 for agreeableness ($K = 123$), and .78 ($SD = .10$) for conscientiousness ($K = 307$). Internal consistency reliabilities are functions of both the number of items in a scale and the item intercorrelations. The *mean* inter-item correlations for personality scales ranged between .12 and .18. The *mean* number of items on personality scales ranged between 20 and 32.

Visweswaran and Ones (2000) also conducted a meta-analysis to estimate coefficients of stability for the Big Five. The frequency weighted mean observed coefficients of stability were: .75 for emotional stability ($K = 221$), .76 for extraversion ($K = 176$), .71 for openness to experience ($K = 139$), .69 for agreeableness ($K = 119$), and .72 ($SD = .13$) for conscientiousness ($K = 193$). The mean number of days between scale administrations ranged between 785 and 331 days. In any event, these coefficients of stability indicate that personality measures tap into relatively stable individual traits. Roberts and DelVecchio (2000), who examined the rank order consistency of personality traits from childhood to old age reported similar findings, concluding that personality traits are consistent over the life course.

Criterion-Related Validity

Ghiselli and Barthol (1953) published the first review of personality scale validities. This first quantitative review of over 100 studies was quite positive in its evaluation of personality test use in personnel selection; the average criterion-related validity summarized across occupations was .23. However, the situationalist view of personality delivered a severe, undeserved blow to personality tests. One leading personality psychologist wrote 'With the possible exception of intelligence, highly generalized behavioral consistencies have not been demonstrated, and the concept of personality traits as broad dispositions is thus untenable' (Mischel, 1968). In an influential review of personality test validities for personnel selection, Guion and Gottier (1965) wrote,

> It is difficult... to advocate with a clear conscience, the use of personality measures in most situations as a basis for making employment decisions about people... It is clear that the only acceptable reason for using personality measures as instruments of decision is found only after considerable research with the measure in the *specific situation* and the *specific purpose* for which it is to be used. (Emphasis added)

However, in the 1990s meta-analyses in the personality domain have demonstrated that a construct-oriented approach uncovers meaningful relations between personality variables and criteria (Barrick & Mount, 1991; Hough et al., 1990; Hough, 1992; Hough & Oswald, 2000; Ones et al., 1993, Salgado, 1997). In their meta-analysis, Barrick and Mount (1991) showed that conscientiousness scales predicted a variety of criteria with notable validities. The validity for predicting performance ratings was over .20. More importantly, conscientiousness was the only dimension of personality whose validity generalized across jobs and settings. Other personality dimensions were found to be valid only for specific occupational groups (e.g., extraversion for sales personnel). Hough (1992) reports that conscientiousness is also a particularly good predictor of law-abiding behavior (avoiding delinquency and counterproductivity). Hough's (1992) work also suggests that if the aim is the prediction of other, different criteria or performance facets, considering conscientiousness sub-dimensions (achievement and dependability) may be useful. Salgado (1997b) meta-analytically cumulated personality scale validities collected from European countries. For the criterion of job performance, the estimated operational validities were .19 for emotional stability and .25 for conscientiousness.

Ones et al. (1993; also see Ones & Visweswaran, 1998) reported criterion-related validities for integrity tests (primarily measuring conscientiousness, but also agreeableness and emotional stability). In a comprehensive meta-analysis, Ones et al. (1993) used 665 validity coefficients across 576,460 data points to investigate whether integrity test validities were generalizable and to estimate differences in validity due to potential moderating influences. Results indicated that integrity test validities are substantial for predicting job performance and counterproductive behaviors on the job such as theft, disciplinary problems, and absenteeism. In predictive studies, conducted using applicant data, the validity for predicting overall job performance was .41. For the criterion of counterproductive behaviors, admissions produced much higher correlations than external criteria, and concurrent studies often seemed to overestimate predictive validity (Ones et al., 1993). Nonetheless, Ones et al. (1993) found that the mean operational predictive validity of integrity tests was positive across situations and is substantial (.39 for overt tests and .29 for personality-based tests).

Taken together, both the recent primary and the meta-analytic evidence indicates that for the prediction of job performance and counterproductivity, conscientiousness is the personality dimension that generates noteworthy operational validities. Based on the evidence, human resource practitioners and researchers are now more optimistic about the potential of personality variables in personnel selection than ever before.

One question of paramount importance involves the influences of social desirability on criterion-related validity. Practitioners have long been wary of personality measures especially for fear of applicants faking good on their responses. There are four potential hypotheses regarding the role of social desirability in using personality scales and integrity tests in personnel selection. Social desirability can function as (1) a predictor, (2) a moderator, (3) a mediator, or (4) a suppressor variable. These four roles cover all the different roles that social desirability can play in personnel selection situations.

Ones and Viswesvaran (1998) reviewed evidence for each of these. Correlations with externally measured performance criteria were found to be small enough to be considered negligible. Thus, social desirability is not a predictor. Further, since there are negligible relationships between social desirability and job performance, social desirability cannot play a mediator role in personnel selection systems using personality measures (Ones, Viswesvaran & Reiss, 1996). Hough et al. (1990) specifically examined the criterion-related validities of personality scales and the effect of response distortion on those validities. To examine whether nonrandom response, social desirability, poor impression, and self-knowledge (the four response validity scales) moderated the validities of the ABLE content scales, Hough et al. (1990) conducted a series of analyses. Their results led to the conclusion that social desirability did not moderate the validities. Finally, in examining the potential suppressor role of social desirability, Ones et al. (1996) showed that partialling social desirability from personality measures does not have any impact on the criterion-related validities of the Big Five variables. The partialling process left the validities intact. From these results, it appears that social desirability does not attenuate the criterion-related validities of personality dimensions. Ones and Viswesvaran (1997) have reported very similar results for integrity tests. Therefore, there is ample evidence that criterion-related validities of personality scales are unaffected by social desirability. Hough and Ones (in this volume) detail other studies from this area.

Incremental Validity

Personality measures are, for the most part, uncorrelated with ability tests (Ackerman & Heggestad, 1997); only openness to experience shows moderate correlation with ability. This implies that most personality scales have promise for incremental validity. There have been a number of primary study examinations of incremental validity of personality measures over cognitive validity measures (e.g., Day & Silverman, 1989), which have suggested that personality scales, particularly conscientiousness, can increment the validity of ability measures.

In order to examine the incremental validity of integrity tests for overall job performance compared to other noncognitive measures, Ones and

Viswesvaran (1998a) sought meta-analytically established criterion-related validities for the same criterion reported in refereed journals. The noncognitive predictors included were structured and unstructured interviews (McDaniel, Whetzel, Schmidt & Maurer, 1994), biodata measures (Rothstein, Schmidt, Erwin, Owens & Sparks, 1990), assessment centers (Gaugler, Rosenthal, Thornton & Bentson, 1987), personality scales (Barrick & Mount, 1991), and interests (Hunter & Hunter, 1984). They relied on the meta-analytic results of Ones et al. (1993) for integrity test validities.

Based on meta-analyses reporting personality scale validities and intercorrelations among predictors, Ones and Viswesvaran (1998a) computed the multiple correlations of combining the noncognitive measure with a cognitive ability measure. The criterion-related validity of cognitive ability was taken as .51 (based on Hunter, 1980). The multiple R of combining an integrity test and a cognitive ability measure was .65 for medium complexity jobs. The incremental validity of integrity tests over cognitive ability measures was computed to be .14. Interestingly, other personality predictors exhibited incremental validities in the .01 to .05 range. Schmidt and Hunter's (1998) analysis also led to the same conclusions as Ones and Viswesvaran (1998a). However, it is important to note that these findings were for the criterion of overall job performance (Ones & Viswesvaran, 1998a; Schmidt & Hunter, 1998) and training performance (Schmidt & Hunter, 1998). When the criterion of interest is counterproductive behaviors, conscientiousness scales also provide incremental validity (Ones & Viswesvaran, 2001).

Salgado (1998) reported additional evidence for the incremental validity of the Big Five. Using a European database, he found that conscientiousness showed incremental validity over GMA by, 11%. He also found that emotional stability showed a 10% percent increase in validity. Furthermore, he found that for emotional stability the incremental validity was moderated by the type of occupation. He found 38% percent increase in validity for military occupations, while the increase was 7% for civilian occupations.

Group Differences

Of various demographic groups examined in the personality and work psychology literatures, the larger body of studies exist for gender (rather than race or ethnic groups). In fact, several qualitative and meta-analytic reviews have examined gender differences in personality (e.g., Feingold, 1994; Hall, 1984; Maccoby & Jacklin, 1974).

Feingold (1994), on the issue of personality differences between the genders, reported results for self-esteem, internal locus of control, and assertiveness. Higher scores were found for men (standardized effect sizes were .12, .12 and .08, respectively). (A more current meta-analysis of gender differences on self-esteem scales has reported a difference of .21 standard deviation units favoring males – Kling, Hyde, Showers & Buswell, 1999.) On anxiety scales, women scored .26 standard deviations higher than men. Feingold (1994) also presented a meta-analysis of gender differences on personality scales based on 13 major adult personality inventory norms reported in test manuals. He used the Big Five dimensions of personality (Costa & McCrae, 1992, 1995a, 1995b; Goldberg, 1990, 1993) and its facets to organize results. On neuroticism facets of anxiety and impulsiveness, women scored higher (by .27 and .04 standard deviation units, respectively). On order facet of conscientiousness, women scored .07 standard deviation units higher. On openness to ideas, men scored .13 standard deviation units higher. On agreeableness facets of trust and tender-mindedness (nurturance), women scored considerably higher (.25 and 1.07 standard deviation unit differences, respectively). Interestingly, on the three facets of extraversion different patterns of gender differences were found. Men scored considerably higher on assertiveness (a difference of .49 standard deviation units). Women scored somewhat higher on gregariousness (sociability; a difference of .14 standard deviation units). There were smaller differences between men and women on the activity facet of extraversion (a difference of .09 standard deviation units).

In a smaller scale investigation of gender differences on 11 personality inventories used in personnel selection in the US, Hough (1998) reported negligible gender differences for most personality variables she examined. There were three exceptions. On dependability scales, women scored higher by .27 standard deviation units (a small to moderate difference). On intellectance scales (openness to experience), men scored higher by .27 standard deviation units. The largest differences were found for rugged individualism scales (masculinity–femininity; a difference of 1.74 standard deviation units). The largest primary (rather than meta-analytic) investigation of gender differences for a work-related personality variables was carried out for integrity tests. Across 680,675 job applicants (316,359 females and 364,316 males), Ones and Viswesvaran (1998b) reported that females scored .16 standard deviations higher than males on overt integrity tests. The data for this study was collected in the US.

There is little work on race and ethnic group differences on personality scales. Perhaps one reason for this has been the large racial differences found on cognitive ability and related measures used in personnel selection that may have consumed the research efforts of investigators concerned with adverse impact. Though not a meta-analysis or a comprehensive review, the only quantitative overview of racial differences on personality scale scores was reported by Hough (1998). Across 11 personality inventories used in personnel selection in the US, Hough (1998) reported negligible race differences for most personality variables she examined. In general, race differences were even smaller than the gender differences she found (see above). There were a few exceptions though. She reported moderate black–white differences on affiliation and intellectance scales, where whites scored .31 and .28 standard deviation units higher than blacks. Hispanic Americans scored considerably higher than whites on response distortion scales (mean standardized difference of .60). Native Americans scored moderately lower than whites on adjustment (emotional stability) scales.

Ones and Viswesvaran (1998b) examined race differences on overt integrity tests by comparing mean scores of blacks (108,871), Hispanics (59,790), Asians (n = 13,594), and Native American (n = 2,601) with those of whites (n = 481,523). All differences were found to be trivial. Blacks scored .04 standard deviations lower than whites. Hispanics scored .14 standard deviations higher than whites. Asians scored .04 standard deviations higher than whites. Native American scored .08 standard deviations higher than whites. Ones and Viswesvaran (1998b) concluded that racial differences on overt integrity tests were trivial. They stated 'group differences of this trivial magnitude are not likely to be the *cause* of any discernible adverse impact in organizations where integrity tests are used'.

In the most recent examination of race differences in the US context, Goldberg et al. (1998) conducted a primary study using data from two adjectival Big Five measures. Using a large sample of (N = 3,629) American adults, these authors found that demographic variables (gender, age, ethnic/racial status, and educational level) correlated, on average, between 0.08 and 0.10 with the Big Five personality dimensions. Unfortunately, Goldberg et al. (1998) chose to index racial group differences using correlation coefficients. There is a significant drawback to using correlations rather than standardized mean differences in comparing groups; correlations are very sensitive to the proportions of subjects in each group being studied (in this case whites and each minority group). If sample sizes for the groups under study are not equal, the correlation coefficient computed is a severe *underestimate* of the relationships under study. In the Goldberg et al. (1998) study, the racial distribution of the sample (n = 3,629) was as follows: 10.7% blacks, 5.7% Hispanics, 10.7% Asian Americans, 0.6% Native Americans and 78.1% whites. Therefore, the results reported by Goldberg et al. (1998) for race may be largely attenuated. Note that unlike correlation coefficients, standardized effect sizes see below) are not influenced by proportions of groups in the ethnic categories examined.

Ones and Anderson (1999) quantitatively estimated the magnitude of group differences on some popular personality scale scores used in the UK for personnel selection and placement. Using data from 504 participants, they found that across three personality inventories examined, there were no large gender differences. Ethnic group differences were a bit larger, but still not large enough to cause concern for adverse impact. In general then, it appears that differences on personality measures are much smaller than those found for cognitive ability tests.

4. Job Knowledge Tests

Prevalence

There are several varieties of tests that can arguably be included under this predictor category. In this chapter, we consider three types of tests within job knowledge measures: job knowledge tests, tacit knowledge tests, and situational judgment tests. European surveys (Shackleton & Newell, 1997) suggest that the use of these measures range from 7% in France to 51% in Belgium, with the average being 27%. In the survey of the International Personnel Management Association cited by Gowing and Slivinsky (1994), job knowledge tests were used in 71% of organizations surveyed in the USA. Job knowledge tests have the advantage of face validity and acceptability to different stakeholders (e.g., applicants). Yet, as noted by Hunter and Hunter (1984) and Schmidt and Hunter (1998), the use of job knowledge tests is limited by the fact that they can only be used if the examinees are previously trained for the job.

Measurement and Construct Validity Issues

To what extent is job knowledge transportable across situations? Are there contextual factors that moderate the relevance of job knowledge across situations? Specifically, in terms of traits, what do job knowledge tests measure? Little research has empirically examined the relationship between job knowledge test scores and scores on other predictors. Ones and Viswesvaran (1998c) reported that a job knowledge test used by a defense manufacturing firm in mid-western United States correlated primarily with cognitive ability scores. Meta-analysis of the criterion-related validity of job knowledge tests suggest that whatever is assessed by these tests has validity that is transportable across situations examined. Research is needed to explore whether the factor structure of the different job knowledge tests that exist in the extant literature have a common core base, and if so, what that common underlying structure is.

Studies that explored the construct validity of job knowledge tests present conflicting findings. For example, Hunter (1986), and Borman, White, Pulakos & Oppler (1991) demonstrated that these tests mediated the relationship between GMA and job performance ratings. Pulakos and Schmitt (1996) found that the correlations between cognitive ability measures and a situational judgment test were small ranging from .07 to .17 (uncorrected). However, McDaniel, Finnegan, Morgeson, Campion and Braverman (1997) found that situational judgment tests and GMA tests were highly correlated, with the average correlation being .53. Moreover, this correlation reached .68 when the situational tests were based on a job analysis but fell to .29 when these tests were not based on a job analysis.

Recently, McDaniel and Nguyen (2001) have meta-analytically explored the evidence concerning the relationship between situational judgment tests and the Big Five personality dimensions as well as between situational judgment tests and job experience. Using a 'bare-bones' meta-analysis, they found that situational judgment tests correlated with agreeableness (observed mean $r = .25$), conscientiousness (observed mean $r = .26$), and emotional stability (observed mean $r = .32$). However, the situational judgment tests did not correlate with extroversion (observed mean $r = .06$), openness to experience (observed mean $r = .13$) and job experience (observed mean $r = .05$).

Criterion-Related Validity

A number of studies have been carried out on the criterion validity of job knowledge tests. In a meta-analysis derived from a large number of correlations reported by Dunnette (1972), Hunter and Hunter (1984) reported on an average validity of .51 ($k = 296$). Hunter and Hunter (1984) found an average corrected validity of .48 ($k = 10$) for predicting performance ratings and .78 ($k = 11$) for predicting work sample performance tests. Dye, Reck and McDaniel (1993), using a large data base consisting of 363,528 subjects and 502 validity studies, found an average operational validity of .45 for predicting job performance ratings and .47 for predicting training success. Dye et al. (1993) also found several moderators of the criterion validity. For example, they found that validity was moderated by job-test similarity and job complexity. In the case of job-test similarity, the findings showed that validity was .62 and .76 for job performance and training success, respectively, for high job-test similarity but the validity was .35 and .46 for job performance and training success, respectively, for low job-test similarity. In the case of job complexity, the results showed that validity was greater for jobs of high complexity than for jobs of low complexity.

The second type of job knowledge measures considered here, the tests of tacit knowledge, are relatively recent and they are based on Sternberg's work on intelligence (Sternberg, 1997; Sternberg, Wagner, Williams & Horvath, 1995). Sternberg reported that the correlations between tacit knowledge and job performance typically ranged from .20 to .40. Along with many other researchers (e.g., Schmidt & Hunter, 1993), we suspect that tacit knowledge measures tap into a particular type of job knowledge.

In connection with the third type of job knowledge measures, McDaniel et al. (1997) meta-analyzed the criterion validity of situational judgment tests. They found an average operational validity of .53 for predicting job performance ratings. Previously, Motowidlo and Tippins (1993) found that a situational inventory that they called low-fidelity simulation showed a criterion validity of. 28.

Incremental Validity

Few studies have reported on the incremental validity of job knowledge tests over GMA tests, although the evidence suggests that they account for variance beyond GMA tests. Schmidt and Hunter (1998) found that the conventional job knowledge tests showed 14% of increase in validity beyond GMA tests for predicting overall job performance ratings. However, in the case of tacit knowledge tests, the findings do not support completely this conclusion. Sue-Chan, Latham and Evans (1997) found that a tacit knowledge test for nurses had no incremental validity beyond GMA for predicting the first year and second year grade-point average.

Group Differences

The findings about subgroup differences for job knowledge tests suggest that there are differences of –0.38 for black–white comparisons (Schmitt et al., 1996). No differences are found between Hispanics and white groups. The results relating to the comparisons between males and females suggest that females perform better than males in job knowledge tests.

Weekley and Jones (1999) investigated group differences in a situational judgment test and found a difference of .85 standard deviations between whites and blacks, favoring whites in a sample of 1,925 (1,800 whites and 125 blacks) retail associates. Hispanics (*n* = 45) scored a quarter standard deviations lower compared to whites. Women scored .30 standard deviations above males (791 males and 1,646 females). In another sample (112 blacks, 199 Hispanics, 614 whites) of hotel employees, blacks scored .52 standard deviations below whites, and Hispanics scored .36 standard deviations below whites. Again women scored .20 standard deviations higher than men (433 males, 584 females). Evidence on bias, adverse impact, differential item functioning, single-group validity, and differential validity, for many different criteria and demographic groups are not available.

5. Work Sample Tests and Simulations

Situational judgment tests covered above can be construed as a low fidelity job simulation. Simulations can be more sophisticated in capturing the psychological and physical aspects of the work settings. We consider work sample tests in this section. Predictors such as assessment centers are covered in a separate section.

Prevalence

Work sample tests have been used for selecting personnel since the first decade of the twentieth century. For example, Münsterberg (1913) described two different work sample tests for selecting drivers and ship pilots. Under the rubric of work sample tests, we include three different tests: work sample tests, video-technology, and virtual reality tests. Obviously, video-based tests and virtual reality tests are currently scarcely used by companies in hiring processes due to the fact that they are personnel selection methods developed very recently and therefore less known than other more classic methods (e.g., GMA tests or personality tests). However, conventional work sample tests are likely to be largely used by companies or at least in a similar way as other older methods. Ryan, McFarland, Baron and Page (1999) reported on the findings of a survey conducted in fifteen countries. They found that video-based tests, work sample tests and simulation exercises are rarely used in personnel selection.

Measurement and Construct Validity Issues

Very little empirical research exists on what constructs are measured by work sample tests. Schmidt and Hunter (1992) present a process model where performance on work sample tests is explained by relationships with general mental ability, experience, and motivation. Ones and Viswesvaran (1998) present correlations between a work sample test and scores on integrity, interviews, and a job knowledge test. They reported that the work sample test correlated .20 with interviews, .07 with an overt integrity test, .27 with a personality-based integrity test and .36 with a job knowledge test.

Given that work sample tests can partly be construed as a method, different work sample tests can be constructed to measure different constructs. However, meta-analyses of the criterion-related validity of work sample tests seem to suggest that there is a common core to all the existing work sample tests. Meta-analytic evidence indicating that work sample tests are valid and generalizable across situations hint at the possibility that the different work sample tests share a common core construct. Just as with interviews, biodata items, and assessment centers, the work sample tests that have been empirically examined in the literature seem to have a common core in that the criterion-related validity appears transportable across situations. Future research is needed to shed more light on this issue.

Video-based tests may have greater face validity than conventional tests. Furthermore, their validity could be improved as the content in the video format is preserved and irrelevant variance related to reading comprehension is removed (Hough & Oswald, 2000).

The third type of simulation that we considered is Virtual Reality Technology (VRT), which is a new technology that has been suggested by Pierce and Aguinis (1997) as an alternative to conventional and video-based technology. VRT is a computer-simulated multisensory environment in which the perceiver feels to be present in an environment generated by a computer. VRT may be used both as a predictor or a criterion. According to, Pierce and Aguinis (1997), an advantage of VRT is that it could enhance the internal and external validity of the measurements. In Europe, a consortium of test publishers from Germany, Italy, Spain and Switzerland has developed a test of virtual reality to select people for dangerous occupations, and they are currently conducting validational studies.

Criterion-Related Validity

There are several meta-analyses on this topic that should be mentioned. An early meta-analysis was by Hunter and Hunter (1984). These authors, using data from Asher and Sciarrino (1974) on verbal work sample tests, reported a validity of .55 for predicting training and .45 for predicting proficiency. They also reported validities of .45 and .62 for predicting the same criteria when motor work sample tests are used. Another very relevant study was carried out by Schmitt et al. (1984), who conducted several meta-analyses of work sample tests using different criteria. Schmitt et al. found that work sample tests predicted job performance ratings (observed $r = .32$, $k = 7$, $n = 384$), achievement/grades (observed $r = .31$, $k = 3$, $n = 95$), and wages (observed $r = .44$, $k = 4$, $n = 1191$).

Robertson and Downs (1989) carried out a third meta-analysis using British studies, in which they examined the criterion validity of work sample tests of trainability. These tests are a sub-type of work sample tests and they are designed to assess how well applicants can learn a new skill. Trainability tests can yield two different, although correlated, scores: a rating of predicted performance in training and an error score. The observed validities were .41 and .48 for ratings and errors, respectively, in predicting training performance. For predicting job performance ratings, trainability tests showed an observed validity of .24. These results seem to show that trainability tests predict training success much better than they predict job performance ratings. Robertson and Downs (1989) also found that

the validity of trainability tests declines over time. Schmidt et al. (1992) suggested that these tests should be better considered as tests of initial training performance, which would explain the decline in validity over time.

The second type of simulations considered here are the video-based tests. As indicated above, these tests are infrequently used in personnel selection. However, in the last few years video-based tests are increasingly used for selecting people, and, in general, the results appear to be supportive of the criterion-validity of these procedures. McHenry and Schmitt (1994) reported two validity studies in which video tests were used. They found observed validities of .34 ($n = 60$) and .40 ($n = 160$) for predicting job performance ratings. Pulakos and Schmitt (1996) found an observed validity of .15 ($n = 467$) using a video test to assess verbal ability. Weekly and Jones (1997) carried out two studies using video-technology. In the first study they found validities of .22 ($n = 787$) and .33 ($n = 684$) for predicting job performance ratings, and in the second they found validities of .35 ($n = 412$) and .24 ($n = 148$). Dalessio and Silverhart (1994) found a validity of .13 ($n = 667$) for predicting turnover. However, not all studies have found positive relationships. Smiderle, Perry and Cronshaw (1994) failed to find criterion validity evidence in a sample of metropolitan transit operators. In a recent meta-analysis, Salgado and Lado (2000) found an operational validity of .49 for video-based tests. Video-based tests may have greater face validity than conventional tests.

Only one study was conducted to estimate the criterion validity of the Virtual Reality Tests. Pamos (1999) reported a concurrent validity study in which a VR-assisted psycho-aptitude test was correlated with some aspects of work behavior. Using a very small sample, he found a correlation of .53 between the distributed attention score and the rating of stress tolerance. The distributed attention score also correlated with the number of incidents headed ($r = .53$). Pamos (1999) also reported significant correlations between number of alarms solved and stress tolerance ($r = .41$) and between the efficiency score and team working rating ($r = .45$). Based on these results, we think that VRT does not substantially improve the criterion validity of other less expensive procedures (e.g., GMA tests, integrity tests). However, VRT may be useful as an alternative to traditional systems to assess job performance, and, used in this way, it may serve as the criterion scores in validational studies, serving as a sort of work sample measure.

Incremental Validity

Schmidt and Hunter (1998) have estimated the incremental validity of work sample tests. They estimated that the gain in validity from adding a work sample test supplementing a GMA test would be .12, which represents 24% of increase in validity. This is probably one of largest amounts of incremental validity shown by a personnel selection procedure. In this review, Schmidt and Hunter did not consider the incremental validity of video-based tests. However, Weekly and Jones (1997) addressed this issue in two studies. In the first study, these researchers found that the video tests accounted for 2.5% of the variance beyond cognitive ability and experience. In a second study, the incremental variance accounted for beyond cognitive ability was 5.7%. The incremental validity average is, therefore, 4.1%, a very modest gain. In another meta-analysis, Salgado and Lado (2000) found that video-tests showed incremental validity over GMA tests. Salgado and Lado estimated that a composite consisting of a GMA test and video-based test could reach a multiple correlation of .57.

Group Differences

The group differences were only estimated for work sample tests. Schmitt et al. (1996) found that work sample tests showed a subgroup effect size of − .38 when blacks and whites are compared, but the effect size is 0 when the comparison is made between Hispanics and whites. Job sample tests apparently produce a slightly favorable effect (.38) for females (Schmitt et al., 1996). Empirical evidence on differential validity, bias, single group validity, potential adverse impact, are scarce.

6. Interviews

Prevalence

Interviews are the most frequently used procedures in personnel selection across all countries. Practically, 100% of selection processes use one or more interviews. However, not all types of interviews are used to the same degree. For example, according to Dipboye (1997), conventional interviews are more commonly used than behavioral interviews (e.g., behavioral description interview, situational interview, structured behavioral interview). Ryan et al. (1999) found that group or panel interviews were less used than one-on-one interviews. There is also evidence that organizations are increasingly using the telephone as a means to conduct selection interviews (Anderson & Fletcher, in press; Schmidt & Rader, 1999; Silvester, Anderson, Haddleton, Cunningham-Snell & Gibb, 2000).

Measurement and Construct Validity Issues

Harris (1998) reviewed the evidence on the construct validity of structured interviews and his main conclusions were that the structured interview might consist of tacit knowledge (job knowledge), abilities, skills, personality and person–organization fit. However, these suggestions are based on indirect

findings and not on the relationship between the structured interview and these other constructs, although some meta-analyses support his conclusions. For example, Huffcutt, Roth and McDaniel (1996) found a corrected average correlation of .40 between interviews and GMA but this value was moderated by degree of structure within the interview, with the correlation decreasing as the degree of structure increased. The results showed a corrected average correlation of .50 for a low degree of structure and .35 for a high degree of structure.

Recently, Salgado and Moscoso (2001) have carried out a comprehensive meta-analysis on the construct validity of structured interviews reported in the literature. They classified interviews into two types using Janz's taxonomy of classifying interviews according to their content: Conventional interviews and structured behavioral interviews. They found that the conventional interview correlated with GMA (rho = .41), experience (rho = .29), emotional stability (rho = .38), extraversion (rho = .34), openness (rho = .30), agreeableness (rho = .26), conscientiousness (rho = .28), and social skills (rho = .46). Structured behavioral interviews correlated with GMA (rho = .28), job experience (rho = .71), job knowledge (rho = .53), emotional stability (rho = .08), extraversion (rho = .21), openness (rho = .09), agreeableness (rho = .14), conscientiousness (rho = .17), social skills (rho = .65), and situational judgment (rho = .46).

Campion, Pursell and Brown (1988) suggested ways in which the psychometric properties of an interview, such as reliability, can be improved. Conway, Jako and Goodman (1995) summarized the interrater and internal consistency reliability estimates of interview scores and found acceptable interrater reliabilities of .67 for high structured interviews (reliability estimates were .37 for low structured interviews). Silvester et al. (2000) have tested the equivalence between telephone and face-to-face semi-structured interviews. They found that applicants received lower ratings when interviewed by telephone than when they were interviewed face-to-face. They also found that applicants did not appear to be as satisfied with telephone interviews as they were with face-to-face interviews.

Criterion-Related Validity

Several meta-analyses assessing the criterion-related validity of interviews have been carried out in the last few years. In these meta-analyses, interviews are usually classified as unstructured and structured, and criterion-related validities are estimated for each group. For predicting job performance, Weisner and Cronshaw (1988) found a corrected validity of .31 for unstructured interviews and .62 for structured interviews. In one of the most comprehensive meta-analyses, McDaniel, Whetzel, Schmidt and Maurer (1994) classified interviews in three types: situational, job-related, and psychological interviews. They found operational validities of .50, .39, and. 29 (.27, .21, and .15, uncorrected) for situational, job-related, and psychological interviews, respectively. Huffcut and Arthur (1994) conducted another relevant meta-analysis in which the interviews were classified into four levels of structure. Huffcut and Arthur found that the corrected validities ranged from .20 to .56, for the lowest and highest level of structure, respectively.

Salgado and Moscoso (1995) examined the criterion-related validity of the behavioral structured interviews (behavior-description, situational, job-related, behavioral structured) and they found an average observed validity of .28. More recently, Schmidt and Rader (1999) assessed the criterion validity of an interview empirically constructed, administered by telephone and scored later based on a taped transcript. Their database consisted of predictive studies that were not included in any other meta-analysis, and they found an observed predictive validity of .19. All validity coefficients commented on above were found using job performance ratings as criterion.

Using training performance as the criterion, McDaniel et al. (1994) found an observed validity of .23. Schuler and his colleagues found that the multi-modal interview (MI), a structured behavioral interview, predicted different criteria (Schuler, 1992, 1997; Schuler and Moser, 1995; Schuler et al., 1995). For example, MI predicted job performance (observed validity = .27), sales and service potential (observed r = .27), and vocational success 4.5 years later.

In the article mentioned above, Schmidt and Rader (1999) meta-analyzed criterion measures not included in previous meta-analyses. They found that the structured interview they studied correlated with production records (rho = .40), sales performance (rho = .24), absenteeism (rho = .19), and with job tenure (rho = .39).

Incremental Validity

Campion, Campion and Hudson (1994) report positive evidence of incremental validity for the interview. According to Schmidt and Hunter's (1998) estimates, the structured interviews resulted in a 24% of increase in validity over GMA validity and the unstructured interviews showed an 8% of increase in validity. Therefore, structured (and behavioral) interviews are one of the personnel selection methods that show larger incremental validity.

Group Differences

Huffcut and Roth (1998) found that the interview appeared to have little negative impact on minorities (d = 0.25) and that high-structure interviews (e.g., behavior description and situational interviews) had a lower impact than low-structure interviews. Latham and Skarlicki (1996) found that behavioral description and situational interviews

were resistant to interviewer bias in minimizing in-group favoritism while the conventional structured interview did show in-group favoritism.

Several studies have examined potential biases that could affect interview scores. Race, gender, age, and attractiveness of the interviewee or interviewer, as well as the interaction between interviewee and interviewer characteristics have been explored. Potential interactions with types of jobs and criteria have been addressed. Unfortunately, the existing empirical evidence is too contradictory for strong inferences to be made at this stage. Future research is needed to shed light on the role of these variables in interview assessment. Similarly very little research exists on bias, differential validity, etc.

7. Biodata

Prevalence

Schmidt et al. (1992) stated that in the United States only 6.8% of firms had ever used biodata in employment decisions, and only .04% indicated that they currently use biodata scales. Shackleton and Newell (1997) estimated that 6% of firms used biodata in all employment decisions and 11% in some cases. Di Milia et al. (1994) found that 19.1% of companies in Australia used biodata. In Europe, the estimates ranged from 0% in Italy to 34% in Belgium, with the average rate being 13%. Ryan et al. (1999) also found that biodata were rarely used by companies in hiring personnel.

Measurement and Construct Validity Issues

Biodata provides a fruitful avenue of research on development of human individuality (Stokes, Mumford & Owens, 1994). Mumford, Stokes and Owens (1990) discuss how studying patterns of life history sheds light on the ecology (as well as ontology) of human individuality. According to these authors, a science of individuality based on traits and cross-sectional data is static, and fails to capture the dynamic interplay between the genetic blueprint of the individual and the environmental processes that act on that genetic blueprint of that individual. Longitudinal analyses are one approach to capture the dynamic development process of individuals. Adolescent life experiences have been found to be predictors of occupational attainment (Snell, Stokes, Sands & McBridge, 1994). In other words, biodata measures can be construed as a proxy for differences in developmental experiences.

The overlap between biodata and interviews (e.g., Dalessio & Silverhart, 1994) has been investigated. Hough and Oswald (2000) report data suggesting that biodata scales used in the United States federal government measure social and cognitive skills. Further, it appears that scales developed in one setting can be made to generalize to other settings (Carlson, Scullen, Schmidt, Rothstein & Erwin, 1999). Dalessio, Crosby and McManus (1996) found that biodata keys and dimensions generalized across two English-speaking countries. Some studies (Hough & Paullin, 1994) suggest that rational, empirical-keying and factor-analytic scoring of biodata items yield comparable results in terms of criterion-related validity whereas other studies (Schoenfeldt, 2001) find that rational and factor-analytic approaches to keying items yield better results compared to empirical keying.

In a factor analysis of a biodata inventory, Mael and Ashforth (1995) found support for four factors. The biodata items could be categorized as rugged, solid citizen, team/group, and achievement orientation. Brown and Campion (1994) investigated the phenomenological meaning of various biodata items and found acceptable levels of interrecruiter reliability in the meanings inferred from items. For example, language and math abilities were inferred from education-related items and physical ability from sports-related items. Leadership and interpersonal skills were imputed using items questioning positions held previously.

Criterion-Related Validity

Several studies have explored the criterion-related validity of biodata. A meta-analysis derived from Dunnette's data (1972, cited by Hunter and Hunter, 1984) showed an average correlation of .34 for predicting job performance. Using military data reported in Vineberg and Joyner (1982), Hunter and Hunter (1984) calculated an operational validity of .20 for predicting global ratings and .29 for predicting suitability. Hunter and Hunter (1984) also found that biodata predicted supervisor ratings (.37), promotion ($r = 0.26$), training success ($r = 0.30$) and tenure ($r = 0.26$). Rothstein, Schmidt, Erwin, Owens & Sparks (1990) carried out a large-sample study in which it was found that validity generalized across organizations, age, gender, education, supervisory experience, and tenure; they found an operational validity of .29.

Brown (1981) meta-analyzed data from 12 US life insurance companies and found an operational validity of .26 for predicting job performance ratings among salesmen. Reilly and Chao (1982) found an average validity of .38. Schmitt et al. (1984), using published studies between 1964 and 1984, found that biodata predicted performance ratings (observed $r = 0.32$), turnover (observed $r = 0.21$), achievement/grades (observed $r = 0.23$), productivity (observed $r = 0.20$), status change (observed $r = 0.33$), and wages (observed $r = 0.53$).

In Europe, Funke, Krauss, Schuler and Stapf (1987) reported a meta-analysis in which biodata were used to predict research achievement in science and technology. They found an average operational validity of .47. Gunter, Furnham and

Drakeley (1993) reported a meta-analysis using British military studies which found an average validity of .21 ($n > 70,000$, $k = 63$). Altink (1991) reported a validity of .40 (uncorrected) for biodata scales using a sample from the Netherlands.

More recently, Bliesener (1996) carried out a meta-analysis concerning the criterion validity of biodata. The study only included articles using biodata which contained purely biographical items and no other types of predictors (e.g., personality scales). Bliesener found an overall observed validity of .30 ($n = 106,302$, $k = 165$). He also found that several methodological moderators affected validity. For example, double cross-validation showed a validity of .50 while external validity or cross validation showed validities of .24 and .28, respectively. Concurrent designs produced higher validity than predictive validity or predictive with selection designs (.35, .29, and .21 respectively). Biodata predicted different criteria. For example, biodata showed a validity of .53 for predicting objective performance, .32 for predicting performance ratings and .36 for predicting training success. In the case of jobs, validity ranged from .23 for sales personnel to .46 for clerks.

Taken together, the results of these meta-analyses suggest that biodata are one of the most valid predictors of personnel selection, and that their validity can generalize across organizations, occupations and samples.

Incremental Validity

Schmidt (1988) reported that a biodata scale (Managerial Profile Record) correlated .50 with cognitive ability. Based on meta-analytic data, Schmidt and Hunter (1998) found that biodata measures provided .01 incremental validity points over general mental ability tests.

Group Differences

Bliesener's (1996) results showed that male and female samples had a different criterion validity, the validity being higher for female samples compared to male samples (.51 vs. .27) for the criterion of overall job performance.

Gandy, Dye and MacLane (1994) reported a black–white difference of .35 standard deviation units favoring whites ($n = 5,758$), while Pulakos and Schmitt (1996) reported a difference of −.05 standard deviation units (favoring blacks) ($n = 357$). Bobko et al. (1999) sample size weighted and averaged these two values: the mean standardized difference between the groups was .33.

8. Assessment Centers (AC)

Prevalence

In general, the percentage of companies using assessment centers for personnel selection is small.

European surveys have shown that the use of AC ranges from 2% in Portugal to 27% in The Netherlands (Dany and Torchy, 1994). According to Shackleton and Newell (1994, 1997), in the case of managerial occupations the percentage of use is greater, ranging from 18.8% in France to 60% in Germany. In Australia, the percentage of companies that use AC for selecting managerial occupations is 58.9% (Di Milia et al., 1994). Levy-Leboyer (1994) reports a lesser use of assessment centers in France and Belgium as compared to the United Kingdom, Germany and the Netherlands.

Measurement and Construct Validity Issues

The construct validity of the AC method remains undetermined. In view of this, Scholz and Schuler (1993) carried out a very comprehensive meta-analysis, exploring the nomological network of ACs ($k = 66$, $n = 22,106$). They found that overall assessment ratings correlated .43 with GMA ($n = 17,373$), .15 with emotional stability ($n = 909$), .14 with extraversion ($n = 1,328$), .30 with dominance ($n = 909$), .40 with achievement motivation ($n = 613$), .41 with social competence ($n = 572$), and .32 with self-confidence ($n = 601$). Lievens (1999a, 1999b) summarized the different factors that affect the construct validity of assessment centers. Collins, Schmidt, Sanchez-Ku, Thomas and McDaniel (1999) found that AC scores could be predicted with cognitive ability and personality scores.

A measurement issue debated in the AC literature is whether dimension factors can be identified from scores across different exercises. Many studies have reported exercise factors (cf. Sackett & Dreher, 1982). Anderson, Payne, Ferguson and Smith (1994) reported that scores cluster more by the method of assessment rather than by content. Shore, Shore and Thornton (1992) suggested that dimension observability would moderate the construct validity of AC scores. Harris, Backer and Smith (1993) stated that if raters had sufficient opportunities to observe, consistency would improve. Kleinmann (1993) tested whether transparent dimensions had more consistency of ratings as well as better construct validity. Although transparency improved convergent validity, problems remained with discriminant validity.

Criterion-Related Validity

The first two meta-analyses relating to the criterion-related validity of assessment center (AC) method were carried out by Schmitt et al. (1984) and Hunter and Hunter (1984). Schmitt et al. found that AC was a good predictor of job performance ratings (observed validity = 0.43, $k = 6$, $n = 394$). They also found that AC predicted achievement/grades (observed $r = 0.31$, $k = 3$, $n = 289$), status change (observed validity = 0.41, $k = 8$, $n = 14361$), and wages (observed $r = 0.21$, $k = 4$, $n = 301$). For their

part, Hunter and Hunter (1984) reported a meta-analysis using the validity coefficients found by Cohen, Moses and Byham (1974). They found that AC predicted promotion (median $r = 0.63$) and performance (.43, corrected for attenuation).

Gaugler, Rosenthal, Thornton and Bentson (1987) carried out a meta-analysis, using a database larger than Hunter and Hunter's (1984) and Schmitt et al.'s (1984) databases. Gaugler et al. found that AC predicted job performance ratings, showing an observed validity of .25 (corrected $r = 0.37$, $k = 44$, $n = 4,180$).

Other relevant validational studies were carried out by Dobson and Williams (1989), Feltham (1988), Wiersma, Van Leest, Nienhuis and Maas (1991), Schuler, Moser and Funke (1994), Jansen and Stoop (1994), and Chan (1996). Dobson and Williams (1989), in a large-scale validation study of the AC method for selecting British Army officers, found an operational validity of .31 for predicting Army training grades and .33 for predicting job performance. Feltham (1988) found an observed validity of .18 for predicting job performance ratings and .11 for predicting potential. This study was a 19-year longitudinal study in the British police. Wiersma et al. (1991) reported the results of a study using the AC method in The Netherlands; they found a correlation of .48 between overall assessment ratings and supervisor ratings of management potential. Also in the Netherlands, Jansen and Stoop (1994) found a validity of .55 (corrected for range restriction) for predicting the present salary. Schuler et al. (1994), in Germany, investigated the moderating effect of the rater–ratee acquaintance on the predictive validity of an AC. Rater–ratee acquaintance varied from 1 month to 30 years. The average observed validity was .37, which fell to .09 when the rater–ratee acquaintance was less than or equal to 2 years, but reached .50 when the rater–ratee acquaintance was greater than two years. Finally, Chan (1996) found that an AC predicted promotability of police in Singapore.

Incremental Validity

Schmidt and Hunter (1998), in their review of 85 years of research in personnel selection, estimated that the AC showed a very small incremental validity beyond GMA tests. According to Schmidt and Hunter, the percentage of increase in validity is 4%. Goffin, Rothstein and Johnston (1996) using data from a sample of managers reported evidence suggesting incremental validity when personality dimensions and biodata scores are combined. Goldstein, Yusko, Braverman, Smith and Chung (1998) found that ACs have incremental validity over cognitive ability.

Group Differences

Goldstein, Braverman and Chung (1993) have found that the written in-basket tests and simulation exercises produced an adverse impact among blacks in comparison to whites, whereas role play exercises produced the reverse effect; in role-play exercises, blacks performed better than whites. Goldstein et al. (1998) have subsequently replicated these results.

9. Other Predictors

In reviewing the different predictors used in personnel selection, we have discussed (1) cognitive ability tests, (2) physical, psychomotor, perceptual ability tests, (3) personality tests, (4) job knowledge tests, (5) work sample tests and simulations, (6) interviews, (7) biodata, and (8) assessment centers. Beyond these predictors reviewed above, several other predictors have been employed in personnel selection. Reference and background checks, recommendation letters, polygraph testing, graphology or handwriting analysis, use of grades, and drug testing (urinalysis, blood testing, hair testing etc.). In this subsection, we briefly review these other predictors.

Prevalence

References are a common method used in personnel selection. In Europe, the prevalence of using references ranges from 66.7% of companies to 100% (Shackleton and Newell, 1994, 1997) or from 47% to 96% (Dany and Torchy, 1994). Similar percentages are reported in surveys conducted in North America and Australia (see Di Milia et al., 1994; Marsden, 1994). For example, Milkovich and Boudreau (1994) suggest that the reference checks are used by virtually all organizations, although Levy-Leboyer (1994) reports a greater reluctance to provide references in France.

Normand, Lempert and O'Brien (1994) report that 87% of major US corporations use some form of drug testing. Usage in other parts of the world is much less common, except for inherently dangerous jobs (e.g., airline pilots, nuclear plant operators).

The use of polygraph has declined since the passage of the Employee Polygraph Protection Act of 1988 in the United States. However, its popularity continues in some countries (e.g., Israel).

Graphology or handwriting analysis has been practically unused across the world, except in a few countries (e.g., France, Israel, Brasil, Switzerland) (see Ryan et al., 1999; Schuler, Frier & Kaufmman, 1993).

Measurement and Construct Validity Issues

Reference reports have different names: reference checks, letters of reference, letters of recommendation, references, or reference statements. In connection with this variability, Loher, Hazer, Tsai, Tilton & James (1997) have suggested that previous research

on references have been atheoretical. Loher et al. (1997) have proposed a conceptual framework for the process of assessment of reference letters. According to Loher et al., the reference process seems to include two communication stages: the message to the informer and the message to the receiver (writer and reader if it is a letter of reference). One problem with reference letters has been that almost all letters are positive in tone. However, some guidelines have been suggested to evaluate reference letters. For example, Aamodt, Bryan and Whitcomb (1993) suggested the use of a model in which the adjectives are identified and classified into five categories (similar to the Big Five). The scores of the individual would be the number of adjectives within each category. In the case of reference letters, the acceptance of candidates have been related to lack of negative information and letter length. Further, the use of specific behavioral examples has been related to better construct validity.

The validity of polygraphs and other mechanical contraptions to assess dissimulation has been challenged (Iacono & Lykken, 1997). Such challenges were at the root of the Federal Polygraph Act in the US, which banned their use by private employers.

Drug testing has emphasized clinical testing of urine, blood and hair samples. Elaborate procedures have been evolved to ensure the integrity of sample and testing processes. Most testing programs apply an initial test such as the immunoassay test, and if positive results were obtained, follow it with more costlier and reliable tests such as gas chromatography.

Measurement of individual characteristics by handwriting analysis also has been challenged. Research studies (e.g., Neter & Ben-Shakhar, 1989) indicate that the predictive validity is more likely due to the content of the written material than due to the style of handwriting. However, attempts have been made to assess traits such as dominance and detail-orientation using the style of handwriting.

A more controversial testing process is the use of genetic screening. With medical advances in behavior genetics suggesting that many characteristics of importance in the workplace have a large heritability component (e.g., Lykken, Bouchard, McGue & Tellegen, 1993), the potential for genetic testing is great. But so are the ethical questions and administration issues. It is definitely an area that personnel selection experts will have to address in the future.

Criterion-Related Validity

Only two meta-analyses have explored the criterion-related validity of references. Reilly and Chao (1982) found a validity of .17 for predicting supervisory ratings. Hunter and Hunter (1984) found that references predicted supervisory ratings ($r = .26$, $n = 5,389$), promotion ($r = .16$, $n = 415$), training ($r = .23$, $n = 1,553$), and tenure ($r = .27$, $n = 2,018$). Additional research concerning the validity of references has been was carried out by Aamondt, Bryan and Whitcomb (1993), who examined the criterion validity of Peres and Garcia's (1962) adjectives categories used in providing references. Aamodt et al. (1993) found that the adjectives associated with mental agility were predictors of graduate school grade point average ($r = 0.32$).

Simmering and Ones (1994) reported on the reliability of urinalysis measures for detecting actual drug use as .76. In a large scale study, Normand, Salyards and Mahoney (1990) estimated the relationships between drug test results and injuries, accidents, absenteeism and turnover ($n = 5,465$). Those testing positive for drugs had 59% higher absenteeism rates than those testing negative. Turnover rate was 47% higher for those testing positive than those testing negative.

Neter and Ben-Shakhar (1989) meta-analytically summarized the validity of graphology. Handwriting analysis had more predictive validity when individuals were required to author a text with actual autobiographical content rather than being asked to copy a predetermined passage.

Five meta-analyses assessed the criterion validity of grades. O'Leary (1980, cited by Hunter and Hunter, 1984) reported a correlation of .21 with promotion ($n = 6,014$), .11 with supervisory ratings ($n = 1,089$), .30 with training ($n = 837$), and .05 with tenure ($n = 181$). Reilly and Chao (1982) found an average validity of .14 for predicting supervisory ratings and .27 for predicting compensation. Hunter and Hunter (1984) found that college grade point average (GPA) predicted supervisory ratings ($r = 0.11$, $n = 1,089$, $k = 10$), promotion ($r = .21$, $n = 6,014$, $k = 17$), training success ($r = .30$, $n = 837$, $k = 3$), but they did not predict tenure ($r = .05$, $n = 81$, $k = 2$). Recently, Roth and his colleagues have carried out two meta-analyses focusing on the relationship between grades and job performance and salary (Roth, BeVier, Switzer and Schippman, 1996; Roth and Clarke, 1998). Roth et al. (1996) found an observed correlation of .16 ($n = 13,984$) for predicting job performance, and .32 when the validity was corrected for criterion unreliability and range restriction. Several variables, such as years between grades and performance, type of organization, education level, source of publication, and source of performance information, moderated the validity. Roth and Clarke (1998), in a meta-analysis of the relationship between grades and salary, found an observed correlation of .18 (corrected for range restriction = .25, $n = 9,759$).

Physiological measures have also been used to assess trustworthiness and deception. Polygraphs were used to assess deception in personnel selection before 1988 (Saxe & Ben-Shakhar, 1999). With the passage of the Employee Polygraph Protection Act of 1988, the use of polygraphs in preemployment testing has been limited to security related jobs in the United States. Iacono and Lykken (1997) report that most psychologists believe that the polygraph has doubtful validity.

Incremental Validity

Little research has investigated the criterion validity of references and even less has checked whether or not references show incremental validity over GMA tests. The exception to this lack of information is Schmidt and Hunter's (1998) review. These authors, using the validity estimates found by Hunter and Hunter (1984) for GMA tests and reference checks, have estimated that references increment validity by 12% beyond GMA tests. Data are needed on the incremental validity of other predictors reviewed in this section.

Group Differences

Group differences, bias, differential validity of these other predictors have rarely been referred to in the literature. It would be profitable for future research to explore these issues.

DESIGNING SELECTION SYSTEMS

Issues in Combining Predictors

Organizations rarely rely on a single predictor for personnel selection. Job analysis for even simple jobs is likely to identify several traits relevant to job performance. When individuals are assessed on several traits, how should the scores be combined? There are two options. The first is a noncompensatory system where the applicant is expected to obtain a minimum score in each predictor. The second is a compensatory system where high scores in one predictor can make up (i.e., compensate) for low scores in another predictor.

A noncompensatory system is used when all predictors are important and the employee cannot compensate the lack of one trait by another. For example, consider the traits visual acuity and cognitive ability for the job of an airline pilot. Both traits are needed. In this instance, the selection can be based on minimum scores on each predictor. Noncompensatory systems can be further classified as multiple hurdle and multiple cut-off systems. In multiple hurdle systems, applicants are assessed on the traits, one trait at a time. Only those who meet the requirements in a trait are assessed in the next trait. This procedure is useful when the costs of the different assessments vary. Organizations tend to administer the least costly assessments first, and the costly assessments are limited to only those who meet the minimum qualifications based on the least costly assessments. In multiple cut-off systems, individuals are assessed on all traits and those who meet the minimum cut-score in all predictors are selected. Multiple cut-off systems are used when it is costly to bring applicants for testing of each predictor (e.g., a national search for engineers). In a compensatory system, the scores from different predictors are combined in one of three ways. The scores may simply be added (i.e., provide unit weights to predictors), or different weights can be assigned to each predictor based on rational arguments. Finally, for optimal prediction, regression weights can be used.

Arthur, Doverspike and Barrett (1996) report on a job-analysis based procedure to weight and combine content-related predictors into an overall score. Schmidt (1971) has argued that simple linear weights are more likely to be generalizable than optimal regression weights. Attempts have been made to combine predictors so as to maximize the reliability of the composite score (Cliff & Caruso, 1998; Li, Rosenthal & Rubin, 1996; Raykov, 1997). When predictors are combined based on their intercorrelations and criterion-related validity, there is the potential for the multiple correlation to be inflated due to capitalization on chance. Cross-validation and shrinkage correction formulae have been developed to estimate the adjusted multiple correlation. The shrinkage formula to be used (Wherry or Cattin) depend on the strategy used in selecting predictors and the questions focused. Raju, Bilgic, Edwards and Fleer (1997, 1999) present a large scale Monte Carlo simulation on the appropriateness of cross-validation and several shrinkage formulae.

Combining predictors to construct a selection system raises several interesting issues. First, we can ask how much increase in predictive power is gained by adding the second predictor to the first. This issue of incremental validity has been discussed earlier in our review of the different predictors. Another issue to consider is the joint effects of group differences in the different predictors combined on the overall adverse impact caused by the selection system. Ones et al. (1993) argued that adding integrity tests to a selection system employing ability tests reduces adverse impact. Sackett and Ellingson (1997) provide a readable summary of issues in this area, concluding that combining predictors with no group differences with one that shows large group differences (e.g., cognitive ability) is likely to reduce adverse impact, but does not erase (or even halve it).

More research is needed on the correlations between the predictors and the criterion as well as the intercorrelations among the predictors to address the impact of combining predictors on the validity of the composite as well as adverse impact assessments. Schmitt, Rogers, Chan, Sheppard and Jennings (1997) attempted to synthesize the existing literature on the intercorrelations among predictors as well as race differences (i.e., primarily white–black differences). Bobko, Roth, and Potosky (1999) present refined estimates for assessing adverse impact of predictor combinations. Obviously, a lot more research is needed before inferences

on potential adverse impact and criterion-related validity of predictor composites are satisfactorily answered.

Group Differences and Banding in Personnel Selection

In discussing group differences, one can distinguish between culture-fair assessment, group differences, adverse impact, discrimination, bias, single-group validity, differential validity, differential item functioning and fairness. These are related, but distinct, concepts. Consider the issue of culture-fair assessment. The assessment of any trait by any method is ground in culture to some extent. As such, some have argued that it is not possible to have culture-free assessments. The degree to which the responses are unique to a particular culture is the culture-loadedness of the test. If culture-loaded tests are used in selection, members of the group on which the items are based might score better than individuals belonging to other cultures. In this aspect, culture's influences on test scores, that are independent of the constructs being measured, may be regarded as contamination.

Note that culture-fair assessment does not imply lack of group differences on traits. Just as there are discernible individual differences, there can be discernible group differences on traits. Groups can be defined based on race, gender, age, or ethnic group. When there are group differences, it is possible that there will be more members of the higher scoring group being selected. When the selection ratios (ratio of those selected to those applied) differ substantially across groups, adverse impact results. That is, the low scoring group has been adversely impacted by the selection procedures.

Certain points need to be kept in mind in discussing adverse impact. First, according to the law in the United States, adverse impact is inferred only if the selection ratio for the protected group is less than 80% (i.e., four-fifths) of the selection ratio for others. Second, just because there are group differences, it does not necessarily mean that there will be adverse impact. Sackett and Roth (1996) present several factors such as selection ratio and within-group variability that affect adverse impact. Third, the existence of adverse impact is not evidence of malevolence or any evil intent. Perhaps what should be kept in mind is that all tests are designed to discriminate; the question is whether they discriminate based on job-relevant traits or on some irrelevant group characteristic.

The issue of bias, in contrast to issues of fairness, is a statistical concept with a precise definition. Predictive bias is defined as the systematic over or under prediction of a criterion. In discussing bias, we need to review discussions of single group validity and differential validity. Single group validity refers to the idea that the predictor is valid for one group but not for the other group. Differential validity states that the predictor is valid in both groups but the magnitude of the validity differs. In discussing single group validity, care should be taken not to overlook the potential for different sample sizes across groups. In the 1960s, a number of studies conducted in the United States found that cognitive ability is a significant predictor for whites but not for blacks. However, the number of blacks included in a validation study is typically less than that of whites. As the sample sizes decrease, there is more error or instability in the estimates, so that smaller samples are not as statistically significant as results for larger samples. Once corrected for differences in sample size, the evidence for single group validity is very weak (Boehm, 1977; Hunter, Schmidt & Hunter, 1979).

In recent years there has been an increasing debate (Cascio, Goldstein, Outtz & Zedeck, 1995; Schmidt & Hunter, 1995) over the use of banding in personnel selection. The rationale advanced for the use of banding is the well-known fact that there is measurement error associated with each observed score. The idea is that scores within a band are all the same – differences between them are probably due to measurement error. Bands are usually formed using the top score in a group of applicants and the standard error of measurement (SEM). Selection can be at random within the bands, or preferential hiring based on other variables can be employed. Another option in the use of bands is to decide whether to compute the bands every time the top score is selected or only after all respondents in the band have been exhausted. The latter is referred to as fixed bands and the former as sliding bands (i.e., the bands slide every time the top score is selected).

Some researchers reject the logic of banding (cf. Schmidt, 1991) on the grounds that just as the differences in scores within a band can be attributed to SEM, the difference between the lowest score in the band and the highest score outside the band can also be attributed to error. For example, consider a test where three candidates scored 98, 90 and 83, respectively. Assume the SEM is 5 and the organization decides to use a 95% confidence interval (i.e., the organization wants to make sure that the conclusion that the person who scored higher than another has more of the trait is at error no more than 5% of the time). In this instance, observed score differences of 10 points can be placed in the same band. On this logic, the organization decides that the candidates who scored 98 and 90 belong in the same band; both will have equal probability of being selected based on test scores. But note that the difference in the scores 90 and 83 can also be due to measurement error. The candidate with a score of 90 is included in the band (with a chance to get hired) whereas the candidate with a score of 83

is denied this opportunity. If it is reasonable to lump scores of 98 and 90 together, it is equally reasonable to lump the scores 90 and 83. Thus, it becomes illogical to defend banding based exclusively on the concept of SEM. Other considerations such as the practical reality of selection have to be invoked (Cascio et al., 1995).

There are also other issues to consider in using bands. The SEM is dependent on the reliability of the test. By using an unreliable test, an organization can generate broad bands (with unreliable tests, the SEM increases). Thus, an organization intent on ensuring enough selected individuals belonging to a low scoring group can achieve its political goals by using unreliable tests (Murphy, 1994; Murphy, Osten & Myors, 1995). Sackett and Roth (1991) present a Monte Carlo simulation of the effects of several other characteristics on the effects of using banding in personnel selection. Truxillo, Bauer and Bauer (1999) present data exploring applicant reactions to the use of banding in personnel selection. As expected several contextual factors affect applicant reactions and more research is needed in this topic.

Special Topics in Selection

We briefly summarize issues in selecting individuals to work in a team context, computerized assessment, and different process models advanced to explain the observed validity and intercorrelations among different predictors. Some of these topics (e.g., team selection) are covered in more detail in other chapters in this Handbook and interested readers are referred to them.

Team Selection

Recent years have seen an increased emphasis on teamwork (Guzzo & Salas, 1995). The growth of knowledge is such that it is becoming increasingly impossible for individuals to function independently of teams (Klimoski & Zukin, 1999). Should selection focus on team skills? Barrick, Stewart, Neubert and Mount (1998) found that variables such as extraversion were related to social cohesion of groups. Stevens and Campion (1994) reported on an instrument to select individuals for teamwork. West and Allen (1997) summarized the predictors of team performance. They report that individuals with similar attitudinal assumptions perform well together in a team. West and Allen also report that for individuals with a collectivist orientation, a group based training is effective whereas for individuals with an individualist orientation, a self-focused training is effective. Still, issues such as whether teams should be staffed with individuals similar in trait levels or with individuals who complement one another in traits, need to be explored more comprehensively (Klimoski & Jones, 1995). The interaction between type of job and team composition needs further investigation. For example,

Barry and Stewart (1997) found that individual team member conscientiousness did not predict effectiveness on a creative task. Further, research on functional relationships between variables at different levels of analysis (e.g., individual difference variables such as ability and team level variable such as team effectiveness) needs to be developed further (cf. Chan, 1998, for a review of underlying issues).

Computerized Assessment

Drasgow and Olson-Buchannan (1999) have edited a book on the use of computers in assessment. The ability to tailor tests more easily has been noted. Issues such as measurement equivalence (Mead & Drasgow, 1993; Finger & Ones, 1999) have been investigated. Speeded tests (or tests where time is a factor) have shown less equivalence than power tests (where ample time is provided to test takers). Computerized assessments have been found to be useful in delivering complex three dimensional stimuli and multimodal stimuli (musical notes etc.). For example, Vispoel (1999) presents an interesting account of using computers to assess aptitude for music. The rapid technological growth suggests that computerized assessment will be an important topic for future research in the coming decades.

Process Models

Decades of research have clearly demonstrated that personnel selection experts can reliably measure individual differences in several traits, and successfully predict performance on several different criteria. The question then raises as to the causal mechanisms or scientific explanations underlying why certain predictors work under certain circumstances. As noted by Schmidt and Kaplan (1971), the maturation of a field is reflected in the types of research questions posed. Once the practical utility of a field is established, experts turn to address causal explanations.

In one of the earlier attempts at developing process models, Hunter (1986) invoked concepts from classical learning theories to suggest that individual differences in cognitive ability predict effectiveness in learning. This in turn, affects performance in work sample tests as well as job performance. The predictions were confirmed when data were cumulated across 14 studies. Barrick, Mount and Strauss (1993) report that the predictive validity of conscientiousness can be explained by the mediating effects of goal setting. Borman, Hanson, Oppler, Pulakos and White (1993) replicate and extend the works of Schmidt, Hunter and Outerbridge (1986) on the role of experience in explaining job performance. Carretta and Doub (1998) examined the role of cognitive ability and prior experience in the acquisition of job knowledge. Campbell, McCloy, Oppler and Sager (1993) propose a model of performance where the different predictors (e.g., ability) affect performance through their effects on either motivation or declarative knowledge or procedural knowledge. McCloy, Campbell and Cudeck (1994) provide empirical support for the hypothesized determinants.

In one of the comprehensive attempts to derive a model that takes into account how ability and personality variables operate to predict job performance, Schmidt and Hunter (1992) developed a path model. In that model, personality variables such as conscientiousness were hypothesized to affect job performance via several mechanisms. First, conscientious individuals were expected to engage in more organizational citizenship behaviors resulting in higher job performance ratings (Orr, Sackett & Mercer, 1989). Second, conscientious individuals are expected to spend more time on the task and less time on day-dreaming. This is hypothesized to result in three effects. First, the increased time spent on the task can increase productivity that can translate into higher job performance ratings. Second, the increased time spent on tasks can be noted by others (e.g., supervisors) and this can yield higher performance ratings. Third, the increased time spent on tasks can facilitate a corresponding increase in job knowledge that in turn can enhance productivity and obtained performance ratings. Several other potential mechanisms have been advanced. Empirical research is needed to test these hypothesized mechanisms and causal paths.

Methodological Advances

In this subsection, we review some of the methodological advances in personnel assessment and selection. We discuss refinements to validity generalization, issues associated with the use of correlation coefficients, and response distortion in psychological assessment. Given that separate chapters have been devoted to meta-analysis, research methods, and measurement in this Handbook, our review is very selective. Further, because the correlation coefficient plays such a central role in personnel selection, we devote more attention to methodological issues surrounding the estimation of a correlation coefficient.

Validity Generalization

The advent of validity generalization (Schmidt & Hunter, 1977) has truly generated a paradigm shift in personnel selection. Schmidt and Hunter (Chapter 3, this volume) cover the essential features of the concept of validity generalization in discussing the methods of meta-analysis. The last two decades have seen many attempts to refine the methods. Schmidt et al. (1993) summarize the refinements in estimating sampling error and accounting for nonlinearities in range restriction correction. Several simulation studies attest to the similarities among the different models.

The Correlation Coefficient

The correlation coefficient has served as a useful index in assessing the appropriateness of a predictor. Recently, some researchers (e.g., Zickar, Rosse & Levin, 1996) have argued that the correlation coefficient is insensitive to rank order changes. Specifically, arguments have been made that a positive correlation coefficient in the applicant sample need not imply a positive correlation in the selected sample. This argument has been made in the context of response distortion by candidates, and claims that the correlation coefficient does not take into account that fakers rise to the top. However, the important point to note is that the correlation coefficient is designed to index the usefulness of a predictor in the population of applicants (not in the selected group of employees).

To estimate the validity in the population of applicants, researchers have developed range restriction correction formulae. Thorndike (1949) distinguished between direct range restriction on the predictor, indirect range restriction on a third variable, and restriction on the criterion. Although all three are likely to occur in the real world context, the linearity assumptions made in the regression analysis preclude correction for more than one type of range restriction. Sackett and Yang (2000) succinctly discussed range restriction in selection and present a conceptual framework. Ree, Carretta, Earles and Albert (1994) presented a computer program to implement Lawley's (1943) multivariate correction for range restriction. Salgado (1997b), using formulae derived by Bobko and Rieck (1980), developed a computer program to estimate the sampling error of range restriction corrected correlation. Aguinis and Whitehead (1997) demonstrated that indirect range restriction could increase the sampling variance of the correlation by as much as 8.5%.

Meta-analytic cumulation of validities has employed artifact distributions. Given that range restriction information is not reported in all individual studies, meta-analysts have compiled distributions of values indexing range restriction (e.g., ratios of restricted to unrestricted standard deviations) from existing literature (e.g., test manuals, national norm samples, etc.). Some researchers (Hartigan & Wigdor, 1989) have questioned the appropriateness of such correction. However, research has shown that making corrections results in better estimates. Sackett and Ostgaard (1994) showed that using national norms in lieu of job-specific applicant pool norms is appropriate for cognitive ability. Ones and Viswesvaran (1999) using a large database of over 85,000 job applicants across 255 jobs demonstrated that for the Big Five personality scores national norms are comparable to job-specific applicant pool standard deviation.

In addition to range restriction, the correlation coefficient is affected by unreliability in the measures correlated. In earlier years, meta-analysts

combined different forms of reliability in one distribution. Schmidt and Hunter (1996) presented cogent arguments for the need to separate the different types of reliability estimates (e.g., interrater, intrarater) and use the appropriate ones for correction in meta-analyses. Viswesvaran, Ones and Schmidt (1996) presented artifact distributions of different types of reliability estimates (interrater, alphas, test–retest) for different dimensions of job performance as well as for overall job performance. Reliability estimates were provided for peer and supervisor ratings separately (Viswesvaran et al., 1996). Rothstein (1990) showed that interrater reliability improved with opportunity to observe. Salgado and Moscoso (1996) compared reliability estimates in civilian and military settings. Conway, Jako and Goodman (1995) presented distributions of reliability estimates for interviewer assessments.

CONCLUSIONS

Personnel selection is a central topic in our field. A review of salient trends in research and practice shows that we have come a long way in the past 100 years. At the turn of the millennium, we stand poised to address the new challenges based on the solid statistical and theoretical advances made to date. Considering that job performance is a concept with multiple facets and elements, and that the main goal of personnel selection, from a professional point of view, is to predict job performance, we have some research suggestions:

1. New studies should be devoted to investigating the criterion-related validity of personnel selection methods for predicting alternative criteria, such as, career progress, income, counterproductivity and organizational delinquency (e.g., absenteeism, theft, substance abuse), tenure, job satisfaction, performance ratings by self, peers, and customers, promotability, leadership, work accidents and injuries, and team efficiency. There is a lot of work to be done.

2. New assessment tools are currently being developed (e.g., video simulations, virtual-reality tests). These new instruments will probably be more accurate in their measurement, have more face validity, and be better accepted by applicants. However, three questions should be answered before generalized implementation of these techniques: (a) What constructs are assessed by these new techniques? (b) What is their criterion validity and what is their incremental validity over the validity of less sophisticated procedures? and (c) What is their cost-effectiveness using multiple criteria, not only job performance criteria, but also total quality criteria (see for example Rynes and

Trank, 1999, for a review of total quality systems and human resources management)?

3. A consensus should be reached concerning the mean reliabilities of the main predictors in personnel selection as well as the typical range restriction ratios found in those studies. A similar consensus should be reached for job performance reliability, and about its facets and elements (e.g., Viswesvaran et al., 1996). This consensus would enhance comparisons between different meta-analyses and would probably produce a clearer description about whether or not the differences found are caused by differences in the studies or by differences in the distributions of the artifactual errors when correction for these statistical artifacts are made.

4. Issues in team selection, assessing team effectiveness, and selection in a global context, need to be thoroughly investigated. The applicability of our predictors across cultures need to be further explored.

5. Very sparse literature exists on topics such as (a) predictor intercorrelations, (b) differential validity for different group, predictor and criteria combinations, (c) bias analysis for different group, predictor and criteria combinations, (d) differential item functioning for different group and predictor combinations, (e) single group validity for different group, predictor, and criterion combinations, and so forth. Future research should attempt to fill the void in the literature.

Despite these research needs to enhance the global practice of personnel selection, there are some research findings from the literature which are cause for optimism. For example, it is now well-established that job performance = f (ability, conscientiousness). Bright and hard-working individuals do better on their jobs. Knowing that ability predicts overall job performance with a validity of .52, and conscientiousness predicts performance with a validity of .23 across jobs and situations is similar to knowing that water on average freezes at 0 degrees Celsius (32 degrees Fahrenheit). The fact that the freezing and boiling points of water vary by altitude does not detract from the usefulness of this information. Further, yes, both ability and conscientiousness are both multidimensional constructs. Yet, knowing that water is made up of hydrogen and oxygen atoms does not make the concept of water scientifically or practically useless!

We have come a long way indeed in personnel selection during the past 100 years. As work psychologists around the globe continue to conduct primary studies as well as meta-analyses for predictors used in different cultures, the emerging picture appears to be that validities for most popular selection tools can be generalized cross-culturally. Indeed, reviewing meta-analytic evidence from multiple countries and writing this chapter has convinced us that ability and some other predictors (e.g., personality-based predictors such as conscientiousness) are generalizably valid across cultures. There appear to be some scientific principles in work psychology that are universally applicable.

REFERENCES

Aamodt, M.G., Bryan, D.A., & Whitcomb, A.J. (1993). Predicting performance with letters of recommendation. *Public Personnel Management, 22*, 81–90.

Ackerman, P.L., & Heggested, E.D. (1997). Intelligence, personality and interests: Evidence for overlapping traits. *Psychological Bulletin, 121*, 219–245.

Aguinis, H., & Whitehead, R. (1997). Sampling variance in the correlation coefficient under indirect range restriction: Implications for validity generalization. *Journal of Applied Psychology, 82*, 528–538.

Almagor, M., Tellegen, A., & Waller, N.G. (1995). The Big Seven model: A cross-cultural replication and further exploration of the basic dimensions of natural language trait descriptors. *Journal of Personality and Social Psychology, 69*(2), 300–307.

Altink, W.M.M. (1991). Construction and validation of a biodata selection instrument. *European Work and Organizational Psychologist, 1*, 245–270.

Anderson, N., & Fletcher, C. (in press). Telephone based selection interviews: A field study modeling interviewer impression formation and decision making. *Journal of Occupational and Organizational Psychology*,

Anderson, N., Payne, T., Ferguson, E., & Smith, T. (1994). Assessor decision making, information processing and assessor decision strategies in a British assessment centre. *Personnel Review, 23*, 52–62.

Arthur, W. Jr., Doverspike, D., & Barrett, G.V. (1996). Development of a job analysis-based procedure for weighting and combining content-related tests into a single test battery score. *Personnel Psychology, 49*(4), 971–985.

Arvey, R.D., Landon, T.E., Nutting, S.M., & Maxwell, S.E. (1992). Development of physical ability tests for police officers: A construct validation approach. *Journal of Applied Psychology, 77*, 996–1009.

Asher, J.J., & Sciarrino, J.A. (1974). Realistic work sample tests: A review, *Personnel Psychology, 27*(4), 519–533.

ASPA (1983). ASPA-BNA Survey No. 45: Employee selection practices. Washington, DC: Bureau of National Affairs.

Baron, H., Ryan, A.M., & Page, R.C. (1998). *Results of an international recruitment and selection study*. Paper presented at the symposium 'Selection practices around the world' in the 24th International Congress of Applied Psychology, San Francisco, CA, August.

Barrick, M.R., & Mount, M.K. (1991). The Big Five personality dimensions and job performance: A meta-analysis. *Personnel Psychology, 44*, 1–26.

Barrick, M., Mount, M.K., & Strauss, J.P. (1993). Conscientiousness and performance of sales representatives: Test of the mediating effects of goal setting. *Journal of Applied Psychology, 78,* 715–722.

Barrick, M.R., Stewart, G.L., Neubert, M.J., & Mount, M.K. (1998). Relating member ability and personality to work-team processes and team effectiveness. *Journal of Applied Psychology, 83*(3), 377–391.

Barry, B., & Stewart, G.L. (1997). Composition, process, and performance in self-managed groups: The role of personality. *Journal of Applied Psychology, 82*(1), 62–78.

Bartram, D. & Baxter, P. (1996). Validation of the Cathay Pacific Airways pilot selection program. *International Journal of Aviation Psychology, 6,* 149–169.

Bevan, S., & Fryatt, J. (1988). *Employee selection in the U.K.* Falmer, Sussex: Institute of Manpower Studies.

Blakeley, B.R., Quiñones, M.A., Crawford, M.S., & Jago, I.A. (1994). The validity of isometric strength tests. *Personnel Psychology, 47,* 247–274.

Bliesener, T. (1996). Methodological moderators in validating biographical data in personnel selection. *Journal of Occupational and Organizational Psychology, 69,* 107–120.

Block, J. (1995). A contrarian view of the five-factor approach to personality description. *Psychological Bulletin, 117,* 187–217.

Bobko, P., & Rieck, A. (1980). Large sample estimators for standard errors of functions of correlation coefficients. *Applied Psychological Measurement, 4,* 385–398.

Bobko, P., Roth, P.L., & Potosky, D. (1999). Derivation and implications of a meta-analytic matrix incorporating cognitive ability, alternative predictors, and job performance, *Personnel Psychology, 52*(3), 561–589.

Boehm, V.R. (1977). Differential prediction: A methodological artifact? *Journal of Applied Psychology, 62*(2), 146–154.

Bond, M.H., Nakazato, H.S., & Shiraishi, D. (1975). Universality and distinctiveness in dimensions of Japanese person perception. *Journal of Cross-Cultural Psychology, 6,* 346–355.

Borkenau, P., & Ostendorf, F. (1990). Comparing exploratory and confirmatory factor analysis: A study of the 5-factor model of personality. *Personality and Individual Differences, 11,* 515–524.

Borman, W.C., Hanson, M.A., Oppler, S.H., Pulakos, E.D., & White, L.A. (1993). Role of early supervisory experience in supervisor performance. *Journal of Applied Psychology, 78,* 443–449.

Borman, W.C., White, L.A., Pulakos, E.D., & Oppler, S.H. (1991). Models of supervisory job performance ratings. *Journal of Applied Psychology, 76,* 863–872.

Brandt, C. (1987). The importance of general intelligence. In S. Modgil & C. Modgil (Eds.), *Arthur Jensen: Consensus and controversy.* New York: Palmer Press.

Brown, B.K., & Campion, M.K. (1994). Biodata phenomenology: Recruiters' perceptions and use of biographical information in resume screening. *Journal of Applied Psychology, 79,* 897–908.

Brown, S.H. (1981). Validity generalization and situational moderators in life insurance industry. *Journal of Applied Psychology, 66,* 664–670.

Bureau of National Affairs (1988). *Recruiting and selection procedures* (May, pp. 17–24). Washington, DC: Bureau of National Affairs.

Campbell, J.P. (1996). Group differences and personnel decisions: Validity, fairness, and affirmative action. *Journal of Vocational Behavior, 49*(2), 122–158.

Campbell, J.P., McCloy, R.A., Oppler, S.H., & Sager, C.E. (1993). A theory of performance. In N.E. Schmitt & W.C. Borman (Eds.), *Personnel selection in organizations* (pp. 35–70). San Francisco, CA: Jossey-Bass.

Campion, M.A., Campion, J.E., & Hudson, J.P. (1994). Structured interviewing: A note on incremental validity and alternative question types. *Journal of Applied Psychology, 79,* 998–1002.

Campion, M.A., Pursell, E.D., & Brown, B.K. (1988). Structured interviewing: Raising the psychometric properties of the employment interview. *Personnel Psychology, 41*(1), 25–42.

Carlson, K.D., Scullen, S.E., Schmidt, F.L., Rothstein, H., & Erwin, F. (1999). Generalizable biographical data validity can be achieved without multi-organizational development and keying. *Personnel Psychology, 52*(3), 731–755.

Carretta, T.R., & Doub, T.W. (1998). Group differences in the role of g and prior job knowledge in the acquisition of subsequent job knowledge. *Personality and Individual Differences, 24*(5), 585–593.

Carretta, T.R., & Ree, M.J. (1994). Pilot-candidate selection method: Sources of validity. *International Journal of Aviation Psychology, 4*(2), 103–117.

Carretta, T.R., & Ree, M.J. (1997). Expanding the nexus of cognitive and psychomotor abilities. *International Journal of Selection and Assessment, 5,* 149–158.

Carretta, T.R., & Ree, M.J. (2000). General and specific cognitive and psychomotor abilities in personnel selection. The prediction of training and job performance. *International Journal of Selection and Assessment, 8,* 227–236.

Carroll, J.B. (1993). *Human cognitive abilities: A survey of factor-analytic studies.* New York, NY: Cambridge University Press.

Cascio, W.F., Goldstein, I.L., Outtz, J., & Zedeck, S. (1995). Twenty issues and answers about sliding bands. *Human Performance, 8*(3), 227–242.

Cellar, D.F., Miller, M.L., Doverspike, D.D., & Klawsky, J.D. (1996). Comparison of factor structures and criterion-related validity coefficients for two measures of personality based on the five factor model. *Journal of Applied Psychology, 81,* 694–704.

Chaiken, S.R., Kyllonen, P.C., & Tirre, W.C. (2000). Organization and components of psychomotor ability. *Cognitive Psychology, 40,* 198–226.

Chan, D. (1996). Criterion and construct validation of an assessment centre. *Journal of Occupational and Organizational Psychology, 69,* 167–181.

Chan, D. (1998). Functional relations among constructs in the same content domain at different levels of analysis:

A typology of composition models. *Journal of Applied Psychology*, 83(2), 234–246.

Cliff, N., & Caruso, J.C. (1998). Reliable component analysis through maximizing composite reliability. *Psychological Methods*, 3(3), 291–308.

Cohen, B., Moses, J.L., & Byham, W.C. (1974). *The validity of assessment centers: A literature review.* Pittsburgh, PA: Development Dimensions Press.

Collins, J., Schmidt, F.L., Sanchez-Ku, M., Thomas, L.E., & McDaniel, M. (1999). Predicting assessment center ratings from cognitive ability and personality. Paper presented at the 14th Annual Conference of the SIOP, Atlanta, Georgia, April 29–May 2.

Conley, J.J. (1985). A personality theory of adulthood and aging. In R. Hogan & W.H. Jones (Eds.), *Perspectives in Personality* (Vol. 1, pp. 81–115).

Conway, J.M., Jako, R.A., & Goodman, D.F. (1995). A meta-analysis of interrater and internal consistency reliability of selection interviews. *Journal of Applied Psychology*, 80(5), 565–579.

Cook, M. (1998). *Personnel selection: Adding value through people* (3rd ed.). West Sussex: John Wiley & Sons.

Costa, P.T. (1996). Work and personality: Use of the NEO-PI-R in industrial/organizational psychology. *Applied Psychology: An International Review*, 45 225–241.

Costa, P.T., & McCrae, R.R. (1985). *The NEO personality inventory manual.* Odessa, FL: Psychological Assessment Resources.

Costa, P.T., & McCrae, R.R. (1988). From catalog to classification: Murray's needs and the five-factor model. *Journal of Personality and Social Psychology*, 55, 258–265.

Costa, P. Jr., & McCrae, R.R. (1992a). *The revised NEO Personality Inventory (NEO PI-R) and NEO Five-Factor Inventory (NEO-FFI) professional manual.* Odessa, FL: Psychological Assessment Resources.

Costa, P.T., & McCrae, R.R. (1992b). Four ways five factors are basic. *Personality and Individual Differences*, 13(6), 653–665.

Costa, P.T. Jr., & McCrae, R.R. (1995a). Domains and facets: Hierarchical personality assessment using the Revised NEO Personality Inventory. *Journal of Personality Assessment*, 64, 21–50.

Costa, P.T. Jr., & McCrae, R.R. (1995b). Solid ground in the wetlands of personality: A reply to Block. *Psychological Bulletin*, 117, 216–220.

Cronbach, L.J. (1970). *Essentials of psychological testing.* NY: Harper & Row.

Dalessio, A.T., Crosby, M.M., & McManus, M.A. (1996). Stability of biodata keys and dimensions across English-speaking countries: A test of the cross-situational hypothesis. *Journal of Business and Psychology*, 10(3), 289–296.

Dalessio, A.T., & Silverhart, T.A. (1994). Combining biodata test and interview information: Predicting decisions and performance criteria. *Personnel Psychology*, 47(2), 303–315.

Dany, F., & Torchy, V. (1994). Recruitment and selection in Europe: Policies, practices and methods. In C. Brewster & Hegewisch (Eds.), *Policy and practice in European human resource management: The Price Waterhouse Cranfield Survey.* London, UK: Routledge.

Day, D.V., & Silverman, S.B. (1989). Personality and job performance: Evidence of incremental validity. *Personnel Psychology*, 42, 25–36.

Di Milia, L., Smith, P.A., & Brown, D.F. (1994). Management selection in Australia: A comparison with British and French findings. *International Journal of Selection and Assessment*, 2, 80–90.

Digman, J.M. (1990). Personality Structure: Emergence of the Five Factor Model. *Annual Review of Psychology*, 41, 417–440.

Digman, J.M., & Takemoto-Chock, N.K. (1981). Factors in the natural language of personality: Re-analysis and comparison of six major studies. *Multivariate Behavioral Research*, 16, 146–170.

Dipboye, R.L. (1997). Structured selection interviews: Why do they work? Why are they underutilized? In N. Anderson & P. Herriot (Eds.), *International Handbook of Selection and Assessment* (pp. 455–473). London, UK: John Wiley & Sons.

Dobson, P., & Williams, A. (1989). The validation of the selection of male British Army officers. *Journal of Occupational Psychology*, 62, 313–325.

Drasgow, F., & Olson-Buchanan, J.B. (Eds.) (1999). *Innovations in computerized assessment.* Mahwah, NJ: Lawrence Erlbaum Associates.

Dunnette, M.D. (1972). *Validity study results for jobs relevant to the petroleum refining industry.* Washington, DC: American Petroleum Institute.

Dye, D.A., Reck, M., & McDaniel, M.A. (1993). The validity of job knowledge measures. *International Journal of Selection and Assessment*, 1, 153–157.

Ellingson, J.E. (1999). Social desirability in personality measurement for personnel selection: Issues of applicant comparison and construct validity. Unpublished doctoral dissertation, University of Minnesota, Minneapolis, MN.

Eysenck, H.J. (1990). Biological dimensions of personality. In L.A. Pervin et al. (Eds.), *Handbook of personality: Theory and research* (pp. 244–276). New York, NY: The Guilford Press.

Eysenck, H.J. (1991a). Dimensions of Personality: The biosocial approach to personality. In J. Strelau & A. Angleitner et al. (Eds.), *Explorations in temperament: International perspectives on theory and measurement* (pp. 87–103). New York, NY: Plenum Press.

Eysenck, H.J. (1991b). Dimensions of personality: 16, 5, or 3? – Criteria for a taxonomic paradigm. *Personality and Individual Differences*, 12, 773–790.

Eysenck, H.J. (1994a). Normality–abnormality and the three-factor model of personality. In S. Strack & M. Lorr et al. (Eds.), *Differentiating normal and abnormal personality* (pp. 3–25). New York, NY: Springer Publishing Co, Inc.

Eysenck, H. (1994b). The Big Five or giant three: Criteria for a paradigm. In C.F. Halverson, Jr. & G.A. Kohnstamm et al. (Eds.), *The developing structure of temperament and personality from infancy to adulthood* (pp. 37–51). Hillsdale, NJ: Lawrence Erlbaum Associates.

Eysenck, H.J. (1998). *Dimensions of personality*. New Brunswick, NJ: Transaction Publishers.

Feingold, A. (1994). Gender differences in personality: A meta-analysis. *Psychological Bulletin, 116*(3), 429–456.

Feltham, R. (1988). Validity of a police assessment centre: a 1–19-year follow-up. *Journal of Occupational Psychology, 61*, 129–144.

Finger, M.S., & Ones, D.S. (1999). Psychometric equivalence of the computer and booklet forms of the MMPI: A meta-analysis, *Psychological Assessment, 11*(1), 58–66.

Fiske, D.W. (1949). Consistency of the factorial structures of personality ratings from different sources. *Journal of Abnormal and Social Psychology, 44*, 329–344.

Fleishman, E.A. (1954). Dimensional analysis of psychomotor abilities. *Journal of Experimental Psychology, 48*, 437–454.

Fleishman, E.A., & Mumford, M.D. (1991). Evaluating classifications of job behavior: A construct validation of the ability requirement scales. *Personnel Psychology, 44*, 523–575.

Fleishman, E.A., & Quaintance, M.K. (1984). *Taxonomies of human performance: The description of human tasks*. New York: Academic Press.

Fleishman, E.A., & Reilly, M.E. (1991). *Human abilities: Their definition, measurement, and job task requirement*. Palo Alto, CA: Consulting Psychologists Press.

Funke, U., Krauss, J., Schuler, H., & Stapf, K.H. (1987). Zur prognostizierbarkeit wissenchaftlich-tecnischer Leistungen mittels Personvariablen: eine meta-analyse der validitat diagnosticher verfahren im bereich forschung und entwicklung. *Gruppendynamik, 18*, 407–428.

Gandy, J.A., Dye, D.A., & MacLane, C.N. (1994). Federal government selection: The individual achievement record. In G.S. Stokes & M.D. Mumford & W.A. Owens (Eds.), *Biodata handbook: Theory, research, and use of biographical information in selection and performance prediction* (pp. 275–309). Palo Alto, CA: Consulting Psychologists Press.

Gaugler, B.B., Rosenthal, D.B., Thornton, G.C., & Bentson, C. (1987). Meta-analysis of assessment center validity. *Journal of Applied Psychology, 72*, 493–511.

Ghiselli, E.E. (1973). The validity of aptitude tests in personnel selection. *Personnel Psychology, 26*, 461–477.

Ghiselli, E.E., & Barthol, R.P. (1953). The validity of personality inventories in the selection of employees. *Journal of Applied Psychology, 37*, 18–20.

Goffin, R.D., Rothstein, M.G., & Johnston, N.G. (1996). Personality testing and the assessment center: Incremental validity for managerial selection. *Journal of Applied Psychology, 81*, 746–756.

Goldberg, L.R. (1990). An alternative 'description of personality': The Big Five factor structure. *Journal of Personality and Social Psychology, 59*(6), 1216–1229.

Goldberg, L.R. (1992). The development of markers of the Big-Five factor structure. *Psychological Assessment, 4*, 26–42.

Goldberg, L.R. (1993). The structure of phenotypic personality traits. *American Psychologist, 48*(1), 26–34.

Goldberg, L.R., Sweeney, D., Merenda, P.F., & Hughes, J.E., Jr. (1998). Demographic variables and personality: The effects of gender, age, education, and ethnic/racial status on self-descriptions of personality attributes, *Personality & Individual Differences, 24*(3), 393–403.

Goldstein, H.W., Yusko, K.P., Braverman, E.P., Smith, D.B., & Chung, B. (1998). The role of cognitive ability in the subgroup differences and incremental validity of assessment center exercises. *Personnel Psychology, 51*(2), 357–374.

Gottfredson, L.S. (1997). Why *g* matters: The complexity of everyday life. *Intelligence, 24*, 79–132.

Gough, H.G., & Heilbrun, A.B. Jr. (1983). *The Adjective Checklist Manual: 1983 Edition*. Palo Alto, CA: Consulting Psychologists Press.

Gould, S.J. (1981). *The mismeasure of man*. New York: Norton.

Gowing, M.K., & Slivinski, L.W. (1994). A review of North American selection procedures: Canada and the United States of America. *International Journal of Selection and Assessment, 2*, 103–114.

Guion, R.M. (1998). *Assessment, measurement, and prediction for personnel decisions*. Mahwah, NJ: Lawrence Erlbaum Associates.

Guion, R.M., & Gottier, R.F. (1965). Validity of personality measures in personnel selection. *Personnel Psychology, 18*(2), 135–164.

Gunter, B., Furnham, A., & Drakeley, R. (1993). *Biodata: Biographical indicators of business performance*. London, UK: Routledge.

Guzzo, R.A., & Salas, E. (Eds.) (1995). *Team effectiveness and decision making in organizations*. San Francisco: Jossey-Bass.

Hall, J.A. (1984). *Nonverbal sex differences: Communication accuracy and expressive style*. Baltimore, Johns Hopkins University Press.

Harris, M.M. (1998). The structured interview: What constructs are being measured? In R. Eder & M.M. Harris (Eds.), *The employment interview: Theory, research and practice* (2nd ed.). Thousand Oaks, CA: Sage.

Harris, M.M., Backer, A.S., & Smith, D.E. (1993). Does the assessment center scoring method affect the cross-situational consistency of ratings? *Journal of Applied Psychology, 78*, 675–679.

Harris, M.M., Dworkin, J.B., & Park, J. (1990). Preemployment screening procedures: How human resource managers perceived them. *Journal of Business and Psychology, 4*(3), 279–292.

Hartigan, J.A., Wigdor, A.K. (Eds.) (1989). *Fairness in employment testing: Validity generalization, minority issues, and the General Aptitude Test Battery*. National Research Council, Commission on Behavioral and Social Sciences and Education Study. Washington, DC: National Academy Press.

Hirsh, H.R., Northrop, L.C., & Schmidt, F.L. (1986). Validity generalization results for law enforcement occupations. *Personnel Psychology, 39*(2), 399–420.

Hogan, J. (1991). Structure of physical performance in occupational tasks. *Journal of Applied Psychology, 76*, 495–507.

Hogan, J., & Hogan, R. (1989). How to measure employee reliability. *Journal of Applied Psychology, 74,* 273–279.

Hogan, J., & Hogan, R. (1991). Levels of analysis in the big five theory: The structure of self-description. Paper presented at the Sixth Annual Conference of the Society for Industrial and Organizational Psychology, St. Louis, MO, April.

Hogan, J., & Quigley, A. (1994). Effects of preparing for physical ability tests. *Public Personnel Management, 23,* 85–104.

Hough, L.M. (1992). The 'Big Five' personality variables-construct confusion: Description versus prediction. *Human Performance, 5,* 139–155.

Hough, L.M. (1998). Personality at work: Issues and evidence. In M. Hakel (Ed.), *Beyond multiple choice: Evaluating alternatives to traditional testing for selection* (pp. 131–159). Hillsdale, NJ: Erlbaum Associates.

Hough, L.M., Eaton, N.K., Dunnette, M.D., Kamp, J.D., & McCloy, R.A. (1990). Criterion-related validities of personality constructs and the effect of response distortion on those validities [monograph]. *Journal of Applied Psychology, 75,* 581–595.

Hough, L.M., & Oswald, F.L. (2000). Personnel selection: Looking toward the future – Remembering the past. *Annual Review of Psychology, 51,* 631–664.

Hough, L., & Paullin, C. (1994). Construct-oriented scale construction: The rational approach. In G. S. Stokes & M.D. Mumford et al. (Eds.) *Biodata handbook: Theory, research, and use of biographical information in selection and performance prediction* (pp. 109–145). Palo Alto, CA: CPP Books.

Huffcutt, A.I., & Arthur, W. (1994). Hunter and Hunter (1984) revisited: Interview validity for entry-level jobs. *Journal of Applied Psychology, 79,* 184–190.

Huffcutt, A.I., & Roth, P.L. (1998). Racial group differences in employment interview evaluations. *Journal of Applied Psychology, 83*(2), 179–189.

Huffcutt, A.I., Roth, P.L., & McDaniel, M.A. (1996). A meta-analytic investigation of cognitive ability in employment interview evaluations: Moderating characteristics and implications for incremental validity. *Journal of Applied Psychology, 81,* 459–474.

Hunter, J.E. (1980). Validity generalization for 12,000 jobs: An application of synthetic validity and validity generalization to the general aptitude test battery (GATB). Washington, DC: US Department of Labor: US Employment Service.

Hunter, J.E. (1986). Cognitive ability, cognitive aptitudes, job knowledge, and job performance. *Journal of Vocational Behavior, 29,* 340–362.

Hunter, J.E., & Hirsh, H.R. (1987). Applications of meta-analysis. In C.L. Cooper & I.T. Robertson (Eds.), *International review of industrial and organizational psychology* (pp. 321–357). Chichester: John Wiley & Sons.

Hunter, J.E., & Hunter, R.F. (1984). Validity and utility of alternate predictors of job performance. *Psychological Bulletin, 96,* 72–98.

Hunter, J.E., Schmidt, F.L., & Hunter, R. (1979). Differential validity of employment tests by race: A comprehensive review and analysis. *Psychological Bulletin, 86*(4), 721–735.

Hunter, J.E., Schmidt, F.L., & Judiesch, M.K. (1990). Individual differences in output variability as a function of job complexity. *Journal of Applied Psychology, 75*(1), 28–42.

Iacono, W.G., & Lykken, D.T. (1997). The validity of the lie detector: Two surveys of scientific opinion. *Journal of Applied Psychology, 82*(3), 426–433.

Jansen, P., & Stoop, B. (1994). Assessment centre graduate selection: Decision processes, validity, and evaluation by candidates. *International Journal of Selection and Assessment, 2,* 193–208.

Jensen, A.R. (1998). *The g factor: The science of mental ability.* Wesport, CT: Praeger.

John, O.P. (1990). The search for basic dimensions of personality: A review and critique. In P. McReynolds & J.C. Rosen (Eds.), *Advances in psychological assessment* (Vol. 7, pp. 1–37). New York, NY: Plenum Press.

Kleinmann, M. (1993). Are rating dimensions in assessment centers transparent for participants? Consequences for criterion and construct validity. *Journal of Applied Psychology, 78,* 988–993.

Klimoski, R., & Jones, R.G. (1995). Staffing for effective group decision making: Key issues in matching people and teams. In R.A. Guzzo & E. Salas (Eds.), *Team effectiveness and decision making in organizations* (pp. 291–332). San Francisco: Jossey-Bass.

Klimoski, R., & Zukin, L.N. (1999). Selection and staffing for team effectiveness. In E. Sundstrom (Ed.). *Supporting work team effectiveness* (pp. 63–91). San Francisco: Jossey-Bass.

Kling, K.C., Hyde, J.S., Showers, C.J., & Buswell, B.N. (1999). Gender differences in self-esteem: A meta-analysis. *Psychological Bulletin, 125*(4), 470–500.

Kranzler, J.H., & Jensen, A.R. (1991). The nature of psychometric g: Unitary process or a number of independent processes? *Intelligence, 15,* 397–422.

Kyllonen, P.C. (1993). Aptitude testing inspired by information processing: A test of the four-sources model. *Journal of General Psychology, 120,* 375–405.

Latham, G.P., & Skarlicki, D.P. (1996). The effectiveness of situational, patterned behaviour, and conventional structured interviews in minimizing in-group favouritism of Canadian francophone managers. *Applied Psychology: An International Review, 45,* 177–184.

Lawley, D.N. (1943). A note on Karl Pearson's selection formulae. *Proceedings of the Royal Society of Edinburgh, 62,* 28–30.

LePine, J.A., Hollenbeck, J.R., Ilgen, D.R., & Hedlund, J. (1997). Effects of individual differences on the performance of hierarchical decision-making teams: Much more than g. *Journal of Applied Psychology, 82*(5), 803–811.

Levine, E.L., Spector, P.E., Menon, P.E., Narayanon, L., & Cannon-Bowers, J. (1996). Validity generalization for cognitive, psychomotor, and perceptual tests for craft jobs in the utility industry. *Human Performance*, 9, 1–22.

Levy-Leboyer, C. (1994). Selection and assessment in Europe. In H.C. Triandis, M.D. Dunnette & L.M. Hough (Eds.), *Handbook of Industrial and Organizational Psychology* (Vol. 4, pp. 173–190). Palo Alto, CA: Consulting Psychologists Press.

Li, H., Rosenthal, R., & Rubin, D.B. (1996). Reliability of measurement in psychology: From Spearman-Brown to maximal reliability, *Psychological Methods*, 1(1), 98–107.

Lievens, F. (1999a). Development of an assessment center. *European Journal of Psychological Assessment*, 15(2), 117–126.

Lievens, F. (1999b). Een generaliseerbaarheidsanalyse van assessment center beoordelingen [A generalizability analysis of assessment center practice]. *Gedrag en Organisatie*, 12(1), 16–31.

Livneh, H., & Livneh, C. (1989). The five-factor model of personality. Is evidence of its cross-measure validity premature? *Personality and Individual Differences*, 10, 75–80.

Loher, B.T., Hazer, J.T., Tsai, A., Tilton, K., & James, J. (1997). Letters of reference: A process approach. *Journal of Business and Psychology*, 11, 339–355.

Lorr, M., & Youniss, R.P. (1973). An inventory of interpersonal style. *Journal of Personality Assessment*, 37, 165–173.

Lubinski, D. (2000). Scientific and social significance of assessing individual differences: 'Sinking shafts at a few critical points'. *Annual Review of Psychology*, 51, 405–444.

Lykken, D.T., Bouchard, T.J., McGue, M., & Tellegen, A. (1993). Heritability of interests: A twin study. *Journal of Applied Psychology*, 78(4), 649–661.

Maccoby, E.E., & Jacklin, C.N. (1974). *The psychology of sex differences*. Stanford, CA: Stanford University Press.

Mael, F.A., & Ashforth, B.E. (1995). Loyal from day one: biodata, organizational identification, and turnover among newcomers. *Personnel Psychology*, 48, 309–334.

Marsden, P.V. (1994). Selection methods in US establishments. *Acta Sociologica*, 37, 287–301.

McCloy, R.A., Campbell, J.P., & Cudeck, R. (1994). A confirmatory test of a model of performance determinants. *Journal of Applied Psychology*, 79, 493–505.

McCrae, R.R. (1989). Why I advocate the five factor model: Joint factor analyses of the NEO-PI with other instruments. In D.M. Buss & N. Cantor (Eds.), *Personality Psychology: Recent Trends and emerging directions*. New York: Springer-Verlag.

McCrae, R.R., & Costa, P.T. (1985). Updating Norman's 'adequacy taxonomy': Intelligence and personality dimensions in natural language and in questionnaires. *Journal of Personality and Social Psychology*, 49(3), 710–721.

McCrae, R.R., & Costa, P.T. (1987). Validation of the five-factor model of personality across instruments and observers. *Journal of Personality and Social Psychology*, 52(1), 81–90.

McCrae, R.R., & John, O.P. (1992). An introduction to the Five Factor model and its applications. *Journal of Personality*, 60, 175–216.

McDaniel, M.A., Finnegan, E.B., Morgeson, F.P., Campion, M.A., & Braverman, E.P. (1997). Predicting job performance from common sense. Paper presented at the 12th annual SIOP Conference, April, St. Louis.

McDaniel, M.A., & Nguyen, N.T. (2001) Situational judgment tests: A review of practice and constructs assessed. *International Journal of Selection and Assessment*, 9.

McDaniel, M.A., Whetzel, D.L., Schmidt, F.L., & Maurer, S. (1994). The validity of employment interviews: A comprehensive review and meta-analysis. *Journal of Applied Psychology*, 79, 599–616.

McHenry, J.J., Hough, L.M., Toquam, J.L., Hanson, M.L., & Ashworth, S. (1990). Project A validity results: the relationship between predictor and criterion domains. *Personnel Psychology*, 43, 335–354.

McHenry, J.J., & Schmitt, N. (1994). Multimedia testing. In M.G., Rumsey, C.B., Walker & J.H. Harris (Eds.), *Personnel selection and classification* (pp. 193–232). Hillsdale, NJ: Erlbaum.

Mead, A.D., & Drasgow, F. (1993). Equivalence of computerized and paper-and-pencil cognitive ability tests: A meta-analysis. *Psychological Bulletin*, 114(3), 449–458.

Michaelis, W., & Eysenck, H.J. (1971). The determination of personality inventory factor patterns and intercorrelations by changes in real-life motivation. *The Journal of Genetic Psychology*, 118, 223–234.

Milkovich, G.T., & Boudreau, J.W. (1994). *Human resource management* (7th ed.). Homewood, IL: Richard D. Irwin.

Mischel, W. (1968). *Personality and Assessment*. New York: Wiley.

Motowidlo, S.J., & Tippins, N. (1993). Further studies of the low-fidelity simulation in the form of a situational inventory. *Journal of Occupational and Organizational Psychology*, 66, 337–344.

Mumford, M.D., Stokes, G.S., & Owens, W.A. (1990). *Patterns of life history: The ecology of human individuality*. Hillsdale, NJ: Lawrence Erlbaum Associates.

Münsterberg, H. (1913). *Psychology and industrial efficiency*. Boston, MA: Houghton Mifflin [Original German version: Psychologie und Wirtschaftsleben. Leizip, Germany: J.A. Barth].

Murphy, K.R. (1994). Potential effects of banding as a function of test reliability. *Personnel Psychology*, 47, 477–496.

Murphy, K.R., Osten, K., & Myors, B. (1995). Modeling the effects of banding in personnel selection. *Personnel Psychology*, 48, 61–84.

Neter, E., & Ben-Shakhar, G. (1989). Predictive validity of graphological inferences: A meta-analytic approach. *Personality and Individual Differences*, 10, 737–745.

Noller, P. Law, H., & Comrey, A.L. (1987). Cattell, Comrey, and Eysenck personality factors compared: More evidence for the five robust factors? *Journal of Personality and Social Psychology*, 53, 775–782.

Norman, W.T. (1963). Toward an adequate taxonomy of personality attributes: Replicated factor structure in peer nomination personality ratings. *Journal of Abnormal and Social Psychology, 66,* 574–582.

Norman, W.T., & Goldberg, L.R. (1966). Raters, ratees, and randomness in personality structure. *Journal of Personality and Social Psychology, 4,* 681–691.

Normand, J., Lempert, R.O., & O'Brien, C.P. (1994). *Under the influence? Drugs and the American work force* (pp. 215–240). Washington, DC: National Academy Press.

Normand, J., Salyards, S.D., Mahoney, J.J. (1990). An evaluation of preemployment drug testing. *Journal of Applied Psychology, 75*(6), 629–639.

Olea, M.M., & Ree, M.J. (1994). Predicting pilot and navigator criteria: Not much more than g. *Journal of Applied Psychology, 79,* 845–851.

O'Leary, B.S. (1980). *College Grade Point Average as an Indicator of Occupational Success: An update.* Washington, DC: US Office of Personnel Management.

Ones, D.S., & Anderson, N. (1999). *Gender and ethnic group differences on personality scales: Some data from the UK.* Paper presented at the annual conference of the Society for Industrial and Organizational Psychology, Atlanta, GA, April.

Ones, D.S., & Viswesvaran, C. (1997). *Empirical and theoretical considerations in using conscientiousness measures in personnel selection.* Paper presented at the fifth European Congress of Psychology, Dublin, Ireland. July 6–11.

Ones, D.S., & Viswesvaran, C. (1998a). Integrity testing in organizations. In R.W. Griffin, A. O'Leary-Kelly & J.M. Collins (Eds.), *Dysfunctional Behavior in Organizations: Vol. 2. Nonviolent Behaviors in Organizations.* Greenwich, CT: JAI Press.

Ones, D.S., & Viswesvaran, C. (1998b). Gender, age and race differences on overt integrity tests: Analyses across four large-scale applicant data sets, *Journal of Applied Psychology, 83,* 35–42.

Ones, D.S., & Viswesvaran, C. (1998c, April). Relationships among integrity, interview, job knowledge and work sample measures: Implications for incremental validity. In D.S. Ones (Chair), *Multiple predictors, situational influences and incremental validity.* Symposium conducted at the annual conference of the Society for Industrial and Organizational Psychology, Dallas, TX.

Ones, D.S., & Viswesvaran, C. (1999). *Job-specific applicant pools and national norms for personality scales: Implications for range restriction corrections in validation research.* Paper presented at the annual conference of the Society for Industrial and Organizational Psychology, Atlanta, GA, April.

Ones, D.S., & Viswesvaran, C. (2001a). Integrity tests and other Criterion-Focused Occupational Personality Scales (COPS) used in personnel selection. *International Journal of Selection and Assessment, 9.*

Ones, D.S., & Viswesvaran, C. (2001b). Personality at work: Criterion-Focused Occupational Personality Scales (COPS) used in personnel selection. In B. Roberts & R.T. Hogan (Eds.), *Applied Personality Psychology.* Washington, DC: American Psychological Association.

Ones, D.S., Viswesvaran, C., & Reiss, A.D. (1996). Role of social desirability in personality testing for personnel selection: The red herring. *Journal of Applied Psychology, 81,* 660–679.

Ones, D.S., Viswesvaran, C., & Schmidt, F.L. (1993). Comprehensive meta-analysis of integrity test validities: Findings and implications for personnel selection and theories of job performance [Monograph]. *Journal of Applied Psychology, 78,* 679–703.

Orr, J.M., Sackett, P.R., & Mercer, M. (1989). The role of prescribed and nonprescribed behaviors in estimating the dollar value of performance. *Journal of Applied Psychology, 74,* 34–40.

Pamos, A. (1999). Virtual reality at a power plant. Technical chapter. In VAT Consortium (TEA, SA – Spain; OS – Italy, Hogrefe verlag – Germany, and GM – Switzerland). *Virtual Reality Assisted Psycho-Aptitude Testing Handbook.* Esprit project no. 22119. Bruxells: The European Commission.

Pearlman, K., Schmidt, F.L., & Hunter, J.E. (1980). Validity generalization results for test used to predict job proficiency and training success in clerical occupations. *Journal of Applied Psychology, 65,* 569–607.

Peres, S.H., & Garcia, J.R. (1962). Validity and dimensions of descriptive adjectives used in reference letters for engineering applicants. *Personnel Psychology, 15,* 279–286.

Pierce, C.A., & Aguinis, H.A. (1997). Using virtual reality technology in organizational behavior research. *Journal of Organizational Behavior, 18,* 407–410.

Pulakos, E.D., & Schmitt, N. (1996). An evaluation of two strategies for reducing adverse impact and their effects on criterion-related validity. *Human Performance, 9,* 241–258.

Raju, N.S., Bilgic, R., Edwards, J.E., & Fleer, P.F. (1997). Methodology review: Estimation of population validity and cross-validity, and the use of equal weights in prediction. *Applied Psychological Measurement, 21*(4), 291–305.

Raju, N.S., Bilgic, R., Edwards, J.E., & Fleer, P.F. (1999). Accuracy of population validity and cross-validity estimation: An empirical comparison of formula-based, traditional empirical, and equal weights procedures. *Applied Psychological Measurement, 23*(2), 99–115.

Raykov, T. (1997). Estimation of composite reliability for congeneric measures. *Applied Psychological Measurement, 21*(2), 173–184.

Ree, M.J., & Carretta, T.R. (1994). The correlation of general cognitive ability and psychomotor tracking tests. *International Journal of Selection and Assessment, 2,* 209–216.

Ree, M.J., & Carretta, T.R. (1997). What makes an aptitude test valid. In R. Dillon (Ed.), *Handbook of Testing* (pp. 65–81). Westport, CT: Greenwood Press.

Ree, M.J., & Carretta, T.R. (1998). General cognitive ability and occupational performance. In C.L. Cooper & I.T. Robertson (Eds.), *International Review of*

Industrial and Organizational Psychology (Vol. 13, pp. 159–184). London, UK: Wiley.

Ree, M.J., Carretta, T.R., Earles, J.A., & Albert, W. (1994). Sign changes when correction for range restriction: A note on Pearson's and Lawley's selection formulas. *Journal of Applied Psychology, 79,* 298–301.

Ree, M.J., & Earles, J.A. (1991). Predicting training success: Not much more than *g. Personnel Psychology, 44,* 321–332.

Ree, M.J., Earles, J.A., & Teachout, M. (1994). Predicting job performance: Not much more than *g. Journal Applied Psychology, 79,* 518–524.

Reilly, R.R., & Chao, G.T. (1982). Validity and fairness of some alternative employee selection procedures. *Personnel Psychology, 35,* 1–62.

Roberts, B.W., & DelVecchio, W.F. (2000). The rank-order consistency of personality traits from childhood to old age: A quantitative review of longitudinal studies, *Psychological Bulletin, 126,* 3–25.

Robertson, I.T., & Downs, S. (1989). Work-sample tests of trainability: A meta-analysis. *Journal of Applied Psychology, 74,* 402–410.

Robertson, I.T., & Makin, P.J. (1986). Management selection in Britain: A survey and critique. *Journal of Occupational Psychology, 59,* 45–57.

Roth, P.L., BeVier, C.A., Switzer, F.S. III, & Schippmann, J.S. (1996). Meta-analyzing the relationship between grades and job performance. *Journal of Applied Psychology, 81*(5), 548–556.

Roth, P.L., & Clarke, R.L. (1998). Meta-analyzing the relation between grades and salary. *Journal of Vocational Behavior, 53*(3), 386–400.

Rothstein, H.R. (1990). Interrater reliability of job performance ratings: Growth to asymptote level with increasing opportunity to observe. *Journal of Applied Psychology, 75,* 322–327.

Rothstein, H.R., Schmidt, F.L., Erwin, F.W., Owens, W.A., & Sparks, C.P. (1990). Biographical data in employment selection: Can validities be made generalizable?. *Journal of Applied Psychology, 75,* 175–184.

Ryan, A.M., McFarland, L., Baron, H., & Page, R. (1999). An international look at selection practices: Nation and culture as explanations for variability in practice. *Personnel Psychology, 52*(2), 359–391.

Rynes, S.L., & Trank, C.Q. (1999). Behavioral Science in the business school curriculum: Teaching in a changing institutional environment, *Academy of Management Review, 24,* 808–824.

Sackett, P.R., Burris, L.R., & Callahan, C. (1989). Integrity testing for personnel selection: An update. *Personnel Psychology, 42,* 491–529.

Sackett, P.R., & Dreher, G.F. (1982). Constructs and assessment center dimensions: Some troubling empirical findings. *Journal of Applied Psychology, 67*(4), 401–410.

Sackett, P.R., & Ellingson, J.E. (1997). The effects of forming multi-predictor composites on group differences and adverse impact. *Personnel Psychology, 50*(3), 707–721.

Sackett, P.R., & Ostgaard, D.J. (1994). Job-specific applicant pools and national norms for cognitive ability

tests: Implications for range restriction corrections in validation research. *Journal of Applied Psychology, 79,* 680–684.

Sackett, P.R., & Roth, L. (1991). A Monte Carlo examination of banding and rank order methods of test score use in personnel selection. *Human Performance, 4*(4), 279–295.

Sackett, P.R., & Roth, L. (1996). Multi-stage selection strategies: A Monte Carlo investigation of effects on performance and minority hiring. *Personnel Psychology, 49*(3), 549–572.

Sackett, P.R., & Wilk, S.L. (1994). Within-group norming and other forms of score adjustment in psychological testing. *American Psychologist, 49,* 929–954.

Sackett, P.R., & Yang, H. (2000). Correction for range restriction: An expanded typology. *Journal of Applied Psychology, 85*(1), 112–118.

Salgado, J.F. (1994). Validez de los tests de habilidades psicomotoras: Meta-analisis de los estudios publicados en Espana (1942–1990). [Validity of psychomotor ability tests: Meta-analysis of studies published in Spain]. *Revista de Psicología Social Aplicada, 4,* 25–42.

Salgado, J.F. (1997a). The five factor model of personality and job performance in the European Community. *Journal of Applied Psychology, 82,* 30–43.

Salgado, J.F. (1997b). Valcor: A program for estimating standard error, confidence intervals, and probability of corrected validity. *Behavior Research Methods, Instruments, and Computers, 29,* 464–467.

Salgado, J.F., & Anderson, N. (2001). Cognitive and GMA testing in the European Community: Issues and evidence. *Human Performance, 14.*

Salgado, J.F., & Lado, M. (2000). Validity generalization of video tests for predicting job performance ratings. Paper presented at the 15th Annual Conference of SIOP, New Orleans, Lousiana, April 14–16.

Salgado, J.F., & Moscoso, S. (1995). Validez de la entrevista conductual estructurada [Validity of structured behavioral interview]. *Revista de Psicología del Trabajo y las Organizaciones, 11,* 9–24.

Salgado, J.F., & Moscoso, S. (1996). Meta-analysis of interrater reliability of job performance ratings in validity studies of personnel selection. *Perceptual and Motor Skills, 83,* 1195–1201.

Salgado, J.F., & Moscoso, S. (1998). Within-setting variability of cognitive tests validity. Departmento of Social Psychology, University of Santiago de Compostela, Spain. Unpublished manuscript.

Salgado, J.F., & Moscoso, S. (2001). *Comprehensive meta-analysis of the construct validity of employment interview: A meta-analysis.* Manuscript submitted for publication.

Saxe, L., & Ben-Shakhar, G. (1999). Admissibility of polygraph tests: The application of scientific standards post-Daubert. *Psychology, Public Policy, and Law, 5*(1), 203–223

Schmidt, F.L. (1971). The relative efficiency of regression and simple unit predictor weights in applied differential psychology. *Educational and Psychological Measurement, 31*(3), 699–714.

Schmidt, F.L. (1988). The problem of group differences in ability test scores in employment selection. *Journal of Vocational Behavior, 33*(3), 272–292.

Schmidt, F.L. (1991). Why all banding procedures in personnel selection are logically flawed. *Human Performance, 4*, 265–278.

Schmidt, F.L., & Hunter, J.E. (1977). Development of a general solution to the problem of validity generalization, *Journal of Applied Psychology, 62*(5), 529–540.

Schmidt, F.L., & Hunter, J.E. (1992). Causal modeling of processes determining job performance. *Current Directions in Psychological Science, 1*, 89–92.

Schmidt, F.L., & Hunter, J.E. (1993). Tacit knowledge, practical intelligence, general mental ability, and job knowledge. *Current Directions in Psychological Science, 2*(1), 8–9.

Schmidt, F.L., & Hunter, J.E. (1995). The fatal internal contradiction in banding: Its statistical rationale is logically inconsistent with its operational procedures. *Human Performance, 8*, 203–214.

Schmidt, F.L., & Hunter, J.E. (1996). Measurement error in psychological research: Lessons from 26 research scenarios. *Psychological Methods, 1*(2), 199–223.

Schmidt, F.L., & Hunter, J.E. (1998). The validity and utility of selection methods in personnel psychology: Practical and theoretical implications of 85 years of research findings. *Psychological Bulletin, 124*(2), 262–274.

Schmidt, F.L., Hunter, J.E., & Caplan, J.R. (1981). Validity generalization results for two job groups in the petroleum industry. *Journal of Applied Psychology, 66*(3), 261–273.

Schmidt, F.L., Hunter, J.E., & Outerbridge, A.N. (1986). The impact of job experience and ability on job knowledge, work sample performance, and supervisory ratings of job performance. *Journal of Applied Psychology, 71*, 432–439.

Schmidt, F.L., & Kaplan, L.B. (1971). Composite versus multiple criteria: A review and resolution of the controversy. *Personnel Psychology, 24*, 419–434.

Schmidt, F.L., Ones, D.S., & Hunter, J.E. (1992). Personnel selection. *Annual Review of Psychology, 43*, 671–710.

Schmidt, F.L., & Rader, M. (1999). Exploring the boundary conditions for interview validity: Meta-analytic validity findings for a new interview type. *Personnel Psychology, 52*(2), 445–464.

Schmit, M.J., & Ryan, A.M. (1993). The Big Five in personnel selection: Factor structure in applicant and non-applicant populations. *Journal of Applied Psychology, 78*, 966–974.

Schmitt, N., & Chan, D. (1998). *Personnel selection.* Thousand Oaks, CA: Sage Publications.

Schmitt, N., Clause, C.S., & Pulakos, E.D. (1996). Subgroup differences associated with different measures of some common job-relevant constructs. In C.L. Cooper & I.T. Robertson (Eds.), *International Review of Industrial and Organizational Psychology* (Vol. 11, pp. 115–139). Chichester, UK: Wiley.

Schmitt, N., Gooding, R.Z., Noe, R.A., & Kirsch, M. (1984). Meta-analyses of validity studies published between 1964 and 1982 and the investigation of study characteristics. *Personnel Psychology, 37*, 407–422.

Schmitt, N., Rogers, W., Chan, D., Sheppard, L., & Jennings, D. (1997). Adverse impact and predictive efficiency of various predictor combinations. *Journal of Applied Psychology, 82*(5), 719–730.

Schneider, B. (1987). The people make the place. *Personnel Psychology, 40*(3), 437–453.

Schoenfeldt, L.F. (2001). From dust bowl empiricism to rational constructs in biographical data. *Human Resources Management.*

Scholz, G., & Schuler, H. (1993). Das nomologische netzwerk des assessment centers: eine meta-analyse. [The nomological network of the assessment center: A meta-analysis]. *Zeitschrift für Arbeits- und Organisations psychologie, 37*, 73–85.

Schuler, H. (1992). Das multimodale einstellungsinterview. [The multimodal employment interview]. *Diagnostica, 38*, 281–300.

Schuler, H. (1997). *Validity of multimodal interview.* Paper presented at the 8th European Congress of Work and Organizational Psychology, 2–5 April, Verona, Italy.

Schuler, H., Frier, D., & Kauffmann, M. (1993). *Personalauswahl im europäischen Vergleich.* Göttingen: Verlag für Angewandte Psychologie.

Schuler, H., & Moser, K. (1995). Die validität des multimodalen interviews. [Validity of multimodal interviews]. *Zeitschrift für Arbeit und Organisations psychologie, 39*, 2–12.

Schuler, H., Moser, K., Diemand, A., & Funke, U. (1995). Validitat eines einstelungsinterviews sur prognose des ausbildungerfolgs. [Validity of an employment interview for the prediction of training success]. *Zeitschrift für Pedagogische Psychologie, 9*, 45–54.

Schuler, H., Moser, K., & Funke, U. (1994). The moderating effect of rater–ratee-acquaintance on the validity of an assessment center. *Paper presented at 23rd International Congress of Applied Psychology*, Madrid, Spain.

Shackleton, V., & Newell, S. (1991). Management selection: A comparative survey of methods used in top British and French companies. *Journal of Occupational Psychology, 64*, 23–36.

Shackleton, V., & Newell, S. (1994). European management selection methods: A comparison of five countries. *International Journal of Assessment and Selection, 2*, 91–102.

Shackleton, V., & Newell, S. (1997). International assessment and selection. In N. Anderson & P. Herriot (Eds.), *International Handbook of Selection and Assessment.* Chichester, UK: Wiley.

Shore, T.H., Shore, L.M., & Thornton G.C. III (1992). Construct validity of self- and peer evaluations of performance dimensions in an assessment center. *Journal of Applied Psychology, 77*, 42–54.

Silvester, J., Anderson, N., Haddleton, E., Cunningham-Snell, & Gibb, A. (2000). A cross-modal comparison of telephone and face-to-face selection interviews in graduate recruitment. *International Journal of Selection and Assessment, 8*, 16–21.

Simmering, M.J., & Ones, D.S. (1994). *Personnel selection strategies for reducing drug and alcohol abuse on the job*. Paper presented at the 23rd meeting of the International Congress of Applied Psychology, Madrid, Spain, July.

Sinangil, H.K., Ones, D.S., & Jockin, V. (1999, April). *Survey of personnel selection tools and techniques in Turkey*. Paper presented at the annual conference of the European Association for Work and Organizational Psychology, Helsinki, Finland.

Smiderle, D., Perry, B.A., Cronshaw, S.F. (1994). Evaluation of video-based assessment in transit operator selection. *Journal of Business and Psychology, 9*, 3–22.

Snell, A.F., Stokes, G.S., Sands, M.M., & McBride, J.R. (1994). Adolescent life experiences as predictors of occupational attainment. *Journal of Applied Psychology, 79*(1), 131–141.

Sternberg, R.J. (1997). Tacit knowledge and job success. In N. Anderson & P. Herriot (Eds.), *International handbook of selection & assessment* (pp. 201–213). London, UK: Wiley.

Sternberg, R.J., Wagner, R.K., Williams, W.M., & Horvath, J.A. (1995). Testing common sense. *American Psychologist, 50*, 912–927.

Stevens, M.J., & Campion, M.A. (1994). The knowledge, skill, and ability requirements for teamwork: Implications for human resource management. *Journal of Management, 20*(2), 503–530.

Stokes, G., Mumford, M., & Owens (Eds.) (1994). *Biodata handbook: Theory, research and use of biographical information in selection and performance prediction*. Palo Alto, CA: Consulting Psychologists Press.

Sue-Chan, C., Latham, G.P., & Evans, M.G. (1997). The construct validity of the situational and patterned behavior description interviews: Cognitive ability, tacit knowledge and self-efficacy as correlated. Joseph L. Rotman Faculty of Management, University of Toronto, Toronto: Canada. *Unpublished manuscript*.

Taylor, P., Mills, A., & O'Driscoll, M. (1993). Personnel selection methods used by New Zealand organizational and personnel consulting firms. *New Zealand Journal of Psychology, 22*, 19–31.

Thacker, J.W., & Cattaneo, R.J. (1987). The Canadian personnel function: Status and practices. *Proceedings of the Administrative Sciences Association of Canada, Supplement 2, Personnel and Human Resources* (pp. 56–66). Toronto, Ontario, Canada.

Thorndike, R.L. (1949). *Personnel selection*. New York: Wiley.

Truxillo, D.M., Bauer, D.M., & Bauer, T.N. (1999). Applicant reactions to test scores banding in entry-level and promotional contexts. *Journal of Applied Psychology, 84*, 322–339.

Tupes, E.C., & Christal, R.C. (1961). *Recurrent personality factors based on trait ratings* (Tech. Rep. No. ASD-TR-61-97). Lackland Air Force Base, TX: US Air Force.

Vineberg, R., & Joyner, J.N. (1982). *Prediction of job performance: Review of military studies*. Human Resources Research Organization: Alexandria, VA.

Vispoel, W.P. (1999). Creating computerized adaptive tests of music aptitude: Problems, solutions, and future directions. In F. Drasgow & J.B. Olson-Buchanan (Eds.), *Innovations in computerized assessment* (pp. 151–176). Mahwah, NJ: Lawrence Erlbaum Associates.

Viswesvaran, C., & Ones, D.S. (2000). Measurement Error in 'Big Five Factors' of Personality Assessment: Reliability Generalization Across Studies and Measures. *Educational and Psychological Measurement, 60*, 224–235.

Viswesvaran, C., Ones, D.S., & Schmidt, F.L. (1996). Comparative analysis of the reliability of job performance ratings. *Journal of Applied Psychology, 81*, 557–574.

Watson, D. (1989). Strangers' ratings of the five robust personality factors: Evidence of a surprising convergence with self report. *Journal of Personality and Social Psychology, 57*, 120–128.

Weekly, J.A., & Jones, C. (1997). Video-based situational testing. *Personnel Psychology, 50*, 25–50.

Weekley, J.A., & Jones, C. (1999). Further studies of situational tests. *Personnel Psychology, 52*(3), 679–700.

Weisner, W.H., & Cronshaw, S.F. (1988). A meta-analytic investigation of the impact of interview format and degree of structure on the validity of the employment interview. *Journal of Occupational Psychology, 61*, 275–290.

West, M.A., & Allen, N.J. (1997). Selecting for teamwork. In N. Anderson & P. Herriot (Eds.), *International Handbook of Selection and Assessment*. pp. 493–506. Chichester: John Wiley & Sons.

Wiersma, U.J., Van Leest, P.F., Nienhuis, T., & Maas, R. (1991). Validiteit van een Nederlands assessment center. [Validity of a Dutch assessment center]. *Gedrag en Organisatie, 6*, 474–482.

Wiggins, J.S., & Pincus, A.L. (1992). Personality: Structure and assessment. *Annual Review of Psychology, 43*, 473–504.

Yang, K., & Bond, M.H. (1990). Exploring implicit personality theories with indigenous or imported constructs: The Chinese case. *Journal of Personality and Social Psychology, 58*, 1087–1095.

Zickar, M.J., Rosse, J., & Levin, R. (1996, April). *Modeling the effects of faking on personality scales*. Paper presented at the annual meeting of the Society of Industrial and Organizational Psychologists, San Diego, CA.

10

Recruitment and Selection: Applicant Perspectives and Outcomes

NEIL ANDERSON, MARISE BORN
and NICOLE CUNNINGHAM-SNELL

This chapter considers selection processes from the applicant's perspective. Contrasting the considerable past attention by work psychologists on organizational decision-making in selection procedures, this chapter reviews an increasingly large body of research which views the process from the applicant's viewpoint. Four major themes of research are reviewed: candidate reactions to selection methods, attribution theory and research in selection, distributive and procedural justice perspectives, and applicant decision-making in the selection process. In two of these four areas, candidate reactions and distributive and procedural justice, recent years have witnessed an exponential growth in the number of published studies, and consequently the present chapter attempts to overview the key findings and themes of enquiry. In the final section of this chapter we develop an empirically testable model of applicant decision-making in the selection process. Identifying five types of general models of decision-making in the work psychology literature (rational-economic, rational-psychological, person–organization fit, individual differences, and negotiation process models), we develop and extend these to put forward a general model of applicant decision-making. This model, based upon five classes of relevant variables (applicant characteristics, applicant reactions, perceived fit between the candidate and the job and the organization, labour market conditions, and organizational and job attractiveness) is proposed as a general model of applicant decision-making. In conclusion, we discuss theoretical and practical implications stemming from this model and the importance of selection research from the applicant's perspective.

I did have a question. Or rather, what I actually have is an Answer. I wanted to know what the Question was ... well, it's a long story ... but the Question I would like to know is the Ultimate Question of Life, the Universe and Everything. All we know about it is that the Answer is Forty-Two. (Adams, *The Hitch Hiker's Guide to the Galaxy* 3, 1982)

MORE THAN 'G' + 'C' = 'P'

In the previous chapter of this Handbook, Salgado, Viswesvaran and Ones (Chapter 9) present a comprehensive summary of the predictive validity of selection methods. Relying heavily on advances in meta-analysis, the authors report generalized average predictor–performance correlations for a wide range of assessment techniques. Such techniques as meta-analysis have contributed significantly to our understanding of the predictive validity of selection methods, and can be singled out as a major advance in the methodological and empirical sophistication of selection research over the last twenty years or so.

It is apparent that selection research has taken strides forwards in contributing to our understanding of the predictive capacities of different selection methods, likely moderator variables, and local recruitment-scenario conditions which impinge upon the accuracy of selection decisions (see also, Murphy, 1996). This ongoing theme of research effort in work psychology has been pursued by many selection researchers in several countries, but especially in the USA where significant advances have been made. Meta-analysis findings aside, however, one danger is to attempt to oversimplify the complex processes involved in selection down to generalized, monolithic 'laws' of cause–effect relations. It is almost too tempting to conclude from an over-simplistic distillation of the mass of validity evidence that selection can be succinctly encapsulated in one all-encompassing formula:

$$g + c = p$$

where g is general intelligence as measured by a cognitive ability test; c is conscientiousness as measured by one dimension of a Big Five-based personality instrument; and p is a unitary rating of overall or composite job performance.

Since g (general intelligence) and c (conscientiousness) have been found to be the most consistently parsimonious predictors across numerous predictive validity studies in both the USA and other countries, the danger is to make the huge inferential leap that this 'headline' predictor–performance coefficient is all one needs to know in order to understand selection fully (see also Guion, 1998). But it would be inaccurate to portray meta-analysis as a grand attempt to distil down the validity evidence to such a generalized formula, and indeed, recently debate has begun to surface around the myriad of moderating and mediating factors which underlie these headline coefficients (e.g., Murphy, 1996; Herriot & Anderson, 1997; Rynes, 1993; Snow & Snell, 1993). However, in placing the primacy of organizational goals above an individual applicant's goals, the almost exclusive concentration by work psychologists upon the organizational perspective in selection can be incited for neglecting candidates themselves as serious decision-makers in the recruitment and selection process.

Murphy (1996) is an important and thought-provoking contribution to this debate. In it he presents a cogently argued case for a more critical stance on g as the panacea predictor in selection, arguing for a 'broader conceptualization of the roles of individual differences' (p. 20) and for more attention to be devoted to a diverse set of noncognitive predictors in selection, such as personality, honesty and integrity, and other factors. If predictor variance (i.e., selection performance) is based not only on cognitive ability, but on noncognitive factors such as motivation, then our current inferences about predictor–criterion relationships may be misleading. Research has shown that attitudes towards selection tests do not provide incremental validity

beyond test scores validity (e.g., Arvey, Strickland, Drauden & Martin, 1990; Barbera, Ryan, Desmarais & Dyer, 1995; Schmitt & Ryan, 1992), but that attitudes towards tests can moderate criterion-related validity (e.g., Barbera et al., 1995; Chan, Schmitt, DeShon, Clause & Dellbridge, 1997; Schmitt & Ryan, 1992).

But selection involves more than merely predicting in statistical terms the suitability of an individual for a job. In essence this is the central and recursive argument of this chapter, as well as to suggest that a wider, more eclectic, applied social psychological perspective to recruitment and selection procedures is essential if one is to fully appreciate the dynamic and bilateral nature of these processes in real life. This chapter contrasts with that of Salgado, Viswesvaran and Ones (Chapter 9) in that it reviews developments in research from a broadly social psychological and candidate-oriented perspective. By necessity, the considerable range of literature covered is diverse, and, indeed, we were forced to be somewhat selective in our coverage due to the sheer volume of studies in some topic areas. However, only where recent and comprehensive reviews have been published have we excluded an area from consideration (and even here in the process of writing this chapter we became aware of other in-progress reviews of some of this material). Hence, we sectionalize this chapter to cover four main themes of research:

- Candidate reactions to selection methods
- Attribution theory and research in selection
- Organizational justice: Distributive and procedural justice
- Applicant decision-making in selection.

The number of individual studies within some of these themes has grown exponentially over recent years (most notably, in candidate reactions and distributive and procedural justice). This is undoubtedly due in part to a more candidate-focused agenda being perused by several prodigiously active researchers both in the USA (e.g., Chan, Gilliland, Ployhart, Ryan, Rynes, Schmit, amongst others) and in Europe (e.g., Robertson, Silvester, etc.). The importance of candidate perceptions, reactions, and decisions has thus been increasingly recognized, and researchers have been eager to rectify any claims of neglecting the candidate's perspective in earlier selection research. Certainly, it is axiomatic that candidates, as well as organizations, reach outcome decisions in selection procedures and it is therefore perhaps somewhat curious that their 'side' of this bilateral decision-making process has received significantly less attention than organizational decisions in selection. This growth has been especially evident over the last 10 or so years, and so this chapter, it is hoped, also acts as an update to, and synergy across, previous reviews in these four areas (e.g., Herriot, 1989a;

Schmitt & Gilliland, 1992; Rynes, 1993; Anderson & Ostroff. 1997; Iles & Robertson, 1997; Gilliland & Steiner, in press; Ryan & Ployhart, 2000).

CANDIDATE REACTIONS TO SELECTION METHODS

The selection literature has increasingly acknowledged that applicants' reactions to procedures are an important aspect of the selection process (e.g., Rynes, 1993; Gilliland & Steiner, in press; Ryan & Ployhart, in press). Reactions to selection may impact on several factors including applicant decision-making, an organization's reputation, and litigation. Research from the applicants' perspective has typically described and compared candidates' reactions to various selection procedures, and in this section we review the extant research into candidate reactions to recruitment and selection procedures. We consider recruitment methods, biodata, psychometric tests, interviews, work samples and assessment centres. Unfortunately, limitations of space prevent us from covering studies into applicant reactions to two other methods, although comprehensive reviews of these have appeared more recently: honesty and integrity testing (e.g., Sackett & Wanek, 1996) and drug testing (e.g., Konovsky & Cropanzano, 1991). In conclusion, we describe and evaluate four theoretical models of applicants' reactions to selection.

Recruitment Methods

Since Rynes, Heneman and Schwab's (1980) review, less research has investigated this issue than one might have ideally hoped. The studies which have been conducted generally suggest important effects in terms of applicant reactions. Taylor and Bergmann (1987), report that whilst job attributes were the most important factor influencing candidates reactions, recruitment activities were important at the interview stage only. This allies with other findings (e.g., Harris & Fink, 1987) which indicate the crucial role that the recruiter has upon candidate reactions. In addition, candidates are prone to extrapolating from recruiter behaviour to infer wider characteristics such as organizational leadership style (Rynes, Bretz & Gerhart, 1991). Finally, in relation to application forms, Saks, Leck and Saunders (1995) reported that candidates reacted more favourably to forms containing no discriminatory questions than to those which do, but more surprising was the finding that candidates also preferred application blanks which included a statement of equal opportunity by the recruiting organization. More research is called for to address candidate reactions to recruitment processes, especially as it is at this early stage that many may decide to self-select-out in order to avoid further time commitments in attending selection procedures with the organization. Scheu, Ryan and Nona (1999) conducted a study involving 98 psychology students to investigate the effectiveness of 10 manufacturing organizations' web-sites as recruiting mechanisms. They found that potential applicants' perceptions of the web-sites influenced their views of the organization and, in turn, their intention to apply to that particular organization.

Biodata

Despite its strong validity (e.g., Hunter & Hunter, 1984; Bliesener, 1996), biodata is rarely used, probably due in part to the larger numbers of applicants needed to make a biodata inventory viable, but also to the poor face validity of biodata as items may have no obvious connection with the job. Indeed, a number of studies have identified that candidates react negatively to the use of biodata for selection purposes as they doubt its accuracy and usefulness (Robertson, Iles, Gratton & Sharpley, 1991; Smither, Reilly, Millsap, Pearlman & Stoffey 1993; Stone & Jones, 1997). For example, Stone and Jones (1997) conducted an experimental study whereby 86 participants were asked to play the role of job applicants and complete a biographical information questionnaire. Half the participants were told the purpose of the questionnaire was as part of a selection decision-making process, the other half were told the questionnaire was for career tracking purposes if they received a job. Results indicated that perceptions regarding the fairness of biodata items (e.g., birth order, marital status, college size, leisure activities) were significantly lower when the data were collected for personnel selection purposes. Exceptions were for biodata items more directly related to job skills (e.g., scholastic standing, grades, job preferences etc.)

Testing

Candidates respond moderately well to cognitive tests (Silvester & Brown, 1993; Steiner & Gilliland, 1996), but tend to rate tests with concrete items as more job-related than abstract tests (Smither et al., 1993; Rynes & Connerley, 1993). In a telephone survey involving 546 participants, Lounsbury, Borrow and Jensen (1989) found that more positive attitudes were associated with employment testing when participants were told how the test related to job performance and when they received feedback on test performance. Positive reactions to computer-based testing have also been reported in the literature (Arvey et al., 1990; Schmitt, Gilliland, Landis & Devine, 1993; Schmidt, Urry & Gugel, 1978). Schmidt et al. (1978) found that the 163 examinees liked computer adaptive testing since it was fast, required them to answer fewer questions, provided immediate feedback, and faster notification of their chances of obtaining a job. Chan, Schmitt and their coworkers at Michigan State University have made a sustained and important contribution to this literature (e.g., Chan, 1997; Chan et al., 1997; Chan, Schmitt, Jennings, Clause & Delbridge, 1998a; Chan, Schmitt, Sacco & Deshon, 1998b; Schmitt & Chan, 1999). They have found, *inter alia* that test-taking motivation is related to subsequent test performance and that black applicants' lower test scores are attributable in part to lower test-taking motivation (Chan et al., 1997; see also, Schmitt & Ryan, 1997), that pre-test reactions (face validity, predictive validity, and fairness perceptions) affected actual test performance (Chan et al., 1998a), and that test taker's perceptions of fairness are influenced by the perceived job relevance of cognitive tests (Chan et al., 1998b). For a concise, applied summary of this area see Schmitt and Chan (1999). Importantly, Schmitt and Ryan (1997) report that the requirement to sit tests did not affect applicant decisions to withdraw from selection for police officer roles in the US, and in another study (Thorsteinson & Ryan, 1997) that the selection ratio did not influence applicants' perceptions of test fairness. Tests are not, however, viewed as favourably as assessment centres, the latter of which are more liked and perceived as being more job relevant by applicants (Macan, Avedon, Paese & Smith, 1994). Applicants tend to react somewhat less favourably to personality tests (e.g., Smither et al., 1993).

In contrast to this now quite extensive research base into candidate reactions to ability tests, fewer studies have examined reactions to other types of test such as attitude testing, personality testing or physical ability testing. Research on personality testing has, though, indicated that candidates react somewhat less favourably to personality tests (e.g., Smither et al., 1993). There are inconsistent findings on the extent to which the provision of an explanation regarding use of a personality test can impact on candidates' reactions to the procedure (cf. Harland, Rauzi & Biasotto, 1995; Fink & Butcher, 1972). Clearly, though, the length and level of detail provided in the explanation will be critical. Two recent studies (Ryan, Greguras & Ployhart, 1996; Kravitz, Stinson & Chavez, 1996) examining physical ability testing have reported the job relevance of these tests to be an important determinant of positiveness of candidate reactions. Finally, research has yet to fully address the implications of growth in the use of internet testing for employment decisions, although early studies have begun this gargantuan task (e.g., Bartram, 1999).

Interviews

A considerable amount of research has explored applicants' reactions to the selection interview (e.g., Harris & Fink, 1987; Powell, 1991; Rynes, 1991; Rynes et al., 1980; Taylor & Bergmann, 1987). In particular, this research has focused on the impact of the personal qualities and behaviour of the interviewer on various outcome variables, such as job offer expectancy, perceived probability of receiving and accepting an offer, and impression of the company. Early research supported the impact of personal qualities such as warmth, sincerity, empathy, and good listening skills on the perceptions and intentions of interviewees (e.g., Harris & Fink, 1987; Rynes, 1991; Rynes et al., 1980). In terms of interviewer behaviour, empirical research suggests that question style, question invasiveness, interviewer job knowledge and informativeness were also found to influence applicants' general reactions to interviews (e.g., Harris & Fink, 1987; Powell, 1991; Rynes & Miller, 1983). However, in an experimental study, Rynes and Miller (1983) found that only 4% of the variance in subjects' willingness to accept a second interview could be attributed to manipulations of recruiter affect and warmth. Similarly, field and experimental studies have found that interviewer effects added little or nothing to the predicted variance on job choice intentions when perceived job attributes were controlled for (e.g., Harris & Fink, 1987; Rynes & Miller, 1983; Taylor & Bergmann, 1987). Harris and Fink (1987) suggest that high correlations between recruiter and job variables in some studies may have resulted in multicolinearity, and therefore reduced the impact of the recruiter variables. Alternatively, the relative effects of recruiter and job characteristics may be determined by the stage of selection. Taylor and Bergmann (1987) found that recruitment activities were related to applicants' intentions to accept offers and perceptions of organizational attractiveness at the initial interview phase, but at subsequent stages in the process job attributes were more predictive of these outcomes.

Positive candidate reactions have been reported to particular interview formats and modes of delivery: patterned behaviour description interviews (Janz & Mooney, 1993) and video conference interviews (Kroeck & Magnusen, 1997), for instance. Conversely, candidates have been found to react less positively to telephone-based than face-to-face interviews (Silvester, Anderson, Haddleton, Cunningham-Snell & Gibb, 1999).

Work Samples

Applicants rate work-sample tests positively, perceiving them as fair, valid and job related (e.g., Smither et al., 1993; Schmitt et al., 1993; Steiner & Gilliland, 1996). Schmidt, Ones and Hunter (1992) found that reactions of both majority and minority applicants to work-sample and written trade tests differed. Both groups found the written tests to be more difficult and less fair.

Assessment Centres

Applicants give favourable ratings to assessment centres (ACs) (e.g., Dodd, 1977; Dulewicz, Fletcher & Wood, 1983), probably due to their apparent job-relatedness, the use of work-sample tests, and the opportunity to meet in person with assessors (e.g., Iles & Robertson, 1997; Macan et al., 1994). For instance, Macan et al. (1994) found that candidates rated ACs more positively than cognitive ability tests (see also the following section on comparisons between method favourableness). But, it is important to note that ACs have also been found to have effects upon candidate self-esteem and psychological well-being (Fletcher, 1991; Robertson et al., 1991), and negatively so for unsuccessful candidates. This suggests the need for further longitudinal research into both candidate reactions *and* psychological impact.

Comparison of Selection Methods

A number of experimental studies have more recently been carried out into applicant reactions to different selection procedures (e.g., Iles & Mabey, 1993; Kravitz et al., 1996; Rynes & Connerly, 1993; Smither et al., 1993). Rynes and Connerly (1993), for example, solicited the reactions of 390 current and future job seekers to 13 selection procedures. They found positive reactions to references and methods with high apparent content validity (e.g., simulations and business-related tests). Personality inventories, drug testing and honesty testing were generally viewed as neutral. Reactions to the interview varied according to interview content, and whether the interviewer represented the line or staff. In Kravitz et al.'s (1996) study, 222 participants rated the fairness, job relevance, appropriateness and invasiveness of 16 tests. The most positive ratings were obtained for interviews, work samples and job skills tests, and the most negative ratings for astrology, graphology and polygraphs.

A few field studies have also been conducted comparing applicants' reactions to different stages of a selection process (e.g., Macan et al., 1994; Robertson et al., 1991; Rosse, Miller & Stecher, 1994; Taylor & Bergmann, 1987). Rosse et al. (1994) conducted a study involving 80 applicants for seasonal jobs at a property management firm and found that attitudes towards selection methods were influenced by the additional measures they are used in conjunction with. Applicants were screened through one of three conditions: interviews only, interviews plus a personality inventory, or interviews, personality inventory and cognitive ability tests. Applicants' reactions were less positive in the interview plus personality condition, whereas the interview only and interview plus both test types were perceived similarly.

Finally, in a field study conducted by Macan et al. (1994), applicants completed a survey of reactions at two stages of a selection process: first after a cognitive ability test ($n = 3,984$) and second, for those progressing through, after an assessment centre ($n = 194$). Controlling for attitudes to the cognitive test, Macan et al. (1994) found that perceptions of face-validity explained 18% of the variance in organizational attractiveness, 16% of the variance in applicants' liking of the job, and together with perceptions of fairness, 22% of the variance in candidates' satisfaction with the selection process. By controlling for reactions to the earlier selection stage, Macan et al. (1994) were more accurately able to identify the impact of the assessment centre per se.

Models of Applicant Reactions to Selection

Following on from these studies, a number of models have been proposed to account for applicants' reactions to the selection process. Four models will be briefly described: Schuler, Farr and Smith (1993), Arvey and Sackett (1993), Iles and Robertson (1997), and Anderson and Ostroff (1997).

Considering Schuler et al. (1993) first, his model of 'social validity' postulates that four components influence the perceived acceptability of selection: the presence of job and organizational relevant information; participation by the applicant in the development and execution of the selection process; transparency of the assessment so that applicants understand the objectives of evaluation process and its relevance to organizational requirements; and the provision of feedback with appropriate content (e.g., open, honest, developmental) and form (e.g., comprehensible, considerate, facilitative). One additional factor is the dynamic personal relationship between the applicant and assessor which has been shown to have an impact on applicants in selection (e.g., Harris & Fink, 1987; Maurer, Howe & Lee, 1992; Rynes et al., 1991).

Arvey and Sackett (1993) proposed that the perceived fairness of the process can be influenced by the content of selection (e.g., job relatedness, thoroughness of knowledge, skills and ability coverage, invasiveness of questions, and ease of faking answers), an understanding of the system development process, the administration of the selection procedures (e.g., consistency, confidentiality, opportunity for reconsideration, and prior information) and the organizational context (e.g., the selection ratio). However, Arvey and Sackett (1993) do not outline how these determinants combine to form perceptions of fairness (Gilliland, 1993).

Iles and Robertson (1997) suggest that the impact of the decision is mediated by reactions to the process. It is suggested that various features of the selection method (e.g., intrusiveness, face validity, job relevance, feedback) influence applicants' cognitive reactions towards the process. These reactions are hypothesized in turn to influence various outcomes (e.g., organizational commitment, self-esteem, job and career withdrawal), moderated by the career stage and personal characteristics of the individual. Whilst this model is useful in highlighting the impact of both the assessment process and the outcome decision, the role of reactions as only mediators of the decision impact is questionable. As noted by James and Brett (1984), mediation implies causal order in which an antecedent (i.e., the decision) must precede the mediating variable (i.e., the reactions to the process). Arguably, reactions to the process can precede communication of the decision, and these pre-decision reactions may have an impact on reactions to the decision and other outcome variables.

The final model is that proposed by Anderson and Ostroff (1997), and extended by Anderson (in press). Whilst it has long been recognized that selection methods can act as pre-entry socialization techniques (e.g., Louis, 1980; Wanous, 1992), there still remains a paucity of research into this question. Anderson and Ostroff (1997) propose a model of 'Socialization Impact' to describe these effects. They put forward an empirically testable, five-domain framework covering information provision, preference impact, expectation impact, attitudinal impact, and behavioural impact. First, they propose that all selection methods convey information to the candidate, either intentionally or unintentionally on the part of the organization. Further, that this information will then be either correctly or incorrectly construed by applicants. Second, that such information is one of several factors which influence candidate preferences for particular methods. Third, that these two forms of impact generate and change candidate expectations of the job role, the organization as an employer, and, more widely, the psychological contract (see, for instance Shore & Tetrick, 1994). Fourth, that selection methods will affect candidate attitudes and beliefs (see also Anderson, in press). The fifth and final type of effect proposed by Anderson and Ostroff (1997) is that of 'behavioural impact'. Ultimately, this is the crucial issue, of course: Do selection methods actually influence subsequent candidate behaviour, not just neutrally predict them? If so, there is the prospect that organizations could design-in socialization impact to their selection methods in order to improve their predictive validity.

Summary and Future Research

What is striking is the chasm between the sophistication and range of these models on the one hand, and the piecemeal nature of existing studies into candidate reactions on the other. Few studies have gone any way beyond preference reactions, yet these eloquent models postulate much longer-term

impacts upon such important variables as candidate psychological well-being, organization commitment, applicant decision-making, and even potential withdrawal from the selection process. Summarizing the mass of individual studies into applicant reactions, it is clear that several factors consistently appear to account for positive or negative reactions. Methods that are perceived as (i) more job-relevant, (ii) less personally intrusive (see also Connerley, Mael & Morath, 1999), (iii) not contravening candidate procedural or distributive justice expectations (see below), and (iv) allowing the candidate an opportunity to meet in person with selectors, are rated more favourably by applicants.

To the layperson these findings would hardly be breathtaking one suspects, yet the sheer volume of studies carried out by work and organizational psychologists is itself indicative of the increasing importance afforded to the applicant's perspective in selection procedures over more recent years. More critically, the most central of questions remain largely unanswered, including whether preference reactions affect candidate job motivation or organization commitment in the longer term, or even applicant decision-making as suggested in some of the models reviewed earlier. Candidate preference and liking may be important short-term considerations, but our research efforts should surely now turn towards these longer-term effects, and thereby to rigorous empirical validation of these reactions models if we are to advance understanding in this area beyond its current state. Such longer-term studies will need to be longitudinal and organizationally based rather than experimental manipulations, and will need to extend beyond relatively simplistic cross-sectional surveys of candidate preferences if they are to begin to shed light upon more fundamental candidate reactions and how the treatment of applicants in the selection process affects their intentions of whether or not to accept subsequent offers of employment.

ATTRIBUTION THEORY AND RESEARCH IN SELECTION

An approach which has received strong theoretical attention, and a steadily increasing amount of empirical attention, has been attribution theory in selection decision-making. Intriguingly, however, almost all of these theory-building papers and empirical studies have been confined to one particular selection method – the interview. In addition, almost all of the applied research into attribution in selection has been conducted relatively recently, mostly from 1990 onwards.

Attribution theory as originally proposed suggests that a person will attribute the behaviour of another either to internal causes (e.g., personality, motivation etc.) or to external causes (situational factors) (Heider, 1958; Weiner, 1985, 1986). As this theoretical framework has been expanded over the years, a number of attribution errors (e.g., fundamental attribution error, actor–observer differences) and more fine-grained categorizations of attribution have been proposed. Since attribution theory concerns observer ascribed causes for observed behaviour, it is understandable that most studies have focused upon interviewer attributions of interviewee behaviour.

Herriot (1981, 1989a) sets out this theoretical framework in the context of employment interviews. He states four propositions, three related to Heider's (1958) covariation principle, and the fourth regarding fundamental attribution error. First, Herriot postulates that falsely high consensus may exist between interviewers and candidates; that is both assume the same expectations are held about each other's behaviour, whereas in reality they will vary, sometimes widely so. Second, he proposes a false assumption of low distinctiveness; that is, that interview behaviour is believed to be representative of behaviour on the job, whereas in fact distinctions will become obvious. Third, the high consistency proposition assumes that behaviour will be consistent across interview situations, whereas again Herriot argues this to be a false belief. The fourth and final point Herriot makes is that both parties may be prone to fundamental attribution error, that is, to incorrectly attribute much of the cause of the other's behaviour to internal dispositional factors instead of to the peculiarities of the interview situation itself. Herriot's theoretical stance is eloquent and worthy of further research, as are several of the directions for future research proffered by Knouse (1989), yet more recent studies have only really begun to unravel some aspects of this rich theoretic stance (see also Silvester & Chapman, 1997 for a wider application of attribution theory to organizational behaviour).

Struthers, Colwill and Perry (1992) examined Weiner's (1985, 1986) attributional model in simulated employment interviews using a 'pencil-and-paper' design to manipulate applicant answers at interview. Interview transcripts manipulated three variables: outcome (positive–negative), locus (internal–external), and stability (stable–unstable). Subjects were 240 first-year psychology students and effects were measured across three dependent variables: interviewer expectations of future job performance (expectancy), emotional reactions (hopefulness), and hiring probability (decision). It was found, in common with much previous real-life interview research, that positive outcome information favoured interviewer expectancy, hopefulness, and hiring probability (see also Tucker & Rowe, 1979). Despite concerns over ecological validity and students acting as surrogates for actual employment interviewers in this particular study, this experiment

is suggestive of the valuable explanatory framework offered by attribution theory.

Silvester (1997) has investigated real-life studies of interview decision-making in the UK. In a review of attribution theory applied to interviewer decision-making Silvester and Chapman (1996) delineate the conditions under which recruiters' attributional biases may have an adverse impact against minority-group candidates. Silvester (1997) examined in detail the attributional statements made by graduate interviewees. Across 35 interviews a total of 1,967 discrete attributional statements were extracted from interview transcripts. These were coded using five key dimensions (stable–unstable, global–specific, internal–external, personal–universal, and controllable–uncontrollable). Results indicated that, on average, between 40 and 80 spoken attributions were made by candidates in these 30-minute interviews. Successful candidates made significantly more stable and personal attributions regarding negative life and career events, but for attributions over positive events, no statistically significant differences were found.

In a carefully designed and conducted study, Ployhart and Ryan (1997) applied both attribution theory and organizational justice theory to candidates' reactions to selection procedures and decisions (see our subsequent review of distributive and procedural justice for details of the latter). Subjects were applicants to a US graduate school in psychology. Questionnaires were mailed at two time points: pre-application, and post-offer. A sample of 297 questionnaires was obtained at time 1, 80 at time 2, to examine the attrition due to self-selection by applicants, a high selection ratio, and dropout between the initial application and final offer phases. In relation to attribution theory, the questionnaire incorporated Russell's (1992) causal dimension scale, as well as scales for justice and candidate intentions regarding acceptance of offers and recommendations, amongst others. It was found that Weiner's (1986) dimension of locus, stability and controllability correlated .39, .38, and .35 respectively with perceptions of outcome fairness. In addition, successful candidates attributed offers to more internal, stable and controllable causes than rejected applicants, a somewhat understandable self-serving bias.

Finally, a study by Ramsay, Gallois and Callan (1997) investigated perceived rule-breaking behaviours by candidates at interview. Audiotapes of actual interviews were rated by recruiters ($n = 60$) on communication skills and hireability of interviewees. Recruiters who perceived interviewees as having broken general interpersonal competence rules tended to attribute such transgressions to situational factors, whereas internal attributions to the candidate were more salient for transgressions of specific interview rules (for instance, interpersonal skills, self-confidence, activity, and self-awareness).

Summary and Future Research

To summarize this small but growing body of studies, it is clear that attributional theory has much to offer our understanding of how interviewers interpret candidate replies and behaviour (cf. Anderson, 1992; Silvester, 1997). Nevertheless, it is a definite shortcoming that existing research seems almost exclusively confined to the selection interview (but, see Arvey et al., 1990, regarding test-takers' attitudes and reactions). Moreover, all of the recent studies have focused upon recruiter attributions of interviewee behaviour, rather than interviewee attributions towards recruiters. Further research is needed into candidate attributions of recruiter behaviour, both at interview and in other face-to-face selection encounters given the possible impact this may have upon candidates. How candidates attribute behaviour by recruiters is an important question, of course, as it may have a direct bearing on how candidates reach decisions in the selection process (see the final section of this chapter). Whether applicants are prone to the same series of biases in attribution as recruiters have been found to be is another avenue for future research, but in terms of the present state of knowledge in this area we are limited by the real lack of research into applicant attributions in selection. Reviewing this approach more widely, research into attributions by both parties in face-to-face selection contexts other than merely the assessment interview (e.g., assessment centres, work samples) is conspicuous by its absence. Attribution research in these contexts would be valuable, for instance in suggesting how assessors' attribution biases may be undermining formal rating dimensions at ACs.

ORGANIZATIONAL JUSTICE: DISTRIBUTIVE AND PROCEDURAL JUSTICE

The application of organizational justice theories has provided a useful framework from which to conceptualize candidates' reactions to selection procedures (Borman, Hanson & Hedge, 1997; Chan, 1997; Gilliland, 1993; Schmitt & Gilliland, 1992). Original justice theories focused on outcome distributions in the form of equity and distributive justice (e.g., Adams, 1965), whereas later theories acknowledged process aspects in the form of procedural and interactional justice (Bies & Moag, 1986; Leventhal, 1980; Thibaut & Walker, 1975). In selection, these two main types of justice equate to the perceived fairness of the selection decision and the perceived fairness of the hiring process respectively. Organizational justice theories contend that the fairness in organizational procedures constitutes an important determinant of work attitudes and behaviours. Here we briefly review

organizational justice theories and the research around the determinants of candidates' reactions to selection justice. We then examine the impact of justice on selection outcomes and the possible impact of culture on justice reactions.

Organizational Justice Theories

Based on the organization justice literature, Schmitt and Gilliland (1992) and Gilliland (1993) presented a number of distributive and procedural rules in selection that may account for candidates' overall perceptions of distributive and procedural fairness in selection. These rules were predicted to have an impact on applicants – both during the hiring process and post-entry into the organization (Gilliland, 1993).

Distributive Justice

Distributive justice focuses on the fairness of outcome distributions and is determined by three distributive rules: equity, equality and need (Adams, 1965; Deutsch, 1975). The primary distributive rule is equity; the extent to which a person's inputs justify the outcome, relevant to a referent comparison (Adams, 1965). In selection, this refers to the extent to which the decision is deserved based on past success, experience and qualifications (Gilliland, 1993). Perceptions of equity arise when the hiring decision is consistent with the applicants' hiring expectation, whereas inequity results from either underpayment (i.e., when a negative outcome is unexpected), or conversely from overpayment (i.e., when a positive outcome is unexpected: Gilliland, 1993). Consistent with Deutsch (1975), Gilliland (1993) postulated two additional distributive justice rules: equality and needs. The equality rule suggests that all individuals should have the same chance of receiving an outcome, and in selection this is only applicable to job-irrelevant characteristics. The needs rule holds that preferential treatment should be given to certain sub-groups (e.g., disabled applicants) which inevitably leads to violation of the equality and equity rules (Gilliland, 1993).

Selection research on distributive justice has focused on the equity rule. There is mixed support for the theory that perceived selection distributive justice arises from a combination of the applicants' hiring expectations and the outcome (cf. Gilliland, 1994; Gilliland & Honig, 1994b). Research on a selection procedure for temporary employment supported the interaction between expectations and hiring decision on distributive justice (Gilliland, 1994); whereas research involving retrospective assessments of hiring expectations for permanent employment was not supportive (Gilliland & Honig, 1994b).

Procedural Justice

Drawing upon the procedural justice literature (e.g., Leventhal, 1980; Bies & Moag, 1986; Thibaut &

Walker, 1975; see also Gilliland & Chan, Chapter 8 in Volume 2 of this Handbook), Gilliland (1993) identified 12 selection procedural justice rules. As shown in Table 10.1, these rules related to the formal characteristic of the process (e.g., job relatedness), rules relating to the information offered during the selection process (e.g., selection informativeness) and rules relating to the interpersonal treatment received (e.g., interpersonal effectiveness).

Initial selection research has largely supported the role of procedural justice in shaping applicants' attitudes towards selection fairness (Cunningham-Snell, 1999; Gilliland and Honig, 1994a; Ployhart, Ryan & Bennett, 1999). For instance, Gilliland and Honig (1994a) conducted a study involving 333 graduates making retrospective ratings of selection experiences, and found that 50% of the variance in perceptions of overall procedural fairness was accounted for by the perceived satisfaction or violation of the following 10 procedural rules: job relatedness, opportunity to perform, consistency bias, ease of faking, feedback, selection information, honesty, interpersonal effectiveness, two-way communication and question propriety. Since the reliability of the overall fairness scale was $\alpha = .85$, Gilliland and Honig (1994a) concluded that the 10 rules account for the majority of variance in overall procedural fairness. Rule salience has been found to vary across different selection methods; Gilliland (1995) found that applicants' primary concern for integrity tests was ease of faking, for ability and work sample tests it was job relatedness, and for interviews the interpersonal effectiveness was most salient.

The Relationship between Procedural and Distributive Justice

Consistent with the organizational justice literature (Greenberg, 1987, 1993; McFarlin & Sweeney, 1992), selection research on the interaction between procedural and distributive justice has found that high procedural justice can mitigate the impact of unfavourable outcomes (Gilliland, 1994; Gilliland & Honig, 1994b). Although Ployhart and Ryan (1998) did not find support for such an interaction, this may have been due to their measuring procedural justice by the artificial manipulation of conditions and to their focus on the administration consistency rule only. There are a number of possible explanations why procedural and distributive justice may in fact interact (see Brockner & Wiesenfeld, 1996), including referent cognition theory (RCT: Cropanzano & Folger, 1989) and attribution theory (Folger, Rosenfield & Hays, 1978). RCT suggests that with fair procedures, recipients of negative decisions are less likely to mentally construct scenarios that would have resulted in a positive outcome. On the other hand, attribution

theory suggests that fair procedures generate the perception of behaviour being internally motivated resulting in less dependency on the anticipated receipt of a favourable outcome. Existing research does not provide a basis for favouring one explanation over another (Gilliland & Beckstein, 1996).

The Impact of Selection Justice

Organizational justice research has demonstrated that fairness perceptions can influence a range of organizational, individual and ethical outcomes (e.g., Greenberg, 1990, 1993; Konovsky & Cropanzano, 1991; McFarlin & Sweeney, 1992). Gilliland (1993) subsequently documented the impact of selection justice on three levels: (i) applicants' attitudes and behaviour during the hiring process, (ii) applicants' self-perceptions, and (iii) attitudes and behaviour post-entry into the organization.

Initial selection research adopting this theoretical perspective has generally supported the impact of selection justice on various outcome measures, such as intention to recommend the organization to others (e.g., Bies & Shapiro, 1988; Gilliland, 1994; Ployhart & Ryan, 1997), self-efficacy (e.g., Gilliland, 1994; Ployhart & Ryan, 1997), anxiety (Cunningham-Snell, 1999), motivation (Cunningham-Snell, 1999), performance expectations (Ployhart & Ryan, 1998); and work performance (Gilliland, 1994). For example, Gilliland (1994) conducted a study involving 260 undergraduate students applying for temporary clerical employment. Manipulations were conducted on the procedural justice rules of job relatedness and explanation for the selection procedure. These manipulations influenced applicants' attitudes during hiring, their self-perceptions and their behaviour post-entry. Rejected participants who were offered an explanation were more likely to recommend the project than those rejected and offered no explanation; job-relatedness had a positive effect on the self-esteem of those accepted and a negative effect on those rejected; and job relatedness influenced post-hire performance. However, the effects on job-performance were short-lived and the explanation manipulation had a negative effect on performance quality.

The importance of examining the impact of justice longitudinally is also increasingly appreciated (e.g., Ployhart & Ryan, 1997, 1998; Thorsteinson & Ryan, 1997). For instance, Ployhart and Ryan (1998) conducted a study involving 283 undergraduate students applying for short-term employment. The consistency of test administration was manipulated in three different testing sessions by (i) giving 85% of applicants less than the official time to complete the test (negative consistency), or (ii) giving 85% of applicants more than the official time (positive consistency), or (iii) giving all applicants the

Table 10.1 *Procedural justice rules*

Rule	Definition	Examples of supporting selection research
Formal characteristics		
Job relatedness	The measurement of constructs relevant to the job	Chan et al. (1998a); Cunningham-Snell (1999); Gilliland (1994, 1995); Gilliland & Honig (1994a); Kluger & Rothstein (1991); Kravitz et al. (1996); Smither et al. (1993)
Opportunity to perform	The opportunity to display knowledge, skills and abilities	Bies & Shapiro (1988); Cunningham-Snell (1999); Gilliland (1995); Gilliland & Honig (1994a); Kluger & Rothstein (1991)
Consistency of administration	The standardization of administrative procedures across people and techniques	Gilliland (1995); Gilliland & Honig (1994a); Ployhart & Ryan (1998)
Information offered		
Performance feedback	The provision of timely and informative feedback regarding selection performance and the outcome	Gilliland (1995); Lounsbury et al. (1989); Gilliland & Honig (1994a)
Selection process information	The adequacy of information provided to applicants regarding the selection process	Cunningham-Snell (1999); Gilliland & Honig (1994a)
Honesty in treatment	The organization's integrity during selection	Gilliland (1995); Gilliland & Honig (1994a)
Interpersonal treatment		
Recruiter effectiveness	The interpersonal effectiveness and interest of the recruiter	Cunningham-Snell (1999); Gilliland (1995); Gilliland & Honig (1994a)
Two-way communication	The extent to which conversation flows in a normal pattern and applicants are given opportunities to ask questions	Cunningham-Snell (1999); Gilliland (1995); Gilliland & Honig (1994a)
Propriety of questions	The appropriateness of the questions asked	Bies & Moag (1986); Gilliland (1995); Gilliland & Honig (1994a)
Additional		
Ease of faking	The extent to which applicants believe information can be distorted in a socially desirable way	Gilliland (1995); Gilliland & Honig (1994a)

correct amount of time. Each testing session involved different applicants. Measures of justice were taken both before selection and after the selection decision. Applicants' outcome fairness perceptions directly influenced post-hire intentions (e.g., recommendation intentions, intentions to volunteer for similar experiments), but the effects of pre-hire process fairness were indirect and mediated through intentions measured before testing.

Research has also considered the extent to which procedural justice reactions moderate selection predictive validity (e.g., Cunningham-Snell, 1999; Thorsteinson & Ryan, 1997). In a laboratory study involving 147 students taking a battery of tests, Thorsteinson and Ryan (1997) measured perceptions of procedural fairness before and after communication of the outcome decision. The criterion scores were high-school and current college grade-point average (GPA). Fairness perceptions measured pre- and post-decision moderated the validity of a cognitive but not personality test. For the cognitive test, higher perceptions of procedural justice yielded higher test validity. Thorsteinson and Ryan (1997) note that two potentially interconnected explanations may account for the finding: negative reactions towards selection may have decreased performance, or, alternatively, applicants may have viewed selection negatively because they felt the process was not predictive of their job performance ability. However, in a field study with predictive validity data on 70 candidates receiving offers of employment following an assessment centre, Cunningham-Snell (1999) did not find support for the moderating role of procedural justice reactions measured pre- or post-decision.

The Impact of Culture on Selection Justice

The majority of selection research adopting an organization justice framework has been conducted in North America, and so the extent to which these findings generalize to other countries remains largely unknown. Because the prevailing social, economic, political, and management environment may impact on applicants' reactions to selection procedures, caution is needed when generalizing the findings from one country to another (e.g., Baron & Janman, 1996; Rynes, 1993). Indeed, issues of selection fairness and adverse impact are considerably more prominent in the United States than in Europe (Dipboye, 1997; Iles & Robertson, 1997; Schuler et al., 1993). Some research has examined the impact of culture on the salience of justice rules in predicting overall fairness reactions to selection procedures. For example, Steiner and Gilliland (1996) conducted a study whereby French and American colleges provided their reactions to 10 selection methods according to seven

justice dimensions (scientific evidence, employer's right to obtain information, opportunity to perform, interpersonal warmth, face validity, widespread use, and respect for privacy). The results indicated significant cultural differences to the extent that the procedural justice dimensions were generally less predictive of overall process favourability for the French students. However, there was some agreement in terms of the most salient dimension being face validity across both cultures. Steiner (2000) similarly found this to be the most salient dimension in a sample of 49 managerial and professional employees from French private, public and quasi-public organizations.

Summary and Future Research

Ultimately, candidates' reactions to procedural and distributive justice are likely to impact on an organization's continued ability to recruit effectively. As demographic changes affect the balance of power between the two parties, the impact of justice reactions on candidates' perceptions of the organization is likely to take on greater significance. Presently, however, much of the research in this area has focused on overall perceptions of procedural and distributive justice, or has focused on a limited number of the justice rules. Future research should pay greater attention to the justice rules to provide more specific insight into which are the critical rules impacting the process. Organizations can then adapt their process in order to generate more positive reactions from candidates.

Future selection research is also required to explore the justice reactions of a more diverse range of candidates. This includes comparing the reactions of groups of candidates with different biographical backgrounds (e.g., minority and majority candidates) and different professional backgrounds (e.g., graduates versus professionals and nonprofessionals with work experience). Steiner's (2000) initial research would indicate that the salience of the justice rules is comparable across graduate and professional applicants; however, further research is required with larger samples and across a range of job types. Further, as organizations increasingly recruit outside their national frontiers, greater insight is required into the justice reactions of candidates from a range of cultures. Presently, research has been conducted in cultures which have generally similar characteristics (Hofstede, 1980), and so research into more diverse cultures would be useful.

Over the past few years, field research and longitudinal studies have been increasing in the selection justice literature, and this remains an important approach for future research. Additionally, applied research exploring the impact of justice reactions to selection on the early socialization process of recruits would usefully add to this area. Research also needs to address the impact of justice reactions relative to the impact of job and organizational characteristics.

Finally, an important avenue for future research will be to explore the role of selection justice in shaping the emergence of the psychological contract. The role of organizational justice in reducing the negative impact of contract violations for longer-tenured employees has been acknowledged (e.g., Arnold, 1996; Rousseau, 1995; Rousseau & Aquino, 1993; Shore & Tetrick, 1994). Applicants' perceptions of selection justice may serve as a salient source of information regarding anticipated employer obligations; fair selection procedures and outcomes may generate expectations of higher levels of contribution in any future relationship with the organization. In their model of organizational careers, Herriot and Pemberton (1996) suggest that the distributive and procedural justice dimensions map onto the two types of psychological contract: transactional and relational. Going beyond Herriot and Pemberton's (1996) model, it is proposed here that in selection, distributive justice may reinforce transactional elements of the contract that focus on specific employment outcomes (e.g., high pay and merit pay), while procedural justice may reinforce the relational components (e.g., career development and loyalty). Through the principle of reciprocity, it may also influence new recruits' perceptions of employee obligations. However, research to date has not examined these possible relationships.

APPLICANT DECISION-MAKING IN SELECTION

In reviewing the decision-making process by candidates it is possible to identify five categories of model and comment on their potential power to explain candidates' decision-making behaviour. We argue that these models differ from each other in the attention paid to rational goals, as opposed to a view of the candidate as driven by emotions and other needs. As emphasized previously, the classical recruitment and selection model pays little if any heed to candidate decision-making processes. It is therefore important to step back initially from propounding a general model of applicant decision-making (although we do this subsequently) to consider the range of models which can be identified in the W/O psychology literature as being potentially relevant to candidate decision-making. We identify five such types of models:

- Rational-economic models
- Rational-psychological models
- Person-organization fit models
- Individual differences models
- Negotiation process models

Rational-Economic Models

First, in turning the focus from organizational decision-making to applicant decision-making, one might straightforwardly pose the question whether individual decision-making mirrors a rational process which is supposedly directed towards maximizing utility (e.g., McFadyen & Thomas, 1997). Indeed, economic models – among which the so-called 'scarred model' and the 'search theoretic model' each using different assumptions on the likelihood of getting a job over time (McFadyen & Thomas, 1997) – assume individuals have precisely this rationality in striving for maximal utility. This economic approach is almost exclusively based on the notion that applicants are rational job seekers and choose between offers purely on economic grounds. Rational-economic models depend upon the concept of a 'reservation wage' – the minimum wage that the individual is prepared to accept. The individual will go on searching for a job until the income offered is higher than the reservation wage. At that point the offer will be accepted.

Over the years some amendments to the basic model have been made, for instance the inclusion of factors such as job-offer probability, the status of the job, and the individual's appreciation of leisure time (McFadyen & Thomas, 1997). However, even with such extensions, economic models remain completely rational in their view of applicant decision-making. Another restriction is that there is no place for individual difference variables – these models merely try to capture general human behaviour and presume there are no individual differences in job-choice behaviour. Nevertheless, psychological research does show a negative relationship between the length of unemployment and the motivation to search, which DeWitte (1993) suggests may result from a strategy of coping with rejection. Finally, from a psychological perspective, the wage criterion is clearly an unnecessarily restrictive one. Not only are there more factors which can be distinguished within the category of 'hard' criteria (e.g., career perspectives), but also a host of 'soft' criteria can be detected too (e.g., an interesting job, independence, new challenges, etc.) In a recent Dutch survey concerning on-the-job-search (Business Publications Arbeidsmarkt, 1999) such 'soft' job characteristics were valued more positively by applicants than 'hard' job criteria.

Rational Psychological Models

A second category of models can be identified which also espouse a rational view of candidate decision-making but which are derived from the applied social and applied cognitive psychology literatures. These models presume a candidate's pursuit of a job will depend on the value or attractiveness of the job multiplied by the probability of obtaining the job. The economic models may be seen to be a special case of this category in that the value or attractiveness of a job is merely defined in monetary terms. Within the category of psychological models, however, the attractiveness may be made up of a host of factors (e.g., the chance to learn new things, the experience of control, career opportunities, job security, opportunity to relate to others, to name a few). Examples of this type of model include *expectancy value models of motivation* (e.g., Feather & O'Brien, 1987; Feather, 1992; Barber, 1998), Soelberg's (1967) *generalizable decision processing model* (see also, Bryant, 1990, and Kahneman & Tversky, 1979), and *critical contact information processing models* (e.g., Behling, Labovitz & Gainer, 1968; Barber, 1998).

Person-Organization Fit Models

This class of models focuses on individual differences in psychological and emotional needs. The emphasis is on the perceived fit between, on the one hand, the individual in terms of his/her personality, norms, values and needs and, on the other hand, the organization's culture, norms and management style (see for instance Kristof, 1996). The assumption is that an individual's decisions during recruitment and selection will primarily be a result of the perceived ability of the organization to satisfy the predominant needs of the individual.

Individual Differences Models

A related but distinct approach emphasizes individual differences between candidates from quite a different perspective. Here, personality differences are put forward as explanatory factors for style differences in job search decision-making behaviour. In trying to predict individual decision-making style during recruitment and selection, a number of personality characteristics have been put forward to predict such style differences. In their review article, Schwab, Rynes and Aldag (1987) mention the following outcomes. In job search, achievement motivation correlates positively with job search intensity, as does self-esteem. Procrastination on the other hand is thought to negatively relate to job search intensity.

Negotiation Process Models

A fifth type of model that can be identified stresses the recruitment and selection process as a social negotiation between two parties, namely the organization and the individual (e.g., Herriot, 1989b). The assumption is that both consider the recruitment and selection process as a negotiation process towards a possible future employment relationship. The model therefore assumes that both partners have comparatively strong bargaining positions and that outcomes can indeed be 'negotiated' through interactions during the selection process (see also Anderson, 1992). Which factors are relevant and salient in the negotiation process depends heavily upon the cultural/societal context. Enacted rights of workers and the strength of trade unions differ greatly across countries. In some Western countries, for example the US and The Netherlands, unemployment is currently at record low levels and it is very difficult for organizations to recruit qualified candidates into job areas of skills shortage. Candidates here are in such a strong market position that demands during the selection process can be pushed higher and higher. In general, it is in the domain of working conditions and remuneration that negotiations will occur.

A General Model of Applicant Decision-making

Having acknowledged these broad types of models, below we present a tentative general model of applicant decision-making in selection (see also Ryan & Ployhart, in press). The model distinguishes five main classes of variables pertinent to applicant decision-making in the specific context of selection procedures (Figure 10.1):

- Applicant characteristics
- Applicant reactions to selection procedures
- Perceived fit between the candidate and the job and organization
- Labour market conditions
- Organizational and job attractiveness

Applicant characteristics can be seen to reflect the individual differences approach in the literature; applicant reactions to selection incorporate the candidate's reactions, attribution and justice research literature reviewed earlier in this chapter; perceived fit echoes the person–organization fit tradition; labour market conditions are linked to issues of the negotiation process model, again reviewed earlier; and finally, in organizational and job attractiveness, economic and rational-psychological models may be recognized.

Applicant Characteristics

Applicant characteristics and self-perceptions are hypothesized to have a direct, main effect upon perceptions of job fit (relationship (1) in Figure 10.1). Such variables as applicant personality, education, qualifications, motivation, career aspirations, self-esteem, and so forth are argued to influence perceived fit, although importantly it will be applicant self-perceptions of these variables which are influential as opposed to independent measures of these variables.

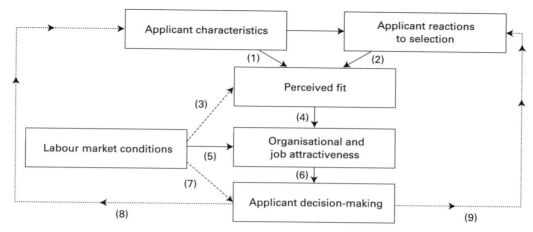

Figure 10.1 *A general model of applicant decision-making. Key: main effect ———; moderating effect ------; feedback effect·········.*

Applicant Reactions to Selection

Applicant reactions to the selection process are similarly hypothesized to have a direct, main effect upon perceived fit (relationship (2) in Figure 10.1). In spite of the considerable volume of research into candidate reactions to selection methods reviewed earlier in this chapter, the precise manner in which these affect applicant outcome decisions is less clear. In general, the more the process is liked – the more informative, relevant, fair, timely and transparent, less intrusive, and more affable the recruiter – the greater the chance of perceived fit (see also Maurer, Hove & Lee, 1992).

Perceived Fit

A distinction can clearly be made between two levels of perceived fit: applicant–job fit, and applicant–organization fit (e.g., Kristof, 1996). Applicant–job fit will be determined primarily by perceptions of congruence between applicant knowledge, skills and abilities (KSAs) and job demands, responsibilities and characteristics. Applicant–organization fit will be more amorphous, being primarily determined by applicant perceptions of value congruence between themselves and the recruiting organization based upon limited exposure to the organization during selection processes (again see Kristof, 1996, for a detailed review). Both levels of fit we hypothesize will be directly influenced by applicant characteristics and applicant reactions (relationships (1) and (2) in Figure 10.1), but will be moderated by candidate perceptions of prevailing labour market conditions (relationship (3) in Figure 10.1). Thus, in a highly competitive labour market with concomitantly high selection ratios (i.e., larger numbers of applicants for fewer jobs), applicants will adjust their criterion level of perceived minimum fit downwards, becoming more willing to accept

greater incongruence and, in addition, to tolerate less preferable treatment in the selection process itself. In labour market conditions which favour the applicant, either due to skill shortages or simply a more general shortage of applicants for positions, applicant reactions become more critical. Here, the issue of perceived fit also becomes more important. Whatever the current labour market conditions, we believe that this issue of perceived fit is one warranting considerably more research in the future by selection psychologists in different countries; indeed, we see it as a crucially important area for future applicant behaviour research.

Labour Market Conditions

Labour market conditions and the position of the candidate within their sector of the market will exert considerable influence on applicant decision-making (e.g., Schwab et al., 1987). These factors will influence candidate expectations of the chance of receiving job offers, in other words. Alternative job opportunities and the labour market status of the applicant confers upon them the prerogative to be more critical and turn down a job offer, or to withdraw from the recruitment process with relative impunity. On the other hand, when labor market conditions are unfavourable for the applicant, a job offer will be more readily accepted. Not only will this class of variables have a moderating effect upon perceived fit as asserted above (relationship (3) in Figure 10.1), it will also have a main effect upon organizational and job attractiveness (relationship (5)), and a moderating effect upon applicant outcome decision-making (relationship (7)). That is, labour market conditions and organizational and job attractiveness are likely to be negatively correlated. In addition, the stronger the candidate believes their own position to be within the labour market for particular recruits, the less immediately attractive will be the organization or job in question. Whilst organization and job attractiveness are hypothesized to have a direct, main effect upon applicant decisions (relationship (6) in Figure 10.1), labour market conditions will moderate outcome decision-making – relationship (7).

Organizational and Job Attractiveness

Organizational and job attractiveness we have already hypothesized will be determined primarily by perceived fit (relationship (4)) and by labour market conditions (relationship (5)). The candidate's perceptions of job demands, responsibilities and characteristics as well as their views of the attractiveness of the organization will also affect these perceptions of fit. In turn, organizational and job attractiveness will exert a direct, main effect upon applicant outcome decisions: that is, to accept or reject an offer of employment or to withdraw from the selection process prior to this (relationship (6) in Figure 10.1). Attractiveness will include both extrinsic factors (career opportunities, training and development, job security, etc.).

Finally, we propose two parallel feedback loops in the model from applicant decision-making to applicant characteristics (relationship (8)), and from decision-making to reactions to selection procedures (relationship (9)). Here we hypothesize that applicant decisions will affect their own perceptions of self-efficacy, particularly where a candidate is able to choose between a number of job offers. Similarly, past experiences of selection processes, and in particular the candidate's own decisions in these processes, will influence their likely reactions to future selection procedures.

To summarize, we propose this model of applicant decision-making as a general schema which includes the main variables and effects which are likely to be present in any selection situation where the candidate feels that they have an opportunity to reach a decision during the process. It is acknowledged that this model is by necessity a simplification of the highly complex and dynamic nature of applicant decision-making but, nevertheless, it contains a number of empirically testable relationships, effects and hypotheses. It is for future research to examine these hypothesized effects in a variety of selection contexts.

CONCLUDING COMMENTS

This chapter has presented an overview of research into applicant reactions and decision-making in the selection process. It has sought to achieve this overview by initially presenting recent findings into three flourishing areas of research: candidate reactions to selection methods, attribution theory and research, and distributive and procedural justice.

From the sheer number of studies presented in these three sections, it is clear that work and organization psychologists with a particular interest in staff selection have been increasingly active in examining the process from a 'candidate's-eye view'; the unifying theme across all of these studies being the implicit assumption that applicant reactions and decisions are an integral part of selection outcomes, and, as such, are therefore worthy of research attention. Building upon this burgeoning range of study findings, the final section reviewed extant models of decision-making from which our general model of applicant decision-making in selection was eventually derived. This model is propounded as an encompassing schema of applicant decision-making capable of being empirically tested in real-life selection scenarios where the focus of any research effort is upon the reactions and decisions of the applicant rather than the organization. It is our sincere hope that this model generates further research into its hypothesized main and moderator effects, or at the very least serves as a general schema of the types of variables and their possible impact upon applicant decision-making in selection processes.

REFERENCES

Adams, J.S. (1965). Inequity in social exchange. In L. Berkowitz (Ed.), *Advances in experimental in psychology*, (Vol. 2, pp. 267–299). New York: Academic Press.'

Anderson, N.R. (1992). Eight decades of employment interview research: A retrospective meta-review and prospective commentary. *European Work and Organizational Psychologist*, 2, 1–32.

Anderson, N.R. (in press). Towards a theory of socialization impact, *International Journal of Selection and Assessment*.

Anderson, N.R., & Ostroff, C. (1997). Selection as socialization. In N. Anderson & P. Herriot (Eds.), *International handbook of selection and assessment*. London: Wiley.

Arnold, J. (1996). The Psychological contract: A concept in need of closer scrutiny? *European Journal of Work and Organizational Psychology*, 5(4), 511–520.

Arvey, R.D., & Sackett, P.R. (1993). Fairness in selection: Current developments and perspectives. In N. Schmitt & W. Borman (Eds.), *Personnel selection in organizations*. San Fransisco: Jossey Bass.

Arvey, R.D., Strickland, W., Drauden, G., & Martin, C. (1990). Motivational components of test-taking. *Personnel Psychology*, 43, 695–716.

Barber, A.E. (1998). *Recruiting employees. Individual and organizational perspectives*. Thousand Oaks, CA: Sage.

Barbera, K.M., Ryan, A.M., Desmarais, L.B., & Dyer, P.J. (1995). *Multimedia employment tests: Effects of attitudes and experiences on validity*. Paper presented at the Tenth Annual Conference of the Society for Industrial and Organizational Psychology, Orlando, FL., USA.

Baron, H., & Janman, K. (1996). Fairness in the assessment centre. In C.L. Cooper & I.T. Robertson (Eds.), *International Review of Industrial and Organizational Psychology* (Vol. 11, pp. 61–113).

Bartram, D. (1999). Testing and the internet: Current realities, issues and future possibilities. *Selection and Development Review, 15*, 3–12.

Behling, O., Labovitz, G., & Gainer, M. (1968). College recruiting: A theoretical basis. *Personnel Journal, 47*, 13–19.

Bies, R.J., & Moag, J.S. (1986). Interactional Justice: Communication criteria of fairness. *Research on Negotiation in Organizations, 1*, 43–55.

Bies, R.J., & Shapiro, D.L. (1988). Voice and justification: Their influence on procedural fairness judgements. *Academy of Management Journal, 31*, 676–685.

Bliesener, T. (1996). Methodological moderators in validating biographical data in personnel selection. *Journal of Occupational and Organizational Psychology, 69*, 107–120.

Borman, W., Hanson, M., & Hedge, J. (1997). Personnel Selection. *Annual Review of Psychology, 48*, 299–337.

Brockner, J., & Wiesenfeld, B.M. (1996). An integrative framework for explaining reactions to decisions: Interactive effects of outcomes and procedures. *Psychological Bulletin, 120*, 189–208.

Bryant, R.R. (1990). Job search and information processing in the presence of nonrational behavior. *Journal of Economic Behavior and Organization, 14*, 249–260.

Business Publications Arbeidsmarkt (1999). *BOA '99. BPA Onderzoek Arbeidsmarkt* [BPA Labour Market Research]. Amsterdam, The Netherlands: VNU Business Publications.

Chan, D. (1997). Racial subgroup differences in predictive validity perceptions on personality and cognitive ability tests. *Journal of Applied Psychology, 82*, 311–320.

Chan, D., Schmitt, N., DeShon, R.P., Clause, C.S., & Delbridge, K. (1997). Reactions to cognitive ability tests: The relationship between race, test performance, face validity perceptions, and test-taking motivation. *Journal of Applied Psychology, 82*, 300–310.

Chan, D., Schmitt, N., Jennings, D., Clause, C.S., & Delbridge, K. (1998a). Applicant perceptions of test fairness: Integrating justice and self-serving bias perspectives. *International Journal of Selection and Assessment, 6*, 232–239.

Chan, D., Schmitt, N., Sacco, J.M., & DeShon, R.P. (1998b). Understanding pre-test and post-test reactions to cognitive ability and personality tests. *Journal of Applied Psychology, 83*, 471–485.

Connerley, M.L., Mael, F.A., & Morath, R.A. (1999). 'Don't ask – Please tell': Selection privacy from two perspectives. *Journal of Occupational and Organizational Psychology, 72*, 505–422.

Cropanzano, R., & Folger, R. (1989). Referent cognitions and task decision autonomy: beyond equity theory. *Journal of Applied Psychology, 74*, 293–299.

Cunningham-Snell, N.A. (1999). Alternative perspectives on selection: Social impact and validation of graduate selection within a multinational oil company. Ph.D. thesis, University of London.

Deutsch, M. (1975). Equity, equality and need: What determines which value will be used as the basis for distributive justice? *Journal of Social Issues, 31*, 137–149.

DeWitte, K. (1993). Gevolgen van langdurige werkloosheid voor het psychisch welzijn: Overzicht van de onderzoeksliteratuur. *Psychologica Belgica, 3*, 1–35.

Dipboye, R.L. (1997). Structured Selection Interviews: Why do they work? Why are they under-utilised? In N. Anderson & P. Herriot (Eds.), *International handbook of selection and assessment* (pp. 455–473). Chichester: Wiley.

Dodd, W.E. (1977). Attitudes towards assessment center programs. In J.L. Moses & W.C. Byham (Eds.), *Applying the assessment center method*, Elmsford, NY: Pergamon Press.

Dulewicz, S.V., Fletcher, C., & Wood, P. (1983). The study of the internal validity of an assessment centre and of participants' background characteristics and attitudes: A comparison of British and American findings, *Journal of Assessment Centre Technology, 6*, 15–24.

Feather, N.T. (1992). Expectancy-value theory and unemployment. *Journal of Occupational and Organizational Psychology, 65*, 315–330.

Feather, N.T., & O'Brien, G.W. (1987). Looking for employment: An expectancy valence analysis of job-seeking behavior among young people. *Journal of Occupational Psychology, 78*, 251–272.

Fink, A.M., & Butcher, J.N. (1972). Reducing objections to personality inventories with special instructions. *Educational and Psychological Measurement, 32*, 631–639.

Fletcher, C. (1991). Candidates' reactions to assessment centres and their outcomes: A longitudinal study. *Journal of Occupational Psychology, 64*, 117–127.

Folger, R., Rosenfield, D., & Hays, R.P. (1978). Equity and intrinsic motivation: The role of choice. *Journal of Personality and Social Psychology, 36*, 557–564.

Gilliland, S.W. (1993). The perceived fairness of selection systems: An organizational justice perspective. *Academy of Management Review, 18*, 696–734.

Gilliland, S.W. (1994). Effects of procedural and distributive justice on reactions to a selection system. *Journal of Applied Psychology, 79*, 691–701.

Gilliland, S.W. (1995). Fairness from the applicant's perspective: Reactions to employee selection procedures. *International Journal of Selection and Assessment, 3*, 11–19.

Gilliland, S.W., & Beckstein, B.A. (1996). Procedural and distributive justice in the editorial review process. *Personnel Psychology, 49*, 669-691.

Gilliland, S.W., & Honig, H. (1994a). Development of the selection fairness survey. Paper presented at the 9th Annual Conference of the Society for Industrial and Organizational Psychology, Nashville, TN, April.

Gilliland, S.W., & Honig, H. (1994b). The perceived fairness of employee selection systems as a predictor of attitudes and self-concept. In S.W. Gilliland (Chair). Selection from the applicant's perspective: Justice and *employee selection procedures.* Symposium presented at the 9th Annual Conference of the Society for Industrial and Organizational Psychology, Nashville, TN, April.

Gilliland, S.W., & Steiner, D.D. (in press). Causes and consequences of applicant perceptions of unfairness. In R. Cropanzano (Ed.), *Justice in the workplace.* Hillsdale, NJ: Erlbaum.

Greenberg, J. (1987). Reactions to procedural injustice in payment distributions: Do the means justify the ends? *Journal of Applied Psychology, 72,* 55–61.

Greenberg, J. (1990). Employee theft as a reaction to underpayment inequity: The hidden cost of pay cuts. *Journal of Applied Psychology, 75,* 561–568.

Greenberg, J. (1993). Stealing in the name of justice: Informational and interpersonal moderators of theft reactions to underpayment inequity. *Organizational Behaviour and Human Decision Processes, 54,* 81–103.

Guion, R.M. (1998). *Assessment, measurement, and prediction for personnel decisions.* Mahwah, NJ: Lawrence Erlbaum.

Harland, L.K., Rauzi, T., & Biasotto, M.M. (1995). Perceived fairness of personality tests and the impact of explanations for their use. *Employee Responsibilities and Rights Journal, 8,* 183–192.

Harris, M.M., & Fink, L.S. (1987). A field study of applicant reactions to employment opportunities: Does the recruiter make a difference? *Personnel Psychology, 40,* 765–783.

Heider, F. (1958). *The Psychology of interpersonal relations.* New York, NY: Wiley.

Herriot, P. (1981). Towards an attribution theory of the selection interview. *Journal of Occupational Psychology, 54,* 165–173.

Herriot, P. (1989a). Attributional effects on interview decisions. In. G.R. Fern & R.W. Eder (Eds.), *The employment interview: Theory research and practice* (1st ed.). California: Sage.

Herriot, P. (1989b). Selection as a social process. In M. Smith & I.T. Robertson (Eds.), *Advances in selection and assessment* (pp. 171–188). Chichester: Wiley.

Herriot, P., & Anderson, N.R. (1997). Selecting for change: How will personnel and selection psychology survive? In N.R. Anderson & P. Herriot (Eds.), *International handbook of selection and assessment.* Chichester: Wiley.

Herriot, P., & Pemberton, C. (1996). Contracting careers. *Human Relations, 49*(6), 757–790.

Hofstede, G. (1980). *Culture's consequences: International differences in work related values.* Beverly Hills CA: Sage.

Hunter, J.E., & Hunter, R.F. (1984). Validity and utility of alternative predictors of job performance. *Psychological Bulletin, 96,* 72–98.

Iles, P., & Mabey, C. (1993). Managerial career development programmes: Effectiveness, availability and acceptability. *British Journal of Management, 4,* 103–118.

Iles, P.A., & Robertson, I.T. (1997). The impact of personnel selection procedures on candidates. In

N. Anderson & P. Herriot (Eds.), *International handbook of selection and assessment.* Chichester: Wiley.

James, L.R., & Brett, J.M. (1984). Mediators, moderators and tests for mediation, *Journal of Applied Psychology, 69,* 307–321.

Janz, T., & Mooney, G. (1993). Interviewer and candidate reactions to patterned behaviour description interviews, *International Journal of Selection and Assessment, 1,* 165–169.

Kahneman, D., & Tversky, A. (1979). Prospect theory: An analysis of decision under risk. *Econometrika, 47,* 263–291.

Kluger, A.N. & Rothstein, H.R. (1991, April). the influence of selection test type on applicant reactions to employment testing. In R.R. Reilly (Chair), *Perceived validity of selection procedures: Implications for organizations.* Symposium conducted at the sixth annual Society for Industrial/Organizational Psychology Conference, St. Louis, MO.

Knouse, S.B. (1989). The role of attribution theory in personnel employment selection: A review of the recent literature. *The Journal of General Psychology, 116,* 183–196.

Konovsky, M.A., & Cropanzano, R. (1991). Perceived fairness of employee drug testing as a predictor of employee attitudes and job performance. *Journal of Applied Psychology, 76,* 698–708.

Kravitz, D.A., Stinson, V., & Chavez, T.L. (1996). Evaluations of tests used for making selection and promotion decisions. *International Journal of Selection and Assessment, 4,* 24–34.

Kristof, A.L. (1996). Person–organization fit: An integrative review of its conceptualizations, measurements, and implications. *Personnel Psychology, 49,* 1–49.

Kroeck, K.G., & Magnusen, K.O. (1997). Employer and job candidate reactions to videoconference job interviewing. *International Journal of Selection and Assessment, 5,* 137–142.

Leventhal, G.S. (1980). What should be done with equity theory? New approaches to the study of fairness in social relationships. In K.J. Gergen, M.S. Greenberg & R.H. Willis (Eds.), *Social exchange: Advances in theory and research* (pp. 27–55). New York: Plenum Press.

Louis, M.R. (1980). Surprise and sense making: What newcomers experience in entering unfamiliar organizational settings. *Administrative Science Quarterly, 25,* 226–251.

Lounsbury, J., Borrow, W., & Jensen, J. (1989). Attitudes toward employment testing: Scale development, correlates, and 'known-group' validation. *Professional Psychology: Research and Practice, 20,* 340–349.

McFadyen, R.G., & Thomas, J.P. (1997). Economic and psychological models of job search behavior of the unemployed. *Human Relations, 50,* 1461–1484.

McFarlin, D.B., & Sweeney, P.D. (1992). Distributive and procedural justice as predictors of satisfaction with personal and organizational outcomes. *Academy of Management Journal, 35,* 626–637.

Macan, T.H., Avedon, M.J., Paese, M., & Smith, D.E. (1994). The effects of applicants' reactions to cognitive ability tests and an assessment center. *Personnel Psychology, 47*, 715–738.

Maurer, S.D., Howe, V., & Lee, T.W. (1992). Organizational recruiting as marketing management: An interdisciplinary study of engineering graduates. *Personnel Psychology, 45*, 807–833.

Murphy, K.R. (1996). Individual differences and behaviour in organizations: Much more than g. In K.R. Murphy (Ed.), *Individual differences and behaviour in organizations*. San Francisco: Jossey-Bass.

Ployhart, R.E., & Ryan, A.M. (1997). Toward an explanation of applicant reactions: An examination of organizational justice and attribution frameworks. *Organizational Behavior and Human Decision Processes, 72*, 308–335.

Ployhart, R.E., & Ryan, A.M. (1998). Applicants' reactions to the fairness of selection procedures: The effects of positive rule violation and time of measurement. *Journal of Applied Psychology, 83*, 3–16.

Ployhart, R.E., Ryan, A.M., & Bennett, M. (1999). Explanations for selection decisions: Applicants' reactions to informational and sensitivity features of explanations. *Journal of Applied Psychology, 84*, 87–106.

Powell, G.N. (1991). Applicant reactions to the initial employment interview: Exploring theoretical and methodological issues. *Personnel Psychology, 44*, 67–83.

Ramsay, S., Gallois, C., & Callan, V.J. (1997). Social rules and attributions in the personnel selection interview. *Journal of Occupational and Organizational Psychology, 70*, 189–203.

Robertson, I.T., Iles, P.A., Gratton, L., & Sharpley, D.S. (1991). The impact of personnel selection and assessment methods on candidates. *Human Relations, 44*, 963–982.

Rosse, J.G., Miller, J.L., & Stecher, M.D. (1994). A field study of job applicants' reactions to personality and cognitive ability testing, *Journal of Applied Psychology, 79*, 987–992.

Rousseau, D.M. (1995). *Psychological Contracts in Organizations*. London: Sage.

Rousseau, D.M., & Aquino, K. (1993). Fairness and implied contract obligations in termination: The role of remedies, social accounts, and procedural justice. *Human Performance, 6*, 135–149.

Russell, D. (1992). The causal dimension scale: A measure of how individuals perceive causes. *Journal of Personality and Social Psychology, 42*, 1137–1145.

Ryan, A.M., Greguras, G.J., & Ployhart, R.E. (1996). Perceived job relatedness of physical ability testing for firefighters: Exploring variations in reactions. *Human Performance, 9*, 219–240.

Ryan, A.M., & Ployhart, R.E. (in press). Applicants' perceptions of selection procedures and decisions: Critical review and agenda for the future, *Journal of Management*.

Rynes, S.L. (1991). Recruitment, job choice, and post-hire consequences: A call for new research directions. In M.D. Dunnette & L.M. Hough (Eds.), *Handbook of industrial and organizational psychology* (2nd ed.). Palo Alto: Consulting Psychologists Press.

Rynes, S.L. (1993). Who's selecting whom? Effects of selection practices on applicant attitudes and behavior. In N. Schmitt & W. Borman (Eds.), *Personnel selection in organizations*. San Fransisco: Jossey-Bass.

Rynes, S.L., Bretz, R.D., & Gerhart, B. (1991). The importance of recruitment in job choice: A different way of looking. *Personnel Psychology, 44*, 487–521.

Rynes, S.L., & Connerley, M.R. (1993). Applicant reactions to alternative selection procedures, *Journal of Business and Psychology, 7*, 261–277.

Rynes, S.L., Heneman, H.G., & Schwab, D.P. (1980). Individual reactions to organizational recruiting: A review. *Personnel Psychology, 33*, 529–542.

Rynes, S.L., & Miller, H.E. (1983). Recruiter and job influences on candidates for employment, *Journal of Applied Psychology, 68*, 147–154.

Sackett, P.R., & Wanek, J.E. (1996). New developments in the use of measures of honesty, integrity, conscientiousness, dependability, trustworthiness, and reliability for personnel selection. *Personnel Psychology, 49*, 787–830.

Saks, A.M., Leck, J.D., & Saunders, D.M. (1995). Effects of application blanks and employment equity on applicant reactions and job pursuit intentions. *Journal of Organizational Behavior, 16*, 415–430.

Scheu, C., Ryan, A.M., & Nona, F. (1999). Company web-sites as a recruiting mechanism: What influences applicant impressions? Paper presented at the 14th Annual Conference for the Society of Industrial and Organizational Psychology, Atlanta, Georgia.

Schmidt, F.L., Ones, D.S., & Hunter, J.E., (1992). Personnel selection. *Annual Review of Psychology, 43*, 627–670.

Schmidt, F.L., Urry, U.M., & Gugel, J.F. (1978). Computer assisted tailored testing: Examinee reactions and evaluations. *Educational and Psychological Measurement, 38*, 265–273.

Schmit, M.J., & Ryan, A.M. (1992). Test-taking dispositions: A missing link? *Journal of Applied Psychology, 77*, 629–637.

Schmit, M.J., & Ryan, A.M. (1997). Applicant withdrawal: The role of test taking attitudes and racial differences. *Personnel Psychology, 50*, 855–876.

Schmitt, N., & Chan, D. (1999). The status of research on applicant reactions to selection tests and its implications for managers. *International Journal of Management Research*, March, 45–62.

Schmitt, N., & Gilliland, S.W. (1992). Beyond Differential Prediction: Fairness in selection. In D. Saunders (Ed.), *New approaches to employee management: Fairness in employee selection* (Vol. 1, pp. 21–46). Greenwich, CT: JAI Press.

Schmitt, N., Gilliland, S.W., Landis, R.S., & Devine, D. (1993). Computer-based testing applied to selection of secretarial applicants. *Personnel Psychology, 46*, 149–165.

Schuler, H., Farr, J., & Smith (1993). The individual and organizational sides of personnel selection and assessment. In H. Schuler, C.J.L. Farr & M. Smith (Eds.), *Personnel selection and assessment: Individual and organizational perspectives*. New Jersey: Lawrence Earlbaum.

Schwab, D.P., Rynes, S.L., & Aldag, R.J. (1987). Theories and research on job search and choice. In K.M. Rowland & G.R Ferris (Eds.), *Research in personnel and human resources management* (Vol. 5, pp. 129–166). Greenwich, Connecticut: JAI Press.

Shore, L.M., & Tetrick, L.E. (1994). The psychological contract as an explanatory framework in the employment relationship. In C.L. Cooper & D.M. Rousseau (Eds.), *Trends in organizational behavior* (Vol. 1, pp. 91–109). Chichester: John Wiley.

Silvester, J. (1997). Spoken attributions and candidate success in graduate recruitment interviews. *Journal of Occupational and Organizational Psychology, 70,* 61–73.

Silvester, J., Anderson, N.R., Haddleton, E., Cunningham-Snell, N., & Gibb, A. (1999). A cross-modal comparison of telephone and face-to-face selection interviews in graduate recruitment. *International Journal of Selection and Assessment, 8,* 16–21.

Silvester, J., & Brown, A. (1993). Graduate recruitment: Testing the impact. *Selection and Development Review, 9*(1), 1–3.

Silvester, J., & Chapman, A.J. (1996). Unfair discrimination in the selection interview: An attributional account. *International Journal of Selection and Assessment, 4,* 63–70.

Silvester, J., & Chapman, A.J. (1997). Asking 'Why?' in the workplace: Causal attributions and organizational behavior. In C.L. Cooper & D.M. Rousseau (Eds.), *Trends in organizational behavior*, Vol. 4. Chichester: Wiley.

Smither, J.W., Reilly, R.R., Millsap, R.E., Pearlman, K., & Stoffey, R.W. (1993). Applicant reactions to selection procedures. *Personnel Psychology, 46,* 49–76.

Snow, C.S., & Snell, S.A. (1993). Staffing as strategy. In N. Schmitt, W. Borman and Associates (Eds.), *Personnel selection in organizations.* San Francisco: Jossey-Bass.

Soelberg, P.O. (1967). Unprogrammed decision-making. *Industrial Management Review, 8,* 19–29.

Steiner, D.D. (2000). Perceptions des méthodes de recrutement en France: La perspective de la justice organisationelle. [Perceptions of selection techniques in France: The organizational justice perspective.] *Psychologie du Travail et des Organisations, 6,* 89–106.

Steiner, D.D., & Gilliland, S.W. (1996). Fairness reactions to personnel selection techniques in France and the United States. *Journal of Applied Psychology, 81,* 134–141.

Stone, D.L., & Jones, G.E. (1997). Perceived fairness of biodata as a function of the purpose of the request for information and gender of the applicant. *Journal of Business and Psychology, 11,* 313–323.

Struthers, C.W., Colwill, N.L., & Perry, R.P. (1992). An attributional analysis of decision-making in a personnel selection interview. *Journal of Applied Social Psychology, 22,* 801–818.

Taylor, M.S., & Bergmann, T.J. (1987). Organizational recruitment activities and applicants' reactions at different stages of the recruitment process. *Personnel Psychology, 40,* 261–285.

Thibaut, J., & Walker, L. (1975). *Procedural justice: A psychological analysis.* Hillsdale NJ: Erlbaum.

Thorsteinson, T.J., & Ryan, A.M. (1997). The effect of selection ratio on perceptions of the fairness of a selection battery. *International Journal of Selection and Assessment, 5*(3), 159–168.

Tucker, D.H., & Rowe, P.M. (1979). Relationship between expectancy, causal attributions, and final hiring decisions in the employment interview. *Journal of Applied Psychology, 64,* 27–34.

Wanous, J.P. (1992). *Organizational entry: Recruitment, selection, orientation and socialization of newcomers* (2nd ed.). Reading, MA: Addison-Wesley.

Weiner, B. (1985). An attributional theory of achievement motivation and emotion, *Psychological Review, 92,* 548–573.

Weiner, B. (1986). *An attributional theory of motivation and emotion.* New York, NY: Springer-Verlag.

11

Cognitive Ability

MALCOLM JAMES REE,
THOMAS R. CARRETTA
and JAMES R. STEINDL*

This chapter reviews the extensive literature examining relations between cognitive ability, especially general cognitive ability (*g*), and occupational performance. We begin with an examination of the structure of ability and the similarity of factor structure for sex and ethnic groups. Next, we identify several methodological issues in the measurement of ability and occupational performance. We then examine the predictive validity of *g* for training and on-the-job performance, and the incremental validity of specific cognitive abilities, job knowledge, and personality. Next, path models are reviewed that document studies examining causal relations among *g*, job knowledge, and occupational performance in training and on the job. We then briefly review the literature on differential validity and predictive bias. In addition, we respond to critics citing methodological and theoretical issues.

Ability is a general term concerning the power or capacity to act financially, legally, mentally, physically, or in some other way. Cognitive ability refers specifically to mental qualification or capacity. The relationship between cognitive ability, especially general cognitive ability (*g*), and occupational performance has long been a subject of theoretical speculation and applied research. Several areas of study have contributed to our understanding of this relationship. These include studies examining the structure of ability, the predictive validity of *g* and other personnel attributes (e.g., specific abilities, job knowledge, personality) for training and on-the-job performance, and causal models of the relations among *g*, job knowledge, and occupational performance.

STRUCTURE OF ABILITIES

Historical Perspective

Speculation on the structure of human abilities can be traced back to Aristotle who distinguished ability (*dianoia*), from the emotional and moral faculty (*orexis*). The French secular philosopher Descartes conceived of ability as *res cogitans*, 'the thing that thinks'.

Peiró and Munduate (1994) report a sixteenth century Spanish treatise by Huarte in 1575 on cognitive and other abilities and work called *Examen de ingenios para las ciencies* (available as Huarte de San Juan, 1991), that was later published in English as *The examination of men's wits: Discovering the*

*The views expressed are those of the authors and not necessarily those of the United States Government, the Department of Defense, or the United States Air Force. Address all correspondence to the first author at Our Lady of the Lake University, Center for Leadership Studies, 411 S. W. 24th Street, San Antonio, Texas 78207. Send electronic mail to reemal@lake.ollusa.edu.

great differences of wits among men and what sort of learning suites best with each genius. Despite these early efforts, the scientific study of human abilities is often traced back to Galton, Binet, Spearman, and the US Army Alpha test of the First World War.

In his view of general and specific abilities, Spearman (1927) proposed that every test measures a general factor (g) common to all tests, and one or more specific factors (s_1 to s_n) that are unique to each test. Spearman often depicted these constructs with overlapping circles. General ability was represented by a large circle and specific abilities by smaller ovals, arrayed radially (for an illustration, see Jensen, 1980: 214; Ree & Carretta, 1998: 162). The amount of overlap between the large circle and small ovals varies, depending on the extent to which a test measured g and one or more specific abilities. Ultimately, Spearman acknowledged what have become known as group factors. These are 'specifics' that appear in more than one test such as verbal or spatial.

Flat and Hierarchical Models of Cognitive Abilities

The structure of ability has been conceptualized in many different ways. For example, Thurstone's (1938) model of Primary Mental Abilities did not include a general factor. It is a flat model. Thurstone proposed there was no general factor and that ability consisted of seven independent 'primary' factors, a position that data later forced him to abandon (Thurstone & Thurstone, 1941). Despite Thurstone and Thurstone's recantation, multiple aptitude theories strongly influenced psychology for several years (Fleishman & Quaintance, 1984; Gardner, 1983; Guilford, 1956, 1959; Sternberg, 1985). The influence of multiple aptitude theories was especially evident in psychometrics, where they led to the development of several multiple ability tests including the Armed Services Vocational Aptitude Battery (ASVAB), the Differential Aptitude Test (DAT), Flanagan Aptitude Tests (FIT-FACT), the General Aptitude Test Battery (GATB), and others.

Despite the popularity of multiple aptitude theories, there has been a growing consensus over the past 50 years that abilities have a pyramidal or hierarchical structure (e.g., Burt, 1949; Vernon, 1950, 1969). Burt (1949) proposed a five-level hierarchy with g at the apex, and successively expanding levels below. From higher to lower, these levels are 'General Intelligence', 'Relations', 'Association', 'Perception', and 'Sensation'. Burt suggested that the second level is made up of broad group factors based on form and content. The successive levels are more numerous and composed of narrower more specialized group factors.

Vernon's (1950, 1969) hierarchical model also has g at its apex. The next level has two broad (i.e., major group) factors of verbal–educational (v: ed) and spatial-mechanical or spatial-perceptual–practical (k:m). These major group factors subdivide into minor group factors that further devolve to specific factors.

Cattell (1971) and Horn (1978) hypothesized a hierarchical model that does not include g. Instead, their model had two factors at its highest point, Gc (i.e., crystallized ability) and Gf (i.e., fluid ability). Hakstian and Cattell (1978) tentatively added four other factors representing memory (Gm), perceptual speed (Gps), retrieval (Gr), and visualization (Gv), but recognized the need for further confirmation. Jager (1967) also proposed several higher-order factors, but his model has not been influential.

Gustafsson (1988) suggested a relationship between the Spearman-type g model and the Cattell–Horn fusion. He suggests that Gf corresponds to g, Gc to v: ed, and Gv to k: m. Gustafsson (1980) supports a portion of this interpretation by finding the loading of Gf on g at .94, a near identity.

Hierarchical models of ability imply higher-order sources as well as several specific lower-order sources. For cognitive ability, the highest-order factor (g) usually accounts for more of the variance than do all of the specific factors combined. To understand the nature of the lower-order factors, it is important to residualize (Schmid & Leiman, 1957), thus removing the effects of g on the lower-order factors. The largest proportion of variance accounted for by a residualized specific factor in representative multiple-ability tests is about 8% (Carretta & Ree, 1996; Ree & Carretta, 1994: Stauffer, Ree & Carretta, 1996). Frequently this 8% is due to specific knowledge, not specific ability. To put this in perspective, g typically accounts for about 30% to 65% of variance depending on the test battery composition. See Jensen (1980, chapter 6) for an informative review.

Fairness and Similarity: Are the Same Factors Measured in All Groups?

Several principles must be considered when addressing the measurement of cognitive abilities in multiple groups. One of these is that the same factors should be measured for all groups. McArdle (1996), for one, has stated that factorial invariance (i.e., equality of factor loadings) should be established before other group comparisons (e.g., mean differences) are considered. McArdle argues that if factorial invariance is not observed, the psychological constructs being measured may be qualitatively different for the groups being compared, thus obscuring the interpretability of other comparisons.

Several studies have been done regarding the similarity of cognitive factors for different race/ethnic, sex, and socioeconomic groups. For example, Michael (1949) found virtually no differences in the cognitive factor structure for blacks and whites on Second World War US Army pilot selection tests. Humphreys and Taber (1973) also found no differences in their comparison of factor structures for high and low socioeconomic status boys from Project Talent. Although the ethnicity of the Project Talent participants was not specifically identified, Humphreys and Taber stated that they believed the ethnic composition of the high and low socioeconomic status groups would differ significantly.

DeFries et al. (1974) compared the structure of ability for Hawaiians of either European or Japanese ancestry. Using 15 cognitive tests, they found the same four factors and nearly identical factor loadings for the two groups.

Michael (1949), Humphreys and Taber (1973), and DeFries et al. (1974) all examined common factors. In contrast, others (Carretta & Ree, 1995; Ree & Carretta, 1995) have used hierarchical models to investigate the comparative structure of cognitive abilities for sex and ethnic groups. In a multi-group cognitive ability factors comparison using a hierarchical model that included g and three lower-order factors of verbal/math, speed, and technical knowledge, Ree and Carretta (1995) noted only small group differences on the verbal/math and speed factors. No significant differences were found for g on ability measures.

Carretta and Ree (1995) compared cognitive-ability factor structures in large samples of young Americans. Their hierarchical model included g and five lower-order cognitive ability factors representing verbal, math, spatial, aircrew knowledge, and perceptual speed. The model showed good fit and little difference for men and women and for all five ethnic groups. Correlations between factor loadings for the sex groups and for all pairs of ethnic groups were very high, approaching $r = 1.0$. Regressions between pairs of groups indicated that there was no mean difference in loadings between males and females or among the ethnic groups. Similar results were observed for sex groups on two cognitive ability and psychomotor ability test batteries (Carretta, 1997b; Carretta & Ree, 1997). Cai, Gong, Dai and Tang (1998) found similarity of cognitive ability factor structure in Chinese living in urban and rural communities. These and previous results (see, for example, Jensen, 1980) present a consistent picture of the near identity of cognitive ability structure for sex and ethnic groups.

Methodological Issues in the Measurement of Ability and Occupational Performance

There are several crucial methodological issues that influence the interpretability of the relations between ability and occupational performance (Carretta & Ree, in press; Ree, 1995). Ree facetiously offered nine rules for doing ability studies wrong. These ability studies are typified by validation studies. The 'rules' are listed below with added comments on what constitutes a more valid approach.

- *Rule 1: Avoid looking in the published literature.* Ignoring the published literature prohibits your research from having a sound theoretical basis (see, for an explanatory example, Schmidt, 1994).

- *Rule 2: Develop unreliable measures of abilities and criteria.* The validity of a measure is limited by a function of the reliability of the variables. Strive to make all your variables reliable (see, for example, Gulliksen, 1950, 1989).

- *Rule 3: Use small, range-restricted samples.* Small, range-restricted samples are the avatar of poor research. Nothing else can do so much to invalidate your conclusions. Whenever possible, correct correlations for range restriction (Lawley, 1943; Ree, Carretta, Earles & Albert, 1994; Thorndike, 1949).

- *Rule 4: Capitalize on chance.* Failing to cross-validate validity findings presents an unacceptable risk to your user. Do not provide false hope that a predictor will work when you are only capitalizing on chance.

- *Rule 5: Use the wrong model of reliability.* Study the psychometric reliability literature (McDonald, 1999). There is an overapplication on coefficient alpha. If you have speeded tests, a test that shows daily variability, or significant learning effects, coefficient alpha will produce inappropriate estimates.

- *Rule 6: Interpret the smallest source of variance in a factor.* Most rotated factors have a widely shared common factor, such as g, as their prime source of variance. Elsewhere (Ree & Carretta, 1998) we have explained this by noting that the mathematics factor is mostly g hence the mathematics factor should be thought of as mostly g and some small amount of M, mathematics. However, most factors are named by their smallest source of variance.

- *Rule 7: Be concerned only with your experiential variable and not with variables to which it may be related.* Human characteristics, especially job-related characteristics, are intercorrelated. Selection on one constitutes indirect selection on all correlated variables. This can have undesirable effects on observed correlations.

For example, the American Psychological Association (1987) recommends that job tenure be considered via partial correlation when conducting validation studies.

- *Rule 8: Disregard group differences.* Do not surprise your user by ignoring differences among groups (Ree, Carretta & Earles, 1999). Analyze and report all correlations and mean and variance differences for all groups with sufficient sample size.
- *Rule 9: Avoid using marker variables.* Marker or reference variables are the generally agreed upon measures of a construct. To know what your variable measures it should be administered along with known marker variables. Appropriate marker variables might include a measure of *g*, conscientiousness, or psychomotor tracking.

SPECIFIC COGNITIVE ABILITIES, KNOWLEDGE, AND NONCOGNITIVE TRAITS

It has often been proposed that the measurement of specific cognitive abilities, knowledge, and noncognitive traits is prerequisite for understanding human characteristics and occupational performance. For example, McClelland (1993) speculated that under some circumstances noncognitive traits such as motivation might be better predictors of job performance than cognitive abilities. Sternberg and Wagner (1993) proposed using measures of tacit knowledge and practical intelligence in place of measures of 'academic intelligence'. They define tacit knowledge as 'the practical know how one needs for success on the job' (p. 2). Practical intelligence is characterized as a more general form of tacit knowledge. Schmidt and Hunter (1993), in a review of Sternberg and Wagner, note that their concepts of tacit knowledge and practical intelligence are redundant with the well-established construct of job knowledge.

ACADEMIC AND OCCUPATIONAL PERFORMANCE

Academic performance is commonly measured using class grades or cumulative grade point average. These measures generally reflect the student's ability to demonstrate the acquisition of knowledge gained in the classroom.

Occupational performance consists of several broad components. Some examples include: (1) possessing the knowledge, skills, and techniques required to perform the job, (2) training and retraining for promotions or new jobs, or just staying current with the changing demands of the 'same' job, and (3) the application of knowledge, skills, and

techniques to achieve organizational goals. We do not discuss models of job performance here as they are presented in other chapters in this volume and elsewhere (Ree & Carretta, 1998).

Academic and Training Measures

The first step in doing a job is to acquire the necessary knowledge and master the required skills. This process begins early during formal education with reading, writing, and arithmetic. Secondary school, college, formal job training, and on-the-job-training provide the opportunity to acquire more specialized job knowledge. General cognitive ability has been shown to be predictive of performance in all of these training settings (Jensen, 1998).

Predictive Utility of g

Many studies have demonstrated the predictive utility of *g* against academic performance. Jensen (1980: 319) provides the following estimates of the validity of *g* for predicting academic success: at elementary school, .6 to .7; at high school, .5 to .6; at college, .4 to .5; and at graduate school, .3 to .4. Jensen further observed that the apparent decrease in the predictiveness of *g* might be the result of artifacts such as range restriction and selective assortment into educational track.

Thorndike (1986) examined the predictive utility of *g* for six high school course grades and found an average correlation of .532. This is consistent with Jensen's (1980) estimates. In his presidential address to the American Psychological Association, McNemar (1964) reported that *g* was the best predictor of school performance in 4,096 studies that used the Differential Aptitude Tests. Additionally, Brodnick and Ree (1995) showed that *g* was a better predictor of college performance than social class.

Measures of general cognitive ability have also been shown to be useful for predicting training performance. For example, Roth and Campion (1992) illustrated the validity of a general ability composite for predicting training success for petroleum process technicians. The validity of the *g*-based composite was .50 after correction for range restriction. Salgado (1995) reported biserial correlations of .38 between a general ability composite and a measure of pilot training success in the Spanish Air Force. His data were not corrected for range restriction. Using cumulative techniques, Salgado demonstrated that there was no variability in the correlations across five classes of pilot trainees.

Jones (1988) used the loadings from the unrotated first principle component of a 10-test multiple-aptitude battery to estimate their *g*-saturation. She then correlated these loadings with the average validity of the 10 tests for predicting training performance for 37 jobs and observed a correlation of .76. Jones also computed the same correlation within each of the four job families (administrative, electronics, general, and mechanical) that encompassed the 37 jobs. No differences were found between the job families. Ree and Earles (1992) subsequently corrected Jones' *g* loadings for unreliability and found the correlation to be .98. Ree and Earles obtained the same value in a replication in a different sample across 150 jobs. Jensen (1998) investigated the source of validity of aptitude tests and concluded 'that *g* is the ubiquitous agent of predictive validity over an extremely wide variety of jobs' (p. 286).

Incrementing the Predictive Utility of *g*

Thorndike (1986) reported the comparative validity of measures of *g* versus specific ability composites for predicting success for about 1,900 enlisted US Army trainees enrolled in 35 technical schools. Specific abilities showed little incremental validity (.03) beyond *g*. Further, on cross-validation the multiple correlations for specific abilities usually shrunk below the bivariate correlation for *g*.

Using a large military sample, Ree and Earles (1991) demonstrated that training performance was more a function of *g* than specific factors. Participants were 78,041 US Air Force enlisted personnel enrolled in 82 job-training courses. Ree and Earles examined whether *g* predicted training performance in about the same way regardless of the kind of job or its difficulty. It might be argued based on Hull's (1928) theory, that although *g* was useful for some jobs, specific abilities were compensatory or more important and therefore, more valid for other jobs. Ree and Earles tested Hull's hypothesis using linear models analysis. They sought to determine whether the relationship between *g* and training performance was the same for all 82 jobs. This was done by first imposing the constraint that the regression coefficients for *g* be the same in each of the 82 equations, and then releasing the constraint and allowing the 82 regression coefficients to be estimated individually. Although there was statistical evidence that the relationship between *g* and the training criteria differed by job, these differences were so small as to be of no practical predictive consequence. The relationship between *g* and training performance was nearly identical across jobs. Using a single prediction equation for all 82 jobs reduced the correlation between *g* and training performance by less than one-half of 1%.

In personnel selection applications, specific ability tests sometimes are given to qualify applicants for jobs based on the assumption that specific abilities are predictive or incrementally predictive. The US Air Force uses such tests for qualifying applicants for training as computer programmers and intelligence operatives. Besetsny, Earles and Ree (1993) and Besetsny, Ree and Earles (1993) examined these two tests to determine if they measured

something other than *g* and if their validity was incremental to *g*. The samples were 3,547 computer programming and 776 intelligence operative trainees and the criterion was training performance. Two multiple regression equations were computed for each group of trainees. The first equation had only *g* and the second had *g* and specific cognitive abilities. The difference in R^2 between these two equations was tested to determine whether specific abilities incremented *g*. Incremental validity gains for the two jobs for specific abilities beyond *g* were .00 and .02, respectively. Although the two tests were designed to measure specific cognitive abilities, they added little or nothing beyond *g*.

In a similar vein, selection interviews are sometimes used in the belief that they measure abilities and characteristics that are incremental to *g*. For example, Walters Miller, and Ree (1993) investigated the validity and incremental validity of an experimental structured interview for selecting US Air Force pilot trainees. Two hundred and twenty-three (223) pilot trainees were administered the Air Force Officer Qualifying Test (AFOQT; Carretta & Ree, 1996), computer-based cognitive and personality tests, and the structured interview. Experienced Air Force pilots who had completed a brief training course in interview techniques served as interviewers. Interview questions were designed to assess trainees' educational background, motivation to fly, self-confidence and leadership, and flying job knowledge. Interviewers rated trainees in each of these areas and on probable success in pilot training, bomber-fighter flying, and tanker-transport flying. The dependent measure in the validation study was a dichotomous passing/failing pilot training outcome score. The average validity of the predictors was as follows: 16 AFOQT tests, .28; computer-based tests, .18; and the seven interview scores, .21. No incremental validity was found for the seven interview scores when they were added to the regression equation containing the AFOQT and computer-based test scores. The lack of incremental validity for the interview scores occurred because they lacked unique predictive variance. Ree and Carretta (1997) subsequently performed linear regression analyses using Walters et al.'s (1993) data to compare full and restricted regression equations for predicting pilot training outcome. These analyses showed that adding the interview scores to a measure of *g* extracted from the AFOQT did not improve prediction. The interview's predictive utility clearly came from the measurement of *g*. As with Besetsny, Earles and Ree (1993) and Besetsny, Ree and Earles (1993), despite the intent of the interview designers to measure unique abilities beyond *g*, the interview failed to do so.

Thorndike (1986) reported Second World War data regarding the incremental validity of specific composites versus *g* for the prediction of passing/

Table 11.1   *Meta-analytic predictive validity of g and a second predictor for training performance*

Predictor	Validity (r)	Multiple R	R−r$_g^1$
g	.56		
Integrity tests	.38	.67	.11
Conscientiousness tests	.30	.65	.09
Employment interviews (Structured and unstructured)	.35	.59	.03
Peer ratings	.36	.57	.01
Reference checks	.23	.61	.05
Job experience (years)	.01	.56	.00
Biographical data	.30	.56	.00
Years of education	.20	.60	.04
Interests	.18	.59	.03

Note: [1] This is the difference between the correlation for g only (.56) and the multiple correlation, R.
Source: Adapted from Schmidt and Hunter (1998). Reprinted by permission. Copyright 1998 American Psychological Association.

failing pilot training for a sample of 1,000 trainees. He found an increment of .05 (.64 vs. .59) for specifics beyond g. Examination of the test content revealed that specific knowledge (i.e., aviation information) was tested and may have accounted for part of the increment.

Along the same lines as Thorndike (1986), Olea and Ree (1994) examined the validity of psychometric g, specific ability, and specific knowledge for predicting several US Air Force pilot and navigator training criteria. Psychometric g, specific ability, and specific knowledge were estimated from the principal components of the Air Force Officer Qualifying Test (AFOQT; Carretta & Ree, 1996). The AFOQT is a multiple aptitude battery that measures g and the five lower-order factors of verbal, math, spatial, perceptual speed, and aircrew knowledge. The samples were approximately 4,000 pilot and 1,400 navigator trainees. All had completed college before entering training. Similar academic and work sample training criteria were available for the pilots and navigators. The criteria for the pilot sample included academic grades, hands-on flying work samples (i.e., flight maneuvers), passing/failing training, and an overall performance composite made by summing the other criteria. The criteria for the navigator sample were academic grades, work samples of day and night celestial navigation, passing/failing training, and an overall performance composite made by summing the other criteria. Similar results were observed for the pilots and navigators. Regression analyses revealed that psychometric g was the best predictor for all pilot and navigator criteria. For the composite criterion, which is the broadest and most meaningful measure of performance, the validity after correction for range restriction was .40 for pilots and .49 for navigators. The non-g measures exhibited an average increment in validity to g of .08 for pilots and .02 for navigators. A closer examination revealed that

the incremental validity found for pilots was the result of specific knowledge about aviation (i.e., aviation controls, instruments, and principles), rather than specific cognitive abilities (i.e., math, perceptual speed, spatial, verbal). Olea and Ree speculated that the lack of incremental validity beyond g for navigators happened because none of the tests included specific knowledge about navigation (i.e., celestial navigation, estimation of course corrections).

Meta-Analyses

Hunter and Hunter (1984) provided a broad meta-analysis of the predictiveness of g for training criteria. Their study included several hundred jobs across many job families as well as re-analyses of data from previous studies. They estimated the true validity of g to be .54 for job training criteria. Levine, Spector, Menon, Narayanan and Cannon-Bowers (1996) conducted a meta-analysis of 52 validation studies totaling 5,872 participants. They estimated the average true validity of g-saturated cognitive tests (see their appendix 2) as .668 for training criteria. In a meta-analysis spanning 85 years of research findings, Schmidt and Hunter (1998) examined the utility of measures of general mental ability (GMA is an alternative abbreviation for g and we use the authors' terminology here) and 18 other commonly used personnel selection procedures (e.g., biographical data, conscientiousness tests, integrity tests, employment interviews, reference checks). They estimated the predictive validity of GMA tests to be .56 for training. The two combinations of predictors with the highest multivariate validity for job training programs were GMA plus an integrity test (mean validity of .67) and GMA plus a conscientiousness test (mean validity of .65). Table 11.1, adapted from Schmidt and Hunter (1998), shows the meta-analytic validity of g and other predictors for training performance. These meta-analyses and other research reviewed demonstrate that *g* predicts both academic and training criteria well.

Linkage between *g* and Occupational Performance

Terman and his collaborators reported some of the earliest results on the relationship between *g* and occupational performance. In a series of publications regarding their studies of gifted individuals, they examined the relationship between ability measured in childhood at about age 11 and adult occupational attainment. Much of the most relevant information regarding these studies is provided in the 35-year follow-up report (Terman & Oden, 1959). Terman and Oden presented occupational data for the gifted participants and showed them to greatly exceed the performance of the general population. The educational attainment and occupational status of the gifted group was very high; over 85% of the male sample was in the professional-managerial job category. The gifted group, on average, had high incomes and exhibited many other indicators of occupational accomplishment. Even though Terman's findings are very informative, they are descriptive rather than predictive or causal in nature. However, their importance should not be dismissed, because they helped to establish the foundation for later research on the relationship between *g* and occupational performance.

Similarly, Eysenck (1998) reported a study by Nyborg who followed the careers of 4,376 middle-aged veterans. Nyborg demonstrated a strong relationship between IQ (a robust *g* surrogate) and earnings. Eysenck provides a very informative chapter (6) entitled 'What is the use of IQ tests?' that is recommended to all studying the practical use of *g*.

Predictiveness of g

As illustrated by Hunter (1983b), the predictiveness of *g* varies systematically as a function of job complexity. Hunter analyzed a large-scale database encompassing 515 occupations collected by the US Department of Labor. These occupations were categorized according to three levels of complexity of data handling (low, medium, and high) and two categories of complexity of dealing with things (simple feeding/offbearing and complex work set-up). As job complexity increased, the validity of *g* also increased. The average corrected validities of *g* were .40, .51, and .58 for the low, medium, and high data complexity jobs. The corrected validities were .23 for the low complexity feeding/offbearing jobs and .56 for the complex set-up work jobs, respectively. Gottfredson (1997) provides a more complete discussion.

Vineberg and Taylor (1972) presented an example of the predictiveness of *g* in a study using the *g*-saturated Armed Forces Qualification Test (AFQT). The AFQT is a composite score consisting of the sum of the two verbal and two math tests from the US military enlistment selection and classification test known Armed Services Vocational Aptitude Battery (ASVAB; Ree & Carretta, 1994.) There were 1,544 US Army enlistees in four jobs: armor, cook, repair, and supply. Job experience ranged from 30 days to 20 years. The job performance criteria consisted of work samples. A significant correlation between ability and job performance was observed. After the effects of education and experience were removed, the partial correlations between *g*, as measured by the AFQT, and job performance were: armor .36, cook .35, repair .32, and supply .38. Vineberg and Taylor also examined the predictiveness of *g* for supervisory ratings for the same four jobs. The validities for supervisory ratings were: armor .26, cook .15, repair .15, and supply .11. These and other similar validities across dissimilar jobs led Olea and Ree (1994) to comment, 'From jelly rolls to aileron rolls, *g* predicts occupational criteria' (p. 848).

Roth and Campion (1992) demonstrated the validity of a general ability composite for predicting job performance for petroleum process technicians. After correction for range restriction, the validity of the *g*-based composite was .37.

Carretta, Perry and Ree (1996) examined the predictiveness of a broad cognitive, psychomotor, and personality test battery against job performance criteria for US Air Force fighter pilots. The 171 F-15 pilots had between 193 to 2,805 post-pilot-training flying hours and between 1 and 22 years of job experience. The job performance criterion was based on supervisory and peer ratings of flying performance, specifically 'situational awareness'. Situational awareness is a broadly defined measure of knowledge of the dynamic flight environment involving perception, forecasting, decision-making, and pilot behavior. After holding experience constant, *g* was predictive of the criterion.

Cumulative evidence clearly shows that *g* predicts current performance. Chan (1996) demonstrated that *g* also predicts future performance. Scores from a highly *g*-loaded test predicted future promotions of officers in the Singapore Police Force; officers who scored higher on the test were more likely to be promoted. Wilk, Desmarais and Sackett (1995) showed that *g* was a major cause of the 'gravitational hypothesis' of job mobility and promotion. They noted 'individuals with higher cognitive ability move into jobs that require more cognitive ability and that individuals with lower cognitive ability move into jobs that require less cognitive ability' (p. 84). Occupational complexity interacts with *g* in job satisfaction. Ganzach (1998) found that *g* was positively associated with job satisfaction, but when job complexity was held constant, the relationship was negative. This is consistent with and expected from the results of Wilk et al. (1995).

Crawley, Pinder and Herriot (1990), in a study of the dimensionality of assessment centers, showed that *g* was predictive of task-related dimensions. The highest correlation for *g*, in their range-restricted sample, was with the task-based problem-solving dimension and the lowest correlation for *g* was with the assertiveness dimension.

Kalimo and Vuori (1991) examined the relationship between measures of *g* taken in childhood and the occupational health criteria of physical and psychological health symptoms and 'sense of competency'. They concluded that 'weak intellectual capacity' during childhood led to poor work conditions and increased health problems.

While Chan (1996) and Kalimo and Vuori (1991) provide information about the relation of *g* to future occupational success, O'Toole (1990) and O'Toole and Stankov (1992) went one step further, examining the relation of *g* to probability of death by vehicular accident or suicide. O'Toole (1990) found that the Australian Army intelligence test was a good predictor of mortality by vehicular accident for Australian military men aged 20 to 44. Lower test scores were associated with higher probability of death by vehicular accident. O'Toole and Stankov (1992) extended O'Toole (1990) to include death by suicide and noted similar results. For example, the mean intelligence score for those who died because of suicide was about .25 standard deviations lower than comparable survivors, and a little more than .25 standard deviations lower for those who died as result of vehicular accident. In addition, survivors were different from decedents on variables related to *g*. Survivors completed more years of education, obtained a greater number of academic degrees, were more likely to be employed in white-collar occupations, and rose to high military rank. O'Toole and Stankov contend 'The "theoretical" parts of driver examinations in most countries act as primitive assessments of intelligence' (p. 715). Blasco (1994) noted that similar studies on the relation of ability to traffic accidents have been performed in Spain and South America.

Although these results provide compelling evidence about the importance of *g*, none of these job performance studies examined the incremental validity of specific abilities or specific knowledge beyond *g*.

Incrementing the Predictiveness of g

McHenry, Hough, Toquam, Hanson and Ashworth (1990) examined the utility of several predictors against multiple job performance criteria for nine US Army jobs. The predictors included *g*, perceptual-psychomotor, spatial, temperament/personality, vocational interest, and job reward preference. The criteria were based on Campbell's job performance model (Campbell, McHenry &

Wise, 1990). General cognitive ability was predictive of all of the job performance factors. It was the best predictor of the first two job performance factors, 'core technical proficiency' and 'general soldiering proficiency', with correlations of .63 and .65 corrected for range restriction. None of the other predictors incremented the validity of *g* by more than .02. For the other job performance factors ('effort and leadership', 'personal discipline', and 'physical fitness and military bearing'), temperament/personality was incremental to *g* or superior to it for prediction. In a study of team performance (as opposed to individual performance), Neuman and Wright (1999) found that the predictiveness of *g* was incremented by personality variables of agreeableness and conscientiousness. These results are consistent with Crawley, Pinder and Herriot (1990). It is noteworthy that the constructs that *g* predicted best are in the first higher-order factor and the constructs that personality predicted well are in the second higher-order factor in the reanalyzed (Ree & Carretta, 1998) Campbell model.

Ree, Earles and Teachout (1994) examined the relative validity of *g* and specific abilities for predicting job performance in a sample of 1,036 US Air Force enlisted personnel from seven blue-collar jobs. The job performance measures included hands-on work samples, job knowledge interviews, and a combination of the two called the 'Walk Through Performance Test'. The job knowledge interviews assessed both declarative and procedural knowledge. The measures of *g* and specific abilities were extracted from a multiple aptitude battery. Multiple regression models were used to compare the predictiveness of *g* and specific abilities for the three criteria. The average validity of *g* across the seven jobs was .40 for the hands-on work sample, .42 for the job knowledge interview, and .44 for the 'Walk Through Performance Test'. The validity of *g* was incremented by the addition of the specific ability measures by an average of only .02. Ree et al.'s (1994) results are very similar to those reported by McHenry et al. (1990).

Linkage Between *g* and Occupational Prestige

Jensen (1980, 1998) has provided a comprehensive review of this area. Based on a study of 444 jobs and scores from the General Aptitude Test Battery, he found an average true correlation of .70 between GATB general ability scores and perceived ranking of job prestige (or 'level'). The correlation of job rank and *g* increases with age, ranging from .50 for younger persons to .70 for middle-aged and older who have established careers. Jensen concluded that *g* plays an important role in job level as well as the level of performance on the job.

Table 11.2   *Meta-analytic predictive validity of g and a second predictor for job performance*

Predictor	Validity (r)	Multiple R	R−r$_g$[1]
g	.51		
Work sample test	.54	.63	.12
Integrity tests	.41	.65	.14
Conscientiousness tests	.31	.60	.09
Structured interviews	.51	.63	.12
Unstructured interviews	.38	.55	.04
Job knowledge tests	.48	.58	.07
Job tryout procedures	.44	.58	.07
Peer ratings	.49	.58	.07
T&E behavioral consistency	.45	.58	.07
Reference checks	.26	.57	.06
Job experience (years)	.18	.54	.03
Bio data	.35	.52	.01
Assessment centers	.37	.53	.02
T&E point method	.11	.52	.01
Years of education	.10	.52	.01
Interests	.10	.52	.01
Graphology	.02	.51	.00
Age	−.01	.51	.00

Note: [1] This is the difference between the correlation for *g* only (.51) and the multiple correlation, *R*.
Source: Adapted from Schmidt and Hunter (1998). Reprinted by permission. Copyright 1998 American Psychological Association.

Meta-Analyses

Schmidt, Gooding, Noe and Kirsch (1984) performed a 'bare bones' meta-analysis (McDaniel, Hirsh, Schmidt, Raju & Hunter, 1986) of the predictive efficiency of *g* for job performance. Schmidt et al., reported an average validity of .248. Ree and Carretta (1998) corrected this value for range restriction and predictor and criterion unreliability using the meta-analytically derived default values in Raju, Burke, Normand and Langlois (1991). After correction, the estimated true correlation between *g* and job performance was .512.

Hunter and Hunter (1984) performed a meta-analysis of hundreds of studies that examined the relationship between *g* and job performance. Across job families that covered a large portion of the American economy, they estimated a mean true correlation of .45.

Building on studies of job performance (Schmidt, Hunter & Outerbridge, 1986) and job separation (McEvoy & Cascio, 1987), Barrick, Mount and Strauss (1994) performed a meta-analytic investigation of the relationship between *g* and involuntary job separation. Barrick et al., found that those with low job performance were more likely to be involuntarily separated. The relationship between *g* and involuntary job separation was *indirect*, and was moderated through job performance and supervisory ratings.

In a meta-analysis that encompassed 85 years of research findings, Schmidt and Hunter (1998) examined the utility of measures of general mental ability (*g*) and 18 other commonly used selection procedures. They estimated the predictive validity of *g* tests to be .51 for job performance (see Table 11.2). The three combinations of predictors with the highest multivariate validity were *g* plus an integrity test (mean validity of .65), *g* plus a structured interview (mean validity of .63), and *g* plus a work sample test (mean validity of .63). Schmidt and Hunter note that the first two combinations have the advantage that they can be used with either entry-level selection or selection of experienced employees. Work sample tests are usually used only with applicants who already have some job experience.

Causal Models

In a major summary of research findings, Hunter (1986) demonstrated that '…general cognitive ability has high validity predicting performance ratings and training success in all jobs' (p. 359). In addition to its predictive validity, the *causal* role of *g* in job performance has been demonstrated. Using data from 14 studies involving 3,264 participants, Hunter (1983a) derived meta-analytically cumulated correlations of *g*, job knowledge, and job performance (supervisory ratings and work sample performance). These correlations were used to develop and test path models of the causal influence of *g* and job knowledge on job performance. Hunter found that the major causal influence of *g* was on the acquisition of job knowledge (standardized path coefficient of .80). In turn, job knowledge had a major causal impact on supervisory ratings (.40) and work sample performance (.56). Ability also had a direct effect on work sample performance (.31). However, no direct effect of g on supervisory ratings was reported; all effects of g on supervisor ratings (.47) were moderated (i.e., indirect). Job knowledge and work sample performance accounted for all of the relationship between g and supervisory ratings in Hunter's model. However, it should be noted that the total direct and indirect causal impact of g was considerable.

Schmidt, Hunter and Outerbridge (1986) extended Hunter (1983a) with the inclusion of on-the-job experience. Schmidt et al., found that experience influenced job knowledge and work sample measures of job performance. Job knowledge and work sample measures of job performance directly influenced supervisory ratings. No *direct* link between g and experience was found; the causal impact of g was entirely indirect.

Borman, White, Pulakos and Oppler (1991) confirmed Hunter's (1983a) model in an additional sample of job incumbents. They made Hunter's model more parsimonious, including sequential causal effects from ability to job knowledge to task proficiency to supervisory ratings. Borman et al. (1991) determined that the paths from ability to task proficiency and from job knowledge to supervisory ratings were not necessary and attributed this to the uniformity of job experience of the participants. Borman, White and Dorsey (1995) subsequently confirmed Borman et al.'s parsimonious model on two additional peer and supervisory samples.

The causal analyses reviewed up to this point were done using subordinate job incumbents. Borman, Hanson, Oppler, Pulakos and White (1993) tested a causal model for supervisory job performance, showing again that ability influenced job knowledge. They also observed a small, but significant, path going from ability to experience. They hypothesized that individuals were given the opportunity to acquire supervisory job experience because they demonstrated high ability. Experience subsequently led to increases in job knowledge, proficiency, and supervisory ratings.

Ree and his colleagues (Ree, Carretta & Doub, 1998/1999; Ree, Carretta & Teachout, 1995) added the construct of prior job knowledge to occupational causal models. They defined prior job knowledge as job relevant knowledge applicants bring to training. Ree et al. (1995) examined the role of g and prior job knowledge on the acquisition of additional job knowledge and work sample performance during military aircraft pilot training. They reported that g had a strong causal influence on prior job knowledge. No direct path was found for g to either of two work sample performance factors (i.e., hands-on flying measures). However, g exerted an indirect influence on the work samples, moderated through job knowledge acquisition. This study also included three sets of sequential classroom training courses. The direct relationship between g and the first sequential training factor was large. The direct relationship of g was almost zero for the second sequential training factor, which builds on the knowledge of the first, and was low positive for the third sequential training factor that introduces substantially new material. Most of the influence of g was expressed indirectly through the acquisition of job knowledge in the sequential training courses. This is consistent with Hunter's (1983a) model.

Based on data from 83 independent studies with a total sample of 42,399 participants, Ree, Carretta and Doub (1998/1999) constructed and tested path models to examine the causal roles of g and prior job knowledge in the acquisition of subsequent job knowledge. Results supported a model where g had a causal influence on both prior and subsequent job knowledge. General cognitive ability had a direct influence on both prior job knowledge and subsequent job knowledge; and also had an indirect effect on subsequent job knowledge through prior job knowledge. The R^2 for predicting subsequent job knowledge was .80 for the model including all 83 jobs.

DIFFERENTIAL VALIDITY AND BIAS

The performance of sex and race/ethnic groups on tests has received much attention, especially when the tests are used for selection into educational, training, and occupational settings (Hartigan & Wigdor, 1989; Jensen, 1980). Two concepts are of particular interest: *differential validity* and *bias*. Differential validity (prediction) occurs when a test's validity is not the same in the majority (usually males or whites) and minority (usually females or race/ethnic minorities) groups. Despite group differences in mean test performance (Carretta, 1997a, 1997b; Hyde, 1981; Jensen, 1980; Maccoby & Jacklin, 1974), there is little convincing evidence that well constructed tests are more predictive of educational, training, or occupational performance for members of the majority group than for members of minority groups.

If the validity coefficient for a test is the same (i.e., not significantly different) for the majority and minority groups, it does not necessarily guarantee that the test is not biased. Despite equal validities for the groups, the regression equations could differ. A common method for examining possible test bias involves the use of a series of regression models. As a first step, some (Jensen, 1980) suggest comparing the equality of the *variance error of estimate* (SE^2_{est}) for the majority and minority groups. The test statistic is a simple ratio of the larger SE^2_{est} divided by the smaller SE^2_{est} and is distributed as F (Jensen, 1980; Reynolds, 1982). If the two values of SE^2_{est} for the two groups are equal, linear models may be used to test the equality of the regression slopes and intercepts (Cleary, 1968; Jensen, 1980). If the values of SE^2_{est} of the regression lines are not equal, some argue (Linn, 1973) that testing linear models is inappropriate; others (Hunter & Schmidt, 1976) do not consider the testing of variance errors of the estimate crucial.

The next step involves testing of linear models. A 'full model' is compared to a 'restricted model' that contains a subset of the variables from the full model. An F statistic is used to evaluate the change in predictive efficiency between the full and restricted models using the hierarchical step-down method described by Lautenschlager and Mendoza (1986). The starting (full) model (Model 1) for each analysis contains separate estimates for the slopes and intercepts for the two groups being compared (e.g., males vs. females). The first restricted model (Model 2) removes the separate slope estimates, and the second restricted model (Model 3) removes the separate intercept estimates. First, Models 1 and 2 are compared to examine for slope bias. If evidence of slope bias is found, the analysis sequence is terminated. If no slope bias is found, the test score is tested for difference in intercepts. Cumulative evidence suggests that the existence of bias is rare (Carretta, 1997; Jensen, 1980; Roberts & Skinner, 1996).

CRITICAL ISSUES

It has been suggested (Murphy, 1996) that relying on a single index to characterize ability means that ability is unitary. This is not necessarily true. Just because the relationship between two measures can be well-summarized by a single number, does not imply that each measure is itself univariate. It implies and means that the two measures covary with each other. For example, consider a typical multiple aptitude battery. If we administer the battery twice and sum the tests within each administration, the correlation of the sums will be nearly 1.0 (see Ree, Carretta & Earles, 1998). In fact, Dawes (1979) showed that a simple composite of two uncorrelated variables will be highly correlated with other weightings of the same two variables.

Some have asserted that we have not devoted much effort to 'understanding' the non-g portions of aptitude tests. However, we have not ignored the potential of non-g factors for prediction, and we have proposed explanations for the non-g portions of the tests in several studies (Earles & Ree, 1991; Olea & Ree, 1994; Ree, Carretta & Doub, 1998/ 1999; Ree, Carretta & Teachout, 1995). Further, critics sometimes ask why we do not enter specifics before g in regression equations to determine if g is incremental to specifics. In Ree and Earles (1991)

and in Olea and Ree (1994), we observed that the distribution of validity for g and specifics did not overlap. The predictive efficiency of g was greater than the most valid specific ability. Note that we specify ability, not personality constructs such as used by McHenry et al., (1990). As noted elsewhere in this chapter, McHenry et al., demonstrated incremental validity of temperament/personality measures beyond g for the training criteria of 'effort and leadership', 'personal discipline', and 'physical fitness and military bearing'. Other investigators have found the same result, perhaps most notably in the large study by McHenry et al. (1990). Further, because g and specific cognitive abilities are *per force* uncorrelated, the matter of which enters the regression in what order is irrelevant.

Individual differences in job performance are important to organizational effectiveness. Campbell, Gasser and Oswald (1996) reviewed the findings on the value of high and low job performance and, using a conservative approach, they estimated that the top 1% of workers produces a return 3.29 times as great as the lowest 1% of workers. Further, they estimated that the value might be from 3 to 10 times the return, depending on the variability of job performance.

The validity of g as a predictor of job performance has long been the topic of research. Gottfredson (1997: 83) argued that '...no other measured trait, except perhaps conscientiousness...has such general utility across the sweep of jobs in the American economy'. When summarizing the finding that specific abilities can be identified and measured, Hattrup and Jackson (1996) concluded that they 'have little value for building theories about ability–performance relationships' (p. 532).

The foundation for occupational performance is dependent on learning the knowledge and skills required for the job, and continues into on-the-job performance and beyond. Our review of the literature clearly shows that g predicts a wide range of occupational criteria including training performance, job performance, lifetime productivity and, finally, early mortality.

REFERENCES

American Psychological Association Division of Industrial-Organizational Psychology (1987). *Principles for the validation and use of personnel selection procedures* (3rd ed.). Washington, DC: Author.

Barrick, M.R., Mount, M.K., & Strauss, J.P. (1994). Antecedents of involuntary turnover due to a reduction in force. *Personnel Psychology, 47*, 515–535.

Besetsny, L.K., Earles, J.A., & Ree, M.J. (1993). Little incremental validity for a special test for Air Force intelligence operatives. *Educational and Psychological Measurement, 53*, 993–997.

Besetsny, L.K., Ree, M.J., & Earles, J.A. (1993). Special tests for computer programmers? Not needed. *Educational and Psychological Measurement, 53*, 507–511.

Blasco, R.D. (1994). Psychology and road safety. *Applied Psychology: An International Review, 43*, 313–322.

Borman, W.C., Hanson, M.A., Oppler, S.H., Pulakos, E.D., & White, L.A. (1993). Role of early supervisory experience in supervisor performance. *Journal of Applied Psychology, 78*, 443–449.

Borman, W.C., White, L.A., & Dorsey, D.W. (1995). Effects of ratee task performance and interpersonal factors on supervisor and peer performance ratings. *Journal of Applied Psychology, 80*, 168–177.

Borman, W.C., White, L.A., Pulakos, E.D., & Oppler, S.H. (1991). Models of supervisory job performance ratings. *Journal of Applied Psychology, 76*, 863–872.

Brodnick, R.J., & Ree, M.J. (1995). A structural model of academic performance, socio-economic status, and Spearman's g. *Educational and Psychological Measurement, 55*, 583–594.

Burt, C. (1949). The structure of the mind: A review of the results of factor analysis. *British Journal of Educational Psychology, 19*, 100–111, 176–199.

Cai, T., Gong, Y., Dai, X., & Tang, Q. (1998). Chinese intelligence scale for young children (CISYC). III: The study of factor structure. *Chinese Journal of Clinical Psychology, 6*, 203–206.

Campbell, J.P., Gasser, M.B., & Oswald, F.L. (1996). The substantive nature of job performance variability. In K.R. Murphy (Ed.), *Individual differences and behavior in organizations* (pp. 258–299). San Francisco: Jossey-Bass.

Campbell, J.P., McHenry, J.J., & Wise, L.L. (1990). Modeling job performance in a population of jobs. Special Issue: Project A: The US Army Selection and Classification Project. *Personnel Psychology, 43*, 313–333.

Carretta, T.R. (1997a). Group differences on US Air Force pilot selection tests. *International Journal of Selection and Assessment, 5*, 115–127.

Carretta, T.R. (1997b). Male–female performance on U.S. Air Force pilot selection tests. *Aviation, Space, and Environmental Medicine, 68*, 818–823.

Carretta, T.R., & Ree, M.J. (1995). Near identity of cognitive structure in sex and ethnic groups. *Personality and Individual Differences, 19*, 149–155.

Carretta, T.R., & Ree, M.J. (1996). Factor structure of the Air Force Officer Qualifying Test: Analysis and comparison. *Military Psychology, 8*, 29–42.

Carretta, T.R., & Ree, M.J. (1997). Negligible sex differences in the relation of cognitive and psychomotor abilities. *Personality and Individual Differences, 22*, 165–172.

Carretta, T.R., & Ree, M.J. (in press). Pitfalls of ability research. *International Journal of Selection and Assessment*.

Carretta, T.R., Perry. D.C. Jr. & Ree, M.J. (1996). Prediction of situational awareness in F-15 pilots. *The International Journal of Aviation Psychology, 6*, 21–41.

Cattell, R.B. (1971). *Abilities: Their structure, growth, and action*. Boston: Houghton Mifflin.

Chan, D. (1996). Criterion and construct validation of an assessment centre. *Journal of Occupational and Organizational Psychology, 69*, 167–181.

Cleary, T.A. (1968). Test bias: Prediction of grades of negro and white students in integrated colleges. *Journal of Educational Measurement, 5*, 114–124.

Crawley, B., Pinder, R., & Herriot, P. (1990). Assessment centre dimensions, personality and aptitudes. *Journal of Occupational Psychology, 63*, 211–216.

Dawes, R. (1979). The robust beauty of improper linear models. *American Psychologist, 34*, 571–582.

DeFries, J.C., Vandenberg, S.G., McClearn, G.E., Kuse, A.R., Wilson, J.R., Ashton, G.C., & Johnson, R.C. (1974). Near identity of cognitive structure in two ethnic groups. *Science, 183*, 338–339.

Earles, J.A., & Ree, M.J. (1991). *Air Force Officers Qualifying Test (AFOQT): Estimating the general ability component* (Al-TP-1991-0039). Brooks AFB, TX: Armstrong Laboratory, Human Resources Directorate, Manpower and Personnel Research Division.

Eysenck, H.J. (1998). *Intelligence*. New Brunswick, NJ: Transaction Publishers.

Fleishman, E.A., & Quaintance, M.K. (1984). *Taxonomies of human performance: The description of human tasks*. Orlando, FL: Academic Press.

Ganzach, Y. (1998). Intelligence and job satisfaction. *Academy of Management Journal, 41*, 526–539.

Gardner, H. (1983). *Frames of mind: The theory of multiple intelligence*. NY: Basic Books.

Gottfredson, L.S. (1997). Why g matters: The complexity of everyday life. *Intelligence, 24*, 79–132.

Guilford, J.P. (1956). The structure of intellect. *Psychological Bulletin, 53*, 267–293.

Guilford, J.P. (1959). Three faces of intellect. *American Psychologist, 14*, 469–479.

Gulliksen, H. (1950). *Theory of mental tests*. NY: Wiley.

Gulliksen, H. (1989). *Theory of mental tests*. Mahwah, NJ: Erlbaum.

Gustafsson, J.E. (1980). *Testing hierarchical models of ability organization through covariance models*. Paper presented at the Annual Meeting of the American Educational Research Association, Boston, April.

Gustafsson, J.E. (1988). Hierarchical models of individual differences in cognitive abilities. In R.J. Sternberg (Ed.), *Advances in the psychology of human intelligence* (Vol. 4, pp. 35–71). Hillsdale, NJ: Lawrence Erlbaum.

Hakstian, A.R., & Cattell, R.B. (1978). Higher-stratum ability structures on a basis of twenty primary abilities. *Journal of Educational Psychology, 70*, 657–669.

Hartigan, J.A., & Wigdor, A.K. (Eds.) (1989). *Fairness in employment testing: Validity generalization, minority issues, and the General Aptitude Test Battery*. Washington, DC: National Academy Press.

Hattrup, K., & Jackson, S.E. (1996). Learning about individual differences by taking situations seriously. In K.R. Murphy (Ed.), *Individual differences and behavior in organizations* (pp. 507–547). San Francisco: Josey-Bass.

Horn, J.L. (1978). Human ability systems. In P.B. Baltes (Ed.), *Life-span development and behavior* (Vol. 1, pp. 211–256). NY: Academic Press.

Huarte de San Juan, J. (1991). *Examen de ingenios para las ciencies* [Examination of wits for the sciences]. Madrid: Espasa Calpe.

Hull, C.L. (1928). *Aptitude testing*. Yonkers, NY: World Book.

Humphreys, L.G., & Taber, T. (1973). Ability factors as a function of advantaged and disadvantaged groups. *Journal of Educational Measurement, 10*, 107–115.

Hunter, J.E. (1983a). A causal analysis of cognitive ability, job knowledge, job performance, and supervisor ratings. In F. Landy, S. Zedeck & J. Cleveland (Eds.), *Performance measurement and theory*. Hillsdale, NJ: Lawrence Erlbaum.

Hunter, J.E. (1983b). *Overview of validity generalization for the U.S. Employment Service* (USES Test Research Report 43.). Washington, DC: U.S. Department of Labor, Employment and Training Administration.

Hunter, J.E. (1986). Cognitive ability, cognitive aptitudes, job knowledge, and job performance. *Journal of Vocational Behavior, 29*, 340–362.

Hunter, J.E., & Hunter, R.F. (1984). Validity and utility of alternative predictors of job performance. *Psychological Bulletin, 96*, 72–98.

Hunter, J.E., & Schmidt, F.L. (1976). A critical analysis of the statistical and ethical implications of various definitions of 'test bias'. *Psychological Bulletin, 83*, 1053–1071.

Hyde, J.S. (1981). How large are cognitive gender differences? A meta-analysis using ω^2 and *d*. *American Psychologist, 36*, 892–901.

Jager, A.O. (1967). *Dimensionen der intelligenz* [Dimensions of intelligence]. Göttingen: Hogrefe, Germany.

Jensen, A.R. (1980). *Bias in mental testing*. NY: The Free Press.

Jensen, A.R. (1998). *The g factor: The science of mental ability*. Westport, CT: Praeger.

Jones, G.E. (1988). *Investigation of the efficacy of general ability versus specific abilities as predictors of occupational success*. Unpublished master's thesis, Saint Mary's University of Texas, San Antonio, TX.

Kalimo, R., & Vuori, J. (1991). Work factors and health: The predictive role of pre-employment experiences. *Journal of Occupational Psychology, 64*, 97–115.

Lautenschlager, G.J., & Mendoza, J. (1986). A step-down hierarchical multiple regression analysis for estimating hypotheses about test bias in prediction. *Applied Psychological Measurement, 10*, 133–159.

Lawley, D.N. (1943). A note on Karl Pearson's selection formulae. *Proceedings of the Royal Society of Edinburgh, section A, 62*, part 1, 28–30.

Levine, E.L., Spector, P.E., Menon, S., Narayanan, L., & Cannon-Bowers, J. (1996). Validity generalization for cognitive, psychomotor, and perceptual tests for craft jobs in the utility industry. *Human Performance, 9*, 1–22.

Linn, R. (1973). Fair test use in selection. *Review of Educational Research, 43*, 139–161.

Maccoby, E.E., & Jacklin, C.N. (1974). *The psychology of sex differences*. Stanford, CA: Stanford University Press.

McArdle, J.J. (1996). Current directions in structural factor analysis. *Current Directions in Psychological Science, 5*, 11–18.

McClelland, D.C. (1993). Intelligence is not the best predictor of job performance. *Current Directions in Psychological Science, 2*, 5–6.

McDaniel, M.A., Hirsh, H.R., Schmidt, F.L., Raju, N.S., & Hunter, J.E. (1986). Interpreting the results of meta-analytic research: A comment on Schmidt, Gooding, Noe, and Kirsch (1944). *Personnel Psychology, 39*, 141–148.

McDonald, R.P. (1999). *Test theory: A unified approach*. Mahwah, NJ: Erlbaum.

McEvoy, G.M., & Cascio, W.F. (1987). Do good or poor performers leave? A meta-analysis of the relationship between performance and turnover. *Academy of Management Journal, 30*, 744–762.

McHenry, J.J., Hough, L.M., Toquam, J.L., Hanson, M.A., & Ashworth, S. (1990). Project A validity results: The Relationship between predictor and criterion domains. *Personnel Psychology, 43*, 335–354.

McNemar, Q. (1964). Lost our intelligence? Why? *American Psychologist, 19*, 871–882.

Michael, W.B. (1949). Factor analyses of tests and criteria: A comparative study of two AAF pilot populations. *Psychological Monographs, 63*, 55–84.

Murphy, K.R. (1996). Individual differences and behavior in organizations: Much more than g. In K.R. Murphy (Ed.), *Individual differences and behavior in organizations* (pp. 3–30). San Francisco: Jossey-Bass.

Neuman, G.A., & Wright, J. (1999). Team effectiveness: Beyond skills and cognitive ability. *Journal of Applied Psychology, 84*, 376–389.

Olea, M.M., & Ree, M.J. (1994). Predicting pilot and navigator criteria: Not much more than g. *Journal of Applied Psychology, 79*, 845–851.

O'Toole, V.I. (1990). Intelligence and behavior and motor vehicle accident mortality. *Accident Analysis and Prevention, 22*, 211–221.

O'Toole, V.I., & Stankov, L. (1992). Ultimate validity of psychological tests. *Personality and Individual Differences, 13*, 699–716.

Peiró, J.M., & Munduate, L. (1994). Work and organizational psychology in Spain. *Applied Psychology: An international review, 43*, 231–274.

Raju, N.S., Burke, M.J., Normand, J., & Langlois, G.M. (1991). A new meta-analytic approach. *Journal of Applied Psychology, 76*, 432–446.

Ree, M.J. (1995). Nine rules for doing ability research wrong. *The Industrial-Organizational Psychologist, 32*, 64–68.

Ree, M.J., & Carretta, T.R. (1994). Factor analysis of the ASVAB: Confirming a Vernon-like structure. *Educational and Psychological Measurement, 54*, 459–463.

Ree, M.J., & Carretta (1995). Group differences in aptitude factor structure on the ASVAB. *Educational and Psychological Measurement, 55*, 268–277.

Ree, M.J., & Carretta, T.R. (1997). What makes an aptitude test valid? In R.F. Dillon (Ed.), *Handbook on testing* (pp. 65–81). Westport, Conn: Greenwood Press.

Ree, M.J., & Carretta, T.R. (1998). General cognitive ability and occupational performance. In C.L. Cooper & I.T. Robertson (Eds.), *International review of industrial and organizational psychology*, *13*, (pp. 159–184). Chichester, UK: John Wiley.

Ree, M.J., Carretta, T.R., & Doub, T.W. (1998/1999). A test of three models of the role of *g* and prior job knowledge in the acquisition of subsequent job knowledge in training. *Training Research Journal*, *4*, 135–150.

Ree, M.J., Carretta, T.R., & Earles, J.A. (1998). In top-down decisions, weighting variables doesn't matter: A consequence of Wilks' theorem. *Organizational Research Methods*, *1*, 407–420.

Ree, M.J., Carretta, T.R., & Earles, E.A. (1999). In validation, sometimes two sexes are one too many: A tutorial. *Human Performance*, *12*, 79–88.

Ree, M.J., Carretta, T.R., Earles, J.A., & Albert, W. (1994). Sign changes when correcting for range restriction: A note on Pearson's and Lawley's selection formulas. *Journal of Applied Psychology*, *79*, 298–301.

Ree, M.J., Carretta, T.R., & Teachout, M.S. (1995). Role of ability and prior job knowledge in complex training performance. *Journal of Applied Psychology*, *80*, 721–780.

Ree, M.J., & Earles, J.A. (1991). Predicting training success: Not much more than *g*. *Personnel Psychology*, *44*, 321–332.

Ree, M.J., & Earles, J.A. (1992). Intelligence is the best predictor of job performance. *Current Directions in Psychological Science*, *1*, 86–89.

Ree, M.J., Earles, J.A., & Teachout, M.S. (1994). Predicting job performance: Not much more than *g*. *Journal of Applied Psychology*, *79*, 518–524.

Reynolds, C.E. (1982). Methods for detecting construct and predictive bias. In R.A. Berk (Ed.), *Handbook of methods for detecting test bias* (pp. 199–227). Baltimore, MD: Johns Hopkins University Press.

Roberts, H.E., & Skinner, J. (1996). Gender and racial equity of the Air Force Officer Qualifying Test in officer training school selection decisions. *Military Psychology*, *8*, 95–113.

Roth, P.L., & Campion, J.E. (1992). An analysis of the predictive power of the panel interview and pre-employment tests. *Journal of Occupational and Organizational Psychology*, *65*, 51–60.

Salgado, J.F. (1995). Situational specificity and within-setting validity variability. *Journal of Occupational and Organizational Psychology*, *68*, 123–132.

Schmid, J., & Leiman, J. (1957). The development of hierarchical factor solutions. *Psychometrika*, *22*, 53–61.

Schmidt, F.L. (1994). The future of personnel selection in the U.S. Army. In M.G. Rumsey, C.B. Walker & J.H. Harris (Eds.), *Personnel selection and classification* (pp. 333–350). Hillsdale, NJ: Erlbaum.

Schmidt, F.L., & Hunter, J.E. (1993). Tacit knowledge, practical intelligence, general mental ability, and job knowledge. *Current Directions in Psychological Science*, *2*, 8–9.

Schmidt, F.L., & Hunter, J.E. (1998). The validity and utility of selection methods in personnel psychology: Practical and theoretical implications of 85 years of research findings. *Psychological Bulletin*, *124*, 262–274.

Schmidt, F.L., Hunter, J.E., & Outerbridge, A.N. (1986). Impact of job experience and ability on job knowledge, work sample performance, and supervisory ratings of job performance. *Journal of Applied Psychology*, *71*, 432–439.

Schmidt, N., Gooding, R.Z., Noe, R.A., & Kirsch, M. (1984). Meta analyses of validity studies published between 1964 and 1982 and the investigation of study characteristics. *Personnel Psychology*, *37*, 407–422.

Spearman, C. (1927). *The abilities of man: Their nature and measurement*. NY: Macmillan – now Palgrave.

Stauffer, J.M., Ree, M.J., & Carretta, T.R. (1996). Cognitive components tests are not much more than g: An extension of Kyllonen's analyses. *The Journal of General Psychology*, *123*, 193–205.

Sternberg, R.J. (1985). *Beyond IQ: A triarchic theory of human intelligence*. NY: Cambridge University Press.

Sternberg, R.J., & Wagner, R.K. (1993). The g-ocentric view of intelligence and job performance is wrong. *Current Directions in Psychological Science*, *2*, 1–5.

Terman, L.M., & Oden, M.H. (1959). The gifted group at mid-life: Thirty-five years' follow-up of the superior child. In L.M. Terman, *Genetic studies of genius*, Vol. V. Stanford, CA: Stanford University Press.

Thorndike, R.L. (1949). *Personnel selection*. New York: Wiley.

Thorndike, R.L. (1986). The role of general ability in prediction. *Journal of Vocational Behavior*, *29*, 322–339.

Thurstone, L.L. (1938). Primary mental abilities. *Psychometric Monographs*, No. 1. Chicago: University of Chicago Press.

Thurstone, L.L., & Thurstone, T.G. (1941). Factorial studies of intelligence. *Psychometric Monographs*, No. 2. Chicago: University of Chicago Press.

Vernon, P.E. (1950). *The structure of human abilities*. NY: Wiley.

Vernon, P.E. (1969). *Intelligence and cultural environment*. London: Methuen.

Vineburg, R., & Taylor, E. (1972). *Performance of four Army jobs by men at different aptitude (AFQT) levels: 3. The relationship of AFQT and job experience to job performance*. Human Resources Research Organization Technical Report 72–22. Washington, DC: Department of the Army.

Walters, L.C., Miller, M., & Ree, M.J. (1993). Structured interviews for pilot selection: No incremental validity. *The International Journal of Aviation Psychology*, *3*, 25–38.

Wilk, S.L., Desmarais, L.B., & Sackett, P.R. (1995). Gravitation to jobs commensurate with ability: Longitudinal and cross-sectional tests. *Journal of Applied Psychology*, *80*, 79–85.

12

The Structure, Measurement, Validity, and Use of Personality Variables in Industrial, Work, and Organizational Psychology

LEAETTA M. HOUGH and DENIZ S. ONES

This chapter describes the evolution of personality taxonomies and proposes a working set of personality taxons for use in conjunction with the Big Five to enhance our understanding of the role of personality in work settings. We also chronicle significant contributions of personality variables in describing and predicting effective work behaviors. We summarize findings describing the importance of personality variables as they relate to career and occupational choice, organizational choice, training, satisfaction, leadership, and occupational health and safety. We also provide a thorough review of (a) methods of assessing personality variables (including the questionnaire method, self and other ratings, biodata, conditional reasoning, virtual reality testing, genetic testing, and neurological testing); and (b) measurement equivalence across different measurement methods, language, and culture. In addition, we summarize research addressing issues related to the use of personality variables, including applicant reactions, mean score differences between groups, intentional distortion (socially desirable responding) and its effect on validity.

INTRODUCTION

Globalization, demographics, and technology have transformed life – at home, at work, at play. Many countries have experienced a transition from a manufacturing economy to a service economy, and for many the information age has replaced the industrial age. Several authors (Dunnette, 1998; Herriot & Anderson, 1997; Jansen, 1997; Kraut & Korman, 1999; Pearlman & Barney, 2000) have cogently described forces changing our economy and marketplaces and the implications of such changes in our world of work and family life.

During the late twentieth century and continuing on today, personality variables and issues related to their use, especially in work settings, have generated a vast amount of research and publication. The importance of personality to industrial, work and organizational (IWO) psychology is now apparent, but this was not always the case. The period from the 1960s to the mid-1980s was a dark age for personality; with a few notable exceptions such as Ghiselli (1966), most IWO psychologists turned their backs on personality measures. A renaissance began in the mid- to late 1980s (see R. Hogan & Roberts, 2001; Hough & Schneider, 1996; McAdams, 1997, for a history of this period).

It was in applied settings that the importance of personality variables became apparent. When personality scales were organized according to constructs, meta-analyses of their criterion-related validities for predicting work-related constructs revealed the importance of personality variables in understanding and predicting work performance. The usefulness of those variables for understanding team performance has also helped bring personality variables into mainstream IWO psychology. Personality variables are now recognized as important in predicting and understanding individual, team, and organizational performance and effectiveness.

In ten short years, personality research has had a significant impact on the practice and science of IWO psychology. Hough (2001) described the impact: More construct-oriented thinking for both predictors and criteria has led to greater accuracy in prediction and understanding of the domain of work performance. Improved job/work analysis methods attend more completely to dimensions of work performance important in our new world of work. Job and work performance models now include task performance and contextual performance, and predictors of performance criteria now include measures of intellectual, social, and emotional intelligence.

Emerging issues and problems require new ways of thinking. In this chapter, we first discuss personality theory and structure, assessment methods, and then summarize the evidence for personality variables in personnel selection. We conclude with a discussion of personality pre- and post-selection. Across these topics, we summarize relevant research, identify emerging issues, and, at times, suggest new ways of thinking about these topics.

PERSONALITY THEORY, STRUCTURE, AND ASSESSMENT

There is little agreement about what personality is – its definitions are many. Moreover, the field abounds with dozens of 'pet' personality variables of varying complexity and breadth. Hundreds of scales have been developed to measure personality variables, many of which measure similar constructs but bear different names and some of which bear the same name but measure different constructs. Without an adequate taxonomy or understanding of the underlying structure of the many constructs and their measures, the science of personality psychology is unable to advance, hindering the intelligent use of personality variables in applied settings.

An adequate taxonomy is important for revealing patterns, understanding research results, enabling predictions, generalizing across events, and communicating efficiently (Fleishman & Quaintance, 1984). Taxonomies are also important for developing construct validity – mapping the relationships, the nomological nets of our variables. In scientific endeavors, lack of good taxonomies is a sign of a young science.

Structure of Personality Variables

Tellegen (1993) distinguishes between theoretical psychological constructs and personality variables identified through analysis of lexical terms (language), referring to the latter as psycholexical dimensions, natural-language constructs, or folk concepts that represent shared personal constructs of personality – person-perceptual schemata – relevant for the assessment of personality. Much taxonomic effort has focused on psycholexical variables; the Five-Factor Model (FFM), for example, has its roots in natural-language constructs. At least two other types of approaches to developing personality taxonomies have influenced our thinking: (a) psychological theory-based taxonomies, and (b) nomological-web clustering.

Lexical Approach

The lexical hypothesis originated with Galton (1884) who proposed that personality traits are captured in the words that people use to describe one another and which are thus encoded in dictionaries. Using Roget's *Thesaurus*, Galton identified and catalogued personality descriptors. Allport and Odbert (1936) continued the project but used *Webster's New International Dictionary* (1925), producing a much more comprehensive list of personality-related words than Galton. Allport and Odbert (1936) classified the words into four categories: personal traits, evaluative, metaphorical, temporary states and moods. They eliminated all words classified into the evaluative, metaphorical, and temporary states and moods categories, as well as words that did not fit into their categories. The reduced list consisted of 4,504 words that people in the English community use in their daily lives to describe and interact with each other.

A list of 4,504 words is, however, much too long to be useful for theoretical or applied purposes. It is hardly an adequate taxonomy, and the research task of identifying a scientifically adequate taxonomy began. The research task continues on today, although many embrace the Five-Factor Model (also called the Big Five) and believe the search can and should end (e.g., Goldberg, 1995). Hundreds of studies using factor analytic or deductive methods to derive the structure of personality were undertaken. In this section we describe the major factor-analytically-derived lexical models that have been derived.

Cattell's Efforts

R.B. Cattell (1943) was the first to attempt to summarize Allport and Odbert's 4,504 personality-related words, although he considered any resulting verbally-defined traits as only a 'preliminary scaffolding' (Cattell, 1945: 70). He maintained that the starting point needed to be the complete trait-variable population; that is, the entire 'surface' of the personality sphere. He, therefore, added several hundred words related to attitudes, interests, types, and syndromes and eliminated several hundred words that he deemed vague, esoteric, or figurative. Through a variety of clinical and mathematical methods he reduced the number to 35 clusters. He obtained peer ratings of 208 men on these 35 clusters and subjected the ratings to factor analysis using the centroid method and rotation to simple structure. Cattell claimed to have identified 12 factors. However, inspection of the factor loadings suggests Cattell over-interpreted his data. A series of additional data gathering and factor-analytic studies ensued.

Cattell developed the *Sixteen Personality Factor Questionnaire* (16PF) to measure what he regards as the fundamental dimensions of normal personality. Unfortunately, neither the 16PF handbook (Cattell, Eber & Tatsuoka, 1970) nor Cattell's many other books, chapters, and articles clarify how the 16 dimensions (15 personality and one cognitive) came to be. Although historically important, there are too many criticisms, failures to replicate, and psychometric inadequacies for Cattell's 15 personality factors to constitute an adequate taxonomy of personality variables (Eysenck, 1991).

Early Five-Factor Models

Although five factors did not appear in the literature until the mid-twentieth century, reanalysis of Edward Webb's data set suggests that underlying his ratings was a *latent* five-factor model that went unrecognized for 80 years until Deary (1996) reanalyzed Webb's data. Webb (1915) concluded he had one general factor – Persistence of Motives or will. Thirty-four years would pass before five factors were identified in personality ratings data.

Fiske (1949) was the first to derive a five-factor model of personality from separate factor analyses of self, peer, and psychologists' ratings of 128 target individuals. He labeled the five factors Social Adaptability, Emotional Control, Conformity, Inquiring Intellect, and Confident Self-Expression.

Tupes and Christal (1961/1992) are credited with identifying the five-factor model in essentially the form that we know it today (Goldberg, 1993). They obtained peer ratings on a subset of Cattell's 35 trait descriptors from eight samples of Air Force and university students. In seven of the eight data sets, factor analyses resulted in five factors that they labeled Surgency, Agreeableness, Dependability, Emotional Stability, and Culture.

The Big Five

A variation of Tupes and Christal's five factors has become known as the Big Five. The Big Five are Extraversion, Conscientiousness, Agreeableness,

Neuroticism (also known as Emotional Stability or Adjustment) and Openness to Experience. (The interested reader is referred to Block, 1995; Digman, 1990; John, 1990a 1990b; John, Angleitner & Ostendorf, 1988; Wiggins & Trapnell, 1997 for detailed descriptions of the history of the Big Five.)

Over the years, many researchers have contributed evidence that the Big Five are robust and generalizable across different types of assessments, rating sources, cultures, language, and gender as well as a variety of factor extraction and rotation methods (e.g., Benet-Martínez & John, 1998; Digman & Takemoto-Chock, 1981; Goldberg, 1990; Katigbak, Church & Akamine, 1996; McCrae & Costa, 1987, 1997b; Norman, 1963b; Ostendorf & Angleitner, 1994; Peabody & Goldberg, 1989; Saucier & Goldberg, 1998; Somer & Goldberg, 1999). A review of this literature (as well as others not cited) shows that variants of the Big Five are found in many studies. Extraversion and Neuroticism are the most robust across studies; with only a few exceptions, these factors are replicated reliably in all studies. Conscientiousness is next in order of stability. There is less empirical evidence for Agreeableness, and even less for Openness to Experience (Ostendorf & Angleitner, 1992). McCrae and Costa (1997b) acknowledge that Openness to Experience is the most controversial of the Big Five among personality psychologists, and, unfortunately, factor analyses have not been especially helpful in defining it. It remains a fuzzy construct, albeit an important one that requires much more research to define.

Goldberg (1990, 1992) developed a list of adjectives now regarded as the standard markers of the Big Five factors, and Costa and McCrae (1985, 1989, 1992) developed a personality questionnaire that has become widely used in measuring the Big Five factors and their facets. McCrae, Costa, their colleagues, and others as well (Costa, Busch, Zonderman & McCrae, 1986; Costa & McCrae, 1988, 1995; Costa, Zonderman, Williams & McCrae, 1985; Hofstee, de Raad & Goldberg, 1992; McCrae & Costa, 1985, 1987, 1989a, 1989b; McCrae, Costa & Busch, 1986; Ostendorf & Angleitner, 1992) systematically related the NEO-PI to most of the major measures of personality, showing that the Big Five accounts for much of the variance in these other respected measures. However, whether or not it accounts for enough of the variance is seriously debated.

The Big Five has provided an important organizing and summarizing function for the field of personality psychology, yet it has engendered, perhaps because of its wide acceptance, considerable criticism. Within the field of personality psychology, Block (1995), Eysenck (1991, 1992), McAdams (1992), Pervin (1994), Tellegen (1993), Waller & Ben-Porath (1987), and Zuckerman

(1992) have criticized it severely. There are advocates and critics in the field of industrial and organizational psychology as well. Barrick and Mount (1991) found the Big Five useful for organizing personality scales into constructs and then meta-analyzing criterion-related validities according to personality construct. However, Hough and her colleagues (Hough, 1989b, 1992, 1997, 1998a; Hough et al., 1990; Hough & Oswald, 2000; Hough & Schneider, 1996; Schneider & Hough, 1995) argue that the Big Five ignore, confound, and obscure understanding of variables when combined into these five broad factors. They argue that important differences exist within the Big Five factors, that these differences are important for predicting and understanding work behavior and effectiveness and that these relationships are obscured when validities are summarized according to the Big Five. A review of meta-analyses concluded the Big Five factors do not correlate highly with job performance (Matthews, 1997). McAdams (1992) summarized the contributions and criticisms of the Big Five saying the 'Big Five may be viewed as one important model *in* personality studies but not the integrative model *of* personality' (1992: 329, italics in original).

Seven-Factor Model

Tellegen (1993) criticized the Big Five factors as an incomplete taxonomy because lexical researchers had eliminated from their lists of words evaluative terms and terms describing temporary states, including moods and emotional activity. This practice eliminated the possibility of identifying affective states and self-esteem variables, variables important to many psychological theories. He and Waller (Tellegen & Waller, 1987, n.d., also summarized in Waller & Zavala, 1993) conducted their own lexical study, adding words referring to self and other evaluation, as well as transitory or temporary feelings. They found seven factors, five of which correspond reasonably well with the Big Five (with some noteworthy differences) and two additional factors – Positive Valence and Negative Valence (not to be confused with Positive Emotionality/Affectivity and Negative Emotionality/Affectivity). Sample descriptors for Positive Valence are special, excellent, outstanding (versus ordinary), hinting of narcissism. Sample descriptors for Negative Valence are bad, evil (versus decent), perhaps reflecting either flaunting or rejecting of a 'bad me'. These two additional factors have been found in the Spanish and Hebrew languages when similarly nonrestrictive criteria are used to select words from the natural language of personality description (Benet & Waller, 1995; Almagor, Tellegen & Waller, 1995). Saucier (1997) also used a wider range of terms and found seven factors, one resembling Negative Valence.

Psychological Theory-Based Approaches

Personality theorists develop and use personality constructs to explain behavior and its causes.[1] Critics of the Five-Factor Model (e.g., Block, 1995; Tellegen, 1993) argue that the factor-analytic-dependent lexical hypothesis results in folk concepts rather than scientific psychological constructs and thus an incomplete and inadequate taxonomy or structure of personality. Critics (e.g., Waller & Ben-Porath, 1987) also argue that the Big Five cannot adequately incorporate other respected personality taxonomies, such as those by Gough (1987), Murray (1938), and Tellegen (1982). Moreover, according to Schneider and Hough (1995), a 'truly scientific personality taxonomy should consist of traits that can be ultimately linked to neuropsychological structures that *cause* behavior' (p. 84, italics in original), a point of view not inconsistent with Allport, Cattell, Eysenck, Gray, Meehl and Tellegen.

Eysenck (1970) proposed three super traits – Neuroticism, Extraversion, and Psychoticism – each with connections to physiological processes. He (1992) argues that his Neuroticism is clearly Neuroticism in the Big Five, his Extraversion is clearly Extraversion in the Big Five, and his Psychoticism is the negative pole of Agreeableness and Conscientiousness in the Big Five. Tellegen (1982, 1985) also proposed a three-factor model and a four-factor model – Negative Emotionality, Positive Emotionality (in the four-factor model this construct splits into Agenic Positive Emotionality and Communal Positive Emotionality), and Constraint – for his 11-scale *Multidimensional Personality Questionnaire* (MPQ; Tellegen, 1982). According to Ackerman and Heggestad (1997) who summarized relationships among the variables in these models, Tellegen's three traits are aligned with Eysenck's three traits as follows: Neuroticism with Negative Emotionality, Extraversion with Positive Emotionality, and Psychoticism with Constraint, although Tellegen would disagree (Tellegen & Waller, n.d.). Neither Tellegen's Absorption scale nor the Big Five factor Openness to Experience are well accounted for in the super three.

Many personality theorists have developed measures of their variables, and most have incorporated psychometric data to refine their measures with the result that, in terms of psychometric quality, personality inventories based on the lexical hypothesis are often indistinguishable from personality inventories based on theory. Thus, the criticism that lexically-based personality inventories lack comprehensiveness can be evaluated empirically without psychometric quality of the scales confounding the results.

Proponents of the Big Five argue their five factors account for most of the variance in these other personality inventories. As described above, McCrae and Costa believe the evidence they have produced supports this claim. However, after close inspection of the studies, the answer is not perfectly clear. For example, Costa and McCrae (1995) compared three- and five-factor solutions of the *Eysenck Personality Profiler* (EPP; Eysenck & Wilson, 1991), *Eysenck Personality Questionnaire* (EPQ; Eysenck & Eysenck, 1991), and NEO-PI-R (Costa & McCrae, 1992), concluding that some EPP scales were misclassified and that the scales could be better understood in terms of the Big Five than Eysenck's three. Although Costa and McCrae (1995) do not provide other solutions, an examination of the eigenvalues indicates little difference between five, six, and seven factors. Murray's (1938) catalog of needs, as operationalized by Jackson's *Personality Research Form* (PRF; Jackson, 1984) is another set of theoretical constructs the Big Five is hypothesized to encompass. Costa and McCrae (1988) factor analyzed the NEO-PI and the PRF and concluded five factors encompassed all of Murray's needs. However, their approach was procrustean; they prespecified five factors, even though they acknowledged that using different criteria for the number of factors would have yielded different solutions. In fact, they noted, as did Block (1995), that an alternate seven-factor solution was possible. Similarly, after regressing each scale of the *California Psychological Inventory* (CPI; Gough, 1987) on the five NEO-PI factors, McCrae, Costa and Piedmont (1993) concluded that the Big Five could account for Gough's constructs. Again, however, after examining the data more closely, a different possibility emerges: seven of the CPI scales had adjusted multiple *R*s below .50, indicating that the CPI either includes constructs not included in the Big Five or the scales included in the NEO do not comprehensively tap the Big Five. A similar situation exists with the *Minnesota Multiphasic Personality Inventory* (MMPI; Dahlstrom, Welsh & Dahlstrom, 1972, 1975). Costa et al. (1985) factor analyzed the MMPI and found nine factors, again suggesting that the Big Five, at least as measured by the NEO, is incomplete.

Personality inventories that were based on theories and hypotheses about personality variables have provided evidence that the following variables are not well accounted for by Big Five factors: masculinity/femininity (Costa et al., 1985; Kamp & Gough, 1986), aggression, hostility, impulsivity and sensation seeking (Zuckerman, Kuhlman & Camac, 1988; Zuckerman, Kuhlman, Joireman, Teta & Kraft, 1993; Zuckerman, Kuhlman, Thornquist & Kiers, 1991), and absorption (Church & Burke, 1994).

Factor analyses of natural language personality descriptors and scales derived from the lexical hypothesis suggest the following variables are not represented in the Big Five model: religiousness, fashionableness, sensuality/seductiveness,

masculinity/femininity, frugality, humor, prejudice, folksiness, and cunning (Saucier & Goldberg, 1998), egotism, conservatism, and morality (Paunonen & Jackson, 2000), positive valence (Almagor, Tellegen & Waller, 1995; Benet & Waller, 1995; Tellegen & Waller, 1987; Waller & Zavala, 1993), negative valence (Almagor, Tellegen & Waller, 1995; Benet & Waller, 1995; Tellegen & Waller, 1987; Saucier, 1997), consideration (Tokar, Fischer, Snell & Harik-Williams, 1999), imaginative and esthetically sensitive (Digman & Inouye, 1986), and verbal expression (Digman & Inouye, 1986).

Nomological-Web Clustering Approach

Hough is unique in the field in arguing for a taxonomy that emerges through clustering of personality variables based on their nomological nets; that is, the web of their relationships to other psychological variables, job performance variables, and other individual difference variables – not just other personality variables. She and her colleagues (Hough, 1989b, 1992, 1997, 1998a; Hough, Eaton, Dunnette, Kamp & McCloy, 1990; Hough & Schneider, 1996; Schneider & Hough, 1995) argue that the pattern of relationships that a variable has with other variables should be similar to other variables that are in the same taxon or construct. Hough thus argues that evidence of construct validity is demonstrated empirically through cluster analysis of the profiles of relationships of the target variables. The emergent taxonomy is not dependent upon a psychological theory, nor is it dependent upon factor analysis of personality variables or relationships between just personality variables. Similar to the periodic table, it is an evolving taxonomy; more taxons can be added. The approach relies on bootstrapping – successive approximations over time and across studies – until a refined taxonomy exists. It is a taxonomy that relies on empirical evidence that the elements or facets in the construct relate similarly to other variables, not just other personality variables. The approach focuses on construct validity; that is, a variable's nomological web, as the key determinant of the adequacy of a taxonomy of personality variables.

After grouping personality variables into constructs according to their relationships with other variables, Hough (1989b, 1992, 1997) concluded that the Big Five model is an inadequate taxonomy for I/O psychologists involved in personnel selection decisions because the factors consist of components that are differentially valid for criteria. She argues that conscientiousness and extraversion are too coarse, too heterogeneous, too fat to serve as good taxons for understanding the relationships between personality variables and other variables. She prefers instead to separate conscientiousness into dependability and achievement,[2] citing her own research

(Hough, 1992) that shows dependability and achievement correlate differently across a variety of criteria, as well as other meta-analytic research that shows the distinction is important for predicting different criteria of managerial effectiveness (Hough, Ones & Viswesvaran, 1998) and for predicting sales performance (Vinchur, Schippmann, Switzer & Roth, 1998). Factor analytic work by Jackson, Paunonen, Fraboni & Goffin (1996) also supports treating achievement as a separate construct. Hough also prefers to separate Extraversion into at least two constructs – surgency (or potency) and affiliation.[3] She and her colleagues (Hough, 1992; Hough et al., 1990; & Hough et al., 1998) provide evidence that surgency and affiliation correlate differently with criteria and that measures of surgency and affiliation correlate differently with personality variables.

Proposed Working Model

While working on a meta-analysis, the present authors were once again aware that many personality scales measure characteristics that are combinations of variables that, depending upon the model or theorist, are considered to be in different constructs. That is, many personality scales are heterogeneous, mixing, for example, items that measure agreeableness with items that measure neuroticism. Similarly, at the facet level, scales are often not pure in terms of the characteristic measured, at least not according to some researchers and theorists.

Recognizing this complexity and wanting to test whether or not such complexity affected the criterion-related validity of constructs that contained such complexity, the present authors devised a set of working taxons, each of which was similar in what it was believed to measure. We then classified most of the existing personality scales into these working taxons, taxons that as data accumulate may merge with other taxons. The proposed working taxons appear in Appendix A organized, when possible, according to Big Five factors and facets.

Our process for classifying existing personality scales was as follows: We reviewed existing taxonomies, scale definitions, and correlations between scales that were available in inventory manuals and published and unpublished sources. We independently classified each scale into one of the working taxons. When we disagreed about the placement of a scale in a taxon, we jointly reviewed the reference materials described above, discussing our reasons for classifying the scale as we had until we agreed upon the taxon to which it should be assigned.

Call for Research and Refinement

As Hough (2001) states:

The new world of work, with its changing prediction needs – from prediction of global job performance for hiring and promotion decisions to more precise placement decisions for project staffing – requires that I/O psychologists change their research approach. What is needed is a database that can be used with synthetic validation models to build prediction equations for specific situations. First, however, I/O psychologists need research data to provide information about the relationships between predictor constructs and criterion constructs... (Hough, 2001: 37)

We propose that the research begins using our newly proposed taxons as the predictor constructs. For example, we suggest that researchers conducting meta-analyses of personality variables, include in their research the relevant taxons from our working model as well as other structural models. Once we have data portraying the nomological web of each working taxon, we can refine the taxons, merging some, perhaps differentiating others even further, bootstrapping until we arrive at more useful taxons – personality constructs that IWO psychologists, and others as well, can use to understand and predict behavior.

When we understand the nomological webs of our variables, we can combine them to form compound variables that have higher criterion-related validity than any of the individual components (Hough, 1997, 1998a, 2001; Hough & Schneider, 1996; Ones & Viswesvaran, 2001). When we have information about the nomological nets of our working taxons, we can synthetically form compound variables to predict behavior for specific, even unique prediction situations.

ASSESSMENT METHODS AND ISSUES

A variety of methods exist for measuring personality constructs and each brings with it concerns and issues to resolve and overcome if personality assessment is to be useful in industrial and organizational settings. Psychometric properties, measurement equivalency between paper-and-pencil and computerized forms, and equivalency of measures translated from one language to another are especially important issues for the questionnaire method of measurement. Other forms of measurement exist, such as others' ratings (obtained via interviews and assessment centers), biodata, conditional reasoning, virtual reality, genetic, and neurological testing. Although much less information is available about some of these other methods of measuring personality variables, we expect some of them will become more popular in the years ahead.

Questionnaire Method

The questionnaire method is, by far, the most often used method for measuring personality. Both self and other assessments of a target individual is commonly done via questionnaire. Psychometric properties, measurement equivalence across administration mode, such as paper-and-pencil versus computer, and measurement equivalence across culture and language have received considerable research attention. In the area of personnel selection, the self-assessment questionnaire method has special issues related to applicant reactions, intentional distortion, mean score differences between groups, and in the United States legal issues resulting from legislation such as the Civil Rights Acts and the Americans with Disabilities Act.

Psychometric Properties

Reliability in the form of stability (test–retest) and internal consistency are important measurement properties; however, they are differentially important for personality scales. Test–retest reliability is important for trait measures but not mood measures or characteristics that vary legitimately with time. Internal consistency is important for measures of mood as well as trait or construct measures. Test–retest reliability is important for compound variables that measure more than one construct although internal consistency is not. Thus, although reliability is an important psychometric property of a scale, the reliability of a scale needs to be evaluated according to what the scale purports to measure.

Viswesvaran and Ones (2000) examined reliability coefficients for scales measuring Big Five factors, that is, trait measures, separately meta-analyzing test–retest and internal consistency reliabilities for measures of each Big Five factor. They found the frequency-weighted mean observed test-retest reliabilities were .75 for Emotional Stability ($K = 221$), .76 for Extraversion ($K = 176$), .71 for Openness to Experience ($K = 139$), .69 for Agreeableness ($K = 119$), and .72 for Conscientiousness ($K = 193$). They found the frequency-weighted mean observed internal consistency reliabilities were .78 for Emotional Stability ($K = 370$), .78 for Extraversion ($K = 307$), .73 for Openness to Experience ($K = 251$), .75 for Agreeableness ($K = 123$), and .78 for Conscientiousness ($K = 307$). They concluded these five personality constructs have similar levels of test–retest reliability and similar levels of internal consistency reliability.

Another important psychometric property of a scale is whether or not the score on a scale is interpreted by comparison to others (normative measurement) or to the self (ipsative measurement). If measurement is normative, then a person's score provides information about how the person scores on the construct compared to other people. Thus a normative measure provides a between-people rank order on the characteristic measured. If measurement is ipsative, then a person's score provides information about how the person scores on the construct relative to how the person scores on other

personality constructs. Thus, an ipsative measure provides a within-person rank order of the personality characteristics in terms of the strength of the characteristics compared to other characteristics of the person. The format of ipsative measures is typically forced choice wherein the choice is between endorsing one characteristic but not others thereby forcing the individual to score lower on one characteristic compared to the other. Normative measures are useful for comparing people and are thus useful for personnel selection. Ipsative and normative measures are both useful for counseling purposes. In recent years, some have advocated the use of ipsative measures for normative purposes (e.g., selection). We find this inadvisable (see also Hicks, 1970).

Measurement Equivalence Across Mode of Administration: Paper-and-Pencil vs. Computer

Many personality scales are available in both paper-and-pencil and computerized versions resulting in a concern about the equivalence of the two administration modes. King and Miles (1995) analyzed the factor structures of four computerized and paper-and-pencil instruments, finding similar latent structures for the two formats. A meta-analysis of means, standard deviations, and correlations between paper-and-pencil and computerized versions of the MMPI found near zero differences in means and standard deviations across studies, and near perfect rank orderings for the two modes of administration (Finger & Ones, 1999). A meta-analysis that controlled for non-independent effect sizes contributing to the study (correlated observations) found a near zero overall effect size when mean scale scores of computerized non-cognitive instruments were compared to mean scale scores of their paper-and-pencil counterparts (Richman, Kiesler, Weisband & Drasgow, 1999). This was true for social desirability (unlikely virtue) scales as well as substantive (content) scales; effect sizes were .01 and .06, respectively.

Although Richman et al. (1999) did not examine effect sizes according to personality construct, they did analyze other potential moderators (i.e., anonymous vs. identity known, alone vs. in a group, backtracking allowed vs. not allowed, and skipping items allowed vs. not allowed) separately for content scales and social desirability scales. Controlling for moderators, there was less distortion on computerized measures of social desirability scales than on paper-and-pencil measures of social desirability (effect size of −.39). That is, anonymity, being alone and able to backtrack and skip items on a computerized version of a social desirability scale resulted in less distortion than in paper-and-pencil format. For substantive scales, however, there was more distortion on computerized measures than on paper-and-pencil substantive scales (effect size of .46) when moderators were taken into account. That is, there was more socially desirable responding on computerized substantive scales than on paper-and-pencil scales. However, conditions of anonymity, being alone and able to backtrack but not skip items reduced the amount of socially desirable responding on computerized versions of substantive scales (Richman et al., 1999).

Persons interested in converting their paper-and-pencil personality scales to computerized format are advised to design their administration such that persons tested on the computer do so alone, can backtrack, and can change their answers. The effect of being able to skip items was statistically significant in the computerized version of the social desirability scales whereas it was not statistically significant for substantive personality scales (Richman et al., 1999). Thus, computerized versions should allow respondents to skip items.

Lack of anonymity in the computerized version of substantive scales results in large distortion compared to paper-and-pencil format, effect size of .62, although lack of anonymity in the computerized version of social desirability scales results in less distortion than in paper-and-pencil format, effect size of −.27 (Richman et al., 1999). In selection situations, anonymity is not possible. However, there are antidotes to distortion in settings where respondents are required to identify themselves along with their responses. When participants expect to defend their responses in an interview, distortion may be reduced (Doll, 1971). Similarly, when participants are informed of the existence of a lie detection scale, distortion may be reduced (Doll, 1971). A meta-analysis of studies that did and did not provide warnings to participants about distorting their responses indicates that warnings reduce distortion, effect size of .23 (Dwight & Donovan, 1998). Thus, direct action can be taken to reduce the distortion on computerized versions of substantive scales that can counteract, at least to some degree, the amount of distortion likely to occur when anonymity is not possible.

If corrections to substantive scale scores are made on the basis of scores on social desirability scales, we urge caution. Results obtained using corrections developed on paper-and-pencil versions may not generalize to computerized versions. However, such corrections may not be necessary in the first place (Hough, 1998b; Ones & Viswesvaran, 1998c).

Measurement Equivalence Across Language and Culture

International and multinational organizations with their global markets, culturally diverse work teams, and expatriate work assignments have meant greater interest in and sensitivity to cultural and language issues. For personality assessment this has resulted in a focus on the meaning and interpretation of words and behavior in different languages and cultures. Translation of written materials from one language to another such that they convey equivalent meaning is exceedingly difficult. Even if the same constructs are relevant, the behavioral indicators may differ. For example, behavioral indicators of potential and effectiveness can vary from culture to culture, resulting in inaccurate assessment and nonvalid predictions (Sinangil, Ones & Viswesvaran, 1998).

Several issues arise when transporting measures across national borders. Availability of tests in the relevant languages, construct equivalence of translated tests across language and culture, relevant norm groups, differences in response styles, and cultural filters that result in misinterpretation of the meaning of a given behavior are but a few of the issues (Nyfield & Baron, 2000).

Several personality inventories originally developed in English have been translated to other languages and have demonstrated similar psychometric properties across cultures (see Barrett & Eysenck, 1984; Katigbak et al., 1996; McCrae & Costa, 1997a; Nyfield & Baron, 2000). Much research on the Big Five personality factors has demonstrated their relevance across several cultures. In spite of strong support for the Big Five factors across several cultures, certain culturally based differences may exist in personality structure and scales (Ghorpade, Hattrup & Lackritz, 1999; Narayanan, Menon & Levine, 1995).

One approach to developing personality scales relevant across cultures is to involve psychologists from many different cultures and languages in all phases of inventory development and validation, a strategy used to develop the *Global Personality Inventory* (Schmit, Kihm & Robie, 2000). This approach focuses on the construct meaning and equivalence across cultures, enhancing the probability of construct equivalence after translation into the other languages – the key criterion for Jackson (1994).

A more fine-grained statistical approach that focuses on item analysis, differential item functioning (DIF), has been used successfully to identify items that operate differently in different languages and cultures (Ellis, 1989; Ryan, Horvath, Ployhart, Schmitt & Slade, 2000). Using Hofstede's (1991) cultural difference dimensions, Ryan et al. (2000) hypothesized item-level differences between countries differing on cultural dimensions, confirming that some items did indeed operate differently in different cultures.

The International Committee on Test Standards has produced a set of stringent standards for translating instruments into another language (Hambleton, 1999). These standards should be followed whenever a personality inventory is translated from one language to another.

Others' Ratings

Others are an important source for personality measurement. Others provide, for example, the assessment of the target individual in interviews, assessment centers, and 360 degree feedback tools. Although in each of these methods the target individual provides the information, the other provides the assessment, interpretation, and integration of the information that forms the description of the target individual. Unfortunately, the criterion-related validity research on interviews and assessment centers is not typically construct-oriented. Thus, we are unable to compare the level of criterion-related validity between self- and other-ratings of personality constructs obtained via the interview or assessment center.

Research with the commonly used questionnaire method does, however, provide such comparisons. Mount, Barrick and Strauss (1994) and Nilsen (1995) found that compared to self-ratings, ratings provided by others have higher validity for predicting job-related criteria. Mount et al. (1994), for example, found that customer ratings of sales representatives' personality characteristics of extraversion, agreeableness, and conscientiousness correlated substantially higher with both supervisor and coworker ratings of the sales representatives' job performance than did self-ratings of those personality characteristics. Working with executives, Nilsen (1995) found that concurrent validities of personality scales for predicting job performance were higher for personality descriptions made by others than for the executives' self-descriptions.

Self-Ratings

In applied settings, the source of much personality measurement is the target individual (the self), wherein the individual provides his or her self-description. The organization uses that information, as well as other information, for personnel selection, placement, promotion, career counseling, training and development, coaching, team building, and so forth. When used for making personnel selection, placement, and promotion decisions, this dependence upon self-description has been the source of much concern, hence research about applicant reactions to its use, effects of intentional distortion on construct and criterion-related validity, and mean score differences between groups. In the United States, the effect of legislation on its use is also a topic of concern.

Applicant Perceptions and Reactions

As the title to this section suggests, reactions to personality testing are relevant primarily in a selection context. After reviewing applicant reaction literature from the period 1985 to 1999, Ryan and Ployhart (2000) concluded the following:

- whether or not applicants are accepted or rejected clearly influences perceptions;

- feedback about cognitive ability test performance affects self-esteem, and the effect is amplified when provided in an interpersonally sensitive manner;
- perceptions vary considerably, universally shared perceptions do not exist;
- perceptions vary depending upon what else is part of the process;
- explanations of why a procedure is used affects perceptions of fairness;
- perceptions may be a function of individual differences (e.g., personality characteristics) as well as test or situation characteristics;
- gender differences have not been systematically examined; and
- self-selection out of a hiring process is not linked to perceptions of the process.

Whereas applicant perceptions about cognitive ability tests appear to interact with race, this is not true for personality tests. Research by Chan and his colleagues (Chan, 1997; Chan, Schmitt, DeShon, Clause & Delbridge, 1997; Chan, Schmitt, Jennings, Clause & Delbridge, 1998; Chan, Schmitt, Sacco & DeShon, 1998) indicates that applicant perceptions of cognitive ability tests may affect test performance. Performance on personality scales, however, is unaffected by applicant perceptions (Chan, 1997).

Mean Score Differences Between Groups

The Big Five personality factors have provided a way of organizing information about a variety of topics, including mean score differences between groups of interest. Hough, Oswald and Ployhart (2001) summarized mean score differences between men and women, whites and blacks, and whites and Hispanics on Big Five personality factors and some Big Five facets as well. They concluded that minimal differences exist between ethnic/cultural groups at the Big-Five factor level, effect sizes ranged from −.21 to +.04. The largest difference was between blacks and whites on Openness to Experience. Blacks score about .2 standard deviations ($d = -.21$) lower than whites. Whites, blacks, and Hispanics score similarly on integrity tests as well (Ones & Viswesvaran, 1998a). The largest mean score differences between different ethnic/cultural groups and whites is on Social Desirability scales. Hispanics score slightly over .50 standard deviations higher ($d = .56$) than whites (Hough, 1998b; Hough et al., 2001).

Some noteworthy differences exist between men and women. Women score about .40 standard deviations higher than men do on Agreeableness. Differences at the facet level of Conscientiousness exist: Women score higher than men on dependability ($d = .22$) but about the same as men on achievement. Differences at the facet level of

Extraversion also exist: women score slightly higher than men on affiliation ($d = .12$) but lower than men on surgency or potency ($d = -.24$). On scales of Rugged Individualism (or masculinity), women score much lower ($d = -1.74$) than men (Hough, 1998b; Hough et al., 2001). On integrity tests, women score somewhat higher ($d = .16$) than men (Ones & Viswesvaran, 1998a).

Older and younger adults (i.e., 40 years of age or older versus younger than 40 years of age) score similarly on Big Five factors, d ranging from $-.02$ to $.21$, (Hough et al., 2001), and they score similarly on integrity tests, $d = . 08$ (Ones & Viswesvaran, 1998a). Only at the facet level of Conscientiousness do noteworthy differences emerge: compared to younger adults, older working adults score almost .50 standard deviations higher ($d = .49$) on dependability and about .25 standard deviations lower ($d = -.24$) on achievement (Hough et al., 2001).

Intentional Distortion

The literature is replete with studies demonstrating that people can, when instructed to do so, distort their responses to self-report items. Thus, it is no surprise that the meta-analysis of differences between honest and directed-faking conditions by Viswesvaran and Ones (1999) shows large mean score differences: .72 standard deviations for within-subjects design studies and .60 standard deviations for between-subjects designs. However, the amount of distortion in naturally occurring applicant settings appears to be less than that in directed faking settings. An examination of effect sizes in studies that compared applicant and incumbent mean scores (e.g., Dunnette, McCartney, Carlson & Kirchner, 1962; T. Hansen & McLellan, 1997; Heron, 1956; Hough et al., 1990; Kirchner, 1962; Michaelis & Eysenck, 1971; Orpen, 1971; Ryan & Sackett, 1987; Schwab & Packard, 1973; Trent, 1987) reveals that distortion in actual applicant settings is not as large as that produced in directed faking studies. On the other hand Rosse, Stecher, Levin and Miller (1998) found applicants ($N = 197$) scored on average .69 standard deviations higher than incumbents ($N = 73$) on Big Five facet-level scales. Interpreting applicant incumbent differences solely due to faking, they noted that the level of distortion found among applicants is similar to that found in directed faking studies. Hough (1998a) reported data from perhaps the largest sample sizes of incumbents and applicants. In three separate samples involving a total of over 40,500 applicants and over 1,700 incumbents, she found significantly less distortion on personality scales than that found in directed faking studies.

Snell, Sydell and Lueke (1999) speculate that ability and motivation to fake are the key determinants of the amount of distortion in an applicant setting. The Hough (1998a) results suggest other factors may operate as well. A warning not to distort, for example, appears to be an important factor. Dwight and Donovan (1998) meta-analyzed studies that compared the amount of distortion with and without such warnings, and found that warnings reduced distortions by about .23 standard deviations. The Hough (1998a) studies all included warnings. When such warnings are removed, distortion increases (Griffith, Frei, Snell, Hammill & Wheeler, 1997).

Effect of Distortion on Validity

Many researchers have investigated the effect of intentional distortion on criterion-related validity. Many (for example, Barrick & Mount, 1996; Christiansen, Goffin, Johnston & Rothstein, 1994; Dicken, 1963; Hough, 1998a; Hough et al., 1990; McCrae & Costa, 1983; Ones & Viswesvaran, 1998b, 1998c; Schwab & Packard, 1973) have found that distortion does not affect criterion-related validity of personality scales. On the other hand, many others (for example, Douglas, McDaniel & Snell, 1996; Dunnette et al., 1962; Ironson & Davis, 1979; Norman, 1963a; Otto & Hall, 1988; Schmit & Ryan, 1992; Schmit, Ryan, Stierwalt & Powell, 1995; Zichar & Drasgow, 1996) have found that intentional distortion seriously affects validity. Others (for example, Dunnette, Paullin & Motowidlo, 1989; Kamp, 1996; Paajanen, 1988) have found distortion affects validity a small to moderate amount.

Hough (1998a) resolved the apparent conflict by stratifying results by employment setting, and categorizing studies into different settings in which motivation to distort is likely to differ. The three types of settings were (a) directed-faking studies (laboratory-type settings), (b) real-life applicant settings (real-life employment selection settings), and (c) employee 'honest' settings (studies involving real employees working for a real organization – job incumbents in research-only settings). Hough summarized the criterion-related validities obtained in each setting, and found that the setting moderated the effect of distortion on criterion-related validity. In directed-faking settings, personality scales have dramatically lower criterion-related validities than those obtained in applicant or incumbent settings. In applicant settings, personality scales have the same or slightly lower criterion-related validity than those obtained from job incumbents in research-only settings. Studies published since Hough's (1998a) analysis (e.g., Jackson, Wroblewski & Ashton, 2000) provide further support for her conclusions. Thus, Schwab and Packard's (1973) statement still applies: The data 'strongly suggest that the conclusions obtained from distortion research on students ... tell us little about what to expect in employee selection and predictive validation studies' (Schwab & Packard: 374).

These findings and conclusions are echoed in research investigating the effects of distortion on construct validity of personality scales. That is, construct validity is negatively affected in directed-faking studies (Ellingson, Sackett & Hough, 1999), but the effect is not as serious in applicant settings (Collins & Gleaves, 1998; Ellingson, Smith & Sackett, 2001; Ones & Viswesvaran, 1998c).

Perhaps the most persuasive evidence that distortion in real-life employment settings does not moderate the validity of personality variables is a comparison of meta-analytically-derived validity based on predictive studies involving applicants with meta-analytically-derived validity based on incumbents. Meta-analyzing validities of personality-based integrity tests for predicting counterproductive behaviors (broadly defined external criteria but not including theft), Ones, Viswesvaran and Schmidt (1993) found predictive validity of $r = .29$ for studies involving applicants, predictive validity of $r = .26$ for studies involving incumbents, and concurrent validity of $r = .29$ for studies involving incumbents. The predictive validities are stable, $K = 62$ and $N = 93,092$ for predictive validity studies involving applicants and $K = 5$ and $N = 37,415$ for predictive validity studies involving incumbents. Meta-analyzing validities of integrity tests for predicting supervisory ratings of overall job performance, Ones et al. (1993) found predictive validity was .41 for studies involving applicants ($K = 23$ and $N = 7,550$). They found $r = .33$ for studies involving incumbents ($K = 90$ and $N = 18,499$).

Data clearly establish that distortion in natural-occurring applicant settings does not moderate the validity of personality scales. Meta-analytic evidence also establishes that social desirability does not function as a predictor, practically useful suppressor, or mediator of the criterion-related validity of personality scales (Ones, Viswesvaran & Reiss, 1996). Echoing earlier research (e.g., Costa & McCrae, 1983; Furnham, 1986), Ones et al. (1996) also concluded that social desirability is related to emotional stability and conscientiousness. These relationships are stable across self-report and observer measures.

Coaching

Only limited research exists on the effects of coaching people how to dissimulate effectively. A well-designed experiment by Alliger, Lilienfeld and Mitchell (1996) found subtle items resistant to coaching and distortion, whereas obvious items could be distorted and done so without detection by measures of social desirability. However, the generalizability of these findings to field settings has not been established. Gough's (1971, 1972, 1994) approach to developing personality scales thus appears to have considerable merit. An effective strategy for developing personality scales characterized by excellent levels of validity and items resistant to distortion is thus probably most successfully accomplished by theory-driven initial item development followed by scale refinement with item-level validity data.

Detection of Distortion

Snell et al. (1999) question the ability of traditional measures of social desirability to detect distortion, thereby questioning the conclusions of research that have used such scales. They argue that different indices of distortion are needed. Meta-analytic evidence, however, indicates that traditional measures of social desirability are very sensitive to respondents' effort to distort responses. Using traditional measures of social desirability, Viswesvaran and Ones (1999) found such scales detected differences in mean scores between honest and faking conditions. Indeed, they found that the effect size in mean score differences between honest and directed-faking conditions for within-subject designs is approximately two to three times greater for social desirability scores than for content scale scores. That is, when instructed to distort, people raise their scores on traditional social desirability scales from two to three times more than the same people raise their scores on content scale scores. On the other hand, Alliger et al. (1996) found that with coaching, research participants could distort their scores on integrity tests consisting of obvious items without detection by traditional social desirability measures, although integrity tests consisting of subtle items were resistant to coached distortion. It is likely that item type – overt versus subtle – may be an important distinction and may operate as a moderator variable in this area. Yet, implications for validity may be minimal; Ones et al. (1993) found integrity tests containing subtle and overt integrity tests to be equally valid in predicting job performance.

Other indices of distortion have been developed and researched. Holden and Hibbs (1995) developed an item-response latency index as an alternative to traditional measures of distortion. Holden (1995, 1998) again used the response latency index to classify people into honest and fake good conditions, and again results were good. Correct classifications ranged from 62 to 74%. The first study suggested that the response latency index correctly classified significantly more people than traditional social desirability scales. However, when only studies that did not capitalize on chance are examined, the data suggest the traditional indices and response latency index yield approximately the same level of classification accuracy. Dwight and Alliger (1997), however, found that a traditional social desirability scale combined with Holden and Hibb's response latency index improved correct classifications into honest, fake good, and coached conditions than either index used alone. Unfortunately, other research (e.g., Vasilopoulos, Reilly & Leaman, 2000) suggests that response time is correlated with familiarity with the applied-for job. Moreover, speed of response to personality items may be readily coached.

Other Concerns

Despite the evidence, concern still exists about distortion in real-life selection situations. One concern is that applicants who distort their self-descriptions rise to the top of the distribution, and in a top-down selection strategy these people are hired first. Rosse, Stecher, Miller and Levin (1998) argue that research should focus on the effect of response distortion on hiring decisions, rather than whether or not intentional distortion attenuates criterion-related validity. Zickar, Rosse, Levin and Hulin (1996) suggest that the correlation coefficient may not be an appropriate index for detecting the effects of distortion in personality tests when used as selection instruments.

We believe the correlation coefficient *is* an appropriate index for evaluating the usefulness of self-description personality measures. We also believe that the myriad of studies and analyses investigating the effects of distortion provide conclusive evidence that distortion in natural-occurring selection settings does not attenuate validity. With coaching, this conclusion may apply only to personality scales consisting of subtle rather than obvious items, although much more evidence is needed before this can be considered a final conclusion. We do recommend the use of warnings against distortion and possibly in some settings consequences for distortion.

Legal Issues in the US

The US Congress has enacted employment legislation that affects the use and defense of employment testing – the Civil Rights Acts and the Americans with Disabilities Act (ADA). A review of federal court cases in the USA involving alleged hiring discrimination against minorities and women from 1978 to 1997 showed that not one case involved alleged discrimination on the basis of using personality or honesty tests (Terpstra, Mohamed & Kethley, 1999). The reason, of course, is that personality scales and honesty tests show small, or no, mean score differences between whites and minority groups. Although some differences exist between men and women, the differences often favor women, the protected group, and overall the differences between men and women across personality characteristics cancel each other out.

The ADA does, however, affect the use of personality tests in employment settings. The ADA prohibits disability-related inquiries of applicants, and it prohibits a medical examination before a conditional job offer. As described by Hough (1998b), personality measures are not necessarily considered medical examinations; the particular circumstances of their development, purpose, administration, and typical setting in which they are administered determine whether or not a test is considered a medical

exam. Personality inventories such as the *Minnesota Multiphasic Personality Inventory* and *Inwald Personality Inventory* can only be administered after a conditional job offer because they are considered medical exams or ask questions prohibited under the ADA. Each item in a personality scale should be examined to evaluate whether or not it is, or is potentially, in violation of the ADA. Harrison Gough, for example, undertook such an examination of the *California Psychological Inventory*, revising or deleting some of its items because of concerns regarding the ADA.

Biodata

Biodata, an abbreviation for biographical data, is a type of item that asks about the respondent's background, experiences, and life history. Research examining the construct validity of biodata scales indicates they measure a variety of individual characteristics, including cognitive abilities, personality characteristics, and physical abilities (Hough, 1989a; Mumford, Snell & Reiter-Palmon, 1994; Mumford & Stokes, 1992; Tenopyr, 1994). Although reviews of the criterion-related validity of biodata scales indicate they are among the best predictors of a wide range of criteria, the reviews were not done (and could not have been done) according to construct, thus limiting the usefulness of the conclusions.

Only recently has research in this area been construct oriented. Mumford and Stokes (1992) item-generation procedures for developing construct valid biodata scales provide researchers with a needed approach. Mumford, Costanza, Connelly and Johnson (1996) described eleven studies in which they examined the construct validity of biodata scales generated using the Mumford–Stokes approach, finding the criterion-related validity of these scales similar to those of traditional empirical keying efforts. We expect that more biodata scales will be developed to measure personality constructs in the future.

Conditional Reasoning

James (1998, 1999) pioneered a new approach to personality measurement – conditional reasoning. The approach assumes that (a) people rely on logical reasoning processes to justify what they do, and that (b) people high on a personality construct tend to use different justifications for their behavior than people low on that construct. Scale development therefore requires identifying the reasoning (flawed though it may be) that people high and low on the target construct use to justify their behavior. For example, people high on achievement motivation tend to attribute success and failure to internal rather than external sources. They also tend to consider demanding tasks, tasks for which success is uncertain, as challenging. Scales for two constructs, achievement motivation and aggression have been developed and researched. Scales for social deviance and social bias are under development (Migetz & James, 1999; Walton, 1999).

Expected patterns of the conditional reasoning measures with organizational criteria have been found. The conditional reasoning scale for aggression correlates negatively with overall job performance (James, 1998; Hornick, Fox, Axton & Wyatt, 1999), and positively with counterproductive work behavior (Burroughs, Bing & James, 1999; Green, 1999; Migetz, McIntryre & James, 1999; Patton, Walton & James, 1999). The achievement conditional reasoning scale correlates positively with scholastic and cognitive ability criteria (James, 1998; Smith, DeMatteo, Green & James, 1995) as well as in-basket performance (Migetz, James & Ladd, 1999). Larger-sample studies in the future, or perhaps a meta-analysis of several small-sample studies, will help resolve some of the variability found across study findings.

One of the advantages of conditional reasoning scales is that intentional distortion is not an issue. One of the disadvantages is that conditional reasoning scales do not tend to correlate highly with self-report scales purporting to measure the same construct, thus leading to concern about what the scales are measuring. Burroughs et al. (1999), for example, found that the aggression scale correlated around .10 to .20 with self-report measures of the same construct, and when factor analyzed the conditional reasoning aggression scale did not load on any factor comprising self-report personality scales. Similarly, Smith et al. (1995) found that the achievement scale correlated about .10 with other measures of achievement, although other studies have found somewhat higher correlations with other self-report measures of the same construct (James, 1999). Another disadvantage of the achievement scale is that it is likely to have adverse impact against some minority groups. It correlates about .40 with measures of cognitive ability, although the aggression scale correlates near zero with measures of cognitive ability (James, 1999).

Other Measurement Methods

This section consists of futuristic methods of measuring personality characteristics. Some are more problematic than are others. Nonetheless, we anticipate research with and operational use of some of these methods.

Virtual Reality

This is a computerized or, more accurately, digitized form of testing. It involves simulation that is highly interactive. With this form of testing come all the problems of construct validity inherent in simulations. Of the three methods in this section, this one will be the most difficult to develop and operationalize. We can only imagine the difficulties involved in developing psychometrically adequate virtual reality measures of personality characteristics.

Genetic Testing

There is growing evidence from research in behavior genetics that personality characteristics have considerable heritability. Heritability estimates range from approximately 30 to 60% for the Big Five and its facets, as well as for other variables – social desirability, constraint, sensation seeking, Type A behavior, job involvement, ego development – and close to 100% for subjective well-being or happiness 'set point' (Bouchard, 1997a,b,c; Bouchard & Hur, 1998; Gilbert & Ones, 1995a,b, 1996, 1998a,b,c,d; Jang, McCrae, Angleitner, Riemann & Livesley, 1998; Lykken, 1997; Lykken & Tellegen, 1996; Newman, Tellegen & Bouchard, 1998; Pederson, 1997; Saudino, 1997; Zuckerman, 1995). Even individual differences in responding to specific situations, often assumed to be environmental effects, are genetically influenced (Phillips & Matheny, 1997). Research by Scarr (1996), for example, suggests that people create their own environments. Such evidence may suggest entirely different tools for measuring personality variables in personnel selection. For example, the cheek swab is now a standard technique for DNA testing (Plomin, 1997). In countries other than the United States, the self-report questionnaire for measuring personality characteristics may become an archaic, twentieth century phenomenon. In the United States, ADA and ongoing senate hearings on genetic information in the workplace are likely to influence the use of DNA testing in US worksites (Maranto, 2000). Nonetheless, DNA research and testing is likely to revolutionize psychological research in the twenty-first century (Plomin & Crabbe, 2000).

Neurological Testing

Other forms of measurement provide exciting new possibilities as well. In psychobiology, for example, brain dopamine activity is 'strongly and specifically associated with trait levels of positive emotionality', that is, extraversion (Depue, Luciana, Arbisi, Collins & Leon, 1994: 485). In the United States, this type of personality measurement would be considered a medical exam under the Americans with Disabilities Act (ADA), thus precluding its use in selection as a pre-job offer screen. It may not, however, preclude its use with incumbents for other purposes, and other countries are not legally affected by US legislation such as the ADA.

PERSONALITY VARIABLES AND PERSONNEL SELECTION: VALIDITIES FOR PREDICTING WORK-RELATED CRITERIA

Construct-oriented research and meta-analyses have changed our thinking about the usefulness of personality variables for industrial and organizational psychology. The focus on *both* personality constructs and criterion constructs has elucidated meaningful relationships between personality characteristics and other variables important to applied psychologists (Hough, 1997, 2001). Today, personality variables are widely accepted. They are now even included as determinants in models of job performance.

Several meta-analyses in the 1990s used the Five-Factor model as the taxonomy for organizing personality scales (e.g., Barrick & Mount, 1991; Tett, Jackson & Rothstein, 1991; Salgado, 1997, 1998) for summarizing validities. In spite of the recognition that the Barrick and Mount (1991) meta-analysis has received (it was the most cited *Personnel Psychology* reference of the 1990s), the level of validity for each of the Big Five factors is not high (Matthews, 1997). Hough (1992, 1997, 1998b, 2001), arguing for a more refined taxonomic structure of personality variables, has criticized the Big Five factors as not yielding validity levels much higher, if at all higher, than those found by Ghiselli (1966) and Schmitt, Gooding, Noe and Kirsch (1984). She argues that we need to understand the nomological web of each facet-level or fine-grained taxon and then, depending upon the criterion construct, form a compound variable of the facet-level variables to predict the criterion. She argues that taxonomic structure used to summarize and examine validities moderates validity of the taxons.

Several other factors moderate the relationship between personality characteristic and work-related criteria: criterion construct, type of job (which may actually be a poor surrogate for criterion construct), criterion measurement method, complexity of job, and validation strategy (Hough & Schneider, 1996). Very likely, validities generalize across some national borders but not all. Importantly, the validity of personality constructs for predicting criteria is incremented when they are used in appropriate combination with other personality constructs to form compound variables (e.g., customer service, integrity, managerial potential scales), some of which Ones and Viswesvaran (2001) refer to as criterion-focused occupational personality scales. When comparing validity of personality variables with validity of other individual difference domains, such as cognitive ability, it is the validity of these compound variables that should be used rather than the validity of a single personality variable.

Validities Using the Big Five Factors

The Barrick and Mount (1991) meta-analysis of criterion-related validities of the Big Five factors for predicting job proficiency, training proficiency, and personnel data is the most cited *Personnel Psychology* article of the 1990s (Hollenbeck, 1998; Mount & Barrick, 1998). An examination of the validities of the Big Five factors for predicting job proficiency show, except for Conscientiousness (mean observed $r = .13$), that the obtained validities are very close to zero, ranging from $-.02$ to $+.06$. Corrected validities are .10, .07, .06, .23, $-.03$ for Extraversion, Emotional Stability, Agreeableness, Conscientiousness, and Openness to Experience, respectively. The median corrected mean validity of the Big Five using the Barrick and Mount results is .07. Although Ghiselli (1966) did not specify the taxonomic structure he used in summarizing criterion-related validities of personality variables for predicting job proficiency, he obtained an *uncorrected* median mean validity of .24 across the jobs he analyzed. Using no taxonomy at all, Schmitt et al. (1984) obtained a corrected mean validity of .21 for predicting job performance ratings. It is difficult to argue from these data that the Big Five taxonomy has yielded the best validities we can obtain in the personality domain. One could conclude from the Barrick and Mount meta-analysis, as some have (Mount & Barrick, 1995), that Conscientiousness is the primary personality variable useful for I/O psychology because it is linked to work performance in more or less all jobs. In a meta-analysis of European studies, Emotional Stability and Conscientiousness linked to work performance in more or less all jobs (Salgado, 1997).

In contrast to the results for the Big Five as the organizing structure, Hough (1992), who used a different taxonomic structure, found higher validities. Two important differences between her taxonomy and the Big Five are her divisions of the Extraversion factor into separate surgency/potency and affiliation constructs, and the Conscientiousness factor into separate dependability and achievement constructs. She reported differential validity for these constructs, as have Vinchur, Schippmann, Switzer and Rother (1998) for sales performance and Hough, Ones and Viswesvaran (1998) for managerial performance. Robertson and Kinder (1993) meta-analyzed 20 *Occupational Personality Questionnaire* (OPQ; Saville & Holdsworth, 1990) validation studies and found higher validities than meta-analyses conducted using the Big Five factors. Importantly, Hough (1992) and Robertson and Kinder (1993) also categorized criteria into constructs. The taxonomic structure of both the predictor and criterion constructs moderates validity of personality variables.

Validities for Predicting Different Criterion Constructs

Our criterion space is now better defined and better understood (e.g., Campbell, 1990; Visweswaran, this volume). It is multidimensional and it is these criterion constructs that are increasingly important in our new world of work. Competency models now direct our attention to concepts such as adapting to change, continuously learning throughout one's work life, transferring knowledge to others, working as a team, innovating, and focusing on customer needs and their satisfaction as important performance areas in a service oriented, information economy (Hough, 2001). Our models of the determinants of job performance now include personality variables (e.g., Borman, White, Pulakos & Oppler, 1991; Pulakos, Schmitt & Chan, 1996; Schmidt & Hunter, 1992). Our performance models now incorporate 'prosocial' (Brief & Motowidlo (1986), 'good citizenship' (Organ, 1988) or 'contextual' (Borman & Motowidlo, 1993) variables as distinguished from task performance (Borman & Motowidlo, 1997; Conway, 1996, 1999; Motowidlo & Van Scotter, 1994). These contextual variables and their definitions are, however, the constructs that are more likely to vary across cultures than are task performance constructs. Only a few studies address contextual variables in work settings outside the US (e.g., Chen, Hui & Sego, 1998; Farh, Earley & Lin, 1997; Lam, Hui & Law, 1999). Construct equivalence of these criterion variables across culture and language is a little researched area and in need of attention in our global workplace.

Many studies establish the usefulness of personality variables for predicting prosocial, good citizenship, or contextual criterion constructs. Examples are J. Hogan, Rybicki, Motowidlo and Borman (1998); Hough (1992); Hough et al. (1990); Konovsky and Organ (1996); McHenry, Hough, Toquam, Hanson and Ashworth (1990); Motowidlo and Van Scotter (1994); Negrao (1997); Organ and Ryan (1995); and Penner, Fritzsche, Craiger and Freifeld (1995). Indeed, personality variables are good, often better predictors of these criterion constructs than, for example, cognitive variables.

Validities of Compound Variables

Compound variables (sometimes called 'emergent' traits) consist of multiple individually homogeneous variables that may or may not all covary (Hough & Schneider, 1996). When compound variables are formed by appropriately weighting and combining homogeneous variables that each correlate with an aspect of the criterion of interest, validity of the compound variable will be higher than any of the individual, homogeneous variables.

Many compound personality variables exist; a few are discussed below. For a more detailed discussion of compound variables that have been formed to predict performance for specific criteria and in specific occupations, see Ones and Viswesvaran (2001).

Integrity

Integrity tests are of two types: overt tests, which directly assess attitudes towards theft and dishonest and illegal acts, and personality-based tests, which are designed to measure personality characteristics that correlate with a broad range of counterproductive behaviors (Sackett, Burris & Callahan, 1989). Ones and Viswesvaran (1998b) summarized previous Ones' meta-analyses of the relations between integrity tests and Big Five variables: true score correlations between integrity tests and Big Five factors are .42 for Conscientiousness, .40 for Agreeableness, .33 for Emotional Stability, .12 for Openness to Experience, and −.08 for Extraversion. Thus, integrity tests are compound variables consisting primarily of Conscientiousness, Agreeableness, and Adjustment.

One of the largest meta-analyses to date (i.e., Ones, Viswesvaran & Schmidt, 1993), shows that integrity tests have excellent validity for predicting broad counterproductive behaviors such as violence on the job, tardiness, and absenteeism as well as overall job performance. They also found several variables moderate the relationship with criteria: type of criteria (self-report vs. external), type of criterion construct (theft vs. absenteeism), type of study (concurrent vs. predictive), and type of work (simple versus complex).

Customer Service Orientation

Meta-analysis of the correlations between customer service scales and measures of Big Five factors reveals that customer service orientation is a compound variable, made up of the same Big Five factors as integrity although the concentrations differ. Ones and Viswesvaran (1996) found true correlations between customer service scales and Agreeableness, Emotional Stability, and Conscientiousness were .70, .58, and .43, respectively. The meta-analytic validity of customer service scales for predicting supervisory ratings of job performance is .31, corrected only for unreliability in the criterion (Frei & McDaniel, 1998). More recently, Ones and Viswesvaran (2001), using a more comprehensive database, examined validities of customer service scales for additional criteria. Customer service scales predict customer service ratings with an operational validity of .34 ($N = 4,401$). The operational validity for counterproductive behaviors was .42 ($N = 740$). They predicted supervisory ratings of overall job performance with an operational validity of .39 ($N = 6,944$).

Emotional Intelligence and Social Competence

Goleman (1995, 1998) defines emotional intelligence (EQ) as impulse control, empathy, self-awareness, social deftness, persistence, zeal, and self motivation, arguing that lack of emotional intelligence is a cause in career derailment and violent crime. His definition of EQ includes social and emotional competencies. It is a model that conceptualizes EQ as a mixture of abilities and personality characteristics. Bar-On (1997) similarly defines emotional intelligence as an aggregate of abilities, competencies and skills, combining mental abilities with personality characteristics. He argues that together EQ and IQ provide a more balanced picture of a person's general intelligence.

Mayer, Salovey and their colleagues (Mayer & Geher, 1996; Mayer & Salovey, 1993; Salovey & Mayer, 1990; Salovey, Mayer, Goldman, Turvey & Palfai, 1995) initially conceptualized emotional intelligence as a mixed model consisting of mental abilities and personality characteristics, similar to the Bar-On and Goleman models. Over time, Mayer and Salovey moved to a mental ability model, focusing on the interactions between emotional and cognitive abilities (Mayer & Salovey, 1997; Mayer, Salovey & Caruso, 2000). They describe the domain of emotional intelligence as consisting of four classes of discrete emotional abilities: (a) skills involving perception and appraisal of emotion; (b) skills involving assimilating basic emotional experiences into mental life (weighing them against each other, and other sensations and thoughts, and allowing them to direct attention); (c) skills involving understanding and reasoning about emotions; and (d) skills involving managing and regulating emotions both in oneself and others (Mayer, Salovey & Caruso, 2000). Their mental ability theory of emotional intelligence postulates that EQ is an intelligence like other mental abilities and that (a) EQ problems (questions) have right or wrong answers, (b) EQ skills correlate with other mental abilities, and (c) the absolute level of EQ increases with age (Mayer, Caruso & Salovey, 2000; Mayer, Salovey & Caruso, 2000).

Davies, Stankov and Roberts (1998) sought to clarify the elusive emotional intelligence construct by examining the relations between measures of emotional intelligence, cognitive abilities, and personality. They found: (a) reliable self-report measures of emotional intelligence tend to load on personality factors, though not necessarily the Big Five factors; (b) most direct, objective measures of emotional intelligence are unreliable; and (c) in spite of low reliabilities, a separate Social Intelligence factor appears to emerge.

Research on social competence suggests that it is a compound variable consisting of social insight, social maladjustment, social appropriateness, social openness, social influence, warmth, and extraversion (Schneider, Ackerman & Kanfer, 1996). Reliable, self-report measures of social insight (e.g., Gough, 1968) and empathy (e.g., R. Hogan, 1968), of course, have a long history, as do situation judgment measures of social intelligence (e.g., Moss, Hunt, Omwake & Woodward, 1955).

Emotionality

The composition of emotionality, often called affectivity, appears controversial. Averill (1997) and Russell and Carroll (1999) conclude that emotionality consists of two bipolar dimensions – evaluation (negative–positive affectivity) and activation (aroused–unaroused). Others (e.g., Ackerman & Heggestad, 1997; Tellegen, 1982, 1985; D. Watson, Clark & Tellegen, 1988) conclude that positive emotionality/affectivity and negative emotionality/affectivity are separate dimensions, roughly similar to Extraversion and Neuroticism, respectively.

Arvey, Renz and T. Watson (1998) present a model of how emotionality interacts with emotional demands of jobs and organizations to trigger emotions and emotional displays, illustrating the impact of emotionality on job performance and coworkers. They differentiate between felt emotion and displayed emotion, pointing out that displayed emotion is not necessarily felt emotion. They refer to emotional work, work that requires displays of particular emotions regardless of felt emotion. Customer service jobs, for example, require an employee to smile and be pleasant, regardless of the rudeness or hostility of the customer and the employee's felt emotion. The basic premise is that jobs differ in the emotions usually triggered by the work itself. They call for job analyses that highlight these differences. They also point out the emotionality/arousal is not necessarily dysfunctional. The key is how one deals with the aroused state.

Emotionality does predict important work-related criteria. Wright and Cropanzano (1998) found negative affectivity correlated .72 with emotional exhaustion (burnout) in social welfare workers, and emotional exhaustion correlated −.27 ($p < .05$) with job performance.

Summary

A taxonomic structure is important for organizing personality characteristics. An examination of the validities of the Big Five factors for predicting work-related criteria indicates it is not a structure that yields the highest levels of predictive validity. A better approach is to build understanding of the web of relationships with other variables of each more fine-grained taxon, and then build broader, compound variables using this information in conjunction with an understanding of the criterion construct to be predicted.

We have proposed a set of working taxons for our field to begin this effort. Admittedly, these taxons need refinement, but understanding our variables at a more molecular level will produce rewards in our changing world of work, in which performance constructs rather than jobs will be the more frequent prediction situation. Formation of compound variables is likely to yield higher validities in many of our future prediction situations. Focusing on greater understanding of the web of relationships of more fine-grained constructs than the Big Five factors will improve our theoretical models and the accuracy of our predictions in applied settings. Given many variables moderate the relationship between personality constructs and criterion constructs, this strategy will ultimately be more practical and yield more accurate predictions.

Variables that moderate the relationship between personality and criterion construct are personality taxonomy, criterion construct, employment setting (applicant versus directed faking), other versus self-description, anonymity, and perhaps item subtlety when coaching has occurred. Mode of administration (computerized versus paper-and-pencil) and intentional distortion in real-life applicant settings do not appear to affect validity of personality scales (especially scales consisting of subtle items). New measurement methods that emerged at the end of the twentieth century, for example conditional reasoning scales, and those that are likely to emerge this century, for example virtual reality testing, genetic testing and neurological testing, face much different issues. Rather than issues regarding intentional distortion, such testing is likely to face construct validity issues, concern about invasion of privacy, and, at least in the US, possible violations of ADA.

PERSONALITY VARIABLES PRE- AND POST-SELECTION: CASCADING EFFECTS

In addition to their usefulness in predicting job performance, personality variables are also crucial in determining who applies for specific jobs, occupations and organizations. Once on the job, personality variables continue to play very important roles in the behavior of employees. The effects of personality variables cascade, influencing virtually all human behavior – individual and group behavior – in organizations. Some disagree with this statement (e.g., Davis-Blake & Pfeffer, 1989). Nonetheless, evidence in the areas of personnel selection, counterproductive work behavior, career and occupational choice, organizational choice, training, job satisfaction, leadership, teamwork, occupational health and safety, work attitudes, motivation, goal commitment and self-set goal setting overwhelmingly leads to the conclusion that personality influences virtually all organizational behavior.

In previous sections of this chapter, we reviewed literature related to personality variables and their relationship to selection and counterproductive work behavior. In the remainder of this chapter, we review work that examines personality variables as they relate to the following areas: career and occupational choice, organizational choice, training, job satisfaction, leadership, and occupational health and safety. This research illustrates the consequences of employee personalities for organizational behavior.

Career and Occupational Choice

Much of vocational and counseling psychology literature is devoted to exploring individual difference variables and their role in achieving and predicting fit between an individual and his or her career or occupational choice. Personality variables are an important part of the equation, resulting in characteristic personality profiles of job applicants for, and employees in, specific occupational groups (Dawis & Lofquist, 1984; Holland, 1997). Personality variables are important in understanding job search and employment, career aspirations, occupational interests, and career choice as well as career indecision.

Personality variables are related to job search and employment. For example, among college students seeking employment, emotional stability, extraversion, conscientiousness, and openness to experience are associated with assertive job hunting (Schmit, Amel & Ryan, 1993) and career search efficacy (Solberg, Good, Fischer, Brown & Nord, 1994). One year after graduation from college, extraversion and conscientiousness predict employment status (De Fruyt & Mervielde, 1999). Among unemployed (but previously employed) workers, conscientiousness is associated with job-seeking frequency (Wanberg, Watt & Rumsey, 1996), and extraversion and conscientiousness are associated with higher levels of networking intensity as well as higher use of other traditional job-search methods (Wanberg, Kanfer & Banas, 2000).

Personality variables, in particular, locus of control and emotional stability related constructs, are also related to career aspirations (O'Brien & Fassinger, 1993; Rainey & Borders, 1997). For example, Mau, Domnick and Ellsworth (1995) used data from the National Education Longitudinal Study of 1988 to investigate the role of locus of control on eighth-grade girls' career aspirations to homemaking versus science/engineering careers. Homemaking aspirations were linked to external locus of control, whereas science/engineering aspirations were linked to internal locus of control. Using the same database, Rojewski and Yang (1997) found that positive self-evaluations (higher self-esteem and internal locus of control) were predictive of career aspiration prestige in grades 8, 10 and 12.

Personality variables are also associated with occupational interests (De Fruyt & Mervielde, 1997; Goh & Leong, 1993; Gottfredson, Jones & Holland, 1993; Schinka, Dye & Curtiss, 1997; Schneider, Ryan, Tracey & Rounds, 1996; Tokar, Vaux & Swanson, 1995). These studies suggest that openness to experience is associated with artistic and investigative interests; extraversion is related to social and enterprising interests; agreeableness is associated with social interests; conscientiousness is related to conventional interests; emotional stability is related to realistic and investigative interests. Perhaps the most intriguing result is the apparent relationship between self-presentation ability and artistic interests (Carson & Mowsesian, 1993).

Personality variables are also related to career choice, although the results are somewhat inconsistent. In a study of 232 civil service employees in 129 jobs, Spector, Jex and Chen (1995) found that individuals who scored high on anxiety tended to be in lower complexity jobs (jobs that were characterized by lower experienced levels of autonomy, task variety, identity and significance). Silver and Malone (1993) examined personality profiles of six occupational groups. They found that relatively high scores on paranoia characterized individuals who were, or were planning to be, accountants, and high scores on hysteria and narcissism characterized the theater/drama group. In a predictive study of college seniors, De Fruyt and Mervielde (1999) found that extraversion, openness, agreeableness, and conscientiousness were related to employment in realistic, social, and enterprising jobs a year later, although the relationships were modest.

There is a body of compelling literature that career indecision is related to neuroticism (e.g., Chartrand, Rose, Elliott, Marmarosh & Caldwell, 1993; Meyer & Winer, 1993; Multon, Heppner & Lapan, 1995). The personality–career indecision link has been studied using both global and facet measures. Betz and Serling (1993), for example, correlated four components of neuroticism (low hardiness, low self-esteem, anxiety, and fear of commitment) to career undecisiveness in three samples of college students. Although all four components of neuroticism correlated with global career indecision, fear of commitment was the strongest correlate. Lucas and Wanberg (1995) investigated the relationships of anxiety and low optimism with three career indecision components (i.e., level of career decidedness, comfort with career decision status, and reasons for career indecision). Correlations were in the expected direction.

A fit or correspondence exists between the personality of incumbents of occupations (as well as applicants to occupations) and the requirements or demands of the particular occupations. Personality is an important contributor to occupational sorting and thus has implications for the composition of applicant and employee pools in organizations.

Organizational Choice

Personality variables shape not only career and occupational decisions, but decisions regarding which organization to work for as well. Schneider's (1987) Attraction–Selection–Attrition (ASA) theory addresses this phenomenon explicitly. ASA postulates that '[a]ttraction to an organization, selection by it, and attrition from it yield particular kinds of persons in an organization' (p. 441).

In a direct examination of the ASA framework, Schneider, Smith, Taylor and Fleenor (1998) examined whether the personality attributes of managers within organizations were more similar to each other than to managers in other organizations. Using archival data from the Center for Creative Leadership of more than 13,000 managers from 142 organizations, Schneider et al. (1998) compared the personalities of managers from the same organization to managers from all the organizations. They found that personalities of managers in the same organization were more homogenous than the personalities of managers across all the organizations. In a similar field study in Great Britain, Jordan, Herriott and Chalmers (1991) examined personality differences (as measured by the 16PF) among four organizations. They found both organizational main effects as well as organization by occupational interaction effects. Future research should further disentangle personality-based links between occupational and organizational choices. A person–environment fit model that incorporates various types of fit (e.g., Kristof, 1996; Kristof-Brown, 2000) may be useful in disentangling relations between personality, occupational choice, and organizational choice.

Although Schneider, Goldstein and Smith (1995) prefer to study ASA in its entirety, future research also needs to examine the separate components of the attraction, selection and attrition process. Knowledge of the relative strengths of attraction versus selection versus attrition in creating personality homogeneity at the organizational level may yield unique applications. For example, attraction has consequences for the composition of the job applicant pool of the organization and hence should be taken into account in recruiting, screening, selection and staffing in general. Attrition, on the other hand, has implications for interventions regarding retention and thus who should be targeted for such interventions.

Personality and Training

Personality variables play an important role in several process and outcome variables in training.

Several meta-analyses and path analyses shed insight on the relationship of personality variables to training-related variables such as motivation to learn, reactions to training, post-training self-efficacy, skill acquisition, acquisition of declarative knowledge, learning and skill transfer, and overall training success. Colquitt, LePine and Noe (2000) conducted a meta-analysis of the relationships between several antecedent variables and several specific, training variables. They included in their analyses four personality variables – conscientiousness, achievement (a facet of conscientiousness in the Big Five model), anxiety (a facet of emotional stability), and locus of control. Other meta-analyses included these and other personality variables, as well as more global training success criteria.

According to the Colquitt et al. (2000) meta-analysis, motivation to learn is related to several personality variables. Anxiety (opposite of emotional stability) was the highest correlate of motivation to learn, with mean corrected $r = -.57$ ($k = 3$, $N = 242$). The mean corrected correlation between internal locus of control and motivation to learn was .46 ($k = 33$, $N = 309$). Conscientiousness and achievement (a facet of conscientiousness in the Big Five model) were also highly correlated with motivation to learn, mean corrected r = .38 ($k = 3$, $N = 388$) for conscientiousness and mean corrected $r = .35$ ($k = 2$, $N = 244$) for achievement.

Colquitt et al. (2000) examined relations between personality variables and reactions to training. Anxiety was again negatively related ($r = -.23$, $k = 2$, $N = 174$). They found conscientiousness was negatively and negligibly related to reactions to training, mean corrected $r = -.06$ ($k = 1$, $N = 139$), but achievement (a facet of conscientiousness in the Big Five model) was positively and moderately related ($r = .20$, $k = 3$, $N = 558$). The mean corrected correlation between internal locus of control and reactions to training was $-.18$ ($k = 2$, $N = 125$). All of these results are, however, based on small sample sizes and very few studies.

Colquitt et al. (2000) also examined the relationships between the personality variables and skill acquisition and declarative knowledge. They found anxiety was negatively related to both skill acquisition (mean corrected $r = -.15$, $k = 4$, $N = 368$) and acquisition of declarative knowledge (mean corrected $r = -.17$, $k = 8$, $N = 1070$). However, they found conscientiousness was related to neither skill acquisition nor declarative knowledge (mean corrected $r = -.05$, $k = 6$, $N = 839$ for skill acquisition and $r = -.01$, $k = 3$, $N = 725$ for acquisition of declarative knowledge). They found achievement was related to skill acquisition but essentially unrelated to declarative knowledge, corrected mean $r = .17$ ($k = 2$, $N = 356$) for skill acquisition and $r = .07$ ($k = 4$, $N = 610$) for declarative knowledge. Also surprising were the results for locus of control. Internal locus of control was negatively related to

the acquisition of declarative knowledge ($r = -.21$, $k = 7$, $N = 924$) and unrelated to skill acquisition ($r = -.04$, $k = 7$, $N = 386$). Perhaps some of these results are due to the small sample sizes and few studies included in the meta-analysis. For example, in contrast with the Colquitt et al. (2000) meta-analytic findings, in a large path analytic study, Borman et al. (1991) found that dependability (a facet of conscientiousness in the Big Five model) had a path coefficient of .14 ($N = 4,362$) with job knowledge (declarative knowledge).

Personality variables appear to exert influences on post-training attitudes and behavior as well. In Colquitt et al.'s (2000) meta-analysis, achievement, conscientiousness, and anxiety correlated with post-training self-efficacy, for achievement mean corrected $r = .22$ ($k = 2$, $N = 318$), for conscientiousness mean corrected $r = .19$ ($k = 1$, $N = 82$), and for anxiety mean corrected $r = -.47$ ($k = 2$, $N = 144$). Internal locus of control was, however, unrelated to post-training self-efficacy (corrected mean $r = .00$, $k = 5$, $N = 309$). In terms of transfer of training, Colquitt et al.'s (2000) results indicate conscientiousness correlated .29 ($k = 1$, $N = 80$) with it and that internal locus of control correlated negatively with transfer of training (mean corrected $r = -.27$, $k = 2$, $N = 125$). Again, as previously noted, the sample sizes are small and the studies few, thereby limiting the confidence in the generalizability of these results.

Several meta-analyses and quantitative reviews have summarized correlations between personality variables and *overall* training success. Barrick and Mount (1991) and Salgado (1997) reported corrected mean validities for Big Five personality variables and training proficiency. Their training proficiency criterion included training performance, work sample performance, and time to complete training. Barrick and Mount (1991) found notable correlations for extraversion (true score $r = .26$, $N = 3,101$), conscientiousness (true score $r = .23$, $N = 3,585$), and openness to experience (true score $r = .25$, $N = 2,700$). Salgado's (1997) meta-analysis suggested that except for extraversion, the other Big Five variables correlated with training success at useful levels, estimated true validity of these four variables ranged from .17 to .24. However, his meta-analysis was based on studies conducted in European communities and was smaller than the Barrick and Mount meta-analysis.

Hough (1992) also summarized personality correlates of overall training success. Her training success criterion included instructor ratings, grades, field test scores, and completion of training. She found the following. Mean observed r for achievement (a facet of the Big Five conscientiousness construct) was .21 ($N = 1,160$); mean observed r for dependability (a facet of the Big Five conscientiousness construct) was .11 ($N = 4,710$);

mean observed *r* for emotional stability was .12 (*N* = 8,685); mean observed *r* for agreeableness was .08 (*N* = 988); mean observed *r* for potency (the energy level and dominance facets of extraversion in the Big Five model) was .07 (*N* = 8,389); mean observed *r* for intellectance (same construct as Big Five openness to experience) was .02 (*N* = 8,744); and mean observed *r* for locus of control was .28 (*N* = 225). The Barrick and Mount (1991) and Hough (1992) summaries yield some interesting similarities and differences. Both found conscientiousness predictive of training success. However, whereas Barrick and Mount found openness to experience to be a useful predictor of training success, Hough did not. Whereas Barrick and Mount found extraversion to be a useful predictor of training success, Hough found it only somewhat useful. Although Hough found emotional stability a useful predictor of training success, Barrick and Mount did not. Except for openness to experience, Hough's (1992) and Salgado's (1997) results are more similar than either one is to Barrick and Mount's (1991) results.

Ones, Viswesvaran and Reiss (1996) meta-analyzed relations between social desirability scales and training performance. They reported the operational validity (corrected for unreliability in the criterion alone) of social desirability scales for predicting instructor ratings of training success was .22 (*N* = 4,547). Ones et al., suggested that self-enhancement ability may be an aspect of social competence and those individuals who distort their responses in a socially desirable direction may be the same individuals who can impress instructors through successful interpersonal interactions during their training periods.

Ones and Viswesvaran (1998b) meta-analyzed the relations between integrity (a compound variable) and training performance for newly hired employees participating in job training. Training performance was measured by either objective tests (75% of their data) or supervisory ratings of training success (25% of their data), both obtained at the end of the training period. They found an operational validity of .38 (*N* = 2,364), indicating a substantial link between the integrity construct and performance in job training. As described earlier, integrity is a compound variable consisting of conscientiousness, agreeableness, and emotional stability (Ones & Viswesvaran, 1998b). It is thus likely to correlate at a higher level with training performance given the relations between conscientiousness, agreeableness, emotional stability, and training success found in the Hough (1992) and Salgado (1997) studies.

Overall, most of the results suggest that neuroticism (opposite of emotional stability) interferes with learning and thus training success whereas conscientiousness (dependability and achievement) facilitates learning and thus training success. Less

clear are the roles of extraversion and openness to experience in employee learning and training. Future work will need to explore why different quantitative summaries of the literature (e.g., Barrick & Mount, 1991; Colquitt et al., 2000; Hough, 1992, Salgado, 1997) have come to differing conclusions regarding the role of these personality constructs in training.

Finally, although personality determinants of training motivation, skill acquisition, training performance, success etc., have proliferated in the literature, studies of personality variables in interactionist models (disposition by treatment interactions) are surprisingly absent. Future research should explore such models for different training content areas (see also Campbell & Kuncel, Chapter 13 of this volume).

Personality and Job Satisfaction

What makes employees love or hate their jobs? Much of IWO psychology literature has responded to this question by studying organizational variables such as job characteristics (skill variety, task identity, task significance, autonomy, feedback), role variables (role ambiguity and role conflict) and pay. Personal antecedents of job satisfaction have been limited primarily to demographic variables, most notably gender and age. However, important insights can be gleaned from considering personality variables as antecedents of job satisfaction. Evidence from three lines of research support the usefulness of this approach.

First, longitudinal data show job satisfaction remains stable over time. Staw and Ross (1985) obtained longitudinal data from over 5,000 men and found stability of job satisfaction over a period of five years. Even when individuals changed jobs or employers, job satisfaction remained stable (Staw & Ross, 1985), suggesting that personality variables might be responsible for the cross-situational consistency in job satisfaction. Staw and Ross (1985) wrote '[j]ob attitudes may reflect a biologically based trait that predisposes individuals to see positive or negative content in their lives.... Differences in individual temperament,... ranging from clinical depression to a very positive disposition, could influence the information individuals input, recall, and interpret within various social situations, including work' (p. 471).

Second, genetic data suggest that personality variables may affect job satisfaction. Arvey, Bouchard, Segal and Abraham (1989) used a sample of monozygotic twins reared apart to partition genetic vs. environmental influences on job satisfaction. The intraclass correlation coefficient for monozygotic twins reared apart directly estimates heritability. They found that heritability of job satisfaction was approximately .30. Arvey et al. (1989) suggested that relatively stable personality traits were responsible for the genetic basis of job satisfaction.

Third, direct studies of the relations between personality constructs and job satisfaction indicate personality variables influence job satisfaction. These studies have examined the relationship of job satisfaction to the Big Five dimensions of personality, negative and positive affectivity, and core self-evaluations (positive self-concept).

In a provocative longitudinal study ($N = 118$), Judge, Higgins, Thoreson and Barrick (1999) showed that Big Five measures completed in childhood correlated with adult job satisfaction (intrinsic career success). Conscientiousness correlated most highly with job satisfaction (observed $r = .40$). Childhood neuroticism correlated $-.22$ with adult job satisfaction. Regression analyses, however, indicated that childhood neuroticism did not explain incremental variance over conscientiousness. As might be expected, regression analyses using adult personality data showed stronger relations with job satisfaction.

In an early study, affective disposition (negative–positive affectivity) was linked to job satisfaction (Staw, Bell & Clausen, 1986). Since then, there have been multiple studies examining the relationship between negative and positive affectivity with job satisfaction (e.g., Brief, Burke, George, Robinson & Webster, 1988; Levin & Stokes, 1989; Necowitz & Roznowski, 1994; Watson & Slack, 1993). Thoresen and Judge (1997) presented a meta-analysis of these studies and other studies. They found that correlations corrected for unreliability were $-.40$ ($k = 41$) for negative affectivity, and $.52$ ($k = 29$) for positive affectivity.

Core self-evaluations or positive self-concept is a compound personality variable composed of (a) self-esteem, (b) generalized self-efficacy, (c) locus of control, and (d) emotional stability (Judge, Locke & Durham, 1997). According to a meta-analysis of core self evaluations and job satisfaction (Judge & Bono, 2001), the correlations (corrected for unreliability) are sizable. Specifically, job satisfaction correlates .26 with self-esteem ($N = 20,819$), .45 with generalized self-efficacy ($N = 12,903$), .32 with internal locus of control ($N = 18,491$), and .24 with emotional stability ($N = 7,658$). Judge and Bono (2001) suggest that these traits may be the principle dispositions underlying job satisfaction.

Taken together, these three lines of research indicate that job satisfaction is at least partially personality based. Recent research leaves little doubt about which personality traits underlie job satisfaction. However, except for research by Brief (1998), Motowidlo (1996), Spector (1997), and Weiss and Cropanzano (1996), there is little in the literature describing the process mechanisms by which personality constructs influence job satisfaction. Future research should address *how* personality constructs influence job satisfaction.

Personality and Occupational Health and Safety

The relevance of personality variables to occupational health has received extensive attention in the literature. Studies have examined Type A behavior (e.g., Ganster, 1987; Lee, Ashford & Jamieson, 1993), locus of control (e.g., Spector, 1998), and hardiness (Cox & Ferguson, 1991), among others. Perhaps not surprisingly neuroticism and negative affectivity have been found to relate to stressors and psychological distress (e.g., Hart, Wearing & Headey, 1995; Moyle, 1995). In this section we focus on personality variables in a specific area of occupational health: work-related accidents. (See Hart and Cooper, in Volume 2, Chapter 5 of this *Handbook*, for a review of the role of personality variables in burnout, stress–strain relationships, and other organizational safety variables.)

During World War I, Greenwood and Woods (1919) observed that accidents were not evenly distributed among British munitions factory workers. Their explanation of unequal initial liability formed the basis of much research directed at accident proneness, which Greenwood and Woods termed 'an affair of personality'. In a 1926 study of 13 factories, Newbold (1927) also came to the conclusion that accidents were partially the result of 'personal tendency'. Since then, studies examining the relationships between personality traits and accidents have proliferated. During the past decade, researchers have aimed to identify which personality characteristics increase workers' liability for accidents. For example, in a longitudinal study of offshore oil and gas platform workers ($N = 360$), Sutherland and Cooper (1991) found neuroticism and Type A personality correlated with accident involvement. In a sample of blue collar workers ($N = 362$), Iverson and Erwin (1997) found that positive and negative affectivity predicted, in the expected direction, occupational injury over a year. Interested readers are referred to the narrative reviews of C. Hansen (1988; 1989), Porter (1988), Lester (1991), and Lawton and Parker (1998) for details of this literature.

Four groups of researchers have meta-analyzed the relations between personality variables and accidents. Arthur, Barrett and Alexander (1991) meta-analyzed relations between vehicular accidents and locus of control, conscientiousness (regard for authority), emotional stability (low levels of distress), and general activity level (which according to Arthur et al. is aggression, depression and withdrawal). The mean observed r between vehicular accidents (a negative outcome) and internal locus of control was $-.20$ ($N = 1,909$), for conscientiousness r was $-.16$ ($N = 3,242$), for general activity level r was $-.07$ ($N = 7,137$), and for emotional stability r was $-.02$ ($N = 3,106$). For professional drivers, correlations between vehicular accidents and conscientiousness and general activity level were higher than for nonprofessional drivers. For professional drivers, mean observed r was $-.28$ ($N = 635$) for conscientiousness (regard for authority) and $-.22$ ($N = 674$) for general activity level. Robertson and Clarke (1999) reported a meta-analysis of relations between accident involvement and four personality variables: conscientiousness, emotional stability, extraversion, and agreeableness. The mean observed correlation between accident involvement (a negative outcome) and dependability was $-.17$ ($N = 3,845$), $-.16$ ($N = 4,927$) for agreeableness, $-.09$ ($N = 5,959$) for emotional stability, and $+.06$ ($N = 2,450$) for extraversion. Salgado (2000) reported a meta-analysis of the Big Five dimensions of personality and accidents (a negative outcome). Operational validities were $-.08$ ($N = 2,121$) for emotional stability, $-.06$ ($N = 2,094$) for conscientiousness, $-.04$ ($N = 2,341$) for extraversion, $-.01$ ($N = 1,540$) for agreeableness, and $+.09$ ($N = 1,660$) for openness to experience. Ones and Viswesvaran (1998b) meta-analyzed correlations between integrity (a compound variable consisting of conscientiousness, agreeableness, and emotional stability) and accidents on the job (a negative criterion). They found an operational validity of $-.52$ ($N = 759$). Corrections were made for range restriction and unreliability in the criterion, and accident data from all studies contributing to the meta-analysis were obtained from organizational records.

The results of these meta-analyses suggest that employees who are low on integrity (conscientiousness, agreeableness, and emotional stability) are likely to be involved in accidents. These data suggest that personality variables are an important factor in work-related accidents. Undoubtedly, other variables, including organizational influences, are also likely to contribute to work-place safety or lack thereof.

Personality and Leadership

Within the field of psychology, thousands of studies are devoted to the topic of leadership (Bass, 1990). However, researchers from many other fields have also studied leadership. Unlike psychologists, most of these researchers focus on unique characteristics of individual leaders. Psychologists more often focus on the communalities among leaders.

Within IWO psychology, Stodgill's (1950) authoritative review concluded that the 'findings suggest that leadership is not a matter of passive status, or of the mere possession of some combination of traits' (Stodgill, 1950: 66), leading to skepticism about personality and leadership. For the next approximately fifty years, situational theories of leadership dominated the field. In recent years however, new research, primarily based on meta-analyses where the influences of statistical artifacts (sampling error, unreliability, and so forth) are

corrected for, has caused a reconsideration of trait-based views of leadership. Careful thinking about the dependent variables has also helped. Indeed, the role of personality variables depends upon what is meant by leadership (Ones, Hough & Viswesvaran, 2000). The relations between personality characteristics and dependent variables such as leadership perceptions, leadership emergence, leadership effectiveness, overall job success of leaders, and managerial level have been meta-analyzed with interesting results.

In a meta-analysis of individual differences variables and leadership perceptions, Lord, De Vader, and Alliger (1986) found that emotional stability and extraversion were correlated with leadership perceptions (corrected r's $= .24$ and $.26$; and N's $= 1,085$ and $1,701$, respectively). In a more recent meta-analysis, Judge, Bono, Ilies and Werner (2000) found that emotional stability and extraversion are also correlated with leadership emergence (corrected r's $= .19$ and $.34$, respectively), as are conscientiousness and openness to experience (corrected r's $= .34$ and $.24$, respectively). When in a group, individuals who are extraverted, emotionally stable as well as conscientious and open to experience will emerge as leaders. According to the Judge et al. (2000) meta-analysis, effective leaders also display these qualities. Corrected correlations (corrected for unreliability in both predictor and criterion variables) with leadership effectiveness were $.23$ for extraversion, $.26$ for emotional stability, $.24$ for openness to experience and $.15$ for conscientiousness. Effective leaders were also agreeable, corrected $r = .23$ (Judge et al., 2000).

When all aspects of managerial performance are considered (e.g., training success and overall job performance, as well as leadership effectiveness), conscientiousness typically predicts overall performance. Barrick and Mount (1991) found that in US studies, conscientiousness had a true score correlation of $.22$ ($N = 10,058$) with the combined set of criteria for managers. Salgado (1997) found that in European studies, the true score correlation of conscientiousness with the same combined set of criteria was $.16$ ($N = 987$). Results were less consistent for extraversion and emotional stability. In US studies, the true score correlation of extraversion with the combined set of criteria was $.18$ ($N = 11,335$) (Barrick & Mount, 1991), whereas in European studies, the correlation was $.05$ ($N = 987$) (Salgado, 1997). In US studies, the true score correlation of emotional stability with the combined set of criteria was $.08$ ($N = 10,324$) (Barrick & Mount, 1991), whereas in European studies $r = .12$ ($N = 987$) (Salgado, 1997).

Results from a comprehensive meta-analysis by Hough, Ones and Viswesvaran (1998) suggest that facets of extraversion (i.e., energy level and dominance) and conscientiousness (i.e., achievement) may be more potent in explaining variance in managerial job performance than global Big Five variables. In reaching positions of leadership, all facets of extraversion, emotional stability, and achievement appear to be important (Hough et al., 1998).

Contrary to earlier conclusions, personality variables are relevant to leadership. Results from recent meta-analyses have revived trait approaches. Although complex, linkages between personality variables and many different leadership behaviors exist. Meta-analytic data consistently establish the importance of personality variables for leadership behavior.

Summary of Personality Pre- and Post-Selection

It has been over a decade since Davis-Blake and Pfeffer (1989) declared dispositional effects in organizational research 'just a mirage'. As we illustrated for career and occupational choice, organizational choice, training, occupational health and safety, job satisfaction, and leadership, work on personality variables and their effects beyond personnel selection is thriving. Indeed, 'rumors of the death of dispositional research are vastly exaggerated' (House, Shane & Herold, 1996: 203). Future work examining the influence of personality variables pre- and post-selection is likely to benefit individuals and organizations. We agree with Schneider (1996), a research agenda on the role of personality in work behavior should include, but not be limited to, personnel selection.

CONCLUSIONS

The importance of personality variables for work is obvious. They influence career and occupational choice, organizational choice, as well as reaction to testing programs employers use to select employees. Once hired, personality variables influence most of what happens at work including: (a) learning and training processes and outcomes; (b) health and safety on the job; (c) satisfaction with one's job, coworkers, and supervisors; and (d) which people emerge as leaders as well as which ones are effective as leaders.

Evidence clearly shows that personality variables predict behavior and performance in training and on the job, although the particular taxonomic structure of the personality and criterion variables moderates these relationships. Our review suggests that the level of validity obtained using the Big Five factors can be improved. We proposed a working set of personality taxons for conducting and summarizing future research. Compound variables, such as integrity tests and customer service orientation tests improve on the validity of individual personality variables. Once the nomological webs of our working taxons are understood, we can form new compound variables, synthesizing them for new, even unique prediction situations, and producing validities higher than any single taxon. Our changing world of work demands that our field responds to the need to predict performance for small numbers of people performing new and different configurations of work in new and different settings.

Personality measurement today is typically done with a self-report questionnaire. One of the most frequent concerns with self-report is intentional distortion. Although intentional distortion does affect validity in directed faking settings (e.g., fake good studies), it does not appear to affect validity in real-life applicant settings.

Personality testing is changing, eliminating many of the issues involved in self-reports. Some of the newer technologies, however, such as conditional reasoning, virtual reality testing, genetic testing, and neurological testing, bring a new set of measurement, legal, and ethical problems and issues to solve.

A new research agenda is at hand.

NOTES

1 There are several theoretical perspectives or paradigms within which issues related to personality are researched and discussed. A review of major textbooks on personality suggest the major approaches are (a) psychoanalytic/psychodynamic, (b) trait/dispositional, (c) emotions, (d) behavioral/learning, (e) object relations/ego psychology, (f) phenomenological/humanistic, (g) social cognitive, and (h) cognitive/information processing (Emmons, 1989; Mayer, 1995). We refer the interested reader to these texts for in-depth discussions of the many theoretical positions in personality psychology.

2 Hough's achievement construct is similar to Tellegen's (n.d.) achievement construct and White's (1959) effectance motivation. It is thus a part of Tellegen's (n.d.) higher-order factor Agentic Positive Emotionality, not the Big Five factor Conscientiousness. Hough's dependability construct is a component of Tellegen's (n.d.) higher-order factor Constraint under which may be a general inhibition system similar to Gray's (1982) psychobiological Behavioral Inhibition System.

3 Hough's affiliation construct is similar to Tellegen's (n.d.) Communal Positive Emotionality.

REFERENCES

Ackerman, P.L., & Heggestad, E.D. (1997). Intelligence, personality, and interests: Evidence for overlapping traits. *Psychological Bulletin, 121,* 219–245.

Alliger, G.M., Lilienfeld, S.O., & Mitchell, K.E. (1996). The susceptibility of overt and covert integrity tests to coaching and faking. *Psychological Science, 7,* 32–39.

Allport, G.W., & Odbert, H.S. (1936). Trait-names: A psycho-lexical study. *Psychological Monographs, 47* (211).

Almagor, M., Tellegen, A., & Waller, N.G. (1995). The Big Seven Model: A cross-cultural replication and further exploration of the basic dimensions of natural language trait descriptors. *Journal of Personality and Social Psychology, 69,* 300–307.

Arthur, J. Jr., Barrett, G.V., & Alexander, R.A. (1991). Prediction of vehicular accident involvement: A meta-analysis. *Human Performance, 4*(2), 89–105.

Arvey, R.D., Bouchard, T.J., Segal, N.L., & Abraham, L.M. (1989). Job satisfaction: Environmental and genetic components. *Journal of Applied Psychology, 74*(2), 187–192.

Arvey, R.D., Renz, G.L., & Watson, T.W. (1998). Emotionality and job performance: Implications for personnel selection. *Research in Personnel and Human Resources Management, 16,* 103–147.

Averill, J.R. (1997). The emotions: An integrative approach. In R. Hogan, J. Johnson & S. Briggs (Eds.), *Handbook of personality psychology* (pp. 513–541). San Diego: Academic Press.

Bar-On, R. (1997). *The Emotional Quotient Inventory (EQ-I): Technical Manual.* Toronto, Canada: Multi-Health Systems.

Barrett, P.T., & Eysenck, S.B.G. (1984). The assessment of personality factors across 25 countries. *Personality and Individual Differences, 5,* 615–632.

Barrick, M.R., & Mount, M.K. (1991). The big five personality dimensions and job performance: A meta-analysis. *Personnel Psychology, 44,* 1–26.

Barrick, M.R., & Mount, M.K. (1996). Effects of impression management and self-deception on the predictive validity of personality constructs. *Journal of Applied Psychology, 81,* 262–272.

Bass, B.M. (1990). *Bass and Stogdill's handbook of leadership: Theory, research, and managerial applications* (3rd ed.). New York, NY: The Free Press.

Benet, V., & Waller, N.G. (1995). The Big Seven Factor Model of personality description: Evidence for its cross-cultural generality in a Spanish sample. *Journal of Personality and Social Psychology, 69,* 701–718.

Benet-Martínez, V., & John, O.P. (1998). *Los Cinco Grandes* across cultures and ethnic groups: Multitrait multimethod analyses of the big five in Spanish and English. *Journal of Personality and Social Psychology, 75,* 729–750.

Betz, N.E., & Serling, D.A. (1993). Construct validity of fear of commitment as an indicator of career indecisiveness. *Journal of Career Assessment, 1,* 21–34.

Block, J. (1995). A contrarian view of the five-factor approach to personality description. *Psychological Bulletin, 117,* 187–215.

Borman, W.C., & Motowidlo, S.J., (1993). Expanding the criterion domain to include elements of contextual performance. In N. Schmitt & W.C. Borman (Eds.), *Personnel selection in organizations* (pp. 71–98). San Francisco: Jossey-Bass.

Borman, W.C., & Motowidlo, S.J. (1997). Task performance and contextual performance: The meaning for personnel selection research. *Human Performance, 10,* 99–109.

Borman, W.C., White, L.A., Pulakos, E.D., & Oppler, S.H. (1991). Models of supervisory job performance ratings. *Journal of Applied Psychology, 76,* 863–872.

Bouchard, T.J. Jr. (1997a). Inheritance of authoritarianism and other social attitudes. In S. Scarr (Chair), *Genetics and personality: The search for why we think, act, and feel the way we do.* Presidential symposium conducted at the 9th Annual Convention of the American Psychological Society, Washington, DC.

Bouchard, T.J. Jr. (1997b). Genetic influence on mental abilities, personality, vocational interests and work attitudes. In C.L. Cooper & I.T. Robertson (Eds.), *International review of industrial and organizational psychology,* Chichester: John Wiley.

Bouchard, T.J. Jr. (1997c). The genetics of personality. In K. Blum & E.P. Noble (Eds.), *Handbook of psychiatric genetics.* Boca Raton, FL: CRC Press.

Bouchard, T.J. Jr., & Hur, J. (1998). Genetic and environmental influences on the continuous scales of the Myers-Briggs Type Indicator: An analysis based on twins reared apart. *Journal of Personality, 66,* 135–149.

Brief, A.P. (1998). *Attitudes in and around organizations.* Thousand Oaks: CA: Sage Publications, Inc.

Brief, A.P., Burke, M.J., George, J.M., Robinson, B.S., & Webster, J. (1988). Should negative affectivity remain an unmeasured variable in the study of job stress? *Journal of Applied Psychology, 73*(2), 193–198.

Brief, A.P., & Motowidlo, S.J. (1986). Prosocial organizational behaviors. *Academy of Management Review, 11,* 710–725.

Burroughs, S.M., Bing, M.N., & James, L.R. (1999). Reconsidering how to measure employee reliability: An empirical comparison and integration of self-report and conditional reasoning methodologies. In L.J. Williams & S.M. Burroughs (Chairs), *New Developments Using Conditional Reasoning to Measure Employee Reliability.* Symposium conducted at the 14th Annual Conference of the Society for Industrial and Organizational Psychology, Atlanta.

Campbell, J.P. (1990). Modeling the performance prediction problem in industrial and organizational psychology. In M.D. Dunnette & L.M. Hough (Eds.), *Handbook of industrial and organizational psychology* (Vol. 1, 2nd ed., pp. 687–732). Palo Alto: Consulting Psychologists Press.

Carson, A.D., & Mowsesian, R. (1993). Self-monitoring and private self-consciousness: Relations to Holland's vocational personality types. *Journal of Vocational Behavior, 42,* 212–222.

Cattell, R.B. (1943). The description of personality: Basic traits resolved into clusters. *Journal of Abnormal and Social Psychology, 38,* 476–506.

Cattell, R.B. (1945). The description of personality: Principles and findings in a factor analysis. *American Journal of Psychology, 58,* 69–90.

Cattell, R.B., Eber, H.W., & Tatsuoka, M.M. (1970). *Handbook for the Sixteen Personality Factor Questionnaire*

(16PF). Champaign, IL: Institute for Personality and Ability Testing.

Chan, D. (1997). Racial subgroup differences in predictive validity perceptions on personality and cognitive ability tests. *Journal of Applied Psychology, 82*, 311–320.

Chan, D., Schmitt, N., DeShon, R.P., Clause, C.S., & Delbridge, K. (1997). Reactions to cognitive ability tests: The relationships between race, test performance, face validity perceptions, and test-taking motivation. *Journal of Applied Psychology, 82*, 300–310.

Chan, D., Schmitt, N., Jennings, D., Clause, C.S., & Delbridge, K. (1998). Applicant perceptions of test fairness: Integrating justice and self-serving bias perspectives. *International Journal of Selection and Assessment, 6*, 232–239.

Chan, D., Schmitt, N., Sacco, J.M., & DeShon, R.P. (1998). Understanding pre-test and post-test reactions to cognitive ability and personality tests. *Journal of Applied Psychology, 83*, 471–485.

Chartrand, J.M., Rose, M.L., Elliott, T.R., Marmarosh, C., & Caldwell, S. (1993). Peeling back the onion: Personality, problem solving and career decision-making style correlates of career indecision. *Journal of Career Assessment, 1*, 66–82.

Chen, X., Hui, C., & Sego, D.J. (1998). The role of organizational citizenship behavior in turnover: Conceptualization and preliminary tests of key hypotheses. *Journal of Applied Psychology, 83*, 922–931.

Christiansen, N.D., Goffin, R.D., Johnston, N.G., & Rothstein, M.G. (1994). Correcting the 16PF for faking: Effects on criterion-related validity and individual hiring decisions. *Personnel Psychology, 47*, 847–860.

Church, A.T., & Burke, P.J. (1994). Exploratory and confirmatory tests of the Big Five and Tellegen's Three- and Four-Dimensional models. *Journal of Personality and Social Psychology, 66*, 93–114.

Collins, J.M., & Gleaves, D.H. (1998). Race, job applicants, and the five-factor model of personality: Implications for black psychology, industrial/organizational psychology, and the five-factor theory. *Journal of Applied Psychology, 83*, 531–544.

Colquitt, J.A., LePine, J.A., & Noe, R.A. (2000). Toward an integrative theory of training motivation: A meta-analytic path analysis of 20 years of research. *Journal of Applied Psychology, 85*(5), 678–707.

Conway, J.M. (1996). Additional construct validity evidence for the task-contextual performance distinction. *Human Performance, 9*, 309–329.

Conway, J.M. (1999). Distinguishing contextual performance from task performance for managerial jobs. *Journal of Applied Psychology, 84*, 3–13.

Costa, P.T. Jr., Busch, C.M., Zonderman, A.B., & McCrae, R.R. (1986). Correlations of MMPI factor scales with measures of the five-factor model. *Journal of Personality Assessment, 50*, 640–650.

Costa, P.T. Jr., & McCrae, R.R. (1985). *The NEO Personality Inventory Manual*. Odessa, FL: Psychological Assessment Resources.

Costa, P.T. Jr., & McCrae, R.R. (1988). From catalogue to classification: Murray's needs and the five-factor model. *Journal of Personality and Social Psychology, 55*, 258–265.

Costa, P.T. Jr., & McCrae, R.R. (1989). The *NEO-PI/NEO-FFI manual supplement*. Odessa, FL: Psychological Assessment Resources.

Costa, P.T. Jr., & McCrae, R.R. (1992). *Revised NEO Personality Inventory (NEO PI-R) and NEO Five-Factor Inventory (NEO-FFI)*. Professional manual. Odessa, FL: Psychological Assessment Resources.

Costa, P.T. Jr., & McCrae, R.R. (1995). Primary traits of Eysenck's P-E-N-system: Three-and five-factor solutions. *Journal of Personality and Social Psychology, 69*, 308–317.

Costa, P.T. Jr., Zonderman, A.B., Williams, R.B., & McCrae, R.R. (1985). Content and comprehensiveness in the MMPI: An item factor analysis in a normal adult sample. *Journal of Personality and Social Psychology, 48*, 925–933.

Cox, T., & Ferguson, E. (1991). Individual differences, stress and coping. In C.L. Cooper & R. Payne (Eds.), *Personality and stress: Individual differences in the stress process* (pp. 7–30). Chichester: Wiley.

Dahlstrom, W.G., Welsh, G.S., & Dahlstrom, L.E. (1972). *An MMPI handbook. Volume I: Clinical interpretation*. Minneapolis: University of Minnesota Press.

Dahlstrom, W.G., Welsh, G.S., & Dahlstrom, L.E. (1975). *An MMPI handbook. Volume II: Research applications*. Minneapolis: University of Minnesota Press.

Davies, M., Stankov, L., & Roberts, R.D. (1998). Emotional intelligence: In search of an elusive construct. *Journal of Personality and Social Psychology, 75*, 989–1015.

Davis-Blake, A., & Pfeffer, J. (1989). Just a mirage: The search for dispositional effects in organizational research. *Academy of Management Review, 14*(3), 385–400.

Dawis, R.V., & Lofquist, L.H. (1984). *A psychological theory of work adjustment*. Minneapolis: University of Minnesota Press.

De Fruyt, R., & Mervielde, I. (1997). The five-factor model of personality and Holland's RIASEC interest types. *Personality and Individual Differences, 23*, 87–103.

De Fruyt, F., & Mervielde, I. (1999). RIASEC types and Big Five traits as predictors of employment status and nature of employment. *Personnel Psychology, 52*, 701–727.

Deary, I.J. (1996). A (latent) big five personality model in 1915? A reanalysis of Webb's data. *Journal of Personality and Social Psychology, 71*, 992–1005.

Depue, R.A., Lucianna, M., Arbisi, P., Collins, P., & Leon, A. (1994). Dopamine and the structure of personality: Relation of agonist-induced dopamine activity to positive emotionality. *Journal of Personality and Social Psychology, 67*, 485–498.

Dicken, C. (1963). Good impression, social desirability, and acquiescence as suppressor variables. *Educational and Psychological Measurement, 23*, 699–720.

Digman, J.M. (1989). Five robust trait dimensions: Development, stability, and utility. *Journal of Personality, 57*, 195–214.

Digman, J.M. (1990). Personality structure: Emergence of the five-factor model. *Annual Review of Psychology*, *41*, 417–440.

Digman, J.M., & Inouye, J. (1986). Further specification of the five robust factors of personality. *Journal of Personality and Social Psychology, 50*, 116–123.

Digman, J.M., & Takemoto-Chock, M.K. (1981). Factors in the natural language of personality: Re-analysis and comparison of six major studies. *Multivariate Behavioral Research, 16*, 149–170.

Doll, R.E. (1971). Item susceptibility to attempted faking as related to item characteristics and adopted fake set. *Journal of Psychology, 77*, 9–16.

Douglas, E.F., McDaniel, M.A., & Snell, A.F. (1996). The validity of non-cognitive measures decays when applicants fake. *Academy of Management Proceedings*.

Dunnette, M.D. (1998). Emerging trends and vexing issues in industrial and organizational psychology. *Applied Psychology: An International Review, 47*(2), 129–153.

Dunnette, M.D., McCartney, J., Carlson, H.E., & Kirchner, W.K. (1962). A study of faking behavior on a forced-choice self-description checklist. *Personnel Psychology, 15*, 13–24.

Dunnette, M.D., Paullin, C., & Motowidlo, S.J. (1989). *Development and validation of the Kelly Applicant Profile for use in screening candidates for positions with Kelly assisted living services* (Institute Report No. 170 and Memorandum). Minneapolis, MN: Personnel Decisions Research Institutes, Inc.

Dwight, S.A., & Alliger, G.M. (1997). *Using response latencies to identify overt integrity test dissimulators*. Paper presented at the 12th Annual Meeting of the Society for Industrial and Organizational Psychology, St. Louis.

Dwight, S.A., & Donovan, J.J. (1998). *Warning: Proceed with caution when warning applicants not to dissimulate (revised)*. Presented at the 13th Annual Meeting of the Society for Industrial and Organizational Psychology.

Ellingson, J.E., Sackett, P.R., & Hough, L.M. (1999). Social desirability correction in personality measurement: Issues of applicant comparison and construct validity. *Journal of Applied Psychology, 84*, 155–166.

Ellingson, J.E., Smith, D.B., & Sackett, P.R. (2001). Investigating the influence of social desirability on personality factor structure. *Journal of Applied Psychology, 86*, 122–133.

Ellis, B.B. (1989). Differential item functioning: Implications for test translations. *Journal of Applied Psychology, 74*, 912–921.

Emmons, R.A. (1989). The big three, the big four, or the big five? *Contemporary Psychology, 34*, 644–646.

Eysenck, H.J. (1970). *The structure of human personality* (3rd ed.). London: Methuen.

Eysenck, H.J. (1991). Dimensions of personality: 16, 5, or 3? – Criteria for a taxonomic paradigm. *Personality and Individual Differences, 12*, 773–790.

Eysenck, H.J. (1992). Four ways five factors are *not* basic. *Personality and Individual Differences, 13*, 667–673.

Eysenck, H.J., & Eysenck, S.B.G. (1975). *Manual of the Eysenck Personality Scales (EPS Adult)*. London: Hodder & Stoughton.

Eysenck, H.J., & Eysenck, S.B.G. (1991). *Manual of the Eysenck Personality Questionnaire*. San Diego, CA: EdITS.

Eysenck, H.J., & Wilson, G.D. (1991). *The Eysenck Personality Profiler*. London: Corporate Assessment Network, Ltd.

Farh, J., Earley, P.C., & Lin, S. (1997). Impetus for action: A cultural analysis of justice and organizational citizenship behavior in Chinese society. *Administrative Science Quarterly, 42*, 421–444.

Finger, M.S., & Ones, D.S. (1999). Psychometric equivalence of the computer and booklet forms of the MMPI: A meta-analysis. *Psychological Assessment, 11*, 58–66.

Fiske, D.W. (1949). Consistency of the factorial structures of personality ratings from different sources. *Journal of Abnormal and Social Psychology, 44*, 329–344.

Fleishman, E.A., & Quaintance, M.K. (1984). *Taxonomies of human performance: The description of human tasks*. Orlando, FL: Academic Press, Inc.

Frei, R.L., & McDaniel, M.A. (1998). Validity of customer service measures in personnel selection: A review of criterion and construct evidence. *Human Performance, 11*, 1–27.

Furnham, A. (1986). Response bias, social desirability and dissimulation. *Personality and Individual Differences, 7*, 385–400.

Galton, F. (1884). Measurement of character. *Fortnightly Review, 36*, 179–185.

Ganster, D.C. (1987). Type A behavior and occupational stress. In J.M. Ivancevich & D.C. Ganster (Eds.), *Job stress: From theory to suggestion* (pp. 61–84). New York: Haworth Press.

Ganster, D.C. (1995). Interventions for building healthy organizations: Suggestions from the stress research literature. In L. R. Murphy, J.J. Hurrell Jr., et al. (Eds.), *Job stress interventions* (pp. 323–336). Washington DC: American Psychological Association.

Gellatly, I.R. (1996). Conscientiousness and task performance: Test of cognitive process model. *Journal of Applied Psychology, 81*(5), 474–482.

Ghiselli, E.E. (1966). *The validity of occupational aptitude tests*. New York: John Wiley & Sons.

Ghorpade, J., Hattrup, K., & Lackritz, J.R. (1999). The use of personality measures in cross-cultural research: A test of three personality scales across two countries. *Journal of Applied Psychology, 84*, 670–679.

Gilbert, J.A., & Ones, D.S. (1995a). *Heritability of conscientiousness: Implications for personnel selection, employee training, compensation, and job performance*. Paper presented at the 103rd Annual Convention of the American Psychological Association, New York City.

Gilbert, J.A., & Ones, D.S. (1995b). *Heritability of emotional stability: A meta-analytic investigation*. Paper presented at the 103rd Annual Convention of the American Psychological Association, New York City.

Gilbert, J.A., & Ones, D.S. (1996). *Heritability of Type A Behavior: Implications for stress and occupational health*. Paper presented at the 104th Annual Convention of the American Psychological Association, Toronto.

Gilbert, J.A., & Ones, D.S. (1998a). *Heritability of extraversion: Implications for I/O psychology*. Paper presented at the 13th Annual Conference of the Society for Industrial and Organizational Psychology, Dallas.

Gilbert, J.A., & Ones, D.S. (1998b). *Heritability of job involvement: Implications for I/O psychology*. Paper presented at International Congress of Psychology Conference, San Francisco.

Gilbert, J.A., & Ones, D.S. (1998c). *Heritability of social desirability: A meta-analysis*. Paper presented at the 106th Annual Convention of the American Psychological Association, San Francisco.

Gilbert, J.A., & Ones, D.S. (1998d). *A meta-analytic investigation of the heritability of openness to experience*. Paper presented at the 106th Annual Convention of the American Psychological Association, San Francisco.

Goh, D.S., & Leong, F.T.L. (1993). The relationship between Holland's theory of vocational interest and Eysenck's model of personality. *Personality and Individual Differences, 15*, 555–562.

Goldberg, L.R. (1990). An alternative 'description of personality': The big five factor structure. *Journal of Personality and Social Psychology, 59*, 1216–1229.

Goldberg, L.R. (1992). The development of markers of the Big-Five factor structure. *Psychological Assessment, 4*, 26–42.

Goldberg, L.R. (1993). The structure of phenotypic personality traits. *American Psychologist, 48*, 26–34.

Goldberg, L.R. (1995). What the hell took so long? Donald W. Fiske and the Big-Five factor structure. In P.E. Shrout & S.T. Fiske (Eds.), *Personality research, methods and theory: A festschrift honoring Donald W. Fiske* (pp. 29–43). Hillsdale, NJ: Lawrence Erlbaum Associates.

Goleman, D. (1995). *Emotional intelligence: Why it can matter more than IQ*. New York, NY: Bantam Books.

Goleman, D. (1998). *Working with emotional intelligence*. New York, NY: Bantam Books.

Gottfredson, G.D., Jones, E.M., & Holland, J.L. (1993). Personality and vocational interests: The relation of Holland's six interest dimensions to the five robust dimensions of personality. *Journal of Counseling Psychology, 40*, 518–524.

Gough, H.G. (1968). *The Chapin Social Insight Test manual*. Palo Alto, CA: Consulting Psychologists Press.

Gough, H.G. (1971). The assessment of wayward impulse by means of the Personnel Reaction Blank. *Personnel Psychology, 24*, 699–677.

Gough, H.G. (1972). *Manual for the Personnel Reaction Blank*. Palo Alto, CA: Consulting Psychologists Press.

Gough, H.G. (1987). *Manual: The California Psychological Inventory*. Palo Alto, CA: Consulting Psychologists Press.

Gough, H.G. (1994). Theory, development, and interpretation of the CPI Socialization scale. *Psychological Reports, 75*, 651–700 (Supplement).

Gray, J.A. (1982). *The neuropsychology of anxiety: An enquiry into the function of the septo-hippocampal system*. Oxford: Oxford University Press.

Green, P.D. (1999). *The visual-oral conditional reasoning test: Predicting scholastic misconduct and deception*. Unpublished doctoral dissertation, University of Tennessee, Knoxville.

Greenwood, M., & Woods, H.M. (1919). *A report on the incidence of industrial accidents with special reference to multiple accidents* (Industrial Fatigue Research Board Report No. 4). London: Her Majesty's Stationery Office.

Griffith, R.L., Frei, R.L., Snell, A.F., Hammill, L.S., & Wheeler, J.K. (1997). Warning versus no warnings: Differential effect of method bias. In G. Alliger (Chair), *Faking matters*. Symposium presented at the 12th Annual Conference of the Society for Industrial and Organizational Psychology, St. Louis.

Hambleton, R.K. (1999). *Guidelines for adapting educational and psychological instruments and establishing score equivalence*. Bulletin of the International Test Commission and International Association for Cross-Cultural Psychology.

Hansen, C.P. (1988). Personality characteristics of the *accident* involved employee. *Journal of Business and Psychology, 2*(4), 346–365.

Hansen, C.P. (1989). A causal model of the relationship among accidents, personality and cognitive factors. *Journal of Applied Psychology, 74*, 81–90.

Hansen, T.L., & McLellan, R.A. (1997). Social desirability and item content. In G.J. Lautenschlager (Chair), *Faking on non-cognitive measures: The extent, impact, and identification of dissimulation*. Symposium conducted at the Annual Meeting of the Society of Industrial and Organizational Psychology, St. Louis, MO.

Hart, P., Wearing, A.J., & Headey, B. (1995). Police stress and well-being: Integrating personality, coping and daily work experiences. *Journal of Occupational and Organizational Psychology, 68*(2), 133–156.

Heron, A. (1956). The effects of real-life motivation on questionnaire response. *Journal of Applied Psychology, 40*, 65–68.

Herriot, P., & Anderson, N. (1997). Selecting for change: How will personnel and selection psychology survive? In N. Anderson & P. Herriot (Eds.), *International handbook of selection and assessment* (pp. 1–34). Chichester, England: Wiley.

Hicks, L.E. (1970). Some properties of ipsative, normative and forced-choice normative measures. *Psychological Bulletin, 74*, 167–184.

Hofstee, W.K.B., de Raad, B., & Goldberg, L.R. (1992). Integration of the big five and circumplex approaches to trait structure. *Journal of Personality and Social Psychology, 63*, 146–163.

Hofstede, G. (1991). *Cultures and organizations: Software of the mind*. London: McGraw Hill.

Hogan, J., Rybicki, S.L., Motowidlo, S., & Borman, W.C. (1998). Relations between contextual performance, personality, and occupational advancement. *Human Performance, 11*, 189–207.

Hogan, R. (1968). Development of an empathy scale. *Journal of Consulting and Clinical Psychology, 33,* 307–316.

Hogan, R.T., & Roberts, B. (2001). Personality and I/O psychology. In B. Roberts & R.T. Hogan (Eds.), *Applied personality psychology: The intersection of personality and I/O psychology* (pp. 3–16). Washington, DC: American Psychological Association.

Holden, R.R. (1995). Response latency detection of fakers on personnel tests. *Canadian Journal of Behavioural Science, 27,* 343–355.

Holden, R.R. (1998). Detecting fakers on a personnel test: Response latencies versus a standard validity scale. *Journal of Social Behavior and Personality, 13,* 387–398.

Holden, R.R., & Hibbs, N. (1995). Incremental validity of response latencies for detecting fakers on a personality test. *Journal of Research in Personality, 29,* 362–372.

Holland, J.L. (1997). *Making vocational choices: A theory of vocational personalities and work environments* (3rd ed.). Psychological Assessment Resources: Odessa, FL.

Hollenbeck, J.R. (1998). *Personnel Psychology's* citation leading articles: The first five decades. *Personnel Psychology, 51,* introduction.

Hornick, C.W., Fox, K.A., Axton, T.R., & Wyatt, B.S. (1999). The relative contribution of conditional reasoning and multiple intelligence measures in predicting firefighter and law enforcement officer job performance. In L.J. Williams & S.M. Burroughs (Chairs), *New developments using conditional reasoning to measure employee reliability.* Symposium conducted at the 14th Annual Conference of the Society for Industrial and Organizational Psychology, Atlanta.

Hough, L.M. (1989a). Biodata and the measurement of individual differences. In T.W. Mitchell (Chair), *Biodata vs. personality: The same or different classes of individual differences?* Symposium presented at the 4th Annual Meeting of the Society for Industrial and Organizational Psychology, Boston.

Hough, L.M. (1989b). Development of personality measures to supplement selection decisions. In B.J. Fallon, H.P. Pfister & J. Brebner (Eds.), *Advances in industrial organizational psychology* (pp. 365–375). Holland: Elsevier Science Publishers.

Hough, L.M. (1992). The 'big five' personality variables – construct confusion: Description versus prediction. *Human Performance, 5,* 139–155.

Hough, L.M. (1997). The millennium for personality psychology: New horizons or good old daze. *Applied Psychology: An International Review, 47,* 233–261.

Hough, L.M. (1998a). Effects of intentional distortion in personality measurement and evaluation of suggested palliatives. *Human Performance, 11,* 209–244.

Hough, L.M. (1998b). Personality at work: Issues and evidence. In M. Hakel (Ed.), *Beyond multiple choice: Evaluating alternatives to traditional testing for selection* (pp. 131–166). Hillsdale, NJ: Lawrence Erlbaum Associates.

Hough, L.M. (2001). I/Owes its advances to personality. In B. Roberts & R.T. Hogan (Eds.), *Applied personality psychology: The intersection of personality and I/O psychology* (pp. 19–44). Washington, DC: American Psychological Association.

Hough, L.M., Eaton, N.K., Dunnette, M.D., Kamp, J.D., & McCloy, R.A. (1990). Criterion-related validities of personality constructs and the effect of response distortion on those validities [Monograph]. *Journal of Applied Psychology, 75,* 581–595.

Hough, L.M., & Oswald, F.L. (2000). Personnel selection: Looking toward the future – remembering the past. *Annual Review of Psychology, 51,* 631–664.

Hough, L.M., & Schneider, R.J. (1996). Personality traits, taxonomies, and applications in organizations. In K.R. Murphy (Ed.), *Individual differences and behavior in organizations* (pp. 31–88). San Francisco: Jossey-Bass.

Hough, L.M., Ones, D.S., & Viswesvaran, C. (1998). Personality correlates of managerial performance constructs. In R.C. Page (Chair), *Personality determinants of managerial potential, performance, progression and ascendancy.* Symposium conducted at the 13th Annual Convention of the Society for Industrial and Organizational Psychology, Dallas.

Hough, L.M., Oswald, F.L., & Ployhart, R.E. (2001). Determinants, detection, and amelioration of adverse impact in personnel selection procedures: Issues, evidence, and lessons learned. *International Journal of Selection and Assessment, 9,* 1–43.

House, R.J., Shane, S.A., & Herold, D.M. (1996). Rumors of the death of dispositional research are vastly exaggerated. *Academy of Management Review, 21*(1), 203–22.

Ironson, G.H., & Davis, G.A. (1979). Faking high or low creativity scores on the Adjective Check List. *Journal of Creative Behavior, 13,* 139–145.

Iverson, R.D., & Erwin, P.J. (1997). Predicting occupational injury: The role of affectivity. *Journal of Occupational and Organizational Psychology, 70*(2), 113–128.

Jackson, D.N. (1984). *Personality Research Form Manual* (3rd ed.). Port Huron, MI: Research Psychologists Press.

Jackson, D.N. (1994). Construct validation issues in test translation. Invited address presented at Bowling Green State University Conference, *Evaluating alternatives to traditional testing for selection,* Toledo.

Jackson, D.N., Paunonen, S.V., Fraboni, M., & Goffin, R.D. (1996). A five-factor versus six-factor model of personality structure. *Personality and Individual Differences, 20,* 33–45.

Jackson, D.N., Wroblewski, V.R., & Ashton, M.C. (2000). The impact of faking on employment tests: Does forced choice offer a solution? *Human Performance, 13,* 371–388.

James, L.R. (1998). Measurement of personality via conditional reasoning. *Organizational Research Methods, 1*(2), 131–163.

James, L.R. (1999). *Use of a conditional reasoning measure for aggression to predict employee reliability.* Invited address at the 14th Annual Conference of the Society for Industrial and Organizational Psychology, Atlanta.

Jang, K.L., McCrae, R.R., Angleitner, A., Riemann, R., & Livesley, W.J. (1998). Heritability of facet-level traits in a cross-cultural twin sample: Support for a hierarchical model of personality. *Journal of Personality and Social Psychology*, *74*, 1556–1564.

Jansen, P.G.W. (1997). Assessment in a technological world. In N. Anderson & P. Herriot (Eds.), *International Handbook of selection and assessment* (pp. 125–145). Chichester, England: Wiley.

John, O.P. (1990a). The 'Big Five' factor taxonomy: Dimensions of personality in the natural language and in questionnaires. In L.A. Pervin (Ed.), *Handbook of personality: Theory and research*. New York: Guilford Press.

John, O.P. (1990b). The search for basic dimensions of personality. In P. McReynods, J.C. Rosen & G.J. Chelune (Eds.), *Advances in psychological assessment* (pp. 1–37). New York: Plenum Press.

John, O.P., Angleitner, A., & Ostendorf, F. (1988). The lexical approach to personality: A historical review of trait taxonomic research. *European Journal of Personality*, *2*, 171–203.

Jordan, M., Herriot, P., & Chalmers, C. (1991). Testing Schneider's ASA theory. *Applied Psychology: An International Review*, *40*(1), 47–53.

Judge, T.A., & Bono, J.E. (2000). Five-factor model of personality and transformational leadership. *Journal of Applied Psychology*, *85*(5), 751–765.

Judge, T.A., & Bono, J.E. (2001). Relationship of core self-evaluations traits – self esteem, generalized self-efficacy, locus of control, and emotional stability – with job satisfaction and job performance: A meta-analysis. *Journal of Applied Psychology* [Short Note], *86*, 80–92.

Judge, T.A., Bono, J.E., Ilies, R., & Werner, M. (2000). *Personality and leadership: A review*. Paper presented at 15th Annual Conference of the Society for Industrial and Organizational Psychology, New Orleans.

Judge, T.A., Higgins, C.A., Thoresen, C.J., & Barrick, M.R. (1999). The Big Five personality traits, general mental ability, and career success across the life span. *Personnel Psychology*, *52*(3), 621–652.

Judge, T.A., Locke, E.A., & Durham, C.C. (1997). The dispositional causes of job satisfaction: A core evaluations approach. *Research in Organizational Behavior*, *19*, 151–188.

Judge, T.A., Martocchio, J.J., & Thoresen, C.J. (1997). Five-factor model of personality and employee absence. *Journal of Applied Psychology*, *82*(5), 745–755.

Kamp, J.D. (1996). Personal communication, May 30, 1996.

Kamp, J.D., & Gough, H.G. (1986). *The Big Five personality factors from an assessment context*. Paper presented at the 94th annual convention of the American Psychological Association, Washington, DC.

Katigbak, M.S., Church, A.T., & Akamine, T.X. (1996). Cross-cultural generalizability of personality dimensions: Relating indigenous and imported dimensions in two cultures. *Journal of Personality and Social Psychology*, *70*, 99–114.

King, W.C. Jr., & Miles, E.W. (1995). A quasi-experimental assessment of the effect of computerizing noncognitive paper-and-pencil measurements: A test of measurement equivalence. *Journal of Applied Psychology*, *80*, 643–651.

Kirchner, W.K. (1962). 'Real-life' faking on the Edwards Personal Preference Schedule by sales applicants. *Journal of Applied Psychology*, *46*, 128–130.

Konovsky, M.A., & Organ, D.W. (1996). Dispositional and contextual determinants of organizational citizenship behavior. *Journal of Organizational Behavior*, *17*, 253–266.

Kraut, A.I., & Korman, A.K. (1999). The 'DELTA Forces' causing change in human resource management. In A.I. Kraut & A.K. Korman (Eds.), *Evolving Practices in Human Resource Management* (pp. 3–22). San Francisco: Jossey-Bass.

Kristof, A.L. (1996). Person-organization fit: An integrative review of its conceptualizations, measurement, and implications. *Personnel Psychology*, *49*(1), 1–49.

Kristof-Brown, A.L. (2000). Perceived applicant fit: Distinguishing between recruiters' perceptions of person-job and person-organization fit. *Personnel Psychology*, *53*(3), 643–671.

Lam, S.S.K, Hui, CH., & Law, K.S. (1999). Organizational citizenship behavior: Comparing perspectives of supervisors and subordinates across four international samples. *Journal of Applied Psychology*, *84*, 594–601.

Lawton, R., & Parker, D. (1998). Individual differences in accident liability: A review and integrative approach. *Human Factors*, *40*(4), 655.

Lee, C., Ashford, S.J., & Jamieson, L.F. (1993). The effects of Type A behavior dimensions and optimism on coping strategy, health, and performance. *Journal of Organizational Behavior*, *14*(2), 143–157.

LePine, J.A., Hollenbeck, J.R., Ilgen, D.R., & Hedlund, J. (1997). Effects of individual differences on the performance of hierarchical decision-making teams: Much more than *g*. *Journal of Applied Psychology*, *82*(5), 803–811.

Lester, J. (1991). *Individual difference in accident liability: A review of the literature* (Contractors' Report No. 306). Crowthorne, UK: Transport and Road Research Laboratory.

Levin, I., & Stokes, J.P. (1989). Dispositional approach to job satisfaction: Role of negative affectivity. *Journal of Applied Psychology*, *74*(5), 752–758.

Lord, R.G., de Vader, C.L., & Alliger, G.M. (1986). A meta-analysis of the relations between personality traits and leadership perceptions: An application of validity generalization procedures. *Journal of Applied Psychology*, *7*(3), 402–410.

Lucas, J.L., & Wanberg, C.R. (1995). Personality correlates of Jones' three-dimensional model of career indecision. *Journal of Career Assessment*, *3*, 315–329.

Lykken, D. (1997). Happy is as happy does. In S. Scarr (Chair), *Genetics and Personality: The Search for Why We Think, Act, and Feel the Way We Do*. Presidential symposium conducted at the 9th Annual Convention of the American Psychological Society, Washington, DC.

Lykken, D., & Tellegen, A. (1996). Happiness is a stochastic phenomenon. *Psychological Science, 7,* 186–189.

Maranto, D.B. (2000, Nov./Dec.). Congress considers genetic information in the workplace. *Psychological Science Agenda.* Washington, DC: American Psychological Association.

Matthews, G. (1997). The Big Five as a framework for personality assessment. In N. Anderson & P. Herriot (Eds.), *International handbook of selection and assessment* (pp. 475–492). Chichester, England: Wiley.

Mau, W., Domnick, M., & Ellsworth, R.A. (1995). Characteristics of female students who aspire to science and engineering or homemaking occupations. *Career Development Quarterly, 43,* 323–337.

Mayer, J.D. (1995). A framework for the classification of personality components. *Journal of Personality, 63,* 819–878.

Mayer, J.D., & Geher, G. (1996). Emotional intelligence and the identification of emotion. *Intelligence, 22,* 89–113.

Mayer, J.D., & Salovey, P. (1993). The intelligence of emotional intelligence. *Intelligence, 17,* 433–442.

Mayer, J.D., & Salovey, P. (1997). What is emotional intelligence? In P. Salovey & D.J. Sluyter (Eds.), Emotional development and emotional intelligence. New York: Basic Books.

Mayer, J.D., Caruso, D.R., & Salovey, P. (2000). Emotional intelligence meets traditional standards for an intelligence. *Intelligence, 27*(4), 267–298.

Mayer, J.D., Salovey, P., & Caruso, D. (2000). Models of emotional intelligence. In R.J. Sternberg (Ed.), *Handbook of intelligence* (pp. 396–420). New York: Cambridge University Press.

McAdams, D.P. (1992). The five-factor model *in* personality: A critical appraisal. *Journal of Personality, 60,* 329–361.

McAdams, D.P. (1997). A conceptual history of personality psychology. In R. Hogan, J. Johnson & S. Briggs (Eds.), *Handbook of personality psychology* (pp. 3–39). San Diego: Academic Press.

McCrae, R.R., & Costa, P.T. Jr. (1983). Social desirability scales: More substance than style. *Journal of Consulting and Clinical Psychology, 51,* 882–888.

McCrae, R.R., & Costa, P.T. Jr. (1985). Comparison of EPI and Psychoticism scales with measures of the five-factor model of personality. *Personality and Individual Differences, 6,* 587–597.

McCrae, R.R., & Costa, P.T. Jr. (1987). Validation of the five-factor model of personality across instruments and observers. *Journal of Personality and Social Psychology, 52,* 81–90.

McCrae, R.R., & Costa, P.T. Jr. (1989a). Reinterpreting the Myers-Briggs Type Indicator from the perspective of the five-factor model of personality. *Journal of Personality, 57,* 17–40.

McCrae, R.R., & Costa, P.T. Jr. (1989b). The structure of interpersonal traits: Wiggin's circumplex and the five-factor model. *Journal of Personality and Social Psychology, 56,* 586–595.

McCrae, R.R., & Costa, P.T. Jr. (1997a). Conceptions and correlates of openness to experience. In R. Hogan, J. Johnson & S. Briggs (Eds.), *Handbook of personality psychology* (pp. 825–847). San Diego: Academic Press.

McCrae, R.R., & Costa, P.T. Jr. (1997b). Personality trait structure as a human universal. *American Psychologist, 52,* 509–516.

McCrae, R.R., Costa, P.T. Jr., & Busch, C.M. (1986). Evaluating comprehensiveness in personality systems: The California Q-Set and the five-factor model. *Journal of Personality, 54,* 430–446.

McCrae, R.R., Costa, P.T. Jr., & Piedmont, R.L. (1993). Folk concepts, natural language, and psychological constructs: The California Psychological Inventory and the five-factor model. *Journal of Personality, 61,* 1–26.

McHenry, J.J., Hough, L.M., Toquam, J.L., Hanson, M.A., & Ashworth, S. (1990). Project A validity results: The relationship between predictor and criterion domains. *Personnel Psychology, 43,* 335–353.

Meyer, B.W., & Winer, J.L. (1993). The Career Decision Scale and neuroticism. *Journal of Career Assessment, 1,* 171–180.

Michaelis, W., & Eysenck, H.J. (1971). The determination of personality inventory factor pattern and intercorrelations by changes in real-life motivation. *Journal of Genetic Psychology, 118,* 223–234.

Migetz, D.Z., & James, L.R. (1999). *Current and new directions in conditional reasoning measurement.* University of Tennessee. Unpublished manuscript.

Migetz, D.Z., James, L.R., & Ladd, R.T. (1999). *A validation of the conditional reasoning measure of achievement motivation and fear of failure.* Paper presented at the 14th annual conference of the Society for Industrial and Organizational Psychology, Atlanta, GA.

Migetz, D.Z., McIntyre, M., James, L.R. (1999). Measuring reliability among contingent workers. In L.J. Williams & S.M. Burroughs (Chairs), *New developments using conditional reasoning to measure employee reliability.* Symposium conducted at the 14th Annual Conference of the Society for Industrial and Organizational Psychology, Atlanta.

Moss, F.A., Hunt, T., Omwake, K.T., & Woodward, L.G. (1955). *Social Intelligence Test manual.* Washington, DC: Center for Psychological Service.

Motowidlo, S.J. (1996). Orientation toward the job and organization: A theory of individual differences in job satisfaction. In K. R. Murphy (Ed.), *Individual differences and behavior in organizations* (pp. 175–208). San Francisco: Jossey-Bass.

Motowidlo, S.J., & Van Scotter, J.R. (1994). Evidence that task performance should be distinguished from contextual performance. *Journal of Applied Psychology, 79,* 475–480.

Mount, M.K., & Barrick, M.R. (1995). The Big Five personality dimensions: Implications for research and practice in human resource management, *Research in Personnel and Human Resource Management, 13,* 153–200.

Mount, M.K., & Barrick, M.R. (1998). Five reasons why the 'Big Five' article has been frequently cited. *Personnel Psychology, 51*, 849–857.

Mount, M.K., Barrick, M.R., & Strauss, P.P. (1994). Validity of observer ratings of the Big Five personality factors. *Journal of Applied Psychology, 79*, 272–280.

Moyle, P. (1995). The role of negative affectivity in the stress process: Tests of alternative models. *Journal of Organizational Behavior, 16*(6), 647–668.

Multon, K.D., Heppner, M.J., & Lapan, R.T. (1995). An empirical derivation of career decision subtypes in a high school sample. *Journal of Vocational Behavior, 47*, 76–92.

Mumford, M.D., Costanza, D.P., Connelly, M.S., & Johnson, J.F. (1996). Item generation procedures and background data scales: Implications for construct and criterion-related validity. *Personnel Psychology, 49*, 361–398.

Mumford, M.D., Snell, A.F., & Reiter-Palmon, R. (1994). Personality and background data: Life history and self-concepts in an ecological system. In G.S. Stokes, M.D. Mumford & W.A. Owens (Eds.), *Biodata handbook: Theory, research, and use of biographical information in selection and performance prediction* (pp. 583–625). Palo Alto, CA: Consulting Psychologists Press.

Mumford, M.D., & Stokes, G.S. (1992). Developmental determinants of individual action: Theory and practice in applying background measures. In M.D. Dunnette & L.M. Hough (Eds.), *Handbook of industrial and organizational psychology*, 2nd ed., Vol. 3 (pp. 61–138). Palo Alto: Consulting Psychologists Press.

Murray, H.A. (1938). *Explorations in personality.* New York: Oxford University Press.

Narayanan, L., Menon, S., & Levine, E.L. (1995). Personality structure: A culture-specific examination of the Five-Factor Model. *Journal of Personality Assessment, 64*, 51–64.

Necowitz, L.B., & Roznowski, M. (1994). Negative affectivity and job satisfaction: Cognitive processes underlying the relationship and effects on employee behaviors. *Journal of Vocational Behavior, 45*(3), 270–294.

Negrao, M. (1997). On good Samaritans and villains: An investigation of the bright and dark side of altruism in organizations. Unpublished manuscript. University of South Florida, Tampa, FL.

Newbold, E.M. (1927). Practical applications of the statistics of repeated events. *Journal of the Royal Statistical Society, 92*, 487–535.

Newman, D.L., Tellegen, A., & Bouchard, T. (1998). Individual differences in adult ego development: Sources of influence in twins reared apart. *Journal of Personality and Social Psychology, 74*, 985–995.

Nilsen, D. (1995). *Investigation of the relationship between personality and leadership performance.* Unpublished doctoral dissertation, University of Minnesota.

Norman, W.T. (1963a). Personality measurement, faking, and detection: An assessment method for use in personnel selection. *Journal of Applied Psychology, 47*, 225–241.

Norman, W.T. (1963b). Toward an adequate taxonomy of personality attributes: Replicated factor structure in peer nomination personality ratings. *Journal of Abnormal and Social Psychology, 66*, 574–583.

Nyfield, G., & Baron, H. (2000). Cultural context in adapting selection practices across borders. In J.F. Kehoe (Ed.), *Managing selection in changing organizations* (pp. 242–268). San Francisco: Jossey-Bass.

O'Brien, K.M., & Fassinger, R.E. (1993). A causal model of the career orientation and career choice of adolescent women. *Journal of Counseling Psychology, 40*, 456–469.

Ones, D.S., Hough, L.M., & Viswesvaran, C. (2000). Personality predictors of performance for managers and executives. In L.M. Hough & D.S. Ones (Co-Chairs), *Personality and performance in leadership positions: Presidents, CEO's and managers*, symposium conducted at the 108th annual conference of the American Psychological Association, Washington, DC.

Ones, D.S., & Viswesvaran, C. (1996). *What do pre-employment customer service scales measure? Explorations in construct validity and implications for personnel selection.* Paper presented at the 11th Annual Conference of the Society for Industrial and Organizational Psychology, San Diego, CA.

Ones, D.S., & Viswesvaran, C. (1998a). Gender, age, and race differences on overt integrity tests: Results across four large-scale job applicant data sets. *Journal of Applied Psychology, 83*, 35–42.

Ones, D.S., & Viswesvaran, C. (1998b). Integrity testing in organizations. In R.W. Griffin, A. O'Leary-Kelly & J.M. Collins (Eds.), *Dysfunctional behavior in organizations: Vol. 2, Nonviolent behaviors in organizations* (pp. 243–276). Greenwich, CT: JAI.

Ones, D.S., & Viswesvaran, C. (1998c). The effects of social desirability and faking on personality and integrity assessment for personnel selection. *Human Performance, 11*, 245–269.

Ones, D.S., & Viswesvaran, C. (2001). Personality at work: Criterion-focused occupational personality scales (COPS) used in personnel selection. In B.W. Roberts & R.T. Hogan (Eds.), *Applied personality psychology: The intersection of personality and I/O psychology* (pp. 63–92). Washington, DC: American Psychological Association.

Ones, D.S., Viswesvaran, C., & Reiss, A.D. (1996). Role of social desirability in personality testing for personnel selection: The red herring. *Journal of Applied Psychology, 81*, 660–679.

Ones, D.S., Viswesvaran, C., & Schmidt, F.L. (1993). Comprehensive meta-analysis of integrity test validities: Findings and implications for personnel selection and theories of job performance [Monograph]. *Journal of Applied Psychology, 78*, 679–703.

Organ, D.W. (1988). *Organizational citizenship behavior: The good soldier syndrome.* Lexington, MA: Lexington Books.

Organ, D.W., & Ryan, K. (1995). A meta-analytic review of attitudinal and dispositional predictors of organizational citizenship behaviour. *Personnel Psychology, 48*, 775–802.

Orpen, C. (1971). Fakability of the Edwards Personal Preference Schedule in personnel selection. *Personnel Psychology, 24,* 1–4.

Ostendorf, F., & Angleitner, A. (1992). On the generality and comprehensiveness of the five-factor model of personality: Evidence for five robust factors in questionnaire data. In G.V. Caprana & G.L. van Heck (Eds.), *Modern personality psychology: Critical reviews and new directions.* London & New York: Prentice Hall Harvester-Wheatsheaf.

Ostendorf, F., & Angleitner, A. (1994). The five-factor taxonomy: Robust dimensions of personality description. *Psychologica Belgica, 34–4,* 175–194.

Otto, R.K., & Hall, J.E. (1988). The utility of the Michigan Alcoholism Screening Test in the detection of alcoholics and problem drinkers. *Journal of Personality Assessment, 52,* 499–505.

Paajanen, G.E. (1988). *The prediction of counterproductive behavior by individual and organizational variables.* Unpublished doctoral dissertation, University of Minnesota.

Patton, T.W., Walton, W., & James, L.R. (1999). Measuring personal reliability via conditional reasoning: Identifying people who will work reliably. In L.J. Williams & S.M. Burroughs (Chairs), *New developments using conditional reasoning to measure employee reliability.* Symposium conducted at the 14th Annual Conference of the Society for Industrial and Organizational Psychology, Atlanta.

Paunonen, S.V., & Jackson, D.N. (2000). What is beyond the Big Five? Plenty! *Journal of Personality, 68,* 821–835.

Peabody, D., & Goldberg, L.R. (1989). Some determinants of factor structures from personality-trait descriptors. *Journal of Personality and Social Psychology, 57,* 552–567.

Pearlman, K., & Barney, M.F. (2000). Selection for a changing workplace. In J.F. Kehoe (Ed.), *Managing Selection Strategies in Changing Organizations* (pp. 3–72). San Francisco: Jossey-Bass.

Pederson, N. (1997). Beyond heritability for personality: Do genetic effects for personality explain genetic variance for other measures? In S. Scarr (Chair), *Genetics and personality: The search for why we think, act, and feel the way we do.* Presidential symposium conducted at the 9th Annual Convention of the American Psychological Society, Washington, DC.

Penner, L.A., Fritzsche, B.A., Craiger, J.P., & Freifeld, T.R. (1995). Measuring the prosocial personality. In J. Butcher & C.D. Spielberger (Eds.), *Advances in personality assessment* (Vol. 10). Hillsdale, NJ: LEA.

Pervin, L.A. (1994). Further reflections on current trait theory. *Psychological Inquiry, 5,* 169–178.

Phillips, K., & Matheny, A.P. (1997). Evidence for genetic influence on both cross-situation and situation-specific components of behavior. *Journal of Personality and Social Psychology, 73,* 129–138.

Plomin, R. (1997). Search for specific genes in personality. In S. Scarr (Chair), *Genetics and personality: The search for why we think, act, and feel the way we do.* Presidential symposium conducted at the 9th Annual Convention of the American Psychological Society, Washington, DC.

Plomin, R., & Crabbe, J. (2000). DNA. *Psychological Bulletin, 126,* 806–828.

Porter, C.S. (1988). Accident proneness: A review of the concept. In D.J. Oborne (Ed.), *International reviews of ergonomics: Current trends in human factors research and practices* (Vol. 2, pp. 177–206). London: Taylor & Francis.

Pulakos, E.D., Schmitt, N., & Chan, D. (1996). Models of job performance ratings: An examination of ratee race, ratee gender, and rater level effects. *Human Performance, 9,* 103–119.

Rainey, L.M., & Borders, L.D. (1997). Influential factors in career orientation and career aspiration of early adolescent girls. *Journal of Counseling Psychology, 44,* 160–172.

Richman, W.L., Kiesler, S., Weisband, S., & Drasgow, F. (1999). A meta-analytic study of social desirability distortion in computer-administered questionnaires, traditional questionnaires, and interviews. *Journal of Applied Psychology, 84,* 754–775.

Robertson, I., & Clarke, S. (1999). *Personality and accident involvement: Implications for personnel selection.* Paper presented at the 14th Annual Conference of the Society for Industrial and Organizational Psychology, Atlanta.

Robertson, I.T., & Callinan, M. (1998). Personality and work behavior. *European Journal of Work and Organizational Psychology, 7,* 321–340.

Robertson, I.T., & Kinder, A. (1993). Personality and job competences: The criterion-related validity of some personality variables. *Journal of Occupational and Organizational Psychology, 66,* 225–244.

Rodgers, M.D., & Blanchard, R.E. (1993, May). *Accident proneness: A research review.* Technical Report DOT/FAA/AM-93/9.

Rojewski, J.W., & Yang, B. (1997). Longitudinal analysis of select influences on adolescents' occupational aspirations. *Journal of Vocational Behavior, 51,* 375–410.

Rosse, J.G., Stecher, M.D., Levin, R.A., & Miller, J.L. (1998). The impact of response distortion on preemployment personality testing and hiring decisions. *Journal of Applied Psychology, 83,* 634–644.

Russell, J.A., & Carroll, J.M. (1999). On the bipolarity of positive and negative affect. *Psychological Bulletin, 125,* 3–30.

Ryan, A.M., Horvath, M., Ployhart, R.E., Schmitt, N., & Slade, L.A. (2000). Hypothesizing differential item functioning in global employee opinion surveys. *Personnel Psychology, 53,* 531–562.

Ryan, A.M., & Ployhart, R.E. (2000). Applicants' perceptions of selection procedures and decisions: A critical review and agenda for the future. *Journal of Management, 26,* 565–606.

Ryan, A.M., & Sackett, P.R. (1987). Pre-employment honesty testing: Fakability, reactions of test takers, and company image. *Journal of Business and Psychology, 1,* 248–256.

Sackett, P.R., Burris, L.R., & Callahan, C. (1989). Integrity testing for personnel selection: An update. *Personnel Psychology, 42,* 491–529.

Salgado, J.F. (1997). The five factor model of personality and job performance in the European Community. *Journal of Applied Psychology, 82*(1), 30–43.

Salgado, J.F. (1998). Big Five personality dimensions and job performance in Army and civil occupations: A European perspective. *Human Performance, 11*(2–3), 271–288.

Salgado, J.F. (2000). *The Big Five personality dimensions as predictors of alternative criteria.* Paper presented at the 15th Annual Conference of the Society for Industrial and Organizational Psychology, New Orleans.

Salovey, P., & Mayer, J.D. (1990). Emotional intelligence. *Imagination, Cognition and Personality, 9*(3), 185–211.

Salovey, P., Mayer, J.D., Goldman, S.L., Turvey, C., & Palfai, T.P. (1995). Emotional attention, clarity, and repair: Exploring emotional intelligence using the Trait Meta-Mood Scale. In J.W. Pennebaker (Ed.), *Emotion, disclosure, and health* (pp. 135–154). Washington, DC: American Psychological Association.

Saucier, G. (1997). Effects of variable selection on the factor structure of person descriptors. *Journal of Personality and Social Psychology, 73*, 1296–1312.

Saucier, G., & Goldberg, L.R. (1998). What is beyond the Big Five? *Journal of Personality, 66*, 495–524.

Saudino, K.J. (1997). Moving beyond the heritability question: New directions in behavioral genetic studies of personality. *Current Directions in Psychological Science, 6*, 86–90.

Saville & Holdsworth (1990). *Occupational Personality Questionnaire manual.* Esher, UK: Saville & Holdsworth.

Scarr, S. (1996). How people make their own environments: Implications for parents and policy makers. *Psychology, Public Policy, and Law, 2*, 204–228.

Schinka, J.A., Dye, D.A., & Curtiss, G. (1997). Correspondence between five-factor and RIASEC models of personality. *Journal of Personality Assessment, 68*, 355–368.

Schmidt, F.L., & Hunter, J.E. (1992). Development of a causal model of processes determining job performance. *Current Directions in Psychological Science, 1*, 89–92.

Schmit, M.J., Amel, E.L., & Ryan, A.M. (1993). Self-reported assertive job-seeking behaviors of minimally educated job hunters. *Personnel Psychology, 46*, 105–124.

Schmit, M.J., Kihm, J.A., & Robie, C. (2000). Development of a global measure of personality. *Personnel Psychology, 53*, 153–193.

Schmit, M.J., & Ryan, A.M. (1992). Test-taking dispositions: A missing link? *Journal of Applied Psychology, 77*, 629–637.

Schmit, M.J., Ryan, A.M., Stierwalt, S.L., & Powell, A.B. (1995). Frame-of-reference effects on personality scale scores and criterion-related validity. *Journal of Applied Psychology, 80*, 607–620.

Schmitt, N., Gooding, R.Z., Noe, R.A., & Kirsch, M. (1984). Meta-analysis of validity studies published between 1964 and 1982 and the investigation of study characteristics. *Personnel Psychology, 37*, 407–422.

Schneider, B. (1987). The people make the place. *Personnel Psychology, 40*(3), 453–453.

Schneider, B. (1996). Whither goest personality at work? Overview of the special issue on 'Work and personality'. *Applied Psychology: An International Review, 45*(3), 289–296.

Schneider, B., Goldstein, H.W., & Smith, D.B. (1995). The ASA framework: An update. *Personnel Psychology, 48*, 747–773.

Schneider, B., Smith, D.G., Taylor, S., & Fleenor, J. (1998). Personality and organizations: A test of the homogeneity of personality hypothesis. *Journal of Applied Psychology, 83*(3), 462–470.

Schneider, P.L., Ryan, J.M., Tracey, T.J.G., & Rounds, J. (1996). Examining the relation between Holland's RIASEC model and the interpersonal circle. *Measurement and Evaluation in Counseling and Development, 29*, 123–133.

Schneider, R.J., Ackerman, P.L., & Kanfer, R. (1996). To 'act wisely in human relations': Exploring the dimensions of social competence. *Personality and Individual Differences, 21*, 469–481.

Schneider, R.J., & Hough, L.M. (1995). Personality and industrial/organizational psychology. In C.L. Cooper & I.T. Robertson (Eds.), *International review of industrial and organizational psychology* (Vol. 10, pp. 75–129). New York: Wiley & Sons.

Schwab, D.P., & Packard, G.L. (1973). Response distortion on the 'Gordon Personal Inventory' and the 'Gordon Personal Profile' in a selection context: Some implications for predicting employee tenure. *Journal of Applied Psychology, 58*, 372–374.

Silver, C.B., & Malone, J.E. (1993). A scale of personality styles based on DSM-III-R for investigating occupational choice and leisure activities. *Journal of Career Assessment, 1*, 427–440.

Sinangil, H.K., Ones, D.S., & Viswesvaran, C. (1998). Personnel selection in other countries: Some thoughts on the role of culture. Paper presented at the International Congress of Applied Psychology, San Francisco, CA.

Smith, M., DeMatteo, J.S., Green, P., & James, L.R. (1995). *A comparison of new and traditional measures of achievement motivation.* Paper presented at the annual meeting of the American Psychological Association, New Orleans, LA.

Snell, A.F., Sydell, E.J., Lueke, S.B. (1999), Towards a theory of applicant faking: Integrating studies of deception. *Human Resources Management Review, 9*, 219–242.

Solberg, V.S., Good, G.E., Fischer, A.R., Brown, S.D., Nord, D. (1995). Career decision-making and career search activities: Relative effects of career search self-efficacy and human agency. *Journal of Counseling Psychology, 42*, 448–455.

Somer, O., & Goldberg, L.R. (1999). The structure of Turkish trait-descriptive adjectives. *Personality Processes and Individual Differences, 76*, 431–450.

Spector, P.E. (1997). *Job satisfaction: Application, assessment, causes, and consequences.* Thousand Oaks, CA: Sage Publications, Inc.

Spector, P.E. (1998). A control model of the job stress process. In C.L. Cooper (Ed.). *Theories of Organizational Stress* (pp. 153–169). London: Oxford University Press.

Spector, P.E., Jex, S.M., & Chen, P.Y. (1995). Relations of incumbent affect-related personality traits with incumbent and objective measures of characteristics of jobs. *Journal of Organizational Behavior, 16,* 59–65.

Staw, B.M., Bell, N.E., & Clausen, J.A. (1986). The dispositional approach to job attitudes: A lifetime longitudinal test. *Administrative Quarterly, 31*(1), 56–77.

Staw, B.M., & Ross, J. (1985). Stability in the midst of change: A dispositional approach to job attitudes. *Journal of Applied Psychology, 70*(3), 469–480.

Stodgill, R.M. (1950). Leadership, membership and organization. *Psychological Bulletin, 47,* 1–14.

Sutherland, V.J., & Cooper, C.L. (1991). Personality, stress and accident involvement in the offshore oil and gas industry. *Personality and Individual Differences, 12*(2), 195–204.

Tellegen, A. (1982). *Brief manual for the Multidimensional Personality Questionnaire.* Unpublished manuscript, Department of Psychology, University of Minnesota.

Tellegen, A. (1985). Structures of mood and personality and their relevance to assessment anxiety with an emphasis on self-report. In A. Tuma & J. Maser (Eds.), *Anxiety and the anxiety disorders* (pp. 681–706). Hillsdale, NJ: Erlbaum.

Tellegen, A. (1993). Folk concepts and psychological concepts of personality and personality disorder. *Psychological Inquiry, 4,* 122–130.

Tellegen, A., & Waller, N.G. (1987). *Re-examining basic dimensions of natural language trait descriptors.* Paper presented at the 95th Annual Convention of the American Psychological Association, New York.

Tellegen, A., & Waller, N.G. (n.d.). Exploring personality through test construction: Development of the *Multidimensional Personality Questionnaire.* Unpublished manuscript.

Tenopyr, M.L. (1994). Big Five, structural modeling, and item response theory. In G.S. Stokes, M.D. Mumford & W.A. Owens (Eds.), *Biodata handbook: Theory, research, and use of biographical information in selection and performance prediction* (pp. 519–533). Palo Alto, CA: Consulting Psychologists Press.

Terpstra, D.E., Mohamed, A.A., Kethley, B. (1999). An analysis of federal court cases involving nine selection devices. *International Journal of Selection and Assessment, 7,* 26–34.

Tett, R.P., Jackson, D.N., & Rothstein, M. (1991). Personality measures as predictors of job performance: A meta-analytic review. *Personnel Psychology, 44,* 703–742.

Thoresen, C.J., & Judge, T.A. (1997). *Trait affectivity and work-related attitudes and behaviors: A meta-analysis.* Paper presentation at the 105th annual convention of the American Psychological Association, Chicago, IL.

Tokar, D.M., Fischer, A.R., Snell, A.F., & Harik-Williams, N. (1999). Efficient assessment of the Five-Factor Model of personality: Structural validity analyses of the NEO Five-Factor Inventory (Form S). *Measurement and Evaluation in Counseling and Development, 32,* 14–30.

Tokar, D.M., Vaux, A., & Swanson, J.L. (1995). Dimensions relating Holland's vocational personality typology and the five-factor model. *Journal of Career Assessment, 3,* 57–74.

Trent, T. (1987). *Armed forces adaptability screening: The problem of item response distortion.* Paper presented at the 95th Annual Convention of the American Psychological Convention, New York City.

Tupes, E.C., & Christal, R.E. (1992). Recurrent personality factors based on trait ratings. *Journal of Personality, 60,* 225–251.

Vasilopoulos, N.L., Reilly, R.R., & Leaman, J.A. (2000). The influence of job familiarity and impression management on self-report measure scale scores and response latencies. *Journal of Applied Psychology, 85,* 50–64.

Vinchur, A.J., Schippmann, J.S., Switzer, F.S., & Roth, P.L. (1998). A meta-analytic review of predictors of job performance for salespeople. *Journal of Applied Psychology, 83,* 586–597.

Viswesvaran, C., & Ones, D.S., (1999). Meta-analyses of fakability estimates: Implications for personality measurement. *Educational and Psychological Measurement, 59,* 197–210.

Viswesvaran, C., & Ones, D.S. (2000). Measurement error in 'Big Five Factors' personality assessment: Reliability generalization across studies and measures. *Educational and Psychological Measurement, 60,* 224–235.

Waller, N.G., & Ben-Porath, Y.S. (1987). Is it time for clinical psychology to embrace the Five-Factor Model of personality? *American Psychologist, 42,* 887–889.

Waller, N.G., & Zavala, J.D. (1993). Evaluating the Big Five. *Psychological Inquiry, 4,* 131–134.

Walton, W.R. (1999). *Development of a conditional reasoning scale for social deviance.* University of Tennessee. Unpublished manuscript.

Wanberg, C.R., Kanfer, R., & Banas, J.T. (2000). Predictors and outcomes of networking intensity among unemployed job seekers. *Journal of Applied Psychology, 85,* 491–503.

Wanberg, C.R., Watt, J.D., & Rumsey, D.J. (1996). Individuals without jobs: An empirical study of job-seeking behavior and reemployment. *Journal of Applied Psychology, 81,* 76–87.

Watson, D., & Slack, A.K. (1993). General factors of affective temperament and their relation to job satisfaction over time. *Organizational Behavior and Human Decision Processes, 54*(2), 181–202.

Watson, D., Clark, L.A., & Tellegen, A. (1988). Development and validation of brief measures of positive and negative affect: The PANAS scales. *Journal of Personality and Social Psychology, 54,* 1063–1070.

Webb, E. (1915). Character and intelligence. *British Journal of Psychology Monographs, 1*(3), 1–99.

Webster's *New International Dictionary* (1925). 2nd unabridged edition. Springfield, MA: Merriam.

Weiss, H.M., & Cropanzano, R. (1996). Affective events theory: A theoretical discussion of the structure, causes and consequences of affective experiences at work. In B.M. Staw & L.L. Cummings (Eds.), *Research in organizational behavior: An annual series of analytical essays and critical reviews*, Vol. 18 (pp. 1–74).

White, R.W. (1959). Motivation reconsidered: The concept of competence. *Psychological Review, 66,* 297–333.

Wiggins, J.S., & Trapnell, P.D. (1997). Personality structure: The return of the Big Five. In R. Hogan, J. Johnson & S. Briggs (Eds.), *Handbook of personality psychology* (pp. 737–765). San Diego: Academic Press.

Wright, T.A., & Cropanzano, R. (1998). Emotional exhaustion as a predictor of job performance and voluntary turnover. *Journal of Applied Psychology, 83,* 486–493.

Zickar, M.J., & Drasgow, F. (1996). Detecting faking on a personality instrument using appropriateness measurement. *Applied Psychological Measurement, 20,* 71–87.

Zickar, M.J., Rosse, J.G., Levin, R.A., & Hulin, C.L. (1996). Modeling the effects of faking on personality tests. Unpublished manuscript.

Zuckerman, M. (1992). What is a basic factor and which factors are basic? Turtles all the way down. *Personality and Individual Differences, 13,* 675–682.

Zuckerman, M. (1995). Good and bad humors: Biochemical bases of personality and its disorders. *Psychological Science, 6,* 325–332.

Zuckerman, M., Kuhlman, D.M., & Camac, C. (1988). What lies beyond E and N?: An analysis of scales believed to measure basic dimensions of personality. *Journal of Personality and Social Psychology, 54,* 96–107.

Zuckerman, M., Kuhlman, D.M., Joireman, J., Teta, P., & Kraft, M. (1993). A comparison of three structural models for personality: The Big Three, the Big Five, and the Alternative *Five. Journal of Personality and Social Psychology, 65,* 757–768.

Zuckerman, M., Kuhlman, D.M., Thornquist, M., & Kiers, H. (1991). Five (or three) robust questionnaire scale factors of personality without culture. *Personality and Individual Differences, 9,* 929–941.

APPENDIX: WORKING TAXONS

Part 1   Compilation of Personality Measures Using the Big Five Dimensions and their Facets

Inventory	Scale	Scoring direction
	EMOTIONAL STABILITY (ES)	
• **Global ES Measures**		
Adjective Checklist	Ideal self	+
Adjective Checklist	Personal adjustment	+
Arrow-Dot Test (subtest of IES Test)	Ego strength	+
Bernreuter Personality Inventory	Neuroticism B1-N	−
Comrey Personality Scales	Emotional stability vs. neuroticism	+
Descriptive Adjective Inventory	Emotional stability	+
Eysenck Personality Questionnaire	Emotional stability	+
Eysenck Personality Questionnaire	Neuroticism	−
GAMIN	Nervousness (freedom from such feelings)	−
Goldberg Five Factor Markers	Factor IV: Emotional stability	+
Hilson Career Satisfaction Index	Stress patterns (global)	+
Hilson Career Satisfaction Index	Stress symptoms	+
Hogan Personality Inventory	Adjustment	+
Hogan Personality Inventory	HIC – no guilt	+
Hogan Personality Inventory	HIC – no somatic complaints	+
Inventory of Factors	Depression	−
Inventory of Factors	Emotional stability	−
Inwald Personality Inventory	Depression	−
Inwald Personality Inventory	Illness concerns	−
Inwald Personality Inventory	Obsessive personality	−
Inwald Personality Inventory	Phobias	−
Inwald Personality Inventory	Unusual experiences/thoughts	−
Minnesota Multiphasic Personality Inventory	Hypochondriasis	−
Minnesota Multiphasic Personality Inventory	Depression	−
Minnesota Multiphasic Personality Inventory	Hysteria	−
Minnesota Multiphasic Personality Inventory	Psychasthenia (obsessive)	−
Minnesota Multiphasic Personality Inventory	Schizophrenia	−
Minnesota Multiphasic Personality Inventory	Ego strength	+
Minnesota Multiphasic Personality Inventory	College maladjustment	−
Minnesota Multiphasic Personality Inventory	Post traumatic stress disorder	−
Minnesota Multiphasic Personality Inventory	Fears	−
Minnesota Multiphasic Personality Inventory	Obsessiveness	−
Minnesota Multiphasic Personality Inventory	Depression	−
Minnesota Multiphasic Personality Inventory	Health concerns	−
Minnesota Multiphasic Personality Inventory	Bizarre mentation	−
Multidimensional Personality Questionnaire	Stress reaction	−
NEO PI-R	Neuroticism	−
NEO PI-R	Facet – depression	−
NEO PI-R	Facet – vulnerability	−
Occupational Personality Questionnaire	Worrying	−
Personal Characteristics Inventory	Emotional stability	+
PDRI ABLE	Emotional stability	+
Self-Description Inventory (Ghiselli)	Perceived maturity	+
Sixteen Personality Factor	Factor C: Emotional stability – affected by feelings/emotionally stable	+
Sixteen Personality Factor	Factor O: Apprehension – self-assured apprehensive, guilt prone	−
Sixteen Personality Factor	Q4: Tension – relaxed vs. tense (high ergic tension)	−
Thurstone Temperament Schedule	Stable	+
Youth Attitude Questionnaire Drug Study	Psychological health	+

(Contd.)

Part 1 *Contd.*

Inventory	Scale	Scoring direction
• ES Facet: Self-Esteem		
Adjective Checklist	Self-confidence	+
Bernreuter Personality Inventory	Confidence F1-C	+
GAMIN	Inferiority (freedom from such feelings)	+
Guilford–Martin Personality Inventory	Self-confidence (inferiority feelings)	+
Hogan Personality Inventory	HIC – good attachment	+
Hogan Personality Inventory	HIC – self-confidence	+
Inwald Personality Inventory	Family conflicts	–
Minnesota Multiphasic Personality Inventory	Low self-esteem	–
Minnesota Multiphasic Personality Inventory	Family problems	–
PDRI ABLE	Self-esteem	+
Self-Description Inventory (Ghiselli)	Self-assurance	+
State Farm – Opinion Inventory	Adjustment	+
• ES Facet: Low Anxiety		
Gordon Personal Profile-Inventory	Emotional stability	+
Gordon Personal Profile-Inventory	Hypersensitivity	–
Hogan Personality Inventory	HIC – not anxious	+
Inwald Personality Inventory	Anxiety	–
Jackson Personality Inventory	Anxiety	–
Minnesota Multiphasic Personality Inventory	Anxiety (MAS)	–
Minnesota Multiphasic Personality Inventory	Anxiety	–
NEO PI-R	Facet – anxiety	–
Omnibus Personality Inventory	Anxiety level	–
Sixteen Personality Factor	Anxiety (global)	–
State Trait Anxiety Inventory (Spielberger CPP)	Trait anxiety	–
Taylor Manifest Anxiety Scale	Total score	–
• ES Facet: Even Tempered		
Guilford-Martin Personality Inventory	Cycloid – labile within normal range	+
Hogan Personality Inventory	HIC – calmness	+
Hogan Personality Inventory	HIC – even tempered	+
Inwald Personality Inventory	Hyperactivity	–
Jackson Personality Inventory	Calmness	+
Occupational Personality Questionnaire	Relaxed	+
Sixteen Personality Factor	Undemonstrative, deliberate vs. excitable, impatient	+

EXTRAVERSION (EX)

Inventory	Scale	Scoring direction
• Global EX Measures		
Bernreuter Personality Inventory	Introversion B3-I	–
Comrey Personality Scales	Extroversion vs. introversion	+
Descriptive Adjective Inventory	Surgency	+
Eysenck Personality Questionnaire	Extroversion	+
Eysenck Personality Questionnaire	Surgency	+
Foreign Service Questionnaire	Social isolation	–
Goldberg Five Factor Markers	Factor I: Surgency	+
Inventory of Factors	Social introversion–extraversion	–
Inwald Personality Inventory	Loner type	–
Minnesota Multiphasic Personality Inventory	Social introversion	–
Myers Briggs Type Indicator	Extraversion vs. introversion	+
NEO PI-R	Extraversion (reserved vs. affectionate; sober vs. fun-loving; unfeeling vs. passionate)	+
Personal Characteristics Inventory	Extraversion	+
Personality Research Form	Exhibition	+
Sixteen Personality Factor	Factor F: Liveliness – sober vs. happy-go-lucky	+
Sixteen Personality Factor	Extraversion (global)	+
State Farm Personnel Survey	Extraversion–introversion	+

(Contd.)

Part 1 *Contd.*

Inventory	Scale	Scoring direction
• EX Facet: Dominance		
Adjective Checklist	Exhibition	+
Beckman Scales	Ascendance/submission	+
Bernreuter Personality Inventory	Dominance B4-D	+
California Psychological Inventory	Social presence	+
Edwards Personal Preference Schedule	Dominance	+
Foreign Service Questionnaire	Self-potency	+
GAMIN	Ascendance	+
Gordon Personal Profile-Inventory	Ascendancy	+
Guilford-Zimmerman Temperament Survey	Ascendancy	+
Hogan Personality Inventory	Ascendance	+
Hogan Personality Inventory	HIC – leadership	+
Inwald Personality Inventory	Lack of assertiveness	−
Kuder Preference Inventory	Directing others	+
Manifest Needs Questionnaire	Dominance	+
Multidimensional Personality Questionnaire	Social potency	+
NEO PI-R	Facet – assertiveness	+
Occupational Personality Questionnaire	Persuasive	+
Occupational Personality Questionnaire	Controlling	+
Personality Research Form	Dominance	+
PDRI ABLE	Dominance	+
Sixteen Personality Factor	Factor E: Dominance – humble vs. assertive	+
State Farm Personnel Survey	Ascendance–submission	+
State Farm – Opinion Inventory	Dominance	+
Thurstone Temperament Schedule	Dominant	+
• EX Facet: Sociability		
Adjective Checklist	Affiliation	+
Bernreuter Personality Inventory	Sociability F2-S	+
California Psychological Inventory	Sociability	+
Gordon Personal Profile-Inventory	Sociability	+
Guilford-Zimmerman Temperament Survey	Sociability	+
Hogan Personality Inventory	HIC – entertaining	+
Hogan Personality Inventory	HIC – likes crowds	+
Hogan Personality Inventory	HIC – likes parties	+
Hogan Personality Inventory	HIC – likes people	+
Hogan Personality Inventory	Sociability	+
Jackson Personality Inventory	Sociability	+
Kuder Preference Inventory	Active in groups	+
Life Style Inventory	Affiliative	+
Manifest Needs Questionnaire	Affiliation	+
Minnesota Multiphasic Personality Inventory	Social discomfort	−
NEO PI-R	Facet – gregariousness	−
Occupational Personality Questionnaire	Outgoing	+
Omnibus Personality Inventory	Social extroversion	+
State Farm – Opinion Inventory	Sociability	+
Thurstone Temperament Schedule	Sociable	+
• EX Facet: Activity/Energy Level		
Comrey Personality Scales	Activity vs. lack of energy	+
GAMIN	General activity	+
Guilford-Zimmerman Temperament Survey	General activity	+
Jackson Personality Inventory	Energy level	+
Jenkins Activity Survey	Speed impatience	+
NEO PI-R	Facet – activity	+
Occupational Personality Questionnaire	Active	+
PDRI ABLE	Energy level	+
Thurstone Temperament Schedule	Vigorous	+

(Contd.)

Part 1 *Contd.*

Inventory	Scale	Scoring direction
OPENNESS TO EXPERIENCE (OE)		
• **Global OE Measures**		
Adjective Checklist	Creative personality	+
Eysenck Personality Questionnaire	Culture	+
Goldberg Five Factor Markers	Factor V: Intellect	+
Hogan Personality Inventory	Intellectance	+
Multidimensional Personality Questionnaire	Absorption	+
NEO PI-R	Openness to experience	+
Personal Characteristics Inventory	Openness	+
Personality Research Form	Sentience	+
State Farm – Opinion Inventory	Intellectance	+
• **OE Facet: Complexity**		
Baron-Welsh Art Scale	Preference for complexity	+
Jackson Personality Inventory	Complexity	+
Kelly Role Construct Repertory Test	Cognitive complexity	+
Omnibus Personality Inventory	Complexity	+
• **OE Facet: Culture/Artistic**		
Hogan Personality Inventory	HIC – cultural taste	+
NEO PI-R	Facet – esthetics	+
Occupational Personality Questionnaire	Artistic	+
Omnibus Personality Inventory	Estheticism	+
• **OE Facet: Creativity/Innovation**		
Hogan Personality Inventory	HIC – generate ideas	+
Jackson Personality Inventory	Innovation	+
NEO PI-R	Facet – fantasy	+
Occupational Personality Questionnaire	Innovative	+
• **OE Facet: Change/Variety**		
Adjective Checklist	Change	+
Edwards Personal Preference Schedule	Change	+
Hogan Personality Inventory	HIC – experience seeking	+
Kuder Preference Inventory	Familiar and stable situations	–
NEO PI-R	Facet – actions	+
Occupational Personality Questionnaire	Change oriented	+
Personality Research Form	Change	+
• **OE Facet: Curiosity/Breadth**		
Hogan Personality Inventory	HIC – curiosity	+
Jackson Personality Inventory	Breadth of interest	+
• **OE Facet: Intellect**		
Gordon Personal Profile-Inventory	Original thinking (Gordon Personal Inventory)	+
Hogan Personality Inventory	HIC – intellectual games	+
Kuder Preference Inventory	Working with ideas	+
NEO PI-R	Facet – ideas	+
Occupational Personality Questionnaire	Conceptual	+
Omnibus Personality Inventory	Theoretical orientation	+
Personality Research Form	Understanding	+
AGREEABLENESS (A)		
• **Global A Measures**		
California Psychological Inventory	Amicability	+
Descriptive Adjective Inventory	Agreeableness	+
Eysenck Personality Questionnaire	Agreeableness	+
Goldberg Five Factor Markers	Factor II: Agreeableness	+
Guilford-Martin Personality Inventory	Cooperativeness	+

(Contd.)

Part 1 *Contd.*

Inventory	Scale	Scoring direction
Hogan Personality Inventory	HIC – easy to live with	+
Hogan Personality Inventory	Likability	+
Inwald Personality Inventory	Interpersonal difficulties	–
NEO PI-R	Agreeableness	+
Personal Characteristics Inventory	Agreeableness	+
PDRI ABLE	Cooperativeness	+
Self-Description Inventory (Ghiselli)	Sociometric popularity	+

• A Facet: Nurturance

Adjective Checklist	Nurturance	+
Comrey Personality Scales	Empathy vs. egocentrism	+
Edwards Personal Preference Schedule	Nurturance	+
Hogan Personality Inventory	HIC – sensitive	+
Hogan Personality Inventory	HIC – caring	+
NEO PI-R	Facet – altruism	+
NEO PI-R	Facet – tender-minded	+
Occupational Personality Questionnaire	Caring	+
Personality Research Form	Nurturance	+

CONSCIENTIOUSNESS (C)

• Global C Measures

Arrow-Dot Test (subtest of IES Test)	Superego	+
California Psychological Inventory	Work orientation	+
Descriptive Adjective Inventory	Conscientiousness	+
Eysenck Personality Questionnaire	Conscientiousness	+
Goldberg Five Factor Markers	Factor III: Conscientiousness	+
Hogan Personality Inventory	Prudence	+
Jenkins Activity Survey	Job involvement	+
NEO PI-R	Conscientiousness	+
NEO PI-R	Facet – self-discipline	+
Occupational Personality Questionnaire	Forward planning	+
Occupational Personality Questionnaire	Conscientious	+
Personal Characteristics Inventory	Conscientiousness	+
Protestant Ethic	No scales specified	+
Sixteen Personality Factor	Factor G: Rule consciousness – expedient	+
Sixteen Personality Factor	Q3: Undisciplined, follows own urges vs. control (high self-sentiment)	+
Sixteen Personality Factor	Self control (global)	+

• C Facet: Achievement

Adjective Checklist	Achievement	+
California Psychological Inventory	Achievement via conformance	+
Edwards Personal Preference Schedule	Achievement	+
Hogan Personality Inventory	HIC – mastery	+
Jenkins Activity Survey	Drive/competitiveness	+
Life Style Inventory	Competitive	+
Life Style Inventory	Perfectionistic	+
Life Style Inventory	Achievement	+
Manifest Needs Questionnaire	Achievement	+
Multidimensional Personality Questionnaire	Achievement/hard work	+
NEO PI-R	Facet – competence	+
NEO PI-R	Facet – achievement striving	+
Occupational Personality Questionnaire	Achieving	+
Personality Research Form	Achievement	+
PDRI ABLE	Work orientation	+
Self-Description Inventory (Ghiselli)	Achievement motivation	+
Self-Description Inventory (Ghiselli)	Initiative	+

(Contd.)

Part 1 *Contd.*

Inventory	Scale	Scoring direction
• C Facet: Dependability		
Gordon Personal Profile-Inventory	Responsibility	+
Hogan Personality Inventory	HIC – avoids trouble	+
Jackson Personality Inventory	Responsibility	+
NEO PI-R	Facet – dutifulness	+
PDRI ABLE	Conscientiousness	+
State Farm – Opinion Inventory	Dependability	+
• C Facet: Moralistic		
Hogan Personality Inventory	HIC – moralistic	+
Hogan Personality Inventory	HIC – virtuous	+
• C Facet: Cautiousness/Impulse Control		
vs. Risk Taking/Impulsive		
Arrow-Dot Test (subtest of IES Test)	I (id)	–
Gordon Personal Profile-Inventory	Cautiousness	+
Guilford–Zimmerman Temperament Survey	Restraint	+
Hogan Personality Inventory	HIC – impulse control	+
Jackson Personality Inventory	Risk taking	–
Multidimensional Personality Questionnaire	Control/impulsivity	–
Multidimensional Personality Questionnaire	Harm avoidance/danger seeking	–
NEO PI-R	Facet – deliberation	+
NEO PI-R	Facet – impulsiveness	–
Occupational Personality Questionnaire	Decisive	–
Omnibus Personality Inventory	Impulse expression	–
Personality Research Form	Harm avoidance	+
Personality Research Form	Impulsivity	–
Inventory of Factors	Rhathymia (impulsivity)	–
Thurstone Temperament Schedule	Impulsive	–
• C Facet: Order		
Adjective Checklist	Order	+
Comrey Personality Scales	Orderliness vs. lack of compulsion	+
Edwards Personal Preference Schedule	Order	+
Jackson Personality Inventory	Organization	+
NEO PI-R	Facet – order	+
Occupational Personality Questionnaire	Detail conscious	+
Personality Research Form	Order	+
• C Facet: Persistence		
Adjective Checklist	Endurance	+
Edwards Personal Preference Schedule	Endurance	+
Personality Research Form	Endurance	+

Part 2   Compilation of Compound Variable Measures Using Big Five Dimensions as Organizing Reference

Big Five variables	Inventory	Scale	Scoring direction
+ ES + EX	**Optimism**		
+ES +EX	California Psychological Inventory	Self-acceptance	+
+ES +EX	California Psychological Inventory	Well-being	+
+ES +EX	Foreign Service Questionnaire	Optimism	+
+ES +EX	Guilford-Martin Personality Inventory	Depression	–
+ES +EX	Guilford-Zimmerman Temperament Survey	Emotional stability	+
+ES +EX	Hogan Personality Inventory	HIC – no depression	+
+ES +EX	Hogan Personality Inventory	HIC – no social anxiety	+

(Contd.)

Part 2 *Contd.*

Big Five variables	Inventory	Scale	Scoring direction
+ES +EX	Jackson Personality Inventory	Social confidence	+
+ES +EX	Multidimensional Personality Questionnaire	Well-being	+
+ES +EX	NEO PI-R	Facet – positive emotions	+
−ES −EX	NEO PI-R	Facet – self-consciousness	−
+ES +EX	Occupational Personality Questionnaire	Socially confident	+
+ES +EX	Occupational Personality Questionnaire	Optimistic	+
+ES +EX	Personality Research Form	Play	+
+ES +EX	Sixteen Personality Factor	Factor H: Social boldness – shy vs. venturesome, socially bold (Parmia)	+
+ES +OE	**Intraception**		
+ES +OE	Adjective Checklist	Intraception	+
+ES +OE	California Psychological Inventory	Psychological mindedness	+
+ES +OE	Edwards Personal Preference Schedule	Intraception	+
+ES +OE	Guilford-Zimmerman Temperament Survey	Thoughtfulness	+
+ES +OE	Jackson Personality Inventory	Social astuteness	+
+ES +OE	NEO PI-R	Facet – feelings	+
+ES +A	**Trust**		
+ES +A	Comrey Personality Scales	Trust vs. defensiveness	+
+ES +A	Gordon Personal Profile-Inventory	Personal relations (Gordon Personal Inventory)	+
+ES +A	Hogan Personality Inventory	HIC – Trusting	+
−ES −A	Inwald Personality Inventory	Guardedness	−
−ES −A	Inwald Personality Inventory	Undue suspiciousness	−
+ES −A	Multidimensional Personality Questionnaire	Alienated/unfriendly world	−
−ES −A	Minnesota Multiphasic Personality Inventory	Cynicism	−
−ES −A	Minnesota Multiphasic Personality Inventory	Paranoia	−
−ES −A	NEO PI-R	Facet – angry hostility	−
+ES +A	NEO PI-R	Facet – trust	+
+ES +A	Omnibus Personality Inventory	Personal integration	+
−ES −A	Personality Research Form	Defendance	−
+ES +C	**Self-Control**		
+ES +C	Adjective Checklist	Self control	+
+ES +C	California Psychological Inventory	Law enforcement orientation	+
+ES +C	California Psychological Inventory	Self-control	+
+ES +C	California Psychological Inventory	Tough mindedness	+
+ES +C	Guilford-Martin Personality Inventory	Objectivity	+
+ES +C	Guilford-Zimmerman Temperament Survey	Objectivity	+
+ES +C	Hogan Personality Inventory	Self-control (impulse control)	+
+ES +C	Occupational Personality Questionnaire	Emotional control	+
+ES +C	Occupational Personality Questionnaire	Tough minded	+
−EX +OE	**Reflective**		
−EX +OE	Omnibus Personality Inventory	Thinking introversion	+
−EX +OE	Youth Attitude Questionnaire Drug Study	Introverted artist	+
−EX +OE	Inventory of Factors	Thinking introversion–extraversion	+
−EX +OE	Thurstone Temperament Schedule	Reflective	+
−EX +OE	Occupational Personality Questionnaire	Behavioral	+
−EX +A	**Modesty**		
+EX −A	California Psychological Inventory	Narcissism	−
−EX +A	Edwards Personal Preference Schedule	Abasement	+
−EX +A	NEO PI-R	Facet – modesty	+
−EX +A	Occupational Personality Questionnaire	Modest	+
−EX +A	Personality Research Form	Abasement	+

(Contd.)

Part 2 *Contd.*

Big Five variables	Inventory	Scale	Scoring direction
+EX +A	**Warmth**		
+EX +A	Edwards Personal Preference Schedule	Affiliation	+
+EX +A	Jackson Personality Inventory	Interpersonal affect emotions	+
+EX +A	Jackson Personality Inventory	Empathy	+
+EX +A	Multidimensional Personality Questionnaire	Social closeness	+
+EX +A	NEO PI-R	Facet – warmth	+
+EX +A	Occupational Personality Questionnaire	Affiliative	+
+EX +A	Personality Research Form	Affiliation	+
+EX +A	Sixteen Personality Factor	Factor A: Warmth – reserved vs. outgoing	+
−EX −A	Sixteen Personality Factor	Factor L: Suspicious – vigilance vs. trusting	−
+EX +C	**Ambition**		
+EX +C	Adjective Checklist	Dominance	+
+EX +C	California Psychological Inventory	Dominance	+
+EX +C	California Psychological Inventory	Gough's leadership index	+
+EX +C	Gordon Personal Profile-Inventory	Vigor, energy	+
+EX +C	Hogan Personality Inventory	Ambition	+
+EX +C	Hogan Personality Inventory	HIC – competitive	+
+EX +C	Hogan Personality Inventory	HIC – identity (status)	+
+EX +C	Inwald Personality Inventory	Type A personality	+
+EX +C	Jenkins Activity Survey	Overall	+
+EX +C	Minnesota Multiphasic Personality Inventory	Dominance	+
+EX +C	Minnesota Multiphasic Personality Inventory	Type A	+
+EX +C	Occupational Personality Questionnaire	Competitive	+
+ EX−C	**Autonomy**		
+EX −C	Edwards Personal Preference Schedule	Autonomy	+
−EX +C	Hogan Personality Inventory	HIC – not autonomous	−
+EX −C	Adjective Checklist	Autonomy	+
+EX −C	Manifest Needs Questionnaire	Autonomy	+
+EX −C	Omnibus Personality Inventory	Autonomy	+
+EX −C	Occupational Personality Questionnaire	Independent	+
+EX −C	Personality Research Form	Autonomy	+
+EX −C	Sixteen Personality Factor	Q2: Zestful, liking group action vs. reflective, individualism, internally restrained	+
+ OE +A	**Tolerance**		
+OE +A	California Psychological Inventory	Tolerance	+
+OE +A	Jackson Personality Inventory	Tolerance	+
+OE +A	Jackson Personality Inventory	Tolerance (when getting to know someone)	+
−OE −A	Minnesota Multiphasic Personality Inventory	Religion (rigidity, inflexibility, difficulty getting along with people)	−
−OE −A	Minnesota Multiphasic Personality Inventory	Authoritarianism (F scale)	−
−OE +C	**Traditionalism**		
+OE −C	California Psychological Inventory	Flexibility	−
−OE +C	Hogan Personality Inventory	HIC – not spontaneous	+
−OE +C	Inwald Personality Inventory	Rigid type	+
−OE +C	Life Style Inventory	Conventional	+
−OE +C	Multidimensional Personality Questionnaire	Traditionalism/authoritarianism	+
+OE −C	NEO PI-R	Facet – values	−
−OE +C	Occupational Personality Questionnaire	Traditional	+

(Contd.)

Part 2 *Contd.*

Big Five variables	Inventory	Scale	Scoring direction
+OE −C	Omnibus Personality Inventory	Religious orientation (hi scores, skeptical of religion)	−
−OE +C	Personality Research Form	Cognitive structure (negatively scored)	+
−OE +C	PDRI ABLE	Traditional values	+
+OE −C	Sixteen Personality Factor	Q1: Openness to change – conservative vs. experimenting	−
−OE +C	Youth Attitude Questionnaire Drug Study	Conservative–traditional philosophy	+
+OE −C	Youth Attitude Questionnaire Drug Study	Sensation seeking/flexibility	−
+A −C	**Lack of Aggression**		
−A −C	Adjective Checklist	Aggression	−
+A +C	Adjective Checklist	Deference	+
−A −C	Edwards Personal Preference Schedule	Aggression	−
+A +C	Edwards Personal Preference Schedule	Deference	+
+A +C	Guilford-Martin Personality Inventory	Agreeableness	+
+A +C	Guilford-Zimmerman Temperament Survey	Friendliness	+
+A +C	Guilford-Zimmerman Temperament Survey	Personal relations	+
+A +C	Hogan Personality Inventory	HIC – no hostility	+
+A +C	Jackson Personality Inventory	Cooperativeness	+
+A +C	Kuder Preference Inventory	Avoiding conflict	+
−A −C	Multidimensional Personality Questionnaire	Aggression	−
+A +C	NEO PI-R	Facet – straightforwardness	+
+A +C	NEO PI-R	Facet – compliance	+
+A +C	Omnibus Personality Inventory	Altruism	+
−A −C	Personality Research Form	Aggression	−
+ES + EX +C	**Fair and Stable Leadership**		
+ES + EX +C	California Psychological Inventory	Managerial potential	+
+ES + EX +C	Gordon Personal Profile-Inventory	Self-esteem (sum of ascendancy, responsibility, emotional stability, and sociability)	+
+ES +EX +C	Hogan Personality Inventory	Managerial potential	+
+ES +EX +C	Managerial Potential Report (Reid)	Total score	+
+ES +EX +C	Management Success Profile (London House)	Total score	+
+ES +EX +C	Self Description Inventory (Ghiselli)	Supervisory ability	+
−ES +EX −C	**Self-Destructive Autonomy**		
− ES +EX −C	Hilson Career Satisfaction Index	Drug/alcohol abuse	+
− ES +EX −C	Inwald Personality Inventory	Alcohol use	+
− ES +EX −C	Inwald Personality Inventory	Drugs	+
− ES +EX −C	Inwald Personality Inventory	Substance abuse	+
− ES +EX −C	Minnesota Multiphasic Personality Inventory	Addiction Potential Scale (APS) (Jim Butcher)	+
− ES +EX −C	Minnesota Multiphasic Personality Inventory	Hampton alcohol scale	+
− ES +EX −C	Minnesota Multiphasic Personality Inventory	Holmes alcohol scale	+
− ES +EX −C	Minnesota Multiphasic Personality Inventory	Hoyt and Sedlacek alcohol scale	+
− ES +EX −C	Minnesota Multiphasic Personality Inventory	MacAndrew alcohol scale	+
− ES +EX −C	Minnesota Multiphasic Personality Inventory	Rosenberg alcohol scale	+
+ES +A +C	**Socialization**		
+ES +A +C	California Psychological Inventory	Responsibility	+
+ES +A +C	California Psychological Inventory	Socialization	+
−ES −A −C	California Psychological Inventory	Delinquency	−
+ES +A +C	Comrey Personality Scales	Social conformity vs. rebelliousness	+
−ES −A −C	Eysenck Personality Questionnaire	Psychoticism	−
−ES −A −C	Hilson Career Satisfaction Index	Aggression/hostility	−
−ES −A −C	Hilson Career Satisfaction Index	Anger/hostility patterns (global – both attitudes and behavior)	−

(Contd.)

Part 2 *Contd.*

Big Five variables	Inventory	Scale	Scoring direction
−ES −A −C	Hilson Career Satisfaction Index	Disciplinary history	−
+ES +A +C	Hogan Personality Inventory	Reliability	+
+ES +A +C	Hogan Personality Inventory	Service orientation index	+
−ES −A −C	Inwald Personality Inventory	Antisocial attitudes	−
−ES −A −C	Inwald Personality Inventory	Driving violations	−
−ES −A −C	Inwald Personality Inventory	Trouble with the law	−
−ES −A −C	Minnesota Multiphasic Personality Inventory	Anger	−
−ES −A −C	Minnesota Multiphasic Personality Inventory	Antisocial practices	−
−ES −A −C	Minnesota Multiphasic Personality Inventory	General social maladjustment scale	−
−ES −A −C	Minnesota Multiphasic Personality Inventory	Psychopathic deviate	−
+ES +A +C	Minnesota Multiphasic Personality Inventory	Social responsibility	+
−ES −A −C	Minnesota Multiphasic Personality Inventory	Sociopathy (Spielberger-Florida project)	−
+ES +A +C	Personnel Decisions International – Employment Inventory	Performance	+
+ES +A +C	PDRI – ABLE	Non-delinquency	+
+ES +A +C	Personnel Reaction Blank	Total score	+
−ES −A −C	Personnel Selection Inventory (London House)	Violence	−
−ES −A −C	Personnel Selection Inventory (London House)	Drub abuse	−
−ES −A −C	Personnel Selection Inventory (London House)	Composite	−
−ES −A −C	PDRI – Youth Attitude Questionnaire Drug Questionnaire	Rebellious/deviant attitudes and behavior	−
+EX +OE −C	**Thrill Seeking**		
+EX +OE −C	Hogan Personality Inventory	HIC – thrill seeking	+
+EX +OE −C	NEO PI-R	Facet – excitement seeking	+
+EX +OE −C	Sensation-Seeking Scale (Zuckerman)	Total score	+
+EX +A +C	**Democratic**		
+EX +A +C	Occupational Personality Questionnaire	Democratic	+
+ES +EX +OE +C	**Achievement via Independence**		
+ES +EX +OE +C	California Psychological Inventory	Achievement via independence	+

Part 3   Compilation of Other Measures

Inventory	Scale	Scoring direction
Masculinity (Rugged Individualism)		
California Psychological Inventory	Femininity	−
Comrey Personality Scales	Masculinity vs. Femininity	+
GAMIN	Masculinity	+
Guilford-Zimmerman Temperament Survey	Masculinity	+
Minnesota Multiphasic Personality Inventory	Masculinity – Femininity	−
Omnibus Personality Inventory	Masculinity/Femininity	+

13

Individual and Team Training

JOHN P. CAMPBELL and
NATHAN R. KUNCEL

The objectives of this chapter are to identify and discuss critical issues pertaining to training design, trainee characteristics, the assessment of training effects, and the identification of critical training needs, with particular relevance to the dynamics of the twenty-first century global economy. All training issues are framed by the parameters of the aptitude/treatment interaction. Within this framework there are at least three major linkages in the path from training to organizational effectiveness and they should not be mislabeled. Alternative approaches to training design exist but it is argued that they must all consider certain 'universals' that cannot be avoided or finessed. Also, trainee individual differences always play a critical role in determining training outcomes and research in this domain is expanding; particularly with regard to the motivational determinants of mastery and transfer. Finally, the literature exhibits considerable consensus in the labeling of critical training needs for the new century. This array of identified needs is discussed in terms of current R&D that is being brought to bear on them.

For the purposes of this chapter, training is defined as a planned intervention that is designed to enhance the *determinants* of individual job performance, when the individual functions independently or as a member of a team. Individual job performance is conceptualized as in recent research on performance modeling (e.g., Borman & Motowidlo, 1993; Campbell, Gasser & Oswald, 1996; Murphy, 1989); that is, performance is defined as behaviors or actions that are judged relevant for the organization's goals and that can be scaled in terms of the level of the individual's contribution they represent. For virtually any position, job, or occupation, performance is multidimensional and it is reasonable to think in terms of the major performance factors as describing the critical dimensions along which an individual job holder should be trying to excel.

Given a sample of job holders, individual differences in performance on each of the factors are a function of multiple determinants. Campbell,

McCloy, Oppler and Sager (1993) argued that it is useful to think of direct and indirect determinants and that there are three kinds of direct determinants: knowledge, skill, and volitional choice behavior. Consequently, performance on a particular factor can be improved only by enhancing job relevant knowledge, job relevant skill, or developing more advantageous choice behavior (e.g., choosing to come to work more often, choosing to expend more effort, or choosing to expend effort for a more sustained period of time).

Individual differences in each of the direct determinants are in turn a function of multiple indirect determinants, one of which is training and instruction. Other indirect determinants are such things as abilities (i.e., relatively stable traits) or interventions of a 'motivational' nature (e.g., new reward systems, threats, etc.). There could also be interactive effects. Training then is an attempt to enhance performance relevant knowledge, skill, and/or choice behavior via instruction.

A similar explication applies to team training. Obviously there are different types of teams varying from the very traditional work group to the very autonomous, highly cross-trained, self-managed, high performance work team (Guzzo & Shea, 1992). There is nothing necessarily mysterious about teamwork or team self management. It is simply that the determinants of team performance that are responsive to a training intervention may also involve interactive effects among the knowledges, skills, and choice behaviors of its members, as well as individual levels of knowledge, skill, and choice. The question of how to enhance both the individual effects and the interactive effects via training is the team training issue.

Defined in the above way, this chapter will be limited to learning-based interventions that are, in some sense, formally designed to enhance particular performance determinants. Consequently, other important learning-based experiences such as the organizational socialization process or informal training will not be discussed, even though many of the principles of training design apply to these experiences as well. Also, the general domain of management development has been discussed in another chapter and will not be explicitly addressed here.

OBJECTIVES

The objectives of this chapter are to (1) review and discuss the major issues pertaining to: the design of training for individuals and teams, the instructional conditions that influence training effects, the interactive effects of learner characteristics, and the problem of transfer of training; (2) summarize the research literature on the evaluation of training effects; and (3) summarize the literature on the identification of specific critical training needs. That is, what are the most important substantive training needs that have broad relevance for the world of work.

The information reviewed comes from theory, research, and practice and we will try to identify implications for all three as we go along. Also, we will try to be explicit about those aspects of theory, research, or practice that are universal in nature and those that may incorporate some degree of cross national specificity.

TWO MAJOR ISSUES

Two major issues underlie any attempt to design or implement training, evaluate its effects, develop training theory, or conduct R&D type research on training issues. One concerns the universality of the aptitude – treatment interaction and the other is the ubiquitous criterion problem.

The Aptitude – Treatment Interaction (ATI)

Cronbach (1957) and Cronbach and Snow (1977) made the ATI a virtual icon for research on training and instruction. The principal message is that all trainees are not alike and some of the characteristics where people differ are correlated with training achievement. That is, even though everyone is given the same training experience (i.e., the 'treatment'), some people will do better than others as a function of having more or less of the 'aptitude' (e.g., cognitive ability, need for achievement, anxiety, self efficacy, level of previously acquired knowledge and skill, level of interest in the material, etc.). Further, the magnitude of the correlation may differ across samples that have had different treatments (i.e., instructional programs). The ATI of most interest is the case where X (the aptitude) and Y (the criterion variable) are measured in the same way in each group and the regression lines cross. The major implication is that to maximize aggregate gain across all groups, the same training program should not be given to everyone. Ideally, trainees should be 'assigned' to programs based on their X score (which also could be a weighted or unweighted composite of $x_1 + x_2 +... x_k$). This problem is formally equivalent to personnel placement and classification (when jobs or job levels are treatments) and to the assignment problem in linear programming (e.g., when different locations or routes are treatments). The most extreme case is to provide a different training experience for each individual, which would be optimal, but expensive. However, Cronbach and Gleser (1965) showed that, if the correlations across treatments are different, then the gain in aggregate achievement grows exponentially with the number of treatments. It is a potentially powerful phenomenon. Some are of the opinion that the significant advances in instructional technology in just the last few years and prospects for even more startling development in the next 5 to 10 years will realize the power of the exponent sooner rather than later (e.g., Jensen, 1998). It could very well be in the form of multi-media intelligent tutoring systems which could customize the training experience down to 'virtually' the optimal level, and at a reasonable price.

Cronbach's presidential address to the American Psychological Association in 1956 pointing to the potential power of the ATI (Cronbach, 1957) filled the instructional world with hope, and many attempts were made to find useful ATIs, primarily in education (Cronbach & Snow, 1977; Snow,

1989; Snow & Lohman, 1984). Two ATIs have been found with some consistency. The most frequent has been the interaction of general cognitive ability and the 'structure' of the instructional program when more structure means more instructor guidance, more detailed objectives for the learner, more explicit specifications for the content to be taught, and more frequent feedback (Snow, 1989). High ability people do better with low structure and vice versa for low ability individuals, although the variance accounted for by the interaction has not been large. The second ATI is represented by the interaction of trainee anxiety or self-efficacy and the degree of program structure. High anxiety and low self-efficacy individuals tend to do better in more structured programs.

In general however, a relatively narrow range of ATIs has been investigated, and primarily in education settings. The individual differences variable is almost always general cognitive ability or one of a few personality variables, and treatment differences have been largely limited to the 'structure' parameter. Consequently, the research yield has been limited in terms of its value to organizational training. As will be discussed in a later section, the picture has begun to change a bit with regard to individual differences in trainee motivation. However, as we noted some time ago (Campbell, 1988), the potentially powerful interaction of initial individual differences in trainee knowledge and skill with differences in instructional content is still given scant attention in organizational training. It tends to be one size fits all with little regard for differences in the initial state of the learner's knowledge, skill, or characteristic choice behavior. A reasonable hope is that more versatile computerized tutoring systems will change this situation. We believe it is a truism to assert that there are always relevant individual differences in trainees and that there are always potential differences in training programs. Consequently, the ATI represents a universal set of questions that apply to any training effort. That is, what individual differences correlate with training achievement? What treatment differences are the most relevant? What interactions might be likely? What should the dependent variable be?

The Criterion (Dependent Variable) Problem

Training is implemented for certain purposes, however appropriate or inappropriate they might be or from whatever theoretical perspective they came. This begs the question of the extent to which the program did, or did not, accomplish its objectives; and if not, why not. Consequently, the need for the assessment of training effects is a major issue, regardless of culture, national economic system, industry sector, or one's preferred instructional

theory. Following the definition of training being used above, the objectives of training are to increase job knowledge, increase job relevant skill, or enhance individual choice behavior. The criterion issue concerns whether or not the intended changes were accomplished, and to what extent. This is true regardless of whether the desired changes are defined by the organization, the individual, or via a collaboration between the two.

However, Dipboye (1997) and Salas, Cannon-Bowers, Rhodenizer and Bowers (1999) have pointed out that organizations (and individuals) can have other purposes for training as well. For example, training can serve a number of symbolic functions. Organizations can use it to show various audiences that they are concerned about supporting skill improvement among their employees, or appropriately managing a diverse work force, or preventing sexual harassment, or improving supervision and management. Individuals can use training certificates, educational degrees, or even graduate degrees as symbols of accomplishment and status. Both organizations and individuals may use training certification as a way to avoid or aid litigation, as in establishing 'expert' credentials, or for meeting the terms of an out of court settlement by conducting certain types of training (e.g., for reducing sexual harassment). While none of those purposes are necessarily inappropriate and may serve individuals or organizations well, they are not our concern here, except as they might interfere with designing training to improve performance relevant knowledge, skill, or choice behavior.

The framework most often used to think about the training criterion problem is still the Kirkpatrick (1959, 1996) classification of possible measures into four types: (1) *reactions*, or trainee self-reports of training effectiveness; (2) *learning*, or independent end-of-training measures of knowledge, skill or attitudinal change; (3) *behavior*, or measures of performance back in the job setting (i.e., the transfer issue); and (4) *results*, or assessment of improvements in organizational outcomes that have direct implications for the 'business purpose' and the organization's viability. Unfortunately, these four 'types' have never been all that well-specified (Alliger, Tannenbaum, Bennett, Traver & Shotland, 1997). For example, reactions may refer to global judgments of how much the individual liked the program, to specific opinions about the relevance of the content or the usefulness of the training methods, or to judgments about the expertise of the staff. Learning may refer only to knowledge acquisition or it may also refer to mastery of demonstrable skills or changes in measured attitudes. It is also not clear whether behavior refers to assessment of the same variables specified by the learning criteria, except that they are assessed in the job setting, or whether it refers to the assessment of job performance itself, not its determinants.

As noted by many observers (e.g., Alliger et al., 1997; Salas & Cannon-Bowers, 2001; Salas et al., 1999), there has not been much research directed at modeling training achievement itself. Certainly it has not kept pace with recent research and theory on the nature of job performance (Borman & Motowidlo, 1993; Campbell, 1999; Campbell, McCloy, Oppler & Sager, 1993; Hedge & Borman, 1995). For example, there is only a modest amount of data pertaining to the interrelationships among multiple measures of training achievement. Alliger et al. (1997) present meta-analysis results from 34 studies. One clear finding is that global trainee reactions are not correlated with learning or mastery, or with much of anything else for that matter. Similar results from educational settings (Greenwald, 1997; McKeachie, 1997), call into question the indiscriminate use of student/trainee evaluations for various purposes. Estimates of the correlations among the other Kirkpatrick criterion types have not been well established. However, it may be a futile task and not worth the investment, given the underspecification of the types themselves and the virtual lack of any specifications for how they should be interrelated.

What Kirkpatrick refers to as *learning* is really the core concern of training. A measure of learning is not an intermediate surrogate for performance in the job setting or for indices of unit or organizational effectiveness (i.e., 'results'). By any of the design models to be discussed below, the *direct* objectives of training programs are not to improve the *overall* job performance of individuals or to increase profitability or return on investment for the organization. Learning goals can be stated in terms of changes in knowledge, skill, choice behavior, or even attitudes, but no one training program can include all the determinants of individual job performance (some are not amenable to training), and bottom line or results indices have multiple determinants in addition to the performance of individuals. There is considerable discussion in the practitioner literature about the need to link training activities to the return on investment (ROI) for training costs (e.g., Parry, 1996; Phillips, 1996; Purcell, 2000). In every published discussion of this issue to date, the difficulty of controlling for alternative explanations is largely ignored and obtaining a valid metric for both costs and benefits is made to sound much too easy.

This is *not* an argument that the totality of individual performance or bottom line indicators of organizational effectiveness are not important. They obviously are. However, whether a program meets its objectives and whether the objectives reflect valid determinants of performance are two different questions. The linkage between competencies learned in training and job performance itself is established by a needs analysis, regardless of whether the linkage is easy to identify (everyone agrees it is 'obvious') or requires a more thorough and detailed investigation. A third question is whether the performance of individuals or teams constitutes a causal determinant of differences in organizational effectiveness. Although one would hope this would not be the case, it is potentially possible to design jobs for individuals or teams that have nothing to do with any relevant organizational goal.

The most reasonable view of these issues is first that the bottom line or results indicators must be construct valid measures of organizational effectiveness, which in the beginning assumes some basic agreement among the stakeholders about the nature of the organization's goals. Next, the prescribed performance roles for individuals and teams, however broad or narrow they are, must be valid determinants of organizational effectiveness. This is a matter for organization, team, and job design. Finally, the objectives of training must address valid determinants of individual or team performance. Once these three questions are answered, *then* we can usefully ask whether a particular training program meets its objectives; and if not, why not. Obviously there are a number of things that can disturb the training achievement to job performance linkage as well as the linkage between individual or team performance and the bottom line. A causal model of this sequence must take such variables into account as well.

UNIVERSALS IN TRAINING DESIGN

Given that the ATI and the criterion issue are always with us, we would like to argue that there are also certain universals in training design that are impervious to national or cultural differences as well as to the current controversies over alternative models of training design. Parts of the discussion draw from Campbell (1988). The list simply identifies a number of issues that must be considered and a set of decisions that must be made before a training program is completed. A fundamental point is that even if these questions and decisions are not considered explicitly, or are aggressively (and misguidedly) rejected as irrelevant, they will still be answered by default, *always*; and can be inferred after the fact from what was actually done.

We still believe that Gagné (1962) was very right when he argued that the most fundamental design issue is the specification of what is to be learned. What new knowledges, skills, beliefs, attitudes, or choice behaviors should the individual exhibit after training that they could not, or would not, exhibit before. In our terminology this is the specification of the *training program* objectives. Every training intervention will have them. If not stated explicitly, they can be inferred from what actually happens. This fundamental question is answered by considering three prior issues: goal analysis, job design, and needs assessment.

Job Design and the Organization's Goals

What are the organization's operating goals, and what are their implications for job design? How should jobs be defined and structured to best contribute to goal accomplishment? For example, given certain R&D goals, what kind of R&D operations should there be? What kinds of research positions are needed? Again, if a training program is designed to enhance the determinants of performance on a critical job factor, performance on this factor should, by design, have something to do with the goals of the organization. The responsibility for making sure such a linkage exists goes far beyond the training function (Harris, 1994).

Models and procedures for goal analysis and job design are not within the boundaries of this chapter, but such questions cannot really be avoided. In the training context, they will be answered one way or another, again if only by default. When an organization buys a training program off the shelf from a vendor, it has implicitly asserted that the content of the program does not create goal conflicts and is consistent with the way jobs are designed to meet the organization's goals.

Determining Training Needs

By our definition, training needs reflect current or anticipated deficiencies in determinants of performance that can be remedied, at least in part, by a training intervention. Training needs exist in a number of contexts. For example, current job holders may be deficient in terms of their performance, and the primary purpose of training is to remedy the deficiency. In a different context, if eligibility for promotion is a function of high performance on particular performance components, training on the determinants of those performance components may be offered to, or sought by, anyone wanting to be considered for promotion. Also certain components of performance may be forecasted to be critical in the future; as when new kinds of equipment, will be introduced. For example, what will be the training needs for air traffic controllers when new, and very different, air traffic control systems come on line. Finally, training may be needed for the determinants of performance components that must be executed in totally new environments, as when NASA was faced with training people to drive a car on the moon.

Ideally, a needs assessment would have three major steps: a description of the factors that comprise effective performance, specifications of the determinants of performance on the factors, and identification of the performance determinants that would benefit from a training intervention. Step three could focus on individuals (the traditional person analysis) or on teams, or on forecasted future training needs for everyone in an occupation, or even for everyone entering the labor force (e.g., US Department of Labor's Secretary's Commission on the Achievement of Necessary Skills, 1992). This makes virtually all job analyses and criterion development methods relevant for needs identification.

However, using the available work analysis methods to identify training needs is hampered by several factors. First, while there has been much recent progress in developing descriptive models of work performance (Borman & Motowidlo, 1993; Campbell, McCloy, Oppler & Sager, 1993; Murphy, 1989; Organ, 1997), such efforts are still relatively primitive for purposes of identifying training needs. That is, current models describe a small number of factors that are still very broad in nature. This may be quite valuable for guiding research on personnel selection, but for training purposes we must move down the hierarchy to more specific factor descriptions. In this regard, the most progress has been achieved in describing the components of leadership/supervision (Bass, 1990) management (Borman & Brush, 1993) and now perhaps 'performance as a team member' (Olson, 2000).

Another constraint is that current methods for identifying and mapping performance determinants (KSAs) rests on the judgments of SMEs who are asked to 'link' KSAs to performance factors. Unfortunately, the KSAs themselves, at least those that are potentially trainable, vary from being 'adequately' specified (e.g., requires 'statistical analysis skills at the introductory course level') to being significantly underspecified (e.g., requires good 'writing skills') to being woefully underspecified (e.g., requires high 'adaptability'). Perhaps the worst example of underspecification is to ask an SME to rate the criticality of 'problem solving skill' as a performance determinant. We assert that at its current level of specification, problem solving skill is a virtually meaningless construct for purposes of identifying training needs. More about this later.

Finally, a third difficulty is the crudeness of our methods for identifying the performance determinants that are amenable to a training intervention. That is, what kinds of determinants are trainable and which are not? We may pay too much attention to the obvious suspects, namely specific knowledge deficiencies.

While most job analysis methods operate at too general a level and require SMEs to make too many judgments about very underspecified variables, which reduces their usefulness as methods of training needs analysis, there are methods that address training needs more directly. One of these is the critical incident technique (Anderson & Wilson, 1997) for which relevant observers are asked to consider a potential population of specific performance examples and describe a sample of episodes that reflect very effective and very ineffective performance. The describers can also be asked why the individual was able to exhibit the effective episode or what antecedents led to the ineffective incident. While the inferences about causal determinants are still subject to the errors of human judgment (Morgeson & Campion, 1997), which can never be eliminated completely, the inference is tied to very specific events. The individual is not required to infer linkages between broad constructs or variables and broad factors comprising job performance.

The critical incident technique is sometimes grouped within a broader class of methods generally referred to as cognitive task analysis (CTA) (Chipman, Schraagen & Shalin, 2000). In one sense the literature on CTA, which is now relatively large (Schraagen, Chipman & Shalin, 2000), represents an attempt by cognitive psychology to define work analysis as part of cognitive science since most work is now mental rather than physical. However, most of the CTA analysis techniques are not new and encompass various interviewing formats, observational techniques, and protocol analysis methods. There are many variations of these basic methods from the standard job analysis interview, to software models for eliciting protocols, to interrupted recall techniques for people watching themselves on video tape. Summaries of methods are provided by Annett (2000), Cooke (1994), and Schraagen et al. (2000).

Turf battles aside, CTA does provide certain types of information for specifying training needs that are not addressed by more 'traditional' methods. This occurs because the general goal of CTA is to explain the determinants of expert as compared with novice performance. Consequently, while traditional job analysis attempts to describe the content of a work role and infer the KSAs that would be correlated with individual differences in performance in that role, CTA attempts to address *how* individuals are able to perform work tasks at a particular performance level. To be more specific, how does the expert do it?

The framework for exploring how the expert does it is taken from cognitive science representations of performance determinants. That is, while a CTA begins with a 'traditional' description of the work content, the procedure then attempts to recover information such as the following:

- The way in which the expert/novice translates the prescribed work goals into their own operative goals.
- The mental models experts/novices use to represent their performance requirements and work context.
- The cognitive resources experts/novices use to accomplish the tasks they deem important.

Cognitive resources are usually represented as the relevant knowledge and skill determinants, and the cognitive strategies and strategy selection rules that are used to apply them.

In sum, what individual goals, mental models, cognitive resources, and cognitive strategies do experts use that distinguish them from novices? As outlined by Chipman et al. (2000), there are three principle applications of CTA: specifying the determinants of expert performance for purposes of training and selection; aiding the design of human/system interactions; and analyzing the bases of effective teamwork. The number of bona fide applications of CTA to the specification of training needs is actually quite small. Much more effort has been directed at using CTA for software development to aid decision making, construct control systems, or construct the teaching protocol itself.

One of the most direct applications of CTA methods was the identification of training needs for air traffic controllers reported by Means et al. (1988). Several different analysis methods were used to elicit the goals, mental models, knowledge and skill representations, and cognitive strategies used by a sample of experienced controllers when dealing with simulated control tower ATC job samples at a major airport. The participant experts were first asked to think out loud about how they would deal with a set of air traffic situations as portrayed by the paper copy flight strips. They were then asked to watch a video of a controller working on a simulation of an air traffic scenario. The simulations were run on the ATC training equipment which was identical to the actual equipment and displays used in the tower. Part way through the simulation, the video was stopped and the participant was asked to take over and to verbalize what he was going to do, and why. Then each participant was asked to work through three additional 45-minute simulations using the same equipment. Finally, each participant completed a series of post simulation memory tasks such as recalling and drawing the traffic patterns, recalling the flight strips, and recalling significant events that happened during the scenarios.

The analysis produced considerable protocol information concerning the mental models, cognitive resources, and cognitive strategies that experienced controllers seemed to use. For example, one frequent mental map of the air traffic sector organized planes by the type of problem they represented rather than topographically. Experienced controllers had an amazingly detailed knowledge of what happens in the sector each day, and they engaged in a continual process of prioritizing potential problems extending over a fairly long time frame. It was also the case that experienced controllers had developed some task elements to automaticity. That is, they could do one task automatically (data entry using keyboard) while simultaneously working on a controlled processing task (talking to pilots). These and other findings led directly to training prescriptions to accelerate the development of ATC expertise. The finding that high level of performance is often a function of developing critical tasks to a state of automaticity such that they no longer require attentional resources leads to the prescription that the analysis of high level performance in terms of its consistent versus controlled processing components should be an important part of analyzing training needs (Rogers, Mauer, Salas & Fisk, 1997).

In general, CTA methods build on the more traditional job analysis techniques and do provide additional information about what explains higher level versus novice performance. Unfortunately, it can quickly become time consuming and expensive and is not feasible for all training design problems. However, even a modest amount spent trying to contrast the resources and methods used by novices and experts could provide useful information regarding training needs, keeping in mind at least one major qualification. There are degrees of freedom problems in CTA and the designer must avoid being misled by the idiosyncratic expert.

Specifying Training Objectives

Once training needs are identified, they must be translated into training objectives that lead directly to specifications for training content. Needs assessments as described above are not statements of objectives. Objectives identify what the learner should know or be able to do after finishing the program that he or she could not do before. They are stated in observable terms, and they include some indication of the conditions under which the individual should be able to exhibit them and at what level of proficiency. This is the heart of training design. If the training objectives cannot be specified, it implies that the trainer cannot be clear about what to teach. These statements are often attacked as shopworn rhetoric that is no longer useful (Gordon & Zemke, 2000). Nothing could be further from the truth. It does not matter whether one's orientation is behavior analysis, cognitive science, constructivism, humanism, or consultant of the month dictum. Any training program that is actually implemented will focus, if only by default, on achieving some kind of change that can be exhibited to some level under some set of conditions or constraints. In practice, describing the training objectives explicitly is not an easy task, which may be one reason people tend to avoid it.

An important meta-issue here is that each training objective must incorporate the appropriate 'capability'. For example, a training course for data analysts could formulate objectives having to do with correctly formatting data files and using the proper commands to run standard data analysis software, or it could specify objectives for teaching

analysts how to solve novel analysis problems. The former has to do with the correct execution of certain well-specified steps, while the latter requires problem solving of a specific technical sort. That is, the capabilities to be learned are different. While this is a rather obvious example, the situations when it is not so obvious could lead to a serious misstatement of the training objectives (Gagné, Briggs & Wager, 1988).

Table 13.1 is a suggested framework for highlighting differences among the major types of capabilities that could be the objective of a training intervention. Thinking in taxonomic terms at this stage is intended to help avoid incorporating the wrong capability in the description of a training objective. There is nothing particularly startling about this taxonomy. All are legitimate training objectives and no hierarchy of importance is implied. The distinction between a knowledge capability and a skill capability is the conventional one that distinguishes knowing what to do from being able to actually do it. Sometimes the difference between knowing and doing is small (e.g., computing descriptive statistics) and sometimes it is very large (e.g., resolving conflicts between subordinates, hitting a golf ball). However, the classic instructional design mistake is teaching one but hoping for the other.

The word skill is used in almost as many different ways as the term performance. We have tried to give it a more specific and more useful meaning here. Skills are learned and they reflect the successful application of relevant knowledge capabilities to solve problems or produce outcomes that can be well-specified such that the correct solution or desired outcome is known, and the methods and procedures used to generate successful solutions or outcomes are known as well. For example, there are correct ways to solve linear programming problems, erect the frame for a house, and slalom ski. All of these are well-structured problems to which known procedures can be applied. This does not mean that mastering the methods and procedures (i.e., skills) is easy or that knowledgeable people no longer argue about precisely the best methods to use (e.g., striking a golf ball).

The problem solving capability refers to the application of knowledge and skill to developing solutions for ill-structured problems (Newell & Simon, 1972). That is, there is no a priori correct or best solution; the knowledges and skills that are the most applicable are not completely specifiable; and the problem or goal itself may not be easily identified. All this makes the term problem solving *skill* a bit of an oxymoron. As argued below, the training implications are different for a skill versus problem solving capability. Also, by this definition, effective problem solving is the successful application of acquired knowledge and skill to an ill-structured problem when 'successful' is necessarily a judgment

Table 13.1   *A taxonomy of capabilities that are potentially trainable*

A. Increases in knowledge
   1. Knowledge of labels and facts pertaining to objects, events, processes, conditions, etc.
   2. Knowledge of facts concerning if/then relationships.
   3. Knowledge of rules or procedures for accomplishing specific goals or objectives relative to cognitive, social, or physical behavior.
   4. Knowledge of plans and goals.
   5. Self-knowledge.

B. Increases in observable skills: A skill is defined as the application of knowledge capabilities to solve structured problems or accomplish a specified goal. That is, there are known solutions and known ways of achieving them. The issue is whether the individual can actually apply the knowledge capabilities and achieve the goal
   1. Cognitive skills.
   2. Psychomotor skills.
   3. Physical skills.
   4. Interpersonal skills.
   5. Expressive skills.
   6. Self-management skills.

C. Increases in problem solving skills: Defined as the application of knowledge and skill capabilities to ill-structured problems that is aided by certain strategies; for example
   1. Application of heuristics.
   2. Means–ends analysis.
   3. Pattern matching.
   4. Meta-cognition.
   5. Analogical transfer.

D. Changes in attitudes and beliefs; for example
   1. Self-efficacy.
   2. Organizational commitment.
   3. Racial attitudes.
   4. Sexist beliefs.
   5. Cultural tolerance.

call by knowledgeable people. In this sense, effective problem solving is domain specific. But what else is it? What leads to proficiency in being able to identify problems, specify them in a useful way, identify knowledges and skills that are relevant to the problem as defined, and apply them? Heuristics that can be taught? The ubiquitous 'meta-cognitions'? Or straightforward pattern matching, which makes effective problem solving dependent on the similarity of the current situation to problem situations encountered in the past? These issues are revisited later in this chapter.

Attitudes and beliefs are included in the capability taxonomy because they are the explicit or implicit capabilities of interest in many training programs directed at such things as individual self-efficacy (Gist, 1997), attitudes toward sexual harassment, or beliefs concerning the procedural justice of personnel policies. Two things are important to know about such capabilities. First, the linkage between changes in attitudes or beliefs and the desired (hoped for?) changes in behavior is a complex one (Ajzen, 1985) and far from guaranteed. Second, while the capability specified or implied by the training objective may be an attitude or belief,

the training content itself could include knowledge, skills, or problem solving. For example, men may hold sexist beliefs because (a) they do not know their current beliefs are sexist, (b) they have no non-sexist interpersonal skills relative to interactions with women, or (c) they cannot recognize and deal with new or unique harassment contexts.

In sum, the description of the training objectives is the fundamental step in training design, and probably the most neglected. Producing objectives with the above specifications requires much cognitive effort, and it is difficult to develop very powerful reinforcement contingencies for maintaining such behavior on the part of training designers. It is too much like eating and exercising properly. We know what we should do, but there are always very persuasive people who promise much easier solutions.

Specifying Training Content

The training content is dictated by the training objectives. It is composed of the knowledges, skills, and patterns of choice behavior that the trainee must acquire to be able to meet the objectives. By design, being able to exhibit the objectives is dependent on mastery of the training content. For example, what content must a graduate student master to write a research proposal, make a presentation to a relevant audience, or write down a research question? The distinction between training objectives and training content is important, but sometimes subtle.

Sometimes they are very similar (using a keyboard for word processing) and sometimes they are not (e.g., learning more about your own personality to facilitate acquisition of team member skills). Besides identifying content elements, the sequence in which they are to be learned must also be specified. If the sequence is not clear, either the objectives or the subject matter is not well enough understood (Gagné, Briggs & Wager, 1988).

Content specifications can be determined from three principle sources. One is simply to use expert judgment. People who 'know' the topic specify the training content. Content can also come from more formal theory. For example, in basic skills there are now rather well-developed conceptual descriptions of what arithmetic is (Resnick & Ford, 1981). Closer to home, certain theories of leadership provide a specification of what knowledges and skills must be mastered to enhance leadership performance (Bass, 1990). However, one reason that leadership theory has not progressed further than it has is that a comprehensive substantive model of leadership performance has never really been provided. Training and development will become more powerful as our taxonomies and substantive understanding of performance phenomena grow. We simply need much more research on what constitutes competent performance in various important domains (Glaser & Bassok, 1989).

A major contribution of research in cognitive and instructional psychology to the methodology of content specification is again the application of a wide variety of CTA techniques to elicit the knowledges, skills, and strategies that high level performers use in contrast to novices. Such methods can focus either on the expert protocol to elicit the information, skill, or problem solving capabilities that should be enhanced or on the novice protocol to discern the faults and mistakes ('bugs') that should be corrected or avoided (Schaafstal & Schraagen, 2000).

One CTA technique for representing the training content that seems overemphasized is the elicitation of expert vs. nonexpert semantic networks. That is, participants are asked to consider an array of concepts and procedures, and judge the relative similarity between each possible pair. Once the similarity matrix is obtained, various multidimensional scaling or network analysis techniques (e.g., Pathfinder) can be applied to obtain a dimensional or relational latent structure for the concepts (Goldsmith & Kraiger, 1997; Kraiger, Salas & Cannon-Bowers, 1995; Olson & Biolsi, 1991). A recurring finding is that the similarity matrix is not the same for experts

as it is for novices and a different dimensional or cluster structure is produced. Granted that training and experience can produce changes in such a similarity matrix, it is not clear how this information is useful for training design. The concepts to be clustered usually have very little specification beyond the name or title and the respondents are not asked to generate explanations for their similarity judgments. Relative to the taxonomy of capabilities given in Table 13.1, this procedure focuses only on 'labels', which may not capture the capability specified by the training objectives.

Specifying Instructional Methods and Training Media

Given that a particular body of content is to be learned, the next consideration is the set of instructional methods that should be used to teach or promote mastery of the content. We use the term *instructional methods* to mean the generic teaching methods or learning events that a trainer potentially has available. For example, the direct presentation of information to the student is a generic instructional method, as is simulation. A generic learning method might be executed through any one of several specific techniques, or *media*. For example, information presentation is possible via reading, lectures, or the internet. This is a 'generic' vs. 'brand name' distinction and we would argue that the number of generic methods is relatively few. Table 13.2 is a suggested taxonomy of such methods.

There are two critical features of instructional methods that training design should attempt to optimize (Gagné & Briggs, 1979; Glaser, 1976; Pintrick, Cross, Kozma & McKeachie, 1986). First, the 'capability' incorporated in the training objective and the training content should be represented with as much fidelity as possible by the training method. For example, if the capability is electronic trouble-shooting, and trouble-shooting is specified as an application of known procedures to identify one or more knowable malfunctions (i.e., trouble-shooting skill), then the training method should provide an opportunity for the learner to generate the appropriate application of acquired knowledge to the specified trouble-shooting problems. However, if a course in software design is intended to reflect a problem solving capability, the teaching method should provide a series of novel and incompletely specified problems as stimulus material. In addition, the design must ask whether this training objective is also a function of knowledge and skills that must be mastered before the problem solving capability itself can be addressed. Designing training methods to incorporate the desired capabilities will be successful to the extent that the functional descriptions of the necessary capabilities are (1) valid and (2) substantive enough to guide the training design.

Table 13.2 *Taxonomy of generic instructional methods relevant for occupational training*

1. *Information Presentation.* From traditional lecture to distance learning, probably the most widely used method is simply the presentation of verbal, numerical, figural, auditory information to the learner. However, even though the information presented may include guides and suggestions for how to use the information, the ways in which the information is actually processed is not known.

2. *Modeling.* One very specialized form of information presentation is using a model to demonstrate the desired responses, which could be verbal, social/expressive, psychomotor, or motor. Modeling seems to deserve its own niche because it is the information presentation technique that is most easily directed at a skill capability. The model may be the instructor, a live actor, a video representation, or perhaps even a robot (e.g., the golfer known as Iron Mike).

3. *Information Presentation Plus Provision for Learner Response.* Many instructional techniques attempt to actively engage the learner varying from simply providing the opportunity to ask questions, to more structured question and answer periods, to some form of cooperative learning (Johnson & Johnson, 1975) in which the trainees take turns presenting the material and dealing with questions.

4. *Systematic Response Generation.* A wide range of instructional events require the learner to produce specific kinds of responses that are directly relevant for the training objectives. That is, they are designed to be so, such as solving math problems, responding to instructor questions in foreign language instruction, providing a diagnosis of equipment or system malfunctions, demonstrating how to operate equipment or systems, performing specific physical requirements, etc. The common elements are that an active response is *required* of the learner and the desired response is designed to be directly relevant for the training objectives. Legitimate issues arise over how detailed and structured the response requirement should be and the degree to which the trainee is allowed to make (and possibly learn from) specific errors. Also, there can be disagreement as to how completely the desired responses are 'situated' in a context which comes as close as possible to the job context in which the capability is to be used (Anderson, Reder & Simon, 1996).

5. *Simulation.* Simulation methods are a direct attempt to represent all the relevant elements of the actual job tasks with as much fidelity as possible for the stimulus conditions, the responses, the conditions under which the objectives are to be exhibited, and the difficulty of the requirement for the trainee. Obviously, there can be great variability in the bandwidth and fidelity for the stimulus conditions, response requirements, and contextual features represented by specific simulators.

6. *On the Job Training.* OJT is no longer simulation, it is the actual work context. However, this does not guarantee that the content of the OJT experiences are directly relevant for the training objectives. Just because the method is executed on the job does not absolve the training design of identifying training objectives that are based on valid training needs and ensuring that the content of OJT addresses them. Experience may or may not be the best teacher.

Another principle of method design is that, whatever the capability to be mastered, the learner must be allowed, encouraged, or induced to actively 'produce' that capability during training. Production facilitates both learning and retention (Perry & Downs, 1985; Schmidt & Bjork, 1992). This is as true for a knowledge capability as it is for a physical or cognitive skill. For example, if a training objective concerns knowledge of the new tax law, the training method must induce the trainee to produce or construct that knowledge in one or more ways. So called 'error-based' instructional methods (Ivancic & Hesketh, 1995/1996) attempt to increase cognitive production by requiring the trainees to analyze and correct the source of their own errors. An interesting question is whether such error-based instruction would be differentially effective depending upon the type of capability.

At this point, if the above issues have been addressed, we have arrived at some basic specifications for training objectives, training content, and generic instructional methods. It is only now that the pros and cons of alternative brand names techniques (e.g., specific information presentation media, specific simulators, etc.) become relevant.

While brand names can vary in terms of the validity which they reflect that capability or provide the opportunity to produce the relevant responses, the bulk of the potential utility of a training design has already been captured by the preceding steps. In this regard, it is worth noting that buying the latest brand name techniques is where many instances of training design actually start.

Historically, this is also the point where much of the research on learning and skill acquisition has been concentrated. That is, the training objectives, training content, and generic instructional methods are taken as given and the research questions focus on the optimality of the *learning conditions* incorporated in a specific instructional method. Some of these learning conditions have received a 'new look' in the last 10–20 years.

EFFECTIVE INSTRUCTIONAL CONDITIONS

For purposes of maximizing acquisition, retention and transfer, research questions have revolved around the effectiveness with which instructional methods (a) provide appropriate goals for the learner (trainer-generated, self-generated, or cooperatively determined), (b) provide appropriate guidance for goal accomplishment, (c) provide the opportunity for appropriate kinds of practice, (d) provide the appropriate types of feedback, and (e) keep the learner motivated and interested. These are in fact the classic 'learning principles' (Blum & Naylor, 1968).

The three parameters that have received the broadest attention are goals, practice, and feedback. Issues pertaining to learner interest and motivation go far beyond the instructional method itself and will be discussed later in this chapter as an important domain of individual differences critical for learning.

Goals

As discussed above, the training objectives constitute goals for the training designer; and these objectives are conceptually and substantively distinct from the goals provided to the learner during the period of instruction. The last 30 years have generated a large research literature on goals as a powerful determinant of individual performance (Locke, 2000; Locke & Latham, 1990). While we do not want to recapitulate all of that, it does deal with a number of issues that are particularly relevant for training.

Goals can influence performance via one or more of three general mechanisms (Kanfer, 1990). First, goals can inform people as to where they should direct their efforts. Second, goals can provide the standards or criteria upon which outcomes or rewards are contingent. Third, goals can set the occasion for using different strategies for goal attainment, as when the individual concludes that simply increasing effort will not by itself lead to goal attainment. All three of these mechanisms assume that the individual has made a commitment to the goal.

Within the instructional process itself, goals can be difficult or easy, general or specific, and distal (i.e., the final learning objectives) or proximal (i.e., subgoals for different parts of the instructional sequence). Other things being equal, specific difficult goals, if they are accepted, lead to higher performance. However, in the instructional setting other things may not be equal. Difficult goals may not be accepted because the costs outweigh the benefits of goal attainment and people differ in how they evaluate the positive and negative outcomes of goal attainment (Kanfer, 1990). Also, providing proximal goals too early in instruction or too frequently may direct too much attention away from the mastery process itself (Kanfer, 1990; Kanfer, Ackerman, Murtha, Dugdale & Nelson, 1994). However, despite their attentional costs, specific

proximal goals may be more necessary for low ability or poorly prepared learners as a means for guiding their efforts (Snow, 1989). An important conditional here is that the nature of the proximal goals themselves must not induce low self efficacy for achieving them (Mitchell et al., 1994).

The goals for trainees incorporated in the instructional method may be congruent with or divergent from the 'sense making' goal retranslations made by the trainees themselves (Baldwin & Magjuka, 1997). For example, individuals may see the goals for technology training as a signal that management thinks they are less than competent which in turn has deleterious effects on their commitment and motivation (Klein & Ralls, 1997). In general, the goals communicated to the trainees by the instructional methods are a critical influence on learning and deserve careful attention. Again, it is important to keep in mind that the training objectives are directed at the training designer and are conceptually distinct from the goals presented to the trainees by the instructional methods.

Feedback

There are thousands of citations in the feedback literature and it is a venerable topic in training and instruction. Traditionally, feedback has been seen as having both motivational and informational properties and instructional methods should provide lots of it; that is, feedback is good. Relative to occupational training there have been three influential reviews of feedback research and theory (Balzer, Doherty & Conner, 1989; Ilgen, Fisher & Taylor, 1979; Kluger & DeNisi, 1996), which have provided an increasingly differentiated view of the role feedback plays in instruction.

Feedback can come from several sources (Blum & Naylor, 1968). It can be intrinsic (information generated internally such as when the adjustment to a control 'feels right') or extrinsic (information from external sources); and if extrinsic, it can be primary (based on the individual's self evaluation of external events) or secondary (based on someone else's evaluation of the trainee's performance). The general findings have been that feedback has significant effects on behavior to the extent that all appropriate sources are used (e.g., does the instructional method allow people to monitor their own performance), it is relatively frequent, and it is not delayed. In addition, feedback must be accurate, and accepted as accurate. Acceptance is a function of a number of factors (Ilgen et al., 1979) such as the perceived expertise, reliability, power, and attractiveness of the source. Also, the effects of positive and negative feedback are not equal (positive feedback is generally better). However, negative feedback can have positive effects and positive feedback can have negative effects. For example, if feedback is too frequent it can decrease the perceived validity of the feedback (e.g., the individual begins to question the reasons for all the attention).

The latest review of the feedback literature (Kluger & DeNisi, 1996), and its associated meta analysis of feedback effects on performance, made some provocative hypotheses in an attempt to explain why (a) the effects of feedback were negative in almost 40% of the controlled studies, (b) feedback sign was not a significant moderator of feedback effects, and (c) verbal praise was worse than no feedback at all. In the Kluger and DeNisi review, the critical parameters seemed to be (1) whether increased effort or more knowledge and skill were the critical determinants of performance increments, (2) whether the content of the feedback was a general statement tied to the overall outcome versus being focused on specific performance determinants that could be changed (which they called cue feedback), and (3) the confidence or self-efficacy of the feedback receiver.

In general, they suggest that overall outcome feedback (particularly verbal praise) does not work either because it directs attention away from the task and toward global ego-centered self evaluations or because performance cannot be increased by a simple increase in effort. Virtually the only conditions under which general positive feedback might have positive effects on performance are when effort level is the primary determinant of performance and the learner suffers from low self-confidence; which may be a relatively rare set of conditions for occupational training. It follows that feedback should always be informational (it really has no useful incentive or reward function in the training context) and directed at the specific knowledge and skill determinants of performance. Consequently, negative feedback can contain valuable information that will lead to performance improvement, if the individual is committed to the training performance goals. Goal commitment itself must come from other sources.

Practice

Practice, like feedback, is a venerated learning principle that has generated a large experimental research literature and which has also undergone some rethinking. Perhaps the extreme position is taken by Ericsson and his colleagues (Ericsson & Charness, 1994, Ericsson & Smith, 1991) who argue that the primary determinant of a very high level performance is many years of *deliberate, guided* practice, and not basic aptitudes, which can get one only so far. Deliberate practice is very goal oriented (e.g., Jack Nicklaus asserts that he never made a swing on the golf practice range without a specific goal in mind) and virtually always under expert guidance. In Kluger and DeNisi's terms, the specific cue oriented feedback must be from the most knowledgeable source possible. This assertion has sparked much debate (Howe, Davidson & Sloboda, 1998) over the efficacy of stable traits vs. training and experience as the fundamental determinants of expertise. One element that seems less controversial is the recognition that an important determinant of expert performance often involves the development of critical skills to automaticity via appropriate amounts of practice (Rogers et al., 1997). This again raises the issue of what performance determinants represent consistent skills and how much practice it takes to reach automaticity.

The research cited by Ericsson and Charness to support the value of deliberate guided practice deals primarily with expertise in athletics, the performing arts, or very specialized cognitive skills. It is not clear whether the payoff would be equally large for occupations which are made up of large sets of complex tasks that require very controlled processing.

The type and duration of practice can also be discussed in the context of performance in the training setting versus performance in the actual job setting (Ehrenstein et al., 1997). Schmidt and Bjork (1992) argue that very frequent practice in the training environment may not be optimal, and could even be harmful, for retention and transfer if every practice trial deals with exactly the same task and feedback conditions, and exactly the same context (Arthur et al., 1997; Shute & Gawlick, 1995). This might promote the highest level of skill acquisition in the shortest possible time in the training environment but it could harm retention and transfer for several reasons. First, frequent repetition of the same set of responses to the same task requirements in the training environment may not represent the relevant variation in the transfer situation. Negative transfer could occur. Second, making things 'easy' for the trainee will reduce processing demands during training and detract from the 'production effort' that facilitates long-term storage and retention. Third, providing continual external feedback from secondary sources makes it less likely that individuals will learn to correctly interpret their own performance errors and provide their own feedback, which they must do in the transfer environment. Consequently, practice sessions in training should vary the frequency of feedback, the conditions under which practice trials are conducted, and the nature of the task requirements themselves. Practice also consumes training time and there is always a trade off between time devoted to practice and time devoted to presenting additional training content (Carroll, 1997). Finally, designing practice to minimize learner errors may not be optimal for complex skills that are dominated by controlled processing. Here, errors and the steps taken to correct them can be very beneficial for both retention and transfer (Carlson, Lundy & Schneider, 1992; Frese et al., 1991; Ivancic & Hesketh, 1995/1996).

In sum, the use of goals, feedback, and practice to optimize the effects of instructional methods on acquisition, retention, and transfer incorporates a complex set of contingencies that must be taken into account. Under a broad set of circumstances, certain kinds of goals, feedback strategies, or practice procedures can do more harm than good.

ALTERNATIVE MODELS FOR TRAINING DESIGN

Although we think of the previous list of design parameters as a set of universals, others might see it as something that can be cast against alternatives. Most discussions of alternative 'models' for training design begin with pointed criticism of either the 'traditional approach' (McGehee & Thayer, 1961) or the Instructional Systems Development (ISD) model (Vineberg & Joyner, 1980), which are in fact the primary antecedents of our list of universals.

The traditional approach is said to view the training function as a narrowly constrained micro enterprise that focuses only on the individual trainee as a unit of analysis and only on individual end-of-course performance as the criterion of interest. It does not view the training function as a subsystem within a larger and very complex organizational system, which it obviously is (Kozlowski & Salas, 1997; Noe, 1999).

Instructional Systems Development which grew out of the earlier work of Gagné (1962), Gagné and Briggs (1979), and Glaser (1976) has had its most intense applications in the military services (Vineberg & Joyner, 1980). In its worst light, it is described as based on overly detailed task and needs analyses, specification of a large number of very narrow and specific training objectives that compulsively follow a certain format, and rigid prescriptions for training content. Presumably this presents a very structured experience for the trainee who must move through it in lockstep fashion. According to the current critics (e.g., Gordon & Zemke, 2000), ISD is counter productive in today's world because (1) It is too slow and clumsy and bogs the design process down in almost endless detailed prescriptions; (2) It is not a true science-based technology and cannot make unambiguous substantive prescriptions for how training should be designed. It is simply a long detailed set of procedural steps to follow; (3) It produces bad training designs because it concentrates on procedural checklists, loses sight of the original business purpose (i.e., the critical training needs to be met), and is geared to the slowest and most ignorant trainees, resulting in courses that are dull and uninteresting; and (4) The ISD world view is that the training designer is all knowing and authoritative while the trainee is totally resourceless and needs to be guided every step of the way; and this flies in the face of the obvious fact that many trainees are very resourceful and manage their own learning quite well.

There is probably some truth and much self-serving caricature represented in these current criticisms. Prawat and Worthington (1998) have pointed out that a not uncommon sequence in educational and instructional theory development is that new innovations, while they may be well understood by the original perpetrators, are usually not specified well enough for subsequent users to prevent all manner of misapplication. This will usually generate enough bad examples to energize the critics and generate a backlash. However, 'evidence' for the shortcomings of the traditional models usually consist of vaguely described examples that most would agree represent bad practice. As far as we know, no systematic evidence or documentation exists to substantiate the criticisms.

The alternatives to the traditional models almost always consist of a very sketchily described success story implemented by the critic. However, not all critics of ISD and the traditional model are totally self-serving. Over the past 10–20 years, the most recognizable and thoughtful alternative positions regarding training design seem to be the following.

Design by Participation

This model argues that the most effective training design results from the full participation of trainers and trainees on questions of specifying training needs and objectives, designing course content, and choosing instructional methods. Argyris (1977, 1992) has been the primary advocate of this position which he calls double loop learning. Participation should lead to higher trainee motivation, more relevant specifications of training needs, and more relevant training content. Traditional models are simply too authoritarian or 'theory X'. Participation as a model of training design is also advocated by Wlodkowski (1985) and Knowles (1984). However, Baldwin and Magjuka (1997) argue, on the basis of their own review, that the available evidence simply does not support the central tenets of the participation model. That is, it does not consistently lead to higher achievement of more relevant training goals; and participation may even create expectations that cannot be met.

Self-Design, Constructivism, and the Minimalist Position

Many of the criticisms of ISD in the organizational training literature assert that most individuals are highly motivated to improve their skills and will seek training opportunities to do so virtually on a continuous basis (Carroll, 1997). That is, given half a chance, people will design their own training experiences to meet their needs. Consequently, the responsibility of the organizational training system is to provide resources for people to use as well as to provide opportunities for organizational members to share experiences about how they are trying to meet their training and development needs. Relying on individuals to shape their own training experiences is in part driven by the perception that organizations and jobs are changing so fast that procedures that depend on stability and continuity in jobs are not appropriate.

This position is not unlike the humanist position represented in the debate between Gagné and Kneller (Kneller, 1972) some time ago. That is, trainees should not be constrained by prescribed training objectives and specified content structures for courses and programs. Learning is not analyzable in such terms and imposing such a structure constrains the intrinsic motivation and natural exploratory behavior of individuals and severely limits what individuals achieve.

More recently, a similar position is reflected in educational theory by the constructivist perspective (Forman & Pufall, 1988; Fosnot, 1996). Constructivism is modeled on the theoretical work of Piaget (Rieber, 1992) and asserts that learning benefits most when the students are given information, or placed in a situation, that stimulates their curiosity about why certain things happened in the past, how things work currently, or what will happen in the future. Mastery results from the trainee's subsequent exploration and attempts to construct descriptions or explanations of events and to develop responses (i.e., skills, strategies) that solve the problems about which they are curious. For example, a computerized simulation representing certain technical problems could be used to provide opportunities for the trainee to explore the nature of the problem, hypothesize possible solutions, and evaluate possible solution strategies. It is the active construction of descriptions, explanations, and skilled responses that promote learning.

Elements of the constructivist perspective are also illustrated by the 'minimalist' approach to training design described by Carroll (1997) in the context of teaching new software tools. He sees ISD as a decomposition of the overall training objectives into an exhaustive list of very small and discrete steps which must be presented, demonstrated, practiced, and tested in a specific sequence. Characterized in this way, ISD goes against the tendencies of individuals to get into things quickly, develop their own meaningful understanding of what is to be learned (i.e., sense-making), and learn what they need to know in the context in which they need to know it. Consequently, the training design should start with only the most essential information, embed the capabilities to be mastered in real tasks, rely on trainees to improvise, and perhaps

most importantly, provide quick feedback and corrective help when people make errors. This puts a premium on the anticipation of critical errors by the training design.

The Bottom-Line Systems View

This orientation constantly admonishes the training designer not to forget that the fundamental issue is that training must serve the 'business purpose' and contribute directly to the effectiveness of the organization. All else pales in comparison. The processes used to specify objectives, content, and method should be whatever works. Also, the nuances of content and method are probably overwhelmed by other elements in the training system such as the pretraining climate, the posttraining climate, the organization's real purposes for supporting training, the pretraining motivation of the trainees, the instrumentality of the program for the trainee, and so forth. Consequently, a comprehensive theory of training design must model all of the parameters that might conceivably affect whether or not the program achieves the business purpose.

A Summary of Alternatives

All the seriously stated alternatives raise good points. However, we do not think that our set of universals runs counter to any of them. Certainly the training objectives and the measures used to assess training effects must reflect important goals of the organization. This is a matter for job design and needs analysis. Training needs that speak to important goals could be relatively obvious or it could require extensive effort to specify them. Concomitantly, the organization cannot ignore the requirement that a training program must have the desired effects on the relevant determinants of performance.

Nothing in our discussion of universals precludes self-designed or participatively designed training efforts. It does not require an omnipotent, all knowing 'designer'. We simply want to argue that, even if the training experience is totally self-designed, the same set of specifications and decisions must be made. Relegating them to a black box of the consultant or learner's 'natural instincts' or 'basic intuition' is dangerous.

Nothing in this set of universals says that training content must be dumbed down to the level of the least able trainee or that a very highly structured and detailed set of instructional steps must be used with everyone, or with anyone for that matter. Certainly for many training objectives a constructivist or minimalist approach to choosing training content and training methods would be appropriate. However, our 'model' does assert that even the constructivist, or the marketing oriented consultant, must make their best effort to state as fully as possible what the intended objectives are, and what training content and training methods should be used to address them. These are difficult issues to engage but they are always present and cannot be finessed or dismissed as irrelevant.

INDIVIDUAL DIFFERENCES

Individual differences in training achievement are ubiquitous. That is, it hardly needs arguing that any modestly reliable measure of training achievement will show significant variability across trainees. However, if everyone gets the same training experience, what then accounts for these differences? Research addressing this question has also accelerated during the past 10–15 years, and increasing attention has been devoted to individual differences in cognitive and psychomotor abilities, personality factors, cognitive processes, and numerous properties of individual trainee motivation as predictors of training achievement.

Note that not all such correlations have identical implications. If the predictor variable is a stable trait that is difficult to change then multiple courses and a significant ATI are necessary to realize gain in aggregate achievement, unless selection for training is possible. If the predictor is malleable then main effects are possible.

Cognitive Ability

If prior selection is not extreme and the training content deals with cognitive capabilities then general mental ability (GMA) will predict training achievement (Lohman, 1999); and in general, there will be a modest interaction between GMA and the degree to which the instructional methods provide organization and structure for the learner (Snow, 1989). However this general conclusion is conditional on the performance criterion being a function of controlled processing (i.e., task performance that cannot be automatized). For consistent tasks, end of training performance may be better predicted by specific abilities (Ackerman, 1992). This suggests the distinct possibility of two different ATIs, one that applies during the initial stages and another that applies to the final stages, as when trainees with high versus low specific abilities (e.g., perceptual speed) benefit from different kinds of practice.

Some researchers (e.g., Hannafin, 1992; Jensen, 1998) are relatively optimistic that the recent advances in educational technology and intelligent tutoring systems, and the prospect for ever more startling developments in the future, will provide more opportunities to tailor instruction to individual ability levels and thereby increase the yield from the aptitude x treatment interaction. While the variance in individual achievement may become even greater, *all* learners could potentially attain higher levels than they would under a single treatment.

Motivation

The research on trainee motivation has increased precipitously during the past 15 years, but what does 'motivation' mean in this context? We think a reasonable position to take is that corresponding to the direction, strength, and persistence of volitional behavior, the principal dependent variables of interest are (a) the trainee's decision to attend or not attend the program, (b) the level of attention and effort the trainee decides to invest during training, and (c) whether or not the trainee chooses to finish the program. Consequently, motivation in the training context refers to the independent variables that influence these three choices.

Because it is often not possible to assess individual differences in these choice behaviors directly, a number of investigators (e.g., Colquitt & Simmering, 1998) argue that it is useful to assess individual *intentions* to commit high levels of consistent effort to a particular training program. Such a construct has been labeled *motivation to learn* by Mathieu and Martineau (1997). It represents the classic distinction between the intention to respond and the actual response or behavior (Ajzen, 1985; Ajzen & Fishbein, 1980).

The 'motivational' independent variables that serve as potential determinants of one or more of these three choices are specified by three principal theoretical positions. The *dispositional trait* models see volitional choice as a function of stable behavior tendencies (e.g., a high need for achievement) that lead to individual differences in the characteristic pattern of such choices. *Cognitive expectancy* models focus on certain cognitive evaluations of the current situation such as individual self-efficacy for being able to master the training content, the perceived instrumentality of training completion for obtaining particular outcomes, and the anticipated value (valence) of the salient outcomes. Finally, there is the *behavior analysis* view that the motivational properties of training experiences or outcomes can be known only by their effects, and the specific outcomes that most strongly reinforce the desired choices must be determined empirically.

The perspective that has received the most research attention deals with cognitive judgments in general and Bandura's notion of self-efficacy in particular (Gist, 1997). Self-efficacy, defined as the expected probability of doing well on particular training content, has a consistent positive relationship to training achievement (Mathieu & Martineau, 1997; Mathieu, Martineau & Tannenbaum, 1993). As a main effect, high pretraining self-efficacy is a pervasively good thing. Low self-efficacy should be treated by enhancing prerequisite knowledge and skill, changing course content, or changing the individual self-evaluations themselves.

Pretraining judgments of the instrumentality of training completion for obtaining valued outcomes and the expected value (valence) of those outcomes are sometimes measured directly via self-report methods and sometimes indirectly by being imbedded in self-report measures of training climate, perceived managerial and/or peer support, or organizational commitment (Colquitt, LePine & Noe, 2000). For example, an important component of training climate is the general expectation concerning the instrumentality of training completion for valued outcomes (Rouiller & Goldstein, 1993).

There is considerable evidence documenting the correlation of instrumentality and valence judgments with various representations of motivation to learn (Mathieu & Martineau, 1997). However, these relationships are potentially contaminated by self-report method variance. Using meta-analytically estimated path coefficients, Colquitt et al. (2000) have estimated the effects of cognitive expectancy judgments on training outcomes, as mediated by motivation to learn, and have reported small but significant mediated relationships. The relationships seem robust enough to argue that the training design must also pay attention to trainee instrumentality and valence judgments as main effects on trainee achievement.

Major dispositional or trait characteristics have also been shown to be related to training achievement and to motivation to learn. Measures of achievement motivation consistently yield small positive relationships with measures of training achievement and somewhat larger relationships with motivation to learn (Colquitt et al., 2000; Mathieu & Martineau, 1997). Similar results in the negative direction tend to be true for measures of anxiety and fear of failure (Kanfer & Heggestad, 1997; 1999).

The results for the major personality dimensions (e.g., the Big Five) are not quite so consistent. The Barrick and Mount (1991) meta-analysis showed a generally small positive relationship for conscientiousness and openness to experience with overall measures of training proficiency and training motivation. However, more recent analyses encompassing additional studies (Colquitt et al., 2000) show that conscientiousness may in fact be negatively related to skill acquisition. If personality represents characteristic reactions to various types of goal conditions, then highly conscientious people may spend so much attentional effort on satisfying goals that they neglect the learning task itself (Kanfer & Ackerman, 1989).

Falling between a state versus trait explanation of trainee choice behavior are two components of an individual's orientation toward goal achievement (Dweck, 1986; Dweck & Leggett, 1988). The two dimensions are variously labeled learning (or mastery) orientation and performance (or outcome) orientation, and can be defined experimentally or psychometrically. While Dweck and her colleagues began studying goal orientation in laboratory

settings with school children, the subsequent research in adult training situations has taken an individual differences approach. In this context, it is hypothesized that high scorers on mastery orientation are rewarded by, and interested in, the effort they put into the learning process. They see training as an opportunity to learn something and learning is reinforcing, even if it is difficult and filled with mistakes. They like the mastery process itself (e.g., lots of practice). In contrast, high scorers on performance orientation are rewarded by external recognition for achieving the end-of-course objectives. If the mastery process is effortful and the learner liable for making errors, it is a punishing experience for the performance-oriented, and to be avoided. Mastery-oriented people tend to believe that abilities and skills are malleable and they gravitate toward new training experiences. Performance-oriented people tend to view abilities and skills as difficult to change and they gravitate toward the familiar. Low self-efficacy should really not deter the mastery-oriented while it could be lethal for the performance-oriented.

Several attempts have been made to measure goal orientation via self-reports (e.g., Buttom, Mathieu & Zajac, 1996; Colquitt & Simmering, 1998; VandeWalle, 1997) and to predict training achievement. Conceptually, in occupational training contexts, mastery orientation should be much more adaptive than performance orientation and that has been the general result (Ford et al., 1998). Questions remain however about the construct validity of the current measures, whether mastery and performance orientation are two factors or a bipolar dimension, the degree to which goal orientations are themselves malleable and can be changed (Ames, 1992; Stevens & Gist, 1997), and the domain specificity of mastery versus performance orientation. That is, are individual goal orientations different for different domains of content (e.g., math skills vs. communication skills) or are performance orientation and mastery orientation both unidimensional? The former seems more likely but research has not yet engaged this issue.

TRANSFER OF TRAINING

At this point, a training program with certain explicit or implicit objectives, and employing a particular content structure and set of instructional events, has been provided for a particular trainee sample that exhibits within-group variance on a number of dimensions pertaining to ability and motivation. A major question then arises as to whether the capabilities acquired in training are applied in the job setting such that the relevant components of the individual's performance are improved. This is the traditional form of the transfer of training question. However, throughout the current training literature, the term transfer of training has taken on a number of different meanings that do not have identical implications. Consider the following alternative characterizations.

- Will the capabilities learned in training enhance the job performance components that were the original source of the training needs?
- Will the capabilities learned in training enhance job performance components that are related to, but not the same as, the performance factors that were the original source of training needs (e.g., supervisory performance versus team member performance)?
- Will the capabilities transfer to a new job or new set of performance requirements that are thought to require the same capabilities?
- Will mastery of knowledge capabilities transfer to job situations that require a skill capability?
- Will mastery of knowledge and/or skill capabilities transfer to job situations that require a problem solving capability?
- Will the learned capabilities lead to increases in work group or organizational performance?

These various meanings for transfer are obviously not the same, and while all may be legitimate, using the same terms for all of them creates considerable confusion.

Keeping in mind that training is intended to enhance the direct determinants of one or more components of job performance, we will restrict the term transfer to mean the use of capabilities acquired in training to achieve higher performance on specified performance factors in the actual job setting. Consequently, for example, the term would not be used to describe the generalization of practice on one task to performance on another when both are assessed in the training environment or to the covariation between capabilities mastered in training and the organization's bottom-line effectiveness (e.g., ROI). Again, both are legitimate issues, but lumping all under one collective label makes it too difficult for both researchers and practitioners to 'mean the same thing'.

Given this preferred definition, there are a number of very distinct reasons why the capabilities learned in training might fail to transfer. The trainees simply might not acquire the desired capabilities by the end of training or at least not to the necessary level. Consequently, it *is* important to know whether the training objectives were met, which is the focus of most training evaluation research. It is also possible that trainees acquire knowledge, skills, or attitudes that were not part of the training design (Klein & Ralls, 1997). These may transfer in unknown or perhaps undesired ways (e.g., as a result of their training experience, trainees concluded that management regards them as just low level cogs in a high-tech system).

Even though the intended capabilities were acquired, they are not retained or maintained for any appreciable length of time. Since retention is necessary for transfer to take place, the issue of what instructional methods best facilitate retention of the trainee capabilities are very critical. For example, for a broad range of capabilities the types of practice that maximize end of course mastery vs. retention may be different (Schmidt & Bjork, 1992; Shute & Gawlick, 1995). The optimal feedback protocol may also be different (Carroll, 1997).

If the intended capabilities are in fact mastered and retained, they still may not be transferred if the individual does not recognize the occasions that require them, as in knowing when a particular statistical concept is relevant (e.g., Lehman, Lempert & Nisbett, 1988). Negative transfer could also occur, particularly for automatized or highly practiced skills, if highly developed domains of knowledge, skills, or patterns of choice behavior are wrongly utilized in situations that call for different capabilities. For many capabilities the occasions for their use may be obvious but for others the issue of what instructional methods and conditions best facilitate such recognition is critical.

If capabilities are mastered, retained, and the former trainee recognizes when they are applicable, transfer may still not occur if the support and rewards for using the capability are not sufficient, or use of the capability is in fact punished by peers, supervisors, the management, or some other stakeholder. This is of course the focus of research on the transfer climate (Baldwin & Ford, 1988; Ford & Weissbein, 1997; Rouiller & Goldstein, 1993; Tracey, Tannenbaum & Kavanagh, 1995). For capabilities such as supervisory and management skills it has been shown to be a powerful influence.

Related to the above is a situation in which there is no opportunity to use the learned capabilities, either for actual work flow reasons or because such opportunities are not granted to the trainee by the management (Ford et al., 1992).

Even if the support and rewards for utilizing trained capabilities far outweigh the negative outcomes, and even if the relevant capabilities have been mastered, retained and the individuals fully know when to use them, transfer may still not occur if the individuals choose not to use what they know because of low self-confidence or low self-efficacy (Eden & Aviram, 1995; Gist, 1997; Saks, 1995). Just as self-efficacy can influence end-of-training achievement, it can also attenuate transfer to the work setting if the individual lacks confidence about being able to successfully use what they have learned. Thus the training system must worry both about self-efficacy for completing the course and self-efficacy for using what's learned back in the job setting (Gist, 1997).

Even if the intended capabilities have been retained, the organization supports their use, and individual self-efficacy is fine, individuals could choose not to use the learned capabilities because they believe it would not help their performance. That is, they do not accept the validity of the training objectives. Finally, transfer will not occur if in fact the trained capabilities are not relevant determinants of the critical performance factors. Sometimes the training content and instructional methods could be blamed for what are really mistakes in work design or needs analysis.

If there are multiple distinct reasons for a failure to transfer then there must be multiple distinct remedies. It is a complex issue that is not well-represented by the traditional experimental literature on learning and skill acquisition.

EVALUATIONS OF TRAINING EFFECTS

Probably the most frequently posed question regarding training effects is, 'Did the program work?' However, this implies both a unidimensional criterion and a dichotomous outcome. While there may be a few exceptions, as when the training program is for the sole purpose of learning the location of the nearest fire extinguisher and the trainee either knows the location or does not know it (Sackett & Mullen, 1993), virtually all training programs have more than one objective and most capabilities do not fit the model of a true dichotomy.

Based on the framework used in this chapter, what we would like to know about training effects are the answers to questions such as (1) to what extent did the trainees acquire the capabilities specified by the objectives, (2) to what extent were the capabilities retained over time, (3) to what extent did the learned capabilities transfer to the work setting, and (4) if the specified capabilities were not mastered, or retained, or transferred when the climate was supportive and the occasion was appropriate, why not? Was it because of flawed objectives, inappropriate training content, faulty instructional methods and conditions, unanticipated constraints in the training system, motivational constraints on trainee choice behavior, or deficiencies in prerequisite abilities, knowledge and skills, or dispositional traits?

Historically, what the training literature provides are comparative evaluations of training methods, as in programmed instruction vs. conventional instruction, cooperative learning vs. conventional instruction, multimedia instruction vs. single mode instruction, behavior modeling vs. lecture/discussion, and so forth. It would be much more helpful to summarize research around specific substantive training problems and attempt to specify the optimal training content, instructional methods, learning conditions, and trainee prerequisite characteristics for achieving and retaining the desired capabilities.

To a certain extent, that has begun to happen during the past 10–20 years. As a background for reviewing a major example of need centered research, we would first like to summarize the results of a broad meta analysis of training evaluation results carried out by Carlson (1997).

A Meta-Analysis

Studies were included in the meta-analysis if they (a) dealt with occupationally relative training for normal adults, (b) included one or more actual training interventions, (c) used a control group or both pre and post measures, and (d) permitted the computation of effect sizes. A comprehensive search going back to approximately 1940, yielded 167 studies (42 unpublished) and 574 effect sizes of various kinds. Studies were categorized by decade and the 1970s emerged as the high-water mark for relatively well-controlled training evaluations (70 of the 167). Studies were coded on various moderator variables including type of experimental design, type of criterion measure, the length of time between the conclusion of training and the measurement of training effects, and by the general type of 'instructional' strategy that was used. Unfortunately, they were not coded by substantive differences in training objectives (e.g., training managerial problem solving, interpersonal skills, electronic troubleshooting, etc.).

Across all studies the corrected grand mean for the difference between experimental and control and pre and post measures over all conditions is 1.03 standard deviations. When studies are grouped by type of criterion, the mean effect sizes range from 1.78 SDs for knowledge-based measures to 1.14 to skills-based measures to .52 for 'outcome' measures. The third category refers to job performance-based measures that are not directly parallel to the training objectives (e.g., supervisor ratings of job performance). For criteria categorized as attitudinal (e.g., expressed commitment to the organization), the mean effect size was .43. Studies were also classified into those which used an end-of-training measure and those for which the criterion measure was obtained sometime after training was concluded. The effect sizes for immediate vs. delayed criterion assessment were 1.18 and .76 respectively. While there was considerable variability in the delay period and no information is provided about whether the delayed measure represents transfer or simply retention, the relatively small difference between immediate and delayed effects is reassuring.

The general picture from Carlson's meta-analysis is that training indeed has large effects, on the average, but results are also characterized by considerable variability about the mean, even after corrections for artifacts. Unfortunately, because such variables were not coded, it is not possible to account for this variability via the training objective, the elements of training design, individual differences, organizational systems, or their interactions.

An Example of Objective Centered Research

An example of a research stream that deserves more emulation pertains to instruction in the interpersonal skills relevant for peer leadership, team member performance and supervisory performance. One major milestone was the development, by Goldstein and Sorcher (1974), of a modeling/role play/feedback-based program to teach specific interpersonal skills to supervisors of the so-called hard to employ. The program appeared to reduce turnover and absenteeism to a considerable degree, which led to more widespread use of this kind of program and to a broad range of research efforts (Decker & Nathan, 1985; Kraut, 1976; Latham & Saari, 1979). In general, when well-defined learning points, well-constructed model video tapes, and a variety of role playing practice and feedback opportunities are provided the program will produce significant gains in specific interpersonal skills that are retained and transfer to the work setting. For example, Latham and Saari (1979) facilitated transfer by also training the managers of the trainees and by asking the trainees to try out their newly trained skills back in their work setting and to bring their experiences back to the training sessions for further examination.

Subsequently, other investigators have evaluated the effects of trainer vs. trainee produced training objectives (Hogan, Hakel & Decker, 1986), additional cognitive rehearsal (Decker, 1982), modeling both positive and negative examples of the skill capabilities (Baldwin, 1992), and the incremental value of supplemental training in goal setting vs. training in self-management skill (Gist, Bavetta & Stevens, 1990; Stevens & Gist, 1997). Most recently, May and Kahnweiler (2000) evaluated the incremental effects of additional mastery practice in which each trainee was given intensive one-on-one skills practice with the trainer. Mastery practice improved skill retention but did not increase transfer as assessed by 360 degree feedback techniques. Subsequent interviews suggested that during the transfer measurement period there were actually few opportunities to use the new skills. The results also suggested that the training time and effort needed to master such skills may be seriously underestimated. Many trainees did not achieve the desired level of demonstrable skill by the end of the training, and for those who had the additional 'mastery practice' there was considerable skill loss over a period of just a few weeks. Such findings contrast sharply with the increasing pressure to shorten training times, reduce training costs, and constrain instructional methods to those that are internet deliverable (Pescuric & Byham, 1996).

A brief but reasonable summary of this research record might be that (a) these are difficult skills that probably require more practice than is generally acknowledged, (b) intense one-on-one guided practice from an expert, mental rehearsal, and frequent classroom role play sessions are all valuable, (c) increasing cognitive engagement with the learning objectives by asking trainees to infer the objectives from the model's performance and asking trainees to report on their attempt to use their new skills back at work improve retention and transfer, and (d) variation in models in terms of their levels of proficiency, the content of the scenarios, and the context in which they take place are beneficial for retention and transfer. This body of research also demonstrated that such complex skills have both malleable (i.e., trainable) and trait-like components (e.g., level of introversion/extroversion) which to some degree constrain the efficacy of a training solution (May & Kahnweiler, 2000). The trainable components may also include both skills that are potentially automatizable (e.g., never becoming defensive when criticized) and those which are not (e.g., using negotiating strategies that are optimal for the occasion). Gelfand and Dyer (2000) have also demonstrated the cultural relativity of certain interpersonal skills.

In sum, the field of training would benefit a great deal if more (much more) research focused on how best to achieve particular substantive training objectives that are judged to be broadly important and critical. Consequently, while a worldwide analysis of critical training needs certainly does not exist, a brief summary of the pieces that do exist might be useful.

CURRENT AND FUTURE TRAINING NEEDS

Many observers (e.g., see Howard, Osterman & Carnevale, 1995; Ilgen & Pulakos, 1999; Wilpert, 2000) argue that we are currently in a period of great change, worldwide. Economies are becoming increasingly interdependent, developments in digital and biological technologies are virtually revolutionary in nature, innovation in research and development moves at a faster and faster pace, organizations are trying to redesign themselves to be as knowledgeable and adaptable as possible, and the education and training enterprises are struggling to deal with it all. It is reasonable to ask whether these dynamic events create general training needs that are critical for broad sectors of the global economy. While there is not space here for a lengthy review, we think that the focus of current professional opinion, as expressed in the training and development literature, is reasonably represented by at least the following general training needs:

1. The national educational systems that prepare individuals for work roles vary widely across countries (Ashton, Sung & Turbin, 2000). However, economic globalization is acting to make skill demands more similar across nations. What capabilities, that are amenable to training, are high priority needs for new entrants to the modern work force? These are sometimes referred to as *workforce readiness skills*.
2. People who have entered the labor force recently face the prospect of frequent changes in their work responsibilities over the length of their work life. The nature of organizations and the pace of change will simply demand it. As a result, individuals will need well-developed *skills* in the *self-management* of their own *training* and *career planning*.
3. What are the generic substantive skills that will enhance the individual's *adaptability* to job changes? Are there such *adaptability skills* that can be distinguished from self-directed learning skills and from general dispositions such as openness to experience?
4. Increasingly, people must be able to operate effectively in teams and newly formed work relationships as they move from one work situation to another. What are the *teamwork* capabilities, amenable to training, that are critical determinants of such performance requirements?
5. At virtually all levels of organizations, people are crossing international boundaries to fill jobs and will probably do so at an increasing rate. This situation varies from organizations hiring foreign nationals to fill positions that cannot be filled by the host country labor force, to global organizations sending their own employees to fill positions in their international operations. These are two very different kinds of expatriates. Do they have common training needs? Are there critical training needs that are unique to each? Are there trainable *expatriate skills*?
6. Lastly, what are the *critical leadership capabilities* that will serve organizations well in this new era?

The match between current research and development and this set of critical training issues is very uneven. We will try to summarize where research is attempting to address these issues and where it is not. The emphasis here is on the research literature and not on the sheer availability of training programs that purport to address each of these training needs. Again, the discussion cannot be framed as a point for point match with the above list because some research areas cover more than one of the named training needs, while for others no training literature currently exists (e.g., 'adaptability').

Work Readiness Skills

In the US, over the past 10–15 years, a number of government agencies, public policy groups, and professional organizations have attempted to identify the knowledge and skill capabilities that are critically important for effective performance in the twenty-first century economy. The methods used to identify such capabilities usually involved employer surveys or queries directed at expert panels. Specifications for such employment skills were produced by the National Academy of Sciences (1984), The Secretary's Commission on the Achievement of Necessary Skills (US Department of Labor, 1992), the American Society of Training and Development (Carnevale, Gainer & Meltzer, 1990), the RAND Corporation (Bikson & Law, 1994), the Employability Skills Task Force of the State of Michigan (1989), and the US Office of Technology Assessment (OTA, 1995). A similar effort was conducted in Australia by the National Board of Employment, Education, and Training (1992). In the UK the issues are addressed by the Vocational Education and Training (VET) system and its attempts to develop occupational qualifications standards (Matlay, 1999).

There is considerable communality across these reports and the results have been summarized by O'Neil, Allred and Baker (1997) in terms of the principal categories of knowledge and skill capabilities that emerged. The major categories seen as most critical are the following:

1. The most fundamental is represented by a relatively high level of proficiency in the basic skills of mathematics, reading, expository writing, speaking, and listening. Overall the need is for enhanced writing, math, and communication skills that are appropriate for the technical, fast paced work environment.
2. The second category includes general higher order cognitive skills which have such labels as problem solving and decision making, critical thinking, and creative thinking. Such skills are viewed as critical for the new labor force entrant because of the frequently forecasted need to deal with new problems and adapt to changing conditions.
3. The third category represents attempts to specify the components of interpersonal and teamwork skills that are important for working effectively with coworkers or clients/customers. They include such components as negotiation skill, accepting criticism constructively, and a willingness to participate with others in solving problems or making decisions.
4. The fourth category deals with attitudinal or choice behavior capabilities pertaining to personal dispositions, and includes variables such as being conscientious and responsible, showing motivation and goal commitment, and having high self-esteem. Also included in this

category are self-management and career planning skills.

While there is considerable consensus regarding the labeling of these training needs, the various needs surveys themselves do not provide very much substantive specification for the variables and for how they might be assessed or trained (O'Neil et al., 1997). For example, when attempts were made to develop assessment methods for the SCANS skills, the effort failed because of the lack of content specifications (Nash & Korte, 1997). Overall, much research and development must be done before these kinds of training needs can be addressed systematically.

Self-Directed Learning Skills

While its entry into organizational training discourse might be fairly recent, the concept of self-directed learning (SDL) or self-managed instruction is not new; and as with most such labels, it can be defined broadly or narrowly. In its broadest connotation, self-directed learning can refer to any training experience that is not mandated by an employer, professional association, regulatory body, or so on. Perhaps a more useful construal is to focus on a process of needs assessment, objective setting, course selection, enhancement of trainee (i.e., self-) motivation, and self-assessment of training outcomes that is the responsibility of the individual trainee and over which individuals have total (or near total) discretion. That is, can individuals be their own needs analyst, training designer, and evaluator? An even narrower perspective is to restrict SDL to learning on one's own totally outside the context of available training programs. However, it seems counterproductive to push the concept this far. In the occupational setting, many potential training experiences are available and whether or not the individual utilizes them effectively is an important issue.

Currently, self-directed learning skill is perceived to be critical for a successful employment history in the twenty-first century global economy, regardless of national or cultural boundaries. The literature on SDL is already extensive (London, 1995; Long and Morris, 1995; Schmidt, 2000). The International Self-Directed Learning Symposium is in its fourteenth year (Straka, 1999). Probably the most work on SDL is related to the concern with adult education and lifelong learning within the educational community (e.g., Candy, 1991). A second prominent source is medical education where the fundamental concern is the need to 'keep current' for the rest of one's career after formal training ends (e.g., Miflin, Campbell & Price, 2000). However, as the result of organizational downsizing, attention to SDL among employers is growing (Brockner & Lee, 1995), but is still heavily concentrated on management career planning and development.

For purposes of developing SDL skills, training needs and instructional objectives tend to be modeled in two principal ways. Perhaps the dominant view is that SDL effectiveness is primarily a function of motivational determinants (Brookfield, 1986). For example, individuals will self-manage their own training to the extent that their self-efficacy for being able to do so is high and the perceived instrumentality of successful self-direction for worthwhile outcomes is also high. In addition to such cognitive-expectancy determinants, a motivational model could also include more dispositional determinants and argue that the individual's engagement with SDL is also a function of positive attitudes towards skill improvements for their own sake and individual levels of intrinsic motivation for mastering a particular content area.

A contrasting view is to portray the training objective as the enhancement of specific cognitive skills in needs assessment, training design, and training evaluation. That is, everyone should become their own needs analyst, course designer, and evaluator. Obviously, almost everyone does these things to some extent already. The question is whether such skills have been developed enough to permit the degree of self-directed learning that will be required in the future.

The general issue is whether motivational enhancements or skills training interventions would have the greatest payoff. It seems relatively obvious that both are involved, but that their relative criticality most likely varies as a function of the target group. Many technical/professional incumbents may already be highly motivated to constantly upgrade their skills; and the principal issues are how to do that and how to know if the training objectives have been achieved. In contrast, for such training needs as acquiring basic literacy and communication skills, overcoming low self-efficacy may be a bigger problem.

In adult education in general, as it is modeled and researched from the general education perspective, the concern is primarily with the motivational antecedents of successful SDL and how to generate and sustain self-efficacy, instrumentality, and intrinsic interest (Candy, 1991). Somewhat in contrast, medical education tends to focus on acquiring both SDL skills and the perception that continuing education is instrumental for an effective career in medical practice. The most favored training method for doing this is commonly referred to as problem-based learning, or PBL (Blumberg & Michael, 1992). In our nomenclature, PBL focuses on problem solving capabilities and requires the student to generate the problem definitions (e.g., complex diagnoses), potential solutions, and evaluations of alternative solutions. Supposedly this kind of training experience will promote effective self-management of continuing education.

Grow (1991) and Miflin et al. (2000) argue that it is useful to view the mastery of SDL as a developmental process which must proceed from a very structured instructor-centered training environment to a much more unstructured 'student'-controlled environment. Such a developmental process would permit building both SDL self-efficacy and SDL skills as the training assumes more and more control over their own instructional experience. While such a model may be appropriate for long courses of instruction such as graduate school, professional school, or high level technical training, it may not fit quite as well for occupations which have a much shorter training perspective. In any event, as outlined in our discussion of training universals and individual differences in responses to instruction, both teaching cognitive SDL skills and developing individual motivation for using SDL to obtain valued outcomes are critical considerations.

Research on the effectiveness with which training can improve SDL proficiency is very sparse. For example, while there is evidence that problem-based learning in medical education will provide higher frequencies of SDL behaviors in medical education itself (Blumberg & Michael, 1992), it is still not known whether such training outcomes will lead to more effective continuing education once the physician leaves the university environment (Schmidt, 2000). It is also possible for SDL training to have negative effects. Kossek, Roberts, Fisher and Demarr (1998) assessed the results of an employer-sponsored training program in developing career self-management skills by surveying experimental and control groups both before training and 6–8 months after training. The frequencies (as self-reported) of self-management behaviors such as seeking feedback about one's own performance and acting to increase job mobility were lower for the trained groups than the untrained groups. Over the course of the training itself, self-efficacy for career self-management, attitudes towards feedback seeking, and the perceived instrumentality of training all decreased. An increased awareness on the part the trainee of how much they were *not* now doing and a back-lash against the perceived goals of management for sponsoring such training were offered as explanations.

In sum, training to increase self-directed learning skill is not a simple issue. We must learn much more about what the knowledge and skill structure of SDL really is and how to deal with the complexity of the motivational issues that surround it.

Training the High Performance Team

Attention to team training has grown exponentially during the past 10–20 years. It is driven by at least the perception that the 'high performance team' is a critical element in the design of organizations that will be effective in the global economy. The high performance team, contrasted to the traditional work group, is characterized by a shared commitment to high performance goals, considerable cross-training, and team self-management in the sense that many of the management functions (work scheduling, goal setting, performance monitoring, cost control, etc.) are the collective responsibility of the team. If this organizational form is of increasing importance, and evidence suggests that it is (National Research Council, 1999), then important questions concerning team training needs forcefully present themselves.

Issues concerning team training needs and team performance can be set in a horrifically large literature on group phenomena dealing with theory, research, and practice. For example, within social psychology there is more than a 75-year history of research on the individual, situational, and social process determinants of small group dynamics and performance (e.g., Hare, 1962; McGrath, 1966, 1984; Shaw, 1976; Shepperd, 1993), including a long record of research on individual vs. group problem solving (Hill, 1982; Paulus, 2000), and the effects of participation in decision making on group performance and group member satisfaction (Likert, 1967; Sagie, 1997). Also, much of the literature on leadership and supervision is concerned with the influence of the leader on the attitudes and behavior of the work group members (Maier & Sashkin, 1971). This literature tends to be prescriptive and deals with roles of the leader in setting group goals, maintaining the motivation and commitment of the group members, and facilitating the coordination and problem solving performance of the group. It is these parameters of leader influence that are now prescribed as the responsibility of the team. Finally, a large part of organizational development (OD) is concerned with interventions that change the interpersonal processes in groups and teams. The OD concern for team functioning began with the T-group movement in the 1950s (French & Bell, 1984) and is still very much a part of team development from that perspective (Porras & Robertson, 1992).

The current high performance team concept is a direct descendent of the development of the autonomous work group at Volvo (Walton, 1985) and the study of sociotechnical work systems at Tavistock by Trist and his colleagues (Pasmore et al., 1982; Trist & Bamforth, 1951). The autonomous work group experiments at the Gaines pet food processing plant and the Rushton Coal Mine (Goodman, Devadas & Hughson, 1988) illustrate some critical advantages and disadvantages of self-managed teams as they operate within a larger system.

Taken together, these different streams of research and theory have investigated a wide range of issues regarding the performance and viability of groups and teams. Research and development on the high performance team ignores this long history at its peril.

The high performance team as described above is not the only kind of team with which team training could be concerned (Guzzo & Shea, 1992). For example, a *task force* made up of people who had not previously worked together could be assembled for a brief duration to accomplish a specific purpose. *Advisory* groups or *review* boards made up of people with specific expertise could be in existence for a relatively long period of time but actually operate as a team only for brief periods. Another distinct form is the *action* team which trains more or less continuously but puts its training into practice only for brief periods. Military crews and sports teams are in this category.

These 'types' are illustrative of a number of parameters characterizing teams that are critical for team training design. First, the specific substantive goals the team is to pursue will have an important influence on team training needs. For example, a review board could be responsible for giving the best advice possible or for making actual regulatory decisions. Second, the relative stability of team memberships will influence the extent to which a group of individuals can or should be trained as an intact group. Third, the way in which the contributions of the individual group members are linked together will influence the determination of training needs and training design. Goodman, Lerch and Mukhopadhyay (1994) described the major kinds of within-group linkages, varying from contributions being totally independent (e.g., each team member produces their own output without the need to rely on other team members) to teams in which the efforts of the individual members are sequential, to teams in which there is total interdependence among all team members in real time and a very high level of sustained coordination is required.

Cast against the above considerations, much of the theory and research on team training as reflected in Swezey and Salas (1992b), Cannon-Bowers, Salas, Tannenbaum and Mathieu (1995), Guzzo and Salas (1995), Salas and Cannon-Bowers (1997), and O'Neil, Chung and Brown (1997), is relatively narrow in scope. It tends to be focused on 2 or 3-person teams of the military crew type which have specific prescribed responsibilities for achieving goals that are a function of specific skills. Larger ongoing production, service, or research teams faced with multiple and frequently unstructured problems, and who are liable for long term motivational and goal commitment issues, have not yet received much training research attention. However, it is relatively early in the game and there is much more to come.

In spite of the relative narrowness of the team training literature, it still may be useful to summarize what it has to say about team training needs, without getting too bogged down in boxes and arrows.

Trainable Determinants of Team Performance

If team training needs are defined as determinants of team performance that are amenable to improvement via training, then a substantive model of team performance would be very helpful. However, as is historically the case for the individual, most of the conceptual attention is devoted to the independent variable side, and relatively little to the dependent variable (i.e., the criteria for team performance). In the box and arrow models it tends to be represented simply by a label in a box without further explication. Hackman (1990) may be one of the few exceptions when he builds upon previous small group research and argues there are three principal components of team performance: (1) the degree to which the team accomplishes the substantive goals assigned to it, (2) the degree to which the team provides a rewarding experience for its members such that they choose to remain committed to its goals, and (3) the degree to which the team makes improvements in its skills, resources, and procedures. These three dimensions may have different determinants. Keeping this point in mind, a brief synthesis of the trainable determinants of team performance might look like the following.

The technical knowledge and skill of the individual group members Technical is defined broadly. It could refer to surgical techniques, customer service skill, or physical skills. Cannon-Bowers and Salas (1998) make a distinction between knowledge and skill that is applicable across a range of groups (e.g., knowledge of software applications), versus being highly specific to the work of a particular group. If the within-group skill requirements differ across team member roles then the greater the degree of cross-training the better.

Teamwork knowledge and skill Team work knowledge and skills can have a collective or individual referent. Collective teamwork skills, although they are a function of what individuals do, are skills that require a group unit of analysis when attempting to assess or train them. There are three principal collective skills: (a) appropriate coordination of individual efforts, (b) the appropriate distribution of work load across team members, and (c) appropriate procedures for group problem solving and decision making. Again, labeling them as collective does not mean that individual performance components that facilitate them cannot be identified.

Attempts to specify the domain of individual teamwork knowledge and skill have increased substantially during the past 10 years. Recently, Olson (2000) reviewed these efforts and generated a synthesized set of specification; she then collected several hundred critical incidents from team members in several organizations that used the high performance team design. The question for the participants was to describe examples of effective and

Table 13.3 *A taxonomy of components of individual performance as a team member (from Olson, 2000)*

1. *Fulfilling Team-Related Task Responsibilities.* Takes ownership for and completes assigned tasks according to committed timelines. Demonstrates effort toward team goals. Does not pass work off to others or take shortcuts that compromise quality.
2. *Peer Leadership: Initiating Structure.* Helps to define goals and organize and prioritize tasks. Generates plans and strategies for task completion, identifies resources needed to meet team goals, and shares resources or guides team members to resources to help them complete their tasks.
3. *Peer Leadership: Consideration.* Provides social support and empathy, offers verbal encouragement, and acts respectfully toward other team members, especially when tasks or situations are difficult or demanding. Facilitates cohesion and effective working relationships between team members by acting honestly, communicating openly, and helping to manage or resolve conflicts. Does not embarrass team members in front of others, act impatiently, or blame others.
4. *Training Team Members/Sharing Task Information.* Shares information with team members, provides task explanations and demonstrations, answers questions, and gives timely and constructive feedback to team members. Does not withhold information about team-related tasks.
5. *Team Member Helping/Backup Relief.* Fills in or covers for team members who are overwhelmed or absent. Rearranges own schedule and demonstrates flexibility to help other team members. Puts in extra time and effort to help team members without being asked and without complaining. Does not engage in off-task activities when other team members could use help.
6. *Monitoring Performance.* Observes and is knowledgeable about the performance of other team members. Pays attention to what individual team members are doing. Evaluates progress of self and others and recognizes when team members may need help.
7. *Monitoring Team Effectiveness.* Pays attention to the team's situation, including relevant conditions, procedures, policies, resources, systems, equipment, technology, and level of team accomplishment. Notices and identifies team-relevant problems and obstacles.
8. *Individual Contributions to Problem Solving.* Helps in identifying alternative solutions, strategies, or options for dealing with problems, obstacles, or decisions. Helps in evaluating alternative courses of action, and takes preventive measures to avoid future problems.
9. *Individual Contributions to Workload Distribution/Coordination.* Contributes to and encourages discussion of work distribution, workload balance, potential workload problems, and the sequencing of team member activities. Coordinates own task activities with other team members. Does not make unnecessary requests or overload other team members.

ineffective individual teamwork performance. Different sets of expert panels were then used to either fit the critical incidents to the existing specification of team work skills or to develop a set of teamwork dimensions independently without any reference to previous work. The results of these efforts yielded the revised taxonomy of individual nonteam performance dimensions shown in Table 13.3. The implication is that each of these components' individual contributions to teamwork is trainable, although they might be under varying degrees of motivational control as well (e.g., dimension one).

Accurate and shared mental models For a team to function effectively, the members should have a common and accurate understanding of three principal features of the team: (1) the goals or objectives the team is pursuing, (2) the procedures that the team is to use to accomplish its goals, and (3) the capabilities and behavior tendencies of each group member. That is, the team member should have a shared accurate picture of what each team member can and cannot do.

Obviously there are other determinants of team performance, such as the ability and personality characteristics of the team members, the degree to which it receives management support, the available technology, and so forth. Our emphasis here is on the trainable determinants. However, it may also be the case that individual ability and personality traits may have both interactive and/or main effects on the efficacy with which training can enhance the determinants listed above. To the best of our knowledge, there have been no attempts to model the joint effects of such individual differences and specific training methods on mastery of the trainable capabilities.

Team Training Research

As noted by Salas and Cannon-Bowers (2001), empirical research focused on the effects of team training is relatively sparse, but beginning to accelerate. Two principal research venues have been the performance of two to three-person crews in military aircraft simulators (e.g., Leedom & Simon, 1995; Salas, Fowlkes, Stout, Milanovich & Prince, 1999; Stout, Salas & Fowlkes, 1997) and the performance of commercial aviation (world wide) cockpit crews (Helmreich, Merrill & Wilhelm, 1999; Wiener, Kanki & Helmreich, 1993).

Much of this work is driven by extensive analyses of the causes of aircraft accidents and the findings that faulty communication among crew members, a very hierarchical crew structure which makes crew members reluctant to challenge or question the leader (captain), failure to distribute workloads effectively, and lack of coordination in the problem solving process during emergencies are often the precipitating factors (Foushee, 1984; Orasanu, 1993). The training response in both the military and commercial sectors has been extensive (Wiener et al., 1993). The generic term for the various training programs is Crew Resource Management (CRM) training. Much of the training content for CRM deals with the capabilities related to the individual teamwork skills discussed above. Instructional methods involve information presentation via reading materials, lectures, videotape demonstrations, and small group discussions, and individual skills training via role-playing (Helmreich et al., 1999).

The commercial aviation efforts also incorporate more extensive attempts to address crew coordination, work load distribution, and problem solving capabilities that make use of CRM skills. That is, a second major training procedure, referred to as Line Oriented Flight Training (LOFT) is to place intact crews in the simulator and ask them to fly a complete trip segment (Butler, 1993). The crew must do all the usual tasks but each training session also incorporates unusual or emergency events with which the crew must deal in a coordinated and well-managed way.

The evaluation research record for the CRM and CRM/LOFT courses, while not extensive, is significant. At least as measured by knowledge tests, attitude measures, and both objective and observer rated simulator performance, teamwork skills can be improved via CRM training and there is transfer to the work setting. The commercial aviation data using the LOFT simulations is particularly important because it uses such high-fidelity simulators and has a worldwide industry focus. The cultural backgrounds of the crews do not seem to alter the training objectives, the reactions of the trainees, or the nature of the training-based behavior changes (Helmreich & Foushee, 1993). While everyone agrees the CRM training must be continuously improved and much research is needed, it does represent an example of needs analysis, training design, and program implementation and evaluation that deserves to be imitated.

In contrast to the military and commercial aviation, there is virtually no team training evaluation research dealing with the high performance work team in R&D, production, or service contexts.

Immigrants, Expatriates, and Training

In general, crossing national borders for employment purposes has been going on for centuries and is not unique to the industrial revolution or the information technology revolution. Military conflict, religious conflict, population demographics, and changes in food supplies, as well as economic forces, have all had major influences; and we will certainly not try to deal with such a broad set of issues here. However, even if attention is limited to identifying training needs for individuals who cross national borders only for the purpose of gaining a particular employment opportunity, the target groups are widely varied. They range from technical or management specialists from international organizations who are in the host country for a limited time and limited purpose, to employees of such organizations who take on long-term job assignments in the host country, to technical, professional, or production level people from one country who individually take positions with foreign organizations in another country on a long-term, but not permanent, basis; to individuals who immigrate for employment purposes with the full intention of remaining permanently in the new country. Consequently, the training enterprise could be concerned about everything from a high level corporate executive heading an international subsidiary for a year, to unskilled individuals from one country taking advantage of labor shortages in another. Currently, both phenomena take place in many different parts of the world.

Not surprisingly perhaps, management and technical personnel of international organizations working on temporary assignment in the host country have received the most attention. It has been sufficient to generate at least four literature reviews (Black & Mendenhall, 1990; Deshpande & Viswesvaran, 1992; Kealey & Protheroe, 1996; Ronen, 1989). One consistent finding is that training programs for expatriate managers and technical people have been limited in scope, if they are available at all, and they are not generally based on systematic needs analyses. Most training programs for this kind of expatriate base their designs on prior research and theory pertaining to cross-cultural training (Bhawuk & Brislin, 2000; Kealey & Protheroe, 1996) and view the training goal as successful adjustment to the host country culture.

Within the cross-culture framework, Mendenhall and Oddou (1985) identify the major determinants of successful adjustment as:

- Being able to replace the sources of pleasure and happiness in the home culture with acceptable substitutes available in the host country.
- Developing specific strategies for coping with the stress produced by the new situation.

- Developing high self-efficacy regarding one's technical competence as exhibited in the host country position.
- Developing genuine friendships with host nationals.
- Being willing and able to communicate widely with host nationals, not just a very few people within your immediate work group.
- Having an accurate understanding of the rules, customs, behavioral dispositions, and causal attributions that are characteristic of host nationals.
- Having a capacity to be tolerant of cultural differences with which the expatriate may fundamentally disagree.

The training programs designed to deal with one or more of these determinants tend to focus on four major domains of content: (1) Information about the host country's economy, demographics, and geography; (2) general information about the host country's culture; (3) language skills; and (4) interpersonal skills relevant for cross-cultural interactions. The instructional methods used to develop such capabilities have tended to concentrate on information presentation techniques with varying degrees of trainee involvement ranging from reading on their own to intensive discussions of case problems; and on skills training methods such as modeling/role playing and various types of cultural simulators.

The evaluative research studies have included a variety of criterion measures ranging from knowledge tests, to skills assessment via situational judgment tests and role playing, to expatriate satisfaction surveys, to indicators of whether or not the focal individual 'returned home early'.

Overall, the available results tend to be interpreted positively. However, there is considerable variation across studies that cannot be explained by artifacts, and interpretations should be cautious. The strongest results tend to be for improvements in the accuracy of end-of-training perceptions of the host culture and increases in cultural tolerance, as measured attitudinally. Research on the effects of cross-cultural training on expatriate performance is limited.

Given the almost universal acknowledgment of the adjustment problems that expatriates face, it is surprising that so little attention is paid to the determination of expatriate training needs. A study by Chao and Sun (1997) illustrates the downside of using a general cross-cultural training model rather than identification of specific training needs. In a survey study using interviews, US expatriates in China reported that besides more language skill what they really needed was specific knowledge of the Chinese business culture in which they were working, not the more general aspects of Chinese culture.

If so little training research has been devoted to high level expatriates in multinational firms it is probably not surprising that there is virtually no research on the employment training needs of immigrant groups. The sociological and political issues are important and often framed in terms of assimilation vs. integration vs. isolation (Berry, 1997). Since employment is such a major part of these processes, the training enterprise should have much to contribute.

Leadership Training for the Global Economy

Leadership theory and research produced a vast literature during the twentieth century (Bass, 1990; Yukl & Van Fleet, 1992). We will not attempt to review it here. It is also true that the increasing globalization of national economics during the twenty-first century is forecasted to present some additional performance requirements for the leadership of organizations, wherever in the organization it resides (e.g., Bassi, Cheney & Lewis, 1998; House, Wright & Aditya, 1997; Mobley, Gessner & Arnold, 1999; Smith, 1997). These additional requirements range from dealing with much more rapid changes in technology, competitive pressures, customer preferences, and the parameters of the labor market, to managing the increasing diversity of cultures within the organization, including the management ranks. People from different cultures do bring different value systems to work (England & Harpaz, 1990; Haire, Ghiselli & Porter, 1966; MOW, 1987).

Broadly construed, the major goals of the leadership function in business organizations tend to be transnational or universal. That is, the major goals or desired outcomes of effective leadership are (a) the facilitation of effective unit or organizational goal setting and providing support for their accomplishment, (b) promoting high levels of individual motivation, commitment, and satisfaction, (c) facilitating effective interactions among individuals within teams or units, and (d) increasing the probability that individuals within the organization will set very high goals for themselves, not be reluctant to take on new challenges, and will place the effectiveness of the organization above their own self-interests. We mean this to be a brief amalgamation of the recurring findings in leadership research from the Ohio State and Michigan studies through various instantiations of leadership theory to the more recent refinements in transformational leadership by Bass and his colleagues (Bass, 1997).

Given this very brief characterization, the recent cross-cultural, or transnational, research on leadership suggests that while the major goals that the leadership function is trying to accomplish appear to be universal, the specific things people in leadership roles do to accomplish them have some cultural specificity (e.g., Aycan et al., 2000; Brodbeck et al., 2000; Smith, Misumi, Tayeb, Peterson & Bond, 1989). Even Bass (1997) argues that across national boundaries the ways in which people in leadership roles attain transformational leadership outcomes can be quite different. All of this suggests that while leadership in global organizations may have similar goals across nations and cultures, the knowledges and skills people need to accomplish them are, to a significant extent, a function of the cultural backgrounds of the individuals involved. This in turn suggests that what the leadership training enterprise needs is a synthesis of leadership development and cross-cultural training that is specifically focused on the global organization.

A second issue is the degree to which the determinants of effective leadership performance, relative to the above goals, are amenable to a training intervention. As was noted with regard to interpersonal skills training, significant proportions of variance in leadership performance may be accounted for by ability and personality variables which are not easily altered. For example, Bass (1997) points out that transformational leadership behaviors seem to have a relatively high heritability coefficient as estimated from twin data (e.g., Rose 1995). Again the ATI is always with us and the question is whether ability and personality interact with differences in leadership training strategies or whether the main effect is dominant.

Problem Solving

More effective problem solving is identified as a critical training need, virtually no matter what the context. The term is used easily and often. It is seen as critical for new entrants to the modern work force, effective team work, and effective leadership, at all organizational levels. No list is without a problem solving entry. Unfortunately, if we ask (1) what are the specifications for how to measure individual differences in problem solving, or (2) if we want to train people to be better problem solvers in the work role context what should we teach them?, very few answers are forthcoming.

The theoretical and research literature on problem solving is of course voluminous (e.g., Newell & Simon, 1972). However, it is concerned primarily with identifying the general cognitive strategies that seem to best describe the ways people process information to arrive at problem solutions (e.g., Reeves & Weisberg, 1994). The answers to the two questions posed in the previous paragraph remain illusive, even though a large part of the research literature attempts to distinguish determinants of problem solving performance by experts vs. novices (Chi, Glaser & Farr, 1988).

Virtually everyone working in this area (e.g., Anderson, 1993; Baron, 1993; Bransford, Sherwood,

Vye & Rieser, 1986; Frederikson, 1984) agrees that the most important determinant of effective problem solving is the level of domain specific knowledge and skill acquired by the individual and the degree to which it is organized and structured in ways that mimic the expert. There is no substitute for knowing a lot and having a wide range of experiences in applying such domain specific knowledge and skill to a variety of problems. A major implication is that effective problem solving must be trained within content domains, be it management or plumbing, and that the course content must provide a wide variety of domain relevant practice experiences.

Beyond the domain-specific features, the specifications for problem solving training content are difficult to abstract from the literature. There have been general problem solving courses offered at the university level (e.g., Hayes, 1980; Rubenstein, 1980), for elementary and junior-high-school students (Covington, Crutchfield, Davies & Olton, 1974; Herrnstein, Nickerson, de Sanchez & Swets, 1986), and for managers (e.g., Kepner & Tregoe, 1965). Such courses attempt to teach certain strategies (e.g., means and analysis, reasoning by analogy), heuristics (e.g., always verbalize the problem explicitly), or rules of thumb (e.g., spend more time in problem identification than you think necessary, describe it to as many other people as possible). Relative to such course content, we will assert that evaluative research with adult populations is nonexistent. At this point, we still do not know whether there are domain-free determinants of effective problem solving than can be trained, such that they transfer to the work setting.

The more recent discussions tend to focus on the dispositional side of critical thinking (e.g., Halpern, 1998) and the role of so-called meta-cognition (Kuhn, 2000). The former refers to motivating individuals to always question the conventional wisdoms or expert dicta in a domain and to routinely ask whether alternative problem representations or solutions are possible. The latter is the cognitive psychology label for spending time reflecting upon, or devoting attention to, one's own problem solving efforts. There is consistent evidence from laboratory studies that, other things being equal, meta-cognitive activity is helpful (Berardi-Coletta, Buyer, Dominowski & Rellinger, 1995). However, when things are not equal, we would expect the effects of meta cognition to be greatly over shadowed by differences in domain expertise.

The briefest of summary statements might be that training for effective problem solving (i.e., developing solutions for ill-structured problems) is primarily a function of developing the appropriate domain knowledge and skill, providing opportunities for exploration and practice on a wide variety of context relevant problems, and incorporating appropriate feedback. Beyond the domain-specific features, the development of critical thinking attitudes, the use of meta-cognitive reflection, and the practice of explicit verbalization (of the nature of the problem and possible alternative solutions) have potential for value added. However, after a century of research on problem solving, the efforts to develop training approaches to improve problem solving in the work context seem not to have come very far.

IN CONCLUSION

Training is a critical component of effective human resource management. Its importance, both to individuals and to organizations probably cannot be overstated. The extant training evaluation literature shows that training can have large effects on knowledge and skill acquisition and on attitude change. Also, there is an increasing amount of research on the optimal conditions for learning, the influence of individual differences on learning and transfer, the role of trainee motivation – particularly the influence of self-efficacy, and the unique needs of team training vs. individual training.

However, particularly when cast against the magnitude and scope of the training enterprise, the available fund of relevant research, basic or applied, is relatively small. There simply is not very much. It was startling to learn that a comprehensive search for all published and unpublished studies of training effects yielded only 147 interpretable studies over a 60-year period, and the rate is declining not accelerating (Carlson, 1997). Consequently, we would like to close with some brief comments about where future research investments might be made.

It seems to us that there are three general research issues. The first concerns the development of substantive specifications for critical training needs. If it is true that there are substantive training needs that have considerable criticality and generality across occupations, organizations, industries, or broad segments of the labor force, then this issue goes far beyond the methodological questions of traditional job analysis vs. the critical incident method vs. CTA. The training needs outlined in the previous section seem critical for the global economy and should be given careful attention. However, before that can be done there must be a much fuller substantive specification for such capabilities as teamwork skills, self-managed learning, adaptability, problem solving, and so forth. At present, the specifications are not clear enough to guide training design effectively.

The second issue concerns focusing research on how best to achieve specific, but broadly important, training goals. For example, assuming that a substantive specification for effective self-directed training skills can be given, then what are the most effective ways to acquire such skills? Research

comparing instructional methods should only be for the purpose of developing optimal methods for meeting a particular training need. Although it is certainly not a complete story, the example of research on teaching supervisory interpersonal skills is a reasonable example to follow.

Third, the ways in which trainee individual differences influence training outcomes need even more attention. In the training context, what determines pre- and posttraining self-efficacy, mastery orientation, and instrumentality judgments? How can these aspects of learner motivation be enhanced? Also, if critical training needs can be more fully specified, then it should be possible to tailor training to individual differences in current levels of knowledge and skill. In the real world of adult training it is individual differences in pretraining levels of knowledge and skill, not cognitive abilities that offer the most leverage for capturing ATI effects.

Finally, training methods are being greatly influenced by the advancements in information technology. As noteworthy as these developments have been, the future will be even more startling, by orders of magnitude. However, spectacular as this will be, we believe that it is also true that the universals of training design will remain so. To neglect them will be to waste much of the benefit that technology can and will provide.

REFERENCES

Ackerman, P.L. (1992). Predicting individual differences in complex skill acquisition: Dynamics of ability determinants. *Journal of Applied Psychology, 77,* 598–614.

Ajzen, I. (1985). From intentions to actions: A theory of planned behavior. In J. Kuhl & J. Beckmann (Eds.), *Action control: From cognition to behavior* (pp. 11–39). Berlin: Springer-Verlag.

Ajzen, I., & Fishbein, M. (1980). *Understanding attitudes and predicting social behavior.* Englewood-Cliffs, N.J.: Prentice-Hall.

Alliger, G.M., Tannenbaum, S.I., Bennett, W., Traver, H., & Shotland, A. (1997). A meta-analysis of the relations among training criteria. *Personnel Psychology, 50,* 341–358.

Ames, C. (1992). Classrooms: Goals, structures, and student motivation. *Journal of Educational Psychology, 84*(3), 261–271.

Anderson, J.R. (1993). Problem solving and learning. *American Psychologist, 48,* 35–44.

Anderson, J.R., Reder, L.M., & Simon, H.A. (1996). Situated learning and education. *Educational Researcher, 25*(4), 5–11.

Anderson, P.L., & Wilson, S. (1997). Critical incident technique. In D.L. Whetzel & G.R. Wheaton (Eds.), *Applied measurement methods in industrial psychology.* Palo Alto: CA: Davis-Black.

Annett, J. (2000). Theoretical and pragmatic influences on task analysis methods. In J.M. Schraagen, S.F. Chipman & V.J. Shalin (Eds.), *Cognitive task analysis* (pp. 25–37). Mahwah, N.J.: Lawrence Erlbaum.

Argyris, C. (1977). Double loop learning in organizations. *Harvard Business Review*, September.

Argyris, C. (1992). *On organizational learning*. Malden, MA.: Blackwell.

Arthur, W. Jr., Day, E.A., Bennett, W. Jr., McNelly, T.L., & Jordan, J.A. (1997). Dyadic versus individual training protocols: Loss and reacquisition of a complex skill. *Journal of Applied Psychology, 82*, 783–791.

Ashton, D., Sung, J., & Turbin, J. (2000). Towards a framework for the comparative analysis of national systems of skill formation. *International Journal of Training and Development, 4*(1), 8–25.

Aycan, Z., Kanungo, R.N., Mendonca, M., Yu, K., Deller, J. Stahl, G., & Kurshid, A. (2000). Impact of culture on human resource management practices: A 10-country comparison. *Applied Psychology: An International Review, 49*, 192–221.

Baldwin, T.T. (1992). Effects of alternative modeling strategies on outcomes of interpersonal-skills training. *Journal of Applied Psychology, 77*, 147–154.

Baldwin, T.T., & Ford, J.K. (1988). Transfer in training: A review and directions for future research. *Personnel Psychology, 41*, 63–105.

Baldwin, T.T., & Magjuka, R.J. (1997). Organizational context and training effectiveness. In J.K. Ford, W.J. Kozlowski, K. Kraiger, E. Salas & M.S. Teachout (Eds.), *Improving training effectiveness in work organizations*. Mahwah, N.J.: Erlbaum.

Baldwin, T.T., Magjuka, R.J., & Loher, B.T. (1991). The perils of participation: Effects of choice of training on trainee motivation and learning. *Personnel Psychology, 44*, 51–65.

Balzer, W.K., Doherty, M.E., & O'Connor, R. Jr. (1989). Effects of cognitive feedback on performance. *Psychological Bulletin, 106*, 410–433.

Baron, J. (1993). Why teach thinking? – An essay. *Applied Psychology: An International Review, 42*, 191–237.

Barrick, M.R., & Mount, M.K. (1991). The Big Five personality dimensions and job performance: A meta-analysis. *Personnel Psychology, 44*, 1–26.

Bass, B.M. (1990). *Bass and Stogdill's handbook of leadership*. New York: Free Press.

Bass, B.M. (1997). Does transactional-transformational leadership paradigm transcend organizational and national boundaries? *American Psychologist, 52*, 130–139.

Bassi, L., Cheney, S., & Lewis, E. (1998). Trends in workplace learning: Supply and demand in interesting times. *Training and Development*, 51–87.

Berardi-Coletta, B., Buyer, L.S., Dominowski, R.L., & Rellinger, E.R. (1995). Metacognition and problem solving: A process-oriented approach. *Journal of Experimental Psychology: Learning, Memory, and Cognition, 21*, 205–223.

Berry, J.W. (1997). Immigration, acculturation, and adaptation. *Applied Psychology: An International Review, 46*(1), 5–68.

Bhawuk, D.P.S., & Brislin, R.W. (2000). Cross-cultural training: A review. *Applied Psychology: An International Review, 49*, 162–191.

Bikson, T.K., & Law, S.A. (1994). *Global preparedness and human resources. College and corporate perspectives* (MR-326-CPC). Santa Monica, CA: RAND Corporation, Institute on Education and Training.

Black, J.S., & Mendenhall, M. (1990). Cross-cultural training effectiveness. A review and theoretical framework for future research. *Academy of Management Review, 15*, 113–136.

Blum, M.L., & Naylor, J.C. (1968). *Industrial psychology: Its theoretical and social foundations*. New York: Harper & Row.

Blumberg, P., & Michael, J.A. (1992). Development of self-directed learning behaviors in a partially teacher-directed problem-based learning curriculum. *Teaching and Learning in Medicine, 4*, 3–8.

Borman, W.C., & Brush, D.H. (1993). More progress toward a taxonomy of managerial performance requirements. *Human Performance, 6*(1), 1–21.

Borman, W.C., & Motowidlo, S.J. (1993). Expanding the criterion domain to include elements of contextual performance. In N. Schmitt & W.C. Borman (Eds.), *Personnel selection in organizations* (pp. 71–98). San Francisco, CA: Jossey-Bass.

Bransford, J., Sherwood, R., Vye, N., & Rieser, J. (1986). Teaching thinking and problem solving. *American Psychologist, 41*, 1078–1089.

Brockner, J., & Lee, R.J. (1995). Career development in downsizing organizations: A self-affirmation analysis. In M. London (Ed.), *Employees, careers and job creation: Developing growth-oriented human resource strategies and programs* (pp. 49–70). San Francisco: Jossey-Bass.

Brodbeck, F.C., and 45 others. (2000). Cultural variation of leadership prototypes across 22 European countries. *Journal of Occupational and Organizational Psychology, 73*, 1–29.

Brookfield, S.D. (1986). *Understanding and facilitating adult learning*. San Francisco: Jossey-Bass.

Butler, R.E. (1993). LOFT: Full-mission simulation as crew resource management training. In E.L. Wiener, B.G., Kanki & R.L. Helmreich (Eds.), *Cockpit resource management* (pp. 231–259). CA: Academic Press.

Buttom, S.B., Mathieu, J.E., & Zajac, D.M. (1996). Goal orientation in organizational research: A conceptual and empirical foundation. *Organizational Behavior and Human Decisions Processes, 67*, 26–48.

Campbell, J.P. (1988). Training design for performance improvement. In J.P. Campbell, R.J. Campbell & Associates (Eds.), *Productivity in organizations* (pp. 177–216). San Francisco: Jossey-Bass.

Campbell, J.P. (1999). The definition and measurement of performance in the new age. In D.R. Ilgen & E.D. Pulakos (Eds.), *The changing nature of performance: Implications for staffing, motivation, and development*. San Francisco: Jossey-Bass.

Campbell, J.P., Gasser, M.B., & Oswald, F.L. (1996). The substantive nature of job performance variability. In K.R. Murphy (Ed.), *Individual differences and behavior in organizations*. San Francisco: Jossey-Bass.

Campbell, J.P., McCloy, R.A., Oppler, S.H., & Sager, C.E. (1993). A theory of performance. In N. Schmitt & W.C. Borman (Eds.), *Performance selection in organizations* (pp. 35–70). San Francisco: Jossey-Bass.

Candy, P.C. (1991). *Self-direction for lifelong learning*. San Francisco: Jossey-Bass.

Cannon-Bowers, J.A., & Salas, E. (1998). Team performance and training in complex environments: Recent findings from applied research. *Current Directions in Psychological Science, 7*(3), 83–87.

Cannon-Bowers, J.A., Salas, E., Tannenbaum, S.I., & Mathieu, J.E. (1995). Toward theoretically-based principles of trainee effectiveness: A model and initial empirical investigation. *Military Psychology, 7*, 141–164.

Carlson, K.D. (1997). *Impact of instructional strategy on training effectiveness*. Unpublished Ph.D. Dissertation. University of Iowa, Iowa City, IA.

Carlson, R.A., Lundy, D.H., & Schneider, W. (1992). Strategy guidance and memory aiding in learning a problem-solving skill. *Human Factors, 34*, 129–145.

Carnevale, A.P.O., Gainer, L.J., & Meltzer, A.S. (1990). *Workplace basics*. San Francisco, CA: Jossey-Bass.

Carroll, J.M. (1997). Toward minimalist training: Supporting the sense-making activities of computer users. In M.A. Quiñones & A. Ehrenstein (Eds.), *Training for a rapidly changing workplace: Applications of psychological research* (pp. 303–328). Washington, D.C: American Psychological Association.

Chao, G.T., & Sun, Y.J. (1997). Training needs for expatriate adjustment in the people's republic of china. In D.M. Saunders (Series Ed.) and A. Zeynep (Vol. Ed.), *New approaches to employee management: Vol. 4. Expatriate management: Theory and research* (pp. 207–226), JAI Press.

Chi, M.T.H., Glaser, R., & Farr, M. (Eds.) (1988). *The nature of expertise*. Hillsdale, N.J.: Lawrence Erlbaum.

Chipman, S.F., Schraagen, J.M., & Shalin, V.L. (2000). Introduction to cognitive task analysis. In J.M. Schraagen, S.F. Chipman & V.J. Shalin (Eds.), *Cognitive task analysis* (3–23). Mahwah, N.J.: Lawrence Erlbaum.

Colquitt, J.A., LePine, J.A., & Noe, R.A. (2000). Toward an integrative theory of training motivation: A meta-analytic path analysis of 20 years of research. *Journal of Applied Psychology, 85*, 678–707.

Colquitt, J.A., & Simmering, M.S. (1998). Consciousness, goal orientation, and motivation to learn during the learning process: A longitudinal study. *Journal of Applied Psychology, 83*, 654–665.

Confessore, S.J., & Kops, W.J. (1998). Self-directed learning and the learning organization: Examining the connection between the individual and the learning environment. *Human Resource Development Quarterly, 9*, 365–375.

Cooke, N.J. (1994). Varieties of knowledge elicitation techniques. *International Journal of Human-Computer Studies, 41*, 801–849.

Covington, M.V., Crutchfield, R.S., Davies, L., & Olton, R.M. (1974). *The productive thinking program: A course in learning to think*. Columbus, OH: Merrill.

Cronbach, L.J. (1957). The two disciplines of scientific study. *American Psychologist, 12*, 671–684.

Cronbach, L.J., & Gleser, G.C. (1965). *Psychological tests and personnel decisions* (2nd ed.). Urbana: University of Illinois Press.

Cronbach, L.J., & Snow, R.E. (1977). *Aptitudes and instructional methods*. New York: Irvington.

Decker, P.J. (1982). The enhancement of behavior modeling training of supervisory skills by the inclusion of retention processes. *Personnel Psychology, 35*, 323–332.

Decker, P.J., & Nathan, B.R. (1985). *Behavior modeling training: Principles and applications*. New York: Praeger.

Deshpande, S.P., & Viswesvaran, C. (1992). Is cross-cultural training of expatriate managers effective: A meta analysis. *International Journal of Intercultural Relations, 16*, 295–310.

Dipboye, R.L. (1997). Organizational barriers to implementing a rational model of training. In M.A. Quiñones & A. Ehrenstein (Eds.), *Training for a rapidly changing workplace: Applications of psychological research* (pp. 119–148). Washington, DC: American Psychological Association.

Dweck, C.S. (1986). Motivational processes affecting learning. *American Psychologist, 41*, 1040–1048.

Dweck, C.S., & Leggett, E.L. (1988). A social-cognitive approach to motivation and personality. *Psychological Review, 95*, 256–273.

Eden, D., & Aviram, A. (1993). Self-efficacy training to speed reemployment: Helping people to help themselves. *Journal of Applied Psychology, 78*, 352–360.

Ehrenstein, A., Walker, B., Czerwinski, M., & Feldman, R. (1997). Some fundamentals of training and transfer: Practice benefits are not automatic. In M.A. Quiñones & A. Ehrenstein (Eds.), *Training for a rapidly changing workplace: applications of psychological research* (31–60). Washington, DC: American Psychological Association.

Employability Skills Task Force (1989, October). *Employability skills task force progress report to the Governor's Commission on Jobs and Economic Development and the Michigan State Board of Education*. Lansing, MI: State of Michigan, Office of the Governor.

England, G.W., & Harpaz, I. (1990). How working is defined: National contexts and demographic and organizational role influences. *Journal of Organizational Behavior, 11*, 253–266.

Ericsson, K.A., & Charness, N. (1994). Expert performance: Its structure and acquisition. *American Psychologist, 49*, 725–747.

Ericsson, K.A., & Smith, J. (Eds.) (1991). *Toward a general theory of expertise: Prospects and limits*. Cambridge, England: Cambridge University Press.

Ford, J.K., Quiñones, M.A., Sego, D.J., & Sorra, J.S. (1992). Factors affecting the opportunity to perform trained tasks on the job. *Personnel Psychology, 45*, 511–527.

Ford, J.K., Smith, E.M., Weissbein, D.A., Gully, S.M., & Salas, E. (1998). Relationships of goal-orientation, metacognitive activity, and practice strategies with learning outcomes and transfer. *Journal of Applied Psychology*, 83, 218–233.

Ford, J.K., & Weissbein, D.A. (1997). Transfer of training: An updated review and analysis. *Performance Improvement Quarterly*, 10, 22–41.

Forman, G., & Pufall, P. (Eds.) (1988). *Constructivism in the computer age*. Hillsdale, NJ: Lawrence Erlbaum.

Fosnot, C.T. (1996). Constructivism: A psychological theory of learning. In C.T. Fosnot (Ed.), *Constructivism: Theory, perspectives and practice*. New York: Teachers College Press.

Foushee, H.C. (1984). Dyads and triads at 35,000 feet: Factors affecting group processes and aircrew performance. *American Psychologist*, 39, 885–893.

Frederiksen, N. (1984). Implications of cognitive theory for instruction in problem solving. *Review of Educational Research*, 54, 363–407.

French, W.L. & Bell, C.H., Jr. (Eds.) (1984). *Organizational development: Behavioral science interventions for organization improvement*. Englewood Cliffs, N.J.: Prentice-Hall.

Frese, M., Brodbeck, F., Heinbokel, T., Mooser, C., Schleiffenbaum, E., & Thiemann, P. (1991). Errors in training computer skills: On the positive function of errors. *Human-Computer Interaction*, 6, 77–93.

Gagné, R.M. (1962). Military training and principles of learning. *American Psychologist*, 17, 83–91.

Gagné, R.M., & Briggs, L.J. (1979). *Principles of instructional design*. New York: Holt, Rinehart & Winston.

Gagné, R.M., Briggs, L.J., & Wager, W.W. (1988). *Principles of instructional design* (3rd ed.). New York: Holt, Rinehart & Winston.

Gelfand, M.J., & Dyer, N. (2000). A cultural perspective on negotiation: Progress, pitfalls, and prospects. *Applied Psychology: An International Review*, 49, 62–99.

Gist, M.E. (1997). Training design and pedagogy: Implications for skill acquisition, maintenance, and generalization. In M.A. Quiñones & A. Ehrenstein (Eds.), *Training for a rapidly changing workplace: Applications of psychological research* (pp. 201–222). Washington, DC: American Psychological Association.

Gist, M.E., Bavetta, A.G., & Stevens, C.K. (1990). Transfer training methods: Its influence on skill generalization, skill repetition, and performance level. *Personnel Psychology*, 43, 501–523.

Gist, M.E., Stevens, C.K., & Bavetta, A.G. (1991). Effects of self-efficacy and post-training intervention on the acquisition and maintenance of complex interpersonal skills. *Personnel Psychology*, 44, 837–861.

Glaser, R. (1976). Components of a psychology of instruction: Toward a science of design. *Review of Educational Research*, 46, 1–24.

Glaser, R., & Bassok, M. (1989). Learning theory and the study of instruction. *Annual Review of Psychology*, 40, 631–666.

Goldsmith, T., & Kraiger, K. (1997). Applications of structural knowledge assessment to training evaluation.

In J. Ford, S. Kozlowski, K. Kraiger, E. Salas & M. Teachout (Eds.), *Improving training effectiveness in work organizations*, 4 (pp.73–96). Mahwah, N.J.: Lawrence Erlbaum.

Goldstein, A.P., & Sorcher, M.A. (1974). *Changing supervisory behavior* (pp. 90). New York: Pergoman Press.

Goodman, P.S., Devadas, R., & Hughson, T.L. (1988). Groups and productivity: Analyzing the effectiveness of self-managing teams. In J.P. Campbell, R.J. Campbell & Associates (Eds.), *Productivity in organizations* (pp. 295–327). San Francisco: CA: Jossey-Bass.

Goodman, P.S., Lerch, F.J., & Mukhopadhyay, T. (1994). Individual and organizational productivity: Linkages and processes. In D.H. Harris (Ed.), *Organizational linkages: Understanding the productivity paradox* (pp. 54–80). Washington, DC: National Academy Press.

Gordon, J., & Zemke, R. (2000). The instructional systems design (ISD) approach to instruction design. Is it leading us astray? *Training*, April, 43–53.

Greenwald, A.G. (1997). Validity concerns and usefulness of student ratings of instruction. *American Psychologist*, 52(11), 1182–1186.

Grow, G.O. (1991). Teaching learners to be self-directed. *Adult Education Quarterly*, 41, 125–149.

Guzzo, R.A., & Salas, E. (Eds.) (1995). *Team effectiveness and decision making*. San Francisco, CA: Jossey-Bass.

Guzzo, R.A., & Shea, G.P. (1992). Group performance and intergroup relations in organizations. In M.D. Dunnette & L.M. Hough (Eds.), *Handbook of industrial and organizational psychology* (pp. 269–313). Palo Alto, CA: Consulting Psychologists Press.

Hackman, J.R. (Ed.) (1990). *Groups that work (and those that don't)*. San Francisco, CA: Jossey-Bass.

Haire, M., Ghiselli, E., & Porter, L. (1966). *Managerial thinking: An international study*. New York: Wiley.

Halpern, D.F. (1998). Teaching critical thinking for transfer across domains. *American Psychologist*, 53, 449–455.

Hannafin, M.J. (1992). Emerging technologies, ISD, and learning environments: Critical perspectives. *Education Technology Research and Development*, 40, 49–63.

Hare, A.P. (1962). *Handbook of small group research*. New York: The Free Press of Glencoe.

Harris, D.H. (1994). *Organizational linkages: Understanding the productivity paradox*. Washington, DC: National Academy Press.

Hayes, J.R. (1980). Teaching problem-solving mechanisms. In D.T. Tuma & F. Reif (Eds.), *Problem solving and education: Issues in teaching and research*. Hillsdale, N.J.: Lawrence Erlbaum.

Hedge, J.W., & Borman, W.C. (1995). Changing conceptions and practices in performance appraisal. In A. Howard (Ed.), *The changing nature of work* (pp. 451–481). San Francisco: Jossey-Bass.

Helmreich, R.L., & Foushee, H.C. (1993). Why crew resource management? Empirical and theoretical bases of human factors training in aviation. In E.L. Wiener, B.G. Kanki & R.L. Helmreich (Eds.), *Cockpit resource management* (pp. 3–45). CA: Academic Press.

Helmreich, R.L., Merritt, A.C., & Wilhelm, J.A. (1999). The evolution of crew resource management training in commercial aviation. *International Journal of Aviation Psychology, 9,* 19–32.

Herrnstein, R.J., Nickerson, R.S., de Sanchez, M., & Swets, J.A. (1986). Teaching thinking skills. *American Psychologist, 41,* 1279–1289.

Hill, G.W. (1982). Group versus individual performance: Are N+1 heads better than one? *Psychological Bulletin, 91*(3), 517–539.

Hogan, P.M., Hakel, M.D., & Decker, P.J. (1986). Effects of trainee-generated versus trainer-provided rule codes on generalization in behavior-modeling training. *Journal of Applied Psychology, 71,* 469–473.

House, R.J., Wright, N.S., & Aditya, R.N. (1997). Cross-cultural research on organizational leadership: A critical analysis and a proposed theory. In P.C. Earley & M. Erez (Eds.), *New perspectives in international industrial organisational psychology* (pp. 535–625). San Francisco, CA: New Lexington.

Howard, A., Osterman, P., & Carnevale, A.P. (1995). Human resources and their skills. In A. Howard (Ed.), *The changing nature of work.* San Francisco: Jossey-Bass.

Howe, M.J.A., Davidson, J.W., & Sloboda, J.A. (1998). Innate talents: Reality or myth? *Behavioral and Brain Sciences, 21,* 399–407.

Ilgen, D.R., Fisher, C.D., & Taylor, M.S. (1979). Consequences of individual feedback on behavior in organizations. *Journal of Applied Psychology, 64,* 349–371.

Ilgen, D.R., & Pulakos, E.D. (Eds.) (1999). *The changing nature of performance: Implications for staffing, motivation, and development.* San Francisco: Jossey-Bass.

Ivancic, K., & Hesketh, B. (1995/1996). Making the best of errors during training. *Training Research Journal, 1,* 103–125.

Jensen, A.R. (1998). The g factor and the design of education. In R.J. Sternberg & W.M. Williams (Eds.), *Intelligence, instruction, and assessment.* Mahwah, N.J.: Lawrence Erlbaum.

Johnson, D.W., & Johnson, R.T. (1975). *Learning together and alone: Cooperation, competition, and individualization.* Englewood Cliffs: N.J.: Prentice-Hall.

Kanfer, R. (1990). Motivation theory and industrial/ organizational psychology. In M.D. Dunnette & L. Hough (Eds.), *Handbook of industrial and organizational psychology: Vol. 1. Theory in industrial and organizational psychology* (pp. 75–170). Palo Alto, CA: Consulting Psychologists Press.

Kanfer, R., & Ackerman, P.L. (1989). Motivation and cognitive abilities: An integrative/aptitude-treatment and interaction approach to skill acquisition. *Journal of Applied Psychology, 74,* 657–690.

Kanfer, R., Ackerman, P.L., Murtha, T.C., Dugdale, B., & Nelson, L. (1994). Goal setting, conditions of practice, and task performance: A resource allocation perspective. *Journal of Applied Psychology, 79,* 826–835.

Kanfer, R., & Heggestad, E.D. (1997). Motivational traits and skills: A person-centered approach to work motivation. In L.L. Cummings & B.M. Staw (Eds.), *Research in organizational behavior,* Vol. 19 (pp. 1–57). Greenwich, CT: JAI Press.

Kanfer, R., & Heggestad, E.D. (1999). Individual differences in motivation: Traits and self-regulatory skills. In P.L. Ackerman, P.C. Kyllonen & R.D. Roberts (Eds.), *Learning and individual differences* (pp. 293–314). Washington, DC: American Psychological Association.

Kealey, D.J., & Protheroe, D.R. (1996). The effectiveness of cross-cultural training for expatriates: An assessment of the literature on the issue. *International Journal of Intercultural Relations, 20*(2), 141–165.

Kepner, C.H., & Tregoe, B.B. (1965). *The rational manager: A systematic approach to problem solving and decision making.* New York: McGraw-Hill.

Kirkpatrick, D.L. (1959). Techniques for evaluating training programs. *Journal of ASTD, 13,* 3–9.

Kirkpatrick, D.L. (1996). Invited reaction: Reaction to Holton article. *Human Resources Development Quarterly, 7,* 5–15.

Klein, K.J., & Ralls, R.S. (1997). The unintended organizational consequences of technology training: Implications for training theory, research, and practice. In J.K. Ford, S.W.J. Kozlowski, K. Kraiger, E. Salas & M.S. Teachout (Eds.), *Improving training effectiveness in organizations* (pp. 323–354). Hillsdale, N.J.: Lawrence Erlbaum.

Kluger, A.N., & DeNisi, A. (1996). The effects of feedback interventions on performance: A historical review, a meta-analysis, and a preliminary feedback intervention theory. *Psychological Bulletin, 119*(2), 254–284.

Kneller, G.F. (1972). Behavioral objectives? No! (with a reply by R.M. Gagné). *Educational Leadership, 23,* 394–400.

Knowles, M. (1984). *The adult learner: A neglected species.* Houston, TX: Gulf.

Kossek, E.E., Roberts, K., Fisher, S., & Demarr, B. (1998). Career self-management: A quasi-experimental assessment of the effects of a training intervention. *Personnel Psychology, 51,* 935–962.

Kozlowski, S.W.J., & Salas, E. (1997). In J.K. Ford, S.W.J. Kozlowski, K. Kraiger, E. Salas & M.S. Teachout (Eds.), *Improving training effectiveness in organizations* (pp. 247–287). Hillsdale, N.J.: Lawrence Erlbaum.

Kraiger, K., Salas, E., & Cannon-Bowers, J.A. (1995). Measuring knowledge organization as a method for assessing learning during training. *Human Performance, 37,* 804–816.

Kraut, A.I. (1976). Behavior modeling symposium: Developing managerial skills in modeling techniques: Some positive research findings. *Personnel Psychology, 29,* 325–328.

Kuhn, D. (2000). Metacognitive development. *Current Directions in Psychological Science, 9,* 178–181.

Latham, G.P., & Saari, L.M. (1979). The application of social learning theory to training supervisors through behavioral modeling. *Journal of Applied Psychology, 64,* 239–246.

Leedom, D.K., & Simon, R. (1995). Improving team coordination: A case for behavior-based training. *Military*

Psychology, 7, 109–122. Likert, R. (1967). *The human organization: Its management and value*. New York: McGraw-Hill.

Lehman, R., Lempert, R.O., & Nisbett, R.E. (1988). The effects of graduate training on reasoning: Formal discipline and thinking about everyday life events. *American Psychologist, 43*, 431–442.

Likert, R. (1967). *The human organization: Its management and value*. New York: McGraw-Hill.

Locke, E.A. (July, 2000). Motivation, cognition, and action: An analysis of studies of task goals and knowledge. *Applied Psychology: An International Review, 49*, 408–429.

Locke, E.A., & Latham, G.P. (1990). *A theory of goal setting and task performance*. Englewood Cliffs, N.J.: Prentice-Hall.

Lohman, D.F. (1999). Minding our p's and q's: On finding relationships between learning and intelligence. In P.L. Ackerman, P.C. Kyllonen & R.D. Roberts (Eds.), *Learning and individual differences* (pp. 55–76). Washington, DC: American Psychological Association.

London, M. (Ed.) (1995). *Employees, careers and job creation: Developing growth-oriented human resource strategies and programs*. San Francisco: Jossey-Bass.

Long, H.B., & Morris, S. (1995). Self-directed learning in the business and industry: A review of the literature 1983–93. In H.B. Long & Associates (Eds.), *New dimensions in self-directed learning*. Norman: Public Managers Center, College of Education, University of Oklahoma.

Maier, N.R.F., & Sashkin, M. (1971). Specific leadership behaviors that promote problem solving. *Personnel Psychology, 24*, 35–44.

Mathieu, J.E., & Martineau, J.W. (1997). Individual and situational influences in training motivation. In J.K. Ford, S.W.J. Kozlowski, K. Kraiger, E. Salas, & M.S. Teachout (Eds.), *Improving training effectiveness in organizations* (pp. 193–222). Hillsdale, N.J.: Lawrence Erlbaum.

Mathieu, J.E., Martineau, J.W., & Tannenbaum, S.I. (1993). Individual and situational influences on the development of self-efficacy: Implications for training effectiveness. *Personnel Psychology, 46*, 125–147.

Matlay, H. (1999). Employers' perceptions and implementation of S/NVQs in Britain: A critical overview. *International Journal of Training and Development, 3*(2), 132–141.

May, G.L., & Kahnweiler, W.M. (2000). The effect of a mastery practice design on learning and transfer in behavior modeling training. *Personnel Psychology, 53*, 353–373.

McGehee, W., & Thayer, P.W. (1961). *Training in business and industry*. New York: Wiley.

McGrath, J.E. (1966). *Small group research*. New York: Holt, Rinehart & Winston.

McGrath, J.E. (1984). *Groups, interaction, and performance*. Englewood Cliffs, NJ: Prentice-Hall.

McKeachie, W.J. (1997). Student ratings. *American Psychologist, 52*(11), 1218–1225.

Means, B., Mumaw, R., Roth, C., Schlager, M., McWilliams, E., Gagné, E., Rice, V., Rosenthal, D., & Heon, S. (1988). *ATC training analysis study: Design of the next-generation ATC training system*. Technical Report for the Federal Aviation Administration, Alexandria, VA: HumRRO International.

Mendenhall, M., & Oddou, G. (1985). The dimensions of expatriate acculturation: A review. *Academy of Management Review, 10*(1), 39–47.

Miflin, B.M., Campbell, C.B., & Price, D.A. (2000). A conceptual framework to guide the development of self-directed, lifelong learning in problem-based medical curricula. *Medical Education, 34*, 299–306.

Mitchell, T.R., Hopper, H., Daniels, D., George-Falvy, J., & James, L.R. (1994). Predicting self-efficacy and performance during skill acquisition. *Journal of Applied Psychology, 79*, 506–517.

Mobley, W.F., Gessner, M.J., & Arnold, V. (Eds.) (1999). *Advances in global leadership*. Stanford, CT: JAI Press.

Morgeson, F.P., & Campion, M.A. (1997). Social and cognitive sources of potential inaccuracy in job analysis. *Journal of Applied Psychology, 82*, 627–655.

MOW International Research Team (1987). *The meaning of working*. London and New York: Academic Press.

Murphy, K.R. (1989). Dimensions of job performance. In R. Dillon & J. Pelligrino (Eds.), *Testing: Applied and theoretical perspectives* (pp. 218–247). New York: Praeger.

Nash, B.E., & Korte, R.C. (1997). Validation of SCANS competencies by a national job analysis study. In H.R. O'Neil, Jr. (Ed.), *Workforce readiness: Competencies and Assessment* (pp. 77–102). Mahwah, N.J.: Lawrence Erlbaum.

National Academy of Sciences (1984). *High schools and the changing workplace. The employers' view* (NTIS Report PB84-240191). Washington, DC: National Academy Press.

National Board of Employment, Education and Training (1992, December). *Skills sought by employers of graduates* (Commissioned Report No. 20). Canberra, Australia: Australian Government Publishing Service.

National Research Council (1999). *The changing nature of work: Implications for occupational analysis*. Washington, DC: National Academy Press.

Newell, A., & Simon, H.A. (1972). *Human problem solving*. Englewood Cliffs, N.J.: Prentice-Hall.

Noe, R.A. (1999). *Employee training and development*. Boston: Irwin/McGraw-Hill.

Noe, R.A., & Wilk, S.L. (1993). Investigation of the factors that influence employees' participation in development activities. *Journal of Applied Psychology, 78*, 291–302.

Office of Technology Assessment (1995, September). *Learning to work: Making the transition from school to work* (OTA-EHR-637). Washington, DC: US Government Printing Office.

Olson, A.M. (2000). *A theory and taxonomy of individual team member performance*. Unpublished Ph.D. dissertation. University of Minnesota, Minneapolis, MN.

Olson, J.R., & Biolsi, K.J. (1991). Techniques for representing expert knowledge. In K.A. Ericsson &

J. Smith (Eds.), *Toward a general theory of expertise* (pp. 240–285). Cambridge, England: Cambridge University Press.

O'Neil, H.F. Jr., Allred, K., & Baker, E.L. (1997). Review of workforce readiness theoretical frameworks. In H.R. O'Neil, Jr. (Ed.), *Workforce readiness: Competencies and Assessment* (pp. 3–25). Mahwah, N.J.: Lawrence Erlbaum.

O'Neil, H.F. Jr., Chung, G.K.W.K., & Brown, R.S. (1997). Use of networked simulations as a context to measure team competencies. In H.R. O'Neil, Jr. (Ed.), *Workforce readiness: Competencies and Assessment* (pp. 411–452). Mahwah, N.J.: Lawrence Erlbaum.

Orasanu, J.M. (1993). Decision-making in the cockpit. In E.L. Wiener, B.G. Kanki & R.L. Helmreich (Eds.), *Cockpit resource management* (pp. 137–172). CA: Academic Press.

Organ, D.W. (1997). Organizational citizenship behavior: It's construct clean-up time. *Human Performance, 10,* 85–97.

Parry, S.B. (1996). Measuring training's ROI. *Training and Development,* May.

Pasmore, W., Francis, C., Haldeman, J., & Shani, A. (1982). Sociotechnical systems: A North American reflection on empirical studies of the seventies. *Human Relations, 35,* 1179–1204.

Paulus, P.B. (2000). Groups, teams, and creativity: The creative potential of idea-generating groups. *Applied Psychology: An International Review, 49*(2), 237–262.

Perry, P., & Downs, S. (1985). Skills, strategies, and ways of learning. *Programmed Learning and Educational Technology, 22,* 177–181.

Pescuric, A., & Byham, W.C. (1996). When unveiled 20 years ago, behavior modeling was predicted to do wonders for training. It has. And, now, an enhanced version is keeping up with our changing times. *Training and Development, July,* 25–30.

Phillips, J.J. (1996). ROI: The search. *Training and Development,* February.

Pintrick, P.R., Cross, D.R., Kozma, R.B., & McKeachie, W.J. (1986). Instructional psychology. *Annual Review of Psychology, 37,* 611–651.

Porras, J.I., & Robertson, P.J. (1992). Organizational development: Theory, practice, and research. In M.D. Dunnette & L.M. Hough (Eds.), *Handbook of industrial and organizational psychology* (2nd ed., Vol. 3, pp. 719–822). Palo Alto, CA: Consulting Psychologists Press.

Prawat, R.S., & Worthington, V.L. (1998). Educational psychology: Getting to the heart of the matter through technology. *Applied Psychology: An International Review, 47,* 263–283.

Purcell, A. (2000). 20/20 ROI. *Training and Development,* July.

Reeves, L.M., & Weisberg, R.W. (1994). The role of content and abstract information in analogical transfer. *Psychological Bulletin, 115,* 381–400.

Resnick, L.B., & Ford, W. (1981). *The psychology of mathematics for instruction.* Hillsdale, N.J.: Lawrence Erlbaum.

Rieber, L.P. (1992). Computer-based microworlds: A bridge between constructivism and direct instruction. *Education Technology Research and Development, 40,* 93–106.

Rogers, W., Mauer, T., Salas, E., & Fisk, A. (1997). Training design, cognitive theory, and automaticity: Principles and a methodology. In J.K. Ford, S.W.J. Kozlowski, K. Kraiger, E. Salas & M.S. Teachout (Eds.), *Improving training effectiveness in organizations* (pp. 19–46). Mahwah, N.J.: Lawrence Erlbaum.

Ronen, S. (1989). Training the international assignee. In I.L. Goldstein & Associates (Eds.), *Training and development in organizations* (pp. 417–453). San Francisco, CA: Jossey-Bass.

Rose, R. (1995). Genes and human behavior. *Annual Review of Psychology, 46,* 625–654.

Rouiller, J.Z., & Goldstein, I.L. (1993). The relationship between organizational transfer climate and positive transfer of training. *Human Resource Development Quarterly, 4,* 377–390.

Rubenstein, M.F. (1980). A decade of experience in teaching an interdisciplinary problem-solving course. In D.T. Tuma & F. Reif (Eds.), *Problem solving and education: Issues in teaching and research.* Hillsdale, N.J.: Lawrence Erlbaum.

Sackett, P.R., & Mullen, E.J. (1993). Beyond formal experimental design: Towards an expanded view of the training evaluation process. *Personnel Psychology, 46,* 613–627.

Sagie, A. (1997). Leader direction and employee participation in decision making: Contradictory or compatible practices? *Applied Psychology: An International Review, 46*(4), 387–452.

Saks, A.M. (1995). Longitudinal field investigation of the moderating and mediating effects of self-efficacy on the relationship between training and newcomer adjustment. *Journal of Applied Psychology, 80,* 211–225.

Salas, E., & Cannon-Bowers, J.A. (1997). Methods, tools, and strategies for team training. In M.A. Quiñones & A. Ehrenstein (Eds.), *Training for a rapidly changing workplace: Applications of psychological research* (pp. 249–280). Washington, DC: American Psychological Association.

Salas, E., & Cannon-Bowers, J.A. (2001). The sciences of training: A decade of progress. *Annual Review of Psychology, 52.*

Salas, E., Cannon-Bowers, J.A., Rhodenizer, L., & Bowers, C.A. (1999). Training in organizations: Myths, misconceptions, and mistaken assumptions. *Research in Personnel and Human Resources Management, 17,* 123–161.

Salas, E., Fowlkes, J., Stout, R.J., Milanovich, D.M., & Prince, C. (1999). Does CRM training improve teamwork skills in the cockpit? Two evaluation studies. *Human Factors, 41,* 326–343.

Schaafstal, A., & Schraagen, J.M. (2000). Training of troubleshooting: A structured, task analytical approach. In J.M. Schraagen, S.F. Chipman & V.J. Shalin (Eds.), *Cognitive task analysis* (pp. 57–70). Mahwah, N.J.: Lawrence Erlbaum.

Schmidt, H.G. (2000). Assumptions underlying self-directed learning may be false. *Medical Education, 34,* 243–245.

Schmidt, R.A., & Bjork, R.A. (1992). New conceptualizations of practice: Common principles in three paradigms suggest new concepts for training. *Psychological Science, 3,* 207–217.

Schraagen, J.M., Chipman, S.F., & Shalin, V.J. (Eds.) (2000). *Cognitive task analysis.* Mahwah, N.J.: Lawrence Erlbaum.

Schraagen, J.M., Chipman, S.F., & Shute, V.J. (2000). State-of-the-art review of cognitive task analysis techniques. In J.M. Schraagen, S.F. Chipman & V.J. Shalin (Eds.), *Cognitive task analysis* (pp. 467–487). Mahwah, N.J.: Lawrence Erlbaum.

Shaw, M.E. (1976). *Group dynamics: The psychology of small group behavior* (2nd ed.). New York: McGraw-Hill.

Shepperd, J.A. (1993). Productivity loss in performance groups: A motivation analysis. *Psychological Bulletin, 113,* 67–81.

Shute, V.J., & Gawlick, L.A. (1995). Practice effects on skill acquisition, learning outcome, retention, and sensitivity to relearning. *Human Factors, 37,* 781–803.

Smith, P.B. (1997). Leadership in Europe: Euromanagement or the footprint of history? *European Journal of Work and Organizational Psychology, 6,* 375–386.

Smith, P.B., Misumi, J., Tayeb, M., Peterson, M., & Bond, M. (1989). On the generality of leadership style measures across cultures. *Journal of Occupational Psychology, 62,* 97–109.

Snow, R.E. (1989). Aptitude-treatment interaction as a framework for research on individual differences in learning. In P.L. Ackerman, R.J. Sternberg & R. Glaser (Eds.), *Learning and individual differences: Advances in theory and research* (pp. 13–59). New York: Freeman & Co.

Snow, R.E., & Lohman, D.F. (1984). Toward a theory of cognitive aptitude for learning from instruction. *Journal of Educational Psychology, 76*(3), 347–376.

Stevens, C.K., & Gist, M.E. (1997). Effects of self-efficacy an goal-orientation training on negotiation skill maintenance: What are the mechanisms? *Personnel Psychology, 50,* 955–978.

Stout, R.J., Salas, E., & Fowlkes, J.E. (1997). Enhancing teamwork in complex environments through team training. *Journal of Group Psychotherapy, Psychodrama and Sociometry, 49,* 163–186.

Straka, G.A. (1999). Perceived work conditions and self-directed learning in the process of work. *International Journal of Training and Development, 3,* 240–249.

Swezey, R.W., & Salas, E. (1992a). Guidelines for use in team-training development. In R.W. Swezey & E. Salas (Eds.), *Teams: Their training and performance* (pp. 219–246). Norwood, N.J.: Ablex Publishing Co.

Swezey, R.W., & Salas, E. (Eds.) (1992b). *Teams: Their training and performance.* Norwood, N.J.: Ablex Publishing Co.

Tracey, J.B., Tannenbaum, S.I., & Kavanagh, M.J. (1995). Applying trained skills on the job: The importance of the work environment. *Journal of Applied Psychology, 80,* 239–252.

Trist, E.L., & Bamforth, K.W. (1951). Some social and psychological consequences of the longwall method of coal getting. *Human Relations, 4,* 3–38.

US Department of Labor (1992). *Skills and tasks for jobs: A SCANS report for America 2000.* Washington, DC: US Department of Labor, Secretary's Commission on Achieving Necessary Skills.

VandeWalle, D. (1997). Development and validation of a work domain goal orientation instrument. *Educational and Psychological Measurement, 57,* 995–1015.

Vineberg, R., & Joyner, J.N. (1980). *Instructional system development (ISD) in the armed services: Methodology and application.* (HumRRO Technical Report 80–1). Alexandria, VA: Human Resources Research Organization.

Walton, R.E. (1985). From control to commitment in the workplace. *Harvard Business Review, 63*(2), 76–84.

Wiener, E.L., Kanki, B.G., & Helmreich, R.L. (Eds.) (1993). *Cockpit resource management.* CA: Academic Press.

Wilpert, B. (2000). Presidential Address: 24th International Congress of Applied Psychology, San Francisco, August 9–14, 1998. *Applied Psychology: An International Review, 49,* 3–22.

Wlodkowski, R.J. (1985). *Enhancing adult motivation to learn.* San Francisco: Jossey-Bass.

Yukl, G., & Van Fleet, D.D. (1992). Theory and research on leadership in organizations. In M. Dunnette & L. Hough (Eds.), *Handbook of industrial and organizational psychology* (2nd ed., Vol. 3, pp. 147–198). Palo Alto: Consulting Psychologists Press.

14

Individual Development in the Workplace

CYNTHIA D. McCAULEY and
SARAH A. HEZLETT

An increased emphasis on learning in organizations has enhanced researchers' and practitioners' interest in the dynamics of individual development in the workplace. Three approaches to understanding individual development (behavioral change, self-directed learning, and adult development) are reviewed, and the common elements across these approaches are identified. These elements are used to evaluate six popular individual development practices: 360-degree feedback, executive coaching, developmental assignments, action learning, social support for learning, and communities of practice. This analysis indicates no one practice is a panacea for individual development. Directions for research are suggested and trends that are likely to influence individual development in the workplace in the future are discussed.

Although learning and skill acquisition have been studied by industrial psychologists since the field's inception, relatively little attention has been devoted to understanding individual development in the workplace. The vast majority of research and practice on work-related learning has focused on training, particularly on the design and evaluation of individual training programs. Recent changes in the workplace, however, have altered how learning is viewed. Escalating technological innovation, corporate downsizing, the flattening of organizational hierarchies, an increased use of teams, and rising numbers of temporary and contract employees have been accompanied by a shift in responsibility for learning away from organizations towards employees (Callanan & Greenhaus, 1999; London & Mone, 1999). Learning is no longer viewed as a need that occurs occasionally when a new system is introduced or when a new job is begun, but is viewed as a continuous process (Senge, 1990; Vaill, 1996). Training programs continue to be an important

mechanism for employee learning, but individuals increasingly need to manage their own development, regularly updating and expanding their skills to prepare for future job demands (Callanan & Greenhaus, 1999; London & Mone, 1999). These changes make understanding individual development in the workplace a priority for both researchers and practitioners.

The purpose of this chapter is to review the current state of research and practice related to individual development in the workplace. In the first half of the chapter, three approaches to understanding individual development in the workplace are discussed. In many ways these approaches are distinct, each pursued by different scholars drawing on separate theories and leading to disparate bodies of knowledge and expertise. Yet, despite these differences, the approaches are largely complimentary. At the end of this section of the chapter, we highlight the themes common to each approach, deriving five elements that are critical to individual development in the workplace.

In the second half of the chapter, we provide an overview of six individual development practices that are currently popular. For each practice, we provide a brief description and a summary of related research. We conclude this section of the chapter with an analysis of the practices in terms of the common elements of individual development distilled in the first half of the chapter. Our goal is to illustrate the strengths and limitations of each technique by evaluating the extent to which they facilitate the process of individual development. We do not include training programs in our overview of individual development practices (although training remains a popular current practice) because a separate chapter in this handbook is devoted to the topic of training.

This chapter concludes with some suggestions for 'next steps' for both researchers and practitioners. Methodological challenges associated with studying individual development are outlined in this discussion. Before beginning our review of theory and research on individual development in the workplace, we define what we mean by the construct. In addition, we introduce the issue of cross-cultural differences.

INDIVIDUAL DEVELOPMENT: A DEFINITION

We define individual development in the workplace as the expansion of an individual's capacity to function effectively in his or her present or future job and work organization. In other words, an instance of individual development is an intra-individual change that results in better work performance, today or in the future. The review of a theory of work performance helps illustrate the potential locus of such changes.

According to Campbell and his colleagues (Campbell, 1990; Campbell, McCloy, Oppler & Sager, 1993; Campbell, Gasser & Oswald, 1996), there are eight components of job performance. Each component is a function of declarative knowledge, procedural knowledge, and motivation. Each of these performance determinants are affected by individual difference variables (e.g., ability, personality, and interests), situational variables (e.g., education, training, and experience), and their interaction. Individual development may involve stable changes in any of the proximal or distal individual determinants of work performance. Note that this excludes transient changes in work performance that may arise through temporary changes in motivation, as well as those that stem from alternations in situational factors, such as equipment modifications or changes in working conditions. Referring to Campbell et al.'s model also highlights that individual development is not limited to

changes that affect task performance. The eight performance components include non-technical aspects of work performance, such as facilitation of peer and team performance.

It is worth pointing out that our definition of individual development is similar to the definition of training provided by Goldstein in his chapter in the *Handbook of Industrial and Organizational Psychology* (1991): '...the training process is defined as the systematic acquisition of attitudes, concepts, knowledge, rules, or skills that result in improved performance at work' (p. 508). The likeness is appropriate given the close ties between training and development. There are at least three differences between the two, however. First, in practice, training has tended to focus on formal education that takes place away from the worksite. Individual development utilizes a more diverse array of learning events. Second, the objectives of individual development tend to be broader than those of training. While training often is directed at expanding knowledge, skills, or behaviors related to employees' current jobs, individual development focuses on long-term professional and personal growth (Noe, Wilk, Mullen & Wanek, 1997; Tharenou, 1997a). Finally, individual development will be, at times, unsystematic. Although individual development is stimulated and enhanced through planned initiatives, several theories suggest that individual development is often an on-going, unintentional outcome of work experiences (Dixon, 1994; Marsick & Watkins, 1992).

Individual development also is not synonymous with career development. Career development refers to any organizational initiative designed to help individuals manage their pattern of work experiences and attain their career goals (Russell, 1991). Such programs and experiences may not necessarily result in changes in individual attributes that affect work performance. For example, retirement initiatives and work–family policies (Russell, 1991) may assist individuals in attaining career goals, but are not intended to yield individual development.

Much of the work on individual development in the workplace has been conducted in Western cultures. Most research has been conducted in the United States, the United Kingdom, and Australia. The extent to which the theories and findings on individual development covered in this chapter will transfer to other cultures is largely untested. At the most basic level, the notion of individual development in the workplace is embedded in a number of culture-based assumptions. Some examples include (a) development is primarily an individual phenomenon, (b) most people can develop, (c) personal mastery and advancement is desirable, (d) improvement and progress are normal, (e) being open to change is good, and (f) work is of central importance in life (Hoppe, 1998). These tenets are not universally accepted. For example, individualistic and collectivist cultures tend to differ in how education and learning are perceived. In individual-istic societies, where interpersonal ties are loose and taking care of oneself and one's immediate family is emphasized, learning tends to be seen as lifelong. Education teaches one how to learn, not just how to do. In contrast, in collectivist cultures, where people belong to and protect cohesive in-groups throughout their lifetime, learning is more likely to be viewed as a one time process (Hofstede, 1997). And in 'doing' or action-oriented cultures where people want to actively shape their lives, individuals may feel more committed to pursuing development that will improve their work situations than do individuals in 'being' or acceptance-oriented culture where people believe they should accept what life has given them (Wilson, Hoppe & Sayles, 1996).

In addition to cultural differences that impact whether individual development in the workplace is seen as possible and worthwhile, there are likely cultural differences in comfort with the various individual development practices described in the second section of this chapter. For example, data and measurement are more highly valued in some cultures, which may affect comfort with 360-degree feedback; and seeking support from others is more natural in some cultures, which may influence comfort with coaching relationships or action learning groups (Hoppe, 1998). Throughout the chapter, we point out where research on development has been conducted outside the United States and note the extent to which development practices have been applied outside of the United States.

THREE LENSES ON INDIVIDUAL DEVELOPMENT

There are numerous streams of research relevant to the topic of individual development. We have organized these into three broad groups: behavior change, self-directed learning, and adult develop-ment. Each represents a different approach to understanding individual development in the work-place. Looking through each lens focuses our atten-tion on different research questions, constructs, and parts of the development process. Using all three lenses provides a more comprehensive view for understanding how to enhance individual develop-ment in the workplace.

Behavior Change

The state of our knowledge about behavioral change in work settings is well-articulated by Hellervick, Hazucha and Schneider (1992). They use theory and research on behavior change methods (e.g., behavior modeling, behavior modification),

motivation (e.g., self-regulation, control theory), and training to develop an integrated behavior change framework. According to this framework, there are five steps in the process of behavior change. The first step involves an assessment or needs analysis, which identifies the general nature of the behavior to be changed. In the second step, concrete behavioral objectives are specified. Next, individuals must form strong intentions to attain the behavioral objectives. That is, they must be com-mitted to achieving the change-related goals. During the fourth step, individuals begin to modify their behavior in a specific environment. This envi-ronment may be the same as the one in which new behaviors ultimately will be performed (e.g., the workplace) or be different (e.g., a training pro-gram). Finally, the new or modified behavior is generalized beyond the initial environment and maintained. Hellervik et al. (1992) note that the behavior change process is not always sequential. 'Later' steps may influence 'previous' steps. For example, early success in learning a new behavior may increase self-efficacy and boost commitment to achieving behavioral objectives.

In recent years, the behavioral change framework has been applied to research on the conditions under which feedback interventions lead to changes in behavior. Although the Hellervik et al. (1992) model has not been comprehensively tested, rela-tionships consistent with the model have been observed in a few field studies. (Hazucha, Hezlett & Schneider, 1993; Hezlett and Koonce, 1995).

With its roots in social learning theory, this approach to individual development shares com-mon 'ancestors' with behavior change approaches in clinical settings (e.g., smoking cessation, weight loss). It focuses on replacing currently ineffective behaviors with more effective ones and implicitly views learning as a challenge, where an individ-ual's motivation must be focused, protected, and supported. It emphasizes the importance of specific goals (i.e., a clear picture of the desired behaviors) and the perceived value of achieving those goals. In this view, although an individual's commitment to change is critical, the identification and initiation of the need to change does not necessarily come from the individual. In essence, this approach to develop-ment asks: how can people's behavior be changed to increase their effectiveness at work? The resulting model is prescriptive and process-focused.

The Hellervick et al., framework points to the necessary components of individual development from the behavior change perspective: (a) clear articulation of desired behaviors, (b) employees with high self-efficacy and instrumentality beliefs (i.e., expectations that they can achieve the behav-ioral standards and that achieving them will lead to valued outcomes), (c) learning situations that pro-vide opportunities to see the behavior, try out the behavior, and get feedback and reinforcement, and

(d) a work context that maintains the behavioral standards, continues to provide feedback and reinforcement through self-monitoring and external sources (e.g., supervisors), and minimizes threats to the behavior.

Self-Directed Learning

Self-directed, or continuous, learning involves self-initiated, deliberate, and sustained pursuit of formal and informal learning activities with the goal of increasing career-relevant knowledge and skills (London & Smither, 1999). Several streams of research contribute to the current state of knowledge regarding self-directed learning: maintaining professional competence (Kozlowski & Farr, 1988; Kozlowski & Hults, 1987; Pazy, 1995; Willis & Dubin, 1990), antecedents of participation in development activities (Birdi, Allen & Warr, 1997; Maurer & Tarulli, 1994; Noe & Wilk, 1993), self-management of careers (Hall, 1996), and learning to learn (Cell, 1984; Smith, 1990).

Research within this lens has tended to focus on ascertaining the personal and situational variables that determine participation in developmental activity. Of the individual attributes studied, education (Birdi et al., 1997; Campion, Cheraskin & Stevens, 1994; Kozlowski & Farr, 1988; Tharenou, 1997a, 1997b), management level (Birdi et al., 1997; Noe & Wilk, 1993; Tharenou, 1997b), motivation (Birdi et al., 1997; Noe & Wilk, 1993; Maurer & Tarulli, 1994), and attitudes (Maurer & Tarulli, 1994; Noe & Wilk, 1993; Tharenou, 1997b) have shown the most consistent relationships with participation in development activities. Age, tenure, and the perceived benefits of development have not been consistently linked to pursing development (Birdi et al., 1997; Campion et al., 1994; DeMeuse, 1985; Kozlowski & Farr, 1988; Noe & Wilk, 1993; Tharenou, 1997a, 1997b). Turning to situational variables, most studies have found support from supervisors, or other senior staff, encourages participation in development activities (Birdi et al., 1997; Hazucha et al., 1993; Noe, 1996; Noe & Wilk, 1993; Tharenou, 1997b). In contrast, the evidence is divided on whether support from peers hinders (Maurer & Tarulli, 1994) or facilitates participation in development activities (Birdi et al., 1997). Similarly, the relationship between organizational practices and participation in development activities has varied across studies (Hazucha et al., 1993; Maurer & Tarulli, 1994; Noe & Wilk, 1993; Tharenou, 1997b). Overall, this body of research provides a rich description of the individual and situational characteristics that encourage attempts to develop.

Recent conceptual contributions have begun to expand the focus of self-directed learning theories. Noe, Wilk, Mullen and Wanek (1997) suggested that a decision process mediates the relationship between individual difference variables and participation in learning activities. For example, rather than having a direct impact on participation in development activities, individual variables such as education and management level are predicted to affect the *decision* to pursue learning. Noe et al., noted several extant theories that may capture this decision process, including social learning theory, expectancy theory and the theory of reasoned action. This addition to the basic Person × Situation model represents a more process-oriented view on self-directed learning.

London and Smither (1999) also articulated a more process-focused model of self-directed learning. They propose that continuous learning has several distinct stages: pre-learning (recognizing the need for continuous learning and setting learning goals), learning (acquiring new skills and knowledge and monitoring learning), and application of learning (applying learning in a work context, evaluating learning, and reaping the benefits of learning). Individual and situational variables influence each of the three stages. For example, individuals who are high self-monitors, tend to seek feedback, and have greater openness to experience are predicted to be more likely to recognize the need for development during the pre-learning stage.

Through this lens, learning is viewed as an activity that is pursued by individuals to gain new knowledge and skills. It emphasizes the role of individual differences: some people will naturally pursue development more than others. Some of these individual differences are more stable while others are more malleable. The organization's role in development is to influence the more malleable individual differences (e.g., self-efficacy or feedback-seeking) and to enact the situational variables that support learning. Underlying this lens is the assumption that individuals play an active role in identifying their learning gaps and initiating a process to fill those gaps. The implicit question addressed is: what leads people to become self-directed learners?

The results of research grounded in the Person × Situation model of updating highlights motivation to learn and support from supervisors as key components of individual development. The new conceptual framework proposed by London and Smither (1999) elaborates upon these, suggesting the the necessary components of individual development from the self-directed learning perspective are: (a) changes in the environment (e.g., technology change, deregulation, contingent employment) or the organization (e.g., decentralization, global expansion, quality efforts) which create a gap between the employee's capabilities and current or future job requirements, (b) the individual's ability to recognize this gap (which is enhanced by proclivity toward such activities as self-monitoring and feedback seeking), (c) the motivation and ability to close the gap, and (d) opportunities and support for application of new knowledge and skills. The motivation and ability to close the gap is a function of both the individual (e.g., his or her self-efficacy and mastery orientation) and the situation (e.g., organizational climate for learning, resources available for learning, and empathy and support from coworkers). Application of learning is more likely if there are situational cues to remind employees to use their new knowledge and skills and if this use is reinforced by coworkers and the supervisor.

It is worth noting that studies of participation in development activities have been conducted in the United States (Hazucha et al., 1993; Noe & Wilk, 1993; Maurer & Tarulli, 1994), Australia (Tharenou, 1997b), and the United Kingdom (Birdi, Allan & Warr, 1997). Both management and non-management samples have been studied.

Adult Development

Cognitive interactionist theories of learning (Argyris & Schön, 1974; Dewey, 1938; Kolb, 1984; Mezirow, 1991), constructionist models of cognitive and interpersonal development (Basseches, 1984; Kegan, 1994; Perry, 1970), and studies of managerial learning (Burgoyne & Reynolds, 1997; McCall, Lombardo & Morrison, 1988; Wagner & Sternberg, 1985) have examined how adults continue to develop more complex capacities over time. All of these theories and frameworks point to *experience* – purposive interaction with one's environment – as the medium through which learning occurs. Learning, in this view, is a process of cognitively reorganizing and reconstructing how one understands oneself and the world and using that understanding to guide future action. This learning is developmental to the degree that the reconstructed understanding is more adequate for dealing with complexity, integrates a broader range of dimensions of experience and perspectives upon that experience, and is less egocentric (Basseches, 1984).

Dixon (1994) provides an integrated view of the learning process from the cognitive interactionist perspective. In any experience, a person selectively takes in information from the environment. People are more likely to pay attention to information that is different from their current understanding or from their expectations. They try to make sense of the new information by retrieving meaning structures, which are ways of organizing and relating information. If their existing meaning structures are useful for making sense of the new information, then it will be assimilated into that structure. If the information conflicts with the existing meaning structure, then people feel an internal sense of disequilibrium or dissonance, and work to alter or reconstruct their meaning structures to accommodate the new information. People develop various meaning structures that are connected in networks

(often called 'cognitive maps'). A person's cognitive map represents how he or she makes sense of the world and guides a person's future actions. Some aspects of people's cognitive maps are consciously accessible and intentionally altered, and other aspects are tacit and unintentionally altered. In either case, the process of creating order out of and giving meaning to experiences is what learning is.

This learning-from-experience process is often conceptualized as a learning cycle of having concrete experiences, making observations and reflecting on those experiences, forming concepts and generalizations based on those reflections, and testing those ideas in new situations (Kolb, 1984). Argyris and Schön (1974) added the distinction of single-loop and double-loop learning. In single-loop learning, observation and reflection detects errors in one's initial concepts and these concepts are refined to account for the new information without disrupting the central assumptions of one's meaning structures. In double-loop learning, the central assumptions themselves are examined and challenged, leading to new meaning structures. Further research and inquiry based on theories of adult learning and development have examined elements of the process, such as reflection and transformation of meaning structures, more closely (Hodgetts, 1994; Schön, 1983; Mezirow & Associates, 1990); blocks in the learning process (Argyris, 1991); individual differences in learning styles or approaches (Dalton, 1999; Kolb, 1984; Mumford, 1995); and the outcomes of developmental learning, such as tacit knowledge (Torff & Sternberg, 1998) and levels of cognitive complexity (Basseches, 1984; Lewis & Jacobs, 1992).

From the adult development lens, learning is viewed as an ongoing process that individuals routinely engage in as they interact with their environments. The purpose of learning is to develop more complex and adaptable ways of understanding self and the world. This lens draws attention to *how* people learn, with a particular focus on the cognitive processes involved. It emphasizes the importance of disequilibrating experiences and having the resources for making sense of those experiences (e.g., time for reflection, access to others) – factors that both individuals and organizations can influence. Rather than something individuals and organizations must invest in sustaining, motivation to learn naturally stems from the discomfort associated with dissonant new information. Research in this lens helps answer the question: How do people develop more complex capacities in adulthood?

From the adult development perspective, the factors that enhance individual development include: (a) access to work experiences that are new or different from previous experiences (McCall et al., 1988; Wick, 1989), (b) intentional reflection in and on experiences (Seibert & Daudelin, 1999), (c) reacting to disequilibrating experiences by reexamining the basic assumptions reflected in current meaning structures (Argyris & Schön, 1974), (d) relationships with more-developed mentors and guides (i.e., access to more complex meaning structures) (Schön, 1983; 1987; Torff & Sternberg, 1998), and (e) opportunities to work closely with others in the same field or profession, sharing knowledge and learning collectively (Wenger, 1998).

Elements of Individual Development across Lenses

Each of the three lenses provides a somewhat different perspective on individual development in the workplace. Each emphasizes a particular outcome of individual development: changed behaviors, enhanced knowledge and skills, and transformed understanding that guides future action. The behavior change lens highlights the difficulty of individual development and the role of goals, instrumentality beliefs, and reinforcement in the change process. The self-directed learning lens emphasizes individual differences in the motivation to pursue learning and the situational factors that facilitate continuous learning. The adult development lens highlights interaction with the environment as the source of learning and the cognitive processes involved in development.

However, there are common themes across the different perspectives, and taken together they provide a more complete picture of a workplace that is rich in individual development. These five elements of individual development are: awareness of developmental needs, self-efficacy for learning, new experiences, examination of self-in-experiences, and valuing of individual development. A description of each element and how it is embodied in each development lens is shown in Table 14.1.

DEVELOPMENTAL PRACTICES

We now turn to examining the practice of individual development in the workplace. Six organizational practices aimed at fostering individual development are considered. Four of these are specific development methodologies: 360-degree feedback, coaching, developmental job assignments, and action learning. Two others – enhancing social support for learning and fostering communities of practice – are broader approaches to stimulate and support development throughout an organization.

For each practice, we provide a description, a summary of the state of the practice, and, where possible, an overview of research. At the end of the section, we analyze the practices in terms of the five elements for individual development. We should note that the literature on most of these practices, particularly the four specific development methodologies,

is heavily weighted toward management development rather than development at all levels in an organization.

360-Degree Feedback

The terms 360-degree feedback, multisource feedback, multiple perspective feedback, and multi-rater feedback refer to organizational processes in which employees systematically receive feedback from more than one group of coworkers. The groups providing feedback may include the employee's supervisors, peers, subordinates, and, occasionally, clients. Upward feedback involves supervisors receiving feedback from their subordinates.

Across and within organization, 360-degree feedback systems vary. Differences between systems may be loosely organized into two broad categories: (a) factors associated with the feedback individuals receive, and (b) conditions related to what individuals do after they receive feedback.

Factors that influence the feedback employees receive include the groups (perspectives) who are asked to provide feedback, how specific raters are selected, and the method used to collect the feedback (e.g., paper and pencil, the internet). The content of feedback instruments also differ. Employees may be evaluated in terms of their personality, the extent to which they 'live' the values of their organization, or on their work-related behavior. For each of these kinds of content, raters may be asked to provide feedback on a dozen items or over a hundred. Finally, differences in reporting affect the feedback employees see. Common variations include the level at which results are aggregated (e.g., within vs. across rating perspectives and item level vs. dimension level) and whether the feedback recipient's strongest and weakest areas are highlighted.

After feedback is distributed, 360-degree feedback systems differ on a number of conditions that may affect how the results are used. These include the amount of assistance provided in interpreting feedback and the nature of supplemental resources designed to facilitate development. Some feedback recipients may receive written material providing them with basic information on how to write a development plan, while others may be personally directed to specific learning activities designed to address their particular development needs. Another critical distinction between 360-degree feedback systems are the expectations for feedback recipients. Although individual development is typically a primary objective of 360-degree feedback systems, some organizations use them for performance evaluations. Therefore, some recipients simply are advised to work on their development, while others are held accountable for their results. Overall, 360-degree feedback systems can differ on a large number of variables.

Table 14.1 *Common elements of individual development across three lenses on development*

Element	Behavior change	Self-directed learning	Adult development
Awareness of developmental needs • Knowing in what way an individual's capacities need to be expanded	• Clear articulation of desired behaviors	• Awareness of gaps between current capabilities and current or future job requirements (from self-monitoring and feedback-seeking)	• Reacting to disequilibrating experiences by reexamining the basic assumptions in current meaning structures
Self-efficacy for learning • Belief that one can expand his or her capacity in certain domains	• High expectations from employees that they can achieve the behavioral standard	• Employee self-efficacy and mastery orientation	• Belief that new meaning structures can be created in response to disequilibrating experiences
New experiences • Activities that require individuals to stretch skills or learn new ones	• Learning situations that provide opportunities to try out new behaviors	• Changes in the environment or the organization that create a gap between capabilities and requirements • Opportunities for application of new knowledge and skills	• Access to new or different work experiences • Access to guides with more complex meaning structures
Examination of self-in-experiences • Being intentionally conscious of behaviors, feelings, and thought processes when encountering new experiences	• Self-monitoring and feedback during the aquisition and generalization of new behaviors	• Feedback and situational cues to facilitate the application of knowledge and skills	• Intentional reflection in and on experiences • Opportunities to learn collectively with coworkers
Valuing of individual development • Development is experienced as leading to valued outcomes	• Work contexts that reinforce and minimize threats to new behaviors • High expectations from employees that achieving behavioral standards will lead to valued outcomes	• Support and reinforcement of new knowledge and skills from coworkers and supervisors	• Access to guides with more complex meaning structures • Opportunities to learn collectively with coworkers

The use of 360-degree feedback is relatively widespread ('A twist on performance reviews' 1993; London & Smither, 1995). A recent survey suggests it is used as a tool for developing top executives and other managers by a substantial number of organizations based in the United States and many companies in Europe. Some organizations also use 360-degree feedback with employees who are not managers (Conference Board, 1999). Those interested in implementing a 360-degree feedback system have a number of articles (e.g., Bracken, 1994; Johnson, Olson & Courtney, 1996), chapters (e.g., Bracken, 1996; London, 1995), and books (e.g., Lepsinger & Lucia, 1997; Tornow, London & CCL Associates, 1998; Van Velsor, Leslie & Fleenor, 1997) to turn to for guidance. A clear picture of how to handle non-US implementations is also beginning to emerge (Leslie, Gryzkiewicz & Dalton, 1998).

Although 360-degree feedback has been criticized as an area where research has lagged behind practice, more research has been conducted on this development practice than many others. In addition to studying the psychometric properties of feedback instruments, researchers have studied three issues: (a) feedback recipients' reactions to the process, (b) self–other agreement, and (c) the impact of 360-degree feedback on behavior change.

An early concern about 360-degree feedback was that employees would not accept evaluations from their subordinates or peers. Research suggests this fear is unfounded. Although few studies have investigated reactions to 360-degree feedback, the results indicate attitudes towards receiving feedback from subordinates, peers, and supervisors improve after employees have participated in the process (Bernardin, Hagan & Kane, 1985). Studies focused on single rating perspectives also generally have yielded favorable results. (Antonioni, 1994; Barclay & Harland, 1995; Bernardin, Dahmus & Redmon, 1993; McEvoy & Buller, 1987). Overall, feedback from the sources involved in many 360-degree feedback systems is viewed positively, particularly if the purpose of the feedback is developmental.

Consistent with the basic elements of individual development identified earlier in this chapter, a goal often associated with 360-degree feedback is increasing employees' self-awareness. Research on this topic has generally assumed that better agreement between self- and others' ratings indicate greater self-awareness. Several longitudinal studies have found that the correlation between self- and others' ratings increases after participation in upward and 360-degree feedback (Hazucha et al., 1993; London & Wohlers, 1991). On the other hand, studies examining mean differences between self- and others' ratings have obtained inconsistent results (Atwater, Roush & Fischtal, 1995; Bernardin et al., 1995; Nilsen & Campbell, 1993; Smither, London, Vasilopoulos, Reilly, Millsap &

Salvemini, 1995). By outlining variables that affect the complex process of accurate personality judgment, Funder's (2001) Realistic Accuracy Model suggests it may be unrealistic to expect complete agreement between self- and others' ratings. This model also predicts that there are individual and cultural differences in self-knowledge. Finally, when considering research on self-other agreement in ratings, it is worth noting that rating congruence, self-awareness, and an understanding of what is most crucial to learn or improve are probably not perfectly correlated.

A handful of studies have tested whether upward or 360-degree feedback systems lead to individual development. The results suggest upward feedback encourages development (Hegerty, 1974), particularly for certain groups of feedback recipients. These include individuals who initially received low ratings from their subordinates (Johnson & Ferstl, 1999; Reilly, Smither & Vasilopoulos, 1996; Smither et al., 1995; Walker & Smither, 1999) and those who received lower ratings from their subordinates than they gave themselves (i.e., overraters) (Atwater et al., 1995; Johnson & Ferstl, 1999). Managers who discuss their feedback with their subordinates also tend to receive higher subsequent ratings from them (Walker & Smither, 1999). Most of these studies have demonstrated that the observed improvements are not accounted for by regression to the mean (Atwater et al., 1995; Johnson & Ferstl, 1999; Reilly et al., 1996; Smither et al., 1995; Walker & Smither, 1999). There is some evidence, however, that improvements occur regardless of whether individuals actually receive the initial feedback or merely anticipate that they will (Smither et al., 1995).

Evaluations of 360-degree feedback systems have been mixed. Although Hazucha et al. (1993) observed skill improvement following receipt of feedback, their study lacked a control group, making it impossible to rule out alternate explanations for the observed improvement. Bernardin et al. (1995) observed that peer and subordinate ratings received by feedback recipients improved over time, the ratings made by supervisors did not. In addition, supervisor ratings for those receiving 360-degree feedback did not differ significantly from those for a control group who received feedback only from their supervisors. To summarize, a limited amount of research on the impact of upward and 360-degree feedback on individual development has been conducted. Although not definitive, this research provides some evidence that such feedback may be beneficial for certain individuals. Subordinates' ratings of poor performers and individuals who initially had inflated views of themselves appear to improve over time.

Despite the use of feedback instruments as development tools for nonmanagement employees, research has focused on individuals in leadership positions. Research conducted outside the United States has utilized feedback instruments to investigate cross-cultural differences in the importance and use of skills (Hazucha, Hezlett, Bontems-Wackens & Ronnkvist, 1999).

Executive Coaching

Executive coaching involves a series of one-on-one interactions between a manager or executive and an external coach in order to further the professional development of the manager. Although each coaching initiative is tailored to meet the needs of the participating executive and his or her organization, there are five basic steps in the process.

First, the coaching process is initiated by a member of an organization. One estimate suggests roughly half of coaching interventions are initiated by the executive receiving the coaching (Judge & Cowell, 1997). Human resources (HR) representatives or more senior executives may also suggest that a manager or executive would benefit from coaching. This phase of the coaching process typically culminates in a contracting meeting. During the meeting, the coach, the person being coached, and other organizational stakeholders (e.g., more senior executives, an HR representative) review the basic developmental issues to be addressed and agree upon the scope of the coaching intervention.

The second step in the coaching process is an assessment of the participating executive. The assessment may simply consist of a 360-degree feedback instrument completed by the executive's superiors, peers, and direct reports, but is often more in-depth. The executive may complete several personality inventories and be extensively interviewed by the coach. The coach also often interviews people who regularly interact with the executive, including individuals outside the organization, such as key customers and the executive's spouse and family members.

The third phase of the coaching process has two major components: delivering the results of the assessment to the executive and agreeing upon a course of action. The coach typically shares the results with the executive in an interactive session that may last anywhere from two hours to two days. The coach not only shares information with the executive, but elicits the executive's thoughts and reactions to the feedback. The coach and executive begin identifying areas which are priorities and arrive at an understanding of what developmental actions will be taken.

During the fourth phase of the coaching intervention, the development plan is implemented. Throughout this phase, the coach and executive meet regularly. The content of each meeting can vary widely. In some meetings, the coach may act as a sounding board for initiatives the executive is thinking about implementing. At other times, meetings may be devoted to building skills or analyzing recent situations the executive has encountered. The coach and the executive also may opt to meet periodically with other stakeholders in order to foster an environment which facilitates the executive's development efforts. The implementation phase of the coaching process is the longest, lasting from several months to over a year.

The fifth and final stage of coaching is a follow-up phase. The coach and executive meet less frequently, primarily to help ensure that the executive is still making progress towards his or her development goals.

One way coaching interventions have been differentiated is by the kind of people who participate. Executive coaching was initially developed in order to 'rescue' talented individuals who are in danger of stalling their careers or even losing their jobs because of a particular deficit in their performance. A classic case would be the individual who was promoted into a position of responsibility based on his or her exceptional technical proficiency, but is lacking in interpersonal skills. A second group of individuals who may participate in coaching are high potential managers who need additional development before advancing further up the corporate ladder. Professionals, such as doctors, are also beginning to seek coaching in order to learn how to deal with administrative responsibilities, such as managing finances.

Several authors (Witherspoon and White, 1996; Thach & Heinselman, 1999) have distinguished among coaching interventions based on the nature of the coaching. Peterson (1996) provides the most comprehensive taxonomy, differentiating three types of coaching using six criteria: scope of coverage, the assessment, participant motivation, organizational involvement, frequency of sessions, and follow-up and support.

As a practice, executive coaching is flourishing. It emerged as an outgrowth of leadership development programs in the early 1980s and by 1990 was being offered by many traditional human resource consulting firms (Judge & Cowell, 1997; Hellervick et al., 1992). A recent survey of 900 human resources executives found 71% of polled organizations provided coaching to their employees. Although most of the coaching was supplied by managers or internal consultants, 20% of the firms used external consultants (HR Focus, 1999). Companies outside the United States also utilize executive coaching for their top executives, and, to a lesser extent, other managers. As its label suggests, non-management employees rarely receive executive coaching, either within or outside the United States (Conference Board, 1999).

Descriptions of executive coaching have appeared in the popular press (e.g., Smith, 1993), as well as in professional journals (e.g., Koonce, 1994; Thach & Heinselman, 1999). A special issue of

Consulting Psychology Journal: Research and Practice was dedicated to executive coaching in 1996. Chapters on executive coaching also have been published (e.g., Hayes, 1997; Strickland, 1997), and discussions of the topic have been included in recent chapters on behavior change (Hellervick et al., 1992), leadership development (e.g., Hollenbeck & McCall, 1999), and developmental relationships (McCauley & Douglas, 1998). Books on the general topic of coaching in the workplace have recently begun to appear (e.g., Hudson, 1999; Peterson & Hicks, 1996).

Although there are a number of case studies portraying successful instances of executive coaching (e.g., Diedrich, 1996; Kiel, Rimmer, Williams & Doyle, 1996; Peterson, 1996; Tobias, 1996), little empirical research has been conducted on this practice (Hollenbeck & McCall, 1999; Kilburg, 1996). A few studies have found that coaching participants find their experiences as valuable and effective (Edelstein & Armstrong, 1993; Hall, Otazo & Hollenbeck, 1999). Peterson (1993) found that managers who participated in coaching showed greater improvement on the skills they targeted for development than on those they do not attempt to build. In addition, the behavior of coaching participants was seen as changing by others. While these results are promising, further studies of executive coaching are needed to evaluate its effectiveness as a technique for individual development.

Developmental Job Assignments

A number of studies indicate that a great deal of workplace learning occurs in the course of dealing with the roles, responsibilities, and tasks associated with one's job (McCall et al., 1988; Sternberg, Wagner, Williams & Horvath, 1995; Zemke, 1985). Focusing primarily on managerial jobs, research has indicated that some types of job assignments are more developmental than others (Davies & Easterby-Smith, 1984; Kelleher, Finestone & Lowy, 1986; McCauley, Ruderman, Ohlott & Morrow, 1994). The terms *challenging* and *stretching* have been used to describe assignments that are particularly developmental. Challenging assignments tend to have one or more of the following components: new situations with unfamiliar responsibilities; tasks or projects that require the individual to create change, manage across organizational boundaries, build relationships, or deal with diverse people; and high-level, high-latitude responsibilities (McCauley & Brutus, 1998; McCauley, Ohlott & Ruderman, 1999). These components are positively correlated with job incumbents' reports of on-the-job learning (McCauley et al., 1999).

Equipped with this growing base of knowledge about developmental assignments, organizations have begun to systematically and intentionally use developmental assignments rather than rely solely on their natural occurrence in the workplace. There appear to be three general approaches to using developmental assignments more systematically (McCauley & Brutus, 1998): (a) When choosing people for jobs, the potential development offered by the job is used as one factor in decision making (Clark & Lyness, 1991; Friedman, 1990). For example, if the job contained more new elements for one candidate than for another, the job would be more developmental for this candidate and would thus be a positive in favor of choosing him or her. (b) Specific types of assignments are used as part of a development system (Bonoma & Lawler, 1989; Morrison & Hock, 1986). In these situations, the specific kinds of job experiences needed by individuals in particular career paths or people targeted for higher-level jobs are identified, and job assignments are given over time to ensure that individuals get these experiences. For example, in order to develop a global perspective in its high-potential managers, a company ensures that each of these managers has the opportunity to manage a subsidiary in a foreign country (Seibert, Hall & Kram, 1995). (c) Employees are encouraged to develop within their current jobs by adding challenging opportunities, for example, through special projects, task forces, new responsibilities, and boundary-spanning roles (Lombardo & Eichenger, 1989; McCauley et al., 1999). Organizations may expect managers to help their employees craft a developmental task each year through their formal developmental planning process, or they may provide information about developmental opportunities and expect employees to seek these out on their own.

A recent survey (Conference Board, 1999) suggests that although developmental job assignments are used more extensively in US-based companies, they are a popular tool both within and outside the United States. For top executives and other managers, organizations in the United States and Europe report utilizing developmental job experiences about as often as they use 360-degree feedback. Fewer organizations use developmental job assignments with their non-management personnel (27% in US companies and 19% in non-US companies). A number of resources are available to the practitioner who wants to design developmental assignments for employees (Bonoma & Lawler, 1989; Lombardo & Eichenger, 1989; McCall et al., 1988; McCauley et al., 1999; Wick & Leon, 1993).

As discussed previously, research on developmental job assignments has distinguished what kinds of assignments are particularly developmental. Although systematic use of job assignments for individual development is based on considerable research into the nature of developmental assignments, there has been no research examining the impact or relative value of the three general approaches described above. Researchers have examined the characteristics of individuals who are particularly adept at learning from job experiences (Bunker & Webb, 1992; Dalton & Swigert, 2000; Dechant, 1990; Lombardo & Eichenger, 1996; Spreitzer, McCall & Mahooney, 1997; Van Velsor & Guthrie, 1998). These characteristics include a learning orientation (i.e., learning is central to self-concept), a proactive stance toward problems and opportunities, an ability to engage in critical reflection, and openness to change (McCauley & Brutus, 1998). As is often the case in emerging areas of research, various researchers have labeled and described this learning construct differently (e.g., ability to learn from experience, learning versatility, learning agility). What the various approaches have in common is an emphasis on motivation to learn and on being able to apply a range of learning strategies. This line of research implies that learning from developmental assignments is not automatic; organizations must not only provide challenging job opportunities to employees, but must either select for or develop learning capacities in them.

The impact of race and gender on access to and outcomes from developmental assignments have also received attention in the research literature (Cianni & Romberger, 1995; Ohlott, Ruderman & McCauley, 1994; Morrison, White & Van Velsor, 1992; Ruderman & Hughes-James, 1998). These studies suggest that learning from experience in male-dominated organizations is more complex for women and minorities because there is more ambiguity about causal factors in the situations they encounter (e.g., to what degree is an outcome attributable to their own effort versus others' reaction to their non-dominant status). There is, however, evidence that access to developmental assignments is increasing for women and minorities in US organizations.

Action Learning

Action learning was developed by Revans (1982) as an educational approach that encourages people to apply and generate knowledge from real-world situations. Although there are numerous ways that action learning is practiced, the approach has three main components: problems or issues that have no clear solution, people who will take responsibility for action on the issues, and a group of six or so colleagues (often called a 'set') who support and challenge each other to make progress on problems (Pedler, 1997).

Revans conceptualized learning as a function of programmed knowledge (gained through traditional instruction) and questioning insight (arrived at through critical reflection). Perceiving questioning insight to be the more powerful, but under-utilized, driver of traditional education, Revans made it the focus of his action learning programs. In a typical action learning program, participants are exposed to

theories or knowledge using typical programmed instruction methods. They then apply this new knowledge and knowledge from their previous experiences to a project that has potential value to the organization. These projects focus on complex issues that often involve many stakeholders, such as movement into new markets, the introduction of new technology, reorganizations, and decentralization (Marsick, 1990).

As they are working on the project, participants meet in groups, usually with a facilitator or advisor, to discuss their understanding of the dilemmas they encounter, to question the theories and concepts they are applying in the project, and to discover new ways of thinking or creative alternatives to accomplish their objectives. Through this process of action, debriefing, and feedback with mutual learners, participants gain more in-depth knowledge and effective theories to apply to their work. The approach also assumes that the group debrief methodology encourages enhanced knowledge and skills in group dynamics and in learning-to-learn strategies.

As experience with action learning has grown, how it is used in organizations has evolved in several directions. Action learning may be (a) a component of an individual development program (particularly those designed for management development), (b) part of an organizational change initiative, or (c) part of an ongoing strategy for organizational learning (Marsick & O'Neil, 1999; Dotlich & Noel, 1998). Different uses of action learning emphasize somewhat different components and processes.

Action learning projects as a component of an individual development program often utilize individual projects rather than team projects. Participants still meet in groups or sets to reflect on progress and question strategies, with each project getting some of the group's attention. The projects are usually connected to the participants' current job responsibilities. Dotlich and Noel (1998) describe an internal program at Citibank, and Marsick (1990) describes programs at the Management Institute in Lund, Sweden, that utilize action learning in this manner.

When the action learning program is driven by organizational changes or goals, then team projects serve as the focus of testing and reshaping knowledge in real-world situations. These programs generally serve goals beyond individual development: to provide opportunities to work across units and build internal networks, to bring various perspectives and expertise to bear on an organizational issue, and to institutionalize a particular approach to problem identification and analysis. Vicere and Fulmer (1997) provide a detailed case analysis of this type of action learning initiative at ARAMARK. In addition to focusing on team rather than individual projects, action learning initiatives in this context differ in other ways from those designed primarily for individual development: They generally require participants to work on projects outside of their current responsibilities, tend to focus more on learning about group processes and dynamics, and often end with a recommendation on a course of action that is carried out by the sponsoring business unit (rather than by the project team).

With its beginnings in the UK, the action learning approach has been increasingly applied in Europe, North America, and Australia. A Conference Board survey (1999) reported that 45% of US companies used action learning projects in their management development initiatives, and 9% used this method for nonmanagement employee development. For companies outside the US, the figures were 36% and 11% respectively. There is also evidence that action learning programs are beginning to be used in Asia (Pun, 1997). The pragmatic approach of integrating learning with real work on organizational problems is appealing to companies seeking more tangible results from their investment in employee development (Stern, 1997). Considerable practical knowledge on implementing action learning programs and interventions is available (see Dotlich & Noel, 1998; McGill & Beaty, 1992; Mumford, 1997; Pedler, 1997; Weinstein, 1995).

Initial formal evaluations of action learning programs relied heavily on interviews with program participants. Studies reported in Mumford (1997) and Pedler (1997) found that participants experienced learning in the areas of teamwork, communication, effective management, facilitation skills, self-confidence, self-awareness, self-discipline, and networking. The challenge and reflection experienced in learning sets, access to an advisor or facilitator, and the support of an organizational sponsor were generally cited as the most important process elements in action learning. However, O'Neil, Marsick, Yorks, Niles & Kolodny (1997) identified several tensions experienced by action learning participants: tensions between expectations for learning and delivering tangible results, between time required for learning and for the task, and between team conflict and harmony. More recent research documenting the positive impact of action learning programs have used multiple sources for assessing learning and change (e.g., coworkers and organizational sponsors) and have begun to address the question of transfer of learning from the program to ongoing work (Dilworth & Willis, 1999; Lamm, 2000; Raelin, 1997; Yorks, Lamm, O'Neil, Kolodny, Marsick & Nilson, 1998).

Enhancing Social Support for Learning

There are a number of strategies organizations might use to increase the social support experienced by employees in their work setting. We examine two that have received the most attention in research and practice: encouraging mentoring relationships and developing the support and coaching capacities of supervisors.

Mentoring typically involves a committed, long-term relationship between a more seasoned higher-level employee and a less experienced employee. Mentors give their protégés career-related assistance (e.g., sponsorship, coaching, challenging assignments, and high visibility) and psychosocial support (e.g., advice, encouragement) (Kram, 1983, Noe, 1988). Role-modeling may be a third distinct function mentors provide (Burke, 1984; Johnson & Scandura, 1994). Receiving support from a mentor is associated with higher performance ratings, more recognition, greater compensation, more career opportunities, and more promotions (Burke & McKeen, 1997; Chao, 1997; Dreher & Ash, 1990; Fagenson, 1989; Orpen, 1995; Scandura, 1992; Turban & Dougherty, 1994; Whitely, Dougherty & Dreher, 1991).

One way organizations encourage mentoring is by creating opportunities for interaction between seasoned and inexperienced employees, thus increasing the probability that informal mentoring relationships will evolve. For example, project teams or task forces are purposefully staffed by a mixture of experienced and new employees. Or experts in a particular area are identified as resource people for others to use as consultants or advisors on their projects. A second way to encourage mentoring relationships is by creating formal mentoring programs that pair junior and senior employees and create a structure for their interaction over a specified period of time. Although evaluations of formal mentoring programs have demonstrated positive results (Gaskill, 1993; Noe, 1988; Portwood & Granrose, 1986), there is some evidence that protégés participating in formal mentoring programs benefit less than those who have informal mentoring relationships (Chao, Walz & Gardner, 1992).

A Conference Board survey (1999) found informal mentoring is used by more organizations than formal mentoring. Both informal and formal mentoring is used most extensively at low-to-middle management levels in both US companies (38% use formal, 65% use informal) and companies outside of the US (25% use formal, 47% use informal). Both are used less extensively at executive and nonmanagement levels.

Practitioners have learned a great deal from trying to implement formal mentoring programs, thus advice on how to design effective programs and avoid some of the potential downsides of these programs is available (Kram & Bragar, 1992; Murray & Owen, 1991). A literature review (Douglas, 1997) identified well over one hundred different characteristics of successful mentoring programs; however, these characteristics clustered around five themes: (a) organizational support for the program, (b) clarity of purpose, expectations, and roles, (c) participant choice and involvement, (d) careful selection and matching procedures, and (e) continuous monitoring and evaluation.

A broader idea of 'manager as coach' grew out of the success of external coaching programs and mentoring. This has led to increased attention on developing managers who can coach all of their subordinates (Peterson & Hicks, 1996; Waldroop & Butler, 1996). This approach has several potential advantages over coaching by external experts or mentoring. First, managerial coaching may provide support for development to more employees. Second, since supervisors tend to communicate more frequently with 'typical subordinates' than with their protégés, support for development may be reinforced more regularly through coaching than through mentoring. Third, managerial coaching suggests development is important for all employees, not just those who find or are assigned a mentor.

Organizational strategies for enhancing managerial support and coaching include articulating the payback to managers for spending time developing their subordinates, developing coaching skills among managers, and holding managers accountable for the development of their subordinates (McCauley & Douglas, 1998). Scant attention has been devoted to assessing the impact of manager's coaching on development, but results are encouraging. One study found preparing managers to act as coaches led subordinates to demonstrate substantially more transfer of training (Olivero, Bane & Kopelmane, 1997). And as previously discussed, supervisor support has been linked to greater participation in development activities in the United States, Australia, and the United Kingdom (Birdi et al., 1997; Hazucha et al., 1993; Noe, 1996; Noe & Wilk, 1994; Tharenou, 1997b). Interestingly, a study of both managers and nonmanagers conducted in a Danish bank found no relationship between employees' perceptions of supervisor support (i.e., receiving feedback and being empowered) and supervisor ratings of employees' seeking of feedback and development (London, Larsen & Thisted, 1999). Although several methodological issues may account for this disparate finding, the researchers note that cultural differences also offer a plausible explanation. Compared to their counterparts in other countries, Danish employees may feel more empowered and, thus, may pursue development regardless of how supportive their supervisors are.

Fostering Communities of Practice

'Community of practice' is a concept associated with the Institute for Research on Learning (IRL). Founded in 1987, IRL's goal is to design social architectures that foster learning in workplaces and in schools. The institution has brought together scholars from diverse fields who collaborate with groups and organizations that are seeking to transform themselves into environments for continuous learning; they primarily utilize research-in-action methodologies that combine research and interventions (IRL, 1999).

From IRL's perspective, learning is fundamentally a social activity taking place within communities of practice. Communities of practice are groups of people mutually engaged in a joint enterprise with a shared repertoire of tools, concepts, actions, stories, and historical events (Wenger, 1998). People are members of multiple communities of practice: families, work groups, sports teams, musical groups, volunteer organizations, and so forth. People who are united by a common enterprise develop shared beliefs and ways of doing things as a function of their joint involvement in mutual activity. As individuals gain membership and participate in community activity they develop particular kinds of knowledge and expertise. Learning is this process of contributing to the development of and ongoing participation in a community of practice (Wenger, 1998). In this view, learning is not just the acquisition of knowledge and skills, but the formation of an identity.

According to Wenger (1998), the components of an architecture that fosters communities of practice – and thus enhances learning – are (a) an infrastructure of engagement (e.g., physical spaces that encourage interaction, things to do together, ways of belonging to the community to various degrees, problems that engage energy and creativity, occasions for mutual evaluation, repositories of information and documentation, apprenticeship systems), (b) an infrastructure of imagination (e.g., open spaces; stories and examples; organizational charts; facilities for comparison with other practices; retreats, sabbaticals, and other breaks in rhythm; opportunities and tools for trying things out; play and simulations), and (c) an infrastructure of alignment (e.g., common focus; plans, deadlines, and schedules; information transmission; data collection and measurement).

Numerous research-in-action projects have enacted, tested, and refined the concept and understanding of communities of practice. For example, IRL collaborated with a high-tech company to create a workplace that would support informal interaction and collaboration in teams (Wild, Bishop & Sullivan, 1996). A mobile office environment was designed and implemented. A comparison to two existing workplaces showed that the experimental workplace increased informal learning and interaction substantially. Subsequently, they worked with an office and furniture designer to shift the way they assess their customer sites – from looking at individuals and how they work to looking at the communities and how they work together to create knowledge (IRL, 1999). IRL helped another organization rethink their approach to the development of

Table 14.2 *Elements of development emphasized by each individual development practice*

	360-degree feedback	Executive coaching	Developmental assignments	Action learning	Social support for learning	Communities of practice
Awareness of developmental needs	√	√				
Self-efficacy for learning					√	√
New experiences			√	√		
Examination of self-in-experiences	√			√		
Valuing of learning					√	√

new hires for their nationwide sales force. After analysis of how sales representatives accomplished their most meaningful learning, they recommended a dedicated, field-based, new-hire learning support process, and formal knowledge development activities that integrated work and learning and helped the new hires develop relationships within their work communities (IRL, 1999).

Communities of practice that link experts from across an organization are being nurtured in a number of companies as a vehicle for professional development, transfer of best practice, and quick problem solving (Wenger & Snyder, 2000). For example, DaimlerChrysler supports 'tech clubs', groups of engineers who do not work in the same unit but voluntarily meet regularly to talk about problems related to their own area of expertise. Organizations wanting to incorporate the communities of practice concept into their learning strategies are encouraged to identify potential communities, provide the infrastructure that will support each community, and assess the value of these communities by the impact individual members have back in their units and work teams (Wenger & Snyder, 2000).

An Analysis of Practices in Terms of the Elements of Development

To what degree does each developmental practice provide employees with the elements of development: awareness of developmental needs, self-efficacy for learning, new experiences, examination of self-in-experiences, and valuing of individual development? As shown in Table 14.2 each practice is particularly effective in delivering one or two of the elements. Other elements may be addressed in a specific application of the practice, but are not routinely part of the practice. We draw two implications from the information in Table 14.2. First, when implementing any of these practices, care needs to be taken to build in the elements that are not a natural strength of the practice. And secondly, no one practice is a panacea for individual development. To adequately address all five elements, these practices need to be used together in an integrated way.

Multisource feedback and developmental assignments each focuses intensely on providing one element of development. Upward and 360-degree feedback systems are primarily used as tools for developing awareness of development needs; developmental assignments provide new experiences. Although they each contain a powerful element in the development process, they are in danger of having little impact if other elements are not explicitly considered and built into each practice's implementation.

Well-designed 360-degree feedback systems may improve individuals' awareness of their developmental needs. In developing or adopting the content of a feedback system, organizations identify what behaviors, knowledge, skills, abilities, or other attributes are important for a particular group of employees. When individuals receive upward or 360-degree feedback, they can determine how well they meet these standards. Areas in which individuals receive relatively low ratings, have self-ratings that are highly discrepant from others' ratings, or have divergent ratings from others may be targeted as development needs. It should be noted, however, that 360-degree feedback systems differ in the extent to which feedback recipients are given assistance in interpreting their results and setting developmental objectives. Without assistance from facilitators, support materials, or co-workers, individuals may not reach a clear understanding of how they should direct their development efforts.

Feedback systems are less likely to provide the other four elements of individual development. These can be encouraged by adding supplemental features to the 360-degree feedback process. For example, the self-efficacy of feedback recipients can be bolstered by facilitators or supervisors trained to assist individuals who are discouraged by low ratings or to challenge those who received high ratings to continue to grow. The materials or resources that accompany 360-degree feedback can help individuals select new experiences or situations that will enable them to learn new behaviors. These materials can also suggest strategies and provide tools for receiving ongoing feedback. Finally, options for building valuing individual development into 360-degree feedback systems range from linking behavioral improvements to pay increases or bonuses to communicating an organizational vision that encourages supervisor support for development. These examples highlight that 360-degree feedback systems do not inherently include all of the elements that are central to the process of development.

Similarly, developmental job assignments provide employees with new experiences, but may not deliver the other four elements of development. Developmental assignments, whether created by the organization or crafted by an individual, place employees in situations that expose them to unfamiliar responsibilities, new and dynamic challenges, and the latitude to shape their jobs in ways that will stretch them. Without safeguards and support, however, a new assignment could be overwhelming rather than developmental. To ensure awareness of developmental needs, mechanisms are needed to identify and communicate how the assignment is expected to be developmental for the new incumbent. Self-efficacy can be encouraged by providing the time and resources needed to begin mastering the assignment. Otherwise, self-efficacy can begin to dip, particularly in early stages when performance may be erratic before the learning curve begins a more steady ascent. It also is worth noting that if developmental assignments are reserved for a select group of 'high-potential' employees, this practice could reduce other employees' belief in their own learning capacity. Processes for reflecting on one's experience in the assignment and getting ongoing feedback (e.g., journal writing, intentional time for reflection, formal or informal coaches, ongoing dialogue with the supervisor or others in similar assignments) are necessary for providing the element of examination of self-in-experiences. Finally, ways to show that learning is valued need to be built in to assignments. For example, to maximize learning from developmental assignments, experimentation must be encouraged and reasonable mistakes need to be tolerated and considered part of the learning process.

Compared to 360-degree feedback and developmental assignments, executive coaching and action learning are more multifaceted individual development practices. Each of these practices are strong sources of two of the elements of development. And the remaining elements can be readily built in to these practices, primarily because they both have ongoing learning partnerships at their core.

The primary strengths of executive coaching are building awareness of development needs and facilitating the examination of self-in-experiences. Extensive understanding of development needs is generated during the contracting, assessment, and feedback phases of executive coaching. The input from the coach, superiors, peers, and even family members provide executives with detailed information on their current behaviors and capabilities. Through the contracting meeting, feedback session, and ongoing meetings with the coach stakeholders, executives learn what behaviors are expected of them, models of effective behaviors, and information about the knowledge and skills they need in their current and future jobs.

Coaches also assist executives with the examination of self-in-experiences. Coaching sessions provide executives with the opportunity to step back from experiences and reflect upon them. Through sharing their experiences and insight, coaches can provide executives an objective, new perspective on their experiences. More directly, coaches also can offer executives feedback on their behavior in coaching sessions and on the job.

The other three elements of development – self-efficacy for learning, new experiences and valuing individual development – can readily be added to the coaching process. Skilled coaches can effectively bolster participants' self-efficacy and help executives handle the negative emotions they may experience while learning. Coaching sessions offer executives the opportunity to practice new behaviors in a non-threatening situation. Coaches can also provide the executive with new knowledge and help them plan how to apply it in new situations. And coaches show that they value learning by supporting and encouraging the growth and change that the individual demonstrates over the course of the relationship.

On the other hand, factors outside the coaching session can affect whether the executive experiences self-efficacy for learning and valuing of learning. Executives differ substantially in their initial motivation to develop. Individuals who are told they must participate in coaching and show significant behavior change or lose their jobs may be demoralized. Those faced with an antagonistic work environment may feel that no matter what they do, they will not succeed. Others will find that their new skills, though valued by the coach, are not recognized, reinforced, and rewarded in the organization. Thus, even if all of the key elements of development are present within the coaching intervention, factors in the broader context may not be supportive of development.

Action learning programs excel at providing new experiences and encouraging the examination of self-in-experiences. New experiences in the form of projects are the raw material of action learning programs. In some programs, these are individual projects related to the person's job, and in others, the projects are entirely new, purposefully taking the participant out of his or her realm of expertise. Sometimes these projects even represent areas the organization has never explored before. In team projects, participants also experience working with people from other functions or units of the organization. A methodology for examination of one's experiences through systematic reflection and questioning also is a core part of action learning process. Guided by a facilitator or coach, individuals systematically work with a diverse group of colleagues to reflect on actions, the theories behind those actions, and when the impact of actions point to a need to revise theories.

Awareness of developmental needs, self-efficacy for learning, and valuing of learning can also be readily built in to action learning programs. Although participants are likely to become more aware of their developmental needs as they examine their actions and the theories behind them, action learning groups could more explicitly help members identify their development needs. As with coaching relationships, action learning participants can bolster each other's self-efficacy for learning, and they can support and encourage each other's growth and development. But as we noted with coaching, the learning environment created within an action learning team may not be congruent with the day-to-day work environment, decreasing the impact of the intervention. However, the major threat to learning in action learning programs is an overemphasis on the 'action' component. Teams may feel pressure to complete the project quickly, short-changing their reflective work together. The organization may emphasize action learning more as a strategy to solve its problems rather than a development practice, thus sending a message that they do not place as much value on learning.

The two remaining practices – enhancing social support for learning and fostering communities of practice – tend to emphasize the elements of self-efficacy for learning and valuing of learning. As noted earlier, these practices are broader efforts to support learning throughout an organization, thus creating a context – people who believe they can develop and that development is desirable – that provides the necessary support for more targeted interventions like 360-feedback and developmental assignments. These practices also utilize strategies for embedding the other elements of development (assessment of developmental needs, developmental assignments, and examination of self-in-experience) into the systems and culture of the organization.

FUTURE DIRECTIONS

Suggestions for Future Research

Our recommendations for future research are organized in parallel with the organization of this chapter. We begin by focusing on questions that need to be addressed in order to further build our current models of individual development. We then suggest ways in which research can improve the practice of individual development in the workplace. Finally,

we consider the thorny methodological problems associated with studying change in individuals.

In this chapter, we discussed three major lenses that have been used in examining individual development: behavior change, self-directed learning, and adult development. Five elements critical to development in the workplace were derived: awareness of developmental needs, self-efficacy for learning, new experiences, examination of self-in-experiences, and the valuing of individual development. Although research and practice suggest each of these elements plays an important role in development, further research is needed to ascertain how these elements interact. For example, it is unclear whether the valuing of individual development (e.g., supervisor support) affects development through fostering an awareness of development needs, increasing individual's self-efficacy for learning, encouraging the examination of one's experiences, providing resources needed for development, or a combination of these.

Research also needs to be devoted to understanding the variables that differentiate the lenses. For example, within the self-directed learning lens, individual difference variables have been linked to participation in development activities. Do individual differences, such as education, have a direct influence on participating in new experiences, or do individual difference variables indirectly affect participation by facilitating self-awareness or self-efficacy for learning?

Finally, the role an additional construct plays in individual development needs to be investigated. That construct is content. Research on individual development generally has not taken into consideration *what* employees are learning. To some extent, this has been a methodological necessity. Since each individual may pursue their own learning goals, examining the effectiveness of a particular intervention requires the assumption that individuals who are building their presentation skills learn the same way as those who are attempting to design their first five-year business plan. It seems worthwhile, however, to test this assumption. What kinds of development activities are most likely to lead to what kinds of skill improvement? Are the elements essential for building declarative knowledge the same as those critical for increasing procedural knowledge?

Tackling these three lines of research will help further refine our models and theories of development. The three bodies of research, or lenses, on development reviewed in this chapter provide a great deal of insight into the conditions which foster individual development in the workplace and the situations which may derail it. Recent conceptual contributions have begun to integrate across the different lenses. For example, London and Smither's (1999) model of continuous learning combines the individual and situational variables emphasized by

Table 14.3 *Summary of research needs related to the practice of individual development*

	360-degree feedback	Executive coaching	Developmental assignments	Action learning	Social support for learning	Communities of practice
Descriptive	√√	√√	√√	√√	√√	√√
Individual differences			√			
Group differences	√		√√		√√	
Outcomes						
reactions	√√	√		√√		√
knowledge			√	√		
behavior	√√	√		√	√	
results						

Cells that are blank indicate where training is needed the most; √ indicates some research has been done in this area (1–3 studies); √√ indicates a moderate amount of research has been done in this area.

the self-directed learning lens with the process-focus and social learning theory roots of the behavior change framework. Tesluk and Jacobs' (1998) integrated model of work experience incorporates the Person × Situation approach with a taxonomy of work experiences related to the adult development lens. Empirical tests of these, and other integrative models, are critical to furthering our understanding of the process of development in the workplace.

Research is also needed to improve the practice of individual development in organizations. For each kind of developmental intervention, four basic kinds of research would be helpful. First, descriptive information regarding the use of each practice would aid in setting research priorities. Information about how widespread a practice is outside the United States would be particularly useful to practitioners. Second, understanding how individual difference variables, such as personality and experience, affect reactions and responses to interventions would help practitioners maximize the effectiveness of interventions. Similarly, knowledge of the role of group differences would promote interventions that are equally beneficial for all participants and do not result in adverse impact. Finally, information regarding the outcomes of interventions is essential. Following Kirkpatrick's levels of analysis, we note four possible outcomes: reactions, knowledge, behavior, and results. Reactions pertain not only to 'smile sheets' indicating enjoyment of an intervention, but also to self-reported attitudes. For example, it would be helpful for practitioners to know whether a particular intervention was likely to be successful in building support for the organization's new mission statement or reducing intentions to leave the organization. Table 14.3 graphically indicates where research is most needed for each practice area. Topics that have not been investigated are blank.

In conducting studies evaluating the outcomes of developmental interventions, researchers face a number of challenges. First, finding a control group can be problematic; organizations typically want all or none of a targeted population to participate in an intervention. Some creative solutions to this dilemma already have been identified, such as comparing change on behaviors individuals are and are not trying to develop (Peterson, 1993). Second, psychometric problems abound. To assess what contributes to development, one must reliably measure it. Difference scores often are unreliable. Several recently developed regression techniques help address this problem. Some research, however, suggests that scholars attempting to compare measures made at two points in time may be frustrated by changes in how ratings scales are used. Several studies have found that individuals who are perceived as changing, do not receive higher skill ratings over time (Martineau, 1998). Thus, research also needs to be devoted to studying how to study development.

Trends Relevant to the Practice of Individual Development

Changes in the workplace will continue to challenge and reshape current practices intended to enhance individual development. One major change is the rapid increase in the use of information technologies within and between organizations. Internets and intranets are making it possible to work and learn on-line, decreasing the need for physical proximity and face-to-face interactions with coworkers and colearners. Many of the individual development practices are beginning to make use of these technologies. Processes for the collection and delivery of 360-degree feedback on-line and distance coaching are both currently available. Action learning groups, whose members are often geographically dispersed, are taking advantage of on-line access in the course of project work. Communities of practice are forming on the internet. For example, researchers at IRL are studying SeniorNet, a group of computer-using senior citizens. This research examines the history of how the community has evolved, the current mechanisms for maintaining a robust and growing network community, and the relation between on-line and face-to-face activities within the community (IRL, 1999). In general, the use of new information technologies in current individual development practices is ahead of research information on how these technologies might change the dynamics and impact of the intervention.

The technology-based increase in the use of distance feedback, coaching, assignments, and learning groups has the potential of making these practices more accessible to more employees. Currently, many practices are targeted to high potential employees or to individuals in management positions. Information technology may be a means to lower-cost access to learning opportunities, thus making them less of a scarce resource that has to be reserved for certain individuals in the organization. This is an important outcome to strive for because continuous learning is needed at all levels and corners of an organization.

A second major change is the increased mobility of employees across organizations. Some of this mobility is driven by employees themselves and some by organizations wanting to create more flexible work forces. The image of the loyal employee is being replaced by the 'free agent' employee. In this type of workplace, organizations are motivated to invest in employee development – not in order to reap the long-term benefits of that development as has been the case in the past – but to attract employees as they are needed. An interesting development in response to this change in mobility is the emergence of consortia of organizations (e.g., the Talent Alliance) that attempt to integrate and pool their employee development resources. The consortia members look beyond their current employees as resources. They see all the employees in an industry or a profession as potential employees and seek ways to share joint responsibility for the development of a talented employee pool.

The workplace is also changing as a new generation of post-baby-boomer employees move into organizations. One characteristic of this generation is their expectations for customization (Helgesen, 2000). They have grown up in a world where, as consumers, their choices have been expansive and where products are increasingly tailored to individual needs. They are bringing the expectation for customization to the workplace and expect individual development opportunities that meet their particular needs. The resulting scenario is probably fewer 'standard' developmental interventions that all employees in particular career paths are expected to experience, and more menus of options that employees can access on demand. Consistent with this trend is the suggestion to make funds for development a standard part of employees' benefit packages. Employees could then pursue the development activities that best suited their interests and needs.

Finally, some organizations are beginning to approach individual development in a more integrated, systemic fashion. This approach is characterized by (a) development initiatives that link and integrate the various discrete practice areas, (b) an examination and alignment of various organizational systems that influence development in the workplace (e.g., reward systems, information systems, control systems), (c) linking individual development practices with the organization's strategic goals, (d) an increasing emphasis on organizational cultures that value continuous learning, and (e) thinking about individual, team, and organizational development as simultaneous and overlapping processes. A systemic approach may reflect a stage of organizational development necessary to truly make individual development continuous and a shared responsibility between organizations and their employees.

CONCLUSION

In the past, training was characterized as being dominated by fads (Campbell, 1971). New training techniques were introduced, widely praised and implemented, evaluated with a few empirical studies, criticized, and eventually abandoned when a new technique appeared. All of the individual development practices we have discussed here are currently popular or commonly used in the United States. Are they, too, fads?

Given the emphasis on change in the workplace, is seems likely that the popularity of particular individual development practices will wax and wane. Perhaps, however, we can learn from the history of training and avoid sequentially embracing and discarding individual development practices. Research and practice on individual development already has a firm foundation of theories and models on which to build. As we have demonstrated here, careful evaluation of a practice using these theories and models can yield realistic expectations regarding what it can and cannot accomplish.

REFERENCES

Antonioni, D. (1994). The effects of feedback accountability on upward appraisal ratings. *Personnel Psychology*, 47, 349–356.

Argyris, C. (1991). Teaching smart people how to learn. *Harvard Business Review*, 99–109, May/June.

Argyris, C., & Schön, D.A. (1974). *Theory in practice: Increasing professional effectiveness*. San Francisco: Jossey-Bass.

Atwater, L., Roush, P., & Fischtal, A. (1995). The influence of upward feedback on self- and follower ratings of leaderhip. *Personnel Psychology*, 48, 35–59.

Barclay, J.H., & Harland, L.K. (1995). The impact of rater competence, rater location, and rating correctability on fairness perceptions. *Group and Organization Management, 20,* 39–60.

Basseches, M. (1984). *Dialectical thinking and adult development.* Norwood, NJ: Ablex Publishing.

Bernardin, H.J., Dahmus, S.A., & Redmon, G. (1993). Attitudes of first line supervisors toward subordinates appraisals. *Human Resource Management, 32,* 315–324.

Bernardin, H.J., Hagan, C., & Kane, J.S. (1995). The effects of a 360-degree appraisal system on managerial performance: No matter how cynical I get, I can't keep up. In W.W. Tornow (Chair), *Upward feedback: The ups and downs of it.* Symposium conducted at the annual conference of the Society for Industrial and Organizational Psychology, Orlando, FL, May.

Birdi, K., Allan, C., & Warr, P. (1997). Correlates and perceived outcomes of four types of employee development activity. *Journal of Applied Psychology, 82,* 845–857.

Bonoma, T.V., & Lawler, J.C. (1989). Chutes and ladders: Growing the general manager. *Sloan Mangement Review, 30*(3), 37.

Bracken, D.W. (1994). Straight talk about multi-rater feedback. *Training and Development,* September, 44–51.

Bracken, D.W. (1996). Multisource (360-degree) feedback: Surveys for individual and organizational development. In A.I. Kraut (Ed.), *Organizational surveys* (pp. 117–143). San Franciso: Jossey-Bass.

Bunker, K.A., & Webb, A.D. (1992). *Learning how to learn from experience: Impact of stress and coping.* Greensboro, NC: Center for Creative Leadership.

Burgoyne, J., & Reynolds, M. (1997). *Management learning: Integrating perspectives in theory and practice.* London: Sage.

Burke, R.J. (1984). Mentors in organizations. *Group and Organization Studies, 9,* 353–372.

Burke, R.J., & McKeen, C.A. (1997). Benefits of mentoring relationships among managerial and professional women: A cautionary tale. *Journal of Vocational Behavior, 51,* 43–57.

Callanan, G.A., & Greenhaus, J.H. (1999). Personal and career development: The best and worst of times. In A.I. Kraut & A.K. Korman (Eds.), *Evolving practices in human resource management: Responses to a changing world* of work (pp. 146–171). San Francisco, Jossey-Bass.

Campbell, J.P. (1971). Personnel training and development. *Annual Review of Psychology, 22,* 565–602.

Campbell, J.P. (1990). Modeling the performance prediction problem in industrial and organizational psychology. In M.D. Dunnette & L.M. Hough (Eds), *Handbook of industrial and organizational psychology,* Vol. 1 (2nd ed., pp. 687–732). Palo Alto, CA: Consulting Psychologist Press.

Campbell, J.P., Gasser, M.B., & F.L. Oswald (1996). The substantive nature of performance variability. In K.R. Murphy (Ed.), *Individual differences and behavior in organizations* (pp. 258–299). San Francisco: Jossey-Bass.

Campbell, J.P., McCloy, R.A., Oppler, S.H., & Sager, C.E. (1993). A theory of performance. In N. Schmitt, W.C. Borman & Associates (Eds.), *Personnel selection in organizations* (pp. 35–70). San Francisco, Jossey-Bass.

Campion, M.A., Cheraskin, L., & Stevens, M.J. (1994). Career-related antecedents and outcomes of job rotation. *Academy of Management Journal, 37,* 1518–1542.

Cell, E. (1984). *Learning to learn from experience.* Albany: State University of New York Press.

Chao, G.T. (1997). Mentoring phases and outcomes. *Journal of Vocational Behavior, 51,* 15–28.

Chao, G.T., Walz, P.M., & Gardner, P.D. (1992). Formal and informal mentorships: A comparison of mentoring functions and contrast with nonmentored counterparts. *Personnel Psychology, 45,* 619–636.

Cianni, J., & Romberger, B. (1995). Perceived racial, ethnic, and gender differences in access to developmental experiences. *Group and Organization Management, 20,* 440–459.

Clark, L.A., & Lyness, K.S. (1991). Succession planning as a strategic activity at Citicorp. In L.W. Foster (Ed.), *Advances in applied business strategy,* Vol. 2 (pp. 205–224). Greenwich, CT: JAI Press.

Conference Board (1999). Developing leaders. *HR Executive Review, 7*(1), 1–18.

Dalton, M.A. (1999). *The Learning Tactics Inventory: Facilitator's guide.* San Francisco: Jossey-Bass/Pfeiffer.

Dalton, M.A., & Swigert, S. (2000, April). An exploration of learning versatility within a model of work experience. In C.M. McCauley (Chair), *Developments on development: The process and consequences of continuous learning.* Symposium conducted at the annual conference of the Society for Industrial and Organizational Psychology, New Orleans, LA.

Davies, J., & Easterby-Smith, M. (1984). Learning and development from managerial work experiences. *Journal of Management Studies, 21*(2), 169–183.

Dechant, K. (1990). Knowing how to learn: The 'neglected' management ability. *Journal of Management Development, 9*(4), 40–49.

DeMeuse, K.P. (1985). Employees' responses to participation in an in-house continuing education program. *Psychological Reports, 57,* 1099–1109.

Dewey, J. (1938). *Experience and education.* West Lafayette, IN: Kappa Delta Pi.

Diedrich, R.C. (1996). An iterative approach to executive coaching. *Consulting Psychology Journal: Practice and Research, 48*(2), 61–66.

Dilworth, R.L., & Willis, V.J. (1999). Action learning for personal development and transformative learning. In L. Yorks, J. O'Neil & V.J. Marsick (Eds.), *Action learning: Successful strategies for individual, team, and organizational development* (pp. 75–82). San Francisco: Berrett-Koehler.

Dixon, N.M. (1994). *The organizational learning cycle: How we can learn collectively.* London: McGraw-Hill.

Dotlich, D.L., & Noel, J.L. (1998). *Action learning: How the world's top companies are re-creating their leaders and themselves.* San Francisco: Jossey-Bass.

Douglas, C.A. (1997). *Formal mentoring programs in organizations: An annotated bibliography*. Greensboro, NC: Center for Creative Leadership.

Dreher, G.F., & Ash, R.A. (1990). A comparative study of mentoring among men and women in managerial, professional, and technical position. *Journal of Applied Psychology, 75*, 539–546.

Edelstein, B.C., & Armstrong, D.J. (1993). A model for executive development. *Human Resource Planning, 16*(4), 51–64.

Fagenson, E.A. (1989). The mentor advantage: perceived career/job experiences of protégés versus non-protégés. *Journal of Organizational Behavior, 10*, 309–320.

Friedman, S.D. (1990). Succession systems in the public sector: Lessons from the Oklahoma Department of Correction. *Public Personnel Management, 19*(3), 291–303.

Funder, D.C. (2001). Accuracy in personality judgment: Some research and theory concerning an obvious question. In B.W. Roberts & R. Hogan (Eds.), *Personality psychology in the workplace*. Washington, DC: American Psychological Association.

Gaskill, L.R. (1993). A conceptual framework for the development, implementation, and evaluation of formal mentoring programs. *Journal of Career Development, 20*(2), 147–160.

Goldstein, I.L. (1991). Training in work organizations. In M.D. Dunnette & L.M. Hough (Eds.), *Handbook of industrial and organizational psychology*, Vol. 2 (2nd ed., pp. 507–620). Palo Alto, CA: Consulting Psychologist Press.

Hall, D.T. (1996). Protean careers of the 21st century. *Academy of Management Executive, 10*(4), 9–16.

Hall, D.T., Otazo, K.L., & Hollenbeck, G.P. (1999). Behind closed doors: What really happens in executive coaching. *Organizational Dynamics, 27*(3), 39–53.

Hayes, G.E. (1997). Executive coaching: A strategy for management and organizational development. In A.J. Pickman (Ed.), *Special challenges in career management: Counselor perspective* (pp. 213–222). Mahwah, NJ: Lawrence Erlbaum Associates.

Hazucha, J.F., Hezlett, S.A., Bontems-Wackens, S. & Ronnkvist, A. (1999). In search of the Euro-manager: Management competencies in France, Germany, Italy, and the United States. In W.H. Mobley, M.J. Gessner & V. Arnold (Eds.), *Advances in global leadership*, Vol. 1 (pp. 267–290). Stamford, CT: JAI Press.

Hazucha, J.F., Hezlett, S.A., & Schneider, R.J. (1993). The impact of 360-degree feedback on management skills development. *Human Resource Management, 32*, 325–351.

Hegarty, W.H. (1974). Using subordinate ratings to elicit behavior changes in supervisors. *Journal of Applied Psychology, 59*, 764–766.

Helgesen, S. (2000, May). *The shift to custom work*. Presentation at the annual Friends of the Center Conference, Greensboro, NC.

Hellervik, L.W., Hazucha, J.F., & Schneider, R. J. (1992). Behavior change: Models, methods, and a review of the evidence. In M.D. Dunnette & L.M. Hough (Eds.),

Handbook of Industrial and Organizational Psychology, Vol. 3 (2nd ed., pp. 821–895). Palo Alto, CA: Consulting Psychologists Press.

Hezlett, S.A., & Koonce, B.A. (1995). *Now that I've been assessed, what do I do? Facilitating development after individual assessments*. Paper presented at the IPMA Assessment Council Conference on Public Personnel Assessment, New Orleans, LA, June.

Hodgetts, W. (1994). *Coming of age: How male and female managers transform relationships with authority at midlife*. Unpublished doctoral dissertation. Harvard University Graduate School of Education.

Hofstede, G. (1997). *Cultures and organizations: Software of the mind*. New York: McGraw-Hill.

Hollenbeck, G.P., & McCall, M.W. (1999). Leadership development: Contemporary practices. In A.I. Kraut & A.K. Korman (Eds.), *Evolving practices in human resource management: Responses to a changing world of work* (pp. 172–200). San Francisco, Jossey-Bass.

Hoppe, M.H. (1998). Cross-cultural issues in leadership development. In C.D. McCauley, R.S. Moxley & E. Van Velsor (Eds.), *The Center for Creative Leadership handbook of leadership development* (pp. 336–378). San Francisco: Jossey-Bass.

HR Focus (1999, October). Corporate coaching growing as retention tool, *HR Focus*, 76.

Hudson, F.M. (1999). *The handbook of coaching*. San Francisco: Jossey-Bass.

Institute for Research on Learning (1999). *Institute for Research on Learning*. Palo Alto, CA: Author.

Johnson, J.W., & Ferstl, K.L. (1999). The effects of interrater and self-other agreement on performance improvement following feedback. *Personnel Psychology, 2*, 271–303.

Johnson, J.W., Olson, A.M., & Courtney, C.L. (1996). Implementing multiple perspective feedback: An integrated framework. *Human Resources Management Review, 6*, 253–277.

Johnson, N.B., & Scandura, T.A. (1994). The effect of mentorship and sex-role style on male–female earnings. *Industrial Relations, 33*, 263–274.

Judge, W.Q., & Cowell, J. (1997, July/August). The brave new world of executive coaching. *Business Horizons*, 71–77.

Kegan, R. (1994). *In over our heads: The mental demands of modern life*. Cambridge, MA: Harvard University Press.

Kelleher, D., Finestone, P., & Lowy, A. (1986). Managerial learning: First notes on an unstudied frontier. *Group and Organization Studies, 11*(3), 169–202.

Kiel, F., Rimmer, E., Williams, K., & Doyle, M. (1996). Coaching at the top. *Consulting Psychology Journal: Practice and Research, 48*(2), 67–77.

Kilburg, R.R. (1996). Toward a conceptual understanding and definition of executive coaching. *Consulting Psychology Journal: Practice and Research, 48*(2), 134–144.

Kolb, D. (1984). *Experiential learning: Experience as the source of learning and development*. Englewood Cliffs, NJ: Prentice-Hall.

Koonce, R. (1994, February). One on one. *Training and Development*, 34–40.

Kozlowski, S.W.J., & Farr, J.L. (1988). An integrative model of updating and performance. *Human Performance, 1*, 5–29.

Kozlowski, S.W.J., & Hults, B.M. (1987). An exploration of climates for technical updating and performance. *Personnel Psychology, 40*, 539–562.

Kram, K.E. (1983). Phases of the mentor relationship. *Academy of Management Journal, 26*, 608–625.

Kram, K.E., & Bragar, M.C. (1992). Development through mentoring: A strategic approach. In D. Montross & C. Shinkman (Eds.), *Career development: Theory and practice* (pp. 221–254). Springfield, IL: Charles C. Thomas.

Lamm, S. (2000). *The connection between action reflection learning and transformative learning: An awakening of human qualities in leadership.* Walter F. Ulmer, Jr. Applied Research Award Paper, Center for Creative Leadership, Greensboro, NC.

Lepsinger, R., & Lucia, A.D. (1997). *The art and science of 360-degree feedback.* San Francisco: Pfieffer.

Leslie, J.B., Gryzkiewicz, N.D., & Dalton, M.A. (1998). Understanding cultural influences on the 360-degree feedback process. In W.W. Tornow, M. London & CCL Associates (Eds.), *Maximizing the value of 360-degree feedback: A process for successful individual and organizational change* (pp. 196–216). San Francisco: Jossey-Bass.

Lewis, P., & Jacobs, T.O. (1992). Individual differences in strategic leadership capacity: A constructive-developmental view. In J.G. Hunt & R.L. Phillips (Eds.), *Strategic leadership: A multiorganizational-level perspective* (pp. 121–138). New York: Quorum.

Lombardo, M.M., & Eichenger, R.W. (1989). *Eighty-eight assignments for development in place: Enhancing the developmental challenge of existing jobs.* Greensboro, NC: Center for Creative Leadership.

Lombardo, M.M., & Eichenger, R.W. (1996). *Learning agility: The Learning II Architect.* Greensboro, NC: Lominger Limited.

London, M. (1995). *Self and interpersonal insight: How people gain understanding of themselves and others in organizations.* New York: Oxford University Press.

London, M., Larsen, H.H., & Thisted, L.N. (1999). Relationships between feedback and self-development. *Group and Organization Management, 24*, 5–27.

London, M., & Mone, E.M. (1999). Continuous learning. In D.R. Ilgen & E.D. Pulakos (Eds.), *The changing nature of performance* (pp. 119–153). San Francisco, Jossey-Bass.

London, M., & Smither, J.W. (1995). Can multi-source feedback change perceptions of goal accomplishment, self-evaluations, and performance-related outcomes. Theory-based applications and directions for research. *Personnel Psychology, 48*, 803–839.

London, M., & Smither, J.W. (1999). Career-related continuous learning: Defining the construct and mapping the process. In K.M. Rowland & G.R. Ferris (Eds.), *Research in personnel and human resources management, Volume 17* (pp. 81–121). Greenwich, CT: JAI Press.

London, M., & Wohlers, A.J. (1991). Agreement between subordinate and self ratings in upward feedback. *Personnel Psychology, 44*, 375–390.

Marsick, V.J. (1990). Experience-based learning: Executive learning outside the classroom. *Journal of Management Development, 9*(4), 50–60.

Marsick, V.J., & O'Neil, J. (1999). The many faces of action learning. *Management Learning, 30*(2), 159–176.

Marsick, V.J., & Watkins, K.E. (1992). *Informal and incidental learning in the workplace.* London: Routledge.

Martineau, J.W. (1998). Using 360-degree surveys to assess change. In W.W. Tornow, M. London & CCL Associates (Eds.), *Maximizing the value of 360-degree feedback: A process for successful individual and organizational development* (pp. 217–248). San Francisco: Jossey-Bass.

Maurer, T.J., & Tarulli, B.A. (1994). Investigation of perceived environment, perceived outcome, and person variables in relationships to voluntary development activity by employees. *Journal of Applied Psychology, 79*, 3–14.

McCall, M.W., Lombardo, M.M., & Morrison, A.M. (1988). *The lessons of experience: How successful executives develop on the job.* Lexington, MA: Lexington Books.

McCauley, C.D., & Brutus, S. (1998). *Management development through job experiences.* Greensboro, NC: Center for Creative Leadership.

McCauley, C.D., & Douglas, C.A. (1998). Developmental relationships. In C.D. McCauley, R.S. Moxley & E. Van Velsor (Eds.), *The Center for Creative Leadership Handbook of Leadership Development* (pp. 160–193). San Francisco: Jossey-Bass.

McCauley, C.D., Ohlott, P.J., & Ruderman, M.N. (1999). *Job Challenge Profile: Facilitator's guide.* San Francisco: Jossey-Bass/Pfeiffer.

McCauley, C.D., Ruderman, M.N., Ohlott, P.J., & Morrow, J.E. (1994). Assessing the developmental potential of managerial jobs. *Journal of Applied Psychology, 79*, 544–560.

McEvoy, G.M., & Buller, P.F. (1987). User acceptance of peer appraisals in an industrial setting. *Personnel Psychology, 40*, 785–797.

McGill, I., & Beaty, L. (1992). *Action learning: A practitioner's guide.* London: Kogan Page.

Mezirow, J. (1991). *Transformative dimensions of adult development.* San Francisco: Jossey-Bass.

Mezirow, J., & Associates (1990). *Fostering critical reflection in adulthood: A guide to transformative and emancipatory learning.* San Francisco: Jossey-Bass.

Morrison, A.M., White, R.P., & Van Velsor, E. (1992). *Breaking the glass ceiling: Can women reach the top of America's largest corporations?* (2nd ed.). Reading, MA: Addison-Wesley.

Morrison, R.F., & Hock, R.R. (1986). Career building: Learning from cumulative work experience. In D.T. Hall (Ed.), *Career development in organizations* (pp. 236–273). San Francisco: Jossey-Bass.

Mumford, A. (1995). Four approaches to learning from experience. *Industrial and Commercial Training, 27*(8), 12–19.

Mumford, A. (Ed.) (1997). *Action learning at work.* Aldershot: Gower.

Murray, M., & Owen, M.A. (1991). *Beyond the myths and magic of mentoring: How to facilitate an effective mentoring program.* San Francisco: Jossey-Bass.

Nilsen, D., & Campbell, D.P. (1993). Self-observer rating discrepancies: Once an overrater, always an overrater? *Human Resource Management, 32,* 265–281.

Noe, R.A. (1988). An investigation of the determinants of successful assigned mentoring relationships. *Personnel Psychology, 41,* 457–479.

Noe, R.A. (1996). Is career management related to employee development and performance? *Journal of Organizational Behavior, 17,* 119–133.

Noe, R.A., & Wilk, S.L. (1993). Investigation of the factors that influence employees' participation in development activities. *Journal of Applied Psychology, 78,* 291–302.

Noe, R.A., Wilk, S.L., Mullen, E.J., & Wanek, J.E. (1997). Employee development: Issues in construct definition and investigation of antecedents. In J.K. Ford, S.W.J. Kozlowski, K. Kraiger, E. Salas & M.S. Teachout (Eds), *Improving training effectiveness in work organizations* (pp. 153–189). Mahwah, NJ: Lawrence Erlbaum Associates.

O'Neil, J., Marsick, V., Yorks, L., Nilson, G., & Kolodny, R. (1997). Life on the seesaw: Tension in action reflection learning. In M. Pedler (Ed.), *Action learning in practice* (3rd ed., pp. 339–346). Brookfield, VT: Gower.

Ohlott, P.J., Ruderman, M.N., & McCauley, C.D. (1994). Gender differences in managers' developmental job experiences. *Academy of Management Journal, 37,* 46–67.

Olivero, G., Bane, K.D., & Kopelmane, R.E. (1997). Executive coaching as a transfer of training tool: Effects on productivity in a public agency. *Public Personnel Management, 26*(4), 461–469.

Orpen, C. (1995). The effects of mentoring on employees' career success. *Journal of Social Psychology, 135*(5), 667–668.

Pazy, A. (1995). Professionals' experience of lack of knowledge: A phenomenological study. *Journal of Social Behavior and Personality, 10,* 907–922.

Pedler, M. (Ed.) (1997). *Action learning in practice* (3rd ed.). Brookfield, VT: Gower.

Perry, W.G. (1970). *Forms of intellectual and ethical development in the college years.* New York: Holt, Rinehart & Winston.

Peterson, D.B. (1993). *Skill learning and behavior change in an individually tailored management coaching and training program.* Unpublished doctoral dissertation. University of Minnesota.

Peterson, D.B. (1996). Executive coaching at work: The art of one-on-one change. *Consulting Psychology Journal: Practice and Research, 48*(2), 78–86.

Peterson, D.B., & Hicks, M.D. (1996). *Leader as coach: Strategies for coaching and developing others.* Minneapolis, MN: Personnel Decisions International.

Portwood, J.D., & Granrose, C.S. (1986). Organizational career management programs: What's available?

What's effective? *Human Resource Planning, 9*(3), 107–119.

Pun, A.S.L. (1997). Theory, model and action for managing change: Bridges meets Revans in Hong Kong. *Organization Development Journal, 15*(4), 43–49.

Raelin, J.A. (1997). Individual and situational precursors of successful action learning. *Journal of Management Education, 21,* 368–394.

Reilly, R.R., Smither, J.W., & Vasilopoulos, N.L. (1996). A longitudinal study of upward feedback. *Personnel Psychology, 49,* 599–612.

Revans, R.W. (1982). *The origin and growth of action learning.* Bromley: Chartwell Bratt.

Ruderman, M.N., & Hughes-James, M.W. (1998). Leadership development across race and gender. In C.D. McCauley, R.S. Moxley & E. Van Velsor (Eds.), *The Center for Creative Leadership handbook of leadership development* (pp. 291–335). San Francisco: Jossey-Bass.

Russell, J.E.A. (1991). Career development interventions in organizations. *Journal of Vocational Behavior, 38,* 237–287.

Scandura, T.A. (1992). Mentorship and career mobility: An empirical investigation. *Journal of Organizational Behavior, 13,* 169–174.

Schön, D.A. (1983). *The reflective practitioner.* New York: Basic Books.

Schön, D.A. (1987). *Educating the reflective practitioner.* San Francisco: Jossey-Bass.

Seibert, K.W., & Daudelin, M.W. (1999). *The role of reflection in managerial learning: Theory, research, and practice.* Westport, CT: Quorum.

Seibert, K.W., Hall, D.T., & Kram, K.E. (1995). Strengthening the weak link strategic executive development: Integrating individual development and global business strategy. *Human Resource Management, 34,* 549–567.

Senge, P.M. (1990). *The fifth discipline: The art and practice of the learning organization.* New York: Doubleday.

Smith, L. (1993, Dec 27). The executive's new coach. *Fortune,* 126–134.

Smith, R.M. (1990). *Learning to learn across the lifespan.* San Francisco: Jossey-Bass.

Smither, J.W., London, M. Vasilopoulos, N.L., Reilly, R.R., Millsap, R.E., & Salvemini, N. (1995). An examination of the effects of an upward feedback program over time. *Personnel Psychology, 46,* 1–34.

Spreitzer, G.M., McCall, M.W., & Mahoney, J.D. (1997). Early identification of international executive potential. *Journal of Applied Psychology, 82,* 6–29.

Stern, A.L. (1997, September). Where the action is. *Across the Board,* 43–47.

Sternberg, R.J., Wagner, R.K., Williams, W.M., & Horvath, J.A. (1995). Testing common sense. *American Psychologist, 50,* 912–927.

Strickland, K. (1997). Executive coaching: Helping valued executives fulfill their potential. In A.J. Pickman (Ed.), *Special challenges in career management: Counselor perspectives* (pp. 203–212). Mahwah, NJ: Lawrence Erlbaum Associates.

Tesluk, P.E., & Jacobs, R.R. (1998). Toward an integrated model of work experience. *Personnel Psychology, 51,* 321–355.

Thach, L., & Heinselman, T. (1999, May). Executive coaching defined. *Training and Development,* 35–39.

Tharenou, P. (1997a). Determinants of participation in training and development. In C.L. Cooper & D.M. Rousseau (Eds.), *Trends in organizational behavior,* Vol. 4 (pp. 15–27). New York: John Wiley & Sons.

Tharenou, P. (1997b). Organisational, job, and personal predictors of employee participation in training and development. *Applied Psychology: An International Review, 46,* 112–113.

Tobias, L.L. (1996). Coaching executives. *Consulting Psychology Journal: Practice and Research, 48*(2), 87–95.

Torff, B., & Sternberg, R.J. (1998). Changing mind, changing world: Practical intelligence and tacit knowledge in adult learning. In M.C. Smith & T. Pourchot (Eds.), *Adult learning and development: Perspectives from educational psychology* (pp. 109–126). Mahwah, NJ: Lawrence Erlbaum.

Tornow, W.W., London, M., & CCL Associates (1998). *Maximizing the value of 360-degree feedback: A process for successful individual and organizational change.* San Francisco: Jossey-Bass.

Turban, D.B., & Dougherty, T.W. (1994). Role of protégé personality in receipt of mentoring and career success. *Academy of Management Journal, 37,* 688–702.

Vaill, P.B. (1996). *Learning as a way of being: Strategies for survival in a world of permanent white water.* San Francisco: Jossey-Bass.

Van Velsor, E., & Guthrie, V.A. (1998). Enhancing the ability to learn from experience. In C.D. McCauley, R.S. Moxley & E. Van Velsor (Eds.), *The Center for Creative Leadership handbook of leadership development* (pp. 242–261). San Francisco: Jossey-Bass.

Van Velsor, E., Leslie, J.B., & Fleenor, J.W. (1997). *Choosing 360: A guide to evaluating multi-rater feedback instruments for management development.* Greensboro, NC: Center for Creative Leadership.

Vicere, A.A., & Fulmer, R.M. (1997). *Leadership by design.* Boston, MA: Harvard Business School Press.

Wagner, R.K., & Sternberg (1985). Practical intelligence in real-world pursuits: The role of tacit knowledge. *Journal of Personality and Social Psychology, 49,* 436–458.

Waldroop, J., & Butler, T. (1996). The executive as coach. *Harvard Business Review, 74,* 111–117, November–December.

Walker, A.G., & Smither, J.W. (1999). A five-year study of upward feedback: What managers do with their results matters. *Personnel Psychology, 52,* 393–423.

Weinstein, K. (1995). *Action learning: A journey in discovery and development.* London: Harper Collins.

Wenger, E.C. (1998). *Communities of practice: Learning, meaning, and identity.* Cambridge: Cambridge University Press.

Wenger, E.C., & Snyder, W.M. (2000, January/February). Communities of practice: The organizational frontier. *Harvard Business Review,* 139–145.

Whitely, W., Dougherty, T.W., & Dreher, G.F. (1991). Relationship of career mentoring and socioeconomic origin to managers' and professionals' early career progress. *Academy of Management Journal, 34,* 331–351.

Wick, C.W. (1989). How people develop: An in-depth look. *HR Reporter, 6*(7), 1–3.

Wick, C.W., & Leon, L.S. (1993). *The learning edge: How smart managers and smart companies stay ahead.* New York: McGraw-Hill.

Wild, H., Bishop, L., & Sullivan, C.L. (1996). *Building environments for learning and innovation.* Palo Alto, CA: Institute for Research on Learning.

Willis, S.L., & Dubin, S.S. (Eds.) (1990). *Maintaining professional competence.* San Francisco: Jossey-Bass.

Wilson, M.S., Hoppe, M.H., & Sayles, L.R. (1996). *Managing across cultures: A learning framework.* Greensboro, NC: Center for Creative Leadership.

Witherspoon, R., & White, R.P. (1996). Executive coaching: A continuum of roles. *Consulting Psychology Journal: Practice and Research, 48*(2), 124–133.

Yorks, L., Lamm, S., O'Neil, J., Kolodny, R., Marsick, V.J., & Nilson, G. (1998). Transfer of learning from an action reflection learning program. *Performance Improvement Quarterly, 11*(1): 59–73.

Zemke, R. (1985, August). The Honeywell studies: How managers learn to manage. *Training,* 46–51.

15

Human–Machine Interaction: Usability and User Needs of the System

DAVID J. OBORNE
and KAREN M. ARNOLD

This chapter considers the development and concept of human machine interaction (HMI) from the central viewpoint of the user in the system. Thus, whereas traditional ergonomics and human factors argued for design based on an equivalent interplay between people and their environments, the view propounded in this chapter is for person centrality – the superiority of the user as the controlling feature of any system. Without such a view, the richness of people–environment interactions that is over and above a simple mechanistic transfer of control and information will be lost. People bring to the system a collection of inherent strengths and weaknesses (from such factors as experiences, expectations, motivations, and so on) which themselves will interact with the system to change it. Central to this view is that of the communication acts between system components, and the needs of users within the system. Such features impact on the usability of the system overall and its eventual success. The chapter concludes with a consideration of the changing nature of HMI and of user needs with the changing nature of available technologies and our expectations and abilities.

INTRODUCTION

Recognition of the importance of designing equipment and systems with the user in mind can be traced back many centuries (Marmaras, Poulakakis & Papakostopoulos, 1999). Indeed, common measuring terms such as the 'foot' or the 'hand' confirm the view that those who designed and created new environments and facilities in the past also realised that they were doing so for the benefit of people who were to use them. Furthermore, even the most cursory glance at relatively ancient weaponry, buildings and so on, illustrates that the designers took cognisance of the anthropometric and biomechanic characteristics of their potential users (albeit probably through a process of 'creeping evolution' rather than 'tailored design').

Oborne (1995) has traced the development of more modern person-machine interaction philosophies back to the early days of the last century (and perhaps even earlier), when modern warfare required people (fighting personnel and workers in support industries) to operate at cognitive, emotional, and physical levels that had not previously been needed. New physical environments, in the air, under water, in dark and/or noisy conditions, leading to outcomes such as fear, fatigue, and even physical/emotional breakdown, necessitated careful analyses of the physical environment to ensure that the system did not require more than the operator was able to 'give'.

The philosophies supporting such understanding have changed considerably over the years, as the nature of the systems to be accommodated by users has also changed. During and just after the First World War the primary concern dealt with fatigue and the relationship between the physical environment and the worker, and its impact on the worker's ability actually to perform novel physical tasks (many of which were allied to fighting tasks). Concerns about fatigue and health led, in 1915, to the establishment of the Health of Munitions Workers' Committee that comprised a multidisciplinary team (including physiologists and psychologists) to evaluate the impact of the (poor) physical environment on health and efficiency. Following the conclusion of the war, this Committee was reconstituted as the Industrial Fatigue Research Board (IFRB) to carry out research into fatigue problems in industry. Finally, in 1929 it was renamed the Industrial Health Research Board (IHRB) and its scope broadened to investigate general conditions of industrial employment and the concept of 'industrial efficiency' was included in its remit.

By virtue of the prevailing systems and needs of the time, therefore, the initial concept of more 'modern' ergonomics rested in the area of work efficiency, and on the impact of such features as 'fatigue', 'stress', and 'physical work' (load carrying, rest pauses, etc.)

By the time of the late 1930s and early 1940s (and as a result of the external pressures created by another World War), however, the requirements of system designers had developed further to take cognisance of the new technologies that were rapidly emerging. Thus radar enabled otherwise invisible information to be made perceptible and so provide advanced warning of incoming enemy aircraft. The fighting machines themselves demanded faster, more accurate, and more controlled behaviours than previously had been the case. So the central criteria of ergonomics shifted from physical abilities to a mixture of physical and cognitive ones. From physical fatigue and health and its impact on traditional work to be concerned with perceptual and operational features relating to safety and efficiency.

Following the creation, in the late 1940s, of the formal discipline of Ergonomics (UK) and Human Factors (US), for decades the predominant philosophy was one of the 'man–machine system'. This represented an almost cybernetic approach comprising a closed loop information/control system between the two primary components: 'man' and 'machine'. Thus it was considered that information is transmitted from the machine to the man via displays and (his) perceptual system, and from the man to the machine via (his) effector system and controls. The strength of this view was reinforced by the complexity of emerging systems, particularly those concerning space travel. With it the period described as the 'knobs and dials' era of ergonomics emerged, with emphasis being laid on the design (for effective use) of particularly micro input/output systems. Often, their more macro place within the total system (for example, the space capsule itself or the space programme) was ignored.

Despite the limitations imposed by equating the two primary components in the system, the man–machine system approach provided the major benefit of forcing designers to consider the central role of communication between the components. Particularly due to the emergence of computers and computer-based systems, a realisation of the importance of communication and communication networks entered the ergonomics philosophy. Again, therefore, the force of the subject matter shifted the nature of the subject. The activities of the two simple components, man and machine – as well as those of their separate components (displays, perceptual system, controls, and effector systems) – became subservient to the *inter*action of different individual man–machine systems. Thus the communication became central, as did the *perceived meaning* of the communication. Concern about individual man–machine components gave way to concern about systems – in all their glory. More recently this has expanded further to consider not just physical and organisational systems but also cognitive and social ones (e.g., Carroll, 1996).

In many respects these developments can be viewed as being 'natural' extensions of the sociotechnical systems approach developed in the 1950s and 1960s (see, e.g., Cooper & Foster, 1971; Pasmore & Sherwood, 1978). The basis of this approach is that *all* aspects of the organisation – social, technical, organisational – interact to influence behaviour. Altering any one will affect the efficiency of the other. Whyte (1959) takes three concepts: interaction (the social-interpersonal contacts developed at work), activities (the tasks performed), and sentiments (how the individuals feel about the world about them), and suggests that they are mutually interdependent.

As an example, Kim and Moon (1998) considered the design of customer computer-based interfaces for cyber-banking systems that emphasised emotionality as well as functionality. By varying features such as interface colour, use of clipart, menu dimensions, and so on, they demonstrated significant impacts on such characteristics as perceived trustworthiness and other kinds of emotions. As the authors point out, 'whether or not the casual navigator will become a loyal customer of a particular cyber shopping mall or cyber bank may depend on the first impression of the interface…[so] the emotions aroused by the interface…must be systematically incorporated into the design…' (p. 20).

PERSON CENTRALITY

In parallel with the development of a complete systems approach to the issues of man–machine interactions, in recent years the realisation that the two primary components in the wider organisation ('man' and 'machine' – or 'operator' and 'system') are not equal has led to an argument of bias. That is, that the person in the system (no matter how large or small the system) should be considered to be more 'central' than the rest of the system. People, then, are first amongst equals. Discussing the human–computer interaction domain, for example, Eason (1991) has argued that the traditional man–machine viewpoint 'as a form of conversation between different kinds of participants' misses the rich complexity of the interaction. He points out that we interact with machines not merely to exchange messages but to engage in complex tasks in the real world. So the man–machine interaction has a meaning that is over and above that which can be expressed by simple, straightforward analyses of the component parts.

Wisner (1989) took the argument beyond just interacting with computers to encompass the full domain of ergonomics. He argued that rather than just studying specific 'properties of man', ergonomics and psychology should attempt to 'understand how man uses his own properties in terms of a story, his own story and that of humanity, the part of humanity to which he belongs'. So individual wishes and desires, motives and experiences are brought to a working situation and must be understood when considering the 'fit'. Even such factors as social background and culture play an important role – as discussed above.

So the shift in ergonomics thinking that has emerged in recent years has been towards understanding more the nature of the individual within the system. The original concept of the person and machine being almost equal partners has given way to a view which argues that the partners are not equal; that the person should play a more central role within a working system.

Thus the contemporary philosophy, a person-centred philosophy, views the interaction as one that is controlled and dominated by the operator(s) in the system. Individuals bring to the system a collection of inherent strengths and weaknesses (from such factors as experiences, expectations, motivations, and so on) which themselves will interact with the system to change it. Indeed, sometimes these features will include variability, fallibility and maybe even perversity – any of which are likely to lead to errors and inefficiency. Both the positive and negative facets of the person's input are emphasised in Wisner's words: that operators will use their 'own story' when being asked to control and manipulate events.

Put in another way, with others Branton (1983) has emphasised that human operators in a system inevitably turn it from being a closed-loop system in which information flows from one component to the other with (in theory) maximum efficiency

for correcting deviations within the system, to an open-loop one. Instead of a 'designed' error-correcting system, then, the operator, on the basis of his or her 'mental model' of the system and its operation, effects the deviation corrections. Within this concept the issues of human uncertainty reduction, control and autonomy also need to be considered. From a psychological viewpoint uncertainty reduction plays a major role in everyday life; we attempt to reduce it if for no other reason than to reduce the stressful effects of unpredictability. Of course, like stimulation and arousal, individual attempts to reduce uncertainty are likely to be tempered by some concept of an optimum level. Indeed in many respects life would be very boring if all events were perfectly predictable.

Expressed in mathematical language, certainty and uncertainty concern the probabilities that an event will occur. When taken in conjunction with the 'quasi-mathematical' model of the skilled operator's behaviour, however, they can be seen to play a potentially important role within a person-centred approach. Thus, whereas the approach accepts that quasi-mathematical levels of information are needed to help the operator in making predictions about the likely outcome of actions, reducing uncertainty has important implications for the kind of information that should be provided. Such information will deal with features of the situation in which the operator enters uncertain states, rather than aspects that have more certain outcomes. Branton (1979) puts such arguments to the test in his analysis of the complex issues involved in train driving skills, from which he provides practical recommendations to aid the train driver, including aids to orientation and anticipation skills, improvement of motivation, and environmental enrichment.

Since increased control over a situation improves the likelihood that the events will occur in the desired and expected manner, it is clear that uncertainty reduction is also related to control. The evidence for 'mini-panics' resulting from 'mind wanderings' demonstrates that uncertainty occurs when control is relaxed. For example, Branton & Oborne (1979) undertook a comprehensive observational study of anaesthetists at work. By analysing video recordings, using fast-play techniques, 'head nodding' behaviour could be observed that related to periods of boredom, fatigue, and lack of concentration. At such times the operator entered states of uncertainty and slight panics. Relevant equipment and operational design could have been used to reduce both the incidence and the impact of such episodes.

Discussing the design of computer screens, Branton and Shipley (1986) highlighted the importance of control as an important factor in stress causation and management. They proposed that such technology has propagated a new 'breed' of individuals 'Houston Man':

Perhaps his VDU screen presents an illusory picture of the true condition of any plant or process deemed to be under control? Glued to his screen, how far can he actually control the reality out there? Our interest is not so much in what is actually shown to be on the screen but in what is behind it, in what the display is supposed to represent to the operator. The processes to be controlled are at least one step removed from the controller's direct experience. The stress arises when these displays can no longer be trusted. The very remoteness from the end product generates feelings of helplessness, a condition often reported in the literature on stress. (p. 1)

Thus the traditional ergonomics philosophy of a mechanistic relationship between an operator and a machine can be said to have misperceived a critical perspective of the system in which it is involved – the operator and the attributes which he or she brings to the system in the wider sense. So, rather than concentrating simply on ways of improving the information flow between components within the system, person-centred ergonomics takes as its central point the need to accommodate the human attributes that the person brings to the system. The emphasis is thus on accentuating the positive and reducing the negative effects of the individual's interactions.

Indeed, this missing perspective is especially important in that it suggests how the ergonomics should be considered – particularly the point within the system at which an ergonomics intervention is made and how it is made. To take a very simple example: the design of a control for safe and efficient operation. By emphasising the closed-loop nature of the interaction and the need to design the system to fit the user, traditional ergonomics argues that the control design – the point of the ergonomics intervention – should be made from the viewpoint of the machine's requirements as they impinge on the operator's wishes and abilities. Certainly the operator's abilities are important, but it is the system and its controls and displays that define the interaction and thus the design.

By viewing the interaction from the other side, however, from the viewpoint of the individual, the person-centred approach argues that the intervention into the closed-loop system should be made at the level of the operator. He or she is the component that is designed to activate the system and to maintain its efficient running. Thus the person-centred perception is one in which the operator and his or her abilities define the working system. So the goal is to create supportive dynamic environments that enable individuals to work at their safest and most effective levels; not just to design the environment to 'fit' the person in some static sense.

The current person-centred view (e.g., Oborne, Branton, Leal, Shipley & Stewart, 1993) of man-machine interactions, therefore, provides a more global perspective of the factors that guide the effective operation of complex systems. By viewing the interactions from the centrality of the user and by including into the system all features of the environment (physical, social, and cognitive), Wisner's 'story that the user tries to tell' is more likely to be understood. Systems will then be designed that are both useful and usable by those who are to work with them.

COMMUNICATION

Accepting the centrality of the user in the system, and ensuring that the user can 'tell' his or her 'story' regarding the working system's effective operation, is becoming a more accepted prerequisite of appropriate person–machine interaction design. However, this more recent philosophy still begs a major issue, concerning the nature of the communication that is activated between the user and the system. Somehow the user must be able to 'tell his story', and the need for the system to provide appropriate and meaningful information to the user is crucial to effective operations.

The process underlying communication can perhaps best be understood when one realises that the linguistic origin of the word is the Latin *comunis*, meaning 'common'. One clear characteristic of meaning in human communication therefore, is its 'commonness' – an essential prerequisite being a common understanding by those involved in the communication process. However, this quality of commonness does not necessarily mean that all participants in the communicative process have to have identical understanding of the symbols or thoughts transmitted, so long as some understanding is common to them all. So communication can take place even if the transmitter and receiver do not 'speak the same language' as long as the basic ideas being transmitted in the message are received accurately.

The role of ergonomics, then, is to arrange a situation that enhances the chances of the transmitter and the receiver having a maximum common understanding. Reasons why communication may break down become more apparent when viewing the system from a person-centred viewpoint. First, personalities might be involved. A receiver who dislikes or mistrusts the transmitter could be unreceptive to what is being said. Indeed, the receiver's understanding of the message could well be distorted by negative opinions of the transmitter or by imputed motives. Secondly, even if the receiver is receptive to the message it may become distorted by personal preconceptions ('set'). As Bartlett (1950) has argued, one of the chief functions of the active mind is to 'fill up gaps', that is constantly to try to link new material with older material to make it more meaningful. So a message might be distorted by the receiver placing it in a context in which it is not meant to be placed simply because of a 'set' to the message.

Thirdly, there is the problem of interest and attention. If the receiver is not attending to the message, perhaps because he or she is bored, part of it may easily be missed or misinterpreted. Finally messages can become distorted because of our limited capacity to process the transmitted information. This concept has already been discussed briefly when dealing with our ability to store different stimuli but it also applies to the storage of complex, meaningful material such as ideas and concepts. If the message is too detailed or too long it may overload our memory system and become distorted, lost or simply unable to be retrieved. In summary, therefore, the common channel for communication may be distorted by social influences, by personal attitudes and expectations, by boredom and a lack of interest, or by information overload.

Another feature suggested by the person-centred approach is that of purposivity. In most cases it is self evident that the operator at work performs his or her task with a sense of purpose. He or she has some reason for carrying out the action, some goal to attain: to throw a switch, illuminate a bulb, record a message, or whatever. Without such a purpose the action has no meaning as far as the system is concerned and can be classed as 'random' movements. No amount of ergonomic design will be able to accommodate such behaviours – at least not for any sensible reason other than to ensure that the unpurposeful movements do not damage the system by increasing the likelihood of inefficiency or accidents.

The person-centred approach, therefore, argues strongly that one of the primary features that the individual brings to the system is a sense of purpose, of action. When the purpose is understood it should be possible to begin to design the system in order to facilitate it. Purposivity, then, determines 'set'.

To take one example of this approach: Wright (1986) suggests that a traveller who views an information display board at an airport does so with a preconceived model of the structure of the information in his or her 'mind'. For example, someone may want to access the information in terms of the flight number, the destination, or the time of departure. From their different starting points different individuals may then desire different features from the information: departure gate number, whether the plane is delayed, and so on. Whereas it would be impractical to design a separate airport display board for each individual traveller's expectations, it should be possible to determine the general purpose of the display board for use by the majority of passengers.

By understanding the purpose of the individual at the point of his or her entry into the system, therefore, ergonomists can begin to consider designs that will facilitate this aim, and allow the activities to be carried out most efficiently.

A further feature of the person that can influence 'set' is the individual's ability for prediction. Indeed, the existence of purposivity implies also some concept of prediction and anticipation; to decide to throw a switch, for example, and to perform the cognitive and muscular actions to accomplish the desired goal, one must have a fair idea of the likely outcomes. By implication, therefore, the concept of purposivity also suggests that the user will have some notion of the desired outcome, and thus some 'internal' model of the course of future events. This is an important linkage as far as person-centred ergonomics is concerned. Prediction, and the anticipation which arises from it, concern the operation of the system within the individual's perceived control, and will have major implications also for the nature and the quality of the information required for the task.

Branton (1978) has argued that prediction and anticipation are not merely necessary precursors to efficient operation, but that they also determine the efficiency of the operation. To be able to control the vehicle, the train driver must be able to predict the outcome of his or her actions; the quality of this predictive behaviour (which may be determined in part by the quality of the information supplied) will have considerable bearing on the quality of the task performed.

Finally, there are the features related to interest, boredom and adaptation that are issues concerning how far the operator has an interest in the operation under control. Thus interest is related to purpose insofar as reduced purposivity can lead to reduced interest, and reduced interest can lead to reduced awareness of the environment.

A deeper analysis of the construct, however, leads us to consider not so much interest *per se* but the reason for the interest in the job being undertaken. Thus it has been argued that interest is expressed through stimulus-seeking behaviour. The work of investigators like Sherrington, Granit and Von Békésy, for example, shows that the nervous system adapts and habituates quite rapidly to any prolonged and unvaried stimulation, leading to cortical inhibition of stimuli and extinction of responses. Boredom, a result of reduced interest can soon lead to a reduced ability to perceive and respond to important stimuli, and adaptation to the stimuli can have similar effects.

Branton (1978) recognised that this problem could arise when considering the performance of high-level tasks. As he observed, if individuals are starved of this stimulus variation within their environment they will actively seek it from elsewhere, probably through mind wanderings and day dreaming (Branton & Shipley, 1986).

USABILITY

Associated with the concept of the user being at the centre of the person–machine system is that of usability. This is an issue that has had a variety of inputs – particularly in more recent years with the development of interactive software. Lin, Choong & Salvendy (1997) define usability as 'the ease with which a software product can be used to perform its designated task by its users at a specific criterion'. Such a definition, loose as it is, places usability firmly into the domain of the product itself – the extent to which it can be used by an individual for productive output. Indeed, in their literature review of the topic, Lin et al. (1997) provide other definitions of usability (from one created by the International Standards Organization, 1993, to others provided by a range of authors – e.g., Shackel, 1991; Preece, 1993; Eason, 1984; Chapanis, 1991). All, again, place the emphasis on the system, its effective use and the extent to which the design facilitates ease of use. In the definitions supplied there is little evidence for an emphasis on the *synergistic* nature of the system or of the importance of understanding the needs of the user in the system as a *prerequisite* for designing for effective use. This issue will be considered later.

Shackel (1991) defined usability as 'the capability in human functional terms to be used easily and effectively by the specified range of users, given specified training and support, to fulfil the specified range of tasks, within the specified range of environmental scenarios'. A more specific definition, provided by the ISO (1993) considers usability in more operational terms: [usability is] 'the quality of use: the effectiveness, efficiency and satisfaction with which specified users achieve specified goals in particular environments'. In relation to software design Bevan (1999) traces a number of similar definitions through a variety of different ISO specifications that combine a range of product attributes from both internal and external (to the product) perspectives. ISO 9241-11 (1998), for example, replaces the term 'efficiency' with 'productivity' and takes a slightly user-centric view of usability. It includes concepts of:

- *Effectiveness* – relating the user's goals or subgoals to the accuracy and completeness with which these goals are achieved.
- *Productivity* – relating the level of effectiveness to the expenditure of resources (including physical effort, time, materials, or financial).
- *Satisfaction* – the 'comfort' and 'acceptability of the use' of the product.

None of the above, of course, relates specifically to a *user-centric* view of HMI; all the features place the product at the centre and define its usability in operational terms. Nevertheless, this is an extremely important aspect of ensuring that the product/system matches the abilities and needs of the user.

Bevan (1999) argues that there are four user-centre design activities that need to take place at all stages of a project to ensure, as much as possible, usability. These are to:

- Understand and specify the context of use, which leads to
- Specify the user and the organisational requirements, which leads to
- Product design solutions, which leads to
- Evaluate the designs against the requirements.

If the final stage indicates that the product meets the users requirements, then the process is completed; otherwise it is repeated. The sequence by which these stages are performed, and the level of detail required, depends on the nature of the product and the system. The process, then, involves specification, prototype development, testing, and evaluation. This process is fundamental to usability testing processes described by others. For example, Carter (1999) describes the 'usability first' principle which 'goes beyond a mere [sic] concern for the user and concerns itself with all of the facets of usability both for the user and for the developers'. Similarly Hasdogan's user model approach (1996) argues that the process involves users and designers developing 'models' of each other's behaviours, and testing to evaluate the extent to which they match.

Usability, then, refers to the process of ensuring that systems designed for the user can be used as intended; that they are effective, able to be learned easily, flexible, and acceptable to all who have to use them. Each of these functional definitions of usability requires, in some way, that the product/systems being designed are tested against some predetermined usability criteria. This begs the question, of course, of the nature of the testing that needs to be carried out.

Stanton and Young (1998) describe a range of methods that can be used within ergonomics contexts and discuss the nature of the situations in which they may be used appropriately. Earlier, Stanton and Baber (1996) had reduced the selection of appropriate methods to four basic factors, one or more of which will determine which methods are appropriate:

- The stage of the design process
- The form that the product takes
- Access to end users
- Pressure of time.

Using a questionnaire approach, Stanton and Young investigated the likelihood of using each of 27 methods at different stages in the design process. Their results demonstrated clear preferences for some kinds of methods over others. Thus checklists were rated as significantly easier to use than simulation, guidelines than prototyping, and interviews than mock-ups. Baber and Mirza (1996) report that product designers tend to restrict their methods to interviews, observation and checklists, confirmed by Stanton and Young as probably being due to the ease of applying the methods. The concept of and need for usability, then, concerns as much the methods as the reason for using them.

Hasdogan (1996) presents an interesting categorisation of ergonomics and usability testing methods. Based on his framework for modelling the user described earlier, Hasdogan argues that there are essentially three groups of models that the designer uses when attempting to determine the nature of user input. These are:

1. *Empirical models* which are based on the kind of 'desktop' data collected by designers from such sources as guidelines, published material, data resources, and so on.
2. *Experimental models* which use 'live users' to study the usage process using representatives of the user population or 'the designer himself and/or some of his colleagues' acting out usage'.
3. *Scenario-based models* that are based on 'formal or informal story lines relating to users, usage, the usage environment and usage circumstances of the product of interest'.

Taking these three model groups, and examining them in terms of the better-understood models of physical, cognitive, consequence and psychosocial models, Hasdogan presents a useful table of the different kinds of usability testing methods available. This is shown in Table 15.1, although the all-important psychological models are rather sparsely covered.

Working outside of the standard HCI methods, and returning more to the fundamental tenets of usability, Lin et al. (1997) present a useful framework for usability (in particular user interface) testing. Basing their arguments on human information processing, they identify eight features that are important:

- *Compatibility*: Both stimulus–response (S–R – Fitts & Seeger, 1953) and cognitive compatibility (e.g., Oborne, 1995) are important to ensure that the outcome of any control action are compatible with user expectations of that action. As Lin et al., argue, the mediating processes can be conceived more generally as reflecting the operator's mental model of the task.
- *Consistency*: This directly improves user performance and satisfaction and comprises both *internal* (within a system) and *external* (between systems) consistency. Without consistency the user must learn new responses each time.
- *Flexibility*: The interface must be able to adapt to users' needs; different users have different needs, skills, experiences, and so forth.

- *Learnability*: The learning process will be enhanced and the result retained for longer with well-designed and well-organised interfaces.
- *Minimal action*: On the face of it this criterion is quite obvious – users should undertake fewest actions to achieve a goal. However, rigid adherence to this may, paradoxically, reduce learnability particularly the experiential kind of learning that often occurs when understanding the structures and functions of new systems.
- *Minimal memory load*: Mental workload is strongly represented by working memory load. As Lin et al. argue, 'the less that users need to learn, the faster they can learn it'.
- *Perceptual limitation*: Perceptual organisation is the process by which people understand and represent relationships between apparently different stimulus elements. There is a considerably literature on the structure of such organisation, embodied within the Gestalt principles. The Gestalt school's predictions provide some very simple suggestions as to how information ought to be arranged for easy presentation, based on the argument that people organise stimuli during perception into 'wholes' or *gestalts*, that possess features of their own that are not obvious from an examination of their individual parts. The principles of *proximity*, *similarity*, *common fate*, *good continuation*, *area*, *symmetry*, and *simplicity* are discussed in detail by Oborne (1995).
- *User guidance*: A system with good user guidance will, almost by definition, improve the learnability of the system as well as decrease the mental workload of users. Thus less 'effort' will be needed by users to undertake designated tasks.

Lin et al. then related these eight features to the information processing stages at which they take place: perceptual, central cognitive, and action, and developed a useful framework for determining usability at each of these stages, as shown in Table 15.2.

USER NEEDS

The discussion so far has extended the concept by embracing the centrality of the user within the design process. User centrality implies understanding not only the needs of users but also their very mode of 'operation'. Users are sentient beings with wishes, desires, motivations, and varied abilities (both between and within users). Notwithstanding this, the prime movement towards users has been to establish and reinforce the concept of usability which is one that emphasises the need to design for the users' *ability* to operate the system effectively, rather than his or her needs and motivations within

Table 15.1   *Matrix of usability options adapted from Hasdogan (1996)*

Mode	Empirical models	Experimental models	Scenario-based models
		Models in practice	
Physical models		• Trials • Observation • Self-modelling	
Anthropometric	• Charts • Templates • Manikins • Recommendations • Computerised models	• Dynamic anthropometry	
Biomechanical	• Strength charts • Computerised man models	• Fatigue measurement	
People with special needs	• Recommendations	• Criteria groups	• Least competent user scenarios related to special needs
Cognitive models	• Protocols • Trials • Self-modelling		
Sensory models	• Sensory and motor data • Recommendations re controls/displays		
Cognitive process models	• Motion stereotypes		• Mental process scenarios
Users' mental models	• Metaphors	• Eye movement recordings • Concept mapping	• User stereotypes • Metaphors
Performance models	• User test results	• Protocols • Trails • Self-modelling	• Scenarios on a working simulation • Worst case scenarios
Task models		• Task network models • Task simulations	• Task analysis
Consequence models	• Accident data • Health hazards	• Discomfort surveys	• Accident misuse, worst case, 3rd party scenarios • Fault tree analysis • Failure mode and effect analysis • Preliminary hazard analysis
Psychosocial models	• Sales reports • Market research results	• Subjective questioning • Panels • Questionnaires	
Demographic	• Demographic data		
Psychographic	• Psychological/habitation surveys		• Life-style profiling

Table 15.2   *Stages in usability processing, adapted from Lin et al. (1997)*

Human information processing	Perceptual stage	Cognitive stage	Action stage
Compatibility	x	x	x
Consistency	x	x	x
Flexibility		x	
Learnability		x	
Minimal action			x
Minimal memory load		x	
Perceptual limitation	x		
User guidance		x	

the system. Usability, then, must be considered to be a subfeature of user centricity within the systems designer's conceptual environment. In other words it focuses on system, rather than user, centricity. To redress the balance, more consideration is required towards understanding the needs of users as they impact on the system design and this is the purview of user needs analysis.

Many studies have demonstrated the effectiveness of involving users in system design. For example, Damodoran (1996) summarised the impact as:

- Improved quality of the system arising from more accurate user requirements;
- Avoiding costly system features that the user did not want or cannot use;
- Improved levels of acceptance of the system;
- Greater understanding of the system by the user resulting in more effective use;
- Increased participation in decision-making in the organisation.

At the same time, and to ensure that the above benefits do accrue from accommodating user needs, she emphasises the need for *proper* user involvement in the design process – rather than mere tacit involvement: 'The users should be able to influence design, not merely "rubber stamp" it'. Indeed, even simple 'involvement' is insufficient to achieve successful systems; the quality and experience of the participation are crucial determinants of success. Damodoran further argues that users often find themselves in one of two difficult positions when becoming involved in user needs trials (from Hedberg, 1975): either as 'hostage' of the situation whose development is eventually blocked by the design team, in which case the potential users 'operate in a way that promotes "social comfort" and mutual esteem but limits real communication' (as Damodoran points out, this kind of role is particularly damaging because it fails to deliver any of the benefits of user involvement while sustaining the delusion that users are represented in the design team); or as 'propagandist', where the users begin to adopt the designer's view of the design process which can lead to 'indoctrination' – thus the users no longer represent the 'views' of the target group

but begin to adopt those of the 'designers', and, 'Over time there appears to be a tendency for such indoctrinated "representatives" to perceive user problems and issues from an IT perspective'.

To overcome these kinds of problems, Domodoran argues for a 'user involvement infrastructure' that supports a network of users with assigned roles and responsibilities, consultative procedures and user education. Such a network can be developed, she argues, using:

- Membership of steering/advisory committees
- Membership of design teams
- Membership of problem-solving groups
- Consultation with individuals/groups
- Prototypes/simulations
- Quality assurance procedures.

Although important for both the validity and reliability of the information obtained, simply taking such steps belies another extremely important question relating to the effective interpretation of user needs: who are the users who should be represented within this (or any other kind of) framework?

Such a question can be considered at a range of levels. At its simplest, those who ultimately will operate the product or system the end users can be said to represent the 'real' users. However the situation is far more complex and involves almost all people who interact with the product/service at some time in its life – from development, through production, use, maintenance, and so on. Each role (Domodoran, 1996) will have a different 'need' from the system. The problem facing the designer, of course, is that designing to accommodate both the needs and usability features of one group of users may detrimentally affect the design for another group. Different mental models, motivations for use, and even abilities can lead to different conceptualisations of the product and thus interaction with it. Bailey (1994), for example, represents the problem in the following way: three people are asked to classify a group of kitchen utensils. One may classify them functionally as spoons, knives, forks, and so on; another may classify them in terms of the material from which they are built, such as plastic, wood, or metal; and the third may classify the utensils according to size: large, medium, small. Each of the three classifications is accurate, but each represents a different 'view' of this particular 'world'. Each, therefore, would lead to different user needs due, largely, to the differences in the user groups.

Based on such conceptualisation, Valero and Sanmartin (1999) provide an empirical way to determine the separate user groups that need to be considered in design. This is based on detecting commonality between potential users by using subjective distances between different concepts. In this way they were able to demonstrate groups of users (of a student information server) in the population (of students) that maintained their own, identifiable, information structures.

Whether the user groups have been determined by empirical/statistical means, along the lines of Valero and Sanmartin's procedure, or by more 'intuitive' means (by considering the different kinds of 'roles' in the system, such as that espoused by Domodoran), the issue finally becomes one of ensuring that appropriate methods are employed to obtain and understand the information supplied by the users. As discussed earlier, a wide range of techniques are available with some more appropriate than others in different circumstances. These techniques can be classified according to their nature (information extraction and statistical analysis), and to their mode of action (with groups of users working together vs. separately).

In relation to methods that use groups of users together, these include workshops and focus groups, panel studies, and brainstorming sessions. Methods with groups of users individually include questionnaires, observation, interviews, ratings diary studies, and attribution analysis. Techniques with individual users include projective techniques (including the semantic differential, repertory grid, sentence completion, and description evaluation), verbal protocols and content analysis, and user trials.

HMI FOR THE FUTURE

This chapter has considered the evolution and concept of the branch of science that deals with people–environment interactions. Human–machine interaction, human–computer interaction, ergonomics, human factors all attempt to understand how best to design the world to fit the needs of those who interact with it. However, the evolution has demonstrated that neither the question posed (whatever is the question) nor the answer supplied is simple. All interactions that involve people are complex events that contain both physical and psychological elements interacting in different ways at different times and with different people. Usability, user needs and user perceptions are all features that should be

considered within design, just as much as the environmental and physical characteristics of the system.

Although such requirements are gradually being realised in the research output of workers in this area, there is a need for more understanding of the impact of subjective variables on the operability of the overall system. Just as social interactions are affected in significant ways by individual attributions that are developed, both internal and external, so are physical interactions with aspects of the environment. How we perceive an object plays a large role in how we interact with it; how we feel about a system (perhaps a work-based system) plays a large role in how we operate within it, and so on. Thus there is need for more to be done to investigate the reciprocal interaction between cognitions and emotions and environmental/equipment design. In this, user needs and perceptions are crucial.

Equally important, and frequently overlooked, is the impact of communication within the system. All interactions physical and social – are based on the communication of information between actors. Indeed, traditional ergonomics that invoked the man–machine system concept did so on the basis of the communication links between man and machine (controls) and machine and man (displays). Modern technology, however, is itself communication based and the systems developed impact directly on more traditional communication structures. Just as communicating by telephone interferes with the transmission and reception of nonverbal communication, so modern system-based applications such as electronic commerce or remote (tele-) working impact on the existing (and often well understood) communication structures. Indeed, since communication provides information, and since information is often perceived as 'power' and 'control' it soon becomes clear that communication (and the impact of the system on existing communication structures) is a significant facet of man and machine interaction that must not be ignored. If communication structures change, then work and all of the organisational structures surrounding it will also change.

The centrality of users within the system has been considered from two viewpoints: those of the user's ability to use the system and the user's needs from the system when doing so. A range of techniques exists to enable relevant information to be extracted from different kinds of users in order that these criteria can be better understood for the system being developed. Before declaring success, however, there is a final aspect of the issue that must be considered, which relates to the nature of the system and its interaction with the expressed needs of different kinds of users.

The impression may have been gained that users and systems, once defined, can be considered to be relatively static entities. In the design of a computer interface, for example, once the user needs for functionality, operability, learnability, usability, and so on, have been appropriately analysed and understood, it could easily be assumed that what was once a problem is probably no longer present. The interface will have been designed for optimum use by the user. With modern technologies and systems, however, the issue is far from being resolved. The reason for this concerns the very nature of user needs, in that they reflect the user's 'cognitive model' within the design and evaluation process. Thus, as the user interacts more frequently and more effectively with the system, the individual's needs will change – often in uncertain and unpredictable ways (Oborne, 1995).

The question is perhaps better understood by nuclear physicists following the proposition of the 'Uncertainty Principle' by Heisenberg in the 1930s. Heisenberg was concerned with measuring the behaviour of atoms but concluded that it is not possible to measure their behaviour without affecting them: 'Every subsequent observation ... will alter the momentum (of the atom) by an unknown and indeterminable amount such that after carrying out the experiment our knowledge of the electronic motion is restricted by the uncertainty relation'. The same is also true, unfortunately, for human behaviour. As soon as the user enters the system and exerts and influences the subsequent behaviour of the system (including the human operator) will be affected in an uncertain manner. In short, the system that was so carefully designed becomes, effectively, a different system with new issues relating to usability and needs.

A simple example of this effect could be seen in the development of a new piece of software say a word processor. If the software is conceived by the user to be the digital analogue of a typewriter, enabling words and text (and even diagrams and graphs) to be entered onto a an electronic 'page', then the needs and usability issues will revolve around these kinds of features. With use and experience, however, other features incorporated into the software may be explored and exploited, taking the software away from being simply a digital typewriter to creating a text processing environment, with summarising features, textual analysis options, and so on. The original design, therefore, although still appropriate, is limited and its usability and utility *as the designer anticipated* will be reduced. In this case, user experience (which often cannot be examined *before* a new concept arises) changes the very nature of the product or service being designed.

The modern development of information and communication technologies (ICTs) has exacerbated this issue to more extreme effect. Thus initially fairly simple technologies involving computer-based networking (such as e-mail) have created major and global changes in living and working relationships that would not have been considered just a decade ago (and thus would not

have been examined from a usability/user needs perspective). Oborne and Arnold (2000), for example, have demonstrated significant changes that take place within organisational structures when ICTs (at whatever level of complexity) are introduced. These changes, which include the implied integration of otherwise external bodies such as families, clients and competitors, organised labour, and so on into the internal structure of the organisation, have inevitable impacts on both those who work in the organisation and those who interact with the organisation from 'outside'.

Thus, from the viewpoint of design, the very act of introducing new products or systems will impact on the needs of those who interact with them to such an extent that, once an interaction has occurred, the user's mental model of opportunities will change radically – and the whole cycle may need to be revisited. Because of the dynamic interaction between people and the system, therefore, it is likely that the designer's job is never done; the 'output' of usability and user needs shifts as the 'input' of the human–machine interaction develops.

REFERENCES

Baber, C., & Mirza, M.G. (1996). Ergonomics and the evaluation of consumer products: Surveys of evaluation practices. In N.A. Stanton (Ed.), *Human factors in consumer product design*. London: Taylor & Francis.

Bailey, K.D. (1994). *Typologies and taxonomies: An introduction to classification techniques*. London: Sage.

Bartlett, F.C. (1950). Programme for experiments on thinking. *Quarterly Journal of Experimental Psychology, 2*, 145–152.

Bevan, N. (1999). Quality in use: Meeting user needs for quality. *The Journal of Systems Software, 49*, 89–96.

Branton, P. (1978). The train driver. In W.T. Singleton (Ed.), *The study of real skills. Vol I: The analysis of practical skills*. Lancaster: MTP Press.

Branton, P. (1979). Investigation into the skills of train-driving. *Ergonomics, 22*, 155–164.

Branton, P. (1983). Process control operators as responsible persons. Invited paper to symposium on Human Reliability in the Process Control Centre, Institution of Chemical Engineers, Manchester, April.

Branton, P., & Oborne, D. (1979). A behavioural study of anaesthetists at work. (With D.J. Oborne). In D.J. Oborne, M.M. Gruneberg & J.R. Eiser (Eds.), *Research in psychology and medicine*. London: Academic Press.

Branton, P., & Shipley, P. (1986). VDU Stress: Is Houston Man addicted, bored or mystic? Paper presented to International Scientific Conference on Work with Display Units, Stockholm. May.

Carroll, J.M. (1996). Becoming social: Expanding scenario-based approaches to HCI. *Behaviour and Information Technology, 15*, 266–275.

Carter, J. (1999). Incorporating standards and guidelines in an approach that balances usability concerns for developers and end users. *Interacting with Computers, 12*, 179–206.

Chapanis, A. (1991). Evaluating usability. In B. Shackel & S. Richardson (Eds.), *Human factors for informatics usability*. Cambridge: Cambridge University Press.

Cooper, R., & Foster, M. (1971). Sociotechnical systems. *American Psychologist, 26*, 467–474.

Damodoran, L. (1996). User involvement in the systems design process – a practical guide for users. *Behaviour and Information Technology, 15*, 363–377.

Eason, K.D. (1984). Towards the experimental study of usability. *Behaviour and Information Technology, 3*, 133–143.

Eason, K.D. (1991). Ergonomic perspectives on advances in human–computer interaction. *Ergonomics, 34*, 721–742.

Fitts, P.M., & Seeger, C.M. (1953). S–R compatibility: Spatial characteristics of stimulus and response codes. *Journal of Applied Psychology, 46*, 199–200.

Hasdogan, G. (1996). The role of user models in product design for assessment of user needs. *Design Studies, 17*, 19–33.

Hedberg, B. (1975). Computer systems to support industrial democracy. In E. Mumford & H. Sackman (Eds.), *Choice and computers*. Amsterdam: North Holland.

ISO (1993). *ISO CDS 9241-11: Guidelines for specifying and measuring usability*.

ISO (1998). ISO/IEC FCD 9126-1 *Software product quality. Part 1: Quality model*.

Kim, J., & Moon, J.Y. (1998). Designing towards emotional usability in customer interfaces trustworthiness of cyber-banking system interfaces. *Interacting with Computers, 10*, 1–29.

Lin, H.X., Choong, Y.-Y., & Salvendy, G. (1997). A proposed index of usability: A method for comparing the relative usability of different software systems. *Behaviour and Information Technology, 16*, 267–278.

Marmaras, N., Poulakakis, G., & Papakostopoulos, V. (1999). Ergonomic design in ancient Greece. *Applied Ergonomics, 30*, 361–368.

Oborne, D.J. (1995). *Ergonomics at work: Human factors in design and development*. Chichester: John Wiley & Sons.

Oborne, D.J., & Arnold, K.M. (2000). Organizational change in the Information Society: Impact on skills and training. *Industry and Higher Education, 14*, 125–133.

Oborne, D.J., Branton, R., Leal, F., Shipley, P., & Stewart, T. (1993). *Person-centred ergonomics: A Brantonian view of human factors*. London: Taylor & Francis.

Pasmore, W.A., & Sherwood, J.J. (Eds.) (1978). *Sociotechnical systems: A sourcebook*. California: University Associates Inc.

Preece, J. (Ed.) (1993). *A guide to usability: Human factors in computing*. Wokingham: Addison-Wesley.

Shackel, B. (1991). Usability – context, framework, definition, design and evaluation. In B. Shackel & S. Richardson (Eds.), *Human factors for informatics usability*. Cambridge: Cambridge University Press.

Stanton, N.A., & Baber, C. (1996). Factors affecting the selection of methods and techniques prior to conducting a usability evaluation. In P.W. Jordan, B. Thomas, B.A. Weerdmeester & I.L. McClelland (Eds.), *Usability evaluation in industry*. London: Taylor & Francis.

Stanton, N.A., & Young, M. (1998). Is utility in the mind of the beholder? A study of ergonomics methods. *Applied Ergonomics, 29*, 41–54.

Valero, P., & Sanmartin, J. (1999). Method for defining user groups and user-adjusted information structures. *Behaviour and Information Technology, 18*, 245–259.

Whyte, W.F. (1959). An interaction approach to the theory of organizations. In M. Haire (Ed.), *Modern organisational theory*. New York: John Wiley.

Wisner, A. (1989). Fatigue and human reliability revisited in the light of ergonomics and work psychopathology. *Ergonomics, 32*, 891–898.

Wright, P. (1986). Phenomena, function and design: Does information make a difference? In D.J. Oborne (Ed.), *Contemporary Ergonomics*. London: Taylor & Francis.

16

Prevention of Human Errors in the Frame of the Activity Theory

ANNE-SOPHIE NYSSEN
and VÉRONIQUE DE KEYSER

In this chapter, we will discuss error prevention tools in the frame of the Russian Activity Theory, concentrating on three tools: error reporting systems, training simulators and operator aids. The Activity Theory will lead us to describe these tools not just as artifacts or material but as instruments based on the principle of mediation between the person and the work object. We will define human error and the process of causal attribution by which it is marked and argue the need to evaluate how error prevention tools support activity, interact with general work dimensions, affect culture and produce changes in the people working.

There are more and more innovations designed to prevent human errors. Some are prototypes; others are already used by organizations and we can follow their impact on safety. These include: training programs using new tools such as simulators, accident reporting systems, operators' aids, selection techniques, and so on. However, most of these techniques focus on active errors committed by workers rather than contextual conditions. They are implemented in isolation rather than articulated in a safety program; they are often context-free rather than adapted to a particular work situation. As Reason (1997) pointed out, these error prevention tools often ignore the developments that have occurred over the last 20–30 years in safety and cognitive areas. Research results reveal that the context in which accidents evolve plays a major role in human performance. Human errors have multiple causes: personal, task-related, situational and organizational. Usually there is a chain of causes, and it is more the result of a social judgment to attribute an accident to human error rather than an objective search process (Cook & Woods, 1994).

Errors should therefore be considered as the result of mismatched conditions within a sociotechnical system. Further, in dynamic environments, human behavior cannot be termed error without taking into account the history of the person and context. The expression 'cognition in the wild' proposed by Hutchins (1995) is about locating cognitive activity in context, where context is not fixed but dynamic. All the behaviors and ways of interacting should be considered together with the task requirements and resources available at that particular time to define an error. There is nothing new in the idea of studying behavior in context. The 'activity' theory developed in Russia in the late 1920s is markedly contextual. Kaptelinin (1996) pointed out six general principles central to 'activity' theory:

- *Unity of consciousness and activity*. The human mind emerges through human interaction with his or her environment.
- *Object-orientedness*. Activity is defined as object-oriented behavior, tied to a social–material environment.

- *Hierarchization of activity.* The structure of the activity must be organized hierarchically according to the object of the activity. At the upper level, an overall motive is set; motives are objects, materials or ideals that express a need. Then a series of subordinated actions are produced and executed to satisfy goals in a top-down manner until the lowest level, directly linked to muscular activities. The hierarchy is usually described as going from thought to muscular action. Currently, we think that there is another dimension involved going from conscious thought to automated behavior. This hierarchical structure is useful in understanding errors. Human errors can be differentiated according to different levels of activity regulation. Knowledge errors are located at the higher levels of regulation; action of execution at the lower level. This is integrated in different approaches to human errors – for example the taxonomies based on Rasmussen's skill, rule, knowledge classification (Rasmussen, 1982, 1987a; Reason 1987a,b); the analysis of action slips (Norman, 1981; Reason & Mycielska, 1982); the taxonomies oriented to the action process (Rouse & Rouse, 1983), and the study of errors in complex problem solving (Dörner, 1987).
- *Internalization–externalization.* According to Vygotsky (1962), any higher mental function necessarily goes through an external stage in the development because it is initially, at some point, a social function. As such, and unlike other authors like Piaget (1958, 1959), Vygotsky considers internalization as a social process. Of course, internalization transforms the process itself and changes its structure and functions (Wertsch, 1985).
- *Mediation.* Human activity is mediated by external tools (such as computers, language, books etc.) and internal tools (such as heuristics) which shape the way people act and greatly influence their cognitive development.
- *Development.* Every phenomenon has to be understood and described in terms of its development process and not as such in its existing form.

Activity theory was seen in Russia not just as a descriptive science of work behavior but as a prescriptive science that should contribute to work design. In recent years, it has contributed to an original approach to the concept of tools as a mediator between the person and the work object. Numerous US and West European researchers have carried this approach further (action theory: Frese & Zapf, 1994; Nardi, 1996). In France, Rabarbel (1993) developed a framework for the analysis and design of activities using instruments based on the principle of mediation; he differentiated the artifact from the instrument. The artifact is the envelope, either material or symbolic, of the instrument; by itself, it is powerless. The concept of instrument integrates the person's use, appropriation and adaptation of the raw material in doing a task. It can be very different from the formal use prescribed by the designer. Activity theory conceives the instrument as a mediator between the person and the work object; the instrument changes the work object. The person has an impact on the instrument but the instrument also has an impact on the person by changing action and control strategies and transforming knowledge distribution between people and equipment. This consideration is one of the main assumptions of Distributed Cognition (Norman, 1991; Zhang & Norman, 1994).

In this chapter, our focus will be upon the examination of techniques of error prevention using the concept of tool as a mediator between the person and the activity in order to assess their relevance. At the first level, error prevention techniques are developed by designers to satisfy a specific goal. An example is a diagnosis aid that must help practitioners to diagnose diseases. At the second level, tools must support human activities in context; practitioners must be able to use the aid in their daily activities. It is only when this requirement is met that the artifact becomes a tool of prevention that facilitates activity in context, supports knowledge acquisition and, in turn, reduces human error without creating new forms of risk. Because errors are drawn from our research in anesthesiology, most of the discussion is about prevention techniques in anesthesia, but the results apply to other domains such as in aviation and the nuclear power plant using similar prevention techniques. We will deal with three classes of techniques: (1) error reporting systems, (2) training simulators, and (3) technological operator aids. The principal goal of the reporting systems is to create a database and identify the risk of accidents, but they also change current ideas about error and develop a culture. At a first level, simulators attempt to train people but they also change operators' knowledge about cognition or metaknowledge. The first goal of technological aids is to improve human performance, but they also transform control strategies or action regulation in terms of Russian activity theory.

ERROR REPORTING SYSTEMS

Most high-risk systems have been plagued by the problem of human error (Hollnagel, 1993). In some cases reporting forms have been designed to collect information about human performance, and this measure is, in many countries, required by insurance companies. In general, the reporting form includes a detailed report of the incident, a classification of the nature of the incident and an appreciation of the contributory factors (Aviation Safety Reporting System (ASRS); Runciman, Webb, Lee & Holland, 1993). The method is often based on self-reporting and the potential for bias exists. A study carried out in an Australian hospital (Currie, Pybus & Torda, 1989) using such a technique shows that in 80% of the reported cases, the accidents described involve nurses and are limited to problems which are relevant to them. Another bias comes from what psychologists call the 'fundamental attribution error' that makes people focus more on the personal rather than the situational factors when seeing someone performing badly (Ross & Anderson, 1982). Given such bias, the reports cannot be used as a statistical basis for estimating accident probability. The utility of this technique of reporting systems is in gathering sensitive information about the mechanisms of failure.

In general, reported incidents are reviewed for common characteristics and classified into one of the three categories: human error, equipment failure and other complications. Within each category, the type of error or failure is broken down into subcategories reflecting the underlying causal processes of failure. Errors, for instance, can have different forms, different psychological origins, occur in different parts of the system. The choice of the subcategories reflects the definition that the designer has of an error. Hollnagel (1998) has reviewed the different taxonomies of human errors that have been developed over the last twenty years. Schematically, we can differentiate three forms of taxonomy: the slots, the diagrams, and the scenarios. Each reflects a different model of causality of human errors which, in turn, will have practical implications on the remedial actions that result from analyses of the reporting techniques. The three forms of taxonomies appeared successively and today coexist. Figure 16.1 shows the evolution of the conception of causality together with the elements of the definition taken into account in the technique.

In recent years, a consensus has appeared to consider error as a symptom rather than a cause. Psychologists agree to define human error as the failure of a planned action to achieve the desired outcome – without the intervention of some unforeseeable event (Leplat, 1985; Reason, 1990). There are three elements in this definition: (a) errors only appear in a goal-oriented activity that incorporates both the goal and the means to achieve it, (b) they imply, to some degree, the nonattainment of the goal, and (c) they should have been potentially avoidable (Frese & Altmann, 1989). This definition is different to a technical approach, which defines error as the violation of a rule or standard. Since human beings can voluntarily violate a prescribed procedure, this would not be considered as an error by cognitive psychologists (Reason, 1990).

Table 16.1 *Omission–commission classification*

Error of omission	Errors of commission
Entire task or a step in task	Selection error (select wrong control, misposition control, wrong command...)
	Error of sequence
	Time error (too early, too late)
	Qualitative error (too little, too much)

Source: Based on Swain and Guttman (1983).

The 'Slots'

The traditional form of taxonomy used in reporting systems classifies human error into categories, giving error the status of technical failure and evaluating the probability of its appearance. The categories are usually predetermined according to some theoretical base. Table 16.1 depicts a classical example of this form of taxonomy developed by Swain and Guttman (1983). Human error is defined as a behavioral deviation from a prescribed course of action, and this approach to human error has been widely used in nuclear power plant industries. Underlying cognitive processes are ignored as well as the context and environment in which errors occur. Classes can also be formed iteratively during the review of the reports. This is often the case when the collection of reports pursues a pragmatic goal such as the assessment of new technology. In general, classes here will be constructed on the basis of extensive field observations. In the assessment of a new drug delivery system in anesthesia, for instance, the following categories have been developed through observation of anesthetists' interactions with the system: wrong syringe placement, mode confusion, error of encoding. Here the idea is not to create general or abstract error categories, but rather to specify critical interaction in the design process that affects the passage from the artifact to the instrument status for the new performance aid.

In recent years, psychologists, influenced by the development of cognitive science, have looked farther in an attempt to discover more generic error types. The concept of hierarchical structure of action was first used by Rasmussen (1982) to analyze errors in the field. Reason (1987b) developed a taxonomy that differentiates between skill-based (SB), rule-based (RB) and knowledge-based (KB) errors. At the skill-based level, when we carry out routine, highly practiced tasks in an automatic way, *slips* and *lapses* occur when the actions fail to go as planned but the plan is adequate. An example may be when a practitioner forgets to turn on the ventilator after he is interrupted by a telephone call. Slips refer to more observable actions. Lapses are more internal events.

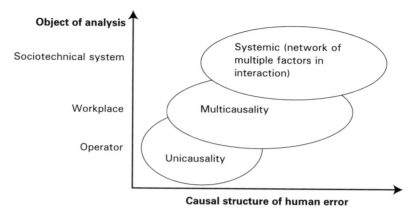

Figure 16.1   *Evolution of thinking about causality of human error*

At the rule-based level, when we apply learned rules of the kind 'if – then', *mistakes* can occur when wrong decisions are made in the assignment of plans (misapplication of good rules, application of bad rules or failure to apply good rules). The action may conform to the plan but the plan is performed in a wrong situation. For example, a practitioner can misdiagnose a disease but apply the good associated treatment. Typical rule-based errors occur when some information is ignored or processed incorrectly and preexisting solutions that have been successful before are applied.

At the knowledge-rule level, when we resort to slow and effortful thinking after the failure of the preexisting solutions, *mistakes* can occur when there is a lack of knowledge about the facts linked to the tasks and the tools to carry out these tasks. Errors often occur because the information processing capacity is limited. Examples of errors described by Dörner (1987) are the treatment of dynamic phenomena as statics, and the perception of different entities as more similar than they actually are.

There are other error taxonomies that have been influential. Rasmussen (1987a) differentiates errors according to their dependence on the mental operations implied in the task. The following categories exist: (a) detection of a demand, (b) observation, search for information; (c) identification of a system state; (d) development of a goal and strategic decisions, including prognosis of future events; (e) generation of plans, decision to select a particular plan; (f) procedure; (g) execution and monitoring the plan. Errors can occur at each step, but there can be more than one error step in the same failure process. For example, practitioners can fail to detect relevant input and then misdiagnose the problem.

The use of 'slot' taxonomies to classify data from reporting systems provides a global indication about the occurrence of human errors. It has been largely used by the media to claim that 80–90% of accidents involve human error and by the engineers to replace human beings by automation. The approach has had some impact on the way human error is perceived.

The Context

In the current slot taxonomy, error is classified into predetermined categories without information about the context in which it occurred. Several researchers proposed to cross different dimensions; classifying human performance with reference to task elements (time, locus of occurrence) in order to identify patterns or task elements that have more potential for errors. However, errors are still classified according to their mode: what was wrong, not why. As Rasmussen (1987b) pointed out, in order to have an explicative value, the attributes adopted to define the task elements must be precise enough to define the characteristics of the internal mode of regulation of human behavior as well. This cannot be practically realized in ad hoc reporting systems. There is a need for a careful analysis of human behavior activity in context with the help of observations and interviews to define the attributes of performance elements for which a reporting system can be devised.

Mutually Exclusive Categories

This is far from being met in the slot taxonomies presented; as mentioned earlier, different error steps can coexist in the same event. In addition, the three level of performance are not mutually exclusive. For instance, injection of drugs by a practitioner is carried out at the SB level. The choice of the drug, taking into account the patient state, occurs at the RB or KB level. In these conditions, classifying an error according to the level of performance can be difficult. In addition, the result of such a taxonomy based on psychological theory can be hard for the people concerned to use.

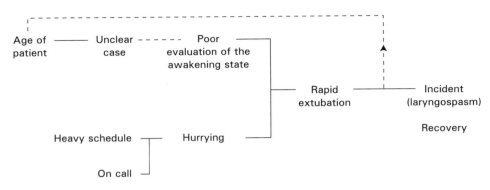

Figure 16.2   *Hypothetical causal structure of incident*

Error Determination

Few taxonomies clearly specify the rules by which they determine the attribution of an error. There are several categories of standard that can be used. An error can be labeled as such by reference to a predefined model of task performance. This is limited to tasks for which a detailed knowledge about problem situations and how to solve them is available. Another standard is the comparison with standard operating procedures. For instance, in medicine it is not possible to predict all the varieties of the problem situation, but there exist some standards of care that provide some guides for activity in some conditions. A third approach is called the neutral observer criteria by De Keyser and Woods (1990). It was developed regarding the dynamics and uncertainty of modern work situations, and is an empirical approach that compares practitioner behavior during the incident to the behavior of similar practitioners at various points in the same evolving situation.

For these reasons, slot taxonomies in reporting systems could be inadapted. The error process is too complex to be classified into one single independent category. Moreover, 'human error is not a distinct category of human performance' (Cook & Woods, 1994: 304). Attribution of error, as we said before, is more the result of a social judgement rather than an objective analysis.

The 'Diagram'

An alternative for classifying errors is to use diagrams to describe the sequence of failures. The method consists of reconstituting graphically, in branching form, a series of causal combinations, starting from an event and searching (as far upstream as possible) its causes. First, researchers used the method to quantify human factors by calculating the probabilities of occurrence of branches, causes and events. They adopted a technical approach to error. Progressively, their goal

became preventive and diagrams were used mainly to emphasize the multicausal aspect of accidents. In France, the causal tree diagram, created in the 1970s by the Institute National Français de Recherche Scientifique (Krawsky, Monteau & Szekely, 1981) refers to the Failure Tree method formalized by Bell Telephone and adopted by the aerospace industry (Boeing, 1993). It is a clinically oriented method based on two main phases: the construction of the tree and its qualitative evaluation.

The tree is constructed by seeking out those events which, singly or in combination, could lead to occurrence of the index event (previously defined). The process is then repeated in order to define each of the basic events. The time axis of the tree moves from left to right approaching the index event. The resulting event is considered to be the consequence of the preceding events. The examination of accident analyses often reveals sequences of actions aimed at recovering unusual situations. Moyen, Quinot, and Heimfert (1980) called these 'vicariant actions'. If successful, they should allow the elimination of the problem, but when they fail they create a new, unexpected condition that will, in turn, have to be remedied. Figure 16.2 gives an example of a causal tree drawn up from our data collected in anesthesia.

Because no harm actually came to the patient in this case, no trace of such a case would be found in most institutions, unless systematic collection (e.g., for Quality Conferences) was in effect. It seems (and seemed to peer experts who evaluated the incident in quality conferences) that the failure here consists of a poor evaluation of the patient's awakening state. It may seem simpler merely to attribute this case to human error and stop here. The causal tree formalism, however, reveals a more complicated story about human performance. Moving back through the tree, it can be noticed that there are more events linked to the organization of work, and fewer events linked to the anesthetists' actions. Certain of these events constitute latent states present within the organization before the incident, others are active errors. It is through their interaction that the problem situation arises.

As slot taxonomies, diagram techniques have some bias which in turn has an impact on the way people perceive error.

Frame Definition

No well-established rules define how far the retrospective search for causes should proceed. The time of the retrospective analysis depends on the specific events of each accident and on the sources of information available (for instance, two years for Three Mile Island and nine years for Challenger). The technique can be easily used by the people concerned. For instance, in a textile factory, operators were trained to the diagram technique in order to improve accident analyses (De Keyser, 1981). First, they constructed very rich trees illustrating the latent factors which lead to human errors. Then, the retrospective search shortened and the analysis of the causes stopped when responsibilities were distributed. This illustrates the relation between a technique and its use in context. It shows the importance of linking research and remedial actions in order to maintain the use of a technique in the long term.

Singularity

One criticism often directed at the diagram technique is that a causal tree based on a clinical method only provides a singular set of facts and circumstances. In spite of this limit, a well-conducted clinical analysis remains a precious source of information. As opposed to a simple repertoire of circumstances and events leading to the production of an accident, the tree allows not only the representation, in a schematic manner, of the causal chains that exist between events, but it also reveals where and how the means of improving reliability can be applied. By applying this technique in a systematic manner to a wide variety of cases, we can locate typical configurations of accidental sequences, which will allow safety diagnoses without waiting for errors or accidents to arise.

Knowledge of the System

Constructing diagrams requires profound knowledge of the work situation and of the relevant models of human decision making. Close cooperation between several professional disciplines is necessary.

The 'Scenarios'

In recent years, several investigators have looked farther into the idea of the multicausality of accidents to question the extent to which the interaction of factors are important influences on accidents compared to events or histories (Caroll, 1995;

Cook, Woods & Miller, 1998). In other words, does thinking about accidents' characteristics tell us about why accidents and human errors occur at work. For example, in order to understand the significance of someone's behavior at work, knowing about the associated factors is certainly important, but what may be much more relevant is the 'history' of the person and his context, how the event developed over time. This approach is also emphasized within dynamic work environments such as anesthesia where every particular situation configuration demands a different adjustment and tuning from the anesthetist. Human behavior cannot be termed error by referring to some procedure as is usually done in rule-dominated domains such as a power plant. All the behaviors and ways of interacting should be considered with the task requirements and resources available *at that time*.

Inspired by ecological theories (Woods, 1995), some researchers have applied the use of scenarios to describe accidents. The unit of analysis is then semantic. The idea is to provide a description of the environment that was directly relevant to the conducting of the behavior. The scenarios capture the relationship between the environment and the activity and how this unfolds over time. From this perspective, it is the constant processes of interaction between the person and the environment that is important, rather than particular characteristics of the person or the environment at any particular time. It is clear that a person's behavior or decision-making can be explained by each event that precedes it, but much more significant is the whole episode and history of the person's involvement with the organization and the task. The major challenge is to distil the reported histories into a smaller number of scenarios containing the critical issues concerning accident analyses. Cook et al. (1998) have used the technique to collect a corpus of cases in anesthesia illustrating some generic cognitive difficulties. Researchers also looked for recurrence occurrence and used data from field observations and discussions to filter out the relevant scenarios.

One immediate implication of this taxonomy approach is that the initial assessment using formal categories and showing human error as the major cause of accidents should perhaps be supplemented by techniques that can assess behavior in context. A further implication is that understanding the relationship between actors' behavior and task requirements gives us vital information about how and when to intervene to improve the man–machine–task system.

However, as in the case of the other kinds of taxonomy, the technique based on scenario has some limitations.

Objectivity

The wealth and especially the strictness of the procedure depend essentially on the objectivity and shrewdness of the analyst. In fact, bias cannot be

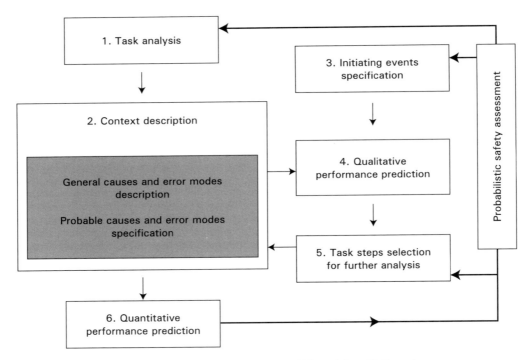

Figure 16.3 *General method for performance prediction. (Adapted from Hollnagel [1998] p. 226.)*

excluded and the analyst works without a safety guard.

Predictivity

By definition, each story is unique, each case special, so it is difficult to combine the data and draw predictions. CREAM is a tool developed by Hollnagel (1998) for combining descriptive and explicative analysis of error. The method provides six steps in order to achieve a quantitative performance prediction (Figure 16.3), and insists on the fact that it is not always necessary to obtain a quantitative prediction. 'If the performance prediction identifies potentially critical tasks or actions and if the failure modes can be identified, then it is perhaps not necessary to quantify beyond a conservative estimate'. CREAM is probably the most ambitious attempt, currently, to capture 'erroneous actions' in a context; it shows explicit links between this context, the internal and external antecedents, the possible error modes and their consequences. It is a method, a group of very detailed classification schema, and a systematic and contextual model of human performance all in one. However, it is difficult to evaluate the use of the method in terms of the appropriation that the user makes of the artifact in order to create an instrument. In fact, there is still a lack of empirical data concerning its use. The main foreseeable pitfall is its operationalization. The technique is complex and highly time-consuming and we can fear that these constraints render its added value partly inaccessible in routine use. However, the technique should help to explore some aspects of human reliability by confronting the theoretical framework proposed by the author with empirical data.

TRAINING SIMULATORS

Prevention of human error represents a major consideration of the use of training simulators. Simulators are mainly used in high risk domains where operators cannot be trained in the real world for safety, economic, or deontological reasons. They are also used in training operators who must perform adequately on their first exposure to critical situations. For instance, some medical situations occur rarely, and anesthesia trainees do not have the potential to encounter those during their training. The anesthesia simulator provides the possibility for such practical training: it confronts trainees with incidents and enhances their recognition and regulation of rare incidents in real time. The analysis of skills required in responding to critical situations is important to construct effective training programs, but the possibilities of collecting and analyzing data in the real system are rare.

Today, modern simulators are used more and more to study human performance, which raises different problems with such a research use (Flexman & Stark, 1987; Leplat, 1989; Sanders, 1991). First, the performance parameters used for assessment in simulators must be related to the quality of performance in context. The difficulty comes from the fact that performance parameters in context are not always accessible. For instance, accuracy and speed of diagnosis certainly reflect doctors' expertise, but recent research has shown that there is also a need for various other competencies in medicine which strongly influence performance on the job (Xiao, 1994; Nyssen & Javaux, 1996; Gaba, Howard, Flanagan, Smith, Fish & Boney, 1998). These performance parameters are not easy to identify; they must be inferred from in-depth analyses of human performance in context. Second, even if the simulated situation is perceived as stressful by the operator, it does not include all the organizational constraints and emotional aspects under which operators perform in the real system.

Thus, results of performance assessment in simulators must be tempered by data from field studies. Although several studies deal with the use of simulators for training, empirical data are still rare. In anesthesia, we investigated practitioner performance on two kinds of training simulators, screen-based and full-scale simulators, and compared it with data from field studies (De Keyser & Nyssen, 1999; Nyssen, 1999a). Results showed that simulator's characteristics influence operator performance. We observed that, in anesthesia simulators, the simulated surgical act is generally much shorter than in similar real operations with some of the anesthetist acts having a quasi immediate effect, whilst others have a realistic duration. These distortions are much more important in screen simulators than in full-scale simulators, and they have different consequences on training. Internalization of duration is prevented, which it means that in simulators time adaptation requires attentional resources and actions have to be planned and executed in a conscious way – looking for external temporal reference systems. In naturalistic situations, regular durations are internalized, which spares cognitive resources for unexpected events and contextual changes.

Also, higher dynamicity in simulated situations, especially in screen simulators, entails a specific mode of control of the situation, which is more reactive than anticipatory. This means a change in temporal perspectives; a reduction of the anticipation span usually associated with having fewer patient variables to take into account.

Usually, also, simple order is preserved. This is immediately related to the causal model underlying the simulation. For instance, a sequence such as 'action A preceeds B and has an effect on C',

referring to the relations between patient variables and anesthetist actions, is found in naturalistic situations as well as in simulators. But complex order including multiple and conflicting constraints, parallel plans to follow with interferences and interruptions found in naturalistic situations is never simulated (Nyssen & Javaux, 1996). In fact, simulators do not teach the complexity and the variability of the real world; they use regular predictable problem situations. Sources of variability such as patient variability and medical team variability can be introduced in the simulated situations, but they are far removed from the complexity found in naturalistic situations.

By definition, a training session is a kind of classical theater play with unity of time, location and action. Past, present, and future are shrunk into a very short time interval. The briefing tries to reconstitute the history of the case, but it concerns only the patient, not the monitoring systems or the medical team or previous cases this team has already encountered in the past. Even though the present is rather realistic, there is no future beyond the training session; it removes any consequences or social stakes associated with the case. This is excellent from a training point of view, for it gives trainees the opportunity to learn from errors without any risk for the patient. But of course, this is not the real world.

Simulator Validity and the Role of Psychologist

The use of simulators either for training or research raises the issue of ecological validity and fidelity. Ecological validity refers to the degree to which we can generalize and transfer the results of a simulator study to naturalistic situations. Fidelity refers to the degree of accuracy with which the simulator reproduces the system and its environment. First, it was thought that increasing physical and functional fidelity of the simulator improved the validity of the training program. However, several studies showed that lower fidelity computer devices could be useful in training (Jentsch & Bowers, 1998; Salas, Bowers & Rhodenizer, 1998). Schwid (1996) has found that the use of a screen-based simulator improves retention of medical guidelines better than standard textbook review. Other research has shown more effective transfer of training under low scene detail rather than complex scene detail (Taylor, Lintern, Koonce, Kunde, Tschopp & Talleur, 1993). Up to now, simulator designers, taking advantage of simulator technology development, have attempted to achieve complete representation of real systems. However, the main function of a simulator is not to duplicate reality, but to enhance learning. Simulator design should be determined according to the training goal. The emphasis has mainly been put on the acquisition by trainees of procedural knowledge and problem-solving skills to control rare and potentially serious incidents (for aviation see Gabba, Fish & Howard, 1994). However, as we said before, naturalistic decision researchers have shown that in modern systems, dynamicity and uncertainty appear to be the major difficulties for decision-makers. Operators deal rather with situation assessment and verification of the hypothesis than with applying some predefined response.

Furthermore, some critical features of the real system such as organizational aspects are difficult to simulate, rendering simulation useless as a training tool. Thus, the simulator training goals should be determined according to an analysis of human performance in naturalistic settings rather than pre-defined criteria. The concept of *psychological fidelity* summarizes this new approach to simulator design. Psychological fidelity is the extent to which simulated situations reproduce similar psychological conditions of action to naturalistic situations, enhancing the learning of skills involved in naturalistic situations (Baker & Marshall, 1989; Leplat, 1989; Grau, Doireau & Poisson, 1998). Psychological fidelity stems from similarity between the conditions of action rather than similarity between technical or functional characteristics per se. Because the conditions of action cannot be derived exclusively from formal task models, they must be determined through activity analysis. In addition, activity analysis defines the training and learning functions to be supported by the simulator. Simulated situations appear, not as templates of reality, but as knowledge mediators between the trainees and reality.

Samurçay and Rogalski (1998) have described this mediation process. According to these authors, simulated situations are always a simplification of naturalistic situations; but the instructor, with adequate knowledge, may compensate for this. The role of the psychologist in a simulator team will be to enhance this knowledge (Nyssen & De Keyser, 1998). Training simulators too often 'assume' rather than 'observe' decomposition of naturalistic situations, which can lead to a premature focalization of performance, which inturn can create an inappropriate prioritization of the training issues. From our point of view, a key element for the psychologist is to collect and compare data on human performance from various sources, from the field and from simulators (Nyssen, 2000). The goal is not to improve the physical or functional fidelity of the simulators; rather, the juxtaposition of data allows a better understanding of the cognitive demands of the task situation, the sources of errors and the potential of preventive measures in either training or other improvements of the man–machine system. At the same time, the results of such a research process swinging from field situations to simulated situations can serve to guide the ongoing evaluation

of the training programs. It can also be part of the improvement of the learning process as well as that of training the instructors.

Too often, simulator instructors are domain experts who do not exploit recent scientific findings in the training, learning and cognitive areas. The psychologist can help the instructor to assess the trainees' states of knowledge and skill, to create appropriate simulated situations, to provide extrinsic feedback, to draw attention to the learners' self-monitoring behaviors during the debriefing. The reciprocal relationship between psychologist and instructor will in turn improve the effectiveness of the training program.

In Finland, the VTT Automation team formed by psychologists and nuclear power plant simulator instructors has developed a simulator training method (Analysis of Way of Acting, AWA). The method includes tools such as diagrams and tables which provide general frames for the description of a specific task situation, give criteria for the observation and evaluation of the crew's activity, and offer informative ways of giving feedback to the subjects. The method is subject-centered, contextual and emphasizes the dynamicity of activity. According to Hukki and Norros (1998), the main training goal in the simulator should be the promotion of situatively adequate ways of acting. Appropriate description of the problem situation is important; it is the first step of the AWA method. The situation is not described in the form of a predetermined course of action but from the point of view of choice of actions and critical information available for decision-making. This conceptual effort is in direct line with Scandinavian tradition, which has always been very close to the field. It stems initially from the Russian activity theory since the simulator must improve knowledge about operators' modes of regulation. But the method also has French roots: Hukki and Norros have stressed the importance given by the subjects to the *interpretation* of the situation in the *course of action*. The subjects have to be able to make sense of the situation which is not given beforehand and emerges from interactions during the simulation process. This emphasis on emerging subjective meaning is also shared with Harré and Gillet (1994) and Theureau (1996). Theureau is considered, in France, as the father of this psychological hermeneutic school, and has introduced, with Pinski, the concept of the *course of action* as the subjective and dynamic construct of a goal-oriented activity.

OPERATOR AIDS

This is a technique of error prevention in which much innovation has been offered in the past but, for a variety of reasons, their use in context has not always been effective. Among these reasons, we can cite (O'Moore, 1995):

- *A large mismatch between aid support and user's real problems.* For example, in medical health, the majority of aid systems are designed for diagnosis while practitioners mainly encounter difficulties with prognosis and therapy.
- There is a *communication gap* between potential users and computer science and the role of the aid is often unclear for the user.
- *No coherent design philosophy exists*, for instance the method of knowledge representation may be inappropriate.
- *Organizational issues are disregarded.* Thus, the complex environment where the system is used is not taken into account; neither its dynamicity and uncertainty.

Aid in itself is a rather general term. It refers to various technical systems which can be very different in their capacity of aid and man–machine co-operation. The device can work like a black box, independently of the user. One finds applications which are very similar to traditional technology. The computer takes charge of certain operators' tasks such as numerical or logical computation without any strong interaction with the users. Other systems can aid operators' actions, reasoning and evaluation. They are in continuous interaction with operators' activities and, of course, real-time systems. For example, in the prototype of an intelligent car, an intelligent system (Generic Intelligent Driver Support, GIDS, Michon, 1993) evaluates the degree of help required by the driver according to the traffic on the road and the driver's working load. It is in such creations, still in the experimental stage, that we can gauge the extent to which researchers dream of the day when joint cognitive systems (Woods, 1986) come into being and we will see systems where a natural agent – a man – and an artificial agent – a computer – interact favorably in their environment. The theory of distributed cognition, which analyses this joint cognitive system, refutes the notion of help as such. In fact, taken literally, this term fixes the distribution of the roles between humans and artifacts. The system they form is permanently adapting and organizing itself. Take the example of memory 'aids' used in cockpits, Hutchins (1995: 153) noted that:

> to call a specific artifact a 'memory aid' for the pilots is to mistake the cognitive properties of the reorganized functional system for the cognitive properties of one of its human components. This artifact does not help pilots remember speeds; rather they are part of the process by which the cockpit system remembers its speeds.

In this conception, nothing is an aid *a priori*, but each artifact can become one at a given time, according to the context and the requirements of the action.

Recent accident investigations revealed that the current generation of automated devices may have created new kinds of failure modes in the human–machine system by having changed the nature of operators' roles in the process. The operators have become system managers who are monitoring systems and who intervene only when changes are necessary or unanticipated situations occur. This has removed the operator from the loop of control, decreasing system awareness, especially if feedback on the automation and behavior is limited (Sarter & Woods, 1994, 1995; Woods, Johannesen, Cook & Sarter,1994). In fact, it has to be noted that the more autonomous the machine, the more difficult it is to penetrate. It is clear that the amount of information on the screen ceases to increase, but the complexity of the system makes it difficult to give an explicit representation of the functional information on the interface all the time. Some relevant sensorial information (auditive or tactile) has been taken away from the human operator's work environment. The speed of the process also adds to its complexity; Bainbridge (1987) insists on the difficulty operators encountered when controlling machines which operate faster than themselves and possibly function very differently. In these working conditions the supervision and diagnostic role is particularly unsettling for the human operator.

Even if the growing complexity of installations means that from now on assistance is unavoidable in managing them, it does not justify the current drift, which is an increase in aid at all levels. In numerous companies, aid is proliferating despite remaining unused, and sometimes this leads to serious dysfunctions. An example is the Socrates software which had to be taken out of service in the French National Railways because it disrupted passengers services so much. This drift can be explained by the joint action of three factors: (1) technological market push, (2) fear of human error, and (3) inadequate conception of aid. Often overlooked is the fact that new devices create new demands for the individual and the group of practitioners responsible for operating and managing these systems. These demands can include new and modified tasks (setup, initialization, operating sequences etc.) as well as new cognitive demands. There are new knowledge requirements (e.g., how the device functions), new communication tasks (instructing the automated device), new management tasks (finding the relevant data on the menu), and new attentional demands (tracking the automated device state and performance).

The presence of these demands generates a risk of new forms of error and failure that can be classified under the term '*design-induced*'. For example, in anesthesia, there is no longer any doubt about the value of integrated monitoring systems which bring together all the patient's vital parameters onto one screen and can be configured to the anesthetist's needs. However, these artifacts have not always been developed taking into account the anesthetist's real activity; sometimes even the most elementary ergonomic rules such as encoding, readability, information layout and so on are not respected (Nyssen, 1999b). Finally and most importantly, although these artifacts are in principle designed to cope with problem situations more easily, they are in fact rarely conceived for incidents; their use at the time of the crisis often creates problems (such as access to relevant information which is hidden). It is one of the ironies of automation referred to by Bainbridge as *Clumsy Automation*; and every industrial sector is subject to this kind of technological evolution. We use as an example to illustrate this type of problem an air catastrophe, that of the A320 at Mont St. Odile near Strasbourg in 1992, which led to the death of 87 people (Monnier, 1992):

On January 20, 1992, an Airbus A320 flown by the airline Air Inter crashed at night on Mont St. Odile near Strasbourg, leaving 87 victims. The administrative inquiry following the accident did not highlight the technical failure of the aircraft, certainly no more so than in the air disasters which have implicated Airbus aircraft in the past few years. In fact, the most likely hypothesis accepted not so much by the administrative as by the judicial inquiry, centers on an error of the type committed by a pilot, or a problem of 'situation awareness'. At the moment of approach, believing to be in auto-pilot descent mode FPA (or FLIGHT PATH ANGLE, a vertical descent mode coupled with horizontal navigation mode TRK or TRACK in the A320), the pilot appears to have entered a descent input of 3.3. This should, in that case – FPA mode active – have led to a rather normal descent angle of 3.3°. But, the auto-pilot was not in FPA descent mode: in order to comply with radar guidance at the moment of approach, the pilots had changed the horizontal navigation mode to HDG (or HEADING), and this mode happens to be coupled automatically with vertical descent mode V/S (or VERTICAL SPEED): the vertical descent mode had changed from FPA to V/S, this being unnoticed by either of the pilots. The 3.3 input entered on approach (that is, after the selection of horizontal mode) no longer meant a descent angle of 3.3° (corresponding roughly to a descent rate of 700 to 800 feet per minute) but a much faster rate of 3,300 feet per minute. Altitude was lost five times faster than expected and this was not detected by the pilots. As a consequence, the airplane hit Mont St. Odile at 18h 20 local time, killing 87 people. The VCR black box containing the communication of the pilot and copilot shows that up to the moment of impact and, in spite of certain displays on the FCU and the PFD (primary flight display) screen, the crew were unaware of the imminence of the catastrophe. Because they were unaware of the situation, we can

say that the initial auto-pilot mode error had been replaced by one of fixation, the two members of the flight crew being insensitive to certain information appearing on their screens. Furthermore, the complexity of the on-board flight aids has increased to the extent of forming, for some pilots, an impenetrable layer of computer technology which prevents prediction of the aircraft's behavior and awareness of the actual situation. (De Keyser & Javaux, 1996)

Regarding these unintended side effects of technology development, several researchers indicated the need to reevaluate the human–machine interaction at a fundamental level (Norman, 1993; Sheridan, 1995). The concept of human-centered design (HCD) or user-centered technology refers to this attempt. The fundamental principles of such new design approaches are: involvement of practitioners in the design process, action-centered design, and error management. We will briefly discuss each of these principles.

Involvement of the Target Users in the Design Process

The idea of involving users or domain experts in the design process is not really original, but its application is often limited in practice to some particular design stages. It suffices to refer to the conception cycle described by Wickens (1992) to be convinced. At the beginning of the cycle, potential users rarely converse with designers. It is the 'human factors professionals' who provide the designers with the frame of reference concerning the task, the work environment and the users' needs. As the prototype is developed, the users are more easily included in the design process, especially for the validation of the prototype. This integration exists in various forms: questionnaires, and observation of human–computer interactions in either experimental or actual work situations. At the end of the design process, the functionality of the product, and sometimes its impact on the work situation, is assessed in real use for some time. This phase is particularly important to identify how operators shape the artifact to function as an instrument. The approach consists of keeping a record of the human-aid interactions and continuously comparing and analyzing the planned project with the real one. If a mismatch is observed between the users' needs hypothesis and the actual operations in context, a change should be implemented either in the product or in the work situation in order to prevent the occurrence of design-induced errors. But, at this late stage, changing the product becomes unfeasible and procedures or training measures constitute, most of the time, the protective measures that ensure safety. Note that the principle of integrating the target users in the design process is only partly applied because of the time limits of the design project.

Action-Centered Design

From an HCD perspective, aid systems should be designed to support operators in doing a task safely and efficiently in real work situations. Thus, the basis for development should not be the technology per se, but rather the operators' needs in context under resource and time constraints. The approach is to carry out an activity analysis to identify what would be useful in the field of activity in order to improve safety and efficiency. Support for activity can be considered at various levels and leads us to some questions:

1. At the mental strategy level – does the artifact support strategies used by the operators in context to perform the task?
2. At the regulation level – does the artifact increase the potential regulation of activity under any circumstances? Does it minimize the risk of operators' detachment? From an HCD perspective, aid design is not only about how the artifact supports some tasks, but also how it increases operators' control or regulation of activity. This view meets the activity theory idea that people who have control can do better because they can choose adequate strategies to deal with the situation.
3. At the cognitive task level – does the artifact support the operators' decision-making during times of highest and lowest workloads? Which steps in the decision-making process are supported and are those the most difficult for the operator in context?
4. At the work situation level – does the artifact support the system performance? Does it support coordinated activity?

The level of individual and social acceptability of the artifact in the workplace will depend on the answers to these questions. Because many aids are not used in context, several researchers proposed to carry out the quality assessment of the product in parallel with the integration assessment (Brender, Talmon, Nykänen, McNair, Demeester & Beuscart, 1995). This, in turn, leads to the realization that the design process should be a dynamic process (Rasmussen, Pejtersen & Goodstein, 1994; Wickens, Gordon & Liu, 1997); that is, a continuing design refinement as we learn more about the mutual shaping that goes on between artifacts and users in context.

Error Management

Because it is impossible to prevent all possible human errors, human-centered design should support error management (Frese, 1991); that is, to increase both system error resistance and system error tolerance. Traditionally, the goal of software designers and industrial engineers is to reduce the occurrence of errors. In contrast, an error management strategy attempts both to reduce the number of errors and to limit the adverse consequences of those errors that still occur. Error management includes two principal ideas: error resistance and error tolerance.

An error resistant system is one in which it is very difficult for a human operator to make an error (Billings, 1997). Design resistance includes, for instance, forcing functions which limit a sequence of user actions along particular paths, or electronic checklists which assist in the complex task. However, as we said before, the use of new devices makes unpredictable errors possible. Tools such as alarms that help people to detect errors are critical to prevent the propagation of the error within a system, thus avoiding negative consequences. For this reason, several researchers pointed out that error detection and error handling are as important as error prevention. The term *system tolerance* describes the capacity of the system to avoid the negative consequences of an error. Within a work situation, large numbers of errors are committed every day, but only very few of them have bad consequences because most are caught by the various defenses that protect the system and restrict propagation along possible accident trajectories.

Some tolerant design measures include tools that enhance detection of errors, that increase operators' understanding of the system, that limit the system in some acceptable mode, that monitor people's activities, that interpose safety barriers, and so on. In Reason's (1997) model of organizational accidents, the necessary condition for an accident is the rare conjunction of a set of holes in the multiplicity of defenses. The author makes an important distinction between latent conditions and active failures. Latent conditions are pathogen conditions that can be present within the system for many years before they combine with local circumstances that promote active error by the individual and penetrate the system's layers of defenses. Since no-one can foresee all the potentials for accidents, the system's defenses have always some weaknesses, allowing propagation of the accident within the system. Understanding how these defenses can break down is important if we want to understand how they shape operators' activities in context and increase the complexity of the system.

CONCLUDING REMARKS

When producing error prevention tools, a procedure for doing something is developed materially. When using these tools afterwards, people change as do the work situations. Up to now, industrial engineers have attempted to solve the problem of human error by automation. The idea has been that the less people actually do, the fewer errors they commit. Recently, emphasis has been put on accident reporting systems, training simulators and aid supports. These are certainly good practices, but these tools are also more than just material for error prevention. They affect culture and also produce changes in the people working. For this reason, it is important to assess error prevention tools in context, just like other tools, and evaluate what short and long-term effects they have on the general work situation. Russian activity theory has been a useful theory, both in terms of studying the activity with instruments in real environments and in providing a structured approach to assessing tools designed to support activity. In contrast to the pure engineering perspective, here tools are not only seen as artifacts or material, but as instruments as they are used by people for doing something effectively and safely.

Thus, there is a need to analyze activity in context in order to identify the users' needs within resources and constraints. Too often, error prevention tools are designed without any precise idea of the actual activity in the real environment. This may lead to some wrong perceptions about the critical performance issues for the worker in the real system which, in turn, may lead to the development of irrelevant tools. Being used in a work situation, the tool changes the way of doing things (e.g., the work dimension may improve after error analyses, mental functions may be trained, help may be provided). Thus, there is a need to evaluate how the tools interact with general work dimensions and what effect they have on the work situation. As a result, a feedback loop should connect tool designers with workers in order to refine tool development as we learn more about the man–instrument interaction and adaptation. The feedback loop is also important to motivate people to further use the instrument. Finally, error management measures encompass error prevention.

What makes errors undesirable within a system is their negative consequences, not the error per se. Indeed, errors have several advantages. They can help people to understand a process, to explore and discover some part of it, to realize that they do not know something, improving people's metaknowledge about their control strategies. From a developmental perspective, error plays an influential role. This gives a different orientation to design, the principal goal being to limit the path leading to bad consequences within the system. We see that the integration of concepts and findings between human factors, industrial engineers and work psychologists is the basic principle for the progress of the design.

ACKNOWLEDGMENTS

This work was supported by the Belgian State, Prime Minister's Federal Offices for Scientific, Technical and Cultural Affairs, Interuniversity Poles of Attraction Programme and Worker Protection in the Area of Health Programme, Phase II.

REFERENCES

ASRS. Federal Aviation Administration, Office of System Safety, Safety Data. http://nasdac.faa.gov/safety_data.

Bainbridge, L. (1987). Ironies of automation. In J. Rasmussen, K. Duncan & J. Leplat (Eds.), *New technology and human error*. London: Wiley.

Baker, S., & Marshall, E. (1989). Simulators for training and the evaluation of operator performance. In L. Bainbridge & S.A.R. Quintanilla (Eds.), *Developing skills with information technology*. Chichester, UK: John Wiley & Sons.

Billings, C.E. (1997). *Aviation automation: The search for a human-centered approach*. Mahwah, New Jersey: Lawrence Erlbaum.

Boeing Commercial Airplane Group (1993). *Accident prevention strategies: removing links in the accident chains: Commercial Jet Aircraft world wide operations 1982–1991* (Boeing Airplane Safety Engineering B-210B). Seattle, WA: Author.

Brender, J., Talmon, J., Nykänen, P., McNair, P., Demeester, M., & Beuscart, R. (1995). On the evaluation of system integration. In E.M.S.J. van Gernip & J.L. Talmon (Eds.), *Assessment and evaluation of information technologies in medicine* (pp. 189–209). IOS Press.

Caroll, J.M. (1995). *Scenario-based design*. New York: Wiley & Sons.

Cook, R.I., & Woods, D.D. (1994). Operating at the sharp end: The complexity of human error. In M.S. Bogner (Ed.), *Human error in medicine*. Hillsdale: Erlbaum.

Cook, R., Woods, D., & Miller, C. (1998). *A tale of two stories: Constrasting views of patient safety*. Report from a workshop on Assembling the Scientific Basis for Progress on Patient Safety. National Patient Safety AMA.

Currie, M., Pybus, D.A., & Torda, T.A. (1989). A prospective study of anaesthetic critical events: A report on a pilot study of 88 cases. *Anaesthesia & Intensive Care, 16*, 98–100.

De Keyser, V. (1981). La démarche participative en sécurité. *Bulletin de Psychologie*, xxxiii (344), 479–491.

De Keyser, V., & Javaux, D. (1996). Human factors in aeronautics. In F. Bodart & J. Vanderdonckt (Eds.), *Proceedings of the Eurographics Workshop, Design, Specification and Verification of Interactive Systems '96*. Vienna: Springer-Verlag Computer Science.

De Keyser, V., & Nyssen, A.S. (1999). The management of temporal constraints in naturalistic decision making. The case of anaesthesia. In G. Klein & E. Salas (Eds.), *Linking expertise and naturalistic decision making*, Vol 4, chap. 10.

De Keyser, V., & Woods, D.D. (1990). Fixation errors: Failure to revise situation assessment in dynamic and risky systems. In A.G. Colombo & A. Saiz de Bustamente

(Eds.), *Systems reliability assessment*. ECSC, EEC, EAEC: Brussels and Luxembourg.

Dörner, D. (1987). On the difficulties people have in dealing with complexity. In J. Rasmussen, K. Duncan & J. Leplat (Eds.), *New technology and human errors*. London: Wiley.

Flexman, R.E., & Stark, E.A. (1987). Training simulators. In G. Salvendy (Ed.), *Handbook of industrial and engineering work* (pp. 1012–1037). New York: John Wiley.

Frese, M. (1991). Error management or error prevention: Two strategies to deal with errors in software design. In H.J. Bullinger (Ed.), *Human aspects in computing: Design and use of interactive systems and work with terminals*. Amsterdam: Elsevier Science.

Frese, M., & Altmann, A. (1989). The treatment of errors in learning and training. In L. Bainbridge & S.A.R. Quintanille (Eds.), *Developing skills with information technology*. London: John Wiley & Sons.

Frese, M., & Zapf, D. (1994). In H.C. Triandis, M.D. Dunnette & L.M. Hough (Eds.), *Handbook of industrial and organizational psychology*, Vol. 4 (2nd ed.). Palo Alto, CA: Consulting Psychologists Press.

Gaba, D., Fish, K., & Howard, S. (1994). *Crisis management in anesthesiology*. New York: Churchill Livingstone.

Gaba, D., Howard, S., Flanagan, B., Smith, B., Fish, K., & Boney, R. (1998). Assessment of clinical performance during simulated crises using both technical and behavioural ratings. *Anesthesiology*, 89, 8–18.

Grau, J., Doireau, P., & Poisson, R. (1998). Conception et utilisation de la simulation pour la formation: Pratiques actuelles dans le domaine militaire. *Le Travail humain*, 61(4), 361–385.

Harré, R., & Gillet, G. (1994). *The discursive mind*. Thousand Oaks, CA: Sage.

Hollnagel, E. (1993). Models of cognition: Procedural prototypes and contextual control. *Le travail humain*, 56, 1/1993, 27–57.

Hollnagel, E. (1998). *Cognitive Reliability and Error Analysis Method. CREAM*. Oxford, New York & Tokyo: Elsevier.

Hukki, K., & Norros, L. (1998). Subject-centred and systemic conceptualization as a tool of simulator training. *Le Travail humain*, 61(4), 313–331.

Hutchins, W.E. (1995). *Cognition in the wild*. Cambridge, M.A.: MIT Press.

Jentsch F., & Bowers, C.A. (1998). Evidence for the validity of PC-based simulations in studying aircrew coordination. *The International Journal of Aviation Psychology*, 8(3), 243–260.

Kaptelinin, V. (1996). Activity theory: Implications for Human-Computer interaction. In B.A. Nardi, *Context and consciousness* (pp. 103–116). Cambridge: MIT Press.

Krawsky, G., Monteau, M., & Szekely, J. (1981). La Méthode I.N.R.S. *d'Analyse des Accidents, Outil de Gestion de la Sécurité. Psychologie du travail*, 13.

Leplat, J. (1985). *Erreur humaine, fiabilité humaine dans le travail*. Paris: Armand Colin.

Leplat, J. (1989). Simulation and simulators in training: Some comments. In L. Bainbridge & A. Ruiz

Quintanilla (Eds.), *Developing skills with information technology* (pp. 277–291). London: Wiley & Sons.

Michon, J.A. (1993). *Generic Intelligent Driver Support: A comprehensive Report on GIDS*. London, UK: Taylor & Francis.

Monnier, A. (1992). *Rapport préliminaire de la Comission d'enquête administrative sur l'accident du Mont Saint-Odile du 20 janvier 1992*. Paris, France: Ministère de l'Equipement du Logement, des Transports et de l'Espace.

Moyen, D., Quinot, E., & Heimfert, M. (1980). Exploitation d'analyses d'accidents du travail à des fins de prévention. *Le travail humain*, 42(2), 255–274.

Nardi, B.A. (1996). *Context and Consciousness*. Cambridge: MIT Press.

Norman, D. (1981). Categorization of action slips. *Psychological Review*, 88, 1–15.

Norman, D.A. (1991). Cognitive artifact. In J.M. Caroll (Ed.), *Designing interactions*. Cambridge, MA: Cambridge University Press.

Norman, D.A. (1993). *Things that make us smart: Defending human attributes in the age of the machine* (pp. 97–109). Reading, M.A.: Addison-Wesley.

Nyssen, A.S. (1999a). Training simulators in anesthesia: Towards a hierarchy of learning situations. *Proceedings of Human Computer Interactions International 99*. Munich, Germany, August 22–26, 1999. Vol. 1, 890–894.

Nyssen, A.S. (1999b). *Anesthésistes et patients devant le risque d'erreur: Développement d'une méthodologie d'évaluation des systèmes informatisés de contrôle et de surveillance*. Rapports de recherche, Service de la Politique Scientifique belge, ST/12/011.

Nyssen, A.S. (2000). Analysis of human errors in anaesthesia: Our methdological approach: from general observations to targeted studies in laboratory. In C. Vincent & B.A. De Mol (Eds.), *Safety in Medicine* (pp. 49–63). London: Pergamon.

Nyssen, A.S., & Javaux, D. (1996). Analysis of synchronization constraints and associated errors in collective work environments. *Ergonomics*, 39, 1249–1264.

Nyssen, A.S., & De Keyser V. (1998). Improving training in problem solving skills: Analysis of anesthetist's performance in simulated problem situations. *Le travail humain*, 61(4), 387–401.

O'Moore, R. (1995). The conception of a medical Computer System. In E.M.S.J. van Gennip & J.L. Talmon (Eds.), *Assessment and Evaluation of Information Technologies in Medicine*. Amsterdam: IOS Press.

Piaget, J. (1958). La lecture de l'expérience. *Etudes d'épistémologie génétique*, 5, Paris: PUF.

Piaget, J. (1959). *La formation du symbole chez l'enfant* (2nd ed.). Neuchatel, Delachaux et Niestlé.

Rabarbel, P. (1993). Représentations dans des situations d'Activités instrumentées. In A.W. Fassina, P. Rabarbel & D. Dubois (1993). *Représentations pour l'action*. Toulouse: Octares Eds.

Rasmussen, J. (1982). Human errors: A taxonomy for describing human malfunction in industrial installation. *Journal of Occupational Accidents*, 4, 311–335.

Rasmussen, J. (1987a). Cognitive control and human error mechanisms. In J. Rasmussen, K. Duncan & J. Leplat (Eds.), *New technology and human error* (pp. 53–61). Chichester, UK: Wiley.

Rasmussen, J. (1987b). The definition of human error and a taxonomy for technical system design. In J. Rasmussen, K. Duncan & J. Leplat (Eds.), *New technology and human error* (pp. 23–30). Chichester, UK: Wiley.

Rasmussen, J., Pejtersen, A.M., & Goodstein, L.P. (1994). *Cognitive systems engineering*. New York: John Wiley & Sons.

Reason, J. (1987a). A preliminary classification of mistakes. In J. Rasmussen, K. Duncan & J. Leplat (Eds.), *New technology and human error* (pp. 15–22). Chichester, UK: Wiley.

Reason, J. (1987b). Generic error-modelling system (GEMS): A cognitive framework for locating common human error forms. In J. Rasmussen, K. Duncan & J. Leplat (Eds.), *New technology and human error* (pp. 63–83). Chichester, UK: Wiley.

Reason, J. (1990). *Human error*. Cambridge: Cambridge University Press.

Reason, J. (1997). *Managing the risks of organizational accidents*. Hampshire, UK: Ashagte.

Reason, J., & Mycielska, K. (1982). *Absent-minded? The psychology of mental lapses and everyday errors*. New York: Prentice-Hall.

Ross, L., & Anderson, C.A. (1982). Shortcoming in the attribution process: On the origins and maintenance of erroneous social assessments. In D. Khaneman, P. Slovic & A. Tversky (Eds.), *Judgment under uncertainty heuristics and biases*. Cambridge: Cambridge University Press.

Rouse, W.B., & Rouse, S.H. (1983). Analysis and classification of human error. *IEEE Transactions on Systems, Man and Cybernetics, SMC-13*, 539–549.

Runciman, W.B., Webb, R.K., Lee, R., & Holland, R. (1993). System failure: An analysis of 2000 incidents reports. *Anaesthesia a Intensive Care, 21*, 684–695.

Salas, E., Bowers C.A., & Rhodenizer, L. (1998). It is not how much you have but how you use it: Towards a rational use of simulation to support aviation training. *The International Journal of Aviation Psychology, 8*(3), 197–208.

Samurçay R., & Rogalski, J. (1998). Exploitation didactique des situations de simulation. *Le Travail humain, 61*(4), 333–359.

Sanders, A.F. (1991). Simulation as a tool in the measurement of human performance. *Ergonomics, 34*(8), 995–1025.

Sarter, N.B., & Woods, D.D. (1994). Pilot interaction with cockpit automation II: An experimental study of pilot's model and awareness of the Flight Management System (FMS). *International Journal of Aviation Psychology, 4*, 1–28.

Sarter, N.B., & Woods, D.D. (1995). Strong, silent, and out-of-the-loop: Properties of advanced (cockpit) automation and their impact on human-automation interaction. *CSEL* Report-95-TR-01. Columbus, Ohio State University.

Sheridan, T.B. (1995). Human centred automation: Oxymoron or common sense? Lecture delivered at industrial summer school on Human-centered Automation, Saint-Lary, France.

Swain, A.D., & Guttman, H.E. (1983). *Handbook of Human reliability Analysis with Emphasis on Nuclear Power Plant Applications*. NUREG/CR-1278, Albuquerque N.M., Sandia National Laboratories.

Schwid, M.D. (1996). Graphical Anesthesia Simulators Gain Widespread Use. *APSF Newsletter*, 32–34.

Taylor, H.L., Lintern, G., Koonce, J.M., Kunde, D.R., Tschopp, J.M., & Talleur, D.A. (1993). Scene content, field of view and amount of training in first officer training. In R.S. Jensen (Ed.), *Proceedings of the 7th International Symposium on Aviation Psychology* (pp. 753–757), Columbus: Ohio State University.

Theureau, J. (1996). Course of action analysis and ergonomics design. Paper presented at the Workshop on Work and learning in transition. San Diego, January.

Vygotsky, L.S. (1962). *Thought and language*. Cambridge, MA: MIT Press.

Wertsch, J.V. (1985). *Vygotsky and the social formation of mind*. Cambridge, MA: Harvard University Press.

Wickens, C.D. (1992). *Engineering Psychology and Human Performance*. New York: HarperCollins.

Wickens, C.D., Gordon, S.E., & Liu, Y. (1997). *An introduction to Human Factors engineering*. New York: Longman.

Woods, D. (1986). Paradigms for intelligent decision support. In E. Hollnagel, G. Mancini & D. Woods (Eds.), *Intelligent Decision Support in Process Environments* (pp. 153–173). Berlin: Springer-Verlag.

Woods, D.D. (1995). Towards a theoretical base for representation design in the computer medium: Ecological perception and aiding in human cognition. In J. Flasch, P. Hancocock, J. Caird & K. Vicente (Eds.), *Global Perspectives on the Ecology of Human-Machine Systems* (Vol. 1, pp. 157–188). Hillsdale, NJ: Lawrence Erlbaum.

Woods, D., Johannesen, L., Cook, R., & Sarter, N. (1994). *Behind human error: Cognitive Systems, Computers, and Hindsight. State of the Art Report*. CSERIAC SOAR, Dayton, OH.

Xiao, Y. (1994). *Interacting with complex work environments: A field study and planning model*. Unpublished thesis, Department of Industrial Engineering, Toronto, Ontario, Canada.

Zhang, J., & Norman, D.A. (1994). Representations in Distributed Cognitive Tasks. *Cognitive Science, 18*, 87–122.

17

Utility Analysis: A Review and Analysis at the Turn of the Century

PHILIP L. ROTH, PHILIP BOBKO and HUNTER MABON

Utility analysis is based on the assumption that the behavior of individuals has important economic implications for organizational performance and that these implications can be modeled in order to aid in organizational decision-making. Such an approach is consistent with current managerial thinking embodied in the human capital measurement movement, and thus it appears to be a timely concern. We briefly trace the historical development of single attribute utility analysis through the Brogden–Cronbach–Gleser utility model, and suggest that utility analysis can aid decision-making in the consideration of a wide variety of organizational interventions. Within this approach, there are many approaches to measuring the standard deviation of job performance in dollars. In contrast, there has been much less emphasis in utility analysis on multiple attribute utility analysis. We highlight this approach and its advantages as an alternative to traditional single attribute utility analysis. Finally, the acceptance of utility analysis is a key concern to both practitioners and researchers at the turn of the century. We suggest conceptual attention to determining the definition of the area, and theoretical models that help applied psychologists understand the acceptance process.

Applied psychologists and human resource managers are often faced with important decisions about which programs or interventions they should implement in organizations. These decisions include whether to implement a new system where no human resource management (HRM) system currently exists, and whether or not to replace an existing human resource system with a new system. In both cases, the decision-maker is faced with processing a very large amount of data. This information can include the expected effect size of the intervention, the number of people affected, the amount of time the affected people will stay with the organization, the value of the job performance to the organization, the costs of the intervention, and so on. In addition to individual-level performance and costs, decision-makers may also be concerned with the impact of turnover, the potential for adverse impact of the selection system, and the image that the organization projects to applicants that are not hired. Such a large amount of information is very difficult for decision-makers to process in a systematic manner. Utility analysis (UA) (e.g., Cronbach & Gleser, 1965) helps decision-makers overcome information-processing limitations and make higher quality decisions.

Formally stated, the purpose of UA is to aid in understanding the implications of applied psychology/human resource management decisions or processes. As such, it is often considered a decision aid for applied psychologists and managers. It offers an important set of advantages over non-aided decision-making. These advantages include use of mathematical models to combine information; being able to index the value of planned organizational changes in metrics that decision-makers can comprehend; and sensitivity analyses to see if decisions still 'make sense' after varying some aspects of the situation.

In order to stimulate the use of, and research about, this family of decision aids by applied psychologists, we trace the history and development of current UA models, including methods for estimating the standard deviation of job performance in dollars, as well as acceptance of these models by managers. While we attempt to review much of the body of UA work, we pay particular attention to multi-attribute utility analysis and the acceptance of UA by decision-makers. We believe these issues are likely to be more important as UA research and application enters the next century. However, we briefly note an assumption of UA and its convergence ideas from the human capital movement.

A KEY ASSUMPTION OF UA

The major philosophical assumption underlying UA is that humans and human performance have value to an organization and this value should be estimated. It is interesting to note that this assumption converges with ideas from the human capital measurement movement as many organizations (in Europe and the US) espouse the view that a well-organized human resource management effort can lead to considerably improved corporate financial outcomes. In fact, many companies have found that the human element in the production of goods and services has increased dramatically, and that for many companies it is the dominating production resource.

One manifestation of this way of thinking is how many companies are now valued on major stock exchanges. Traditionally, market value was based heavily on book value; that is, the value of the material assets of the organization. The ratio of market value to book value is still fairly low in traditional heavy industry, while attaining unprecedented levels in new knowledge-intensive organizations. Flamholz and Main (1999) show that the ratio for US Steel was 2 in 1997, while that of Intel Corp was 6 and Microsoft 17. The difference between book value and market value is clearly some sort of evaluation of the intellectual capital within the organization; in the case of Microsoft this intellectual capital is valued at 16 times that of the material assets. The gap between market value and book value has consequently given rise to an intense interest in evaluating intellectual capital and determining its components (Edvinsson & Malone, 1997; Pfeffer, 1997; Stewart, 1997; Sveiby, 1997; Lazear, 1998).

A second manifestation of this trend is that some organizations are trying to estimate the value of their human assets. These organizations have published Human Resource Audits for a number of years, and perhaps the first company in the world to attempt to assess its intellectual capital was the Swedish financial giant Skandia which produced a supplement to its 1994 annual report on this topic. We believe that such manifestations of the trend of placing importance on human contributions and estimating their influence on key organizational outcomes is consistent with UA. As a result, we suggest that estimating the value of applied psychological interventions to the organization is quite timely and suggest links between the human capital movement and UA later in the chapter. First, let us turn to the history of traditional UA models.

HISTORY AND DEVELOPMENT OF MAJOR UTILITY MODELS

The history and development of applied psychology utility models occurred in two relatively distinct streams of research. We first detail the development of the Brogden–Cronbach–Gleser utility model, and label this stream of research as single attribute utility analysis in order to note that decision-makers are seeking to model the effect of some decision on a single dependent variable (e.g., job performance). Later we also describe multi-attribute utility analysis as a way to model the effects of a decision on multiple dependent variables.

Single Attribute Utility Analysis

Perhaps the most frequently used and cited utility analytic model is labeled the Brogden–Cronbach–Gleser model. It is fruitful to consider some of the precursors to that model. In so doing, we focus on the situation where one predictor (say, X) is used in a single stage to hire individuals. Presumably, there is an ordinal (often presumed linear) relation between scores on the selection instrument (X) and scores on some criterion measure (or composite) of interest (say, Y). As will be seen below, a selection test will have some utility to the organization if its use increases the value to the organization of those who are selected using this test relative to the use of some other test, or even no test at all. As will be seen and discussed throughout, 'value' can be assessed and operationalized in a variety of ways (e.g., performance levels, dollar worth of performance levels, and so forth).

Some Notation

The single stage selection system involves a cutpoint on the predictor (X), above which people are selected and below which individuals are not selected. The percentage of individuals scoring above the cutpoint, that is the percentage of individuals selected, is referred to as the selection ratio (*s.r.*). Generally speaking, lower selection ratios (more selectivity), will result in greater utility of those individuals selected, although practical considerations (i.e., a particular number of jobs needing to be filled) might constrain optimization on this dimension. Further, as already noted, it is generally assumed that there is a linear relation between X and job performance (or the value of that job performance), Y. The Pearson product-moment correlation between Y and X will simply be denoted here as r.

Taylor-Russell Utility

The notion of utility as described early in the twentieth century by Taylor and Russell (1939) involves the dichotomous use of both the predictor and the criterion. Dichotomizing the predictor (X) is consistent with the assumption that a cutpoint is determined for a selection test, and only individuals above that cutpoint are selected. Thus, most models of utility dichotomize X (although see discussion later of the notion that top choices might turn down the organization's offer). The distinctive aspect of Taylor–Russell utility comes in the assumption that performance is dichotomous. This might make sense if one is interested in performance that is acceptable or not, or in performance that meets a particular standard, or not, and so forth.

If X and Y are both dichotomous, and n decisions are made, then four possibilities arise:

1. A person is above the cutpoint on X (and is presumably hired) and performs acceptably (call the number of outcomes of this type, a).
2. A person is below the cutpoint on X and, had that person been hired, would not have performed acceptably (call the number of outcomes of this type, b).

Note that from the organization's vantage, both of the above outcomes are 'good' in that a 'correct' decision has been made. The remaining two possibilities are 'errors' (and conform to the notion of Type I and Type II errors in classical hypothesis testing).

3. A person is above the cutpoint on X (and is presumably hired) but does not perform acceptably (call the number of outcomes of this type, c). These outcomes are sometimes called false positives.

4. A person is below the cutpoint on X but, had that person been hired, would indeed have performed acceptably (call the number of outcomes of this type, d). These outcomes are sometimes called false negatives.

Overall, then, $a + b + c + d = n$. Further, $a + b$ decisions are 'good' from the organization's point of view, while $c + d$ decisions are errors of some type. Thus, it makes sense to consider the ratio

$$U_1 = \frac{a + b}{a + b + c + d} \qquad (17.1)$$

as an index of utility, because it provides the proportion of decisions made using the selection system that were not in error. This makes good theoretical sense when the performance measure (Y) is dichotomous.

Operationally, however, an organization would not have empirical estimates of the value of b and d above. For example, the number of people falling in the second category, b, assumes we know what would happen on the job performance dimension for a person who was never hired. Thus, another ratio of utility is

$$U_2 = \frac{a}{a + c} \qquad (17.2)$$

This index makes more sense from a practical point of view (because data can be obtained to estimate both a and c). The value of U_2 provides an index of the proportion of individuals hired using the test X who eventually perform successfully.

One of the contributions of Taylor and Russell was to provide theoretical estimates of the values of U, based upon assumptions of bivariate normality on X and Y. The estimates of U_1 and U_2 are a function of (1) the degree of selectivity (*s.r.*), (2) the validity (r_{xy}), and (3) the base rate percentage of individuals in the applicant pool who would have performed acceptably.

For example, suppose that 30% of the individuals in the applicant pool would have performed acceptably (i.e., 30% of the individuals will perform acceptably if hiring is random). Suppose the validity of the test is .35 and the selection ratio is .50. Then, the Taylor–Russell tables indicate that if one uses the selection test, 40% of the selected individuals will perform acceptably – an increase of 10% over the base rate. Or, if the company can afford to be more selective and the selection ratio is .05, then 58% of the individuals selected would perform acceptably. In general, as the validity increases and the selection ratio decreases, the proportion of successful performers increases. Indeed, a glance at Taylor and Russell's tables indicates that both events (high r, low $s.r.$) must occur to yield maximum benefit of the selection test. That is, if the selection ratio is high (low selectivity) then increases in the validity will not generate much of an increased selection advantage. However, increments in a test's validity will be relatively beneficial when the $s.r.$ is low. The overall points are:

- If one is interested in dichotomous outcomes, then a practical estimate of test utility is the percentage of selected individuals who will succeed on the job.
- The Taylor–Russell tables allow the user to estimate those percentages and compute the increase in such a percentage, compared to a baseline percentage of acceptable performers.
- The utility index is a function of both the validity (r) and the selection ratio ($s.r.$).

Lawshe et al.'s Approach

Lawshe and others (e.g., Lawshe, Bolda, Brune & Auclair, 1958) provided a variant of the Taylor–Russell approach that focused on parsing the selection test scores (X) into five ordinal categories (the top 20% of the scores on X, the next 20%, and so forth). These authors then computed expectancy charts that provide the percentage of individuals who would perform acceptably, as a function of their five-category status on the selection test. Once again, these expectancies depend upon the validity of the selection test and the overall base rate for performance. For example continuing with the illustration above, suppose that the validity of a selection test is .35 and that 30% of all applicants would be expected to acceptably perform the job. In this instance, 49% of the individuals scoring in the top 20% on X would be expected to perform acceptably; 42% of the individuals scoring in the next 20% on X would be expected to perform acceptably; and so forth. (Indeed, 30% of the individuals scoring in the lowest 20% on X would be expected to perform acceptably – no better than the base rate.) The reader is referred to Guion (1965) for a rare, yet clear, detailed exposition of these expectancy charts.

It is important to realize that both the Taylor–Russell approach and the Lawshe et al., expectancy charts treat performance as a dichotomous variable. In one sense, this is a fairly generalizable manner of thinking. For example, although we have used acceptable vs. nonacceptable performance as our descriptor of the variable Y, it might be just as appropriate to use something such as superior vs. not superior performance (if superior performance potential was the priority of the selection system).

On the other hand, a dichotomous performance variable is also potentially limiting. Such a variable presupposes that incremental performance beyond a certain standard of performance is of no additional value to the organization. Of course, this does not logically make sense, in that really superior performers are often 'worth their weight in gold' relative to performers who meet set performance standards (for example, consider the worth of a Michael Jordan to a professional basketball team). This leads to the next two approaches to utility analyses – which exploit performance scales (Y) as continuous variables.

Naylor-Shine Approach

Once again, let X represent a selection test, or composite of tests, used in single stage selection (Naylor & Shine, 1965). Assume Y (performance or performance value) is scored continuously and that there is a linear relation between X and Y indexed by the correlation, r_{xy}. For ease of exposition, assume that both X and Y are standardized in the applicant population, such that $\bar{X} = \bar{Y} = 0$ (and the respective standard deviations are 1.0). Intuitively, it should be clear that if an organization selects everyone who applies, then the expected average level of performance will be equal to the overall applicant mean (i.e., zero). However, suppose that r_{xy} is greater than zero and that one engages in some top-down selection using X. The positive validity means that, on average, individuals selected on the basis of X will perform a bit (or possibly much) greater on Y than if all applicants were selected. In other words, $\bar{Y}$ for the selected individuals should be greater than $\bar{Y}$ overall (i.e., zero).

Indeed, assuming that X and Y are bivariate normal, and given a particular cutpoint on X (i.e., a selection ratio less than 1.0), one can compute the average Y score for those individuals selected. This is precisely the approach taken by Naylor and Shine (1965). The result is that

$$\bar{Y}_{\text{selected}} = \text{gain in performance} = r_{xy} \frac{\lambda}{s.r.} \quad (17.3)$$

where r_{xy} is the validity of the test X against the criterion Y, $s.r.$ is the selection ratio, and lambda (λ) is the height of the standard normal curve at the selection cutpoint. (Note that this result can be proved by integrating the product of X and the density function for a standard normal distribution from the range $X =$ cutpoint to $X =$ infinity. The proof proceeds using integral calculus and is not provided here.) Note also that the expression in Equation 17.3 is labeled 'gain in performance' and not just 'predicted performance for those selected'. This is because the comparison value – the average predicted performance when hiring everyone who applies – is zero. Thus, the predicted performance of those selected is the same as the predicted *gain* via selection.

It is instructive to look at both the form of Equation 17.3, as well as its components. Indeed, this is an amazing result for a variety of reasons. Notice, for example, that the selection ratio ($s.r.$) is in the denominator. This makes sense in that (consistent with the Taylor–Russell approach), the more selective an organization can afford to be, the higher the predicted performance of its eventual selectees. The reader is reminded that the formula immediately above assumes standard scores, so it is often written using z-score notation (i.e., $\bar{Y}$ is replaced by the man of Z_y).

The factor λ is statistically interesting. Thorough tables of the normal distribution will also provide values of λ (to repeat, this is the height of the theoretical standard normal curve at the selection cutpoint). If one selects 50% of the applicants, then λ is at its maximum value because that is the top of the bell-shaped curve. This value is about .399. As organizations become more selective (i.e., *s.r.* less than .50), the value of λ is reduced. However, the net gain from selection does not go down because the value of *s.r.* goes down faster than the value of λ. Thus, as organizations become more selective, the ratio $\lambda/(s.r.)$ increases, as does the net gain from selection.

Another intuitively appealing facet of Equation 17.3 is that r_{xy} appears in the numerator. This makes sense in that the gain from selection is increased as the validity of the selection test increases. One of the amazing aspects of the appearance of r_{xy} in the numerator is that it is *not* squared. That is, students of statistics are often taught that the magnitude of a correlation is interpreted by first computing r^2 (and that r^2 represents the proportion of variation in X associated with variation in Y). Although this is correct, note that the value of r must first be squared. This is somewhat depressing, because the value of r is almost always less than 1.0, and squaring r results in an even smaller value. In contrast, the Naylor–Shine statement about utility gain is important in that r_{xy} appears as a straightforward, linear factor and does not need to be squared. Thus, a test with validity .50 is twice as 'useful' as a test with validity .25; the test with validity of .50 is also 50% as good as a perfectly valid test.

It should also be noted that the net gain from selection is in whatever metric that Y is measured in. Thus, the metric might be linked to some performance outcome such as units sold/repaired, dollars, or other theoretically constructed metric of choice. The notion of utility metrics is considered later.

Brogden and Cronbach-Gleser Approach

The Naylor–Shine approach exploits the fact that performance (and performance value) might be continuous. The question becomes, however, exactly what does it mean to say that the average performance score of those selected is, for example, .23 standardized units greater than if individuals were randomly selected? The response to this question is often provided by using a dollar metric.

Thus, equations for gain in utility are often presented in terms of economic (dollar) value. This is consistent with Brogden and Taylor's (1950) 'dollar criterion' concept; that is, the notion that organizational programs, behavior, and decisions might best be couched in overall dollar influence on the organization.

A typical equation found in the Brogden–Cronbach–Gleser approach is:

$$\$ \text{ gain in utility} = \frac{N_s \, r_{yx} \, (\$D_y)\lambda}{s.r.} - \frac{N_s \, C}{s.r.}$$

(17.4)

where N_s represents the number of individuals selected, r_{yx} is the validity coefficient, *s.r.* is the selection ratio, λ is the height of the standard normal curve at the selection cutpoint, C is the per person cost of testing, and $\$D_y$ is the standard deviation of performance, in dollars, in the applicant population.

This result was presented by Brogden (1949) and elaborated upon by Cronbach and Gleser (1965). The Brogden–Cronbach–Gleser approach is associated with a dollar value metric. This makes sense given Brogden's interest in a dollar criterion. However, the focus on dollars is also interesting in light of the fact that Cronbach and Gleser's derivations do not assume a dollar metric attached to the outcome Y. Indeed, Cronbach and Gleser (see their Appendix 1) explicitly use a metric free payoff (e) in their derivations, although they do incorporate the cost of testing in their equations, so dollar values are implied. Once again, it is helpful to consider the form and factors in Equation 17.4. Specifically, the second term on the right hand side of the equation (involving cost of testing) is straightforward and is simply a way of stating the overall cost of testing in terms of the number of individuals selected. Typically, this second term is small relative to the first term (positive gain across all persons selected), even when the cost of testing is substantial, as for example in the case of assessment center selection (e.g., Cascio & Ramos, 1986).

The first term on the right-hand side of Equation 17.4 makes sense in many ways. Notice that the entire right-hand side of Equation 17.3, $r \lambda /(s.r.)$, is directly incorporated in Equation 17.4! Thus, dollar utility gain is a direct function of the mean performance of those individuals selected such that hiring the highest predicted performers results in the highest utilities. Any approach to hiring that deviates from hiring from the top scores downward until all jobs are filled (e.g., banding deviates from this approach) will result in lower levels of utility. The additional two terms in Equation 17.4 make sense, as well. That is, whatever the dollar gain from testing, it is multiplied by N_s, the number of individuals selected. After all, utility gain accrues for each person selected from a valid system. The value of D_y is the remaining additional factor. Its estimation has been the subject of much research and discussion (considered below). At this point, it is best to consider D_y as a critical scaling function that translates mean expected performance (à la Naylor–Shine) into dollar performance. Indeed, D_y is the reason that gain is expressed in dollars – all other terms in the first, positive, factor of Equation 17.4 are metric free. The capital 'S' in 'SD_y' is replaced with a dollar sign to emphasize this fact.

As was the case with Equation 17.3, (1) as organizations become more selective (i.e., *s.r.* decreases), the dollar gain from the selection system increases and (2) dollar gain is a direct function of the validity coefficient, r_{yx}.

The numerical value estimate of D_y is often a very large number (e.g., in the tens of thousands of dollars). Thus, even small validity coefficients can result in significant estimates of overall dollar utility.

Speaking of validity coefficients, Equation 17.4 can be readily modified to fit the situation where one wants to know the gain in utility over some prior selection system. That is, as presented, Equation 17.4 represents the gain in utility over random selection. If there was a prior system in place, then one replaces r with the increase in validity relative to the new system ($r_{new} - r_{old}$); similar replacements occur with the cost of testing term (as per Schmidt, Mack & Hunter, 1984).

Equation 17.4 is really a very simple regression in disguise; it can be proved using basic theory in linear regression analysis (cf. Bobko, 1995). One simply assumes, as was also done by Cronbach and Gleser, that there is a linear relationship between performance value and test scores, and that the variables are bivariate normal – the latter assumption is necessary to derive the presence of the factor $\lambda/(s.r.)$.

The estimate provided by Equation 17.4 has been expanded upon and modified over the years, generally due to cost-accounting issues and the time value of money. For example, the above utility estimates are often gathered with a one-year perspective (e.g., what is that standard deviation, across individual worth per year, in the applicant pool?). However, if one is hired using a selection test, then presumably the benefits from the selected individual accrue to the organization for as long as the person remains in that job. Thus, Equation 17.4 is often multiplied by the average number of years a new hire is expected to stay in the job. Of course, as time issues become more long term, then the projected dollar benefit to an organization needs to be discounted for the time value of money, so Equation 17.4 has been further modified via discounting factors. Other possible factors have included corporate tax rates and the fact that better performers might need higher salaries (generally labeled 'variable costs'). These factors have been implemented

by Boudreau and his colleagues and can be applied to selection and nonselection scenarios. Russell, Colella and Bobko (1993) have also suggested that D_y may also change over time.

Moving the Brogden–Cronbach–Gleser Model Beyond Selection

The measurement of utility has concentrated heavily upon the selection process for two reasons. The first is that the terminology and measurement techniques, as already shown, have been refined over a period of fifty years, and the second is that it is primarily within this area that utility theory has been applied in practice. Macan and Highhouse (1994) show that just under 50% of all utility applications relate to selection, with training accounting for a further 25%. It should not be forgotten, however, that utility theory can be applied to any human resource intervention involving the flow of personnel through the company (Cascio, 2000). Boudreau and Berger (1985) illustrate this in their model of acquisitions and separations. In general, it is possible to express these interventions in utility terms when it comes to areas such as recruitment, training, discrimination, well-being or rehabilitation programs, compensation, turnover or downsizing.

Recruitment relates to utility in that different techniques might be expected to provide different base ratios and selection ratios. This will influence the total costs of staffing in a manner not envisioned by Cronbach and Gleser (1965). The role of recruitment in staffing utility analysis was first modeled by Boudreau and Rynes (1985). Boudreau and Rynes (1985) and Martin and Raju (1992) show that recruitment decisions can substantially alter selection utility values in a variety of ways. This model was further developed by Law and Myors (1993) and de Corte (1994, 1995).

Training utility is a further area where some progress has been made. A model for the cost–benefit analysis of training was provided by Cullen, Sawzin, Sisson and Swanson (1978), while a more specific utility approach was presented by Cascio (1991). Other studies are by Schmidt, Hunter and Pearlman (1982) and Mathieu and Leonard (1987). The basic model, as defined by Cascio, is that d_t, referred to as effect size (e.g., the actual difference in performance between trained and untrained in standard units), replaces $r_{xy}\lambda/s.r.$ Marginal utility then becomes, following previous terminology:

$$\text{\$ gain in utility} = N_S\, d_t\, (\$D_y) - C \qquad (17.5)$$

where C is the total cost of the training intervention.

A further complication in this model is that of obtaining objective criterion data. For this reason, Cascio considers that d_t should be corrected for attenuation and computed as d/r_{yy}, where r_{yy} is the reliability of the criterion measure, for instance the inter-rater reliability of two superiors.

It is often difficult to obtain an accurate value of d_t; the best, although seldom realized, situation is when before and after measures can be obtained for both trained and untrained individuals. In the absence of this specific data, companies should aim at performing some form of meta-analysis where the combined experience of previous studies can be used and a value for expected utility improvements after training can be obtained. An approach to such a meta-analysis may be found in Birati and Tziner (1999) in which they discuss different training outcomes, capital budgeting, and company goals.

Discrimination is also an area where utility theory can be applied, although once again the empirical research is limited. A study by Faley, Knapp, Kustis and Dubois (1999) investigated the cost of sexual harassment in the US Army by estimating the costs for productivity reduction, each specific incident, absenteeism, replacement and transfer costs. They conclude that sexual harassment costs the Army in excess of $250 million per year.

Regarding the utility of compensation systems, two empirical studies (Trevor, Gerhart & Boudreau, 1997; Williams & Livingstone, 1994) show that the relationship between employee performance and voluntary turnover is curvilinear, in that low and high performers have greater turnover than average performers. Adapting the Boudreau and Berger (1985) separation/acquisition utility model, Boudreau, Sturman, Trevor and Gerhart (1999) show that a strategy with differentiated salary increases reflecting high and low performance generates the highest total utility as soon as SD_y reaches the conservative level of 40% of salary, whereas utility quickly increases as SD_y tends towards the 100% level. A further point is that these differences will not normally be apparent when traditional accountancy principles are applied. In the battle to win the talent war, this kind of study is of clear practical significance.

Another applied aspect of other utility models concerns downsizing. Here the principles applied to selection go into reverse. If a company is faced with a downsizing situation, management will normally be interested in the severance of those who perform poorly; that is, individuals with the lowest utility. There may, however, be ethical and in some countries legal restrictions when it comes to this approach. In studies by Mabon (1996) and Mabon and Westling (1996), a general model for downsizing was developed where it was shown that the outcome of a downsizing process will be very different if the goal is to reduce total utility, total salary costs or total headcount. Salary and utility distributions within the organization also play a part, as does the correlation between them. An empirical study of a large insurance company (Mabon & Westling, 1996) showed, inter alia, that the correlation

between salary and utility was zero, as was that between salary and age/tenure. It was also shown that a financial breakeven point from the viewpoint of the company would be achieved by offering those accepting severance somewhere between 63% and 110% of present salary, depending on whether the object was to reduce headcount, utility or total payroll. Companies tend to announce the need to downsize by, say, 10% and announce that they have set aside a large sum of money to cover the costs of this reduction. Closer inspection often shows that they often have little idea what this involves or what they really are trying to achieve. The downsizing model developed in the above studies makes it possible to approach this sensitive area in a more analytical way.

So far in this section we have considered various examples of how utility can be used to analyze various types of HR interventions other than in selection. A further consideration is that there may be an *interaction* between interventions that should be taken into account when a cost–benefit analysis is being performed. This need was pointed out by Steffy and Maurer (1988) where they call for the use of stochastic models to analyze the mix of human resource interventions (e.g., selection, training and compensation) which will give the best rate of return. Unfortunately, little work has been done on this complicated issue and we encourage such work in the future.

DEVELOPMENT AND COMPARISON OF METHODS OF ESTIMATING SD_Y

Equations 17.4 and 17.5 assumed that the standard deviation of performance across individuals (SD_y) was known (in fact, because the value is often considered in a dollar metric we also used the symbol $\$D_y$). The estimation of SD_y has been an historical stumbling block to use of the Brogden et al. model (Cascio, 1992; Schmidt, Hunter, McKenzie & Muldrow, 1979). The lack of ability to estimate SD_y made the model unusable as a good decision aid for many years. The development of the global estimation procedure by Schmidt and colleagues (Schmidt et al., 1979) opened an entirely new stream of research using the Brogden et al. model. Following development of this procedure, research in UA in general, and SD_y estimation in particular, increased dramatically in the 1980s and early 1990s as a substantial number of articles compared the psychometric properties of various approaches, and this topic was viewed as a 'hot' research area. Development of new approaches to estimating SD_y and evaluation of existing approaches has waned in the middle and later 1990s as other issues, such as acceptance of UA recommendations by managers, have received more attention. We review the literature on estimating SD_y in some detail as it is a critical part of using the BCG model (see also Boudreau, 1991).

Preliminary, but Important Issues for SD_y Estimation

Before considering specific estimation techniques, it seems critical to focus effort on determinants of the overall metric of estimation. Traditionally, UA researchers have believed that managers would like to see this variable modeled in dollars (e.g., Boudreau, 1983; Cronshaw & Alexander, 1985). This assumption has given rise to a stream of research on how to express dollar gains best, by incorporating a variety of financial variables and formulae (e.g., Cronshaw, Alexander, Wiesner & Barrick, 1987). Within this stream, researchers have discussed when it is best to use these approaches (Cascio & Morris, 1990) and when to avoid these approaches (Schmidt, Hunter & Coggins, 1988). Interestingly, we are unaware of much empirical research on the metric that private-sector managers would prefer to use. So far, the approaches seem to be related to the types of organizations, their missions, and the types of decision being made.

Most applications of UA in applied psychology use dollars as the metric to measure the increase in the value of job performance (e.g., Burke & Frederick, 1984; Cascio & Ramos, 1986). Consequently, SD_y is estimated in terms of dollars (or other currencies). Other organizations prefer to think of performance increases in different terms. Researchers have questioned the use of dollars for military (Bobko, Karren & Kerkar, 1987) and law enforcement organizations (Barrick, Barrett, Doverspike, Robison & Grubs, 1990). For example, dollars do not readily lend themselves to naturally expressing the increase in performance of tank commanders (Eaton, Wing & Mitchell, 1985) or other military occupational specialties as their mission is to maximize combat effectiveness. Likewise, the mission of most police officers is not primarily financial in nature (Barrick et al., 1990). Some researchers in this area have focused on approaches such as the Superior Equivalents Technique to understand how many superior performers it would take, rather than average performers, to maintain a given level of effectiveness (Eaton et al., 1985). Finally, some researchers suggest that utility can be expressed solely in terms of percentage of increase in output (Hunter & Schmidt, 1983). Determining the appropriate metric to facilitate decision-making appears to be an important issue in one's choice of SD_y estimation techniques as it might influence the reliability and acceptance of UA estimation (Bobko et al., 1987).

Most applications of UA in applied psychology tend to base their estimates of SD_y on the value of output (e.g., the global estimation procedure or some cost accounting approaches) or use salary as a proxy for the value of output (e.g., percentage of salary rules and CREPID). An alternative approach may be suggested by examining the human capital movement noted above.

Cascio (1998: 16) defines human capital as 'the knowledge, skill and capability of individual employees to provide solutions to problems that customers think are important'. The sting is in the tail of this definition; an 'outside-in' approach rather than the opposite (as is traditionally used in UA). When it comes to measuring human capital, it is clear that more work has been done in creating a theoretical framework. Cascio (1998) gives the practical advice that one should keep it simple with a limited number of measures. Measure only what is strategically important, as well as activities which produce intellectual wealth. If Cascio's definition is accepted, measures of human capital are closely related to customer satisfaction. As measures, he proposes innovation, employee attitudes and inventories of knowledgeable employees.

A different approach to the measurement of intellectual capital more firmly based in Industrial/Organizational psychology is that of attempting to link human resource metrics to the broader strategic goals of the company (see Boudreau & Ramstad, 1997; Boudreau, 1998). In a framework called the PeopleSCAPE Model (later PeopleSCOPE) Boudreau and colleagues show how clusters of human attributes such as capability, opportunity and motivation can be used to act positively to 'Moments of Truth' in their day-to-day activities. This in turn contributes to key business processes and in achieving value propositions. The contention is that human resource specialists can work with their resources from below and that they, in a two-way process, will meet the overriding commercial demands of the organization and arrive at a *modus vivendi* for handling decisive situations at work.

The suggestions by Cascio and Boudreau provide interesting ideas to individuals interested in UA. They suggest an 'outside-in' approach to UA. This is markedly different than the traditional approach in applied psychology where one starts with the tasks of the job and then estimates the impact on the organization. Instead, utility analysts may wish to look outside to customers and key strategic goals and then demonstrate utility toward achieving those elements. Such thinking represents an alternative value base for utility analysts and one that has not received a great deal of attention. It also represents an approach where one interacts with decision-makers to determine what is important to them rather than prescribing what dependent variable (e.g., performance of job tasks) they should focus on and the metric they should use.

In sum, the initial choice of a 'value base' for performance is a conceptual issue that should not be taken lightly. One has a variety of choices, some of which have received comparatively little attention in traditional UA applications. In addition, as will be seen, the value base that an SD_y technique starts with appears to influence what other SD_y techniques its results converge with.

Researchers and practitioners may also wish to consider decision-maker reaction to SD_y estimation processes and results. Although some researchers have emphasized the importance of getting decision-makers involved in the UA process (Rauschenberger & Schmidt, 1987), there has been relatively little empirical research on this issue. We note the limited research on managerial reactions to SD_y estimation in procedures in this section and devote a later section of the chapter to acceptance of recommendations and results from the entire UA decision process.

Traditional Methods of Estimating SD_y in Applied Psychology

Global Estimation Procedure

The global estimation procedure developed by Schmidt and Hunter stimulated innovation and facilitated a great deal of UA research (Schmidt et al., 1979). The procedure was designed on the basis of basic research in the judgment and decision-making literature (Schmidt et al., 1979; Roth, 1993, 1994a) and calls for subject matter experts, usually immediate supervisors, to make a series of estimates of the value of job performance in dollars. Originally, the experts were asked to estimate the dollar value of performance of workers (or applicants depending upon the purpose of estimation) performing at the 50th percentile, the 85th percentile, and the 15th percentile. The ordering was important as this process is based on the fractile estimation process from the judgment and decision-making literature. Research suggests subjects can make such estimates on a variety of variables and that such estimates are generally conservative (Roth, 1993). Researchers generally attribute this to the anchoring and adjustment heuristic (Kahneman, Slovic & Tversky, 1982). This heuristic models the process by which judges make an estimate of the middle of a distribution and then are 'anchored' to it and do not move far enough away from it in subsequent estimates of percentiles of the distribution.

Researchers computed two estimates of SD_y from judges' estimates. The first estimate is the difference between the 85th and 50th percentiles and the second estimate is between the 15th and 50th percentiles. If these estimates are not significantly different, they provide support for the proposition that they came from a normal distribution and they may be averaged for the overall estimate of SD_y (Schmidt et al., 1979) (see also Bobko et al., 1987). We note that lack of a significant difference is a necessary, but not sufficient, condition for normality of the value of job performance in dollars.

Several things are noteworthy about the global estimation procedure. First, it was designed to be an estimate, and complete accuracy down to the last dollar was not expected. This assumption is consistent with UA viewed as a way of modeling the likely influence of a decision. Further, perfect accuracy is not needed for most applied psychological applications of UA. Most applications have compared different selection or training interventions *within* a given job or job family (e.g., Schmidt et al., 1984; Weekley, Frank, O'Connor & Peters, 1985).

The global estimation procedure appears to be potentially conservative for a variety of reasons. As noted above, judges are instructed to use the generally conservative approach that mirrors the fractile literature from judgment and decision-making research. The findings from this research are completely consistent with more purely psychometric research (Judiesch, Schmidt & Hunter, 1992). These researchers found that judges started the estimation process, typically, by basing their estimates of the value of the 50th percentile of performance on mean wages. This is interesting because mean wages will nearly always be less than the value of job performance at the 50th percentile for profit producing firms (thus, the starting point of the estimation process is inherently conservative). Judges then tended to use a mental model in which they multiplied the 50th percentile times by some amount (depending upon judge and job). The implication is that given the downward bias in the starting point of the estimation process and the multiplicative mental model of most judges, estimates of SD_y are highly likely to be downwardly biased (or conservative).

There is another completely independent reason the global estimation procedure is conservative. The procedure applies to the applicant pool for a selection decision, but judges may implicitly base their estimates on incumbents (who are likely to have a smaller SD_y than applicants) (Bobko et al., 1987). Thus, the procedure may be doubly conservative for typical applications of UA in applied psychology. Further, when decision-makers are estimating SD_y across multiple jobs or across multiple functional areas in an organization (e.g., operations and HRM), the accuracy of the global estimation method versus the accuracy of other utility estimation practices in other areas may become important. For example, conducting a UA to compare modifying a selection system for one job versus instituting a training program for another job may make accurate SD_y estimation more salient.

Finally, it is useful to recall that the global estimation procedure generally does a good job of matching straightforward accounting estimates of the standard deviation of job performance in dollars for certain jobs. Jobs with one major dimension of job performance, such as the performance of insurance salespeople or insurance claim processors, show a fairly strong correspondence between global estimates of SD_y and accounting SD_y 'criteria' (Bobko, Karren & Parkington, 1983; DeSimone, Alexander & Cronshaw, 1986).

Researchers have also noted some other interesting results while using the global estimation procedure. Several researchers have had judges make logically inconsistent estimates of percentiles (Bobko et al., 1983; Roth, Pritchard, Stout & Brown, 1994). For example, some judges will have a larger estimate for the 50th percentile of performance than the 85th percentile of performance. Typically, researchers delete these judges from further analysis. Also of concern are large variations around the estimates for a given percentile. For example, the average 15th percentile estimate might be $14,837, but the standard deviation might be $13,148 with a minimum of −$24,000 and a maximum of $120,000 (Bobko et al., 1983). Such a large level of 'within-cell variation' (Bobko et al., 1983) has caused researchers to question if all judges are using a similar set of dimensions to estimate value (Orr, Sackett & Mercer, 1989) or if there are a variety of frames of reference (Mathieu & Tannenbaum, 1989).

Researchers have also found negative values of performance at the 15th percentile (e.g., Burke & Frederick, 1984). In one study, the judges explicitly noted and discussed that this level of performance would be associated with economic losses (Mathieu & Tannenbaum, 1989). Such findings are interesting in and of themselves as applied psychology interventions such as selection systems, reward structures, and so on, may be able to help organizations deal with these issues.

The research literature has not sufficiently considered the process by which judges estimate the percentiles of performance (Bobko et al., 1987). Do judges use rectangular (not normal) distributions when estimating SD_y or do they think of particular people as they make percentile estimates? We have learned that focusing judges on the *loss* of money associated with various levels of performance can tend to increase the size of estimates relative to *gains* of hiring someone at the same level of performance (Bobko, Shetzer & Russell, 1991). However, there is a great deal of research waiting to be done on how judges make estimates of the percentiles of performance.

Percent of Salary Rules

A second, and conceptually different, approach to estimating SD_y was developed using salary as an index of the value of the performance of a particular job to an organization. This is conceptually distinct from using the value of the goods and/or services of a worker as noted above in the global estimation procedure. It rests on the assumption that the salary of the job is tied to the value of performance. The original work in this area suggested that

SD_y could be conservatively estimated as 40% of mean salary (Hunter & Schmidt, 1983; Schmidt & Hunter, 1983). Some research suggests such a value can be markedly conservative (Becker & Huselid, 1992), although managers may prefer this method to other methods such as CREPID (Hazer & Highhouse, 1997). One limitation of this approach is that it does not naturally lend itself to examining the negative values associated with low levels of performance.

Standard Deviation of Production (SD_p)

Research on the standard deviation of employee output developed simultaneously with the 40% of salary rule, and the two streams of research are naturally related (see Schmidt & Hunter, 1983). The purpose of SD_p is to allow researchers to estimate the standard deviation of output as a percentage of mean output. Thus, 'output' is the basis for estimation rather than salary. The first meta-analytic investigation suggested that SD_p was approximately 15% of mean output for piecerate systems of compensation, and 20% for nonpiecerate systems of compensation (Schmidt & Hunter, 1983). This investigation was interesting because it showed that SD_p (and SD_y) can be influenced by characteristics/procedures of the organization such as pay structure. However, this investigation was based primarily on blue collar & semi-skilled jobs (Schmidt & Hunter, 1983). Thus, it was difficult to determine if job complexity was related to SD_p. Later work corrected these figures for research artifacts and found that job complexity was related to SD_p. SD_p is 19%, 32%, and 48% of mean output, corrected for range restriction and reliability, for low, medium, and high complexity jobs (Hunter, Schmidt & Judiesch, 1990). Researchers should be careful to take complexity into account in their own estimation of SD_p to achieve the most accurate UA figures possible.

Cascio-Ramos Estimate of Performance in Dollars (CREPID)

A second salary-based approach to estimating SD_y was developed by Cascio and Ramos (1986) and called the Cascio–Ramos Estimate of Performance in Dollars (CREPID). The approach assumes that an organization's compensation system reflects current market forces for a job, and that the economic value of a job is reflected best by salary (Cascio, 1987).

The procedure outlines eight major steps for implementation. First, identify the major activities of the job (each activity comprising more than 10% of the total work time). Second, rate each activity in terms of time/frequency and importance. Third, multiply frequency and importance ratings to achieve an overall rating of the importance of each activity. Fourth, assign dollar values to each activity.

This is done by taking the average rate of pay for the job and aportioning this pay according to the percentage of overall importance in step 3. Fifth, rate the performance of each employee on a 0–200 scale for each activity. Sixth, multiple the rating (expressed as a decimal number) by the activity's dollar value. At this point, the researcher has a number for the value of each activity for each employee. Seventh, compute the overall dollar value for each employee's performance by adding the values for each activity. Eighth, compute the mean and SD of the value across all employees in the job.

CREPID, as other approaches, has both its strengths and limitations. First, it takes more managerial time and commitment to implement than other procedures. However, this may be a way to get managers participating in the estimation process and could have positive attitudinal outcomes as noted below. Second, CREPID does not typically allow negative economic values for low levels of job performance and the associated thinking about such values. Third, CREPID is a straightforward process that has been well-documented (e.g., Cascio, 1987).

Superior Equivalents and System Effectiveness Techniques

The superior equivalents and systems effectiveness techniques were developed for UA in situations in which decision-makers did not naturally evaluate performance in dollars, but some dollar based measure of SD_y was needed (Eaton et al., 1985). For example, the performance of tank commanders might not easily be evaluated in a dollar metric.

The superior equivalents technique asks judges to estimate the number of superior performers (85th percentile) it would take to produce the same performance level of a given number of average performers. For example, a military unit might normally have 17 tanks and the job in question might be 'tank commander'. Supervisors of such units might estimate that 10 superior tank commanders and tanks could function just as effectively. To obtain SD_y, the ratio of the number of average performers to the number of superior performers has the constant of subtracted from it and the result is multiplied by the value of an average performer (e.g., salary and benefits of an average performer). Perhaps the most interesting aspect of this approach is not that it can ultimately achieve a dollar value, but to remind one that utility can be assessed in metrics such as the ratio of average to superior performers (rather than just dollars per se). This approach may help decision-makers determine how to manage the increased performance due to better selection or training.

The systems effectiveness technique is a relatively straightforward application of the work done on SD_p. Essentially, Eaton et al. (1985) suggest calculating SD_p and then multiplying this value by the value of the *entire system* of human resources and technology that is required for job performance. For example, one might calculate SD_p as being .20 for tank commanders and then multiple this times the value of $300,000 per year for the yearly cost of the tank and its support system. Again, the most interesting part of this technique is not necessarily that one can find a way to express gains in dollars, but that researchers may want to use the value of a *system* of resources rather than merely salary.

Raju–Burke–Normand Approach

Many of the difficulties involved in having expert judges directly estimate SD_y via the global estimation procedure led a group of researchers to formulate a different approach to the SD_y problem (Raju, Burke & Normand, 1990). These researchers algebraically transformed the Brogden et al. model; instead of SD_y being the judged parameter of interest, they suggested multiplying the standard deviation of the criterion (e.g., a supervisory performance rating) by the factor A, which is some form of valuation for the job (e.g., salary). The advantage of this approach is that it removes the need for direct estimation of SD_y. However, it appears to shift the issue of valuation and estimation to determining what to use as the scaling factor A. A more detailed debate of this procedure is found in other sources (Judiesch, Schmidt & Hunter, 1993; Raju, Burke, Normand & Lezotte, 1993), and an interesting application of this approach is found in Morrow, Jarrett and Rupinski (1997).

Comparison of Procedures

There is a substantial literature comparing the results of approaches to estimating SD_y. While the results of such studies have been documented elsewhere (Boudreau, 1991), we briefly cover these issues to ensure that the reader is familiar with the results of the major methods to estimating SD_y. We also note the limited research on judges' attitudes toward the procedures.

The literature on comparing the results of various approaches seems to suggest that SD_y estimation methods using the same basis to job valuation tend to converge. Both CREPID and the percentage of salary rules use salary as an index, and their results tend to be similar in several key studies. For example, the CREPID value for SD_y was $7,700 and the 40% of salary rule value was $8,489 in a study of convenience store managers (Weekley et al., 1985). Interestingly, the result for the global estimation procedure was $13,967. In a study of district-level managers the value for CREPID was $12,170 and the value for the 40% of salary rule was $14,567 (Edwards, Frederick & Burke, 1988). In the same study, a variant of global estimation procedure yielded an estimate of $63,326. Thus, we note that output based methods of estimating SD_y do not tend to converge with the salary based approaches.

Another key study also suggests that output based procedures also tend to converge, though the tendency is not quite as pronounced as for salary based measures. Two researchers estimated SD_y for the job of route salesperson for a soft-drink company (Greer & Cascio, 1987). They found the global estimation procedure yielded an estimate of $14,636 while the cost accounting estimate was $15,864. The CREPID estimate was $8,988. In other cases, the global estimation procedures is markedly less than the cost accounting procedure (Mayer, 1982). In one case, the global estimation procedure was larger than criterion values (computed from actual values in a simulation designed to help train managers) (Reilly & Smither, 1985).

In contrast to psychometric comparisons, the perceptions and attitudes of managers toward the various methods of estimating SD_y have received very little research attention. The typical treatment of this issue is for researchers to note that managers may like the underlying logic of CREPID or the ease of the 40% rule (e.g., Weekley et al., 1985). The lack of attention is somewhat surprising given that UA may be viewed as a decision-aid or system to support decision-making, and managerial use of such an aid may depend on its acceptability.

One study found that the perceived accuracy of CREPID ratings was 3.58 on a 5-point scale, while the accuracy of the estimates made for the global estimation procedure was 2.82 (Edwards et al., 1988). The difference in perceived accuracy of these ratings may be partially due to the nature of the estimated numbers. CREPID ratings are inputs to the computation of SD_y and these values are highly similar to other personnel systems that managers are fairly used to processing (e.g., performance appraisal systems). In contrast, the estimates for the global estimation procedure are measures of the value of output and are closer to the output of the SD_y estimation process. In contrast to perceived accuracy, ratings of feasibility/doability on a 5-point scale (in which five was the highest rating) were 2.81 for global estimation procedure and 2.11 for CREPID (Edwards et al., 1988).

Other studies of the perceived accuracy of estimates show results near the middle of response scales. For example, mean accuracy was reported to be 2.77 for the global estimation procedure (on a 5-point scale) for account executives and 3.15 for mechanical foreman supervisors (Day & Edwards, 1987). Also, perceived accuracy of the global estimation procedure for insurance salespeople were slightly below the middle of a 7-point scale (Roth et al., 1994). These ratings must be taken in context as judges were asked to make ratings of *their* estimates before aggregation with other estimates and final estimates were known. Finally, returning to the study by Day and Edwards (1987), CREPID was preferred over the global estimation procedures by approximately 80% of judges (Day & Edwards, 1987).

Recommendations for Use

We make some recommendations for use of SD_y procedures. First, organizational decision-makers should consider the metric of valuation. If it is dollars, typical approaches such as the global estimation procedure or CREPID are worth considering. If valuation is not dollars, multi-attribute effectiveness points (described below) or SD_p approaches may have merit. Second, decision-makers should consider their approach to valuing the job. If it is salary based, we note that the 40% of salary rule and CREPID provide similar estimates. Thus, applied psychologists may wish to weigh issues such as the participation in CREPID as a way to get managers involved or the percentage of salary rules as a way to efficiently make estimates. If researchers are more inclined toward output, the global estimation procedure or SD_p may be appropriate. However, we note that the issue of managerial acceptance of the entire UA calculation (not just the SD_y reaction) should also be considered.

Finally, we note that the communication of numeric values obtained from UA requires some thought. In this regard, at least two issues are important to managers. First, UA values tend to be rather large when calculated over a period of years for a moderate to large work force (Boudreau, 1983). Second, managers may be skeptical that they will ever realize UA gains. We suggest that researchers or practitioners consider putting the large UA gains in the context of their total human resource costs over similar years. This proportioning will help temper UA feedback. And we suggest that UA gains be characterized as 'pre-managed' gains. That is, managers must have a strategy of how to achieve the estimated economic gains if they want them to appear in the bottom line.

Multi-Attribute Utility Models

Multi-attribute utility analysis (MAU) is a second conceptually distinct family of approaches to UA that may deserve more attention within the realm of HR UA. This attention seems warranted given that MAU approaches offer a number of unique advantages as a decision aid itself, as well as a method to facilitate research on managerial decision processes. Unfortunately, the authors are not aware of any MAU utility analyses carried out in HR. Given this state of affairs (and a much wider understanding of single attribute UA in works such as Boudreau, 1991), we review the work of MAU in some depth to disseminate this information. We also note the MAU is generally less overtly quantitative and formula based. Thus, our review of this topic is conceptual in nature.

Background

MAU developed in a parallel and independent manner to the traditional applied psychology UA as embodied in the Brogden et al. model. As noted above, traditional UA approaches have focused on one outcome such as increases in job performance (e.g., Cascio & Ramos, 1986) or, occasionally, on turnover reduction cost savings (e.g., Schmidt & Hoffman, 1973). In contrast, MAU may be defined as a set of procedures to guide decision-making that integrate *multiple* outcomes from a course of action into a single value that represents the usefulness of that course of action (Roth & Bobko, 1997: 342). As such, attributes may be thought of as key outcome variables that will help decision-makers model the effect of a given course of action. For example, an applied psychologist might be concerned with the choice of a selection device (e.g., cognitive ability test versus a structured interview). The psychologist might want to include attributes such as the value of job performance in dollars, adverse impact against protected groups, applicant reactions, and organizational image in the community. MAU could incorporate all four attributes in UA. Alternatively, a decision-maker could use ideas from the human capital movement to define attributes (as we will note below). The ability of MAU to handle multiple outcomes makes it a good choice to use with the human capital approach.

The focus on single vs. multiple attributes within UA approaches is probably attributable to the fields from which the approaches developed, and problems the two approaches were designed to address. As noted, traditional approaches to UA in applied psychology have focused on modeling the effect of a decision (e.g., use of a cognitive ability test or an interview) on the basis of a single attribute such as job performance. Given the historical importance of predicting job performance for industrial/organizational psychologists, this implicit emphasis on performance is not surprising. It is also interesting to note that the pioneering work on this approach was conducted in the 1960s and before, thus it originated before the rise of equal employment opportunity law and programs and applicant reaction research.

MAU approaches developed primarily during the 1960s and 1970s, though from completely different origins. For example, Multi-Attribute Utility Technology (MAUT) was developed out of experimental psychology and integrated with the program evaluation literature (Edwards & Newman, 1982). Past uses have included decisions about land use on the California coast (Edwards, 1977), evaluating school desegregation plans (Edwards, 1979), and evaluating energy policies for then West Germany (Edwards & von Winterfeldt, 1987).

There is also a body of work by Bob Pritchard and colleagues (e.g., Pritchard, 1990) on ProMES, the Productivity Measurement and Enhancement System. While ProMES was designed to be used as a productivity measurement system for multifaceted jobs, it also provides an elegant approach to MAU (Roth, 1994b).

Two key issues are interesting to note about these, and other, applications of MAU. Most organizational decisions are likely to have an influence on multiple outcomes and will affect multiple constituencies or groups. For example, land-use decisions will affect members of the business community, environmentalists, and citizens. In addition, each group may have distinctly different policies or priorities that influence their views. For this reason, Ward Edwards, the primary developer of MAUT, assumed multiple constituencies may exist, and that they may have different policies that will result in different MAUT systems (Edwards, 1977). Further, he assumed that development and discussion of the different policies and priorities between groups will facilitate overall compromise between groups and superior decision-making.

Advantages of MAU

MAU has important advantages over a single attribute utility approach. As noted above, applied psychologists and managers faced with selection decisions may wish to model performance increases due to selection methods, degree of adverse impact against protected groups, organizational image, and so forth, into decision-making. While the above statement is somewhat obvious to most readers, its implications are important. From a practitioner view, management can see the influence of multiple factors on decisions, thereby reflecting the reality of managerial decision-making.

Movement in our field on attributes beyond task performance may also make UA relevant to a wider variety of organizational interventions. While UA has traditionally been available to guide decisions on employee selection and training, other programs may need a more multidimensional evaluation system. Examples of such programs may include Employee Assistant Programs and employee monitoring programs. Employee Assistance Programs designed to help substance abusers may have several important outcomes such as increased performance from some employees, lowered chance of accidents, or they may also influence attitudes toward the organization such as job satisfaction and organizational justice perceptions. Employee monitoring programs, such as computers designed to monitor various aspects of transportation worker behavior (e.g., average speed of a truck, miles off shortest distance, etc.), may also have multiple outcomes.

MAU may be especially applicable to global enterprises. MAUT assumes that there may be multiple constituencies and each constituency may have different attributes or weights to attributes that result in different 'policies'. As more firms merge or become global, they transcend one culture and its priorities and assumptions. For example, different cultures (and organizations) may have differing views on the primacy of work and family. Such priorities might translate into differences in willingness to relocate for international assignments (and expatriate programs). Likewise, differing cultures might view predictors of job performance in very different lights. For example, handwriting analysis is widespread in Europe, but relatively rare in the US. Examining these differences through MAU may prove enlightening to practitioners and may stimulate interesting research on cross-cultural policy differences. MAUT approaches offer a way to systematically deal with this concern (Edwards & Newman, 1982).

The metric or unit of analysis of the 'payoff function' is a very interesting issue in MAU. As noted, traditional UA approaches such as the BCG model typically use dollars as the appropriate metric to aid decision-making. The logic has been that managers are likely to think in dollars (Boudreau, 1983; Cronshaw & Alexander, 1985; Cronshaw et al., 1987). MAU has used what we will term 'effectiveness' points. As we note below in more depth, MAU allows applied psychologists and managers to use an alternative metric that may increase managerial acceptance of UA.

MAU is not without its disadvantages. The primary disadvantage is that there are a larger number of potentially difficult judgments. Decision-makers could easily be asked to double or triple the number of judgments compared to traditional Brogden et al., approaches. Thus, MAU may require more managerial commitment than traditional approaches. Another disadvantage is that MAU approaches have also not been tested as often in the private sector and the authors are not aware of any use of MAU for applied psychology or human resource management decision-making (even though there is a voluminous literature on their application in other areas). Thus, cutting-edge applications may have relatively little guidance from previous HR applications.

Implementing MAU

We provide an overview of how to implement MAU, through an example, in this chapter in order to facilitate its use in applied psychology decision-making. We chose to focus on the Productivity Measurement and Enhancement System (ProMES) for two reasons. First, there are some useful conceptual properties to this system, such as attribute weighting (which will be discussed below) and there is a clear literature on using ProMES (e.g., Pritchard, 1990; Roth & Bobko, 1997). We also note there is good documentation for using MAUT (Edwards & Newman, 1982). We suggest using the following five steps to implementing either MAU technique.

Early preparation There are three primary activities that need to be accomplished during this stage.

The first activity is to note the purpose of the decision. For example, the organization may need to determine which selection device to use to select manager trainees. The second activity is to delineate the alternatives that the decision-makers are willing to consider. The third activity involves identifying multiple constituencies. Continuing our example, decision-makers may wish to evaluate cognitive ability tests vs. a structured description interview. We choose to keep our comparisons relatively simple in this case to make sure our illustration is clear; thus we assume a single constituency of HR managers for selecting manager trainees in our example.

Defining attributes As noted above, an attribute is a key variable that will help decision-makers model the effect of a given course of action. Some individuals conceptualize this as an objective of the decision (Edwards & Newman, 1982), a consequence of decision-making (Keeney & Raiffa, 1976), or an outcome of the decision-making process (Roth & Bobko, 1997).

We suggest the choice of attributes should involve the following criteria. First, attributes should be measurable in some objective, possibly subjective manner. Second, the attributes should be parsimonious. That is, they should be relatively small in number (e.g., three to eight), but cover the major outcomes of a decision that will delineate one alternative from another. Third, the attributes should avoid overlap with each other. Attributes that 'cover' highly similar outcomes can lead to 'overweighting' a particular set of outcomes. Fourth, attributes should be easily understandable to the decision-makers (Keeney & Raiffa, 1976).

Attributes for our continuing example of selecting manager trainees might include: validity, adverse impact, and organizational image. Note that these attributes should be defined by the decision-makers and show how *they* think about the decision. Thus, the MAU approach is focused on being a descriptive decision aid, rather than a prescriptive aid such as the Brogden et al. model. We also note that the same situation and different decision-makers could lead to different attributes, such as the economic value of job performance in dollars (instead of validity), ethnic group differences (instead of adverse impact), and so on. In fact, decision-makers from the human capital movement may be more interested in modeling the influence of a decision on key employee knowledge, customer satisfaction, and so forth. Finally, we note that there are a variety of group approaches to defining attributes and other steps in the process which are covered in detail elsewhere (Roth & Bobko, 1997).

Constructing measures Each attribute must be measured by one or more indicators (Pritchard, 1990), or 'location measures' in MAUT terminology. In

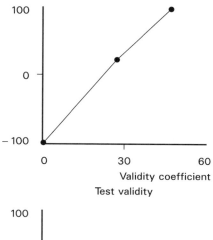

Test validity

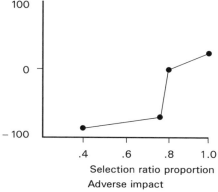

Adverse impact

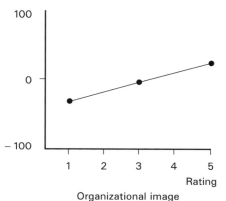

Organizational image

Figure 17.1 *Multi-attribute contingencies*

Continuing with our example, decision-makers might choose the following measures for the attributes noted in step:

- *Validity* Measure: mean corrected correlation between predictor and job performance from meta-analytic literature.
- *Adverse impact* Measure: the ratio of the black selection rate to the white selection rate.
- *Organizational image* Measure: mean rating of organizational image of public relations and HR departments on a 5-point Likert scale.

The measures may vary greatly, but should also be consistent with how decision-makers view the attributes. For example, fairly sophisticated HR decision-makers might wish to monitor the ratio of the black selection rate to the white selection rate (as per Bobko, Roth & Potosky, 1999). As this measure moved further from 1.0 and closer to .00 it would indicate lower selection rates for blacks than for whites. A particularly salient value on this measure would be .80, which would signify 'adverse impact' given the 4/5ths rule of employment law. This outcome would be important in the context of our example because cognitive ability tests are typically associated with large group differences and adverse impact at many selection ratios (Sackett & Wilk, 1994).

Estimating utility functions The major task facing UA researchers in this step is to construct a function that relates each measure to overall utility. MAUT and ProMES use somewhat different approaches to accomplish this and we refer interested readers to Edwards and Newman (1982) for MAUT approaches and Pritchard (1990) for ProMES approaches. We continue with the ProMES approach and note that researchers generally call the utility functions 'contingencies' and use the metric of effectiveness points on the vertical axis to allow a combination of the measures into one score for each decision alternative (e.g., behavior description interview and cognitive ability test). Hypothetical contingencies for our continuing example may be found in Figure 17.1.

One of the interesting characteristics of ProMES contingencies is the scale for effectiveness. Typically, 100 points is the most positive value that an indicator score could be associated with. Minus 100 is the worst value, indicating the most harmful level that any indicator score could achieve. Note that decision-makers are not required to use either 100 or −100, but often these values are used to start the scaling process as noted in Pritchard (1990). The zero point on the effectiveness scale delineates levels of indicators that help the organization function effectively vs. those levels of the indicator that hurt organizational effectiveness.

These values and the shape of the contingency contain a great deal of information. The adverse

either case, the process is highly similar in that applied psychologists must assign numbers to accurately represent the attributes. Interested readers are referred to Pritchard (1990) for more detail. Decision-makers will also need to define minimum and maximum values for each indicator based on their judgment and experiences. We will note this process below.

impact contingency tells us that the proportion of 1.0 (black and white selection ratios are the same) is worth 20 effectiveness points or roughly a fifth of the effectiveness of a validity of .60 (on the validity contingency). There is not much of an increase in effectiveness from .8 to 1.0 (as effectiveness values only change from 0 to 20), but there is a large drop in effectiveness after the ratio drops below .80. The reason for this drop is that *prima facie* evidence of adverse impact occurs at this level. Subsequent drops in the proportion are associated with less effectiveness until ratios of .4 or less are very harmful.

Contingencies may be linear or non-linear. Figure 17.1 shows that decision-makers believe that increases in organizational image and validity are linearly related to increased effectiveness of the selection system. However, the contingency for adverse impact is markedly nonlinear such that there is a large loss of points when *prima facie* adverse impact occurs. The shape of the contingency function of managerial policy may depend strongly on the organization's values and strategies.

Making a decision   The final step is to use the MAU system to recommend a decision. This is done by assigning numeric scores to the measures/indicators, finding the associated effectiveness values, and combining these values to give each decision option a score. Continuing with our example, manager trainee might be considered a job of moderate complexity. We assign scores to the indicators by examining the selection literature. For cognitive ability, the indicator values are .53 for validity (Hunter & Hunter, 1984) and an image rating of 3.5. The ratio of selection rates is complex and may be estimated by noting that the black–white *d* score on jobs of medium complexity is .72 ($K = 18$, $N = 31,990$) (Roth, BeVier, Bobko, Switzer & Tyler, 1999). Assuming a selection rate of approximately .25 for the majority group, the minority group selection rate is .085 (Sackett & Ellingson, 1997). Thus, the ratio of these rates is .34. The indicators would be associated with the effectiveness values for validity, image, and adverse impact as follows: $81 + 5 - 90 = -4$. Thus, the overall effectiveness for the cognitive ability test option is relatively low.

The interview validity can be estimated by combined structure levels 2–4 of the structure definition used by Huffcutt and Arthur (1994) which yields a validity of .48 ($K = 99$, $N = 11,344$) and the organizational image rating might be 4.5. We estimate the ratio of selection rate as above by noting a black–white *d* of .22 (Huffcutt & Roth, 1998) for the interview. A majority selection rate of .25 and a *d* of .20 are associated with a minority rate of .192 or a ratio of .77. Thus, the effectiveness scores are $68 + 15 - 60 = 23$ total points for the interview. Thus, the decision aid suggests that the interview is associated

with higher overall effectiveness even though we might consider its validity to be slightly lower. Note also that the recommended decision might change depending upon the contingency functions for validity and adverse impact. We briefly note that sensitivity analysis (Boudreau, 1991), Monte Carlo analysis (Rich & Boudreau, 1987), and so on, can be applied to values of the indictors as well as effectiveness values.

Research Issues

MAU offers a wide variety of both applied and basic research opportunities. One such opportunity is to capture managerial decision policies toward HR interventions. While single attribute UA has prescribed how to model the influence of a selection or training intervention on job performance, MAU allows investigation of what attributes managers actually want to use in decision-making. Thus, we can tailor our decision aid to the needs of managers rather than tell them what to model. Also of great interest is using MAU to examine managerial policy issues such as the value of performance increases versus adverse impact concerns. This is an important issue, as selection researchers have extensively analyzed the performance implications of various selection systems, yet other researchers note that managers are concerned with adverse impact and legal exposure (De Corte, 1999; Hoffman & Thornton, 1997). We purposefully chose these variables in our example to illustrate this important issue. We find it interesting that no one has explicitly conceptualized or modeled the 'trade-off' between these two variables as a function of managerial policies.

There are also many interesting psychometric research opportunities embedded in the use of MAU. First, what metric do decision-makers prefer to use in UA (e.g., dollars vs. effectiveness 'points')? We return to this issue below. Second, MAU researchers may examine issues of how one weights utility functions in MAU. Various MAU approaches use different methodologies to arrive at these weights and we refer the interested reader to Roth and Bobko (1997) for more coverage of these issues. Third, different types of groups could be used in various steps in the design process (Roth & Bobko, 1997). For example, nominal groups, consensus groups, delphi groups, and so on could affect the nature of information incorporated in MAU and might also influence managerial satisfaction with the decision-making process.

ACCEPTANCE OF UA RESULTS

Acceptance of UA by decision-makers appears to be the major issue facing UA researchers at the turn of the century. As noted above, the 1980s and early 1990s were associated with a great deal of research into the psychometric properties of SD_y estimates and inclusion of economic parameters in UA models. However, all the psychometric and modeling research may not be particularly useful unless decision-makers accept and use the results of UA. This focus on the psychological nature of how decision-makers view UA is (or should be) leading towards a different approach to UA research. While previous research relied on complex modeling, acceptance research will generally require the use of more grounded psychological theories and methods to analyze how and why decision-makers accept or ignore UA. We first discuss current acceptance research and then suggest future research directions in this area consistent with Roth, Segars & Wright (1999).

Empirical Acceptance Research

The first major study of acceptance was conducted in the late 1980s (Florin-Thuma & Boudreau, 1987). These researchers examined acceptance of UA by three managers in a small business. The focus was on the implementation of an employee feedback system for the amount of ice cream served to customers. Some of the most interesting findings suggested that decision-makers underestimated the magnitude of the overserving problem and seriously underestimated the ability of the feedback program to fix it. The lack of attention to the problem was particularly notable given that (a) the UA estimates for using feedback were largely objective, (b) subjective estimates made by the decision-makers suggested the same course of action, and (c) the subjectively estimated impact of the feedback intervention on other aspects of the business such as customer and employee satisfaction would not have changed the recommended course of action. These results might be partially explained by the relatively inexperienced managers, but are somewhat puzzling given the economic consequences of using feedback.

Empirical acceptance research lay dormant until the mid-1990s when two studies focused on the field on acceptance. The researchers conducted a pair of laboratory studies in which managers played the role of a senior corporate officer responsible for human resource management. In the first study, Latham and Whyte (1994) presented managers with validity information, validity + expectancy table information, validity + utility information, or validity + expectancy table + utility information. The study found that managers reported much higher levels of commitment to a human resource management decision when presented with just validity information rather than any condition with utility information (Latham & Whyte, 1994). The authors interpreted this result as suggesting that managers appear to be negatively influenced by utility information.

The results of the previous study were extended by having a well-known expert make a video-tape and be available to answer questions about utility analysis (Whyte & Latham, 1997). The new study found that the 'improved' utility condition also received lower acceptance ratings than validity-only conditions. While Latham and Whyte (1994) found fairly negative reactions to UA, several other researchers have found different results. Two researchers presented a number of managers with a transcript between an HRM official and a company president concerning utility analysis (Hazer & Highhouse, 1997). They found that acceptance for UA information was above the mid-point for all UA conditions and that use of the 40% of salary rule was associated with higher levels of acceptance than CREPID. Thus, there appeared to be more UA acceptance than in the Latham and Whyte studies. However, one should note that acceptance results were moderate and not high.

Another study also tends to suggest that acceptance of UA is not quite as negative as implied by Latham and Whyte. Two researchers distributed a vignette to groups of managers, executive MBAs, members at a Society for Human Resource Management meeting, and a few acquaintances of undergraduates in which a consultant used UA when recommending an organizational change (Beckstein & Gilliland, 1996). The results across all respondents suggested there were no differences among a no-UA condition, a simple UA condition with just a Brogden et al., UA, and a complex condition in which variables costs, taxes, and discounting were added to the traditional UA.

A different set of researchers sought to replicate and extend previous work (Carson, Becker & Henderson, 1998). They found that they could not replicate the effect of lower acceptance of UA in one sample using Latham and Whyte's procedures and measures. MBA and Executive MBA students using the same materials as Latham and Whyte (1994) rated the validity and validity + utility studies at similar moderate levels of acceptance. Carson et al. (1998) hypothesized that the *way* in which information was presented was important. They conducted a second study in which they compared a validity condition and a validity + utility to a revised utility condition in which they modified the UA materials to make them more concise and user-friendly. Results suggested that the revised 'user-friendly' utility condition was viewed more favorably than the other two conditions.

There is one other study that is relevant to acceptance of UA estimates. While most studies in this area have asked managers to react to vignettes of HR decisions involving the use of validity or validity + UA information, Sturman (2000) used a Monte Carlo simulation to address an acceptance related issue. One of the most notable aspects of utility analysis is that they are associated with very large estimates of the economic benefits of a particular human resource management intervention (e.g., selection or training). This is true of the Latham and Whyte studies when one examines their stimulus materials as well as other UA applications. Sturman simulates the influence of several economic variables, employee flow variables and so on on the magnitude of UA estimates. His results suggest that simple UA estimates from the Brogden–Cronbach–Gleser formula decrease dramatically (often from 70–90%) when critical economic and employee flow behaviors are incorporated in the analysis. The decrease in magnitude of the UA estimates may have interesting implications for acceptance of these estimates in future empirical work.

In summary, current empirical research suggests that UA acceptance is usually in the low (Latham & Whyte, 1994) to moderate range (Carson et al., 1998; Hazer & Highhouse, 1997). Further, it is primarily based on laboratory research and suggests that UA may not be highly esteemed by decision-makers primarily in laboratory settings.

Critique and Suggestions for Future Research

Perhaps the most interesting reflections on UA acceptance research are not what is present in it, but what is missing from it. We suggest attention to several different fundamental issues. First, none of the previous researchers defined the acceptance domain. That is, we do not have a working definition of the area that we are studying. One definition is that the acceptance domain includes 'the psychological processes and behaviors prior to conducting a given UA as well as decision-makers' use of UA, reactions to UA, or feelings about UA following a utility analysis' (Roth et al., 1999). Thus, the domain includes psychological processes *before* decision-makers have decided to engage in or calculate a UA. The domain also includes reactions to UA after the presentation of UA. Interestingly, UA acceptance research has largely ignored the half of the domain in which decision-makers are deciding whether to use UA. Thus, an entire part of the acceptance domain appears to be neglected at present.

Second, current acceptance work is rather atheoretical. Simply put, most of the reviewed articles focus on managerial reactions with little theory to guide them. Within this criticism, the work also fails to focus on well-known psychological constructs. Current conception of the dependent variable is that one is interested in 'managerial reactions' (Hazer & Highhouse, 1997: 107) or 'preferences regarding whether to implement a psychologist's recommendations' (Latham & Whyte, 1994: 38). An explicit focus on constructs such as confidence, beliefs, or links to actual behavior does not appear.

Future UA acceptance research should examine several relevant theories. The portion of the domain that concerns whether to use UA appears to be studying how to make decisions: with a decision aid such as UA or unaided decision-making. Image theory (e.g., Beach, 1996) within the judgment and decision-making literature focuses on the process of choice and may offer important insights. The notion of acceptance after calculation or presentation of UA may be more amenable to dual process theories in the message persuasion literature (Chaiken, Wood & Eagley, 1996). These theories suggest that persuasive messages may be processed in different ways. Central processing involves use of a heavily cognitive emphasis on logical analysis of decision alternatives, while peripheral processing involves use of heuristics, biases, and rules of thumb to react to persuasive messages. The type of processing and underlying mechanisms may be useful to generate relevant constructs and understanding of the psychological processes involved in UA acceptance. We certainly do not suggest these are the only relevant theories, but they provide two salient examples.

Third, we suggest there are other key variables that should be included in future analyses. One example is the variable of 'participation in' UA. There is some literature on participation reviewed in other parts of the UA literature (Roth & Bobko, 1997; Roth et al., 1999). Current acceptance research appears to set participation at a very low level, as judges are only allowed to listen to the results instead of getting involved in the decision to use UA, estimation of parameters such as SD_y (or the choice of how to estimate SD_y), whether to include economic variables in UA, how to use sensitivity analysis, and so forth. Another interesting variable is the trust that decision-makers might have in selection experts (consultant or in-house). Again, the prior studies do not allow development of trust as there appears to be no enduring relationship with the UA expert.

SUMMARY AND CONCLUSION

The research in UA in the last portion of the twentieth century has provided a number of important and interesting findings and tools for industrial/organizational psychologists and HR managers. Traditional single attribute UA allows researchers and managers to model the impact of psychological interventions on job performance to help decision-makers choose a superior course of action. Multi-attribute UA allows the same individuals to model the influence of psychological interventions on a variety of outcomes and may facilitate the use of human capital movement ideas in UA. While the acceptance of UA recommendations appears to be in the low to moderate range, we look forward to advances in acceptance research that take this stream of research out of the laboratory, focus on constructs, and examine key variables such as participation. Finally, we find it fascinating that major trends such as the analysis of human capital in the business world are examining similar issues to UA. That is, that human resource-related variables are key to high performance organizations. All told, we hope that UA research in this century allows us to learn as much as did UA research in the last.

REFERENCES

Barrick, M., Barrett, G.V., Doverspike, D., Robison, S., & Grubs, L. (1990). Central tendency and its impact on three SDy procedures: A case study. *Journal of Occupational Psychology, 63*, 265–258.

Beach, L.R. (1996). *Decision making in the workplace: A unified perspective.* Mahwah, NJ: Erlbaum.

Becker, B.E., & Huselid, M.A. (1992). Direct estimates of SDy and implications for utility research. *Journal of Applied Psychology, 77*, 227–233.

Beckstein, B.A., & Gilliland, S.W. (1996). The applicability of utility analysis: When do utility estimates influence decisions. Paper presented at the 11th Annual Meeting of SIOP, San Diego, CA.

Birati, A., & Tziner, A. (1999). Economic utility of training programs. *Journal of Business and Psychology, 14*, 155–164.

Bobko, P. (1995). *Correlation and regression: Principles and applications for management and industrial/organizational psychology.* New York: McGraw-Hill.

Bobko, P., Karren, R.J., & Kerkar, S.P. (1987). Systematic research needs for understanding supervisory-based estimates of SDy in utility analysis. *Organizational Behavior and Human Decision Processes, 40*, 69–95.

Bobko, P., Karren. R.J., & Parkington, J.J. (1983). Estimation of standard deviations in utility analysis: An empirical test. *Journal of Applied Psychology, 68*, 170–176.

Bobko, P., Roth, P.L., & Potosky, D. (1999). Derivation and implications of a meta-analytic matrix incorporating cognitive ability, alternative predictors and job performance. *Personnel Psychology, 52*, 561–589.

Bobko, P., Shetzer, L., & Russell, C. (1991). Estimating the standard deviation of professors' worth: The effects of frame and presentation order in utility analysis. *Journal of Occupational Psychology, 64*, 179–188.

Boudreau, J.W. (1983). Economic considerations in estimating the utility of human resource productivity improvement programs. *Personnel Psychology, 36*, 551–576.

Boudreau, J.W. (1991). Utility analysis for decisions in human resource management. In M. Dunnette & L. Hough (Eds.), *Handbook of industrial and organizational psychology*, Vol. 2 (2nd ed. pp. 621–745). Palo Alto, CA: Consulting Psychologists Press.

Boudreau, J.W. (1998). Strategic human resource management measures: Key linkages and the PeopleVantage Model. *Journal of Human Resource Costing and Accounting, 3*, 21–40.

Boudreau, J.W., & Berger, C.J. (1985). Decision-theoretic utility analysis applied to employee separations and acquisitions. *Journal of Applied Psychology Monograph, 70*, 581–612.

Boudreau, J.W., & Ramstad, P. (1997). Measuring intellectual capital: Learning from financial history. *Human Resource Management, 36*, 343–356.

Boudreau, J.W., & Rynes, S. (1985). Role of recruitment in staffing utility analysis. *Journal of Applied Psychology, 70*, 354–366.

Boudreau, J.W., Sturman, M., Trevor, C., & Gerhart, B. (1999). *Is it worth it to win the talent war? Using turnover to evaluate the utility of performance-based pay.* Working paper 9–06. Center for Advanced Human Resource Studies, School of Industrial and Labor Relations, Cornell University.

Brogden, H. (1949). When testing pays off. *Personnel Psychology, 2*, 171–185.

Brogden, H., & Taylor, E. (1950). The dollar criterion: Applying the cost accounting concept to criterion construction. *Personnel Psychology, 3*, 133–154.

Burke, M.J., & Frederick, J.T. (1984). Two modified procedures for estimating standard deviations in utility analyses. *Journal of Applied Psychology, 69*, 482–489.

Carson, K.P., Becker, J.S., & Henderson, J.A. (1998). Is utility really futile? *Journal of Applied Psychology, 83*, 84–96.

Cascio, W.F. (1987). *Costing Human Resources: The Financial Impact of Behavior in Organizations.* Boston: Kent.

Cascio, W.F. (1991). *Costing Human Resources: The Financial Impact of Behavior in Organizations* (3rd ed.). Boston: Kent.

Cascio, W.F. (1992). Assessing the utility of selection decisions: Theoretical and practical considerations. In N. Schmitt, W.C. Borman & associates (Eds.), *Personnel selection in organizations.* San Francisco: Jossey-Bass.

Cascio, W.F. (1998). The future world of work: Implications for human resource costing and accounting. *Journal of Human Resource Costing and Accounting, 3*(2), 9–19.

Cascio, W.F. (2000). *Costing Human Resources: The Financial Impact of Behavior in Organizations* (4th ed.). Boston: Kent.

Cascio, W.F., & Morris, J.R. (1990). A critical reanalysis of Hunter, Schmidt & Coggin's (1988) 'Problems and pitfalls in using capital budgeting and financial accounting techniques in assessing the utility of personnel programs.' *Journal of Applied Psychology, 75*, 410–417.

Cascio, W.F., & Ramos, R.A. (1986). Development and application of new method for assessing job performance in behavioral/economic terms. *Journal of Applied Psychology, 71*, 20–28.

Chaiken, S., Wood, W., & Eagley, A.H. (1996). Principles of persuasion. In E.T. Higgins & A.W. Kruglanski

(Eds.), *Social psychology: Handbook of basic principles*. New York: Guilford. pp. 702–742.

Cronbach, L., & Gleser, G. (1965). *Psychological Tests and Personnel Decisions* (2nd ed.). Urbana, IL: University of Illinois Press.

Cronshaw, S.F., & Alexander, R.A. (1985). One answer to the demand for accountability: Selection utility as an investment decision. *Organizational Behavior and Human Decision Processes*, 35, 102–118.

Cronshaw, S.F., Alexander, R.A., Wiesner, W.H., & Barrick, M.R. (1987). Incorporating risk into selection utility: Two models for sensitivity analysis and risk simulation. *Organizational Behavior and Human Decision Processes*, 40, 270–286.

Cullen, J., Sawzin, S., Sisson, G., & Swanson, R. (1978). Cost effectiveness: A model for assessing the training investment. *Training and Development Journal*, 32(1), 24–29.

Day, R.R., & Edwards, J.E. (1987). A comparative study of multiple SDy estimation procedures. Paper presented at the Academy of Management Meetings in NewOrleans, LA.

de Corte, W. (1994). Utility analysis for the one-cohort selection-retention decision with a probationary period. *Journal of Applied Psychology*, 79, 402–411.

de Corte, W. (1995). Cutoff scores that optimize the utility of a fixed quota of successful employees selection decision. *International Journal of Selection and Assessment*, 3, 1–10.

de Corte, W. (1999). Weighing job performance predictors to both maximize the quality of the selected workforce and control the level of adverse impact. *Journal of Applied Psychology*, 84, 695–702.

DeSimone, R.L., Alexander, R., & Cronshaw, S.F. (1986). Accuracy and reliability of SDy estimates in utility analysis. *Journal of Occupational Psychology*, 59, 93–102.

Eaton, N.K., Wing, H., & Mitchell, K.J. (1985). Alternative methods of estimating the dollar value of performance. *Personnel Psychology*, 38, 27–40.

Edvinsson, L., & Malone, A. (1997). *Intellectual Capital, Realising Your Company's True Value by Finding its Hidden Brainpower*. New York: Harper Business.

Edwards, W. (1977). Use of multi-attribute utility measurement for social decision-making. In D. Bell, R. Keeney & H. Raiffa (Eds.), *Conflicting Objectives in Decisions* (pp. 247–321). New York: Wiley.

Edwards, W. (1979). Multi-attribute utility measurement: Evaluating desegregation plans in a highly political context. In B. Perloff (Ed.), *Evaluation Interventions: Pros & Cons* (pp. 13–54). Beverly Hills: Sage.

Edwards, J.E., Frederick, J.T., & Burke, M.J. (1988). Efficacy of modified CREPID SDys on the basis of archival organizational data. *Journal of Applied Psychology*, 73, 529–535.

Edwards, W., & Newman, J.R. (1982). *Multiattribute Evaluation*. Beverly Hills: Sage.

Edwards, W., & von Winterfeldt, D. (1987). Public values in risk debates. *Risk Analysis*, 7, 141–158.

Faley, R., Knapp, D., Kustis, G., & Dubois, C. (1999). Estimating the organizational costs of sexual harassment:

The case of the U.S. Army. *Journal of Business and Psychology*, 13, 461–484.

Flamholz, E., & Main, E. (1999). Current issues, recent advancements and future directions in human resource accounting. *Journal of Human Resource Costing and Accounting*, 4(1), 11–20.

Florin-Thuma, B.C., & Boudreau, J.W. (1987). Performance feedback utility in small organization: Effects of organizational outcomes and managerial decision *processes. Personnel Psychology*, 40, 693–713.

Greer, O.L., & Cascio, W.F., (1987). Is cost accounting the answer? Comparison of two behaviorally based methods for estimating the standard deviation of job performance in dollars with a cost-accounting-based approach. *Journal of Applied Psychology*, 72, 588–595.

Guion, R. (1965). *Personnel Testing*. New York: McGraw-Hill.

Hazer, J.T., & Highhouse, S. (1997). Factors influencing manager's reactions to utility analysis: Effects of SDy method, information frame, and focal intervention. *Journal of Applied Psychology*, 82, 104–112.

Hoffman, C., & Thornton, G.C. (1997). Examining selection utility where competing predictors differ in adverse impact. *Personnel Psychology*, 50, 455–470.

Huffcutt, A.I., & Arthur, W., Jr. (1994). Hunter and Hunter (1984). revisited: Interview validity for entry level jobs. *Journal of Applied Psychology*, 79, 184–190.

Huffcutt, A.I., & Roth, P.L. (1998). Racial group differences in interview evaluations. *Journal of Applied Psychology*, 83, 288–297.

Hunter, J.E., & Hunter, R.F. (1984). Validity and utility of alternative predictors of job performance. *Psychological Bulletin*, 96, 72–98.

Hunter, J.E., & Schmidt, F.L. (1983). Quantifying the effects of psychological interventions on employee job performance and work-force productivity. *American Psychologist*, 38, 473–478.

Hunter, J.E., Schmidt, F.L., & Judiesch, M.K. (1990). Individual differences in output variability as a function of job complexity. *Journal of Applied Psychology*, 75, 28–42.

Judiesch, M.K., Schmidt, F.L., & Hunter, J.E. (1992). Estimates of the dollar value of employee output in utility analyses: A test of two theories. *Journal of Applied Psychology*, 77, 234–251.

Judiesch, M.K., Schmidt, F.L., & Hunter, J.E. (1993). Has the problem in judgment been solved? *Journal of Applied Psychology*, 78, 903–911.

Kahneman, D., Slovic, P., & Tversky, A. (1982). *Judgment Under Uncertainty: Heuristics and Biases*. Cambridge: Cambridge University Press.

Keeney, R.L., & Raiffa, H. (1976). *Decisions with Multiple Objectives; Preferences and Value Trade-offs*. New York: Wiley.

Latham, G.P., & Whyte, G. (1994). The futility of utility analysis. *Personnel Psychology*, 47, 31–46.

Law, K., & Myors, B. (1993). Cutoff scores that maximize the total utility of a selection program: Comment on Martin and Raju's (1992). procedure. *Journal of Applied Psychology*, 78, 736–740.

Lawshe, C., Bolda, R., Brune, R., & Auclair, G. (1958). Expectancy charts II, their theoretical development. *Personnel Psychology, 11*, 545–560.

Lazear, E. (1998). *Personnel Economics for Managers*. New York: Wiley.

Mabon, H. (1996). The cost of downsizing in an enterprise with job security. *Journal of Human Resource Costing and Accounting, 1*(1), 31–58.

Mabon, H., & Westling, G. (1996). Using utility analysis in downsizing decisions. *Journal of Human Resource Costing and Accounting, 1*(2), 43–72.

Macan, T., & Highhouse, S. (1994). Communicating the utility of human resource activities: A survey of I/O and HR professionals. *Journal of Business and Psychology, 8*, 425–436.

Martin, S., & Raju, N. (1992). Determining cutoff scores that optimize utility: A recognition of recruiting costs. *Journal of Applied Psychology, 77*, 15–23.

Mathieu, J.E., & Leonard, R.L. (1987). Applying utility concepts to a training program in supervisory skills: A time based approach. *Academy of Management Journal, 30*, 316–335.

Mathieu, J.E., & Tannenbaum, S.I. (1989). A process tracing approach toward understanding supervisors' SDy estimates: Results from five job classes. *Journal of Occupational Psychology, 62*: 249–256.

Mayer, R.S. (1982). An evaluation of alternative methods of estimating the standard deviation of job performance to determine the utility of a test in a fixed treatment sequential employee selection process. Wayne State University: unpublished doctoral dissertation.

Morrow, C.C., Jarrett, M.Q., & Rupinski, M.T. (1997). An investigation of the effect and economic utility of corporate wide training. *Personnel Psychology, 50*, 91–119.

Naylor, J., & Shine, L. (1965). A table for determining the increase in mean criterion score obtained by using a selection device. *Journal of Industrial Psychology, 3*, 33–42.

Orr, J.M., Sackett, P.R., & Mercer, M. (1989). The role of prescribed and nonprescribed behaviors in estimating the dollar value of performance. *Journal of Applied Psychology, 74*, 34–40.

Pfeffer, J. (1997). Pitfalls on the road to measurement: The dangerous liaison of human resources with the ideas of accounting and finance. *Human Resource Management, 36*, 357–365.

Pritchard, R.D. (1990). *Measuring and Improving Organizational Productivity*. New York: Praeger.

Raju, N.S., Burke, M.S., & Normand, J. (1990). A new approach for utility analysis. *Journal of Applied Psychology, 75*, 3–12.

Raju, N.S., Burke, M.S., Normand, J., & Lezotte, D.V. (1993). What would be if what is wasn't? Rejoinder to Judisesch, Schmidt, and Hunter (1993). *Journal of Applied Psychology, 78*, 912–916.

Rauschenberger, J.M., & Schmidt, F.L. (1987). Measuring the economic impact of human resource programs. *Journal of Business & Psychology, 2*, 50–59.

Reilly, R.R., & Smither, J.W. (1985). An examination of two alternative techniques to estimate the standard deviation of job performance in dollars. *Journal of Applied Psychology, 70*, 651–661.

Rich, J.R., & Boudreau, J.W. (1987). The effects of variability and risk in selection utility analysis: An empirical comparison. *Personnel Psychology, 40*, 55–84.

Roth, P.L. (1993). Research trends in judgment and their implications for the Schmidt-Hunter global estimation procedure. *Organizational Behavior and Human Decision Processes, 54*, 299–319.

Roth, P.L. (1994a). Group approaches to the Schmidt-Hunter global estimation procedure. *Organizational Behavior and Human Decision Processes, 59*, 428–451.

Roth, P.L. (1994b). Using the ProMES approach for multi-attribute utility analysis. *Journal of Business & Psychology, 9*, 69–80.

Roth, P.L., BeVier, C.A., Bobko, P., Switzer, F.S., III, & Tyler, P. (1999). Ethnic group differences in cognitive ability in employment and educational settings: A meta-analysis. Unpublished manuscript: Clemson University.

Roth, P.L., & Bobko, P. (1997). A research agenda for multi-attribute utility analysis in Human Resource Management. *Human Resource Management Review, 7*, 341–368.

Roth, P.L., Pritchard, R.D., Stout, J.D., & Brown, S.H. (1994). Estimating the impact of variable costs on SDy in complex situations. *Journal of Business & Psychology, 8*, 437–454.

Roth, P.L., Segars, A.H., & Wright, P.M. Utility analysis acceptance research: A review and analysis. Manuscript submitted for publication.

Russell, C.G., Colella, A., & Bobko, P. (1993). Expanding the context of utility: The strategic impact of personnel selection. *Personnel Psychology, 46*, 781–801.

Sackett, P.R., & Ellingson, J. (1997). The effects of forming multi-predictor composites on group differences and adverse impact. *Personnel Psychology, 50*, 707–721.

Sackett, P.R., & Wilk, S.L. (1994). Within-group norming and other forms of score adjustment in preemployment testing. *American Psychologist, 49*, 929–954.

Schmidt, F.L., & Hoffman, B. (1973). Empirical comparison of three methods of assessing utility of a selection device. *Journal of Industrial and Organizational Psychology, 1*, 13–22.

Schmidt, F.L., & Hunter, J.E. (1983). Individual differences in productivity: An empirical test of estimates derived from studies of selection procedure utility. *Journal of Applied Psychology, 68*, 407–414.

Schmidt, F.L., Hunter, J.E., & Coggins, T.D. (1988). Problems and pitfalls in using capital budgeting and financial accounting techniques in assessing the utility of personnel programs, *Journal of Applied Psychology, 73*, 522–528.

Schmidt, F.L., Hunter, J.E., & Judiesch, M.K. (1990). Individual differences in output variability as a function of job complexity. *Journal of Applied Psychology, 75*, 28–42.

Schmidt, F.L., Hunter, J.E., McKenzie, R.C., & Muldrow, T.W. (1979). Impact of valid selection procedures on work-force productivity. *Journal of Applied Psychology, 64,* 609–626.

Schmidt, F.L., Hunter, J.K., & Pearlman, K. (1982). Assessing the economic impact of personnel programs on work force productivity. *Personnel Psychology, 35,* 333–347.

Schmidt, F.L., Mack, M.J., & Hunter, J.E. (1984). Selection utility in the occupation of US park ranger for three modes of test use. *Journal of Applied Psychology, 69,* 490–497.

Steffy, B., & Maurer, S. (1988). Conceptualizing and measuring the economic effectiveness of human resource activities. *Academy of Management Review, 13,* 271–286.

Stewart, T. (1997). *Intellectual Capital.* New York: Doubleday.

Sturman, M.C. (2000). Implication of utility analysis adjustments for estimates of human resource intervention value. *Journal of Management, 26,* 281–299.

Sveiby, K. (1997). *The New Organisational Wealth. Managing and Measuring Knowledge-Based Assets.* San Francisco: Berret-Koehler.

Taylor, H., & Russell, J. (1939). The relationship of validity coefficients to the practical effectiveness of tests in selection. *Journal of Applied Psychology, 23,* 565–578.

Trevor, C., Gerhart, B., & Boudreau, J.W. (1997). Voluntary turnover and job performance: Curvilinearity and the moderating influence of salary growth and promotions. *Journal of Applied Psychology, 82,* 44–61.

Weekley, J.A., Frank, B., O'Connor, E.J., & Peters, L.H. (1985). A comparison of three methods of estimating the standard deviation of performance in dollars. *Journal of Applied Psychology, 70,* 122–126.

Whyte, G., & Latham, G. (1997). The futility of utility analysis revisited: When even an expert fails. *Personnel Psychology, 50,* 601–610.

Williams, C., & Livingstone, L. (1994). Another look at the relationship between performance and voluntary turnover. *Academy of Management Journal, 37,* 269–298.

18

Cross-Cultural Industrial and Organizational Psychology: A Critical Appraisal of the Field and Future Directions

ZEYNEP AYCAN
and RABINDRA N. KANUNGO

This chapter aims at critically evaluating the theory, methodology and scope of cross-cultural industrial and organizational psychology (I/O) research in the past twenty years with a specific emphasis on future directions for the field. In the theory section, we discuss the extent to which and the ways in which the sociocultural context influences organizational phenomena *vis-à-vis* other contexts that are both internal and external to organizations. Also discussed in this section are issues such as the level of theory, the assumptions of linearity and the unilateral effect of culture on organizations, and the conceptualization and operationalization of culture. The next section concerns the methodological issues including the atheoretical nature of research, level of measurement and data analysis, methods of data collection, and sampling. In the final section, four areas of research which are underrepresented in cross-cultural I/O literature are discussed: fairness in employment practices, workforce development, improvement of the quality of work life, and organizational development. It is argued that, compared to traditional research topics of cross-cultural I/O psychology (e.g., leadership, motivation, work values, etc.), these topics are more central to the field, more related to improvement of human potential and conditions at work, and better able to guide practices in various cultural contexts.

The next millennium will witness an increase in economic activity on a global scale. In our business dealings, we will encounter people of different nations across real and virtual borders. In this world order, understanding the impact of culture on various aspects of organizations and their practices will become more critical than ever to increase synergy, productivity and welfare of the workforce within and across countries. Not unlike other fields of psychology, I/O has flourished mainly in a North American and Western European cultural context.

An upsurge of interest in cross-cultural perspectives to I/O psychology has been mainly due to changing economic and social conditions, such as workforce diversity, widespread business activity beyond national borders, the availability of telecommunications across cultures, and global competition (Erez, 1994). Despite the increasing necessity of understanding the role of culture in workforce development and productivity, the volume of research in the cross-cultural I/O psychology has not reached the level to guide practice. The first comprehensive review of research in the cross-cultural I/O field was conducted by Barrett and Bass (1976) which was followed by reviews by Drenth and Groenendijk (1984), Triandis (1994), Erez (1994), and Hui and Luk (1997). The two decades that have passed between the first and the last review did not witness a substantial advancement in theory, methodology and scope of research in cross-cultural I/O psychology. In this chapter, a critical appraisal of 20 years of research will be presented and future directions for the next 20 years will be discussed.

PAST AND FUTURE TWENTY YEARS OF CROSS-CULTURAL I/O RESEARCH: THEORY, METHODOLOGY, AND SCOPE

Theoretical Issues

There has not been a significant advancement in theory development in cross-cultural I/O field (cf. Erez, 1994). The majority of research has been concerned with testing US-based theories in various cultural contexts. Moreover, research is dominated by the reductionist perspective in which behaviour is examined in isolation from multiple forces of environment. Theories of cross-cultural psychology should adopt a multidisciplinary and interactionist perspective, because behavior takes place in a complex system (i.e., organizations) which operates under the influence of multiple forces of the environment that are both internal and external to the organization. The challenge is to disentangle the contribution of the sociocultural context from other internal and external contextual forces.

The internal context includes a number of organizational characteristics such as size, type of work, industry and production, type of workforce, technology, and stage of development. The environment that is external to the organization includes the political, legal, educational, institutional, and sociocultural context. Among these multiple forces that influence behaviour in organizations, the sociocultural context has only a limited effect. Therefore, the challenge of I/O psychology is to examine the *extent to which* and the *way in which* culture influences individual and group phenomena in organizations. In other words, we are beyond the question of 'whether or not' culture influences organizational phenomena; the more relevant questions now are 'to what extent' and 'how'. Theory development is much needed to tackle these questions.

Let us first discuss the role of culture in shaping organizational practices *vis-à-vis* other contextual forces. In this context, we consider organizational practices as the ways in which organizations choose to structure various job functions and control and guide the workforce who fulfills these functions. As stated above, both internal and external forces influence organizational practices. Therefore, practices such as decision-making, control and coordination, leadership, participation, job design, management and motivational practices, organizational attitudes, and many others may differ vastly from one organization to another even within the same sociocultural context. Organizational practices may influence an individual employee's behaviour such as his/her performance, intention to turnover, absenteeism, and attitudes towards the job and to the organization. Organizational practices along with individual employee behaviour determine some of the key organizational outcomes including an organization's performance, growth rate, and effectiveness in managing its human resources.

The variance in organizational practices within and across cultures has been a topic of wide interest among scholars in the organizational theory and development fields. Since the early 1960s comparative management studies of organizations around the world focused on noncultural factors that influence organizational structure and practices across cultures. Among the most popular noncultural approaches was that of the 'contingency' approach. There were four main theses within the contingency approach. The first thesis, which is referred to as 'logic of industrialization', asserted that industrialization has a homogenizing effect on organizations around the world (Harbison & Myers, 1959). According to this thesis, organizations in industrialized societies increase in their specialization, size and complexity which will bring managerial decentralization, professionalism and constitutionally formalized management. The underlying assumption in this approach is that organizations go through the same stages of industrial and technological development, and those which are at the same level of industrialization converge in their organizational processes irrespective of the political, economic and cultural context.

The second thesis within the contingency approach is called the 'technological implications' by Parker, Brown, Child and Smith (1977). In this approach, technological advancement and automation leads to transformation of social relations and attitudes at work (e.g., more control over work schedule and work processes, increased emphasis on developing social networks, etc.) (e.g., Blauner, 1964; Dore, 1973). Hickson and his colleagues (1969, 1974) developed the third thesis in contingency approach. In this 'culture-free contingency theory of organizational approach', the most important determinants of organizational structure were the contextual elements such as size of the organization, industry, and dependence on other organizations. In their large-scale comparative study, Hickson and associates found that size was positively related with specialization and formalization, whereas dependence was positively related with centralization. The final thesis in the contingency approach was originated by Chandler (1962) in which the role of strategic development was highlighted. In this view, organizational processes and practices vary as the organization progresses through three main strategic developmental stages. In these stages, organizations transform from small, less hierarchical and domestic to large, complex, professional and international. This transformation has implications on practices such as planning, diversification, and role differentiation.

Another strand of the noncultural approach to organizations stems from the political-economy perspective. In this perspective, the nature of a country's sociol-economic system has greater bearing on organizations than other contingencies. In this paradigm, the influence of the two major forms of economic systems of production, namely capitalism and socialism, are contrasted. Organizations in the same sociopolitical systems were assumed to have similar characteristics, especially with respect to organizational objectives, control strategies, and the degree of centralization and decision-making.

The final noncultural approach, namely the 'societal effect approach' (SEA), is an extension of the contingency paradigm (cf. Sorge, 1991). SEA as a process theory focuses on the way in which an organization is constituted socially by its environment (Maurice, 1979). This approach takes into account the social context within which organizations operate, with specific emphasis on the educational system, the system of industrial relations, and the role of the state. Maurice, Sorge and Warner (1980) stated that:

> organizational processes of differentiation and integration consistently interact with process of educating, training, recruiting, and promoting manpower, so that both develop within an institutional logic that is particular to a society, and bring about nationally different shapes of organizations. (p. 59)

In their comparative analysis of organizations in Western Europe, the authors found differences in hierarchical differentiation, the level of flexibility and coordination, and supervisory practices, which they traced back to different paths of socialization through the education system and different industrial relations traditions.

Critics of the noncultural approaches are concerned with its deterministic orientation as well as an underestimation of the role of culture in explaining organizational phenomena. Some authors who take a more holistic and interactionist perspective suggest that culture influences some aspects of organizational practices more than others. For instance, Tayeb (1988) found that while contingency variables influenced 'formal' characteristics of organizations (e.g., centralization, specialization, span of control, etc.), cultural variables influenced the 'interpersonal' aspects such as power and authority structure, delegation, consultation, and communication patterns. Drenth and Groenendijk

(1984: 1223) also suggested that, compared to 'formal organizational characteristics', cultural factors influence 'organizational processes' (i.e., the way in which organizations function). They illustrated this point with an example: formalization (i.e., the presence of written rules) is a formal organizational characteristic, whereas the extent and the manner in which organizational members follow these rules are included in organizational processes which are more prone to the influence of culture (p. 1224). In support of this view, Child and Keiser (1979) found that size predicted greater formalization in management job definitions in both British and German companies, but British managers received role definitions via written documents, whereas German managers receive them from their superiors.

Others, such as Child (1981) asserts that culture has a moderating effect on organizations. That is, even though the contingent factors help determine the organizational structure, culturally driven preferences influence the exercise of choice between alternative structures (Child, 1981: 318). As in the case of Japan, the effect of industrialization on organizations is not homogenous in every country: 'in every country there emerges an amalgamation of cultural traditions and ramifications of industrialization characteristics of it alone' (Dahrendorf, 1968, cited in Child, 1981: 334). Similarly, within the capitalist systems there is vast variety among organizational and management practices. For example, trade union movements (which have strong implications on organizations) in Britain, France, and the United States are fundamentally different despite the similarity in their socio-economic system (i.e., capitalism) (cf. Gallie, 1978). Delmestri (1997) compared Italian and German organizations to test propositions of the SEA, and concluded that 'while national institutions have a binding and supportive effect on firms, there is no one best institutional solution but only a range from which to choose' (p. 97). Child and Keiser (1979) compared British and German companies, and found that arguments of contingency approaches gained support with respect to only a limited number of relationships such as that between size and formal structural characteristics. These authors argued that similarities in the socio-economic system resulted in similar organizational objectives, but the way in which these objectives were materialized differed. Child (1981) concluded that:

> the contingency argument was seen to be moderated by culturally related influences in the areas of decision making, managerial roles, and behavioral expectations. Relations with contextual factors become weaker and less consistent as one moved from the structural to the role and behavioral levels. (p. 316)

Figure 18.1 (after Aycan, 2000) is a heuristic device that recapitulates the discussions up to this

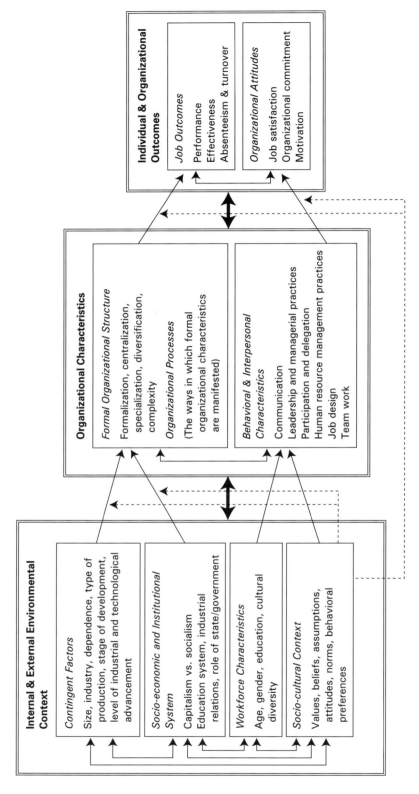

Figure 18.1 *A model of multiple and interacting forces that influence organizations. (Source: Aycan, 2000.)*

point. In the first column, internal and external contextual forces discussed by noncultural and cultural perspectives were summarized. In the second column, organizational structure and processes were presented. This framework proposes an interactionist perspective where contextual and organizational characteristics are assumed to interact within themselves as well as with one another. The figure also depicts the direct and moderating effects of the sociocultural context on organizations.

The last column in the figure presents individual and organizational outcomes. There is limited research on the relationship between formal organizational structure and organizational attitudes in the literature (cf. Porter & Lawler, 1965). Earlier studies (e.g., Porter & Lawler, 1965) suggest that there is a curvilinear relationship between organizational size and job satisfaction. Also, formalization (Crozier, 1964), complexity (Chonko, 1982) and diversification (Hackman & Oldham, 1980) seems to generate job dissatisfaction. These studies have to be replicated in different cultural contexts to see whether or not culture moderates the relationship between organizational structure and attitudes. For instance, one could expect formalization to yield job satisfaction in high uncertainty-avoiding cultures. Child and Keiser (1979) found that although German managers have formal role definitions taken over from their superiors, they exhibited more job satisfaction compared to their British counterparts who receive formal role definitions in a written format. The authors attributed these findings to differences in cultural norms. Similarly, the relationship between behavioral/interpersonal characteristics within an organization and organizational attitudes may not be the same in every cultural context; for instance, research shows that participation yields more satisfaction and commitment. However, culture may moderate this relationship as it influences both the meaning and form of participation as well as employees' reactions to it.

In summary, a mandate of future cross-cultural I/O psychologists is to adopt a multidisciplinary perspective in theory development. Research in the areas of organizational theory and development has much to offer to our theoretical formulations. Organizational phenomena take place under a highly complex context of interacting forces, and advancement in knowledge is possible only if we systematically study the role of the sociocultural context *vis-à-vis* others. This calls for development of mid-range and cross-level theories. In organizational research, cross-level theories which relate the macro-level predictors (e.g., organizational or cultural constructs) with micro-level criteria (e.g., individual behavior) are commonplace (Klein, Dansereau & Hall, 1994; Rousseau, 1985). Although this approach has substantial explanatory power of organizational phenomena, the challenge is to determine the level of theory to which the

study findings are generalized (Rousseau, 1985). If the theory is at the group (or cultural) level, there is an assumption of homogeneity among group members with respect to their position on the theoretical construct; whereas if the theory is at the individual level, then there is assumed heterogeneity among group members (Brett, Tinsley, Janssens, Barsness & Lyttle, 1997). The level of theory is of great importance as it determines the level of measurement and data analysis. As will be discussed in the next section, inconsistency among the levels of theory, measurement and data analysis is the major source of biases such as the reversal paradox and ecological fallacy (cf. Brett et al., 1997).

Future research should compare direct vs. moderating effects of culture on different aspects of organizations. In theory development, Lyttle, Brett, Barsness, Tinsley and Janssens' (1995) three approaches to cross-cultural research could be adopted.

In the first approach, culture is treated as the main effect (Type I hypothesis), and is construed as the main cause of observed differences among human groups. In other words, culture is conceptualized as an antecedent construct predicting certain behaviors or attitudes in a particular group. Researchers who adopt this perspective attribute mean-level differences in observed behavior to cultural variations. This perspective has limitations as it overlooks alternative hypotheses which may be based on differential interpretations, functioning and/or structuring of constructs under study and their relationships among one another. In the second approach culture is treated as the moderator (Type II hypothesis), acknowledging that constructs may be related in a nonuniform way across cultures. However, the assumption still remains that constructs have similar meanings and function in similar ways in different cultural groups. Type II research attributes differences in the strength and magnitude of relationships among constructs to cultural variations. Finally, in the third approach culture is treated as the source of emic meanings and constructs (Type III hypothesis). This approach is very different from the others in that the research starts out by examining the culture-specific meanings of constructs. Conceptual, structural and functional equivalences across cultures are not assumed but tested.

Future theories should also question the linearity assumption and unilateral effect of culture on organizations. Complexity theorists (Dooley, 1997; Gregersen & Sailer, 1993; Mendenhall & Macomber, 1997) challenged the linearity assumption in organizational research. The adoption of Newtonian assumptions of linearity in social sciences results in the development of methodologies that examine organizational phenomena irrespective of the effect of time (cf. Roberts & Boyacigiller, 1984). The predictor–criterion relationship in organizations is time-bound, and this should be acknowledged and reflected especially in cross-cultural I/O research. Furthermore, there may not be a one-way relationship between culture and organizations. Organizations are part of culture, and therefore whatever happens in organizations has significant implications for culture. Roberts and Boyacigiller (1984: 468) caution us 'against the error of viewing environments as one-way causal influences on organizations'. They recommend that we must direct our attention to reciprocal relationships between organizations and their contexts. Organizational socialization, for instance, can be as different and yet as powerful as the family socialization in shaping one's values, assumptions, attitudes and behavior. The bidirectional relationship between context and organizations is reflected in Figure 18.1 by the thick arrows.

The final issue of concern in theory development is the way in which culture is conceptualized and operationalized. One of the most frequently cited conceptualizations of culture in cross-cultural research is that of Kluckhohn (1951):

> culture consists in patterned ways of thinking, feeling and reacting, acquired and transmitted mainly by symbols, constituting the distinctive achievements of human groups, including their embodiments in artifacts; the essential core of culture consists of traditional (i.e., historically derived and selected) ideas and especially their attached values. (p. 86)

Viewing cultures in these generic terms, a culture's manifestations can be observed at three different levels. At the most basic individual level, it manifests as the internal work culture operating within an organization. It is a pattern of shared managerial beliefs and assumptions about organizational characteristics as presented in Figure 18.1. These beliefs and assumptions about organizational process and work behavior determine managerial practice within the organization (Schein, 1992). Two other levels of cultural manifestation influence this internal work culture (column 2 in Figure 18.1): the institutional corporate-level culture and the societal-level culture (Kanungo & Jaeger, 1990; Kanungo, Aycan & Sinha, 1999). The institutional-level culture is determined by the demands of the external economic, political, legal and other contingent factors shown in the first column of Figure 18.1. The societal-level culture is influenced by the demands of the sociocultural environment in which the organization operates (Figure 18.1, column 1).

In the majority of I/O research, cross-cultural differences are analyzed by using cultural dimensions at these three levels. This may not be the only approach, but a convenient one, because cultural dimensions at each of the three levels show validity – they are at the right level between generality and detail; they establish a link among individual, organizational and societal-level phenomena; and

they are easy to communicate. A closer look at Figure 18.1 suggests that the individual and organizational outcomes (column 3) are influenced by culture variables manifested at each of the three levels described above. Because of such influences of culture on outcome variables, I/O psychologists have come to realize that any uncritical adaptation of organizational practices and techniques evolved in the context of western cultural values may not be effective in other sociocultural environments. These changes in the attitudes of I/O psychologists have resulted in more in-depth and systematic studies of culture and its dimensions. At the same time, these changes have also triggered a search for culture-fit models to have a better understanding of how cultural variables may explain effectiveness of different organizational practices in different cultures. One such model of culture fit (see Figure 18.2), as proposed by Kanungo and his associates (Kanungo & Jaeger, 1990; Mendonca & Kanungo, 1994; Mathur, Aycan & Kanungo, 1996; Aycan, Kanungo & Sinha, 1999), asserts that both the sociocultural environment and the enterprise environment affect the internal work culture and human resource management (HRM) practices.

The model of culture fit presented in Figure 18.2 asserts that the internal work culture is composed of managerial beliefs and assumptions about two fundamental organizational elements: the task and the employees. Managerial assumptions pertaining to the task deal with the nature of the task and how it can be best accomplished; those pertaining to the employees deal with the employees' nature and behavior. Managers implement HRM practices based on their assumptions on the nature of both the task and the employees. However, two other levels of culture forces shape these managerial assumptions.

On the one hand, task-driven assumptions are influenced by the institutional level culture as shaped by enterprise characteristics including ownership status (private vs. public sector), industry (e.g., service vs. manufacturing), market competitiveness, and resource availability (e.g., human and technological resources). For instance, ownership status has a bearing on assumptions and beliefs regarding the goal of task accomplishment: public organizations emphasize social gain, whereas private organizations emphasize profit as their goal. Market conditions and industry may influence the beliefs with respect to the way in which a task is accomplished: in manufacturing industry, the process is more important than the result, whereas in service industry and R&D units the emphasis is on results rather than the process (Hofstede, 1991). Similarly, market competitiveness forces organizations to be more pragmatic rather than normative in their task orientation (Hofstede, 1991).

On the other hand, employee-related assumptions are influenced by the characteristics of the societal-level culture. A significant amount of research

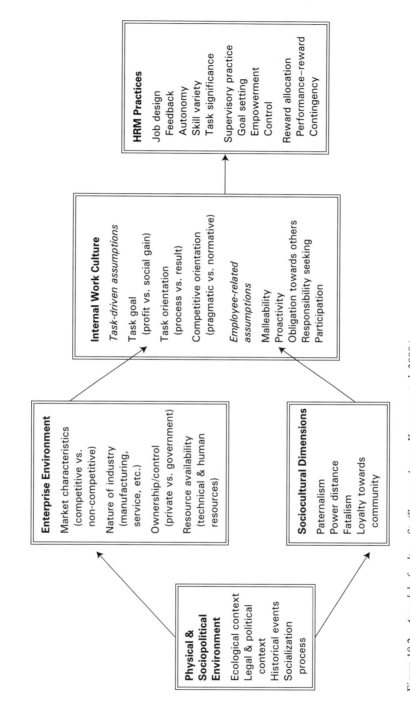

Figure 18.2 *A model of culture fit. (Source: Aycan, Kanungo et al. 2000.)*

has been devoted to the identification of salient societal-level culture dimensions (e.g.,individualism/collectivism) (Hofstede, 1980; Triandis, 1982; Trompenaars, 1994; Schwartz, 1994; Smith, Dugan & Trompenaars, 1996). Managerial assumptions about what employees are like and how they are socialized to behave depend on managers' perceptions of how the society is characterized in terms of these value dimensions.

The model of culture fit as presented in Figure 18.2 was tested by Mathur, Aycan and Kanungo (1996) and Aycan, Kanungo and Sinha (1999). The Mathur et al. (1996) study demonstrated the influence of the institutional enterprise-level culture (using ownership variable) on both internal work culture and HRM practices keeping societal-level culture constant. The more recent Aycan, et al. (2000) study has identified the influences of the sociocultural environment on the internal work culture and HRM practices in a 10-country comparison.

METHODOLOGICAL ISSUES

In this section, limitations and drawbacks of methodologies that are used in cross-cultural I/O psychology will be discussed.

The Atheoretical Nature of Research

The majority of research is characterized as being atheoretical with *post hoc* cultural interpretations (cf. Berry, 1997). Brett et al.'s (1997) 'one-way' and 'n-way' approaches to research can remedy this problem to a certain extent. In the one-way approach, research starts with an in-depth exploration of a particular culture. The goal is to examine the ways in which the identified cultural characteristics influence the relationships among variables in the mid-range theory. This approach helps the researcher to develop *a priori* predictions about the relationship of particular cultural dimensions with other variables of interest. The last step in this approach is to test the generalizability of hypothesized relationship between cultural dimensions and other variables in different cultural contexts. The *n*-way approach starts with an in-depth exploration of multiple cultural contexts. Here, the research is conducted by a multinational team who first investigates the relevance of research question in respective cultures. Then comes the development of emic models and constructs which is followed by a dialogue that involves comparison of emic and etic aspects of research models. Despite their differences, in both approaches, prior in-depth cultural analysis allows the researcher to provide *a priori* rather than *post hoc* cultural explanations.

The Levels Issue

The second problem area in cross-cultural I/O research is related to the level of measurement and analysis. As discussed in the previous section, consistency between theory (the level at which findings are generalized), measurement (the level at which data are collected) and analysis (the level at which data are analyzed) is a very important requirement in cross-cultural research. If a theory is defined at the group or national level, the assumption of homogeneity among group members must be tested before aggregating data from individuals. Even then, the question remains as to whether or not it is appropriate to aggregate individual-level data to make statistical analysis and interpretations at the collective level. The issue has both empirical and conceptual sides. On the empirical side, individual-level analysis (i.e., global correlations computed at the individual level regardless of the culture they come from) usually yields different or opposite results compared to group-level analysis (i.e., ecological correlations based on averaged scores of individuals in each culture). Difference in the magnitude of relationships is attributed to the 'ecological fallacy' (Hofstede, 1980), whereas the reversal of the relationships (e.g., a positive correlation between variables at the group level turning into a negative one at the individual level) is attributed to the 'reversal paradox' (Messick & van der Geer, 1981). In cross-cultural I/O research, it is advisable to test the hypothesized relationships at both individual and collective levels (Brett et al., 1997). If the pattern of relationships among variables differs from one culture to another, then cultural moderation should be considered.

The level issue has also a conceptual side. Because culture, both at the societal and organizational levels, is conceptualized as a collective phenomenon, its operationalization should also be at the collective level. The common practice is to collect data from individuals on their attitudes, values and preferences and aggregate them to have a group score; this raises the question of whether or not the 'whole is the sum of its parts'. This approach assumes homogeneity among parts which may not necessarily be true. There may be two ways to minimize the bias that is introduced with this approach: using 'participant as observant' techniques, and triangulating results with data obtained from unobtrusive measures. In the first approach, respondents are asked to indicate how they perceive prevailing values in their society or organizations. Therefore, they are used as key informants of their collective. This approach was first proposed by Sinha and Verma (1987). In a recent study, Aycan, Kanungo and Sinha (1999) found that, when contrasted with the classical 'respondents as participants' approach (i.e., asking respondents about their own values), the 'respondents as observers' approach yielded more robust results especially when social desirability is a serious threat. In order to support individual-level data, another suggestion is to collect data also from more macro-level sources such as archives, symbols (e.g., language, proverbs, titles, slogans, public symbols of leaders, etc.), documents of organizational communication, human resource policies and practices, company mission and vision statements, and so on (for more examples of unobtrusive data, see House, Wright & Aditya, 1997). Finally, to test theories whose unit of analysis is individual, measures that assess cultural constructs at the individual level should be preferred (Sego, Hui & Law, 1997).

Cross-cultural I/O psychology can greatly benefit from utilizing a relatively recent yet useful data analytical technique to address the level issue. This technique, referred to as Within and Between Analysis (WABA) (e.g., Dansereau, Alutto & Yammarino, 1984; Yammarino & Markham, 1992), is developed with the aim of '…avoiding the "fallacies of wrong level"' (Yammarino, 1998: 204). WABA is primarily used in multi-level theory testing. It helps to determine the level of analysis that a theory holds as well as the relationships defined within the theory.

Methods of Data Collection

The techniques discussed above minimize not only inconsistencies across levels of theory, measurement and analysis, but also biases resulting from common method variance or response biases. Such biases are more prevalent in quantitative methods in general, and in survey methods in particular. Measurement equivalence issues in cross-cultural research have been well-documented by numerous scholars including Triandis (1994), Drenth and Groenendijk (1984), Berry, Poortinga, Segal and Dasen (1992), van de Vijver and Leung (1997a, 1997b), and Usunier (1998). Among the best-known problems of measurement equivalence in cross-cultural organizational research are those briefly summarized as follows:

- *Conceptual equivalence.* When translating research instruments from one language to another, linguistic as well as conceptual equivalence should be established. Survey measures may contain concepts which may have different meanings in different cultural contexts, such as leadership, motivation, participation, fairness, and so on. It is highly challenging and yet necessary to establish conceptual equivalence as the first crucial step in any cross-cultural research. Adopting a qualitative approach at this stage is most useful.
- *Measurement unit equivalence.* Cross-cultural research should also ensure that the measures have common origins. For instance, some intelligence tests cannot be applied validly in different cultural contexts due to variations in their sources of origin (cf. van de Vijver & Leung, 1997a, 1997b). When there is no measurement

unit equivalence, comparing scores from the same test across cultures is meaningless.
- *Metric equivalence.* This type of equivalence is concerned with the extent to which psychometric properties of measures used in different cultural contexts are similar. This type of equivalence can be considered as a special case of structural equivalence (van de Vijver & Leung, 1997a, 1997b). Another issue under metric equivalence is related to the comparability of response scales. The distance between scale scores may vary vastly across cultures, simply because some cultures have fewer or more terms to express gradation and there are discrepancies in the values attached to each score (Sood, 1990).
- *Response style equivalence.* There are differential norms for using the response-set in different cultures. In some cultures such as Asia, respondents prefer to use the midpoints of the response than the extreme scores. In collectivist cultures, responses may reflect social desirability more often than in individualist cultures. Moreover, bilinguals who respond in English tend to give more extreme responses compared to responses in their native language.

Reliance on quantitative methodologies is a reflection of the positivist paradigm in social sciences. Brett et al. (1997) argue that qualitative methodologies with an interpretive rather than positivist stance are more appropriate for cross-cultural I/O research. The interpretive perspective acknowledges that there are multiple realities which are socially constructed (Brett et al., 1997). In order to comprehend unique cultural characteristics, one has to study the historical, social, political, economical and institutional systems of cultures in depth prior to research design and data collection. The in-depth understanding of culture makes it easier to establish conceptual, functional, structural, and methodological equivalences among variables across various cultural contexts. Among the qualitative methodologies that are available to study organizational phenomena are case studies, participant observation, ethnographic approach, discourse analysis, and content analysis of company documents (Cassell & Symon, 1994; D'Iribarne, 1997; Forster, 1994; Marshall, 1994; Mayer & Tuma, 1990; Punnett & Shenkar, 1995). As discussed in the previous section, time is a crucial factor to be included in theory and research of cross-cultural I/O psychology (Roberts & Boyacigiller, 1984), simply because culture is not a fixed or stable phenomenon but a dynamic network of interacting forces. Cultures do change over time, but this change takes place slowly. It is stimulated by numerous factors including resocialization resulting from first-hand and/or second-hand (via media) exposure to other cultures, changing demographics and values in society, the level of industrial development, and so on. Event history analysis

(Mayer & Tuma, 1990; Yamaguchi, 1991) is a useful tool to examine the influence of time on the observed cross-cultural variance. Through event history analysis, it would be possible to attribute changes in organizations to either cultural factors or contingent ones (e.g., technology, size, market competition) or both.

Sampling

Due to limited time and resources, the majority of research in cross-cultural I/O psychology relies on convenient sampling of countries, organizations, and respondents. Although pragmatic considerations cannot be underestimated in sampling, they should not replace or supercede theoretical considerations. The sampling strategy should reflect both the unit of theory and the purpose of the cross-cultural study. If the unit of theory is at the collective level (e.g., culture or organization), then sampling should aim at enhancing within-collective homogeneity (Brett et al., 1997). The sampling strategy also depends on the purpose of the study. In the selection of cultures, convenient sampling could be preferred when the study is an exploratory one; random sampling is more appropriate when the purpose is to test the generalizability of hypothesized relationships; and a systematic sampling strategy is favored when the study is theory-driven (cf. van de Vijver & Leung, 1997a, 1997b). In systematic sampling, 'most similar system design' (i.e., a selection of cultures which are similar in certain cultural dimensions) is preferred, if the purpose is to examine the impact of a particular cultural dimension on an outcome variable. In contrast, 'most different system design' is more appropriate if the aim is to test the generalizability of the relationship between two or more variables in diverse cultural contexts.

In the selection of cultures, an ongoing debate is to what extent 'culture' is equal to 'country' or 'nation'. Ronen (1986) argues that culture and nation are two distinct concepts, and that the unit of analysis should be culture rather than nation. He provides several instances in which culture has been divided into nations (as in some African states), colonial powers arbitrarily draw national boundaries, or several cultures have been subsumed into a single political entity, such as the former Soviet Union. On the other hand, Tayeb (1988) asserts that the concept of 'culture' must be narrowed and replaced by 'national character'. She suggests that future organizational research should be cross-national as this reflects the view that organizations are influenced by other national institutions besides culture.

Particular to the cross-cultural I/O research is the additional challenge of selecting organizations. As discussed in the previous section, organizations' internal and external environments have a substantial influence on what goes on in the organizations. That is why organizations vary in many respects within the same cultural context. In cross-cultural studies, this variety is even more aggravated

because countries differ in their level, history and type of industrialization, legislative system, labor relations, socio-economic system, and role of government – all of which have substantial implications for organizations. In order to minimize the confounding effect of these external and internal contingencies, cross-cultural studies must try to draw matched samples. That is, if possible, countries should be matched with respect to the level of industrialization and other institutional characteristics. Organizations, on the other hand, must be matched with respect to their size, sector, industry, type of production, technology, and workforce characteristics. One of the best ways to control for the effects of organizational characteristics is to collect data from subsidiaries of multinational firms as has been done in Hofstede's (1980) study. The main objection to this approach is its lack of representativeness of organizational culture in a given country. Against this criticism, Hofstede (1980) argued that being atypical did not matter as long as multinational subsidiaries are atypical in the same way in every country. However, a subsidiary of a US-based multinational is less atypical in Canada than it is in Turkey. It is appropriate to use multinational subsidiaries in various countries if it is proven that they represent the modal organizations in their respective countries to the same extent.

The final issue regarding sampling concerns respondents. Because respondents' demographic characteristics (e.g., age, gender, education, socio-economic status, urban–rural background, religiosity, etc.) influence their values, attitudes, assumptions and behavioral preferences, respondents must also be as similar as possible across selected countries and organizations.

Finding matched samples at different levels (i.e., cultural, organizational, individual) is an almost impossible task to achieve. There are two ways to ease this task. First, with an increasing number of countries, organizations and individuals involved in cross-cultural studies, the error variance due to confounding effect of macro and micro contingencies could be randomized (see, House et al., 1997; Smith, Dugan & Trompenaars, 1996). Second, the effects of confounding variables could be statistically controlled upon data collection of main as well as confounding effects (Aycan, Sinha & Kanungo, 1999; van de Vijver & Leung, 1997a, 1997b).

SCOPE: CROSS-CULTURAL I/O RESEARCH TOPICS THAT HAVE POTENTIAL TO CONTRIBUTE TO HUMAN AND NATIONAL DEVELOPMENT

The most popular cross-cultural topics in previous reviews as well as in the majority of published research include motivation, leadership, work-related values, management style, teamwork, expatriation, and organizational diversity. However, these topics do not fully represent the range of issues that 'really matter'. Hui and Luk (1997: 400) also call for studies to '...substantially expand the breadth and depth of research in the field', but this should be done with a purpose other than just to satisfy academic curiosity. Cross-cultural I/O research should expand its scope to address the issues that are more directly related to improvement of human potential and conditions at work, such as fairness in employment practices, workforce development, improvement of the quality of work life, and organizational development. These are the four broad categories under which I will discuss future cross-cultural research.

Fairness in Employment Practices

Fairness in staffing implies providing an equal opportunity to all members of society to be employed in jobs where they can fully utilize their knowledge, skills and abilities. Therefore, fairness has major implications for unemployment, underemployment, and representation of women and the disabled in the workforce. In this section, we will discuss the ways in which culture influences the approaches and methods of recruitment and selection, and workforce integration of women and the disabled.

Cross-Cultural Approaches to Staffing

Culture influences the process of recruitment and selection in many ways, such as attitudes towards selection and testing, the purpose that staffing serves, and the perceived fairness and appropriateness of criteria and methods that are used in the process. The first theme of cross-cultural variation is the attitude towards 'selection' and 'testing'. In the North American context, selection is a one-way process whereby applicants are tested by employers to predict their future work behavior. However, in the European context, selection is a mutual agreement and negotiation between the organization and the candidate (Roe, 1989). In some European countries such as Italy, France, Sweden and Portugal, the very issue of testing has a negative connotation, because it is perceived as an invasion of privacy, violating the individuals' rights to control their own careers, and creating a barrier to the wholistic representation of oneself (cf. Levy-Leboyer, 1994; Shackleton & Newell, 1997; Shimmin, 1989; Sparrow & Hiltrop, 1994).

The main purpose of recruitment and selection also varies across cultures. In North America, strategic human resource planning is geared towards recruiting the right number of people with the best qualifications to do the job. In India and Eastern Europe, organizations hire more employees than needed to combat poverty and unemployment (Herriot & Anderson, 1997; Sinha, 1997). In paternalistic cultures such as those in the Pacific

and Southeast Asia (Aycan & Kanungo, 1998; Kim, 1994), organizations protect employees by providing long-term employment. In such cultural contexts, the strategic goal of organizations is to meet societal as well as economic needs.

The criteria for selection should be perceived as relevant to the job as well as predictive of future performance. In the US, some of the most commonly cited criteria for selection include education, past experiences, personality traits, and cognitive skills. There is a paucity of cross-cultural research on the appropriateness of such selection criteria in other cultural contexts. However, the limited existing research sheds doubt on the appropriateness of criteria such as education. Rousseau and Tinsley (1997) argue that the knowledge and skills that are acquired by formal education may not be the best predictors of performance in countries where education is either not available for everyone, or is insufficient to prepare individuals for the workforce. Few studies show that criteria for selection are more interpersonal than individual: for example, in Japan, team members' favorable opinions about the candidate (Huo & Von Glinow, 1995); in Islamic Arab countries, agreeableness, good interpersonal relations and trustworthiness (Ali, 1989); in India, belonging to the same 'in-group' as the manager (e.g., the same family or homeland) (Sinha, 1997); and in Latin America, positive attitudes towards family life (Cassens, 1966 cited in Barrett & Bass, 1976) are the frequently used selection criteria.

Followed by the establishment of criteria, the next step in selection is to determine the method of recruitment and selection. Fairness is related to the candidates' perception of the appropriateness of recruitment channels, questions that are asked in application forms, and job previews. Word-of-mouth is a common method of announcing a job opening in cultures where in-group members are favored. Some questions which are directed to candidates in job application forms (e.g., marital status, religious and family background, physical appearance, etc.) could be perceived as offensive in some cultures rather than others. In job previews, a detailed description of a specific job position will not be a requirement of an ideal recruitment process in cultures (e.g., Japan) where 'generalists' are preferred over 'specialists' (Huddleston, 1990).

The method of selection used in different countries has attracted some cross-cultural research attention, but countries included in such studies were mainly North American and Northwest European. In these studies (Levy-Leboyer, 1994; Shackleton & Newell, 1991, 1997; Steiner & Gilliland, 1996), biodata is one of the least common, whereas interview is one of the most common methods of selection. References or recommendations are commonly used in the majority of countries for different reasons and in varying weights. For instance, in the UK, the US and Australia, recommendations are used as a final check, whereas there is heavy reliance on this method in South Eastern European countries and India (Sinha, 1997; Triandis & Vassiliou, 1972).

In North American literature, studies on the predictive validity of various selection methods have increased in number over recent years. However, the social validity (i.e., perceived fairness and acceptability of a particular practice) is an issue which is mainly overlooked in cross-cultural literature. For instance in a study by Steiner and Gilliland (1996), French compared to American participants perceived written ability tests to be less impersonal, and personality tests to be more offensive in violating their privacy.

The brief review in this section clearly shows that there are cross-cultural variations in various aspects of the recruitment and selection process. Several authors (e.g., Herriot & Anderson, 1997; Shackleton & Newell, 1997; Triandis & Bhawuk, 1997) have suggested that some of these variations could be attributed to culture. Future cross-cultural I/O research on staffing could be guided by the following propositions:

- *Proposition 1a*   In cultures high on individualism, universalism, specificity, and achievement orientation, (1) applicants hold more positive attitudes towards 'selection' and 'testing', (2) the main purpose of the recruitment and selection process is to predict future job performance and work behavior, (3) recruitment is achieved through formal channels with the aim of providing everyone an equal chance of employment, (4) selection criteria are based on job-related and technical competence, (5) preferred methods of selection are scientifically validated, objective, and in written test format, (6) such tests measure psychological traits and technical competencies that are related to tasks, (7) which are predetermined and well-specified by the employing organization.
- *Proposition 1b*   In cultures high on collectivism, particularism, diffuseness, and ascription orientation, (1) applicants hold less positive attitudes towards 'selection' and 'testing', (2) the main purpose of recruitment and selection process is to provide employment to those in need and to in-group members who have some potential to perform well on the job, (3) recruitment is done through informal channels (e.g., networking, word-of-mouth, recommendations, etc.), (4) selection criteria are based mainly on interpersonal competence and skills as well as ascribed status (social class, group membership, etc.), (5) preferred methods of selection are socially validated, subjective, and face-to-face, (6) assessment is about the general knowledge of the job, (7) which is broadly defined and open to further negotiation.

Cross-Cultural Approaches to Workforce Integration of Women and the Disabled

The cross-cultural literature lacks systematic research on cultural forces that influence integration of women and the disabled in the workforce. In almost every region of the world, women and the disabled are underrepresented in the workforce and discriminated against in employment practices. Future cross-cultural I/O research should identify the characteristics of the sociocultural context which foster and hinder workforce integration of underrepresented groups. Let us first discuss the status of women.

According to a UN report (1995), all around the world women are discriminated against in employment practices (e.g., pay, occupational status, career advancement), and this is mainly due to women's constraints by their family-related responsibilities. Although women of the world share similar experiences in work and family domains, cross-cultural differences may explain the magnitude of discrimination and conflict between work and family. Research (cf. Adler & Izraeli, 1994; Konek & Kitch, 1994; Lewis & Lewis, 1996) attributes women's difficulties in gaining equal access to work and career advancement to three main factors. First, the most significant difficulty stems from juggling family and work responsibilities. In all cultures, a woman's priority is her family. However, societal expectations and norms influence the ways in which women make career-related choices. For instance, in Indonesia, Japan and China, women do not feel that they have to make a choice between career and family (Korabik, 1994; Steinhoff & Tanaka, 1994; Wright & Crockett-Tellei, 1994). This is due to two reasons: women do not have any choice but to participate in the workforce right after schooling, and they receive childcare support from extended family members.

Western women, on the other hand (e.g., especially from the US, the UK, Germany and France), feel a strong pressure to choose between career and family (Antal & Krebsbach-Gnath, 1994; Fagenson & Jackson, 1994; Hammond & Holton, 1994; Serdjenian, 1994). In many of the collectivist cultures, women's family responsibilities include taking care of extended family members, in-laws and aging parents which add to women's work load (e.g., Chan & Lee, 1994; Krishnaraj & Chanana, 1989). Another cross-cultural difference is the childbearing norm. In France, the majority of career women opt for not having children (Serdjenian, 1994), whereas this is not an option for Israeli women (Izraeli, 1994).

A second difficulty for women to gain access to the workforce is the attitudes towards women and work. In the majority of organizations around the world, male managers hold negative attitudes towards women, although this is less noticeable in some countries such as Indonesia, Singapore and Turkey (Aycan, 1998; Chan & Lee, 1994; Wright & Crockett-Tellei, 1994). A common belief is that women are ill-equipped cognitively and psychologically for being successful in business. This belief is mainly the product of the socialization of women. For instance, in many of the traditional cultures, women are socialized to be shy, unassertive, dependent, passive, and obedient to all males in their lives. In China 'it is a virtue if woman has no ability' (Korabik, 1994: 117). Women, themselves, as well as others in society, internalize these norms through socialization and develop unfavorable attitudes towards women's abilities and potential. Women in traditional societies are cut off from male networks which are instrumental in career advancement. In Japan and Taiwan, for instance, evening gatherings in pubs or clubs among male employees are highly popular. However, women cannot join them because of their conservative socialization (Cheng & Liao, 1994; Steinhoff & Tanaka, 1994). Another source of negative attitude towards women's work is due to the concern about women's and men's changing status in the family. In traditional societies, woman's work is perceived to be a result of the husband's failure to take care of the family. It is also feared that economic power will increase women's power in the family (Aycan, 1998).

Finally, women lack the necessary support from their families and organizations within which they work. One of the most important sources of support is the spouse. In collectivist cultures, spousal support is very rare, especially when it comes to the actual sharing of household chores (i.e., 'instrumental support'). Even though the husband wishes to share the housework, the negative perception of such males in society (i.e., woman-like, submissive, passive, nonauthoritarian) prevents him from doing it at all or doing it in public. Support is also rare in organizations. Family-friendly work schedules and daycare facilities are lacking in many organizations. However, in paternalistic and collectivist cultures, managers are more tolerant and understanding of women's family responsibilities (cf. Kanungo & Aycan, 1998).

Future cross-cultural I/O research should investigate the ways in which the cultural context influences women's integration into the workforce. The cultural dimensions that are closely related to this topic may include individualism/collectivism and traditionalism/modernism in sex-role ideology (Williams & Best, 1990).

- *Proposition 2* Women in collectivist and traditional cultures are expected to experience: (1) more work-family conflict due to responsibilities to care for children and other family members, (2) negative attitudes toward integration of women into the workforce and career

advancement, and (3) less support from their husbands compared to those in individualistic and modern cultures.

Integration of the disabled into the workforce has attracted very little cross-cultural research attention. Future research should examine societal attitudes towards the disabled and the ways in which they are socialized. In societies where there is an overwhelming concern with 'what others think' (e.g., collectivist societies), there seems to be a tendency for families to hide their disabled children at home to avoid others' pity and to hide their own guilt and shame. Fatalism could be associated with the way in which the disabled are treated. In fatalistic cultures, families may believe that having a disabled child is a punishment from God (or bad *karma*) which they must endure. Fatalism may also foster the belief that there is nothing one can do to improve the life conditions of the disabled. Therefore, less effort is put into their training and rehabilitation for workforce integration. In an experiment by Katz, Hass and Bailey (1988), it was found that people expected the disabled to behave in a passive and dependent manner. When such expectations are violated (i.e., when the disabled behaved in a confident, assertive and achievement-oriented manner), subjects in the experiment declined to help them. Expectations about disabled people's behavior and attitudes towards them have implications for society's efforts in assisting the disabled in gaining access to the workforce. Cross-cultural studies should examine such norms and attitudes as well as other factors which foster and hamper the integration of the disabled into the workforce.

Workforce Development

Workforce development is concerned with practices that help employees improve their performance and capabilities. In I/O psychology, such practices are discussed under the topic of performance management, an area which has attracted very little cross-cultural research attention despite the critical role that culture plays in many aspects of the process. In this section, the impact of culture on performance management will be discussed in two areas: performance evaluation and development.

Performance Evaluation

The first challenging issue in performance evaluation is concerned with determining performance dimensions. Criterion development and measurement has been an issue of ongoing debate among I/O psychologists (Altink, Visser & Castelinjs, 1997; Guion, 1997). There is neither a uniform description of 'performance' nor consensus on dimensions of performance (Campbell, Gasser & Oswald, 1996). The criterion problem is magnified at the cross-cultural level because both the definition and the salient dimensions of 'good performance' are culture-bound. In their review article, Arvey and Murphy (1998) presented recent theoretical developments in modeling performance, including that of Campbell et al. (1996), Viswesvaran (1996), and Borman and Motowidlo (1993). According to some of the major theoretical formulations, the most salient dimensions of performance are job-specific knowledge and proficiency, communication competence, effort, mentorship/supervision, quality of output, productivity, interpersonal competence/ teamwork facilitation, and administrative competence. Cross-cultural replications of these dimensions have yet to be explored.

What constitutes good performance in various cultural contexts? A partial answer to this question was given by expatriation literature. Literature shows that local and parent company managers implement different emphases when evaluating expatriate performance (e.g., Arthur & Bennett, 1997; Sinangil & Ones, 1997). Another strand of cross-cultural research on performance criteria comes from the leadership literature. In collectivist, high power distance and paternalistic cultures, employee-centeredness, self-sacrificing behavior, team integration, and competence in administration are considered to be dimensions of leadership effectiveness (cf. Sinha, 1995).

Existing literature deals with performance criteria of those at the managerial or leadership level. However, criteria for the employees at the lower levels have not been systematically examined across cultures. Performance orientation in individualist cultures creates an evaluation system which is based on employee productivity, timeliness, quality of output, and job-specific knowledge and proficiency. More emphasis is placed on the end-product (e.g., outcomes) rather than the process. As such, performance criteria are objective, tangible and observable (Harris & Moran, 1996; Sinha, 1985). In collectivist and high power distance cultures, employee loyalty is valued more than productivity. Outcomes are important, but social and relational criteria, which are more subjective, have been weighted more heavily in evaluating employees. Such criteria include good human nature, harmony in interpersonal relations, trustworthiness, respectful attitude, loyalty and deference towards superiors, effort and willingness to work, awareness of duties and obligations, gratitude, organizational citizenship, conformity, and contribution to team maintenance (e.g., Blunt & Popoola, 1985; Kim, Park & Suzuki, 1990; Negandhi, 1984; Singh, 1981; Sinha, 1990; Triandis, 1994).

- *Proposition 3* In collectivist, high power distance, paternalistic, and low performance-oriented cultures, interpersonal competencies (harmonious interpersonal relations, team work

facilitation, respect, loyalty and positive attitude towards superiors, etc.) and process (e.g., effort, motivation, goal-directed behavior) are emphasized more than task-related competencies and outcomes (successful task completion) in evaluating employee performance. The reverse order of priority is observed in individualistic, low power distance, and performance-oriented cultures.

Like other employee assessment processes, performance evaluation suffers from the difficulty of establishing reliable and valid methods of evaluation. The difficulty stems mainly from inaccuracies and biases that are involved in the evaluation process. In this section, cross-cultural variations in performance appraisal methods and evaluation biases will be reviewed. Let us first discuss the purpose of performance appraisal. According to Cleveland, Murphy and Williams (1989), the primary reasons for performance appraisal include providing feedback on strengths and weaknesses of employees, and recognition of individual differences in performance. Unlike individualistic cultures, collectivist cultures downplay individual differences. Triandis and Bhawuk (1997) posit that the primary purpose of performance evaluation in collectivist cultures is to justify decisions on compensation and promotion. According to Sinha (1994), appraisal is used to control and instill loyalty. Performance evaluation is done less frequently (because the primary purpose is not to provide feedback) and its timing coincides with salary adjustment and promotion periods.

In high power distance cultures, performance evaluation may serve the purpose of reinforcing the authority structure; performance is usually evaluated by superiors (immediate supervisor, manager and/or several levels up) (Davis, 1998; Harris & Moran, 1996). In such an evaluation system, the authority structure is clearly defined and reinforced. Because performance appraisal is a top-down, unilateral process, evaluation of superiors by subordinates is difficult to employ in high power distance cultures. Therefore, the 360-degree performance appraisal method that is popular in the US is not appealing in such cultures (Davis, 1998). In collectivist cultures, the 360-degree evaluation may disturb group harmony due to constant monitoring of the behavior of one's colleagues. Accuracy of such evaluations is also jeopardized because in-group favoritism and loyalty prevent assignment of low performance ratings to one's colleagues and superiors.

- *Proposition 4a* In individualist, performance-oriented and low power distance cultures, (1) the primary purpose of performance evaluation is to enhance performance by providing feedback on employee strengths and weaknesses, (2) performance evaluation is done systematically once or twice a year, (3) standard forms of performance evaluation are used to encourage objective assessment of employees by multiple sources.

- *Proposition 4b* In collectivist, low performance-oriented and high power distance cultures, (1) the primary purpose of performance evaluation is to support promotion and compensation decisions, to reinforce loyalty and authority structure, (2) performance evaluation is done prior to personnel decisions, (3) performance appraisal is usually done by superiors only who base their evaluations on observations and opinions of colleagues.

One of the barriers to obtaining reliable performance evaluation is rating errors, the most pervasive of which include attribution and leniency errors. The accuracy of performance appraisal is a function of attributing the correct reasons for success and failure. Cross-cultural variations in attribution and evaluation biases are well-documented; for instance, Kashima and Triandis (1986) found that Japanese subjects attributed their failures to lack of ability. This finding was contrary to the predictions of 'self-serving' bias, and it was renamed the 'self-effacement' bias. Similarly, Fry and Ghosh (1980) showed that Indian Asians attributed their success to luck, and failure to lack of ability. In a collectivist context, those who engage in self-effacement gain acceptance by peers, whereas pride from success yields disapproval (Bond, Leung & Wan, 1982; Stipek, Weiner & Li, 1989). Yu and Murphy (1993) and Farh, Dobbins and Cheng (1991) conducted studies which demonstrated Chinese workers' negative leniency bias towards themselves. In other words, they rated themselves lower than the ratings they received from their supervisors and peers. This is referred to as 'modesty bias'.

- *Proposition 5* In individualistic cultures, self-serving bias in performance evaluation occurs more frequently than 'self-effacement' or 'modesty bias', while the reverse holds true for collectivist cultures.

The final topic in this performance evaluation section is related to the communication of performance feedback. Culture has a bearing on the way in which feedback is given and received. Regardless of cultural context, performance-related feedback is not easy to give or receive, especially when the feedback is of a negative nature. However, in some cultures where the distinction between life and work space is blurred (i.e., associative/diffuse cultures, Trompenaars, 1994), feedback on one's job performance is perceived as feedback on ones' personality. Triandis (1994: 119) stated that 'in associative cultures, it is difficult to criticize, since it is inevitably seen as equivalent to a rejection of the person'.

One of the most fruitful and as of yet overlooked areas of cross-cultural research is social anxiety which could explain negative feedback avoidance in collectivist cultures. According to Leary and Kowalski (1995: 6), 'social anxiety occurs when people become concerned about how they are being perceived and evaluated by others'. Collectivism could elevate such concerns, because everyone's behavior is monitored by others, and people's opinions are of primary importance as they have direct implications on an in-group's acceptance or rejection. A different but related line of research shows that people from collectivist cultures are more easily embarrassed than those from individualistic cultures (e.g., Edelmann & Neto, 1989). Therefore, it is reasonable to expect that people avoid negative performance feedback in collectivist cultures to save face. On the other hand, positive feedback on performance is also not well-taken in collectivist cultures. Triandis (1994) argues that positive feedback serves the purpose of facilitating interpersonal relations, and, as such, it may be necessary at the initial stages of entry to the group. Once group acceptance is ensured, there is less need to give positive feedback. Positive feedback to individual performance could also disturb group harmony as it may induce jealousy and resentment among those who did not receive such feedback. Also, in collectivist cultures, positive feedback is expected to come from the outside. If a manager praises his/her own employees, then it could be perceived as self-serving.

If neither negative nor positive feedback is appreciated, then it implies that no feedback could be the most preferred condition in collectivist cultures. There is at least one empirical research to support this position. Bailey, Chen and Dou (1997) showed that Japanese and Chinese employees did not take any initiative to seek feedback on individual performance. This was attributed to three reasons. First, as previously mentioned, there is avoidance to receiving both negative and positive feedback. Second, seeking feedback on individual performance is perceived as '...vulgar self-centeredness' (Bailey & Chen, 1997: 611). Therefore, feedback on *group* performance could be valued and preferred more than that on individual performance. Finally, in collectivist cultures, high-context communication patterns are prevalent (Gibson, 1997), and performance-related information could be embedded in contextual cues. As such, contextual cues could provide indirect, implicit and subtle messages about performance to prevent conflicts that may result in communicating information in a direct and confrontational manner.

- *Proposition 6a* In collectivist, associative, high-context and low performance-oriented cultures: (1) giving and receiving feedback on the group rather than individual performance is preferred, (2) individuals avoid seeking both negative and positive feedback, and (3) the manner in which feedback is given is indirect, subtle, and nonconfrontational.

- *Proposition 6b* In individualist, abstractive, low-context and high performance-oriented cultures: (1) giving and receiving feedback on individual as well as group performance is preferred, (2) individuals seek to receive performance feedback, and (3) the manner in which feedback is given is direct, explicit, and confrontational.

Performance Development

The final phase in performance management is dedicated to improvement of performance. Some of the most frequently administered practices to improve performance include performance-based rewards, training, and coaching/mentoring. In this section, the cross-cultural literature on each of these practices will be reviewed.

Are rewards contingent upon performance? The answer depends on the cultural context. Aycan et al. (2000) found that in collectivist and fatalist cultures, there is weak performance-reward contingency due to a number of factors. First, in fatalist cultures managers believe that employees are not malleable, and therefore they do not see any rationale behind rewarding employees as a means of changing their behavior. Secondly, individualist cultures administer the norm of equity in allocating rewards. Therefore, there is one-to-one correspondence between performance and rewards, whereas reward allocation in collectivist culture depends on contingencies other than performance (see, Erez, 1997; Hui & Luk, 1997; Leung, 1997; Smith & Bond, 1993 for reviews on distributive justice). Finally, in collectivist cultures, rewarding the group as a whole is preferred rather than rewarding individual members (Gluskinos, 1988). As mentioned in the previous section, individual gratification may result in disturbed group harmony and resentment.

Another issue that is related to performance-reward contingency are the types of rewards that are salient in various cultural contexts. The discussion on reward allocations in the cross-cultural literature mostly centers around economic rewards. However, noneconomic rewards that satisfy needs for affiliation and recognition are more likely to occur in collectivist and high power distance cultures (Mendonca & Kanungo, 1994). Kim, Park and Suzuki (1990) posit that 'social rewards' such as friendship outside the working group or choice of a person as a working partner are more salient in Korea and Japan than in the US. In high power distant and paternalistic cultures, approval by the 'authority' or 'father figure' could be the most important and salient reward for good performance. Future research should examine what constitutes a 'reward' in different cultural contexts. It may be because of the differences in definitions of 'reward'

that research cannot find performance-reward contingency in some countries.

- *Proposition 7a* In collectivist, high power distance and low performance-oriented cultures, (1) there is weak correspondence between performance and economic rewards, (2) performance-related rewards can be non-economic, such as approval by group members and supervisors, and (3) group rewards are appreciated more than individual rewards for good team performance.
- *Proposition 7b* In individualist, low power distance, and high performance-oriented cultures, (1) there is high performance-reward contingency, and (2) individual rather than (or in addition to) group rewards are expected upon good team performance.

The second practice to enhance performance is training. One of the first questions to ask is whether or not training needs are determined on the basis of performance outcomes, which seems to be the case in individualist and performance-oriented cultures. For instance, in US firms, performance evaluation gives feedback on areas in which employees need training to enhance their performance. However, decisions on what kind of training is given to whom are determined haphazardly in organizations where a performance evaluation system is not well-established. Sinha refers to this lack of a systematic approach in identifying training needs as 'adhoc-ism' (1994: 735). Training topics are usually based on supervisors' recommendations. In low performance-oriented and high power distance contexts, decisions on who will participate in training are based on criteria other than job performance. Employees who maintain good relations with higher management are sent to attractive training programs (i.e., training overseas or in resorts) as a reward for their loyalty (Sinha, 1997). Because training is given as a favor or reward, trainees give highly favorable feedback about the effectiveness of their training which can be misleading.

The effectiveness of such training depends on both the content and process. Earley (1994) asserted that individualism/collectivism impacted the way in which information was used during the process of training. In his experiment on Chinese and American participants, he found that group-focused training, where the focus was on collective self and enhancement of in-group capability, was more effective in improving self-efficacy and performance for Chinese participants. On the other hand, individual-focused training which emphasized personal capability and private self was more effective for American participants. Future cross-cultural research on training should examine the influence of culture on criteria that are used to assess training needs and effectiveness, as well as content and methods of training that are most effective in improving performance.

- *Proposition 8* In individualistic, performance-oriented and low power distance cultures, compared to collectivist, low performance-oriented and high power distance cultures, (1) performance-related criteria are used more to assess training needs and effectiveness, and (2) training programs that are designed to improve individual, rather than group, capabilities yield better performance outcomes.

The next practice in performance development is coaching and mentoring, which involves a personalized relationship with the employee to enhance performance. Mentors are older and more experienced people who provide guidance to employees; they are '...paternalistic and serve in a "godparent" role' (Munchinsky, 1997: 200). The roles of a mentor include modeling correct behavior, setting clear performance standards and goals with the employee, coaching, monitoring and giving constructive feedback on performance, and making necessary adjustments to tasks and the work environment to improve performance (Cascio, 1991; Mendonca & Kanungo, 1990). Mentors work with and for employees. According to Mendonca and Kanungo (1994), high power distance is not compatible with mentorship. In high power distant cultures, superior–subordinate relationships are not personalized, and managers are not usually participative in goal-setting. However, mentorship is more likely when high power distance is combined with paternalism. In paternalistic cultures, superior–subordinate relationships are personalized, and managers guide employees in professional as well as personal matters (Aycan & Kanungo, 1998).

- *Proposition 9* Mentorship and coaching are more likely to occur in paternalistic cultures than in high power distance cultures where there is an authoritarian leadership structure.

Quality of Work Life

Quality of work life (QWL) is related to organizational conditions and practices that aim at promoting employee's mental and physical health, safety and satisfaction. Although this is one of the most important topics which is directly related to employee well-being and development, it has not attracted adequate attention in cross-cultural I/O psychology literature. Cascio and Thacker (1994: 19) propose that organizational practices such as employee participation and involvement, job enrichment, democratic supervision, and safety practices improve quality of work life. Whether or not similar practices would also improve QWL in non-western cultural contexts should be examined by future cross-cultural research. Organizational practices that are geared towards improving quality of work life can be divided into practices which

promote physical health and others which promote psychological health. Culture may influence both of these practices.

A safe work environment is one which is free from accidents and does not pose a threat to employee health. There are certain conditions under which accidents are more likely to occur; the most prevailing reasons being a lack of the necessary job-related training and failure to comply with rules (Wagenaar & Hudson, 1998). The two cultural dimensions which may be related to workplace safety are fatalism and universalism/particularism. In fatalistic cultures, people are inclined to believe that things will happen no matter what one does to prevent them (cf. Kanungo & Aycan, 1998). This assumption may be related not only to religious and other spiritual beliefs (e.g., *karma*), but also to life conditions which create a sense of helplessness (e.g., poverty, over population, etc.). Fatalism, therefore, is expected to hinder occupational practices that promote workplace safety. The universalism/particularism dimension could also be related to safety. In particularistic cultures, rules are not for everyone to adhere to; those who have certain privileges (e.g., high status officers, acquaintance of the boss, etc.) are freed from rules and regulations. Therefore, accidents due to rule violations are more likely to occur in particularist cultures compared to the universalist ones.

- *Proposition 10* In fatalist and particularist cultures, industrial accidents are more likely to occur compared to in nonfatalist and universalist cultures.

Organizational practices that aim at promoting psychological health may be more prone to the influence of culture. Satisfaction, involvement (as opposed to alienation), and low occupational stress are the most frequently cited indicators of quality of work life (e.g., Buunk, Jonge, Ybema & Wolff, 1998; Kanungo, 1990; Warr, 1987). According to Warr (1987), there are nine critical environmental factors that influence psychological health at work: opportunity for control, opportunity for skill use, challenging goals, variety, environmental clarity, availability of monetary sources, physical security, opportunity for interpersonal contact, and valued social position. The ability to generalize this finding is limited to a certain cultural context which is mainly individualistic, low power distant and achievement-oriented. The underlying purpose of such practices is to achieve self-actualization through job enrichment. However, research has shed doubt on the validity of the job enrichment model (Hackman & Oldham, 1980) in nonwestern cultural contexts (Shamir & Drory, 1981; Triandis, 1994; Erez, 1994; Mendonca & Kanungo, 1994). Psychological health in collectivist and high power distance cultures may be influenced more by interpersonal aspects of the work, such as a sense of belonging, acceptance by peers and superiors, harmony in interpersonal relations, paternalistic supervision, and so on. A wholistic approach to quality of work life requires inclusion of family-related stressors. For instance, in collectivist cultures where individuals have to fulfill responsibilities to their aging parents and extended family members, the work–family conflict is expected to be one of the major predictors of workplace psychological health.

- *Proposition 11* In individualistic and achievement-oriented cultures, psychological health at work is expected to be influenced by task-related factors, whereas in collectivist and less achievement-oriented cultures, it is expected to be influenced by relational and family-related factors.

Organizational Development

Organizational development (OD) is a process of planned change in organizations towards improvement of organizational efficiency and employee productivity (Huse, 1980; Porras & Robertson, 1994). Some of the most popular practices of OD include total quality management (TQM), management by objectives (MBO), technology transfers, sensitivity training or T-groups, organizational culture change, 360-degree performance evaluation, and job enrichment and enlargement. In each of these practices, what get changed during OD are not only organizational practices, but also organizational values.

OD practices are based on a particular human model which is egalitarian, participative, confrontational, rational, risk-taking, collaborative, articulate, and trusting (Tannenbaum & Davis, 1969, cited in Jaeger, 1986). Underlying this model (and therefore OD practices) are the following values: low power distance, medium individualism, low uncertainty avoidance, low masculinity (because it is important to express and articulate feelings), achievement-orientation, and context-independence (Jaeger, 1986; Kedia & Bhagat, 1988; Tata & Prasad, 1998). The efficiency of OD practices is ensured to the extent that underlying values and assumptions in each practice fit the values and assumptions of the cultural context.

Hui and Luk (1997) reviewed some of the OD interventions and practices in various cultural contexts, and concluded that many of them failed due to the mismatch between the OD and the sociocultural values. For instance, autocratic values in sub-Saharan Africa, bureaucratic rigidity, fatalism and centralized control in Arab countries, obedience to authority and the tendency to resign in the face of difficulty in the Philippines, and an unfavorable attitude towards open discussion and confrontation in Singapore were cultural barriers to successful implementation of OD practices (Hui & Luk, 1997: 391–394).

Literature is rife with examples of US-based practices whose applicability in other countries have proven to be constrained by the cultural context, and OD practices are no exception. Prior to their application, an infrastructural change may be necessary to ensure the fit between the value structure of the OD practice and the sociocultural context. What is meant by 'infrastructural' change is modification of either the OD practice to fit into the values of the culture of application, or the people to fit into the values of the imported practice. In the latter case (i.e., workforce change), training, leadership, coaching and mentorship become critical to the preparation of a workforce for the new application. In a Turkish textile factory, the Japanese management system had been fully integrated into the organization only after the preparation of the workforce for 18 years. In another Turkish factory in automated industry, the 360-degree performance evaluation system has been implemented successfully only after two years of meetings between superiors and subordinates, and training programs (Aycan, 1999). In these examples, successful implementation of OD practices was ensured, but it was at the expense of changing individual and organizational values. In such cases, the question goes beyond that of a scientific one, such as whether or not one can change the values of the workforce, to an ethical one in considering whether or not one is entitled to change the values of the workforce to implement OD practices.

An alternative to ensure the fit is to modify OD practices to fit into the values of the workforce. In this case, the most appropriate way to change an OD practice is to indigenize it. Some of the best examples of indigenization include Japan's quality circles (cf. Hui & Luk, 1997), and India's nurturant–task leadership style (Sinha, 1980). In these examples, task and performance management is accomplished in a collectivist manner where values related to in-group harmony and nurture are maintained with an emphasis on task accomplishment. This method is what Singh-Sengupta (1998: 21) refers to as 'integrative indigenization' rather than 'protected and closed indigenization' (i.e., concepts, theories and methods without national origins get rejected). Future cross-cultural research should engage in systematic investigation of values and assumptions underlying western OD practices, and the ways in which such practices could be integrated into local sociocultural contexts.

CONCLUSION

In this chapter, a brief overview of the last 20 years of cross-cultural I/O research has been presented and specific proposals formulated for future research. This evaluation suggests that the field suffers from a lack of theory-driven research. Research, so far, has been characterized by comparative studies of various organizational practices by using convenient samples and methods. The accumulation of knowledge from such research is not sufficient to provide insights into the role of culture in explaining organizational phenomena. It is recommended that future research should adopt a multidisciplinary and an interactionist perspective to reflect the complex environment within which organizations function. The challenge for future studies is not only to identify cultural characteristics that are relevant to various organizational phenomena, but also to examine *the extent to which* and *the ways in which* culture *vis-à-vis* other contextual forces influence individual and group behavior in organizations. To handle the complexities involved in cross-cultural I/O research, innovative methodologies must be developed that allow in-depth understanding of cultures and organizations.

In summary, the multiple challenges that await cross-cultural I/O researchers in the next 20 years should not be discouraging. The academic pressure for more research and more publications makes it certainly more difficult, but not impossible to do good research. As one of the most dynamic and promising fields of psychology, cross-cultural I/O psychology has much to offer to individual, organizational and national development. To serve this purpose, the field needs rigorous research conducted by multinational, multidisciplinary and multiprofessional teams.

REFERENCES

Adler, N.J., & Izraeli, D.N. (Eds.) (1994). *Competitive frontiers: Women managers in a global economy* (pp. 3–22). Cambridge: Blackwell.

Ali, A.J. (1989). A comparative study of managerial beliefs about work in the Arab states. *Advances in International Comparative Management*, *4*, 95–112.

Altink, W.M.M., Visser, C.F., & Castelinjs, M. (1997). Criterion development: The unknown power of criteria as communication tools. In N. Anderson & P. Herriot (Eds.), *International handbook of selection and asssessment* (pp. 287–302). Chichester, England: John Wiley & Sons.

Antal, A.B., & Krebsbach-Gnath, C. (1994). Women in management in Germany: East, west and reunited. In N.J. Adler & D.N. Izraeli (Eds.), *Competitive frontiers: Women managers in a global economy* (pp. 206–223). Cambridge: Blackwell.

Arvey, R.D., & Murphy, K.R. (1998). Performance evaluation in work settings. *Annual Review of Psychology*, *49*, 141–168.

Arthur, W., & Bennett, W. (1997). A comparative test of alternative models of international assignee job performance. In Z. Aycan (Ed.), *Expatriate management: Theory and research* (pp. 141–172). Connecticut: JAI Press.

Aycan, Z. (1998). Kadinlarin is hayatinda basarilarini etkileyen faktorler [Factors which influence career advancement of women in Turkey]. *Human Resources*, *2*(7), 82–90.

Aycan, Z. (1999). *Organizational culture and human resource management practices in 'Anatolian Tigers'.* Paper presented at the 7th National Congress on Management and Organizations, Istanbul, May.

Aycan, Z. (2000). Cross-cultural industrial and organizational psychology: Contributions, past developments and future directions. *Journal of Cross-Cultural Psychology*, *31*(1), 110–128.

Aycan, Z., & Kanungo, R.N. (1998). *Paternalism: Towards conceptual refinement and operationalization.* Paper presented at 14th International Congress of Cross-Cultural Psychology, USA, August.

Aycan, Z., Kanungo, R.N., Mendonca, M., Yu, K., Deller, J., Stahl, J., & Kurshid, A. (2000). Impact of culture on human resource management practices: A ten-country comparison. *Applied Psychology: An International Review*, *49*(1), 192–220.

Aycan, Z., Kanungo, R.N., & Sinha, J.B.P. (1999). Organizational culture and human resource management practices: The model of culture fit. *Journal of Cross-Cultural Psychology*, *30*(4), 501–527.

Bailey, J.R., Chen, C.C., & Dou, S.G. (1997). Conceptions of self and performance-related feedback in the US, Japan and China. *Journal of International Business Studies*, *3rd qtr*, 605–625.

Barrett, G.V., & Bass, B.M. (1976). Cross-cultural issues in industrial and organizational psychology. In M.D. Dunnette (Ed.), *Handbook of industrial and organizational psychology* (pp. 1639–1686). Chicago: Rand McNally.

Berry, J.W. (1997). An ecocultural approach to the study of cross-cultural industrial/organizational psychology. In P.C. Earley & M. Erez (Eds.), *New perspectives on international industrial/organizational psychology* (pp. 130–148). San Francisco: The New Lexington Press.

Berry, J.W., Poortinga, Y.H., Segal, M.H., & Dasen, P.R. (1992). *Cross-cultural psychology: Research and applications*. New York: Cambridge.

Blauner, R. (1964). *Alienation and freedom*. Chicago/London: University of Chicago Press.

Blunt, P., & Popoola, O.E. (1985). *Personnel management in Africa*. Reading, MA: Addison Wesley Longman.

Bond, M.H., Leung, K., & Wan, K.C. (1982). How does cultural collectivism operate? The impact of task and maintenance contributions on reward distribution. *Journal of Cross-Cultural Psychology*, *13*, 186–200.

Borman, W.C., & Motowidlo, S.J. (1993). Expanding the criterion domain to include elements of contextual performance. In N. Schmitt and W.C. Borman (Eds.), *Personnel selection in organizations* (pp. 71–98). San Francisco: Jossey-Bass.

Brett, J.M., Tinsley, C.H., Janssens, M., Barsness, Z.I., & Lyttle, A.L. (1997). New approaches to the study of culture in industrial/organizational psychology. In

P.C. Earley & M. Erez (Eds.). *New perspectives on international industrial/organizational psychology* (pp. 75–130). San Francisco: The New Lexington Press.

Buunk, B.P., Jonge, J., Ybema, J.F., & Wolff, C.J. (1998). Psychosocial aspects of occupational stress. In P.J.D. Drenth, H. Thierry & C.J. de Wolff (Eds.), *Handbook of work and organizational psychology: Vol. 2. Work psychology* (pp. 145–182). East Sussex: Psychology Press.

Campbell, J.P., Gasser, M.B., & Oswald, F.L. (1996). The substantive nature of job performance variability. In K.R. Murphy (Ed.), *Individual differences and behavior in organizations* (pp. 258–299). San Francisco: Jossey-Bass.

Cascio, W.F. (1991). *Applied psychology in personnel management* (4th ed.). Englewood Cliffs, NJ: Prentice-Hall.

Cascio, W.F., & Thacker, J.W. (1994). *Managing human resources*. Canada: McGraw-Hill Ryerson.

Cassell, C., & Symon, G. (Eds.) (1994). *Qualitative methods in organizational research*. London: Sage.

Chan, A., & Lee, J. (1994). Woman executives in a newly industrialized economy: The Singapore scenario. In N.J. Adler & D.N. Izraeli (Eds.), *Competitive frontiers: Women managers in a global economy* (pp. 127–142). Cambridge: Blackwell.

Chandler, A. (1962). *Strategy and structure*. Cambridge, MA: MIT Press.

Cheng, W., & Liao, L. (1994). Women managers in Taiwan. In N.J. Adler & D.N. Izraeli (Eds.), *Competitive frontiers: Women managers in a global economy* (pp. 143–159). Cambridge: Blackwell.

Child, J. (1981). Culture, contingency and capitalism in the cross-national study of organizations. In L.L. Cummings & B.M. Staw (Eds.), *Research in organizational behavior* (Vol. 3, pp. 303–356). Greenwich, CT: JAI Press.

Child, J., & Keiser, A. (1979). Organizations and managerial roles in British and West German companies: An examination of the culture-free thesis. In C.J. Lammers & D.J. Hickson (Eds.), *Organizations alike and unlike: International and interinstitutional studies in the sociology of organizations* (pp. 251–272). London: Routledge & Kegan Paul.

Chonko, L.B. (1982). The relationship of span of control sales representatives' experienced role conflict and role ambiguity. *Academy of Management Journal, 25*, 452–456.

Cleveland, J.N., Murphy, K.R., & Williams, R.E. (1989). Multiple uses of performance appraisal: Prevalence and correlates. *Journal of Applied Psychology, Feb.*, 130–135.

Crozier, M. (1964). *The bureaucratic phenomenon*. Chicago: University of Chicago Press.

Dansereau, F., Alutto, J.A., & Yammarino, F.J. (1984). *Theory testing in organizational behavior: The variant approach*. Englewood Cliffs, NJ: Prentice-Hall.

Davis, D.D. (1998). International performance measurement and management. In J.W. Smither (Ed.), *Performance appraisal* (pp. 95–131). San Francisco: Jossey-Bass.

Delmestri, G. (1997). Convergent organizational responses to globalization in the Italian and German machine-building industries. *International Studies of Management and Organization, 27* (3), 86–109.

D'Iribarn, P. (1997). The usefulness of an ethnographic approach to the international comparison of organizations. *International Studies of Management and Organization, 26*, 30–47.

Dooley, K.J. (1997). A complex adaptive systems model of organization change. *Nonlinear Dynamics, Psychology and the Life Sciences, 1*, 69–97.

Dore, R. (1973). *British factory – Japanese factory*. London: Allen & Unwin.

Drenth, P.J.D., & B. Groenendijk (1984). Work and organizational psychology in cross-cultural perspective. In P.J.D. Drenth, H. Thierry, P.J. Willems & C.J. De Wolff (Eds.), *Handbook of work and organizational psychology* (Vol. 2, pp. 1197–1230). New York: Wiley.

Earley, P.C. (1994). Self or group? Cultural effects of training on self-efficacy and performance. *Administrative Science Quarterly, 39*, 89–117.

Edelmann, R.J., & Neto, F. (1989). Self-reported expression and consequences of embarrassment in Portugal and U.K. *International Journal of Psychology, 24*, 351–366.

Erez, M. (1994). Toward a model of cross-cultural industrial and organizational psychology. In H.C. Triandis, M.D. Dunnette & L.M. Hough (Eds.), *Handbook of industrial and organizational psychology*, 2nd ed. (Vol. 4, pp. 559–608). Palo Alto, CA: Consulting Pychologists Press.

Erez, M. (1997). A culture-based model of work motivation. In P.C. Earley & M. Erez (Eds.), New perspectives on international industrial/organizational psychology (pp. 193–243). San Francisco: The New Lexington Press.

Fagenson, E.A., & Jackson, J.J. (1994). The status of women managers in the United States. In N.J. Adler & D.N. Izraeli (Eds.), *Competitive frontiers: Women managers in a global economy* (pp. 388–404). Cambridge: Blackwell.

Farh, J., Dobbins, G.H., & Cheng, B. (1991). Cultural relativity in action: A comparison of self-rating made by chinese and U.S. workers. *Personnel Psychology, 44*(1), 129–147.

Forster, N. (1994). The analysis of company documentation. In C. Cassell & G. Symon (Eds.), *Qualitative methods in organizational research* (pp. 147–166). London: Sage.

Fry, P.S., & Ghosh, R. (1980). Attributions of success and failure: Comparison of cultural differences between Asian and Caucasian children. *Journal of Cross-Cultural Psychology, 11*, 343–363.

Gallie, D. (1978). *In search of the new working class*. London: Cambridge University Press.

Gibson, C.B. (1997). Do you hear what I hear? A framework for reconciling intercultural communication difficulties arising from cognitive styles and cultural values. In P.C. Earley & M. Erez (Eds.), *New perspectives on international industrial and organizational psychology* (pp. 335–362). San Francisco: The New Lexington Press.

Gluskinos, U.M. (1988). Cultural and political considerations in the introduction of Western technologies: The Mekorot project. *Journal of Management Development*, 6, 34–46.

Gregerson, W., & Sailer, L. (1993). Chaos theory and its implications for social science research. *Human Relations*, 46, 777–802.

Guion, R. (1997). Criterion measures and the criterion dilemma. In N. Andreson & P. Herriot (Eds.), *International handbook of selection and assessment* (pp. 287–302). Chichester, England: John Wiley & Sons.

Hackman, J.R., & Oldham, G.R. (1980). *Work redesign*. Reading, MA: Addison-Wesley.

Hammond, V., & Holton, V. (1994). The scenario for women managers in Britain. In N.J. Adler & D.N. Izraeli (Eds.), *Competitive frontiers: Women managers in a global economy* (pp. 224–242). Cambridge: Blackwell.

Harbison, F., & Myers, C.A. (Eds.) (1959). *Management in industrial world*. New York: McGraw-Hill.

Harris, P.R., & Moran, R.T. (1996). *Managing cultural differences* (4th ed.). Houston: Gulf.

Herriot, P., & Anderson, N. (1997). Selecting for change: How will personnel and selection psychology survive? In N. Anderson & P. Herriot (Eds.), *International handbook of selection and assessment* (pp. 1–38). Chichester England: John Wiley & Sons.

Hickson, D.J., Hinings, C.R., McMillan, C.J., & Schwitter, J.P. (1974). The culture-free context of organization structure: A tri-national comparison. *Sociology*, 8, 59–80.

Hickson, D.J., Pugh, D.S., & Pheysey, D.C. (1969). Operations technology and organization structure: An empirical reappraisal. *Administrative Science Quarterly*, 14, 378–397.

Hofstede, G. (1980). *Culture's consequences*. California: Sage.

Hofstede, G. (1991). *Cultures and organizations: Software of the mind*. London: McGraw-Hill.

House, R.J., Wright, N.S., & Aditya, R.N. (1997). Cross-cultural research on organizational leadership: A critical analysis and a proposed theory. In P.C. Earley & M. Erez (Eds.), *New perspectives on international industrial/organizational psychology* (pp. 130–148). San Francisco: The New Lexington Press.

Huddleston, J.N. (1990). *Gaigin Kaisha: Running a foreign business in Japan*. Armour, NY: Sharp.

Hui, H., & Luk, C.L. (1997). Management and organizational behavior. In J.W. Berry, M.H. Segall & Ç. Kagitçibasi (Eds.), *Handbook of cross-cultural psychology: Vol. 3. Social behavior and applications* (rev. ed.) (pp. 371–412). Needham Heights, MA: Allyn & Bacon.

Huo, Y.P., & Von Glinow, M.A. (1995). *Managing human resources across the Pacific Ocean: A tri-national comparison of staffing practices*.

Huse, E.F. (1980). *Organization development and change* (2nd ed.). St. Paul, MN: West.

Izraeli, D.N. (1994). Outsiders in the promised land: Women managers in Israel. In N.J. Adler &

D.N. Izraeli (Eds.), *Competitive frontiers: Women managers in a global economy* (pp. 301–324). Cambridge: Blackwell.

Jaeger, A.M. (1986). Organization development and national culture: Where's the fit? *Academy of Management Review*, 11, 178–190.

Kanungo, R.N. (1990). Culture and work alienation: Western models and eastern realities. International *Journal of Psychology*, 25, 795–812.

Kanungo, R.N., & Aycan, Z. (1998). *Test of the Model of Culture Fit: A 10-country comparison*. Paper presented at 24th International Congress of Applied Psychology, USA, August.

Kanungo, R., Aycan, Z., & Sinha, J.B.P. (1999). Socio-Cultural Environment, Work Culture and HRM Practices: The Model of Culture Fit. In J.C. Lasry (Eds.), *Latest contributions to cross-cultural psychology* (pp. 269–286). Lisse: Swets & Zeitlinger.

Kanungo, R.N., & Jaeger, A.M. (1990). Introduction: The need for indigenous management in developing countries. In A.M. Jaeger & R.N. Kanungo (Eds.) *Management in developing countries* (pp. 1–23). London: Routledge.

Kashima, Y., & Triandis, H.C. (1986). The self-serving bias in attributions as a coping strategy: A cross-cultural study. *Journal of Cross-Cultural Psychology*, 17, 83–97.

Katz, I., Hass, R.G., & Bailey, J. (1988). Attitudinal ambivalence and behavior toward people with disabilities. In H.E. Yuker (Ed.), *Attitudes toward persons with disabilities* (pp. 47–57). New York: Springer.

Kedia, B.L., & Bhagat, R.S. (1988). Cultural constraints on transfer of technology across nations: Implications for research in international and comparative management. *Academy of Management Review*, 13(4), 559–571.

Sinangil, H., & Ones, D.S. (1997). Empirical investigations of the host country perspective in expatriate management. In Z. Aycan (Ed.), *Expatriate Management: Theory and Research* (pp. 173–206). Connecticut: JAI Press.

Kim, U.M. (1994). Significance of paternalism and communalism in the occupational welfare system of Korean firms. In U. Kim, H.C. Triandis, Ç. Kağitçibaşi, S. Choi & G. Yoon (Eds.), *Individualism and collectivism*. Thousand Oaks, CA: Sage.

Kim, K.I., Park, H.J., & Suzuki, N. (1990). Reward allocations in the United States, Japan and Korea: A comparison of individualistic and collectivistic cultures. *Academy of Management Journal*, 33, 188–198.

Klein, K.J., Dansereau, F., & Hall, R.J. (1994). Levels issues in theory development, data collection, and analysis. *Academy of Management Review*, 19, 195–229.

Kluckhohn, C. (1951). The study of culture. In D. Lerner & H.D. Lasswell (Eds.), *The policy sciences*. Stanford, CA: Stanford University Press.

Konek, C.W., & Kitch, S.L. (1994). *Women and careers*. Thousand Oaks, CA: Sage.

Korabik, K. (1994). Managerial women in People's Republic of China. In N.J. Adler & D.N. Izraeli (Eds.),

Competitive frontiers: Women managers in a global economy (pp. 114–126). Cambridge: Blackwell.

Krishnaraj, M., & Chanana, K. (1989). *Gender and the household domain*. India: Sage.

Leary, M.R., & Kowalski, R.M. (1995). *Social anxiety*. New York: The Guilford Press.

Leung, K. (1997). Negotiation and reward allocations across cultures. In P.C. Earley & M. Erez (Eds.), *New perspectives on international industrial/organizational psychology* (pp. 640–675). San Francisco: The New Lexington Press.

Levy-Leboyer, C. (1994). Selection and assessment in Europe. In H.C. Triandis, M.D. Dunnette & L.M. Hough (Eds.), *Handbook of industrial and organizational psychology* (2nd ed., Vol. 4, pp. 173–190). Palo Alto, CA: Consulting Pychologists Press.

Lewis, S., & Lewis, J. (Eds.) (1996). *The work-family challenge rethinking employment*. Cambridge: Sage.

Lyttle, A.L., Brett, J.M., Barsness, Z.I., Tinsley, C.H., & Janssens, M. (1995). A paradigm for confirmatory cross-cultural research in organizational behaviour. In L.L. Cummings & B.M. Staw (Eds.), *Research in Organizational Behaviour*, Vol. 17 (pp. 167–214). Greenwich: Jai Press Inc.

Marshall, H. (1994). Discourse analysis in an occupational context. In C. Cassell & G. Symon (Eds.), *Qualitative methods in organizational research* (pp. 91–106). London: Sage.

Mathur, P., Aycan, Z., & Kanungo, R.N. (1996). Work cultures in Indian organizations: A comparison between public and private sector. *Psychology and Developing Societies*, 8(2), 199–223.

Maurice, M. (1979). For a study of the 'social effect': Universality and specificity in organization research. In C.J. Lammers & D.J. Hickson (Eds.), *Organizations alike and unlike: International and interinstitutional studies in the sociology of organizations* (pp. 42–60). London: Routledge & Kegan Paul.

Maurice, M., Sorge, A., & Warner, M. (1980). Social differences in organizing manufacturing units: A comparison of France, West Germany and Britain. *Organization Studies*, 1, 59–86.

Mayer, K.U., & Tuma, N.B. (Eds.) (1990). *Event history analysis in life course research*. Madison, W.I.: University of Wisconsin Press.

Mendenhall, M.E., & Macomber, J.H. (1997). Rethinking the strategic management of expatriates from a nonlinear dynamics perspective. In Z. Aycan (Ed.), *New approaches to employee management* (pp. 41–62). Greenwich: Jai Press.

Mendonca, M., & Kanungo, R.N. (1990). Performance management in developing countries. In A.M. Jaeger & R.N. Kanungo (Eds.), *Management in developing countries* (pp. 223–251). London: Routledge.

Mendonca, M., & Kanungo, R.N. (1994). Managing human resources: The issue of cultural fit. *Journal of Management Inquiry*, 3(2), 189–205.

Messick, D.M., & van der Geer, J.P. (1981). A reversal paradox. *Psychological Bulletin*, 90, 582–593.

Munchinsky, P.M. (1997). *Psychology Applied to Work*. Pacific Grove, CA: Brooks/Cole Publishing Co.

Negandhi, A.R. (1984). Management in the third world. *Advances in International Comparative Management*, 1, 123–154.

Parker, S.R., Brown, R.K., Child, J., & Smith, M.A. (1977). *The sociology of industry*. London: Allen & Unwin.

Porter, L.W., & Lawler, E.E. (1965). Properties of organizational structure in relation to job attitudes and job behaviour. *Psychological Bulletin*, 81, 23–51.

Porras, J.I., & Robertson, P.J. (1994). Organizational development: Theory, practice and research. In M.D. Dunnette & L.M. Hough (Eds.), *Handbook of industrial and organizational psychology* (2nd ed., Vol. 3, pp. 719–822). Palo Alto, CA: Consulting Psychologists Press.

Punnett, B.J., & Shenkar, O. (Eds.) (1995). *Handbook for international management research*. Oxford: Blackwell.

Roberts, K.H., & Boyacigiller, N.A. (1984). Cross-national organizational research: The grasp of the blind man. In B.M. Staw & L.L. Cummings (Eds.), *Research in organizational behaviour* (pp. 423–475). Connecticut: Jai Press Inc.

Roe, R.A. (1989). Designing selection procedures. In P. Herriot (Eds.), *Assessment and selection in organizations*. Chichester, England: John Wiley.

Ronen, S. (1986). *Comparative and multinational management*. New York: Wiley.

Rousseau, D.M. (1985). Issues of level in organizational research: Multi-level and cross-level perspectives. *Research in Organizational Behavior*, 7, 1–37.

Rousseau, D.M., & Tinsley, C. (1997). Human resources are local: Society and social contracts in a global economy. In N. Anderson & P. Herriot (Eds.), *International handbook of selection and assessment* (pp. 39–62). Chichester, England: John Wiley & Sons.

Schein, E.H. (1992). *Organizational culture and leadership* (2nd ed.). San Francisco, CA: Jossey-Bass.

Schwartz, S.H. (1994). Cultural dimensions of values: Towards an understanding of national differences. In U. Kim, H.C. Triandis, C. Kagitcibasi, S.C. Choi & G. Yoon (Eds.), *Individualism and collectivism: Theoretical and methodological issues* (pp. 85–119). Thousand Oaks, CA: Sage.

Sego, D.J., Hui, C., & Law, K.S. (1997). Operationalizing cultural values as the mean of individual values: Problems and suggestions for research. In P.C. Earley & M. Erez (Eds.), *New perspectives on international industrial/organizational psychology* (pp. 148–160). San Francisco: The New Lexington Press.

Serdjenian, E. (1994). Women managers in France. In N.J. Adler & D.N. Izraeli (Eds.), *Competitive frontiers: Women managers in a global economy* (pp. 190–205). Oxford: Blackwell.

Shackleton, N.J., & Newell, S. (1991). Management selection: A comparative survey of methods used in top British and French companies. *Journal of Occupational Psychology*, 64, 23–36.

Shackleton, N.J., & Newell, S. (1997). International assessmant and selection. In N. Anderson & P. Herriot (Eds.), *International handbook of selection and assessment* (pp. 81–96). Chichester, England: John Wiley & Sons.

Shamir, B., & Drory, A. (1981). A study of cross-cultural differences in work attitudes among three Israeli prison employees. *Journal of Occupational Behavior, 2,* 267–282.

Shimmin, S. (1989). Selection in a European context. In P. Herriot et al. (Eds.), *Assessment and Selection in Organizations: Methods and practice for recruitment and appraisal.* Chichester, England: Wiley.

Singh, R. (1981). Prediction of performance from motivation and ability: An appraisal of the cultural difference hypothesis. In J. Pandey (Ed.), *Perspectives on experimental social psychology in India.* New Delhi: Concept.

Singh-Sengupta, S. (1998). Towards integrative indigenization: I/O psychology research in India. *Cross-Cultural Psychology Bulletin, 32*(2), 16–21.

Sinha, J.B.P. (1980). *The nurturant task leader.* New Delhi: Concept.

Sinha, J.B.P. (1985). Psychic relevance of work in Indian culture. *Dynamic Psychiatry, 91,* 134–141.

Sinha, J.B.P. (1990). *The cultural context of leadership and power.* New Delhi: Sage.

Sinha, J.B.P. (1994). Cultural embeddedness and the developmental role of industrial organizations in India. In H.C. Triandis, M.D. Dunnette & L.M. Hough (Eds.), *Handbook of industrial and organizational psychology* (2nd ed., Vol. 4, pp. 727–764). Palo Alto: Consulting Psychologists Press.

Sinha, J.B.P. (1995). *The cultural context of leadership and power.* New Delhi: Sage Publications.

Sinha, J.B.P. (1997). *A Cultural Perspective on Organizational Behavior in India.* New Approaches.

Sinha, J.B.P., & Verma, J. (1987). Structure of collectivism. In C. Kagitcibasi (Ed.), *Growth and progress in Cross-Cultural Psychology* (pp. 123–129). Lisse: Swets & Zeitlinger.

Smith, P.B., & Bond, M.H. (1993). *Social psychology across culture.* New York: Harvester Wheatsheaf.

Smith, P.B., Dugan, S., & Trompenaars, F. (1996). National culture and the values of employees: A dimensional analysis across 43 nations. *Journal of Cross-Cultural Psychology, 27*(2), 231–264.

Sood, J.H. (1990). Equivalent measurement in international market research: Is it really a problem? *Journal of International Consumer Marketing, 2*(2), 25–41.

Sorge, A. (1991). Strategic fit and the societal effect: Interpreting cross-national comparisons of technology, organization and human resources. *Organization Studies, 12,* 161–190.

Sparrow, P., & Hiltrop, J.M. (1994). *European Human Resource Management in Transition.* Hemel Hempstead: Prentice-Hall.

Steiner, D.D., & Gilliland, S.W. (1996). Fairness reactions to personnel selection techniques in France and United States. *Journal of Applied Psychology, 81*(2), 134–142.

Steinhoff, P.G., & Tanaka, K. (1994). Women managers in Japan. In N.J. Adler & D.N. Izraeli (Eds.), *Competitive frontiers: Women managers in a global economy* (pp. 79–100). Cambridge: Blackwell.

Stipek, D., Weiner, B., & Li, K. (1989). Testing some attribution-emotion relations in the People's Republic of China. *Journal of Personality and Social Psychology, 56,* 109–116.

Tannenbaum, R., & Davis, S.A. (1969). Values and organizations. *Industrial Management Review, 10,* 67–83.

Tata, J., & Prasad, S. (1998). Cultural and structural constraints in total quality management implementation. *Total Quality Management, 9*(8), 703–711.

Tayeb, M. (1988). *Organizations and national culture.* London: Sage.

Triandis, H.C. (1982). Review of culture's consequences: International differences in work-related values. *Human Organization, 41,* 86–90.

Triandis, H.C. (1994). Cross-cultural industrial and organizational psychology. In H.C. Triandis, M.D. Dunnette & L.M. Hough (Eds.), *Handbook of industrial and organizational psychology* (2nd ed., Vol. 4, pp. 103–172). Palo Alto, CA: Consulting Psychologists Press.

Triandis, H.C., & Bhawuk, D.P.S. (1997). Culture theory and the meaning of relatedness. In P.C. Earley, & M. Erez (Eds.), *New perspectives on international industrial/organizational psychology* (pp. 13–53). San Francisco: The New Lexington Press.

Triandis, H.C., & Vassiliou, V.A. (1972). Interpersonal influence and employee selection in two cultures. *Journal of Applied Psychology, 56,* 140–145.

Trompenaars, F. (1994). *Riding the waves of culture.* Illinois: Irwin.

United Nations (1995). *The world's women 1995: Trends and statistics.* New York: United Nations.

Usunier, J.-C. (1998). *International and cross-cultural management research.* Thousand Oaks: Sage.

Van de Vijver, F., & Leung, K. (1997a). *Methods and data analysis for cross-cultural research.* Thousand Oaks, CA: Sage.

Van de Vijver, F., & Leung, K. (1997b). Methods and data analysis of comparative research. In J.W. Berry, Y.H. Poortinga & J. Pandey (Eds.), *Handbook of cross-cultural psychology* (Vol. 1, pp. 257–301). Needham Heights, MA: Allyn & Bacon.

Viswesvaran, C. (1996). *Modeling job performance: Is there a general factor?* Presented at 11th Annual Meeting of the Society of Industrial and Organizational Psychology, San Diego, CA.

Wagenaar, W.A., & Hudson, P.T.W. (1998). Industrial safety. In P.J.D. Drenth, H. Thierry & C.J. de Wolff (Eds.), *Handbook of work and organizational psychology: Vol.2. Work psychology* (pp. 65–88). East Sussex: Psychology Press.

Warr, P.B. (1987). *Work, unemployment, and mental health.* Oxford: Clarendon.

Williams, J.E., & Best, D.L. (1990). *Sex and psyche.* Newbury Park, CA: Sage.

Wright, L., & Crockett-Tellei, V. (1994). Women in management in Indonesia. In N.J. Adler & D.N. Izraeli (Eds.), *Competitive frontiers: Women managers in a global economy* (pp. 57–78). Cambridge: Blackwell.

Yamaguchi, K. (1991). *Event history analysis.* Newbury Park, CA: Sage.

Yammarino, F.J. (1998). Multivariate aspects of the Variant/WABA approach: A discussion and leadership illustration. *Leadership Quarterly, 9* (2), 203–238.

Yammarino, F.J., & Markham, S.E. (1992). On the application of within and between analysis: Are absence and effect really group-based phenomena? *Journal of Applied Psychology, 77,* 168–176.

Yu, J., & Murphy, K.R. (1993). Modesty bias in self-ratings of performance: A test of cultural relativity hypothesis. *Personnel Psychology, 46*(2), 357–363.

19

Toward a Globalized Conceptualization of Organizational Socializations

TALYA N. BAUER and SULLY TAYLOR

This targeted review points to globalizing trends and forces and the need to expand our notion of organizational socialization to encompass global workforce issues. The purpose of this chapter is to review specific socialization literature that is relevant to a global perspective of organizational socialization, not to review all of the socialization research which exists to date. Much of the socialization theory development and empirical testing has been carried out within US firms and within the US or other Western cultures. This is a potential shortcoming in this area if present theories do not generalize to other countries and/or cultures. Propositions are offered in reference to information seeking and organizational tactics in a global context.

Most observers of the changing nature of business point to globalization as one of the most important factors affecting how business will be conducted in the new millennium, if not *the* most important (Bartlett & Ghoshal, 1998; *The Economist*, 1995; Toyne & Nigh, 1997; Yip, 1995). As the recent spate of cross-border mergers and alliances – Daimler/Chrysler; Renault/Nissan; ATT/British Telecom – clearly show, the pressure of global customers, the need for additional or complementary resources, and the increasing deregulation of markets requires local firms to build global presence (Yip, 1995). Organizations must become key players in all areas of the world in order to remain a key player in a local area. Structurally, these global firms are also leveraging their international presence by devolving global responsibility to those units of the corporation best able to fulfill them, regardless of geographic location (Bartlett & Ghoshal, 1998). A global firm that insists on retaining all critical tasks in one central location when other units can perform the function better is

doomed. This raises the profile of local employees, both managerial and technical.

At the same time, the nature of industries has undergone a radical shift. The basis of the fastest growing industries today is not natural resources, but knowledge (Bartlett & Ghoshal, 1998; Hambrick, Nadler & Tushman, 1998; Hamel, 1999; Nohria & Ghoshal, 1997; Pfeffer, 1998). Thus, firms are also globalizing in order to access the best people worldwide who can produce the knowledge they need to create competitive advantage (Pfeffer, 1998). The attraction and retention of talent worldwide is therefore the key to success in the fastest growing industries today, from software to entertainment.

These globalization forces, as well as the move to knowledge-based industries, result in four pressures on how these firms deal with socialization of newcomers. First, a substantial number of an organization's employees may be in a country which is not their home country. While Nestlé has long dealt with this reality, it is a relatively new one for most US firms. GE, for example, now finds that only

200 of its 23,000 international consumer-finance division employees are US nationals (*The Economist*, September 18, 1999: 25). Thus the approaches to socialization used by these companies need to be reexamined as more and more of their employees are working outside their home country. Second, the criticality of these foreign employees to the functioning of the firm has increased as the firm's strategic assets and decision-making responsibilities have been excentralized; that is, decision-making is now made in the unit and at the level most appropriate, rather than simply centralized or decentralized (Bartlett & Ghoshal, 1998; Taylor, Beechler & Napier, 1996). In Dow Chemical, for example, the heads of four of its 13 business lines are now located outside the US. The importance of the socialization of employees abroad has thus gained greater competitive salience. Third, because so many firms now rely on knowledge as the basis of their competitiveness, their ability to socialize newcomers has become a key part of attracting and retaining this talent. If they do this well, they are likely to become an employer of choice and keep the precious human resources – and the important networks they create with other employees, customers and suppliers – they have worked so hard to recruit.

Yet increasingly, as argued above, these precious human resources may not exist within their home countries, but rather are becoming located about the world, from Zurich to Sydney to Santiago. Finally, globalization has also led to increasing immigration as transportation has become cheaper and borders more permeable. The US workforce is now comprised of 12% immigrants (US Census Bureau, 1998), and in high technology industries in the US, the percentage of technical personnel who are foreign-born is growing. Germany now faces a new reality in which 8.7% of its workforce is of non-German descent (Federal Statistical Office Germany, 1998). Even Japan, long a bastion of monoculturalism, has witnessed increasing immigration, both legal and illegal, of Middle Eastern and Asian people over the last decade. Thus, even in the home country that houses their corporate headquarters and major operations, many global firms are facing much greater cultural and ethnic diversity today than in the past.

The purpose of this chapter is to examine how a global perspective of organizational socialization informs present theory and empirical research. The reality of an increasingly global workplace has prompted theorizing about the implications of organizational socialization internationally (e.g., Bauer, Morrison & Callister, 1998; Chao, 1997; Feldman, 1997; Morrison, Bauer, Callister & Ben-Rechav, 1998). Empirical research, however, has lagged far behind on this topic. While a limited number of studies have been conducted in nonWestern cultures, the vast majority of organizational socialization

research has been limited to predominantly Western cultures such as the United States and Great Britain. The chapter will first briefly define socialization, and then examine why internationalization of socialization is important to the development of sound theories and research in the field. The fourth section examines the influence of culture on management processes such as socialization, and offers a conceptual model of cultural dimensions that will be utilized throughout the chapter. The fifth, and largest, section draws on extant socialization literature to examine how culture may affect theories and results, and offers propositions to guide future research in testing and expanding our current understanding in the field. The final section suggests future lines of inquiry to broaden, strengthen and refine our present understanding of socialization to ensure that it is truly applicable in the multiple cultural and sociopolitical environments in which global firms operate today.

SOCIALIZATION

One purpose of this chapter is to review specific socialization literature that is relevant to a global perspective of organizational socialization, not to review all of the socialization research which exists to date; exhaustive reviews of the literature exist elsewhere (e.g., Bauer et al., 1998; Fisher, 1986; Wanous & Collela, 1989), as do targeted reviews of the literature (e.g., Anderson & Ostroff, 1997; Feldman, 1997). Rather than repeat those reviews here, our goal is to highlight areas of socialization which have the potential to stimulate future research. We hope to do this by targeting gaps in our understanding of the global nature of organizational socialization. We will delineate trends and areas where future research may be fruitful in obtaining a greater understanding of how the study and practice of organizational socialization is informed by the globalization of business.

Before conducting this review, it is first necessary to establish our definition of organizational socialization. Organizational socialization is the process where a new member learns and adapts to the value system, the norms, and the required behavior patterns of an organization, society, or group (Schein, 1968). In other words, it is the process of newcomers becoming 'broken in' and 'learning the ropes' of functioning within the organization once entering it (Fisher, 1986). More specifically,

> Organizational socialization is the process by which an individual comes to appreciate the values, abilities, expected behaviors, and social knowledge essential for assuming an organizational role and for participating as an organizational member. (Louis, 1980: 229–230)

It is seen as a joint process, involving organizations seeking to influence and shape new members, and employees who want to define an acceptable role for themselves within the organization (Fisher, 1986). Organizational socialization occurs whenever employees change roles or cross boundaries within or across organizations (Van Maanen & Schein, 1979). As noted by Bauer et al. (1998) in their review of the literature, it should be especially pronounced when individuals experience new jobs, new organizations, and new cultures. The present review adopts Feldman's (1976) working definition of newcomer socialization. Feldman proposes that not only do newcomers come to learn the culture and values of their new job settings as Van Maanen (1975) proposed, but that newcomers must also learn to adjust to their new work environment and develop work skills.

INTERNATIONALIZING SOCIALIZATION RESEARCH

The pressures on socialization approaches within global firms require that scholars studying this management issue redouble their efforts to examine the theories and empirical results generated thus far. This is particularly necessary because so much of the theory development, as well as empirical testing, has been carried out within US firms and within the USA or other Western cultures. This raises several concerns often voiced by international management scholars concerning the applicability of theories developed in the US to other contexts (Adler & Boyacigiller, 1996; Boyacigiller & Adler, 1991; Early & Mosakowski, 1996). First, are our models fully specified? In particular, have our models captured all relevant constructs, or has the restricted context in which the theories were developed led us to overlook certain constructs? A purely emic (within one culture) approach to theory development (Berry, 1990) often leads to myopia concerning what variables are important, or even what variables exist. For example, Hofstede (1980) in the development of his widely used framework of cultural values used Western subjects, and found four dimensions of culture. However, Asian scholars and others subsequently found that these were not sufficient, and in further work with Asian respondents unearthed a fifth dimension of culture distinct from the original four dimensions (Hofstede & Bond, 1988). Can we be sure that the theories concerning socialization developed in the West, and the organizational practices derived from them, are indeed complete in capturing all relevant aspects of the phenomena?

Second, are our interpretations of the constructs correct in other cultures (Earley & Mosakowski, 1996; Teune, 1990)? The idea of functional equivalents needs to be examined closely lest we try to measure constructs in the same way across cultures, only to find that we have mis-specified. As Osland and Osland (1999) argue, to study leadership in West Africa a researcher should study tribal chiefs rather than business people, since business is regarded as a less important activity and is often headed by foreigners anyway. In the case of socialization, this could result in a need to look at the functional equivalents of such constructs as sources of information.

Finally, are the relationships between constructs that we have specified robust across societies? Are the causal mechanisms the same, the direction of influence the same, the strength of the relationships the same (Earley & Mosakowski, 1996)? For example, research on social loafing has shown that the phenomenon is not observed in collectivist cultures (e.g., mainland China) while it is in individualist cultures (Gabrenya, Latane & Wang, 1983, 1985; Earley, 1989, 1993). In addition, are we examining all of the relevant levels of analysis for socialization in different societies (Osborn, Hagedoorn & Baugh, 1999)? While interdisciplinary studies can also be very valuable in increasing our awareness of alternative possibilities, testing our theories of management internationally also forces us to reconsider important theoretical linkages that have been supported only by research in a narrow range of cultural contexts.

All of these concerns point to the need for socialization scholars to question whether the socialization content and processes identified by research carried out almost exclusively within an Anglo-Saxon context will be applicable in other cultural contexts. The organizations within which socialization has been studied have been largely Western as well, ignoring, for example, the ways in which socialization occurs in Chinese state-owned firms, overseas Chinese companies, and African companies. It is quite likely that very fundamental re-formations of the construct of socialization will have to be undertaken as a result of research in other cultural and organizational settings, and this will lead to better specified models that have a more legitimate claim to being a universal theory of socialization, rather than an 'emic' construct based on Western cultural values and organizations.

CULTURE AND MANAGEMENT RESEARCH

In order to examine how theories of socialization, and hence practices derived from them, may be influenced by differences in cultural contexts, we must first establish a basis for discussing or categorizing the cultural differences both researchers and international firms may encounter as they operate abroad. Our assumption is that socialization goals and processes must be acceptable to the newcomers involved in order to be effective, and that one of the key influences on acceptability is the culture in which the newcomer was raised. Culture not only influences individual preferences, but also perception. While we acknowledge that the economic-political context may be as important as culture (Child & Markoczy, 1993), for the purposes of this chapter we will mostly focus on the role culture may play in determining the effectiveness of socialization approaches.

As Triandis (1998) has noted:

Cultures include unstated assumptions about the way the world is. Members of cultures believe that their ways of thinking are obviously correct, and need not be discussed.... The most interesting aspect of culture is that basic assumptions are not questioned. They influence thinking, emotions, and actions without people noticing that they do. (p. 9)

Values are an obvious outgrowth of these basic assumptions, and societies can be studied based on values. Values,

(1) are concepts or beliefs, (2) pertain to desirable end states or behaviors, (3) transcend specific situations, (4) guide selection or evaluation of behavior and events, and (5) are ordered by relative importance. Values, understood this way, differ from attitudes primarily in their generality or abstractness (feature 3) and in their hierarchical ordering by importance (feature 5). (Schwartz, 1992: 4)

Newcomer socialization is likely to be highly influenced by culture because it involves 'desirable end states' (goals) and 'selection or evaluation of behavior and events' (processes or tactics).

Many frameworks for comparing the values held by one society with another have been proposed (Hofstede, 1980; Kluckhohn & Strodtbeck, 1961; Parsons & Shils, 1951; Trompenaars & Hampden-Turner, 1998; Schwartz, 1992). Osland and Osland (1999) point out that there is a core of about 22 dimensions which most of these frameworks focus on, but that there is no single best framework for discussing etic (between cultures) differences. Moreover, as Osland and Bird (2000) point out, we must be careful in how we use these frameworks, as even within one culture a value (e.g., collectivism) can be salient in one situation (e.g., work) but 'trumped' by another value in another situation (e.g., family). Boyacigiller, Kleinber, Phillips and Sackmann (1996) have also raised concerns about the utilization of cultural frameworks given the wide number of subcultures to which any one individual belongs. We recognize the importance of these concerns about using cultural frameworks, and encourage researchers in newcomer socialization to address these issues in the studies carried out to test theories of socialization internationally. Nevertheless, we will use a cultural framework to

examine how newcomer socialization may in fact be impacted by the globalization of business.

We draw on Schwartz's framework for comparing cultures as it is exceptionally well-grounded in theory and empirical research collected from individuals in 20 countries (see Schwartz, 1992, for a full description; Earley & Mosakowski, 1996; Schwartz & Bilsky, 1987), and it encompasses many of the cultural dimensions of other frameworks. In his framework, Schwartz finds there are two major bipolar value dimensions (Figure 19.1).

The first basic dimension places a higher-order type combining stimulation and self-direction values in opposition to one combining security, conformity and tradition values. We call this dimension openness to change vs. conservation. It arrays values in terms of the extent to which they motivate people to follow their own intellectual and emotional interests in unpredictable and uncertain directions vs. preserving the status quo and the certainty it provides in relationships with close others, institutions, and traditions.

The second basic dimension combines power, achievement, and hedonism values in opposition to one combining universalism and benevolence values (including a spiritual life). We call this dimension self-enhancement vs. self-transcendence. It arrays values in terms of the extent to which they motivate people to enhance their own personal interests (even at the expense of others), vs. the extent to which they motivate people to transcend selfish concerns and promote the welfare of others, close and distant, and of nature (Schwartz, 1992: 43–44). These two broad, bipolar dimensions of culture can be identified with 10 motivational value types: universalism, benevolence, achievement, power, self-direction, stimulation, hedonism, security, conformity, and tradition (Schwartz, 1992; Schwartz & Bilsky, 1987). The full model is presented in Figure 19.1. These value types will be more fully described as we develop our propositions below.

Before turning to our propositions, however, a dimension of culture not fully covered by Schwartz's model but of importance to a discussion of socialization research is the concept of *time*. Time has been proposed by a variety of scholars as a key differentiator between cultures. How individuals view time is partially dependent on whether they belong to a 'being' or a 'doing' culture (Kluckhohn & Strodtbeck, 1961). Time perceptions also influence how tasks are performed: monochronically (one at a time) or polychronically (several at a time) (Hall & Hall, 1990). Finally, Hofstede and his colleagues describe different orientations to performance and goals, and named this 'long-term versus short-term orientation or Confucian Dynamism' (Hofstede & Bond, 1988). It is this long-term–short-term way of differentiating time that we will argue is particularly important in the study of newcomer socialization across countries.

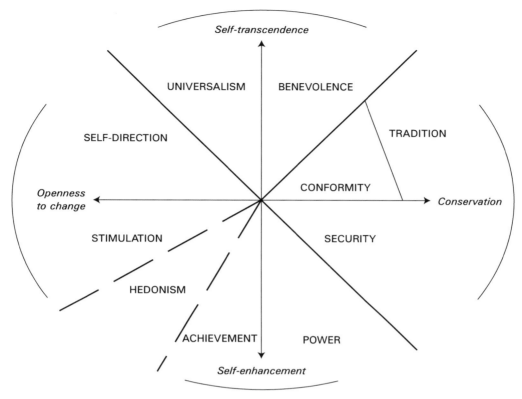

Figure 19.1   *Theoretical model of relations among motivational types of values, higher order value types, and bipolar value dimensions. (Source: This figure originally appeared in Schwartz, S.H. [1992]. Universals in the content and structure of values: Theoretical advances and empirical tests in 20 countries.* Advances in Experimental Social Psychology, 25, *p. 45. Reprinted by permission from Academic Press, Inc.)*

Newcomer Socialization Propositions

We will now examine how the goals, tactics, and information seeking of newcomer socialization may differ significantly across cultures. We will use this to offer propositions that may be drawn on to guide future research in this area. These propositions are probably most useful as beginning orientations to be used in qualitative research to help build grounded theory in this area (Glaser & Strauss, 1967). A summary of the propositions is given in Table 19.1.

Goals

The ultimate goals or outcomes of socialization have not been widely studied, but Fisher (1986) described socialization as a process involving learning and change. The five types of learning and change delineated in her review are (1) preliminary learning; (2) learning to adapt to the organization; (3) learning organizational values, goals, culture; (4) learning work group values, norms, and friendships; (5) learning how to do the job, needed skills and knowledge; and (6) personal change relating to identity, self-image, and motive structure.

A scale by Chao, O'Leary-Kelly, Wolf, Klein and Gardner (1994) is one of the first works to identify and examine different content areas (goals of socialization) that may be learned during organizational socialization (see Taormina, 1994 for another recent socialization scale which focuses on the process of socialization). Building upon previous socialization literature, Chao et al. (1994) proposed and empirically supported six socialization dimensions: performance proficiency, politics, language, people, organizational goals/values, and history. Performance proficiency refers to the degree to which an individual has mastered the required knowledge, skills and abilities of his or her job. The politics dimension refers to the individual's success in gaining information regarding formal and informal work relationships and power structures within the organization. Language refers to the individual's knowledge of the

Table 19.1   *Summary of research propositions*

Proposition 1   In societies in which business organizations are highly embedded in state structures, newcomer socialization will include a goal of learning about the external power structures surrounding the firm.

Proposition 2   In societies in which the conservation value orientation is predominant, organizations will emphasize the company's history as a socialization goal, and newcomers will expect such an emphasis.

Proposition 3   In long-term oriented societies, the goals of newcomer socialization will differ in the short term from the goals of socialization in short-term societies.

Proposition 4   In societies high on conservation, there will be a propensity by both organizations and newcomers to favor highly institutionalized, serial tactics of socialization.

Proposition 5   In societies that are high on self-direction, socialization processes will be comprehensive, broad and in-depth, and reflective of expectations of hard work.

Proposition 6   In societies high on conservation, there will be a weak or nonexistent negative relationship between institutionalized tactics of socialization and role innovation.

Proposition 7   In societies high on self-transcendence, newcomer socialization will favor both collective and divestiture tactics.

Proposition 8   In high self-transcendent, benevolent societies there will be a higher use of indirect means of socialization by newcomers.

Proposition 9   In societies high on self-transcendence and benevolence, newcomer socialization will utilize unstructured tactics.

Proposition 10   In societies high on conservation, organizations will discourage, and newcomers will not exhibit, high levels of self-directed information seeking that is not organizationally sanctioned.

Proposition 11   In societies where tacit knowledge of employees is recognized and valued, there will be a higher emphasis on socialization approaches appropriate to its transmission to newcomers.

profession's technical language as well as acronyms, slang, and jargon unique to the organization. The dimension of people involves the degree to which an individual has established successful and satisfying work relationships with organizational members. Organizational goals and values are the degree to which individuals understand the goals of their work groups and organization. Finally, history refers to the degree to which individuals know an organization's traditions, customs, myths and rituals (or a firm's organizational culture) (for a review of the culture literature see Ashkenasy and Jackson's chapter in Volume 2 of this Handbook). Taken together, these six dimensions are one conceptualization of socialization. We will use this useful conceptualization as a general framework for the potential 'goals' of socialization which organizations and individuals may have in different organizations and in different countries.

As noted by Chao et al. (1994), the goals of newcomer socialization found for their sample are representative of socialization for many individuals, and the emphasis on different goals can be predicted to vary across cultural contexts. For example, the goals are exclusively focused on internal organizational objectives which may be appropriate domestically within a given country. Yet globally, drawing on Child and Markoczy (1993), the economic-political milieu in which a firm operates may make goals external to the organization as important to newcomer socialization as internal ones. For example, in the People's Republic of China the interweaving of the state with the business enterprise is vast, and hence a newcomer is as likely to need to understand the political power structures in which the organization

exists as much as the internal political structure of organization members (Chen, 1995; van Kemenade, 1997). All organizations in China have a Communist Party representative, for example, whose own status within the party and local government agencies is key to how the firm functions.

This external orientation may be as important to 'learning the ropes' for a newcomer in an organization in China as is learning all the internal goals, yet it receives little or no attention from Western theorists. It may be that the relative independence of business organizations from state structures in the US in particular, and the West generally, has led to a bias toward specifying goals that are mostly internal to the organization. We should also note that, in the West, industry may affect the extent to which external constituencies are important to the socialization of newcomers. In the oil industry, for example, getting to know government agencies and politicians may be an exceedingly important political goal for some newcomers. However, as a generality, US business operates relatively independently of direct participation by government agents in day-to-day operations. This leads us to our first proposition:

- *Proposition 1*   In societies in which business organizations are highly embedded in state structures, newcomer socialization will include a goal of learning about the external power structures surrounding the firm.

In addition to adding to the goals that may be important in newcomer socialization, research done internationally is likely to find that the salience of different goals differs by cultural context. For example, organizations in societies that put a great deal of weight on the conservation end of the value dimension (Schwartz, 1992) will honor tradition, and expect organization members to be embued with the organization's history, traditions and customs. Thus the history goal of socialization (Chao et al., 1994) in such cultures will receive greater weight in societies at the conservation end of the value dimension. Therefore salience of newcomer goals that may be affected by culture can be offered:

• *Proposition 2* In societies in which the conservation value orientation is predominant, organizations will emphasize the company's history as a socialization goal, and newcomers will expect such an emphasis.

An important aspect of culture that we believe will be important in testing the universality of our theories and findings on organizational socialization is the concept of time. In particular, the orientation of a society to the short-term rather than the long-term (Hofstede & Bond, 1988) can be seen as influencing the process of newcomer socialization. Whereas in most studies conducted in the West socialization outcomes are measured at one, three and six months (e.g., Bauer et al., 1998), socialization in other societies is seen as a process that takes a much longer time. For example, Rohlen (1988) describes the socialization of new management recruits in a Japanese bank as a process by which the recruits learn to become members of a family. His description is illuminating:

> Large Japanese companies are distinctly different from the contract-based, machine-like work organization familiar to Westerners. Where we maintain order by separating the employee's personal life from his business life, the Japanese incorporate the two into one grand system. In this light, the rigorous training programs for new employees make sense. By participating in the programs, recruits learn the values of the 'family' they are about to enter, values that in many ways conflict with those found in other parts of Japanese society. (Rohlen, 1988: 134)

An emphasis on the long-term in business in general, and the employment relationship in particular in certain cultures, is likely to influence companies in these societies to manage socialization of newcomers differently in at least two ways. First, certain goals may not even be considered in the first year or so of employment of an individual. As Pucik (1984, 1989) has demonstrated, evaluations of job performance for most management personnel in Japanese companies are carried out frequently but with little repercussion for the first 10 years of the employee's employment. The company views these years as an apprenticeship period during which the employee is gaining the job skills that he or she will use over the course of the next 25 years or so in performing job tasks important to the company. However, the

person's '*ningen kankei*' (relationships with people) are considered very important from the first day of employment, and the purpose of extensive training programs with cohorts who joined the company the same year (many Japanese companies traditionally hire new management employees only once a year) is to build the social network among the group, imbue them with the company's values and history, and develop their 'people' skills in general. As can be seen from this one example, the goals of socialization at the time demarcations used in the West are likely to differ across cultures, and in addition, different, longer time demarcations altogether may need to be devised for some societies. This leads to a final proposition:

• *Proposition 3* In long-term oriented societies, the goals of newcomer socialization will differ in the short-term from the goals of socialization in short-term societies.

Two general streams of literature have dominated organizational socialization research over the past 20 years. We will review work on organizational socialization tactics as defined by Van Maanen and Schein (1979) to examine what organizations do to help in the socialization of new organizational members. In addition, we will review work that addresses newcomer proactivity during socialization (especially information seeking). These two perspectives characterize the 'Interactionist Perspective' referred to by Reichers (1987) and others. The interactionist perspective refers to the interplay between newcomers and insiders during organizational entry and beyond. It has been hypothesized (e.g., Reichers, 1987), and initial work (e.g., Bauer & Green, 1998) supports the view, that the behaviors of insiders and newcomers are both important to varying degrees at different points in the adjustment process. Organizational insiders implement socialization tactics and often serve as the sources of information.

Tactics

Van Maanen and Schein's (1979) organizational socialization tactics have been heavily studied. Jones (1986) designed separate scales for each of the six tactics outlined by Van Maanen and Schein, and his research found that the scales were highly correlated with one another. Based on these initial results, he proposed that the six tactics be arranged on a single continuum, where at one end lay highly institutionalized approaches (e.g., sequential, formal, clear) and at the other end lay highly individualized approaches (e.g., random, informal, ambiguous). This continuum has been supported by subsequent research (e.g., Allen & Meyer, 1990; Ashforth & Saks, 1996; Baker & Feldman, 1990; Jones, 1986; Laker & Steffy, 1995). In general research on Van Maanen and Schein's (1979) ideas that different tactics result in different socialization outcomes have also been supported. Researchers have found that tactics reflecting an individualized approach are more likely to produce an innovative orientation toward one's role, and that tactics reflecting an institutionalized approach tend to result in custodial orientations (Ashforth & Saks, 1996; Baker & Feldman, 1990; Jones, 1986; King & Sethi, 1992; Mignerey, Rubin & Gorden, 1995; West, Nicholson & Rees, 1987).

Bauer et al. (1998) report that, in addition to examining the effects of organizational tactics on newcomer role orientation, several Western-based studies have found positive relationships between institutionalized tactics and attitudinal outcomes such as organizational commitment (Allen & Meyer, 1990; Ashforth & Saks, 1996; Jones, 1986; King & Sethi, 1992), job satisfaction (Ashforth & Saks, 1996; Baker & Feldman, 1990; Jones, 1986; Zahrly & Tosi, 1989), intentions to remain (Ashforth & Saks, 1996; Jones, 1986), and role clarity (Jones, 1986; King & Sethi, 1992). In addition, negative relationships with self-efficacy (Jones, 1986) and work/family conflict (Zahrly & Tosi, 1989) have been found.

Bauer et al. (1998) posit that it appears there may be a trade-off between innovation and commitment and that organizations may need to sacrifice one for the other. They cite examples of both Jones (1986) and Allen and Meyer (1990) who found that institutionalized tactics were positively related to newcomer commitment yet negatively related to role innovation. However, Allen and Meyer (1990) did not find these relationships after new employees were on the job past one year. Major and Kozlowski (1997) studied students in internships and found that those low in self-efficacy maintained the status quo while those high on self-efficacy were less dependent upon insiders for information and were therefore predicted to be more innovative. These findings suggest that institutionalized tactics may reduce role innovation initially, but that over time this effect dissipates and/or that individual and situational characteristics may augment or limit innovation. This interpretation, which is somewhat speculative, warrants additional research across cultures.

Another important area in this regard is tactic 'preferences'. It may be that newcomers prefer institutionalized socialization tactics because these tactics relieve some of the performance pressure and ambiguity associated with socialization. Typically, when newcomers enter an organization as part of a cohort and receive formal, sequential training, they receive structured information that facilitates sense-making (Jones, 1986). Newcomers are likely to prefer this situation over one that provides less structured information. However, this preference for institutionalized tactics may not last beyond the early period of newcomer adjustment (as indicated by the findings of Allen & Meyer, 1990). The implications of newcomers' preferences for different types of socialization tactics is an issue that deserves future research attention. Just as newcomers' attitudes have been shown to be influenced by the degree of 'fit' between their values and the values of the organization (Chatman, 1991), their attitudes may also be affected by the similarity between their preferences with respect to various socialization tactics and the tactics actually adopted by their organization.

The tactics of organizational socialization are also likely to be affected by the culture in which they are deployed. The preference for institutionalized tactics over highly individualized approaches, for example, will be influenced by the degree to which the society falls toward the conservation rather than the openness to change end of the value spectrum (Schwartz, 1992). Societies high on openness to change, for example, are more likely to emphasize self-direction and stimulation. Consequently, socialization tactics that favor individualized approaches, and are random, informal and ambiguous, are more likely to be both tolerated and desired by newcomers. In high conservation societies, there is an emphasis on tradition, conformity and security, which would make institutionalized socialization tactics more acceptable. As mentioned previously, institutionalized tactics facilitate sense-making by making information structured (Jones, 1986). In addition, we can predict that organizations in societies high on conservation will be more likely to adopt serial rather than disjunctive socialization, where experienced members of the organization serve as role models for newcomers (Van Maanen & Schein, 1979). Because serial socialization emphasizes stability and identification with insiders, it is consistent with the conservation emphasis on conformity and group identity. (Note that serial socialization is also probably highly influenced by the degree of self-transcendence of the society, discussed below). This leads to a fourth proposition concerning socialization:

- *Proposition 4* In societies high on conservation, there will be a propensity by both organizations and newcomers to favor highly institutionalized, serial tactics of socialization.

Individuals in cultures in which activity is primarily directed toward self-directional goals, which are related to ambition, success, and influence (Schwartz, 1992) are likely to work hard, be high achievers, and maximize their time at work. (This is closely related to Kluckhohn and Strodtbeck's, 1961, concept of 'doing' versus 'being' cultures.) Individuals whose activity is primarily directed toward hedonism, which is defined as '...pleasure or sensuous gratification for oneself (pleasure, enjoying life)' (Schwartz, 1992: 8), are likely to work only as much as needed to be able to live (Adler, 1997). We expect that a company functioning in a 'doing' mode will define successful socialization processes as comprehensive, broad and in-depth, and utilizing criteria and performance measures reflecting expectations of hard work. It is also possible that a company functioning in a hedonistic culture may not even define successful socialization. This leads to a further proposition:

- *Proposition 5* In societies that are high on self-direction, socialization processes will be comprehensive, broad and in-depth, and reflective of expectations of hard work.

The robustness of the findings of studies concerning socialization tactics and outcomes such as organization commitment and job satisfaction, described previously, may be challenged by international studies of these relationships. For example, in societies such as Japan that are high on conservation (Doi, 1973; Nakane, 1970; Rohlen, 1978), individual role innovation is probably less prized than role conformity in work settings. Hence, the negative relationship between institutionalized tactics and role innovation found by both Jones (1986) and Allen and Meyer (1990) may be much weaker than in their studies, or even nonexistent. Role innovation is simply not seen as a positive organizational behavior in such societies, and consequently the socialization tactic used has little effect on whether individual role innovation occurs or not. The same sort of reexamination of relationships must occur for the other outcomes, since such things as local labor market norms of high mobility (Singapore) (Putti & Chong, 1985), or extremely low mobility (e.g., China) (Chen, 1995) may affect such things as organizational commitment. Because of the plethora of such cultural effects, only one example proposition will be offered rather than an exhaustive list:

- *Proposition 6* In societies high on conservation, there will be a weak or nonexistent negative relationship between institutionalized tactics of socialization and role innovation.

There are likely to be systematic differences in socialization tactics between organizations in highly self-transcendent cultures and those in highly self-enhancement oriented cultures. These two dimensions are related to the concepts of individualism and collectivism often used by other culture theorists (Hofstede, 1980; Kluckhorn, & Strodtbeck, 1961; Triandis, 1998). We can expect that relative to organizations within self-enhancement cultures, which will tend to be individualistic, those within self-transcendent cultures will be more likely to adopt collective forms of socialization, where newcomers are put through a common set of experiences as a group (Van Maanen & Schein, 1979). We also predict that organizations within collectivist cultures will be more likely to utilize the divestiture tactic, whereby the organization 'seeks to deny and strip away personal characteristics of the recruit' (Van Maanen & Schein, 1979: 250).

This tactic is consistent with the downplaying of individual identity within collectivist cultures and is certainly supported by research on organizational socialization in highly collectivist societies such as Japan (Rohlen, 1978). As mentioned previously, serial tactics of socialization are more likely to be used in self-transcendent societies that are also high on conservation, as the emphasis on collectivism leads to high identification with insiders.

- *Proposition 7* In cultures high on self-transcendence, newcomer socialization will favor both collective and divestiture tactics.

The tactics newcomers use to obtain information important to their socialization may also be influenced by the culture in which they live. Settoon and Adkins (1997) found that seeking information from family and friends predicted socialization outcomes early on but not later, and Morrison (1993a, 1995) found a predilection by newcomers to use direct tactics rather than indirect tactics to obtain technical information. However, these results must be reexamined in light of other cultures. For example, in societies such as Mexico or some other Latin American countries, there is a heavy reliance on family connections both to obtain a position in a firm and to make contact with a potential employer (Kras, 1994; Osland, De Franco & Osland, 1999). 'Nepotism is an accepted practice in many organizations, partly because employers may feel members of the same family are a safer bet (an issue of trust) or because people are somewhat obligated to find jobs for relatives' (Osland, De Franco & Osland, 1999: 225). These societies tend to be toward the self-transcendence end of the value dimension, and toward the benevolence aspect of self-transcendence. Self-transcendence is an overall prosocial value type, and benevolence '...focuses on concern for the welfare of close others in everyday interaction' (Schwartz, 1992: 11), whereas the universalism aspect of self-transcendence favors '...understanding, appreciation, tolerance, and protection for the welfare of all people and for nature' (Schwartz, 1992: 12). The concern for close others, particularly family, in making decisions about what organization to enter, as well as the reliance on these family members for information, contacts, and advice on organizational adjustment, is much greater in societies emphasizing the self-transcendence and benevolence end of the scale. Moreover, it is likely that the trust in the information of close others (particularly other family members) may be much higher than trust in the information of non-connected others. Fukuyama (1996), in his book on the relationship between trust and social capital, has pointed out that the ability to trust 'strangers' who are not part of one's family is much lower in societies where there is less social capital. Taken together, this indicates that newcomers may both rely more heavily as well as longer on family and close friends for information about their job in high self-transcendent and benevolent societies than in self-enhancement, achievement-oriented societies. This leads to a further proposition:

- *Proposition 8* In high self-transcendent, benevolent societies there will be a higher use of indirect means of socialization by newcomers.

Socialization tactics will also be influenced by the degree to which a society is self-transcendent and benevolent in another way. In benevolent societies, there will be a tendency towards particularism, in which rules are important yet adaptable to circumstances (Hofstede & Bond, 1988; Trompenaars & Hampden-Turner, 1998). Relationships with friends or family members will affect one's obedience to laws. The social contract is not detailed, and the strength of the relationship maintains commitment. In universalistic societies (Schwartz, 1992; Trompenaars & Hampden-Turner, 1998), on the other hand, laws are for everyone at all times. Since in benevolent or particularist societies the psychological contract is intentionally unstructured, we predict that organizations in these societies will adopt unstructured tactics that are flexible, and reduce the use of written and formal components of the social-psychological contract. This leads us to the following proposition:

- *Proposition 9* In societies high on self-transcendence and benevolence, newcomer socialization will utilize unstructured tactics.

Information Seeking

Individuals entering new organizations engage in what has been termed 'sense-making' (Louis, 1980; Weick, 1995) to understand the new work and social roles they must fulfill to become fully functioning members of their new work group and/or organization. Organizational socialization researchers have predominantly studied information seeking as the primary form of newcomer proactivity and sensemaking. Research has shown that where information comes from, how much is gathered, and how frequently it is sought all matter to organizational outcomes such as job satisfaction, commitment, intentions to remain, and/or performance issues (e.g., Morrison, 1993a, 1993b; Ostroff & Kozlowski, 1992). Researchers have also found that information seeking patterns are fairly similar over time (e.g., Callister, Kramer & Turban, 1999; Morrison, 1993a, 1993b; Ostroff & Kozlowski, 1992). On the other hand, several studies have found that information seeking was unrelated to many of these same outcomes when other constructs were included as predictors (e.g., Ashford & Black, 1996; Bauer & Green, 1998; Kramer, 1995; Mignerey et al., 1995).

Studies in the United States do demonstrate predictable patterns in the relative frequency with which newcomers seek various types of information. Researchers have found that newcomers seek technical and referent information more than social and normative information. Morrison (1993a) also found that as time went on newcomers tended to seek less technical, normative, and social information, while they sought more referent and feedback information.

Newcomers also tend to vary their use of information seeking tactics and sources depending on information type. For example, Morrison (1993a, 1995) found that newcomers use direct tactics, such as inquiry, more than indirect tactics, such as monitoring, to obtain technical information, but that indirect tactics were used more than direct tactics to obtain other types of information that were less urgent and more sensitive. In addition, newcomers have been found to rely upon supervisors more than peers to obtain technical, referent and feedback information, and peers more than supervisors to obtain social information (Morrison, 1993a). Settoon and Adkins (1997) found that seeking information from family and friends predicted socialization outcomes early on; but that later, information sought from supervisors and coworkers was all that mattered. Researchers have also shown that newcomers tend to obtain more information through active means than through passive means (Comer, 1991; Morrison, 1995), highlighting the potential importance of proactive information seeking. All of this research was conducted in the United States.

Brett, Feldman and Weingart (1990) found that newcomers were more likely to seek feedback at six months after joining their new organizations to the extent that they had felt well adjusted at three months, whereas transferees were more likely to seek feedback at six months after their transfers to the extent that they had felt poorly adjusted at three months. The authors proposed that new hires seem to need to feel confident and accepted before they will seek feedback, whereas individuals who are changing jobs seek feedback only when they feel that they are *not* adjusting well.

Researchers have also begun to investigate forms of proactive behavior other than information seeking. Ashford and Black (1996), for example, studied a range of such behaviors along with information seeking. They conceptualized socialization as a process whereby newcomers temporarily lose feelings of control, and then attempt to regain control by being proactive. In support of this argument, they found that newcomers' desire for control was related not only to information seeking, but also to socializing, networking, negotiating job changes, and positive framing. Overall, the results of this study provided limited support for the authors' control-seeking perspective, suggesting that desire for control may be one factor motivating newcomers to be proactive, but not the primary factor.

Saks and Ashforth (1996) also investigated a range of proactive behaviors, but in contrast to

Ashford and Black (1996) they adopted a behavioral self-management framework. The behaviors that they investigated included self-observation, self-goal setting, self-reward, self-punishment, and rehearsal. Although the results from that study were mixed, they provide at least some support for the idea that self-management behaviors reduce anxiety during the first month of employment and relate to indicators of effective socialization at six months. Additional studies on the impact of self-management behaviors are clearly needed.

The main approach to the study of information seeking has been to ask newcomers how frequently they seek information from a variety of sources such as coworkers, managers, manuals, and observation (e.g., Bauer & Green, 1998; Morrison, 1993a, 1993b). Typically these studies have been longitudinal, and researchers have assessed changes in information seeking across time (typically one, three, and six months post-entry).

Information seeking is an area of newcomer socialization which has received increasing attention. It is based on the premise that newcomers in organizations worldwide will exhibit proactivity in their socialization process, as well as an equal desire for sense-making. As cited earlier, Comer (1991) and Morrison (1995) both found that newcomers tend to obtain more information through active means than through passive means. Moreover, newcomers will seek different types of information at different stages of the socialization process to gain different types of information (Morrison, 1993a, 1995). Yet the premise that newcomers will exhibit proactivity at all is based on a value on openness to change and self-enhancement (Schwartz, 1992). Moreover, it is based on the premise that individuals feel they have control over their environment, an attitude which studies in anthropology have shown to vary a great deal across cultures (Kluckhohn & Strodtbeck, 1961). Consequently, are the results of many of the studies on information seeking by newcomers only applicable within societies that are high on openness to change and self-enhancement? The idea of the newcomer as an active participant in his or her socialization may be, in fact, an anathema in some societies that favor conformity very highly, such as Korea or Japan. Indeed, it is possible that in some organizations, regardless of cultural setting, seeking information can be dangerous to your health, such as the former KGB, the FBI, or Iraqi President Hussein's government! In short, being proactive during socialization is not necessarily a positive action that will enhance the integration and acceptance of the individual.

What is most likely, however, is that the areas in which proactivity is encouraged by the organization may be more highly constrained in Eastern countries than in the West. In Asia, seeking out information from unknown others higher in the organizational hierarchy, for example, may be seen as a serious breach of the norms, and penalized. In the West, such behavior may be seen as taking initiative, and applauded. In addition, withholding of information from others may be influenced by culture. In Japan, for example, the emphasis on conservation has led to a system of lifetime employment (now waning) which enabled organizational members to seek and receive high degrees of technical information from job incumbents because newcomers were not seen as threatening to jobholders (Koike, 1978, 1987). This leads us to a further example proposition:

- *Proposition 10* In societies high on conservation, organizations will discourage, and newcomers will not exhibit, high levels of self-directed information seeking that is not organizationally sanctioned.

The kind of information newcomers seek as well as the tactics they use to obtain information is likely to be highly influenced by their cultural background. The kind of knowledge sought has been divided into technical and referent information vs. social and normative information. Yet research from other societies suggests that this division may not capture all the types of knowledge important to newcomers, particularly those who are in non-Western countries. As Nonaka and Takeuchi (1995) describe in their book *The Knowledge Creating Firm*, in Japan there is a much greater recognition of the value of tacit knowledge over explicit knowledge (Polyani, 1958, 1966). Tacit knowledge exists in a nonverbalized form among organization members and within workgroups, and has been described as 'personal, context-specific, and therefore hard to formalize and communicate. Explicit or "codified" knowledge, on the other hand, refers to knowledge that is transmittable in formal, systematic language' (Nonaka & Takeuchi, 1995: 59).

Work in the field of organizational learning has found that the tacit knowledge existing in 'communities of practice' can be of great value, but is best communicated through stories told by 'knowers' (Brown & Duguid, 1991). Nonaka and Takeuchi (1995) argue that in Japan, and to some degree in other Asian cultures, there is a greater recognition of the value of this tacit knowledge and of the need to find effective means of sharing it among organizational members. Research in international joint ventures supports this view. Asian joint venture partners seek more tacit knowledge relative to Western partners (Inkpen, 1998; Lyles & Salk, 1996; Si & Bruton, 1999). This indicates that our theories of socialization may not be fully specified in terms of the constructs concerning the kind of knowledge sought or needed by newcomers, or that existing categories (e.g., technical knowledge) need to be further refined to reflect this difference in tacit vs. explicit knowledge seeking by newcomers.

- *Proposition 11* In societies where tacit knowledge of employees is recognized and valued, there will be a higher emphasis on socialization approaches appropriate to its transmission to newcomers.

This chapter has argued that newcomer socialization needs to be examined in other cultural contexts than the US. This is important because business itself is globalizing and managing more and more employees in other societies, and because good management science demands that we test the universality of our theories and empirical results. We have discussed how we believe major theories and findings in the present organizational socialization literature may be affected by differences in cultural values across societies. While we have not analyzed at equal length the effect of the economic and political structures on socialization, these too may be found to have profound influence on both the variables and relationships specified by present theories. As a growing number of scholars test propositions such as those offered in this chapter (such as Taormina & Bauer, 2000), the field in general will be enriched.

FUTURE RESEARCH

There are areas we have not addressed in this chapter that also deserve attention from future researchers. The socialization of expatriates, discussed by Sinangil and Avallone in Chapter 17, Volume 2 of this Handbook, is a particular case of socialization that is growing in importance as firms become more globalized, and is of interest to socialization (e.g., Black, 1992). In addition, we need to address the phenomenon of repeat expatriates – is socialization the same in the second assignment as in the first? – as well as the phenomenon of inpatriates, managers sent to headquarters from foreign affiliates. An even larger group, 'global travelers', also needs to be studied. These are employees hired and socialized into a firm, who slowly but increasingly find that their jobs become internationalized, with considerable foreign travel and interaction with fellow employees in other countries. This in essence represents a new job, yet little attention has been paid to the socialization of these employees who are crossing geographic boundaries to carry out tasks with fellow employees in other countries. Differences in socialization approaches between different parts of the firm may assume greater importance as the number of 'global travelers' increases. Finally, the increasing cultural and ethnic diversity faced by companies in their home countries, discussed in the introduction to this chapter will lead to a greater need to study how approaches to socialization used primarily for a culturally homogeneous group of newcomers must be modified to address the variety of goals and tactics a heterogeneous group brings to the process. The findings from testing propositions such as those given in this chapter will be helpful to all these avenues of research in the years to come.

We would like to finish with a suggestion that researchers draw on both qualitative and quantitative methods to examine organizational socialization in other cultural contexts. A vast majority of socialization research in recent years has been based on survey research. There are two problems with a reliance on such approaches in international research. First, as Harpaz (1996) shows, utilizing survey research across cultures must address questions such as functional equivalency, metric equivalency, translation, sampling in countries with multiple cultural groups (e.g., Switzerland), and the cultural acceptability of different measurement instruments. A particularly effective way of addressing these challenges is to use a decentralized-collective research method which draws researchers from different nations and cultures to jointly participate in all aspects of a study from the formulation, design, development, implementation, to the data analysis of a given project (Drenth & Wilpert, 1980; Harpaz, 1996).

The second problem with using survey research was discussed earlier in this chapter, namely the increased likelihood of missing variables and relationships not specified in previous theories and research conducted in the West. For this reason it is particularly important for organizational socialization researchers to utilize inductive methods of research to capture the phenomenon as it is manifested in other cultures, rather than beginning with preconceived notions based on existing theory (Wright, 1996). Again, working with a multicultural team of researchers is likely to aid this process by providing other viewpoints on methodological approaches, interpretations of observations, and generation of hypotheses.

ACKNOWLEDGMENT

We would like to thank Donald Truxillo for his helpful comments on an earlier version of this chapter.

REFERENCES

Adler, N.J. (1997). *International dimensions of organizational behavior* (3rd ed.). Boston, MA: PWS/Kent.

Adler, N.J., & Boyacigiller, N. (1996). Global management in the 21st century. In B. Punnet & O. Shenkar (Eds.), *Handbook for international management research* (pp. 537–558). Cambridge, MA: Blackwell.

Allen, N.J., & Meyer, J.P. (1990). Organizational socialization tactics: A longitudinal analysis of links to newcomers' commitment and role orientation. *Academy of Management Journal, 33*, 847–858.

Anderson, N., & Ostroff, C. (1997). Selection as socialization. In N. Anderson & P. Herriot (Eds.), *International handbook of selection and assessment* (pp. 413–440). New York: John Wiley & Sons.

Ashford, S.J., & Black, J.S. (1996). Proactivity during organizational entry: A role of desire for control. *Journal of Applied Psychology, 81*, 199–214.

Ashforth, B.E., & Saks, A.M. (1996). 'Socialization tactics: Longitudinal effects on newcomer adjustment. *Academy of Management Journal, 39*, 149–178.

Baker, H.E., III, & Feldman, D.C. (1990). Strategies of organizational socialization and their impact on newcomer adjustment. *Journal of Managerial Issues, 2*, 198–212.

Bartlett, C., & Ghoshal, S. (1998). *Managing across borders: The transnational solution.* Boston: Harvard Business School Press.

Bauer, T.N., & Green, S.G. (1998). Testing the combined effects of newcomer information seeking and managerial behavior on socialization. *Journal of Applied Psychology, 83*, 72–83.

Bauer, T.N., Morrison, E.W., & Callister, R.R. (1998). Organizational socialization: A review and directions for future research. In G.R. Ferris (Ed.), *Research in personnel and human resources management*, Vol. 16 (pp. 149–214). Greenwich, CT: JAI Press.

Berry, J. (1990). Imposed-etics, emics, and derived-etics: Their conceptual and operational status in cross-cultural psychology. In T.N. Headland, K.L. Pike & M. Harris (Eds.), *Emics and etics: The insider/outsider debate.* Newbury Park, CA: Sage.

Black, J.S. (1992). Socializing American expatriate managers overseas: Tactics, tenure, and role innovation. *Group and Organization Management, 17*, 171–192.

Boyacigiller, N., & Adler, N. (1991). The parochial dinosaur: Organizational science in a global context. *Academy of Management Review, 16*(2), 262–290.

Boyacigiller, N., Kleinberg, J., Phillips, M., & Sackmann, S. (1996). Conceptualizing culture. In B. Punnet & O. Shenkar (Eds.), *Handbook for international management research* (pp. 157–208). Cambridge, MA: Blackwell.

Brown, J., & Duguid, P. (1991). Organizational learning and communities-of-practice: Toward a unified view of working, learning, and innovation. *Organization Science, 2*(1), 40–57.

Brett, J.M., Feldman, D.C., & Weingart, L.R. (1990). Feedback-seeking behavior of new hires and job changers. *Journal of Management, 16*, 737–749.

Callister, R.R., Kramer, M., & Turban, D. (1999). Feedback seeking following career transitions. *Academy of Management Journal, 42*, 429–438.

Chao, G.T. (1997). Complexities in international organizational socialization. *International Journal of Selection and Assessment, 5*, 9–13.

Chao, G.T., O'Leary-Kelly, A.M., Wolf, S., Klein, H.J., & Gardner, P. (1994). Organizational socialization: Its content and consequences. *Journal of Applied Psychology, 79*, 730–743.

Chatman, J.A. (1991). Matching people and organizations: Selection and socialization in public accounting firms. *Administrative Science Quarterly, 36*, 459–484.

Chen, M. (1995). *Asian Management Systems.* London and New York: Routledge.

Child, J., & Markoczy, L. (1993). Host-country managerial behaviour and learning in Chinese and Hungarian joint ventures. *Journal of Management Studies, 30*, 611–631.

Comer, D.R. (1991). Organizational newcomers' acquisition of information from peers. *Management Communication Quarterly, 5*, 64–89.

Doi, T. (1973). *The anatomy of dependence.* Tokyo: Kodansha International.

Drenth, P., & Wilpert, B. (1980). The role of 'social contracts' in cross-cultural research. *International Review of Applied Psychology, 29*(3): 293–306.

Earley, C., & Mosakowski, E. (1996). Experimental international management research. In B.J. Punnett & O. Shenkar (Eds.), *Handbook for international management research* (pp. 83–114). Cambridge, MA: Blackwell.

Earley, P.C. (1989). Social loafing and collectivism: A comparison of United States and the People's Republic of China. *Administrative Science Quarterly, 34*, 565–81.

Earley, P.C. (1993). East meets West meets Mideast: Further explorations of collectivistic and individualistic work groups. *Academy of Management Journal, 36*, 319–48.

The Economist (1995). A Survey of multinationals: Big is back. Supplement, June 24–30, 1–22.

The Economist (1999). Jack Welch, GE and creative destruction. September 18–23, 23–26.

Federal Statistical Office, Germany (1998). http://www.statistik-bund.de/basis/e/erwerb/erwerbtxt.htm.

Feldman, D.C. (1976). A contingency theory of socialization. *Administrative Science Quarterly, 21*, 433–452.

Feldman, D.C. (1997). Socialization in an international context. *International Journal of Selection and Assessment, 5*, 1–8.

Fisher, C.D. (1986). Organizational socialization: An integrative review. In K.M. Rowland & G.R. Ferris (Eds.), *Research in Personnel and Human Resource Management* (Vol. 4, pp. 101–145) Greenwich, CT: JAI Press.

Fukuyama, F. (1996). *Trust.* New York: Free Press.

Gabrenya, W.K. Jr., Latane, B., & Wang, Y. (1983). Social loafing in cross-cultural perspective. *Journal of Cross-cultural Psychology, 14*, 368–84.

Gabrenya, W.K., Jr., Latane, B., & Wang, Y. (1985). Social loafing on an optimizing task: Cross-cultural differences among Chinese and Americans. *Journal of Cross-cultural Psychology, 16*, 223–242.

Glaser, G., & Strauss, A. (1967). *The discovery of grounded theory: Strategies for qualitative research.* Chicago: Aldine Publishing.

Hall, E.T., & Hall, M.R. (1990). *Understanding cultural differences.* Yarmouth, ME: Intercultural Press.

Hambrick, D., Nadler, D., & Tushman (1998). *Navigating change.* Boston: Harvard Business School Press.

Hamel, G. (1999). Bringing silicon valley inside. *Harvard Business Review*, Sept.–Oct., 70–86.

Harpaz, I. (1996). International management survey research. In B. Punnet & O. Shenkar (Eds.), *Handbook for international management research* (pp. 37–62). Cambridge, MA: Blackwell.

Hofstede, G. (1980). *Culture's consequences: International differences in work related values.* Beverly Hills, CA: Sage.

Hofstede, G., & Bond, M. (1988). The Confucius Connection: From cultural roots to economic growth. *Organizational Dynamics*, Spring: 4–21.

Inkpen, A. (1998). Learning and knowledge acquisition through International Strategic Alliances. *Academy of Management Executive*, 12(4): 69–80.

Jones, G.R. (1986) Socialization tactics, self-efficacy, and newcomers' adjustments to organizations. *Academy of Management Journal*, 29, 262–279.

King, R.C., & Sethi, V. (1992). Socialization of professionals in high-technology firms. *Journal of High Technology Management Research*, 3, 147–168.

Kluckhohn, F., & Strodtbeck, F. (1961). *Variations in value orientations.* Evanston, IL: Row, Peterson.

Koike, K. (1978). Japan's industrial relations. *Japanese Economic Studies*, Fall: 42–90.

Koike, K. (1987). Human resource development and labor-management relations. In K. Yamamura & Y. Yasuba (Eds.), *The political economy of Japan*, Vol. 1. Stanford, CA: Stanford University Press.

Kramer, M.W. (1995). A longitudinal study of superior-subordinate communication during job transfers. *Human Communication Research*, 22, 39–64.

Kras, E. (1994). *Modernizing Mexican management style: With insights for U.S. companies working in Mexico.* Las Cruces: Editts.

Laker, D.R., & Steffy, B.D. (1995). The impact of alternative socialization tactics on self-managing behavior and organizational commitment. *Journal of Social Behavior and Personality*, 10, 645–660.

Louis, M.R. (1980). Surprise and sense making: What newcomers experience in entering unfamiliar organizational settings. *Administrative Science Quarterly*, 25: 226–251.

Lyles, M., & Salk, J. (1996). Knowledge acquisition from foreign parents in international joint ventures: An empirical examination in the Hungarian context. *Journal of International Business Studies*, 27(5): 877–904.

Major, D.A., & Kozlowski, S.W.J. (1997). Newcomer information seeking: Individual and contextual influences. *International Journal of Selection and Assessment*, 5, 16–28.

Mignerey, J.T., Rubin, R.B., & Gorden, W.I. (1995). Organizational entry: An investigation of newcomer communication behavior and uncertainty. *Communication Research*, 22, 54–85.

Morrison, E.W. (1993a). Longitudinal study of the effects of information seeking on newcomer socialization. *Journal of Applied Psychology*, 78, 173–183.

Morrison, E.W. (1993b). Newcomer information seeking: Exploring types, modes, sources, and outcomes. *Academy of Management Journal*, 36, 557–589.

Morrison, E.W. (1995). Information usefulness and acquisition during organizational encounter. *Management Communication Quarterly*, 9, 131–155.

Morrison, E.W., Bauer, T.N., Callister, R.R., & Ben-Rechav, G.G. (1998). *Implications of international socialization.* Paper presented at the Western Academy of Management, International Division, Istanbul, Turkey.

Nakane, C. (1970). *Japanese Society.* Berkeley: University of California Press.

Nohria, N., & Ghoshal, S. (1997). *The differentiated network: Organizing multinational corporations for value creation.* San Francisco: Jossey-Bass.

Nonaka, I., & Takeuchi, H. (1995). *The knowledge-creating company.* New York: Oxford University Press.

Osborn, R., Hagedoorn, J., & Baughn, C. (1999). *The mythology and reality of cross-disciplinary international research.* Paper presented at the conference on Mastering the International Business Research Dimension, Center for Global Business Studies, St. Mary's University, San Antonio, Texas, October.

Osland, J., & Bird, A. (2000). Beyond sophisticated stereotyping: A contextual model of cultural sense-making. *Academy of Management Executive*, February.

Osland, J., De Franco, S., & Osland, O. (1999). Organizational implications of Latin American culture: Lessons for the expatriate manager. *Journal of Management Inquiry*, 8(2), 219–234.

Osland, J., & Osland, O. (1999). *Mastering international qualitative research.* Paper presented at the conference on Mastering the International Business Research Dimension, Center for Global Business Studies, St. Mary's University, San Antonio, Texas, October.

Ostroff, C., & Kozlowski, S.W.J. (1992). Organizational socialization as a learning process: The role of information acquisition. *Personnel Psychology*, 45, 849–874.

Parsons, T., & Shils, E. (1951). *Toward a general theory of action.* Cambridge, MA: Harvard University Press.

Pfeffer, J. (1998). *The human equation.* Boston, MA: Harvard Business School Press.

Polanyi, M. (1958). *Personal knowledge.* Chicago: University of Chicago Press.

Polanyi, M. (1966). *The tacit dimension.* London: Routledge & Kegan Paul.

Putti, J., & Chong, T. (1985). American and Japanese management practices in their Singapore subsidiaries. *Asia Pacific Journal of Management*, 2(2), 106–114.

Pucik, V. (1984). White-collar human resource management in large Japanese manufacturing firms. *Human Resource Management*, 23(3), 257–276.

Pucik, V. (1989). Managerial career progression in large japanese manufacturing firms. *Research in Personnel and Human Resources Management*, Suppl. 2, JAI Press: 257–276.

Reichers, A.E. (1987). An interactionist perspective on newcomer socialization rates. *Academy of Management Review*, 12, 278–287.

Rohlen, T. (1978). The education of a Japanese banker. *Human Nature Magazine*, 1(1), 22–30.

Rohlen, T. (1988). The education of a Japanese banker. In D. Okimoto & T. Rohlen (Eds.), *Inside the Japanese system*. Stanford: Stanford University Press.

Saks, A.M., & Ashforth, B.E. (1996). Proactive socialization and behavioral self-management. *Journal of Vocational Behavior, 48*, 301–323.

Schein, E.H. (1968). Organizational socialization and the profession of management. *Industrial Management Review, 9*, 1–16.

Schwartz, S. (1992). Universals in the content and structure of values: Theoretical advances and empirical tests in 20 countries. *Advances in Experimental Social Psychology, 25*, 1–61.

Schwartz, S., & Bilsky, W. (1987). Toward a universal psychological structure of human values. *Journal of Personality and Social Psychology, 53*, 550–62.

Settoon, R.P., & Adkins, C.L. (1997). Newcomer socialization: The role of supervisors, coworkers, friends and family members. *Journal of Business and Psychology, 11*, 507–516.

Si, S., & Bruton, G. (1999). Knowledge transfer in international joint ventures in transitional economies: The China experience. *Academy of Management Executive, 13*(1): 83–90.

Taormina, R.J. (1994). The Organizational Socialization Inventory. *International Journal of Selection and Assessment, 2*, 133–145.

Taormina, R.J., & Bauer, T.N. (2000). Organizational socialization in two cultures: Results from the United States and Hong Kong. *International Journal of Organizational Analysis, 8*, 263–290.

Taylor, S., Beechler, S., & Napier, N. (1996). Toward an integrative model of strategic international human resource management. *Academy of Management Review, 21*(4), 959–985.

Teune, H. (1990). Comparing countries: Lessons learned. In *Comparative methodology*. London: Sage.

Triandis, H. (1998). Vertical and horizontal individualism and collectivism: Theory and research implications for international comparative management. In J. Cheng & R. Peterson (Eds.), *Advances in international comparative management*. Stamford, CT: JAI Press.

Toyne, B., & Nigh, D. (1997). The future development of international business inquiry. In B. Toyne & D. Nigh (Eds.), *International business, an emerging vision* (pp. 673–683). Columbia, S.C.: The University of South Carolina Press.

Trompenaars, F., & Hampden-Turner, C. (1998). *Riding the waves of culture* (2nd ed.). New York: McGraw Hill.

U.S. Census Bureau (1998). *Current population reports special studies* (pp. 23–195), Profile of the Foreign-Born Population in the United States, 1997. www.census.gov/population/www/socdemo/foreign.htm/

Van Kemenade, W. (1997). *China, Hong Kong, Taiwan, Inc.: The dynamics of a new empire*. New York: Knopf.

Van Maanen, J. (1975). Police socialization: A longitudinal examination of job attitudes in an urban police department. *Administrative Science Quarterly, 20*, 207–228.

Van Maanen, J., & Schein, E.H. (1979). Toward a theory of organizational socialization. In B.M. Staw (Ed.), *Research in organizational behavior* (Vol. 1, pp. 209–264). Greenwich, CT: JAI Press.

Wanous, J., & Colella, A. (1989). Organizational entry research: Current status and future directions. In K.M. Rowland & G.R. Ferris (Eds.), *Research in personnel and human resource management* (Vol. 7, pp. 59–120). Greenwich, CT: JAI Press.

West, M.A., Nicholson, N., & Rees, A. (1987). Transitions into newly created jobs. *Journal of Occupational Psychology, 60*, 97–113.

Weick, K. (1995). *Sensemaking*. Thousand Oaks, CA: Sage.

Wright, L. (1996). Qualitative international management research. In J. Punnet & O. Shenkar (Eds.), *Handbook for international management research* (pp. 63–81). Cambridge, MA: Blackwell.

Yip, G. (1995). *Total global strategy*. Englewood Cliffs: Prentice-Hall.

Zahrly, J., & Tosi, H. (1989). The differential effect of organizational induction process on early work role adjustment. *Journal of Organizational Behavior, 10*, 59–74.

20

Expatriate Management

HANDAN KEPIR SINANGIL
and DENIZ S. ONES

We provide an overview of research that has been conducted on expatriates over the past five decades. It is our aim to highlight some of the key findings in expatriate management and to provide a critical appraisal of research needs. We first review who expatriates are. Then we discuss two main complementary IWO psychology interventions: expatriate staffing (e.g., expatriate selection; personality-based predictors; criterion-related validities) and training (e.g., cross-cultural training; culture assimilators; effectiveness of training interventions). A discussion of the criterion domain for expatriates follows. This section considers (1) expatriate satisfaction and early returns, (2) adaptation and adjustment, and (3) job performance. We conclude this chapter with a discussion of three emerging areas: (1) non-work and family considerations, (2) women expatriates, and (3) the host country perspective. We also offer an evaluation of expatriate management research.

There have been rapid increases in globalization of business (Black & Gregersen, 1999; Ohmae, 1991, 1995). The United States alone has more than 3,500 multinational companies, 25,000 companies with overseas branches or affiliates, and around 40,000 companies doing business abroad on a sporadic basis (Prentice, 1990). Accompanying this trend, advanced technology has resulted in ease of communication and travel, creating the 'Global Village.'

During the late twentieth century, the phenomenon of globalization has meant interdependence of economies, political systems and cultures. Organizations have increased their overseas operations. This means relying more heavily on their experts and managers as 'expatriates.' Many of the key positions in the overseas operations of multinational companies are filled with parent company or third country nationals.

Increasing numbers of employees are being sent on international assignments (Black, 1988; Dollins, 1999; Tung, 1982; see Forster 2000, for a dissenting opinion). In the early 1980s, Adler (1984a, 1984c) found that 600 multinational companies surveyed employed 13,338 expatriates. The number of business people who go overseas has considerably increased in the last 20 years, more than in any other period in history. Annually, over 100,000 expatriates are relocated to work in the United States (Micco, 1998). A recent survey of over 250 human resource managers and international relocation experts found that organizations continue to rely on expatriates (Windham International, 1999). The same survey reported that 41% of corporate revenues are generated away from the home country. As Shackleton and Newell (1997) note: 'Adopting an international strategy for global expansion is likely to lead to the extensive use of expatriate managers.' (p. 82). This is especially the case in developing countries.

Management of expatriate personnel is a crucial ingredient for achieving success in the global marketplace (Black & Gregersen, 1999). Particularly for multinational companies (MNCs), successful expatriate management has significant impact for the bottom-line (Adler, 1987; Mendenhall & Oddou, 1985; Naumann, 1992; Stroh & Caligiuri, 1998). Overseas operations of multinational companies have increasingly become the real profit centers of these firms (Bartlett & Ghoshal, 1989), highlighting the importance of expatriates. From an individual point of view, expatriate assignments can have important implications for career prospects of expatriates (Grant, 1997). An increasing emphasis is being placed on getting international experience for senior managers who are expected to make the crucial decisions for multinational companies (Adler & Bartholomew, 1992; Porter, 1990).

In this chapter, we provide a selective overview of research that has been conducted on expatriates over the past five decades. It is our aim to highlight some of the key findings in expatriate management and to provide a critical appraisal of research needs. We first review who expatriates are. Then, we discuss two main complementary IWO psychology interventions: expatriate staffing and training. A discussion of the criterion domain for expatriates follows. This section considers (1) expatriate satisfaction and early returns, (2) adaptation and adjustment, and (3) job performance. We conclude this chapter with a discussion of three emerging areas: (1) non-work and family considerations, (2) women expatriates, and (3) the host country perspective. Finally, an evaluation of expatriate management research is offered.

WHO ARE EXPATRIATES?

Since ancient times, nations and businesses have been sending members of their own groups to other parts of the world. Some familiar examples include armies, crusaders, traders, missionaries, ambassadors and most recently the personnel of multinational companies. All of these people can be subsumed under the generic term 'expatriate.' Expatriates are individuals who go overseas to accomplish a job-related goal. This aspect differentiates an expatriate from a tourist or an international student. On the other hand, top company officials traveling overseas to sign an agreement are not considered expatriates because they are very much like tourists in terms of their contact with a new culture, which does not require a period of adjustment. Another distinction that needs to be made is between a sojourner and an expatriate. Sojourners include international students, refugees, guest workers, asylum seekers, and *expatriates* who eventually leave the foreign country upon completion of their task (Berry, Poortinga, Segall & Dasen, 1992; Church, 1982). Thus, sojourner is a more encompassing term than expatriate. Aycan and Kanungo (1997) offered a definition for expatriates as 'employees of business and government organizations who are sent by their organization to a related unit in a country which is different from their own, to accomplish a job or organization-related goal for a pre-designated temporary time period of usually more than six months and less than five years in one term' (p. 250).

Expatriates tend to be CEOs, executives, managers and professionals (Tung, 1981), affirming the highly complex nature of jobs performed by expatriates. A high degree of responsibility is another hallmark of expatriate jobs, particularly for expatriates of multinational companies. Perhaps the most important element that distinguishes expatriate jobs from other high complexity and high responsibility jobs is an added element of complexity by the intercultural environment in which these jobs are performed.

One key question in expatriate management is how to ensure expatriate success in global assignments. The answer to this question has involved suggestions for better expatriate selection, training, and other interventions (Bird & Dunbar, 1991; for Black & Gregersen, 1991a, 1991b; Black, Mendenhall & Oddou, 1991; Kealey, 1989). We next offer an overview of this literature.

EXPATRIATE STAFFING

All good employment practices start with good recruiting and selection. Given the increasingly important role that expatriates play in the generation of multinational profits, there is pressure to select the best employees to manage overseas operations (Wilson & Dalton, 1998). According to a recent survey, 92% of MNCs make expatriate selection decisions based on managerial recommendations; over half do not use any structured procedures; and less than 10% do not use any type of screening (Human Resource Institute, 1998). This is despite a very large body of literature in IWO psychology supporting the use of systematic assessments in selection of employees to maximize future job performance and minimize undesirable behaviors (e.g., counterproductivity) and outcomes (undesirable turnover).

There may be two reasons for this: First, in most cases, individuals being sent on expatriate assignments are already employees with the organization. Hence, expatriation may be viewed as a placement rather than a selection decision. Second, research specifically on expatriate selection has had a checkered history. There is much literature on factors relevant for expatriate adjustment, but there is little consistency across studies regarding which variables should be measured and/or what their associated magnitudes of predictive validity are.

Most studies in this literature have focused on the high failure rates among expatriates, especially American personnel overseas (O'Boyle, 1989; Tung, 1987). Are personal characteristics important for expatriates? Are there individual differences factors that contribute to an expatriate's adjustment? Job performance? Early returns? Can personality variables be used in expatriate selection and assignments?

The first large-scale systematic selection evaluations for expatriates were carried out during the early days of the Peace Corps. The Peace Corps was established in 1961 as a way of having Americans serve overseas, particularly aiding in the development efforts of foreign countries. Early on, personality testing and panel interviews were used. During training, clinical psychologists and field officers provided evaluations of overseas suitability. At the end of the training, appointments were made for suitable candidates (Adler, 1991). There are several accounts of the Peace Corps selection experiments (e.g., Dicken, 1969; Dicken & Black, 1965; Harris, 1973, 1975). Partly because of its less than stellar record in predicting success, the Peace Corps abandoned its selection procedure in 1970. Over the years the Peace Corps has moved to a system of 'self-selection,' the result being increased terminations and greatly reduced overseas success (Adler, 1991). Basing their conclusions on the Peace Corps evaluations of suitability, researchers (Harris, 1973; Harris & Harris, 1972) have concluded that personality-based assessments of potential expatriates were not likely to be fruitful.

No large-scale systematic applications or evaluations of selection have been carried out for diplomats and international scholars. Selection for overseas duties seems to have been determined by informal judgments of potential adjustment and effectiveness, as well as willingness to relocate. Mumford (1983) states 'People are selected for overseas assignment based on technical skills, availability and other factors, but not on their ability to get along overseas. Even in the world of diplomacy, people are not sent overseas because they are adaptable, empathic, persevering, patient and courteous ....' (p. 95). Nevertheless, there have been a few standardized instruments developed for predicting expatriate adjustment for other occupational groups. In the United States armed services, a 'Navy Overseas Adjustment Scale' was developed in the 1970s to predict adjustment of service people to other cultures. For technical assistance personnel, selection for expatriate assignments has not been a high priority issue in the US. However, the Canadian International Development Agency has been actively using and evaluating selection devices. Most findings have focused on intercultural communication competence (Kealey, 1989; Kealey & Ruben, 1983; Ruben & Kealey, 1979).

As for multinational expatriates, in the early 1970s, 80% of expatriates were selected on the basis of recommendations and 48% of companies were relying on the personnel department for evaluations (Miller, 1972). Although most companies recognized that interpersonal skills were important

for overseas success, only 5% of companies surveyed formally assessed interpersonal competence and relational abilities (Tung, 1981). One selection method that has been used for expatriate selection by businesses, albeit not to a great extent, is the assessment center. Assessment centers usually include some evaluative component of personality. However, even in the last decade, Hogan and Goodson (1990) have lamented 'unfortunately, many companies do not realize the potential bottom-line impact of expatriate success and fall short in their efforts' (p. 50).

Despite poor or nonexistent practices in selecting expatriates, the academic literature on the topic has burgeoned. Most papers have been rather speculative and non-empirical. Many of these studies have focused on various aspects of personality, though as noted by Ones and Viswesvaran (1998), few acknowledge the personality roots of these proposed predictors. For example, Copeland and Griggs (1988) suggest that the person selected for overseas duties should have 'breadth.' They list seven necessary components of 'breadth', which include: (1) hardness like water; (2) resourceful independence through people; (3) curiosity; and (4) positive regard for others. According to Brislin (1981) six characteristics are important for intercultural adjustment and success: (1) intelligence, essentially the familiar concept of cognitive ability; (2) task orientation, including conscientiousness, responsibility, persistence, diligence; (3) tolerant personality, including patience, tolerance for ambiguity, nondogmatism, nonauthoritarianism, large cognitive width, and cognitive flex; (4) strength of personality, including self-esteem, integrity, security, loyalty, courage and self-concept; (5) relations with others, including empathy, sociability, warmth, consideration, extraversion, nonjudgmentalness; and (6) potential for benefiting from cross-cultural experience, reflecting openness to change and the ability to accept and use feedback. Hammer, Gudykunst, and Wiseman (1978) proposed four dimensions for predicting intercultural adjustment: communication competence (which included respect, nonjudgmentalness, empathy, self-orientedness), ability to deal with stress, establishing interpersonal relationships, and tolerance for ambiguity. Mendenhall and Oddou (1985) named four factors that they thought would predict success: (1) self-orientedness, including self-esteem, self-confidence, and mental adjustment; (2) others orientedness, including ability to interact with others, develop relationships, and willingness to communicate; (3) perceptual dimension, including ability to understand why foreigners behave the way they do, and being nonjudgmental; and (4) cultural toughness, an environmental dimension which suggests that depending on the expatriate's culture of origin, some cultures are more difficult to adjust to than others (i.e., a moderator effect by cultural distance between the original culture of the expatriate and the host culture). A clear theme that emerges from an extensive review of this literature is that most predictors suggested by authors can be grouped under the umbrella of the Big Five dimensions of personality (Ones & Viswesvaran, 1997).

Apart from theoretical arguments about the relevance of personality constructs (Ones & Viswesvaran, 1997; Ronen, 1989), both rated importance of various personality-related characteristics for overseas success by a number of sources (e.g., by expatriates themselves, Arthur & Bennett, 1997, and by host country nationals, Sinangil & Ones, 1997), and traditional criterion-related validity studies for specific scales have been reported (e.g., Peace Corps studies, e.g. Ezekiel, 1968; Harris, 1973; Mischel, 1965). Among others, the following traits have received attention as potential predictors of overseas behaviors: tolerance (Miller, 1972), interpersonal cultural sensitivity (Byrnes, 1966), open-mindedness, sensitivity to power (Ezekiel, 1968), and authoritarianism or dogmatism (Smith, 1966).

Arthur and Bennett (1995) examined the relative importance of factors perceived to contribute to expatriate success. Expatriates from various countries and organizations rated the importance of 54 attributes identified to be relevant for overseas success. Five factors were identified for effective performance in international assignments. These dimensions were family situation, flexibility/ adaptability, job knowledge and motivation, relational skills, and extra-cultural openness. However, our understanding of the host country managers' perceptions of the factors critical to expatriate performance remain limited (Sinangil & Ones, 1996).

A number of studies have examined the criterion-related validities of various predictors for overseas adjustment, performance and early returns. Unfortunately, most criterion-related validity work on using personality variables for predicting overseas work behaviors has been discouraging. This is in sharp contrast to both theoretical arguments about the importance of personality (e.g., Ones & Viswesvaran, 1997; Ronen, 1989) and empirical findings from studies obtaining ratings from multiple sources (e.g., Arthur & Bennett, 1995, 1997; Sinangil & Ones, 1997). The first systematic evaluations of the criterion-related validities of personality variables for expatriate behaviors overseas were conducted in the 1960s in the context of the Peace Corps studies. Work on Peace Corps evaluations of suitability led to the conclusion that personality-based assessments of potential expatriates were not likely to be fruitful (Harris, 1973, 1975). Other empirical studies were also quite discouraging (e.g., David, 1972; Dinges, 1983). Several researchers commenting on this earlier literature concluded that 'Measured [personality] traits are not good

predictors' (Brislin, 1981, p. 52), 'A review of the literature leaves one with the impression that the prediction of an individual's ability to adapt in a foreign environment is an extremely difficult, if not impossible task' (Benson, 1978), and 'Prediction of effectiveness based on personality tests, however rarely produced outcomes that are better than those based on random selection' (Deller, 1997).

There are several reasons for questioning the reportedly poor and mostly non-significant criterion-related validities of personality variables for overseas behaviors. These have included predictor-related problems, methodological problems, and criterion problems. In the next few paragraphs, we take up the first two issues. Later in the chapter, we turn our attention to the criterion problem.

One reason research on expatriate selection has been confusing and discouraging is the lack of a unifying theoretical framework to organize the personality variables studied. Indeed, most researchers have chosen to use home-grown scales for measuring personality variables. The use of nonstandardized personality measures mirrors the lack of a theoretical framework in this area.

It is no surprise that researchers reviewing this literature have written: 'A review of the literature leaves one with the impression that the prediction of an individual's ability to adapt in a foreign environment is an extremely difficult, if not impossible task' (Benson, 1978). Byrnes (1966) commented there is '… little data to indicate that there's an overseas type' (p. 106). We believe that this early pronouncement was premature and only partially correct. We concur that personality type is not likely to explain expatriate behavior, but theoretically grounded continuous personality variables, measured using well-developed, standardized nonclinical personality inventories are likely to be of much use in predicting expatriate success components and thereby have utility in expatriate selection (see Ones & Viswesvaran, 1997, for the theoretical case for using personality constructs in expatriate selection).

Earlier criterion-related validity studies, when conducted, have suffered from methodological shortcomings, including statistical power problems, sampling problems, measurement problems and analysis problems. (See Chapter 2 in this volume for further elaborations on these methodological points.) The empirical examinations of criterion-related validities of personality-related variables for overseas behaviors have been plagued by small sample research (typical Ns less than 30), creating a statistical power problem, where fairly substantial criterion-related validities were rejected as non-significant. Sampling has also been an issue. With the exception of a small number of recent studies, criterion-related validity studies have sampled Peace Corps and Aid Agency volunteers. However, criterion-related validities need to be empirically examined using expatriate business people, rather than volunteers. The context of volunteerism could be drastically different from expatriate work in for-profit organizations. The problem of small and/or inappropriate samples in this area has been compounded by other statistical artifacts such as poor measurement reliability, and inattention to the effects of restriction in range. Both measurement error and range restriction attenuate criterion-related validities and obscure personality-expatriate success criteria.

An analysis-related issue that has misled researchers in predicting expatriate behaviors has been a misplaced focus on R^2 in regression analyses. Typically, researchers have carried out regression analyses where the influences of several predictors on a criterion have been examined and the R^2 has been taken as proof of the small/nonexistent effects of person-based predictors. These researchers interpret R^2 as the proportion of the variance in the dependent variable that is explained by the independent variables. 'The "percent variance accounted for" is statistically correct but substantively erroneous. This is because R^2 (and all other indices of percentage variance accounted for) are related only in a very nonlinear way to the magnitudes of the effect sizes that determine their impact in the real world'. (Hunter & Schmidt, 1990, p. 199). The multiple R should be the index reported and interpreted for accurate conclusions. Expatriate management researchers should avoid using variance-based estimates because these estimates are 'deceptive and misleading and should be avoided' (Hunter & Schmidt, 1990, p. 201; see pp. 199–202 for a full explication of why variance-based estimates are to be avoided).

Given the predictor-related problems and methodological problems outlined above, it is not surprising that the use of personality variables were virtually abandoned for expatriate selection. Indeed, Mischel's own work with the Peace Corps data, and his evaluation of other Peace Corps studies were partially responsible for his later assertions about little cross-situational consistency of behavior and belief in the potency of 'situation' variables in the prediction of behavior (Mischel, 1965, 1968). Following in the footsteps of Mischel, other authors have also remarked, 'Much of the variance in performance abroad can be attributed to factors in experiences during training and especially during the early stages of life in the second country, and … less of the variance can be accounted for by the character structure and deeper personality factors of the individual' (Guthrie, 1975, p. 97). Similar conclusions have been reached by David (1972), Dinges (1983) and Harris (1973).

However, a number of recent criterion-related validity studies have produced more promising results, largely because greater attention has been directed to both theoretical issues and methodological problems (e.g., Caligiuri, 2000a, 2000b; Dalton & Wilson, 2000; Deller, 1998; Sinangil & Ones, 1995, 1997). That is, recent empirical work using the Big Five measures paints a rosier picture than previous research on the validity and utility of measuring personality among potential expatriates (Caligiuri, 2000a; Sinangil & Ones, 1995; Wilson & Dalton, 2000). The general findings from these newer studies appear to indicate that the personality determinants of expatriate early returns, job performance, adjustment and other criteria are quite different. For example, Sinangil and Ones (1998) found that the Prudence scale of the Hogan Personality Inventory (measuring the dependability facet of conscientiousness) is a poor predictor of expatriate job performance, but is a valid predictor of overseas counterproductive behaviors. Most of these studies have also found that personality variables predictive of expatriate adjustment include emotional stability (Caligiuri, 1995); whereas, for job performance, ambition and aspects of openness to experience were predictive (Deller, 1998; Sinangil & Ones, 1995, 1998).

While criterion-related validity studies address the question of what personality variables act as determinants of overseas behaviors, they do not address the question of what managers or selection decision makers consider to be important. In recent years, in evaluating the suitability of expatriates for overseas assignments, managers appear to be attending to personality factors when selecting expatriates. A policy-capturing study indicated that among American managers, conscientiousness was perceived to be the most important personality factor for judgments about: (1) completion of overseas assignment, (2) adjustment, (3) interpersonal relations with host country nationals, and (4) overseas job performance (Ones & Viswesvaran, 1999). Openness to experience was perceived to be important for completion of overseas assignments. Similar work needs to be carried out for non-American managers who select expatriates, in order to ascertain the generalizability of findings.

In closing this section, we would like to comment on an often-encountered criticism in the expatriate selection research. Many researchers lament that businesses seem to be operating on the premise that technical expertise is the most important criterion for selection (Mendenhall & Oddou, 1985). Academic and practitioner literature is replete with calls not to use technical skills as the basis for selecting expatriates. We prefer interpreting this literature to mean that organizations should not make expatriate selection decisions based *solely* on technical expertise (Ones & Viswesvaran, 1997). Rather, technical expertise should be considered as one factor in a selection system that includes other variables such as personality. There is ample evidence that ability, knowledge and skills are valid predictors of performance in any performance domain (e.g., Kuncel, Hezlett & Ones, 2001; Schmidt & Hunter, 1992; Viswesvaran & Ones, in press) and for the complex environment that expatriates operate in, we see cognitive ability and technical skills as crucial determinants of overseas job performance.

There are some areas of staffing that have, to date, received little research attention. For example, examinations of recruiting strategies are glaringly absent from the literature. Similarly, potential expatriate reactions to MNC staffing practices is another area of research that needs to be explored. We see these as two fruitful avenues for future research.

TRAINING OF EXPATRIATES

Bhawuk and Brislin (2000) define cross-cultural training as formal efforts for preparing people for living in other cultures. Sophisticated cross-cultural training introduces potential expatriates to the differences between cultures in social interactions and requires them to practice cross-culturally suitable behaviors. (There are also training programs which aim to prepare expatriates for repatriation, but the page limits on this chapter's length prevent us from reviewing repatriation literature here.)

Cross-cultural training is viewed as an effective intervention to prevent expatriate failures (e.g., Black & Mendenhall, 1990; Earley, 1987). Both expatriates and their partners are positively predisposed to cross-cultural training (Brewster & Pickard, 1994). According to Black and Mendenhall (1990), cross-cultural training improves cultural awareness, interpersonal adjustment, and managerial effectiveness. Similarly, Brislin and Yoshida (1994) note that improving interpersonal relations and job success are two main goals of cross-cultural training.

Cross-cultural training is a human resources intervention that has been with us for the past 50 years. The early work in the area has focused on reducing culture shock by shocking the participants in a training session and then having them discuss cultural differences. Culture shock refers to 'an occupational disease of people who have suddenly been transported abroad...precipitated by the anxiety that results from losing all your familiar signs and symbols of social discourse' (Oberg, 1960, p. 177). The consequences of culture shock can be both psychological (e.g., depression and psychosis) as well as psychosomatic (e.g., headaches, diarrhea, insomnia) (see Furnham and Bochner's, 1986, book on the topic for a more detailed discussion). Our understanding of culture shock has been enriched by Triandis' (1994) conceptualization of cultural determinants of culture shock. Culture shock is likely to be experienced more severely when the cultural distance between the cultures is large (Mumford, 1998), when there is a

history of conflict between cultures involved, when the language proficiencies of the host and the expatriate are poor, and when they know little of each others' cultures (Triandis, 1994). In training that utilizes 'shocking' the participants, 'losing familiar signs and symbols of social discourse' is experienced during training.

This type of approach to cross-cultural training is a result of the realization that lecture as a training method may not be the most effective approach in cross-cultural training. Experiential training methods proliferated during the 1960s (Harrison & Hopkins, 1967). Lecture approaches are geared toward passive learning and it was argued that active learning using experiential exercises would be more effective. The rationale behind this expectation was that expatriates have 'to confront situations that are charged with emotion, and they need to develop "the emotional muscle" which is needed in intercultural interactions' (Bhawuk & Brislin, 2000, p. 168). Experiential exercises and simulations have aimed to emotionally involve the trainees. Another theme spanning several experiential exercises (Kolb, 1976), area simulations (Trifonovitch, 1977) and Kraemer's cultural self-awareness model (Kraemer, 1973, 1974) has been the recognition that we all operate under the assumptions of our own culture.

One popular cross-cultural training method has been the culture assimilator. Culture assimilators consist of critical incidents of cross-cultural interactions and ways of avoiding misunderstandings. The trainees read each critical incident and are provided with alternatives, outlining courses of action that can be used to avoid misunderstandings between the two cultures. One of the alternatives reflects the point of view of the expatriate's culture, another reflects the view of the foreign culture. Other alternatives are less appropriate. For each alternative, explanations are provided on the appropriateness of the behavior (why an alternative is to be preferred), on separate sheets of paper. (See Triandis, 1995, for a detailed description.) Culture assimilators can be a suitable, self-study tool for expatriates preparing for their overseas assignments. However, many are culture specific (specific to a particular home and host culture) and hence tend to be expensive and difficult to develop. (See Albert, 1983, for a list of available culture assimilators.) Effectiveness of culture specific assimilators appear to be for enhancing interpersonal relations (e.g., Chemers, 1969; Fiedler, Mitchell & Triandis, 1971; Gudykunst & Hammer, 1983; Malpass & Salancik, 1977; Tolbert, 1990), rather than improving performance (Mitchell & Foa, 1969). Further, we would like to observe that most culture assimilators have been developed more than 25 years ago and they are now likely to be quite outdated.

Other early cross-cultural training methods have included the cultural analysis system (Lee, 1966) and the contrast-American methods (Stewart, 1966). The former casts business problems faced by expatriates in terms of both the home and host culture. Trainees are asked to observe their own cultural values regarding the problem at hand. Training concludes by redefining the problem without reference to the expatriate's cultural values. In the contrast-American method, trainees observe behaviors opposite to those found in the trainee's own culture. They are coached to identify their own cultural values, contrast these with other cultural values and apply the understanding they acquire to cross-cultural interaction problems. Both methods recognize the culture bound nature of cross-cultural communication and aim to have participants recognize their own cultural values. The same goal is echoed in culture-general assimilators (Brislin & Bhawuk, 1999), where topics such as 'self-awareness and sensitivity training that allow one to learn about himself or herself in preparation for interaction with any culture' (Brislin & Pedersen, 1976) are covered. Research on the effectiveness of the culture general assimilators is reviewed in Landis and Bhagat (1996).

Black and Mendenhall (1990) have suggested that cross-cultural training interventions should be based on social learning theory principles (Bandura, 1977) and behavior modification training could be more effective in preparing expatriates for overseas assignments. In a study comparing the effectiveness of Japanese culture assimilator, behavioral modeling training, a combination of the two methods and no training at all, for the criterion of learning, Harrison (1992) found that the combination method produced the highest effect. Replication studies would be welcome in this area.

Recently, theory-based culture assimilators have been developed (Bhawuk, 1995, 1998). The main feature of this training method is the conceptualization of training stages as intercultural expertise development. Surprisingly lacking from the culture assimilator literature are methods utilizing ubiquitous multimedia technology. Other under-researched areas in the cross-cultural training literature include post-arrival training (Selmer, Torbiorn & de Leon, 1998) and expatriate career development (Selmer, 1999).

Deshpande and Viswesvaran (1992) reported a meta-analysis of the literature on the effectiveness of cross-cultural training. Across 21 empirical studies, a total of 1,611 subjects were used to investigate the effects of cross-cultural training on the effectiveness of expatriate managers on five criteria (self-development, perception, relationship, adjustment, and performance). In other words, effects of training on self-development, perceptions, relations with host country nationals, adjustment and job performance were examined. The effect sizes were strongest for self-development (corrected r with training $= .56$) and weakest for performance (corrected r with training $= .39$).

Despite the evidence that cross-cultural training is worthwhile, at the beginning of 1990s, only approximately 25% of MNCs offered pre-departure cross-cultural training to expatriates and their families (Black & Gregersen, 1991a, 1991b). A more recent survey by Andersen Consulting found that among the best 32 of Fortune 500 companies, 94% offered language training programs, and 69% offered other cross-cultural training to expatriates (Cuthill, 1997). Among 250 organizations from multiple industries, 63% offered cross-cultural training to their international assignees (Windham International, 1999). The gap between research and practice in this area is unfortunate (Aryee, 1997). Perhaps, we IWO psychologists, need to champion our methods better.

There are three research areas that are in need of attention in expatriate training. First, much empirical work tends to focus on trainee reactions or learning. Data are needed to support the transfer of training to behavior during expatriate assignments. Further, the positive consequences of cross-cultural training for organizational outcomes await empirical documentation. Second, cross-cultural training research has tended to focus on main effects. The possibility that there may be treatment by aptitude interactions in this area needs to be explored. For example, the differential effectiveness of cross-cultural training for high and low attitudinally and behaviorally open individuals (see Caligiuri, Jacobs & Farr, 1999, for the development of such a scale) could be examined. Also, a potential expatriate's ability to learn could produce treatment by aptitude interaction effects. Third, cross-cultural training has been evaluated using haphazard criteria. The criterion problem that has hampered expatriate selection research is also a relevant issue for expatriate training.

CRITERIA FOR EXPATRIATES

Expatriate failures are expensive (Adler, 1986; Guzzo, Noonan & Elron, 1994; Ronen, 1989; Stone, 1991; Wederspahn, 1992). Expatriate selection is predicated on the premise of selecting from a pool of applicants those who are likely to be more successful on their assignment (compared to those not selected). Training programs are designed to improve expatriate success rates. Thus, it is important to know what that construct of 'expatriate success' entails.

The criteria have been the Achilles heel in most expatriate research. The expatriate literature has also been afflicted with poor conceptualizations and measurement of criteria (see also Caligiuri, 1997; Hannigan, 1990; Ones & Viswesvaran, 1997).

Many authors maintain that the ultimate criterion in expatriate selection is overseas effectiveness, which Hammer (1987) defines as 'achieving desirable ends or goals.' This definition of effectiveness is similar to the definition of overall job performance in traditional selection research. Others have conceptualized effectiveness as multidimensional. Hawes and Kealey (1979) use a three-factor model. Their dimensions of overseas effectiveness were intercultural interaction, professional effectiveness, family/personal adjustment and satisfaction. Many studies have also used early returns from the country of assignment as a measure of expatriate success. Conceptualizing success as tenure or failure as turnover is ill-advised. Turnover is not part of the job performance domain and tenure is not a measure of job success (Campbell, 1990).

There are linkages between expatriate adjustment, job performance, satisfaction, and early returns (Church, 1982). For example, Tung (1981) found that expatriates' failure to complete overseas assignments was influenced by problems with expatriate and/or spousal adjustment to host culture. The same finding was echoed in the more recent expatriate management literature (Kraimer, Wayne & Jaworski, 2001; Shaffer & Harrison, 1998; Sinangil & Ones, 1997; Triandis, 1994). However, these constructs are not interchangeable and researchers should not pretend that they are.

The problem of the criterion has been almost a more vexing issue in the expatriate literature (e.g., Benson, 1978) than it has been in most domestic (within-culture) studies in industrial/organizational psychology (Campbell, Gasser & Oswald, 1996; Viswesvaran, 1993). The well-known problem in studying expatriate 'success' stems from the numerous ways of operationalizing what success and failure mean.

The list of criteria (dependent variables) utilized to index success for expatriates includes job performance, satisfaction, adaptation, adjustment, completion rate, premature returns, culture shock, role shock, overseas effectiveness, professional effectiveness, interpersonal effectiveness, acculturation and overseas success. This laundry list of criteria is problematic for a few reasons. First, the list includes content and process variables. That is, variables such as culture shock and acculturation describe a process and thus cannot be indicative of 'success.' Second, criteria are traditionally used to serve mainly two purposes: (1) they are used to select and reject interventions (mainly selection and training interventions), and (2) they are used to evaluate overall effectiveness. Some of the criteria listed above (e.g., satisfaction) may be inappropriate for both purposes.

We next review research on expatriate adjustment, job performance, satisfaction, and early returns to clarify the conceptual and empirical boundaries of each construct. We hope what will become clear is that expatriate satisfaction, adjustment, adaptation, job performance and completion of overseas assignments are distinct, but causally related constructs.

Expatriate Satisfaction and Early Returns

Unfortunately, as noted above, expatriate management treats expatriate satisfaction, organizational commitment, overseas adjustment, acculturation, assimilation, job performance, effectiveness, and early returns as though they are proxies for the same construct (Aycan, 1997a; Hannigan, 1990; Ones & Viswesvaran, 1997). In addition most research in expatriate management uses self-report measures, further confounding the constructs being tapped with the measurement method (Caligiuri, 1997; Ones & Viswesvaran, 1997).

A meta-analysis of studies that have measured job satisfaction among the expatriates found that the same set of variables that are related to job satisfaction among domestic workers are also related to job satisfaction among expatriates (Alampay, Beehr & Christiansen, 2000). Such variables included task self-efficacy, job level, skill variety, role ambiguity (negative), task identity, task significance, role discretion, job feedback and mentoring. Expatriate satisfaction can be conceptualized as a determinant of expatriate adjustment (Dunbar, 1992), and ultimately completion of overseas service.

Much research has highlighted the high rate of expatriate early returns. Especially, extremely high costs associated with early expatriate returns, has focused further attention on this area (e.g., Kraimer et al., 2001). Expatriation is an expensive proposition. On average, two and half times more money is spent for expatriates compared to hiring locally (McGoldrick, 1997). Birdseye and Hill (1995) noted that the direct costs of sending an expatriate on an international assignment can be as high as $220,000.

Interestingly, North American expatriates have been reported to have higher early return rates than Western European expatriates (Brewster, 1991; Selmer, 1999). Although failure rates among North American expatriates may be improving (Harzing, 1992), a study of European multinationals found an extremely low early return rate continuing for expatriates of European origin (Price Waterhouse, 1997).

In within-country analyses, turnover intentions predict actual turnover (e.g., Mobley, 1982). Withdrawal cognitions also predict expatriate turnover (Garonzik, Brockner & Siegel, 2000; Naumann, 1992, Shaffer & Harrison, 1998). However, most expatriate management research is in agreement that one of the chief determinants of early returns involves inability to adjust. This is a line of research that concentrates on intercultural adaptation and adjustment.

Garonzik et al. (2000) studied non-work-related outcomes and perceived procedural fairness as predictors of premature expatriate departures. In two studies, expatriates were more likely to think seriously about prematurely departing when their non-work outcomes (i.e., non-work adjustment) were unfavorable. However, all current favorability and early turnover intentions were more strongly related when perceived procedural fairness was low. In other words, organizations can focus on their institution's procedural fairness in their attempts to curb premature returns. There appears to be value to using findings from the literature on psychological contracts in understanding expatriate behaviors (Guzzo et al., 1994).

Expatriate Adaptation and Adjustment

Adaptation and adjustment are related but distinct concepts. An early conceptualization of adjustment from Brislin (1981) defined adjustment as 'satisfaction, perceived acceptance from hosts, ability to function during everyday activities without severe stress' (p. 271). In contrast, adaptation is a construct that includes adjustment as a dimension, and hence involves much more than just the ability to function without adverse effects of stress in daily activities. The dimensions of adaptation have been identified as adjustment, identification with hosts, cultural competence, and role acculturation (Briody & Beeber Crisman, 1991; Taft, 1977). Further, recent research (e.g., Aycan & Berry, 1996; Berry, 1992; Searle & Ward, 1990; Ward, 1996) indicates that adaptation is the outcome of the acculturation process. Adaptation signifies changes in the expatriate in response to environmental demands. The process of adaptation can result in reaction, adjustment, or withdrawal.

Interestingly, until recently, there was no widely accepted definition of what was meant by expatriate adjustment. Largely based on the work of Black, Stephens, Gregersen, Mendenhall, Oddou and colleagues, the past two decades have seen a convergence of what is meant by adjustment. Expatriate adjustment refers to the psychological comfort expatriates feel with regard to the host culture within which they are operating (Gregersen & Black, 1990). Black and Stephens (1989) proposed three facets of expatriate adjustment: work adjustment, interaction adjustment, and expatriate general adjustment. Work adjustment measures the degree to which the expatriate feels psychologically comfortable in his or her overseas work role (Black, 1988), as it 'requires some degree of adjustment to new work tasks and responsibilities' (Gregersen & Black, 1990, p. 463). Interaction adjustment measures the degree to which the expatriate feels comfortable interacting with host country nationals (Black, 1988). This aspect of adjustment is perhaps closest to the intercultural effectiveness construct that cross-cultural psychologists use (Church, 1982). General adjustment measures the degree to which the expatriate feels comfortable in the new living environment, including adjustment to housing, food, shopping, etc. (Black & Stephens, 1989).

Research examining the factor structure of expatriate adjustment measures and their nomological nets is in its infancy. In addition, there is confusion in the literature as to whether work adjustment, interaction adjustment, and expatriate general adjustment are truly facets of a general overarching construct or whether they are causal determinants of one another. On one hand, there is work substantiating the tripartite factor structure of the Black and Stephens (1989) measure. On the other hand, Kraimer et al. (2001) maintain that general expatriate adjustment mediates the link between interactions and work adjustment. A recent meta-analysis found nine studies reporting correlations among facets of expatriate adjustment (Alampay et al., 2000). The unreliability corrected correlation between general adjustment and interactional adjustment was .60 ($N = 1,813$, $K = 9$). General adjustment and work adjustment were related at a lower level (unreliability corrected correlation = .43, $N = 1,813$, $K = 9$). Interestingly, the relationship between work adjustment and interaction adjustment was the weakest, .37 ($N = 1,586$, $K = 8$). Interaction adjustment and general adjustment are not synonymous with work adjustment for expatriates (Alampay et al., 2000).

There appears to be a large amount of specific variance associated with each of the facets of expatriate adjustment. Bolstering this view, somewhat different nomological nets for each of the adjustment facets have been reported in a comprehensive, yet small-scale meta-analysis (Alampay et al., 2000). General adjustment is correlated most highly with spouse general adjustment (corrected correlation = .64). Moderate corrected correlations are found between general adjustment and interpersonal skills (.24), general self-efficacy (.28), social efficacy (.29), role discretion (.37), frequency of interactions with host country nationals (.23), and spouse interaction adjustment (.42). Interaction adjustment is most highly correlated with frequency of interactions with host country nationals (corrected correlation = .56). Moderate relationships are found between interaction adjustment and general self-efficacy (.34), number of months on assignment (.23), spouse interaction adjustment (.38), and spouse general adjustment (.37). And finally, work adjustment is most closely related to general self-efficacy (.43), role discretion (.44), role ambiguity (− .42), and role conflict (− .46). Moderate relationships are found between work adjustment and frequency of interactions with host country nationals (.28), frequency of interactions with home headquarters (.19), and family adjustment (.35).

Somewhat unfortunately, adjustment has frequently been employed as the sole criterion of overseas success. We would like to posit that a distinction needs to be made between a criterion and a determinant of a criterion. Expatriate adjustment is analogous to the construct of handling stress in the domestic IWO literature. Just as those who can handle stress well can avert the decline of their psychological health, adjustment may be expected to prevent deterioration of expatriate job performance. But is adjustment a component or a determinant of expatriate job performance?

We believe that much can be gained by clearly delineating adjustment and expatriate job performance (see also Aycan, 1997a, 1997b). We maintain that adjustment is best conceptualized as a proximal determinant of both early returns and expatriate job performance. In other words, adjustment is relevant to expatriate job performance probably only as a determinant. Adjustment is not an end in itself, but rather a part of a process that allows the expatriate to be able to focus on and carry through the tasks of the job that he/she has been sent to perform.

Expatriate Job Performance

An important consideration that tends to get overlooked by the expatriate management literature is that expatriates are in the country of their assignment for performing a job (Shaffer & Harrison, 1998). It is surprising that the criterion of job performance has attracted the least amount of attention of all variables studied in relation to expatriates. Most studies examine predictors of adjustment, acculturation, adaptation, early returns, or variables hypothesized to be important determinants of 'overseas success.' This has been the case despite complaints from multinational managers of 'high failure rates and *low job performance* (emphasis added)' (Boyacigiller, 1991). According to Copeland and Griggs (1985) a large portion of expatriates who do complete their overseas assignments are marginally effective or ineffective in their job performance.

Throughout the last decade, great progress has been made in enhancing our understanding of the meaning of job success in domestic contexts. For example, the work of Campbell and colleagues (Campbell, 1990; Campbell et al., 1996; Campbell, McCloy, Oppler & Sager, 1993; Campbell, McHenry & Wise, 1990) relies on an eight component taxonomy for job performance across jobs. In a similar vein, Viswesvaran and colleagues (Viswesvaran, 1993; Viswesvaran & Ones, 2000; Viswesvaran, Ones & Schmidt, 1996; Viswesvaran, Schmidt & Ones, 1994) have relied on a nine-dimensional hierarchical model with a general factor at the apex of the hierarchy. In this model, all measures of job performance are conceptualized to be construct deficient manifestations of the

general factor. Other performance models also exist and can be described using different levels of hierarchy and composites from the Campbell or Viswesvaran, Schmidt, and Ones models (e.g., Borman & Brush, 1993; Borman & Motowidlo, 1993; Organ, 1994).

This emerging literature is applicable to defining and measuring expatriate job performance which can then guide practice in assessing expatriates and offer solutions to the criterion problem in evaluating expatriate selection and training efforts in multinational organizations. That is, we expect that mostly the same taxonomy of job performance components will apply to expatriate managers and other international assignees. The eight dimensions of Campbell and the nine dimensions of Viswesvaran et al. are meant to apply across jobs, settings, and industries with specific content and aspects of each dimension varying across jobs. For expatriates, critical incidents for the dimensions will be different. That is, when expatriates are the focus, the content of these dimensions will need to be anchored using critical incidents specific to the job, but the overall taxonomy and structure of the job performance domain will remain essentially unchanged.

Hough and Dunnette (1992) were among the first to provide behavioral dimensions for effective expatriate job performance and adjustment to living abroad, using the critical incidents methodology. They examined the behavioral dimensions critical for effective performance in international assignments. Data were collected from expatriate and repatriate managers working for a multinational telecommunications firm and their spouses. Hough and Dunnette (1992) identified 121 critical incidents of expatriate behaviors. Eleven critical dimensions of expatriate success were identified: adjustment to living abroad, adjustment to foreign business practices, establishing/maintaining business contacts, knowledge of foreign language, spouse and family support, technical competence, working with others, communicating/persuading, initiative/effort, company support and factors relevant for accepting foreign assignments.

Our reading of Hough and Dunnette's work suggests that while accepting foreign assignments, spouse and family support, knowledge of foreign language, adjustment to living abroad and company support might be important *determinants* of job performance, they are not part of the criterion domain of interest (i.e., job performance). On the other hand, establishing and maintaining business contacts, technical competence, working with others, communicating and persuading, initiative and effort may be construed as different dimensions of expatriate job performance. This conceptualization of the job performance construct is congruent with the recent emerging industrial-organizational psychology literature in this area (e.g., Campbell, 1990; Campbell et al., 1996; Viswesvaran, 1993;

Table 20.1   *Working model of expatriate job performance*

Job performance dimension	Description
Establishing and maintaining business contacts	Identifying, developing, using and maintaining business contacts to achieve goals
Technical performance	Task performance
Productivity	Volume of work produced by the expatriate
Working with others	Proficiency in working with others, assisting others in the organization
Communicating and persuading	Oral and written proficiency in gathering and transmitting information; persuading others
Effort and initiative	Dedication to one's job; amount of work expended in striving to do a good job
Personal discipline	The extent to which counterproductive behaviors at work are avoided
Interpersonal relations	The degree to which the expatriate facilitates team performance; supports and champions others in the organization and unit
Management and supervision	Proficiency in the coordination of different roles in the organization
Overall job performance	Composite of all dimensions of expatriate job performance described above; also refers to the general non-halo factor that is hierarchically extracted from ratings of job performance dimensions (Viswesvaran, 1993)

Note: Descriptions are distilled from Campbell et al. (1996), Hough and Dunnette (1992), Ones and Viswesvaran (1997), Viswesvaran and Ones (2000) and Viswesvaran et al. (1996).

Viswesvaran et al., 1996). However, there are a number of job performance dimensions that are likely to hold across domestic and expatriate jobs, which were not incorporated into the Hough and Dunnette (1992) study. These are personal discipline (Campbell, 1990; Viswesvaran, 1993), interpersonal relations (Campbell, 1990; Viswesvaran, 1993), management and supervision (Campbell, 1990; Viswesvaran, 1993), and productivity (Viswesvaran, 1993).

Table 20.1 presents a potential model of expatriate performance components. This is a *working model* of expatriate job performance dimensions largely drawn from Campbell et al. (1996), Hough and Dunnette (1992), Ones and Viswesvaran (1997), Viswesvaran and Ones (2000), and Viswesvaran et al. (1996). Caligiuri (1997) has also presented a model of expatriate performance. Her model distinguishes between four dimensions of expatriate performance: (1) technical performance; (2) contextual/prosocial performance; (3) contextual/managerial performance (e.g., training and developing subordinates); and (4) expatriate specific performance (e.g., language and cultural proficiency).

We should note that the job performance dimensions presented in Table 20.1 (or those presented by Caligiuri, 1997) are not expected to be orthogonal for expatriates. There is meta-analytic evidence from studies conducted in the domestic context that over 50% of the variance in the job performance construct is attributable to a general factor across the dimensions (Viswesvaran, 1993; Viswesvaran & Ones, 2000). The positive manifold anticipated in the matrix of job performance dimension intercorrelations is a manifestation of this general factor. A similar positive manifold can be expected in modeling expatriate job performance.

A consideration in obtaining ratings is the source of the rating. A major problem in expatriate job performance research has been the use of self-report instruments to measure the constructs. While self-ratings are important in their own right, they do not constitute a good criterion against which IWO psychologists can evaluate their predictors or training interventions. For expatriates, two more relevant sources for performance ratings are home country supervisors and host country national co-workers (Zeira & Banai, 1985). To date, little research has utilized either source. Although most authors writing on expatriate management and cross-cultural IWO psychology recognize the relevance and importance of the host country national perspective, only a handful of studies have actually used performance evaluations obtained from host country nationals. (There are a few notable exceptions [e.g., Kealey, 1989; Kraimer et al., 2001; Sinangil & Ones, 1997; Zeira & Banai, 1985].) This is unfortunate because host country nationals have a greater opportunity to observe expatriate performance on a daily basis. Previous research has shown that the opportunity to observe performance is critical in improving the psychometric quality of job performance ratings (Rothstein, 1990). We hope that the publication of this chapter will spur research on measuring expatriate job performance using multiple perspectives. In the day and age of 360-degree feedback interventions, this, hopefully, is no longer regarded as an unattainable ideal.

EMERGING ISSUES IN EXPATRIATE MANAGEMENT

Non-Work Considerations: Spouse and Family

The failure of family and spouse to adjust to the international environment is one of the non-work dimensions which has been shown to negatively affect expatriate job performance and increase the likelihood of early overseas returns (Black & Gregersen, 1991a, 1991b; Tung, 1981). These results are not limited to Western expatriates. Fukuda and Chu's (1994) study reports that family adjustment problems are ranked number one in explaining early returns for Japanese expatriates.

However, little research has attempted to determine the precise role of the spouse and family in relation to expatriate adjustment and more importantly expatriate job performance. According to Black et al.'s (1991) model of international adjustment, the degree of expatriate adjustment to work, interaction with host nationals, and general environment is affected by both individual and organizational skills, some of which affect all areas of adjustment while others only relate to specific areas. Organizational issues related to adjustment include organizational culture, social support, logistical help, and role factors such as clarity, discretion, novelty, and conflict. Individual skills or issues include self-efficacy, interpersonal skills, and perception skills. Two areas of non-work variables cited as important to expatriate adjustment are cultural novelty and family-spouse presence/adjustment. Black and Stephens (1989) suggest that the major advantage of married expatriates is the social support provided by the spouse.

There are potentially two aspects to social support for an expatriate manager. The first aspect revolves around the general emotional and psychological support provided by in-country family members. This type of support would be expected to most directly affect individual skills such as self-efficacy. The second aspect of social support would involve providing a cultural haven to the expatriate manager.

The ability of spouse and family to provide social support is likely to depend on *their* degree of adjustment. Several studies suggest that the inability to interact successfully with host country nationals can lead to isolation, loneliness, inadequate adjustment, and premature return from assignment (Tung, 1988). In a preliminary examination of spousal adjustment, Black and Gregersen (1991b) found that cross-cultural training, social support networks, acceptable standard of living, cultural novelty, and early involvement in selection predicted positive spousal adjustment.

As mentioned earlier, family and spouse adjustment is related to positive outcomes such as avoiding early returns and improved adjustment and job performance (Caligiuri, Joshi & Lazarova, 1999; Tung, 1999). Shaffer and Harrison (1998) considered the role of family context factors in expatriates' decisions to return early from their assignments. Testing their model with a sample of 224 expatriates and their spouses, they found support for direct, indirect, and moderating effects of family responsibility, spouse adjustment, and spouse overall satisfaction on withdrawal cognitions.

An initial meta-analysis confirmed that spouse adjustment is related to expatriate job performance (Alampay et al., 2000). This finding can be explained by a spillover theory (Caligiuri, Hyland, Joshi & Bross, 1998), where non-work and work life are related because affective responses from one domain 'spill over' into the other. The role of children in expatriate adjustment remains an unaddressed area.

Women in Expatriate Management

The numbers of women in expatriate management have traditionally been low. Further, despite the increasing numbers of women in management in general, the numbers of expatriate women have remained low. In the early 1980s, about 3% of US expatriates and 1% of Canadian expatriates were female (Adler, 1984a, 1984b, 1984c, 1979). More recent research indicates that these figures might have crept up to about 5% to 10% (Arthur & Bennett, 1997; Caligiuri, 1997). Current estimates suggest that between 5% and 12% of expatriates are women (Black, Gregersen, Mendenhall & Stroh, 1999; Tung, 1987).

Traditionally, three reasons have been put forth for the low number of female expatriates: (1) women are not interested in international careers; (2) organizations refuse to send women employees abroad for fear of poor job performance in foreign cultures; and (3) foreign cultures discriminate against women (Adler, 1987). Adler (1993) suggested that women might not be selected for expatriate positions because those making selection decisions believe in these three prevalent myths that prevent them from hiring females.

Some recent research attention has been directed at examining each of these three points. Virtually all studies addressing the first potential myth have found that women are interested in international assignments and indicate that they would be likely to accept expatriate positions (Stone, 1991; Stroh, Varma & Valy, 2000). Concerning the second myth, while organizations report that they are no less likely to send female expatriates than their male counterparts, expatriate women report the opposite to be true (Stroh et al., 2000). The third potential myth, that women are met with hostility in foreign cultures, has also been investigated (e.g., Westwood & Leung,

1994). One of the reasons for the smaller number of women expatriates may have to do with the perceptions of some cultures being particularly hostile to women in work environments.

There appears to be tremendous corporate resistance to selecting female employees for overseas assignments. Survey evidence suggests that about half of multinationals hesitate to select women for expatriate positions (Adler, 1984a, 1987; Thal & Cateora, 1979) and about 70% of multinationals cite foreigner prejudice as the reason behind their decisions not to send female expatriates (Adler, 1987).

Are foreign work environments, especially in certain parts of the world such as Asia and the Middle East, more hostile to female expatriates? Are multinational organizations justified in shying away from female expatriates? In our own recent research, we examined women expatriates' performance ratings *vis-à-vis* their male counterparts in Turkey. Performance ratings were supplied by Turkish co-workers. Results indicated that for most dimensions of job performance, female expatriates were rated slightly higher than males. Further, female expatriates displayed somewhat higher overall adjustment ($m = 7.33$, sd = 1.12) compared to male expatriates ($m = 6.93$, sd = 1.23). Interestingly, the only effect size that indicated slightly higher ratings for males was on technical competence ($d = .12$). Women expatriates were generally rated by host country nationals more highly than their male counterparts in terms of their overall job performance (Sinangil & Ones, 1999). The main conclusion from the line of research addressing the low number of female expatriates is that while women are interested in expatriate positions and host country nationals may be welcoming to female expatriates, for whatever reason organizations appear to be hesitant in sending women on such assignments.

In this area, from a practice perspective, the message to multinationals and human resource managers is clear: Do not assume (based on stereotypes and perceptions) that female expatriates will perform poorly on international assignments and will be perceived poorly by host country nationals in male dominant cultures. In this day and age, there is not justifiable reason for excluding or limiting women from expatriate assignments. Caligiuri and Cascio (1998) discuss strategies for maximizing the likelihood of success of women expatriates.

Host Country Perspective

Expatriate assignments involve balancing of multiple and often conflicting goals. The balancing act needs to take into account the home organization and culture as well as the host country perspective. The values, beliefs, and attitudes of the host culture represent a part of the puzzle that can advance understanding of factors that contribute to expatriate adjustment and overseas job performance.

Unfortunately, very little research has been conducted to understand the host country perspective in expatriate management. Even though most authors writing on expatriate management and cross-cultural industrial psychology appear to recognize the relevance and potential importance of host country national perspective in understanding expatriate psychological states and behaviors overseas, only a handful of studies have actually studied perceptions and evaluations of the host country nationals. Further, these few studies have been limited in their scope to western/industrialized countries, and are already likely outdated in today's rapidly evolving global economy.

Zeira and Banai (1985) were the first to investigate the 'expectations of host country organizations concerning desired selection criteria for expatriate managers' (p. 37) and to compare these expectations with those of headquarters and the expatriate managers. They reported the frequencies of endorsement for 14 selection criteria for expatriate managers as perceived by host country organizations. Similarly, Pazy and Zeira (1985) examined the compatibility of host country professionals' expectations with those of parent-country managers. The focus of this second investigation was trainees' effectiveness. Zeira and Banai (1985) prefaced their exploratory study as a precursor to 'sophisticated multivariate analysis this topic deserves' (p. 40).

Unfortunately, it does not appear that many 'sophisticated' or in depth analyses of the host country perspective have taken place in the subsequent literature. Kealey (1989) used local peer ratings of effectiveness in transferring skills and knowledge for Canadian technical advisors posted to developing countries. His findings are perhaps the most comprehensive in suggesting that peer (local/host country) ratings of overseas job performance can provide us with a better understanding of the factors contributing to acculturation stress (culture shock), adjustment, job performance, and early returns. Adding to our small pool of knowledge about the host country perspective, Black and Mendenhall's (1990) comprehensive review of cross-cultural training effectiveness noted five studies (Landis, Brislin & Hulgus, 1985; Randolph, Landis & Tzeng, 1977; Weldon, Carlston, Rissman, Slobodin & Triandis, 1975; Worchel & Mitchell, 1972) where host national group measures were used in assessing learning.

In an attempt to address the gap in knowledge of the host country perspectives in expatriate management, Sinangil and Ones (1997) reported a series of three studies. Three parts from a large-scale project were used to investigate (a) factors that host country nationals (HCN) perceive to be important for expatriate success, (b) the relevance of their appraisals of these factors in their expatriate coworkers for important criteria (expatriate adjustment to living abroad and intentions to complete the assignment), and (c) the criterion-related validities of expatriate characteristics for host country national ratings of job performance. Data from 220 matched pairs of expatriates working in Turkey and their Turkish co-workers were used.

The purpose of the first part of our study was to empirically examine factors that host country nationals perceive to contribute to international assignee success. Confirmatory factor analysis indicated that five factors adequately explained the data. These factors were: (1) job knowledge and motivation; (2) relational skills; (3) flexibility/adaptability; (4) extra-cultural openness; and (5) family situation. For host country coworkers, the job knowledge and motivation dimension was found to be the most important factor, and the least important factor was family situation. The second part of the study examined the relationships between host country national ratings (HCN ratings) of expatriates on these five broad categories of attributes of success and (a) expatriate adjustment, and (b) intentions to stay in the country of assignment. HCN ratings on the five dimensions of expatriate success attributes correlated moderately but consistently with expatriate adjustment to living abroad and expatriate intentions to stay. The third part of our study examined the criterion-related validities of expatriate characteristics for predicting HCN ratings of nine job performance dimensions as well as for overall job performance. Criterion-related validities of expatriate background variables (e.g., age, experience), adjustment to living abroad, and ethnocentric attitudes were computed. Across different job performance dimensions, adjustment to living abroad emerged as the best predictor of HCN ratings. Previous expatriate performance and language knowledge proved to be particularly poor predictors of HCN job performance ratings.

Two major weaknesses continue to afflict research in expatriate management: (1) single-source ratings; and relatedly (2) the problem of common method variance. Too often only data are obtained solely from expatriates. It should come as little surprise then that results from much expatriate management research have been biased by shared method variance (see Ones & Viswesvaran, 1997 for an elaboration of this problem.) In IWO psychology research it has become increasingly clear that self-ratings of performance do not converge well with ratings from other sources (Harris & Schaubroeck, 1988). On the other hand, correlations among peers and supervisors, and subordinates approximate interrater reliabilities within one source (e.g., Harris & Schaubroeck, 1988; Viswesvaran et al., 1996; Viswesvaran, Ones & Schmidt, 1997). In the expatriate management literature, Kealey (1989) presented similar findings. One should be careful not to use self reports of job performance or its dimensions in validating or

researching determinants of these constructs, as such a practice is likely to result in predictors that are quite (if not completely) different from ones that would be found to contribute to success if host country nationals (peer and subordinate) or head quarters/supervisor ratings are used. We beg expatriate management researchers to use non-self-report criteria.

Future research on expatriates should examine the host country perspective in other cultures. Both home headquarters and host country data can fruitfully be employed and should be used in expatriate management research. We are convinced that better understanding of the host country national perspective from this research can aid in personnel selection and training that is in line with host country expectations. Using multiple measurements of the same constructs is a hallmark of good science. Research on expatriates has reached a point where measurements using multiple perspectives and multiple levels of analysis are likely to be most useful.

CONCLUSIONS

Although expatriate failure rates and adjustment have been studied and written about for over 50 years, much of the empirical work on expatriates has lacked in rigor until recently. In addition to the extensive reliance on self-report measures discussed above, another weakness in the literature has been reliance on cross-sectional research designs. While cross-sectional research designs can be useful, longitudinal research can uniquely answer questions. We are hopeful that given the increasing rate of globalization of work, we will start seeing longitudinal studies in expatriate management.

Our other hopes for the expatriate management literature involve expanding the findings from mostly Western expatriates to expatriates from other parts of the world (e.g., Japanese expatriates working in North America) and to other occupational groups (non-managerial, non-professional guest workers). Thanks to the Internet and other technological advances, there are unprecedented opportunities for collaboration among researchers and practitioners who are in different parts of the world. Collecting data in international contexts is progressively getting easier. IWO psychologists can be on the cutting edge of such research. Our traditional strengths in measurement should serve us well. For expatriate management, the state of the art research is around the corner; let us just hope that practice follows.

ACKNOWLEDGMENTS

We extend our deepest appreciation to Chockalingam Viswesvaran for his suggestions for revisions.

REFERENCES

Adler, N.J. (1979). Women as androgynous managers: A conceptualization of the potential for American women in international management. *International Journal of Intercultural Relations*, 3, 407–435.

Adler, N.J. (1984a). Expecting international success: Female managers overseas. *Columbia Journal of World Business*, *14*, 79–85.

Adler, N.J. (1984b). Women do not want international careers: And other myths about international management. *Organizational Dynamics*, *13*(2), 66–79.

Adler, N.J. (1984c). Women in international management: Where are they? *California Management Review*, *26*, 78–89.

Adler, N.J. (1986). *International dimensions of organizational behavior*. Belmont, CA: PWS-Kent.

Adler, N.J. (1987). Pacific basin managers: A Gaijin, not a woman. *Human Resource Management*, *26*, 169–191.

Adler, N.J. (1991). *International dimensions of organizational behavior* (2nd ed.). Boston: PWS-Kent.

Adler, N.J. (1993). Competitive frontiers: Women managers in the triad. *International Studies of Management and Organization*, *23*(2), 3–23.

Adler, N.J., & Bartholomew, S. (1992). Managing globally competent people. *Academy of Management Executive*, *6*, 52–65.

Alampay, R.H., Beehr, T.A., & Christiansen, N.D. (2000). *Antecedents and consequences of employees' adjustment to overseas assignments*. Unpublished manuscript.

Albert, R.D. (1983). The intercultural sensitizer or culture assimilator: A cognitive approach. In D. Landis & R.W. Brislin (Eds.), *Handbook of intercultural training: Issues in training methodology* (Vol. 2, pp. 186–217). New York: Pergamon.

Arthur, W., Jr., & Bennett, W., Jr. (1995). The international assignee: The relative importance of factors perceived to contribute to success. *Personnel Psychology*, *48*, 99–114.

Arthur, W.A., & Bennett, W.B. (1997). A comparative test of alternative models of international assignee job performance. In D.M. Saunders (Series Ed.) & Z. Aycan (Vol. Ed.), *New approaches to employee management: Vol. 4. Expatriate management: Theory and research* (pp. 141–172). Greenwich, CT: JAI Press.

Aryee, S. (1997). Selection and training of expatriate employees. In N. Anderson & P. Herriot (Eds.), *Handbook of selection and appraisal*. London: Wiley.

Aycan, Z. (1997a). Acculturation of expatriate managers: A process model of adjustment and performance. In D.M. Saunders (Series Ed.) & Z. Aycan (Vol. Ed.), *New Approaches to Employee Management: Vol. 4. Expatriate management: Theory and research*. Greenwich, CT: JAI Press.

Aycan, Z. (1997b). Expatriate adjustment as a multifaceted phenomenon: Individual and organizational level predictors. *International Journal of Human Resource Management*, *8*(4), 434–456.

Aycan, Z., & Berry, J.W. (1996). Impact of employment-related experiences on immigrants' psychological well-being and adaptation to Canada. *Canadian Journal of Behavioral Science*, *28*, 240–251.

Aycan, Z., & Kanungo, R.N. (1997). Current issues and future challenges in expatriate management. In D.M. Saunders (Series Ed.) & Z. Aycan (Vol. Ed.), *New approaches to employee management* (pp. 245–260). Greenwich, CT: JAI Press.

Bandura, A. (1977). *Social learning theory*. Englewood Cliffs, NJ: Prentice-Hall.

Bartlett, C.A., & Ghoshal, S. (1989). *Managing across borders: The transnational solution*. Boston, MA: Harvard Business School Press.

Benson, P.G. (1978). Measuring cross-cultural adjustment: The problem of criteria. *International Journal of Intercultural Relations*, *2*, 21–36.

Berry, J.W. (1992). Acculturation and adaptation in a new society. *International Migration*, *30*, 69–85.

Berry, J.W., Poortinga, Y.H., Segall, M.H., & Dasen, P.R. (1992). *Cross-cultural psychology: Research and applications*. New York: Cambridge University Press.

Bhawuk, D.P.S. (1995). The role of culture theory in cross-cultural training: A comparative evaluation of culture-specific, culture-general, and theory-based assimilators. Unpublished doctoral dissertation, University of Illinois at Urbana-Champaign.

Bhawuk, D.P.S. (1998). The role of culture theory in cross-cultural training: A multimethod study of culture-specific, culture-general, and culture theory-based assimilators. *Journal of Cross-Cultural Psychology*, *29*(5), 630–655.

Bhawuk, D.P.S., & Brislin, R.W. (2000). Cross-cultural training: A review. *Applied Psychology*, *49*(1), 162–191.

Bird, A., & Dunbar, R. (1991, Spring). Getting the job done over there: Improving expatriate effectiveness. *National Productivity Review*, 145–156.

Birdseye, M.G., & Hill, J.S. (1995). Individual, organizational/work and environmental influences on expatriate turnover tendencies: An empirical study. *Journal of International Business Studies*, *26*, 787–813.

Black, J.S. (1988). Work role transitions: A study of American expatriate managers in Japan. *Journal of International Business Studies*, *19*, 277–294.

Black, J.S., & Gregersen, H.B. (1991a). Antecedents to cross-cultural adjustment for expatriates in Pacific Rim assignments. *Human Relations*, *44*, 497–515.

Black, J.S., & Gregersen, H.B. (1991b). The other half of the picture: Antecedents of spouse cross-cultural adjustment. *International Journal of Intercultural Relations*, *22*, 461–477.

Black, J.S., & Gregersen, H.B. (1999). The right way to manage expats. *Harvard Business Review (March-April)*, 52–62.

Black, J.S., Gregersen, H.B., Mendenhall, M.E., & Stroh, L.K. (1999). *Global assignments*. Boston, MA: Addison-Wesley.

Black, J.S., & Stephens, G.K. (1989). The influence of the spouse on American expatriate adjustment and intent to stay in Pacific Rim overseas assignments. *Journal of Management*, *15*, 529–544.

Black, J.S., & Mendenhall, M. (1990). Cross-cultural training effectiveness: A review and a theoretical framework for future research. *Academy of Management Review, 15*(1), 113–136.

Black, J.S., Mendenhall, M., & Oddou, G. (1991). Toward a comprehensive model of international adjustment: An integration of multiple theoretical perspectives. *Academy of Management Review, 16*(2), 291–317.

Borman, W.C., & Brush, D.H. (1993). More progress toward a taxonomy of managerial performance requirements. *Human Performance, 6*(1), 1–21.

Borman, W.C., & Motowidlo, S.J. (1993). Expanding the criterion domain to include elements of contextual performance. In N. Schmitt & W.C. Borman (Eds.), *Personnel selection in organizations.* San Francisco, CA: Jossey-Bass.

Boyacigiller, N. (1991). The international assignment reconsidered. In M. Mendenhall & G. Oddou (Eds.), *Readings and cases in international human resource management* (pp. 148–155). Boston, MA: PWS-Kent.

Brewster, C. (1991). *The management of expatriates.* London: Kogan Page.

Brewster, C., & Pickard, J. (1994). Evaluating expatriate training. *International Studies of Management and Organization, 24*(3), 18–35.

Briody, E.K., & Beeber Chrisman, J. (1991). Cultural adaptation on overseas assignments. *Human Organization, 50*(3), 264–282.

Brislin, R.W. (1981). *Cross-cultural encounters: Face-to-face interaction.* New York: Pergamon Press.

Brislin, R.W., & Bhawuk, D.P.S. (1999). Cross-cultural training: Research and innovations. In J. Adamopoulos & Y. Kashima (Eds.), *Social psychology and cultural context* (pp. 205–216). Thousand Oaks, CA: Sage.

Brislin, R.W., & Pedersen, P. (1976). *Cross-cultural orientation programs.* New York: Gardner.

Brislin, R.W., & Yoshida, T. (1994). *Intercultural communication training: An introduction.* Thousand Oaks, CA: Sage.

Byrnes, F.C. (1966). Role shock: An occupational hazard of American technical assistants abroad. *The Annals of the American Academy of Political and Social Science,* 95–108.

Caligiuri, P.M. (1995). Individual characteristics related to effective performance in cross-cultural work settings (expatriate). Unpublished doctoral dissertation, The Pennsylvania State University, PA.

Caligiuri, P.M. (1997). Assessing expatriate success: Beyond just 'being there.' In D.M. Saunders & Z. Aycan (Eds.), *New approaches to employment management, Vol. 4* (117–140). Greenwich, CT: JAI Press.

Caligiuri, P.M. (2000a). The Big Five personality characteristics as predictors of *expatriate's* desire to terminate the assignment and supervisor-rated performance. *Personnel Psychology, 53*(1), 67–88.

Caligiuri, P.M. (2000b). Selecting expatriates for personality characteristics: A moderating effect of personality on the relationship between host national contact and cross-cultural adjustment. *Management International Review, 40,* 61–80.

Caligiuri, P.M., & Cascio, W.F. (1998). Can we send her there? Maximizing the success of western women on global assignments. *Journal of World Business, 33*(4), 394–416.

Caligiuri, P.M., Hyland, M., Joshi, A., & Bross, A. (1998). A theoretical framework for examining the relationship between family adjustment and expatriate adjustment to working in the host country. *Journal of Applied Psychology, 83,* 598–640.

Caligiuri, P.M., Jacobs, R.R., & Farr, J.L. (1999). The attitudinal and behavioral openness scale: Scale development and construct validation. *International Journal of Intercultural Relations, 56,* 1–22.

Caligiuri, P.M., Joshi, A., & Lazarova, M. (1999). Factors influencing the adjustment of women on global assignments. *The International Journal of Human Resource Management, 10*(2), 163–179.

Campbell, J.P. (1990). Modeling the performance prediction problem in Industrial and Organizational Psychology. In M.D. Dunnette & L.M. Hough (Eds.), *Handbook of Industrial and Organizational Psychology* (Vol. 1, 2nd ed., pp. 687–732). Palo Alto, CA: Consulting Psychologists Press.

Campbell, J.P., Gasser, M.B., & Oswald, F.L. (1996). The substantive nature of job performance variability. In K.R. Murphy (Ed.), *Individual differences and behavior in organizations* (pp. 258–299). San Francisco: Jossey-Bass.

Campbell, J.P., McCloy, R.A., Oppler, S.H., & Sager, C.E. (1993). A theory of performance. In N. Schmitt & W.C. Borman (Eds.), *Personnel selection in organizations.* San Francisco, CA: Jossey-Bass.

Campbell, J.P., McHenry, J.J., & Wise, L.L. (1990). Modeling job performance in a population of jobs. *Personnel Psychology, 43,* 313–333.

Chemers, M.M. (1969). Cross-cultural training as a means of improving situational favorableness. *Human Relations, 22,* 531–546.

Church, A.T. (1982). Sojourner adjustment. *Psychological Bulletin, 9*(3), 540–572.

Copeland, L., & Griggs, L. (1985). *Going international: How to make friends and deal effectively in the global marketplace.* New York: Random House.

Copeland, L., & Griggs, L. (1988). The internationable employee. *Management Review, 77,* 52–53.

Cuthill, S. (1997). *Global Best in Class Study: Summary Report.* Arthur Andersen and Bennett Associates, Andersen Worldwide, SC.

Dalton, M., & Wilson, M. (2000). The relationship of the Five-Factor Model of Personality to job performance for a group of Middle Eastern *expatriate* managers. *Journal of Cross-Cultural Psychology, 31*(2), 250–258.

David, K.H. (1972). Intercultural adjustment and applications for reinforcement theory to problems of culture shock. *Trends, 4*(3), 1–64.

Deller, J. (1997). Expatriate selection: Possibilities and limitations of using personality scales. In D.M. Saunders (Series Ed.), & Z. Aycan (Vol. Ed.), *New approaches to employee management: Vol. 4 Expatriate management: Theory and research.* Greenwich, CT: JAI Press.

Deller, J. (1998, August). *Personality scales can make a difference in expatriate selection: The case of Germans working in Korea.* Paper presented at the International Congress of Applied Psychology, San Francisco, CA.

Deshpande, S.P., & Viswesvaran, C. (1992). Is cross-cultural training of expatriate managers effective: A meta-analysis. *International Journal of Intercultural Relations, 16*(3), 295–310.

Dicken, C.F. (1969). Predicting the success of Peace Corps community development workers. *Journal of Consulting and Clinical Psychology, 33*(5), 597–606.

Dicken, C.F., & Black, J.D. (1965). Predictive validity of psychometric evaluations of supervisors. *Journal of Applied Psychology, 49*(1), 34–47.

Dinges, N. (1983). Intercultural competence. In D. Landis & R. Brislin (Eds.), *Handbook of intercultural training, Vol. 1* (pp. 176–202). New York: Pergamon Press.

Dollins, I. (1999, Winter). 1998 Global Relocation Survey: Current trends regarding expatriate activity. *Employment Relations Today,* 1–11.

Dunbar, E. (1992). Adjustment and satisfaction of expatriate U.S. personnel. *International Journal of Intercultural Relations, 16,* 1–16.

Earley, P.C. (1987). Intercultural training for managers: A comparison of documentary and interpersonal methods. *Academy of Management Journal, 30,* 685–698.

Ezekiel, R. (1968). The personal future and Peace Corps competence. *Journal of Personality and Social Psychology Monograph, 8,* 2 (pt.2).

Fiedler, F.E., Mitchell, T.R., & Triandis, H.C. (1971). The culture assimilator: An approach to cross-cultural training. *Journal of Applied Psychology, 55,* 95–102.

Forster, N. (2000). The myth of the 'international manager'. *International Journal of Human Resource Management, 11*(1), 126–142.

Fukuda, K., & Chu, P. (1994). Wrestling with expatriate family problems: Japanese experiences in East Asia. *International Studies of Management and Organizations, 24,* 36–47.

Furnham, A., & Bochner, S. (1986). *Culture shock: Psychological reactions to unfamiliar environments.* London: Methuen.

Garonzik, R., Brockner, J., & Siegel, P.A. (2000). Identifying international assignees at risk for premature departure: The interactive effect of outcome favorability and procedural fairness. *Journal of Applied Psychology, 85*(1), 13–20.

Grant, L. (1997, April). That overseas job could derail your career. *Fortune, 135,* 166.

Gregersen, H.B., & Black, J.S. (1990). A multifaceted approach to retention in international assignments. *Group and Organization Studies, 15,* 461–485.

Gudykunst, W.B., & Hammer, M.R. (1983). Basic training design: Approaches to intercultural training. In D. Landis & R.W. Brislin (Eds.), *Handbook of intercultural training: Issues in theory and design: Vol. 1* (pp. 118–154). Elmsford, NY: Pergamon.

Guthrie, G.M. (1975). A behavioral analysis of culture learning. In R.W. Brislin, S. Bochner & W.J. Lonner (Eds.), *Cross-cultural perspectives on learning* (pp. 95–115). New York: Sage and Wiley/Halstead.

Guzzo, A.R., Noonan, A.K., & Elron, E. (1994). Expatriate managers and the psychological contract. *Journal of Applied Psychology, 79*(4), 617–626.

Hammer, M.R. (1987). Behavioral dimensions of intercultural effectiveness: A replication and extension. *International Journal of Intercultural Relations, 11,* 65–88.

Hammer, M., Gudykunst, W.B., & Wiseman, R.L. (1978). Dimensions of intercultural effectiveness: An exploratory study. *International Journal of Intercultural Relations, 4*(2), 382–393.

Hannigan, T.P. (1990). Traits, attitudes, and skills that are related to intercultural effectiveness and their implications for cross-cultural training: A review of the literature. *International Journal of Intercultural Relations, 14,* 89–111.

Harris, J.G. (1973). A Science of the South Pacific: Analysis of the character structure of the Peace Corps volunteer. *American Psychologist, 28,* 232–247.

Harris, J.G. (1975). Identification of cross-cultural talent: The empirical approach of the Peace Corps. *Topics in Culture Learning, 3,* 66–78.

Harris, M.M., & Schaubroeck, J. (1988). A meta-analysis of self-supervisor, self-peer, and peer-supervisor ratings. *Personnel Psychology, 41,* 43–62.

Harris, P.R., & Harris, D.L. (1972). Training for cultural understanding. *Training and Development Journal, 26,* 8–10.

Harrison, J.K. (1992). Individual and combined effects of behavior modeling and the culture assimilator in cross-cultural management training. *Journal of Applied Psychology, 77,* 952–962.

Harrison, R., & Hopkins, R.L. (1967). The design of cross-cultural training: An alternative to the university model. *Journal of Applied Behavioral Science, 3,* 431–460.

Harzing, A.K. (1992). The persistent myth of high expatriate failure rates. *The International Journal of Human Resource Management, 6*(2), 457–474.

Hawes, F., & Kealey, D.J. (1979). *Canadians in development: An empirical study of adaptation and effectiveness on overseas assignment.* Communication Branch Briefing Center, Canadian International Development Agency.

Hogan G.W., & Goodson J.R. (1990). The key to expatriate success. *Training and Development Journal, 44*(1), 50–53.

Hough, L.M., & Dunnette, M.D. (1992, August). US managers abroad: What it takes to succeed. In R. Guzzo (Chair), *Expatriate assignments: Identifying candidates, managing retention, and strategic roles.* Symposium conducted at the 52nd annual meeting of Academy of Management, Las Vegas.

Human Resource Institute (1998). *Comprehensive personnel management report: Global staffing* (Research Report). St. Petersburg, FL.

Hunter, J.E., & Schmidt, F.L. (1990). *Methods of meta-analysis: Correcting error and bias in research findings.* Newbury Park, CA: Sage.

Kealey, D.J. (1989). A study of cross-cultural effectiveness: Theoretical issues, practical applications. *International Journal of Intercultural Relations, 13,* 387–428.

Kealey, D.J., & Ruben, B.D. (1983). Cross-cultural personnel selection criteria, issues, and methods. In D. Landis & R.W. Brislin (Eds.), *Handbook of intercultural training, Vol. I* (pp. 155–175). New York: Pergamon.

Kolb, D. (1976). *Learning style inventory.* Boston: McBer.

Kraemer, A. (1973). *Development of a cultural self-awareness approach to instruction in intercultural communication* (Technical Report No. 73–17). Arlington, VA: HumRRO.

Kraemer, A. (1974). *Workshop in intercultural communication: A handbook for instructors* (Technical Report No. 74–13). Arlington, VA: HumRRO.

Kraimer, M.L., Wayne, S.J., & Jaworski, R.A. (2001). Sources of support and expatriate performance: The mediating role of expatriate adjustment. *Personnel Psychology, 54.*

Kuncel, N.R., Hezlett, S.A., & Ones, D.S. (2001). A comprehensive meta-analysis of the predictive validity of the Graduate Record Examinations: Implications for graduate student selection and performance. *Psychological Bulletin, 127,* 162–181.

Landis, D., & Bhagat, R. (Eds.) (1996). *Handbook of intercultural training.* Newbury Park, CA: Sage.

Landis, D., Brislin, R.W., & Hulgus, J.F. (1985). Attributional training versus contact in acculturative learning: A laboratory study. *Journal of Applied Social Psychology, 15,* 466–482.

Lee, J.A. (1966). Cultural analysis in overseas operations. *Harvard Business Review, 44*(3), 106–144.

Malpass, R.S., & Salancik, G.R. (1977). Linear and branching formats in culture assimilator training. *International Journal of Intercultural Relations, 1*(2), 76–87.

McGoldrick, F. (1997, Summer). Expatriate compensation and benefit practices of U.S. and Canadian firms: Survey results. *International HR Journal,* 13–17.

Mendenhall, M., & Oddou, G. (1985). The dimensions of expatriate acculturation: A review. *Academy of Management Review, 10*(1), 39–47.

Micco, L. (1998, February). Study: Homesickness of foreign-born executives too often is overlooked. *HR News,* 12.

Miller, E.L. (1972). Overseas assignment: How managers determine who is to be selected. *Michigan Business Review,* May 1972, 12–19.

Mischel, W. (1965). Predicting the success of Peace Corps volunteers in Nigeria. *Journal of Personality and Social Psychology, 1*(5), 510–517.

Mischel, W. (1968). *Personality and assessment.* New York: Wiley.

Mitchell, T.R., & Foa, U.G. (1969). Diffusion of the effect of cultural training of the leader in the structure of heterocultural task groups. *Australian Journal of Psychology, 21,* 31–43.

Mobley, W.H. (1982). *Employee turnover: Causes, consequences, and control.* Reading, MA: Addison-Wesley.

Mumford, D.B. (1998). The measurement of culture shock. *Social Psychiatry and Psychiatrical Epidemiology, 33,* 149–154.

Mumford, S.J. (1983). The cross-cultural experience: The program manager's perspective. In D. Landis & R.W. Brislin (Eds.), *Handbook of intercultural training: Vol. II* (pp. 82–99). New York: Pergamon.

Naumann, E. (1992). A conceptual model of expatriate turnover. *Journal of International Business Studies, 3,* 499–531.

Oberg, K. (1960). Culture shock: Adjustment to new cultural environments. *Practical Anthropology, 7,* 177–182.

O'Boyle, K. (1989, December 11). Grappling with expatriate issues. *The Wall Street Journal,* p. B1.

Ohmae, K. (1991). *The borderless world: Power and strategy in the interlinked economy.* New York, NY: Harper.

Ohmae, K. (1995). *The end of the nation state: The rise of regional economies.* New York, NY: Free Press.

Ones, D.S., & Viswesvaran, C. (1997). Personality determinants in the prediction of aspects of expatriate job success. In D.M. Saunders (Series Ed.), & Z. Aycan (Vol Ed.), *New approaches to employee management: Vol. 4 Expatriate management: Theory and research* (pp. 63–92). Greenwich, CT: JAI Press.

Ones, D.S., & Viswesvaran, C. (1998). The effects of social desirability and faking on personality and integrity assessment for personnel selection. *Human Performance, 11,* 245–271.

Ones, D.S., & Viswesvaran, C. (1999). Relative importance of the Big Five Dimensions of Personality for expatriate selection. *Human Performance, 12,* 275–294.

Organ, D.W. (1994). Organizational citizenship behavior and the good soldier. In M.G. Rumsey, C.B. Walker & J.H. Harris (Eds.), *Personnel selection and classification* (pp. 31–68). Hillsdale, NJ: Erlbaum.

Pazy, A., & Zeira, Y. (1985). Compatibility of expectations in training parent-country managers and professionals in host-country organizations. *International Studies of Management and Organization, 15,* 75–93.

Porter, M.E. (1990). *The competitive advantage of nations.* New York: The Free Press.

Prentice, R. (1990). The muddled state of Title VII's application abroad. *Labor Law Journal,* September, 633–640.

Price Waterhouse (1997). International assignments: European policy and practice: 1997/98, Europe.

Randolph, G., Landis, D., & Tzeng, O.C. (1977). The effects of time and practice upon culture assimilator training. *International Journal of Intercultural Relations, 1,* 105–119.

Ronen, S. (1989). Training the international assignee. In I.L. Goldstein (Ed.), *Training and development in organizations* (pp. 417–453). San Francisco: Jossey-Bass.

Rothstein, H.R. (1990). Interrater reliability of job performance ratings: Growth to asymptote level with increasing opportunity to observe. *Journal of Applied Psychology, 75,* 322–327.

Ruben, B.D., & Kealey, D.J. (1979). Behavioral assessment of communication competency and the prediction of cross-cultural adaptation. *International Journal of Intercultural Relations, 3*, 15–47.

Schmidt, F.L., & Hunter, J.E. (1992). Development of a causal model of processes determining job performance. *Current Directions in Psychological Science, 1*, 89–92.

Searle, W., & Ward, C. (1990). The prediction of psychological and sociocultural adjustment during cross-cultural transitions. *International Journal of Intercultural Relations, 14*, 449–464.

Selmer, J. (1999). Adjustment to Hong Kong: US v European expatriates. *Human Resource Management Journal, 9*(3), 83–93.

Selmer, J., Torbiorn, I., & de Leon, C.T. (1998). Sequential cross-cultural training for expatriate business managers: Pre-departure and post-arrival. *The International Journal of Human Resource Management, 9*(5), 831–840.

Shackleton, V., & Newell, S. (1997). International assessment and selection. In J. Anderson & P. Herriot (Eds.), *International handbook of selection and assessment*. West Sussex, England: John Wiley.

Shaffer, M.A., & Harrison, D.A. (1998). Expatriates' psychological withdrawal from international assignments: Work, nonwork, and family influences. *Personnel Psychology, 51*, 87–118.

Sinangil, H.K., & Ones, D.S. (1995). *Turkiye'de calisan yabanci yoneticilerin kisilik ozellikleri ve bunlarin kriter gecerligi* [Personality characteristics of expatriates working in Turkey and the criterion-related validities of these constructs]. Unpublished paper, Marmara University, Istanbul, Turkey.

Sinangil, H.K., & Ones, D.S. (1996, April). Expectations of Turkish managers from their expatriate co-workers. In D.S. Ones & C. Viswesvaran (Co-Chairs), *Frontiers of international I/O psychology: Empirical findings for expatriate management*. Symposium conducted at the annual meeting of Society for Industrial and Organizational Psychology, San Diego, CA.

Sinangil, H.P., & Ones, D.S. (1997). Empirical investigations of the host country perspective in expatriate management In D.M. Saunders (Series Ed.), & Z. Aycan (Vol Ed.), *New approaches to employee management: Vol. 4 Expatriate management: Theory and research* (pp. 173–205). Greenwich, CT: JAI Press.

Sinangil, H.K., & Ones, D.S. (1998, August). *Personality correlates of expatriate adjustment in Turkey*. Paper presented at the International Congress of Applied Psychology, San Francisco, CA.

Sinangil, H.K., & Ones, D.S. (1999, April). *Women expatriates in Turkey*. Paper presented at the annual conference of the European Association for Work and Organizational Psychology, Helsinki, Finland.

Smith, M.B. (1966). Explorations in competence: A study of Peace Corps teachers in Ghana. *American Psychologist, 21*, 555–566.

Stewart, E. (1966). The simulation of cultural differences. *Journal of Communication, 16*, 291–304.

Stone, R.J. (1991). Expatriate selection and failure. *Human Resource Planning, 14*, 9–18.

Stroh, L.K., & Caligiuri, P.M. (1998). Increasing global competitiveness through effective people management. *Journal of World Business, 33*, 1–16.

Stroh, L.K., Varma, A., & Valy, S. (2000). Women and expatriation: Revisiting Adler's findings. In M.J. Davidson & R.J. Burke (Eds.), *Women in management: Current research, Issue II*. London: Paul Chapman.

Taft, R. (1977). Coping with unfamiliar cultures. In N. Warren (Ed.), *Studies in cross-cultural psychology: Vol. 1* (pp. 121–153). London: Academic Press.

Thal, N.L., & Cateora, P.R. (1979). Opportunities for women in international business. *Business Horizons, 22*, 21–27.

Tolbert, A.S.S. (1990). Venezuelan culture assimilator: Incidents designed for training US professionals conducting business in Venezuela. Unpublished doctoral dissertation, University of Minnesota.

Triandis, H.C. (1994). *Culture and social behavior*. New York: McGraw-Hill.

Triandis, H.C. (1995). Culture specific assimilators. In S. Fowler & M. Mumford (Eds.), *Intercultural sourcebook (Vol. 1)*. Yarmouth, ME: Intercultural Press.

Trifonovitch, G. (1977). On cross-cultural orientation techniques. In R.W. Brislin (Ed.), *Culture learning: Concepts, applications, and research* (pp. 213–222). Honolulu, HI: University of Hawaii Press.

Tung, R.L. (1981). Selecting and training of personnel for overseas assignments. *Columbia Journal of World Business, 16*, 68–78.

Tung, R.L. (1982). Selection and training procedures of US, European, and Japanese multinationals. *California Management Review, 25*, 57–71.

Tung, R.L. (1987). Expatriate assignments: Enhancing success and minimizing failure. *Academy of Management Executive, 1*, 117–126.

Tung, R.L. (1988). *The new expatriates: Human resources abroad*. Cambridge, MA: Ballinger.

Tung, R.L. (1999). Expatriates and their families abroad. In J. Engelhard & W.A. Oechsler (Eds.), *International management: Effects of global changes on competition, corporate strategies, and markets*. Betriebswirtschaftlicker Verlag Dr.: Wiesbaden.

Viswesvaran, C. (1993). *Modeling job performance: Is there a general factor?* Unpublished doctoral dissertation, University of Iowa, Iowa City, IA.

Viswesvaran, C., & Ones, D.S. (2000). Perspectives on models of job performance. *International Journal of Selection and Assessment, 8*(4), 216–226.

Viswesvaran, C., & Ones, D.S. (in press). Agreements and disagreements on the role of General Mental Ability (GMA) in Industrial, Work and Organizational Psychology. *Human Performance*.

Viswesvaran, C., Ones, D.S., & Schmidt, F.L. (1996). A comparative analysis of the reliability of job performance ratings. *Journal of Applied Psychology, 81*, 557–594.

Viswesvaran, C., Ones, D.S., & Schmidt, F.L. (1997). *Supervisor–peer convergence in rating aspects of contextual job performance [Abstract]*. Proceedings of the fifth European Congress of Psychology, Dublin, Ireland.

Viswesvaran, C., Schmidt, F.L., & Ones, D.S. (1994, April). Examining the validity of supervisory ratings of job performance using linear composites. Paper presented in F.L. Schmidt (Chair), *The construct of job performance*. Symposium conducted at the ninth annual meeting of the Society of Industrial and Organizational Psychologists, Nashville, Tennessee.

Ward, C. (1996). Acculturation. In D. Landis & R. Bhagat (Eds.), *Handbook of intercultural training* (pp. 124–147). Newbury Park, CA: Sage.

Wederspahn, G.M. (1992). Costing failures in expatriate human resources management. *Human Resource Planning, 15*, 27–35.

Weldon, D.E., Carlston, D.E., Rissman, A.K., Slobodin, L., & Triandis, H.C. (1975). A laboratory test of effects of culture assimilator training. *Journal of Personality and Social Psychology, 32*, 300–310.

Westwood, R., & Leung, S. (1994). The female expatriate manager experience: Coping with gender and culture. *International Studies of Management and Organization, 24*(3), 64–85.

Wilson, M.S., & Dalton, M.A. (1998). *International success: Selecting, developing, and supporting expatriate managers*. Center for Creative Leadership, NC.

Wilson, M.S., & Dalton, M.A. (2000). The relationship of the Five-Factor Model of Personality to job performance for a group of Middle Eastern expatriate managers. *Journal of Cross-Cultural Psychology, 31*(2), 250–257.

Windham International (1999). *Global Relocation Trends 1999 Survey Report*. Jointly prepared by the National Foreign Trade Council and the Institute for International Human Resources. Http://www.windhamint.com.*article/index.html*

Worchel, S., & Mitchell, T.R. (1972). An evaluation of the effectiveness of the culture assimilator in Thailand and Greece. *Journal of Applied Psychology, 56*, 472–479.

Zeira, Y., & Banai, M. (1985). Selection of expatriate managers in MNCs: The host-environment point of view. *International Studies of Management and Organization, 15*, 33–51.

Author Index to Volume 1

Subject Index to Volume 1